MW01202047

Family Names of the Island of Newfoundland

Family Names of the Island of Newfoundland

E.R. SEARY

with the assistance of Sheila M.P. Lynch

Corrected Edition edited by
William J. Kirwin

J.R. Smallwood Centre for Newfoundland Studies
Memorial University of Newfoundland
St. John's Newfoundland

McGill-Queen's University Press
Montreal & Kingston • London • Chicago

©   J.R. Smallwood Centre for Newfoundland Studies
ISBN 978-0-7735-1782-0 (cloth)
ISBN 978-0-7735-6741-2 (ePDF)

Legal deposit third quarter 1998
Bibliothèque nationale du Quebec

First edition published November 1977
Reprinted 1978, 1980, 1984, 1988, 2015

Printed in Canada on acid-free paper

This book has been published with the financial
assistance of the J.R. Smallwood Centre for
Newfoundland Studies.

McGill-Queen's University Press acknowledges the
financial support of the Government of Canada through
the Canada Book Fund for its activities. We also
acknowledge the support of the Council for the Arts for
our publishing program.

Seary, E.R. (Edgar Ronald), 1908–1984
    Family names of the island of Newfoundland
    Corrected ed.
    Includes bibliographical references.
    ISBN 978-0-7735-1782-0 (cloth)
    ISBN 978-0-7735-6741-2 (ePDF)
    1. Names, Personal – Newfoundland. 2. Onomastics –
    Newfoundland. 3. Newfoundland – Genealogy.
    I. Kirwin, W.J., 1925– II. Lynch, Sheila M.P. III. Title.
    CS2389.S42 1998   929.4'2'09718   C98-900674-3.

This book was typeset by Acappella in 10/12 Times Roman.

To the Chancellor, President, Regents, Senate, Faculty, Staff, and Students of the Memorial University of Newfoundland in grateful acknowledgement of over twenty years of friendship and collaboration.

Contents

Preface

THIS STUDY OF NEARLY THREE THOUSAND FAMILY NAMES of Newfoundland has grown out of an earlier, and still continuing, work on the place names of the island as it became increasingly obvious that no definitive account of the place names could be produced until much more was known about the family names since so many places, both features and settlements, bear them. But as the study progressed, its ancillary role faded somewhat to give way to its own intrinsic fascinations: in finding families which had been associated with one place since their residence in Newfoundland had been first recorded, or had subsequently migrated to other places, in the settlement of ethnic groups in particular areas, in the traditions of men, often deserters from the navies of Britain and France, changing their names to avoid detection, in the discovery of new sources of information, of names apparently not recorded elsewhere, of changes made to unusual names, whether foreign or not, to accommodate them to Newfoundland tongues, of almost forgotten episodes in Newfoundland history such as the landing from Ireland of convicts in 1789 and of impressed men in ?1811.

That it is deficient and imperfect in many regards will doubtless become as apparent to its readers as it is to those who have worked on it, but it is hoped that in its present state it will not be looked on as more than an introductory, pilot chart, subject to later amplification and correction. Certainly, in due course, names which are now of unknown origin and meaning will be explained, and information will often replace conjecture as the flow of family and public papers into the Provincial Archives swells.

The aims of the book are set out in the Introduction, but it is hoped, too, that it will be a source of pleasure to the descendants of those "that have left a name behind"; for if one thing has been made clear in its preparation, it is the deep and enduring pride that Newfoundlanders have in their forebears and families.

Inevitably in a work of this kind one incurs many heavy debts of obligation – to one's predecessors in the field of research and to those who have given more immediate help. The extent of the former will be seen in the Bibliography, the latter I am happy to acknowledge here.

The President and Regents of the University by appointing me Henrietta Harvey Professor of English gave me the opportunity of concentrating on my research free from the claims of teaching and administration, and to them and to the Canada Council I am grateful for support towards the costs of research and publication.

Still within the University, I have received unstinted help of many kinds from many colleagues. Dr. D.G. Pitt, Head of the Department of English Language and Literature, and Drs. G.M. Story, W.J. Kirwin, J.D.A. Widdowson and Mrs. Joan Halley have, as always, been generous with counsel and concern, and information from their vast stores of Newfoundland lore and lexicology. Drs. H. Halpert, K. Matthews, J. Mannion and T. Nemec have made available replies to questionnaires on family histories and traditions (among other things) by students in the Departments of Folklore, History, Geography and Sociology. To Dr. Matthews I am also grateful for a copy of the typescript of his "A 'Who was Who' of Families engaged in the Fishery and Settlement of Newfoundland, 1660–1840." The University Librarian and Miss Agnes O'Dea, Head of the Centre for Newfoundland Studies, have placed their resources at my disposal. Lord Taylor of Harlow was instrumental in procuring copies of the Telephone Directories of the United Kingdom for me. Drs. D.G. Alexander, A.G. Macpherson and R. Barakat have provided information on books and manuscripts, J. Hewson, H.J. Paddock and V. Bubenik on linguistic matters.

The following student assistants, among others, were responsible from time to time for extracting names from documents of one kind and another and for reducing the raw material to usable order: Patricia Delaney, Susan Hoddinott, Robert Joy, Jennifer Mercer, Margot Metcalfe, Colin Penney, Helen Peters, Mary Rowsell, Richard Seary and Noel White.

Two other internal debts will be acknowledged later.

Colleagues elsewhere have been helpful in special ways.

Professor R.M. Wilson, of the University of Sheffield, among other kindnesses, provided access to material prepared by P.H. Reaney for inclusion in *A Dictionary of British Surnames* but omitted therefrom for reasons given in the Introduction. Professor R.M. Savory of the University of Toronto provided interpretations of names from Syria-Lebanon, as did Dr. Fwan-Wai So of Okemos, Michigan, for Chinese names.

Other informants and correspondents have given items of family history and I have relied heavily on the Hon. R.F. Sparkes for information about families and names in northern Newfoundland.

Librarians and archivists have given freely of their professional skills and knowledge and I am particularly indebted to the Provincial Archivist, Mr. F. Burnham Gill, his Cataloguer, Mr. J.P. Greene, and his Chief of Research, Mr. David Davis; to Mr. Gordon Foley, the late Registrar-General of the Division of Vital Statistics, Newfoundland; to Mrs. I. Pridmore, archivist of the United Society for the Propagation of the Gospel, London; and to the staffs of the Hunter Library, St. John's, the British Library, the Priaulx Library, Guernsey, and the Library of the University of Sheffield.

Authors and publishers of works I have quoted from have generously given permission for their use: Routledge and Kegan Paul Ltd. for P.H. Reaney's *The Origin of English Surnames* and *A Dictionary of British Surnames*; the Clarendon Press for Miss E.G. Withycombe's *The Oxford Dictionary of English Christian Names* and E. Ekwall's *The Concise Oxford Dictionary of English Place-Names*; John Murray (Publishers) Ltd. for E. Weekley's *Surnames* and *The Romance of Names*; The New York Public Library for G. Black's *The Surnames of Scotland*; Dr. B. Cottle for *The Penguin Dictionary of Surnames*; Dr. E. MacLysaght for *The Surnames of Ireland* and *Irish Families*; and Professor W.G. Hoskins for "The Homes of Family Names." These and other works to which I have referred are described in the Bibliography.

Finally, it is my great pleasure to pay tribute to three people who have completely identified themselves with this study since its inception. Sheila Lynch not only took as her special interest the Early Instances, directing the student assistants and putting the information they gathered into the form in which it appears in the Dictionary, but also brought a sharp eye and an accurate memory to the revisions of early drafts and took care of the administration of the project. Marion Kelly produced an almost impeccable typescript from a frequently difficult manuscript. Both brought to the study personal knowledge of families and places. Without their help it would have been less comprehensive and accurate and its completion long-delayed. My wife's contribution is hardly to be measured in quantitative terms, but for her care and comfort over the years I remain her lasting debtor.

I have previously recognized the deficiencies and imperfections inherent in this work. It remains to be said that I hold myself solely responsible for those which could conceivably have been avoided.

E.R.S.
Memorial University of Newfoundland
December 1975

Editor's Preface

FAMILY NAMES HAS GAINED MANY READERS since its first appearance in 1977. The work, prepared by E.R. Seary, a leader in the scholarly research in the Department of English even up to his death in 1984, gives a special kind of overview of the history of Newfoundland society because of its attention to people whose names appeared in records since the 1630s and formed the body of the population listed in the *Official List of Electors* [St. John's, 1955]. The entry for each surname treated presents brief documented details on families bearing that name and, in the process, references to individual family members noted during those three centuries. Much other useful information is also recorded incidentally. The original personal name files assembled by E.R. Seary are deposited in the Memorial University of Newfoundland Folklore and Language Archive.

In preparing this revision, requested of the late G.M. Story and me in March, 1993, by the Division of University Relations, Memorial University, my esteem for E.R. Seary's creation, scholarship, and organizational strengths has steadily increased. With that respect always in mind, I asked myself what material in the book should be left in its original form and what changes should I be bold to make. The revision presented here incorporates three sets of "Addenda and Corrigenda" included by Seary in the 1978 and 1980 reprints of *Family Names*, along with a number of penciled corrections in his personal copy. The very minor errors in spelling, punctuation, italics, dates, numbers, and points of consistency discovered in the course of checking the text have been corrected. Information about family histories submitted to me by researchers and details contained in subsequent published studies not available to Seary have been added to the text. The following correspondents who submitted information to the author and to me have corrected and improved the entries: F.G. Adams, A.W. Adey, S. Alcoe, R. Andersen, Mrs. M. Artiss, E.G. Baird, R. Benteau, H. Clarke, G.J. Cranford, F. Cater, D.V. Harbin, H.G. Harnett, A.J. Hearn, D. Hippern, A. Horwood, D.E.J. Kelland, G.C. Lacey, R.J. Lahey, D.A. Macdonald, W.J. Moore, S. O'Dea, R.D. Pepper, J.P. Pollis, S. Prince, Mrs. J. Rickert, J. Ritcey, E.C. Smith, P.E.L. Smith, G.W. Sodero, G.R. Thomas, G.S. Thomas, H.M. Tizzard, B. Wadden, and W.J. Walsh. A small number of further references useful in Newfoundland name studies have been added to the Select Bibliography. For necessary electronic, keyboarding, and editing contributions I am grateful to Trevor Porter and Jacob Larkin. G.P. Jones, head of the Department of English Language and Literature, Memorial University, and Robert Hollett have provided assistance at every stage of the preparation.

Members of the board of the Smallwood Foundation became interested in supporting the publication of this reset edition in 1996. Since the Director of the Smallwood Centre, Ronald Rompkey, took an active role in approaching publishers, he was able to conclude an agreement with McGill-Queen's University Press to publish Seary's book. The University and I owe him a great debt of gratitude for concluding these arrangements.

The work, with these infrequent changes and additions, cannot be considered a wholesale revision. Anthroponymic research appearing after the cut-off date of 1977 has not been systematically undertaken by any followers of Seary. The masses of names data published in histories and journals in the last two decades have not been sifted to permit the valuable information they contain to be added to the *Family Names* entries. Nevertheless, Seary's names stock based on the 1955 electors *List* and his 1977 historical and etymological record continue to supply invaluable factual information to scholars and to individuals looking into their families' background. This work of mine is intended to be a successor respectful of the other notable publications initiated and carried out by E.R. Seary and his colleague G.M. Story.

William J. Kirwin

Note on the Author

THE ENTRY IN THIS VOLUME UNDER HIS NAME puts it with characteristic understatement and succinctness: "Seary, rare at St. John's since 1953." Edgar Ronald Seary was indeed rare, but there was much more to him than that. Born in Sheffield, England, in 1908 and educated at Firth Park Grammar School, he graduated from the University of Sheffield in 1929 with an honours degree in English Language and Literature and then proceeded to the M.A. (1930) and the Ph.D. (1933). He was Research Scholar and Fellow of the University from 1930 to 1932.

Before his arrival at Memorial University of Newfoundland in 1953 as professor of English, Seary had been Lektor in the Dolmetscher-Institut of the Handelschochschule, Mannheim, in 1933 and lecturer and senior lecturer in English at Rhodes University, Grahamstown, South Africa, 1935–51. (During the Second World War, he served in the South African Artillery and the Army Education Service.) He was subsequently professor and head of the Department of English in the College of Arts and Science, Baghdad, 1951–53. When he later became head of the English department at Memorial University (1954–70), he exercised his considerable experience in developing rigorous academic programs and exacting standards of scholarship.

Recognizing the University's responsibility for scholarship in Newfoundland studies, Professor Seary fostered work not only in language and literature but in folklore, local history, biography, the publication of early texts, the study of place names – and, of course, family names. His own work on Newfoundland family names was accomplished during his tenure as Henrietta Harvey Professorship of English from 1970 and continued, following his retirement in 1978, when he became professor emeritus. In the course of his career he exerted a profound influence on a generation of undergraduate and graduate students in English and helped establish Newfoundland studies as a worthy academic pursuit. Apart from his academic leadership at Memorial University, he was president of the Canadian Linguistic Association (1960–62), and of the Association of Canadian University Teachers of English (1963–64). He was made a fellow of both the Royal Historical Society and the Society of Antiquaries. He received the Canadian Centennial Medal in 1967 and honorary degrees from both the University of Sheffield (Litt.D., 1971) and Memorial University (D.Litt., 1973). He died in 1984.

In addition to the present volume and his numerous contributions to journals and encyclopedias, Dr. Seary's publications and collaborations include *A Biographical and Bibliographical Record of South African Literature in English, South African Short Stories, Names of the Northern Peninsula, Reading English* (with G.M. Story), *The Avalon Peninsula of Newfoundland: An Ethno-Linguistic Study* (with G.M. Story and W.J. Kirwin), and *Place Names of the Avalon Peninsula of the Island of Newfoundland*. This last volume, together with *Family Names of the Island of Newfoundland*, will remain fundamental to any further work in the field.

Ron Rompkey
June 1998

Introduction

I RANGE AND AIMS

THE FAMILY NAMES OF NEWFOUNDLAND, like its place names, are part of the great European inheritance of the island, deriving from those races which over the last three to four hundred years have contributed to its settlement: English, Irish, Scots, French and Channel Islanders in the forefront, followed among others by Welsh, Germans, Scandinavians, Spanish and Portuguese, and from further afield by Maronites from Lebanon and Chinese. The Micmac Indians of Newfoundland have adopted surnames from French, English and Irish.

The names studied in this work occur in the *Official List of Electors 1955*, chosen since it presented a comprehensive list of names and the localities with which they were linked before the massive resettlement of families in the 1960s led to the abandonment of communities in which some had had their homes for generations, but with which their ties will soon be lost. From it were excluded, however, the names of transients such as members of the armed forces and of the Royal Canadian Mounted Police, of doctors and nurses, which are no longer found in such contemporary documents as Telephone Directories. Occasionally a name has become extinct by death or migration since 1955, but where there is evidence of its earlier occurrence it has been included.

For each name an attempt has been made in the first place to present its geographic origin in England, Scotland, Ireland, France or wherever it may be or, as frequently happens, in more than one of these countries; its linguistic origin or origins which are not necessarily the same as its geographic origin as, for example, in those English and Irish surnames which derive from French surnames and place names; and its meaning or interpretation. Names in parenthesis at the end of this section, such as Reaney, Cottle, Black, MacLysaght, etc., refer to authorities from whom the foregoing information has been drawn in whole or in part or who may provide additional information. The note *"see"* followed by a surname in capitals, or a surname in capitals in the text, draws the reader's attention to further information on the surname under discussion; *"see also"* usually draws attention to other names of similar origin or meaning.

Secondly, as far as possible, an attempt has been made to give the particular associations of each name, especially with the counties of England, Ireland and Scotland, citing the authorities from whom information has been drawn.

Thirdly, for Newfoundland, family and local traditions about surnames have been given when known, though many of them are not substantiated, and indeed are often contradicted, by documentary evidence which follows in the section Early Instances. The traditions are included not so much for their authenticity, but because they form an integral part of the lore of the island.

Early Instances contain, for the most part, the first occurrence of a family name in a particular community as found in documents listed in the Select Bibliography, Sections 3 and 4.

The modern status and common location of each name and place names associated with it follow.

It will be seen, then, that the main purpose of this study has been simply to answer such questions as Where does a name come from? What does it mean? How long has it been recorded in Newfoundland? With what part of Newfoundland has it been particularly associated? It is not intended to be a genealogy of Newfoundland, but it may provide a stimulus and a starting-point for more histories of Newfoundland families, of which at present there are all too few, though they are the foundations on which the social historian must build much of his work, or indeed for that much needed Dictionary of Newfoundland Biography.

II SOURCES OF INFORMATION

The four main national sources of Newfoundland names, England, Ireland, Scotland and France, all possess recent, scholarly dictionaries of their surnames from which this work has inevitably and gratefully drawn heavily.

1. England and Wales

In England, the study of surnames can be traced from William Camden, *Remaines concerning Britaine* (1605), but works down to the beginning of the twentieth century may be generally ignored except for citations of names omitted from modern works, since fancy and guesswork rather than evidence are frequently the basis of their etymologies, and where evidence is given it is inadequate in both substance and detail. Only with C.W. Bardsley, *A Dictionary of English and Welsh Surnames* (1901), were the principles of the study of surnames firmly established. In Reaney's words, "He insisted on the need for the collection of as many early examples of the surname as possible, dated and localized, on which the etymology must be based." But since Bardsley's day, as Reaney notes, more evidence has become available and "a marked advance [has been made] in our knowledge of the English language, particularly in the history of its dialects, personal-names and place-names." Thus armed, P.H. Reaney was able to compile *A Dictionary of British Surnames* (1958), although, as he comments in his Preface, "A complete Dictionary of Surnames cannot yet be produced, partly because for many of the large number of surnames surviving material is at present scanty or lacking, partly because of the high cost of such a production. This has meant a strict economy in examples and in exposition and the elimination from the first draft of some 100,000 words and 4,000 names." Happily for future students of British surnames, at the time this is being written in 1975, Professor R.M. Wilson of the University of Sheffield, who had read the proofs of the first edition of the *Dictionary* for Reaney, is preparing a new edition, freed from the stringencies which had beset Reaney himself.

Other works useful in the study of English surnames are Reaney, *The Origin of English Surnames* (1967), an analysis of names based largely but not exclusively on material from his *Dictionary*, in which he discusses such topics as the classification of names, names from French and other European places, names of relationship, names from native personal names, names of office and occupation, nicknames, and the growth and distribution of names; two volumes by Ernest Weekley, *The Romance of Names* (1914, 4th edition 1928) and *Surnames* (1916, 1936); E.G. Withycombe, *The Oxford Dictionary of English Christian Names* (1945, 1950), valuable for its references to surnames drawn from Christian names; and Basil Cottle, *The Penguin Dictionary of Surnames* (1967), which in many entries is often no more than a condensation of Reaney's *Dictionary* – without the evidence, as Cottle acknowledges – yet in others offers new and often entertaining commentary, introduces names not found in Reaney, has a succinct and useful introduction, and all in all is the most convenient, cheap guide for the common reader. For the many surnames drawn from place names, E. Ekwall, *The Concise Oxford Dictionary of English Place-Names* (1936, 1960), the county volumes of the English Place-Name Society, and the Society's *English Place-Name Elements* (1956) by A.H. Smith are necessary references.

The local origins of English and Scots surnames are found in H.B. Guppy, *Homes of Family Names in Great Britain* (1890), in which, county by county (in England), he discusses and lists names associated with each. The lists show names in the classes General (30–40 counties), Common (20–29 counties), Regional (10–19 counties), District (4–9 counties), County (2–3 counties) and Peculiar (confined mostly to one county and sometimes, indeed, to a particular town). An Alphabetical List of English and Welsh Names and an Alphabetical List of the Most Frequent of Scottish Names show distribution by counties (and by more general areas usually in Scotland), based on the names of farmers extracted from Kelly's Post Office Directories. The names are counted in a system of proportional numbers per 10,000 of the farmers in each county, except where the relative frequency is less than 7 per 10,000.

Chapter XVII of Reaney's *Origin of English Surnames* contains an appraisal of Guppy's achievement and limitations which has recently been amplified by W.G. Hoskins, "The Homes of Family Names" in *History Today*, Vol. XXII, No. 3, March 1972. Hoskins writes:

After eighty years it remains the only book in the field. It was a massive undertaking; and, like all pioneer works, it has serious faults, as we discover in seeking to extend the range of our knowledge. Guppy believed that, despite the rapid extension of communications in his lifetime, certain classes of people remained pretty well fixed in or near their ancient place of origin. But he chose his social class too carefully and narrowly: he regarded what he called "the Old English Yeomen" as the most stable section of the community, the least affected by foreign immigrants, the most bound to a locality through their land. He therefore limited his counting to the farmer-class in nineteenth-century directories; and he produced some extremely interesting and, at times, valuable results. ...

[But] Guppy's method and his sources were too selective. To count only the farming class and no other; to use only late nineteenth-century directories and no other source: this is to invite results that are either rather obvious at times and at other times misleading. When we break this subject of surname-distribution down into a single parish, or a single family, using the widest range of sources that are available in local and central records, we begin to see that the subject is infinitely more complicated than Guppy had supposed, and that to examine the problem at only one period of time gives us a very limited and simplified picture.

The article from which the foregoing passage has been quoted is extended into a chapter of the revised edition of Hoskins's *Local History in England* (1972).

Of particular interest to the student of English surnames in Newfoundland are the works of C. Spiegelhalter and K. Matthews. Spiegelhalter, "A Dictionary of Devon Surnames" (mimeograph 1958), contains those names which were "found in the county before the sixteenth century [and] ... survived long enough to appear in Parish Registers," with derivations, as he warns, "which apply only to Devon, [since] in other parts of England many of the names have a very different origin." Matthews, "A 'Who was Who' of Families engaged in the Fishery and Settlement of Newfoundland, 1660–1840" (typescript 1971), investigates "the overseas commerce of Devon and Dorset, with an emphasis upon the Newfoundland fishery," ranges in fact beyond Devon and Dorset, and provides information on some five thousand surnames.

G.M. Miller, *BBC Pronouncing Dictionary of British Names* (1971), "includes titles, family names (i.e. surnames), certain Christian names (or personal first names), place names, those of institutions and societies, and adjectival forms of proper names, drawn from England, Wales, Scotland, Northern Ireland, the Isle of Man, and the Channel Islands – the last appearing in a separate appendix." The pronunciation of personal names is based on family usage, that of place names, for the most part, on local usage with variants wherever they occur. The inclusion of names from the Channel Islands, an area much neglected in both English and French studies of surnames and place names, with distinctions made of the pronunciation of Jersey and Guernsey in special cases, makes the book of especial value for this present work.

2. Ireland

Reaney had included a number of surnames of Ireland in his *A Dictionary of British Surnames*, but E. MacLysaght found his treatment of them less than satisfactory because of omissions, the inclusion of names which are Irish but not British, and particularly in the mode of dealing with "those English names which have been widely used as the anglicized form of Irish surnames: there is no indication in the entries for Collins, Farren, Moore or Traynor (to take four examples at random) that these are anything but exclusively English ..."

MacLysaght's own work had been partly anticipated by Sir Robert E. Matheson, *Special Report on Surnames in Ireland* (1909) and Patrick Woulfe, *Irish Names and Surnames* (1923), but *The Surnames of Ireland* (1969, revised paperback edition 1973), based on but expanded beyond the names in his *Irish Families* (1957), *More Irish Families* (1960), *Supplement to Irish Families* (1964) and *Guide to Irish Families* (1964), is the only authoritative study. Not only does MacLysaght interpret names, except in the special case of surnames like Ryan, derived from old personal names of obscure meaning which are left without comment, but more often than not also names the areas with which they are particularly associated. His introduction and the notes which follow it are essential to an understanding of the complexities and idiosyncrasies of Irish nomenclature. The edition of 1973 contains several additional names and occasional further or different comment on those in the edition of 1969, but nowhere indicates that any changes have been made.

3. Scotland

G.F. Black, *The Surnames of Scotland* (1946), studies their origin, meaning and history with a long, introductory essay, but rarely provides information on their location in modern times and does not always distinguish obsolete from current names. "Many names explained here," he writes, "have not survived as surnames, but it is never safe to say of any given name that it is extinct. Within recent years some surnames described in public print as no longer existing have brought forth indignant letters of protest from bearers of such names vigorously denying their extinction." However, in this work, for the most part, only surnames known as current from other evidence have been identified as "of Scotland."

4. France and the Channel Islands

A. Dauzat, *Dictionnaire étymologique des Noms de Famille et Prénoms de France* (1951, 1969), has superseded earlier work, though A. Dauzat and C. Rostaing, *Dictionnaire étymologique des Noms de Lieux en France* (1963), sometimes contains supplementary material. As their titles suggest, neither work discusses names of the Channel Islands. However, Marion G. Turk, The *Quiet Adventurers in America Channel Island Settlers in the American Colonies and in the United States* (1975), a genealogical study, provides about three hundred names found in Newfoundland, considerably more than the number in G.M. Miller, referred to above.

5. Other Countries

E.C. Smith, *American Surnames* (1969), is a comprehensive survey of more than 7,000 of the surnames of those many countries and races from all over the world which by immigration have contributed to the population of the United States. Many more, some 22,000 in all, are briefly explained in his *New Dictionary of American Family Names* (1956, 1973). His *Treasury of Name Lore* (1967) discusses many different aspects of names and his *Personal Names A Bibliography* (1952), though now in need of revision, is still an essential work of reference.

B.O. Unbegaun, *Russian Surnames* (1972), contains a chapter on Surnames of European Origin which includes a section of surnames of Jewish origin.

Two German works, Heintze-Cascorbi, *Die deutschen Familiennamen* (1882, 7th edition 1933, reprinted 1967), and M. Gottschald, *Deutsche Namenkunde* (1931, 4th edition 1971), have scholarly introductions but suffer in the studies of individual names from systems of crabbed abbreviations which make them virtually unintelligible to all but specialist readers.

6. Newfoundland

Reaney opened the introduction to *A Dictionary of British Surnames* with the remark that "The purpose of a Dictionary of Surnames is to explain the meaning of names, not to treat of genealogy and family history." But in the context of Newfoundland where families may be said to have made a new start in life, more often than not, it seems, completely severing their ties with the country of their origin, there appears to be justification not only for explaining the meaning of names but also for adducing evidence and traditions of their incidence here. They are to be found in a wide variety of documents, manuscript and printed, in many collections and locations. Some of the more interesting and important are described in the following pages.

A mass of information is contained in Colonial Office papers relating to Newfoundland, now preserved in the Public Record Office, London. They include dispatches and reports from the captains of the Newfoundland convoys and governors of Newfoundland to the Board of Trade and Plantations and later to the Secretary of State for the Colonies, and correspondence with the governors.

In 1675, the commander of the convoy, Sir John Berry, was commissioned to report on the state of the island and to collect statistics, and in fact took the first census of its inhabitants thus providing the first major collection of family names. His successors made similar reports which, like his, are collected in Colonial Office Series I, Colonial Papers General Series (CO 1). Rogers, pp. 82–86, discusses the importance of the role of the captains and summarizes the contents of Sir W. Poole's report of 1677.

Other papers are valuable for the names of magistrates, justices of the peace and constables, of grand and petty jurors, of plaintiffs and defendants in litigation, and especially for two lists, the first (CO 194.38) containing the names and places of origin of sixty-three or sixty-four Irish convicts (one name is repeated), who were landed at Petty Harbour and Bay Bulls in 1789, probably to provide cheap labour (Rogers, p. 140), the second (CO 194.51) containing the names of seventy-two impressed men who sailed from Ireland in ? 1811 perhaps as reinforcements for ships of the Royal Navy at a time when relations between Britain and the United States were to lead to the War of 1812. The fate of the group of Irish convicts is revealed in a communication from Professor R.J. Lahey, 6 Dec 1977:

Governor Milbanke regarded this [the transportation of the convicts to Newfoundland] as an unprecedented event (Milbanke to the Secretary of the Admiralty, 9 September 1789, Adm. 1/472, f. 334) and seventy-four of the men and six of the women landed were sent by him to England (Milbanke to the Secretary of the Admiralty, 24 October 1789, Adm. 1/472, ff. 340–341).

It will be noted that the number of convicts differs in CO 194.38 and Adm. 1/472 and that the latter document includes women.

Typescript copies of correspondence from 1780 to 1825, the D'Alberti Transcripts, (so named after two sisters who made them, not always with flawless accuracy), are in the Centre for Newfoundland Studies of the Memorial University of Newfoundland.

Four documents which appear to have been prepared for the governor for submission to the Colonial Office in the latter years of the eighteenth and the early years of the nineteenth century, though only one (CO 199.18) bears a Colonial Office reference, provide information on family names associated with St. John's and vicinity, Trinity Bay, Conception Bay and Bonavista.

"An Account of Inhabitants residing in the Harbour and District of St. John's 1794/ 1795," (referred to in this study as Census 1794–5), in the Hunter Library, St. John's, gives the names, occupations, length of residence in Newfoundland, and numbers in the families both kin and servants, of 801 householders, made up of 652 in St. John's, 53 in Petty Harbour, 49 in Torbay, 34 in Portugal Cove and 13 on Bell Island.

"A Return of the Number of Houses, Inhabitants, Fishing Rooms, Rents of Rooms, etc. in the District of Trinity, Nfld. in the Winter of 1800 and 1801 ...," (referred to as Census Trinity B.), housed in the Provincial Archives, gives the names of some 225 fishermen in seventeen communities.

A "Return of Possessions held in Conception Bay" of 1805 (CO 199.18), a microfilm copy of which is in the Provincial Archives, known as the "Plantation Book," enumerates no less that 575 persons in possession of land, stages and other properties around Conception Bay, with descriptions of the properties and, most important for this study, the date of a family's first acquiring property. From it may be learned, to mention only a few instances, that Andrewses held property at Port de Grave before 1658 and at Harbour Grace before 1675, Badcocks at Bay Roberts before 1663, Bishops there before 1689, and Dawes at Port de Grave as early as 1595.

A "Register of Fishing Rooms, Bonavista Bay, 1806," (referred to as Bonavista Register), of which the original is in the Hunter Library and a copy in the Provincial Archives, contains the names of about ninety owners and occupiers of fishing rooms in the district.

The archives of the United Society for the Propagation of the Gospel in Foreign Parts, London, contain a number of petitions, addresses and similar documents, signed by inhabitants of Bonavista, Ferryland, Harbour Grace and Bay Bulls between ? 1772 and 1802, usually urging the need for a missionary or schoolmaster, though in 1791 the Society received a request from Harbour Grace for the removal of the missionary there, James Balfour. Some of these documents were sent in the first place to the Governor of Newfoundland.

But by far the richest source of family names in the U.S.P.G. archives is a copy of nineteen sheets of "Baptisms solemnized in the Parish of Twillingate in the island of Newfoundland in the Years 1816–17–18 and 19–20–21–22 and 23," containing 485 entries, not only from Twillingate but also from Change Islands, Fogo, Herring Neck and other settlements, with an affidavit: "I the Rev T. G. Langharne do make oath and declare that these sheets do contain a copy of the Register kept in my House at Twillingate. Sworn before me this twentysixth day of Sep 1823. R[ichard] A[lexander] Tucker. C[hief] J[ustice]." There is no indication of the purpose of the copy or at whose request it was made.

In Newfoundland itself there have been irreparable losses of historical material in the past from indifference, carelessness and irresponsibility, but there yet remains, to take St. John's alone, a formidable mass of manuscript papers, the most fruitful of all sources for family names being over one hundred copies of baptismal, marriage and rare death registers of the Anglican, Methodist, Roman Catholic, Congregational, Presbyterian and Reformed Episcopal churches, from most parts of the island, for varying periods usually up to 1890 or 1891, the earliest being the Anglican baptismal registers for Trinity and the Cathedral, St. John's, which date from 1753. Most of the copies were made in the 1940s by local clergy, schoolmasters and others. They were housed in the former Provincial Department of Public Health and Welfare (hence the reference DPHW), later the Department of Health, Division of Vital Statistics, until their transfer to the Provincial Archives in 1974. A numerical index of the registers, showing denomination, kind and dates, appears in the Bibliography under the heading DPHW. They are now being supplemented by copies of more Roman Catholic registers, such as those from Harbour Grace (HGRC), King's Cove (KCRC) and the Cathedral (now Basilica) parish of St. John's (BRC), which often state the place of birth or residence in Ireland of brides and bridegrooms.

It should be noted that only the earliest instance of a family name in a particular place has been extracted from the registers, and that many registers which may be found scattered in parishes around the island have not been examined.

The Folklore and Language Archive and the Departments of History, Geography and Sociology of the Memorial University of Newfoundland have records of oral traditions, both family and local, of changes of name and of the time and circumstances of arrivals in

Newfoundland, collected by student informants usually from older members of the family or community. A number of theses, some completed, others in progress, frequently dealing with special areas of Newfoundland, are also rich in family and place nomenclature.

Printed sources of information are many and various. They include later census returns, almanacs, directories, newspapers published in St. John's and other towns (most useful for notices of death and obituaries which often give the place of birth of the deceased), other periodicals, histories, collections of biographies, and the writings of travellers in Newfoundland.

Manuscript, typescript, mimeographed and printed sources used in the preparation of this book are all named in the Bibliography.

A final source of information has been found in inscriptions on gravestones mostly in St. John's.

III SURNAMES – SOME GENERAL CONSIDERATIONS

1. Their Rise

The function of a surname (byname or, in its original sense, nickname, which is *an ekename* – an additional name) is to distinguish and identify persons bearing the same personal (given, first, Christian, baptismal, font) name. Though some men adopted surnames for themselves, Reaney has demonstrated that it was the need of officialdom in a complex society to know, for example, who owed service to the king, who was subject to taxation, who was concerned in the letting or conveyancing of land, who were criminals, that made accurate identification of individual persons essential. From early, wordy descriptions, the one-word surname at length evolved which, as will be seen later, falls into one or more of four classes.

Surnames, simply as additional names, are known to have existed in England before the Norman Conquest, and Reaney maintains that some Normans had hereditary surnames, that is, family names, before they came to England, though Dauzat attributes the formation of family names in France only from the thirteenth century. Be that as it may, surnames became hereditary in England only in the three hundred years following the Conquest, from the eleventh to the fourteenth century, spreading from the upper classes slowly to the common people.

The earliest surnames recorded in Scotland, in the twelfth century, were those of Normans which had already become hereditary in England. Only in the sixteenth century did surnames begin to become hereditary in Wales.

"Ireland," according to MacLysaght, "was one of the earliest countries to evolve a system of hereditary surnames: they came into being fairly generally in the eleventh century, and indeed a few were formed before the year 1000. ... At first the surname was formed by prefixing Mac to the father's Christian name or O to that of a grandfather or earlier ancestor. Names with the prefixes Mac and O, apparently surnames, will be found in records relating to centuries before the tenth, but these were ephemeral not hereditary."

2. Their Kinds

The surnames of the countries of Western Europe, those additional, identifying names given to our ancestors, fall into four classes which, following Reaney and Cottle, may be described as:

(i) Surnames of relationship, taken from, or based on, the first name of an ancestor;
(ii) Local surnames, recording localities or places where ancestors originated, held land, or lived, whether specifically designated or not;
(iii) Surnames of rank, status, office and occupation;

(iv) Surnames from nicknames, descriptive of the ancestor's physical appearance, disposition, relationship, occupation, notable feats and performances, and miscellaneous traits and qualities.

Reaney shows, however, that "a single modern name may belong to more than one class" and, it should be added, may have more than one source of origin within a class, as well as having more than one linguistic origin.

An important national characteristic of surnames lies in the proportions of each of the four classes to the whole body of names: for while surnames of relationship form the largest class in Ireland, Wales and the Highlands of Scotland, local surnames form the largest in England and the smallest in Ireland. In France, Dauzat observed the great preponderance of local names in the Basque country as opposed to a majority of old baptismal names in the northeast, in Lorraine. E.C. Smith, *Treasury of Name Lore,* sketches the characteristics of surnames in some fifty races, countries and cultures.

A brief account of each class follows. More extensive treatment will be found in the sources named above, especially Reaney and Cottle.

(i) Surnames of Relationship

By far the commonest surnames of relationship are those from the personal name of a male ancestor (patronymics), though surnames from the personal name of an ancestress (matronymics, metronymics) also occur.

Personal names in Britain derive from various stocks, the first in point of time being those of the Britons (the Celtic ancestors of the Welsh, Cornish and Bretons), which are either native or taken and adapted to Celtic usage from the names of Roman invaders. Among the native names are Cadwallad(e)r from Welsh *cad* – battle and *gwaladr* – leader, Caradoc from Welsh *Caradawg* – amiable, which has given the surname Craddock, Gavin from Welsh *Gwalchmai* – ? hawk of the plain, a surname and still a common baptismal name in Scotland, Howel from Welsh *hywel* – eminent, Llewel(l)yn from Welsh *llyl* – leader, Lloyd from Welsh *llwyd* – grey, Madoc from Welsh *mad* – fortunate, which has given the surnames Maddock(s), Maddox, Meredith from Welsh *Maredudd* with the second element *iudd* – lord, and Morgan from Welsh *mor* – sea and ? bright. From the Latin are Arthur (? Latin *Artorius*), Cai or Kay (Latin *Caius*), one of the sources of the surname Kay, Evan (? Latin *Johannes*) and Owen (? Latin *Eugenius*).

After about 400 A.D,, the invasions of the Angles, Saxons and Jutes brought two kinds of Germanic personal names to Britain: simple (single-element, monothematic) names and compound (double-element, dithematic) names. Old English simple names which have survived as surnames include *Bisceop* (Bishop), *Brūn* (Brown), *Cniht* (Knight), *Goda* and its feminine form *Gode* (Good), *Hwīta* (White), *Scot* (Scott) and *Swift* (Swift).

It is, however, the compounds that are particularly characteristic of Germanic names. They consist of two elements which may or may not have some significance in relation to each other, as is seen in such Old English names of "good augury" as *Ethelweard* – noble protector (surviving in the surname Aylward), *Ethelbert* – noble bright (Albert, Albright), *Ēadmund* – prosperity protector (Edmond, Edmund), *Ēadweard* – prosperity guard (Edward), and *Ēadwine* – prosperity friend (Edwin). But an early convention of showing relationship by having in a child's name an element of the father's (and sometimes of the mother's) name led to the creation of compounds, most of which can be translated but yield such meaningless and often contradictory combinations as peace-wolf, war-peace, brown-famous, dawn-powerful and victory-beauty. The "meaning" of compound names, it seems, had no more significance for the Anglo-Saxons than that of most baptismal names today.

The ninth and early tenth centuries in Britain were marked by further invasions and settlement, first by the Danes and secondly by Norwegians from Ireland, which led to the introduction of more Germanic names, both simple and compound, but with Scandinavian spellings and some new elements. One popular name *Ketill* – (sacrificial) cauldron, which has survived in the surname Kettle, formed an element in a compound name *thorketill* – (the god) Thor's cauldron, from which no less than twenty surnames have evolved including Turtle and Tuttle.

The last great influx of personal names followed the Norman Conquest of 1066, the invaders and later immigrants bringing with them gallicized forms of Old German and Scandinavian names, Norman and Breton names, and names from other parts of France, biblical names and saints' names. The Germanic names introduced by the Normans have been the source of a vast body of baptismal names, both masculine and feminine, many of them surviving with numerous variations in surnames, such as Archibald, Aylmer, Bardolph, Bertram, Drew, Geoffrey, Gervase, Gilbert, Goddard, Guy, Henry, Hugh, Maud, Maynard, Miles, Ralph, Raymond, Richard, Robert, Roger, Roland, Rosamond, Walter and William. Few of the Old English personal names withstood this onslaught, the survivors being, as Withycombe suggests, either names of saints (Edward, Edmund, Hilda, Mildred) or of former kings (Alfred, Edward, Edgar, Ethelbert). With the extension of Norman influence beyond England, their names came to be prominent also in the nomenclature of Scotland and Ireland.

In brief, the upshot of these invasions was that the old Celtic names of the Britons became mostly confined to Wales and the Welsh Border counties, while in England, Norman and French names virtually superseded those from Old English and Scandinavian.

The following demonstration, adapted from Cottle, shows how in English usage, personal names became surnames:

(a) The personal name may be left as it is: Andrew.

(b) The Middle English genitive (possessive) singular inflexion *-es* may be added to show the relationship: Andrewes – (son) of Andrew, though sometimes the possessive may denote "servant of" or "dweller in the house of."

(c) The genitive form may be modernized by omission of the e: Andrewes > Andrew's > Andrews – son of Andrew. This form of the relationship is usually passed over silently in the Dictionary.

(d) The relationship may be made even clearer by the addition of *-son*: Robert's son > Robertson.

(e) A pet-form or diminutive of the personal name made without a suffix may be used: Rob, though the pet-form may not always show an obvious link with the personal name, as in the obsolete forms: *Hob, Dob, Nob*. These, usually with the genitive inflexion *-(e)s* or with *-son*, have given such surnames as Robb, Robson, Hobb(e)s, Hobson, Dobb(s), Dobson, Nobbs. Similarly, pet-forms of Richard: Rich(ie), Rick, Hick and Dick, and of Roger: Hodge and Dodge, and those of other common personal names, have given rise to numerous surnames.

(f) A pet-form or diminutive may have one or more diminutive suffixes added to it, not necessarily of the same linguistic oriqin as the personal name, giving double and even treble diminutives. English *-cock* and *-kin* (the latter of German, Dutch or Flemish origin) occur singly. French *-el, -et, -in, -on, -ot, -un* may occur singly or in such combinations as *-elin, -elot, -inot*, and may be added to the full name or to a pet-form.

The form *-cock*, not only a diminutive suffix but like *-kin* also used as equivalent to *-son*, has given such surnames as Adcock (from Adam), Alcock (from some names beginning with *Al-*), Badcock, Battcock (from Old English *Bada* or from *Bat*, a pet-form of Bartholomew), Han(d)cock (from Henry), Wilcock (from William); *-kin* has given Adkin, Atkin (from Adam), Batkin (from Bartholomew), Hodgkin (from Roger), Hopkin (from Robert) and Tomkin (from Thomas). The French diminutive suffixes have given such surnames as Robin, Roblin, Roblett (from Robert), Parnell (from

Peter), Rawlin (from Old French *Raoul*), Bartlett, Batten (from Bartholomew), Hamlin (from old German *Haimo*), and Wakelin (from Old German *Walho* or *Walico*). Reaney, *Origin*, has further discussion of -*cock* (which may have other origins), -*kin* and of the French diminutive suffixes.

(g) A genitive suffix in -*es* or -*s* may be added to the pet-form: Hobb(e)s, or to the double diminutive: Robins.

(h) -*son* may be added to the diminutive: Robson, or to the double diminutive: Hopkinson.

The prefix *Fitz*-, in both English and Irish usage, is an Anglo-Norman formation from Latin *filius*, Old French *fils*, Anglo-Norman *fis* (pronounced fits) – son, attached to Norman names to show descent. It has no equivalent in French usage.

Though not necessarily indicative of noble descent as an examination of Fitz-names in the *Dictionary of National Biography* shows, Fitz- has been used in England since the time of Henry VIII to denote natural sons of royalty: Henry Fitzroy (of Henry VIII), Charles Fitzcharles, Charles (and others) Fitzroy (of Charles II), James Fitzjames (of James, Duke of York, later James II), and Adolphus and George Fitzclarence (of William, Duke of Clarence, later William IV).

In the Gaelic languages, -*son* is represented by the prefixes *Mac* in Scots and Irish and *Ap* in Welsh, though some names have both a Gaelic and an anglicized form: MacAndrew, Andrews; MacFergus, Fergus(s)on; MacHugh, Hewson; MacMaster, Masterson; MacFeeters, Peterson. The prefix *O* before Irish names means grandson or descendant of So-and-so.

Black maintains that Mac is "wrongly contracted" to Mc or M', but MacLysaght remarks more moderately, "The practice of differentiating between Mac and Mc (not to mention the now almost obsolete M') is fortunately dying out." Cottle's ruling that O should never be followed by an apostrophe is not upheld by MacLysaght's practice.

MacLysaght draws attention to the fact that Mac and O were widely dropped in Irish names during the period of British supremacy from the seventeenth to the late nineteenth century but were generally resumed after the establishment of the Gaelic League in 1893, except in rare instances in such names as Murphy (the commonest surname in Ireland), Connolly, Donnelly, Doyle, Foley, Hogan, Kennedy, Nolan, Quinn and Sheridan.

It may perhaps be not inappropriate here to draw attention to MacLysaght's many examples of the anglicization of Irish names, not only of relationship, by processes that he recognizes as translation, mistranslation or pseudo-translation. By translation, Bane has become White, (Mac) Gillespie – Bishop, (O)Drought – Bridgeman, (Mac) Cullin – Holly, (O)Monaghan and MacEvanny – Monks. By mistranslation, (O)Lacken and (O)Lohan have become Duck, (O)Fahey – Green(e), (O)Quilty – Woody, (O)Quigg – Fivey. By pseudo-translation, MacClave and (O)Lavin have become Hand, (O)Conroy – King, (O)Deeny – Peoples, (O)Fee – Hunt, Duane – Kidney, (O)Loan(e) – Lamb(e), (O)Quirke – Oates.

Welsh *Ap* in the anglicized form of names becomes initial P as in Price from *Ap Rhys* and Powell from *Ap Howell*, or initial B as in Bevan from *Ap Evan* and Bowen from *Ap Owen*.

Generally speaking, the baptismal name or names and the surname are sufficient to identify an individual person, but in communities where surnames are few and baptismal names tend to be limited, a further means of showing relationship is sometimes used to establish identity by describing a child as (the son or daughter) "of" the father or a woman as (the wife) "of" her husband. The practice is usually informal and oral but it has received quasi-official sanction in Newfoundland in *Electors* 1955 where, in the community of Cupids, for example, among the Laracys, Mary is distinguished from Mary "of Frank," Michael from Michael "of Thos." and Thomas from Thomas "of Rich."; and among the Powers, John "of R" is distinguished from John "of Wm.," Michael from Michael "of M," Patrick F. from Patrick "of Pat," and Thomas L. from Thomas "of Pat." Withycombe notes: "There are even parts of England (notably Yorkshire and Staffordshire) where, within living memory, the poorer classes seldom used their surnames except in legal documents, &c., men being known by such appellations as 'Tom o' Dick o' Mary's.'"

(ii) Local surnames

The second group of surnames in England, those derived from the names of places (toponymics) and of localities (locatives), identified a man by his place of birth, origin, residence past or present, or work, and range from the widest description, one of the cardinal points, to the narrowest, a field, a tree, a bush. Their variety is almost limitless and the following examples are necessarily selective. Some may also have other derivations.

Hence, in some sort of descending order, we have such names as North – the man from the North, the man living on the north side of the village, and similarly South with Southern and other variants, East and West, with Western and Westren traced by Guppy oddly enough only in Devon.

Countries, territories, duchies, provinces and counties have given England and English, a rare Scotland and the common Scott, Ireland and Irish, Wales and Walsh and Welsh. France is rare, but Frank, Francis and French are common enough. Germany has given German, Jarman, Jermyn and other variants and Turkey, Turk. Other territories have given Flanders and Fleming; Norman(d) from Normandy; Freston and Frisby from Friesland; Brabazon, Brabbin and Bremner from Brabant; Brittain, Britten from Brittany; Champney(s) from Champagne; Loring from Lorraine; Pickard from Picardy; Portwain and Portwine from Poitou; and Lombard from Lombardy. English counties have given Cheshire, Cornwall with Cornwallis and Cornish, Derbyshire, Devon and Devenish, Hampshire, Lancashire and especially Wiltshire which has some seventeen variants.

English towns and cities have given, among others, Bedford, Bristow(e) from the old form of Bristol, Bristol as a surname being from Burstall (Yorkshire ER) or Birstal (Yorkshire WR), Cambridge, Gloster from Gloucester, Lancaster, Leicester with several variants, Nottingham, Rochester, Salisbury and York(e), but these are far exceeded by surnames from names of villages which are often insignificant and even lost or unidentified. Some of these village names like Aston, Eaton, Middleton, Norton and Sutton, originally names of farms, are so widespread and common that they offer no evidence, without other support, of the origin of the bearer of the name.

Many French place names, chiefly in the modern departments of Calvados, Eure, La Manche and Seine-Inférieure, have been the source of English surnames such as Bullen from Boulogne, Charteris from Chartres and Dangerfield from Angerville. Reaney, *Origin,* counted two hundred and forty-three such surnames with one hundred and ninety-four drawn from places in Normandy. Surnames from Belgian towns include Danvers from Antwerp (Anvers in French), Bridges from Bruges by translation, Ga(u)nt from Ghent, Luke from Libge (Luik in Flemish) and Dipper from Ypres. Germany has given Cullen from Cologne and Lubbock from Lubeck, and from farther afield Baghdad has given Baldock from *Baldac,* the name of the city in Old French, transferred to a manor in Hertfordshire owned and named by the Knights Templars. A sea, the Adriatic, is the ultimate source of the surnames Adrain, Adrian and Adrien, from Latin *Hadrianus,* the name of a Roman emperor adopted by several popes including Nicholas Breakspear (d. 1159), the only English pope. Strange denotes any stranger, foreigner or newcomer.

Places of residence or work, frequently within or near a city, town or village, could be defined narrowly by names of man-made objects, whence such surnames as Abbey, Alcott (old cottage), Armitage (hermitage), Backhouse (bakehouse), Bain(e)(s) (public baths), Bamford (ford with a bridge), Barry (rampart), Bell (an inn), Biggin (building, house), Booth (hut, shed), Bower (dwelling, chamber, woman's room), Bridge(s) and Briggs (bridge), Brough (fort), Brougham and Burton (homestead or farm near a fort), Burgh and Bury (fort, manor), Cal(de)cott (cold cottage), Carfax (crossroads), Chambers, Church and Kirk(e), Cote and Coate(s) (cottage, hut) and Northcott, Southcott and Westcott, Chester and Castle (Roman site or Norman castle), Foss (ditch or the Roman road called the Fosse Way), Gate(s) and Yates (gate, road, street), Hall, Lane, Lodge (hut, cottage), Malthus (malthouse), Mill(s), Newbolt (new building), Newton (new place, farm, homestead, village), Rowe (of houses, cottages), Stanbury (stone fort), Staple(s) (pillar, post), Street (Roman road), Travers and Travis (crossing, tollbridge, tollgate).

But the great mass of local surnames reminds us that England in Old English and post-Conquest times was essentially rural and agricultural and that places were often seen through countrymen's eyes and named after countrymen's ways. Hence we have names from physical features such as brooks, becks, springs, wells, fords, fields, marshes, heaths and hills, from characteristics of pieces of land, from farms and farm buildings, from crops and from haunts of birds and animals, but no class reveals such variety as those names associated with woods and trees.

There are broad generics that have given surnames like Lea, Lee, Leigh (wood, clearing, glade, field, pasture), Wood(s), Woodland, Atwood (at the wood), Firth, Frith, Hirst, Hurst (wood, woodland), as well as such narrower names as Greenwood, Smallwood, Underwood, or Staveley and Yardley (wood or clearing for staves and poles), Whaley (wood by a road) and Whalley (wood by a hill), but most prominent are the surnames containing names of individual kinds of trees of which a selection follows.

The *alder* has given: Alder, Ollerenshaw (copse with alders), Ellerbeck (alder brook), Ellerker (alder marsh), Allerton, Ellerton (alder farm), Vernay, Vernon (both from a Gaulish word for alders), Aldridge (dairy farm in the alders or ridge of alders). The *apple*: Apperley, Appleby, Applegarth, Appleton, Pomeroy (all meaning roughly apple orchard, the last from Old French). The *ash* has given at least twenty-four names including Dash(wood), Nash (at the ash), Aske and, from Old French, Frain. The *aspen*: Aspinal (spring in the aspens), Aspley (aspen wood). The *beech*: Beech, Boughton (place in the beeches), Beckwith (beech wood), Fay (beech tree, from Old French). The *birch*: Birch, Birk, Bir(k)beck (stream in the birches), Birtles (birch hills), Birkenshaw (copse with birches, a name with over twenty variants), Barclay and Berkeley (birch wood). The *box*: Box, Bexley, Boxley (box-tree wood), Boxwell (spring in the box trees). The *chestnut*: Chaston (chestnut tree, from Old French). The *crab-apple*: Crabtree. The *elm*: Elm(e)s, Nelm(e)s (at the elms), Elmore (river bank with elms). The *hawthorn*: Hawthorne, Thorn(e), Haythornthwaite (clearing with hawthorns). The *hazel*: Haslam (at the hazels), Haslip (hazel valley), Haswell (spring in the hazels), Hazeldene, with several variants (hazel valley), Hazelgrove, Hazelhurst, Hazelwood (all hazel wood). The *lime*: Lind, Lindall (lime-tree valley), Lindfield (lime-tree wood), Lindridge (lime-tree ridge), Lindsell (hut in the lime trees). The *maple*: Mapledoram (maple-tree homestead), Mapleton (place in the maples), Mapperley (maple wood), Mapplebeck (brook in the maples). The *nut*: Nutbeam (nut tree), Nutley (nut wood), Nuttall (nook where nuts are found). The *oak*: Oak(e), Oakes, Oakden and Ogden (both oak valley), Oakley (oak wood), Oakford, Oakhill, No(a)kes (at the oaks), Acland (oak land), Acton, Aughton (both oak farm), Askew (oak wood), Chesnay, Chesney (both oak grove, from Old French). The *pear*: Perry (pear tree), Purley (pear-tree field). The *plum*: Plum(p)tre(e) (plum tree), Plumley (plum-tree field), Plumpton (plum-tree farm). The *rowan*: Rowan, Rowntree. The *sallow* or *willow*: Sale, Sallows, Salford, Salton (farm in the sallows), Selbourne (stream in the sallows), Selby (sallow farm), Welford, Wilford (ford in the willows), Widley (willow clearing), Widmer (pool in the willows), Willen (at the willows), Willey (willow wood), Willoughby (farm in the willows), Willows, Withey (willow), Withycombe (willow valley), Withnell (hill with willows). The *yew*: Ewbank (hillside with yews), Ifield (field or open country with yews), New (at the yew tree).

Local surnames are by no means uncommon in Scotland, France and elsewhere, but MacLysaght frequently remarks on their rarity in Ireland. He notes the following Irish (as opposed to English, Scots and French) local names: Ardagh from Ardagh (Cos. Donegal, Limerick, Longford) – high field; Brosnan ? from Brosna (Co. Kerry), a river name; Cappock from Cappock (Co. Louth) – plot of land; Corbally, Corballis from Corbally, Corballis (Co. Louth and elsewhere) – odd town; Craughwell from Craughwell (Co. Galway) – hill of plunder; (O)Delargy ? from Ir. *learg* – plain, slope; Drumgoole, Drumgold from *Dromgabhail* (Co. Louth), "whence the modern name Drumgoolestown"; Finglas from Finglas (Co. Dublin) – clear stream; Galbally from Galbally (Co. Limerick) – foreigner's town; Glanny, Glenny from Ir. *an Ghleanna* – of the glen; Lusk from Lusk (Co. Dublin) – cave; Maghery from Ir. *an Mhachaire* – of the field; (O)Moher from Ir. *mochar* – place overgrown with brushwood; (O)Malmona, Mulmona, partially translated as Moss, from Ir. *móin*, genitive *móna* – moorland, turf bog; Mullock ? from Meelick (Co. Galway); Powderley from Powerlough (Co. Meath); Rath from Rath (Cos. Clare, Offaly) – ringfort; Santry from Santry (Co. Dublin); Scollard, a locative of unascertained meaning; Slane(y) from Slane (Co. Meath); Sruffaun, semi-translated as Bywater, from Ir. *sruth* – stream; Swords from Swords (Co. Dublin), ? from Ir. *sord* – pure spring or well; Trim from Trim (Co. Meath) – town of the ford of the elder tree.

(iii) Surnames of Rank, Status, Office and Occupation

Though fewer than surnames derived from relationship or places, surnames in England of this third group also show a wide range. Some may have other origins, may be capable of more than one interpretation, and may belong to categories besides those in which they appear here. Some, especially those of high rank and status or associated with the Church, are likely to be nicknames from the original bearer having played a part in a pageant or religious play and, with a final *-s* as in Clarges, Parsons and Vicars, may denote *servant of* rather than *son of*. Not infrequently, the same rank, office or occupation may have more than one name sometimes, though not invariably, drawn from English and French, as in the pairs Bishop and Veck (Old French *l'eveske*, wrongly divided, as Cottle shows, as *le vesk*), Monk and Moyne (Old French *moi(g)ne*), and King and Roy (Old French *roi*). Metonyms, whereby occupations are denoted by the names of objects made, sold or used as, for example, Bacon for bacon-seller, Fish for fisherman or fish-seller, Boot for bootmaker and Glass for glazier, are not uncommon.

The following lists, extracted for the most part from surnames in Cottle and usually with his interpretations and comments, show something of their extent, though most variants have been omitted.

The Church: Abbot(t); Bishop, Veck; Cannon (canon); Chapl(a)in; Clarges (servant of the clergyman); Clark(e) (especially a cleric in minor orders and therefore not necessarily celibate); Deacon (next below a priest and officially celibate); Dean; Frater (in charge of the monastic refectory); Frere, Friar; Maidment (maidens' or ? nuns' servant); Monk, Moyne; Nunn; Pardner (pardoner, a licensed seller of indulgences); Parsons; Pope; Priest; Prior; Sexton (sacristan); Vicar(s).

Rank and Status, which range from the highest (except for the emperor which occurs, however, in the Channel Islands as Lemprière) to the lowest: King, Roy; Prince; Duke; Earl(e); Bar(r)on; Lord; Vavasour (feudal tenant next below a baron); Knight; Templar (Knight Templar, a member of the military religious order founded to protect pilgrims to the Holy Land); Bachelor (young knight); Childe (youth awaiting knighthood); Squire (esquire, young gentleman attending a knight); Franklin(g) (franklin, free citizen, gentleman), Yeoman (attendant with rank between squire and page, later a small freeholder); Page; Paget (little page); Marshall (a title as in Earl Marshal, the eighth of the great offices of state, or an occupational name: farrier, groom, blacksmith); Alderman (alderman, head of a guild); Burgess, Portman (citizen, freeman, inhabitant of a borough); Senior (lord of a manor); Tiddeman (head of ten householders); Frank, Freebody, Freeman (freeborn man); Tennant (tenant); Dring (young man, later a free tenant holding land by service, rent and military duty); Sargent (tenant by military service below the rank of knight); Thain(e) (tenant by military service); Knape, Ladd, Mann, and from the Celtic Vassal and Vassar (servant, lowborn man); Bond, Swan(n) (peasant); Thew (serf, slave).

Officers of Royal or Noble Households: Bailey (a title ranging from king's officer, crown official, keeper of a royal building, to sheriff's deputy, agent or bailiff); Burl(e) (cup-bearer, butler); Butler (wine-steward, butler); Cater, Purves (purveyor for a household); Chamberlain, Chambers, Usher (private attendant of a king or lord, or one in charge of private rooms); Constable (chief executive officer of a king's court); Farmer, Grave, Spence(r),

Spender, Stewart (all steward but with differing duties, farmer, for example, being a tax-collector or bailiff, grave a property-manager); Grieve (originally governor of a province, but later overseer, manager, bailiff); Horder (treasurer); Legat(t) (legate, ambassador, deputy); Napier (keeper of the table-linen); Pant(h)er (keeper of the pantry); Wardrobe, Wardrop(e) (keeper of the robes and clothes).

Minor Officials and Servants: Ambler (keeper of ambling horses or mules); Palfrey(man) (keeper of palfreys, ladies' saddle-horses); Runciman (keeper of the nags); Baine (attendant at the public baths); Beadle, Wagstaff (beadle); Bridgeman, Bridger, Punter (bridgekeeper); Catchpole ("chase-fowl," one who seized poultry in lieu of debts, tax-gatherer, official making arrests on warrants for debts); Conner (inspector, examiner of, for example, ale); Ewer (water-bearer, the servant who brought ewers, basins, of water for guests to wash their hands at table); Gaylor (gaoler); Hornblower, Waghorn (official who summoned men to work by blowing a horn); Lardner (official in charge of the larder or of pig food such as acorns and mast in the forest); Massinger, Galpin, Trotter (messenger); Mew (keeper of the mew, hawks' cage); Parker (park-keeper, ranger); Pinder, Pound(er) (impounder of stray animals); Reeve (reeve, chief magistrate, bailiff); Roadknight (mounted servant); Sa(w)yer (assayer); Sheriff (reeve of a shire); Todhunter (official fox-catcher); Toller, Tolman (toll-collector, tax-gatherer); Guard, Ward(e), Spier, Veil, Wait(e), Wakeman (watchman); Warren(d)er, Warner (warrener, game-keeper); Weather (keeper of wethers).

Military Affairs: Archer, Bowman; Arrowsmith (maker of iron arrow-heads); Armour (armourer), Ballester (crossbowman); Banner(man) (standard-bearer, herald); Beamer, Trumper (trumpeter); Bowyer (maker of bows), Stringer (maker of strings for bows); Fletcher (maker of arrows); Hansard (maker of cutlasses, daggers); Homer (maker of helmets); Mang(n)ell (operator of the mangonel, catapult); Quarrell (maker of the crossbolt, arrow); Scutt (scout, spy); Sworder (maker of swords); Taberer (drummer).

Law: Bailey (bailiff); Beadle; Dempster, Judge (judge); Gaylor (gaoler); Lawman; Plater (pleader, advocate); Reeve (reeve, chief magistrate); Sheriff (reeve of a shire); Sargent (officer of the courts); Sizer (juryman); Spickernell (sealer of the King's writs in Chancery); Sumner (summoner, officer citing and warning people to appear in court).

Medicine: Leach, Mayer, Physick (doctor, physician); N(o)urse (nurse); Pestell, Pothecary (druggist); Surgeon.

Seafaring: Ashman (shipman, sailor, pirate); Boatswain; Marner, Murdoch (from Scots Gaelic) (mariner); Seaman, Shipman, Waterman (sailor); Shipwright.

Country Life: As with local names, surnames from rural and agricultural pursuits preponderate over those from other trades and occupations. Farmer appears not to have acquired its present sense of one who "farms" land, whether as tenant or owner, until the end of the sixteenth century, but a number of terms served in its stead: Ackerman, Husband and Younghusband, Tiller, Tillman. A noteworthy group consists of names ending in -*art*, -*(h)ard*, -*ert*, and -*ward*, signifying herdsman or keeper especially of animals: Calvert (calf-herd); Colthard (colt-herd); Coward (cow-herd); Oxnard (oxen-herd); Forward, Hoggard (swineherd); Geldard (keeper of the geldings); Gossard (goose-herd); Herd; Shepherd (sheep-herd), Stoddart (keeper of the stud), to which may be added: Buck(man) (keeper of goats or stags); Bull(ock); Femister (sheep- or cow-herd); Foreman (swineherd); Tegg (shepherd); Vacher (cow-herd). Hayward was the guardian of fences, hedges and enclosures and controlled straying cattle.

Other names relating more or less closely to farm work include: Ashburner (maker of potash for fertiliser by burning ashes of wood, weeds and straw); Bean (grower of beans); Beeman (beekeeper); Col(e)man, Collier (charcoal-burner); Copestake, Hacker, Talboys, Woodger, Woodyer (woodcutter); Day (dairy-man or -maid); Driver, Drover; Sumner (packhorse man); Carter, Jagger, Leader, Tranter, Wain (carter, driver); Fewster (maker of saddle-trees); Forest(er), Kidder, Woodman, Woodward (wood-keeper, forester); Gardner, Garner (gardener); Groom, Steadman (farm-worker); Hewer (maker of hoes, mattocks, etc.); Mather (mower); Osler (bird-catcher); Pallister (fence-maker); Plowman, Ploughman; Sixsmith (scythe-maker), Sucksmith (ploughshare-maker); Thresher.

Hunting has given: Hunt(er); Huntsman; Gravenor, Grosvenor (great or chief huntsman); Chase, Venner (hunter); Fowler, Falconer, Hawk(er), Ostridge (hawker or falconer); Otter (otter-hunter); Trainer, Trapp (trapper).

Three major industries, the provision of food, clothing and shelter, and trades associated with them have given

Food: Ayler, Garlick (seller of garlic); Baker, Baxter, Backhouse, Cakebread, Fournier, Pester, Wafer, Whitbread (all bakers though some specialized); Bacon and Hogsflesh (pork butcher); Balmer, Spicer (seller of spices); Boucher, Butcher, Flesher, Maskery (butcher); Brasseur, Brewer, Brewster (brewer); Cannell (seller of cinnamon); Cheese, Cheeseman, Cheesewright, Furmenger, Ring (maker or seller of cheese); Cook(e), Lequeux (cook); Cooper, Cowper, Hooper, Tubman (maker of casks); Crocker, Potter (potter); Duck (breeder or seller of ducks); Fish(er), Petcher, Pike (fishmonger); Flanner (maker of pies, pancakes); Flower, Miller, Milner, Millman, Millward, Molyneux (miller); Garnet(t) (seller of pomegranates); Ginger (seller of ginger); Herring (seller of herring); Peppercorn, Culpepper, Peever, Pepper, Piper (seller of pepper); Pottinger (maker of soup, broth); Poulter (poulterer); Saffron (grower or seller of saffron); Salter (salt-worker or dealer); Service, Tapper, Taverner (seller of ale); Stockfish (seller of dried cod); Tripe (seller of tripe); Vinter (wine-merchant); Wort (greengrocer).

Clothing: Aguilar, Needler (needle-maker); Barker, Tanner, Leather, Skinner, Whittier (tanner, leather-worker); Blaxter (bleacher); Boot, Cordiner, Le Sueur, Sewer, Soutar (bootmaker); Buckler (buckle-maker); Butner, Button (button-maker); Capper (cap-maker); Chaucer (maker of hose, breeches, etc.); Clothier, Draper (cloth-maker); Dexter, Dyer, Lister (dyer); Flaxman (flax-grower or preparer of flax for linen); Fuller, Voller, Tucker, Walker, Tessler, Tozer (preparer of cloth by fulling, bleaching or teazing); Garland (maker of metal garlands or chaplets); Girdler (maker of girdles, belts); Glover (maker of gloves); Kemper, Kempster (comber of flax or wool); Packer (? of wool); Parminter, Taylor, Snider, Sloper (tailor); Sacker, Secker (maker of sackcloth); Pilcher (maker of pilches, outer garments of skin with the hair, later of leather or wool); Plumer (seller of plumes, feathers); Quaif(e) (maker of skullcaps); Ring (jeweller); Sharman, Shearer, Shirer (shearer or cutter of superfluous nap off woollen cloth); Silk (weaver or seller of silk); Simister (sempstress); Slaymaker (maker of slays used in weaving); Spindler, Trinder (maker of spindles); Tisserand, Weaver, Webb(er), Webster (weaver); Wimple (maker of wimples, veils); Wooller, Woolman (wool merchant).

Shelter: Wright (carpenter, joiner, craftsman); Carpenter; Joiner; Dauber, Parget(t)er (plasterer); Garnet(t) (maker of hinges); Locksmith, Lockyer (locksmith); Glaisher, Glass, Verrier, Window (glazier); Hillier, Rover, Tyler, Shingler, Slater, Spooner, Tillman (maker of tiles of wood, slate, etc.); Reader, Thatcher, Thaxter, Theaker, Sedgman (thatcher); Jenner (architect, master mason); Machen, Mason (mason); Painter, Stainer (painter); Limer, Whiter (white-washer); Workman (builder).

The worker in metal, the smith, has given a variety of forms from different sources: *An*gove (*the* smith) (Cornish); Faber, Feaver (Latin); Farrar, Fearon (French); and Goff(e) (Welsh, Breton, Cornish); in Scotland Caird, Gow (Scots Gaelic). Specialist trades have given: Arrowsmith (maker of iron arrowheads); Brownsmith (worker in copper or brass); Goldsmith, Offer (goldsmith); Greensmith (worker in copper); Shoesmith, Horsenail (maker of horseshoes); Locksmith, Lockyer (locksmith); Naismith (cutler); Sixsmith (scythe-maker); Sucksmith (maker of ploughshares); Whitesmith (tinsmith); Wildsmith (wheel-wright). The occurrence of the commonest of the smiths, the blacksmith, the worker in iron (the black metal as opposed to tin, the white metal), as a surname is supported uniquely by Lower in *Patronymia Britannica* 1860, though omitted from his *English Surnames*, 4th edition, 1875.

Other workers and dealers in metal include: Bloomer (maker of bloomers, iron or steel ingots); Brasher, Brazier (brazier, brassfounder); Calderon (maker of cauldrons); Cutler; Frobisher (furbisher, polisher of arms and armour); Ironmonger; Leadbeater, Plumb, Plummer (worker in lead); Rower, Wheeler, Wheelwright (wheelwright); Silver (silversmith); Steele (worker in steel); Tinker (tinker, metalworker); Latter, Turner (maker of, or worker with, a lathe).

The wright, the craftsman, the maker, has given not only the generic Wright but several specialist names including: Cartwright, Cheesewright, Plowright (maker of ploughs), Sievewright, Shipwright, Wainwright (wagon-builder), Wheelwright.

Miscellaneous trades and occupations: Banister, Coffin, Hott(er), Ripper (basket-maker); Barrell (barrel-maker); Bessemer (maker of besoms, brooms); Brayer (pestle-maker); Bushell (maker of bushel-vessels); Carver, Marbler (sculptor); Chandler (candle-maker or dealer); Cutter (tailor, barber, ? wood or stone cutter); Ferrier, Ferry (ferryman); Harberer (lodginghouse-keeper); Horner (maker of horn objects); Kilner (worker at a lime kiln); Latimer (interpreter); Lavender, Washer (laundry-(wo)man); Lodder (beggar); Miner; Minter (moneyer, coiner); Pegler (patcher, mender); Peutherer (maker of pewter vessels, etc.); Pott(er) (maker of crockery, metal pots, bells); Porter (gate- or door-keeper); Poyser (maker of scales); Purser (maker of pouches); Quilter (maker of quilted mattresses or coverlets); Raper, Roper (rope-maker); Ratter (ratcatcher); Retter (net-maker); Ridler, Sevier, Sievewright (sieve-maker); Ringer (bellringer); Scrivener (writer, copier, scribe, clerk); Soper (soap-maker); Taper (taper or candle maker); Tasker (task or piece worker as opposed to a day-labourer); Teacher; Trouncer (cudgel-maker); Ulman (oil-dealer); Wain (wagon-builder); Waxman (dealer in wax); Witcher (maker of chests).

Trading: Barter (barterer, exchanger); Chapman, Vender, Marchant (merchant); Mercer (merchant, especially dealer in luxury fabrics); Warman (dealer in wares); Farman, Pedlar, Pakeman (pedlar, hawker); Groser (wholesaler); Huxter (petty trader); Shopper (shopkeeper).

Entertainment: Champion, Kemp, Player (athlete); Crowther, Fiddler (fiddler); Dancer, Sailer, Hopper, Leaper, Tripper (dancer); Harper; Hollier, Hollister (brothel-keeper); Juggler; Luther (lute-player); Piper, Whistler (whistler, piper, flautist); Poyner (boxer); Restler (wrestler); Root, Rutter, Salter (player on the rote or psaltery); Rymer, Sangster, Singer, and in Scotland Baird (bard, minstrel, singer).

Like local surnames, occupational surnames are common enough in Scotland, France and other countries but again somewhat infrequent in Ireland in Irish names. Among those given by MacLysaght are:

The Church: Mac Anaspie, Gillespie (bishop); Mac Dagney, (O)Dane (dean); Mac Evanny, (O)Manahan, (O)Minogue, (O)Monaghan (monk).

Rank and Status: (O)Conroy (king); (O)Flahavan, (Mac)Glavin, (O)Lahiff, (O)Tuohy (ruler); (Mac)Kiernan, Mac Ternan, (O)Tierney (lord); (O)Herlihy (underlord); Mac Evilly, Eddary (knight); (Mac)Nally (poor man).

Military Affairs: (O)Feeny, (O)Hourihan, (O)Loan(e), (O)Loonan(e) (soldier, warrior); (O)Trohy (foot soldier); (O)Morchoe (sea-warrior).

Law: (Mac)Abraham, (Mac)Brehany (judge).

Medicine: Mac Alee, (O)Hickey (doctor, physician).

Seafaring: Mac Glinchy (mariner); (O)Moriarty, Mac Morrow, Murtagh (navigator).

Miscellaneous: Mac Ateer (craftsman); (O)Clery (clerk); Mac Cloughry (stonemason); (O)Drought (bridgeman); Mac Evoy (woodman); Mac Scollog (farmer); Gow (smith); (O)Anglim, (O)Graddy (champion); Cushnahane (defender); (O)Driscoll (intermediary); (O)Cuddihy (helper); Mac Glo(w)ry (spokesman); Mac Feely (chessplayer); (O)Riordan (royal bard); Mac Shanaghy (storyteller); (O)Markey (rider); (O)Timoney (driver); Weir (steward); (O)Scully (student); (O)Spillane (scythe ?-maker).

(iv) Surnames from nicknames

By far the largest groups of surnames derived from nicknames in England are those drawn from physical appearance and disposition. Animal names are common in, and may belong to, both groups. Much smaller groups describe relationship, strangeness in a community, occupation, notable feats, performances as in plays and pageants, wealth and poverty, time of birth or baptism, rent, and idiosyncrasies often of expression.

Nicknames of physical appearance denote beauty, deformity and ugliness, size which is often associated with strength, girth, and especially complexion and colour of hair.

Old French *bel, biau, beau* and Old English *feger* – fair, beautiful, handsome, have given besides Beale, Bell, Bew and Fair and their many variants several compound names such as Belcher (beautiful face), Beldham (fair lady), Belham (fine man), Bellamy (handsome friend), Bellmain (beautiful hand), Fairbairn (beautiful child), Fairbrother, Fairfax (beautiful hair), Fairfoot, Fairhead and Fairman. Bright, Sheer(e) and Trett also denote beauty. Standaloft, Standeven, Straight and Upright indicate characteristic posture.

Deformity and ugliness are seen in Bossey and Crooke (hunch-backed), Crookshank (bow-legged), Crump and Scaife (crooked), Beckett (little beak), Caddick (decrepit), Courtenay (short nose), Gammon and Smallbones (short-legged), Murch (dwarf), Smollett (little head), Shorthose (short neck), Godsmark (plague spot), Grealey (pock-marked), Lazar and Lepper (leper), while names of parts of the body such as Dent (tooth), Foot, Hand, Legg(e), Head, Tester (head), Shanks, Thum and Tooth may also indicate some abnormality. Baldness is denoted by Ball, Ballard, Caffin, Callow, Casbolt, Cave, Cavell, Chaff(e), Nott, and Snowball (bald patch).

Size and sometimes strength are seen in Bigg, (Le) Grand, Grant (big), Gully (giant), Leng, Long, Longfellow, Longman, Much, Storr and Stout. Fitch and Lank denote tallness or thinness. Smallness is seen in Bass, Bassett, Little, Littlejohn, Pettit, Short, Shortman, Small.

Girth and fatness are seen in Broad, Bradman (broad man), Bro(a)drib, ? Dodd, Fatt, Giffard (bloated), Le Gros, Gross, Kipps (son of the fat one), Metcalfe (meat-calf, a calf fattened for food), Pauncefoot and Puddephat (round belly), Round, Thick (thickset), and Whalebelly.

Complexion and colour of hair are denoted by Blake, Blanchard, Blank, Blundell, Blunt, Frost, Snow, White (white, fair, light, pale) and Whitehead, Whitlock; Black, with Blake in its opposite sense from white, (black) and Blacklock; Brooman, Brown(e), Browning, Brownjohn, Burnett, Dark(e), Dunn(e), Swart (brown, dark); Gray, Grey (grey) and Harlock (hoary lock); Read(e), Rousell, Rudd, Russell, Sorrell (red).

Resemblance to animals is seen in Bird, Bott (toad), Bull and Farr (bull), Bullock, Coote ("bald as a coot"), Corbin, Corbett and Raven (raven-haired), Crowe, Fox and Todd (fox), Gelding, Grew (crane), Luttrell (otter), Paddock (toad, frog), Partridge, Rook(e), Ruddick (robin), Teale (teal, duck), Titmuss (titmouse), Vidler (wolf-face), Wigg (beetle), Woodcock.

Nicknames descriptive of disposition denote many aspects of temper, mood and morals and the high or low regard in which a person was held.

Goodness: Bonham, Bonner, Good and Goodbody, -child, -enough (!), -fellow, -lad, Godsal (good soul, honest man).

Cheerfulness, Happiness: Bligh, Blythe, Carless (without care), Gay, Merriman, Merry, Root, Sealey, Tait.

Love, Loyalty, Friendship: Darling, Drury, Leaf, Leveson, Love, Luff, Marrow, Paramour, Sweet and Sweetman, – apple, -ing, Truelove, Wellbeloved, Dowsett; Comfort, Faithful, Friend, Bonamy, Goodwin, Leuty, Trigg(e), True, Trueman, Wine, Winn.

Bravery, Boldness, Resolution: Bream, Durant, Fear (ultimately from Old French *F(i)er* – bold, fierce, proud), Hardy, Keen, Manley, Snell, Standfast, Sturdy, Whatman, Wheat, Wight, Ventris (adventurous).

Strength, Austereness: Starke, Sterne, Stiff, Stith.

Liveliness, Briskness: Baud, Crank, Gaylord, Kedge, Quick, Ready, Sharp(e), Smart, Spark(e)(s), Volant, Warme.

Courtesy: Curtis, Fane, Gent, Gentle, Gentleman, Hendy.

Nobility: Free, Fry(e), Large (generous), Noble.

Truthfulness: Vardy, Verity.

Wisdom, Sagacity: Glew, Prudhomme, Sage, Secrett, Ware, Wise, Wiseman, Wake, Witty.

Mildness, Guilelessness: Coy, Daft, Fine, May, Mildmay, Maiden, Meek(e), Simple, Still.

Pride: Proud, Proudfoot, Rank.

Wildness, Savagery, Ferocity, Cruelty: Buffard, Grill, Purchase, Rama(d)ge, Redwood, Savage, Sturdy, Tempest, Tyson, Wild(e), Wildblood, Wroth.

Deceitfulness, Craftiness, Cunning: Fage, Gabb, Gain, Pratt, Pretty, Quant, Yapp.

Greed: Bevin (drink wine), Gulliford, Greedy.

Laziness: Dolittle, Dormer, Drane (drone), Gotobed, Idle, Sleeper, Tardew.

Foolishness: Follett, Follenfant, Giddy, Gigg, Samways, Tott.

Miserliness: Miskin, Penny, Pennyfeather, Treasure.

Prodigality: Scattergood.

Sensuality: Bairnsfather, Blandamore, Crawcour, Fullalove, Lickerish, Spendlove, Toplady, Toplass.

Qualities associated with animals: Agnew (lamb), Best (beast), Brock (badger), Buck, Bull, Bullock, Cheever and Chivers (goat), Cock, Coote ("daft as a coot"), Cuckow, Conning (rabbit), Caddow and Dawe (jackdaw), Doe, Dove, Drake (dragon), Fawn, Finch, Fowle, Fox, Hart, Hawke, Hind, Hogg, Jay(e), Keat (kite), Lamb, Lappin(g) (rabbit), Lovell (little wolf), Martyr (weasel), Mutton, Papigay (parrot), Peacock, Pidgeon, Pigg, Pink (finch), Pinnock (hedge-sparrow), Pullan (colt), Purcell (little pig), Puscat, Raven, Roe, Roebuck, Scarfe (cormorant), Sparrow, Speck and Speight (woodpecker), Squirrel, Stirk and Stott (bullock), Turtle (dove), Veal(e) (calf), Wildbore (wild boar), Wilder (wild animal), Wildgoose, Wolf(e).

Minor groups of nicknames.

Relationship: Ayer (heir), Cousen (cousin, nephew, relation), Samson (dame's son), Dobell (twin), Eame and Yemm (son of the uncle), Elder, Senior, Fillary and Fitzroy (king's son), Foster (foster parent or child), Maufe (-in law), Neave (nephew), Odam (son- or brother-in-law), Old (senior), Soane (son, junior), Suckling, Twinn, Widdowson, Young, Younger. To these may be added names denoting a stranger, newcomer or foreigner: Guest, Newcom(b)(e), Newman, Strange.

Occupation: Balhatchet (executioner), Boutflour (miller), Brennan (burn hand, the official who executed the penalty or his victim), Dixey (chorister), Fish (fishmonger), Golightly, Rideout and Trotter (messenger), Goodall (brewer of good ale), Hollowbread (baker of holy bread), Kellogg (pork butcher), Knatchbull (butcher), Shotbolt (archer), Stroulger (astrologer), Tazewell (efficient teaser of cloth), Tredgett (juggler), Warr (warrior).

Notable feats:

In Pageants and Plays: Bishop, Pope, Postle (apostle), Saint, Virgin, Prof(f)it(t) (prophet), Baron, Earle, Duke, Lord, King, Roy.

Of Strength: Armstrong, Strongitharm (strong in the arm), Bradfer and Bradford (arm of iron), Fortman (strong hand), Ironside, Shakeshaft, Shakespeare, Strong, Turnbull, Vigours (vigorous).

Of Agility: Harfoot (hare foot), Rawbone (roe leg), Skeat (swift), Skipper (dancer), Springer (jumper).

Of Singing: Lark, Nightingale, Wrenn.

Of Travel: Palmer, Pilgrim and Peregrine (pilgrim), Parsley (cross the water), Passmore (cross sea).

Of Scholarship: Beauclerk (fine scholar).

Idiosyncrasies:

Of Expression: Bonger (Good day!), Bonser (Good sir!), Debney (God bless!), Drinkale (Drink health, luck!), Fettiplace (Make room!), Godbear (God be here!), Godsave (God's sake!), Good(d)ay, Goodspeed ([May] God prosper [you]!), Goodyear, Pardew (By God!), Purefoy (By [my] faith!).

Other: Belch, Drinkwater, Startup, Woodruff (user of woodruff, a sweet-scented herb), Scarlett (from favourite colour), Tabard (sleeveless coat), Toy(e) (close-fitting cap).

Time of Birth or Baptism: Averill (April), Christmas, Feverel (February), Midwinter, Pentecost, Winter.

Wealth, Poverty: Bean (not worth a bean), Brockless (without breeches), Moneypenny (many a penny), Poor, Rich(e).

Rent: ? Farthing, ? Hal(f)penny, ? Hallmark (half mark), ? Shilling.

Surnames from nicknames of physical description appear to predominate in this class in Scots, Irish and Welsh. The following are illustrative: MacKenzie (Scots comely), Cam (Scots crooked, cross-eyed, one-eyed), Cameron (Scots crooked or hooked nose), Campbell (Scots wry or crooked mouth), Cashen (Irish bent), Kennedy (ugly head), MacLeod (Scots ugly), Meikle (Scots big), Meiklejohn (big John), Moir (Scots big), Vaughan (Welsh small); Boyd (Scots ? yellow-[haired]), Corcoran (Irish purple-[faced]), Duff (Scots, Irish black), Gough (Welsh red), Gwynn and Wynn (Welsh white), Lloyd (Welsh grey), MacGlashan (Scots, Irish grey or grey-green), MacIlroy (Scots, Irish red), Moyle (Cornish bald), Voyle (Welsh bald).

3. *Their Linguistic Origins*

It will have been apparent in the foregoing accounts of the rise and kinds of surnames that countries are not dependent on their own linguistic resources, but that from the circumstances of history – invasion, conquest, settlement, and the affairs of ordinary men – the surnames of England derive not only from English origins but also notably from French, that the surnames of Ireland derive not only from Irish but also from English, Scots and French. The nature of this indebtedness has been suggested already in the discussion of surnames of relationship and local surnames; here it may be convenient to examine it in relation to French in surnames of rank, status, office and occupation and in surnames from nicknames, within the limits of the preceding lists.

In *The Making of English*, Henry Bradley summarized the kinds of objects and ideas chiefly denoted by the words that came into the English vocabulary from French during the two centuries following the Norman Conquest. He writes:

Readers of *Ivanhoe* will remember the acute remark which Scott puts into the mouth of Wamba the jester, that while the living animals – *ox, sheep, calf, swine, deer* – continued to bear their native names, the flesh of those animals as used for food was denoted by French words, *beef, mutton, veal, pork, bacon, venison.* The point of the thing is, of course, that the "Saxon" serf had the care of the animals when alive, but when killed they were eaten by his "French" superiors.

He finds a similar significance in the French origin of *master, servant, butler, buttery, bottle, dinner, supper, banquet,* of terms relating to law, government and property, of titles of nobility with the exception of *earl,* and of many of the terms relating to military matters.

The relevance of these observations to the origin of surnames will readily be seen though the dichotomy is by no means absolute.

In surnames associated with the Church, four groups may be distinguished but with no suggestion that those from French, though greater in number, imply any superiority in the hierarchy. The groups are those from Old English: Abbott, Pope, Priest; from Old French: Cannon, Chapl(a)in, Clarges, Clark(e), Dean, Frere, Friar, Pardner, Parsons, Sexton (sacristan), Vicars; from Old English or Old French: Deacon, Nunn, Prior; and the pairs of names, one from Old English, the other from Old French: Bishop and Veck, Monk and Moyne.

In surnames derived from rank and status, King from Old English and Roy from Old French exist side by side; but with the exception of Earl(e) and Lord other titles of nobility are from Old French. Names associated with chivalry are Knight and Childe from Old English, Bachelor and Squire from Old French.

In the ranks below the nobility and knighthood, names of roughly equivalent status from Old English and Old French frequently occur as in Old English Freebody, Freeman and Old French Frank, Franklin; Portman and Burgess; Thain(e), Dring (from Old Norse) and Sargent, Tennant. But names denoting servants, peasants and serfs, such as Knape, Ladd, Mann, Swan(n) and Thew are wholly English.

Most names of officers of royal or noble households are from Old French, exceptions being Burl(e), Grieve, Horder and Stewart from Old English and Grave from Old Norse. Among minor officials and servants, names from Old French are slightly more numerous than those from Old English.

In military affairs, names from Old French outnumber names from Old English roughly two to one, with Beamer and Bowman from Old English respectively equivalent to Trumper and Archer from Old French.

Names from law are almost equally divided between English and French. In medicine only Leech has survived from Old English; in seafaring only Marner from Old French.

When, however, Bradley goes on to assert that "In industrial civilization the French-speaking strangers were no doubt greatly superior to the native population, and it is probably for this reason that nearly all the commonest designations of classes of tradesmen and artisans are of French origin," the evidence of surnames hardly bears him out.

English has provided rather more surnames associated with the preparation and storage of food than French, though there are several equivalent terms. Usually surnames from English are more common, as with Baker and Baxter opposed to Fournier; Brewer and Brewster opposed to Brasseur; Cheeseman and Cheesewright opposed to Furmenger; Cook opposed to Lequeux; and Miller, Milner and Millman opposed to Flower and Molyneux. Exceptions, however, are found in French Bacon opposed to English Hogsflesh and Butcher to Flesher.

The preparation of raw materials for and the making and sale of clothing have given many more surnames from English than from French, not least because of such groups in English as Barker, Tanner, Leather, Skinner, Whittier; Dexter, Dyer and Lister; Fuller, Tucker, Walker, Tessler and Tozer; and Webb(e), Webber, Webster and Weaver; but three common surnames derive from French: Boot, Draper and especially Taylor.

Similarly, surnames from the provision of shelter are predominantly English because of the groups associated with roofing: Hillier, Rover, Tyler, Shingler, Spooner and Tiller opposed to French Slater; and Reader, Thatcher, Thaxter, Theaker and Sedgman. English Wright has equivalents in French Carpenter and Joiner. Mason is of French origin.

As was shown above, the smith has given a number of surnames from different linguistic sources, but English Smith, as Cottle comments, is "Easily the commonest surname in England and Wales (though Jones is far ahead in Wales alone), Scotland and USA, and [was] the fifth in Ireland in 1890." To Smith have to be added names from specialist trades such as Arrowsmith, Goldsmith, etc., though the first element in Sucksmith is French.

Other workers in metal have given such pairs of names as English Naismith and French Cutler, Leadbeater and Plumb, Latter and Turner, but for the most part the rest are of English origin.

Like the smith, the wright has also given several surnames from specialist trades, all of which are English.

Miscellaneous trades and occupations show slightly more English than French names and few equivalent names from both languages. Trading has given especially Chapman from Old English, but other common names such as Barter, Marchant and Mercer are from Old French. Names from entertainment appear to be almost equally derived from English and French origins.

Surnames from country life are predominantly from English sources, exceptions including Vacher, Talboys, Summer, Tranter, Fewster, Gardner, Garner, Osler and Pallister, with Femister, Copestake and Sucksmith combining French and English elements. In hunting, Old English has given Hunt, Hunter, Fowler, Hawker, Otter and Trapp, Old French Gravenor, Grosvenor, Chase, Venner, Falconer, Ostridge and Trainer.

Surnames from nicknames are derived from Old English (with a sprinkling from Middle English and Old Norse) and from Old French in the ratio of two to one, with nicknames denoting physical appearance and disposition making the largest groups in both languages. Equivalent names are rare except for those denoting beauty, baldness and girth. Those denoting beauty have been given above. Baldness is denoted by Ball, ? Ballard, Callow, Casbolt, Nott and Snowball from English and Caffin, Cave, Cavell and Chaff(e) from French; and girth by Broad, Bradman, Brodrib, Fatt, Kipps, Metcalfe, Puddephat, Thick and Whalebelly from English and Giffard, Le Gros, Gross, Pauncefoot and Round from French. It is perhaps not without significance in the relations between the two races that only in the group denoting wildness, savagery, ferocity and cruelty do nicknames from French outnumber those from English, French giving Buffard, Purchase, Rama(d)ge, Savage, Sturdy, Tempest, and Tyson, English Grill, Redwood, Wild(e), Wildblood and Wroth.

IV THE SURNAMES OF NEWFOUNDLAND

1. National Origins

As was indicated at the beginning of this Introduction, several races have contributed to the stock of Newfoundland surnames, but an attempt to provide statistical information on their national origins presents some difficulty since many names belong to more than one national group. Some, like those with the prefix O and Murphy, Connolly, Ryan and Hogan, for instance, are indubitably and solely Irish, but a seemingly Scots surname like Campbell, besides having been introduced into Ireland by immigrants, may also have an Irish origin. Similarly such names as Brennan, Canning and Collins may be English as well as Irish, and some like Black, Brown(e), Cook(e), Col(e)man and Murray, whatever their linguistic origins, are surnames of England, Scotland and Ireland. Martin, to take one example, is common to England, Scotland, Ireland, France and Germany. The phenomenon will be found in scores of entries in the Dictionary.

With it in mind, the following estimates may be made. Of some 3,000 surnames in Newfoundland, 2,130 or 71 per cent of the total are surnames of England and Wales, 1,200 or 40 per cent of Ireland, 530 or 17.66 per cent of Scotland, 300 or 10 per cent of the Channel Islands, and 260 or 8.7 per cent of France. Another 120 or 4 per cent are surnames of probably thirteen other countries, those of Germany with 30 or 1 per cent being the most numerous. For reasons shown in Part II of the Introduction, the number of surnames of Scotland may be greater than that given here. In addition, the Dictionary contains over two hundred variants of surnames apparently not recorded elsewhere, some of which, it would seem, are peculiar to Newfoundland. Variants of French (including Basque, Breton and Channel Islands) names number roughly 109, of Irish names 62, of English names 35. The more interesting are discussed below.

How to determine whether a surname with multiple national origins is of England, Ireland, Scotland or elsewhere in any one instance is often impossible without knowledge of the history of the family, though some kinds of external evidence may be not without validity.

Certain baptismal names, though not an infallible guide, often provide a clue as with names of saints and popes common in Irish Catholic families: Patrick, Joseph, Bernard, Augustine, Francis, Ignatius, Michael, Lawrence, Leo, Pius, Gregory, Ambrose and Dominic. Baptismal names from the Old Testament tend to occur in Protestant families and may therefore as a rule be taken as English: Adam, Abraham, Isaac, Jacob, Moses, Solomon and Samuel, as may such names from miscellaneous sources as Chesley, Reginald, Harold, Leslie, Alfred and Harvey. Common Welsh names – David, Lloyd, Owen, Scots – Alexander, Angus, Archibald, Donald, Duncan, Malcolm, and German – Karl (or Carl) and Otto are less trustworthy as guides to nationality because of their use by people with no Welsh, Scots or German connections. A few French baptismal names are in use: Arsène, Baptist(e), Lucien, Narcisse anglicized as Narcissus, Romieu as Romeo, and Remy as Remi, but most families of French extraction have adopted the same names as those used by Irish Catholics.

A second kind of evidence, though limited in its range, is in the spelling of the surname with a final -e. Although Cottle states that Cook is "A good old surname that ought not to have the snobbish -e," and that in Earle "the -e is pointless" (though in other names like Brooke and Greene he finds grammatical justification for it), the fact remains that in Irish usage the form with final -e is the only one recognized by MacLysaght for Brooke, Browne, Cooke, Deane, Foote, Locke, Moore, Sharpe among others, and usually for Dunne, and so may indicate an Irish rather than an English name.

Thirdly, the location of families either in particular settlements or in wider areas of Newfoundland may be indicative of the national origins of their surnames. Parts of the South Coast were settled by men from metropolitan France and St. Pierre, parts of the West Coast also by French and Acadians. Hence, when such names as Billard and Blanchard, which are of both England and France, occur in these areas, the question of French origins may well be raised. Curtis, a surname of England and Ireland, occurs at Virgin Arm and Campbellton in the Twillingate area and also at Trepassey. Since the first two settlements consist of families which have almost wholly English surnames, it may be assumed that Curtis there is also likely to be English; but at Trepassey, where surnames are practically all Irish, there it is likely to be Irish. Similarly, Colbert, a surname of England, France and Ireland, in the context of St. Michaels and Bauline on the Southern Shore of the Avalon Peninsula is much more likely to be Irish than French or English.

When they are applicable, all three of the preceding types of evidence should of course be taken into consideration.

The best evidence of all, however, occurs when a family has remained in one location since its first days in Newfoundland – Andrews and Dawe in Port de Grave, Burt in Old Perlican, Badcock and Bradbury in Bay Roberts and many more – and documentary evidence in wills, registers, inscriptions on gravestones, obituary notices and elsewhere attests an early member as of Waterford, Glasgow, Exmouth or wherever the family has sprung from.

2. Surnames from England and Wales

The following estimate of the contributions of the counties of England to the stock of Newfoundland surnames is based for the most part on the numbers counted by Guppy as described earlier in this Introduction. Where a surname in Guppy's lists occurs in more than one county, that with the highest score is credited with it, though the ascription of a surname to a particular county by this process may not always reflect its origin as a surname of Newfoundland. The number for Devon includes many additional names noted by Spiegelhalter, but had similar studies for Cornwall, Dorset, Somerset, Hampshire and Gloucester been available, the order of frequency might well have been changed. Names having the same highest score for more than one county are reckoned in the total for all the counties concerned. A few names in other counties have been taken from other sources. No county affiliation has been found for more than five hundred names.

In order of descending frequency, then, with the reservation made above, surnames from English counties and the broader regions of North and South Wales rank thus:

Rank	County or Region	Number of Surnames	Percentage of 2130 English & Welsh Surnames in Newfoundland
1	Devon	468	21.9
2	Dorset	119	5.6
3	Somerset	88	4.1
4	North Wales 18		
	South Wales 20		
	Monmouth 22	60	2.8
5	Cornwall	55	2.6
6	Northumberland	47	2.2
7	Wiltshire	41	1.9
8	Yorkshire WR	38	1.8
9	Gloucestershire	36	1.7
10a	Derbyshire	35	1.6
10b	Lancashire	35	1.6
12	Hampshire	33	1.5
13a	Cheshire	31	1.5
13b	Kent	31	1.5
15	Sussex	30	1.4
16a	Nottinghamshire	27	1.2
16b	Suffolk	27	1.2
18	Warwickshire	25	1.1
19a	Leicestershire and Rutland	24	1.1
19b	Worcestershire	24	1.1
21	Durham	23	1.1
22a	Cumberland and Westmorland	22	1.0
22b	Norfolk	22	1.0
22c	Staffordshire	22	1.0
22d	Yorkshire ER, NR	22	1.0

The remaining thirteen counties have each contributed less than one per cent.

In the circumstances of Newfoundland's trade with the West Country, there is no wonder that Devon with such ports as Exmouth, Plymouth, Barnstaple and Bideford should head the list with such a commanding lead. Nearby counties, Dorset, Somerset, Cornwall, Wiltshire and Gloucestershire, with such ports as Poole, Weymouth, Bridport, Bridgwater, Falmouth and Bristol, also appear in the first ten though the combined total of their surnames falls far short of those from Devon. What is surprising and unexplained is the comparatively large number of names from the north of England, especially from Northumberland, Yorkshire WR and Lancashire, unless the answer is to be found in the influence of men from the agricultural West Country who migrated to the industrial North in search of employment during the Industrial Revolution; for the North was always remote from trade with Newfoundland and Newfoundland had no obvious industrial attractions except in mining to a small extent.

Accounts of the connections between the West Country and Newfoundland are to be found in the writings of Prowse, Rogers, Lounsbury, McLintock, and for the Avalon Peninsula especially in Seary, Story and Kirwin, as listed in the Bibliography.

Most English surnames have remained unchanged in Newfoundland though a number of minor variants may be observed, some of which no doubt may also occur in England.

The commonest is simply a change in spelling which does not, however, indicate a change in pronunciation: Berg for Bergh, Bridal for Bridle or Bridel(l), Coaker for Coker, Gaden for ? Gayden, Myrden for Murden, Petten for Petton, Willar for Willer. Others by a change of vowel or consonant suggest a local phonetic spelling: Ashbourne for Ashburn, Bavis for Beavis, Bavidge for Bev(e)ridge or Babbage, Crimp for Crump, Critch for Crutch, Cullihall for Collihole, Enwood for Inwood, Gidge for Gedge, Hindy for Hendy, Keeping for Kippin(g), Mesh for Mash, Nippard for Neppard, Peckford for ? Pickford, Roost for Rust, Tuffin for Tiffen, Combden for ? Compton, Crisby for Grisby, Durdle for ? Turtle, Skeard for Skarth, Vater(s) for Faytour or Fetters.

Vowels and consonants may also be added or deleted, sometimes it seems to replace an unknown or unfamiliar name by a name which is a familiar word, sometimes to form a name more easily pronounced than the English original: Regular for Regler, Colford for ? Cullyford, Normore for Narramore, Lomond for ? Lowman, Sansford for ? San(d)ford, Shinnicks for Senneck or Sinnocks, Stansbury for Stanbury, Kinden for ? Kingdon, Kinslow for Kingslow, Taplin for Tam(p)lin or Tambling. The inclusion of a vowel between two consonants to form a bridge or transitional syllable is shown in English usage in the forms Whiteaway for Whiteway, Hoddinott for Hodnett, the first of which is preserved in Newfoundland speech, the second in the Newfoundland form of the name.

The inclusion or exclusion of initial H, a phenomenon by no means unusual in many dialects of English, is shown in Newfoundland in such forms as Hedderson for ? Edison, Hallingham for Allingham, Hefford for Efford, Inder for Hender.

The relationship between names formed by these processes and their English originals is for the most part fairly readily recognizable, but more complex changes create variants more distantly removed from the originals in, for example, such names as Coveyduck for Cob(b)ledick and Spingle for Spigurnel or Spickernell.

In addition, the following surnames preserved in Newfoundland, though known or presumed to be of English origin, do not appear to have been recorded or discussed by any of the authorities on surnames consulted in this study, except that those marked by G, M, K, have been recorded, though not interpreted or discussed, by Guppy, Matthews or Kirwin.

Abery, Ansford

Batterton, Beason, Belben and Belbin (M), Bigsby and Bixby (M), Bingle, Breckon, Brentnall, Briffett, Broydell, Brumsey

Channing (G), Chapter, Clatney, Comben, Comby and Cumby, Connock, Cornick, Coxworthy, Crant, Crickard, Critchell, Crowdell, Cullimore (G), Curnell

Dewland (M), Dewling, Dinney, Dowden, Duder, Dunford (G), Durdle

Eales (M), Ebbs, Ezekiel

Fagner, Feener, Fiander, Finney (G), Fizzard (M), Fost, Fowlow, Fradsham, Framp, Frecker

? Gamberg, Genge, Goobie (M), Go(o)sney, Granter, Gullage Guzzwell (M)

Hancott, Harnum, Hattie, Hefferman, Hefferton, Hepditch and Hipditch (G), ? Herlidan, Hewardine, Hiscott, Hobey (G), Hollett, Hounsell (G), Hoven, Hubley, Hurdle, Husk, Hustin(s)

Jestican

Karn (G), Kearley

Lamswood (M), Langer (M), Lanning, Lash, Lavis, Layden, Learning, Leawood, Lethbridge, Lingard (G), Lushman, Lydall, Lythcott, Lyver

Mavin, Maybee, Melendy and Melindy, Mifflen and Mifflin (K), Minty (G), Mosdell, Motty, Mowday, Murcell, Mutford

Newhook, Noftall and Noftle

Penwell and Penwill, Pinhorn, Pippy, Polem, Pushie, Pynn (M)

Ringman

Scaplen (M), Shambler (M), Sheaves, Spurvey, Strangemore, Stride and Stryde (G), Strugnell (M)

Trelegan, Tremills, Trimm

Vincer, Vineham

Walkins, Welcher, Whiffen and Whiffin, Wigh, Wimbleton, Wornell, Worthman

Yabsley, Yarn

? Zillman

For various reasons, a not uncommon one by deserters from the Royal Navy being to avoid detection, some families have changed their surnames: Chapter to Shapter, Crisby to Martin and again to Crisby, Hoddinott to Holmes and again to Hoddinott, Cuff to Matchem, Peyton to Penton, Rexford to Rixon, Samson to Sansome. In three instances, the change appears to have led to the creation of an entirely new name: Padley to Paddle, Terrifield to Torraville, Warrington to Waddleton.

3. *Surnames from Ireland*

In *The Surnames of Ireland* (1969, 1973), MacLysaght has given information on over 4,000 names of which 1,200 have been traced in Newfoundland. The repetition of some names in more than one county or province gives a gross total of 1,339 names which may be broadly analysed thus:

Rank	Province	Number of Surnames	Percentage of 1,339 Irish Surnames in Newfoundland
1	Ulster	414	30.9
2	Munster	329	24.6
3	Leinster	301	22.5
4	Connacht	174	13.0
	General	66	4.9
	Unspecified	55	4.1

The number of surnames from Ulster is perhaps unexpectedly large, but no single county in the province ranks in the first ten of all counties, probably because from its total of 414 names as many as 174 are given for Ulster in general.

The order of descending frequency by counties showing more than one per cent of 1,339 surnames is as follows:

Rank	County	Number of Surnames	Percentage of 1,339 Irish Surnames in Newfoundland
1	Cork (Munster)	120	9.0
2	Tipperary (Munster)	64	4.8
3	Clare (Munster)	58	4.3
4	Kilkenny (Leinster)	57	4.3
5	Galway (Connacht)	56	4.2
6	Wexford (Leinster)	54	4.0
7	Kerry (Munster)	50	3.7
8	Limerick (Munster)	48	3.5
9	Waterford (Munster)	47	3.5
10	Dublin (Leinster)	44	3.3
11	Donegal (Ulster)	37	2.8
12	Antrim (Ulster)	35	2.6
13	Mayo (Connacht)	31	2.3
14	Down (Ulster)	30	2.2
15	Tyrone (Ulster)	29	2.2
16	Armagh (Ulster)	28	2.1
17	Fermanagh (Ulster)	23	1.7

Rank	County	Number of Surnames	Percentage of 1,339 Irish Surnames in Newfoundland
18	Sligo (Connacht)	22	1.6
19	Monaghan (Ulster)	21	1.6
20a	Offaly (formerly King's) (Leinster)	20	1.5
20b	Derry (Ulster)	20	1.5
22a	Leix or Laoighis (formerly King's) (Leinster)	18	1.3
22b	Meath (Leinster)	18	1.3
22c	Roscommon (Connacht)	18	1.3
22d	Westmeath (Leinster)	18	1.3
26	Cavan (Ulster)	17	1.3
27	Louth (Leinster)	16	1.2
28a	Kildare (Leinster)	14	1.0
28b	Leitrim (Connacht)	14	1.0

All thirty-two counties have contributed to the stock of Irish names in Newfoundland, but Cos. Carlow, Longford and Wicklow have provided less than one per cent.

A detailed analysis of surnames in Ireland, with particular reference to numerical strength and distribution, is to be found in Matheson.

· Accounts of Irish emigration in general are to be found in Redford and W. F. Adams, of emigration to and settlement in Newfoundland in McLintock, Mannion, Rogers, and Seary, Story and Kirwin, as listed in the Bibliography.

Surnames of Ireland are common almost everywhere in Newfoundland with the most frequent and the largest concentrations in communities throughout the Avalon Peninsula except along the shores of Trinity Bay.

About ninety surnames of Ireland have been changed in Newfoundland, but most of the changes have been of little significance: Coady for Cody, Dorsey for Dorcey, Gleason for Gleeson, Guilfoyle for Gilfoyle, Keefe for Keeffe, Meaney for Meany, Shanahan for Shannahan. A few changes show the intrusion of a transitional syllable (not unknown in Ireland in, for example, Branigan for Brangan, Berrigan for Bergen, and noted also in England): Darrigan for Dargan, Hartery for Hartry, Hennebury for Henebry, S(h)ugarue for S(h)ugrue. Sometimes the spelling of an unstressed vowel is changed: Hannifan for Hanifin, Hannihan for Hanahan, Hoben for Hoban, Laffin for Laffan, Merner for Mernagh, ? Shiner for Shinnagh. Other variants, apparently unknown to MacLysaght, include Alyward for Aylward, Mahaney and Mehaney for ? Mahony, Milley for Millea, Monster for Munster, O'Donald for O'Donnell, Reardigan and Reddigan for ? Redahan, Kilfoy for ? Gilfoyle, Caravan for Kerevan, Sesk for Sisk, Handrigan for ? Hanrahan.

The prefix O often appears to have been retained or dropped indiscriminately. Mac has usually been retained. Names which are known or believed to be Irish, but are not in MacLysaght, are Clance, Galgay, ? Hanton, McAbee, ? Shortis, ? Stamp, Strapp.

Accounts of the Irish in Newfoundland are to be found in W. F. Adams, Beaudoin, Harvey, Lounsbury, McLintock, Mannion, Nemec, Prowse, Rogers, Seary, Story and Kirwin, and Seary, as listed in the Bibliography.

4. Surnames from Scotland

Evidence for the number and distribution of surnames from Scotland in Newfoundland is less satisfactory than that for names from England and Ireland. Many Scots names are found in Ireland, especially in Ulster, and so may have been introduced into Newfoundland as Irish rather than Scots; and of a total of some 530 names identified as Scots by Black, only 353 are given a location by Guppy who, moreover, frequently gives a broad region – South of the Forth and Clyde, North of Scotland, Scottish Border Counties – rather than a county as the home of a name.

The following analysis is therefore at best inadequate and tentative.

1	Unspecified	62
2	South	52
3	Ayrshire	39
4	Scattered	20
5a	Aberdeenshire	19
5b	Dumfriesshire	19
5c	Perthshire	19
8	Lanarkshire	17
9a	Argyllshire	16
9b	Galloway (Kirkcudbrightshire and Wigtownshire)	16

Eighteen counties and three regions contributed one to ten names and eight counties made no contributions whatever.

If a conclusion may be drawn, it is that the southern and southwestern counties have made the greatest contribution to the stock of Scots surnames in Newfoundland, whether they were introduced directly or via Ireland. Scots names concentrated in the southwest of Newfoundland, most of them introduced by settlers from Nova Scotia, may, however, account for more widespread origins.

Most Scots surnames have remained unchanged, though a few variants have been observed: Clayson for Clason, Jewer for ? Dewar, McCrate for ? MacCraith, Manderton for Manderston, Mootrey and Mutrey for Moutray, Mourne for ? Mouren, Patry for Petrie, Roost for Roust (Rust).

The following, known or believed to be Scots, are not given in Black: Dustan, Etsell, McAbee (if not Irish).

Historians appear to have neglected the impact of Scots settlement in Newfoundland.

5. *Surnames from France*

The contribution of French surnames (excluding those traced in the Channel Islands) to Newfoundland has come from many parts of the country, but apparently in no great numbers from any particular area. The number of names which are obviously Breton or Basque, for example, is remarkably small.

Without exception, all have lost any diacritical marks (accents, cedilla, diaeresis) they may have had, and about half of the two hundred or so have undergone some change or other either to make them easier on the English (or Irish) tongue or to attempt a phonetic spelling of a strange-sounding name.

The following examples, though not exhaustive, will serve to show the kinds of changes that have taken place: Benteau for Beneteau, Bonia for Bon(n)ier, Brockerville for Brocqueville, Cammie for Camin, Cormey for Cormier, Cornect for Cornec (Breton), Cuza for ? Cuzin, Deluney for Delaunay, Devoe for ? Devau, Dubie for Dub(a) (Breton), Duffenais and Duffney for Dufresnay, Dutrey for Dutre(u)il, Etchegary for Etchegaray (Basque), Figary for ? Figuier, Fushell for Fusil, Hawco for Hautcoeur, Jesseau and Jesso for Chasson, Kerfont for Kerfot (Breton), Kerrotret for Kérobert (Breton), Lagatdu for Lagade(u)c (Breton), Lasaga and Lasage (pronounced lisigar, with the accent on the first syllable) for Lissagaray or Lissaragay (Basque), Madore for Madamour, Morassie and Morazie for Morancé, Necho and Nicho for Nicaud, Presh(y)on and Presuyon for Perrichon or Perruchon, Pygas for Pigasse, Remo for Rémon(d) or Rémont, Rhymes for Rheims,

Robere for Robert, Rouzes for Rouzé, Rubia for Roubieu, Taleck for Tal(l)ec (Breton), Thomey for ? Thomieu, Tibbo for T(h)ibaud, Tricco for Tricot.

A few surnames have been translated into English or Irish: Aucoin to O'Quinn, Benoît to Bennett, Le Blanc to White, Le Jeune to Young.

No record has been found of the following names which are known, believed or appear to be French: Beaucage, Berniquez, Desbarats, Gaultois, Kerfot, Lecountre.

The South and West Coasts of Newfoundland have been the main areas of French settlement: the South Coast receiving settlers from metropolitan France and St. Pierre, the West Coast also from Acadia and the east coast of the Northern Peninsula of Newfoundland, a part of what was once the French Shore.

Accounts of the French in Newfoundland are to be found in Prowse and Rogers, as listed in the Bibliography.

6. *Surnames from the Channel Islands*

As far as is known, no comprehensive study of the surnames of the Channel Islands exists and the following list has been compiled from such sources as Turk, Miller, the Telephone Directories of Guernsey and Jersey and family traditions. It will be noticed that names are of both English and French origin, that some also belong to metropolitan France, and that some have acquired Newfoundland variants. Where possible, surnames have been allotted to Guernsey (G), Jersey (J), most of the remainder tend to belong to both islands (G&J); though a few have not been precisely located.

Ahier (J), Alexander (J), Allen, Anderson (G), Andrews (G), Anthony, Archer, Avery (G)

Bailey, Baker (G), Barber (G), Barrett (J), Battiste for Batiste, Beason, Beeso, Beson for Bisson (G&J); Beauchamp for Beauchamps , Beaucamp; Beaudoin for ? Baudin; Beckett for Becquet (J); Begin for Beghin; Bell, Bennett (J), Bernard (G), Berry, Berteau, Bignall, Bishop, Blundell, Boone (G), Borden for Bourdon (J), Bow(d)ridge for Bowdedge, Bowdidge (G), Brake (G), Breton, Broughton, Brown(e); Bullen for Bollen, Balleine (J), Burgess, Burt (J), Bussey for Bussy (J)

Cain (J), Carey (G), Carter (G), Caswell (G), Cave (G), Chalker (G), Champion, Chinn (J), Cleal (G), Clemen(t)s (J), Colley, Collins, Cook, Cooper, Corbet(t), Corbin (G), Cornish (J), Cross

Darby (J), Davey (G), De Gruchey (J), Dennis (G), Dorey, Drew (J), Durant (J), Durand (G), Duval, Dyer (G)

Edmonds (G), Efford, English, Ereaut

Falle (J), Farnham, Fe(a)ver, Ferry (J), Fillatre (J), Filleul, Fillier for Filleul, Fisher, Foley (G), Follett, Fontaine (J), Forcey and Forsey (G), Francis (G), Freeman (G), Fresne for Le Fresne (J), Fuller (G)

Gale, Garnier (J), Gilbert (G), Giles, Gill, Gillam (J), Godden (J), Godfrey, Gosse (G), Graham (J), Grandy for Grandin (J), Gray, Greeley for Le Gresley (J), Green (G), Greenslade (G), Gr(o)uchy, Gushue (J)

Hacquoil (J), Haines, Hallett (J), Hamen, Hardy, Hart, Harvey, Harview for Hervieu, Haskell, Hawco for Hacquoil, Hayes (G), Hellier, Henry, Hicks, Hill, Hilliard, Homer (G), Hooper (G), Howell (G), Howlett, Hoyle (J), Hubbard (J), Huelin (J), Hughes, Hurrell

Jackson, James, Jarvis, Jefferies for Jeffreys (G), Johnson (G), Jones
Knight

Lacey (G), La Cour(ce) (J), Lainey, Lainez for Lainé, Lambert, La Page for Le Page, Lawrence, ? Learning (G), Le Blanc for Le Blancq, Le Coq for Le Cocq, Drew, Le Drew for Le Dru (J), Lee, Le Feuvre, Le Fresne for (Du) Fresne (J), Le Grow for Le Gros (J), Lelievra for Lelievre (G), Le Mee, Le Messurier, Le Moine for Le Moisne, Leonard, Le Quant for Le Quesne and Cain (J), Le Riche (J), Le Roux (J), Le Roy, Le Selleur (J), Le Shana for Le Shanu (J), Le Tiec (J), Le Valliant for Le Vaillent (J), Lilly, Loveridge, Lowe, Lucas

Macey for Macé, Mass(e)y etc. (G), Mainwaring (J), Manning, Marquis, Martin, Masters, Matthews for Mathews, Mauger, Maybee ? for Mabey (G), Messervey (J), Michael(s) for Mi(t)chel(l), Middleton (G), Mitchell, Moody, Morrell, Morrissey (J), Mosler for Moser, Mott for Motte (J), Motty for Mottee or Mottie (J), Moyse (J), ? Murrin

Neale for Neal(e) and Neil formerly Neel (J), Neville (J), Nicholas, Nicholle, Nightingale, Noel (J), Noftall, Noftle for Naftel (G), Norman

Oliver and Olivier, Osborne, Osmond, Owen(s) (G), Ozon for Ozanne (G)

Pack (?G), Page for Le Page, Palmer, Paquette for Pacquet (J), Parrott, Pasha and Pasher for Perchard, Payne for Paine, Peddle (J), Pelley for (Le)Pelley (G), Pennell (J), Penn(e)y (G), Perchard (J), Perrett for Perrot (G), Perrier (J), Perrin (J), Perry (J), Petitpas (J), Phillips (G), Picco(tt) for Picot, Pidgeon, Pieroway for Pirouet, Pike (G), Pinel (J), Pippy for Peppy or Pipet (J), Poirier (J), Pollard, Poulain, Poullett for Poulet (J), Powell, Price (G), Prideaux, Prince (J), Puddester for Poingdestre (J), Pullin for Poulain

Quinn

Radford (G), Randell for Randall (G), Read, Reed, Redman (G), Remo for Remon (J), Renouf, Rich, Richard (J), Richards (G), Richardson, Robbins, Robert(s), Robin, Robinson (G), Roche, Rodgers for Roger (G), Rolands for Rowlands, Rousseau, Rowe (G), Rowsell (G)

Sacrey for Sacré (J), St. Croix, St. George (G), Salter, Sam(p)son (G), Sanders (G), Savage (G), Savery for ? Sauvary (G), Sharp, Shepherd, Short, Simmon(d)s, Simon, Skinner, Smith (G), Soper (J), Stafford (G), Steele (J), Stephens (G), Stone (G), Stoodley (J), Strong (J)

Taylor, Tessier, Thistle for Touzel, Thomas, Thomey for Thoume, Toms, Tompkins (J), Touching(s) for Tostevin (G), Touzel (J), Turner

Udle

Vincent, Viscount for (Le)Vesconte (J), Vivian, Vokey (J), Voutier for Vautier,

Walker, Wallis, Walters, Way (G), Webber, Welsh (G), Wheadon (G), White, Whiteley (J), ? Widger, Williams, Wright

Young

The name Hacquoil was changed to Clement and back to Hacquoil.

The South Coast of Newfoundland has been the main area of settlement by Channel Islanders, though there were a number of early settlers in Conception Bay in the seventeenth century.

The relations between Newfoundland and the Channel Islands are discussed in Prowse, Rogers, Le Messurier and Fay, as listed in the Bibliography.

7. *Surnames from Syria-Lebanon*

A small group of surnames is associated with the emigration from Syria and Lebanon to Newfoundland of a number of Maronite families in the late nineteenth or early twentieth century. Members of the sect, a leading Christian community in Lebanon, speak Arabic but use Syriac in their liturgy. Since Lebanon achieved independence in 1943, a convention has been established that the President of the republic should be a Maronite, the Prime Minister a Sunni Moslem, and the Speaker of the Chamber of Deputies a Shia Moslem.

From humble beginnings in Newfoundland as small dealers and pedlars (when they were known locally and popularly, together with Jews and any other dark-skinned people, as "Tallies," ? Italians), the Maronites have established themselves as prosperous and respected members of the community, though they seem to have been overlooked in local studies.

Their surnames in Newfoundland are anglicized versions of mainly Christian Arabic names, though some are of uncertain origin, apparently non-Arabic, and have defied interpretation. The list may be incomplete.

Abbass, Abbiss, Alexander, Alteen, Andrews, Basha, Boulos, Carbage, Faour, Gaultois, Gosine, Hemeon, Herro, Joseph, Kawaja, Markarian, Michael(s), Noah, Sabb, Sapp, Sheehan, Simon, Tooton, Tuma.

8. *Surnames from Other Countries*

Among the minor contributors to the stock of Newfoundland surnames, mostly in the twentieth century, Germany comes first with some thirty, a number of which have undergone anglicization on much the same lines as those of France: Arns for ? Arends, Fralic and Frelich for Frölich, Ingerman for Ingermann, Kippenhuch for ? Köpenick, Kreiger for Krieger or Krüger, Langins for ? Langhans, Riteman for ? Riedemann, Rittemann or Rüttemann, Sidel for ? Seidel, Wentzell for Wen(t)zel. Rompkey from Ramgen has followed an arbitrary course.

Scandinavian surnames appear to have remained largely unchanged except for the loss of the diaeresis in Swedish names ending in -*ström*: Baxstrom, Edstrom, Lindstrom; Danish Westergaard has been reduced to Westguard.

The handful of surnames from Portugal, Spain, Holland, Hungary and Switzerland appear to be in their original forms.

Russian-Jewish surnames have remained virtually unchanged: Ferman for Furman(ov), Melamed for Melamud, Perlin for Pérlin, or simplified: Levitz for Levitskij.

E.C. Smith, *American Surnames*, notes that few Chinese names have been changed in America since they present no difficulties in pronunciation. One name, however, may have several interpretations. In Newfoundland they include: Au, Chong, Chow, Ding, Fong, Hong, Jim, Kung, Lem, Ling, Mok, Ping, Wing (also English), Wong, Ying, and probably others. The circumstances of their introduction into Newfoundland are obscure.

9. *Surnames of the Micmac Indians*

Micmac Indians from the Canadian mainland were known in Newfoundland as early as 1661. They assisted the French in their invasions in the seventeenth and eighteenth centuries, and had begun to settle in Bay d'Espoir ? by 1765, in White Bear Bay, and in St. George's Bay by 1783. They eventually made their main settlements on the Conne River in the east arm of Bay d'Espoir and in the Stephenville area.

In his "Report on the Micmac Indians at Bay d'Espoir," 1908, Sir. W. MacGregor, then governor of Newfoundland, doubted whether there was a "single pure-blooded Micmac on the Island"; and it seems probable that their surnames, of French, English and Irish origins, adopted ? about the middle of the nineteenth century, derive from the European fathers of half-breeds. Another suggestion, given some support by the name Juk(e)s, otherwise unknown in Newfoundland and now obsolete, ? after J. B. Jukes (1811–1869), geological surveyor of Newfoundland in 1839–40, is that Micmacs adopted the surnames of hunters and explorers for whom they acted as guides.

The surnames include: Barrington, Beaton (Montagnais), Bernard, Brazil, Burke, Bushey, Collier, Drew, Gallant, Glode, Hinks, Hoskins, Jeddore, Joe, John, Juk(e)s, Lewis, Louis, Macdonald, Martin, Matthew(s), Michel, Mitchell, Paul, Poullett, Stride.

Accounts of the Micmacs in Newfoundland are by Millais, MacGregor, Rogers and Speck, as listed in the Bibliography.

Select Bibliography

1. GENERAL WORKS – PRINTED

Adams, W.F. *Ireland and the Irish Emigration to the New World from 1815 to the Famine* (Yale University Press, New Haven 1932; reissued Russell, New York 1967).

Arthur, W. *An Etymological Dictionary of Family and Christian Names* (Sheldon, New York 1857; reissued Gale, Detroit 1969).

Barber, H. *British Family Names* (Elliot Stock, London 1903; reissued Gale, Detroit 1968).

Bardsley, C.W. *A Dictionary of English and Welsh Surnames* (Oxford University Press, London 1901).

Baring-Gould, S. *Family Names and their Story* (Seeley, London 1910; reissued Gale, Detroit 1969).

Beaudoin, J. *See* Gosselin, A.

Black, G.F. *The Surnames of Scotland* (The New York Public Library, New York 1946).

Bradley, H. *The Making of English* (Macmillan, London 1904 and many later reprints).

Brocklebank, J. *Affpuddle in the County of Dorset* (Bournemouth 1968).

Carew, B.M. *The Life and Adventures of Bamfylde Moore Carew* (Exeter 1745).

Chapuy, P. *Origine des Noms patronymiques français* (Dorbon-Aîné, Paris [1934]).

Charnock, R.S. *Ludus Patronymicus* (Trübner, London 1868; reissued Gale, Detroit 1968).

Cottle, B. *The Penguin Dictionary of Surnames* (Penguin Books, Harmondsworth 1967, 2nd edition 1978).

Coulson, J. *The Saints* (Hawthorn Books, New York 1958).

Dauzat, A. *Dictionnaire étymologique des Noms de Famille et Prénoms de France* (Larousse, Paris 1951, 1969).

– et Ch. Rostaing *Dictionnaire étymologique des Noms de Lieux en France* (Larousse, Paris 1963).

DNB Dictionary of National Biography [to 1900] edited by L. Stephen and S. Lee. 63 vols; Supplement, 3 vols; Index and epitome. (Oxford University Press, London 1885–1903). Additional supplements for the 20th century. *Concise DNB*, 2 vols, 1952, 1961. In Progress.

EDD Wright, J. *The English Dialect Dictionary* (Oxford University Press, London 1898–1905).

Ekwall, E. *The Concise Oxford Dictionary of English Place-Names* (Clarendon Press, Oxford 1936, 4th edition 1960).

Ewen, C.H.L. *A History of Surnames of the British Isles* (Kegan Paul, London 1931; reissued Gale, Detroit 1968).

– *A Guide to the Origin of British Surnames* (Gifford, London 1938; reissued Gale, Detroit 1969).

Fägersten, A. *The Place-Names of Dorset* (Lundequistska Bokhandeln, Uppsala 1933).

Fowkes, R.A. "Welsh Naming Practices, with a Comparative Look at Cornish" *Names* 29, 4, December 1981, 265–72.

Garis, Marie de *English-Guernsey Dictionary* (La Société Guernesiaise, Guernsey 1967).

Gosselin, A. *Les Normands au Canada. Journal d'une Expédition de D'Iberville* [par l'abbé Jean Beaudoin] (Évreux 1900).

Gottschald, M. *Deutsche Namenkunde* (1931, 4th edition Gruyter, Berlin 1971).

Gover, J.E.B., A. Mawer and F.M. Stenton *The Place-Names of Devon* (English Place-Name Society. Part I Vol. VIII Cambridge University Press, Cambridge 1931; Part II Vol. IX Cambridge University Press, Cambridge 1932).

Groome, F.H. *Ordnance Gazetteer of Scotland* 6 vols. (Jack, Edinburgh Vol. I 1882, Vols. II, III, IV 1883, Vol. V 1884, Vol. VI 1885).

Guppy, H.B. *Homes of Family Names in Great Britain* (Harrison, [London] 1890).

Hanks, P., F. Hodges, with D.L. Gold *A Dictionary of Surnames* (Oxford University Press, Oxford 1988).

Heintze, A. and P. Cascorbi *Die deutschen Familiennamen* (1882, 7th edition 1933; reprinted Georg Olms Verlagsbuchhandlung, Hildesheim 1967).

Hill, J.S. *The Place-Names of Somerset* (Bristol 1914).

Horwood, A. *Captain Harry Thomasen* ([W & G Baird, Antrim, N.I.] 1973).

Hoskins, W.G. "The Homes of Family Names" *History Today* 22, 3, March 1972, 189–94.

– *Local History in England* (revised edition Longman, London 1972).

Illustrated Road Book of Ireland (Automobile Association of Ireland, Cork and Dublin, 2nd edition 1966).

Le Maistre, F. *Dictionnaire Jersiais-Français* (Don Balleine Trust, Jersey 1966).

Long, H.A. *Personal and Family Names* (Hamilton, London 1883; reissued Gale, Detroit 1968).

Lower, M.A. *English Surnames* (4th edition, 2 vols. John Russell Smith, London 1875; reissued Gale, Detroit 1968).

MacLysaght, E. *Irish Families* (Hodges Figgis, Dublin 1957).

- *More Irish Families* (O'Gorman, Galway and Dublin 1960).

- *Supplement to Irish Families* (Genealogical Book Company, Baltimore [1964]).

- *A Guide to Irish Surnames* (Genealogical Book Company, Baltimore [1964]).

- *The Surnames of Ireland* (Irish University Press, Shannon 1969; revised paperback edition 1973).

Mansion, J.E. ed. *Harrap's Standard French and English Dictionary*, part one French-English with Supplement (1962) (Harrap, London etc. 1934, revised edition 1940).

Matheson, R.E. *Special Report on Surnames in Ireland* (His Majesty's Stationery Office, Dublin 1909).

Matthews, C. M. *English Surnames* (Weidenfeld, London 1966).

Miller, G.M. *BBC Pronouncing Dictionary of British Names* (Oxford University Press London 1971).

OED A New English Dictionary on Historical Principles [now generally known as *The Oxford English Dictionary*] edited by J.A.H. Murray and others (Clarendon Press, Oxford 1888–1933).

Reaney, P.H. *A Dictionary of British Surnames* (Routledge, London 1958), 2nd edition revised by R.M. Wilson (Routledge, London 1975), 3rd edition with corrections and additions by R.M. Wilson (Routledge, London 1991).

- *The Origin of English Surnames* (Routledge, London 1967).

Redford, A. *Labour Migration in England 1800–1850* (Manchester University Press 1926; 2nd edition revised by W.H. Chaloner 1964).

Smith, A.H. *English Place-Name Elements* (English Place-Name Society. Part I Vol. XXV, Part II Vol. XXVI, Cambridge University Press, Cambridge 1956).

Turk, M.G. *The Quiet Adventurers in America Channel Island Settlers in the American Colonies and in the United States* (Printed by Genie Repros, Cleveland, Ohio 1975).

- *The Quiet Adventurers* [Channel Islanders] *in Canada* (Printed by Harlo Press, Detroit, Michigan 1979).

Unbegaun, B.O. *Russian Surnames* (Clarendon Press, Oxford 1972).

Weekley, E. *The Romance of Names* (Murray, London 1914, 4th edition 1928).

- *Surnames* (Murray, London 1916, 3rd edition 1936).

Withycombe, E.G. *The Oxford Dictionary of Christian Names* (Clarendon Press, Oxford, 1st edition 1945; 2nd edition 1950, reprinted with corrections 1971).

Woulfe, P. *Irish Names and Surnames* (Gill, Dublin 1923).

2. GENERAL WORKS – OTHER THAN PRINTED

CO Colonial Office, Great Britain. See under Newfoundland – Other than Printed.

Reaney Notes   Material prepared by P. H. Reaney for inclusion in *A Dictionary of British Surnames* but omitted therefrom, in the Library of the University of Sheffield.

Spiegelhalter, C. "A Dictionary of Devon Surnames" (Mimeograph 1958). Typescript in the W. P. Rock Library, Barnstaple.

Stevens, Charles "Catalogue of Jersey Family Names" (Typescript 1970).

Visscher, N. *Carte Nouvelle contenant la Partie d'Amérique la plus Septentrionale et l'ile de Terre Neuve* [about 1680]. Map.

3. NEWFOUNDLAND – PRINTED

Adams, F.G. *The Adams Family of Pennywell Path* [St. John's] (Robinson-Blackmore, St. John's [? 1969]).

Anspach, L.A. *A History of the Island of Newfoundland* (London 1819).

Bowring See Keir

Devine, M.A. and M. J. O'Mara *Notable Events in the History of Newfoundland* (St. John's 1900).

Devine, P. K. *Ye Olde St. John's, 1750–1936* (Newfoundland Directories, St. John's 1936).

- and J.T. Lawton *Old King's Cove* (1944).

Electors 1955 Official List of Electors [St. John's 1955] The Electoral Districts as constituted in 1955 were: Bell Island, Bonavista North, Bonavista South, Burgeo and La Poile, Burin, Carbonear-Bay de Verde, Ferryland, Fogo, Fortune Bay and Hermitage, Gander, Grand Falls, Green Bay, Harbour Grace, Harbour Main, Humber East, Humber West, Labrador North, Labrador South, Placentia East, Placentia West, Port au Port, Port de Grave, St. Barbe, St. George's, St. John's Centre, St. John's East, St. John's North, St. John's South, St. John's West, St. Mary's, Trinity North, Trinity South, Twillingate, White Bay North, White Bay South.

Fay, C. R. *The Channel Islands and Newfoundland* (Heffer, Cambridge 1961).

Feild, E. "Newfoundland Journal of a Voyage of Visitation ... on the Coast of Labrador and round the whole

Island of Newfoundland in the year 1849" *Church in the Colonies*, XXV, July 1850.

Gazetteer of Canada. Newfoundland and Labrador (Canadian Permanent Committee on Geographical Names, Ottawa 1968; 2nd ed., *Newfoundland*, Ottawa 1983).

Harvey, M. *Text Book of Newfoundland History* (Collins, London and Glasgow, 2nd edition 1890).

Hibbs, R. (ed.) *Newfoundland Who's Who* (R. Hibbs, St. John's 1927, 1930, 1937). *See also* THOMS, J. R.

Howley, J.P. *The Beothucks, or Red Indians* (Cambridge University Press, Cambridge 1915; Facsimile reprint Coles, Toronto 1974; AMS Reprint, New York 1979).

Howley, M.F. *Ecclesiastical History of Newfoundland* (Doyle and Whittle, Boston 1888).

Hutchinson's Newfoundland Directory, for 1864–5 (McConnan, St. John's 1864).

In the Privy Council. In the Matter of the Boundary between the Dominion of Canada and the Colony of Newfoundland in the Labrador Peninsula. 9 vols. and atlas [London 1927].

Job, R.B. *John Job's Family* (Telegram Printing Co., St. John's 1953). *See also* Newfoundland – Other than Printed.

Keir, D. *The Bowring Story* (John Lane, London 1962).

Le Messurier, H.W. "The Early Relations between Newfoundland and the Channel Islands" *The Geographical Review* 2, 6, December 1916, 449–57.

Lounsbury, R.G. *The British Fishery at Newfoundland 1634–1763* (Yale University Press, New Haven 1934).

Lovell 1871. *Lovell's Province of Newfoundland Directory for 1871* (Lovell, Montreal 1871).

Lovell 1877. Rochfort, J. A. *Business and General Directory of Newfoundland* (Lovell, Montreal 1877).

MacGregor, W. "Report ... on a Visit to the Micmac Indians at Bay d'Espoir [1908]" *Colonial Reports Miscellaneous No. 54* (His Majesty's Stationery Office, London 1908).

McLintock, A.H. *The Establishment of Constitutional Government in Newfoundland 1783–1832. A Study in Retarded Colonization* (Longmans, London 1941).

Mannion, J.J. *Irish Settlements in Eastern Canada* (Toronto University Press, Toronto 1974).

Millais, J.G. *Newfoundland and its Untrodden Ways* (Longmans, London 1907).

Mott, H.Y. *Newfoundland Men* (Cragg, Concord, N.H. 1894).

Nemec, T.F. "The Irish Emigration to Newfoundland" *Newfoundland Quarterly* 69, 1, July 1972, 15–24. *See also* Newfoundland – Other than Printed.

Newfoundland and Labrador Genealogical Society Newsletter, Vol. 1, No. 1 (St. John's 1985), continued by *Newfoundland Ancestor* Vol. 4, No. 1 (St. John's 1987–).

Newfoundland Who's Who. See Hibbs, R. and Thoms, J.R.

NEWSPAPERS AND PERIODICALS
The following newspapers and periodicals, mostly of the nineteenth century, are held in the Hunter Library, the Library of the Memorial University of Newfoundland and the Provincial Archives, frequently in broken runs. *Banner of Temperance*, St. John's; *Carbonear Mercury*; *Carbonear Sentinel and Conception Bay Advertizer*; *Carbonear Star and Conception Bay Journal*, later *Star and Newfoundland Advocate*; *Conception Bay Mercury*, Harbour Grace; *Daily News*, St. John's; *Evening Telegram*, St. John's; *Harbour Grace and Carbonear Weekly Journal*; *Newfoundland Almanac*; *Newfoundland Indicator*, St. John's; *Newfoundland Mercantile Journal*, St. John's; *Newfoundland Patriot*, St. John's; *Newfoundland Quarterly*, St. John's; *Newfoundlander*, St. John's; *Public Ledger*, St. John's; *Royal Gazette and Newfoundland Advertiser*, St. John's; *Times,* St. John's; *Weekly Herald and Conception Bay General Advertizer (Harbour Grace Weekly Herald)*.

Official List of Electors 1955
See *Electors 1955.*

Prowse, D.W. *A History of Newfoundland* (Macmillan, London and New York 1895).

Rogers, J.D. *A Historical Geography of the British Colonies. Vol. V – Part IV Newfoundland* (Clarendon Press, Oxford 1911).

Seary, E.R. *Place Names of the Avalon Peninsula of the Island of Newfoundland* (University of Toronto Press for the Memorial University of Newfoundland, Toronto 1971).

Seary, E.R., G.M. Story and W. Kirwin *The Avalon Peninsula of Newfoundland: An Ethno-linguistic Study* (National Museum of Canada Bulletin No. 219 Anthropological Series No. 81, Ottawa 1968).

Smallwood, J.R. (ed.) *The Book of Newfoundland*, 6 vols. Vols. I and II (St. John's 1937); Vols. III and IV (St. John's 1967); Vols. V and VI (St. John's 1975).

– *I Chose Canada* (Macmillan of Canada, Toronto 1973).

Speck, F.G. *Beothuk and Micmac* (Museum of the American Indian Heye Foundation, New York 1922).

Thomas, A. *The Newfoundland Journal of Aaron Thomas*, edited by Jean M. Murray (Longmans, London 1968).

Thomas, G.R. "Some Acadian Family Names in Western Newfoundland" *Onomastica Canadiana* 62, December 1982, 23–34.

– "French Family Names on the Port-au-Port Peninsula,

Newfoundland" *Onomastica Canadiana* 68, December 1986, 21–33.

Thoms, J R. (ed.) *Newfoundland Who's Who* (E. C. Boone Advertising, St. John's 1968). *See also* HIBBS, R.

Whiteley, W.H. *James Cook in Newfoundland 1762–1767* (Newfoundland Historical Society Pamphlet No. 3, [St. John's] 1975).

Wix, E. *Six Months of a Newfoundland Missionary's Journal from February to August 1835* (2nd edition, Smith, Elder, London 1836).

4. NEWFOUNDLAND – OTHER THAN PRINTED

"A Return of the Number of Houses, Inhabitants ... in the District of Trinity ... 1800 and 1801." *See* Census Trinity B.

"An Account of Inhabitants residing in the Harbour and District of St. John's 1794 and 1795." *See* Census 1794–5.

Belbin-Harris Family Papers 1796–1906 (Provincial Archives).

Butler, Gary R. "Supernatural Folk Belief Expression in a French-Newfoundland Community: A Study of Expressive Forms, Communicative Process, and Social Function in L'Anse-à-Canards" (Memorial University Ph.D. diss. 1985).

Bonavista Register. "Register of Fishing Rooms, Bonavista Bay, 1806" (Hunter Library, St. John's; copy in Provincial Archives).

Button (Old Perlican) Family Papers 1780, 1787, 1880 (Provincial Archives).

Carnell Family Papers. *See* Collier etc.

Casey, G.J. "Traditions and Neighbourhoods: The Folklife of a Newfoundland Fishing Outport [Conche]" (Memorial University of Newfoundland M.A. thesis 1971).

Census 1794–5. "An Account of Inhabitants residing in the Harbour and District of St. John's 1794/1795" A census, or ? a copy thereof, apparently prepared for the Colonial Secretary's Office, in the Hunter Library, St.

John's. A copy, with different pagination, by D. J. Fox, 1962.

"An Index to the Names in An Account ...," with a brief introductory note, by W. J. Kirwin and J. Feltham (Department of English Language and Literature, Memorial University of Newfoundland, Xerograph 1968).

Census Trinity B. "A Return of the Number of Houses, Inhabitants, Fishing Rooms, Rents of Rooms, etc. in the District of Trinity, Nfld. in the Winter of 1800 and 1801 ..." (Provincial Archives).

CO. COLONIAL OFFICE, GREAT BRITAIN

CO 1 State Papers Colonial in the Public Record office, London, including Reports from Sir John Berry 1675, Captain Russell 1676 and Sir W. Poole 1677, etc.

CO 194.24 folio 298 Original Correspondence 1744.

CO 194.38

CO 194.51

CO 199.18 "Return of Possessions held in Conception Bay 1805, the 'Plantation Book'" (Microfilm in Provincial Archives).

Collier, Carnell, Gill, Harris (St. John's) Family Papers 1792, 1816, 1834, 1845 (Provincial Archives).

Connors, Michael, Butcher of St. John's Personal Papers 1856-61 (Provincial Archives).

D'Alberta. Transcripts of correspondence, 1780–1825, between the governors of Newfoundland and the Colonial Office, with other material (Centre for Newfoundland Studies, Memorial University of Newfoundland).

DPHW. Department of Public Health and Welfare, St. John's

Newfoundland Registrar-General/Register of Vital Statistics. Baptismal, Marriage and Death Registers of the Anglican, Methodist, Roman Catholic, Congregational, Presbyterian and Reformed Episcopal Churches, usually to 1890 or 1891. Copies in the Provincial Archives, St. John's. The following list is based on the Parish Index prepared by the Provincial Archives.

B = Births   M = Marriages   D = Deaths

DPHW Vol. No.	Parish	Denomination	Registers Available	
22	St. John's Cochrane Street	Methodist	BM	1890–91
22	St. John's George Street	Methodist	BDM	1882–91
23	St. John's	Congregational	B	1780–1891
			M	1802–92
			D	1844–91

DPHW Vol. No.	Parish	Denomination	Registers Available	
24	St. John's	Presbyterian	B	1837–91
			M	1842–91
			D	1879–90
24	Harbour Grace (With Registers of Pastors 1858–1901)	Presbyterian	B	1880–1920
25	St. John's St. Patrick's	Roman Catholic	B	1880–91
26	St. John's Cathedral	Anglican	B	1870–92
26A	"	"	B	1849–70
26B	"	"	B	1796–1848
26C	"	"	B	1753–91
26D	"	"	M	1835–91
26E	"	"	M	1754–1834
27	St. John's St. Mary's	"	BM	1859–91
28	St. John's St. Thomas's	"	B	1868–92
29	"	"	B	1856–68
30	"	"	B	1830–40
30A	"	"	M	1830–92
31	Witless Bay, Ferryland	"	B	1885–91
31	Petty Harbour (with some returns for Aquaforte, Ferryland and Renews)	"	B	1820–91
		"	M	1824–91
32	Pouch Cove	Methodist	B	1841–91
32	"	Anglican	B	1882–91
			M	1841–91
33	Topsail	"	BM	1880–91
33	Foxtrap	"	B	1825–91
			M	1827–91
34	Brigus, Cupids	Methodist	B	1801–55
35	(With one entry dated 1813)		B	1855–70
36	"	"	B	1870–91
36A	"	"	M	1837–92
37	North River, Port de Grave	Reformed Episcopal	B	1884–91
37	Brigus, Salmon Cove	Anglican	B	1860–91
38	"	"	M	1860–91
38	Port de Grave	"	B	1859–91
38	"	"	M	1860–91
39	Bay Roberts	Methodist	BM	1884–91
39	Port de Grave	"	B	1834–91
39A	Clarkes Beach	"	M	1837–90
40	Bay Roberts	Anglican	B	1859–91
			M	1860–91
41	Spaniard's Bay	"	BM	1860–91
42	Harbour Grace	Roman Catholic	B	1866–91
42A	"	"	M	1866–89
43	"	Methodist	B	1819–91
44	"	Anglican	B	1854–90
	"	"	B	1880–90
45	"	"	B	1880–90

DPHW Vol. No.	Parish	Denomination	Registers Available	
			M	1890–91
	Harbour Grace South	Anglican	M	1877–91
45A	Harbour Grace	"	M	1776–1833
45B	Harbour Grace	Anglican	M	1831–90
46	Carbonear	"	BM	1860–91
47	"	Roman Catholic	B	1870–91
48	"	Methodist	B	1793–1848
49	"	"	B	1848–70
50	"	"	B	1870–91
50A	"	"	M	1794–1891
51	Freshwater (Carbonear)	"	BM	1883–91
52	Blackhead, Bay de Verde	"	B	1852–92
52A	"	"	B	1816–52
52B	"	"	M	1816–91
53	Western Bay	"	B	1873–91
			M	1877–91
54	Northern Bay	Roman Catholic	B	1838–61
54A	"	"	M	1838–91
55	Lower Island Cove	Methodist	BM	1850–91
56	Bay de Verde	Anglican	BM	1860–91
57	"	Roman Catholic	B	1880–92
	Northern Bay	"	B	1862–91
57A	Bay de Verde	"	M	1880–91
58	Old Perlican	Methodist	B	1816–91
58A	"	"	M	1816–91
59	Hants Harbour	Methodist	B	1875–91
			M	1825–91
59A	"	"	B	1824–74
60	Heart's Content	"	B	1877–85
	(At beginning of Register: Baptisms, sheets 1–4, parish of Winterton, sheets 1–3, parish of Heart's Content; Marriages, sheets 1–6).		M	1878–91
	Heart's Content			
	(Includes entries for Scilly Cove [now Winterton],	Anglican	B	1873–91
	New Perlican, Heart's Content)		M	1879–91
61	New Harbour	Reformed Episcopal	BM	1885–90
61	Green's Harbour			
	(The Reformed Episcopal Church, parish of New Harbour, became affiliated with the Methodist Church at Green's Harbour; entries for the New Harbour parish are distributed irregularly among those for the Methodist	Methodist	B	1867–90
	Church parish of Green's Harbour)		M	1874–90
61	Whitbourne	Anglican	BD	1889–91
61	Heart's Delight			
	(Baptisms recorded at beginning of Register, sheets 1–14; Marriages towards the back of Register,	"	B	1883–92
	sheets 1–10)		M	1879–94
62	New Harbour	Anglican	B	1861–91
			M	1862–91
63	Trinity	"	B	1860–91

DPHW Vol. No.	Parish	Denomination	Registers Available	
64	Trinity	Anglican	B	1823–60
64A	"	"	B	1753–1823
64B	"	"	M	1757–1839
64C	"	"	M	1839–91
65	Trinity East	"	B	1869–91
			M	1876–91
66	Catalina	Methodist	BM	1864–92
67	"	Anglican	B	1834–91
			M	1833–91
68	Random	Anglican	B	1880–91
68	Britannia, Trinity South	Methodist	BM	1883–91
68	Bird Island Cove (Elliston)	"	B	1890–91
			M	1891
68	Hillview, Little Heart's Ease	"	B	1890–92
69	Bonavista	"	B	1869–91
70	"	Anglican	M	1786–1891
71	"	"	B	1786–1891
71A	"	"	B	1845–91
72	"	Methodist	B	1817–69
72A	"	"	M	1822–91
73	King's Cove	Anglican	B	1845–91
73A	"	"	B	1834–48
			M	1838–91
74	Brooklyn	"	BM	1879–91
75	Greenspond	"	B	1851–69
76	"	"	B	1815–50
77	"	Methodist	BM	1862–92
78	"	Anglican	B	1870–90
78A	"	"	M	1815–90
79	Badger's Quay	"	B	1862–92
			M	1862–1902
80	Glovertown	Methodist	B	1883–91
			M	1884–91
80	Musgravetown	"	B	1871–91
			M	1873–91
80	Wesleyville	Methodist	BM	1884–91
81	Salvage	Anglican	B	1865–93
82	Fogo	"	B	1860–91
83	"	"	B	1840–60
83A	"	"	M	1841–90
83	Change Islands	"	B	1856–91
			M	1854–91
84	Carmanville	Methodist	B	1888–91
84	Fogo	"	B	1861–91
			M	1862–91
84	Musgrave Harbour	"	B	1873–91
			M	1874–91
85	Herring Neck	Anglican	BM	1850–91
86	Twillingate	"	B	1880–93
86	Moreton's Harbour (Exploits)	"	B	1841–92

DPHW Vol. No.	Parish	Denomination	Registers Available	
87	Moreton's Harbour (Exploits)	"	M	1842–91
88	Twillingate	Methodist	B	1842–91
89	"	"	M	1889–91
89A	"	"	M	1867–89
89	Herring Neck	"	BM	1878–90
89	Moreton's Harbour	"	BM	1874–91
90	Nipper's Harbour	"	B	1874–90
91	Little Bay Islands	"	B	1865–91
			M	1867–91
92	Exploits	"	B	1858–91
			M	1859–91
93	Bonne Bay, St. Barbe	Anglican	B	1853–91
			M	1871–91
94	Englee	Methodist	BM	1883–91
94	St. Anthony	"	BM	1873–90
95	Bonne Bay, St. Barbe	Methodist	B	1873–90
			M	1874–90
95	Flowers Cove	"	B	1874–93
			M	1874–90
95	Northwest River	"	B	1882–91
96	Bay of Islands	Presbyterian	BM	1876–91
96	"	Anglican	B	1863–92
	(With entries for 1839, 1842, 1848, 1857, 1858)		M	1870–91
96	Bay St. George	Anglican	B	1870–91
97	Channel	Methodist	BM	1862–91
98	Petites	"	B	1857–91
99	Rose Blanche	Anglican	BM	1860–91
100	Burin	"	BM	1860–91
101	Burgeo	"	BM	1842–91
101	Channel	"	M	1883–87
102	Hermitage	"	B	1843–91
102A	"	"	M	1844–90
102A	Belleoram	"	M	1879–91
102A	Fortune	Methodist	B	1877–91
			M	1842–90
103	Belleoram	Anglican	B	1878–91
103	Pool's Cove	Congregational	B	1874–91
			M	1888–91
104	Harbour Breton	Anglican	B	1850–91
			M	1850–88
105	Flat Islands	Methodist	BM	1873–91
105	Sound Island	"	B	1850–91
106	Fortune	"	B	1877–91
106	Garnish	"	B	1885–92
			M	1887–91
106	Grand Bank	"	B	1859–92
			M	1817–92
107	Lamaline	Anglican	BM	1860–91
108	Burin	Methodist	B	1860–91
108A	"	"	B	1833–60

DPHW Vol. No.	Parish	Denomination	Registers Available	
108A	Grand Bank	"	B	1817–59
109	Burin	"	M	1850–85
110	Harbour Grace	Anglican	B	1775–1807
111	"	"	B	1807–30
112	"	"	B	1830–59
113	Battle Harbour, Labrador	"	B	1847–81
114	"	"	M	1850–82
115		Interdenominational	B	1842–69
116		"	B	1870–79
117		"	B	1880–90

Dillon, V.M. "The Anglo-Irish Element in the Speech of the Southern Shore of Newfoundland" (Memorial University of Newfoundland M.A. thesis 1968).

Fleming, M.A. Papers 1838– (Provincial Archives).

Garland, Charles (Harbour Grace) Wills 1810 (Provincial Archives).

Gill Family Papers. See Collier etc.

Goodfellow, James (St. John's) Papers 1833–93 (Provincial Archives).

Greene, J.P. "A Preliminary Inventory of the Records in the Provincial Archives of Newfoundland and Labrador" 1970.

– "Supplement" to the above, edited by D. J. Davis, Vol. I, No. 2 1972.

Halpert, H. See Memorial University of Newfoundland.

Harris Family Papers. See Belbin and Harris, and Collier etc.

Higgins J.G. (St. John's) Papers 1810–95 (Provincial Archives).

Jackman (Renews) Family Papers (Provincial Archives).

Jeans (Catalina) Family Papers 1834–1917 (Provincial Archives).

Job (St. John's) Family Papers 1761–1952 (Provincial Archives). See also Newfoundland – Printed.

McCrae, Frank (Harbour Grace) Scrap Book (Provincial Archives).

Matthews. Matthews, K. "A 'Who was Who' of Families engaged in the Fishery and Settlement of Newfoundland, 1660–1840" 1971. See also Memorial University of Newfoundland.

MUN. Memorial University of Newfoundland MUN Folklore 1314 Questionnaires on Newfoundland Folklore, Family Names, etc., collected by H. Halpert, 1967, in the Folklore and Language Archive. MUN Geography 149 Papers on Newfoundland Geography, collected by J. J. Mannion. MUN History 150 Papers on Community and Regional Studies, collected by K. Matthews.

Nemec, T.F. "The History, Ecology and Organization of a Newfoundland Anglo-Irish Outport Fishery [Trepassey]" (University of Michigan Ph.D. thesis, presented 1975).

– "A Selected Bibliography of Sources on Newfoundland Society and Culture" 1974. See also Newfoundland – Printed.

Newhook (New Harbour) Family Papers (Provincial Archives).

O'Donnell, Mary (St. John's) Papers (Provincial Archives).

Parsons (Harbour Grace) Family Papers 1807–1957 (Provincial Archives).

Pinsent-Williams (St. John's) Family Papers (Provincial Archives).

"Register of Fishing Rooms, Bonavista Bay, 1806." See Bonavista Register.

Registry Crown Lands. "Registry of Sales of Crown Lands, Oct 1831–Feb 1880" (Provincial Archives).

"Return of Possessions held in Conception Bay" See CO 199.18.

Swain, N.H. "The Reverend Charles Lench" (Provincial Archives).

Tilley (Elliston) Family Papers (Provincial Archives).

Tucker (Port de Grave) Family Papers 1770–1958 (Provincial Archives).

USPG (formerly SPG) United Society for the Propagation of the Gospel, London.

– C/CAN/NFL Box 1, Folio 219 Item 67b 4 Nov 1791. Rev . Harries to Sec. SPG. Subscribers for support of clergyman at Ferryland.

– 1. 221. 107 11 Nov 1791 Petition from inhabitants of Bonavista to Archbishop of Canterbury for a schoolmaster.

- 1. 221. 109 31 Oct 1792 [Same]
- 1. 221. 111 5 Nov 1793 [Same] for a missionary
- 1. 224. 129 27 Nov 1791 Petition of inhabitants of Harbour Grace to Sec. SPG for removal of the missionary, James Balfour.
- 1. 224. 133 10 Jul 1792 [Same] for a missionary to succeed James Balfour, removed from office.
- 1. 224. 134 24 Jul 1792 [Same] to the Rev. Mr. Harris, St. John's, re retention of Mr. Lampen as schoolmaster.
- 1. 224. 138 18 Nov 1801 [Same] to Sec. SPG for a missionary.
- 1. 224. 139 18 Nov 1821 Petition of the Churchwardens of Harbour Grace for a missionary.
- 2. 225. 140 31 Oct 1792 Abraham Akerman to Sec. SPG.
- 2. 225. 142 25 Oct 1793 George Bemister to Sec. SPG.
- 2. 226. 153 19 Dec 1798 Signatories to letter of thanks to Gov. Waldegrave for exertions about the Church [St. John's].
- 2. 230. 193 9 Jan 1810 Rev. L. A. Anspach to Sec. SPG.
- 2. 230. 196 1 Nov 1810 [Same].
- 2. 232. 214 24 Oct 1811 Rev. D. Rowland to Sec. SPG.
- 3. 239. 350 "Baptisms solemnized in the Parish of Twillingate in the Island of Newfoundland in the Years 1816–17–18 and 19–20–21–22 and 23." [Copy, 19 pages].
- 3. 241. 432 [No date, about 1772–5] Petition from inhabitants of Bay Bulls to Molineux Shuldham, governor of Newfoundland.
- 3. 241. 423 6 Oct 1793 Address to Sir Richard King from inhabitants of Bay Bulls.
- 3. 241. 425 12 Dec 1795 George Welsh to Archbishop of Canterbury.
- 3. 241. 433 3 Oct 1802 Petition for a missionary from inhabitants of Bay Bulls to James Gambier, governor of Newfoundland.
- 3. 241. 436 8 May 1810 George Rennell to Sec. SPG.
- 3. 241. 437 23 Jun 1810 Gerrard Ford, Bonavista, to Sec. SPG.
- 3. 241. 440 22 Nov 1811 Thomas Plumleigh, Brigus, to Rev. L.A. Anspach.

Verge, Thomas (Trinity) A master-servant agreement, Trinity, 17 Oct 1811 (Provincial Archives).

Whiteley, W.H. Papers 1858–1922 (Provincial Archives).

Williams (St. John's) Family Papers *See* Pinsent.

Woodley, Nathaniel, planter of St. John's and wife Papers 1823–66 (Provincial Archives).

NOTES FOR THE USE OF THE DICTIONARY

See Introduction, especially I Range and Aims and II Sources of Information.

As far as possible, abbreviations have been avoided, particularly those of the names of English, Irish and Scots counties which may not be readily familiar to North American readers. The major exception is in the citation of authorities used in Early Instances, such as titles of newspapers and periodicals which are easily recognizable, and such forms as DPHW, USPG, CO etc. Documents and authorities used are listed in the Bibliography.

Old English or Anglo-Saxon (O.E. or A.S.) is English as it was used from the earliest writings to about 1100 A.D.

Middle English (M.E.) is English as it was used from about 1100 A.D. to 1450 A.D.

A few symbols used in Old English and Old Norse spellings, but now obsolete, have been modernized.

An asterisk * indicates a postulated form.

Variant spellings of place names, such as Heart's Content and Hearts Content, Musketta and Mosquito, Scilly and Silly Cove in general derive from documents in which they are found.

The titles, Newfoundland Archives, and Provincial Archives, are used to denote the institution which in its publications refers to itself variously as Newfoundland and Labrador Provincial Archives, Provincial Archives of Newfoundland and Provincial Archives of Newfoundland and Labrador.

Dictionary of Newfoundland Family Names

A

ABBASS, a surname of Syria-Lebanon, from the Arabic – one who frowns, probably confused with ABBISS.

In Newfoundland: ? Introduced about 1890–1900.

Modern status: Unique, at Marquise (*Electors* 1955).

ABBISS, a surname of Syria-Lebanon, from the Arabic - morose, sullen, austere, probably confused with ABBASS.

In Newfoundland: ? Introduced about 1890–1900.

Modern status: Rare, at Buchans (*Electors* 1955).

ABBOTT, a surname of England, Ireland and Scotland, from Old English *abbod* later *abbot* - abbot, the head of an abbey of monks. Some Abbotts believe their name to be derived from MACNAB. (Reaney, Cottle, Black, MacLysaght).

Traced by Guppy in Devon, Dorset, Essex, Nottinghamshire, Oxfordshire and Suffolk, and by MacLysaght in Dublin.

In Newfoundland:

Early instances: ———, of St. John's, killed by the French, ? 1705 (CO 194.22); Thomas, of St. John's, 1706 (CO 194.22); William, fisherman of St. John's or Petty Harbour, about 1739-43 (CO 194.11); Richard, son of Elizabeth Abbot(t) of Bonavista, about 1765 (CO 194.16); Richard Abbott, of Bay Bulls, 1793 (USPG); Matt., proprietor and occupier of fishing room at Trinity, Winter 1800–01 (Census Trinity B.); James Abbot, of Harbour Grace Parish, 1817 (Nfld. Archives HGRC); Richard Abbott, planter of Bayleys Cove (Bonavista B.), 1817 (DPHW 72); James, of Careless (now Kerleys) Harbour, 1820, of Ragged Harbour (unspecified), 1822 (Nfld. Archives KCRC); William, of Catalina, 1823 (Nfld. Archives KCRC); James, of British Harbour, 1832 (Nfld. Archives KCRC); George, of Millers Passage, 1835 (DPHW 30); Thomas, fisherman of Carbonear, 1848 (DPHW 49); John, of Doting Cove, 1858 (DPHW 83); John, fisherman of North West Arm (now Lockston), 1860 (DPHW 63); John, married at Rose Blanche, 1861 (DPHW 99); John, of Robinson's Head (St. George's B.), 1870 (DPHW 96); William, fisherman of Bay de Verde, 1871 (Lovell); William, fisherman of Burin, 1871 (Lovell); Jeremiah and John, fishermen and servants of Port au Bras, 1871 (Lovell); John and Thomas, fishermen of Springfield (Brigus district), 1871 (Lovell).

Modern status: Widespread, especially at St. John's, Doting Cove and Bonavista.

Place names: Abbots Pond 43-30 57-50, Abbott Cove 49-32 55-18, ——— Pond 49-32 55-17, ——— Rock 46-50 55-49.

ABERY, a surname of England, apparently not recorded elsewhere, from the English place name Avebury (Wiltshire), which is locally so pronounced. (Ekwall).

In Newfoundland: Of Berkshire origin, at St. John's since 1925.

ABRAHAM, a baptismal name and surname of England, Ireland and Scotland, and a surname of France. In England, Scotland and France, it is of Hebrew origin but not confined to Jews. The name of the patriarch was first *Abram* – high father, later changed to *Abraham* – father of a multitude. In Ireland, however, Abraham is an anglicization of *Mac an Bhreitheamhan* - son of the judge. (Withycombe, Reaney, Cottle, MacLysaght, Dauzat).

Traced by Guppy in Huntingdonshire and Lincolnshire, and by Matthews in Devon, Dorset and Hampshire.

In Newfoundland:

Early instances: ———, of Quidi Vidi, 1703 (CO 194.3); Thomas, of Newfoundland, 1704 (CO 194.3); William, ? fisherman of Port de Grave, 1782 (Nfld. Archives T22); George, arrived in St. John's, 1816 (CO 194.60).

Modern status: After being apparently obsolete, the name was revived by the appointment of the Rt. Rev. Philip Selwyn Abraham as coadjutor bishop of Newfoundland in 1937. Now very rare and scattered.

Place names: Abrahams Cove 48-31 58-55, ——— Sail Point 48-56 57-29.

ACKERMAN, ACREMAN, AKERMAN, variant forms of a surname of England, from Old English *æcermann* – farmer, husbandman, ploughman. In France (Alsace), Akerman is of German origin. (Reaney, Cottle, Dauzat).

Traced by Matthews in Dorset.

In Newfoundland:

Family tradition: Two brothers, John and Thomas, were shipwrecked off the coast of Newfoundland about ? 1870 and settled, Thomas in Fair Island and John in Trinity Bay (MUN Folklore).

Early instances: Stephen Akarman, merchant of Bay Bulls, 1680 (Prowse); Gabr[i]el Akerman, clerk of Fogo, 1780 (D'Alberti 6); Abraham, missionary at Bonavista, about 1783-1821 (USPG, CO 194.64); Sam, servant at Battle Harbour (Labrador), 1795 (MUN Hist); Mary, of Vere (now Fair) Island, 1830, born ? 1812 (DPHW 76); William, planter of Brigus, 1837 (DPHW 34).

Modern status: Especially in the Bonavista North district, including Fair Island up to about 1959-63, when members of the family settled in Centreville.

ADAMS, a surname of England and Ireland with Adam and MacAdam scattered in Scotland, and Adamson common in the north of England and south of the Forth and Clyde. In England it means "son of Adam," a baptismal name from Hebrew *Adam* – red; in Ireland (Co. Down), it is a synonym of Aidy and Eadie. See also ADE, AIKEN. (Reaney, MacLysaght).

Guppy found the name widespread, especially in Devon, Shropshire and Staffordshire.

In Newfoundland:

Family traditions: William (1800-82) was the first settler of Upper Island Cove (MUN Geog.). Thomas, from Devon, settled at Come-By-Chance in 1822 (MUN Geog.).

Early instances: Sam., of Ferryland, 1675, of Caplin Bay (now Calvert), 1676 (CO 1); J[ohn], planter of St. John's, 1703 (CO 194.3); Samuel, J.P. of Placentia district, about 1730-35-1753 (CO 194.9, 13); William, member of court at St. John's, 1751 (CO 194.13); James, in possession of property, Adams Cove, 1796 (CO 199.18); Michael and Co., lessees of land at Harbour Grace, 1798 (CO 199.18); William, occupier of fishing room at Trinity, Winter 1800-01 (Census Trinity B.); William, proprietor of fishing room at Old Perlican, Winter 1800-01 (Census Trinity B.); Adams and Palmer, in salmon fishery at Indian Burying Place, 1804 (CO 194.45); Phillip, planter of Fogo, 1808 (MUN Hist.); John Addams, of Brigus, 1816 (Nfld. Archives L165); Thomas Adams, planter of Twillingate, 1820 (USPG); Dinah, of Joe Batts Arm, 1821 (USPG); Thomas, of Little Belle Isle (now Little Bell Island), 1825 (DPHW 26B); William, planter of Jigging Hole (Trinity North district), 1842 (DPHW 64B); John, planter of Salmon Cove (now part of South River), 1846 (DPHW 34); George, of Round Harbour (Twillingate district), 1851 (DPHW 86); John, fisherman of Great Burin, 1860 (DPHW 108); Thomas, fisherman of North Harbour (Placentia B.), 1871 (Lovell).

Modern status: Widespread, especially at St. John's, Milton and elsewhere in the Trinity North district, and at Upper Island Cove, Old Perlican and Burin.

Place names: Adams Cove 47-52 53-05, —— Head 47-45 54-01, —— Islands 49-06 58-21, —— Pond 47-32 52-53.

ADDERLEY, a surname of England, from the English place name Adderley (Shropshire). (Bardsley).

In Newfoundland: Rare, at Corner Brook.

ADE, a surname of England and France; in England, a pet form of the baptismal name Adam (*See* ADAMS), in France, where it is also an old baptismal name, from a Germanic source ? *adal* – noble. (Reaney, Dauzat 69).

In Newfoundland:

Family tradition: The Ades of Long Pond, Manuels, the only family of the name, believe themselves to be of Irish stock, though Ade is not recorded in MacLysaght, Woulfe or Matheson.

Early instances: Michael Aide, of Harbour Grace Parish, 1818 (Nfld. Archives HGRC); Mary Anne, of St. John's, 1843 (DPHW 26D); Maria, of Harbour Grace, 1870 (Nfld. Archives HGRC); John, of St. John's, 1871 (Lovell).

Modern status: At Long Pond, Manuels.

ADEAUX. *See* AUDEAUX

ADEY, a surname of England, a pet form of *Ade* (Adam) (*See* ADAMS). (Reaney).

Traced by Matthews in Devon and Dorset.

In Newfoundland:

Family tradition: The Adeys of Hants Harbour, Old Perlican and Twillingate came to Newfoundland with the firm of Robert Slade of Poole (Dorset) in the early 1700s. The Adeys of Adeytown moved from Hants Harbour about 1873. Some family sources give Bristol, where the name is still found, as their home about 1850. Adey has been confused with EDDY, to which some Adeys changed their name in 1950. (A.W. Adey).

Early instances: Stephen Ad(e)y, of Bay de Verde, 1791 (DPHW 64); Isaac Ady, proprietor of fishing room at Old Perlican, Winter 1800-01 (Census Trinity B.); Martin and James, proprietors, and Isaac, occupier of fishing rooms at Hants Harbour, Winter 1800-01 (Census Trinity B.); W. Adey, in salmon fishery at Fogo, 1808 (CO 194.48); James Ady, fisherman of Trinity, 1821 (DPHW 64); John Aidey, of Catalina, 1822 (DPHW 70); Martin Adey, fisherman of Seal Cove (now New Chelsea), 1849 (DPHW 59A); William Addy, farmer of Salmon Cove (now part of South River), 1850 (DPHW 34); William, of Foster's Point (Trinity B.), 1883 (DPHW 68).

Modern status: Especially in the Trinity North district, at Adeytown and Clarenville.

Place names: Adeyto(w)n 48-05 53-56, Adies Pond 49-25 55-17, —— River 49-31 57-06.

AHERNE, a surname of Ireland, *Ó hEachthigheirn,* Ir. *each* – steed, *tighearna* – lord. (MacLysaght).

MacLysaght states that at the present time the name is almost confined to Cos. Cork and Limerick, and that in Co. Waterford the English name HEARN is used as a synonym, though some persons named Hearn may be English immigrants.

In Newfoundland:

Early instances: Maurice Ahern, sergeant in the Royal Newfoundland Regiment, 1797 (D'Alberti 6); John, from Cove (for Cobh) Parish (Co. Cork) married at St. John's, 1806 (Nfld. Archives BRC); William Aheron, of Harbour Grace Parish, 1815 (Nfld. Archives HGRC); Patrick Ahearn, of Kings Cove, 1828 (Nfld. Archives KCRC).

Modern status: The name seems to have been rare in Newfoundland and is now obsolete; but some Ahernes here are also said to have changed their name to Hearn. Rev. Sr. M. de Sales Ahearn was a nun in the Mercy Convent, St. John's, 1955 (*Electors* 1955).

AHIER, an old Jersey (Channel Islands) surname formerly Ahyi or Ayi. See also AYERS. (Le Maistre).

In Newfoundland:

Family tradition: John, of Fortune, married about 1870 (MUN Hist.).

Modern status: At Grand Bank (*Electors* 1955), and Burin Bay Arm.

AIKEN, AITKEN, AITKIN(S), Scots forms of the English and Irish surname ATKINS, a pet-form of Adam (See ADAMS). In addition in Ireland Aiken may have sometimes been used for O'Hagan, *Ó hAogáin.* (Reaney, Black, MacLysaght).

Guppy traced Aitken in Lanarkshire and adjacent counties; MacLysaght Aiken in northeast Ulster.

In Newfoundland:

Modern status: All forms are rare and scattered with small concentrations of Aitken in Botwood, Grand Falls and Deer Lake.

AINSWORTH, a surname of England from the English place name Ainsworth (Lancashire). (Bardsley).

Traced by Guppy in Lancashire and Shropshire, with Hainsworth in Yorkshire ER, and by Matthews in Dorset and Hampshire.

In Newfoundland:

Early instances: Samuel and William, drummers at St. John's, 1774 (DPHW 26C); Charles Answorth, of Trinity (Trinity B.), 1812 (DPHW 64).

Modern status: At St. John's from Accrington (Lancashire) since 1953.

AITKEN, AITKIN(S). *See* AIKEN

AKERMAN. *See* ACKERMAN

ALBERT, a baptismal name and surname of England and France, from an Old German personal name containing the elements *noble* and *bright.* (Withycombe, Reaney, Dauzat).

In Newfoundland: The present Alberts of St. John's are believed to be of French origin, formerly Aubert, but came to Newfoundland from London, England, in 1941. (Family).

ALCOCK, a surname of England and Ireland, from the English baptismal name Al[l]an or some other short name in *Al-,* plus *-cock,* "a kind of affectionate or diminutive suffix," "meaning ... probably 'boy' or 'servant,' for *cock* was used as a nickname for one who strutted like a cock and became a common term for a pert boy, being used of scullions, apprentices and servants." (Reaney *Origin,* pp. 211-13). See COX.

Guppy traced Alcock in Nottinghamshire and Staffordshire; MacLysaght in Co. Waterford since the late 17th century.

In Newfoundland:

Early instances: Mansfield, of Harbour Grace, 1801 (CO 199.18); Robert, of Leading Tickles, 1853 (DPHW 86).

Modern status: Somewhat rare and scattered but with small concentrations at St. John's and Leading Tickles. As the name of a transient at Gander in *Electors* 1955 it appeared in the variant Alcoe, borne by a descendant of Charlotte Alcock who, on leaving Newfoundland for New Brunswick, changed her name to Alcoe "because Alcock was a vulgar name." Reaney notes the pronunciation Coeburn for Cockburn and Coeshott for Cockshott. (Dr. Shirley Alcoe, great-granddaughter of Charlotte).

Place name: Alcock Island 49-31 55-25.

ALDERDICE, ALLARDYCE, surnames of Scotland and Ireland, from the old barony of Allardice in the parish of Arbuthnott, (Kincardineshire). Allardyce, Allardice and Allardes are the usual Scots forms, Alderdice in Cos. Antrim and Armagh, Ireland. (Black).

In Newfoundland:

Family traditions: Frederick Charles Alderdice, born in Belfast, came to St. John's in 1886 (MUN Folklore). James Allardyce, from Aberdeen, came to St. John's in 1929 (Family).

Modern status: Rare, at St. John's.

ALDRICH, a surname of England with at least eight variant forms, usually derived from Old English personal names containing the elements *elf* and *ruler* or *noble* and *ruler*; or from the English place name Aldridge (Staffordshire, Buckinghamshire), or from an unidentified place in or near Worcester. (Reaney). See also ELDRIDGE, ETHERIDGE and OLDRIDGE.

Guppy traced Aldrich, Alldridge in Berkshire, Gloucestershire, Hertfordshire, Norfolk, Suffolk and Surrey, with the comment that "Alldridge is the usual form in all these counties except in Norfolk and Suffolk, where it is associated with Aldrich." Spiegelhalter traced a further variant OLDRIDGE to the English place names in Devon, and Matthews traced Alridge in Dorset and Hampshire.

In Newfoundland:

Early instances: Edward Aldridge, of Fortune, 1765 (CO 194.16); Christopher, major in Royal Newfoundland Regiment, 1795 (CO 194.41); Butler, Commissioner of roads from Conception Bay to Trinity Bay, 1834 (*Newfoundlander* 19 Jun 1834); ———, of Grand Bank, 1840-41 (MUN Hist); Louisa Allridge, of Carbonear, 1858 (DPHW 49).

Modern status: Aldrich introduced in 1961.

Place names: Aldridge Head and Rock 47-37 57-35.

ALEXANDER, a baptismal name and surname of England, Scotland, Ireland, Jersey (Channel Islands) and Syria-Lebanon, from the Greek personal name meaning "defender of men." (Withycombe, Reaney, Black, Turk).

Guppy traced Alexander in Wiltshire, Kent, Northumberland, Norfolk and found it scattered in Scotland; Spiegelhalter traced it in Devon; Matthews in Dorset and Jersey (Channel Islands); MacLysaght in Cos. Antrim and Down, adding that "less than a century ago fourteen synonyms of it were recorded in Ulster birth registrations." Cottle remarks that it became "current in Scotland after English-born

Queen Margaret named a son Alexander, and Alexanders II and III reigned 1214-85; hence generic name *Sandy* for a Scot."

In Newfoundland:

Early instances: Stephen, of Newfoundland, ? 1706 (CO 194.24); William, from Campbelltown (Argyleshire), Scotland, merchant of Bonavista, 1817, died ? 1828 (Nfld. Archives KCRC, *Royal Gazette* 9 Sep 1828); James, of Lymington (Hampshire), at St. John's, 1836 (DPHW 26D); ———, merchant of Sandy Point (St. Georges B.), 1849 (Feild); John, born 1865 at Wick (Caithness), at St. John's, 1883, later at Bonavista (MUN Folklore); Andreas, of Harbour Grace, 1867 (Nfld. Archives HGRC); John, fisherman of Indian Head (St. Georges B.), 1871 (Lovell), originally of Chezzetcook (Nova Scotia), ? of French stock, at Kippens, ? 1900 (MUN Folklore).

Modern status: Almost exclusively on the West Coast and especially at Stephenville and Kippens.

Place names (not necessarily from the surname): Alexander (formerly Bloody) Bay 48-43 53-56, ——— Island 49-38 55-40, ——— Rock 49-47 55-10, and localities in Labrador.

ALLAN, ALLEN, baptismal names and surnames of England, Ireland and Scotland, Allen of the Channel Islands, of various origins. In England, and sometimes in Scotland and Ireland, they derive from Old French *Alain, Alein*, old Breton *Alan*, "the name of a Welsh and Breton saint, which was popular with the Bretons who came over with the conqueror, particularly in Lincolnshire" (Reaney). "But early Breton stem *Alamn* – suggests an origin in Germanic tribal [name] *Alemann* – All men, as in French name for Germany" (Cottle). In Scotland it may also derive from the Old Gaelic name *Ailéne* or *Ailin*, from *ail* – rock. In Ireland it may derive from both the foregoing, or from *Ó hAillín* in Cos. Offaly and Tipperary, or it may be a synonym of Hallinan in Tipperary. (Withycombe, Reaney, Cottle, Black, MacLysaght, Turk).

Guppy found Allan in Northumberland and Southern Scotland, Allen widespread in England, with a further variant, Allin, in Devon and Oxfordshire. Matthews found Allen widespread in Devon, Dorset and Somerset.

In Newfoundland:

Family tradition: Four Allen brothers from Portugal Cove lived at Topsail in 1822 (MUN Hist.).

Early instances: Joseph Allen, of St. John's, 1705 (CO 194.3); Thomas Allan, surgeon (? of Newfoundland), ? 1753 (CO 194.3); John Allen, of

St. John's, 1772 (DPHW 26C); Richard, of Burin, 1780 (D'Alberti 6); James and Robert, in fishery at Portugal Cove, 1794-5 (Census 1794-5); George, born at Greenspond, 1804 (DPHW 76); John, from Kill Parish (Co. Waterford), married at St. John's, 1808 (Nfld. Archives BRC); Richard, of Harbour Grace Parish, 1812 (Nfld. Archives HGRC); Alexander, from Montroac, Scotland (unidentified), of St. John's, died 1844, aged 53 (Times 18 Dec 1844); William Allan, surgeon, from Greenock, of Brigus and later the Barrens, 1850 (Nfld. Patriot 26 Jan 1850); Cyrus Allen, of Woody Island (Placentia B.), 1851 (DPHW 105); James, of Herring Neck, 1854 (DPHW 85); James, fisherman of Green Cove (Twillingate district), 1855 (DPHW 85); John, fisherman of Bird Island Cove (now Elliston), 1857 (DPHW 72); George, fisherman of Carbonear, 1858 (DPHW 49); John, fisherman of Burin, 1871 (Lovell); Richard, farmer of Flatrock (St. John's), 1871 (Lovell); Samuel, fisherman of Great Jervis, 1871 (Lovell); James, fisherman of Haystack, 1871 (Lovell); Richard, of Petty Harbour, 1871 (Lovell); John, of Bay of Islands, 1871 (Lovell).

Modern status: In *Electors* 1955, Allan is much rarer than Allen, with small concentrations at Flatrock (where the Allans may be of Irish descent), St. John's and Jacques Fontaine. Allen has concentrations at St. John's, Woody Island (Placentia B.), Mount Moriah and Curling.

Place names (not necessarily from the surname): Allan Brook 49-09 58-01, 50-44 57-13, —— Cove 47-42 56-18, —— Head 47-42 56-19, —— Rock 46-52 55-48, Allan's Island 46-51 55-48, —— Cove Brook 47-42 56-17, Allen Bank 46-59 55-06, —— Rock 47-21 54-17, —— Shoal 47-36 53-59, 52-04 55-39, Allens Brook 48-58 58-03, —— Cove 49-50 56-31, —— Pond 48-00 54-36.

ALLARDYCE. *See* ALDERDICE

ALLEY, a surname of England and Ireland, from an Old Scandinavian and Old English personal name *Alle, Alli,* found in Domesday Book (Reaney), or, according to Spiegelhalter from the English place names Allaleigh (Devon) or, following Weekley, from (dweller) at the lee or clearing (Reaney, Weekley *Romance,* Spiegelhalter, MacLysaght 73).

Traced by Spiegelhalter in Devon and by MacLysaght as formerly numerous in Cos. Kildare and Leix, but now rare.

In Newfoundland:

Early instances: John, of Corbin (Fortune B.), 1835 (DPHW 30); Nicholas, of Crabbes, 1871 (DPHW 96).

Modern status: Essentially a West Coast name, especially at St. David's and in *Electors* 1955 at St. Fintan's.

ALLINGHAM, a surname of England and Ireland, from the English place name Allingham (Kent), found in Ballyshannon (Co. Donegal) since 1613 and later in Co. Leitrim. See also HALLINGHAM. (Bardsley, MacLysaght).

In Newfoundland:

Early instances: J., of Co. Donegal, now of St. John's, 1834 (*Newfoundlander* 25 Sep 1834); William, fisherman of Brandy Islands (St. Barbe district), 1869 (DPHW 93).

Modern status: At Brig Bay and Flowers Cove.

AL(L)STON, surnames of England and Scotland, from the Old English personal name *Æthelstān* – noble stone; or from other Old English names containing the elements *elf, old, temple* or *stone;* or from the English place names, Alston (Lancashire, Devon, Cumberland, Somerset) or Alstone (Gloucestershire). Black suggests that the Scots surname derives from Alston (Cumberland). (Reaney, Cottle).

Alston traced by Guppy in Suffolk, by Spiegelhalter in Devon, and by Black in Glasgow, Ayrshire and Lanarkshire.

In Newfoundland:

Early instance: John W. Alston, of Liverpool, married at St. John's, 1858 (DPHW 23).

Modern status: Allston, of West Bergholt (Essex), at St. John's since 1954.

ALSOP, a surname of England and Scotland from the English place name Alsop en le Dale (Derbyshire). (Reaney).

Al(l)sop traced by Guppy in Derbyshire, Nottinghamshire and Staffordshire, by Matthews in Devon, and by Black in Aberdeen.

In Newfoundland:

Early instance: Robert Jr., merchant of St. John's, 1812 (CO 194.57). Modern status: Unique, at St. John's.

ALTEEN, a surname of Syria-Lebanon.

In Newfoundland:

Family tradition: ——, from Ryshya, Lebanon, emigrated to Canada about 1900, settled in the Maritimes and moved to Newfoundland about 1939 (Family).

Modern status: At Corner Brook and Grand Falls.

ALYWARD, ? a Newfoundland variant of AYLWARD.
  In Newfoundland:
  Modern status: At Cape Broyle (*Electors* 1955), St. John's and Grand Falls.

AM(M)INSON, ? Newfoundland variants of the surname of England Amison – son of *Amice*, *Ami(s)*, from Latin *amicus* – friend, later slave. (Withycombe, Reaney).
  In Newfoundland: At St. John's since about 1870 (Family).

ANDERSON, a surname of England, Scotland, Ireland and Guernsey (Channel Islands), – son of Andrew (See ANDREWS). (Reaney, Turk).
  Traced by Guppy especially in the north of England, by Matthews in Devon, and by Black "over a good part of Scotland." MacLysaght describes Anderson as "one of the most numerous English names in Ireland" especially in northeast Ulster.
  In Newfoundland:
  Early instances: John and William, traders who sustained losses when St. Pierre was surrendered to the French in 1763 (CO 194.16); John, cooper of Petty Harbour, about 1767 (Census 1794-5); Richard, of Trinity Bay, 1775 (DPHW 64); James, of St. John's, 1800-17 (CO 194.59, DPHW 26B); Henry, of Salmon Cove (now part of South River), 1806 (DPHW 34); Anderson and Comer, merchants of Adams Cove, 1816 (CO 194.57); John, planter of British Harbour, 1820 (DPHW 64); William, of Tilton Harbour (now Tilting), 1822 (Nfld. Archives KCRC); Elizabeth, of Fortune, 1823 (DPHW 106); Thomas, of New Harbour (Trinity B.), 1825 (Nfld. Archives KCRC); Thomas, of Harbour Grace Parish, 1828 (Nfld. Archives HGRC); Elizabeth, of Burgeo Islands, baptized 1830, aged 16 (DPHW 30); R., from Waterford, arrived at Harbour Grace, 1833 (*Carbonear Star* 22 May 1833); Robert, of Couteau, 1835 (DPHW 30); John, of Cupids, 1840 (DPHW 34); William, of Nippers Harbour, 1843 (DPHW 86); Thomas, fisherman of West Point (Burgeo-La Poile district), 1843 (DPHW 101); Joseph, of Caplin Cove (Trinity B.), born 1845 (DPHW 59A); Edward and family, of Upper Burgeo, 1849 (Feild); William (1846-99), born at Girvan (Ayrshire), doctor at Port de Grave, 1867, died at Heart's Content (MUN Folklore); William, of Otter Point (Burgeo-La Poile district), 1847, (DPHW 101); Catherine, of Grates Cove, 1849 (DPHW 58); Mary, of Hants Harbour, 1849 (DPHW 59); Edward, of Scilly Cove (now Winterton), 1857 (DPHW 59); William, of Petites, 1857 (DPHW 98); Charles, fisherman of Rose Blanche, 1860 (DPHW

99); John, born 1855 at Saltcoats (Ayrshire), came to Newfoundland 1875 (Mott); Thomas, of Channel, 1871 (Lovell); Eli, fisherman of Codroy and Rivers, 1871 (Lovell); Benjamin and John, fishermen of Grand Bruit, 1871 (Lovell); William Jr., fisherman of Great Barrisway, 1871 (Lovell); George, James and William, fishermen of Hatters Point (Burgeo district), 1871 (Lovell); Robert, fisherman of Logy Bay, 1871 (Lovell).
  Modern status: Especially on the South and West Coasts.
  Place names: Anderson Island 49-42 54-44; —— Lookout 47-54 57-56; Billy Anderson Shoal 47-37 58-02; Andersons Brook 47-41 53-18, —— Cove 47-36 55-07, —— Pond 47-41 53-19.

ANDRE, a surname of England, ? from a French form of Andrew, *Andri*, though the possibility that it is a variant of the French surname André should not be ruled out. (See ANDREWS). (Reaney, Dauzat).
  In Newfoundland: Rare, at Corner Brook West and Too Good Arm.

ANDREWS, a surname of England and Ireland – son of Andrew, and as Andrew of Scotland, Andros or Andrews of Guernsey (Channel Islands), from the baptismal name of Greek origin meaning "manly." It is also the anglicized form of the Lebanese surname Andrea, and in Ireland sometimes a synonym of MacAndrew, Gaelic *Mac Aindriu* (Withycombe, Reaney, MacLysaght, Turk).
  Guppy found Andrews widespread in southern and western counties, especially Dorset, Hampshire and Wiltshire, and Andrew especially in Cornwall and Devon. MacLysaght found Andrews "fairly numerous in Dublin and north-east Ulster, rare elsewhere." Black describes Andrew as "common in Scotland, both as a forename and as a surname. Its popularity, no doubt, is due to its being the name of Scotland's patron saint."
  In Newfoundland:
  Family traditions: Samson, from Odcombe (Somerset), settled at Richards Harbour in 1867 and later moved to François (MUN Hist.). Ablain Andrea, from Hadeth el Joubbe (Lebanon), settled at St. John's about 1890 (Family).
  Early instances: John, of Port de Grave, 1763, but property "in possession of the Family for 105 years or upwards," that is, before 1658 (CO 199.18); John, Francis and Mary, of Harbour Grace, 1765, but property "possest by the Family for upwards of 90 years," that is, before 1675 (CO 199.18); Elias, boatkeeper of St. John's, 1681 (CO 1); Ambrose, of

Petty Harbour, 1703, of St. John's, 1708 (CO 194.3, 4); Charles, of Silly Cove (now Winterton), 1793 (DPHW 64); Charles, of Brigus, 1809 (DPHW 34); Aaron, planter of Hants Harbour, 1826 (DPHW 58); John, of Greenspond, 1831 (DPHW 76); Garland, of Upper Gully (now Gullies), 1832 (DPHW 30); Aron Andries or Andrews, planter of Crocker's Cove, 1833 (DPHW 48); —— Andrews, of Woody Island (Placentia B.), 1835 (Wix); James, of Grand Bank, 1838 (DPHW 109); Henry, of Widmore (Somerset), married at St. John's, 1839 (DPHW 26D); Henry, servant at Maggotty Cove, 1840 (DPHW 26B); Henry Andrew, planter of Trinity, 1841 (DPHW 64B); William Andrews, of Nippers Harbour, 1847 (DPHW 86); William, fisherman of Cupids, 1851 (DPHW 34); Eli, of Lower Island Cove, 1860 (DPHW 55); Thomas, George, John and Peter, planters of Cape Island (Bonavista B.), 1871 (Lovell); Stephen, planter of Cat Harbour (now Lumsden), 1871 (Lovell); Edward, fisherman of Chance Cove (Trinity B.), 1871 (Lovell); Aaron, fisherman of Heart's Desire, 1871 (Lovell); James, fisherman of New Bay (Notre Dame B.), 1871 (Lovell).

Modern status: Widespread, especially at St. John's, Ship Cove (Port de Grave), Winterton, Point Leamington and Bonavista North district.

Place name: Andrews Pond 48-14 54-09, surprisingly unique.

ANGEL(L), surnames of England, Angel formerly a baptismal name as in Hardy's Angel Clare, of England, from a flattering or sarcastic nickname derived from Latin *angelus* – messenger, angel. Cottle suggests that it may also be a sign-name – at the sign of the Angel (inn), or from confusion with the surname Angle, or for one who played this (easy) part in a religious play. (Withycombe, Reaney, Cottle).

Matthews found Angel associated with Paignton and Plymouth (Devon) and Bristol.

In Newfoundland:

Early instances: Samuell Angell, of Petty Harbour, ? 1706 – about 1725 (CO 194.7, 24); Samuel Angel, fisherman of St. John's, 1790, 1794-5, "born in Newfoundland" (DPHW 26D, Census 1794-5); Thomas, of Fermeuse, 1800 (D'Alberti 2); Thomas, merchant and J.P., of Bay Bulls, 1817 (CO 194.60); Samuel, of Petty Harbour, married at St. John's, 1822 (Nfld. Archives BRC); George, of Greenspond, 1823 (DPHW 76); James, born Halifax (Nova Scotia), 1838, to St. John's, 1850 (Mott); George Thomas Angell, of Trinity, 1857 (DPHW

26D); Benjamin Angel, fisherman at English Harbour (Trinity B.), 1871 (Lovell); Edmund, fisherman of Goulds, 1871 (Lovell); Isaac, telegraph operator at Heart's Content, 1871 (Lovell).

Modern status: Angel at St. John's and Grand Falls, Angell at Noggin Cove.

Place names (not necessarily from the surname): Angels Cove 47-00 54-09; Angel Head 48-56 53-39.

ANSFORD, a surname of England, from the English place name Ansford (Somerset). (Ekwall), or ? a variant of Handsford or Hansforth. See HANSFORD.

Early instance: William, of Harbour Breton, died 1915, aged 76. (Harbour Breton Anglican Church Records per D.A. MacDonald).

In Newfoundland: Rare, at Port aux Basques (*Electors* 1955).

ANSTEY, a surname of England, from the English place name Anstey (Devon, Dorset, Hampshire, Hertfordshire, Wiltshire) or Ansty (Warwickshire). (Reaney).

Guppy traced Anstey in Bedfordshire, Gloucestershire, Wiltshire and Dorset, and to a less extent in Devon.

In Newfoundland:

Family traditions: —— Anstey, from Ansteys Cove, near Torquay (Devon), of Little Bay Islands, about 1817 (MUN Folklore). Samuel Ansty, of Grand Beach (Burin district), 1841 (MUN Hist.).

Early instances: Nicholas Anstis (? a variant of Anstey), of Newfoundland, ? 1706 (CO 194.24); Charles Ainstey, of Twillingate, 1768 (MUN Hist.); Anne Ansty, of Greenspond, 1829 (Nfld. Archives KCRC); John, of Vere (now Fair) Island, 1830 (DPHW 76); Charles, fisherman of Bluff Head (Twillingate), 1840 (DPHW 88); William, of Leading Tickles, 1845 (DPHW 86); Elizabeth, of Grand Bank, 1852 (DPHW 106); John, fisherman of Merritts Harbour, 1857 (DPHW 85); Charles Anstey, of Petites, 1859 (DPHW 98); Beria, of Birchy Island, 1859 (DPHW 42); Joseph, of Black Island, 1859 (DPHW 42); Elizabeth, of Fortune, 1860 (DPHW 106); Thomas, of Little Harbour (Twillingate district), 1861 (DPHW 88); Jane, of Purcells Harbour, 1878 (DPHW 89).

Modern status: At Corner Brook and in the Twillingate district, especially Cottle's Island, Summerford, Back Harbour and Northside, and in the Burin district.

Place names: Anstey Point 47-33 54-51, —— Cove 49-39 55-49; Ansteys Brook 49-44 56-52.

ANTHONY, a baptismal name and surname of England, Wales and Ireland, Ant(h)oine of France, Anthony and Ant(h)oine of the Channel Islands, from the Latin personal name *Antonius*, of unknown origin, the name of many saints. Withycombe comments on the spelling and pronunciation: "The intrusive *h* in the spelling *Anthony* was a later development, and seems not to appear before the late 16th century. It may have been the result of false etymologizing, for Camden (1605) derives the name from Greek *anthos* [flower]. The *h* is, of course, silent, but there is some danger nowadays of a spelling pronunciation (already in use in USA), and the older spelling is to be preferred." (Reaney, Withycombe, Turk).

Guppy found Anthony mostly in South Wales, and in smaller numbers in Norfolk, Derbyshire and Devon; MacLysaght in Waterford since the 17th century.

In Newfoundland:

Family traditions: Joseph (1808-76), born at Cupids, married at Seldom Come By (MUN Hist.). Jesse, of Roberts Arm about 1870 (MUN Folklore). John and Samuel, of Pelleys Island about 1870 (MUN Folklore).

Early instances: As an English or Irish family name: Matthew Antony, of Trinity Harbour, 1682 (CO 1); Matthew Anton[y], of St. John's Harbour, 1703 (CO 194.3); Matthew Anthony, of Scilly Cove (now Winterton), 1706 (CO 194.4); Henry, of Port de Grave, 1803, but property "in possession of the Anthony's family for upwards of 80 years," that is, before 1723 (CO 199.18); Mary, of Cupids, 1770 (CO 199.18); Henry, carpenter of Torbay, 1794-5, born in Newfoundland (Census 1794-5); R., of Gasters, 1801 (CO 199.18); Joseph, of Bay Roberts, 1805 (DPHW 34); Pat Antony, of Harbour Grace Parish, 1806 (Nfld. Archives HGRC); Margaret, from Piltown (Co. Kilkenny), married at St. John's, 1830 (Nfld. Archives BRC); Elizabeth Anthony, of Chamberlains, 1838 (DPHW 26D); Henry, of Round Harbour (Twillingate district), 1842 (DPHW 86); John Antony, of Exploits Burnt Island, 1843 (DPHW 86); Henry, planter of Salmon Cove (now part of South River), 1847 (DPHW 34); Mary Anthony, of Clarke's Beach, 1860 (DPHW 38); Ananias and Job, fishermen of Kelligrews, 1871 (Lovell); William (? 1873-90), of Blaketown (DPHW 61).

As a French family name: John Anthoine, magistrate of Fortune Bay, 1811 (D'Alberti 21); John ? Antheine, merchant of Jersey Harbour, 1819 (DPHW 109); Anne Antoni, from Cape Breton, married at Kings Cove, 1829 (Nfld. Archives KCRC);

Francis Anethoine, merchant of Upper Burgeo, 1842 (DPHW 101); R. and F. Anthoine, J.P.'s, Fortune Bay district, 1844 (*Nfld. Almanac*).

Modern status: At St. John's, Roberts Arm, Pelleys Island, Upper Gullies; in small number at several communities in Conception Bay and elsewhere.

Place name (not necessarily from the surname): Anthony Island 48-12 53-28.

ANTLE, a variant of the English surname for which Reaney provides the forms Anketell, Ankettle, Anquetil, Ankill, Antell and Antill, from the Norman form of an old Norse personal name *Ásketill*. (Reaney). See also HASKELL.

Guppy traced Antell and Matthews Antle in Dorset; Anquetil is found in Guernsey and Jersey; Antill in Kent.

In Newfoundland:

Family traditions: ——, from Kent, England, emigrated to Brigus (Conception B.); the family later moved to Griguet, then Northern Arm (Botwood) (MUN Folklore). William Antile, of Bryants Cove, 1836 (MUN Hist.).

Early instances: William and widow, of Brigus, 1782, property "in possession of the Family for upwards of 80 years," that is, before 1702 (CO 199.118); John, proprietor and occupier of fishing room, Turks Cove (Trinity B.), winter 1800-01 (Census Trinity B.); William, planter of Cupids, 1827 (DPHW 34); Robert Antle or Antill, of Harbour Grace Parish, 1835 (Nfld. Archives HGRC); ——, on the *Five Brothers* in the seal fishery out of Port de Grave, 1838 (*Newfoundlander* 29 Mar 1838); John, fisherman of Crockers Cove (Carbonear), 1859 (DPHW 49); Jacob, of Harbour Grace, 1869 (Nfld. Archives HGRC); George Antell and Barney Antle, fishermen of Bay of Islands, 1871 (Lovell); Thomas Antle, of Northern Arm (now part of Botwood), 1886 (DPHW 92).

Modern status: At Victoria, Fox Cove and Mortier, St. John's and Botwood.

Place names: Antles Island 49-12 53-30, Antill Cove (Labrador) 52-13 55-40.

APPLEBY, a surname of England, from Old English *æppel* and Old Norse *by* – (dweller at the) apple-farm, or from the English place name Appleby (Westmorland, Leicestershire, Lincolnshire). (Bardsley, Cottle).

Traced by Guppy in Northumberland, Yorkshire NR and ER, Derbyshire, Durham and Essex.

In Newfoundland:

Family tradition: The Applebys of Path End and Lewins Cove (Burin district) (*Electors* 1955), subsequently at St. John's, probably arrived about 1880. (Family).

Early instances: ——, planter and merchant, from Exeter (Devon), at Renews in the mid-18th century (Matthews).

Modern status: Rare, at St. John's, Lewins Cove and Burin Bay Arm.

APPLIN, a surname of England, from a double diminutive of *Ab*, a pet-form of the baptismal name *Abel* – ? son. (Withycombe, Reaney).

Guppy traced the name only in Somerset.

In Newfoundland:

Early instances: Richard, of Scilly Cove (now Winterton), 1832 (DPHW 59); John Appleton, fisherman of Flowers Cove, 1871 (an error in the *Directory* for Applin) (Lovell); John, fisherman of Flowers Cove, 1874 (DPHW 95).

Modern status: In the St. Barbe district especially at Shoal Cove West.

ARCHER, a surname of England, Scotland, Ireland and the Channel Islands, from Middle English and Old French – (a notably skilled) bowman. Black maintains that it is an English rather than a Scottish surname, and that there were few families of the name in Scotland until recently. (Reaney, Cottle, MacLysaght, Black, Turk).

Guppy found the name widespread, especially in Derbyshire, Cumberland, Westmorland and Buckinghamshire, and also in Devon, Essex, Gloucestershire, Nottinghamshire and Staffordshire; Matthews at Poole (Dorset), South Devon and Bristol; and MacLysaght in Kilkenny since the 13th century.

In Newfoundland:

Early instances: Christopher, of St. John's, 1703, 1730 (CO 194.3, 9); Richard, constable, Trinity district, ? 1730-32 (CO 194.9); William, from Kestow (Devon) (unidentified), deserted apprenticeship at St. John's, 1836 (*Times* 8 Jun 1836); John, planter of Harbour Grace, 1838 (DPHW 43).

Modern status: In *Electors* 1955, at Aguathuna, now only in St. John's and district.

ARCHIBALD, a baptismal name and surname of England, Scotland and Ireland, from an Old German personal name containing the elements *precious* and *bold*. On its use in Scotland for Gaelic GILLESPIE, Black quotes Harrison: "Archibald was adopted by the Scots as a lowland equivalent of Gillespie

because the *bald* was mistakenly supposed to mean "hairless," "shaven," "servant," and therefore to be equivalent to Gaelic *gille* – servant, shaven one, monk." (Withycombe, Reaney, Cottle, Black).

MacLysaght remarks that Archibald or Archbald was a very early name in east Leinster.

In Newfoundland:

Early instances: ——, co-occupier of fishing room, Riders Harbour (Trinity B.), Winter 1800-01 (Census Trinity B.); Edward Mortimer, barrister, Chief Clerk and Registrar of the Supreme Court, St. John's, about 1835-44 (DPHW 26B, *Nfld. Almanac*), Frank Howard (1859-92), born Guysborough County (Nova Scotia), came to St. John's to work for Melvel Archibald, bootmaker, in 1879, and was later, ? from 1881, in business at Harbour Grace (Mott).

Modern status: At Harbour Grace.

ARKLIE, a surname of Scotland, associated with Forfarshire (now Angus). (Black).

In Newfoundland:

Family tradition: James, born at Crieff (Perthshire), from Glasgow to Botwood, 1911, thence to St. John's, but the family associations are with Manchester (Lancashire) in the 18th century (Family).

Modern status: At Grand Falls and Botwood.

ARMSTRONG, a surname of England, Scotland and Ireland, from the self-explanatory nickname; and in Ireland also as the anglicized form of Lavery and TRAINOR. (Reaney, MacLysaght).

Guppy found Armstrong especially common in Northumberland, Westmorland, Cumberland and Durham and in the counties of Southern Scotland; and MacLysaght "very numerous throughout Ulster." Matthews also traced it in Devon and Waterford.

In Newfoundland:

Early instances: Andrew, constable of Ferryland district, ? 1730-32 (CO 194.9); ——, a clergyman of St. John's, 1760 (DPHW 26C); William, of Bay Bulls, 1793 (USPG); William, merchant of Trepassey, 1797 (CO 194.39); William, lessee of land in vicinity of St. John's, 1803-05 (CO 194.45); James, of Witless Bay, 1804 (Nfld. Archives BRC); Thomas, of Harbour Grace Parish, 1829 (Nfld. Archives HGRC); Edward, of Old Perlican, 1835 (DPHW 58); Jacob, of Harbour Grace, 1868 (Nfld. Archives HGRC); Edward, fisherman of Lance Cove (now Brownsdale), 1871 (Lovell); Thomas, fisherman of La Manche (Ferryland district), 1871 (Lovell).

Modern status: Scattered.

ARNOLD, a baptismal name and surname of England, Wales and Ireland, from an Old German personal name containing the elements *eagle* and *power*, or from the English place name Arnold (Yorkshire ER, Nottinghamshire). See also ARNOTT, HARNETT. (Withycombe, Reaney, MacLysaght).

Guppy traced the name especially in South Wales, Monmouthshire, and south Midland counties; Spiegelhalter in Devon; MacLysaght in Dublin and northeast Ulster.

In Newfoundland:

Early instances: Joseph, of Sherborne (Dorset), apprentice of Henry Brooks of Bay Bulls, 1752 (Dorset County Record Office per Kirwin); George, defendant before Supreme Court, St. John's, 1810 (CO 194.50); Pat, from Co. Waterford, married at St. John's, 1811 (Nfld. Archives BRC); Archibald Arnolds, of Bonavista, 1816 (D'Alberti 26); J. Arnold, cooper of St. John's, 1820 (D'Alberti 30); John (1817-93), born in England, went to Greenspond with brother William in 1836, thence to Traytown (MUN Geog.); Charles, of Exploits Burnt Island, 1844 (DPHW 86); William, fisherman of Bloody (now Alexander) Bay, 1871 (Lovell); Thomas, fisherman of Indian Arm (Bonavista B.), 1872 (DPHW 80).

Modern status: Scattered, especially at Traytown (Bonavista B.).

Place names (not necessarily from the surname): Arnold Cove 46-37 53-33, 49-32 55-05; Arnolds Cove 47-45 54-00; —— Pond 48-38 53-39.

ARNOTT, a surname of England, Scotland and Ireland; in England a variant of ARNOLD, in Scotland and Ireland from the Scots place name Arnot (Kinross-shire). See also HARNETT. (Reaney, Black).

MacLysaght notes the townland Ballyarnott (Co. Antrim). Matthews records Arnard, Arnaud, captains of Plymouth (Devon), Arno, captains of Dartmouth (Devon), Arnott, captains of Dartmouth (Devon) and Poole (Dorset).

In Newfoundland: Other variants recorded of transients in *Electors* 1955 are Arnaud (also a French family name) and Arnett.

Early instances: James, of St. John's, 1812, 1817 (CO 194.52, 59); Archibald, of Bonavista, 1821 (CO 194.64); Jean Arnaud, a Frenchman, married at St. John's, 1855 (DPHW 23).

Modern status: Rare, at St. John's and Kelligrews.

ARNS, ? a variant of the German surname *Arends*, from a personal name containing the elements *eagle* and *rule*, similar to ARNOLD.

In Newfoundland: At St. John's.

ARTIS(S), surnames of England, from the French place name *Artois*, an old province of northern France, capital Arras. (Reaney).

In Newfoundland:

Modern status: Unique, at Corner Brook (*Electors* 1955), and St. John's.

ASH, a surname of England, and as Ashe of Ireland, denoting (the dweller by the) ash-tree, or from the English place names Ash (Derbyshire, Devon, Dorset, Herefordshire, Kent, Shropshire, Somerset, Surrey, Hampshire) or Nash (Herefordshire, Shropshire). See also NASH. (Reaney, Ekwall).

Guppy traced Ash in Staffordshire and Buckinghamshire; Spiegelhalter in Devon, where as Ashe it is the name of nineteen places; MacLysaght as Ashe in Cos. Meath and Kildare.

In Newfoundland:

Early instances: Nicholas, of Carbonear, 1776, but property "in possession of the Family for upwards of 98 years," that is, before 1678 (CO 199.18); Abraham, of St. John's, 1705 (CO 194.3); John, of Harbour Grace, 1775, but property "in possession of the Family for upwards of 61 years," that is, before 1714 (CO 199.18); Richard, proprietor and occupier of fishing room at Trinity (Trinity B.), Winter 1800-01 (Census Trinity B.); John, proprietor and occupier of fishing room at Old Perlican, Winter 1800-01 (Census Trinity B.); Henry, planter of Hants Harbour, 1819 (DPHW 58); William, of Caplin Cove (Harbour Grace district), 1827 (DPHW 43); Henry, planter of Salmon Cove (now Champneys), 1831 (DPHW 64B); William, from Kenton (Devon), of St. John's, died 1833 (*Royal Gazette* 5 Nov 1833); Richard, shipmaster of Trouty, 1838 (DPHW 64B); Elizabeth, of Dildo, ? about 1868 (*Evening Telegram* 21 Feb 1964); Solomon, of Crockers Cove (Carbonear), 1871 (Lovell).

Modern status: Scattered, especially at Carbonear, Harbour Grace, Hants Harbour and St. John's.

Place name (not necessarily from the surname): Ashe Rocks (Labrador) 59-53 64-02.

ASHBOURNE, a surname of England, from an English river name – (dweller by the) stream where ash-trees grow, or from the English place name Ashbourne (Derbyshire) or Ashburton, formerly Ashbourne (Devon). (Ekwall).

Spiegelhalter traced Ashburn, Ashburton in Devon.

In Newfoundland:

Family tradition: Two brothers were captured by pirates and landed in Newfoundland (Family).

Early instances: John Ashborn, of Twillingate, 1867 (Nfld. Archives HGRC); Thomas Ashburn, planter of South Islands, Twillingate, 1871 (Lovell).

Modern status: In the Twillingate district.

ASHFORD, a surname of England, from the English place name Ashford (Devon, Derbyshire, Shropshire). (Reaney).

Guppy traced Ashford in Cornwall, Devon, Suffolk and Warwickshire.

In Newfoundland:

Early instances: Thomas, member of court at St. John's, 1751 (CO 194.13); John, of Bay de Verde, 1774 (CO 199.18); William Aishford, of Catalina, 1833 (DPHW 67); William Ashford, member of the Board of Road Commissioners for the area Ragged Harbour to Bird Island (Trinity B.), 1857 (*Nfld. Almanac*): Charles, fisherman of Sagona [Island], 1852 (DPHW 104); Charles, fisherman of Rose Blanche, 1860 (DPHW 99).

Modern status: At Harbour Breton, Gaultois, Rose Blanche, Hallstown and Glendale.

ASHLEY, a surname of England – (dweller by the) ash-tree wood or clearing; or from the English place name Ashley in fifteen counties including Devon. (Cottle).

Traced by Guppy only in Shropshire, but by Spiegelhalter also in Devon.

In Newfoundland:

Early instances: John, cooper, and John, fisherman, at St. John's, 1871 (Lovell).

Modern status: At St. John's, and formerly at Upper Coast Trepassey (*Electors* 1955).

ASHMAN, a surname of England, from the Old English occupational name and nickname *æscmann* – shipman, sailor, pirate. (Reaney).

Traced by Guppy in Somerset and by Reaney also in Essex.

In Newfoundland:

Early instances: George, of St. John's, 1816 (DPHW 26B); Thomas, married at St. John's, 1833 (Nfld. Archives BRC); Thomas, merchant of Herring Neck, 1871 (Lovell).

Modern status: At St. John's (*Electors* 1955).

ASKEW, a surname of England, from the English place name Aiskew (Yorkshire NR), or (dweller in or near the) oakwood. (Reaney, Cottle).

Traced by Guppy in Cambridgeshire and Derbyshire.

In Newfoundland:

Family tradition: One family only in St. John's from Wandsworth (Surrey), 1920 (Family).

Modern status: Rare, at St. John's.

ASPELL, a surname of England and Ireland; in England from the English place names Aspall (Suffolk) or Aspal (Lancashire), or (dweller in the) valley overgrown with aspens, or (dweller on the) aspen hill. In Ireland, Aspell is a variant of Archbold (Archibald) in east Leinster. (Bardsley, Ekwall, MacLysaght).

In Newfoundland:

Early instances: John Aspbell, married in the Northern District, 1814 (Nfld. Archives BRC); Michael Aspel or Aspal, of Harbour Grace Parish, 1815 (Nfld. Archives HGRC); John Asbell, Aspell or Asple, of Riders Harbour, 1815 (Nfld. Archives KCRC); Patrick Asbell, of Hearts Content, 1819 (Nfld. Archives KCRC); Mary Anne Aspell, from Waterford, of St. John's, 1823 (Nfld. Archives BRC); Richard, of Adamstown (Co. Wexford), married at St. John's, 1828 (Nfld. Archives BRC); Robert, of St. John's, 1832 (DPHW 26D); Mary Aspel, occupier of a fishing room in Newfoundland before 1833 (Exeter Library Archives per Kirwin); Anna, of Harbour Grace, 1866 (Nfld. Archives HGRC); Andrew and James Aspell, fishermen of Cape Broyle, 1871 (Lovell); James, planter of Brigus, 1871 (Lovell).

Modern status: Rare, at St. John's, Admiral's Cove and Bay Bulls.

ATKINS, a surname of England and Ireland, a diminutive of Adam. (*See* ADAMS and also AIKEN, ATKINSON). (Reaney, MacLysaght).

Guppy found Atkins (Adkins) widespread, especially in Oxfordshire, Northamptonshire and Warwickshire; Matthews maintains a Devon and Dorset origin; MacLysaght found Atkins especially in Co. Cork.

In Newfoundland:

Early instances: Stephen, keeper of Mr. Butler's castle at Cupids Cove, 1675 (CO 1); Henry, merchant of St. John's, 1736 (CO 194.10); Eliz., laundress of Petty Harbour, 1794-5, "born in Newfoundland," (Census 1794-5); Thomas Atkin, from St. Patricks Parish, Dublin, married at St. John's, 1811 (Nfld. Archives BRC); Dianna, born at Emmanuels (? Manuels), 1812 (DPHW 30); Richard, of Garia, 1859 (DPHW 98); James and William, planters and fishermen of Grates Cove, 1871 (Lovell); Richard, of Rose Blanche, 1871 (Lovell).

Modern status: Small concentrations at St. John's and Bell Island.

ATKINSON, a surname of England and Ireland, son of Atkin. (*See* ADAMS and also AIKEN, ATKINS). (Reaney, MacLysaght).

Guppy found Atkinson widespread and especially in Durham, Cumberland and Westmorland. MacLysaght found it mainly in Ulster.

In Newfoundland: Of Devon origin (Matthews).

Modern status: Scattered.

AT(T)WOOD, surnames of England – (dweller) at the wood. (Reaney).

Traced by Guppy in Worcestershire and Bedfordshire, and by Matthews in Devon.

In Newfoundland:

Early instances: Esau, proprietor of fishing room at Pond Island, Greenspond Harbour, 1778 (Bonavista Register 1806); James Henry, from England, of St. John's, 1810 (D'Alberti 20, 21); Elizabeth, baptized at Pool's Island, 1830, aged 12 (DPHW 76); John, planter of Salvage, 1846 (DPHW 72).

Modern status: Somewhat rare, but especially associated with Corner Brook, Badgers Quay and Safe Harbour.

Place name: Attwoods Island 49-06 53-37.

ATWILL, the Devon and Somerset variant of the English surname Atwell – (dweller) by the stream or spring. See also WELLMAN, WELLON, WELLS. (Reaney).

In Newfoundland:

Early instances: —— Attwell, of Quidi Vidi, 1703 (CO 194.3); Walter Atwell, planter of Fogo, 1808 (MUN Hist.); William Atwill, farmer of Brookfield Road, St. John's, 1840 (DPHW 26B); Richard Atwell (1828-72) from Broadhempston (Devon), master mason of St. John's (General Protestant Cemetery, St. John's).

Modern status: Rare, at St. John's.

ATWOOD, *See* ATTWOOD

AU, a Chinese name with a variety of meanings: hook, unit of measurement. (So).

In Newfoundland:

Modern status: At St. John's.

AUCHINLECK, a surname of Scotland from the Scots place name Auchinleck (Ayrshire). (Black).

In Newfoundland:

Modern status: At St. John's.

AUCOIN, a surname of France, from an Old German personal name containing the elements *temple* and *friend.* (Dauzat).

In Newfoundland: Aucoin has sometimes been hibernicized to O'Quinn. (*See* QUINN).

Tradition: Four Aucoins, Séverin, Tassien, Isaac and Constant, sons of Raphaël Aucoin, of Chéticamp, N.S., arrived in Newfoundland in 1847. Tassien and Constant settled at Stephenville, Séverin at St. George's, and Isaac in the Codroy Valley where another branch of Aucoins, Mesmin and Onésime, also settled about 1848. (G.R. Thomas).

Modern status: Stephenville area especially Kippens.

A(U)DEAUX, ? Newfoundland variants of the surname of France Audoux – son of a (pea) pod, a nickname, or son of the sweet and gentle one. (Dauzat).

In Newfoundland:

Modern status: At Placentia (*Electors* 1955).

AUGOT, ? a Newfoundland variant of the surname of France Auguet – the watchman, look-out. (Dauzat).

In Newfoundland:

Modern status: At Harbour Breton.

AUGUSTUS, a baptismal name and rare surname of ? Portugal and England, 5 in London Telephone Directory 1962, from the Latin *augustus* – venerable, consecrated, cited by Bardsley from the register of St. George's Church, Hanover Square, London, 1772: "Married Isaac Augustus and Rebecca Rawlins," where presumably it is a Jewish name. However, by Lord Hardwick's Marriage Act of 1753, Jews and Quakers were not obliged to be married in the Church of England after that date. (Withycombe, Bardsley).

In Newfoundland:

Family tradition: Dominic, from Oporto, Portugal, was a stowaway on a fish-carrier running between Ramea and Oporto; on reaching Ramea he commenced work with the Penny firm there, about 1918. Later, his brothers Jeremiah and Julio came and settled in Ramea (Family).

Early instances: George, of St. John's, 1795 (CO 194.41). In the French form, Auguste: Eugene, of Fortune, a Methodist, 1852 (DPHW 106).

Modern status: At Ramea.

AUSTEN, AUSTIN(S), surnames of England, Ireland and Scotland, common diminutive mediaeval forms of the baptismal name Augustine, held by two saints. In Scotland, Austin may also be an anglicization of the Gaelic *Uisdean*. (Withycombe, Reaney, MacLysaght, Black).

The name is common in the Midlands and south of England: "Austin is the more frequent form, Austen being found mostly in Kent and Dorsetshire" (Guppy). MacLysaght remarks that Austin, on record in Ireland since the early 14th century, "is now fairly numerous but not closely identified with any particular area."

In Newfoundland: Matthews maintains that the Austins in the more northern parts are from Dorset, the Austens of St. John's from Devon.

Early instances: William Austin, of Trinity, 1803 (DPHW 64); Elinor, from Carrick (Co. Tipperary), married at St. John's, 1811 (Nfld. Archives BRC); John, of Fogo Harbour, 1817 (Nfld. Archives KCRC); John, of Harbour Grace Parish, 1823 (Nfld. Archives HGRC); William, from Moreton Hampstead (Devon), ? of St. John's, 1832 (DPHW 31); Virtusus, of Old Perlican, 1857 (DPHW 58); Samuel, assistant lighthouse keeper at Cape Pine, 1857 (*Nfld. Almanac*); William, fisherman of Round Harbour (Fogo), 1871 (Lovell); William, of King's Cove, 1874 (DPHW 90).

Modern status: Austen, at St. John's; Austin, especially at Brownsdale and Snooks Arm.

AVERY, a surname of England and of Guernsey (Channel Islands), from a French pronunciation of the English baptismal name Alfred. It is one of the few surnames from this baptismal name. Spiegelhalter would also derive it from the French place name Avaray (Loir-et-Cher). (Withycombe, Reaney, Cottle, Spiegelhalter, Turk).

Traced by Guppy in Sussex, Buckinghamshire, Somerset and Devon.

In Newfoundland: Matthews maintains that the Averys in Newfoundland are of Devon stock.

Family tradition: Nathan, from England, settled at Lance Cove (now Brownsdale) about 1820 (MUN Hist.).

Early instances: William, of Bonavista, 1793 (DPHW 70); ——, owner of fishing room at Keels before 1805 (Bonavista Register 1806); Mary, of Grates Cove, 1830 (DPHW 58); William, of Deadman's Bay (Bonavista North district), 1838 (DPHW 76); Thomas, member of Board of Road Commissioners for Ferryland district, 1844 *(Nfld. Almanac)*; Newman, of Catalina, 1857 (DPHW 67); John, of Fox Harbour (Trinity B.), 1858 (DPHW 59A); James, a trader of Old Bonaventure, 1871 (Lovell).

Modern status: At St. John's, Deep Bight, Southport, Long Beach, Hillview, all in the Trinity North district, and Grates Cove.

AYERS, AYRE(S), AYRIS, surnames of England and Scotland, Ayres, Eyres of Ireland, of various derivations: from words in Middle English, Old French etc. from Latin *heres* – heir; from an Old English personal name; from the Scots place name, Ayr; ? as an anglicization of the Jersey (Channel Islands) family name AHIER. (Reaney, Cottle, Black, MacLysaght).

Guppy traced Ayre in Devonshire, Ayres in Berkshire.

In Newfoundland:

Early instances: Roger Ayres, of Port de Grave, 1681 (CO 1); John, of Bonavista, 1708-09 (CO 194.4) Christopher Ayre, of Plymouth, married at St. John's, 1831 (DPHW 26D); George, merchant of Hants Harbour, 1834 (DPHW 59A); Thomas Ayres, of South Taunton (Devon), deserted from service of William Brown, Southside, St. John's, 1835, aged about 21 (*Ledger* 5 May 1835); Elizabeth Ayres, of Fortune, 1853 (DPHW 106); Phillip Ayers, of Meadow (Burin district), 1860 (DPHW 107); ? same as Philip, fisherman of Lamaline, 1871 (Lovell); Charles Robert (1819-89), born Exeter (Devon), arrived in Newfoundland, 1832 (Mott).

Modern status: Ayers in Corner Brook; Ayre in St. John's and scattered; Ayris unique, at St. John's.

AYLES, a surname of England ? from an Old English personal name *Ægel*, found as an element in several English place names: Aylesbeare (Devon), Aylesford (Kent), Aylestone (Leicestershire); or ? from Middle English *egle* – loathsome, troublesome. (Ekwall, Reaney Notes).

Guppy traced the name only in Hampshire, but Matthews found it associated with Dorset.

In Newfoundland:

Early instances: James, of Bonavista, 1804 (DPHW 70); Robert, from Poole (Dorset), son-in-law of Robert Pack of Carbonear, merchant of Carbonear, 1831, died 1851 (*Newfoundlander* 15 Sep 1831, *Weekly Herald* 22 Jan 1851); Charles, of Pool's Island, 1852 (DPHW 76); John, fisherman of Swain's Island, 1871 (Lovell).

Modern status: Somewhat rare, at Port Rexton, and at Mockbeggar, Bonavista, and Summerfield (Bonavista South district).

Place name: Bob Ayles Pond 47-48 53-17.

AYLWARD, a surname of England and Ireland, from an Old English personal name containing the elements *noble* and *protector*, sometimes confused with another personal name containing the elements *elf* and *guard* which has given the family names Al(l)ward and Elward. According to MacLysaght, Elward is a synonym of Aylward in the Carrick-on-Suir area. (Reaney, MacLysaght). *See also* ELLARD, ALYWARD.

Matthews associates Aylward with Devon and Kilkenny, MacLysaght with Waterford.

In Newfoundland:

Family traditions: Michael Alward, from Co. Kilkenny, settled at St. John's in 1850 (MUN Folklore). James Aylward, from Keels (Bonavista B.), early settler of Kings Cove, about 1784 (Devine, *Old King's Cove*).

Early instances: John Alyard, boatkeeper of St. John's, 1681 CO 1); Robert Allword, boatkeeper of St. John's, 1682 CO 1); James Aylward, of Bonavista, married at Kings Cove, 1803 (Nfld. Archives BRC); Catherine, of Keels, married at Kings Cove, 1803 (Nfld. Archives BRC); Richard, from Sleveross (? for Slieverue) (Co. Kilkenny), married at St. John's, 1804 (Nfld. Archives BRC); John, from Co. Kilkenny, fisherman of St. John's, deceased 1811 (*Royal Gazette* 17 Oct 1811); James, from Ramsgate, England, married at St. John's, 1817 (Nfld. Archives BRC); James, of Greenspond, 1817 (Nfld. Archives KCRC); Mary, of Harbour Grace Parish, 1822 (Nfld. Archives HGRC); Sally, of Plate Cove (Bonavista B.), 1824 (Nfld. Archives KCRC); Sera, of Tickle Cove (Bonavista B.), 1827 (Nfld. Archives KCRC); Honora, of Joe Batts Arm, 1827 (Nfld. Archives KCRC); Mary, of Co. Kilkenny, married at Ragged Harbour (unspecified), 1829 (Nfld. Archives KCRC); ——, teacher of Petty Harbour, 1839 (*Newfoundlander* 1 Aug 1839); James and Edward Aylwart, butchers of Harbour Grace, 1842 (Nfld. Archives T98); Catherine Ailworth, of Dog Cove (Bonavista B.), 1850 (Nfld. Archives KCRC); Joseph Ailworth or Aylward, of Stock Cove (Bonavista B.), 1850 (Nfld. Archives KCRC); William Aylword, Ailworth, Elward or Alward, of Knights Cove (Bonavista B.), 1852 (Nfld. Archives KCRC); Catherine Aylward, of Cotterels Island (Bonavista B.), 1856 (Nfld. Archives KCRC); Bridget, of Burnt Island (Bonavista B.), 1857 (Nfld. Archives KCRC); Anne Ailworth, of Gooseberry Island (Bonavista B.), 1866 (Nfld. Archives KCRC); Margaret Aylward, of Indian Arm (Bonavista B.), 1867 (Nfld. Archives (KCRC); John, fisherman of Fermeuse, 1871 (Lovell); John, planter of Little Fogo Island, 1871 (Lovell).

Modern status: Widespread, especially at St. John's, Knight's Cove, St. Brendan's and Fischot.

AYRE(S). *See* AYERS

AYRIS. *See* AYERS

B

BABB, a surname of England, from the Old English personal name *Babba*, whence, for example, Babbacombe (Devon); or a pet-form of the baptismal name Barbara, from the Greek meaning "strange," "foreign"; or from a nickname, Middle English *babe* – infant, young child. (Withycombe, Reaney).

Traced by Spiegelhalter in Devon.

In Newfoundland:

Family tradition: Thomas (1813–), from Devon, settled at Bryants Cove, 1828 (MUN Folklore, MUN Geog.).

Early instances: John Bab(b), of St. John's, 1681, 1682 (CO 1); Thomas Babb, of Carbonear, 1784 (CO 199.18); John, of Low Point (Conception B.), 1797 (CO 199.18); Thomas, of Newton Abbot (Devon), landowner at St. John's, 1798 (D'Alberti 8); Anne Babbs, of Harbour Grace Parish, 1806 (Nfld. Archives HGRC); Bridget Babb, of Heart's Content, 1819 (Nfld. Archives KCRC).

Modern status: Especially at Harbour Grace and Bryants Cove.

BABBITT, a surname of England, a diminutive of the baptismal name Barbara (*see* BABB), or ? sometimes confused with BOBBETT. (Cottle).

In Newfoundland:

Early instance: John Babbit, of Pick Heart (Burin district), 1831 (DPHW 109).

Modern status: Unique, at St. John's (*Electors* 1955).

BABSTOCK, a surname of England (1 in London Telephone Directory), ? from an unidentified English place name, Babstock – *Babba*'s place or outlying farm. *See* BABB.

In Newfoundland:

Early instances: William Babstock, from Somerset, of King's Cove, 1826 (Nfld. Archives KCRC); William Bapstock, of Salvage, 1835 (DPHW 76); George Babstock, of King's Cove, 1838, of Amherst Cove, 1844 (DPHW 73A); Thomas, fisherman of Happy Adventure, 1867 (DPHW 80); William, of Barrow Harbour (Bonavista B.), 1871 (Lovell); George, fisherman of Sailor's Island, 1871 (Lovell); George, fisherman of Heart's Content, 1879 (DPHW 60).

Modern status: Particularly associated with Happy Adventure, Eastport and St. John's.

BADCOCK, a surname of England, from a compound of *Bat[e]*, a pet-name for Bartholomew, from the Hebrew – "son of *Talmai*," "abounding in furrows," and *cock* (*see* ALCOCK), or from an Old English personal name *Bada*. *See* also BATTCOCK, with which confusion is not unlikely, and BARTLE, BARTLETT, BATEMAN, BATES, BATTEN. (Withycombe, Reaney).

Guppy traced the name in Devon, Berkshire and Somerset.

In Newfoundland:

Early instances: William, of Bay Roberts, 1767, but property "in possession of the Family for upwards of 104 years," that is, before 1663 (CO 199-18); William, constable of Carbonear district, ? 1730, 1732 (CO 194.9); William, of Harbour Grace, 1792 (USPG); John, of St. John's, 1796 (CO 194.39); John and Michael, traders, Thomas, trader and planter, and Peter, fisherman of Brigus South, 1871 (Lovell).

Modern status: Especially associated with Bay Roberts, Shearstown and St. John's.

BAGG(S), surnames of England, Bagge of Ireland, from an Old German or Old English personal name, or from Middle English *bagge* – (maker of) bag(s), or for a beggar. (Reaney, MacLysaght).

Guppy traced Bagg in Somerset; Spiegelhalter traced Baggs and Badge in Devon, MacLysaght traced Baggs in Co. Waterford.

In Newfoundland:

Family traditions: The family name was originally Banks and Captain William Baggs who sailed from Poole (Dorset) about 1685 and settled at Broad Cove (Conception B.) was a descendant of Lady Mary Banks (died 1661), who occupied the family residence Corfe Castle (Dorset) for the royalists at the outbreak of the Civil War and withstood two sieges until 1646 when the castle was betrayed by an officer of the garrison (MUN Folklore, DNB). Joseph, son of Captain William Baggs, moved to Spaniards Bay, died, aged 90 (Tradition). William and Stephen, from Poole (Dorset), of Spaniards Bay, 1775 (MUN Geog.).

Early instances: Robert Baggs, of St. John's, 1705 (CO 194.22); William, of Upper Island Cove, 1775 (CO 199.18); Joseph Bagg, of Broad Cove

(North Shore, Conception B.), 1776 (CO 199.18); Joseph, of Adams Cove, 1797 (CO 199.18); Richard Baggs, of Northern Cove (Spaniards B.), 1802 (CO 199.18); Joseph, juror of Greenspond, 1804 (D'Alberti 14); Anne, of Harbour Grace Parish, 1806 (Nfld. Archives HGRC); Thomas Bag, of Ivers Parish (Co. Wexford), married at St. John's, 1820 (Nfld. Archives BRC); Henry Baggs, of Bonavista, 1825 (Nfld. Archives KCRC); John Bagg, of La Hune Bay, 1830 (DPHW 30); Hugh, of Oar Bay, 1835 (DPHW 30); John Baggs, of Biscayan Cove, 1839 (DPHW 26B); Hugh Bagg, of Deer Island (Burgeo-La Poile district), 1842 (DPHW 101); John, of Channel, 1843 (DPHW 101); H., inspector of pickled fish, La Poile, 1844 (Nfld. Almanac); Joseph Baggs, schoolmaster of Trinity (Trinity B.), 1849 (DPHW 64B); John Bagg, fisherman of Cape La Hune, 1856 (DPHW 102); Joseph, teacher of Pouch Cove, 1857 (Nfld. Almanac); John, of Bluff Head (Twillingate), 1861 (DPHW 88); Jeremiah Baggs, farmer of Bryants Cove, 1871 (Lovell).

Modern status: Bagg at Dog Cove and Cape La Hune; Baggs at St. John's, Adams Cove and elsewhere in Conception Bay, in the Burgeo district, at Bluff Head Cove and elsewhere in the Twillingate district.

Place names: Bagg Cove 47-33 56-50, —— Head 47-33 56-47, 49-33 55-17, —— Pond 47-33 56-48; Baggs Head 47-41 58-08, —— Hill 47-49 58-17, —— Island 47-36 57-36, 47-39 54-10.

BAILEY, a surname of England, Scotland, Ireland and the Channel Islands from the term *baillie*, now obsolete in England, but still used in Scotland of a chief magistrate, a sheriff and an alderman; or from the English place name Bailey (Lancashire). (Reaney, Black, Turk).

Guppy found Bailey widespread, especially in Hampshire, Staffordshire and Oxfordshire; he notes that Bayly is a rare form, mostly found in Cheshire, Staffordshire and Sussex, and that Baillie is scattered in Scotland. MacLysaght found Bailey and Bailie numerous in all provinces except Connacht.

In Newfoundland:

Family traditions: James Bayl(e)y (1797–), from Poole (Dorset) married at Harbour Grace, 1820 (MUN Folklore). John Bailey, of Lark Harbour, 1849 (MUN Hist.). John, from Ireland settled at Harbour Main, about 1860 (MUN Folklore). ——, Bayley, of Coachman's Cove, ? about 1860 (MUN Folklore).

Early instances: Richard Bayly, of Bay de Verde, 1675 (CO 1); John, of Barrow Harbour, 1676 (CO 1); John Bailey, fisherman of Trinity, 1758 (DPHW 64);

David Bayly, of Bonaventure, 1777 (DPHW 64); Samuel, juror of St. John's, 1789 (CO 194.38); John Bailey, of Salmon Cove (now Champneys), 1792 (DPHW 64); C., of Petty Harbour, 1794-5 (Census 1794–5); John, of Heart's Content, 1799 (DPHW 64); James Baily, from Co. Wexford, married at St. John's, 1812 (Nfld. Archives BRC); James, of Harbour Grace Parish, 1814 (Nfld. Archives HGRC); Richard Bayley, planter of Bonavista, 1821 (DPHW 64); James Bayly, planter of Cupids, 1827 (DPHW 34); Thomas Baily, planter of Ship Cove (now part of Port Rexton), 1830 (DPHW 64B); James Bail(e)y, planter of British Harbour, 1831 (DPHW 64B); John Baillie, of Bay of Islands, 1835 (DPHW 30); George Bayly, planter of Cat Cove (Trinity North district), 1846 (DPHW 64B); William Bailey, fisherman of Fogo, 1849 (DPHW 83); William Bayley, of Seal Cove (now New Chelsea), 1852 (DPHW 59); Augustus, of Ferryland, 1860 (DPHW 31); Jacob Bayly, of Harbour Grace, 1867 (Nfld. Archives HGRC).

Modern status: Widespread, especially at St. John's, Corner Brook, New Chelsea, Port Rexton and other parts of the Trinity North district.

Place names: Bailey Cove 49-45 56-53; Baileys Point 49-28 57-55; Bayleys Cove 48-39 53-07.

BAINE(S), surnames of England and Scotland, Bain, Bayne of Ireland, from Old English *bān* – bone which in the north of England and in Scotland became *bain*, a nickname, usually in the plural; or from Middle English *beyn* – straight, direct or ready to serve, hospitable, always singular; or from Gaelic *bàn* – fair, white, always singular; or from Middle English *bayne*, French *bain* – (attendant at the public) bath. (Reaney, Black, MacLysaght).

Guppy traced the name in Lancashire, Leicestershire and Rutland, Nottinghamshire, Sussex and Yorkshire WR. He notes that in Lancashire and Yorkshire WR Baynes is frequently found.

In Newfoundland:

Early instances: Robert Baine & Co., from Greenock, Scotland, began business in Port de Grave, 1780, with Robert, Archibald and Walter Baine as partners; later James Lang entered the partnership which became Lang, Baine & Co., 1817. In ? 1801, the firm transferred its headquarters to St. John's, to become Baine, Johnston & Co., after the introduction of a new partner, William Johnston, by 1817 (MUN Hist.); John Baines, fisherman of Salmon Cove (now Champneys), 1871 (Lovell); Michael, of Current Island (St. Barbe district), 1873 (MUN Hist.).

Modern status: Baine is now obsolete and Baines survives (*Electors* 1955) only at Shoal Cove West (St. Barbe district).

Place name: Baine Harbour 47-22 54-54.

BAIRD, a surname of Scotland and Ireland, believed by Cottle and MacLysaght, for example, to be derived from the Gaelic *bárd* – bard, but by Black to be derived from a Scots place name.

Guppy traced Baird in the Glasgow district; MacLysaght found it numerous in Cos. Antrim and Down (Ulster).

In Newfoundland:

Family tradition: Samuel Woods Baird (1817–99), born Waterford, Ireland, of Scots descent, settled in Twillingate in 1843 as a blacksmith and subsequently became customs officer at Tilt Cove in 1868, and stipendiary magistrate at Greenspond 1880 and Fogo 1891-7. (Eleanor G. Baird). James (1832–1909), of Long Pond, Manuels (MUN Folklore).

Early instances: Phillip Beard, of St. John's Harbour, 1677, 1682 (CO 1); Matthew, of Bay Bulls, 1681, 1682 (CO 1); James Baird, born at Saltcoats (Ayrshire) in 1828, came to Newfoundland, 1844 (*Nfld. Quarterly* Jun 1903); Daniel (and others), fishermen of Freshwater Bay (St. John's), 1871 (Lovell); Josiah, fisherman of Long Harbour (Fortune B.), 1871 (Lovell); Samuel, fisherman of Round Harbour (Fogo), 1871 (Lovell); James, merchant of North Island, Twillingate, 1877 (Lovell).

Modern status: Especially at St. John's, Long Pond, Manuels, Grand Falls and Gander.

Place name: Bairds Cove (St. John's).

BAKER, a surname of England, Ireland and Guernsey (Channel Islands) from the Old English occupational name *bæcere* – baker. (Reaney, Turk).

Guppy found the name widespread in England, especially in Monmouth, Suffolk, Surrey and Sussex. It is also widespread in Devon (Matthews) and in Ireland (MacLysaght). BAXTER (formerly in St. John's, *Electors* 1955) from Old English *bæcestre*, the feminine of *bæcere* is found mainly in East Anglia.

In Newfoundland:

Family traditions: —— Baker, the name was later changed to UPSHALL, from Wales to Harbour Buffett, thence to Little Harbour in the early 19th century (MUN Folklore). James Baker, of Dancing Cove, early 19th century (MUN Folklore). John, fisherman of La Poile, 1862 (MUN Hist.). —— of Kite Cove

(now Laurenceton), from England via Barbados, ? about 1860–5 (MUN Folklore).

Early instances: John, of Fermeuse, 1675 (CO 1); Benjamin, of Ferryland, 1681 (CO 1); Edward, of Conception Bay, 1706 (CO 194.4); G., of Placentia, 1724 (CO 194.7); George, of St. John's, 1756 (DPHW 26C); John, fisherman of Trinity (Trinity B.), 1758 (DPHW 64); Edward, of Port de Grave, 1765 (CO 199.18); Guy, of Harbour Main, 1766 (CO 199.18); George, of Bishop's Cove, 1776 (CO 199.18); Thomas, of Harbour Grace, 1782 (CO 199.18); Francis, of Carbonear, 1783 (CO 199.18); William, of Bonavista, 1789 (DPHW 70); John, proprietor and occupier of fishing room at Scilly Cove (now Winterton), Winter 1800–01 (Census Trinity B.); John, of Baker's Estate (St. John's), 1803 (D'Alberti 13); Richard, of Holyrood, 1804 (CO 199.18); Richard, of Burin district, 1808 (D'Alberti 18); Thomas, planter of Northern Cove (Spaniards B.), 1820 (DPHW 43); William, from Kilbarryhalden Parish (Co. Waterford), married at St. John's, 1822 (Nfld. Archives BRC); John, of Barr'd Islands, 1823 (USPG); William, planter of Heart's Content, 1823 (DPHW 64B); William, planter of Bird Island Cove (now Elliston), 1823 (DPHW 72); Thomas, planter of Hants Harbour, 1824 (DPHW 58); Henry, planter of Spaniards Bay, 1825 (DPHW 43); Ellen, of Herring Neck, 1829 (Nfld. Archives KCRC); Joseph, of Hearts Ease, 1830 (Nfld. Archives KCRC); Jonathan, of Bay d'Este (now East Bay, La Poile Bay) at Shelter Point, 1835 (DPHW 30); John, of Black Island (Twillingate district), 1843 (DPHW 86); Edward, of Exploits Burnt Island, 1848 (DPHW 86); John, fisherman of Brunette, 1851 (DPHW 104); Sarah, of Fox Harbour (Trinity South district), 1852 (DPHW 59); James, of Harbour Mille, 1855 (DPHW 104); Israel, blacksmith of Mose Ambrose, 1856 (DPHW 104); James, planter of Blanchet (Burin-Fortune B. district), 1856 (DPHW 104); Simon, of Catalina, 1857 (DPHW 67); James, of Sagona, 1857 (DPHW 104); Robert, of Garia, 1858 (DPHW 98); Caroline, of English Harbour, 1859 (DPHW 104); George, planter of Rencontre East, 1859 (DPHW 104); John, fisherman of Path End, Burin, 1861 (DPHW 100); John, of Fogo, 1861 (DPHW 82).

Modern status: Widespread.

Place names: Baker Brook 49-09 56-10, —— Cove 47-50 54-07, —— Head 46-40 53-27, —— Lake 49-08 56-10, —— Point 47-25 53-54, 47-50 54-07, Bakers Brook 49-39 57-58, 47-45 58-17, 49-39, 57-58, —— Cove 47-45 58-17, —— Island 47-35 53-14, 47-36 58-50, —— Ledge 47-37 58-41, —— Loaf (peak) 48-11 53-32, —— Point

47-38 58-35, —— Spit (sand point) 47-45 58-17, —— Loaf Island 48-42 53-43, Ashley Baker Island 48-30 53-50.

BALDWIN, a surname of England and Ireland, from an Old German personal name with the elements *bold* and *friend*, "a popular Flemish name, common in England both before and after the Conquest" (Reaney). In Ireland, where it is also found in the variant Baldon and came from Germany via Flanders, it is occasionally [in Co. Donegal] used as an anglicized form of *Ó Maolagáin*, normally Mulligan, Ir. *maol* – bald (MacLysaght). "Balding is sometimes a late development of Baldwin" (Reaney). *See also* BUDDEN. (Reaney, MacLysaght).

Guppy traced the name in Buckinghamshire, Gloucestershire, Hertfordshire, Lancashire, Norfolk, Suffolk and Warwickshire, Spiegelhalter in Devon, and MacLysaght found it "well established in Waterford and neighbouring counties before 1500" and in Donegal.

In Newfoundland:

Early instances: Mary and Richard, planters in Newfoundland, 1724 (CO 194.7); Richard, planter of Placentia, 1724 (CO 194.8); Mary and William Balding, of Harbour Grace, 1765 (CO 199.18); Edward, of Port de Grave, 1791 (CO 199.18); David, of Small Point (Conception B.), 1794 (CO 199.18); James Baldwin, of Trinity Parish (Co. Waterford), married at St. John's, 1805 (Nfld. Archives BRC); Edward Baldwyn, of Pouch Cove, 1817 (DPHW 26B); David Balden, of Pouch Cove, 1819, spelled Baldon in 1833 (DPHW 26D); John Baldwin, of Pouch Cove, 1822 (DPHW 26B); James Baldwyn, of St. John's, 1825 (DPHW 26B); Isaac Balding, of Pinchard's Island, 1850 (DPHW 76); William Baldwin, fisherman of Otterbury (Carbonear), 1855 (DPHW 49); John, fisherman of Barrasway Cove (Fortune Bay-Burin district), 1858 (DPHW 102); John Baldwyn, fisherman of Carbonear, 1858 (DPHW 49).

Modern status: Scattered, but especially at Pouch Cove and Victoria.

Place names: Baldwin (Bailey) Cove 49-45 56-53, Baldwin Shoal 47-36 57-38, The Baldwin (island) 47-36 57-39, East Baldwin Rock, Middle —— ——, West —— —— 47-34 59-08; Harry Baldwin's Pond 47-47 53-19.

BALL, a surname of England and Ireland, from an Old Danish personal name, or from various Old and Middle English and Old French words with such meanings as plump, ball, bald, bald place, knoll, or from the English place name Ball (Cornwall). (Reaney, Cottle, Spiegelhalter).

Guppy found the name widespread, Spiegelhalter in Devon, and MacLysaght scattered in Ireland, mainly in Leinster and Ulster.

In Newfoundland:

Early instances: William, fisherman of St. John's or Petty Harbour, about 1739–43 (CO 194.11, 24); Richard, J.P., Ferryland district, 1750 (CO 194.12); James, of Harbour Grace Parish, 1817 (Nfld. Archives HGRC); George, planter of Cuckold's Cove (now Dunfield), 1824 (DPHW 64B); Patrick, of Harbour Grace, 1830 (Nfld. Archives HGRC); Richard, from ? Falmouth, married at St. John's, 1835 (Nfld. Archives BRC); Henry, from Waterford, married at St. John's, 1838 (Nfld. Archives BRC); John, of Grand Bank, 1840 (DPHW 109); William, of Exploits Burnt Island, 1843 (DPHW 86); Elizabeth, of Kings Cove Parish, 1847 (Nfld. Archives KCRC); Abraham, fisherman of Rencontre, 1850 (DPHW 102); George, of Trinity (unspecified), 1856 (Nfld. Archives KCRC).

Modern status: Scattered, especially at Stanhope, Northern Arm and elsewhere in the Gander district and Deer Lake.

Place names (not necessarily from the surname): Ball Island 47-09 55-04, —— Point 49-31 55-04; Captain Ball Rock 46-42 55-47.

BALLAM, a surname of England, from the English place name Baylham (Suffolk). (Reaney).

Traced by Guppy in Dorset.

In Newfoundland: Early instance: Charles Ballen or Balham or Ballow, of Fair Islands, 1846, 1849, 1851 (DPHW 76).

Modern status: Formerly at Lower Island Cove (MUN Hist.); at Shearstown, Curling and St. John's.

BALLARD, a surname of England and Ireland, from Middle English *ballard* – a bald-headed man; in Ireland distinct from BOLLARD. (Reaney, MacLysaght).

Guppy traced the name in Worcestershire and Kent, Spiegelhalter in Devon and Matthews in Dorset.

In Newfoundland:

Early instances: Michael, merchant of St. John's, 1736 (CO 194.10); Robert Jr., of Bay Bulls, 1802 (USPG).

Modern status: Somewhat rare and scattered.

Place name: Cape Ballard 46-47 52-57.

BALLETT, a surname of England ? from the Old Norse personal name *Balli* from ? *ballr* – dangerous; or ? a variant of the French surname Ballet, a diminutive of *bal* – a dancer, player of a musical instrument used at dances. (Reaney Notes, Dauzat).

In Newfoundland:

Family tradition: —— Ballette was a French settler at Harbour Main before 1750 (MUN Hist.).

Early instances: Joseph Ballet, (Ballot in 1835), planter of Ship Cove (now part of Port Rexton), 1833 (DPHW 64B); Richard Ballet, of Trinity (unspecified), 1855 (Nfld. Archives KCRC).

Modern status: At Port Rexton and Canada Harbour (*Electors* 1955).

BALSOM, a variant of the English surnames Balsham and Balson, Balsham from the English place name Balsham (Cambridgeshire), Balson from Balstone (Devon) or Balsdon (Cornwall). (Reaney Notes, Spiegelhalter) .

Traced by Spiegelhalter in Devon.

In Newfoundland:

Family tradition: George, Joseph and Jonathan Balsom were the earliest settlers at Dark Cove, now part of Clarenville (MUN Hist.).

Early instances: Henry Balsam, of Hants Harbour, 1827 (DPHW 59); John, of Scilly Cove (now Winterton), 1828 (DPHW 59); John Balsom, of Random Arm, 1858 (DPHW 59A); Robert Balsam, fisherman of Bay de l'Eau, 1871 (Lovell); Maria, of Heart's Ease, 1876 (Nfld. Archives KCRC).

Modern status: Especially at Clarenville.

BAMBRICK, a surname of England and Ireland, of uncertain origin, ? from the English place name Bamborough (Northumberland) or ? from the Scots place name Bambreich (unidentified). (Reaney Notes, MacLysaght).

Traced by MacLysaght in Co. Leix since 1600.

In Newfoundland:

Early instances: James, ? of St. John's, 1822 (CO 194.55); James, from Conran (Co. Kilkenny) married at St. John's, 1828 (Nfld. Archives BRC); Thomas, from Co. Kilkenny, teacher of St. John's, died 1848, aged 31 (*Royal Gazette* 22 Aug 1848); James Bambric, of Bay of Islands, 1871 (DPHW 96).

Modern status: At Placentia (*Electors* 1955), and St. John's.

Place name: Bambrick Street (St. John's).

BAMBURY, a surname of England, from the English place name Banbury (Devon, Oxfordshire) (Spiegelhalter). MacLysaght notes a surname of

Ireland, Bambery, which he derives from the English place name Bamburgh (Northumberland), "mainly found in Kerry."

Spiegelhalter traced Bambury, Banbury in Devon; Guppy traced Banbury in Devon and Cornwall.

In Newfoundland:

Family tradition: The Bambury family is said to have moved from England to St. Lawrence and thence to Pool's Cove (MUN Hist.).

Early instances: Bambury, Bamberry, captain in the seal fishery, 1833, 1837 (*Newfoundlander* 8 Aug 1833, 16 Mar 1837); Robert Banbury, fisherman of Burin, 1871 (Lovell); Joseph and Mentor Banbury, fishermen of Pool's Cove (Fortune B.), 1871 (Lovell); Samuel Bambury, planter of Bay du Nord, 1877 (Lovell).

Modern status: At Pool's Cove.

BANCROFT, a surname of England, from the English place name Bancroft (Cambridgeshire, Northamptonshire). (Cottle).

Guppy traced Bancroft in Cheshire, Derbyshire and Yorkshire WR.

In Newfoundland:

Early instance: James Frederick (1855–1929), teacher at Bay Roberts, first president of the Newfoundland Teachers' Association, 1890, collector of customs at Bonne Bay, 1891, from whom the present Bancrofts in Newfoundland are descended (*NTA Journal* Dec 1965).

Modern status: At St. John's.

BANFIELD, a surname of England and Ireland; in England a variant of Bam[p]field, Bamfylde, from the English place name Bampfylde Lodge (Devon) – ? bean and field (Spiegelhalter); in Ireland, Banfield and Banville are Co. Wexford variants of BONFIELD. (Spiegelhalter, Bardsley, MacLysaght).

Traced by Guppy only in Herefordshire; by Matthews in Devon, Dorset and Bristol; and by MacLysaght in Co. Wexford.

In Newfoundland:

Family tradition maintains a Cornish origin in the belief that Anstey's Cove, near Torquay (Devon), is in Cornwall (MUN Folklore). —— Anstey *née* Banfield, of Anstey's Cove (Devon) settled at Grand Bank about 1800 (MUN Folklore).

Early instances: ——, son of a wheelwright of Suffolk, England, was shipwrecked in St. George's Bay in 1844. He settled at Cow Cove (near Cow Head) as servant to one of the planters there (Feild); Stephen Bamfield, of Garnish, 1850 (DPHW 104);

James, fisherman of Bay L'Argent, 1857 (DPHW 104); William Banfield, of Sandy Point (St. George's district), 1871 (Lovell).

Modern status: Essentially a South Coast name, especially associated with Bay L'Argent and Garnish.

BANIKHIN (Bannikin in *Electors* 1955), a surname of the Ukraine.

In Newfoundland: The name was introduced by Frank Banikhin, born in the Ukraine in 1888. He emigrated to the North West Territories about 1907, came to Newfoundland in 1917 and died in 1970 (MUN Folklore, *Daily News* 3 Jan 1970).

Modern status: At St. John's.

BANKS, a surname of England, Ireland and Scotland, in England and Scotland – (dweller by a) bank, slope, hillside; in Scotland also from a Scots place name Banks (Orkney); in Ireland often a pseudo-translation of (O)Brohan, *Ó Bruacháin* – ? corpulent. (Reaney, Black, MacLysaght). *See* BAGGS.

Traced by Guppy in Derbyshire, Lancashire, Lincolnshire, Northamptonshire and Yorkshire NR and ER, by Spiegelhalter and Matthews in Devon, and by MacLysaght in Co. Offaly.

In Newfoundland:

Early instances: Cyril, of Bay de Verde, 1716 (CO 199.18); Nicholas, fisherman of St. John's, 1794–5 (Census 1794–5); George, of Fogo, 1805 (D'Alberti 15); George, miner of Tilt Cove, 1871 (Lovell).

Modern status: Scattered, but still found in Fogo, and with a concentration at Seal Cove, Hampden and Bear Cove (White Bay South district).

Place name: Banks Cove (Fogo Island) 49-43 54-18.

BANNISTER, a surname of England and Ireland, from Old French *banastre* – basket(-maker) or banished man, or ? from Old French *balestier* – crossbowman. (Reaney, Cottle, MacLysaght 73).

Traced by Guppy especially in Sussex and also in Lancashire, by Spiegelhalter in Devon, and by MacLysaght in Cos. Carlow and Cork.

In Newfoundland:

Early instances: John Ban[n]ister or Banester, of Trinity Bay, 1784 (DPHW 64); John Bannister, proprietor of fishing room at Trinity, Winter 1800–01 (Census Trinity B.); Robin Banister, planter of British Harbour, 1823 (DPHW 64); John Ban[n]ister, planter of Ship Cove (now part of Port Rexton), 1826 (DPHW 64B); William Banister, planter of Salmon Cove (now Champneys), 1827 (DPHW 64B);

William, seaman of Robin Hood (now part of Port Rexton), 1855 (DPHW 64B).

Modern status: Scattered, with small concentrations at Port Rexton and British Harbour.

BARBAN, a surname of Germany ? from the Russian surname Barabanov – from *baraban* – drum. (Unbegaun).

In Newfoundland:

Modern status: At St. John's since 1947.

BARBER, BARBOUR, surnames of England, Scotland, Ireland, Barber of Guernsey (Channel Islands) and Barbour especially, but not exclusively, associated with Scotland and Ireland, Anglo-French *barbour* giving Barbour and Old French *barbier* giving Barber. "Formerly the barber was also a regular practitioner in surgery and dentistry" (OED). (Reaney, Black, Turk).

Guppy traced Barber in eight counties, especially in Cheshire, and Barbour south of the Forth and Clyde. MacLysaght found both forms in Dublin since the 13th century, though now mainly in Ulster.

In Newfoundland:

Family traditions: The earliest Barbours came from Devon or from France *via* Scotland (MUN Folklore). Benjamin Barbour (1809–91), born at Greenspond, moved to Pinchard's Island about 1824, on Cobbler's Island about 1843, and at Newtown (Bonavista B.), 1878 (MUN Folklore).

Early instances: Joseph Barber, of Newfoundland, convicted of destroying birds and their eggs and publicly whipped, 1792 (D'Alberti 4); Richard, proprietor and occupier of fishing room at Old Perlican and co-occupier of one at Grates Cove, Winter 1800–01 (Census Trinity B.); George, juror at Greenspond, 1804 (D'Alberti 14); John, of Ship Cove (now part of Port Rexton), 1816 (DPHW 64); Benjamin, born at Greenspond, baptized, aged 54, 1830 (DPHW 76); Benjamin, born at Pinchard's Island, baptized, aged 20, 1830 (DPHW 76); George Barbour, planter of Salmon Cove (now Champneys), 1831 (DPHW 64B); Robert Barber, from Galloway (Wigtownshire and Kirkcudbrightshire), Scotland, book-keeper of St. John's since 1804, died 1837, aged 54 (*Newfoundlander* 19 Jan 1837, *Times* 18 Jan 1837); Thomas, fisherman of Robin Hood (now part of Port Rexton), 1854 (DPHW 64B); Benjamin, planter of Inner Islands (now Newtown), 1871 (Lovell).

Modern status: Barbour is particularly associated with Newtown and other settlements in the Bonavista and Trinity North districts, and with St. John's. Barber is very rare.

Place names: Barber's Island 49-12 53-31, Barbours Head 49-11 58-00.

BARCLAY, a surname of England, Scotland and Ireland, from the English place names Berkeley (Gloucestershire), Berkley (Somerset) or Barklye (Sussex). (Reaney, Black, MacLysaght 73).

Found widespread by Guppy in Scotland, especially around Kilmarnock; by Spiegelhalter in Devon; and, usually as Barkley, by MacLysaght in Ulster.

In Newfoundland:

Early instances: John, sergeant in the 98th Regiment, married at St. John's, 1816, given grant of land on road leading to Lady Pond, Harbour Grace, 1819 (DPHW 26D, D'Alberti 29); John, of Perlican (unspecified), 1839 (*Newfoundlander* 31 Oct 1839).

Modern status: Unique, at Bay Roberts.

BAR[E]FOOT, BARFITT, surnames of England, Barfoot of Scotland, from Old English *bær* and *fōt* – bare-footed, "used of friars, pilgrims and those doing penance" (Reaney); in Scotland also from Scots place names, Barfod (Renfrewshire) and Berford (Black).

Guppy traced Barfoot in Hampshire, Matthews Barefoot in Poole (Dorset), Spiegelhalter Barfitt in Devon.

In Newfoundland:

Early instances: Jane Barfit, born 1815, baptized at Pool's Island, 1830 (DPHW 76); George Barfoot, of Pool's Island, 1836 (DPHW 76); George Barfit, of Grates Cove, 1860 (DPHW 56); William Barefoot, fisherman of Pool's Island, 1871 (Lovell).

Modern status: Scattered, with a small concentration of Barfitt at Long Beach (Southern Arm, Random Sound).

BARGERY, a rare surname of England (6 in London Telephone Directory 1962), ? from the French family name Bergerie, *bergerie* – (dweller near, worker at the) sheep-farm, sheep fold. (Reaney Notes, Dauzat).

In Newfoundland:

Family tradition: Winston Bargery, of Pelley's Island, ? about 1877 (MUN Folklore).

Early instance: J. Barjery, sergeant, killed in French attack on St. John's, 1705 (Prowse 262).

Modern status: Rare, at Grand Falls.

BARKER, a surname of England, Scotland and Ireland, from Old French *berk[i]er* – shepherd, or

Middle English *barker* – tanner (Reaney), one who stripped bark from trees and prepared it for the tanner (Black, Cottle, MacLysaght 73). Compare Newfoundland usage in bark-pot, barking-kettle etc.

Guppy found the name widespread, especially in Yorkshire, Derbyshire and Lincolnshire, Spiegelhalter in Devon, and Matthews in Devon and Dorset. MacLysaght found it numerous in Leinster and Ulster.

In Newfoundland:

Family tradition: Robert ("French Bob") came from Le Havre, France, and settled in Coachman's Cove in the late 18th or early 19th century. His descendants are at Windsor (MUN Folklore).

Early instances: Thomas, inhabitant of Newfoundland, 1730 (CO 194.23); John, of St. John's, 1819 (DPHW 26D); Catherine, of Tickle Cove (Bonavista B.), 1819 (Nfld. Archives KCRC); Samuel, of Open Hole (now Open Hall), 1829 (Nfld. Archives KCRC); John, of Corbin (Fortune B.), 1835 (DPHW 30); Elizabeth, of Harbour Grace Parish, 1844 (Nfld. Archives HGRC); Samuel, of Plate Cove (Bonavista B.), 1859 (Nfld. Archives KCRC); Elizabeth, of Indian Arm (Bonavista B.), 1865 (Nfld. Archives KCRC); Maria, of Harbour Grace, 1867 (Nfld. Archives HGRC); John, fisherman at Mingo (? for Mings Bight), 1871 (Lovell).

Modern status: Especially at Open Hall, Coachman's Cove and Windsor.

BARNABLE, a surname of England, ? a variant of Barnabé, Barnaby, Barneby, from Barnaby, the English form of the baptismal name Barnabas, from the Hebrew – "son of exhortation or consolation"; or ? a Newfoundland variant of the Irish surname Barneville or Barnewall, Ir. *de Bearnabhal*, from the French place names Banneville or Barneville (Calvados). (Withycombe, Reaney Notes, MacLysaght *MIF*).

MacLysaght traced Barneville, Barnewall in Co. Meath and elsewhere in the Pale since 1300.

In Newfoundland:

Family tradition: Two brothers Barnable came to Ferryland in the early 19th century (MUN Folklore).

Early instances: James, John and Peter, fishermen at Ferryland, 1871 (Lovell).

Modern status: At Renews, Ferryland and St. John's.

BARNES, a surname of England, Ireland and Scotland; in England from residence near or work at the barn[s], or from the English place name Barnes (Surrey), or son of *Barne*; in Ireland as a synonym of BARRON and of (O)Bardon in Co. Wexford; in Scotland from the Scots place name Barnes (Aberdeenshire). *See also* BEARN[E]S. (Reaney, Cottle, Black, MacLysaght).

Guppy found the name widespread especially in Wiltshire, Hampshire, Dorset, Cumberland and Westmorland; Spiegelhalter and Matthews in Devon; MacLysaght "in small numbers in all provinces ."

In Newfoundland:

Family tradition: ——, from Dorset, a veteran of Waterloo (1815), was the first settler at Harbour Mille about 1820 (MUN Folklore).

Early instances: Thomas Barne(s), of St. John's, 1676 "20 years in Newfoundland in 1680," that is, since 1660 (CO 1); John Bairnes, fisherman of Trinity (Trinity B.), 1757 (DPHW 64); Robert Barnes, trader who sustained losses when St. Pierre was surrendered to the French in 1763, of Placentia district 1774 (CO 194.16, 24); Richard, of New Perlican, 1769 (DPHW 64); Thomas, admiral of the port of Greenspond, 1776 (CO 194.33); George, of English Harbour, 1789 (DPHW 64); Bridget Barns, from Tintern (Co. Wexford), married at St. John's, 1811 (Nfld. Archives BRC); John Barnes, one of 72 impressed men who sailed from Ireland to Newfoundland, ? 1811 (CO 194.51); John, boat-master of Adam's Cove, 1816 (CO 194.57); William, of Harbour Grace, 1817 (D'Alberti 27); Martha, of Harbour Grace Parish, 1817 (Nfld. Archives HGRC); James, of Fogo, 1821 (USPG); William Barns, from Blandford (Dorset), married at St. John's, 1821 (Nfld. Archives BRC); William Barnes, planter of Brigus, 1825 (DPHW 34); Thomas, planter of Old Perlican, 1830 (DPHW 58); Thomas, of Harbour Mille, 1827 (DPHW 30); Samuel, born at English Harbour East, baptized 1835, aged 16 (DPHW 30); John, planter of Trouty, 1838 (DPHW 64B); Richard, planter of Salmon Cove (now Champneys), 1837 (DPHW 64B); Robert, of Broom Cove (Bonavista South district), 1842 (DPHW 73A); Mary, of Rencontre, 1848 (DPHW 26D); James, fisherman of Herring Neck, 1850 (DPHW 85); James, of Stone Harbour, 1853 (DPHW 85); Abraham, of Frenchman's Cove (Fortune B.), married 1857, aged 26 (DPHW 104); Joseph, of Black Currant Islands (Twillingate district), 1862 (DPHW 86).

Modern status: Widespread and numerous, especially at St. John's and Harbour Mille.

Place name: Barnes Island 49-44 54-17.

BARNET[T], surnames of England, Ireland and Scotland, from residence near land cleared by burning, or from English place names Barnet (Hertfordshire, Middlesex), Barnett Farm (Surrey); in Scotland, as popular forms of the personal name Barnard or Bernard, popularized by St. Bernard of Clairvaux. (Reaney, Black).

Guppy traced Barnett in Buckinghamshire, Cheshire, Herefordshire, Leicestershire, Rutlandshire and Staffordshire, Spiegelhalter in Devon, Matthews in Somerset, MacLysaght in Ulster.

In Newfoundland:

Early instances: Andrew Barnet, of Lower Road, St. John's, 1780 (D'Alberti 6); John Barnett, arrived at St. John's, 1816 (CO 194.60); William Barnet, of Harbour Grace Parish, 1821 (Nfld. Archives HGRC).

Modern status: Rare, in the Placentia East and West districts (*Electors* 1955).

Place name: Barnet Island 49-41 54-26.

BARNEY, a surname of England, from the English place name Barney (Norfolk), or (dweller on the) barley or barn island. (Cottle).

In Newfoundland:

Early instances: Thomas, of Pittdown (Co. Kilkenny), married at St. John's, 1821 (DPHW 26D); Richard Barny, merchant of St. John's, 1844 (DPHW 26B).

Modern status: Rare, at Woody Point and Shoal Cove West (*Electors* 1955).

BARR, a surname of England, Ireland and Scotland; in England from Middle English *barre* – barrier, gateway, obstruction (? weir) in a stream or from Welsh *bar* – top, summit, referring to Barr Beacon, or from French place names Barre-en-ouche (Eure) or, perhaps, Barre-de-Samilly (La Manche), or from Old French *barre* – bar or stake, a nickname for a tall, thin man or for a maker of bars; in Scotland from Scots place names Barr (Ayrshire, Renfrewshire); in Ireland, from the preceding. (Reaney, Black, MacLysaght).

Traced by Guppy in the Glasgow district and by MacLysaght especially in northeast Ulster.

In Newfoundland:

Early instances: William, fisherman of Port de Grave, 1775 (Nfld. Archives T22); Ninian, minister of ? Blackhead (Conception B.), 1822, of Old Perlican, 1823 (DPHW 52A, 58); Patrick, from Co. Carlow, married at St. John's, 1827 (Nfld. Archives KCRC); Robert, of St. John's, 1837 (DPHW 26B); Frank de la Barre, pilot on Northwest River (Gander Lake), 1903 (Millais).

Modern status: Rare, at St. John's.

BARRETT, a surname of England, Ireland and Jersey (Channel Islands), from Old French *barat*, Middle English *bar(r)at*, *bar(r)et(te)* – traffic, commerce, deception, fraud; contention, strife, "from any of which a nickname could arise," or Old French *barrette* – (maker of) cap(s), bonnet(s). (Reaney, MacLysaght, Turk).

Guppy found Barratt, Barrett widespread, with Barrett the usual form; MacLysaght found Barrett in Co. Cork and the Mayo-Galway area.

In Newfoundland:

Family traditions: John (about 1728–), ? of Poole (Dorset), settled at Bread and Cheese Cove (now Bishops Cove) (MUN Folklore). Robin, from England, settled at Trepassey in the early 18th century; he later moved to Woody Island (Placentia B.) (MUN Folklore).

Early instances: John, of St. John's, 1705 (CO 194.22); Abraham, of Torbay/ Portugal Cove, 1708 (CO 194.4); John Barrat, from Poole (Dorset), planter of Old Perlican, 1709 (CO 194.4); John, constable, Trinity district, ? 1730 (CO 194.9); Sarah, of Bread and Cheese Cove (now Bishops Cove), 1755 (CO 199.18); Alexander Barret, fisherman of Trinity, 1760 (DPHW 64); Mary Barrett, of Harbour Grace, 1765 or earlier (CO 199.18); John of Holyrood, 1794 (CO 199.18); Abram, of Otterbury (Carbonear), 1800 (CO 199.18); John, of Harbour Main, 1803 (CO 199.18); William, of Kings Cove, 1819 (Nfld. Archives KCRC); Jacob, planter of Careless (now Kerleys) Harbour, 1822 (DPHW 64); Edward, of Ragged Harbour (unspecified), 1825 (Nfld. Archives KCRC); Patrick, planter of Freshwater (Carbonear), 1828 (DPHW 48); Edward, from Co. Wexford, married at Trinity (unspecified), 1828 (Nfld. Archives KCRC); Edward, from Killmacthomas (Co. Waterford), married at Catalina, 1828 (Nfld. Archives KCRC); William, planter of Olims (Brigus-Cupids district), 1837 (DPHW 34); Jane Elizabeth, of Sibley['s] Cove, 1850 (DPHW 58); William, of Keels, 1859 (Nfld. Archives KCRC); Stephen Barret, of Stock Cove (Bonavista B.), 1860 (Nfld. Archives KCRC); Robert Barrett, fisherman of Bay Roberts, 1860 (DPHW 38); Anne, of Plate Cove (Bonavista B.), 1868 (Nfld. Archives KCRC).

Modern status: Widespread, especially at St. John's, Old Perlican, Bishop's Cove, Spaniards Bay, Woody Island and Fleur de Lys.

Place names: Barrett Rock 47-23 54-15; Tim Barret Cove, ―― ―― Rock 47-24 53-52.

BARRIAULT, ? Newfoundland variant of the French surname *Barritault*, itself a variant of *Bariteau* – nickname for a worker in a bolting-mill. (Dauzat).

In Newfoundland:
Modern status: At Mount Moriah.

BARRINGTON, a surname of England, Ireland and of the Micmacs of Newfoundland, from the English place name Barrington (Cambridge, Gloucestershire and Somerset), or from the French place name Barentin (Seine-Maritime), or in Ireland occasionally as an anglicized form of *Ó Bearáin*. *See* BARRON. (Speigelhalter, MacLysaght).

Traced by Guppy only in Somerset, by Spiegelhalter in Devon, by MacLysaght in Cos. Cork and Limerick.

In Newfoundland:

Family tradition: ――, from Nova Scotia, came to Newfoundland to survey telegraph line from Swift Current to Bay d'Espoir, about 1880–90. Thomas Francis, son of above, was born at Piper's Hole (now Swift Current), about 1900.(MUN Folklore).

Early instances: John, of Kings Cove, 1815 (Nfld. Archives KCRC); Michael, married at St. John's, 1838 (Nfld. Archives BRC); ――, in seal fishery, 1832–55 (*Newfoundlander* 15 Mar 1832, 15 Nov 1855); Mrs. E. and Mrs. Sarah, widows of St. John's, 1871 (Lovell); John, a Micmac Indian trapper, 1905, one of the first settlers at Swift Current, who apparently followed the practice of guides taking the name of an employer, had hunting grounds "on the eastern side of [the] Tolt" 48-01 54-40, and lived to be 103 years of age (Millais).

Modern status: At St. John's, Swift Current and Badger.

BARRON, a surname of England, Scotland and Ireland, from Early Middle English and Old French *barun* – baron, sometimes from rank or title, or from service in a baronial household, or from the courtesy title applied to certain freemen of London, York and the Cinque Ports, but also as a nickname, proud or haughty as a baron; in Scotland, also from small baronies, and for land-owners "who had a certain amount of jurisdiction over the population of their lands"; in Ireland, for MacBarron, and for *Ó Bearáin* (*see* BARRINGTON). (Reaney, Black, MacLysaght).

Bar(r)on was traced by Guppy in Lancashire and Yorkshire NR and ER; by Spiegelhalter and Matthews in Devon; by Black in Angus; and by MacLysaght in Waterford-Kilkenny.

In Newfoundland:

Early instances: Laurence, of Placentia, 1794 (D'Alberti 5); Michael, ? of St. John's, 1799 (CO 194-3); Martin Barren, from Roar Parish (Co.

Kilkenny), married at St. John's, 1803 (Nfld. Archives BRC); James Barren or Barron, of Harbour Grace Parish, 1806 (Nfld. Archives HGRC); Michael Barron, from Tintern (Co. Wexford), married at St. John's, 1814 (Nfld. Archives BRC); Thomas, from Co. Waterford, of New Harbour (Trinity B.), 1815 (Nfld. Archives KCRC); Thomas, of Tickle Harbour (now Bellevue), 1817 (Nfld. Archives KCRC); Thomas, of Riders Harbour, 1817 (Nfld. Archives KCRC); William, of St. Mary's, 1822 (D'Alberti 32); Mary Barren, of Torbay, married at St. John's, 1830 (Nfld. Archives BRC); Edward Barrens, of Kings Cove, 1839 (Nfld. Archives KCRC); John Barron, teacher of Portugal Cove, 1839 (*Newfoundlander* 1 Aug 1839); Stephen, from Co. Wexford, teacher of Renews, 1841, 1845 (Dillon, *Nfld. Quarterly* Dec 1911); Robert, of Broomclose (Bonavista B.), 1845 (DPHW 73); William, from Kelgubanate Parish (unidentified) (Co. Waterford), of St. John's, died 1849, "70 years an inhabitant of St. John's," that is, since 1779 (*Nfld. Patriot* 8 Sep 1849); Anastasia, of Stock Cove (Bonavista B.), 1850 (Nfld. Archives KCRC); Patrick, of Keels, 1860 (Nfld. Archives KCRC); Maria, of Harbour Grace, 1870 (Nfld. Archives HGRC).

Modern status: Widespread, especially at St. John's, St. Joseph's (Placentia) and Holyrood.

BARROW, a surname of England, from Old English *bearu* – (dweller by the) grove, or Old English *bearg* – (dweller by the) hill, or from the English place name in several counties. (Reaney).

Traced by Guppy in Lancashire, Kent and Sussex, and by Spiegelhalter in Devon.

In Newfoundland:

Early instances: Petter, ? labourer of St. John's, 1779 (CO 194.34); Edward, of Greenspond, 1828 (DPHW 76); Edward, fisherman of Freshwater Bay (Bonavista), 1871 (Lovell); James, farmer of Holyrood, 1871 (Lovell); Edward, of Gambo, 1876 (Nfld. Archives KCRC).

Modern status: Rare, with small concentration at Middle Brook (Bonavista North).

Place names: Barrow Cove 49-21 55-02, Barrow Harbour 48-40 53-39, Barrow Rock 47-35 55-23.

BARRY, a baptismal name and surname of England, Ireland and Scotland, from Old French *barri* – rampart, later applied to the suburb below the rampart or from the French place name in various localities; also in Ireland for *Ó Báire* or *Ó Beargha*; and in Scotland from the Scots place name Barry (Angus). (Withycombe, Reaney, Black, MacLysaght).

Found by Spiegelhalter in Devon, by Matthews in Dorset, and by MacLysaght widespread in Ireland "though still more numerous in Munster than elsewhere."

In Newfoundland:

Early instances: Redmond, of Bay de Verde, 1730 (CO 194.23); ——, of St. John's, 1766 (DPHW 26C); Patrick, of Trinity Bay, 1783 (DPHW 64); William, fisherman of Torbay, 1794–5, "20 years in Newfoundland," that is, since 1774–5 (Census 1794–5); Michael, shoreman of St. John's, 1794–5, "16 years in Newfoundland," that is, since 1778–9 (Census 1794–5); Margaret Barrey, of Bonavista, 1798 (DPHW 70); Edward Barry, joint purchaser of fishing room on Pond Island (Greenspond Island), 1799 (Bonavista Register 1806); David, from Waterglass Hill (Co. Cork), married at St. John's, 1803 (Nfld. Archives BRC); Sara, of Trepassey, 1807 (Nfld. Archives BRC); Mary, from city of Cork, married at St. John's, 1807 (Nfld. Archives BRC); N., of Harbour Grace Parish, 1812 (Nfld. Archives HGRC); Edward, from Cork, gunner on H.M.S. *Pike*, died at St. John's, 1817, aged 47 (*Nfld. Mercantile Jour.* 30 May 1817); Mary, of Kings Cove Parish, 1838 (Nfld. Archives KCRC); James, of Harbour Grace, 1866 (Nfld. Archives HGRC); Lawrence and Thomas, planters of Red Island (Placentia B.), 1871, from Port Royal (Long Island, Placentia B.) (Lovell, MUN Hist.); John, planter of Bay of Islands, 1871 (Lovell).

Modern status: Widespread, especially at St. John's and Red Island.

Place names: Barry Brook 48-20 58-41, —— Point 46-56 53-33, Barry's Brook 49-16 54-29, 50-09 56-09, —— Cove 50-09 56-08, —— Pond 47-45 53-17, 50-08 56-09, —— Ponds 49-16 54-23, —— Cove Point 50-06 56-06, 50-09 56-08.

BARTER, a surname of England and Ireland, an occupational name from the same source as BARRETT – barterer, exchanger, or as a nickname – squabbler. (Cottle). Another possible origin is from the surname of France Bartaire, a variant of *bretaire* – one who stutters, stammers. (Dauzat). Also an anglicized form of Bortheyre (originally Basque), also attested in St. Pierre (Thomas, "French Fam. Names").

Traced by Spiegelhalter and Matthews especially in Devon, and by MacLysaght "associated exclusively with Co. Cork."

In Newfoundland:

Family tradition: William (1794–1869) and Amos (1795–1852), fishermen of Bay de Verde, from England in early 19th century (MUN Geog.).

Early instances: Andrew, of St. John's, 1706 (CO 194.22); Charles, fisherman of Cape La Hune, 1852 (DPHW 102); James, fisherman at Charles Brook (White B.), 1871 (Lovell).

Modern status: Scattered on the South Coast, especially at Cape La Hune and on the West Coast at Mainland, Bay de Verde, and St. John's. Some Barters of the West Coast are believed to be of French origin.

Place names: Barters Brook 49-27 57-45, Barters Pond 49-26 57-49.

BARTLE, a surname of England, a diminutive of the baptismal name Bartholomew. (Withycombe, Bardsley). *See* BADCOCK and *also* BARTLETT.

Traced by Guppy in Nottinghamshire and Cornwall.

In Newfoundland:

Modern status: Rare, at Grand Falls.

BARTLETT, a surname of England, a double diminutive of the baptismal name Bartholomew. (Reaney). *See* BADCOCK *and also* BARTLE.

Traced by Guppy especially in Dorset, and also in Oxfordshire, Somerset, Northamptonshire, Kent, Gloucestershire, Devon and Cornwall.

In Newfoundland:

Family traditions: Robert, of Anchor Point, ? about 1750 (MUN Hist.). James (1778–1845), from Higher Lytchett (? either Lytchett Matravers or Lytchett Minster, Dorset), settled at Trinity (Trinity B.), 1791 or 1798 (MUN Folklore). Thomas, from Lancashire to Fortune about 1850. (P.E.L. Smith).

Early instances: John Bartlet, of St. John's, 1708 (CO 194.4); James and Arthur Bartlett, of Newfoundland, 1730 (CO 194.22, 23); Francis, of Bay Roberts, 1766 (CO 199.18); Edward and John, ? of Fogo, Twillingate or Tilton (now Tilting), 1771 (CO 194.30); Thomas Bartlett, of Port de Grave, 1778 (CO 199.18); John and William, of Brigus, 1780 (CO 199.18); John, of Turk's Gut (now Marysvale, 1803 (CO 199.18); Caleb, of Carbonear, 1813 (DPHW 48); Joana Bartlet, of Harbour Grace Parish, 1821 (Nfld. Archives HGRC); William Bartlett, servant at Quirpon, 1821 (D'Alberti 31); William, carpenter of Ferryland, 1823 (DPHW 31); Thomas, of Bear's Cove (Harbour Grace), 1824 (DPHW 43); John, planter of Bull Cove, 1824 (DPHW 34); Isaac, of Cupids, 1828 (DPHW 34); Thomas, from Poole (Dorset), married at Riders Harbour, 1829 (Nfld. Archives KCRC); Richard, of Whitechurch (Dorset), deserted from establishment of Alan Goodridge at Renews, 1835 (*Ledger* 11 Sep 1835); John, of King's Cove, 1835

(DPHW 73); John, of Knight's Cove, 1839 (DPHW 73); Samuel, planter of Salmon Cove (now Champneys), 1841 (DPHW 64B); Robert, of Three Arms Island, 1843 (DPHW 86); Robert, of Ward's Harbour (now Beaumont North), 1848 (DPHW 86); Jane, of Torbay, 1850 (DPHW 26D); John, of Amherst Cove (Bonavista district), 1850 (DPHW 73); Samuel, fisherman of Northside Trinity, 1853 (DPHW 64B); William, of Channel, 1857 (DPHW 98); Henry, fisherman of Goose Cove, Trinity, 1857 (DPHW 64B); William, fisherman of Bareneed, 1860 (DPHW 38).

Modern status: Widespread, especially at Marysvale and neighbouring settlements, Bell Island, St. John's, Coombs Cove and Rattling Brook.

Place names: Bartlett Rock 47-01 55-09, Bartlett's Cove 49-38 55-54, —— Harbour 50-57 57-00, —— Pond 51-26 55-37, —— River 51-28 55-40, —— Steady Pond 51-26 55-39.

BARTON, a surname of England and Ireland, from a widespread English place name, or (dweller at the) barley farm or at a farm kept for the lord's use. (Cottle, MacLysaght).

Traced by Guppy especially in Gloucestershire and also in Derbyshire, Hampshire, Kent, Lancashire, Lincolnshire, Sussex and Wiltshire, by Spiegelhalter in Devon, and by MacLysaght in Co. Kildare.

In Newfoundland:

Early instances: John, of St. John's, 1794–5 (Census 1794–5); Patrick, from Carrick on Suir (Co. Tipperary), married at St. John's, 1827 (Nfld. Archives BRC); Thomas, fisherman of Carbonear, 1857 (DPHW 49); John and Richard, fishermen of Petty Harbour, 1871 (Lovell).

Modern status: Rare and virtually limited to the Goulds, near St. John's.

Place name: Barton (locality) 48-13 53-54.

BASHA, a surname of Syria and Lebanon, reflecting the Arabic pronunciation of Turkish *Pasha*, ultimately from Persian *padshah* – emperor, sovereign.

In Newfoundland:

Early instance: Benjamin, of Harbour Grace, 1908 (Nfld. Archives HGRC).

Modern status: Scattered, at St. John's, Bell Island and Corner Brook.

BASKERFIELD, a surname of England, a variant of Baskerville, as in Conan Doyle's *The Hound of the Baskervilles*, from the French place name Bascherville (Eure). (Reaney).

Guppy traced Baskerville in Cheshire.

In Newfoundland:

Modern status: Rare, at Heatherton (St. Georges district).

BASS, a surname of England from the Old French *bas(se)*, Middle English *bass, base, bace* – low, of small height; a man with short legs; or from Old English *bærs*, now *bass* – a fish. (Reaney). See also BASSETT.

Guppy traced Bass in Essex, Leicestershire and Rutlandshire.

In Newfoundland:

Early instances: Thomas Bass, of Bonavista, 1792, 1793 (USPG); James Base, of Twillingate, 1822 (USPG).

Modern status: Unique, at St. John's.

BASSETT, a surname of England and Ireland from the Old French *basset* – of low stature, diminutive of *bas*. *See* BASS. (Reaney).

Guppy traced Bassett in Cornwall, Kent and Staffordshire; Spiegelhalter and Matthews in Devon; MacLysaght found it in Ireland since the 13th century, but "not closely associated with any particular area."

In Newfoundland:

Early instance: Robert, farmer of Pouch Cove, 1871 (Lovell).

Modern status: Rare, at St. John's.

BASTOW, a surname of England, from the English place name Bairstow (Yorkshire WR). (Reaney).

In Newfoundland:

Family tradition: Introduced about 1850 from Torbay (Devon) to St. John's (MUN Folklore).

Early instances: John, farmer, and William, labourer of St. John's, 1871 (Lovell); Marldon Allan (1855–1935), died at St. John's (General Protestant Cemetery).

Modern status: At St. John's.

BATEMAN, a surname of England and Ireland, meaning servant of Bartholomew, "a type of surname formerly common in Yorkshire." (Reaney). *See* BADCOCK.

Traced by Spiegelhalter in Devon and by Matthews in Somerset; MacLysaght found it "fairly numerous in Co. Cork since the 17th century."

In Newfoundland:

Early instances: Joseph, of Trinity (Trinity B.), 1805 (DPHW 64); Charles, fisherman of Indian Harbour (La Poile district), 1871 (Lovell); Francis, of Bay Roberts, 1915 (Nfld. Archives HGRC).

Modern status: Southwest Coast, especially at Channel.

BATES, a surname of England and Ireland, a pet-form of the baptismal name Bartholomew (*see* BADCOCK), or from northern Middle English *bat* – boat(man), or from Old Norse *bati* – (dweller by the) fat pasture. (Reaney).

Guppy found Bates widespread, especially in Leicestershire, Rutlandshire, Warwickshire and Kent, Matthews in Dorset, and MacLysaght "quite numerous in Dublin and North Ulster." A tradition at Duncannon, Co. Wexford, maintains that some old members of the family came to Newfoundland. (Halley).

In Newfoundland:

Early instances: H.C. Bate, St. John's, 1797 (D'Alberti 6); William Baitt, of Trinity (Trinity B.), 1798 (DPHW 64); Thomas Bates, planter of Twillingate, 1820 (USPG); Thomas, of St. John's, 1821 (CO 194.64); Thomas, from Clonmel (Co. Tipperary), married at St. John's, 1821 (Nfld. Archives BRC); Charles, missionary at Old Perlican, 1830 (DPHW 58); Charles, planter of Hants Harbour, 1831 (DPHW 59A); Thomas, of Kings Cove Parish, 1838 (Nfld. Archives KCRC); Laurence, of St. John's, 1839 (Nfld. Archives BRC); James, of Merritts Harbour, 1846 (DPHW 86).

Modern status: Rare, with a small concentration at Happy Adventure.

Place name: Bates Pond 48-33 53-30.

BATH, a surname of England, from the English place name Bath (Somerset) or Bathe Barten (Devon), or from Old English *bæth* – (dweller by a) spring (used for bathing), or ? a variant of BATT. (Spiegelhalter, Reaney Notes).

Guppy traced the name in Kent and Cornwall, Spiegelhalter and Matthews in Devon.

In Newfoundland:

Family tradition: Two brothers, alleged sheep-stealers, came to Newfoundland in the mid-16th century, and may have changed their name to Bath, from their place of origin. One brother is said to have settled on the Horse Islands, the other in Central Newfoundland (MUN Folklore). —— Bath, is said to have been one of the first settlers in Twillingate at Jenkins Cove (*Nfld. Quarterly* Dec 1905).

Early instances: Thomas, of Trinity Harbour, 1722 (CO 194.30); Thomas, planter of Fogo, 1808 (MUN Hist.); John, planter of Twillingate, 1821 (USPG); John Bath or Batt, of Twillingate, 1822

(Nfld. Archives KCRC); John, of Herring Neck, 1842 (DPHW 86).

Modern status: Especially at Burnt Island Tickle and other settlements in the Twillingate district and on Horse Islands (*Electors* 1955).

BATSON, a surname of England, – son of Bate (*see* BATES) or Batt (*see* BATT), or from the English place names Batson, Bason (Devon) (Spiegelhalter), or a variant of BATSTONE. (Reaney).

Traced by Spiegelhalter in Devon and by Matthews in Dorset.

In Newfoundland:

Early instances: William, of English Harbour, 1807 (DPHW 64); John, of St. John's, 1817 (DPHW 26D); Charles, of Nippers Harbour, 1845 (DPHW 86).

Modern status: Rare, with a small concentration at English Harbour and at other settlements in the Trinity North district.

BATSTONE, a surname of England, ? from Bason or Batson (Devon), both earlier *Bad(d)astone*, or a variant of BATSON. (Spiegelhalter).

Traced by Spiegelhalter in Devon.

In Newfoundland:

Family tradition: The family is believed to have come from Wales and settled in Green Bay, in English Harbour (Trinity Bay) and English Harbour East and West (Fortune Bay) (MUN Folklore).

Early instances: John Baston, of St. John's, 1759 (DPHW 26C); William Bestone, of Trinity Bay, 1773 (DPHW 64); John Baston, of English Harbour, 1794 (DPHW 64); J. Badstone, cooper of St. John's, 1820 (D'Alberti 30); James Bastone, planter of Salmon Cove (now Champneys), 1832 (DPHW 64B); Mary Ann Batstone, of Quidi Vidi, 1846 (DPHW 26D); James, of Jackson's ? Arm, 1859 (DPHW 92); Charles and Robert, planters of Nippers Harbour, 1871 (Lovell).

Modern status: At Nippers Harbour and other settlements in Green Bay, Corner Brook, St. John's and English Harbour (Trinity Bay), where is also BATSON (*Electors* 1955), but neither form is apparently recorded in English Harbour East and West (Fortune Bay).

BATT, a surname of England, from *bakke* – bat, a nickname, or from one of the meanings of BATE(S), or a variant of BATH. (Reaney).

Guppy traced Batt in Somerset, Batts in Oxfordshire; Spiegelhalter traced Batt in Devon.

In Newfoundland:

Early instances: Joseph Batt, sentenced to receive fifteen lashes for stealing a pair of shoes and buckles valued at seven shillings and sixpence at Bonavista about 1754 (Pedley); Joseph Batts, of Bonavista, 1792 (USPG); Thomas Batt, shoemaker of St. John's, 1806 (CO 194.45); Bridget, of Goran (unidentified), married at Fortune Harbour, 1831 (Nfld. Archives KCRC); John, of Open Hall, 1835 (DPHW 73A); James, planter of Herring Neck, 1850 (DPHW 85); Benjamin, fisherman of Stone Harbour, 1852 (DPHW 85).

Modern status: A West Coast name, in the Corner Brook area.

Place names: Batt Cove 49-39 55-47, Joe Batt's Arm 49-44 54-10, —— —— Brook 49-04 54-41, —— —— Point 49-45 54-09, —— —— Pond 48-58 54-46, Batts Cove 49-48 56-50, —— Island 47-40 54-07.

BATTCOCK, a surname of England, a pet-form of Bartholomew. *See* BADCOCK, with which confusion is not unlikely.

Traced by Reaney Notes in Devon as Batecock in 1339.

In Newfoundland:

Especially associated with Brigus South (*Electors* 1955), where, however, the name is BADCOCK in Lovell (1871).

BATTEN, a surname of England, a diminutive of the baptismal name Bartholomew. (Reaney). *See* BADCOCK.

Guppy traced Batten and Batting in Devon and Cornwall.

In Newfoundland:

Early instances: Arthur Batten or Battin, of Harbour Grace, 1675 (CO 1); John Batten, juror of St. John's, 1750 (CO 194.12); Samuel Batton, of Port de Grave, 1768 (CO 199.18); William, in possession of land at Bareneed, 1783 (D'Alberti 2); William Batten, of Foxtrap, 1832 (DPHW 30); John, fisherman of Pick Eyes, 1844 (DPHW 39).

Modern status: Associated especially with St. John's, Foxtrap and Bareneed and other settlements in the Port de Grave district.

Place name: Battens Pond 47-33 53-23.

BATTERTON, a surname of England, apparently not recorded elsewhere, ? from the English place names Betterton (Berkshire) or Batherton (Cheshire). (Ekwall).

In Newfoundland:

Early instances: Nicholas, married at Greenspond, 1833 (Nfld. Archives KCRC); Nicholas, of

Pinchers Island (Bonavista B.), 1856 (Nfld. Archives KCRC); Nicholas, of Cape Freels, 1859 (Nfld. Archives KCRC); James, married at Cottells Island (Bonavista B.), 1870, of Kings Cove, 1894 (Nfld. Archives KCRC).

Modern status: At Kings Cove and St. John's.

BATTISTE, ? a Newfoundland variant of the surname of the Channel Islands Batiste (St. John the Baptist).

In Newfoundland:

Early instance: John, fisherman of Channel, 1871 (Lovell).

Modern status: At Channel-Port aux Basques and Mouse Island.

BAULD, a surname of England from the Middle English *ballade* – rotund, corpulent, later bald, or a short form of the Old German personal names *Baldwin* (*see* BALDWIN) or *Baldric* or Old English **Beald*. (Reaney).

In Newfoundland:

Modern status: Almost entirely concentrated at Clarke's Head (Fogo).

Place name: Cape Bauld 51-38 55-26.

BAVIDGE, ? a variant of the surnames of England Bavridge or Beveridge from Old French *bevrege*, Middle English *beuerage* – drink, liquor for consumption, to bind a bargain, or of Babbage, found in the Devon place name Babbages which is probably to be associated with the family of Henry *Bobich*, recorded in 1330. (Reaney, Reaney Notes, Bardsley, Gover).

Guppy traced Babbage in Devon.

In Newfoundland: One family in St. John's, from the north of England, about 1890.

BAVIS, ? a Newfoundland variant, apparently not recorded elsewhere, of the English surname Beaves, Beavis, Bevis etc., from the French place name Beauvais (Oise), or from Old French personal names containing the elements *beau* – fine and *fiz* – son. *See also* BEAUFIELD. (Reaney).

In Newfoundland:

Early instances: James Beavis, married at St. John's, 1833 (Nfld. Archives BRC); John Baviss, fisherman of Brule, Long Island (Placentia B.), 1871 (Lovell); James Bavis, fisherman of Renews, 1871 (Lovell); John and John Jr., of Renews to Cape Race area, 1871 (Lovell); Thomas, labourer of St. John's, 1871 (Lovell).

Modern status: Scattered and somewhat rare, with small concentrations at Jerseyside and Renews.

BAXTROM, ? a surname of Scotland, not recorded by Black, ? of Swedish origin, from Swedish *bakström* – (dweller by the) backward current.

In Newfoundland: At St. John's, from Scotland, since about 1870.

BEALES, a surname of England, from the Old French *bele* – beautiful, used also as a woman's name, or from the English place name Beal (Northumberland, Yorkshire WR). (Reaney).

Guppy traced Beal(e) in Kent, Leicestershire, Rutlandshire, Surrey, Yorkshire NR and ER, and Beales in Norfolk; Spiegelhalter found Beal(e), Beall in Devon; and Matthews found B(e)ale(s) in Devon, Dorset and Guernsey.

In Newfoundland:

Early instances: Joshua Beal, grand juror, St. John's, 1762 (CO 194.5); Richard Beales, married at Labrador, 1881 (Nfld. Archives HGRC).

Modern status: At Curling.

BEANLAND(S), surnames of England, ? from the English place names Beanlands (Park) (Cumberland), or ? variants of the surname of England, Beenlan or Beenlen, recorded only by Matthews in the 18th century in Devon, of unknown origin but possibly from an unidentified Devon place name. (Reaney Notes, Matthews).

Traced by Matthews in Devon and by family in Nelson (Lancashire).

In Newfoundland:

Early instances: Philip Beenlen, churchwarden of Harbour Grace, 1791 (USPG); Philip Beinlin, merchant of St. John's, 1798 (DPHW 26B).

Modern status: One Beanland at Flat Bay (St. Georges) (*Electors* 1955), Kenneth Beanlands at St. John's, 1971, since 1964.

BEARN(E)S, variants of the surname of England BARNES.

In Newfoundland:

Early instances: —— Bearnes, widow of St. John's, 1681 (CO 1); William Bearns, of Devil's (now Job's) Cove, 1812 (*Royal Gazette* 11 Jun 1812); George, of Old Perlican, 1828 (DPHW 58); William Bearns, of Ashburton (Devon), married at St. John's, 1829 (*Royal Gazette* 1 Sep 1829); Seragh, of Harbour Grace Parish, 1834 (Nfld. Archives HGRC); William, planter of Brigus, 1837 (DPHW 31).

Modern status: Rare, at St. John's.

BEASLEY, BEAZLEY, surnames of England and Ireland, from the English place names Beesley (Lancashire) or Higher Besley Farm (Devon). (Spiegelhalter, Reaney).

Guppy traced Bazely, Bazley in Northamptonshire, Beesley in Berkshire and Lancashire; Spiegelhalter found Beasley and B(e)azley in Devon. MacLysaght comments that Beasley has been found in Ireland since the mid-17th century.

In Newfoundland:

Early instances: G. and J. Beazley, inhabitants of Burin, 1805 (D'Alberti 15); Miles Beasly, of Harbour Grace Parish, 1821 (Nfld. Archives HGRC); Mrs. Beasley, teacher of Spoon Cove, 1857 (*Nfld. Almanac*); Gabriel Beazley, fisherman of Sound Island (Placentia B.), 1871 (Lovell).

Modern status: Rare, and especially at Wandsworth, Big Salmonier and other settlements in the Burin district.

BEASON, a surname of England of unascertained meaning; with BEESO, BESON, ? variants of the French (Normandy) and Channel Islands (Guernsey and Jersey) surname BISSON – (dweller in the) bush, bushy country, or a seller of *bisse* – very fine linen. (Dauzat, Turk).

In Newfoundland:

Family tradition: The Beasons who arrived at Joe Batts Arm between 1811 and 1816 were Irish (MUN Hist.). (The name does not appear in MacLysaght, Woulfe or Matheson).

Early instances: John Beeson, from St. Malo (Ille-et-Vilaine), married at St. John's, 1762 (DPHW 26D); Philip Besom, from Jersey (Channel Islands), in possession of property at Harbour Grace, 1776 (CO 199.18); Francis Bes(s)on, of Holyrood, 1792 (CO 199.18); John Besom, of Mint Cove (Spaniards Bay), 1803 (CO 199.18); Cora Beeson, of Harbour Grace Parish, 1816 (Nfld. Archives HGRC); Mary Beezo, of Harbour Grace Parish, 1822 (Nfld. Archives HGRC); William Bessom, fisherman of Codroy, 1845 (DPHW 101).

Modern status: Beason in small numbers at Corner Brook, Grand Falls and Norris Arm; Beson at Windsor, Grand Falls and Corner Brook; Beeso at Bell Island and Holyrood (*Electors* 1955).

BEATON, a surname of England, from the Middle English baptismal name *Beton*, a diminutive of *Bete* (Beatrice), "still used as a Christian name in Cornwall in 1630," and as a rare male baptismal name (presumably from the family name) in Newfoundland at the present time. It has also been used by the Montagnais Indians of Newfoundland. (Reaney, Speck, Bardsley).

Traced by Spiegelhalter in Devon.

In Newfoundland:

Family tradition: One of the four families of Ship Cove (now Botwood) in 1881 (MUN Folklore).

Early instances: ——, ? seaman, 1839 (*Newfoundlander* 4 Jul 1839); Alfred, fisherman of Exploits River, 1871 (Lovell); William, of Harbour Grace Parish, 1882 (Nfld. Archives HGRC). A Montagnais family of the surname Beaton hunted in the lower Exploits River area (Speck).

Modern status: Scattered and especially at Norris Arm.

Place name: Beatons Point 49-05 55-19.

BEAUCAGE appears to be a surname of French origin, but is not recorded by Dauzat as either a surname or a place name.

In Newfoundland:

Modern status: Unique, at Windsor.

BEAUCHAMP, a surname of England, Beauchamps of France and the Channel Islands, and Beaucamp of the Channel Islands from the French place name Beauchamps (La Manche, Somme), also anglicized as BEECHAM. (Reaney, Turk).

In Newfoundland:

Early instances: John Beauchamp 1846 or Beecham 1850, fisherman of Bareneed (DPHW 39).

Modern status: Rare, at Rencontre West (*Electors* 1955) and Port aux Basques.

BEAUDOIN, a surname of France, and ? as Baudin etc., of the Channel Islands, from the Germanic personal name *Baldo* or from the Old French *baud* – happy, from the Germanic *bald* – bold. (Dauzat, Turk).

In Newfoundland:

Modern status: At Bartlett's Harbour, Ferolle Point (*Electors* 1955) and Reef's Harbour.

BEAUFIELD, ? a Newfoundland variant of the French surname Beaufils, *beau* – fine, *fils* – son, as in BAVIS. (Dauzat).

In Newfoundland:

Family tradition: ——, from France, settled on the French Shore ? about 1870 (MUN Folklore).

Modern status: At Raleigh, Ship Cove (White B.) (*Electors* 1955), and St. John's.

BEAZLEY. *See* BEASLEY

BECK, a surname of England and Ireland, from the French place name Bec, in various localities; or from Middle English *bekke* – (dweller by the) brook, common in the north of England and Scotland but not in the south of England; or from Old English personal names **Becca*, from *becca* – pick-axe, or *Beocca*; or from Old French *bec* – beak, bill of a bird, a nickname. In Ireland Beck may also be an anglicization of *Ó Béice*. (Reaney, MacLysaght).

Traced by Guppy in Norfolk and by Spiegelhalter in Devon, and by MacLysaght mainly in Ulster.

In Newfoundland:

Early instances: Henry, ? of St. Lawrence, captured a French banker, 1814 (Prowse); Thomas, of St. John's, 1821 (CO 194.64); Henry, of St. Lawrence, 1826 (DPHW 106); Henry, of Sound Island (Placentia B.), 1835 (DPHW 30); Robert, fisherman of Rose Blanche, 1843 (DPHW 101).

Modern status: Scattered, especially at St. Lawrence and Swift Current.

Place name: Beck Bay 47-30 56-11.

BECKETT, a surname of England and Ireland, Becquet of Jersey (Channel Islands), a diminutive of Old French *bec* – little beak or mouth, as in BECK, or from the English place names Beckett (Devon, Berkshire). (Reaney, Turk).

Traced by Guppy in Cheshire, Norfolk and Nottinghamshire, by Spiegelhalter in Devon, and by MacLysaght in northeast Ulster and Dublin.

In Newfoundland:

Early instances: ? Elizabeth Becket, proprietor and occupier of fishing room at Old Perlican, Winter 1800–01 (Census Trinity B.); Thomas, of Harbour Grace Parish, 1808 (Nfld. Archives HGRC).

Modern status: Especially at Old Perlican.

BECKFORD. *See* BICKFORD

BEECHAM, a variant of BEAUCHAMP.

Guppy traced Beacham in Somerset, Beecham in Lincolnshire.

In Newfoundland:

Early instances: John, of Port de Grave, 1769 (CO 199.18); John Beauchamp 1846 or Beecham 1850, fisherman of Bareneed (DPHW 39).

Modern status: Rare, at Hillview (*Electors* 1955) and Bareneed.

BEEHAN, a variant of the surname of Ireland (O)BEHAN, Beaghan, Ir. *Ó Beacháin,* ? from Ir. *beach* – bee. (MacLysaght).

MacLysaght found the name especially associated with Co. Kerry and Co. Kildare and vicinity.

In Newfoundland:

Early instances: Thomas, of Bay Bulls district, 1805 (Nfld. Archives BRC); William, from Ballyhane (Co. Wexford), married at St. John's, 1819 (Nfld. Archives BRC); Moses Behan, of Harbour Grace Parish, 1831 (Nfld. Archives HGRC); Patrick, fisherman of Cupids, 1871 (Lovell).

Modern status: Beehan, rare, at Cupids (*Electors* 1955) and St. John's; Behan, unique, at Gander.

BEER, a surname of England, from Old English *bǣr* – (dweller near a) swine pasture, or, more commonly, from the English place names Beare, Beara (18) or Beer(a) or Beere (17) (Devon) from Old English *bearu* – grove; or, occasionally, from Old English *bera* – bear (the animal). (Reaney).

Traced by Guppy, Spiegelhalter and Matthews in Devonshire, and by Matthews also in Dorset and Hampshire.

In Newfoundland:

Early instances: J. Bear, of St. John's, 1811 (CO 194.52); George Beere or Beer, fisherman of Freshwater Bay (St. John's), 1818 (DPHW 26B); John Beere or Beer, of Windsor Lake, 1831 (DPHW 26B); I.J. Beer, of Fogo, 1843 (DPHW 83).

Modern status: Rare, at St. John's.

BEESO. *See* BEASON

BEGG, a surname of Ireland, from the Irish *beag* – small, or, in Ulster, a variant of the English surname Bigge. (MacLysaght).

MacLysaght traced Begg in Dublin and adjacent Leinster counties, Beggs mainly in northeast Ulster.

In Newfoundland:

Modern status: Rare, at Holyrood and Topsail (*Electors* 1955).

BEGIN, a variant of the surname of the Channel Islands, Beghin, or of France, Bég(u)in, from French *béguin* – member of a religious sect of the 13th century. (Dauzat, Miller).

In Newfoundland:

Early instances: John ? Bejan, of St. John's, 1775 (DPHW 26C); Francis Beginn, fisherman of Cape Ray, 1871 (Lovell); Frank Began, early settler at Stephenville Crossing, 1909 (MUN Hist.).

Modern status: One at Buchans (*Electors* 1955).

BEHAN. *See* BEEHAN

BELBEN, BELBIN, surnames of England, of unknown origin.

Traced by Matthews in Poole (Dorset) and Christchurch (Hampshire).

In Newfoundland:

Early instances: William Belbin (about 1777–1866) moved from Conception Bay to Seal Cove (now New Chelsea) about 1818 (Nfld. Archives T51); Benjamin, of Grand Bank, 1829 (DPHW 106); Charles, of Lamaline, 1831 (DPHW 109); Susanna Belban, of Grates Cove, 1849 (DPHW 58); John Belbin, fisherman of Russell's Cove (now New Melbourne), 1853 (DPHW 59A).

Modern status: Belben at Glenburnie, Belbin scattered but especially at New Chelsea.

Place name: ? Bellburns 50-20 57-32.

BELL, a surname of England, Ireland, Scotland and the Channel Islands, a pet-form of Isabel, or from Old French *bel* – beautiful, or from Old English *belle* – bell, ie. bellman or bellringer, or one who lives at the sign of the Bell or by the church or town bell. (Reaney, Turk).

Guppy found the name widespread especially in Northumberland and Co. Durham and in the Scots Border counties, especially Dumfriesshire; Matthews and Spiegelhalter in Devon; and MacLysaght "among the ten most numerous names in Ireland," especially in Cos. Londonderry, Antrim, Down and Armagh.

In Newfoundland:

Family tradition: George, of Grand Bank (about 1788–1861) (MUN Hist.).

Early instances: Robert, ? labourer of St. John's, 1779 (CO 194.34); James, missionary of Fogo, 1820 (CO 194.64); John, school teacher of Harbour Grace, 1871 (Lovell); Samuel K., MLC (1854–1930), of Grand Bank, buried at St. John's (General Protestant Cemetery).

Modern status: At St. John's, elsewhere rare and scattered.

Place name (not necessarily from the surname): Bell Brook 48-57 57-57.

BELLAMY, a surname of England, from Old French *bel ami* – fair friend. (Reaney).

Traced by Guppy in Lincolnshire, Nottinghamshire and Huntingdonshire and by Spiegelhalter in Devon.

In Newfoundland:

Early instances: Henry, of St. John's, 1819 (DPHW 26D); Henry, of Maggotty Cove, 1822 (DPHW 26B); William Bellaney, of Harbour Grace, 1812 (Nfld. Archives HGRC).

Modern status: Rare, at St. John's (*Electors* 1955).

BELLOWS, a surname of England, from Middle English *below* – bellows (-blower). (Reaney).

In Newfoundland:

Family tradition: From Sheffield, England, about ? 1860 (MUN Folklore).

Early instances: Thomas, of Trinity, 1818 (DPHW 64); Robert, of Greenspond, 1829 (DPHW 76); Joseph, planter of Ship Cove (now part of Port Rexton), 1831 (DPHW 64B); George, of Freshwater (Trinity B.), 1876 (DPHW 65).

Modern status: At St. John's, Humber East and West districts and Dunfield.

BEM(M)ISTER, surnames of England, from the English place name Beaminster (Dorset), so pronounced locally. (Reaney).

Traced by Matthews in Poole (Dorset) and Christchurch (Hampshire).

In Newfoundland:

Family traditions: John Bemister (1747–1832), probably the first Bemister to winter in Carbonear, started the family which survived there until recently, and was buried at Corfe Mullen (Dorset) (MUN Folklore). William Henry, from Brighton (Sussex), settled at St. John's between 1865–1875 (MUN Folklore).

Early instances: George, schoolmaster of Bonavista, 1791 (USPG); William Bemister, from Christchurch (Hampshire), planter of Green Bay, deceased 1814 (*Royal Gazette* 10 Nov 1814); Thomas Beaminster, of Greenspond, 1815 (DPHW 76); W.W. Bemister, of Harbour Grace, 1817 (D'Alberti 27); Edward, planter of Freshwater (Carbonear), 1823 (DPHW 48); Reuben, of New Perlican, 1859 (DPHW 59A); William, of Hare Bay (Bonavista B.), 1871 (Lovell).

Modern status: At St. John's and Ragged Harbour (Fogo district).

BENDALL, BENDELL, surnames of England, from the English place name Benthall (Shropshire). (Reaney).

Guppy traced Bendall in Suffolk and Bentall in Essex.

In Newfoundland:

Early instances: Paul Bendle, in possession of property and fisherman of Torbay, 1794–5, "40 years in Newfoundland," that is, since 1754 (Census 1794–5); Sarah Anne Bendall, of St. John's, 1834 (DPHW 26D); Thomas Bendel, of Haystack, Long Island (Placentia B.), 1836 (DPHW 30); Henry Bendle, fisherman of Northern Gut (now North River, Conception B.), 1849 (DPHW 39); William B.

Bendall, J.P., Labrador, 1857 (*Nfld. Almanac*); Henry Bendell, fisherman of The Scrape (Port de Grave), 1860 (DPHW 38); Thomas, of Harbour Buffett, 1871 (Lovell).

Modern status: Rare, especially at Otterbury (Port de Grave).

BENGER, a surname of England, from the Old French personal name *Berengier*, Old German *Beringar*, containing the elements *bear* and *spear*. (Reaney).

Traced by Matthews in Bideford (Devon) and Waterford, Ireland.

In Newfoundland:

Early instances: James, inhabitant of St. John's, 1700, "for 10 years," that is, since 1690 (CO 194.2); James, of Ferryland, 1708 (CO 194.4); William Benguss, of Quidi Vidi, 1709 (CO 194.4); Israel Benger, planter of Little Catalina, 1824, of Plate Cove, 1833, of King's Cove, 1836, of Amherst Cove, 1843 (DPHW 64B, 70, 73A).

Modern status: Rare, especially at Middle Amherst Cove (Bonavista South district).

BENMORE, ? a surname of Scotland (not recorded by Black), ? from the Scots place names Benmore (Argyllshire), Ben More (Perthshire, Sutherland, the Hebrides, Isle of Mull) – great hill.

In Newfoundland: At St. John's since ? early 20th century (Family).

BENNETT, a surname of England, Ireland, Scotland, Bennet of Jersey (Channel Islands), from the Old French *Beneit*, *Beneoit*, Latin *Benedictus* – blessed, "a common christian name from the 12th century." (Reaney, Turk).

Guppy found Bennett widespread in England (with Bennetts in Cornwall). Bennet is the common form in Scotland (Black) and in the north of England (Cottle). In Ireland, Bennett has been prominent in Kilkenny and adjacent counties since the 14th century.

In Newfoundland: Bennett has sometimes replaced the French family name BENOIT as at Daniel's Harbour, Stephenville, Isle Valen and Port au Bras.

Family traditions: John, an Irishman of Harbour Main, 1755 (MUN Hist.). Mary Ann (1799–1842), of Fortune (MUN Hist.). Robert (1819–97), from England, of Molliers (Grand Bank) (MUN Hist.). John, from Cutmer's Bridge, St. Ives (Cornwall), settled at Bell Island about 1825 (MUN Folklore). Joshua (1850–) of Petites (MUN Geog.).

Early instances: William Bennet, of St. John's, 1675 (CO 1); Peter Bennett, of Bay de Verde, 1676 (CO 1); John, of Old Perlican, 1708 (CO 194.4); William, of Green Cove (Torbay), about 1758 (Exeter Archives per Kirwin); Stephen, of Harbour Grace, 1791 (USPG); Stephen, of Colliers, 1798 (CO 199.18); William, of Fortune, 1802 (Surrogate Court, Fortune Bay 1802–19, 1821, p. 9, PANL GN5/1/C/1, per P.E.L. Smith); William and John, of Carbonear, 1804 (CO 199.18); William, Jr. of Fortune, 1811 (Surrogate Court, Fortune Bay 1802–19, 1821, p. 125, per P.E.L. Smith); Phillip, of Brigus, 1818 (Nfld. Archives L165); Samuel, from Co. Wexford, married at Tilton Harbour (now Tilting), 1819 (Nfld. Archives KCRC); William, merchant of Adam's Cove, 1819 (DPHW 52A); William, from Davidstown Parish (Co. Wexford), married at St. John's, 1820 (Nfld. Archives BRC); John, of Great Bell Isle (now Bell Island), 1827 (DPHW 26B); Philip, servant of Cupids, 1827 (DPHW 34); C.H., landowner of New Harbour (Trinity B.), 1836 (Nfld. Archives L172); William, of Western Bay, 1841 (DPHW 58); John, of Fogo, 1842 (DPHW 83); John Bennit, of Northern Bay, 1845 (DPHW 54); Peter Remon Bennet, of Upper Burgeo, 1850 (DPHW 101); Samuel Bennett, fisherman of Port au Bras, 1860 (DPHW 100); Henry, fisherman of Northwest Cove (Burgeo-La Poile district), 1860 (DPHW 99); Michael, of Sandy Point (St. George's district), 1870 (DPHW 96).

Modern status: Widespread, with remarkable concentrations at St. John's, Stephenville Crossing and St. Paul's (St. Barbe district) (*Electors* 1955).

Place names: Bennets High Island 49-08 53-34, —— Low Island 49-07 53-34, Bennett Bank 47-17 54-20, Bennett or Benoit's Cove 49-01 58-08, Bennett Cove 47-38 58-36, —— Hill 47-05 55-47, —— Cove Sunker 47-37 58-36, Grassy Bennet Islands 49-12 53-30.

BENNING, a surname of England, ? from the Old English personal name *Beonna* as in the place names Beningbrough (Yorkshire NR), Long Bennington, Benniworth (Lincolnshire). (Bardsley, Ekwall).

Traced by Guppy in Berkshire.

In Newfoundland:

Early instances: Clement, of Burin, 1832 (*Newfoundlander* 26 Jan 1832); Clement, of St. John's, 1857 (*Newfoundlander* 12 Feb 1857); Henry, sub-collector of customs, Lamaline, 1871 (Lovell); Lewis, fisherman of Port au Port, 1871 (Lovell).

Modern status: Rare, at Grand Falls (*Electors* 1955) and Gander.

BENOIT(E), surnames of Newfoundland, including the Micmacs, from the baptismal names and surnames of France *Benoît(e)*, usually from Latin *benedictus* – blessed but occasionally a translation of the Hebrew *Baruch*. (Dauzat).

In Newfoundland: Benoit has sometimes been replaced by BENNETT. Some Benoits at Stephenville came from France in the early 20th century, some at Conne River from France via St. Pierre.

Family traditions: Michael (about 1810–80), born in Cape Breton, settled at Red Brook (Ruisseau Rouge) (Port au Port Peninsula) (MUN Folklore). Four brothers, Luc, George, Paul and Isaac, from Arichat, N.S., settled in the vicinity of St. George's Bay in 1850. (G.R. Thomas). Luc's descendants settled at Point à Luc, Red Brook and Stephenville (MUN Geog.). Charles and John, of Cow Head, 1873 (MUN Hist.). Family of Henry moved to Lourdes, between 1894 and 1904 (MUN Hist.). John, early settler at Stephenville Crossing, 1909 (MUN Hist.). Albert, from St. George's, early settler at Stephenville Crossing, 1909 (MUN Hist.).

Early instances: Laurence and Paul, farmers of Head of Bay d'Espoir, 1871 (Lovell); Constant (and others), fishermen of Indian Head (St. George's B.), 1871 (Lovell); John and Ben, Micmacs at Conne River, 1872 (MacGregor); Benjamin, farmer of Codroy, 1877 (Lovell).

Modern status: Benoit, widespread on the South and West coasts especially at Conne River and St. Alban's and throughout the Port au Port district; Benoite, at St. Joseph's (Fortune B.) (*Electors* 1955) and in the Burgeo-La Poile district.

Place names: Benoit River 48-42 58-40, Benoit's Cove 49-01 58-08.

BENSON, a surname of England and Ireland – son of *Benn* (Bennet) diminutive of Benedict, or from the English place names Benson, Bensington (Oxfordshire). (Reaney). *See* BENNETT.

Guppy traced Benson in Cumberland, Westmorland, Essex, Lancashire and Yorkshire, Spiegelhalter and Matthews in Devon, MacLysaght in Belfast and Dublin.

In Newfoundland:

Family traditions: Levi (1836–76), of Grates Cove and Hickman's Harbour, 1856 (MUN Geog.). Hezekiah, from Grates Cove, one of the earliest settlers of St. Jones Within (MUN Hist.).

Early instances: Thomas, of Carbonear, 1770 (CO 199.18); Joseph, of Harbour Grace Parish, 1809 (Nfld. Archives HGRC); Isaac, of St. John's, 1810 (DPHW 23); George, of Grates Cove, 1829 (DPHW 58); Charles, of Upper Burgeo, 1851 (DPHW 101); Reuben, of Old Perlican, 1859 (DPHW 85); Hezekiah, fisherman, and David, planter of Random Sound, 1871 (Lovell).

Modern status: Scattered, with greatest concentrations at St. John's.

BENTEAU, a Newfoundland variant of the French surname Beneteau itself a variant of Benoît (*see* BENOIT), sometimes confused with *benneteau* – (maker or seller of) small basket(s). (Dauzat).

In Newfoundland:

Family tradition: The Point May branch came from St. Malo, *via* St. Pierre (Raphael Benteau).

Modern status: In the Burin district at Lord's Cove, Allan's Island and Point May (*Electors* 1955).

BENTLEY, a surname of England and Ireland, from the English place name in several counties, or (dweller near the) clearing overgrown with bent-grass. (Cottle, Ekwall, MacLysaght 73).

Guppy traced the name in Dorset, Derbyshire, Kent, Lancashire, Nottinghamshire, Staffordshire and Yorkshire; Spiegelhalter and Matthews in Devon; MacLysaght in Cos. Clare and Limerick since the seventeenth century.

In Newfoundland:

Early instance: David and William, fishermen of St. John's, 1871 (Lovell).

Modern status: Rare, at St. John's.

BERESFORD, a surname of England and Ireland, from the manor and township of Beresford (Staffordshire). (Bardsley, MacLysaght).

Guppy traced Beresford, Berrisford in Staffordshire and Derbyshire. MacLysaght found the name first in Ulster, later in Waterford.

In Newfoundland:

Early instances: Mary, of Kings Cove Parish, 1841 (Nfld. Archives KCRC); Thomas Berrisford, of Gooseberry Island (Bonavista B.), 1859 (Nfld. Archives KCRC); Anastasia Beresford, of Cotterels Island (Bonavista B.), 1856 (Nfld. Archives KCRC); Johanna, of Open Hall, 1893 (Nfld. Archives KCRC).

Modern status: Scattered.

BERG, ? for Bergh, a surname of England, from Old English *beorg* – (dweller by the) hill. (Reaney).

In Newfoundland:

Modern status: Rare, at Manuels.

BERGERON, a surname of France, widespread in Normandy, French *bergeron* – little shepherd, shepherd-boy. (Dauzat).

In Newfoundland:
Modern status: One family in Corner Brook.

BERKSHIRE, a surname of England from the English county – (the man from) Berkshire.
In Newfoundland: The family came to Newfoundland in 1826 (MUN Folklore).
Early instance: William Birkshire, fisherman of Bay L'Argent, 1871 (Lovell).
Modern status: Especially at Corner Brook.

BERNARD, a baptismal name and surname of England, Ireland, France, Guernsey (Channel Islands), and of the Montagnais or Micmacs of Newfoundland, ultimately from an Old German personal name containing the elements *bear* and *brave*; in Ireland also as a synonym of Barnane, a family name of West Cork, Ir. *Ó Bearnáin*. (Withycombe, Reaney, MacLysaght, Dauzat, Turk). *See* NARDINI.
Spiegelhalter traced the name in Devon.
In Newfoundland:
Early instances: James, of St. John's, 1800 (DPHW 26D); Frank and M., fishermen of Cod Roy and Rivers, 1871 (Lovell); John, a Micmac hunter, 87 years of age in 1905, that is, born about 1818, had hunting grounds at Middle Ridge and Glenwood (Millais); Stephen, a Micmac hunter, had hunting grounds at Sandy Pond and Shoe Hills Ridge, 1906 (Millais); Joseph, variously described as a Micmac or Montagnais, chief at Conne River from Labrador, 1872 (MacGregor); Stephen, a son of the foregoing, married a Scot, Rose McDonald (*see* MACDONALD), at Conne River, 1872 (MUN Folklore).
Modern status: Somewhat rare and scattered.
Place names: Bernard Brook 48-00 55-36, Bernards Brook 48-36 55-09.

BERNIQUEZ, a surname of French Canada, not in Dauzat.
In Newfoundland:
Modern status: At St. John's since about 1952.

BERRIGAN, a variant of the surname of Ireland (O)Bergin, *Ó hAimheirgin*, lately contracted to *Ó Beirgin*, from the Irish *aimhirgin* – wondrous birth, now associated with Co. Leix. (MacLysaght).
In Newfoundland:
Early instances: John Bergen, from Rohaspack [sic] Parish (Queen's Co., now Co. Leix), married at St. John's, 1814 (Nfld. Archives BRC); John Bergan, from Donomore (Co. Kilkenny), married at St. John's, 1820 (Nfld. Archives BRC); John Berigan, of Harbour Grace Parish, 1821 (Nfld. Archives HGRC);

Duggan and Berrigan, of St. John's, 1831 (*Newfoundlander* 12 May 1831); Mary Baragan, from Belisle (now Bell Island), married at St. John's, 1832 (Nfld. Archives BRC); Martin Beragan or Berrigan, of Kings Cove Parish, 1841 (Nfld. Archives KCRC); Abby Bergan, of Keels, 1864 (Nfld. Archives KCRC); James Berrican (1819–1891), from Waterford, Ireland, cooper of Carbonear, 1871 (Lovell, R.C. Cemetery Carbonear).
Modern status: At Ferryland (*Electors* 1955), now at St. John's.

BERRY (or Bury), a surname of England, Ireland, Scotland, France, and Jersey (Channel Islands), from OE *burh*, dative *byrig* – fort, surviving in English place names Berry Pomeroy (Devon), Bury St. Edmunds (Suffolk) and Bury (Huntingdonshire, Lancashire); or from Middle English *beri* etc. – (servant at the) manor-house; or from Old English *būr* or *burh* – (dweller by an) enclosure near the bower, or near the fort. In Ireland sometimes also a synonym of (O)Beary, *Ó Béara* in Co. Offaly; in Scotland also a variant of Barrie; in France, from the place name Berry (district and former duchy). (Reaney, MacLysaght, Dauzat).
Guppy found Berry widespread, Spiegelhalter and Matthews traced it in Devon, and MacLysaght describes it as "fairly numerous in Ireland, but widely scattered."
In Newfoundland:
Early instances: William and George, Protestant inhabitants of Torbay, 1822 (D'Alberti 32); John, of St. John's, 1829 (Nfld. Archives BRC); John, of Northern Bay, 1852 (DPHW 54).
Modern status: Rare and virtually restricted to Sandy Point (St. George's district) (*Electors* 1955).

BERT, a surname of England from the Old French baptismal female name *Berthe*, or Old German *Berhta, Berta* – bright; or for BURT (Reaney).
In Newfoundland:
Family tradition: ——, from South Wales settled at Bunyan's Cove (Bonavista B.) (MUN Folklore).
Modern status: At Windsor and Norris Arm (*Electors* 1955).

BERTEAU, a surname of France and of ? Jersey (Channel Islands), from an Old German personal name containing the elements *berht* – bright, renowned and *waldan* – to rule. (Dauzat).
In Newfoundland:
Early instances: Francis, from Channel Islands, settled at Burin, ? about 1850 (MUN Folklore); his

son Francis C. (1856–), born at Burin, was educated at Victoria College, Jersey, and became Comptroller and Auditor-General of Newfoundland, 1898 (*Nfld. Quarterly* June 1903); Joseph Barteau, from Nova Scotia, of Bryants Cove (Conception B.), 1914 (Nfld. Archives HGRC).

Modern status: Rare, at Bryants Cove and St. John's (*Electors* 1955).

BESAU, BESAW, BESSEY, BESSO, Newfoundland variants of the French surnames, *Bès*, *Bessey*, *Besseau* etc. – (dweller by the) plantation of birch-trees, or confused with BEASON, BESON. (Dauzat); or French dialect *besson* – twin (Thomas, "French Fam. Names"). Bessey may also be a surname of England.

In Newfoundland:

Early instances: Nimrod Bessey, fisherman of Quirpon, 1871 (Lovell); Alexander, of Island Bay (White Bay), 1872 (DPHW 94).

Modern status: Scattered, with Besau on Bell Island, Besaw on the Port au Port Peninsula, Bessey at Raleigh and nearby communities in the extreme north of Newfoundland, and Besso at Holyrood.

BESON. *See* BEASON

BESSEY, BESSO. *See* BESAU

BEST, a surname of England and Ireland, from the Old French *beste* – beast, "used of a brutal, savage man, in earlier examples often connoting stupidity or folly," or for a keeper of beasts, a herdsman. (Reaney).

Guppy traced the name in Dorset and Cornwall, Spiegelhalter and Matthews also in Devon; but MacLysaght states that "The Irish Bests came from Kent, England, and settling in Leinster in the 17th century became prominent in Carlow and adjacent counties. The name is now mainly found in Cos. Antrim, Armagh and Tyrone due to more recent immigrations from England."

In Newfoundland:

Early instances: John, juror ? of St. John's, 1750 (CO 194.12); Marks, from Dorchester, married at St. John's, 1812 (Nfld. Archives BRC); George, of Brigus, 1812 (DPHW 34); Mrs., buried at Carbonear, 1821 (D'Alberti 22); William, of Bonavista, 1824 (DPHW 70); Henry, of Torbay, 1833 (DPHW 26D); George, cooper of Henley Harbour (Labrador), 1843 (DPHW 43); Thomas, fisherman of Fogo, 1845 (DPHW 83); John, of Greenspond, 1854 (DPHW 76); George Jr. and Sr. and John, fishermen and planters of Merasheen, 1871 (Lovell); James, fisherman of Isle Valen, 1871 (Lovell).

Modern status: Widespread, especially at St. John's, Southern Harbour, Tack's Beach, Merasheen and other settlements in Placentia Bay and Wesleyville.

Place name: Best's Harbour 47-35 54-13.

BEVERL(E)Y, surnames of England, from the English place name Beverley (Yorkshire ER). (Cottle).

In Newfoundland:

Early instances: Charles William Beverly, of St. John's, 1817 (DPHW 26D); Thomas Beverley, of Bay of Islands, 1819 (DPHW 30); Thomas, of Harbour Island (Bay of Islands), 1849 (Feild).

Modern status: Beverley, rare, at Curling (*Electors* 1955), Beverly, unique, at Curling.

BHNISCH, a family name of Holland, ? from Czech.

In Newfoundland: Very rare in St. John's, from Amsterdam, 1924.

BICKFORD, Beckford, surnames of England from the English place names Bickford, Beckaford and Beckford (Devon) or Beckford (Gloucestershire), or Bickford (Somerset). Bardsley cites both forms. *See also* PICKFORD.

Bickford was traced by Guppy in Staffordshire, and by Spiegelhalter and Matthews in Devon.

In Newfoundland:

Early instances: Robert Beckford, boatkeeper of St. John's, 1681 (CO 1); William, of Salvage, 1681 (CO 1); Marke Bickford, boatkeeper of Petty Harbour, 1682 (CO 1); John Beckford, boatkeeper of St. John's, 1682 (CO 1); Henry, of Lance Cove (Bell Island), 1827 (DPHW 70).

Modern status: Bickford, on Bell Island, especially at Bickfordville (*Electors* 1955); Beckford now obsolete.

Place names: Bickfordville (Bell Island); Beckford Cove 47-23 54-31; —— Head 46-54 53-54; —— Shoal 46-53 53-53.

BICKHAM, a surname of England, from the English place name Bickham which occurs six times in Devon. (Bardsley, Spiegelhalter).

Spiegelhalter traced Bickham in Devon.

In Newfoundland:

Early instances: Thomas, of St. John's, 1828 (DPHW 26D); Walter, from Ashburton (Devon), of St. John's, deceased, 1833 (*Royal Gazette* 22 Jan 1833).

Modern status: At Harbour Grace.

BIDDISCOMBE, a surname of England, ? from the English place name Bittiscombe (Somerset) which, according to Reaney and Bardsley, is also the source of the family name Biddlecombe. Matthews traced Biddecombe in Devon.

In Newfoundland:

Early instances: John Bedlecome, Bidleson or Biddlecom (spelt Middlecom, 1681, Mildcum, 1682), of Old Perlican, 1675–76, 77 (CO 1); William Bedlecome or Biddlecombe, of Bonavista, 1800 (DPHW 70); George Biddiscombe, of St. John's, 1827 (DPHW 26B); William Bilicum, of Kings Cove Parish, 1852 (Nfld. Archives KCRC); Thomas Billicomb or Biddlecombe, of Plate Cove (Bonavista B.), 1858, 1868 (Nfld. Archives KCRC).

Modern status: Very rare, at Logy Bay, Portugal Cove and St. John's.

BIDGOOD, a surname of England of obscure origin containing Old English elements meaning *pray* and *God*. (Weekley).

Traced in Devon by Spiegelhalter and Matthews.

In Newfoundland:

Early instances: Benjamin, juror of St. John's, 1751 (CO 194.13); Philip, in possession of property, in fishery, at Petty Harbour, 1765, 1794–5, born in Newfoundland (Census 1794–5, DPHW 26C); Joseph Bedgood, of Fortune, 1853 (DPHW 106).

Modern status: At Petty Harbour and St. John's.

BIGGIN(S), surnames of England and Ireland, from the Middle English *bigging* – dwelling-place, home, "used also of an outbuilding as distinct from a house," or also from the English place names in six counties. In Ireland as (O)Biggane or Biggins, *Ó Beageáin* and *Ó Bigín*, Ir. *beag* – little. (Reaney, Cottle, MacLysaght).

Guppy traced the name in Derbyshire, Mac-Lysaght in Munster (where it has been largely superseded by Little(ton), and as Beggan(e) in Ulster.

In Newfoundland:

Early instance: James Biggins, of Daniel's Harbour, 1873 (MUN Hist.)

Modern status: Biggin at Daniel's Harbour and Spirity Cove, Biggins at Port Saunders.

BIGGS, a surname of England, from Middle English *bigge* – large, strong, stout, or ? from an unidentified place name (Reaney) or also from Old Norse stems meaning *build* and *inhabitant*. (Cottle).

Guppy traced Biggs in Buckinghamshire, Leicestershire, Rutlandshire, and Monmouthshire, Spiegelhalter in Devon and Matthews in Dorset.

In Newfoundland:

Early instances: Jeremiah, plaintiff before Supreme Court, 1810 (CO 194.50); Joseph, fisherman of Adam's Cove, 1829 (DPHW 52A); Frances, of Pouch Cove, 1850 (DPHW 32); James, fisherman of Bareneed, 1871 (Lovell); John, cooper of Carbonear, 1871 (Lovell).

Modern status: Rare, in St. John's and Riverhead (St. Mary's).

BIGNELL, a surname of England, from the English place names Bickerhall (Somerset) or Bickerhill (Warwickshire). (Bardsley, Ekwall).

Bicknell was traced by Guppy in Somerset; Bignell by Matthews in Devon and Jersey (Channel Islands).

In Newfoundland:

Early instance: Charles Bignall, fisherman of Change Islands, 1847 (DPHW 83).

Modern status: Rare, at Leading Tickles (*Electors* 1955), Fogo, Badger and St. John's.

BIGSBY, BIXBY, surnames of England from ? an unidentified place name or ? Bigby (Lincolnshire). Matthews traced Bixby in Somerset.

In Newfoundland:

Early instance: James Bigsby, of Indian Islands (Fogo), 1858 (DPHW 83).

Modern status: Bixby at Stag Harbour, Salt Pond (Gander district), St. John's; Bigsby at Change Islands (*Electors 1955*).

BILES, a surname of England, from Old English *bile* – bill, beak of a bird, "used both as a nickname ... and as a topographical term 'dweller at the beaklike projection, promontory, hill'" (Reaney).

In Newfoundland:

Modern status: At St. Anthony.

BILLARD, BILLIARD, surnames of England and France, in England ? from an Old English personal name *Bilheard* containing the elements *spear* and *strong* (Weekley); in France from an Old German personal name containing the elements *bili* – soft, lovable and *hard* – hard, strong, or from the apheresis of the baptismal name and surname Robillard, a contraction of Robert. Dauzat denies an association with the game. (Weekley *Surnames*, Dauzat).

In Newfoundland:

Family tradition: Doreen (1840–1902), of Bay Bulls Arm (now Sunnyside), married 1856 (MUN Geog.).

Early instances: Robert, ? of St. John's, 1768

(DPHW 26C); Gabriel, fisherman of Red Island (Burgeo), 1840 (DPHW 101); Gabriel, John, Martin and Samuel, fishermen of Grand Bruit, 1871 (Lovell); Jean Belliard, of Port au Choix, 1873 (MUN Hist.).

Modern status: Billard, especially at Grand Bruit, Margaree and other settlements in the Burgeo-La Poile district, and at St. John's (*Electors* 1955); Billiard (*Electors* 1955) or Billard (*Telephone Directory* 1971) at Port au Choix.

BILLINGS, a surname of England, from the Old English personal name *Billing*, or from the English place name, Billing (Northamptonshire). (Reaney).

Billing(s) was traced by Guppy in Buckinghamshire and Cornwall; Billing by Spiegelhalter in Devon.

In Newfoundland:

Early instances: Edward, fisherman of Fortune Harbour (Exploits B.), 1871 (Lovell); David, fisherman of Isle Valen, 1871 (Lovell); John, cooper of St. John's, 1871 (Lovell).

Modern status: Rare, at Placentia, St. Kyran's, Cottrell's Cove and Brighton (*Electors* 1955).

BINDON, a surname of England and Ireland, from the English place name, Bindon (Dorset), or (dweller at the place) inside the hill. (Cottle, Ekwall).

MacLysaght comments that "Though the Bindons first settled in Co. Tipperary in 1580 the family has since the following century been prominently associated with Co. Clare."

In Newfoundland:

Early instance: William, of St. John's, 1842 (DPHW 29).

Modern status: Rare, at St. John's.

BINGLE, ? a surname of England from the English place name Bingwell (Devon).

In Newfoundland:

Modern status: Rare, at Deer Lake.

BIRD, BYRD, surnames of England and Ireland, from the Old English *bridd* – bird, a nickname or an occupational name for a bird-catcher, or sometimes for woman, damsel, sempstress; in Ireland as a synonym by pseudo-translation of Heany, Hegney, Henaghan and MacEneany, from the Irish *éan* – bird. (Reaney, Cottle, MacLysaght).

Guppy found Bird widespread in the Midlands and south of England; Byrd in Worcestershire; Spiegelhalter found Bird in Devon.

In Newfoundland:

Early instances: Michael Bird, of St. John's, 1814 (D'Alberti 24); Joseph, salmon fisherman of Bonne Bay from 1808 (D'Alberti 31); —— , merchant of Forteaux, 1822 (CO 194.65); George, of Harbour Grace Parish, 1822 (Nfld. Archives HGRC); Jonathan, of Rock Cove (Bay de l'Eau), 1835 (DPHW 30); Charles, fisherman of Trinity (Trinity B.), 1846 (DPHW 64B); Jonathan, of Wreck Cove (Fortune B.), 1850 (DPHW 104); Thomas H., watchmaker of Grand Bank, 1863 (MUN Hist.), of Burnt Island (Burgeo district), 1871 (Lovell); John, Joseph and William, fishermen of Little Placentia (now Argentia), 1871 (Lovell); John, planter of Rose Blanche, 1871 (Lovell); William, fisherman of English Harbour (Fortune B.), 1879 (DPHW 103).

Modern status: Bird at Diamond Cove and Rose Blanche (*Electors* 1955); Byrd, scattered.

BIRMINGHAM, a surname of England and as Bermingham of Ireland, in England from the English place name, Birmingham (Warwickshire), in Ireland "one of the great Anglo-Norman families," *de Bermingham* (MacLysaght).

Spiegelhalter traced the name in Devon; MacLysaght in Cos. Galway and Kildare.

In Newfoundland:

Early instances: Roger, of Toads (now Tors) Cove, 1802 (Nfld. Archives BRC); Richard, of Harbour Grace Parish, 1811 (Nfld. Archives HGRC); Ellen, of Wicklis (for Witless) Bay, married at St. John's, 1830 (Nfld. Archives BRC).

Modern status: Rare, at St. John's and Petty Harbour.

BISHOP, a surname of England, Scotland, Ireland and the Channel Islands, from the Old English personal name *Bisc(e)op*, or "a nickname for one with the appearance or bearing of a bishop, or a pageant name from the custom of electing a boy-bishop on St. Nicholas's Day" (Reaney), or one who worked in the household of a bishop; in Ireland, as a synonym by translation of MacAnespie and GILLESPIE. (MacLysaght, Black, Reaney, Cottle, Turk).

Guppy and Matthews found the name widespread, especially in the southwest of England.

In Newfoundland:

Family traditions: Ned, ? from Fogo, planter of Swain's Island, 1836 (MUN Hist.). Chris., from Colliers, of Coley's Point, about 1863 (MUN Hist.).

Early instances: Thomas, of Salvage, 1681 (CO 1); Robert, in possession of property at Bay Roberts, "possess'd by the Family for upwards of 80 years," that is, before 1689 (CO 199.18); Henery, of Brigus, 1708–09 (CO 194.4); Joseph, fisherman of St. John's or Petty Harbour, about 1739–43 (CO 194.11, 24); John, of St. John's, 1770 (DPHW 26C); Henry, of (Upper) Island Cove, 1785 (CO 199-18); John, of Back Cove (Port de Grave), 1786 (CO 199.18); Henry, constable at Trepassey, 1800 (D'Alberti 11); William, proprietor and occupier of fishing room at New Harbour (Trinity B.), Winter 1800–01 (Census Trinity B.); George, of Fogo, 1803 (D'Alberti 13); Richard, of Burin, 1804 (D'Alberti 14); Robert, from Bradport (? for Bridport) (Dorset), married at St. John's, 1807 (Nfld. Archives BRC); James, of Bonavista, 1810 (DPHW 70); John, of Greenspond, 1815 (DPHW 70); John, given possession of Hobb or Hibb's Hole Island Rock for purpose of fishery, 1818 (D'Alberti 28); Richard, planter of Cupids, 1824 (DPHW 34); John, of Change Islands, 1832 (DPHW 30); Edward, of Pinchard's Island, 1835 (DPHW 76); John, planter of Bradley's Cove, 1837 (DPHW 52A); John, fisherman of Burnt Head (Conception B.), 1842 (DPHW 26); Hannah, of Torbay, 1846 (DPHW 26D); John, of Long Pond (Conception B.), 1847 (DPHW 26D); Jacob, of Petty Harbour, 1852 (DPHW 31); John, planter of Mose Ambrose, 1854 (DPHW 104); Edward, of English Harbour (Fortune B.), 1855 (DPHW 104); William, of Muddy Hole, 1858 (DPHW 83).

Modern status: Widespread, especially at St. John's; at Burnt Head, Pick Eyes, Upper Island Cove and other settlements in Conception Bay; at Heart's Delight and Cavendish (Trinity Bay); and Point La Haye (St. Mary's Bay).

Place names: Bishop Rock 49-31 55-04, Bishop's Cove 47-38 53-13, —— Gully 47-43 53-18, —— Harbour 48-41 53-38, —— Island 49-09 53-32, —— Islands 49-49 54-07, —— Islet 49-50 54-05, —— Pond 47-32 53-27, —— Ponds 47-24 53-24, —— Rock 49-56 55-27. Bishops Falls 49-01 55-30, however, was named to commemorate the visit of Bishop Inglis of Nova Scotia to the Exploits River in 1827.

BIXBY. *See* BIGSBY

BLACK, a surname of England, Scotland and Ireland, from the Old English *blæc*, Middle English *blāke* – black, dark-complexioned, but often confused with Middle English *blāk(e)*, from Old English *blāc* – bright, shining; pale, wan, thus giving two contradictory meanings. *See* BLAKE. (Reaney, Cottle). In Ireland, it is also used as a translation or synonym of DUFF and Kilduff. (Reaney, MacLysaght, Black).

The name was traced by Guppy in Northumberland, Leicestershire and Rutlandshire, by Spiegelhalter in Devon, and by MacLysaght especially in Ulster. It is fairly general in Scotland.

In Newfoundland:

Early instances: Henry and Patrick, in possession of fishing room at Gooseberry Island, before 1806 (Bonavista Register 1806); John, of St. John's, 1822 (CO 194.65); David, of Bonavista, 1822 (Nfld. Archives KCRC); Martha, of Harbour Grace Parish, 1822 (Nfld. Archives HGRC); William, of Pinchard's Island, 1833 (DPHW 76); Henry, of Burn Island (Bonavista B.), 1862 (Nfld. Archives KCRC); William and Ambrose, fishermen of Bay of Islands, 1871 (Lovell).

Modern status: Very rare, at Gander (*Electors* 1955) and St. John's.

Place name: Black's Island 49-12 53-30; The Black Family (rocks)(Labrador) 55-10 59-04.

BLACKIE, a surname of Scotland, diminutive of BLACK; probably also confused with Blaikie, BLAKEY. (Black).

In Newfoundland:

Early instance: Joseph Blackey, fisherman of Barr'd Islands, 1871 (Lovell).

Modern status: Rare, at Gander.

BLACKLER, a surname of England, from the English place name Blackler (Devon). (Reaney).

Spiegelhalter and Matthews traced the name in Devon.

In Newfoundland:

Family tradition: Joseph, from Twillingate, early settler at Springdale, 1880 (MUN Hist.).

Early instances: Richard, fisherman of St. John's, 1794–5, "30 years in Newfoundland," that is, 1764–5 (Census 1794–5); Edward Blackellor, of Toad's (now Tors) Cove, 1771 (DPHW 26C); Thomas Blackler, from Denbury (Devon), boatkeeper of St. John's, deceased, 1813 (*Royal Gazette* 16 Dec 1813); J., of Bay Bulls, 1844 (*Nfld. Almanac*); Thomas, of Bay Roberts, 1859 (DPHW 32); John, Matthew and Samuel, fishermen of Mobile, 1871 (Lovell); Amos and James, fishermen of Twillingate, 1871 (Lovell).

Modern status: Somewhat rare and scattered, but at Mobile and Springdale.

BLACKMORE, a surname of England, from the English place names Blackmoor (Dorset, Hampshire, Devon) or Blackmore (Hertfordshire, Essex) or Blakemoor (Devon). (Cottle, Ekwall).

Guppy traced the name in Devon and Somerset, Matthews also in Dorset.

In Newfoundland:

Family tradition: Patrick Blackmore, from Hull, England, to Pinchard's Island, in the 18th century (MUN Folklore).

Early instances: Henry Blackmoor, boat-owner of Bonavista, 1781 (D'Alberti 2); Jean Blackmore, of Greenspond, 1817 (Nfld. Archives KCRC); Patience, of Pinchard's Island, 1830 (DPHW 76); Martin, clergyman of Burgeo, 1843, of Bay Roberts, 1858 (DPHW 26D); Bridget, of Black Island (Bonavista B.), 1850 (Nfld. Archives KCRC); Catherine, of Gooseberry Island (Bonavista B.), 1850 (Nfld. Archives KCRC); Philip, of Channel, 1871 (Lovell); Patrick, fisherman of Inner Island (Bonavista B.), 1871 (Lovell); Reuben, fisherman of Twillingate, 1871 (Lovell); William, fisherman of Wolf Bay (La Poile), 1871 (Lovell).

Modern status: Widespread, especially at Newtown and other settlements in Bonavista North and St. John's.

BLACKWOOD, a surname of England, Scotland and Ireland, – (dweller by the) dark wood, or from the English and Scots place name, Blackwood (Yorkshire ER and WR, Dumfriesshire, Lanarkshire). (Reaney, Black, MacLysaght 73).

Traced by MacLysaght in Ulster.

In Newfoundland:

Family tradition: The Blackwoods came to Newfoundland from Edinburgh in the early 19th century and settled on Swain's Island, whence they moved to the mainland and settled in various communities around Bonavista Bay (MUN Folklore).

Early instances: Ebenezer, of Bonavista, 1826 (DPHW 70); Andrew (about 1821–78), hairdresser from Greenock, started business at St. John's in 1840 (*Times* 13 May 1840, General Protestant Cemetery, St. John's).

Modern status: Widespread, especially in St. John's, and Brookfield and other settlements in the Bonavista North district.

BLAGDON, a surname of England – (dweller in the) dark valley, as in the English place names Blackden (Cheshire) and Blagdon (Northumberland), or (dweller by the) black hill as at Blagdon (Devon, Somerset) and Blagden Farm (Essex). (Reaney).

Matthews traced Blagdon and Spiegelhalter Blackden in Devon.

In Newfoundland:

Family traditions: Emma (1842–1935), of Boxey

(MUN Geog.), —— ? from Bristol, of Little Bay West (Fortune B.), ? about 1870 (MUN Folklore).

Early instances: John, married at St. John's, 1760 (DPHW 26D); John, of Red Cove (Fortune B.), 1854 (DPHW 104); James, planter of Coomb's Cove (Fortune B.), 1871 (Lovell).

Modern status: Essentially a South Coast name, and especially at Boxey and Coomb's Cove.

BLAIR, a surname of England, Scotland and Ireland, from a number of places in Scotland so called. (Black).

Guppy traced the name in Northumberland, Durham, Ayrshire and Perthshire, MacLysaght especially in northern Ulster.

In Newfoundland:

Early instances: Matthew, member of grand jury at St. John's, 1780 (D'Alberti 6); Henry (about 1847–1926), from Aberfoyle, Scotland, of St. John's (General Protestant Cemetery, St. John's).

Modern status: Rare, at St. John's.

BLAKE, a surname of England, Ireland and Scotland; in England and Scotland of the same dual origin as BLACK; in Ireland for *de Bláca* or more correctly *le Bláca* – black, or for Blowick, *Ó Blathmhaic*, Ir. *blath* – fame, *mac* – son in Cos. Mayo and Fermanagh. (Reaney, Black, MacLysaght).

The name was traced by Guppy in the south of England, especially in Wiltshire, Cornwall, Berkshire and Oxfordshire, by Matthews and Spiegelhalter in Devon, and by MacLysaght in Cos. Galway, Kildare, Mayo and Fermanagh.

In Newfoundland:

Family tradition: Ellen, of Bay de Verde, died 1866 (MUN Geog.).

Early instances: T., of Placentia, 1724 (CO 194.8); John Garrett, J.P., of Trinity (Trinity B.), 1753 (CO 194.13); John, married at St. John's, 1769 (DPHW 26D); John, of Great Belle Isle (now Bell Island), 1770 (DPHW 26C); Philip, from Wexford Town, married at St. John's, 1804 (Nfld. Archives BRC); Mary, from Ferryland, married at St. John's, 1819 (Nfld. Archives BRC); Ralph, of Bay of Islands, 1819 (D'Alberti 29); Thomas, planter of Herring Neck, 1820 (USPG); James, fisherman of Twillingate, 1821 (USPG); John Bleak or Blake, planter of Hants Harbour, 1821 (DPHW 58); James Blake, of Ship Island (Bonavista), 1843 (DPHW 76); Charles, fisherman of Gander Bay, 1850 (DPHW 83); Henry, fisherman of Bonne Bay, 1851 (DPHW 102); Robert, of Green Cove (Twillingate), 1853 (DPHW 85);

Henry, fisherman of Greep Head, 1853 (DPHW 85); Francis and Solomon, fishermen of Barr'd Islands (Fogo), 1871 (Lovell); Henry, fisherman of Bay d'Este (East B., Fortune B.), 1871 (Lovell); John, of Change Islands, 1871 (Lovell); Thomas, of Blake-town, 1888 (DPHW 61).

Modern status: Widespread, especially in the Fogo and Twillingate districts.

Place names: Blake Rock 49-41 54-44, Blaketown 47-29 53-34.

BLAKELY, a surname of England and Ireland, Blackley in Scotland, – (dweller by the) black, dark wood or clearing, or from the English place name Blackley (Lancashire) pronounced Blakeley. (Reaney).

MacLysaght traced the name in Cos. Cavan, Monaghan and Antrim, Black in Dumfriesshire.

In Newfoundland:

Modern status: Rare, at St. John's.

BLAKEY (Blaikie), a surname of Scotland, a diminutive of BLAKE, probably also confused with BLACKIE. *See also* BLACK. (Reaney).

Guppy traced Blakey in Yorkshire WR.

In Newfoundland:

Early instance: James Blaikie or Blackie (1776–1838), from Roxburghshire, magistrate for St. John's district, 1810, deceased 1838 (D'Alberti 20, *Star and Conception Bay Journal* 6 Jun 1838, *Times* 6 Jun 1838).

Modern status: Rare, at St. John's.

BLANCHARD, a surname of England and France, from the Old German personal name *Blanchard*, Old French *Blanchart* etc. – whitish, ? white-haired, or from *blanc* – brilliant, bright and *hard* – hard, strong. (Reaney, Dauzat).

Traced by Guppy in Lincolnshire and Yorkshire ER and NR and by Spiegelhalter in Devon.

In Newfoundland:

Family tradition: ——, second settler at Bear Cove (White B.), from France, early 19th century (MUN Folklore). Charles and wife Henrietta, of Margaree, N.S., settled in St. George's in 1845. (G.R. Thomas).

Early instances: Richard, of Bay de Verde, 1776 (CO 199.18); William, of Bay of Islands, 1835 (DPHW 30); ——, of Gillams Cove (Bay of Islands), 1849, aged 90, "having lived there for nearly 70 years," that is, since about 1779 (Feild); Thomas, of Back Cove (White B.), 1864 (DPHW 94); Timothy, fisher-man of Flat Bay (St. George's B.), 1871 (Lovell); Michael, farmer of Codroy, 1877 (Lovell).

Modern status: Especially at Shallop Cove, Gillams and McIvers and other settlements on the West Coast.

Place names: Blanchard Cove 47-24 55-37, Blanchard Shoal 47-22 55-48.

BLANCH(E), baptismal names and surnames of England and France, from the French feminine baptismal name Blanch(e). (Withycombe, Bardsley, Dauzat).

In Newfoundland:

Early instance: Thomas and Michael Blanch, inhabitants of Placentia, 1794, 1800 (D'Alberti 5, 11).

Modern status: Blanch(e), rare, at Jerseyside.

BLANDFORD, a surname of England, from the English place name, Blandford (Dorset), or (dweller by the) ford of the gudgeons. (Cottle, Ekwall).

Traced by Guppy in Gloucestershire and by Matthews in Dorset and Devon.

In Newfoundland:

Family traditions: John Bennet (1830), from Poole (Dorset), came to Twillingate about 1852 (MUN Folklore). Davis, from Greenspond, settled at Clode Sound (later renamed Port Blandford after him) in 1888 (MUN Hist.).

Early instances: Thomas, servant at Battle Harbour (Labrador), 1795 (MUN Hist.); Davies, of Greenspond, 1837 (DPHW 76); James, fisherman of Fogo, 1847 (DPHW 83); Esau, of Herring Neck, 1849 (DPHW 26D); Joseph, planter of Stone Harbour, 1851 (DPHW 85); James, fisherman of Hare Bay (Fogo), 1851 (DPHW 83); Thomas, planter of Salt Harbour, 1852 (DPHW 85); Joseph, fisherman of Bay of Islands, 1871 (Lovell); Charles, labourer of St. John's, 1871 (Lovell).

Modern status: Scattered, especially at Ship Island (Twillingate district) and St. John's.

Place names: Port Blandford 48-21 54-09, Blandford's Cove 51-53 55-25.

BLOOMFIELD, a surname of England, from the French place name Blonville-sur-Mer (Calvados), now apparently changed to BROOMFIELD. (Reaney).

Traced by Guppy in Norfolk, Suffolk and Essex, and by Spiegelhalter in Devon.

In Newfoundland:

Early instance: James Hayes, of Poole (Dorset), married at St. John's, 1832 (DPHW 26D).

Modern status: Rare, at St. John's, Shalloway Cove (Bonavista North district) and Roddickton (*Electors* 1955).

Place name: Bloomfield 48-23 53-54.

BLUNDELL, a surname of England, Blondel in the Channel Islands and France, from the Old French *blondel*, diminutive of *blond* – fair; also a personal name. (Reaney, Turk).

Traced by Guppy in Lancashire and Bedfordshire, and by Spiegelhalter in Devon.

In Newfoundland: Blundell has sometimes been changed to BLUNDON.

Family tradition: John Blundell, from Channel Islands settled at Bay de Verde in the 19th century (MUN Folklore).

Early instances: John Blundle, of Catalina, 1822 (DPHW 70); Thomas, of Harbour Grace Parish, 1827 (Nfld. Archives HGRC); Mary, of Bay de Verde, 1829 (Nfld. Archives BRC); Mary Jane Blondell, of Hickman's Harbour, 1879 (DPHW 60).

Modern Status: Rare, at Hickman's Harbour.

BLUNDON, a variant of Blunden, a surname of England and Ireland, of unascertained origin, ? the English place name Blunsdon (Wiltshire). (Reaney, MacLysaght 73).

Spiegelhalter traced Blunden in Devon, MacLysaght in Co. Kilkenny since the mid-seventeenth century.

In Newfoundland: BLUNDELL has sometimes been changed to Blundon. The Blundons of Bay de Verde are believed to be of a number of unrelated families.

Family traditions: Stephen, from Bay de Verde was the first permanent settler of Hickman's Harbour in 1799. His descendants are said to have changed their name to Blundell, despite the contrary tradition that Blundell was changed to Blundon (MUN Hist.). Kitty, from Bay de Verde, was an early settler at Daniels Cove (Trinity B.), in 1836 (MUN Hist.).

Early instances: Thomas, of Bay de Verde, 1778 (CO 199.18); —— Blunden, of St. John's, 1784 (DPHW 23); John, occupier of fishing room at Grates Cove, Winter 1800–01 (Census Trinity B.); Elizabeth Blundon or Blunden, of Harbour Grace Parish, 1810 (Nfld. Archives HGRC); Catherine Blunden from Waterford City, of St. John's, 1813 (Nfld. Arhives BRC); John Blundon or Blunden, planter of Catalina, 1820 (DPHW 72); Ann Blunden, of Ragged Harbour (unspecified), 1826 (Nfld. Archives KCRC); William Blundon, planter of Lower Island Cove, about 1851 (DPHW 55); Priscilla, of Rix Harbour, 1860 (DPHW 59); Alfred, of Random South, 1860 (DPHW 59); Elizabeth, of Hants Harbour, 1860 (DPHW 59); John, fisherman of Indian Islands (Fogo), 1871 (Lovell).

Modern status: Widespread in the Conception Bay-Trinity Bay areas, especially at Bay de Verde and Shoal Harbour.

Place names: Blundon's Island 49-33 54-14, —— Point 48-22 53-53, —— Siding 48-21 53-54.

BLYDE, (variant of Bly, Blythe, Bligh etc.) surnames of England and Ireland, from the English place names Blyth (Northumberland, Nottinghamshire) or Blythe (Warwickshire), or from a nickname from Old English *blithe* – gentle, merry, or from an unrecorded personal name derived from it. (Reaney, Cottle, MacLysaght).

Guppy traced Blyth in Essex, Norfolk, Yorkshire ER and NR, Spiegelhalter in Devon. MacLysaght traced Bligh, Bly(the) in Connacht and elsewhere.

In Newfoundland:

Early instances: Robert Blyth, married at St. John's, 1770 (DPHW 26D); J. Bligth, ? of St. John's, 1810 (CO 194.50).

Modern status: Rare, at St. John's.

BOBBETT, BOBBITT, surnames of England, diminutives of the English nickname Bob, from the baptismal name Robert (*see* ROBERTS). (Bardsley).

Bardsley traced Bobbett in Somerset.

In Newfoundland:

Family tradition: The Bobbetts of Milltown came from Dorset to Great Jervis whence they moved to Milltown in 1900 (MUN Hist.).

Early instances: Matthew Bobbitt, fisherman of Pass Island (Burin district), 1844 (DPHW 102); John, fisherman of Round Harbour, 1850 (DPHW 104); William Bobbit, of Burgeo, 1852 (DPHW 101); John Bobbitt, fisherman of Bay Despair, 1852 (DPHW 104); Thomas, fisherman of Rose Blanche, 1860 (DPHW 99).

Modern status: Bobbett, at Gaultois and Channel; Bobbitt, in the Fortune Bay and Hermitage district (*Electors* 1955).

Place names: Bobbett Cove 47-55 55-45, Bobbit Point 47-37 55-57.

BOGGAN, a surname of Ireland, (O)Bog(g)an, *Ó Bogáin*, Ir. *bog* – soft. (MacLysaght). Mainly associated with Cos. Donegal and Wexford (MacLysaght).

In Newfoundland:

Early instances: Ann Boggin, from Breen Parish (Co. Wexford), married at St. John's, 1816 (Nfld. Archives BRC); Michael Boggan, from Davidstown (Co. Wexford), married at St. John's, 1829 (Nfld. Archives BRC); J., of St. John's, 1831 (*Newfoundlander* 29 Dec 1831); Thomas Bogan, of Little Placentia (now Argentia), 1871 (Lovell); John and

William Boggin, farmers of Topsail, 1871 (Lovell).
  Modern status: Rare, at Topsail.

BOLAND, a surname of Ireland (O)Bolan(d), *Ó Beolláin*, formed from a Norse personal name, with "The addition of the D at the end of the name ... an anglicized affectation" (MacLysaght); or ? an anglicization of the French family names Bol(l)and, Bouland containing the elements *boll* – friend, brother and *land* – country; or as Bol(l)and from the English place name Bowland (pronounced Bolland) (Lancashire). (Dauzat, Bardsley, Ekwall). There may possibly be confusion with BULLEN.
  Traced by MacLysaght in Cos. Connacht and Clare and by Bardsley in Lancashire and neighbouring counties.
  In Newfoundland:
  Family tradition: —— Bouland (now Boland), of Caplin Cove (now Calvert), 1815 (MUN Geog.).
  Early instances: Margarita Bolan, born in Newfoundland, baptized in Waterford, 1753 (St. Patrick's Parish Records, Waterford per Kirwin); Sarah, of Ochre Pit Cove, 1780 (CO 199.18); William, fisherman of St. John's, 1794–5, "18 years in Newfoundland," that is, since 1776–7 (Census 1794–5); Daniel, from Waterford Diocese, married at St. John's, 1799 (Nfld. Archives BRC); ——, of Harbour Grace, 1808 (D'Alberti 18); William Bolan, from Kiltecly (unidentified) (Co. Limerick), cooper of Harbour Grace, 1813 (*Royal Gazette* 18 Feb 1813); John Boland, ? Northern Bay, 1838 (DPHW 54); Garrett Thomas, from Ireland, ? of Renews, 1841 (Dillon); Charles Joseph Boland, of Fair Island (Bonavista B.), 1858 (DPHW 75); Moses and Edward Bolan, fishermen of Bay of Islands, 1871 (Lovell); John, fisherman of Ferryland, 1871 (Lovell); James Boland, farmer of Holyrood, 1871 (Lovell).
  Modern status: Boland, widespread especially at St. John's, Calvert, Outer Cove, Curling, Newtown and Lamaline and also Bowland at St. John's (*Electors* 1955).

BOLGER, BULGER, surnames of England and Ireland, (though MacLysaght recognizes only the form Bolger), from Old French *boulgier* – maker of leather wallets or bags, or for (O)Bolger, *Ó Bolguidhir*, Ir. *bolg* – belly and *odhar* – yellow. (Reaney, MacLysaght).
  Matthews traced Bolger (Bulger) in Devon, MacLysaght found Bolger "closely associated with south east Leinster (Co. Wexford) and ... rarely found elsewhere."
  In Newfoundland:

  Early instances: Phillip Bulger, labourer of St. John's, 1794–5, "19 years in Newfoundland," that is, 1775–6 (Census 1794–5); Edward, from Bay Bulls, married at St. John's, 1798 (Nfld. Archives BRC); Mary Bulger alias Condon, from Cloneen Parish (unidentified), married at St. John's, 1803 (Nfld. Archives BRC); Benjamin, planter of Twillingate, 1822 (USPG); Simon, of Harbour Grace Parish, 1823 (Nfld. Archives HGRC); Michael, of Kings Cove, 1825 (Nfld. Archives BRC); Nicholas, of Trinity, 1833 (Nfld. Archives KCRC); Thomas, from Middle Cove (? St. John's district), married at St. John's, 1839 (Nfld. Archives BRC); Michael, of Carbonear, 1857 (*Newfoundlander* 23 Apr 1857); Jacob, of Harbour Grace, 1867 (Nfld. Archives HGRC).
  Modern status: Bolger, somewhat rare, especially at Torbay and St. John's; Bulger at Trepassey Upper Coast and St. John's.

BOLLARD, a surname of Ireland, of which MacLysaght comments: "Of Dutch origin, this name came to Ireland in the early seventeenth century, and soon became prominent in the commercial life of Dublin. The quite distinct Norman name Ballard goes back to early mediaeval times."
  In Newfoundland:
  Early instances: Robert, clerk of the Church, St. John's, 1771 (DPHW 26C); Robert Jr., of Placentia, 1803 (D'Alberti 12); Robert, miner of La Manche (Placentia B.), 1871 (Lovell); James and Steven, of Woody Island (Placentia B.), 1871 (Lovell).
  Modern status: At Windsor (*Electors* 1955), but now spelled Ballard (Telephone Directory 1970).

BOLT(S), surnames of England, from Old English *bolt* – (maker of) bolts, bars, or ? a nickname for a short, heavy person. (Reaney).
  Traced by Guppy in Devon.
  In Newfoundland:
  Family tradition: The Bolts of Tack's Beach received their name from a deserter who changed his name on bolting from the Royal Navy (R.F. Sparkes).
  Early instances: William Bolt, married at St. John's, 1801 (DPHW 26D); Thomas, of Waterford Bridge, married at St. John's, 1836 (Nfld. Archives BRC); Captain Christopher, from Sidmouth, England, married at St. John's, 1848 (*Royal Gazette* 18 Jan 1848); Richard H., from Devon, of St. John's, died 1849, aged 33 (*Royal Gazette* 8 May 1849); Samuel and Thomas, planters of Tack's Beach, 1871 (Lovell).

Modern status: Bolt, on the South Coast, especially at Grand Le Pierre; Bolts at Tack's Beach (*Electors* 1955).

BOND, BOUNDS, surnames of England, and Bond only of Ireland, from Old English *bonde* etc. – husbandman, peasant, churl, later unfree tenant, serf, or from an old Scandinavian personal name. (Reaney, MacLysaght).

Guppy traced Bond in Devon, Somerset, Lancashire, Norfolk, Suffolk and Staffordshire, and Bounds in Herefordshire; MacLysaght found Bond in small numbers in all the provinces except Connacht.

In Newfoundland:

Early instances: Thomas Bound, of Bonavista, 1787 (DPHW 70); Samuel Bond, of St. John's, died ? 1795 (CO 194.40); Cox and Bound, operators of salmon fishery at Round Harbour, 1804 (CO 194.45); John, of Greenspond, 1814 (DPHW 76); Richard, from Southampton, England, planter of Oderin, deceased 1816 (*Nfld. Mercantile Journal* 11 Sep 1816); John Bond, of Garnish, 1827 (DPHW 106); William, of Lamaline, 1829, of Grand Bank, 1830 (DPHW 109); Thomas Bound, of Red Cliff Island (Bonavista B.), 1831 (DPHW 70); John Bond, planter of Bradley's Cove, 1833 (DPHW 52A); Thomas Bound, of Open Hall, 1834 (DPHW 73A); Isaac Bounds, planter of Ochre Pit Cove, 1841 (DPHW 52A); George Bound, of Pinchard's Island, 1841 (DPHW 76); Uriah Bond, fisherman of Lower Burgeo, 1844 (DPHW 101); John Bounds, of Shoe Cove (Twillingate), 1849 (DPHW 86); Sarah Bond, of Frenchman's Cove (Burin), 1853 (DPHW 106); Robert, born at St. John's, 1857 (Mott); Uriah, fisherman of La Poile, 1860 (DPHW 99); Henry, the Hermit of Bay Bulls Big Pond, in Newfoundland from about 1863 to 1871 (*Evening Telegram* 29 Mar 1965).

Modern status: Bond, widespread on the South Coast; Bounds, rare, at Lower Island Cove (*Electors* 1955), but Bowns in Telephone Directory 1971.

Place name: Bond Lake 49-01 56-11.

BONFIELD, a surname of England and Ireland, from the French place name Bonneville (Normandy). *See* BANFIELD. In Ireland Banville is a Co. Wexford variant of Bonfield. (Reaney, MacLysaght).

Guppy traced the name in Hertfordshire, MacLysaght found it "mainly associated with Cos. Limerick and Clare."

In Newfoundland:

Early instances: Edmund Pearce Banfill, ? of Dartmouth (Devon), in possession of land in St.

John's, 1795 (Exeter Archives per Kirwin); Patrick Barvill or Banvell, of Harbour Grace Parish, 1823 (Nfld. Archives HGRC); Nicholas Banville, ? of Northern Bay, 1842 (DPHW 54); Maria J. Bansfield, of Harbour Grace, 1869 (Nfld. Archives HGRC); George Banfil, of Northern Bight (now Hillview, Trinity B.), 1880 (DPHW 68).

Modern status: Unique, at Heart's Content (*Electors* 1955).

BONIA, a surname of Newfoundland, ? a variant of the French surname

Bon(n)ier, containing the elements *bon* – good and *hari* – army. (Dauzat).

In Newfoundland:

Early instance: Thomas, captain, born at Placentia, 1856 (*Nfld. Quarterly* Sep 1903).

Modern status: Somewhat rare, and associated especially with North Harbour and other settlements in St. Mary's Bay, and at Pasadena (*Electors* 1955).

BONNELL, a surname of England, ? from the English place name Bonehill (Staffordshire), or ? from the French surname Bonnel. (Bardsley, Dauzat).

Traced by Bardsley in Staffordshire.

In Newfoundland:

Family tradition: From England to Lord's Cove about 1800, thence to Lamaline (MUN Folklore).

Early instances: William Bonnel, of Lamaline, 1829 (DPHW 106); Philip Bunnel, agent at Cupids, 1830 (DPHW 34); Saul Bonnell, of Fortune, 1841 (DPHW 106); Saul Bonnel, of Petites, 1859 (DPHW 98); Saul Bonnell, of Meadows, 1860 (DPHW 107); Robert Bonnall, of Muddy Hole (Burin district), 1860 (DPHW 107); Richard Bonnell, fisherman of Burin, 1871 (Lovell); George and Robert, of Lord's Cove (Burin), 1871 (Lovell); Benjamin (and others), of Muddy Hole (now Maberly), 1871 (Lovell); Samuel, of Channel, 1877 (Lovell).

Modern status: Especially at Lamaline, Taylor's Bay, Calmer and other settlements in the Burin district, and at St. John's.

Place name: Bonnels Point 47-31 57-20.

BONNER, a surname of England, Scotland and Ireland, from the Old French *(de)bonnaire*, Middle English *boner(e)*, *bonour* – gentle, courteous. (Reaney, Cottle).

Traced by Guppy in Herefordshire and Surrey, by Spiegelhalter in Devon and by MacLysaght in North Ulster as a variant of Bonar, a Scots form, and in Co. Limerick.

In Newfoundland:

Early instance: Alice, of Heart's Content, 1871 (Lovell).

Modern status: Rare, at Carbonear (*Electors* 1955) and St. John's.

BOOMER, a surname of England, of unknown origin, ? from the French surname Boulmer, a contracted form of Boulommier or Boulonmier (Dauzat).

Traced by Reaney Notes in Rothwell (Yorkshire WR in 1664).

In Newfoundland:

Early instance: Willard, motorman, married Gracey L. King of Fortune, and moved there about 1909 (Methodist Baptisms, Fortune 1909, per P.E.L. Smith).

Modern status: Rare, at Fortune.

BOONE, BOWN(E), BOWN(E)S, surnames of England, Boone of Guernsey (Channel Islands), BOWN of Scotland, from the French place name Bohon (La Manche). *See also* BOWEN. (Reaney, Black, Turk).

Guppy traced Boon in Staffordshire, Bown in Somerset and Derbyshire; Spiegelhalter traced Boon(e) in Devon; and Matthews traced Boon(e) in Devon and Dorset and Bown in Dorset and Cornwall.

In Newfoundland:

Family tradition: Harriet Boone (1826–1903), of Salmon Cove (now South River), formerly of Port de Grave (MUN Geog.).

Early instances: John Boon, of Petty Harbour, 1675 (CO 1); Abraham Boone, in possession of property at Port de Grave, 1784, but property "possessed by the Family for 61 years or upwards," that is, since before 1723 (CO 199.18); Robert Bown, of Newfoundland, 1730 (CO 194.23); John, married at St. John's, 1765 (DPHW 26D); John ? Boon, juror of Greenspond, 1804 (D'Alberti 14); —— Boon, joint owner of fishing room at Salvage, 1806 (Bonavista Register 1806); John, of Bareneed, 1816 (Nfld. Archives L165); John, servant of Brigus, 1827 (DPHW 34); James Bown, of St. John's, 1834 (*Newfoundlander* 3 Apr 1834); John Bowne, of Greenspond, 1836 (DPHW 76); John Boon, fisherman of Ferryland, 1838 (DPHW 31); John Boon(e), fisherman of Pouch Cove, 1843 (DPHW 32); Thomas Boone, of Bareneed (died at Seldom Come By, 1897), missionary at Twillingate, 1843 (MUN Hist., DPHW 26B); Charles, fisherman of Seldom Come By, 1853 (DPHW 83).

Modern status: Boone, widespread, especially at Cottrells Cove, South River and St. John's; Bown(e) in the Fogo district; Bown(e)s, rare.

Place name: Boone Point 47-19 52-46.

BORDEN, a surname of England, from the English place name Borden (Kent) or an anglicization of the French surnames Bourdin or Bourdon, or of the Jersey (Channel Islands) surnames Bo(u)rdon. (Bardsley, Dauzat, Turk).

In Newfoundland:

Family tradition: The Bordens of Twillingate and of Corner Brook since the 1920s are probably of French origin (MUN Folklore).

Early instances: J., of St. John's Harbour, 1703 (CO 194.3); —— of Twillingate, 1768 (MUN Hist.); John Boarden or Bourden, planter of Twillingate, 1820 (USPG).

Modern status: At Jenkin's Cove, Virgin Arm (*Electors* 1955), Corner Brook, Carter's Cove and Windsor.

BORGEN, a surname of Norway – dweller in or near a fortified castle. (E.C. Smith).

In Newfoundland:

Early instance: Johan (1894–1972), whaling captain, from Norway, associated with Newfoundland and Labrador from 1937 to 1972, settled at St. John's in 1943 (*Daily News* 19 Jan 1972).

Modern status: Rare, at St. John's.

BOULOS, a surname of Syria-Lebanon, the Christian Arabic form of Paul (*see* PAUL).

In Newfoundland: Introduced in the early 20th century.

Modern status: At Stephenville, Millertown Junction, Deer Lake and St. John's.

BOURGEOIS, a surname of France, – burgess, designating first the inhabitant of a free town, later a citizen. *See* BURGESS. (Dauzat).

In Newfoundland:

Tradition: The families of Bourgeois on the West Coast are ... probably all descendants of Charles-Raymond, a native of France who, having married an Acadian, settled at St. George's. It is also a family name of Acadia, of the Magdalen Islands through which many Acadian settlers to Newfoundland passed, and of St. Pierre. (G.R. Thomas).

Early instance: Eugene, fisherman of Indian Head (St. George's B.), 1871 (Lovell).

Modern status: A West Coast name, especially at Kippens.

BOURNE, a surname of England and Ireland, from Old English *burna*, Old Norse *brunnr* – (dweller by the) stream, or from the English place names Bourn (Cambridge), Bourne (Hampshire, Lincolnshire) etc. (Reaney, MacLysaght).

Traced by Guppy in several counties, especially Shropshire, Staffordshire, Sussex and Wiltshire, by Spiegelhalter in Devon, and by MacLysaght in Ireland since the 16th century, mainly Cos. Dublin and Kildare.

In Newfoundland:

Early instances: Christopher, servant at Battle Harbour (Labrador), 1795 (MUN Hist.); John, in possession of fishing room at Grouts Island, Greenspond, 1806 (Bonavista Register 1806); John, tried in Supreme Court, 1822 (CO 194-65); Valentine Born, of St. John's, 1828 (DPHW 26B); John Bourne, of Gooseberry Island (Bonavista B.), 1830 (DPHW 76); John Gervas Hutchinson Bourne, Chief Justice of Newfoundland, 1839 (DPHW 26B); Catherine Borne, of King's Cove, 1855 (Nfld. Archives KCRC); George Burn, ? from Upway (Dorset), married at Harbour Breton, 1859 (DPHW 104); John, of Harbour Grace, 1867 (Nfld. Archives HGRC).

Modern status: Scattered, especially at St. John's.

BOUTCHER, BUTCHER, surnames of England, Scotland and Ireland, and Boucher of France, from Old French *bo(u)chier* – butcher. (Reaney, Dauzat).

Guppy traced Boucher in Worcestershire, Butcher in Huntingdonshire, Kent, Norfolk, Shropshire, Suffolk and Wiltshire; Spiegelhalter traced Boucher and Butcher in Devon; MacLysaght traced Boucher "on record in Ireland since the 13th century [but] now mainly found in Cos. Cork and Waterford."

In Newfoundland:

Family tradition: The Boutchers of Kingwell, since the early 19th century, and later of Spencer's Cove, Beaver Pond and Carbonear, are of French origin (MUN Folklore).

Early instances: Alexander Boucher, from Greenock, merchant of St. John's, 1801 (CO 194.43), died 1816 (*Nfld. Mercantile Journal* 7 Dec 1816); Roger Boucher or Butcher, of Burin, 1814 (D'Alberti 24); Margaret Butcher, born at Paddy Pond [Poor's] Cove, baptized at Haystack, 1836 (DPHW 30); John, of Greenspond, 1850 (DPHW 76).

Modern status: Boutcher, at Kingwell and Spencer's Cove; Butcher, rare and scattered.

BOUZAN(E), BOUZANNE, ? variants of the French surnames Bo(u)zon etc., from ? a German personal name containing the element *bos* – wicked, or ? from an unidentified French place name. (Dauzat).

In Newfoundland:

Family tradition: Michael Bouzane, younger son of landowners at La Bouzanne (unidentified), about 30 miles northwest of Paris, ran away to sea and settled in Western Bay about 1850. His sons moved to Little Bay (Green Bay) to work in the newly-discovered copper mines in 1878 (MUN Geog.).

Early instances: Thomas Bouzan, of Harbour Grace Parish, 1829 (Nfld. Archives HGRC); Thomas Boozane, of ? Northern Bay, 1842 (DPHW 54); Michael Beausany, of ? Northern Bay, 1856 (DPHW 54); Michael (and others) Boozan, fishermen of Western Bay, 1871 (Lovell).

Modern status: Bouzan(e), scattered, especially at St. Patrick's (Green B.) and in the Grand Falls district; Bouzanne, at St. John's and Corner Brook.

BOVARD, a surname of France, variant of Bouvard, from an old baptismal name, from a German personal name containing the elements *bov* – boy and *hard* – hard, strong; as Bovaird, a family name of Ireland, "formerly quite numerous in Co. Donegal, now rare," where the Bovairds were probably Huguenot refugees. (Dauzat, MacLysaght).

In Newfoundland:

Modern status: At St. John's from Ireland since 1952. (Family).

BOWDEN, a surname of England, Scotland and Ireland, in England from the English place name Bowden (17 in Devon according to Reaney, 20 according to Spiegelhalter, as well as in other counties including Roxburghshire for the Scots surname), or (dweller on the) curved hill or above the hill; in Ireland, a variant of Boden, of the same origin or the anglicization of a rare Irish name *Ó Buadáin*. (Reaney, Black, MacLysaght).

Guppy traced Bowden in Cheshire, Cornwall, Derbyshire and Devon, Boden in Staffordshire and Boaden in Cornwall; Spiegelhalter traced Boden, Bowden in Devon; MacLysaght associates Boden with Co. Kildare.

In Newfoundland:

Early instances: William, of Fermeuse, 1677 (CO 1); —— Boden, of Quidi Vidi, 1703 (CO 194.3); John Bowden, of Newfoundland, ? 1706 (CO 194.24); Richard Bawden, of Quidi Vidi, 1708 (CO 194.4); Andrew Bauden, fisherman of St. John's or Petty Harbour, about 1739–43 (CO 194.11, 24); William Bowden, of St. John's, 1751 (CO 194.13); Edward, seaman of Bay Bulls, 1780 (D'Alberti 6);

William Bo(w)den, of St. John's, 1780 (D'Alberti 6); John, of Petty Harbour, 1819 (DPHW 26B); —— Boden, of Ferryland, 1831 (*Newfoundlander* 26 May 1831); George Bowden, carpenter of Brigus, 1833 (DPHW 34); Robert, baker of Harbour Grace, 1871 (Lovell); Richard, of Rencontre, 1871 (Lovell).

Modern status: At St. John's.

BOWD(E)RING, Newfoundland variants of the surnames of Ireland Bowdern, Bowdren, probably from an Anglo-Norman place name Boderan (untraced). (MacLysaght). MacLysaght traced Bowdern, Bowdren in Co. Waterford.

In Newfoundland:

Family tradition: Bowdrings among the early settlers on Bell Island, with which the name is still and almost entirely associated (MUN Hist.).

Early instances: Pat Bowderan, from Temple Michael (Co. Cork), married at St. John's, 1813 (Nfld. Archives BRC); John, Medoph and Patrick Bowdering, fishermen of Bell island, 1871 (Lovell).

Modern status: Bowdering, unique, at St. John's; Bowdring, at Bell Island and St. John's.

BOW(D)RIDGE, Newfoundland variants of the surname of England Bowdi(t)ch etc., from the English place name Bowditch (Dorset), or variants of the surnames of Guernsey (Channel Islands) Bowdedge, Bowdidge (Bardsley after Lower, Turk).

In Newfoundland:

Early instances: Thomas Bowditch or Bowdrich, carpenter of Grand Bank, 1822 (DPHW 109, MUN Hist.); George Bowdridge, of Upper Burgeo, 1848 (DPHW 101); William Bowdige, of Harris Cove (Exploits district), 1857 (DPHW 92).

Modern status: Rare, Bow(d)ridge in the Burgeo-La Poile district; Bound(e)ridge, at St. John's (*Electors* 1955).

Place name: Bowdridge Shoal 46-51 55-42, 47-37 58-33.

BOWE, a surname of Ireland, a variant of (O)Bogue, *Ó Buadhaigh*, Ir. *buadhach* – victorious. "Bogue is the usual anglicized form in Co. Cork, Bowe mainly in Cos. Kilkenny and Waterford, Bowes and Bowie in the midland counties." (MacLysaght).

In Newfoundland: Believed to be of Scots origin and later of Co. Wexford or Kilkenny (Family).

Family tradition: ——, born 1844, of the Goulds (St. John's South district) (Family).

Early instances: John, shoreman of St. John's, 1794–5, "12 years in Newfoundland," that is, since 1782-3 (Census 1794–5); John Bow, from Lisdowny

Parish (Co. Kilkenny), married at St. John's, 1803 (Nfld. Archives BRC); Miss, of Ferryland, married at St. John's, 1808 (Nfld. Archives BRC); John, of Trepassey, married at St. John's, 1808 (Nfld. Archives BRC); Nicholas Bow(e) or Boe, of Harbour Grace Parish, 1819, of Harbour Grace, 1830 (Nfld. Archives HGRC); William Bowe, of Trinity, 1829 (Nfld. Archives KCRC); William, fisherman of Cupids, 1871 (Lovell); John Bow, farmer of Goulds, 1871 (Lovell).

Modern status: Rare, at the Goulds.

Place names: Bowes Brook 47-41 53-18, —— Long Pond 47-42 53-17, —— Round Pond 47-42 53-17.

BOWEN, a surname of Wales, England and Ireland, from the Welsh *ap Owein* – son of Owen; or in Ireland sometimes for Bolane; sometimes probably confused with BOWN (*see* BOONE). (Reaney, MacLysaght).

Traced by Guppy in Herefordshire, Shropshire, Worcestershire and South Wales.

In Newfoundland:

Early instances: John, ? of St. John's, 1755 (DPHW 26C); Thomas Bowens, fisherman of Trinity (Trinity B.), 1760 (DPHW 64); Mary Bowen, of St. Mary's, married at St. John's, 1837 (Nfld. Archives BRC); John, of Red Cliff Island (Bonavista B.), 1851 (DPHW 73A).

Modern status: At St. Mary's and Red Cliff, Southern Bay and Winter Brook (Bonavista South district).

BOW(E)RING, surnames of England, from Old English **buring*, from *būr* – bower, dwelling, chamber, woman's room. *See also* BOWERS. (Reaney, Cottle).

Traced by Guppy in Somerset, by Spiegelhalter in Devon, and by Matthews in Dorset.

In Newfoundland:

Family tradition: James Bowering (1794–1861), from Chard (Somerset), settled at Coleys Point, 1812 (MUN Geog.).

Early instances: —— Bowring and others, plaintiffs before Supreme Court, 1810 (CO 194.50); Benjamin, from Moreton Hampstead (Devon), established business in St. John's, 1811 (*Nfld. Quarterly*, Autumn 1911).

Modern status: Especially at St. John's, and in the Port de Grave and Trinity North districts.

Place names: Bowring Cove (Labrador) 52-39 55-48, Bowring Park, St. John's.

BOWER(S), surnames of England, Scotland and Ireland, from the English and Scots place name Bower in Somerset, Sussex and Peebleshire etc. (Reaney), or from the French place name Bures (Normandy) (Spiegelhalter); or from the Old English *būr* – bower, dwelling, chamber, woman's room (*see also* BOWERING); or a variant of Bowyer, Middle English *bowyere* – maker of or trader in bows; or, in the form Bower only, a surname of Ireland, "a mistranslation [more obvious in the variant Boar] of MacCullagh, Ir. *Mac Cú Uladh* or *Mac Con Uladh* – hound of Ulster." (Reaney, MacLysaght).

Bower traced by Guppy in Cheshire, Derbyshire and Nottinghamshire, by Spiegelhalter in Devon, and by MacLysaght in Ulster; Bowers traced by Guppy in Staffordshire and by Spiegelhalter in Devon.

In Newfoundland:

Early instances: John Bowers, tailor of St. John's, 1794–5, "16 years in Newfoundland," that is, since 1778–9 (Census 1794–5); Joseph Bower(s), from Bristol, of Harbour Grace, died 1787 (Nfld. Archives L172, CO 194.36); James Bowers, fisherman of Coleys Point, 1842 (DPHW 39); John Bower, of Nipper's Harbour, 1844 (DPHW 86); William, of Indian Burying Place, 1845 (DPHW 86); Robert, fisherman of Salmon Cove (now Champneys), 1847 (DPHW 64B); Isaac and James, fishermen of (Lower) Island Cove, 1871 (Lovell); Frank and James, fishermen of Jacksons Arm (Fogo), 1871 (Lovell).

Modern status: Bowers at Green Bay, Corner Brook, Grand Falls and St. John's.

Place name: ? Bower Ledge 47-44 55-45.

BOWLES, a surname of England and Ireland, from the French place name Bouelles (Seine-Inférieure), or in Ireland also a variant of (O)Boyle, *Ó Baoighill*, of uncertain origin but probably derived from a root word in modern Irish *geall* – pledge. *See also* BOYLE(S). (Reaney, MacLysaght).

Traced by Guppy in Wiltshire and Kent, by Spiegelhalter in Devon, and by MacLysaght in Ulster.

In Newfoundland:

Early instances: Henry, fisherman of Lower Burgeo, 1848 (DPHW 101); Henry and James, fishermen at Coppett (Burgeo district), 1871 (Lovell).

Modern status: In Burgeo-La Poile district, especially Ramea and Burgeo and in the Burin district.

BOWMAN, a surname of England, Scotland and Ireland, from Old English *bōga* – bow and *mann* – man, – bowman, archer, but in North Ulster it is said to be a variant of Beaumont. (Reaney, Black, MacLysaght).

Traced by Guppy in Cambridgeshire, Durham and Hertfordshire, by Spiegelhalter in Devon, by Black especially in western Scotland, and by MacLysaght in Limerick and Ulster.

In Newfoundland:

Early instances: Rev. Mr. Bowman arrived from London at St. John's, 1839 (*Newfoundlander* 14 Nov 1839); William Bo(w)man, of Harbour Grace Parish, 1827, 1828 (Nfld. Archives HGRC); Anna Bowman, of Harbour Grace, 1866 (Nfld. Archives HGRC).

Modern status: Rare, at St. John's, Carbonear and Bishops Falls.

BOWN(E)(S). *See* BOONE

BOWRIDGE. *See* BOW(D)RIDGE

BOWRING. *See* BOWERING

BOYCE, a surname of England, Ireland and Scotland, from French *bois* – (dweller in or near the) wood; or from a German personal name *Boio*, Old English **Boia* – young man, servant, knave, rogue, lad. In Donegal and West Ireland it is an anglicized form of *Ó Buadhaigh*, Ir. *buadhach* – victorious. (Reaney, MacLysaght).

Traced by Guppy in Norfolk, Somerset, Worcestershire, by Spiegelhalter in Devon, and by MacLysaght in various counties in Ireland.

In Newfoundland:

Early instances: William Boyss, inhabitant of Conception Bay, 1706 (CO 194.4); William Boyce, of Carbonear, 1708–9 (CO 194.4); William, of Harbour Grace Parish, 1834 (Nfld. Archives HGRC); William, fisherman of Red Island (Burgeo district), 1844 (DPHW 101); William, of ? Northern Bay, 1847 (DPHW 54); John Boyes, fisherman of St. John's, 1859 (DPHW 29); John and William Boyce, of Harbour Breton, 1871 (Lovell).

Modern status: Rare, at St. John's and Jersey Harbour.

BOYD(E), surnames of Scotland and Ireland, from Gaelic *buidhe* – yellow (-haired), or from the Scots place name, (the island of) Bute. (Reaney, Black, MacLysaght).

Traced by Guppy in Southern Scotland and by MacLysaght in Ulster.

In Newfoundland:

Early instances: Peter Boyd, of Conception Bay,

1706 (CO 194.4); John, of St. John's, 1822 (D'Alberti 32); Thomas Boyed, from Co. Waterford, married at St. John's, 1824 (Nfld. Archives BRC); John Boyd, Wesleyan minister of Brigus, 1830 (DPHW 34); Joseph, born at St. John's, 1835 of a Co. Wexford family (Mott); John, from Glasgow, Scotland, of St. John's, died 1851, aged 63 (*Weekly Herald* 21 Jul 1851); Joseph, of Old Perlican, 1871 (Lovell); Aaron, Robert and Thomas, miners of Tilt Cove, 1871 (Lovell); James Boyd, a fisherman, and John Boyde, planter of Twillingate, 1871 (Lovell); Andrew Boyde, of Tizzard's Harbour, 1874 (DPHW 89).

Modern status: Boyd, especially at Tizzard's Harbour, and Boyde at Summerford.

BOYDEN, a surname of England, from the personal names in Old French **Bodin*, in Old German *Baudin*. (Reaney).

In Newfoundland:

Modern status: At Sandy Point (St. George's district).

BOYLE(S), surnames of Ireland and Scotland; in Ireland (O)Boyle, *Ó Baoighill*, of uncertain origin but probably derived from a root word in modern Irish *geall* – pledge; in Scotland either of the preceding origin or, according to Black, from the French place name "Boyville, otherwise Boeville or Beauville, near Caen," or Bovelles (Seine-Inférieure). *See also* BOWLES. (MacLysaght, Black).

Traced by MacLysaght in northwest Ireland and by Black especially in Ayrshire and Wigtownshire.

In Newfoundland:

Early instances: Johana Boyle, married at St. John's, 1832 (Nfld. Archives BRC); George Boyles, of St. John's, 1833 (DPHW 26D); Margaret Boyle, from Goran (unidentified) (Co. Kilkenny), married at St. John's, 1836 (Nfld. Archives BRC); Catherine, of Harbour Grace Parish, 1838 (Nfld. Archives HGRC); Robert, of Pinckers (? for Pinchards) Island, 1845 (Nfld. Archives KCRC); Patrick and Thomas, fishermen of Witless Bay, 1871 (Lovell); George Boyles, farmer of Bay Bulls Road, 1871 (Lovell).

Modern status: Scattered.

BOZEC, ? a variant of the French family name Bouige, Bouzige, Bouzigue (Dauzat).

In Newfoundland:

Family tradition: Yves LeBozec, Guilvinec, canton of Quimper, Brittany (b. about 1860), settled at L'Anse à Canard in 1888 (Thomas, "French Fam. Names").

Modern status: In the Port au Port district.

BRACE, a surname of England of obscure origin, probably from the English place name Brace (Shropshire). (Bardsley). Bardsley traced the name in early records in Buckinghamshire, Shropshire, Somerset and Worcestershire; Matthews associates it with Ipplepen (Devon).

In Newfoundland:

Family traditions: ——, from Old Perlican, settled at Greens Harbour, about 1835 (MUN Hist.); ——, from England or ? Quidi Vidi, settled at Chance Cove (Trinity B.), about 1838 (MUN Folklore); ——, from Ireland, settled at St. John's, about 1875 (MUN Folklore).

Early instances: Thomas, of Quidi Vidi, 1753 (DPHW 26C); George, of St. John's, 1806 (CO 194.45); George, of Twillingate, 1810 (CO 194.49); W., gaoler at Harbour Grace, 1844 (*Nfld. Almanac*); William, of Green's Harbour, 1858 (DPHW 59A).

Modern status: Especially at Greens Harbour and Chance Cove (Trinity B.), St. John's and Bishop's Falls.

BRACKEN, a surname of England and Ireland; in England from the place name Bracken (Yorkshire ER) (Bardsley); in Ireland, as (O)Bracken, *Ó Breacáin*, Ir. *breac* – speckled. (Bardsley, MacLysaght).

Traced by MacLysaght on the Kildare-Offaly border.

In Newfoundland:

Early instances: ? Pat Brechin, fisherman of St. John's, 1794–5, "11 years in Newfoundland," that is, since 1783–4 (Census 1794–5); ? Stephen Brecken, of Harbour Grace, 1859 (DPHW 43).

Modern status: Rare, at Bell Island (*Electors* 1955).

BRADBROOK, a surname of England – (dweller by the) broad brook. (Reaney).

In Newfoundland:

Modern status: Rare, at Ship Cove (Burin district), Belleoram and St. John's.

BRADBURY, a surname of England from the English place name Bradbury (Durham). (Reaney).

Traced by Guppy in Derbyshire, Staffordshire and Yorkshire WR.

In Newfoundland:

Family tradition: Some Bradburys came to Newfoundland from Bristol (MUN Hist.).

Early instances: Abraham, of Jugler's Cove (Bay Roberts), 1784, property "possess'd by the Family for 80 years," that is, since 1704 (CO 199.18); John, of St. John's, ? 1705 (CO 194.22); Isaac, of Harbour

Grace, 1750 (CO 199.18); Abraham, of Collibou Tickle (Labrador), 1787, of Battle Harbour (Labrador), 1789 (MUN Hist.); Jacob and Jonathan, fishermen of Torbay, 1794–5 (Census 1794–5); Susanna, of Bay Roberts, 1828 (Nfld. Archives HGRC); James, fisherman of Beachy Cove (Port de Grave), 1860 (DPHW 38); Charles, planter, John and Joseph, fishermen of Coleys Point, 1871 (Lovell); Isaac and William, fishermen of (Upper) Island Cove, 1871 (Lovell); Jacob (and others) Bradberry, of Portugal Cove, 1871 (Lovell).

Modern status: Widespread, especially at St. John's and in the Harbour Grace, Port de Grave districts.

BRADLEY, a surname of England, Ireland and Scotland, from the common English place name, or (dweller in or near the) broad wood or clearing; in Ireland usually a synonym of (O)Brallaghan, *Ó Brollacháin* – "from Brollach, an Old Irish personal name presumably derived from *brollach* – breast" (MacLysaght); in Scotland from the lands of Braidlie (Roxburghshire) or as an anglicized form of O'Brolachan, as in Irish usage. (Reaney, Cattle, MacLysaght, Black).

Guppy found Bradley widespread especially in Nottinghamshire, Lancashire and Shropshire,

In Newfoundland:

Early instances: William Bradley, of Carbonear, 1675 (CO 1); Richard, of Bonavista, 1787 (DPHW 70); John, of St. John's, 1798 (DPHW 26D); Joseph Bradly, from Bantry (Co. Cork), married at St. John's, 1821 (Nfld. Archives BRC); William Bradley, planter of Western Bay, 1826 (DPHW 52A); Henry, fisherman of Cupids, 1849 (DPHW 34); William, of Salvage, 1855 (DPHW 73A); John, of Muddy Hole (now Maberly), 1858 (DPHW 83); John, fisherman of Brooklyn (Bonavista B.), 1871 (Lovell); George and Thomas, dealers of Burin, 1871 (Lovell).

Modern status: Scattered, especially at St. John's and Eastport.

Place names: Bradley Rock 47-45 53-11, 49-42 54-47; Bradleys Cove 47-52 53-04.

BRADSHAW, a surname of England and Ireland from the English place name Bradshaw (Derbyshire, Lancashire, Yorkshire WR), or (dweller in or near the) broad copse, thicket or small wood. (Bardsley, Cottle).

Guppy found Bradshaw widespread, especially in Northamptonshire and Lancashire and MacLysaght states that the name "was well established in Ireland in the early seventeenth century and has since been

mainly found in Cos. Tipperary and Oriel [Cos. Armagh and Monaghan are parts of South Down, Louth and Fermanagh] as well as in Dublin and Belfast."

In Newfoundland:

Early instances: Francis, J.P. at Trepassey, 1792 (D'Alberti 4), at Bay Bulls, 1802 (USPG), and at Placentia, 1817 (CO 194.60); Richard, of Gaultois, 1871 (Lovell); Henry, of St. John's, 1871 (Lovell).

Modern status: Scattered.

BRADY, a surname of England, Ireland and Scotland; in England from Old English *brād* – broad, with *ēage* – eye, broad eye (a nickname), or with *ēg* – island – (dweller on or by the) broad island, or with *(ge)hæcg* – enclosure (dweller in or near the) broad enclosure (Reaney); in Ireland (Mac)Brady, *Mac Bradáigh*, possibly Irish *bradach* – spirited, from *brad* – urging, or sometimes for (O)GRADY – (Reaney, MacLysaght, Black).

Traced by MacLysaght in Cos. Cavan, Leitrim and Clare.

In Newfoundland:

Early instances: Thomas, of St. John's, 1787 (DPHW 26C); John, of Domino (Labrador), 1833, died 1834 (*Newfoundlander* 1 Aug 1833, 2 Jan 1834); John, of Harbour Grace Parish, 1830 (Nfld. Archives HGRC); John, of ? Northern Bay, 1838 (DPHW 54); Luke, fisherman of Fortune, 1860 (DPHW 106); Michael, farmer of Little Placentia (now Argentia), 1871 (Lovell); Thomas, fisherman of Red Head Cove (Trinity B.), 1871 (Lovell).

Modern status: At St. John's, Red Head Cove, Bay de Verde and Fortune.

BRAGG, a surname of England, from Middle English *brag(ge)* – brisk, lively, brave, mettlesome, proud, arrogant. (Reaney, Cottle).

Traced by Guppy in Devon.

In Newfoundland:

Family tradition: Mary (? 1769–1831), of Grand Bank (MUN Hist.).

Early instances: William, born at Chard (Somerset), 1799, baptized at Trinity (Trinity B.), 1817 (DPHW 64); William, of Perlican (unspecified) (Trinity B.), married at St. John's, 1803 (Nfld. Archives BRC); John Brag, married in the Northern district, 1814 (Nfld. Archives BRC); Mills Bragg(e), of Pouch Cove, 1814 (DPHW 26B); Joseph Bragg, of Fortune Bay, 1815 (D'Alberti 25); Joseph Brag, born in 1816 at Pointe Blanche, baptized in 1830 at Port aux Basques (DPHW 30); Catherine, of Broad Cove (now Duntara), married at King's Cove, 1827 (Nfld. Archives KCRC); Elizabeth Bragge, of Pouch

Cove, 1835 (DPHW 26D); John Bragg, of Port aux Basques, 1845 (DPHW 30); James, of ? Northern Bay, 1839 (DPHW 54); Charles, of Greenspond, 1841 (DPSW 76); William, fisherman of Seal Islands (Burgeo), 1871 (Lovell).

.Modern status: Scattered, especially at Pouch Cove

Place names: Brag Cove 47-16 55-52, —— Point 47-16 55-52, —— Rock 47-39 58-52, Bragg's Island 48-56 53-40.

BRAIN, a surname of England, Scotland and France; in England and possibly Scotland from Old English *brægen* – brain, used of 'intellectual power' in 1393, or ? from Middle English *brain* – furious, mad. Reaney rejects Weekley's suggestion of a Celtic origin and Black's of a local derivation. In France, Brain is a contraction of Berain, a popular form of *Benignus*, the name of the apostle of Burgundy in the second century. (Reaney Notes, Weekley *Surnames*, Black, Dauzat).

Traced by Guppy in Dorset, Gloucestershire and Wiltshire.

In Newfoundland:

Modern status: Rare, at Grand Falls.

BRAKE, a surname of England and Guernsey (Channel Islands), from Old English *bræc*, Middle English *brake* – (dweller by the) copse, thicket. (Reaney, Turk).

Traced by Guppy in Dorset and Somerset, and by Spiegelhalter in Devon.

In Newfoundland:

Family traditions: Patrick, married at Spanish Room (Mortier B.), 1867 (MUN Hist.). Edward M. (1837–1911), barrelmaker from England, was the first settler of Meadows (Bay of Islands) about 1861 (MUN Geog.).

Early instances: Ralph, from ? Yeominster (Dorset), inhabitant of Bay of Islands for 60 years, that is, since before 1780, until his death in 1842, at age 82, leaving his son Edward and nine other sons living in the area; his wife Jane died 1819 (Feild; PRO C. 108/69, Chancery, Masters Exhibits, per Philip E.L. Smith); John, schoolmaster of the School of Industry, St. John's, 1805,–06,–10 (D'Alberti 17, CO 194.45, 49); John and Philip ? Bracke, of Jean de Bay, 1871 (Lovell); Philip, of Spanish Room, 1871 (Lovell); George, of Muddy Hole (Burin district), 1871 (Lovell).

Modern status: Widespread, especially at Trout River and Meadows.

Place names: Brake Cove 49-32 58-03, Brake (or Brake's) Point 48-58 57-55, Brake's Cove 49-08 58-06.

BRANSFIELD, a surname of Ireland, from an unidentified English place name (MacLysaght).

Traced by MacLysaght in Cos. Waterford and Cork.

In Newfoundland:

Early instances: John and Richard, of Crocker's Cove, 1804 (CO 199.18); John, of Harbour Grace Parish, 1806 (Nfld. Archives HGRC); David, ? of Western Bay, 1841 (DPHW 54); Maurice, from Co. Cork, ? of Port de Grave, 1844 (*Indicator* 24 Aug 1844); Richard, fisherman, Richard, teacher of Carbonear, 1871 (Lovell); Richard, fisherman of St. John's, 1871 (Lovell).

Modern status: At St. John's.

BRANTON, a surname of England, from the English place names Branton (Yorkshire WR) or Braunton (Devon). (Reaney).

Traced by Spiegelhalter in Devon.

In Newfoundland:

Early instance: John, fisherman of Scilly Cove (now Winterton), 1850 (DPHW 59A).

Modern status: Scattered, especially at Thornlea.

BRAY(E), surnames of England, Ireland, Scotland and France; in England and sometimes in Ireland and Scotland from the English place name Bray (Berkshire, Devon and, according to MacLysaght, Cornwall), or (dweller by the) brow of a hill or from Cornish *bregh* – fine, brave (Spiegelhalter); or in Scotland from the Scots place name Brae; or in Ireland from *Ó Breaghdha* – a native of Bregia, a territory in Munster; in France, from the French place name Bray (Normandy), or from Old French *brai* – mud, or Old French *brai* – cry, noise. (Reaney, Black, MacLysaght, Dauzat).

Traced by Guppy in Cornwall, Devon, Herefordshire; by MacLysaght as "formerly well known in Munster."

In Newfoundland:

Family tradition: Richard Bray(e) came to Harbour Grace from ? Yorkshire or ? Devon in the early 19th century (MUN Folklore).

Early instances: Thomas Bray, of Harbour Grace Parish, 1808 (Nfld. Archives HGRC); John, of St. John's, 1810 (CO 194.50); Thomas, from Co. Kilkenny, married at St. John's, 1833 (Nfld. Archives BRC); Robert C., of Harbour Grace died 1834 (*Newfoundlander* 2 Jan 1834).

Modern status: Bray, at St. John's, Braye, at Corner Brook and Grand Falls.

Place name: Bray Lake (Labrador) 54-19 66-13.

BRAZIL, a surname of Ireland and of the Micmacs of Newfoundland, *Ó Breasail* – ? Ir. *bres* – strife. (MacLysaght).

"Mainly a Co. Waterford name" (MacLysaght), but as Brazill, Brasill traced also by Matthews in Devon.

In Newfoundland:

Family tradition: John, cooper of Bristol, in possession of land at Port de Grave before 1729 (MUN Hist.).

Early instances: John, of Harbour Grace, 1776 (CO 199.18); Ann Brazill, of St. John's, 1794–5 (Census 1794–5); Thomas, from Kilmaida (Co. Limerick) (unidentified), shoreman of Little Placentia (now Argentia), deceased, 1811 (*Royal Gazette* 19 Dec 1811); John Brazel, from Bray (Co. Wicklow), married at St. John's, 1817 (Nfld. Archives BRC); Anne Brazil, of Trinity, 1818 (Nfld. Archives KCRC); Peter, of Kings Cove, 1822 (Nfld. Archives KCRC); Mary Anne Braseel, Brazell or Brazil, of Fogo Harbour, 1823 (Nfld. Archives KCRC); Cornelius Brazil, of Tilting Harbour (now Tilting), 1825 (Nfld. Archives KCRC); Joseph Brazell (and others), of Spaniards Bay, 1871 (Lovell); James, fisherman of Toads (now Tors) Cove, 1871 (Lovell); Joe Brazil, a Micmac of Conne River, 1905 (Millais).

Modern status: Scattered, especially at St. John's.

Place names: Brazil Pond 47-32 52-51, 48-03 55-59, Brazils Pond 47-35 53-24.

BREAKER, a surname of England, ? a variant of Br(e)acher, from Old English *bræc* – (dweller near a) piece of newly cultivated land. (Reaney).

Guppy traced Bracher in Wiltshire, Matthews traced Breacher, Breaker in Devon.

In Newfoundland:

Early instances: Judith, born at Swain's Island, 1809 (DPHW 76); Abel, from Lymington (Hampshire), of King's Cove, 1822, of Plate Cove (Bonavista B.), 1828 (Nfld. Archives KCRC); James Br(e)aker, planter of Brigus, 1826 (DPHW 34); David Braker, of Greenspond, 1829 (DPHW 76); Stephen Breaker, blacksmith of Harbour Grace, 1871 (Lovell).

Modern status: Rare, especially in the Port de Grave district.

Place names (not necessarily from the surname): Breaker Point 51-34 55-26, The Breaker 49-07 53-34.

BRECKON, a surname ? of England and Wales, ? from the Welsh place name Brecon also known as Brecknock. See also BRENNOCK.

In Newfoundland:

Modern status: At St. John's since 1953.

BREEN, a surname of Ireland, *Ó Braoin*. *See also* BREWIN. (MacLysaght).

Traced by MacLysaght in Cos. Offaly and Roscommon.

In Newfoundland:

Early instances: Thomas Breen, of Placentia, 1794 (D'Alberti 5); John Breene, of St. John's, 1796 (CO 194.39); Margaret, from Suttons Parish (Co. Wexford), married at St. John's, 1803 (Nfld Archives BRC); Michael, from Killiguy (Co. Wexford) (unidentified), fisherman of Portugal Cove, deceased, 1814 (*Royal Gazette* 17 Nov 1814); John, of Harbour Grace Parish, 1814 (Nfld. Archives HGRC); George Breen, born at Brigus, 1824 (DPHW 34); John, from St. Mary's, married at St. John's, 1837 (Nfld. Archives BRC); John, of Indian Arm, 1870 (Nfld. Archives KCRC); James and Michael, of Bell Island (NTS Grey Islands Harbour), 1871 (Lovell); George, farmer of Colliers, 1871 (Lovell); James Breene, John Breen and others, of Cupids, 1871 (Lovell); Lawrence Breen, of Fogo, 1871 (Lovell); Michael, of Logy Bay, 1871 (Lovell); Andrew, of Petty Harbour, 1871 (Lovell); James, of Port de Grave, 1871 (Lovell); John, of Southern Bay (Bonavista B.), 1871 (Lovell).

Modern status: Scattered, especially in the St. John's district.

Place name: Breen Point 48-26 53-35.

BREMNER, a surname of Scotland of which the old form was Brabener, a native of Brabant. "Artisans and traders from Braband [a former duchy of the Netherlands, now divided between the Netherlands and Belgium] settled early at Aberdeen and on the east coast of Scotland." (Reaney, Black).

In Newfoundland:

Early instances: Alexander, of Catalina, 1822 (DPHW 70); Alexander, J.P. for northern districts of the Colony, 1834 (*Newfoundlander* 10 Jul 1834), for the district of Trinity Bay, 1844 (*Nfld. Almanac*); W.A., of Hants Harbour, 1842 (DPHW 59); Robert, bookkeeper of Harbour Grace, 1871 (Lovell); Alexander, trader of Trinity, 1871 (Lovell).

Modern status: At St. John's.

BRENNAN, a surname of England and Ireland, in England "'Burn hand,' a nickname for the official who carried out the harsh punishment of medieval law"; in Ireland (O)Brennan, *Ó Braonáin*, Ir. *braon* – ? sorrow, or for (O)Brannan, *Ó Branáin*, or

(Mac)Brannan, *Mac Branáin*, Ir. *bran* – raven. (Reaney, MacLysaght).

Traced by MacLysaght in Ossory and Cos. Galway, Kerry, Meath, Fermanagh and Roscommon.

In Newfoundland:

Family tradition: Catherine (1849–) born at Kilbride (MUN Geog.).

Early instances: Timothy Branen, of Placentia ? district, 1744 (CO 194.24); John Brenan, fined in court at Harbour Main for being a Roman Catholic and servant to Michael Katon, 1755 (MUN Hist.); Laurence Brennan, ? labourer of St. John's, 1779 (CO 194.34); Michael, fisherman of Petty Harbour, 1794–5, "8 years in Newfoundland," that is, 1786–7 (Census 1794–5); John Brennen, from Ross Parish (Co. Wexford), married at St. John's, 1805 (Nfld. Archives BRC); Robert Brennan, of Harbour Grace Parish, 1806 (Nfld. Archives HGRC); Bridget, of Cape Broyle, married at St. John's, 1813 (Nfld. Archives BRC); James, of New Harbour (Trinity B.), 1817 (Nfld. Archives KCRC); Marcella, from Co. Kilkenny, married at Catalina, 1829 (Nfld. Archives KCRC); Mary, of Joe Batts Arm, 1831 (Nfld. Archives KCRC); W., of Harbour Grace, 1832 (*Newfoundlander* 23 Aug 1832); James Brennen, planter of Western Bay, 1843 (DPHW 52A); William Brennan, of Adams Cove, 1851 (DPHW 52A); Richard Brenan, of Indian Arm, 1857 (Nfld. Archives KCRC); Richard Brenen or Brennan, of Trinity, 1859 (Nfld. Archives KCRC); Walter Brennan, farmer of Cuslett, 1871 (Lovell); James, fisherman and Patrick, farmer of Ferryland, 1871 (Lovell); Robert, of Harbour Breton, 1871 (Lovell); Michael Brennon, of Little Placentia (now Argentia), 1871 (Lovell); Edward Brennan, farmer of Ship Cove (Placentia B.), 1871 (Lovell).

Modern status: Widespread, especially at St. John's, Little Paradise and Ship Cove.

Place names: Brennan Point 47-37 53-57; Brennans Hill 47-42 53-14.

BRENNER, a surname of England, from Old French *brenier* – keeper of the hounds, or from Old Norse *brenna* – to burn, hence a burner of lime, bricks or charcoal. (Reaney).

In Newfoundland:

Early instance: Alexander, of Catalina, 1828 (Nfld. Archives KCRC).

Modern status: Rare, at Corner Brook.

BRENNOCK, with ? a Newfoundland variant BRINNOCK, surnames of Scotland (Brenock) and Ireland (Brannock and Brennock), ? from the Welsh place name Brecknock, "a name introduced into Ireland during the time of the Anglo-Norman invasion, and from there introduced into Galloway" (Black). *See also* BRECKON. (Black, MacLysaght).

In Newfoundland:

Early instances: Bridget Brinnik, married in the Northern district (of Colony), 1814 (Nfld. Archives BRC); Bridget Brennick, of Rider's Harbour, 1820 (Nfld. Archives KCRC); Patrick Brinick, from Co. Kilkenny, married at St. John's, 1824 (Nfld. Archives BRC); John, of Careless (now Kerleys) Harbour, 1825 (Nfld. Archives KCRC); Patrick Brin(n)ick, Brinock or Brunnick, of Trinity, 1827 (Nfld. Archives KCRC); P. Brennack, of St. John's, 1832 (*Newfoundlander* 5 Jan 1832); Patrick Brenick, of Tickle Cove (Bonavista B.), 1856 (Nfld. Archives KCRC); Joseph Brennick, of Ship Cove (now part of Port Rexton), 1857 (Nfld. Archives KCRC); John Brennack, farmer of Petty Harbour, 1871 (Lovell); John Brunnock, fisherman of Baline (Bauline) (Conception B.), 1871 (Lovell).

Modern status: Very rare; Brennock, at Petty Harbour Road, St. John's; Brinnock at Port Rexton (*Electors* 1955).

BRENSON, BRINSON, BRINSTON(E), variants of Brimson, a surname of England, from the French place name Briençun (Normandy). (Reaney).

In Newfoundland:

Family tradition: The community of Garden Cove, Placentia Bay, was started when Hedley Brinston (of English descent) and family moved there from Conception Bay, 1875 (MUN Hist.).

Early instances: Thomas ? Brinston, planter of Scilly Cove (now Winterton), 1826 (DPHW 64B); Ann Brinstone, of ? Sibley's Cove, 1849 (DPHW 58); Henry, of Change Islands, 1853 (DPHW 83); Joseph Brinsen, of Gander Bay, 1854 (DPHW 83); Dinah Brinson, of Hants Harbour, 1857 (DPHW 59); Josiah Brinston, of Sound Island (Placentia B.), 1858 (DPHW 105); Joseph and Samuel Brenson, fishermen of Beaver Cove (Twillingate-Fogo district), 1871 (Lovell).

Modern status: Brenson, especially at Newstead (Twillingate district); Brinson, especially at Change Islands, Frederickton (Fogo district) and Loon Bay (Twillingate district); Brinston, at Swift Current, Arnold's Cove and Garden Cove; and Brinstone at Petries and Curling.

BRENT, a surname of England, from the English place names, South Brent (Devon) or East Brent

(Somerset), or (dweller on, in or near the) high, steep or burnt (place). (Reaney, Cottle).

Traced by Spiegelhalter in Devon.

In Newfoundland:

Early instances: George, of Bonavista, 1677 (CO 1); John, of Fair Islands (Bonavista B.), 1681 (CO 1); Thomas, of Swain's Island, 1831 (DPHW 76).

Modern status: At Botwood.

Place names: Brent Cove 47-42 56-20, 49-56 55-43; —— Islands 51-16 55-57; —— Rock 51-15 55-57; —— Cove Head 47-43 56-20, 49-58 55-42; Brent's Cove 49-56 55-43.

BRENTNALL, a surname of England, ? from the English place name Brent Knoll (Devon). (Ekwall).

In Newfoundland:

Modern status: At Dark Cove West (Bonavista B.).

BRENTON, a surname of England, from the English place name Brenton (Devon), or ? a variant of BRINTON. (Ekwall, Guppy).

Traced by Guppy in Cornwall and by Spiegelhalter in Devon.

In Newfoundland:

Early instances: Edward, civil servant and judge of the Supreme Court of Newfoundland, 1826, died 1845 (Prowse); Thomas, of Greenspond, 1829 (DPHW 76); Job, of Swain's Island, born ? 1824, baptized 1830 (DPHW 76); Thomas, fisherman of Mortier Bay, 1860 (DPHW 100); John, fisherman of Burin, 1860 (DPHW 100); William, fisherman of Port au Bras, 1871 (Lovell); James, servant of Rushoon, 1871 (Lovell).

Modern status: Especially in the Burin and White Bay North districts.

BREON, a surname of France, from the French place name Bréon (Mayenne) (Dauzat); likely an anglicized form of the St. Pierre BRIAND (Thomas, "French Fam. Names").

In Newfoundland:

Family tradition: Francois, from France, settled at St. Pierre in the 1850s; he later moved to Fortune (MUN Folklore).

Early instance: Frank, fisherman of Fortune, 1877 (DPHW 106).

Modern status: At Marystown and Grand Bank.

BRETON, a surname of England, France and the Channel Islands, especially Jersey, the Breton – a man from Brittany, or, also in England, the Briton – a Welshman or a Strathclyde Briton. *See also* BRETT. (Reaney, Cottle, Dauzat, Turk).

In Newfoundland:

Early instance: Phillip Le Breton, sailmaker for Newman and Co., Gaultois, 1875. (Newman Papers per D.A. Macdonald).

Modern status: At Point Riche (*Electors* 1955).

Place names: ? Harbour Breton 47-30 55-48, Breton Reef 50-55 57-09.

BRETT, BRITT, surnames of England and Ireland, of the same origin as BRETON. (Reaney).

Brett traced by Guppy in Nottinghamshire and Sussex; by Spiegelhalter in Devon and by Matthews also in Hampshire, Dorset and the Channel Islands; Brett, Britt by MacLysaght mainly in Cos. Waterford, Tipperary and Sligo. "In Ireland since the twelfth century" (MacLysaght).

In Newfoundland:

Family traditions: William Britt (1790–1876), from Christchurch (Hants), settled at Barr'd Islands in the early 19th century (MUN Hist.). ? Samuel Brett from ? Poole (Dorset), settled at Moreton's Harbour about ? 1830 (MUN Folklore), MUN Hist.).

Early instances: Patrick Britt, from Waterford, in Newfoundland, 1773 (*Waterford Arch. & Hist. J.* per Kirwin); William Britt or Brett, of Trinity, 1796, occupier of fishing room there, Winter 1800–01 (Census Trinity B., DPHW 64); John Britt, sergeant in Royal Newfoundland Regiment, 1797 (D'Alberti 6); Patrick, from Waterford, fisherman of Carbonear, 1799, deceased 1813 (CO 199.18, *Royal Gazette* 24 Jun 1813); Thomas, of Rider's Harbour, 1803 (DPHW 64); Thomas, of Kerley's Harbour, 1807 (DPHW 64); John, of Harbour Grace Parish, 1809 (Nfld. Archives HGRC); Anne Brett alias Grenvill, of Quidi Vidi, 1810 (Nfld. Archives BRC); Elizabeth Britt, of Harbour Grace, 1811 (Nfld. Archives BRC); Mary Brite, of Bonavista, 1812 (Nfld. Archives BRC); Margaret Britt, of St. John's, 1814 (Nfld. Archives BRC); James, from Tramore (Co. Waterford), married at St. John's, 1815 (Nfld. Archives BRC); Margaret, of Catalina, 1821 (Nfld. Archives KCRC); William, planter of Joe Batts Arm, 1821 (USPG); Mary, of British Harbour, 1832 (Nfld. Archives KCRC); Mary, of Caplin Cove (Port de Grave), 1834 (*Newfoundlander* 23 Jan 1834); Samuel, of Moreton's Harbour, 1843 (DPHW 86); George, of Cat Harbour (now Lumsden), 1859 (Nfld. Archives KCRC); Elisha, of Lawn, 1871 (Lovell); Edward Brett, planter of Twillingate, 1871 (Lovell).

Modern status: Britt, at St. Andrews; Brett, widespread, especially at St. John's, Joe Batts Arm, Moreton's Harbour and Lewisporte.

BREWER, a surname of England, from Middle English *brewere* – brewer, or from the French place name Bruyère (Calvados). (Reaney).

Guppy found Brewer widespread, especially in Cornwall, Gloucestershire and Monmouth; Spiegelhalter traced it in Devon.

In Newfoundland:

Early instances: Joseph Sr., agent or merchant in Conception Bay, 1784 (D'Alberti 2); James, of St. John's, 1804 (Nfld. Archives BRC); William, from Devon, married at St. John's, 1829 (Nfld. Archives BRC); William, of Newell's Island, 1838 (DPHW 76); Patrick Breuor, of Ship Cove (Trinity B.), 1866 (Nfld. Archives KCRC); Thomas, planter of Bay de East, 1871 (Lovell); Edward Jr., fisherman and Edward Sr., planter of Burin, 1871 (Lovell); James, fisherman of Clattis Harbour, 1871 (Lovell); John Brewers, fisherman of North Bay (French Shore), 1871 (Lovell).

Modern status: At St. John's and dispersed elsewhere, especially Epworth.

Place name: Brewer Island 57-10 61-20.

BREWIN, a rare surname of England, recorded by Bardsley who sees it as a variant of BROWN; but in Newfoundland more probably a variant of the Irish family names (O)Bruen or (O)BREEN, *Ó Braoin*. (MacLysaght).

MacLysaght traced Bruen in Co. Roscommon.

In Newfoundland:

Modern status: Rare, at St. John's.

BRIAN(D), (O)BRIEN, BRYAN(T), surnames, in one or more of the preceding variants, of England, Scotland, Ireland and France, from a Breton personal name containing the element *bri* – height, dignity, esteem (Dauzat, Black), or from a "Keltic (Old Welsh/Irish) name containing the element *bre* – hill" (Cottle), of similar form and significance. *See also* BRYNE. (MacLysaght, Reaney).

As a baptismal name "*Brian* or *Bryan* has from early times been a favourite in Ireland on account of the national hero *Brian Boroimhe*; but it was, during the Middle Ages, equally popular in England... [when] for several centuries it was a favourite, as the many common surnames derived from it testify... It survived in Yorks[hire], Westmorland, Cheshire, Lanc[ashire] until the 18th century, but gradually fell into disuse and came to be regarded as an exclusively Irish name. It is still used in Brittany and has come back into use in England during the present century" (Withycombe).

As a family name in England, Reaney, who gives twelve variants, maintains that in the south it is a Breton personal name introduced by the Normans, and, according to Black, "by Bretons who were among the Normans in the invasion of England," but in the north "it is O[ld] Ir[ish] *Brian*, brought by Norsemen from Ireland...to Cumberland and across the Pennines into Yorkshire."

In Scotland, Black cites the forms Brian, Brien and Bryan, and ascribes the Breton origin to them, as does Dauzat for the French forms Brian, Briand, Briant, Briend.

In Ireland, MacLysaght sees the family O Brien, *Ó Briain* "deriving from the family of King Brian Boru," but notices that O'Brien may also be a synonym of O'Byrne (*see* BYRNE), of Bryan, and of MacBryan, *Mac Braoin*.

Guppy found Bryan widespread, especially in Leicestershire and Rutlandshire and Oxfordshire, Bryant especially in Somerset and Wiltshire. Spiegelhalter traced Brian, Bryan(t) in Devon. Matthews traced Brien, Bryan in Ireland, Devon and Dorset, Briant and Bryant in Devon.

MacLysaght found O'Brien "now very numerous in other provinces as well as Munster, being the fifth most numerous name in Ireland," Bryan "The name of a prominent Anglo-Norman family settled in Co. Kilkenny," and MacBryan, sometimes changed to O'Brien in Cos. Fermanagh and Cavan.

In Newfoundland:

Family traditions: Daniel Bryan (1770–   ), from Burnchurch (Co. Kilkenny) (unidentified), settled at Tilting about 1791 (MUN Folklore). John O'Brien, from Co. Waterford, settled at Cape Broyle in 1793 (MUN Folklore). John (1803–75), from Co. Wexford, settled at Topsail in 1833 (MUN Geog.). Briand at Mainland, from Brittany via St. Pierre (Thomas, "French Fam. Names").

Early instances: Denis Bryen, of Newfoundland, 1730 (CO 194.23); James Bryan, fisherman of ? Fermeuse, 1752 (CO 194.13); Harvey, of St. John's, 1758 (DPHW 26C); Roger, of Bay de Verde, 1774 (CO 199.18); John, of Torbay, 1775 (DPHW 26C); Mary, of St. Mary's, 1780 (D'Alberti 6); John Brien, of Trinity, 1785 (DPHW 64); Cornelius Bryan or Brien, fisherman of Bay Bulls, 1788–91 (CO 194.38); Charles O'Brien, from Rathfriland (Co. Down), Irish convict landed at Petty Harbour or Bay Bulls, 1789 (CO 194.38); William Bryan, of Brigus, 1790 (CO 199.18); William, of Carbonear, 1790 (CO 199.18); John, of Musketta (now Bristol's Hope), 1792 (CO 199.18); Catherine, of Colliers, 1793 (CO 199.18); John, of Western Bay, 1794 (CO 199.18); James, of Placentia, 1794 (D'Alberti 5); Ed Bryant, in possession and occupier of fishing room at Heart's Delight, Winter 1800–01 (Census Trinity B.); Timothy Bryan, of Chapel Cove (Conception B.), 1801 (CO 199.18); James Brien, from Co. Kilkenny, married at King's Cove, 1803 (Nfld. Archives BRC); John Brian or Brine, of Harbour Grace Parish, 1806 (Nfld. Archives HGRC); James Brian, tenant at will of fishing room at Turkish Cove (Keels), 1805 (Bonavista Register 1806); Lambert Bryant, magistrate of Ferryland district, 1812 (D'Alberti 22); Anne Bryan, of Tilton Harbour (now Tilting), 1815 (Nfld. Archives KCRC); William, of Bonavista, 1815 (Nfld. Archives KCRC); John, of Fogo Harbour, 1815 (Nfld. Archives KCRC); Patrick, from Co. Wexford, married at Trinity, 1818 (Nfld. Archives KCRC); Mary, of Keels, 1819 (Nfld. Archives KCRC); Sylvester Brien, from Old Ross (Co. Wexford), married at Fogo Harbour, 1823 (Nfld. Archives KCRC); Timothy Bryan, of Ferryland, 1827 (Nfld. Archives BRC); Anastasia, from Inistioge (Co. Kilkenny), married at Harbour Grace, 1829 (Nfld. Archives BRC); Ellen, of Riders Harbour, 1830 (Nfld. Archives KCRC); Ellen, of Ship Cove (unspecified), 1830 (Nfld. Archives KCRC); Maurice Bryan or Brine, of Broad Cove (now Duntara), 1831 (Nfld. Archives KCRC); James O'Brien, of New Harbour (Trinity B.), 1832 (Nfld. Archives KCRC); Mrs. Brien, of Harbour Grace, 1832 (*Newfoundlander* 23 Aug 1832); Honora O'Brian, of Joe Batts Arm, 1833 (Nfld. Archives KCRC); Mary Brien, of Fermeuse, 1834 (Nfld. Archives BRC); Margaret Bryan, of Trepassey, 1839 (Nfld. Archives BRC); John Brien, ? of Northern Bay, 1839 (DPHW 54); James, of Catalina, 1842 (DPHW 67); Sarah Bryant, ? of Sibleys Cove or of Scilly Cove (now Winterton), 1850 (DPHW 58, 59); Thomas Briant, of Hants Harbour, 1857 (DPHW 52A); Mary Bryan, of Stock Cove (Bonavista B.), 1857 (Nfld. Archives KCRC); John ? Briens, of Indian Arm, 1864 (Nfld. Archives KCRC); Annie O'Brien, schoolteacher of Ram's Islands (Placentia B.), 1871 (Lovell).

Modern status: Brien, especially at St. John's; Bryant, especially at St. John's and Trinity districts; Bryan, especially at Island Harbour (Fogo); Brian, at Low Point (Conception B.), St. Pauls and Grand Falls; Briand at Mainland (Port au Port district); O'Brien, widespread, especially at St. John's, Cape Broyle, Bell Island and Topsail.

Place names: Brians Pond 50-15 57-23; Briens 47-24 53-07; —— Pond 47-23 53-16; Bryan Island 53-16 55-43; Bryans Hole 48-26 54-00; Bryant Islands 59-23 63-33 (Labrador); —— Pond 46-56 55-19; Bryants Cove 47-40 53-11; —— Cove Pond 47-40 53-12.

BRIDAL, ? a Newfoundland variant of the English surname Bridle or Bridel(l), from Old English *bridel* – maker of) bridle(s). *See also* BROYDELL. (Reaney).

Matthews traced Bridle, Bridall as captains at Poole and Weymouth (Dorset).

In Newfoundland:

Early instances: William Bridel, married at St. John's, 1807 (Nfld. Archives BRC); John Bridle, of Carbonear, 1811 (DPHW 48); Nicholas, of St. John's, 1840 (DPHW 26B); George, of Greenspond, 1871 (Lovell); Charles, of St. Jacques, 1871 (Lovell).

Modern status: At Brooklyn (Bonavista B.)

BRIDGEMAN, a surname of England and Ireland, the dweller by or keeper of the bridge. In Ireland it is associated with (O)Drought, "an anglicization of two Irish names, *Ó Drochtaigh* of Leinster, and *Ó Droichid* (from *droichead* – bridge) of Cos. Limerick and Clare, now usually made Bridgeman." (Reaney, MacLysaght). *See also* BRIDGER, BURGE.

Traced by Guppy as Bridgman in Devon.

In Newfoundland:

Early instances: Richard, of St. John's, 1780 (D'Alberti 6); Patrick Bridgman, of Kings Cove, 1822 (Nfld. Archives KCRC); Samuel Bridgeman, native of Newton Abbot (Devon), of St. John's, deceased, 1858, aged 58 (*Newfoundlander* 13 Aug 1857, General Protestant Cemetery, St. John's); Patrick Bridg(e)man, of Black Island (Bonavista B.), 1850, of Shole's Cove (unspecified), 1856, of Dog Cove (Bonavista B.), 1858, of Gooseberry Island (Bonavista B.), 1862, of Cottells Island, 1869 (Nfld. Archives KCRC); Patrick, planter of Shoal Harbour (Bonavista B.), 1871 (Lovell).

Modern status: At St. Brendans.

BRIDGER, a surname of England, the dweller by or keeper of the bridge. *See also* BRIDGEMAN, BURGE. (Reaney, Cottle).

Traced by Guppy in Hampshire and Sussex and by Spiegelhalter in Devon.

In Newfoundland:

Family traditions: James, from Ireland settled at Twillingate in the late 19th century (Family). Sarah (1859–1901), born at Ship Cove (now part of Port Rexton) (MUN Geog.).

Early instances: William, planter of Twillingate, 1817 (USPG); John, fisherman of Herring Neck, 1850, of Salt Harbour, 1851 (DPHW 85); James, fisherman of Change Islands, 1852, of Hall's Bay, 1854 (DPHW 83, 86).

Modern status: Especially at Brighton (Green B.) and Paradise (Twillingate district).

(O)BRIEN. *See* BRIAN(D)

BRIFFETT, ? a Newfoundland variant of surnames of England and France, for the English surname Breffitt, a variant of Brevetor, from the Old French, Middle English *brevet* – (the bearer of) "'an official or authoritative message in writing' especially Papal indulgences" (Reaney), or, obscurely by Weekley as (dweller at the) brae foot; or ? for the French surnames Brefort, Breffort, a nickname for a short man, or ? for Brif(f)aud, Briffault, a nickname for a glutton (Dauzat).

In Newfoundland:

Family traditions: Augustus Jean Briffett came from St. Malo as a stowaway to Harbour Grace, whence he moved to Greenspond, Bloody Bay (now Glovertown, Alexander Bay) and Flippers Cove (now ? Rosedale, Alexander Bay) (MUN Folklore). Eloil Briffett is said to have settled at Bryant's Cove by 1869 where the family remained until 1935 when they moved to Boston, Mass. (MUN Hist.).

Early instances: A[u]gustus John Brifet, of Greenspond, 1856 (DPHW 76); Augustus Breffit, fisherman of Bloody Bay, 1871 (Lovell); Leval Briffett, fisherman of Bryant's Cove, 1871 (Lovell).

Modern status: Especially in the Bonavista North district.

BRIGHT, a surname of England, from Old English *beorht* – bright, beautiful, fair. *See also* BURT. (Reaney).

Found widespread by Guppy, especially in Shropshire, Essex, South Wales and Hampshire, and by Spiegelhalter in Devon.

In Newfoundland:

Early instances: Thomas, of St. John's, 1766 (DPHW 26C); Francis, of Bonavista, 1792 (USPG); Martin, of Hants Harbour, 1851 (DPHW 59); Jasper, fisherman of Carbonear, 1854 (DPHW 49); Sarah, of Catalina, 1860 (DPHW 67); Benjamin, fisherman of Heart's Delight, 1871 (Lovell); Jasper, fisherman of Victoria, 1871 (Lovell).

Modern status: Rare.

BRIEN. *See* BRYNE

BRINNOCK. *See* BRENNOCK

BRINSON, BRINSTON(E). *See* BRENSON

BRINTON, a surname of England and Scotland, from the English place name Brinton (Norfolk), or ? a variant of BRENTON; in Scotland, from an unidentified place name Brinton (Bardsley, Black).

Traced by Matthews as captains in Dorset and Devon.

In Newfoundland:

Family tradition: Andrew and family, of Moreton's Harbour, about 1840–60 (MUN Hist.).

Early instances: Thomas, of Burin, 1805 (D'Alberti 15); Richard, fisherman of Port au Bras, 1860 (DPHW 100); William, fisherman of Burin, 1871 (Lovell).

Modern status: Especially at Norris Arm and Marystown South.

BRITT. *See* BRETT

BROADBENT, a surname of England, (dweller by the) broad grassy plain. (Reaney).

Traced by Guppy in Yorkshire WR.

In Newfoundland:

Modern status: Rare, at Corner Brook.

BRO(A)DERS, Broder in MacLysaght, surnames of Ireland, *Ó Bruadair,* "from a Norse forename" (MacLysaght). *See also* BRODERICK and BROTHERS.

Traced by MacLysaght in Cos. Cork and Kilkenny.

In Newfoundland:

Early instances: Jane Broders married in Newfoundland about 1759 (St. Patrick's Parish Records, Waterford, per Kirwin); John Broaders, of Bay de Verde, 1793 (CO 199.18); Daniel Browders, proprietor and occupier of fishing room at Grates Cove, Winter 1800–01 (Census Trinity B.); William Bro(a)ders, planter of Fogo, 1805 (D'Alberti 15); Thomas Broders, of Harbour Grace Parish, 1814 (Nfld. Archives HGRC); William, of Tilton Harbour (now Tilting), 1819 (Nfld. Archives KCRC); Bridget Brawders, from Toads (now Tors) Cove, married at St. John's, 1820 (Nfld. Archives BRC); Jeremiah Broders, of Trinity, 1820 (Nfld. Archives KCRC); Michael, of Riders Harbour, 1820 (Nfld. Archives KCRC); James Broders or Browders, of Hearts Content, 1825 (Nfld. Archives KCRC); William Broders, from Youghal (Co. Cork), of Kings Cove, 1826 (Nfld. Archives KCRC); Thomas Brawders, of Broad Cove (? now Duntara), 1829 (Nfld. Archives KCRC); —— Broders, of Cape Cove (Bonavista B.), 1829 (Nfld. Archives KCRC); Thomas, ? of Northern Bay, 1838 (DPHW 54); David Brawders, of Greenspond, 1849, Haywards Cove (Bonavista B.), 1857 (Nfld. Archives KCRC); David, of Black Island (Bonavista B.), 1850 (Nfld. Archives KCRC); Daniel Broaders or Brawders, of Cottles Island (Bonavista B.), 1859, of Shoels Cove (unspecified), 1863 (Nfld.

Archives KCRC); Elizabeth Broders, of Harbour
Grace, 1870 (Nfld. Archives HGRC); John Broaders,
fisherman of Point Verde (Placentia B.), 1871
(Lovell).

Modern status: Broders, at Tilting, Fogo;
Broaders, at St. John's and Bay de Verde.

BROCKERVILLE, a Newfoundland variant of the
surname of France, Brocquevielle. (Dauzat).
In Newfoundland:
Modern status: At Lawn.

BROCKIE, a surname of Scotland, of uncertain
origin. (Black).
In Newfoundland:
Modern status: Rare, at Buchans.

BROCKLEHURST, a surname of England from the
English place name Brocklehurst (Lancashire) – the
badger hole in the wood. (A. H. Smith).
Traced by Guppy in Cheshire and Derbyshire.
In Newfoundland:
Early instance: Charles B., accountant of St.
John's, 1871 (Lovell).
Modern status: At St. John's.

BROCKWAY, a surname of England, (dweller by
the) road near the brook. (Reaney).
Traced by Matthews as captains at Poole
(Dorset).
In Newfoundland:
Early instances: William, of Greenspond,
baptized 1830, aged 21 (DPHW 76); Henry, fisherman
of Burnt Island, Burgeo, 1871 (Lovell).
Modern status: At Benoits Cove, Curling and
Corner Brook.

BROD(E)RICK, surnames of England and Ireland, in
England ? from the personal name *Baldric*, from Old
German *Baldarich*, containing the elements *balda* –
bold and *ricja* – rule, "introduced into England at the
time of the Norman Conquest" (Withycombe); in
Ireland, *Ó Bruadair*, "from a Norse forename"
(MacLysaght). *See also* BROADERS and BROTHERS.
(Bardsley, MacLysaght).
Traced by Matthews as captains in Dorset, Devon
and Cornwall; by MacLysaght in Cos. Cork and
Kilkenny.
In Newfoundland:
Family tradition: John (1832–1894), of
Freshwater (Carbonear) (MUN Geog.).
Early instances: Andrew Broderick, of St. John's,
17S1 (DPHW 26C); William, of Lower Island Cove,

1802 (CO 199.18); William Brod(e)rick, of Harbour
Grace Parish, 1806 (Nfld. Archives HGRC); Samuel
Broderick, of Grates Cove, 1819 (Nfld. Archives
BRC); James Broderick or Brawdrick, of Kings
Cove, 1819 (Nfld. Archives KCRC); Anistasia [sic]
Bro(a)d(e)rick, of Cape Cove (Bonavista B.), 1831
(Nfld. Archives KCRC); William Broderick, ? of
Northern Bay, 1840 (DPHW 54); Catherine, of
Harbour Grace, 1867 (Nfld. Archives HGRC).
Modern status: Especially at St. John's, Grates
Cove, St. Brendans and Freshwater (Carbonear).

BRODERS. *See* BROADERS

BRODIE, BRODY, surnames of Scotland and Ireland
from the Scots place name Brodie (Moray) or for the
Irish surname (O)Brollaghan, *Ó Brollacháin*, "from
Brollach, an Old Irish personal name presumably
derived from *brollach* – breast." (MacLysaght).
(Reaney, Black).
Black found Brodie "long located in the province
of Moray," and Guppy traced it in Northumberland
and south of the Forth and Clyde. MacLysaght
found (O)Brallaghan mainly in Cos. Derry, Tyrone
and Donegal.
In Newfoundland:
Early instance: Peter McBride Brodie, of St.
John's, 1852 (DPHW 26D).
Modern status: Brodie, rare, at St. John's; Brody,
rare, at St. John's (*Electors* 1955).

BRODRICK. *See* BRODERICK

BRODY. *See* BRODIE

BROGAN, a surname of Ireland, *Ó Brógáin*, of un-
certain origin. (MacLysaght).
Traced by MacLysaght in North Connacht.
In Newfoundland:
Modern status: Rare, at St. John's.

BROKENSHIRE, one of Reaney's 23 variants of the
surname of England, Birkenshaw, from the place
name Birkenshaw (Yorkshire WR).
Traced, as Brokenshire, by Spiegelhalter in
Devon; as Birkinshaw or Burkinshaw by Guppy in
Lincolnshire and Yorkshire WR.
In Newfoundland:
Early instance: Mark Brokenshire, of Brigus,
1818 (Nfld. Archives L165).
Modern status: Rare, at St. John's, from Ontario,
since 1967.

BROMLEY, a surname of England, from the English place names Bromley (Essex, Hertfordshire, Kent, Staffordshire) or Bremley or Brimley (Devon). (Reaney).

Traced by Guppy in Essex, Northamptonshire and Shropshire, by Spiegelhalter in Devon.

In Newfoundland:

Family tradition: John Bromley, ? of Welsh descent, came to Conche from "Conche in Marne," that is, Conches (Eure), in the early 19th century (MUN Geog.).

Early instances: Patrick, shoreman of St. John's, 1794–5, "22 years in Newfoundland," that is, since 1772–3 (Census 1794–5); John Bromly, married on the French Shore, 1839 (Nfld. Archives BRC); James, of Durrell's Arm, 1861 (DPHW 88); John, fisherman of Conche, 1871 (Lovell); Henry (and others), fishermen of Pistolet, 1871 (Lovell).

Modern status: At St. John's and in the White Bay North district.

BROOK(E)(S), surnames of England, Scotland and Ireland, from the English place name Brook (Kent, Rutland) or Brooke (Norfolk), or (dweller near a) stream or water-meadow. (Reaney, Cottle, Black, MacLysaght, Guppy).

All forms are widespread south of Cheshire-Lincolnshire; Brooke in Ulster since the sixteenth century.

In Newfoundland:

Early instances: Richard Brookes, boatkeeper of Bay Bulls, 1681 (CO 1); Thomas Brooks, of St. John's, 1705 (CO 194.22); Phillip, of Hants Harbour, 1708–09 (CO 194.4); Robert, of St. Mary's, 1720 (D'Alberti 7); Benjamin, operator of salmon fishery at Twillingate, 1808 (CO 194.48); Samuel, of Trinity (Trinity B.), 1833 (DPHW 64B); Thomas, fisherman of Ward's Harbour, 1871 (Lovell).

Modern status: Somewhat rare and scattered.

Place names (not necessarily from the surname): Brook Harbour 49-22 55-14; —— Point 47-29 55-47, 49-06 58-23; Brookes Point 49-45 54-10.

BROOKING(S), surnames of England – dweller by the brook.

Traced by Guppy and Spiegelhalter in Devon.

In Newfoundland:

Early instances: Arthur Holdsworth Brooking, of St. John's, 1803 (D'Alberti 13); Robert, surrogate for Trinity district, 1816 (CO 194.57); Richard Brooking(s), planter of Old Perlican, 1835 (DPHW 58); Augustus Brooking, fisherman of Bay of

Islands, 1871 (Lovell); Edward, fisherman of Bloody Bay (now Alexander Bay), 1871 (Lovell).

Modern status: Brooking, scattered, especially at Petley; Brookings, especially at Old Perlican.

BROOKS. *See* BROOK(E)(S)

BROOMFIELD, a surname of England and Scotland, from the English place name Broomfield (Essex, Kent, Somerset) or Bromfield (Cambridgeshire, Shropshire) or a common place name in Scotland, or (dweller near the) broom-covered open-land. (Reaney). *See also* BLOOMFIELD.

Traced by Guppy in Hampshire and by Spiegelhalter in Devon.

In Newfoundland:

Early instances: James, of Salmon Cove (now Champneys), 1787 (DPHW 64); William, apprentice of Battle Harbour (Labrador), 1795 (MUN Hist.); John, of St. John's, 1815 (DPHW 26B); Anne Brumfield, from St. John's, married at King's Cove, 1821 (Nfld. Archives KCRC); Thomas, of Castle Cove (Bonavista B.), 1837, of Keels, 1842 (DPHW 73); Stephen, of Dog Cove (Bonavista B.), 1850, of Hayward's Cove, 1857 (Nfld. Archives KCRC); John Bro(o)mfield, of Cottells Island, 1870, of Dock Cove (Cottells Island), 1872 (Nfld. Archives KCRC); Thomas Broomfield, of Flat Island (Burin district), 1873 (DPHW 105).

Modern status: At St. John's, Port Elizabeth and St. Brendan's.

Place name: Broomfield Island (Labrador) 54-13 58-14.

BROPHY, a surname of Ireland *Ó Bróithe*, of obscure origin.

Traced by MacLysaght in mid-Leinster.

In Newfoundland:

Early instances: John, publican of St. John's, 1794–5, "25 years in Newfoundland," that is, 1769–70 (Census 1794–5); Daniel, from Castlecorner (for Castlecomer) (Co. Kilkenny), married at St. John's, 1801 (Nfld. Archives BRC); Mary, married at Harbour Grace Parish, 1816 (Nfld. Archives HGRC), John, from Thurles (Co. Tipperary), married at Ragged Harbour (now Melrose), 1819 (Nfld. Archives KCRC); John, of Bonavista, 1828 (Nfld. Archives KCRC); John and Matthew, fishermen of Fermeuse, 1871 (Lovell); Patrick, farmer of Goulds Road (Brigus district), 1871 (Lovell); Stephen, of Witless Bay, 1871 (Lovell); John, of Daniel's Harbour, 1873 (MUN Hist.).

Modern status: Especially at Riverhead (Fermeuse), Daniel's Harbour, St. John's and Harbour Main district.

BROTHERS, a surname of England and Ireland; in England from Old English *brothor* – brother, "used in M[iddle] E[nglish] of a kinsman and a fellow member of a guild or corporation"; in Ireland, *Ó Bruadair*, "from a Norse forename" (MacLysaght). *See also* BROADERS and BRODERICK. (Reaney, MacLysaght).

Traced by Spiegelhalter in Devon and by MacLysaght in Cos. Cork and Kilkenny.

In Newfoundland:

Early instances: Richard Brothers (1757–1824), born at Placentia, an enthusiast (*DNB*); Thomas Broathers, of St. John's, 1797 (D'Alberti 6); Michael and James Brothers, of Fermeuse, 1797 (D'Alberti 7); Thomas, of Harbour Grace Parish, 1806 (Nfld. Archives HGRC); Joanna, of Harbour Grace, 1869 (Nfld. Archives HGRC); Anthony and James, fishermen of Toads (now Tors) Cove, 1871 (Lovell).

Modern status: Especially at Admirals (Fermeuse) and Groais Islands.

Place name: Brothers Island 49-32 54-17.

BROUGHTON, a surname of England and the Channel Islands, from a common English place name, or (dweller at the) place on the brook, or hill, or the farm or enclosure near a fort or manorhouse. (Ekwall, Cottle, Turk).

Traced by Guppy in Lincolnshire and by Spiegelhalter in Devon.

In Newfoundland:

Modern status: Rare, at Brigus.

BROWN(E), surnames of England, Scotland and Ireland, Brown of the Channel Islands, from an Old English personal name *Brūn*, or from Old English or Old French for one with brown hair or complexion; or, in Scotland, for *Mac a'Chriuthainn* from Gaelic *briteamh(ain)* – brehon, breive, judge, or for *M'Ille dhuinn* – son of the brown lad. (Reaney, Cottle, Black, MacLysaght, Turk).

In England, the form Browne tends to indicate "a rise in the social scale," (Guppy, Cottle), but it is the usual form in Ireland.

Widespread in England, Scotland and Ireland.

In Newfoundland:

Family traditions: Patrick Browne came from Kilkenny to Sound Island about 1820 (MUN Folklore). Henry Smith, of Jersey (Channel Islands), changed his name to Brown after deserting from HMS

Renown in Burin Harbour and settled in Rock Harbour (MUN Folklore). ——, from England, settled at Cow Head (St. Barbe) in the 1850s (MUN Folklore).

Early instances: Andrew Brown, of Toads (now Tors) Cove, 1676 (CO 1); John Browne, of Petty Harbour, 1677, 1682 (CO 1); John Brown, inhabitant of Newfoundland, 1704 (CO 194.3); Madam, of St. John's, 1720–45 (B.M. Carew); Edward, of Placentia, 1725 (CO 194.8); 1725 (CO 194.8); William, ? of Harbour Main, 1750 (CO 194.12); John, of Quidi Vidi Cove, 1771 (CO 194.18, 30); John and Richard, of Fogo, Twillingate or Tilton (now Tilting), 1771 (CO 194.30); John, of Great Belle Isle (now Bell Island), 1771 (DPHW 26C); William, of Bay Bulls, 1786 (DPHW 26C); Hugh W.B., fisherman of Port de Grave, 1789 (Nfld. Archives T22); William, J.P. of Bonavista, 1791 (USPG); John, of Kerleys Harbour, 1794 (DPHW 64); John, from Tintern (Co. Wexford), married at St. John's, 1797 (Nfld. Archives BRC); William, of Harbour Grace, 1799 (CO 199.18); John, J.P. of Mortier, 1800 (D'Alberti 11); Ann, proprietor and occupier of fishing room at Trinity (Trinity B.), Winter 1800–01 (Census Trinity B.); Robert, of Mint Cove (Spaniards B.), 1803 (CO 199.18); Nicholas and William, of Fogo, 1803 (D'Alberti 13); William, from Poole (Dorset), of King's Cove, 1804 (Bonavista Register 1806); James, of Burin, 1805 (D'Alberti 15); Richard, of Trouty, 1812 (DPHW 64); Henry, of Greenspond, 1815 (DPHW 76); William, planter of Bailey's Cove, 1817 (DPHW 72); Ann, of Joe Batts Arm, 1821 (USPG); Henry, fisherman of Old Perlican, 1822 (DPHW 58); Michael Browne, of Gooseberry Island (Bonavista B.), 1825 (Nfld. Archives KCRC); Honora Brown, of Carbonear, 1829 (Nfld. Archives BRC); A., of Tilting Harbour (now Tilting), 1829 (Nfld. Archives KCRC); Henry, of Salvage, 1830 (DPHW 76); Thomas, baptized at Pool's Island, 1830, aged 18 (DPHW 76); Mary, baptized at Vere (now Fair) Island, 1830, aged 18 (DPHW 76); ——, of Brigus, 1831 (*Newfoundlander* 24 Nov 1831); Peter, of Bird Island [Cove] (now Elliston), 1832 (Nfld. Archives KCRC); William, of Cat Harbour (now Lumsden), 1832 (DPHW 76); Henry, of Lance Cove (now Brownsdale), 1833 (DPHW 58); Elizabeth, of Chapels Cove (? Conception B.), 1835 (Nfld. Archives BRC); Marianne, born at Paddy Pond [Poor's] Cove, baptized at Haystack (Long Island, Placentia B.), 1836 (DPHW 30); George H., from Montgomery, Wales, Lieut. in Nfld. Veteran Company, died 1837 (*Nfld. Patriot* 27 May 1837); John, of Catalina, 1838 (DPHW 67); Henry, ? of

Northern Bay, 1841 (DPHW 54); Joseph, planter of Norman's Cove, 1842 (DPHW 72); Joseph, fisherman of Grole, 1846 (DPHW 102); John, fisherman of Stone Harbour, 1852 (DPHW 85); Samuel, of Dog Cove (Bonavista B.), 1854, of Hayward's Cove, 1857 (Nfld. Archives KCRC); John, fisherman of Smith Sound, 1855 (DPHW 64B); George, lighthouse keeper at Point of Beach, 1856 (*Newfoundlander* 23 Oct 1856); James Browne, of Sound Island (Placentia B.), deceased 1856 (*Newfoundlander* 21 Aug 1856); Alexander D. Brown, born at Dundee, 1855, to St. John's, 1877 (Mott); George, of Mose Ambrose, 1857 (DPHW 104); Rachel, of Herring Neck, 1857 (DPHW 85); John, fisherman of Thoroughfare, 1858 (DPHW 64B); James, fisherman of Green Cove (Twillingate), 1859 (DPHW 85); John, Of Rose Blanche, 1860 (DPHW 99); James, fisherman of Burin Bay, 1861 (DPHW 108); Jane Browne, of Indian Arm, 1865 (Nfld. Archives KCRC); Joseph Brown, of Western Head (Pistolet B.), 1867 (DPHW 94); Luke (1797–1869), from Wexford, died at Ferryland (Dillon); Charles, of Redbrook (St. George's B.), 1870 (DPHW 96).

Modern status: Brown, widespread; Browne, especially at St. John's.

Place names (not necessarily from the surname): Brown Cove 47-02 55-11, 47-39 58-22, 47-40 58-36; —— Harbour 47-16 55-19; —— Head 47-39 54-19; —— Islands 48-57 53-31; —— Islet (Labrador) 55-22 59-52; —— Lookout 47-20 55-13; —— Mead 48-10 53-57; —— Shoal 50-11 57-38; —— Cove Point 47-40 58-37; Brown's Arm 49-16 55-10; —— Cove 49-38 56-49; —— Island 49-07 53-35; —— Neck 52-58 55-53; —— Pond 49-15 57-36, 49-37 56-05; —— Cove Barrens 49-38 56-53; Brownsdale 48-02 53-07; —— Cove 48-02 53-07; Browns Store House 49-09 53-31; Brown Store Islet 48-43 53-44.

BROWNRIGG, a surname of England, Ireland and Scotland, from the English place name Brownrigg (Cumberland), or (dweller on the) brown ridge. (A.H. Smith, Bardsley, MacLysaght).

In Newfoundland:
Early instance: John, of St. John's, 1829 (DPHW 26D).
Modern status: Rare, at St. John's and Corner Brook.

BROYDELL, ? a surname of England, of unknown origin, unless ? a variant of BRIDAL.
Traced in Liverpool, England.

In Newfoundland:
Family tradition: Harry from Liverpool, England, settled in Newfoundland in 1845 (MUN Folklore).
Modern status: In the Burin district.

BRUCE, a surname of England, Scotland and Ireland, from a French place name ? Briouze (Orne) or ? Le Brus (Calvados). (Reaney, Cottle).

Traced by Guppy in Durham and in much of Scotland except the north; by Spiegelhalter and Matthews in Devon; and by MacLysaght in Ulster since the early 18th century and in Co. Cork previously.

In Newfoundland:
Family tradition: ——, from France, settled on the west coast (MUN Folklore).
Early instances: William, J.P. at Placentia, 1753 (CO 194.13); Robert, of St. John's, 1758 (DPHW 26C); Jane, of Quidi Vidi, 1836 (DPHW 26D); Edward and William, fishermen of Long Harbour (Placentia B.), 1871 (Lovell); Daniel (and others), of Rams Island (Placentia B.), 1871 (Lovell).

Modern status: At St. John's, and in the Placentia East, Port au Port districts.

Place names (not necessarily from the surname): Bruce Cove (Labrador) 52-22 55-59; —— Lake (Labrador) 53-16 66-50; —— Pond 47-47 53-18, 48-20 55-34; —— Cove Rock 48-45 53-49; —— Pond Gully 47-47 53-18.

BRUFF, phonetic variant of Brough, a surname of England and Scotland, from the English place name Brough (Derbyshire, Nottinghamshire, Westmorland, Yorkshire ER and NR). "All ancient camps (Old English *burg*) usually Roman, and pronounced *Bruff* or *Broof*" (Reaney); or, in Scotland, also from place names Overbrough and Netherbrough. (Reaney, Black).

Traced by Guppy in Derbyshire and Staffordshire; by Black in the Orkneys and Perthshire.

In Newfoundland:
Early instance: Isaac, fisherman of Cape Broyle, 1871 (Lovell).
Modern status: Rare, at St. John's and in the Ferryland district.

BRUMSEY, a surname ? of England, ? from an unidentified English place name.
In Newfoundland:
Modern status: Rare, at Stephenville.

BRUSHETT, a surname of England, from *brush* – broom, undergrowth, heather and – *ett* – head, a nickname. In France the surname Br(o)usset, denotes one who makes bundles of firewood or who lives in a locality so named from the prevalence of undergrowth, brushwood, bushes. (Weekley *Surnames*, Dauzat).

In Newfoundland:

Early instances: George Brushet, of Bonavista, 1792 (USPG); George, planter of Catalina, 1843 (DPHW 72); John Brussell (? for Brushett), labourer of Gaultois, 1852 (DPHW 104); George and others Brushett, of Burin, 1871 (Lovell); John, fisherman of Port au Bras, 1871 (Lovell).

Modern status: Especially in the Placentia West, Burin, Fortune Bay and Hermitage districts.

BRYAN(T). *See* BRIAN

BRYNE, or Brine, ? variants of BRIAN, BRIEN, etc. and BYRNE.

Guppy traced Brine in Dorset, Matthews also in Devon.

In Newfoundland:

Early instances: John Brine, fisherman of St. John's, 1794–5, "30 years in Newfoundland," that is, 1764–5 (Census 1794–5); John, of Trinity Bay, 1777 (DPHW 64); Timothy Bryne, from Mountrath (Queen's Co. now Co. Leix) and John, from Co. Dublin, Irish convicts landed at Petty Harbour or Bay Bulls in 1789 (CO 194.38); Robert Brine, butcher of Quidi Vidi, 1794–5 (Census 1794–5); Robert, butcher of Bell Island, 1794–5 (Census 1794–5); John, of Trinity, 1795 (DPHW 64); Robert, of Bonavista, 1814 (DPHW 70); Mary, of Kings Cove, 1816 (Nfld. Archives KCRC); William, of Greenspond, 1817 (Nfld. Archives KCRC); Margaret, of Tilton Harbour (now Tilting), 1817 (Nfld. Archives KCRC); William, of Fogo, 1817 (Nfld. Archives KCRC); William, of Joe Batts Arm, 1817 (Nfld. Archives KCRC); James, from Old Ross (Co. Wexford), 1818 (Nfld. Archives BRC); Patrick, of Ship Cove (now part of Port Rexton), 1819 (DPHW 64); Maurice Brine or Bryan, of Broad Cove (now Duntara), 1820 (Nfld. Archives KCRC); Daniel Brine, of Harbour Grace Parish, 1821 (Nfld. Archives HGRC); Robert, of Catalina, 1822 (DPHW 70); Anne, of Logy Bay, 1823 (Nfld. Archives BRC); Juliana, of Fortune Harbour, 1830 (Nfld. Archives KCRC); James, of Harbour Grace, 1831 (Nfld. Archives HGRC); John, planter of Salmon Cove (now Champneys), 1837 (DPHW 64B); James, of Greenspond, 1846 (DPHW 26D); Elizabeth, of Hearts Ease, 1855 (Nfld. Archives KCRC); Mary, of Tickle Cove (Bonavista B.), 1860 (Nfld. Archives KCRC); Sarah, of

Heart's Content, 1860 (DPHW 26D); William, of Bluff Head Cove, 1861 (DPHW 88).

Modern status: Brine, at Catalina, but elsewhere apparently replaced especially by Brien.

Place name: ? Brine Islands 47-27 53-57.

BUCHANAN, a surname of Scotland and Ireland, from the Scots place name Buchanan (Stirlingshire). (Cottle, Black).

Traced by Guppy in the Glasgow district and by MacLysaght in Ulster.

In Newfoundland:

Early instances: Thomas, of Placentia, about 1730–35 (CO 194.9); Archibald, J.P. of St. John's, 1789–98 (CO 194.41, 42); George, merchant of Trinity (Trinity B.), died 1834 (*Newfoundlander* 25 Dec 1834); Arthur, doctor at Heart's Content, 1871 (Lovell).

Modern status: Rare, at St. John's.

BUCK, a surname of England and Scotland, from Old English *bucca* – he-goat or *bucc* – stag, a nickname, or for a dealer in venison or a goat-herd, or from Old English *bōc* – (dweller by the) beech-tree. (Reaney, Cottle, Black).

Traced by Guppy in Norfolk, Suffolk and Nottinghamshire; by Spiegelhalter in Devon and by Matthews also in Dorset.

In Newfoundland:

Early instances: Edward, ? servant of Little Placentia (now Argentia), about 1730–35 (CO 194.9); Nicholas, of Harbour Grace Parish, 1821 (Nfld. Archives HGRC); James, planter, John, Patrick and Robert, farmers of Cats Cove (now Conception Harbour), 1871 (Lovell).

Modern status: Rare, at Conception Harbour, Port Union (*Electors* 1955) and St. John's.

Place name: ? Buck Head 49-14 58-09.

BUCKINGHAM, a surname of England from the English place name Buckingham (Buckinghamshire). (Spiegelhalter).

Traced by Guppy in Devon, Oxfordshire and Suffolk.

In Newfoundland:

Early instances: Mary, of Carbonear, 1775 (CO 199.18); John, appointed magistrate for Conception Bay district, 1817 (D'Alberti 27), J.P. of Carbonear, 1831 (*Newfoundlander* 20 Oct 1831), of the Northern district, 1834 (*Newfoundlander* 10 Jul 1834); John, of Bareneed, 1871 (Lovell).

Modern status: At St. John's and Corner Brook.

BUCKLAND, a surname of England, from an English place name Buckland, that is, book-land, land held by charter, which occurs thirteen times in Devon. (Bardsley, Cottle).

Traced by Spiegelhalter in Devon.

In Newfoundland:

Early instances: William, of Lower Burgeo, 1857 (DPHW 101); Stephen, planter of Harbour Le Cou, 1871 (Lovell); George, fisherman of Mouse Island, 1871 (Lovell); William, fisherman of Ramea Islands, 1871 (Lovell).

Modern status: At Harbour Le Cou (*Electors* 1955) and Burgeo.

BUCKLE, a surname of England and Scotland; in England from Middle English *bokel* – (a maker of) buckle(s); in Scotland from an unidentified place name. (Reaney, Black).

In Newfoundland:

Family tradition: William Buckle, from Lance au Clair (Labrador), moved to Ancher Point, and thence, after his marriage, to Buckle's Point (St. Margaret's Bay). The Buckles of Forteau (Labrador) are said to be his descendants (MUN Hist.).

Early instances: ——, planter of Fogo, 1792 (MUN Hist.); Thomas, of St. John's, ? 1821 (CO 194.64).

Modern status: Scattered, especially at St. John's and Corner Brook.

Place name: ? Buckle Cove (Labrador) 51-43 56-26.

BUCKLER, a surname of England and Scotland, from Old French *bouclier* – maker of buckles, or (fencer with a) buckler – a small round shield worn on the arm. (Reaney, Cottle, Black).

In Newfoundland:

Early instances: William, of Bonavista, 1681 (CO 1); John, of Northern Bay, 1802 (CO 199.18); William, planter of Heart's Delight, 1827, of Seal Cove (now New Chelsea), 1829 (DPHW 59A); Johanna, of Grates Cove, 1844 (DPHW 58); Susan, of Hants Harbour, 1853 (DPHW 59); John (and others),of St. John's, 1871 (Lovell).

Modern status: Rare, at Northern Bay.

BUCKLEY, a surname of England and Ireland, from the English place name Buckley (Somerset, Devon) or Buckleigh (Devon), or (dweller by the) buck clearing; or in Ireland for *Ó Buachalla,* Ir. *buachaill* – boy. (Cottle, MacLysaght).

Traced by Guppy in Cheshire, Derbyshire, Lancashire, Staffordshire, Worcestershire and Yorkshire WR; by Spiegelhalter in Devon, and by MacLysaght in Cos. Cork and Tipperary.

In Newfoundland:

Early instances: William, of Little Harbour (Bonavista B.), 1676 (CO 1); Timothy, lessee of land in the vicinity of St. John's, 1803–05 (CO 194.45); Daniel Buckly, of Harbour Grace Parish, 1809 (Nfld. Archives HGRC); Laurence Buckley, from Fethard (Co. Tipperary), married at St. John's, 1816 (Nfld. Archives BRC); Ellen Buckly, of Brigus by South, 1827 (Nfld. Archives BRC); William, native of Queen's Co. (now Co. Leix), of St. John's, deceased, 1839, aged 36 (*Newfoundlander* 28 Nov 1839, *Times* 27 Nov 1839).

Modern status: At Corner Brook, Buchans, Botwood and St. John's.

Place names: Buckley Cove and Point 48-35 53-55; —— Cove Ponds 48-36 53-54.

BUCKMASTER, a surname of England and ? Ireland from the English place name Buckminster (Leicestershire). (Reaney, Cottle).

Traced by Guppy in Bedfordshire. Two in Dublin Telephone Directory.

In Newfoundland:

Early instance: Pat, butcher of St. John's, 1871 (Lovell).

Modern status: Rare, at St. John's.

Place name: Buckmaster's Field (St. John's).

BUCKWELL, a surname of England and ? Ireland, from the English place name Buckwell (Kent, Sussex). (Reaney Notes).

Traced in London, Nottingham, Dublin and Arklow (Co. Wicklow).

In Newfoundland:

Modern status: Unique, at St. John's.

BUDDEN, a surname of England and ? Scotland; in England ? from the baptismal name Baldwin (*see* BALDWIN), or ? (dweller at the) bottom (of a valley or bay); in Scotland from the Scots place name Budden (Angus). (Weekley *Surnames,* Reaney Notes).

Traced by Guppy in Dorset and Hampshire.

In Newfoundland:

Early instances: George, in fishery at Fortune Bay, 1784 (CO 194.21); William Budden or Buding, from Dorset, married at Fortune Harbour, 1830 (Nfld. Archives KCRC); Janet Budden, from Quebec, married at Bareneed, 1845 (*Royal Gazette* 28 Jan 1845); William, of St. John's, married 1858 (DPHW 23); Richard (and others), fishermen of Heart's

Content, 1871 (Lovell); Charles (and others), fishermen of Perry's Cove, 1871 (Lovell); Stephen, fisherman of Seldom-Come-By, 1871 (Lovell).

Modern status: Scattered, especially at Perry's Cove, Seldom and Sops Arm.

BUDGELL, a surname of England, ? from the Old English personal names *Burgwulf* or *Burghild*. (Spiegelhalter).

Traced by Spiegelhalter in Devon.

In Newfoundland:

Family tradition: A Budgell is said to have left Triton to become the first white settler on Little Bay Islands, about 1825 (MUN Hist.).

Early instances: Giles, of Fleury Bight, 1842, of New Bay Head, 1847 (DPHW 86); Thomas Budgel, of Leading Tickles, 1850, of Triton Harbour, 1852 (DPHW 86); Giles, of Shoe Cove (Twillingate), 1854 (DPHW 86); Elias, fisherman of Burton's Pond (Green B.), 1871 (Lovell); Samuel and Thomas, fishermen of Exploits Burnt Island, 1871 (Lovell); John, farmer of Fortune Harbour, 1871 (Lovell); John, fisherman of Wild Cove (Fogo), 1871 (Lovell).

Modern status: Widespread, especially in the Green Bay, White Bay, Gander and Grand Falls districts.

Place names: Budgell Harbour 49-28 55-24; Budgells Cove 49-33 55-39; —— Ground 49-32 55-32.

BUFFETT, BUFFITT, BURFITT, ? Newfoundland variants of the French surnames Buf(f)et – maker or seller of bellows, or a mighty player on a wind instrument, though Burfitt is also a family name of England from the English place name Burford (Oxford, Shropshire). (Cottle, Dauzat).

Matthews traced Buffett in Dorset as the name of captains and planters.

In Newfoundland:

Early instances: Margaret Bufett, French planter of Placentia, 1714 (CO 194.6); Thomas Buffett, merchant of St. John's, 1762, died ? 1795 (CO 194.15, 40); William, trader who sustained losses when St. Pierre was surrendered to the French in 1763 (CO 194.16); John Burfitt, of Burin, 1805 (D'Alberti 15); Reuben Buffett, of Grand Bank, 1817 (DPHW 109); Mary Ann, of Fortune, 1817 (DPHW 106); Reuben, of Jacques Fontaine, 1819 (DPHW 109); William Beaufort or Beaufit, of Grand Jervis, 1830 (DPHW 30); James Beaufit, of Port aux Basques, 1835 (DPHW 30); John, of Mosquito (Hermitage B.), 1835 (DPHW 30); William, fisherman of Pushthrough, 1845 (DPHW 102); William

Beaufort, of Harbour Le Cou, 1853 (DPHW 101); William Buffett, planter of Jersey Harbour, 1857 (DPHW 104); Snook, planter of Long Harbour (Fortune B.), 1859 (DPHW 104); Snook Buffitt or Beaufit, fisherman of Rose Blanche, 1860 (DPHW 99, 102); Ambrose and Benjamin Buffit, planters of Belleoram,1871 (Lovell); George and Samuel Buffett, fishermen of Garia, 1871 (Lovell); Benjamin (and others), of Lower Burgeo, 1871 (Lovell).

Modern status: Essentially South Coast names.

Place names: Buffet Cove 47-37 55-56; —— Point 47-37 55-57; Jenny Buffet Island 47-40 58-16; Buffett Bank 47-32 54-02; —— Harbour 47-32 54-05; —— Head 47-29 54-05; —— Island 47-32 54-03; —— Point 47-38 56-10; —— Tickle 47-38 56-10; Buffetts Island 47-38 57-34.

BUGDEN, a surname of England, from the English place name Buckden (Huntingdonshire, Yorkshire WR). (Reaney).

Traced by Matthews in Dorset and Hampshire.

In Newfoundland:

Family tradition: Bugdens, early settlers at Heart's Content, moved to Norris Point (Bonne Bay) in the late 1800s (MUN Hist.).

Early instances: Sarah, of Trinity Bay, 1772 (DPHW 64); William, of Trinity (Trinity B.), 1784 (DPHW 64); William Bugdon, servant of Battle Harbour (Labrador), 1795 (MUN Hist.); John Bugden, of English Harbour, 1799 (DPHW 64); Joseph, of Scilly Cove (now Winterton), 1808, of Rider's Harbour, 1814, of Old Perlican, 1816 (DPHW 64); Benjamin, planter of Trouty, 1823 (DPHW 64B); William, clerk of Carbonear, 1831 (DPHW 48); Robert, servant of Bonavista, 1835 (DPHW 72); Thomas, of Haystack, 1836 (DPHW 30); James Bugdon, of Heart's Content, 1860 (DPHW 59); William Bugden, planter of St. Mary's Bay, 1871 (Lovell); James and William, fishermen of Upper Lance Cove (now Brownsdale), 1871 (Lovell).

Modern status: Scattered, including Norris Point and Trinity North district.

Place name: Bugdens Rock 46-59 55-11.

BUGGE, a surname of England, from Middle English *bugg(e)* – hobgoblin, bogy, scarecrow. It is also a common family name in Sweden. (Reaney, Cottle).

Guppy traced Bugg in Dorset.

In Newfoundland:

Modern status: Rare, at St. John's.

BUGLAR, BUGLER, surnames of England, Bugler of Ireland, ? from the English place name Bugley (Wiltshire, Dorset), "not an occupational name" (MacLysaght).

Traced by Guppy in Dorset and by MacLysaght in Co. Clare.

In Newfoundland:

Early instances: John Buglar, mariner, fishing within the plantation of Newfoundland, 1697 (Dorset County Record Office per Kirwin); John, married at Harbour Breton, 1858 (DPHW 104); John Bugler, planter of Jersey Harbour, 1871 (Lovell).

Modern status: Buglar, at Harbour Breton; Bugler, at St. John's and Bay L'Argent.

BULGER. *See* BOLGER

BULGIN, a surname of England, a diminutive of BULL. (Reaney).

Traced by Spiegelhalter in Devon.

In Newfoundland:

Early instances: Adam, Abraham, James and Samuel, fishermen of Twillingate, 1871 (Lovell); Joseph, fisherman of Farmer's Arm (now Summerford), 1881 (DPHW 86).

Modern status: Especially in the Twillingate district.

BULINS, a surname of Latvia.

In Newfoundland:

Modern status: At Corner Brook.

BULL, a surname of England, from Old English *bula* – bull, "occasionally from a[n] [inn] sign" (Reaney).

Traced by Guppy in the Midlands, Wiltshire and Somerset; by Spiegelhalter in Devon and by Matthews also in Dorset.

In Newfoundland:

Family traditions: John, from Christchurch (Hampshire), settled at Salvage in the early 1800s (MUN Folklore). Susan (1821–53), wife of an Englishman at Grand Bank (MUN Hist.).

Early instances: Bull and Kearney, tailors of St. John's, 1794–5, "10 years in Newfoundland," that is, 1784–5 (Census 1794–5); Mary Bull alias Bryan, of Ferryland, married at St. John's, 1817 (Nfld. Archives BRC); Abraham, born at Rencontre, 1819 (DPHW 30); John, of Salvage, 1839 (DPHW 76); Robert, of Exploits Burnt Island, 1844 (DPHW 86); James, fisherman of Fogo, 1853, of Shoal Bay (now Dover), 1858 (DPHW 83).

Modern status: Especially at Eastport.

Place names (not necessarily from the surname):

Bull Arm 47-48 53-51; —— Cove 47-02 55-09, 47-30 53-12, 47-43 56-02; —— Gulch 48-64 53-02; —— Gut (Labrador) 53-45 56-39; —— Head 47-19 52-45; —— Island 47-46 53-47, (Labrador) 52-36 55-44, 52-48 55-48; —— Point 47-27 55-38, 52-37 55-44; —— Pond 47-21 53-22, 47-43 53-14; —— Rock 47-30 53-11; —— Tickle 47-47 53-47; The Bull 47-39 58-32, (Labrador) 52-16 55-35, (Labrador) 52-36 55-44; Bull and Cow 46-46 54-06.

BULLEN, (formerly Boleyn), a surname of England, Ireland and Scotland, Bullen, Bollen, Balleine of Jersey (Channel Islands), from the French place name Boulogne, "the English pronunciation of which was *Bullen* or *Bullin*" (Reaney). (Turk). *See also* BOLAND.

In Ireland since the early 16th century; from the end of the 17th century mainly in Co. Cork (MacLysaght).

Traced by Spiegelhalter in Devon.

In Newfoundland:

Early instances: James Bollen, from Jersey (Channel Islands), planter of Fortune, 1802 (D'Alberti 12); Mary Bullen, born on Bay de l'Eau Island, 1820 (DPHW 30); Henry Bullin, fisherman of Bay Roberts, 1840 (DPHW 39); Mary A. Bolen, of Grand Bank, 1845 (MUN Hist.); Henry Bullen, carpenter of Carbonear, 1849 (DPHW 49); Katherine Bolyn, of St. John's, 1849 (DPHW 26D); John Bullen, of Sagona, 1857 (DPHW 104).

Modern status: Especially at Fortune Bay and Hermitage districts.

Place name: Bullen Rock 47-13 55-03.

BULLEY, a surname of England, from the place names Bouillé (La Manche, Maine-et-Loire, Mayenne), or Bully-en-Brai (Seine-Inférieure), or Bulley (Gloucestershire), or Bulleigh Barton (Devon). "As it means 'bull-clearing,' it was probably common" (Reaney). (Bardsley).

Widespread in Devon.

In Newfoundland:

Family tradition: Edward, and his son Theodore, came from Devon to Sagona Island about 1850, thence to Pass Island (MUN Hist.).

Early instances: William, inhabitant of Newfoundland, ? 1706 (CO 194.24); Samuel, born in Devon, 1730, planter of Southside Hills, St. John's (Nfld. Archives T11); William Bully, fisherman of St. John's or Petty Harbour, about 1739–43 (CO 194.11, 24); Thomas Bulley, of Quidi Vidi, 1771 (CO 194.18, 30); Robert, of Greenspond, 1776 (MUN

Hist.); Joseph, of Petty Harbour, 1826 (DPHW 31); Catherine, of Old Perlican, 1828 (Nfld. Archives BRC); John Bully, from St. Mary's Parish, Devon, married at St. John's, 1839 (Nfld. Archives BRC); George Bulley, from Dawlish, England, of Carbonear, 1845–46 (*Royal Gazette* 22 Jul 1845, DPHW 48); William, fisherman of Sagona Island, 1871 (Lovell).

Modern status: Rare, at Baie Verte and St. John's.

Place name: Bulley's Cove 49-21 55-22.

BULLOCK, a surname of England and Ireland, from Old English *bulluc* – (keeper of a) bull-calf, or a nickname (Reaney).

Traced by Guppy in Berkshire, Cheshire, Cornwall, Gloucestershire, Monmouthshire, Shropshire, Staffordshire, Suffolk and Worcestershire, by Spiegelhalter in Devon and by MacLysaght in Ireland.

In Newfoundland:

Family tradition: The Bullocks moved from Lower Island Cove to Grates Cove in 1790 (MUN Hist.).

Early instances: Richard, of Kelly's Island, 1708–09 (CO 194.4); William, of St. John's, 1795 (CO 194.41); James, proprietor and occupier of fishing rooms at Old Perlican and Grates Cove, Winter 1800–01 (Census Trinity B.); ——, owner of fishing room at Turkish Shore, Keels, before 1805 (Bonavista Register 1806); Thomas, of Harbour Grace Parish, 1806 (Nfld. Archives HGRC); William, planter of Trinity, 1825 (DPHW 64B).

Modern status: Rare, at St. John's.

Place names: Bullock Island 49-43 54-17, Bullocks Point 48-11 53-58.

BUNGAY, a surname of England, from the English place name Bungay (Suffolk). (Bardsley).

In Newfoundland:

Family traditions: —— Bungay, ? a Frenchman, was an early settler at Harbour Main, before 1750 (MUN Hist.). Henry Thomas, born 1871 at Newtown (Bonavista B.) (MUN Hist.). In 1934 the Bungays of Sagona Island moved to Lourdes.

Early instances: William, of Vere (now Fair) Island, 1831 (DPHW 76); Charles, of Lower Burgeo, married 1846 (DPHW 101); John, of Sagona, 1853 (DPHW 104); Jonathan, fisherman of Jersey Harbour, 1853 (DPHW 104); Charles, fisherman of Burin, 1871 (Lovell).

Modern status: Especially in the Burin, Fortune Bay, Hermitage, Bonavista North districts and at St. John's and Lourdes.

Place name: Bungay Rock 47-29 55-42.

BUNTER, a surname of England, of ? Danish or Dutch origin, ? a variant of BOND. (Barber).

In Newfoundland:

Modern status: In the Burgeo-La Poile district.

BURBAGE, BURB(R)IDGE, surnames of England and Ireland (though MacLysaght cites only Burbage), from the English place name Burbage (Derbyshire, Wiltshire, Leicestershire), (Ekwall), possibly confused with BURRAGE and BURRIDGE.

Guppy traced Burbidge in Warwickshire; MacLysaght traced Burbage in Cos. Leitrim and Longford, "on record in Ireland since the sixteenth century."

In Newfoundland:

Early instances: Samuel Burbidge, from Sherborne (Dorset), married at St. John's, 1822 (Nfld. Archives BRC); Joanna Burbridge, of St. John's, married 1850 (DPHW 26D); Alban and Cyrus, fishermen of Burin, 1871 (Lovell); Henry, school teacher of Carbonear, 1871 (Lovell).

Modern status: Burbage at Point Enragée; Burbridge, at Epworth.

BURBRIDGE. *See* BURBAGE

BURCHELL, a surname of England and Ireland, ? from the English place names Birchill (Derbyshire), Birchills (Somerset), Birtle (Lancashire) or Birtles (Cheshire) – birch hill(s). In Ireland, as Burtchaell, "since the seventeenth century associated with Cos. Wicklow and Kilkenny, [but] (spelt Burchill)...now more numerous in Co. Cork" (MacLysaght). (Ekwall, Bardsley).

In Newfoundland:

Early instance: Thomas, of St. John's, 1832 (*Newfoundlander* 3 May 1832).

Modern status: At Flat Bay and St. Teresa (St. George's district) (*Electors* 1955).

BURDEN (or Burdon), surnames of England, Scotland and Ireland, from diminutives of an Old German personal name *Burdo* or Latin *burdo* – mule; or from Old French *bourdon* – pilgrim's staff; or from English place names Great Burdon (Durham), Burdon Head (Yorkshire WR), or Burden (Yorkshire WR); or from Old English *burthegn* – bower-servant, chamberlain; or possibly confused with BURTON. (Reaney, Black).

Traced by Guppy in Dorset and Oxfordshire, by Spiegelhalter in Devon, and by MacLysaght as Burdon, in Cos. Down and Cork.

In Newfoundland:

Family tradition: —— Birdon or Burden, from Dorset or Somerset, at Carbonear before 1800 (MUN Folklore).

Early instances: John, of St. John's or "place adjacent," ? 1706 (CO 194.24); Christopher Burdon, of St. John's, 1759 (DPHW 26C); William Burden, of Fogo, Twillingate or Tilton (now Tilting), 1771 (CO 194.30); Thomas, of Carbonear, 1790 (CO 199.18); Jane, born at Salvage, 1812 or 1813 (DPHW 72); Richard Burden or Burton, of Broad Cove (Bay de Verde), 1819, 1821 (DPHW 52A); John Burden, of Flatrock (St. John's), 1871 (Lovell).

Modern status: Scattered, especially at Carbonear and in the St. Barbe and White Bay North districts.

Place name: Burdens Cove 49-36 56-50.

BURDOCK, a surname of England, a variant of Burdick, in turn a variant of Braddick, from the English place name Breadwick (Devon). The form Burdock is presumably by association with the plant. (Spiegelhalter, Glover).

Traced, as Burdick, by Spiegelhalter in Devon. In Newfoundland:

Modern status: At St. John's and Belleoram.

Place name: Burdock Cove 47-39 55-14.

BURFITT. *See* BUFFETT

BURGE, a surname of England, from Old English *brycg* – (dweller by the) bridge. *See also* BRIDGEMAN, BRIDGER. (Reaney).

Traced by Guppy in Dorset and Somerset. In Newfoundland:

Early instances: William Burge or Burrage, of Trinity (Trinity B.), 1793 (DPHW 64); William Burge, operated salmon fishery at Twillingate, 1808 (CO 194.48), provided lodgings and care for Mary March at Twillingate, 1820 (CO 194.63); Thomas, planter of Bonavista, 1824 (DPHW 72); George, from Bridport (Dorset), accidentally drowned, aged 23 (*Royal Gazette* 6 May 1845); Jacob, of Moreton's Harbour, 1851, of Tizzards Harbour, 1858 (DPHW 86); John and William, of Burin, 1871 (Lovell).

Modern status: At Bonavista, Bishops Falls and in the Twillingate district.

BURGESS, a surname of England, Ireland, Scotland and the Channel Islands, from Old French *burgeis* – inhabitant of a borough, freeman of a borough. *See* BOURGEOIS. (Reaney, Turk).

Guppy traced Burgess in nine counties including Cheshire, Sussex and Devon. In Newfoundland:

Family tradition: —— Burgess on the *Royal George* jumped ship at Crocker's Cove (Carbonear) and settled at Witless Bay (now Whiteway) (Trinity B.), about 1847 (MUN Folklore).

Early instances: Patrick, of St. Mary's, 1792 (D'Alberti 6); Maria Burges, of Twillingate, 1821 (USPG); Henry Burges(s), tailor of Crocker's Cove (Carbonear), 1826 (DPHW 48); William Burgess, of Greenspond, 1827 (DPHW 76); Michael Burges, married at Harbour Grace Parish, 1838 (Nfld. Archives HGRC); Elizabeth Burgess, of St. John's, married 1844 (DPHW 26D); Charles Burges(s), of Carbonear, 1846 (DPHW 48); Charlotte Burges, of Harbour Grace, 1870 (Nfld. Archives HGRC); Henry Burgess, of Witless Bay (now Whiteway), 1874 (DPHW 61).

Modern status: Especially at St. John's, Carbonear and Whiteway.

Place name: Burgess Cove 49-43 55-54.

BURK(E), DE B(O)URKE, surnames of Ireland, BURKE of the Micmacs of Newfoundland, from the English place name Burgh in several counties – fort, manor, hill, mound, in Ireland since the 12th century. (Reaney, MacLysaght).

MacLysaght found the names numerous in all provinces, but least in Ulster. In Newfoundland:

Family traditions: Thomas Burke (about 1722–87), from Waterford, settled at Tilting in 1752. He had three sons, Thomas (1773–99), William (1775–99) and Michael (MUN Geog.). Edmund (about 1755–1848), from Co. Cork, settled at Brigus (MUN Folklore). ——, from Co. Kerry, settled at St. Jacques; later (in 1956) the family moved to Port au Port (MUN Folklore).

Early instances: Arthur Burke, of Newfoundland, ? 1706 (CO 194.24); John Bourk, of Bay Bulls, ? 1753 (CO 194.13); Thomas Burc, shoreman of St. John's, 1794–5, "40 years in Newfoundland," that is, 1754–5 (Census 1794–5); Richard Burk, of Trinity Bay, 1769 (DPHW 64); John ? Burk, of Fogo, Twillingate or Tilton (now Tilting), 1771 (CO 194.30); Aleck Burke, from Clonmell (Co. Tipperary), married at St. John's, 1804 (Nfld. Archives BRC); Michael Bourke, of Fogo Island, 1805 (D'Alberti 15); Edmund Burke, of Harbour Grace Parish, 1806 (Nfld. Archives HGRC); John, deputy naval officer at Trepassey, 1807 (D'Alberti 17); Martin, of Bay Bulls, 1809 (Nfld. Archives BRC); Michael Bourke or Burk, of Carbonear, 1809–15 (DPHW 48); David Burke, one of 72 impressed men who sailed from Ireland to Newfoundland, ? 1811 (CO 194.51); Patt Burk, of Colliers, 1811 (Nfld.

Archives BRC); Thomas Bourke, from Dungarvan (Co. Waterford), planter of Tilting, deceased, 1811 (*Royal Gazette* 17 Oct 1811); John Burke, from Callan (Co. Kilkenny), fisherman of Harbour Grace, deceased, 1814 (*Royal Gazette* 30 Jun 1814); Mary Burk, of Witless Bay, 1817 (Nfld. Archives BRC); John Burke, of Trinity, 1818 (DPHW 64); Anastasia, of Catalina, 1826 (Nfld. Archives KCRC); Robert, of Open Hole (now Open Hall), 1826 (Nfld. Archives KCRC); Elinor, of Joe Batts Arm, 1826 (Nfld. Archives KCRC); Anastasia, of Ragged Harbour (now Melrose), 1827 (Nfld. Archives KCRC); Mary Burk, of Toads (now Tors) Cove, 1830 (Nfld. Archives BRC); Catherine, of Grates Cove, 1835 (Nfld. Archives HGRC); James, of Flat Rock (? St. John's district), 1837 (Nfld. Archives BRC); Francis, of Outer Cove (St. John's district), 1839 (Nfld. Archives BRC); Michael, ? of Northern Bay, 1846 (DPHW 54); Henry Burk, of Eastern Point (Burgeo-La Poile district), 1860 (DPHW 99); Bartholomew Burke, from Gowran (Co. Kilkenny), died at Conche, 1861, aged 36 (Conche Cemetery); widespread in Lovell 1871; Matthew, a Micmac of Conne River, 1872 (MacGregor); Matthew, a Micmac trapper with hunting grounds at Tolt and Piper's Hill Brook, 1900–06 (Millais).

Modern status: Burk, at Stephenville; Burke, widespread especially at St. John's, Tilting and Victoria; DeBourke, DeBurke, at St. John's.

Place names: Burke Island 47-25 53-58, —— —— (Labrador) 52-35 55-43; Jack Burke Brook, —— —— Pond 48-39 58-17; Mother Burke Rock 49-58 55-28; Burkes Cove 47-28 53-12.

BURLEY, a surname of England, from the English place name in several counties including Devon. (Bardsley).

Traced by Spiegelhalter in Devon.

In Newfoundland:

Modern status: At St. John's since 1911, from the north of England. (Family).

BURLING, a surname of England, – son of the cupbearer or butler or ? from the English place names Burling (Essex), Burlings (Lincolnshire), or Birling (Kent, Northumberland). (Ekwall).

In Newfoundland:

Modern status: At St. John's, since about 1920.

BURNELL, a surname of England and Ireland, from Middle English *burnel* from Old French *brunel*, diminutive of *brun* – brown, of complexion, and also a personal name. In Ireland it may occasionally be a synonym of Bernal. (Reaney, MacLysaght).

Traced by Guppy in Buckinghamshire, by Spiegelhalter in Devon, and by MacLysaght in Meath and Dublin since the 13th century.

In Newfoundland:

Early instances: William Burnell or Burnall, of Carbonear, 1814 (D'Alberti 24); Henry Burnell, planter of Brigus, 1829 (DPHW 34); Henry Burnel(l), planter of Trinity (Trinity B.), 1840, of Salmon Cove (now Champneys), 1842 (DPHW 64B); Samuel, fisherman of Cupids, 1871 (Lovell).

Modern status: At St. John's.

Place names: Burnell Beach (Labrador) 52-33 55-44; Burnells Brook 47-06 55-45.

BURNS, a surname of England, Scotland and Ireland, ? from a nickname – burn house, or (dweller by the) burn(s) – stream(s), or from the Scots place name Burnhouse.

"The forefathers of Robert Burns migrated from Burnhouse in Taynuilt to Forfarshire [now Angus] where they were called Campbells of Burnhouse, and later *Burness* or *Burns*... The stress of *Burness* was on the first syllable and as the name was pronounced in Ayrshire as if written *Burns*, Robert and his brother agreed to drop *Burness* and to assume *Burns* in April 1786" (Reaney after Black).

In Ireland, Burns is widely used for O'Beirne, Birrane and BYRNE, and is also the modern form of *Mac Conboirne*. (MacLysaght).

Traced by Guppy in Cumberland and Westmorland and in the Glasgow district and Perthshire; by MacLysaght in Ulster and to a lesser extent in Munster. *See also* BYRNE(S).

In Newfoundland:

Family tradition: Joe, tinsmith of Bonavista and later of Catalina, ? about 1880 (MUN Geog.).

Early instances: James, fisherman of Petty Harbour, 1794–5, "8 years in Newfoundland," that is, 1786–7 (Census 1794–5); Patrick, from Hook (for Hook Head) (Co. Wexford), married at St. John's, 1821 (Nfld. Archives BRC); Patrick, of Harbour Grace Parish, 1821 (Nfld. Archives HGRC); Thomas, of Long Pond, 1841 (DPHW 26D).

Modern status: At Little St. Lawrence, Bay du Nord and Searston.

Place names: Burns Cove (P.O.) 47-24 54-52, —— Head and —— Head Rock 47-01 52-52, —— Point 49-39 54-43, —— Shoal 47-27 53-58; Dick Burns Rock 47-27 53-58; Mother —— Cove 53-35 56-05.

BURRAGE, BURRIDGE, surnames of England, ? from an Old English personal name *Burgru* –

fortress-powerful; or from the English place name Burridge (Devon); or possibly confused with BURBAGE and BURB(R)IDGE. (Reaney).

Burridge traced by Guppy in Dorset; by Spiegelhalter in Devon; Burrage, Burridge also by Matthews in Somerset.

In Newfoundland:

Early instances: William Burrage, of Trinity, 1788 (DPHW 64); E., proprietor and occupier of fishing room at Grates Cove, Winter 1800–01 (Census Trinity B.); John, from England, planter of Trinity, deceased, 1816 (*Nfld. Mercantile Journal* 2 Nov 1816); Anne Burrage alias Locke, of New Harbour (Trinity B.), 1829 (Nfld. Archives KCRC); Richard Burridge, married at Grates Cove, 1830 (DPHW 58); Thomas, of Deadman's Island (between Port aux Basques and Burgeo), 1830 (DPHW 30); Thomas Burrage, of Gates Harbour (near Cape Ray), 1835 (DPHW 30); Thomas Burridge, of Channel, 1842 (DPHW 101); Thomas, mason of St. John's, 1845 (DPHW 26D); Thomas, born at Greenspond, baptized 1853 (DPHW 76); Matilda, of Old Perlican, 1857 (DPHW 58); George Burrage, fisherman of Bonne Bay, 1866 (DPHW 93); William Burridge, fisherman of Seal Island (Garia B.), 1871 (Lovell).

Modern status: Burrage, especially in the Trinity South district; Burridge, at St. John's, Channel and Deer Lake.

BURRESS, a variant of a surname of England and Ireland, Burrows, Burriss etc., – (dweller or employee at the) bower-house. (Reaney).

Guppy traced Burrows in Cornwall, Devon, Somerset, Gloucestershire, Lincolnshire, Nottinghamshire and Suffolk; MacLysaght traced Burrowes, Burris(s) especially in Ulster.

In Newfoundland:

Early instances: John Burross, fisherman of St. John's, 1794–5, "12 years in Newfoundland," that is, 1782–3 (Census 1794–5); Johnston Burrows, from Co. Sligo, Ireland, surgeon of Harbour Grace, 1786, lessee of land at Adams Cove, 1791, physician of Adams Cove, deceased 1814 (CO 194.36, CO 199.18, *Royal Gazette* 13 Jan 1814); Thomas Burress, from Kiluillaheen (unidentified) (Co. Kilkenny), fisherman of St. John's, deceased, 1810 (*Royal Gazette* 11 Oct 1810); Robert Burrow, of Heart's Content, 1819 (Nfld. Archives KCRC); Robert, of Tickle Harbour (now Bellevue), 1829 (Nfld. Archives KCRC); Sarah Burrowes, of Trinity, 1865 (Nfld. Archives KCRC).

Modern status: At Heart's Content and St. John's (*Electors* 1955).

BURRY, a surname of England, from the English place name Bury (Huntingdonshire, Lancashire, Suffolk, Sussex). (E.C. Smith).

In Newfoundland:

Early instances: David Sr., of Greenspond, 1775 (Bonavista Register 1806); David, of Pinchard's Island, 1801 (Bonavista Register 1806); Thomas, of Ragged Harbour (now Melrose), 1816, of New Harbour (Trinity B.), 1825 (Nfld. Archives KCRC); Peter, of Tilton Harbour (now Tilting), 1821 (Nfld. Archives KCRC); Mary, of Riders Harbour, 1829 (Nfld. Archives KCRC); Margaret, born at Cape Island (Bonavista B.), baptized 1830 (DPHW 76); Abraham, fisherman of Port de Grave, 1852 (DPHW 34); Benjamin Burrey Jr., fisherman of English Harbour, 1871 (Lovell); John, miner at La Manche (Placentia B.), 1871 (Lovell); Thomas (and others), of Newell's Island, 1871 (Lovell); Charles and Simon, fishermen of Shoal Cove (Bonavista B.), 1871 (Lovell).

Modern status: Widespread, especially at St. John's, Greenspond and Boyd's Cove.

Place name: Burry's Pond 49-08 53-36.

BURSELL, a surname of England from the English place names Burshill (Yorkshire ER) and Boarshill (Devon).

Traced by Spiegelhalter as Burshell, by Matthews as Bursell, in Devon.

In Newfoundland:

Early instances: G., inspector of pickled fish at Brigus, 1844 (*Nfld. Almanac*); George, master mariner of St. John's, 1846 (DPHW 26B); George, from Paignton (Devon), of St. John's, 1857 (*Newfoundlander* 9 Mar 1857); W.H., schoolteacher of Bay Roberts, 1871 (Lovell).

Modern status: At St. John's.

BURSEY, a surname of England, from the French place name Burcy (Calvados), or from an Old English personal name *Beorhtsige* containing the elements *bright* and *victory*. (Reaney).

Traced by Matthews as captains in Devon.

In Newfoundland:

Family traditions: William Robert (about 1720–80), from Devon, was the first Bursey in Lower Island Cove (MUN Geog.). Joseph (1822–1916), from Devon, settled at Old Perlican in 1834 (MUN Geog.). Brook Cove (now part of Clarenville) was first settled by Burseys (MUN Hist.). Burseys from Manchester settled at Old Perlican in the 18th century (MUN Hist.).

Early instances: John, inhabitant of Newfoundland, ? 1706 (CO 194.24); Michael Bersey, ? of St. John's, 1812 (DPHW 26B); Joseph Bursey, of Old Perlican, 1822 (DPHW 58); William, of Catalina, 1835 (DPHW 67); Charles, planter of Caplin Cove (Bay de Verde), 1845 (DPHW 36); Benjamin Burcey, of Middle Bill Cove, 1848 (DPHW 76); Selina Bursey, of Indian Point (Trinity B.), 1853 (DPHW 59); William Bursey or Bussey, of Grates Cove, 1855 (DPHW 58); Joseph Bursey, of Lower Island Cove, 1856 (DPHW 55); Jane, of Seal Cove (now New Chelsea), 1858 (DPHW 59); Joseph, of Change Islands, 1862 (DPHW 84); John and Richard, fishermen of Clark's Head (Fogo), 1871 (Lovell); Thomas, fisherman of Deer Island (Bonavista B.), 1871 (Lovell); Judith, widow of Russells Cove (now New Melbourne), 1871 (Lovell).

Modern status: Widespread.

BURT, a surname of England, Scotland and Jersey (Channel Islands), from the Old English *beorht* – bright, beautiful, fair. *See also* BRIGHT. (Reaney, Turk).

Traced by Guppy in Dorset, Lincolnshire, Sussex and Wiltshire and by Spiegelhalter in Devon.

In Newfoundland:

Early instances: Margery, of St. John's or Bay Bulls, 1681, "30 years an inhabitant," that is, 1651 (CO 1); Hugh, of Old Perlican, 1675 (CO 1); Anthony, of Silly Cove (now Winterton), 1681 (CO 1); William, inhabitant of Conception Bay, ? 1706 (CO 194.4); Thomas Burtt, planter of St. John's, 1706, of Bell Island, 1708–09 (CO 194.4); William, planter of Brigus, 1708–09 (CO 194.4); Edward Burt, planter of Port de Grave, 1708–09 (CO 194.4); John Burtt, of Carbonear, 1708–09 (CO 194.4); Richard Burt Sr. and Jr., of Old Perlican, 1708–09 (CO 194.4); James, from Winkton (Hampshire) to Old Perlican, 1728 (*Evening Telegram* 11 Aug 1960); John, of Fogo, 1803 (D'Alberti 13); William, of Harbour Grace Parish, 1823 (Nfld. Archives HGRC); Daniel, of Herring Neck, 1820 (USPG); Cornelius Birt, of Bird Island Cove (now Elliston), 1828 (DPHW 72); Robert Burt, of ? Rach (for Wreck) Cove (Bay de l'Eau), 1835 (DPHW 30); Robert, from England, died at Barren Island (now Bar Haven), 1835 (Wix); Richard, of Little Harbour (Twillingate), 1836 (DPHW 88); Thomas, fisherman of Eastern Point (Burgeo-La Poile), ? 1860 (DPHW 99); Robert, planter of Brooklyn (now Lethbridge), 1871 (Lovell); Joseph, fisherman of Great St. Lawrence, 1871 (Lovell); Samuel, fisherman of Moreton's Harbour, 1871 (Lovell); George (and others), of Tizzard's Harbour, 1871 (Lovell); James (and

others), of Twillingate, 1871 (Lovell); William, of Wiseman's Cove (White B.), 1871 (Lovell).

Modern status: Widespread, especially at Virgin Arm, Carter's Cove and elsewhere in the Twillingate district, and at Peter's Arm (Gander district).

Place name: Burts Island 49-41 54-25.

BURTON, a surname of England and Ireland, from a common English place name usually meaning the fort or manor-house enclosure, or the fortified farm; or by confusion with BURDEN. (Cottle).

Guppy found Burton widespread, especially in Nottinghamshire, Spiegelhalter in Devon, and MacLysaght mainly in Co. Donegal.

In Newfoundland:

Early instances: John, of St. John's, 1706 (CO 194.22); ——, constable of Bonavista district, ? 1730 (CO 194.9); John, planter of Fogo, 1780 (D'Alberti 6); William Burton or Barton, of Trinity (Trinity B.), 1788 (DPHW 64); William (and others), of Bonavista, 1792 (USPG); ——, owner of fishing room at Ship Island, Greenspond Harbour, before 1805 (Bonavista Register 1806); Richard Burton or Burden, of Broad Cove (Bay de Verde), 1819 (DPHW 52A); William Burten, planter of Carbonear, 1819 (DPHW 48); Charity Burton, of Joe Batts Arm, 1821 (USPG); Joseph, of Twillingate, 1822 (USPG); Jane Burten, of Harbour Grace Parish, 1828 (Nfld. Archives HGRC); John Burtin, of Kings Cove Parish, 1835 (Nfld. Archives KCRC); Charles Burton, of Famish Gut (now Fairhaven), 1836 (DPHW 30); Abraham, of Ward's Harbour (now Beaumont North), 1842 (DPHW 86); Jonathan, of Fortune, 1852 (DPHW 106); Robert, of Grole, 1855 (DPHW 104); Robert, of Jersey Harbour, 1856 (DPHW 104); John (and others), of English Harbour, 1871 (Lovell); Charles (and others), of Harbour Buffett, 1871 (Lovell); Moses, fisherman of Herring Neck, 1871 (Lovell); William, of Oderin, 1871 (Lovell); Robert, of Rose Blanche, 1871 (Lovell); Mary, widow of Spiller's Cove (Trinity B.), 1871 (Lovell); George, fisherman of Springfield (Brigus district), 1871 (Lovell).

Modern status: Widespread, especially at St. John's, Green Bay, Harbour Buffett (*Electors* 1955), and in the White Bay South district.

Place names: Burton Cove 49-31 55-07, —— —— 49-48 55-50, Burton's Pond 49-48 55-50; —— Cove 49-37 56-52; —— Harbour, —— Head 49-28 55-41; —— Big Pond 49-51 55-50.

BUSH, a surname of England, – (dweller by the) bush or wood. (Cottle).

Traced by Guppy in Essex, Lincolnshire and Norfolk, by Spiegelhalter in Devon, and by Matthews in Dorset.

In Newfoundland:

Early instances: William, fisherman of Trinity (Trinity B.), 1845 (DPHW 64); James, fisherman of Harbour Grace, 1871 (Lovell).

Modern status: At St. John's.

BUSH(E)Y, surnames of England, and of the Micmacs of Newfoundland, from the English place names Bushey (Hertfordshire) or Bush Hays Farm (Devon), or a variant of BUSSEY. *See also* BUSH and PUSHIE.

Traced by Spiegelhalter in Devon.

In Newfoundland:

Family tradition: A Micmac surname in the Springdale area about 1900. A resident of Jackson's Cove (Green Bay) was indifferently known as Joe Bush or Bushey, about 1912 (R.F. Sparkes).

Modern status: At Hampden and Roddickton (White Bay).

BUSSELL, a surname of England, from the Middle English *buyscel*, etc. – bushel, probably for a maker or user of containers holding a bushel, or from Old French *bucel* – a (maker of) small barrel(s). (Reaney).

Guppy traced Bushell in Somerset and Bushel in Yorkshire ER; Spiegelhalter traced Bushell and Bussell in Devon.

In Newfoundland:

Early instances: Michael Bushell, fisherman of St. John's, 1789 (CO 194.38); George Bussell, ? fisherman of Ship Cove (Port de Grave), 1802 (Nfld. Archives T22).

Modern status: Rare, at St. John's, St. Veronica's and St. Albans (*Electors* 1955).

BUSSEY, a surname of England, Bussy of Jersey (Channel Islands), from the French place names Bouce (Orne), Boucey (La Manche) or Bucy-le-Long (Aisne), or from the English place name Bush Hays Farm (Devon). *See* BUSHEY. (Reaney, Spiegelhalter, Turk).

Traced by Spiegelhalter in Devon.

In Newfoundland:

Family tradition: ——, from southwest England, settled in Conception Bay, later moved to St. Lunaire (White B.) (MUN Folklore).

Early instances: John, of Port de Grave, 1775 (CO 199.18); Joseph, in fishery at Fortune Bay, 1784 (CO 194.21); William, of Lower Island Cove, 1788 (CO

199.18); Richard, proprietor and occupier of fishing room at Old Perlican, Winter 1800–01 (Census Trinity B.); Robert Buss(e)y, of St. John's, 1803 (DPHW 26D); Thomas, of Salmon Cove (now part of South River), 1806 (DPHW 34); Anne Bussy, of Harbour Grace Parish, 1806 (Nfld. Archives HGRC); Joseph Bussey, of Cupids, 1824–30 (Dorset County Record Office per Kirwin); James, of Greenspond, 1840 (DPHW 76); William, of Change Islands, 1843 (DPHW 83); John, fisherman of Gander Bay, 1850 (DPHW 83); William Bussey or Bursey, fisherman of Grates Cove, 1851 (DPHW 58); John Bussey, fisherman of Catalina, 1857 (DPHW 70); George, of Caplin Cove and Rip Raps (Brigus), 1871 (Lovell); Charles, of Caplin Cove (Bay de Verde), 1871 (Lovell).

Modern status: Especially in the Port de Grave district and at St. Lunaire (White B.).

BUTCHER. *See* BOUTCHER

BUTLAND, a surname of England, from the English place name Butland (Devon). (Spiegelhalter).

Traced by Spiegelhalter in Devon.

In Newfoundland:

Early instances: John, fisherman of Quidi Vidi, 1731 (CO 194.9); Philip, accountant of St. John's, 1850 (DPHW 29); Thomas, fisherman of Muscle Pond (St. Mary's B.), 1871 (Lovell).

Modern status: At O'Donnells and Mount Carmel.

BUTLER, a surname of England and Ireland, from Old French *bouteillier* – servant in charge of the wine-cellar, usually the head servant. "In some early examples, an officer of high rank nominally connected with the supply and importation of wine." (Reaney). Later examples may be for *bottler* – maker of (leather) bottles.

Guppy found Butler widespread, Spiegelhalter traced it in Devon, MacLysaght found it widespread in all provinces except Ulster. Black comments that Butler appears to have been ousted in Scotland by SPENCE.

In Newfoundland:

Family traditions: Various traditions relate the Butlers to England and Ireland but the Butlers of Curling believe their origins to have been in Holland.

Early instances: James, of Port de Grave, 1760, property "in possession of the Family for 98 years or upwards," that is, before 1662 (CO 199.18); Thomas But(t)ler, of Port de Grave, 1675,–76 (CO 1); John Butler, of Conception Bay [1706], (CO 194.4);

James, of Little Bell Island, 1708–09 (CO 194.4);
John Buttler, of Kellys Island, 1708–09 (CO 194.4);
John Butler, servant of Trinity, 1731 (CO 194.9);
Pearce Buttler, of ? Harbour Main, 1750 (CO
194.12); James, fisherman of St. John's, 1794–5, "41
years in Newfoundland," that is, 1753–4 (Census
1794–5); John and Jane Butler, of Teignmouth
(Devon), owners (by possession) of fishing rooms at
St. John's, 1773 (D'Alberti 6); Richard, servant of
Oderin, 1774 (CO 194.32); James, of Harbour Grace,
1779–80 (D'Alberti 6); William ? Butler, from
Limerick (Co. Limerick), Irish convict landed at
Petty Harbour or Bay Bulls, 1789 (CO 194.38);
Edward, of Northern Bay, 1790 (CO 199.18);
Richard, in fishery at Portugal Cove, 1794–5
(Census 1794–5); John, from Cashel (Co.
Tipperary), married at St. John's, 1798 (Nfld.
Archives BRC); Charles, of Lower Foxtrap, 1800 (CO
199.18); Edmund, occupier of fishing room at Scilly
Cove (now Winterton), Winter 1800–01 (Census
Trinity B.); George, of Gasters, 1801 (CO 199.18);
James Jr., of Cupids, 1804 (CO 199.18); John, of
Bonavista, 1805 (Bonavista Register 1806); Henry,
magistrate of Burin district, 1810 (D'Alberti 20);
James, of Pope's Harbour, 1810 (DPHW 64); Pierce,
from Mulnahoan (for Mullinahone) (Co. Tipperary),
farmer of Golden Grove, St. John's, deceased 1812
(*Royal Gazette* 18 Jun 1812); James, of Filthy (now
British) Harbour, 1813 (DPHW 64); Michael, of
Carbonear, 1814 (D'Alberti 24); John, from Carrick-
on-Suir (Co. Tipperary), planter of Witless Bay,
deceased 1814 *Royal Gazette* (12 May 1814);
Charles, planter of Ireland's Eye, 1818 (DPHW 64);
Mary, from Callan (Co. Kilkenny), married at Riders
Harbour (Trinity B.), 1829 (Nfld. Archives KCRC);
George, of Greenspond, 1829 (DPHW 76); John, of
Middle Bight (now Codner), 1832 (DPHW 30);
William, of Foxtrap, 1832 (DPHW 30); Mary, of
Kings Cove, 1833 (Nfld. Archives KCRC); Thomas
Butler or Butter, shoemaker of Brigus, 1836 (DPHW
34); Anne Butler, of Long Pond, 1837 (DPHW 26D);
James, of Burnt Head (Port de Grave), 1840 (DPHW
39); John, fisherman of Ferryland, 1840 (DPHW 31);
Jacob, of Hibbs Hole, 1844 (DPHW 39); John, of
Robin Hood (now part of Port Rexton), 1850 (DPHW
64B); James, of Muddy Hole (now Maberly), 1851
(DPHW 83); Isaac, of Salmon Cove (now
Champneys), 1853 (DPHW 64B); John, of Green
Cove (Twillingate district), 1855 (DPHW 85); Henry,
of Flat Island (Burin district), 1860 (DPHW 108);
Charles, of Mosquito Cove (Burin district), 1861
(DPHW 108); widespread in Lovell 1871.

Modern status: Widespread.

Place names: Butler Cove 49-30 55-26, 49-31
55-37; —— Head 47-43 53-59; —— Island 47-36
54-08 (Labrador) 52-48 55-49; —— Rock 46-53
55-20, 47-11 54-55; Little Butler Island 47-35
54-08; Butlers Bight 49-30 55-39; —— Pond 47-14
53-02, 47-16 53-18, 49-57 56-11; Butlerville 47-35
53-20.

BUTT, a surname of England, from an Old English
personal name *Butt* or *Butta,* or from Middle
English *butt* – thicker end, stump, "probably used of
a thickset person," or Middle English *butt* – goal,
mark for shooting, used for one who lived near the
archery butts, or, perhaps, an archer. (Reaney).

Traced by Guppy in Devon, Dorset, Gloucestershire and Somerset.

In Newfoundland:

Family traditions: Some Butts moved from the
North Shore of Conception Bay to Pouch Cove
between 1820 and 1835 (MUN Hist.). George
(1779–1864), of Grand Bank (MUN Hist.).

Early instances: Roger Butt, of Carbonear, 1675
(Burt, 1677) (CO 1); John Butt, inhabitant of
Conception Bay, 1706 (CO 194.4); Joseph, of
Crocker's Cove (Carbonear), 1767, property "in
possession of the Family for 61 years," that is, 1706
(CO 199.18); John, born in Newfoundland ? 1720
(Dorset County Record Office per Kirwin); Joseph,
of Clown's Cove (Carbonear), 1747 (CO 199.18);
Thomas, of Blackhead (Bay de Verde), 1750 (CO
199.18); William, of Broad Cove (Bay de Verde),
1750 (CO 199.18); John, of Mosquito (now Bristol's
Hope), 1765 (CO 199.18); George and Thomas, of
Carbonear, 1769 (CO 199.18); Roger, of Freshwater
(Carbonear), 1770 (CO 199.18); William, of
Bradley's Cove, 1785 (CO 199.18); Joseph, of
Bonavista, 1792 (DPHW 70); John, of Northern Cove
(Spaniards Bay), 1802 (CO 199.18); Catherine, of
Harbour Grace Parish, 1807 (Nfld. Archives HGRC);
William and John, of Western Bay, 1814 (D'Alberti
24); George, planter of Adam's Cove, 1817 (DPHW
52A); Henry Butts, planter of Perry's Cove, 1820
(DPHW 48); Richard Butt, of St. John's, 1822 (CO
194.65); George, planter of Chance Cove (now Big
Chance Cove), 1823 (DPHW 64B); Elizabeth Ann,
born at Biscayan Cove (near Pouch Cove), baptized
at Blackhead (Bay de Verde), 1829 (DPHW 52A);
Martin, planter of Gooseberry Cove (unidentified
but ? near Carbonear), 1829 (DPHW 48); Richard, of
Harbour Grace, 1830 (Nfld. Archives HGRC);
William, planter of Blowmedown (Carbonear), 1832
(DPHW 48); Martin, planter of Otterbury (Carbo-
near), 1832 (DPHW 48); James, planter of Northern

Bay, 1837 (DPHW 52A); Hezekiah, fisherman of Salmon Cove (Carbonear), 1838 (DPHW 48); Samuel, of Moreton's Harbour, 1846 (DPHW 86); John, boatkeeper of Catalina, 1852 (DPHW 72); Frances, of Pouch Cove, 1853 (DPHW 32); William, of Ward's Harbour (now Beaumont North), 1855 (DPHW 86); John, of Petites, 1858 (DPHW 98); George, of Cat Harbour (now Lumsden), 1858 (Nfld. Archives KCRC); John Henry, of Exploits, 1859 (DPHW 42); John, of Channel, 1863 (DPHW 97); widespread in Lovell 1871.

Modern status: Widespread, especially at Carbonear and in the Bay de Verde, Humber West and St. John's districts.

Place names: Butt Cove 49-31 55-04; —— Head 47-37 58-38; —— Island 47-37 58-39, (Labrador) 54-33 57-13; —— Shoal 47-36 58-37.

BUTTER(S), surnames of England and Scotland, from Middle English *botor* – bittern, "noted for its 'boom' in the breeding season," or keeper of the buttery, or from Old English *butere* – (maker of or dealer in) butter, (Reaney), or from the English place name Bottor (Devon); or, in Scotland, also from the Scots place name Buttergask (Perthshire). (Reaney, Black, Spiegelhalter).

Butters was traced by Guppy in Lincolnshire, Butter by Spiegelhalter in Devon, Buttar, Butter(s) by Black in Fife and Perthshire.

In Newfoundland:

Early instances: James Butter, ? of St. John's, 1777 (DPHW 26C); Thomas Butter or Butler, shoemaker of Brigus, 1834 (DPHW 34); Charles Butter, of Foxtrap, 1838 (DPHW 26D); James, fisherman of Broad Cove (Bay de Verde), 1845, of Blackhead (Bay de Verde), 1847 (DPHW 52A); John, fisherman of Holyrood, 1853 (DPHW 64B); William, fisherman of Cupids, 1854 (DPHW 34); Peter, fisherman of Spaniard's Bay, 1871 (Lovell); John Butters, carpenter of Harbour Grace, 1877 (Lovell).

Modern status: Butter, at St. John's; Butters, at Brigus and St. John's.

Place names (not necessarily from the surname): Butter Brook 48-10 58-56; —— Cove 47-23 54-30, 47-40 56-02; —— Harbour 47-35 59-06; —— Island (Labrador) 53-34 60-05; —— Rocks (Labrador) 56-47 60-55.

BUTTERWORTH, a surname of England, from the English place names Butterworth (Lancashire), Butterberry, or Buttery (Devon) – the enclosure where butter is made. (Cottle).

Traced by Guppy in Lancashire, by Spiegelhalter in Devon.

In Newfoundland:

Modern status: Rare, at St. John's.

BUTTERY, a surname of England, from Old French *boterie* – originally a place for storing liquor, but early used of a room where provisions are stored, hence the keeper of such a place. (Reaney).

Traced by Guppy in Nottinghamshire, Yorkshire NR, ER.

In Newfoundland:

Early instance: ——, of St. John's, 1722 (CO 194.8).

Modern status: At Grand Bay (Burgeo-La Poile district) (*Electors* 1955).

BUTTON, a surname of England, from Old French *boton* – button (maker), or from the English place names Button (Devon, Gloucestershire) or Botton (Cornwall), or from an Old German personal name *Boto*. (Reaney).

Traced by Guppy in Suffolk, by Spiegelhalter in Devon, and by Matthews also in Dorset.

In Newfoundland:

Family tradition: Richard, of Old Perlican, 1746 (MUN Hist.).

Early instances: Henry, of Trinity Bay, 1770 (DPHW 64); Stephen, of Hearts Content, 1801 (DPHW 64); Thomas, of Vere (now Fair) Island, 1836 (DPHW 76); William, fisherman of Seal Cove (now New Chelsea), 1852 (DPHW 59A); Richard, of Round Harbour, 1852 (DPHW 86); William, fisherman of Hants Harbour, 1854 (DPHW 59A); Thomas, fisherman of Silver Hare Island (now Silver Fox Island), 1871 (Lovell).

Modern status: Especially at St. John's, Old Perlican, Lead Cove and Silver Fox Island.

Place names: Button Island 49-31 55-15; Davy Button Cove 49-40 54-48.

BYRD. *See* BIRD

BYRNE(S), surnames of England and Ireland, *Ó Broin*, Ir. *bran* – raven. *See also* BRIAN, BURNS, BRYNE. (MacLysaght). "Byrne is now one of the most numerous names in Ireland" (MacLysaght).

Traced by MacLysaght especially in Co. Wicklow and by Matthews in Devon.

In Newfoundland:

Early instances: J. Burne, of St. John's, 1704 (CO 194.3); James Byrn, of (Upper) Island Cove, 1773

(CO 199.18); William, of Trinity Bay, 1782 (DPHW 64); Matthew Burn, cooper of Bay Bulls, 1786 (CO 194.36); Joanne Byrne, of Harbour Grace Parish, 1806 (Nfld. Archives HGRC); Lawrence, from Ross (Co. Wexford), married at St. John's, 1809 (Nfld. Archives BRC); James Burne, one of 72 impressed men who sailed from Ireland to Newfoundland ? 1811 (CO 194.51); James Byrn, from Cushing Town (unidentified), Old Ross (Co. Wexford), of Lower Island Cove, deceased 1816 (*Royal Gazette* 16 Jul 1816); John Byrne or Burn, of Kings Cove, 1816, of Bonavista, 1822 (Nfld. Archives KCRC); Bridget Byrne or Burn(s), of Keels, 1819 (Nfld. Archives KCRC); William Byrne, of Greenspond , 1823 (Nfld. Archives KCRC); Cornelius, of Joe Batts Arm, 1825

(Nfld. Archives KCRC); Mary, of Bay de Verde, 1828 (Nfld. Archives BRC); Catherine, of Carbonear, 1828 (Nfld. Archives BRC); Johanna, from Carrick-on-Suir (Co. Tipperary), married at Harbour Grace, 1829 (Nfld. Archives BRC); Martin Burn, of Trinity, 1846 (Nfld. Archives KCRC); Henry, from Devon, married at St. John's, 1847 (*Royal Gazette* 27 Apr 1847); Concilius Byrne or Byrun, ? of Northern Bay, 1850 (DPHW 54); scattered in Lovell 1871.

Modern status: Byrne, widespread, especially at St. John's, Great Paradise, Corner Brook and Conche; Byrnes, at York Harbour and Corner Brook West.

Place names: Byrne Cove, Little —— —— 49-35 54-41.

C

CABLE, a surname of England, from ? an Old English personal name *Ceadbeald* or ? a popular form of the baptismal name Gabriel, or ? from Middle English *caball*, from Latin *caballus* – horse (man). (Reaney Notes, Spiegelhalter, Reaney).

Traced by Spiegelhalter in Devon.

In Newfoundland:

Early instance: Michael, ? of Trinity, 1731 (CO 194.9).

Modern status: At Foxtrap and Peachtown.

CADDIGAN. *See* CADIGAN

CADET, a surname of France, Old French *cadet* – little dog. (Dauzat).

Widespread in France.

In Newfoundland:

Modern status: Rare, at Port au Choix.

CAD(D)IGAN, surnames of Ireland, variants of (O)Cadogan, *Ó Ceadagáin*, ? from Irish *cet* – blow, buffet. (MacLysaght).

Traced by MacLysaght in Co. Cork.

In Newfoundland:

Early instances: Edmond Cadigan, of St. John's, 1802 (Nfld. Archives BRC); Maurice, from Cloyne (Co. Cork), married at St. John's, 1805 (Nfld. Archives BRC); Edmond Cadagan, of Harbour Grace Parish, 1828 (Nfld. Archives HGRC); Patrick Caddigan, of Logy Bay, 1858 (*Newfoundlander* 1 Apr 1858).

Modern status: Caddigan, unique, at Logy Bay Road; Cadigan, at St. John's and Logy Bay Road.

CADMAN, a surname of England – servant of Cade, or from Middle English *cade* – (maker of) cask(s), barrel(s). (Reaney, Bardsley).

Traced by Bardsley in Northern England.

In Newfoundland:

Modern status: Unique, at Grand Falls.

CADWELL, a surname of England, from the English place name Cadwell (Lincolnshire, Devon, Hertfordshire, Oxfordshire). *See also* CALDWELL. (Reaney).

In Newfoundland:

Early instances: William, of Harbour Grace, 1770, property "in possession of the Family for 60 years," that is, 1710 (CO 199.18); John, of Fresh-water (Carbonear), 1761 (CO 199.18); James, fisherman, and Thomas, carpenter of St. John's, 1794–5, "born in Newfoundland" (Census 1794–5); James, of Quidi Vidi, 1822 (D'Alberti 32); William, of Leading Tickles, 1844, of Ward's Harbour (now Beaumont North), 1845 (DPHW 86).

Modern status: at St. John's and Islington (Trinity B.).

CAHILL, a surname of Ireland, *Ó Cathail*, "The personal name *Cathal*, now generally made Charles, means valour" (MacLysaght).

MacLysaght traced (O)Cahill in Cos. Clare, Kerry and Tipperary, Mac Cahill mainly in Cos. Donegal and Cavan.

In Newfoundland:

Early instances: John, of St. John's, 1763 (DPHW 26C); ——, of ? Trinity, 1780 (D'Alberti 6); Edward, of Freshwater (Carbonear), 1791 (CO 199.18); Patrick, of Musketta (now Bristol's Hope), 1795 (CO 199.18); Michael, of Adam's Cove, 1797 (CO 199.18); Edward, from Kilcash (Co. Tipperary), married at St. John's, 1804 (Nfld. Archives BRC); Michael, of Harbour Grace Parish, 1806 (Nfld. Archives HGRC); Elizabeth Cahil alias Keys, of Caplin Cove (unspecified), married at St. John's, 1815 (Nfld. Archives BRC); Thomas Cahill, of Tilton Harbour (now Tilting), 1817 (Nfld. Archives KCRC); Edward, from Grange Parish (unidentified) (Co. Carlow), late of Torbay, 1827 (*Newfoundlander* 19 Dec 1827); Mary Ann Cahil, of Adams Cove, married at St. John's, 1829 (Nfld. Archives BRC); John Cahill, of Carbonear, married at Harbour Grace, 1829 (Nfld. Archives BRC); Michael, of Twillingate, 1829 (Nfld. Archives KCRC); William Cahle of Foxtrap, 1835 (DPHW 30); Sarah Cahill, of Pouch Cove, 1840 (DPHW 30); Michael Cahil, ? of Northern Bay, 1840 (DPHW 54); Luisa Cahil(l), of Harbour Grace, 1866 (Nfld. Archives HGRC); scattered in Lovell 1871.

Modern status: Scattered, especially at St. John's.

Place names: Cahill Point 47-34 52-41, 47-34 52-42, 47-35 55-24.

CAIN, a surname of England, Ireland and Jersey (Channel Islands); in England and Ireland from the Welsh feminine name *Keina*, from Welsh *cain* –

beautiful; or from the Manx personal name *Mac-Cathain* – son of *Cathan*, Manx *cath* – battle, warrior; in England, Ireland and Jersey ? from the French place name Caen (Calvados); or in Ireland for KANE. *See also* CAINES, CANE, KANE, KEAN(E), KEYNES, with which confusion may have occurred. (Reaney, MacLysaght, Turk). *See also* LEQUANT.

Guppy traced Cane and Caine in Hampshire and Sussex, Spiegelhalter traced Cain and Cane in Devon, and MacLysaght traced Cain and Cane in Co. Mayo.

In Newfoundland:

Early instances: Richard, of Harbour Grace, 1800 (CO 199.18); Mary Cain alias Walsh, from Montcoyn (unidentified) (Co. Kilkenny), married at St. John's, 1813 (Nfld. Archives BRC); Samuel Cain, born at Middle Bill Cove (Bonavista North district), 1820 (DPHW 76); James Cain, Kain or Kaine, of Kings Cove, 1821 (Nfld. Archives KCRC); William Cain, of Bonne Bay (Fortune B.), 1835 (DPHW 30); Matthew, of Waterford, died 29 Aug 1851, aged 56, buried at Carbonear (Carbonear R.C. Cemetery); Daniel and Patrick, of Cats Cove (now Conception Harbour), 1871 (Lovell); John, of Marquise, 1871 (Lovell).

Modern status: Somewhat rare, in the Harbour Grace district.

Place names: Cain Pond 48-52 57-57; Cain(e)s Island 47-36 58-42; Cains Point 49-10 55-19.

CAINES, a surname of England, from the French place names Cahaignes (Eure) or Cahagnes (Calvados). *See* CAIN. (Reaney).

Guppy traced Caines and Keynes in Dorset.

In Newfoundland:

Family traditions: ——, from Scotland, settled at St. Barbe, 1847 (MUN Folklore). George, from England, first settler at Shoal Cove East (MUN Hist.). Levi, born in Devon, arrived at St. John's about 1860 (MUN Folklore).

Early instances: William Cains, Kines or Kindes, of St. John's Harbour, 1675, in 1680 "34 years an inhabitant," that is, since 1646, 1681 (CO 1); Joseph, of Greenspond, 1819 (DPHW 76) James, of Lamaline, 1823 (DPHW 109); Joseph, born at Flowers Island, baptized 1830, aged 16 (DPHW 101); John, of Lower Burgeo, 1850 (DPHW 101); James Caines, of Moon's Face (Burgeo-La Poile district), 1855 (DPHW 98); George, fisherman of La Poile, 1860 (DPHW 99); Henry, of Shoal Cove East, 1871 (Lovell); John (and others), of St. John's Island, 1873 (MUN Hist.).

Modern status: Widespread, especially at St. John's, on the South Coast and in the St. Barbe district.

CAKE(S), surnames of England, from Middle English *kake, cake* – (maker of) cake(s), "a comparatively small flattened sort of bread, originally round or oval, usually baked hard on both sides by being turned in the process" (Reaney).

Traced by Guppy in Dorset and by Spiegelhalter in Devon.

In Newfoundland:

Early instances: R. Cake, of Lamaline, 1847 (*Nfld. Almanac*); Joseph, fisherman of East Cul de Sac, 1854 (DPHW 102); George, of Muddy Hole (Burin district), 1860 (DPHW 107); John, fisherman of Little Bay (La Poile B.), 1871 (Lovell).

Modern status: Cake, scattered, including St. John's, Lamaline and Rencontre West; Cakes, rare, at King's Point (Green B.).

CALDWELL, CARDWELL, surnames of England, Caldwell of Scotland and Ireland, Old English *ceald, wielle* – (dweller by the) cold spring or stream, the source of several English place names in a variety of forms, and of Caldwell (Renfrewshire). In Ireland Caldwell is "An English name now generally used as an anglicized form of *Ó hUarghuis* or *Ó hUairisce* (Horish, Houriskey) in Tyrone and of Cullivan and Colavin, *Mac Conluain*, in Co. Cavan." *See also* CADWELL. (Reaney, MacLysaght, Black).

Caldwell traced by Guppy in Lancashire and Ayrshire, by Spiegelhalter in Devon, and by MacLysaght in Cos. Tyrone and Cavan.

In Newfoundland:

Early instances: William Caldwell, sailmaker and Thomas, carpenter of St. John's, 1806 (CO 194.45); Edward, son of George of Greenock, Scotland, died 1885, aged 43 (General Protestant Cemetery, St. John's).

Modern status: Rare, Caldwell at St. John's (*Electors* 1955); Cardwell, at St. John's and Markland.

CALENDAR, CALLANDER, CALLENDER, variants of a surname of England and Scotland, from Old French *calendrier, calendreur* – one who calenders cloth, i.e. passes it through rollers for smoothing, or from the Scots place name Callander (Perthshire). (Reaney, Black).

Callender traced by Guppy in Durham.

In Newfoundland:

Modern status: Rare, Calendar, at St. John's (*Electors* 1955); Callander, at Torbay (*Electors* 1955); Callender, at Carbonear.

CALLA(G)HAN, surnames of Ireland, (O)Callaghan, *Ó Ceallacháin*, ? from Ir. *ceallach* – strife. (MacLysaght).

Traced by MacLysaght in the form (O)Callaghan, in Cos. Cork and Clare.

In Newfoundland:

Early instances: Daniel Callahan, cooper of St. John's, 1730 (CO 194.24); Derby Kallagan, of Harbour Main, 1750 (CO 194.12); William Callaghan, of Port de Grave, 1793 (Nfld. Archives T22); Joana Calahan, from Marcoom Parish (Co. Cork), married at St. John's, 1804 (Nfld. Archives BRC); John Callihan, of Harbour Grace Parish, 1806 (Nfld. Archives HGRC); Daniel Callahan, one of 72 impressed men who sailed from Ireland to Newfoundland, ? 1811 (CO 194.51); Thomas Callaghan, of Belle Isle (now Bell Island), 1812, of Portugal Cove, 1821 (DPHW 26D, D'Alberti 31); Jeremiah, of Fermeuse, 1813 (Nfld. Archives BRC); James Calahan, of King's Cove, 1823 (Nfld. Archives KCRC); Thomas Callahan, of Ragged Harbour (now Melrose), 1825 (Nfld. Archives KCRC); William Calahan, of Gooseberry Island (Bonavista B.), 1825 (Nfld. Archives KCRC); James Callahan, of Keels, 1827 (Nfld. Archives KCRC); Timothy Calahan, from Co. Tipperary, of Bonavista, 1828 (Nfld. Archives KCRC); Matthew Callahan, of Freshwater (Carbonear), 1828 (DPHW 48); Dennis Callaghan, of Carbonear, died 1839 (*Newfoundlander* 31 Oct 1839); Priscilla Callahan, of New Perlican, 1842 (DPHW 59); Martin Calahan, from Co. Waterford, of Harbour Grace, 1844 (*Indicator* 27 Jul 1844); Timothy Callahan, of Indian Island (Fogo district), 1855 (DPHW 83); James, from Co. Waterford, died at Carbonear, 1855, aged 61 (Carbonear R.C. Cemetery); Patrick, of Bay of Islands, 1871 (Lovell); John, tavern-keeper of Harbour Grace, 1871 (Lovell).

Modern status: Callaghan, at Pilley's Island; Callahan, scattered, especially at Corner Brook.

Place names: Callaghan Ground 49-31 55-29; Callaghans Ground 49-29 55-43.

CALLANAN, a surname of Ireland, recorded by Mac-Lysaght as (O)Callinan, *Ó Callanáin*. (MacLysaght).

Fairly widespread, and especially in Co. Cork (Irish Telephone Directory).

In Newfoundland:

Early instances: James J., born at St. John's, 1842 (Mott); Catherine, of Harbour Grace Parish, 1835 (Nfld. Archives HGRC); Maria, of Harbour Grace, 1870 (Nfld. Archives HGRC); John and William Callannan, of Spaniard's Bay, 1871 (Lovell).

Modern status: At St. John's.

CALLANDER. *See* CALENDAR

CALLEN, a surname of Scotland, a variant of Callan, from (Mac)(c)allan – son of Allan. Though not recorded by MacLysaght, Callen may perhaps be also in Ireland a variant of (O)Callan, *Ó Cathaláin*, Gaelic *cathal* – valour, bravery. (Reaney, Black, MacLysaght).

Black traced Callen in Dunoon (Argyll); MacLysaght traced (O)Callan in Cos. Armagh and Monaghan.

In Newfoundland:

Early instances: William ? Callons, of St. John's, 1705 (CO 194.3); George Callan, of St. John's, 1809 (DPHW 23); Edmund Calin, of Harbour Grace Parish, 1833 (Nfld. Archives HGRC); Catherine Callen, of St. John's, 1842 (DPHW 26D).

Modern status: At Norman's Cove and Long Cove (Trinity B.).

CALLENDER. *See* CALENDAR

CALLOWAY, KELLOWAY, surnames of England, ? from the French place name Caillouet (Eure). The family name in turn is the source of the English place name Kellaways (Wiltshire). (Reaney).

Spiegelhalter traced Callaway in Devon, and Guppy traced Kellaway in Dorset.

In Newfoundland:

Early instances: Captain Calloway, of Newfoundland, at Bristol between 1720 and 1740 (Carew); Mrs. Carraway, of Bay Roberts, 1816 (D'Alberti 26); Samuel Callaway, from Devon, aged 21, deserted from the brig *Devon* at St. John's, 1820 (*Nfld. Mercantile Journal* 18 May 1820); Samuel Kellaway, of Greenspond, 1825 (DPHW 76); Joab Killaway, planter of Perry's Cove, 1834 (DPHW 48); Charles Kellaway, of Swain's Island, 1836 (DPHW 76); William Caraway, of Exploits Burnt Island, 1841 (DPHW 86); Thomas Carraway, planter of Little Catalina, 1842 (DPHW 72); James Calloway or Kalloway, fisherman of Pool's Island, 1863 (DPHW 79); Michael Kellway, fisherman of Spout Cove, 1871 (Lovell).

Modern status: Calloway, at St. John's and Hants Harbour; Kelloway, scattered, especially at Perry's Cove and Salmon Cove (Carbonear).

CALVER, a surname of England, from the English place name Calver, (Derbyshire) – ridge for grazing calves. (Reaney, Cottle).

Traced by Guppy in Suffolk.

In Newfoundland:

Early instances: William Bernard, born at St. John's, 1795 (*Daily News* 23 Jun 1971); John, from Ipswich (Suffolk), late of St. John's, 1847 (*Royal Gazette* 30 Nov 1847).

Modern status: At St. John's.

CALVERT, a surname of England, Scotland and Ireland, from Old English *calf* and *hierde* – calf-herd. (Reaney).

Traced by Guppy in Yorkshire and by Mac-Lysaght in Ulster.

In Newfoundland:

Early instances: *See* below under Place Names.

Modern status: Unique, at St. John's.

Place names: Calvert 47-03 52-55; —— Bay 47-03 52-54, formerly Caplin Bay, renamed 1922 after Sir George Calvert, 1st baron Baltimore (? 1580–1632), who planted the colony of Avalon in Newfoundland in 1621–3.

CAMERON, a surname of Scotland and Ireland, in the Highlands of Scotland from the Gaelic *cam-shrón* – wry or hook nose (*See* CAMPBELL), in the Lowlands from the Scots place name Cameron (Fife). (Reaney, Black).

Traced by Guppy in Argyllshire and Perthshire and by MacLysaght in Ulster.

In Newfoundland:

Family tradition: Hugh, from Oban (Argyll), Scotland, settled at Carbonear about 1850 (Family).

Early instances: Alexander, ? of St. John's, ? 1744 (CO 194.32); John, of Harbour Grace Parish, 1829 (Nfld. Archives HGRC); John, of Catalina, 1858 (DPHW 67); Daniel (1816–1887), from Patrick, Scotland, died at St. John's in 1887 (General Protestant Cemetery, St. John's).

Modern status: At St. John's, Carbonear and scattered elsewhere.

CAMMIE, a Newfoundland variant of the surname of France Cami(n), from French *chemin* – (dweller on a country) road (as opposed to one who lives in a street or square in a town or village). (Dauzat).

In Newfoundland:

Modern status: Rare, especially at Benoit's Cove.

CAMP, a surname of England and France; in England, from Old English *campa* – warrior or *camp* – battle; in France from French *champ* – field. (Reaney, Dauzat).

Traced by Guppy in Derbyshire and Hertfordshire, and by Spiegelhalter in Devon.

In Newfoundland:

Early instances: Henry, member of the Board of Road Commissioners for the area from Garnish to Burin, 1857 (*Nfld. Almanac*); Henry, fisherman of Pushthrough, 1871 (Lovell).

Modern status: Scattered.

Place names (not necessarily from the surname): Camp Bay (Labrador) 52-10 55-39, 52-09 55-42; —— Cove 49-53 56-46, 50-07 56-43; —— Hill (Labrador) 56-37 61-34; —— Islands (Labrador) 52-10 55-39; —— Pond 49-57 56-00.

CAMPBELL, a surname of Scotland and Ireland; in Scotland and Co. Donegal from a Gaelic personal name *Caimbeul* – wry or crooked mouth (*See* CAMERON); in Ireland (Co. Tyrone) for *Mac Cathmhaoil*, Ir. *cathmhaoil* – battle chief. *See also* CAUL(E). (Reaney, Black, MacLysaght).

Traced by Guppy especially in Argyllshire and Perthshire, by MacLysaght in Cos. Donegal and Tyrone.

In Newfoundland:

Family tradition: The Campbells of Campbell's Creek, who may have been Acadians, came from Nova Scotia about 1870 (MUN Folklore, MUN Geog.).

Early instances: Colin, of Carbonear, 1702, of St. John's, 1703 (CO 194.2); James, of Salmon Cove (Conception B.), ? 1752 (CO 194.13); Samuel Campbel, of Trinity Bay, 1773 (DPHW 64); Colin Campbell, ? fisherman of Port de Grave, 1775 (Nfld. Archives T22); Alexander, of Harbour Grace, 1811 (D'Alberti 21); Malcolm, of Bonavista, 1816 (D'Alberti 26); James, from St. James Parish (unidentified) (Co. Wexford), married at St. John's, 1836 (Nfld. Archives BRC); John, fisherman of Nipper's Harbour, 1842 (DPHW 88); John, of Little Bay Islands, 1844 (DPHW 86); James, of Trinity, 1857 (Nfld. Archives KCRC); Mrs., schoolteacher at Bay de Verde, 1871 (Lovell); Alex and Archibald, farmers of Codroy and Rivers, 1871 (Lovell); Allen, fisherman of Red Rocks (near Cape Ray), 1871 (Lovell).

Modern status: Widespread, especially at St. John's, Campbell's Creek and elsewhere in the Port au Port district.

Place names: Campbell Hill 47-28 53-12, 49-38 55-48; Mount Campbell 49-34 56-50; Campbells Cove 48-31 58-51; —— Creek 48-31 58-52; —— Gully 47-44 53-22; Campbellton 49-17 54-56.

CANDOW, a surname of Scotland, probably from a Scots place name. Black notes that there was a Candow Park in Aberdeenshire about 1450. (Black).

Traced by Black in Angus and neighbourhood.

In Newfoundland:

Early instance: David, of King's Cove, 1836, of Tickle Cove (Bonavista South), 1838 (DPHW 73A).

Modern status: At St. John's and scattered elsewhere.

CANE, a surname of England and Ireland; in England from ? an Old English personal name *Cana*, or from Old French *cane* – cane, reed, ? for a tall, thin man, or from the French place name Caen (Calvados); or in Ireland for KANE. *See* CAIN. (Reaney, Mac-Lysaght).

Guppy traced Cane and Caine in Hampshire and Sussex, Spiegelhalter traced Cain and Cane in Devon, and MacLysaght traced Cain and Cane in Co. Mayo.

In Newfoundland:

Early instances: Donald, shoreman of St. John's, 1794–5, "22 years in Newfoundland," that is, 1772–3 (Census 1794–5); Thomas, servant of Harbour Grace, 1786 (CO 194.36); Emanuel Canes, of Burgeo Islands, 1830 (DPHW 30); Samuel, of Deadman's Island (between Port aux Basques and Burgeo), 1830 (DPHW 30); Elias Cane, fisherman of Change Islands, 1847 (DPHW 83); Samuel, fisherman of Bonne Bay, 1850 (DPHW 102).

Modern status: Rare, at St. John's.

CANNING, a surname of England and Ireland, ? from the Old English personal name *Can(n)a*, as in Cannington (Devon), or in Ireland also ? for *Ó Canáin*, or as a synonym of (O)Cannon, *Ó Canáin*, Ir. *cano* – wolf-cub. (Guppy, MacLysaght).

Canning was traced by Guppy in Hampshire, Warwickshire and Wiltshire, and by MacLysaght in Cos. Derry, Westmeath and Offaly.

In Newfoundland:

Family traditions: ——, from England, settled at Englee in the early 17th century (MUN Folklore). ——, from Protestant Ireland, settled at Englee in the late 1840s (MUN Folklore). ——, from Denmark *via* Ireland, settled at St. John's about 1816–20 (MUN Folklore).

Early instances: Edward, of St. John's, 1777 (DPHW 26C); John, planter of Freshwater (Carbonear), 1814 (DPHW 48); Samuel, of Lapworth (Warwickshire), died at St. John's, 1827, aged 29 (*Ledger*, V, 459); John, planter of Western Bay, 1830 (DPHW 52A); John, planter of Clown's Cove, 1832 (DPHW 48); Michael, of Ferryland, 1839 (Nfld. Archives BRC); William Cannings, of Muddy Hole (Green B.), 1850 (DPHW 76); Ann Canning, of Canada Bay, 1858 (DPHW 26D); Margaret Cannings,

of Barr'd Island, 1860 (DPHW 87); William, of Brooklyn (Bonavista B.), 1871 (Lovell); Samuel Canning, planter and trader of Witless Bay, 1871 (Lovell).

Modern status: Widespread, especially in the Twillingate and White Bay North districts.

Place names: Cannings Brook 48-39 55-32; —— Cove 48-27 53-51, 48-34 53-55; —— —— Head 48-27 53-50.

CANTWELL, a surname of England and Ireland, from the English place name Kentwell (Suffolk), in Ireland "completely hibernicized from the twelfth century" (MacLysaght). (Bardsley, Ekwall, MacLysaght).

Traced by MacLysaght in Co. Kilkenny.

In Newfoundland:

Early instances: Thomas, from Co. Tipperary, married at St. John's, 1808 (Nfld. Archives BRC); Patrick, of St. John's, 1814 (D'Alberti 24); Thomas, of Harbour Grace Parish, 1816 (Nfld. Archives HGRC); James, of Renews, 1827 (Nfld. Archives BRC); T., lighthouse keeper of Cape Spear, 1847 (*Nfld. Almanac*); Nicholas, farmer of Salmon Cove (now Avondale) and Gasters, 1871 (Lovell); James and Pierce, farmers of Torbay, 1871 (Lovell).

Modern status: Especially at St. John's and Harbour Main.

Place name: Cantwell's Cove 47-32, 52-38.

CARAVAN, KER(R)IVAN, ? Newfoundland variants of the surnames of Ireland, Garavan, *Ó Gairbhín*, Ir. *garbh* – rough, or Carabine, itself a variant of (O)Corribeen, *Ó Coirbín*, ? Ir. *corb* – chariot; or of the French surname Canivenc, Carivenc – seller of penknives. (MacLysaght, Dauzat). MacLysaght traced Carabine and Caravan in Co. Mayo,

In Newfoundland:

Early instances: Edward Canavan, of Trinity Bay, 1771 (DPHW 64); Thomas Keravan or Kerivan, of Bay Roberts, 1781, 1805 (CO 199.18, D'Alberti 15); John Ker(r)ivan, of Cape Cove (Bonavista B.), 1826, of Greenspond, 1829 (Nfld. Archives KCRC); Thomas Kerivan, from Co. Carlow, married at St. John's, 1829 (Nfld. Archives BRC); John, of Tilting Harbour (now Tilting), 1829 (Nfld. Archives KCRC); —— Kerravan, drowned at Flatrock (St. John's district), 1837 (*Newfoundlander* 8 Jun 1837); Patrick (and others) Kerevan, fishermen of Red Island (Placentia B.), 1871 (Lovell); Thomas Kerrivan, of Blackhead (St. John's district), 1871 (Lovell).

Modern status: Caravan, scattered, especially at Bay Roberts; Kerivan, at Point au Mal; Kerrivan, scattered, especially at St. John's and in the Placentia West district.

CARBAGE, a surname of Lebanon, *Kurbaj* (from Turkish) – whip.

In Newfoundland:

Family tradition: Abraham, from Baalbek (Lebanon) to Burin; his family moved to Bell Island after his death (MUN Folklore).

Modern status: At Bell Island.

CARBERRY, a surname of Scotland and Ireland; in Scotland from the Scots place name in Midlothian; in Ireland (Mac) Carbery, *Mac Cairbre*, ? from the personal name *Cairbre* – charioteer, or (O)Carbery, *Ó Cairbre*.

MacLysaght traced (Mac)Carbery in Co. Waterford, (O)Carbery in Co. Westmeath.

In Newfoundland:

Early instances: Richard, fisherman of St. John's, 1794–5, "9 years in Newfoundland," that is, 1785–6 (Census 1794–5); Manuel Carberrey, proprietor and occupier of fishing room at Turk's Cove (Trinity B.), Winter 1800–01 (Census Trinity B.); Richard Carbery, of Carpoon (Quirpon), 1805 (DPHW 64); Mary Carberry, of Trinity Bay, 1806 (Nfld. Archives BRC); Joanna, from Waterford city, of St. John's, 1809 (Nfld. Archives BRC); Richard, of Filthy (now British) Harbour, 1813 (DPHW 64); James, of Harbour Grace Parish, 1816 (Nfld.Archives HGRC); John Carbry, of Heart's Content, 1819 (Nfld. Archives KCRC); William Carberry, planter of (?Old) Bonaventure, 1831 (DPHW 64B); Ellen Carbery, of Heart's Desire, 1832 (Nfld. Archives KCRC); John, planter of Trinity (Trinity B.), 1840, of Ragged Rock Cove, 1843 (DPHW 64B); Jubal, of Burgeons (Burgoynes) Cove, 1858 (DPHW 64B).

Modern status: Scattered, especially at St. John's.

CARD, a surname of England, from an Old English personal name *Cærda* (Spiegelhalter) or from Old French *carde* – (maker of) teasel-head(s) or wool-card(s). (Reaney).

Traced by Spiegelhalter in Devon.

In Newfoundland:

Early instances: Andrew Carde, boatkeeper of St. John's Harbour, 1682 (CO 1); Christopher Card, of Placentia ? district, 1744 (CO 194.22); Samuel, of St. John's, 1762 (CO 194.15); William, planter of Merritts Harbour, 1820 (USPG); James (and others), of Herring Neck, 1871 (Lovell).

Modern status: Scattered, especially at Merritts Harbour.

Place name: Card's Harbour 49-31 55-38.

CARDOULIS, a variant of a surname of an island off Sicily, ? from the Latin *carduelis* – goldfinch, though the family maintains a Greek origin.

In Newfoundland:

Modern status: Rare, at St. John's.

CARDWELL. *See* CALDWELL

CARE, a surname of England, a variant of Kear, from Old English *cæg* – (maker of) key(s). (Reaney).

In Newfoundland:

Early instance: John, fisherman of Cupids, 1836 (DPHW 34).

Modern status: From Folkestone (Kent) since 1954, first at Petty Harbour and later at Goulds (St. John's district).

CAREEN, a variant of a surname of Ireland, most likely (O)Curreen, *Ó Cuirín*, or Creen, *Ó Cuireen*.

MacLysaght traced Curreen in Co. Waterford, Creen in Co. Kerry.

In Newfoundland:

Family tradition: Two brothers, Edward and Philip, came to Point Lance (St. Mary's district) as planters from Dingle (Co. Kerry) (Family).

Early instances: Mary Caren, defendant before Supreme Court, 1810 (CO 194.50); Dennis, from Templorum Parish (Co. Kilkenny), married at St. John's, 1812 (Nfld. Archives BRC); Clement Carien, from Duncormick (Co. Wexford), married at St. John's, 1821 (Nfld. Archives BRC); Edward Caren, of Harbour Grace Parish, 1834 (Nfld. Archives HGRC); Edward, fisherman, and Philip, planter, Carew (? for Careen), of Point Lance, 1871 (Lovell).

Modern status: At Placentia, Branch and Point Lance (*Electors* 1955).

CAREW, a surname of England and Ireland, from the Welsh place name Carew (Pembrokeshire) (Spiegelhalter), or from the French surname Carron – cartwright or wheelwright (MacLysaght), or for CAREY as Carew is sometimes pronounced.

Guppy and Spiegelhalter traced Carew in Devon, MacLysaght in Tipperary.

In Newfoundland:

Early instances: Patrick, of Musketta (now Bristols Hope), 1779 (CO 199.18); Dennis, of St. John's, 1779 (DPHW 26C); Anne, of Witless Bay, married at Bay Bulls, 1805 (Nfld. Archives BRC); Thomas Ca(i)rew, Kereu or Carrew, of King's Cove, 1816 (Nfld. Archives KCRC); Walter Carew, from Shillenall Parish (unidentified) (Co. Tipperary), married at St. John's, 1817 (Nfld. Archives BRC);

Thomas, of Harbour Grace Parish, 1817 (Nfld. Archives HGRC); Judith Cairew, of Ragged Harbour (now Melrose), 1817 (Nfld. Archives KCRC); Michael, of Catalina, 1821 (Nfld. Archives K829 (Nfld. Archives KCRC); Martin Carew, of Torbay, 1836 (Nfld. Archives BRC); James, of Keels, 1860 (Nfld. Archives KCRC); Mary, of Knights Cove, 1863 (Nfld. Archives KCRC); Grace, of Open Hall, 1868 (Nfld. Archives KCRC); scattered in Lovell 1871.

Modern status: Widespread, especially at St. John's, Witless Bay and in the Ferryland district.

CAREY, a surname of England, Ireland and Guernsey (Channel Islands), from the English place name Carey Barton (Devon) after the river Carey – the friendly, pleasant stream; or as the anglicized form of seven Gaelic Irish surnames; or for CAREW; or ? as a variant of the French and Guernsey family name Carré. (Cottle, Bardsley, Ekwall, MacLysaght).

Bardsley describes Car(e)y as "a great West-country surname." Traced by Spiegelhalter in Devon, by Cottle in Somerset; and in Guernsey.

In Newfoundland:

Early instances: Peter, planter of Isle Grole, 1710–15 (CO 194.5); Thomas Cary, constable of Ferryland district, about 1730–32 (CO 194.9); Dennis Car(e)y, mason of St. John's, 1771 (DPHW 26C); Patrick, of Trinity Bay, 1787 (DPHW 64); Darby, from Callan (Co. Kilkenny), Irish convict landed at Petty Harbour or Bay Bulls, 1789 (CO 194.38); Stephen, of Bay Bulls, 1793 (USPG); Thomas, of Bay Roberts, 1798 (DPHW 48); Mary, of Witless Bay, 1806 (Nfld. Archives BRC); Mary, from Ross (Co. Wexford), married at St. John's, 1810 (Nfld. Archives BRC); Pat, of Harbour Grace Parish, 1813 (Nfld. Archives HGRC); Michael, of Catalina, 1824 (Nfld. Archives KCRC); T., member of the Board of Road Commissioners of Bonavista Bay, for the area Keels to Broad Cove (now Duntara), 1844 (*Nfld. Almanac*); Samuel Cary, of Herring Neck, 1845 (DPHW 86); Maurice, of Broad Cove (now Duntara), 1850 (Nfld. Archives KCRC); Mary Anne, of Kings Cove, 1864 (Nfld. Archives KCRC); Henry, of Keels, 1867 (Nfld. Archives KCRC); Johanna, of Open Hall, 1869 (Nfld. Archives KCRC); Mary, of Knights Cove, 1869 (Nfld. Archives KCRC); John, of Fortune Harbour, 1871 (Lovell).

Modern status: Scattered, especially at Fortune Harbour (*Electors* 1955), Windsor, St. John's and in the Ferryland district.

Place names: Carey Island (Labrador) 56-43 61-13; Careys Rock, Cary Rock 48-38 53-24; —— Cove 48-43 53-54; Carys Long Pond 48-23 53-29.

CARLSON, a surname of Sweden – son of Carl.

In Newfoundland:

Family tradition: One family from Sweden, settled at St. John's in the 19th century, the other from Sweden, via Boston (Mass.), settled at St. John's about 1939 (Family).

Modern status: At Gander and St. John's.

CARMICHAEL, a surname of England, Scotland and Ireland, from the Scots place name Carmichael (Lanarkshire) – the fort of Michael. (Cottle, Black).

Guppy found Carmichael in Northumberland and widespread in Scotland, MacLysaght in Ulster.

In Newfoundland:

Early instances: ——, captain of the brig *Alexander*, 1831 (*Newfoundlander* 1 Sep 1831); James, clerk of St. John's, 1871 (Lovell); James Boyd (about 1849–1897), from Dunfermline (Fife), Scotland, died 1897 (General Protestant Cemetery, St. John's); James Adamson (1860–1929), from Scotland, came to Newfoundland in early manhood and settled at St. John's (*Nfld. Who's Who* 1930).

Modern status: At St. John's.

CARNELL, a surname of England, from Old Norman French *carnel*, Old French *crenel* – (the arbalester at the) embrasure (or on the) battlement, or ? for the French family name Carnel. In Newfoundland the name may have been confused with CORNELL. (Reaney).

Traced by Spiegelhalter in Devon.

In Newfoundland:

Family traditions: John, born at Torquay (Devon), 1790, came to St. John's in 1812 as a master millwright to build a flour mill there. His son, Samuel George was the founder of a carriage factory (Nfld. Archives T57, T80). John Carnell or ? Cornell, of Catalina, was one of the first settlers of Flowers Cove, 1850 (MUN Hist.).

Early instances: Abraham, of Back Cove (Port de Grave), 1775 (CO 199.18); John, of Ochre Pit Cove, 1776 (CO 199.18); ——, ? of St. John's, 1806 (CO 194.45); ——, of Northern Bay, 1806 (D'Alberti 16); John, of ? Torbay, 1812 (DPHW 26D); Richard, planter of Western Bay, 1826 (DPHW 52A); John, native of Bishopsteinton (Devon), millwright of Riverhead Mill, St. John's, deceased 1840 (*Nfld. Patriot* 19 Dec 1840); Henry, of Catalina, 1842 (DPHW 26D); John Joseph, of Harbour Grace, 1861 (DPHW 26D); Richard and William, of Indian Islands (Twillingate and Fogo districts), 1871 (Lovell); Joseph, of Musgrave Town (now Musgrave Harbour), 1871 (Lovell).

Modern status: Scattered, especially at St. John's and Flowers Cove.

Place name: Carnell Cove 47-47 55-47.

CARNEY. *See* KEARNEY

CARPENTER, a surname of England and Ireland, from Anglo-French *carpenter* – carpenter; in Ireland usually for Mac Ateer, *Mac an tSaoir*, Ir. *saor* – craftsman, free. (Reaney, Cottle, MacLysaght). Guppy found Carpenter widespread, especially in Oxfordshire and Wiltshire, Spiegelhalter in Devon.

In Newfoundland:

Early instances: John Waldon, married at St. John's, 1758 (DPHW 26D); Nicholas, from Cramlin (Co. Dublin), Irish convict landed at Petty Harbour or Bay Bulls, 1789 (CO 194.38); Richard, servant of Battle Harbour, 1795 (MUN Hist.); John, of Bonavista, 1797 (DPHW 70); Elizabeth, of Kings Cove, 1827, of Keels, 1827 (Nfld. Archives KCRC); George, of Catalina, 1835 (DPHW 67); George, of Little Catalina, 1842 (DPHW 67).

Modern status: Scattered, especially at Little Catalina.

CARR, KERR, surnames of England, Scotland and Ireland, from Middle English *kerr* – (dweller by the) marsh or wet ground overgrown with brushwood (Reaney, Cottle), or ? from Old English *carr* – rock, an element in some English place names, or ? from Cornish *caer* – fort, town (Spiegelhalter), or as the anglicized form of several different Irish surnames (MacLysaght). *See also* CARSON.

Guppy found Carr widespread especially in Northumberland, Cumberland, Westmorland and Yorkshire, and Kerr numerous in the Scottish border counties; Spiegelhalter traced Carr in Devon.

In Newfoundland:

Early instances: William Kerr, of St. John's, 1781 (DPHW 26C); Duggle Carr, soldier of St. John's, 1781 (DPHW 26C).

Modern status: Carr, at St. John's; Kerr, at St. John's and Point au Mal (*Electors* 1955).

CARRIGAN, CORRIGAN, surnames of Ireland, *Ó Corragáin*. (MacLysaght).

Scattered in Ireland.

In Newfoundland:

Early instances: Anstace Corrigan, from Co. Kilkenny "an old offender," married at St. John's, 1811 (Nfld. Archives BRC); Martin Carrigan, of Harbour Grace Parish, 1815 (Nfld. Archives HGRC); Mary Corrigan, of Trinity, 1817 (Nfld. Archives

KCRC); Peter Corrogan, from Sutton's Parish (Co. Wexford), of St. John's, 1828 (*Newfoundlander* 22 May 1828); J. Carrigan, of St. John's, 1832 (*Newfoundlander* 20 Sep 1832); Thomas Currigan, fisherman of Red Island (Placentia B.), 1871 (Lovell); James and Joseph Corrigan, fishermen of Trepassey, 1871 (Lovell).

Modern status: Carrigan, at St. John's; Corrigan, scattered, especially at Trepassey and Red Island.

CARROL(L), surnames of Ireland, either (Mac)Carroll, *Mac Carbhaill*, or (O)Carroll, *Ó Cearbhaill*. MacLysaght). MacLysaght traced (Mac)Carroll in Leinster and Ulster, (O)Carroll in Cos. Kilkenny, Louth and Offaly.

In Newfoundland:

Family traditions: Patrick, settled at Carbonear ? before 1845 (Family). Patrick (1823–), from Garvan (Co. Kilkenny), settled at Conche in 1851 (Casey).

Early instances: John Carroll, of St. John's, 1708 (CO 194.4); Charles Carrol, of Harbour Grace, 1794, property at Bryant's Cove "possess'd by the Family for 50 years," that is, 1744 (CO 199.18); Charles, fisherman of Port de Grave, 1774 (Nfld. Archives T22); Michael, of Musketta (now Bristol's Hope), 1790 (CO William Carroll, shoreman of Torbay, 1794–5, "12 years in Newfoundlandland," that is, 1782–3 (Census 1794–5); Edmond Carral, occupier of fishing room at New Harbour, Winter 1800–01 (Census Trinity B.); C.W., occupier of fishing room at Old Perlican, Winter 1800–01 (Census Trinity B.); Catherine, from Carrick-on-Suir (Co. Tipperary), married at St. John's, 1803 (Nfld. Archives BRC); Bridget Carrol, from Ballyhale (Co. Kilkenny), married at St. John's, 1804 (Nfld. Archives BRC); Anne, of Trepassey, married at St. John's, 1813 (Nfld. Archives BRC); John Carroll, of Kings Cove, 1815 (Nfld. Archives KCRC); Joseph Carrol, of Bonavista, 1815 (DPHW 70); Margaret Carroll, from Co. Kilkenny, married at Fogo Harbour, 1817 (Nfld. Archives KCRC); Margaret, of Ragged Harbour (now Melrose), 1818 (Nfld. Archives KCRC); Thomas, of Greenspond, 1822 (Nfld. Archives KCRC); Thomas, of Trinity, 1825 (Nfld. Archives KCRC); Michael, of Bird Island Cove (now Elliston), 1826 (Nfld. Archives KCRC); Michael, of Fortune Harbour, 1830 (Nfld. Archives KCRC); James Carrell, of Twillingate, 1832 (Nfld. Archives KCRC), James Carrol, of Lower Burgeo, 1834 (DPHW 101); John Carroll, native of Bermuda, of St. John's, died 1848 (*Nfld. Patriot* 5 Jan 1848); James, of Broad Cove (now Duntara), 1850 (Nfld. Archives KCRC); Margaret, of Gooseberry Island (Bonavista B.), 1863 (Nfld. Archives KCRC); widespread in Lovell 1871.

Modern status: Carrol, rare and scattered; Carroll, widespread, especially at Fortune Harbour (*Electors* 1955), St. John's, and in the White Bay North district.

Place names: Carrol Cove (N.W. shore, Straits of Bell Isle, Labrador) 51-41 56-31; —— Hill 49-49 56-34; —— Island (Labrador) 53-27 55-45; —— Point (Labrador) 51-40 56-30; —— Cove (Labrador) 52-10 55-42; Carroll Point 47-45 54-14; Carrolls Cove (St. Carols) 51-23 55-30, (Labrador) 52-09 55-42; Carrols Cove (Labrador) 52-10 55-42.

CARSON, a surname of England, Scotland and Ireland, – (son of the dweller in or near a) marsh, rock or fort (*See* CARR); or for French *garçon* – servant, boy; or a pet-form of names beginning with *Car-*. (E.C. Smith).

Traced in Kircudbrightshire, and by MacLysaght in Ulster.

In Newfoundland:

Early instances: William (1770–1843), M.D., born at "The Billies" (Kirkcudbrightshire), came to Newfoundland in 1808, died at St. John's in 1843 (Nfld. Archives T13, *Nfld. Patriot* 1 Mar 1843); George, fisherman of Harbour Grace, 1871 (Lovell); George, telegraph operator of Heart's Content, 1871 (Lovell).

Modern status: Rare, at Tilting (Fogo district) (*Electors* 1955) and St. John's.

CARTER, a surname of England, Ireland, Scotland and Guernsey (Channel Islands) – maker or driver of carts; in Ireland "sometimes used for MacArthur." (Reaney, Cottle, MacLysaght, Turk).

Widespread in England, including Devon, and Ireland. (Guppy, MacLysaght).

In Newfoundland:

Family tradition: William, of Gaultois, later of Pass Island (Hermitage B.), fog alarm keeper, late 19th century (MUN Hist).

Early instances: John, of Old Perlican, 1675, 1682 (CO 1); ——, of Quidi Vidi, 1703 (CO 194.3); Chris., of St. John's, 1705 (CO 194.22); John Sr. and Jr., of Old Perlican, 1708–09 (CO 194.4); Joseph and Benjamin, in possession of fishing room at Ship Island, Greenspond Harbour, built by the family in 1725 (Bonavista Register 1806); Robert, J.P. for Ferryland, 1738 (D'Alberti 6); ——, of Trinity (Trinity B.), 1779 (CO 194.34); Joseph, of Twillingate, 1814 (Dorset County Record Office per Kirwin); Anne, born at Pool's Island, baptized 1830, aged 6 (DPHW 76); William, of Newell's Island, baptized 1830, aged 31 (DPHW 76); William, of Little

Codroy River, 1835 (DPHW 30); Archibald, fisherman of Transway [? François 1871, below] (Fortune B. – Burin), 1850 (DPHW 102); Edward (and others), of Cape Ray, 1871 (Lovell); George and William, of Channel, 1871 (Lovell); William, of Codroy and Rivers, 1871 (Lovell); Kenneth, merchant of Fogo, 1871 (Lovell); Archibald, planter of François, 1871 (Lovell); Job, of Hare Bay, 1871 (Lovell); Benjamin and Job, of Swain's Island, 1871 (Lovell); Rev. G.W.B., of Topsail, 1871 (Lovell); James (and others), of Witless Bay, 1871 (Lovell).

Modern status: Widespread, especially at St. John's and in the Burgeo-La Poile, Bonavista North and Humber East districts.

Place names: Carter Basin (Labrador) 53-29 59-50; —— Head, —— Head Rock 49-41 54-45; —— Lake 48-35 56-21; Carter's Cove and Head 49-32 54-48; —— Head 49-40 54-46.

CARVILLE, a surname of England, from the French place name Carville (Calvados, Seine-Inférieure). (Reaney, Bardsley).

Traced by Bardsley in Norfolk in the 16th and 17th centuries.

In Newfoundland:

Modern status: Rare, at St. John's and Kippens.

CASE, a surname of England, a variant of Cass, diminutive of the feminine baptismal name Cassandra, popular in the Middle Ages after the Trojan princess. (Reaney, Cottle, Withycombe).

Traced by Guppy in Norfolk and by Spiegelhalter in Devon.

In Newfoundland:

Family tradition: ——, of Welsh ancestry, inhabitant of Salmon Cove (Carbonear) in the 19th century (MUN Folklore).

Early instances: Katherine, of St. John's, 1753 (DPHW 26C); Ananias, of Marshall's Folly (Carbonear), 1830 (DPHW 52A); Hanniah, of Salmon Cove (Carbonear), 1837 (DPHW 48); James, fisherman of Otterbury (Carbonear), 1855 (DPHW 49); Elizabeth, of Carbonear, 1871 (Lovell); Samuel and Thomas, fishermen of Heart's Delight, 1871 (Lovell); Nehemiah, planter of Petty Harbour, 1871 (Lovell).

Modern status: Scattered, especially at St. John's and Salmon Cove (Carbonear).

CASEY, a surname of Ireland, either (Mac) Casey, *Mac Cathasaigh* or (O)Casey, *Ó Cathasaigh*, Ir. *cathasach* – watchful. (MacLysaght).

MacLysaght traced (Mac)Casey formerly in Co. Monaghan, (O)Casey in all provinces (especially

Southwest Munster), except Ulster. "Owing to dropping the prefixes Mac and O, Casey families properly MacCasey are now thought to be O'Casey" (MacLysaght).

In Newfoundland:

Early instances: John, carpenter of St. John's, 1794–5, "8 years in Newfoundland," that is, 1786–7 (Census 1794–5); John, of Trepassey, 1804 (D'Alberti 14); William, of Fogo, 1805 (D'Alberti 15); John, from Lismore (Co. Waterford), married at St. John's, 1808 (Nfld. Archives BRC); James Casay, from Kilfinane (Co. Limerick), shoreman of Trepassey, deceased, 1811 (*Royal Gazette* 26 Dec 1811); Margaret Casey, of Harbour Grace Parish, 1814 (Nfld. Archives HGRC); William Casey or C(e)acy, of Kings Cove, 1815 (Nfld. Archives KCRC); Mary Casey, from Carrick (unspecified), married at Bonavista, 1821 (Nfld. Archives KCRC); Betsy, of Keels, 1822 (Nfld. Archives KCRC); Joanna, of Joe Batts Arm, 1825 (Nfld. Archives KCRC); Mary, of Witless Bay, 1825 (Nfld. Archives BRC); Catherine, of Torbay, 1825 (Nfld. Archives BRC); John Ceacy, of Carbonear, 1828 (Nfld. Archives HGRC); Patrick Casey, of Herring Neck, 1829 (Nfld. Archives KCRC); Patrick, of Bird Island (unspecified), 1832 (Nfld. Archives KCRC); Patrick, of Chamberlains, 1838 (DPHW 26D); William, of Black Island (unspecified), 1845, of Sholes Cove (unspecified), 1855 (Nfld. Archives KCRC); Michael, of Greenspond, 1849 (Nfld. Archives KCRC); Michael, of Dog Cove (Bonavista B.), 1850 (Nfld. Archives KCRC); Ellen Dower *née* Casey, of Conche, 1851 (Casey); Timothy, of Cotterels Island, 1856 (Nfld. Archives KCRC); Mary, of Haywards Cove (Bonavista B.), 1857 (Nfld. Archives KCRC); Mary, of Topsail, 1858 (DPHW 26D); Timothy, of Burnt Island (Bonavista B.), 1860 (Nfld. Archives KCRC); Mary, of Gooseberry Island (Bonavista B.), 1862 (Nfld. Archives KCRC); Peter, of Harbour Grace, 1868 (Nfld. Archives KCRC); scattered in Lovell 1871.

Modern status: Scattered, especially at St. John's and Crouse.

CASHIN, a surname of Ireland (Mac) Cashin, (often O Cashin in Munster), *Mac Caisin*, ? Ir. *cas* – bent or pleasant. (MacLysaght).

MacLysaght traced MacCashin in Co. Leix, O'Cashin in Munster.

In Newfoundland:

Family tradition: John Cashin, from Wexford, came to Newfoundland in 1811 (MUN Folklore).

Early instances: John Cashon, of St. John's, 1778 (DPHW 26C); Joanna Cashin, from Ross (Co.

Wexford), married at St. John's, 1811 (Nfld. Archives BRC); Joann, of Harbour Grace Parish, 1812 (Nfld. Archives HGRC); James, of Keels, 1813 (Nfld. Archives BRC); Richard Cashion, of Kings Cove, 1815 (Nfld. Archives KCRC); Margaret, of Bonavista, 1818 (Nfld. Archives KCRC); John, from Co. Tipperary, of Ragged Harbour (now Melrose), 1819 (Nfld. Archives KCRC); Richard Cashion, Cashin or Cashan, of Gooseberry Island (Bonavista B.), 1822 (Nfld. Archives KCRC); Mary Cashion, from Co. Kilkenny, married at Trinity, 1828 (Nfld. Archives KCRC); Richard Cashin, married at Greenspond, 1830 (Nfld. Archives KCRC); Mary, of Silly Cove (now Winterton), 1832 (Nfld. Archives KCRC); J., of Ferryland, 1844 (*Nfld. Almanac*); Bridget, of Sholes Cove (unspecified), 1855 (Nfld. Archives KCRC); Patrick, of Cottles Island, 1860 (Nfld. Archives KCRC); Martin and Richard, of Cape Broyle, 1871 (Lovell).

Modern status: Scattered, especially at Gambo, Gander and Port au Port.

CASHMAN, a surname of England and Ireland; in England, a catchpoll (Bardsley); in Ireland, the Co. Cork variant of (O)Kissane, *Ó Cíosáin*, Ir. *cíos* – tribute, rent (MacLysaght).

In Newfoundland:

Early instances: John, of Trinity (Trinity B.), 1790 (DPHW 64); William, of Old Perlican, 1821 (DPHW 58), John, of Hants Harbour, 1823 (DPHW 64B); John, of Harbour Grace Parish, 1824 (Nfld. Archives HGRC); James, of Herring Neck, 1829 (Nfld. Archives KCRC); William, of Caplin Cove (Trinity B.), 1829 (DPHW 59A); James, of Fortune Harbour, 1832 (Nfld. Archives KCRC); Thomas, from Co. Waterford, died at Conche, 1851 (Casey).

Modern status: At Heart's Content (*Electors* 1955).

CASSELL, CASTLE, surnames of England, for one who lived near, worked at, paid rent to or performed services for the castle, or from the English place name Castle, which occurs, for example, six times in Devon. (Reaney, Speigelhalter).

Castle traced by Guppy in Berkshirlhalter in Devon.

In Newfoundland:

Early instances: William Cassels, of St. John's, 1780 (D'Alberti 6); William Castle, of Herring Neck, 1855 (DPHW 85); William, of Pike's Arm (Twillingate), 1857 (DPHW 85); James, fisherman of Green Cove (Twillingate), 1857 (DPHW 85); George Cashill (and others), of Great Harbour Deep, 1871

(Lovell); George and James Cassell, of Herring Neck, 1871 (Lovell).

Modern status: Cassell, scattered, especially in the White Bay North and South districts; Castle, at Glendale (*Electors* 1955).

CASWELL, a surname of England and Guernsey (Channel Islands), a variant of Cresswell etc., from Old English *cærse* and *wiella* – (dweller by the) watercress-stream, or from the English place names containing these elements, including Carswell (Berkshire, Devon), Caswell (Dorset, Northamptonshire, Somerset). (Reaney, Turk).

Traced by Guppy in Lincolnshire.

In Newfoundland:

Early instance: John Casswell or Castwell, of Lower Burgeo, 1849 (DPHW 101) .

Modern status: Very rare, at St. John's (*Electors* 1955) and St. Phillips.

CATER, CHAYTER, CHAYTOR, surnames of England, from Old French *achatour*, Middle English *(a)catour* – buyer of provisions for a large household, caterer, or from the English place name Cator (Devon). *See* CHEATER from which some Chaytors in Newfoundland changed their name. (Reaney, Cottle).

In Newfoundland:

Family tradition: John Cater (1824–1869), from Devonshire; John Edwin Cater (1860–1930), moved from Dog Bay (now Horwood) to Grand Falls in 1908 (F. Cater, L. Goulding).

Early instances: Michael Chaytor, carpenter ? of St. John's, 1814 (CO 194.55); James Chater, of Greenspond, 1829 (DPHW 76); George Chaytor, of Chamberlains, 1859 (DPHW 26D); .

Modern status: Cater, at Grand Falls; Chayter, at Botwood; Chaytor, scattered, especially at Flat Island (Bonavista B.) (*Electors* 1955), St. John's and Chamberlains.

CAUL(E), surnames of England and, as MacCall, MacCaul, of Ireland. In England from Middle English *colle* – (maker of a) close-fitting cap worn by women; in Ireland, where Mac is retained, MacCall and MacCaul are anglicized forms of *Mac Cathmhaoil*, Ir. *cathmhaoil* – battle chief, also anglicized as CAMPBELL, and variants of MacCahill (*See* CAHILL). (Reaney, MacLysaght).

MacLysaght traced MacCall, MacCaul in Cos. Tyrone and Armagh.

In Newfoundland:

Early instances: Stephen Caul, of Harbour Grace Parish, 1832 (Nfld. Archives HGRC); Simon,

fisherman of Isle Valen, 1871 (Lovell); David, fisherman of Trinity (Trinity B.), 1871 (Lovell); Margaret Caull, of Kings Cove, 1876 (Nfld. Archives KCRC).

Modern status: Caul, scattered, especially at St. John's and Davis Cove; Caule, at St. John's.

CAVE, a surname of England and Guernsey (Channel Islands), from Latin *calvus*, Old French *c(h)auf* – bald, in England also from the English place name Cave (Yorkshire ER), after a swift (OE *cāf*) stream nearby. *See also* CHAFE, CHAFFEY. (Reaney, Cottle, Ekwall, Turk).

Traced by Guppy in Dorset, Northamptonshire, Oxfordshire, Wiltshire and by Spiegelhalter in Devon.

In Newfoundland:

Early instances: Benjamin Jr., of Fogo, 1803 (D'Alberti 13); Susannah, of Change Islands, 1821 (USPG); Thomas, of Pouch Cove, 1833 (DPHW 26D); ——, on the *Margaret* in the seal fishery out of Bay Roberts, 1838 (*Newfoundlander* 29 Mar 1838); Robert (and others), of St. John's, 1871 (Lovell).

Modern status: Scattered, especially at Bay Roberts and Change Islands.

CEASAR, CEASER, ? Newfoundland variants of the surname of England Cayzer etc., a pageant name ultimately from the Latin *Caesar* – emperor, or ? for the baptismal names and surnames of France César or Césaire, of which the latter represents the name of a saint *Caesarius*, bishop of Arles in the 6th century. (Reaney, Dauzat).

Guppy traced Cesar in Surrey.

In Newfoundland:

Modern status: Very rare; Ceasar, at Burin (*Electors* 1955) and Bulls Cove; Ceaser, at Burin Bay (*Electors* 1955) and Salmonier (Burin district).

CHAFE, a surname of England, a variant of Chaff(e), CAVE etc., from Latin *calvus*, Old French *c(h)auf* – bald. *See also* CHAFFEY. (Reaney).

A Devon name, traced by Guppy as Chave, especially in Tiverton, by Spiegelhalter as Chaff(e), and by Matthews as Chafe.

In Newfoundland:

Early instances: John, of Petty Harbour, 1708 (CO 194.4); John Chaffe, of Bay Bulls, 1708–09, of Petty Harbour, 1720–25 (CO 194.4, 7); —— Chafe, constable of St. John's district, ? 1730 (CO 194.9); Samuel, of St. John's, 1759 (DPHW 26D); Michael Cheeffe, of Harbour Grace Parish, 1819 (Nfld. Archives HGRC); Thomas Chafe, from Devon, life-long resident of Petty Harbour, died 1843, aged 70 (*Nfld. Patriot* 8 Mar 1843, *Royal Gazette* 7 Nov 1843); Abraham, of Quidi Vidi, 1858 (DPHW 29).

Modern status: Especially at St. John's and Petty Harbour.

CHAFFEY, a surname of England, ? not recorded elsewhere, ? a variant of CHAFE, or ? from the English place name Chaffhay Farm (Devon), containing the Old English elements *cealf* – calf and *(ge)hæg* – (? worker at the) calves' enclosure. (Gover).

In Newfoundland:

Early instances: Thomas, of Bonavista, 1803 (DPHW 70); James Cheaffy, of Greenspond, 1838 (DPHW 76); John Chaffey, of Change Islands, 1843 (DPHW 83); Thomas Chaffy, of Amherst Cove (Bonavista B.), 1871 (Lovell); Joseph Chaffey, of Crabbe's Brook, 1871 (Lovell); James, of Shambler's Cove, 1871 (Lovell); Joseph Chaffy, farmer of Codroy, 1877 (Lovell).

Modern status: Scattered, especially in the St. George's and Bonavista South districts.

CHAISSON, a variant, not recorded by Dauzat, of the surname of France Chasson, from the French place name Chasson (Côte-d'Or, Isère etc.). (Dauzat). G.R. Thomas maintains that Chaisson seems to be a peculiarly local Newfoundland form of Chiasson, a family name of Acadia, but offers no interpretation. Neither form is in Dauzat. *See* JESSEAU, JESSO.

In Newfoundland:

Family tradition: Laurent Chiasson (for Chaisson), from France, settled at Margaree (Cape Breton) in the early 19th century. Two grandsons settled in Newfoundland, Nazaire Chiasson, of Chéticamp, N.S., settled at Cape St. George about 1855 (G.R. Thomas) and Julien at Petit Jardin (SW of Stephenville) about 1850–70 (MUN Geog.).

Early instances: —— Chaisson, captain of the *Providence*, 1856 (*Newfoundlander* 22 Sep 1856); Isidore, fisherman of Channel, 1871 (Lovell); O. (and others) Shuisoing, of Cod Roy and Rivers, 1871 (Lovell).

Modern status: Scattered, on the West Coast especially in the St. George's and Port-au-Port districts.

CHALKER, a surname of England and Guernsey (Channel Islands), from Old English *(ge)cealcian* – to whiten, hence a whitewasher; but in Kent and Wiltshire, a dweller on the chalk or at one of the places so-called. *See also* CHAULK. (Reaney, Turk).

Traced in Devon.

In Newfoundland:

Family tradition: George Sr., emigrated to Newfoundland from Dartmouth (Devon) where, it is alleged, he was wanted for sheep-stealing. The family settled at Exploits about 1843, and later at Brigus, George C. Chalker (died 1899) is said to have had Georgetown named after him, though the same claim has been made for George Gushue (MUN Geog.).

Early instance: Thomas, cooper of Brigus, 1834 (DPHW 34).

Modern status: At St. John's.

Place name: Chalker Point 47-55 55-48

CHAMBERS, a surname of England, Scotland and Ireland, "originally official, identical with Chamberlain," "an officer charged with the management of the private chambers of a sovereign or nobleman," but "It was later used of a chamber-attendant, chamber-man, chamber-maid." (Reaney, Black, MacLysaght).

Chambers was found by Guppy widespread especially in Suffolk, and by Spiegelhalter in Devon; MacLysaght found it numerous but scattered, mainly in Ulster and Mayo.

In Newfoundland:

Family traditions: Aaron Chambers came from Scotland with his parents who settled at Deadman's Cove (St. Barbe district), about 1870, and later at Blue Cove (St. Barbe district) (MUN Folklore). James, a Scot, settled at Bear Cove (St. Barbe district) in the late 19th century (MUN Hist.). Charles D., established a business at Harbour Buffett about 1845 (MUN Hist.).

Early instances: John, of Salvage, 1676 (CO 1); William, ? labourer of St. John's, 1779 (CO 194.34); Mary, of Burgeo, married at St. John's, 1828 (DPHW 26D); Alexander, J.P. for the Southern District of the Colony, 1834 (*Newfoundlander* 10 Jul 1834); Ensign William, of the Royal Newfoundland Company, son of Richard, of Peckham (Surrey), died at St. John's, 1857 (*Newfoundlander* 21 May 1857); Abraham (and others), of the Flowers Cove to Point Ferrolle area, 1871 (Lovell).

Modern status: At Bear Cove, Blue Cove, and formerly Barr'd Harbour (*Electors* 1955), all in the St. Barbe district.

Place names: Chambers Cove 46-53 55-27, —— Island 47-37 54-20, —— Point 46-52 55-26, 51-15 56-47.

CHAMPION, a surname of England and the Channel Islands, from the Old French *c(h)ampiun* – a combatant in the campus or arena, one who does battle for another in wager of battle. "In the ordeal by battle, in criminal cases, the accuser and accused took the field themselves, but in disputes about the ownership of land, the actual parties to the suit were represented by 'champions,' in theory their free tenants, but in practice, hired men, professional champions, and very well paid" (Reaney). The name may also be a variant of Champain, from the French province of Champagne. (Reaney, Turk).

Guppy traced Champion in Cornwall, Gloucestershire, Kent and Somerset, Spiegelhalter in Devon.

In Newfoundland:

Early instances: John, of St. John's, 1772 (DPHW 26D); Samuel, proprietor and occupier of fishing room at Old Perlican, Winter 1800–01 (Census Trinity B.); Ann, of Harbour Grace Parish, 1822 (Nfld. Archives HGRC); John, planter of Lower Island Cove, 1850 (DPHW 55); Jemima, of Hants Harbour, 1857 (DPHW 59); Samuel, fisherman of Scilly Cove (now Winterton), 1871 (Lovell).

Modern status: Somewhat rare and scattered, including Lower Island Cove.

CHANCEY, a surname of England, a variant of Chaunc(e)y, ? from a French place name Chançay, Chancé or Chancey. Of Chauncey as a baptismal name, Withycombe writes: "it was the name of the 2nd president of Harvard, Charles Chauncey (1592–1672), some of whose pupils gave it to their children as a Christian name whence it has gradually come into general use as a Christian name in the USA." (Withycombe, Bardsley, Dauzat *Noms de Lieux*).

Traced by Matthews in Dorset.

In Newfoundland:

Early instances: John, fined in court at Harbour Main for being a Roman Catholic servant to Michael Katen, 1755 (MUN Hist.); L., fisherman of Port de Grave, 1781 (Nfld. Archives T22); Lionel, of Harbour Grace, 1793 (D'Albert 5); Lionel, of St. John's, 1802 (D'Alberti 12); Thomas, of Carbonear, 1803 (DPHW 48).

Modern status: At St. John's.

CHANDLER, a surname of England – a maker or seller of candles. (Reaney).

Guppy found Chandler in the south of England, especially in Gloucestershire; Spiegelhalter traced it in Devon.

In Newfoundland:

Early instances: ——, on the *Leamon* in the seal fishery out of Harbour Grace 1853 (*Newfoundlander* 28 Mar 1853); Elizabeth, of Harbour Grace Parish, 1874 (Nfld. Archives HGRC).

Modern status: Rare, at Outer Cove (*Electors* 1955) and Petty Harbour.

Place name: Chandler Reach 48-30 53-47.

CHANNING, a surname of England, ? a variant of C(h)annon, from Old French *chanoine* – canon, a clergyman living with others in a clergy house.

Traced by Guppy in Tiverton (Devon).

In Newfoundland:

Family tradition: From Devon to St. John's ? about 1840 (Family).

Early instance: J. Channings, druggist of St. John's, 1898 (Devine and O'Mara).

Modern status: At St. John's.

CHANT, a surname of England, from Old French *chant* – singing, song, that is, singer, chorister, precentor (Reaney), or for (a man from) Kent (Spiegelhalter).

Traced by Spiegelhalter in Devon.

In Newfoundland:

Early instances: John, married at St. John's, 1765 (DPHW 26D); Oliver, in fishery at Petty Harbour, 1794–5, "8 years in Newfoundland," that is, 1786–7 (Census 1794–5); John, of Bird Island Cove (now Elliston), 1826 (DPHW 70); Mary, of Torbay, 1830 (Nfld. Archives BRC); Charles, fisherman of Little Bay (Burgeo-La Poile district), 1871 (Lovell); John, miner, and Robert, fisherman of Tizzard's Harbour, 1871 (Lovell).

Modern status: At Elliston South and in the Burgeo-La Poile district.

CHAPLIN, a surname of England, from the Old French *chapelain* – priest, clergyman, chantry-priest. (Reaney).

Traced by Guppy in Essex and Norfolk and by Spiegelhalter in Devon.

In Newfoundland:

Early instance: Mark (1855–), tailor of St. John's, 1894 (Mott).

Modern status: Rare, at St. John's and Gambo.

CHAPMAN, a surname of England, Scotland and Ireland, from Old English *cēapmann* – merchant, trader. *See also* CHATMAN, CHIPMAN, CHIPP. (Reaney).

Chapman was found widespread by Guppy, in Devon by Spiegelhalter, mainly in the Lothians and Perthshire by Black, and in all provinces except Connacht by MacLysaght.

In Newfoundland:

Early instances: John, of St. John's, 1681 (CO 1); James, of Battle Harbour (Labrador), 1795 (MUN

Hist.); Patrick, of St. John's, 1822 (CO 194.65); Benjamin, of Harbour Breton, 1828 (DPHW 109); John, of Twillingate, 1828 (*Newfoundlander* 11 Sep 1828); Stephen, of Keels, 1835 (DPHW 73); George B., of Carbonear, died 1844 (*Newfoundlander* 18 Jul 1844); John, member of the Board of Road Commissioners for the Harbour Breton to Connaigre Bay and Hermitage Cove area, 1844 (*Nfld. Almanac*); William, of Castle Cove (Bonavista B.), 1845 (DPHW 73A); Rev. John, of Harbour Grace, 1847, died at Bidale (Yorkshire), 1851 (*Weekly Herald* 30 Apr 1851, *Newfoundlander* 25 Nov 1847); John, agent at Jersey Harbour, 1850 (DPHW 104); Charles, fisherman of Burin, 1871 (Lovell); George, planter of Rencontre, 1871 (Lovell); James (and others), fishermen of Spaniards Bay, 1871 (Lovell).

Modern status: At St. John's, and scattered in the South Coast districts.

CHAPPEL(L), surnames of England, from residence near or service at a chapel, or from the English place names Chapple or Chapel (Devon). *See also* CHAPPELLA. (Reaney, Spiegelhalter).

Guppy traced Chappell in Nottinghamshire and Somerset; Spiegelhalter traced Chap(p)ell, Chapple in Devon.

In Newfoundland:

Early instances: William ? Chappell, of Newfoundland, ? 1706 (CO 194.24); Henery Chapell, of Port de Grave, 1708–09 (CO 194.4); —— Chappel, French planter of Placentia, 1714 (CO 194.6); John Chapel, of St. John's, 1802 (DPHW 26B); Robert Chapple, of Catalina, 1822 (DPHW 70); Robert Chappel(l), of British Harbour, 1842, 1843 (DPHW 64B); Thomas Chappel, fisherman of Twillingate, 1871 (Lovell).

Modern status: Chappel, rare at Goose Arm, and Corner Brook (*Electors* 1955); Chappell, at Salt Pans (Twillingate district); and Chapell, at Stephenville.

Place names: Several places contain Chapel as the specific, but probably only Chapel Cove 47-26 53-09 is from the surname.

CHAPPELLA, ? a variant of the French family name Chapelle, from residence near or service at a chapel. *See also* CHAPPEL(L). (Dauzat).

In Newfoundland:

Modern status: Rare, at Lord's Cove (Burin district).

CHAPTER, a variant, apparently not recorded elsewhere, of the surname of England SHAPTER, from the

English place name Shaptor (Devon), to which some Newfoundland Chapters changed their name.

In Newfoundland:

Early instance: John, labourer of St. John's, 1871 (Lovell).

Modern status: Unique, at St. John's.

CHARD, a surname of England, from the English place name Chard (Somerset). (Cottle).

Traced by Guppy in Somerset and by Spiegelhalter in Devon.

In Newfoundland:

Family traditions: Mark, of Dorset, schoolteacher of Bird Island Cove (now Elliston), about 1815 (MUN Hist.). William, from Chard (Somerset), settled at Coley's Point, about 1830 (MUN Hist.). Samuel, of Devon, fish merchant in Newfoundland about 1850, subsequently in Labrador (MUN Folklore). Abigail Annie (1807–91), of Coley's Point (MUN Geog.).

Early instances: William, of Bonavista, 1821 (DPHW 70); John, baptized at Greenspond, 1830, aged 63 (DPHW 70); Mark, of Bird Island Cove (now Elliston), 1832 (DPHW 70).

Modern status: Scattered, especially in the Bonavista South district.

CHARLES, a baptismal name and surname of England and Ireland, from the Old French personal name *Charles*, from Old German *Karl* latinized *Carolus*, or from the Old English *ceorl* – serf, bondman, countryman, peasant; or from the English place name Charles (Devon); or, in Ireland, as a synonym of (Mac)Corless. (Withycombe, Reaney, Spiegelhalter, MacLysaght).

Traced by Spiegelhalter in Devon.

In Newfoundland:

Early instances: Henry, of St. John's, 1825 (DPHW 26D); William, of Quidi Vidi, 1857 (DPHW 29).

Modern status: Rare, at St. John's.

Place names (not necessarily from the surname): Charles Arm 49-21 55-17, —— Brook 49-20 55-15, —— Island 51-11 56-00, —— Point (Labrador) 53-20 60-10; Charleston 48-23 53-40, —— Bay 48-26 53-36.

CHATMAN, CHETMAN, surnames of ? England, recorded apparently only by Bardsley who describes Chatman as an American variant of CHAPMAN; ? an extended form of the family name Chatt, from the Old French *chat* – cat, i.e. a nickname. CHETMAN may be a variant of the foregoing.

In Newfoundland:

Early instances: Ann Chatman, of Harbour Grace Parish, 1825 (Nfld. Archives HGRC); Simon, of Kings Cove, 1832 (Nfld. Archives KCRC); Stephen, of Keels, 1840 (DPHW 73A); William Chetman, of Keels, 1842 (DPHW 73A); Humphrey Chatman, of Cannings Cove, 1879 (DPHW 74).

Modern status: Chatman, scattered, especially in the Bonavista South district; Chetman, rare at St. John's (*Electors* 1955).

Place name: Chatman Ponds 48-29 53-59.

CHATWOOD, a family name of England, ? from the English place name Chetwood (Buckinghamshire). (Cottle, Ekwall).

In Newfoundland: From Lancashire about 1932.

Modern status: Rare, at St. John's.

CHAULK, a surname of England, from the English place names Bower or Broad Chalke (Wiltshire) or Chalk (Kent), or from residence near a chalk down. *See also* CHALKER. (Reaney).

Spiegelhalter traced Chalk(e) in Devon.

In Newfoundland:

Family traditions: John Chaulk (about 1753–1838), was the first settler of Bird Island Cove (now Elliston) (Murray). William Chalk, from England or Wales, settled at Barr'd Island about 1847, later at Scissors Cove (MUN Folklore).

Early instances: John Chaulk, of Bonavista, 1797 (DPHW 70); Richard Chalk, of Fogo, 1803 (D'Alberti 13); John, of Barr'd Island, 1821 (USPG); John Chaulk, of Bird Island Cove (now Elliston), 1823 (DPHW 70); John Chalk, of Belleoram, 1833 (DPHW 109); William, of Catalina, 1837, of Little Catalina, 1844 (DPHW 67); John, of St. John's, 1856 (DPHW 26D); Richard, of Deadman's Bay (Bonavista B.), 1858 (DPHW 75); Thomas, of Burnt Island (Burgeo-La Poile district), 1871 (Lovell); Robert and William, fishermen of Exploits River, 1871 (Lovell); Abel, of Moretons Harbour, 1871 (Lovell).

Modern status: Widespread, especially in the Burgeo-La Poile, Humber East and Fogo districts.

Place names (not necessarily from the surname): Chalk Rocks 47-46 53-48; Chalk Lake (Labrador) 53-02 64-13; —— Pond 48-26 54-04; Charlie Chaulk's Pond 48-30 54-01.

CHAYTER, CHAYTOR. *See* CATER

CHEATER, a surname of England, from *eschetour* – escheater, an officer appointed to look after the king's escheats, that is, property that reverts to the crown in the absence of legal heirs or claimants. *See*

also CATER for CHAYTOR to which some Cheaters in Newfoundland changed their name. (Reaney).

In Newfoundland:

Family tradition: George Cheater from England in the early 19th century; his son, Charles Cheater, later Chaytor, born at Greenspond, 1854 (MUN Folklore).

Early instances: Moses Cheater, of Fogo, 1781 (D'Alberti 2); William ? Cheeter, ? of St. John's, 1802 (DPHW 26B); George Cheater, of Chamberlains, 1826 (DPHW 26B); George, of Greenspond, 1839 (DPHW 76); Obed., of Eastern Tickle (Fogo district), 1858 (DPHW 83); George, fisherman of Back Cove (Fogo district), 1871 (Lovell); William ? Cheatin, of Flat Island (Bonavista B.), 1871 (Lovell).

Modern status: Rare, at La Scie, Fair Island (Bonavista B.) (*Electors* 1955) and St. John's.

CHEEKE, CHEEKS, surnames of England, from Old English *cē(a)ce* – jaw-bone, "a nickname for one with a prominent jaw" (Reaney). Cheeks appears to be an arbitrary variation.

Cheeke traced by Matthews in Devon, Dorset and Hampshire.

In Newfoundland:

Family tradition: —— Cheek, from the south of England, settled at Torbay in the early 1800s and later moved to St. John's. Some members of the family changed the name to Cheeks (MUN Folklore).

Early instances: John Cheake, boatkeeper of St. John's Harbour, 1682 (CO 1); Roger Cheek, of St. John's, 1751 (CO 194.13); William Cheeks, of Torbay, 1852 (DPHW 32); Marcus Cheek, fisherman of Arnolds Cove, 1871 (Lovell); William Cheeke, of Spanish Room, 1871 (Lovell).

Modern status: Cheeke, at Mooring Cove (*Electors* 1955) and Marystown; Cheeks, at St. John's (*Electors* 1955), Glovertown and Gander.

CHEESEMAN, a surname of England – maker or seller of cheese. (Reaney). *See also* FIRMAGE and FORMANGER.

Guppy traced Che(e)sman in Kent and Lincolnshire.

In Newfoundland:

Early instances: John Cheesman, fisherman of Fox Cove (Burin), 1871 (Lovell); George and Thomas, fishermen of Port au Bras, 1871 (Lovell); John (and others), fishermen of Rushoon, 1871 (Lovell).

Modern status: Scattered, especially at St. John's and in the Burin and Placentia West districts.

Place names: Cheeseman Lake (Labrador) 52-00 62-01; John T. Cheeseman Park 47-38 59-16.

CHERNIN, ? a variant of the surname of France, Cernin, itself a corrupted spelling of Sernin, from *Saturninus,* apostle and martyr of Toulouse of the 3rd century. (Dauzat).

In Newfoundland:

Modern status: Rare, at Corner Brook (*Electors* 1955) and Stephenville.

CHETMAN. *See* CHATMAN

CHEVARIE, a surname of the Magdalen Islands, of ? French origin.

In Newfoundland :

Tradition: Vital, from the Magdalen Islands, settled in St. George's, 1850.

Modern status: Cheverie, unique at Topsail. (G.R. Thomas, Tel. Dir.).

CHIDLEY, a surname of England, from the English place name Chidlow (Cheshire) (Bardsley) or Chudleigh (Devon) (Spiegelhalter).

Traced by Spiegelhalter in Devon.

In Newfoundland:

Early instances: ——, captain of the *Water Lily,* in the seal fishery, 1846 (*Newfoundlander* 19 Mar 1846); George, fisherman of Cape Broyle, 1871 (Lovell); Christopher and Joseph, fishermen of Renews, 1871 (Lovell).

Modern status: At Renews and St. John's.

Place name: Cape Chidley (Labrador) 60-23 64-26.

CHILDS, a surname of England, from Old English *cild* – child, a pet name, or a minor, or a youth awaiting knighthood, or page, attendant, or one who is childish or immature; or from Old English *celde* – (dweller near a) spring (Reaney, Cottle).

Guppy traced Child(e) in Shropshire and Sussex, Childs in Hertfordshire and Sussex; Spiegelhalter traced Child in Devon; and Matthews traced Child(s) in Dorset.

In Newfoundland:

Early instances: Stephen Child, J.P. for Placentia, 1753 (CO 194.13); Thomas Child(s), of St. John's, 1813 (DPHW 26D); Abraham Childs, fisherman of Grand Bruit, 1834 (DPHW 101); James Child, of Rencontre, 1835 (DPHW 30); Bethuna Childs, of Upper Burgeo, 1853 (DPHW 101); George, fisherman of François, 1871 (Lovell); Michael Cheeld, fisherman of Bay of Islands, 1871 (Lovell); Solomon Chiles, fisherman of Bay of Islands, 1871 (Lovell).

Modern status: Scattered, especially at Ramea, Boswarlos and in the Humber West district.

CHINN, CHYNN, surnames of England, Chinn of Jersey (Channel Islands), from Old English *cin* – chin, a nickname "for one with a prominent or long chin or for one with a beard" (Reaney), or from the English place name Ching (Somerset). (Spiegelhalter, Turk).

Guppy found Chinn formerly in Gloucestershire, Spiegelhalter in Devon.

In Newfoundland:

Family tradition: ? Amos Chinn, from England, settled at Twillingate in the 19th century (MUN Folklore).

Early instances: Samuel Chinn, planter of Twillingate, 1818 (USPG); John, of Sandy Point (St. George's district), 1871 (DPHW 96).

Modern status: Chinn, at Hillgrade (Twillingate district) (*Electors* 1955), Corner Brook and Botwood; Chynn, at Seal Rocks (St. George's district) and Deer Lake.

CHIPMAN, a surname of England, a variant of CHAPMAN; or from the English place name Chippenham (Wiltshire). (Spiegelhalter).

Traced by Spiegelhalter in Devon.

In Newfoundland:

Early instances: John, inhabitant of Newfoundland, ? 1706 (CO 194.24); William, of Mint Cove (Spaniard's B.), 1798 (CO 199.18); Edward, married at Fortune Harbour, 1831 (Nfld. Archives KCRC); Frances, of Harbour Grace Parish, 1834 (Nfld. Archives HGRC); Henry, of St. John's, 1857 (DPHW 26D); John, fisherman of Little Bay Islands, 1867 (DPHW 91).

Modern status: Scattered, especially at St. John's, Spaniard's Bay, Corner Brook and Twillingate.

Place name: Chipman Hill 49-37 55-40.

CHIPP, a surname of England, of the same origin as CHAPMAN and CHIPMAN, – (dweller near, or trader in a) market, though Reaney also conjectures a personal name *Chipp* from Middle English *chipp(e)* – small piece of wood chipped or cut off, hence ? one who had damaged or lost his sight from an accident while hewing wood overhead: 'For an old Proverbe is it ledged, He that heweth to hie, with chippes he may lose his sight' (*OED* about 1400). (Reaney Notes, Weekley *Romance*, Bardsley). *See* CHIPPETT.

In Newfoundland:

Family traditions: Solomon, from England, settled at Shoe Cove (Green B.), about 1847; his descendants settled at La Scie (MUN Folklore). ——, from Cornwall, settled at Shoe Cove (Green B.); his descendants settled at Kings Point (MUN Folklore).

Early instance: Isaac, fisherman of Shoe Cove, 1852 (DPHW 86).

Modern status: At Shoe Cove, Middle Arm and Kings Point (Green B. district) and La Scie.

Place name: Chips Hill 49-46 56-00.

CHIPPETT, a surname of England, ? a diminutive of CHIPP.

Traced by Bardsley in early citations in Somerset.

In Newfoundland:

Family traditions: John Chippet, ? a servant of Bryant's Cove, 1847–?1865 (MUN Hist.). Noah Chippett, son of John, of Harbour Grace, ? about 1880 (MUN Folklore).

Early instance: John, of Leading Tickles, 1871 (Lovell).

Modern status: Especially at Leading Tickles. It may be a matter of interest, if not of significance, that Chipp and Chippett both occur predominantly in the same general area of the Green Bay district.

CHISHOLM, a surname of England and Scotland from the Scots place name Chisholm (Roxburghshire). (Bardsley, Black).

In Newfoundland:

Early instance: John Forbes, born at West River (Pictou Co., N.S.), established a bookstore at St. John's in 1858 (Mott).

Modern status: Rare and scattered.

CHISLETT, a surname of England, from the English place name Chislet (Kent) – the gravel place or stream. (Ekwall, Bardsley).

In Newfoundland:

Early instances: James, planter of Island Cove (now Dunfield), 1819, of Heart's Delight, 1823 (DPHW 59A, 64B); Charles, of Bonne Bay (Fortune B.), 1835 (DPHW 30); John, of Round Harbour (Burin district), 1836 (DPHW 106); John, fisherman of Seal Island (Burgeo district), 1846 (DPHW 101); Richard Chislet, of Harbour Le Cou, 1858 (DPHW 98); Charles Chislett, planter of Garia, 1871 (Lovell); John Jr., of West Point (Burgeo district), 1871 (Lovell).

Modern status: Scattered, especially at St. John's and in the Trinity South, Burgeo-La Poile districts.

CHOLOCK, with accent on the second syllable, ? variant of the surnames of France Cholet, Cholot. (Dauzat).

In Newfoundland:

Modern status: Rare, at Clarenville.

CHON, a Chinese name – ? gathered together, ill-health due to old age, container (for measurement).

In Newfoundland:

Modern status: Rare, at St. John's.

CHOW, a Chinese name – to encircle; complete; comprehensive; dense. (So).

In Newfoundland:

Modern status: Unique, at Windsor (*Electors* 1955).

CHOWN, a surname of England, ? the Cornish form of the baptismal name John. (Weekley).

Guppy traced Chow(e)n in Devon.

In Newfoundland:

Early instances: Francis H. Chowen, bookkeeper of St. John's, 1871 (Lovell); Chown, Gibbs & Company, drapers, of St. John's, 1877 (Lovell).

Modern status: Rare, at St. John's.

CHRETIEN, a surname of France, with ? a Newfoundland variant CHRISTIEN, a baptismal name, or a nickname denoting simple-minded and therefore blessed by God, a definition not without similarity to Wordsworth's view: "I have often applied to idiots, in my own mind, that sublime expression of Scripture, that their life is hidden with God" (Letter to John Wilson, June 1802). *See* CHRISTIAN. (Dauzat).

In Newfoundland:

Family tradition: In late 19th century François Chrétien and wife were stationed at Red Island, later settled at La Barre (Thomas, "French Fam. Names").

Modern status: Chretien, at Long Point (Port-au-Port district) (*Electors* 1955); Christian (Cape St. George) (Thomas, "French Fam. Names").

CHRISTIAN, a surname of England and Ireland, from the baptismal name Christian. "In England the masculine name was less frequent than the feminine, which was also common as *Cristina*, the native form" (Reaney). *See* CHRETIEN. (Withycombe).

Traced by Matthews in Hampshire and Dorset and by MacLysaght in northeast Ireland since the 16th century.

In Newfoundland:

Family tradition: George Christian came to Newfoundland from Norway about 1877 (MUN Folklore).

Early instances: Jacob, of Trinity (Trinity B.), 1810 (DPHW 64); Catherine, from Piltown (Co. Kilkenny), married at St. John's, 1821 (Nfld. Archives BRC); William, school teacher of Old Perlican, 1846 Grand Bank, 1871 (Lovell); James, clerk of St. John's, 1871 (Lovell); James Christin, master mariner of St. John's, 1871 (Lovell).

Modern status: Scattered, especially at St. John's.

CHRISTIEN. *See* CHRETIEN

CHRISTMAS, a baptismal name and surname of England, for one born on that day. As a baptismal name "It has now been largely replaced by NOEL" (Withycombe). (Reaney).

Traced by Guppy in Cambridgeshire, Hampshire, Huntingdonshire and Surrey.

In Newfoundland:

Modern status: Rare, at St. John's.

Place names (not necessarily from the surname): Christmas Head 47-41 58-23,

CHRISTOPHER, a baptismal name and surname of England and Ireland, Latin *Christopherus* from Greek – Christ-bearing, "originally a word applied by Christians to themselves, meaning that they bore Christ in their hearts. St. *Christopher* was an early Christian martyr, to whose name was later attached the legend of a gigantic saint who carried the Christ-child across a river, and *Christopher* became an ordinary Christian name. The sight of the image of St. *Christopher* was thought to be a protection from accidents and sudden death for the rest of the day" (Withycombe). (Reaney).

Spiegelhalter traced Christopher(s) in Hampshire; MacLysaght traced Christopher in Co. Waterford.

In Newfoundland:

Early instances: George, of Hants Harbour, 1708–09 (CO 194.4); Thomas, fisherman of Quidi Vidi, 1794–5, "7 years in Newfoundland," that is, 1787–8 (Census 1794–5); Thomas, of St. John's, 1803 (Nfld. Archives BRC); Ned, of Harbour Grace Parish, 1811 (Nfld. Archives HGRC); Robert, planter of Twillingate, 1818 (USPG); Patrick, of Trinity, 1825 (Nfld. Archives KCRC); William, from Clonmel (Co. Tipperary), of St. Mary's (unspecified), deceased 1832 (*Royal Gazette* 22 May 1832); John, of Torbay, 1835 (Nfld. Archives BRC); William, of Ship Cove (now part of Port Rexton), 1857 (Nfld. Archives KCRC); Grace, of Broad Cove (now Duntara), 1866 (Nfld. Archives KCRC); Patrick and William, of Bay of Islands, 1871 (Lovell); Michael (and others), of St. Mary's Bay, 1871 (Lovell); John and William, of Port de Grave, 1871 (Lovell); Bridget, schoolteacher of Topsail, 1871 (Lovell).

Modern status: Scattered, especially at St. John's, Port de Grave, Mall Bay and in the Humber West district.

Place names (not necessarily from the surname): Christopher Island 49-36 54-44; Christopher's Cove (Humber West district).

CHUBB(S), surnames of England, from Middle English *chubbe* – chub (a fish), meaning "'short and thick, dumpy like a chub' or 'of the nature of a chub, dull and clownish'" (Reaney), though Spiegelhalter derives Chubb from an Old English personal name *Ceobba*, a pet-form of *Ceolbeorn* and *Ceolbeorht*.

Guppy traced Chubb in Devon.

In Newfoundland:

Early instances: John Chubb, inhabitant of Newfoundland, 1730 (CO 194.23); David, of Seal Bight (Labrador), 1850 (DPHW 113); John, of Spear Harbour (Labrador), 1851 (DPHW 113); John Chobb, fisherman of Barr'd Islands, 1852 (DPHW 83); Edward Chub, fisherman of Ragged Harbour (now Melrose), 1871 (Lovell); George Chubb, merchant of Carbonear, 1877 (Lovell).

Modern status: Chubb, at Boswarlos; Chubbs, scattered, especially at Carbonear.

CHURCH, a surname of England and Ireland, from residence near, or duties, such as verger, sexton, at the church. (Reaney).

Traced by Guppy in Bedfordshire, Berkshire, Essex, Northamptonshire, by Spiegelhalter in Devon, and by MacLysaght in Ulster since the 17th century.

In Newfoundland:

Early instance: Matthew, plaintiff before the Supreme Court, 1810 (CO 194.50)

Modern status: Rare, at St. John's.

Place names (not necessarily from the surname): Church Cove 47-04 52-52, 48-58 57-59; —— Hill 49-43 54-17; —— Pond 47-42 52-50.

CHURCHILL, a surname of England, from the English place name Churchill (Devon, Somerset, Worcestershire, Warwickshire), or (dweller on the) church-hill. (Reaney).

Traced by Guppy in Dorset and Middlesex, and by Spiegelhalter in Devon.

In Newfoundland:

Family traditions: ——, from Ireland, settled at Bell Island (MUN Folklore). John was one of the first settlers of Coleys Point (MUN Geog.). Philip (1775–1850), whose ancestors came from Belfast, was born at Portugal Cove and was the first settler of Topsail in 1813 (MUN Geog.). Three Churchill brothers, from Devon, came to Newfoundland in the 1850s and settled at Trinity, Notre Dame Bay and Portugal Cove (MUN Folklore).

Early instances: James, of Bay Roberts, 1793, property "possess'd by the Family for 60 years," that is, 1733 (CO 199.18); Nicholas, juror of St. John's, 1777 (CO 194.33); Richard, of Portugal Cove, 1781 (DPHW 26C); Stephen, of Battle Harbour (Labrador), 1787–89 (MUN Hist.); Nicholas, of Ochre Pit Cove, 1806 (CO 199.18); John, of New Harbour (Trinity B.), 1809 (DPHW 64); William, from Ringwood (Hampshire), fisherman of Little Bell Island, deceased 1815 (*Royal Gazette* 14 Dec 1815); Charles William, baptized at Harbour Grace, 1827 (DPHW 43); Joseph, planter of Trinity (Trinity B.), 1837 (DPHW 64B); George, of Kings Cove Parish, 1840 (Nfld. Archives KCRC); Sarah, of Burgeo, 1844 (DPHW 26D); George, of Thoroughfare, 1852 (DPHW 64B); George, fisherman of Rider's Harbour, 1858 (DPHW 64B); Absalom, of Grates Cove, 1860 (DPHW 56); John Jr. and Sr., of Great St. Lawrence (now St. Lawrence), 1871 (Lovell); Philip and Samuel, of Topsail, 1871 (Lovell); Philip, of Twillingate, 1871 (Lovell).

Modern status: Widespread, especially at St. John's.

CHURLEY, a surname of England, according to Bardsley a variant of Chorley, from the English place name Chorley (Cheshire, Lancashire, Somerset, Hertfordshire and Shropshire). (Bardsley, Ekwall).

Matthews traced Chorley in Devon.

In Newfoundland:

Family tradition: Caroline (1818–), of Old Perlican (MUN Geog.).

Early instances: Joanne, of Harbour Grace Parish, 1819 (Nfld. Archives HGRC); James R., planter of Hants Harbour, 1828 (DPHW 59A).

Modern status: Rare, at Old Perlican.

CHYNN. *See* CHINN

CLAIR(E), baptismal names and surnames of France, and ? variants of the baptismal name and surname of England and Ireland CLARE.

In Newfoundland:

Modern status: Clair, at Boyd's Cove (Twillingate district); Claire, unique, at Corner Brook.

Place name: ? L'anse au Clair (Labrador) 51-25 57-04.

CLANCE, ? a variant, apparently unrecorded elsewhere, of the surname of Ireland CLANC(E)Y.

In Newfoundland:

Early instances: Julian Clanse, of Tilton Harbour (now Tilting), 1815 (Nfld. Archives KCRC); Daniel Clance, of St. John's, 1818 (*Nfld. Mercantile Journal* 29 Jul 1819); John, of Harbour Grace Parish, 1824 (Nfld. Archives HGRC); James, of Greenspond, 1845 (Nfld. Archives KCRC); Susan, of Cat Harbour (now Lumsden), 1858 (Nfld. Archives KCRC); Susanna, of Harbour Grace, 1870 (Nfld. Archives HGRC).

Modern status: At La Scie.

CLANC(E)Y, surnames of Ireland, *Mac Fhlannchaidh* – ? ruddy warrior. (Mac-Lysaght).

Traced by MacLysaght in Cos. Clare and Leitrim.

In Newfoundland:

Family tradition: Edward Clancey settled at Exploits in 1825 (MUN Folklore).

Early instances: William Clancey, fisherman of St. John's, 1794–5, "16 years in Newfoundland," that is, 1778–9 (Census 1794–5); Richard Clancy, of Fermeuse, 1798 (Nfld. Archives BRC); William, from Kilcash (Co. Tipperary), married at St. John's, 1798 (Nfld. Archives BRC); Daniel, of Harbour Grace Parish, 1810 (Nfld. Archives HGRC); John, from Co. Waterford, fisherman of St. John's, deceased, 1810 (*Royal Gazette* 29 Nov 1810); Patrick, of Tilting Harbour (now Tilting), 1827 (Nfld. Archives KCRC); James, ? of Northern Bay, 1852 (DPHW 54); Bridget Clancey, of Harbour Grace, 1867 (Nfld. Archives HGRC); John and Michael, fishermen of Caplin Bay (now Calvert), 1871 (Lovell); Edward, fisherman of Exploits Burnt Island, 1871 (Lovell).

Modern status: Clancey, at Corner Brook, Sweet Bay (Bonavista B.) and St. John's; Clancy, at Calvert, Great Brehat (White B.) (*Electors* 1955), Campbellton and St. John's.

Place name: Clancey's Pond 47-08 55-31.

CLARE, a baptismal name and surname of England and Ireland, with Clear as a variant of the surname, from Latin *Clara*, French *Claire* – bright, fair, "a woman's name, common, probably, owing to the popularity of St. Clare of Assisi" (Reaney); or from the English place names Clare (Suffolk) and Clere (Hampshire), but not from Co. Clare (Ireland); or from Old English *clæg* – (a worker with) clay, that is, a clayer or plasterer. See CLAIR. (Withycombe, Reaney, Cottle).

Clare was traced by Guppy in Oxfordshire, Clear by Spiegelhalter in Devon; and Clare and Clear by MacLysaght in Cos. Wexford and Kilkenny.

In Newfoundland:

Early instances: John, of St. John's, 1705 (CO 194.3); Mary, from Graigenamanagh (Co. Kilkenny), married at St. John's, 1812 (Nfld. Archives BRC);

Mary Clear or Clare, of Trinity, 1828 (Nfld. Archives KCRC); Patrick Clare, of Harbour Grace Parish, 1834 (Nfld. Archives HGRC); Moses, miner of Tilt Cove, 1871 (Lovell); John, fisherman of Upper Small Point (now Kingston), 1871 (Lovell); Martin and Thomas Cleare, fishermen of Portugal Cove, 1871 (Lovell).

Modern status: Rare, at Kingston and Beachy Cove (St. John's district) (*Electors* 1955).

CLARK(E), surnames of England, Scotland and Ireland, from Old English *cler(e)c*, Latin *clericus*. "The original sense was 'a man in a religious order, cleric, clergyman.' As all writing and secretarial work in the Middle Ages was done by the clergy, the term came to mean 'scholar, secretary, recorder or penman.'" As a surname, "it was particularly common for one who had taken only minor orders" (Reaney). Clarke "usually stands for O'Cleary in Ireland" (MacLysaght).

The forms Clark and Clarke are widespread and indiscriminate in England; Guppy found Clark dispersed over a large part of Scotland, but rare in the north; MacLysaght traced Clarke in Dublin.

In Newfoundland:

Family tradition: The Clarkes in the Trinity area, Bonaventure and Cuckold's Cove (now Dunfield) came from Devon or Poole (Dorset) about 1525 (MUN Folklore).

Early instances: William Clark, of Crockers Cove (Carbonear), 1775, property "in possession of the Family for 70 years," that is, 1705 (CO 199.18); William of ? St. John's, ? 1706 (CO 194.24); John Clark(e), J.P. for the Bonavista district, ? 1730, 1732 (CO 194.9); John Clark, of Placentia (?district), 1744 (CO 194.24); John, of Carbonear, 1765 (CO 199.18); John and Isaac, of Brigus, 1770 (CO 199.18); John Clarke, fisherman of Port de Grave, 1782 (Nfld. Archives T22); Robert Clark(e), of Trinity Bay, 1782, of Trinity, 1795, of Cuckold's Cove (now Dunfield), 1803 (DPHW 64); Samuel and John Clarke, merchants of Harbour Breton 1803 (D'Alberti 13); John Clark, of Broad Cove (Bay de Verde district), 1804 (CO 199.18); John, of Burin, 1805 (D'Alberti 15); Anne, of Harbour Grace Parish, 1806 (Nfld. Archives HGRC); Pat, one of 72 impressed men who sailed from Ireland to Newfoundland, ? 1811 (CO 194. 51); William, of Twillingate, 1811 (D'Alberti 22); William, of Turk's Cove (Trinity B.), 1814 (DPHW 48); Anne Clarke, of St. John's, 1814 (Nfld. Archives BRC); Bridget, from Waterford City, married at St. John's, 1816 (Nfld. Archives BRC); Flora Clark, of Heart's Content, 1819 (Nfld. Ar-

chives KCRC); Robert Clarke, of British Harbour, 1819 (DPHW 64); Thomas, of Petty Harbour, 181 (DPHW 26B); Robert Clark, of Bonavista, 1821 (DPHW 70); Richard Clarke, of Catalina, 1821 (Nfld. Archives KCRC); Joseph Clark, of Bonaventure (unspecified), 1825 (DPHW 64B); Joseph, of Careless (now Kerley's) Harbour, 1827 (DPHW 64B); James Clarck, of White Hills (St. John's), 1829 (Nfld. Archives BRC); Solomon Clarke, planter of Freshwater (Carbonear), 1830 (DPHW 48); John Joseph from Liverpool, married at St. John's, 1838 (Nfld. Archives BRC); Mary Clark, of Portugal Cove, 1839 (DPHW 26D); William Clarke, of Kings Cove Parish, 1839 (Nfld. Archives KCRC); John Clark, of Island Cove (now Dunfield, 1845 (DPHW 64B); John, of Little River (Burgeo-La Poile), 1847 (DPHW 101); Charles Clarke, of Garia, 1858 (DPHW 98); Joseph Clark, of Lower Island Cove, 1859 (DPHW 55); John, of Harbour Grace, 1869 (Nfld. Archives HGRC); Clark(e) widespread in Lovell 1871.

Modern status: Clark, scattered, especially at St. John's; Clarke, widespread, especially at Little Bay East (Fortune B.), Gilesport (*Electors* 1955), Corner Brook, Dunfield, Little St. Lawrence with large concentrations at Carbonear, Victoria and St. John's.

Place names: Clark Cove (Labrador) 52-39 55-47; —— Lake (Labrador) 53-35 66-35; —— Point 47-34 54-52, 49-18 54-30; —— Rock 50-44 56-10; Clarke Cove 47-53 55-48, 49-41 55-54; —— Head 47-51 55-50; —— Inlet (Labrador) 57-45 61-40; Clarke's Beach 47-33 53-17; —— Cove 49-39 54-35; —— Head 49-18 54-30; —— Pond 47-31 53-19; Clarkes Tickle (Labrador) 56-30 61-18; Clarke's Beach Pond 47-33 53-17; Clarks Brook 47-46 53-14, 49-01 58-08; —— Pond 47-19 53-19.

CLATNEY, a surname of England or Ireland, apparently previously unrecorded, ? from an unidentified place name – burdock island, or ? a variant of Claughney or GLADNEY.

In Newfoundland:

Family tradition: —— Clatney (originally spelt Cleateney), from Ireland, settled at ? Flat Rock (St. John's) about 1889; his descendants moved to Grand Falls (Family).

Early instances: James Claughney, private in the Royal Newfoundland Regiment, 1797 (D'Alberti 7); Daniel Cleatney, married at St. John's, 1832 (Nfld. Archives BRC); John, of Quidi Vidi, 1835 (Nfld. Archives BRC); Daniel Clatney, died at St. John's, 1881, aged 101 years (Devine and O'Mara).

Modern status: Rare, at Grand Falls.

CLAYSON, a variant of the surname of Scotland, Clason, a diminutive of Nicholas; or of the surname of Ireland, Cla(u)sson, itself a variant of MacNicholas. (Black, MacLysaght).

In Newfoundland:

Family tradition: Harry, from Wales, settled at Harbour Buffett before 1900; his descendants moved to Grand Falls (Family).

Modern status: Rare, at Grand Falls.

CLEAL, a surname of England and Guernsey (Channel Islands), ? from the English place name Cleahall (Cumberland) – burdock mound, ? or, from the elements *cle* and *hale* (*halh*) – (dweller at or near the) clay(ey) place. (A.H. Smith, Weekley *Surnames*).

In Newfoundland:

Family tradition: Joseph, from England, settled at Birchy Island (Mortier B.), in 1837 (MUN Hist.).

Early instance: Joseph, servant of Butter's Cove (Mortier B.), 1871 (Lovell).

Modern status: At Marystown and Creston South.

CLEARY, a surname of Ireland, (O)Cle(a)ry, *Ó Cléirigh*, Ir. *cléireach* – clerk. *See* CLARK(E). (MacLysaght).

Traced by MacLysaght formerly in Donegal, at the present time in Munster and Dublin.

In Newfoundland:

Early instances: J. Clary, of Petty Harbour, 1702 (CO 194.3); Stephen Clarey, tailor of St. John's, 1794–5, "34 years in Newfoundland," that is, 1760–61 (Census 1794–5); Simon Cleary, from Nash Parish (unidentified) (Co. Wexford), married at St. John's, 1797 (Nfld. Archives BRC); Andrew, R.C. minister of Placentia, 1810 (CO 194.49); Ann Clary, of Harbour Grace Parish, 1813 (Nfld. Archives HGRC); Ellen Cleary, of Quidi Vidi, 1823 (Nfld. Archives BRC); Patrick, of Cape Cove (Bonavista B.), 1829 (Nfld. Archives KCRC); Patrick, of Moretons Harbour, 1830 (Nfld. Archives KCRC); Patrick, of Bonavista (Nfld. Archives KCRC); Patrick, of Tilting Harbour (now Tilting), 1831 (Nfld. Archives KCRC); Mary, of Trinity, 1831 (Nfld. Archives KCRC); Patt, of White Hills (St. John's), 1836 (Nfld. Archives BRC); Mary Clary, of Harbour Main, 1838 (Nfld. Archives BRC); [Patrick] Cleary, Parish Priest of Bay Bulls, 1856 (*Newfoundlander* 14 Feb 1856); Mary Ann, of Carbonear, 1860 (DPHW 49); Richard, of Harbour Grace, 1866 (Nfld. Archives HGRC); Joseph Clary, of the French Shore, 1868 (Nfld. Archives HGRC); William, planter of Bay of Islands, 1871 (Lovell); Richard, fisherman of Little

Placentia (now Argentia), 1871 (Lovell); John, miner of Tilt Cove, 1871 (Lovell).

Modern status: Scattered, especially at Riverhead (Harbour Grace) and St. John's.

CLEMENS, CLEMENTS, CLEMMENS, surnames of England and Ireland, Clemon(t)s of Jersey (Channel Islands), Clement a baptismal name, from Latin *Clemens*, French *Clement* – mild, merciful, the name of a saint and of several popes, and from the corresponding woman's name *Clemence*, from Latin *clementia* – mildness. In Ireland Clements is also a variant of Mac Clement, *Mac Laghmainn*. (Withycombe, Reaney, Cottle, MacLysaght).

Guppy traced Clement(s) in Devon, Leicestershire and Rutlandshire and South Wales; MacLysaght traced Clements in Cos. Leitrim, Donegal and Derry; Matthews traced Clemen(t)s in Dorset, Gloucestershire and Jersey.

In Newfoundland:

Family traditions: Jim Clement Hacquoil, of Jersey (Channel Islands), deserted from the Royal Navy and settled in Turnip Cove (Fortune B.) as Jim Clement. His change of name was discovered in what proved to be a posthumous search for him as a beneficiary in a relative's will. His descendants thenceforth assumed HACQUOIL as the family name (MUN Hist.). William Clements, from Plymouth, settled at Grand Bank in 1800 (MUN Folklore). John Clement, from Jersey (Channel Islands), merchant of Burgeo, 1865 (MUN Hist.).

Early instances: William Clemens, of Brigus, 1709 (CO 194.4); John Clements, of Juglers Cove (Bay Roberts), 1760 (CO 199.18); John Clement, merchant of Harbour Grace, 1771 (Nfld. Archives L118); John Clements, of Port de Grave, 1782 (Nfld. Archives T22); —— Clemins, widow of Renews, 1784 (D'Alberti 2); John Clements, of Back Cove (Bishop's Cove), 1787 (CO 199.18); John, formerly of Southside, Broad Cove (now St. Philips), 1790 (CO 199.18); ——, of St. John's, 1791 (DPHW 26C); John, of Bryants Cove, 1793 (CO 199.18); William Clemens or Clement, from Christchurch (Hampshire), married at Tilton Harbour (now Tilting), 1817, of Herring Neck, 1829, of Fortune Harbour, 1832 (Nfld. Archives KCRC); William Clements, from Cornwall, of Lance Cove (Bell Island), 1827 (DPHW 70, MUN Hist.); William, of Torbay, 1829 (DPHW 26B); Richard, of Petty Harbour, 1841 (DPHW 26D); Philip Clement, agent of Philip Nicolle, at Lawn, 1846 (*Nfld. Patriot* 29 Apr 1846); Joseph Clements, of Herring Neck, 1850, of Salt Harbour, 1852 (DPHW 85); William Clemens, from Bridport (Dorset), of

Grand Bank, 1853 (DPHW 106, MUN Hist.); James Clements, of Quidi Vidi, 1857 (DPHW 29); Joseph, fisherman of Great Harbour Deep, 1871 (Lovell); Philip Clement, of Little Bay (Burgeo-La Poile district), 1871 (Lovell).

Modern status: Scattered, Clemens at St. John's; Clemmens, at Grand Bank; Clements, at St. John's and in the White Bay North districts.

Place names: Clements Pond 47-36 56-52; —— Cove 47-45 53-11.

CLENCH, CLYNCH, surnames of England and Ireland, from Old English *clenc* – lump, mass, found in several minor place names and meaning (dwelling by the) hill; or ? (dweller by the) ravine or crevice; or for a maker or user of clinches, big nails, rivets. (Reaney, Cottle).

Clinch was traced by Guppy in Kent, by Spiegelhalter in Devon and by MacLysaght in Leinster.

In Newfoundland:

Family traditions: In the 18th century, two brothers came from Leeds, England; one settled probably at Shoal Harbour where Clench is a common family name, the other sailed north (MUN Folklore). One family of Clenches lived at Change Islands, 1880–88, at Beaverton, 1888–1919, at Lewisporte 1919–24 and thereafter at Deer Lake (MUN Folklore).

Early instances: John Clinch, J.P. of Trinity district, 1784 (D'Alberti 2); John, of Trinity, 1786, in possession of property at Bay de Verde, 1802 (DPHW 64, CO 199.18); John, of Salvage, 1806, in possession of a fishing room there (Bonavista Register 1806); Thomas, of Fortune Bay, 1815 (D'Alberti 25); Charles Clintch or Clinch, of Hants Harbour, 1827, 1830, of Caplin Cove (Trinity B.), 1828 (DPHW 59, 59A); William Clench, of Hare Bay, 1841 (DPHW 83); George Clinch, of St. John's, 1858 (DPHW 29); William Clynch, of Ward's Harbour (now Beaumont North), 1854 (DPHW 86); David Clench, of Fortune, 1871 (Lovell); Charles, of Random Sound (Trinity B.), 1871(Lovell).

Modern status: Clench, scattered, especially at Shoal Harbour (Trinity B.); Clynch, rare, at Deer Lake (*Electors* 1955).

Place name: Clench Brook 48-46 56-52.

CLEUETT. *See* CLUETT

CLIFFORD, a surname of England and Ireland – (dweller by the) ford at a cliff, or from the English place name Clifford (Gloucestershire, Herefordshire, Yorkshire WR). In Ireland, Clifford is mainly the anglicized form of *Ó Clumháin*, but in Co. Fer-

managh of (Mac)Crifferty, *Mac Raibheartaigh.* (Reaney, Cottle, MacLysaght).

Traced by Guppy in Gloucestershire and Kent; by MacLysaght in Cos. Fermanagh, Kerry and Cork.

In Newfoundland:

Early instances: Thomas, of Trinity Bay, 1765 (DPHW 64); Thomas, of Trinity (Trinity B.), 1803 (DPHW 64); Honora, from Kilcash (Co. Tipperary), married at St. John's, 1815 (Nfld. Archives BRC); Maria, of Hants Harbour, 1822 (DPHW 58); John Cliffert, of Harbour Grace Parish, 1832 (Nfld. Archives HGRC); James Clifford, of Trouty, 1840 (DPHW 64B); ——, widow of St. John's, 1856 (*Newfoundlander* 11 Dec 1856); James, fisherman of Cuckold's Cove (now Dunfield), 1871 (Lovell); John, fisherman of Fortune, 1871 (Lovell); Francis, fisherman of Spaniard's Bay, 1871 (Lovell).

Modern status: Rare, at Trouty (*Electors* 1955) and St. John's.

CLIFT, a surname of England, a variant of Cliff, from Old English *clif* – (dweller by the) cliff, rock, steep descent, slope, river bank. (Reaney).

Traced by Guppy in Hampshire and by Spiegelhalter in Devon.

In Newfoundland:

Early instances: William Clift or Cleft, of St. John's, 1704 (CO 194.3); John Clift, of Harbour Grace Parish, 1833 (Nfld. Archives HGRC); Alex, auctioneer, and Henry A., barrister of Harbour Grace, 1871 (Lovell).

Modern status: At St. John's.

Place name (not necessarily from the surname): Clift Point 49-34 56-51.

CLINTON, a surname of England, Scotland and Ireland, according to Bardsley from the English place name Glinton (Northamptonshire) or Glimpton (Oxfordshire).

Traced by Guppy in Hertfordshire. MacLysaght found the name rare now, but prominent in mediaeval Irish records.

In Newfoundland:

Early instances: Henry, from Feltham (Middlesex), surgeon, at Harbour Breton, 1837, died there 1855 (DPHW 30; Harbour Breton Anglican Church Records per D.A. Macdonald); Henry, of Jersey Harbour, 1853 (DPHW 106); Charles, merchant of Fox Cove (Bay du Nord), 1877 (Lovell).

Modern status: Rare, at St. John's.

CLOONEY, a surname of Ireland, a variant of (O)Cloney, *Ó Cluanaigh,* Ir. *cluana* – deceitful, flattering, rogue; and in Co. Down a variant of MacLoonie. *See also* CLUNEY. (MacLysaght).

Traced by MacLysaght in Cos. Wexford and Down.

In Newfoundland:

Early instances: Edward, of Chapel's Cove, 1766 (CO 199.18); Martin, from Ross (unspecified) (Co. Wexford), married at St. John's, 1803 (Nfld. Archives BRC); Daniel, defendant before Supreme Court, St. John's, 1810 (CO 194.50); William, fisherman of Little Placentia (now Argentia), 1871 (Lovell); John, fisherman of Middle Bight (now Codner), 1871 (Lovell).

Modern status: Rare, at St. John's.

CLOTHIER, a surname of England, from Old English *clāth* – (maker or seller of) cloth. (Reaney).

Traced by Guppy in Somerset.

In Newfoundland:

Early instances: John Clothier(s), of Trinity Bay, 1765 (DPHW 64); John Clothier and son, occupiers of fishing room, Trinity, Winter 1800–01 (Census Trinity B.); Charles, of Little River (Burgeo-La Poile district), 1841 (DPHW 101); George, fisherman of Barr'd Islands, 1850 (DPHW 83); John, fisherman of Rencontre, 1853 (DPHW 102); Isaac, fisherman of Lower Burgeo, 1871 (Lovell).

Modern status: In the Burgeo-La Poile district.

CLOUSTON, a surname of Scotland, from the Scots place name Clouston (Orkney). (Black).

In Newfoundland:

Family tradition: ? John, came from Scotland to St. John's as foreman stone mason for the Roman Catholic Cathedral about 1857 (MUN Folklore).

Early instances: John, of St. John's, 1840 (DPHW 23); John (1814–92), born at Kirkwall (Orkney), died at St. John's, 1892 (General Protestant Cemetery, St. John's).

Modern status: At St. John's.

CLOUTER, a surname of England, from Old English *clūt* – patch, hence patcher, cobbler, or ? from Old French *cloutier* – nail-smith. (Reaney).

In Newfoundland:

Early instances: —— Clowter, of Bay Bulls, 1682 (CO 1); Henry Clouter, of Bonavista, 1787 (DPHW 70); Thomas, fisherman of Bird Island Cove (now (Elliston), 1814 (Murray); Henry, of Catalina, 1833 (DPHW 67).

Modern status: Scattered, especially in the Trinity North district.

CLOWE, a surname of England, a variant of Clough, from Old English *clōh* – (dweller in a) ravine or deep-sided valley. (Reaney).

Guppy traced Clough in Yorkshire WR.

In Newfoundland:

Early instances: Henry Clow, of Ferryland, 1843 (*Newfoundlander* 23 Feb 1843); Edmund, of St. John's, 1852 (*Newfoundlander* 1 Nov 1852); Marmaduke, of Port aux Basques, married at Ferryland, 1856 (DPHW 31); Robert and Henry, of Harbour Grace, 1871 (Lovell).

Modern status: At Ferryland.

CLUETT, CLEUETT, variants of surnames of England and France, Cluett in England, Clouet, Cleuet in France, ? diminutives from St. Cloud, a French bishop of the 6th century. (Dauzat).

Guppy traced Cluett in Dorset.

In Newfoundland:

Family traditions: Ancestors of the Cluetts escaped the French Revolution by fleeing to England and later settling on the South Coast (MUN Folklore). —— Cluett, from Wales, settled at Belleoram (MUN Folklore). ——, from Devon, to Rose Blanche, later settled at Belleoram (MUN Folklore). John, from Dorchester (Dorset), was the second settler at Belleoram in the early 18th century (MUN Hist.).

Early instances: Thomas Cluet, of Belleoram, 1835 (DPHW 30); John Clewitt, member of the Board of Road Commissioners for the Belleoram to St. Jacques area, 1844 (*Nfld. Almanac*); Charlotte Cluett, of Garnish, 1860 (DPHW 106); William Cluet, fisherman of Cape Fogo, 1871 (Lovell); John Clewett (and others), of Frenchman's Cove (Burin), 1871 (Lovell).

Modern status: Cluett, at Frenchman's Cove, Garnish and Belleoram; Cleuett, rare, at Port aux Basques.

Place names: Cluett Bight 47-37 55-54; —— Head 47-52 55-49; —— Rock 47-36 55-54.

CLUNEY, a surname of England and as Cluny or Clunie of Scotland, in England from the French place name Cluny (Saône-et-Loire), in Scotland from the Scots place name Clunie (Perthshire). There is also the possibility of confusion with the Irish family name CLOONEY. (Reaney, Black).

Spiegelhalter traced Cluney in Devon.

In Newfoundland:

Early instances: Philip Cluny, of Harbour Grace Parish, 1808 (Nfld. Archives HGRC); James, from Co. Wexford, married at St. John's, 1823 (Nfld. Archives BRC).

Modern status: Scattered, especially in the Harbour Main district.

CLYNCH. *See* CLENCH

COADY, a variant of the surname of Ireland Cody, *Mac Óda*, "A Gaelic patronymic assumed by the Archdeacon family who are in Co. Kilkenny since the thirteenth century" (MacLysaght).

In Newfoundland:

Early instances: Michael, of St. John's, 1776 (DPHW 26D); John, servant of Harbour Main, 1779 (MUN Hist.); Keran Cody, of Torbay, 1794–5, "11 years in Newfoundland," that is, 1783–4 (Census 1794–5); John Coady, of Bay Bulls, 1793 (USPG); John Cody, of Portugal Cove, 1794–5 (Census 1794–5); Bridget Coady alias Reardon, from Mullinahone Parish (Co. Tipperary), of St. John's, 1807 (Nfld. Archives BRC); Richard Cody, of Harbour Grace Parish, 1807 (Nfld. Archives HGRC); Anne Codey, of Bay Roberts, married at St. John's, 1808 (Nfld. Archives BRC); William Cody, one of 72 impressed men who sailed from Ireland to Newfoundland, ? 1811 (CO 194.51); Pierce, from Graiguenamanagh (Co. Kilkenny), planter of Bay Bulls, deceased 1813 (*Royal Gazette* 2 Dec 1813); William, of Trinity, 1829 (Nfld. Archives KCRC); John Cod(e)y, of Harbour Grace, 1830 (Nfld. Archives HGRC); William Coadey, of New Harbour (Trinity B.), 1832 (Nfld. Archives KCRC); Bridget Cody, of Fermeuse, married at St. John's, 1832 (Nfld. Archives BRC); Michael Coady, ? of Ferryland, 1838 (*Newfoundlander* 25 Oct 1838); Michael, from Waterford, resident of St. John's for 60 years, that is, since 1784, died 1844 (*Times* 24 Jul 1844); John, of Silly Cove (now Winterton), 1856 (Nfld. Archives KCRC); Nicholas, of Collins Cove (Burin district), 1860 (DPHW 108); widespread on the Avalon Peninsula, Placentia Bay, St. John's in Lovell 1871.

Modern status: Widespread, especially at St. John's and district, Ferryland district and Placentia West district.

COAKER, a variant of the surname of England, Coker, from the English place name Coker (Somerset), "Really the name of the stream at Coker" – crooked river. (Bardsley, Ekwall, Cottle).

Coaker was traced by Guppy in Devon, Coker by Spiegelhalter in Devon, and Coaker, Cooker, Cocker by Matthews in Devon and Bristol.

In Newfoundland:

Early instances: John, of St. John's, 1705 (CO 194.22); Willis, of Scilly Cove (now Winterton), 1885 (DPHW 60).

Modern status: At St. John's.

COATES, a surname of England and Scotland, in England from the English place name Cote(s), Coat(e)(s) in thirteen counties including Coat (Somerset), from Old English *cot(e)* – cottage, shelter, woodman's hut. "In Middle English, when the term was common, the surname may denote a dweller at the cottage(s) or, as it was used especially of a sheep-cote, one employed in the care of animals, a shepherd" (Reaney). In Scotland, Coates is a variant of Coults, from the Scots place name Cults (Aberdeenshire). (Reaney, Cottle, Black).

Guppy traced Coate in Somerset and found Coates widespread especially in Yorkshire.

In Newfoundland:

Early instances: Philip, ? of St. John's, 1795 (CO 194.40); Philip Coats, occupier of fishing room at Trinity (Trinity B.), Winter 1800–01 (Census Trinity B.); William Coates, of Harbour Grace Parish, 1809 (Nfld. Archives HGRC); George Coats, of Fogo, 1821 (USPG); Philip Coates, fisherman of Eddy's Cove (St. Barbe district), 1871 (Lovell); James, clerk of Harbour Grace, 1871 (Lovell); Philip, fisherman of Hare Bay (Fogo district), 1871 (Lovell); Charles Coate (and others), of Upper Gully (now Upper Gullies), 1871 (Lovell).

Modern status: Scattered, especially at Eddie's Cove East, Upper Gullies, Wing's Point and in the Gander district.

COBB, a surname of England and Scotland, Cobbe of Ireland, from an Old English personal name *Cobba*, or ? a diminutive of the baptismal name Jacob, or ? from Old English *cob* – roundish mass, hump (? a nickname), or ? from Cobb, a semicircular pier in Lyme Regis (Dorset) dating from the time of Edward I, (the scene of Louisa Musgrove's fall in Jane Austen's *Persuasion*) – (dweller by the) cobb. (Bardsley, Ekwall, MacLysaght 73).

Traced by Guppy in Dorset, Kent and Nottinghamshire, by Spiegelhalter in Devon, and by MacLysaght in Cos. Leix, Offaly and Kildare.

In Newfoundland:

Early instances: Cobb's Room at Bonavista, 1805 (Bonavista Register 1806); James Cob, of Harbour Grace Parish, 1824 (Nfld. Archives HGRC); Christopher, of Barr'd Islands, 1852, of Indian Island, 1858 (DPHW 83, 84); William, fisherman of Change Islands, 1871 (Lovell); George, fisherman of Joe Batt's Arm, 1871 (Lovell).

Modern status: Scattered, especially at St. John's and Joe Batts Arm.

Place names: Cobb (Station) 47-51 53-58; —— Cove 49-35 54-16; Cobb's Arm 49-37 54-34; —— Pond 48-58 54-38; —— Pool 48-18 58-39.

COBHAM, a surname of England, from the English place name Cobham (Kent, Surrey). (Bardsley).

Traced by Spiegelhalter in Devon.

In Newfoundland:

Modern status: Rare, at Portugal Cove, formerly of Beachy Cove.

COCARELL, a surname of England from Old French *cocherel, cokerel* – cock-seller, poultry-dealer, or from Middle English *cockerell* – young cock (a nickname). (Reaney).

Guppy traced Cockerill, Cockerell in Northamptonshire and Yorkshire NR and ER; Cockerell was traced by Spiegelhalter in Devon and by Matthews in Somerset and Greenock, Scotland.

In Newfoundland:

Early instance: Frank, from Somerset, arrived at Gaultois, 1864, from an inscription on a piece of timber in an old store, once owned by Newman & Co. at Gaultois (MUN Hist.).

Modern status: At Gaultois.

COCHRANE, a surname of Scotland and Ireland from the Scots place name Cochrane (Ayrshire); in Ireland also occasionally a variant of the Irish surname (Mac)Cuggeran, *Mac Cogaráin*, ? Ir. *cogar* – whisper. (Reaney, Black, MacLysaght).

Traced by Guppy especially in Ayrshire and by MacLysaght in Ulster.

In Newfoundland:

Early instances: James, of St. John's, 1764 (DPHW 26C); John Cocrane, of Harbour Grace Parish, 1828 (Nfld. Archives HGRC); Ann Cocheran, from Kingskerswell (Devon), married at St. John's, 1846 (*Royal Gazette* 10 Nov 1846); James Cockran, fisherman of Flatrock (St. John's district), 1871 (Lovell).

Modern status: Especially at St. John's and in the Placentia districts.

Place names: Cochrane Cove 47-24 54-09; —— Pond 47-28 52-51, —— —— 47-33 52-50; —— —— Brook 47-27 52-46; —— —— Park 47-28 52-53.

COCKER, a surname of England, from Middle English *cocken* – to fight, a fighter, a wrangler, or from Middle English *coke* – to put up hay in cocks, a hay maker; or ? a variant of COAKER. (Reaney).

In Newfoundland:

Early instance: From England to St. John's about 1919 (Family).

Modern status: Rare, at St. John's.

CODNER, a surname of England, a variant of Cordner, from Old French *cordonnier* – cordwainer, shoemaker, or from Old French *cordon* – (maker or seller of) cords, ribbons. (Reaney).

Spiegelhalter traced Co(r)dner in Devon.

In Newfoundland:

Early instances: Henry, of Renews, 1676 (spelt Godner in 1681) (CO 1); Bickford, fisherman of St. John's or Petty Harbour about 1739–43 (CO 194.11, 24); William and John, of St. John's, 1751 (CO 194.13); John, in possession of property, and fisherman of Torbay, 17945, "20 years in Newfoundland," that is, 1774–5 (Census 1794–5).

Modern status: At Torbay and St. John's.

Place name: Codner 47-31 53-00.

COE, a surname of England and Ireland; in England from Middle English *co, coo* – jackdaw (Reaney); in Ireland, a variant of (O)Coey, the anglicized form of *Ó Cobhthaigh*, "used by the north Ulster sept, distinct from those usually called COFFEY" (MacLysaght).

Traced by Guppy in Cambridgeshire, Essex, Norfolk and Suffolk. MacLysaght traced (O)Coey in Ulster.

In Newfoundland:

Early instance: ——, captain of the *Wren*, 1856 (*Newfoundlander* 4 Dec 1856).

Modern status: Unique, at St. John's.

COFFEN, COFFIN, surnames of England – maker of baskets or coffers; or a variant of Caffin, Caffyn, from Old French *c(h)auf* – bald; or ? from Welsh *goch* – red, as in GOUGH; or an Old Cornish personal name, *Cophin, Coffin* or *Coffeyn*. (Cottle, Spiegelhalter, Weekley *Surnames*).

Traced by Guppy in Devon.

In Newfoundland:

Family traditions: John Coffin from Southampton, came to White Bay in 1810 and later settled at Joe Batts Arm (MUN Hist.). Elias (1813–83), settled at Channel about 1830 (MUN Geog.).

Early instances: Ann Coffin, of St. John's, ? 1752 (CO 194.13); John, of Bonavista, 1822, of Keels, 1831, of King's Cove, 1834 (DPHW 70, 73A); Robert, of Pinchgut, 1836 (DPHW 30); John, of Joe Batt's Arm, 1842 (DPHW 83); William, of Rencontre East, 1851 (DPHW 104); Ambrose, of Barr'd Islands, 1871

(Lovell); Elias, of Channel, 1871 (Lovell); Robert, planter of Haystack, 1871 (Lovell); Samuel, merchant of Spencers Cove, 1871 (Lovell).

Modern status: Coffen, at St. John's; Coffin, scattered, especially at Joe Batt's Arm.

Place names (not necessarily from the surname): Coffin Cove 47-31 54-05; —— Island 49-28 54-48, (Labrador) 57-34 61-42; —— Point 47-37 58-35; Coffins Cove 47-30 54-28, 47-34 54-23.

COFFEY, a surname of Ireland, *Ó Cobhthaigh,* Ir. *cobhtach* – victorious. *See also* COE. (MacLysaght).

Traced by MacLysaght in Cos. Cork, Galway, Roscommon and Westmeath.

In Newfoundland:

Family tradition: John Coffey, born of immigrant Irish parents at Angel's Cove, about 1845, moved to Cuslett (Mannion).

Early instances: George, of St. John's, 1708 (CO 194.4); Daniel Coffee, of Newfoundland, convicted of destroying birds and their eggs and publicly whipped, 1792 (D'Alberti 4); Maurice Coffee or Caffee, of Bonavista, 1824 (Nfld. Archives KCRC); Michael Coffe, of Harbour Grace Parish, 1833 (Nfld. Archives HGRC); Alice Coffee, of Sound Island, 1871 (Lovell); James, murdered at Spaniard's Bay, 1873 (Devine and O'Mara).

Modern status: Scattered, especially at Cuslett and Angel's Cove.

COFFIN. *See* COFFEN

COFIELD, a surname of England, ? from Old English *colfeld* – open place where charcoal was burnt, as in the English place name Sutton Coldfield (Warwickshire) – hence ? charcoal-burner; or ? from the French place name Colleville (Seine-Inférieure), and thus a variant of the English surname Colvill(e). (Reaney, Ekwall).

In Newfoundland:

Early instances: James Colfield, of St. John's, 1842 (*Newfoundlander* 17 Nov 1842); Thomas Caulfield or Coffield, of Sweet Bay, 1885 (Nfld. Archives KCRC).

Modern status: At St. John's.

COHEN, a Jewish family name – prince or priest, and a surname of Ireland, a variant of Coen, for Coyne, in Connacht and of Cowan in Co. Down, with "usually no Jewish connotation in Ireland" (MacLysaght, E.C. Smith).

In Newfoundland:

Early instances: Edward, of St. John's, 1814

(DPHW 26D); Arthur (1902), born at Lind, England, of Corner Brook, 1937 (*Nfld. Who's Who* 1937).

Modern status: At St. John's, Bell Island and Grand Falls.

COISH, a variant of Cosh, Coy(i)sh, surnames of England and, as (Mac)Cosh, Cush, of Ireland; in England from Middle English *cosche* – small cottage, hut, hovel, or from a French personal name *Coise*; in Ireland for *Mac Coise,* ? Ir. *cos* – foot, leg. "Foote and Legge are used as synonyms of it whether by translation or pseudo-translation" (MacLysaght). (Reaney, Spiegelhalter, MacLysaght).

Spiegelhalter traced Coysh in Devon; MacLysaght traced MacCosh mainly in Co. Antrim, Cush in Co. Tyrone and Oriel.

In Newfoundland:

Family tradition: —— Coish, from England (or Ireland), settled at Ochre Pit Cove; the family thence moved to Indian Island(s), Stag Harbour and other communities (MUN Folklore).

Early instances: Richard Cosh, of Ochre Pit Cove, 1784 (CO 199.18); Jane Coyse, of Cupids, 1828 (DPHW 34); Robert Coish, of Bay de Verde, 1832 (DPHW 30); William Coysh, from Shaldon (Devon), married at St. John's, 1842 (DPHW 26D); James Cosh, of Green's Harbour, 1862 (DPHW 62); Alfred Coish (and others), fishermen of Indian Islands, 1871 (Lovell).

Modern status: Scattered, especially at Bay de Verde and Stag Harbour.

COKES, a variant of, and with the same pronunciation as, COOK.

Spiegelhalter traced Coke in Devon.

In Newfoundland:

Early instances: —— Coke, planter of St. John's, 1701 (CO 194.2); Dewes, of Trinity, 1779, later of St. John's, in Newfoundland since 1763 (CO 194.34, Census 1794–5); George, planter of Lamaline, 1877 (Lovell).

Modern status: At Head of Bay D'Espoir.

COLBERT, a surname of England, Ireland and France, from the Old German personal name *Colber(h)t,* containing the elements *fresh* and *bright.* (Reaney, MacLysaght, Dauzat).

Spiegelhalter traced Coleberd in Devon, MacLysaght found Colbert in Munster since the early 15th century.

In Newfoundland:

Early instances: Michael, of St. John's, 1767 (DPHW 26C); Thomas, of Harbour Grace Parish, 1808

(Nfld. Archives HGRC); Margaret, from Clonmel (Co. Tipperary), married at St. John's, 1814 (Nfld. Archives BRC); Garret, from Caplin Cove (unspecified), married at St. John's, 1818 (Nfld. Archives BRC); Patrick, of Ragged Harbour (now Melrose), 1820 (Nfld. Archives KCRC); John, of Bonavista, 1826 (Nfld. Archives KCRC); Bridget, of Harbour Grace, 1866 (Nfld. Archives HGRC); Garrett (and others), of Caplin Cove (Fogo district), 1871 (Lovell); James (and others), of Jobs Cove, 1871 (Lovell); John and Peter, of Carbonear, 1871 (Lovell).

Modern status: Scattered, especially at Bauline and St. Michael's (Ferryland district), and St. John's.

COLB(O)URN(E), surnames of England, from an Old English personal name *Colbeorn*, or from the English place name Colburn (Yorkshire NR) (Spiegelhalter). In Ireland, Coburn may be a variant of Scots Cockburn or English Colborne since all have the same pronunciation. (Spiegelhalter, MacLysaght).

Spiegelhalter traced Colbo(u)rne in Devon; Matthews in Dorset and the Channel Islands.

In Newfoundland:

Family tradition: In the early 19th century, three brothers came to Newfoundland, one settled in St. John's, one continued to the U.S.A., the third settled at Twillingate and later at Purcell's Harbour (MUN Folklore).

Early instances: John Colborne, of Old Perlican, 1682 (CO 1); John Colbourne, planter of Colburn, of Placentia, 1794 (D'Alberti 5); W. Colbourne, ? of St. John's, 1799 (D'Alberti 10); Mary, of Change Islands, 1821 (USPG); John Colbourn(e), from Sturminster Newton (Dorset), of Twillingate, 1846, died 1857 (*Newfoundlander* 21 May 1846, 8 Oct 1857); James Colburn, on the *Jubilee* in the seal fishery out of Carbonear, 1847 (*Newfoundlander* 25 Mar 1847); Robert Colbourne, of Indian Bight, 1854 (DPHW 92); Andrew Colborn, of Brehat, 1871 (Lovell).

Modern status: Colbourne, scattered, especially in the Green Bay and White Bay North districts; Colburn, unique, at St. John's; Colburne, unique, at Carbonear.

COLE(S), surnames of England, Cole of Ireland and Coles of Scotland, from the Old English personal name *Cola*, from Old English *col* – coal, that is, dark, swarthy, or a diminutive of Nicholas, or from Old English **coll* – (dweller on the) hill; also in Ireland for (Mac)Cool, *Mac (Giolla) Comhghaill* – devotee of St. Comhghal; also in Scotland for

Macdowall, Gaelic *Mac Dhùghaill* – son of Dougal, the black stranger, the Dane. *See* COOL(E). (Reaney, Cottle, MacLysaght, Black).

Guppy found Cole and Coles widespread, with Coles especially in Somerset, Dorset and Devon. Black found Coles in Glasgow, and MacLysaght Cole in Co. Donegal.

In Newfoundland:

Early instances: Richard Cole, of Bonaventure, 1675 (CO 1); John, of Torbay, 1676 (spelt Call in 1681) (CO 1); Richard, of St. John's, 1703 (CO 194.3); ——, of Quidi Vidi, 1703 (CO 194.3); —— Coles, inhabitant of Newfoundland, 1704 (CO 194.3); John Cole, of Colliers, 1778 (CO 199.18); John, of Bonavista, 1789 (D'Alberti 4); William Coles, of Bonavista, 1791 (USPG); Samuel Cole, J.P. for Bay Bulls and Ferryland district, 1792 (D'Alberti 4); N., of Upper Bacon Cove, 1793 (CO 199.18); James and William, of Harbour Grace, 1793 (CO 199.18); Humphrey, of Trinity (Trinity B.), 1810 (DPHW 64); —— Coles, planter of Fogo, 1816 (MUN Hist.); Elias Cole, fisherman of Carbonear, 1818 (DPHW 48); Richard, of Bird Island Cove (now Elliston), 1823 (DPHW 70); John Coal, planter of Crocker's Cove, 1825 (DPHW 48); Stephen Cole, shoemaker of Brigus, 1826 (DPHW 34); Stephen, of Mosquito (now Bristol's Hope), 1828 (DPHW 43); Humphrey, of Round Harbour, 1829 (*Newfoundlander* 26 Nov 1829); John Coles, of Ward's Harbour (now Beaumont North), 1846 (DPHW 86); E. Cole, at Harbour Breton, 1848; Edward or Edwin Coles, son of Joshua and Jemima of Stokenham (Devon), married at Harbour Breton, 1862, aged 24 (Harbour Breton Anglican Church Records per D.A. Macdonald). Philip Cole, of Flatrock (St. John's district), 1860 (DPHW 32); Cole widespread in Lovell, 1871.

Modern status: Cole, widespread, especially at Victoria, Colliers and St. John's; Coles, scattered, especially at Elliston, Deep Bay and St. Barbe district.

Place names: Cole Cove (Labrador) 52-39 55-48; Coles Bank (Labrador) 52-12 55-38, —— Pond 51-00 56-00; John Cole Brook 53-41 57-02.

COLEMAN, a surname of England, Ireland and Scotland. In the north of England, Ireland and Scotland, in the form Colman, it is usually from Old Irish *Colmán*, earlier *Columbán*, from Ir. *colm*, Latin *columba* – dove. It was "adopted by Scandinavians as Old Norse *Kalman*, and introduced into Cumberland, Westmorland and Yorkshire by Norwegians from Ireland" (Reaney). "The name was borne by two hundred and eighteen saints" (Black). In England it may also be from a German personal name, ? Old German *Col(e)man* – the black, swarthy man; or a diminutive of Nicholas; or an occupational name – charcoal-burner. In Ireland, Coleman is *Ó Clumháin*. (Reaney, Black, MacLysaght).

Guppy traced Coleman in the Midlands and Kent and Sussex, Colman mostly in Norfolk and Essex. Spiegelhalter traced Coleman in Devon. MacLysaght found (O)Colman widespread except in Ulster, Coleman in Co. Cork.

In Newfoundland:

Early instances: Michael Colman, fisherman of St. John's, 1794–5 (Census 1794–5); Bartholomew Coleman, proprietor and occupier of fishing room at Trinity (Trinity B.), Winter 1800–01, of Green Island Cove, 1809 (DPHW 64, Census Trinity B.); P., one of 72 impressed men who sailed from Ireland to Newfoundland, ? 1811 (CO 194.51); Patrick, from Lismore (Co. Waterford), of St. John's, 1814 (Nfld. Archives BRC); Timothy, of Harbour Grace Parish, 1816 (Nfld. Archives HGRC); Cornelius, of Greenspond, 1823 (Nfld. Archives KCRC); John, of Ragged Harbour (now Melrose), 1824 (Nfld. Archives KCRC); William Colman, of Keels, 1825 (Nfld. Archives KCRC); John, of Riders Harbour, 1826 (Nfld. Archives KCRC); John, of Cape Cove (Bonavista B.), 1827 (Nfld. Archives KCRC); John, from Co. Cork, of Tilting Harbour (now Tilting), 1829 (Nfld. Archives KCRC); William, of Coblers Island, 1830 (Nfld. Archives KCRC); Eleaner Colmen, of Ferryland, 1835 (DPHW 26D); Michael Coleman, of Bay Bulls, 1837 (Nfld. Archives BRC); Timothy Coalman, ? of Harbour Grace, 1845 (*Newfoundlander* 16 Jan 1845); Peter Coleman, of Silly Cove (now Winterton), 1856 (Nfld. Archives KCRC); John Colman, of Harbour Grace, 1866 (Nfld. Archives HGRC).

Modern status: Scattered, at St. John's, Corner Brook and Isle aux Morts.

Place names: Coleman Island 49-33 53-49; —— Islet 48-56 53-35.

COLERIDGE, a surname of England, from the English place names Coldridge, Coleridge or Corridge (Devon), or (dweller or worker) on the charcoal ridge, the ridge where charcoal is burnt. (Cottle, Spiegelhalter).

Traced by Spiegelhalter in Devon.

In Newfoundland:

Early instance: Samuel, of Catalina, 1834 (DPHW 67).

Modern status: Rare, at Trinity (Trinity B.) and St. John's.

COLES. *See* COLE

COLEY, a surname of England, from the English place name Colhayes (formerly Colehouse) (Devon); or ? a variant of COLLEY, COWLEY. (Spiegelhalter, Gover).

Traced by Spiegelhalter in Devon, and by Guppy in Worcestershire.

In Newfoundland:

Early instance: Matthew, born at Trinity (Trinity B.), 1841 (DPHW 64B).

Modern status: In the Burgeo-La Poile district.

Place name: Coley's Point 47-35 53-16 but not from the surname.

COLFORD, ? a variant, apparently not recorded elsewhere, of the surname of England Cullyford, ? from the English place names Coleford (Devon, Gloucestershire) or Culford (Suffolk), or of the surname of Ireland Colfer, formerly Calfer (Ekwall, E.C. Smith, MacLysaght).

MacLysaght traced Colfer in Co. Wexford.

In Newfoundland:

Early instances: Pat, carpenter in possession of property at St. John's, 1794–5, "16 years in Newfoundland," that is, 1778–9 (Census 1794–5); Mary Colfer, of St. John's, 1804 (Nfld. Archives BRC); Patrick, from Rosegarland (unidentified) (Co. Wexford), married at St. John's, 1812 (Nfld. Archives BRC); Bridget Colfers, of Hearts Content, 1819 (Nfld. Archives KCRC); Patrick Colford or Colfort, of Harbour Grace Parish, 1823 (Nfld. Archives HGRC); Moses Colford, of Kings Cove Parish, 1837 (Nfld. Archives KCRC); Patrick, ? of Northern Bay, 1839 (DPHW 54); Moses, of Burin, 1871 (Lovell); Alexander (and others), of Job's Cove, 1871 (Lovell).

Modern status: Scattered, especially in the St. John's district.

Place name: Colford Lake (Labrador) 54-29 61-51.

COLLETT, a surname of England, Collet of France, a double diminutive of the baptismal name Nicholas, or occasionally in England an aphetic form of acolyte, and in France also from *collet* – (maker or seller of) collar(s), or porter, carrier. (Reaney, Dauzat).

Guppy traced Collett in Oxfordshire and Wiltshire, Collet in Cambridgeshire. Matthews traced Collet in Devon.

In Newfoundland:

Family tradition: Thomas Collett, from Bromsgrove (Worcestershire), about 1815, to St. John's and later to Harbour Buffett (MUN Folklore).

Early instances: John, of St. John's, 1705 (CO 194.22); Thomas, of Petty Harbour, 1824 (DPHW 31); Thomas, of Long Island (Placentia B.), 1836 (DPHW 30); Thomas, of Harbour Buffett, 1838 (DPHW 26B); Phoebe, schoolteacher of Spencer's Cove, 1871 (Lovell).

Modern status: Collett, scattered, especially at Fairhaven and Harbour Buffett (*Electors* 1955).

Place names: Collett Cove, —— —— Island 47-35 54-05.

COLLEY, a surname of England, Ireland and the Channel Islands, from Old English *colig* – coaly, coal-black, hence ? swarthy or ? black-haired, or from the English place name Colley House (Devon), or a variant of COLEY, COWLEY; or also, in Ireland, for MacColley, *Mac Colla*, or a variant of COOLEY. (Reaney, MacLysaght, Turk).

Traced by Guppy in North Wales, by Spiegelhalter in Devon, and by MacLysaght in Cos. Roscommon and Galway.

In Newfoundland:

Early instances: George and James, of St. John's, 1709 (CO 194.4); He(r)bert, of Hants Harbour, 1709 (CO 194.4); Edward, married at Harbour Breton, 1850 (DPHW 104); Rev. E., of Hermitage Bay, 1855, of Grole, 1858 (*Newfoundlander* 17 Dec 1855, 1 Apr 1858).

Modern status: Rare, at Channel.

COLLIER, COLYER, surnames of England, Scotland and Ireland, and Collier of the Micmacs of Newfoundland, from Old English *col* – coal, a maker or seller of charcoal. (Reaney).

Guppy traced Collier in Berkshire, Cheshire and Staffordshire and Collyer usually in Surrey; Spiegelhalter traced Collier in Devon; MacLysaght traced Collier in Ireland since 1305; it is now mainly found in Cos. Carlow, Kilkenny and Wexford.

In Newfoundland:

Family traditions: The Colliers were inhabitants of St. Lawrence and Gaultois as early as 1800 (MUN Hist.). ——, from England to Burnt Woods, Conne River, 1838 (MUN Folklore).

Early instances: George Collier or Collyer, publican of St. John's, 1794–5, "33 years in Newfoundland," that is, 1761–2 (Census 1794–5, CO 194.33); Edward Collier, of Trinity Bay, 1768 (DPHW 64); George, from London, carpenter deserted from the ship *Perseverance*, 1818 (*Nfld. Mercantile Journal* 28 Aug 1818); John, of Codroy Islands, 1835 (DPHW 30); Samuel, of Otter's Point, 1839 (DPHW 101); George, of Bonavista, 1840 (DPHW 70); John, of

Lower Burgeo, 1850 (DPHW 101); Samuel, member of the Board of Road Commissioners for the area of Gaultois, 1857 (*Nfld. Almanac*); Jacob (and others), of Fortune, 1871 (Lovell); George, a Micmac of Conne River, about 1872 (MacGregor).

Modern status: Collier, scattered, especially at St. Alban's; Colyer, rare, at St. John's.

Place names: Collier Bay 47-36 53-42; —— Point 47-36 53-41, 48-32 58-20; —— Rock 46-49 55-44; Colliers 47-28 53-13; —— Arm 47-38 53-44; —— Bay 47-29 53-12; —— Point 47-20 53-10; —— River 47-27 53-15: —— Big Pond 47-24 53-19; Collyers Bight (Labrador) 56-51 61-03; —— Point (Labrador) 56-49 61-06.

COLLINGWOOD, a surname of England, from the English place name Collingwood (Staffordshire) – the wood of disputed ownership. (Reaney).

Traced by Guppy in Durham and Lincolnshire.

In Newfoundland:

Early instances: ——, on the brig *Alarm*, 1838 (*Newfoundlander* 7 Jun 1838); William, born at Poole (Dorset) in 1842, came to St. John's in 1855 (H.P. Smith per Kirwin).

Modern status: At St. John's.

COLLINS, a surname of England, Ireland and the Channel Islands, with Collings also of Guernsey; in England a double diminutive of the baptismal name Nicholas; in Ireland, it is nearly always the anglicized form of *Ó Coileáin*, Ir. *coileán* – whelp, but in west Ulster for *Mac Coileáin*. (Reaney, MacLysaght, Turk).

Guppy found Collins widespread in the Midlands and southwest of England, with Collings characteristic of Cornwall, Devon, Gloucestershire and Somerset where it is also associated with Collins. MacLysaght found Collins especially associated with Cos. Cork and Limerick.

In Newfoundland:

Family traditions: ——, from Ireland, settled at Job's Cove in the early 19th century (MUN Folklore). ——, from London, settled at Grandy's Point, about 1847 (MUN Folklore). John, from London (born 1790) to Newfoundland in 1815, settled at St. Anne's (MUN Folklore). ——, from England, settled at Dover (Bonavista B.) (MUN Folklore). William, from Winchester, settled at Spaniards Bay (MUN Folklore). ——, from the Channel Islands to Bristol's Hope about 1710, later settled at Spaniards Bay (MUN Geog.).

Early instances: John, of St. John's, 1675 (CO 1); James, of Renews, 1681 (CO 1); John and George Collings, fishermen of St. John's or Petty Harbour,

1739–43 (CO 194.11, 24); John Collins, of Bona-
vista, 1791 (USPG); Samuel (and others), of
Placentia, 1794 (D'Alberti 5); Timothy, of Mint
Cove (Spaniard's B.), 1796 (CO 199.18); William,
from Isle of Wight, married at St. John's, 1804
(Nfld. Archives BRC); William, of Burin, 1805
(D'Alberti 17); ——, of Flat Island (Bonavista B.),
1806 (Bonavista Register 1806); Pat, of Bay de
Verde, 1806 (CO 199.18); Jeremiah, enlisted in the
Nova Scotia Regiment at Harbour Grace, 1806–07
(CO 194.46); Mary, of Harbour Grace Parish, 1808
(Nfld. Archives HGRC); Michael, one of 72 im-
pressed men who sailed from Ireland to Newfound-
land, ? 1811 (CO 194.51); Ellen, of Joe Batts Arm,
1815 (Nfld. Archives KCRC); Mary, of Kings Cove,
1815 (Nfld. Archives KCRC); Patrick, of Ragged
Harbour (now Melrose), 1815 (Nfld. Archives
KCRC); John, of Perlican (unspecified), 1815 (Nfld.
Archives KCRC); Michael, from Black Rock (Co.
Cork), of Fogo, deceased 1816 (Royal Gazette 30 Jul
1816); William, of Trinity (Trinity B.), 1816 (DPHW
64); Francis Collin(g)s, of Cuckold's Cove (now
Dunfield), 1828 (DPHW 64B), Francis Collins, planter
of Island Cove (now Dunfield), 1845 (DPHW 64B);
Richard Collins, blacksmith of Carbonear, 1828
(DPHW 48); John, of Harbour Grace, 1828 (Nfld.
Archives BRC); Hannah, of Cape Cove (Bonavista
B.), baptized 1830, aged 29 (DPHW 76); William,
planter of Blowmedown (Carbonear), 1835 (DPHW
48); James, of Catalina, 1836 (DPHW 67); Philip
Powell, of Cashel (Co. Tipperary), died at St. John's,
1837 (Newfoundlander 9 Feb 1837); John Collin(s),
of Old Perlican or Grates Cove, 1838
(Newfoundlander 20 Sep 1838, DPHW 54); James
Collins, of Knight's Cove, 1839 (DPHW 73A);
William, of Otterbury (Carbonear), 1840 (DPHW 48);
Robert Collans, from Dumfries, Scotland, of Bona-
vista, died 1842, aged 26 (Royal Gazette 3 May
1842); Charles Collins, of Round Harbour, 1844
(DPHW 85); Ann of Herring Neck, 1852 (DPHW 85);
William, of Flatrock (Carbonear), 1854 (DPHW 49);
John, of Indian Islands, 1856 (DPHW 83); Charles, of
Garia, 1856 (DPHW 98); John, of Collins Cove
(Burin), 1860 (DPHW 108); Samuel, of Flat Island
(Burin district), 1860 (DPHW 108); William, of Stone
Harbour, 1860 (DPHW 85); widespread in Lovell
1871.

Modern status: Widespread, especially at St.
John's and Hare Bay.

Place names: Collins Cove 47-02 55-10, 47-33
54-24; —— Head 47-50 55-51; —— Lake 49-03 55-
04; —— Ledge 48-11 52-48; Inner —— —— 48-09
52-50; Collins Point (Labrador) 59-41 63-56.

COLLIS, a surname of England and Ireland – son of
Col(l), ? of the same origin as COLE(S) in England.
See also COLSON. (Cottle, MacLysaght).

Traced by Spiegelhalter in Devon and by
MacLysaght in Co. Kerry since 1638.

In Newfoundland:

Early instances: James, from Church Knowle,
Isle of Purbeck (Dorset), planter and dealer of Trinity,
deceased 1828 (*Royal Gazette* 1 Jan 1828); James, of
St. John's, 1836 (DPHW 26B); John S., schoolteacher
of English Harbour (Trinity B.), 1871 (Lovell).

Modern status: At Rencontre East, Trinity
(Trinity B.) (*Electors* 1955) and St. John's.

COLOMBE, a surname of France, from the French
female saint Colombe, martyred at Sens in 273, or
from the nickname – dove. (Dauzat).

In Newfoundland:

Modern status: At Shallop Cove (St. George's
district).

COLSON, a surname of England and France – son of
Col(l), a diminutive of the baptismal name Nicholas.
See also COLE, COLLIS. Also in England ? from the
English place names Colston, Coulson and Coldstone
(Devon). (Reaney, Dauzat).

Traced by Guppy in Suffolk and by Spiegelhalter
in Devon.

In Newfoundland:

Modern status: In the St. George's district and at
Corner Brook.

COLTON, a surname of England, Scotland and
Ireland from the English place names Colaton,
Collaton and Coleton (Devon), Colton (Lancashire,
Norfolk, Somerset and Staffordshire), and also in
Ireland, ? for *Ó Comhaltáin*. (Spiegelhalter, Ekwall,
MacLysaght).

Spiegelhalter traced Co(u)lton in Devon,
MacLysaght in Cos. Armagh, Monaghan, Down,
Louth and Fermanagh and Galway.

In Newfoundland:

Early instances: Patrick, of St. John's, ? 1821 (CO
194.64); John, from Kingskerswell (Devon), married
at St. John's, 1849 (*Royal Gazette* 6 Feb 1849).

Modern status: Rare, at St. John's.

COLYER. *See* COLLIER

COMBDEN, COMBDON, surnames of England, ? from
the English place name Combe Doan (Somerset), or
? variants of COMPTON. *See also* COMBEN, COMBY.

In Newfoundland:

Family tradition: Henry Combden (1830–85), fisherman, was the first Combden to settle on Barr'd Islands, about 1845 (MUN Geog.).

Early instances: Henry Combden, of Barr'd Islands, 1862 (DPHW 84); John, fisherman of Wild Cove (Fogo), 1871 (Lovell).

Modern status: Combden, especially at Barr'd Islands; Combdon, especially at Jackson's Arm.

COMBEN, ? a surname of England, apparently not recorded elsewhere, ? from the English place name Combpyne (Devon), or a variant of COMBDEN, COMPTON, or for the French family name Combin – (dweller in the) little dry valley. *See also* COMBY, COMPTON. (Ekwall, Dauzat).

In Newfoundland:

Early instance: Rev. Charles, Wesleyan minister, of Blackhead, Bay de Verde and Carbonear, 1871 (Lovell).

Modern status: At Grand Bank (*Electors* 1955)

COMBY, CUMBY, surnames of England, ? from the French family and place name Comby – dry valley. *See* COMBEN, COMPTON. (Dauzat).

In Newfoundland:

Family tradition: Michael Cumb, of Bristol, a member of Guy's colony at Cupids, was the first settler at Heart's Content in 1612. Later generations changed the name to Cumby (MUN Folklore).

Early instances: Robert Comby, of Trinity Bay, 1768 (DPHW 64); Thomas Combay, proprietor and occupier of fishing room at Heart's Content, Winter 1800–01 (Census Trinity B.); Elinor Comby, from Prince Edward Island, married at St. John's, 1807 (Nfld. Archives BRC); Thomas Cumby, of Harbour Grace Parish, 1816 (Nfld. Archives HGRC); Levenia Combee, of Scilly Cove (now Winterton), 1857 (DPHW 59); Jacob Combey, fisherman of Griquet, 1871 (Lovell); Robert Cumby, fisherman of Barren Island (now Bar Haven), 1871 (Lovell).

Modern status: Comby, in the Placentia West district, (*Electors* 1955); Cumby, especially in the Trinity South district.

COMERFORD, a surname of England and Ireland, ? from the English place names Comberford (Staffordshire) or Comford (Cornwall), or for the Irish surname Cumiskey, or a variant of the English surname Comfort. (Ekwall, MacLysaght, E.C. Smith).

Traced by MacLysaght in Cos. Kilkenny, Cavan and Longford, "prominent in Ireland since 1210" (MacLysaght).

In Newfoundland:

Early instances: Philip, married at St. John's, 1765 (DPHW 26D); Catherine, of St. John's, 1802 (Nfld. Archives BRC); Ellen Commerford, of Harbour Grace Parish, 1809 (Nfld. Archives HGRC); William Comerford, one of 72 impressed men who sailed from Ireland to Newfoundland, ? 1811 (CO 194.51); Joanna Cummeford, from Co. Kilkenny, married at St. John's, 1811 (Nfld. Archives BRC); James Comerford, from Co. Kilkenny, shoreman of Witless Bay, deceased 1813 (*Royal Gazette* 9 Dec 1813); Michael Cummaford, of Catalina, 1821 (Nfld. Archives KCRC); James and Thomas Comerford, fishermen of Burin, 1871 (Lovell).

Modern status: In the St. John's and St. Mary's districts.

COMPAGNON, also anglicized as COMPANION, a surname of France – fellow-worker. (Dauzat).

In Newfoundland:

Early instance: Prosper Companion, a Frenchman, of Frenchman's Cove (Bay of Islands), 1849 (MUN Hist., Feild).

Modern status: Compagnon and Companion, scattered in the Humber West and Port au Port districts.

COMPTON, a surname of England, from the English place Compton in several west Midland and southern counties, including 8 in Somerset. *See also* COMBDEN, COMBY. (Cottle).

Traced by Guppy in Wiltshire and by Spiegelhalter in Devon.

In Newfoundland:

Early instances: William, merchant or bye-boatkeeper of Petty Harbour, 1777–90 (Innis per Kirwin); John, planter of Twillingate, 1820 (USPG); Thomas, of Barr'd Islands, 1841, of Hooping Harbour, 1864 (DPHW 83, 94); Stephen, of Caplin Cove (Conception B.), 1871 (Lovell); Henry J., fisherman of Griquet, 1871 (Lovell); John, fisherman of Little Bay Island, 1871 (Lovell).

Modern status: Scattered, especially in the White Bay North district.

Place name: Compton Rock 49-37 55-50.

CONDON, a surname of Ireland and France; in Ireland formerly de Caunteton (MacLysaght); in France from the place name Condon (Ain, Drôme, Landes) or Condom (Gers). *See also* CONGDON. (MacLysaght, Dauzat).

Traced by MacLysaght in Co. Cork.

In Newfoundland:

Early instances: David, shoreman of St. John's, 1794–5, "30 years in Newfoundland," that is, 1764–5 (Census 1794–5); Abraham Cundon, of Trinity Bay, 1775 (DPHW 64); Garrett Condon, of Harbour Grace, 1798 (CO 199.18); Mary, from Shenkess Parish (unidentified) (Co. Kilkenny), married at St. John's, 1812 (Nfld. Archives BRC); Bridget Condan, of Ferryland, 1814 (Nfld. Archives BRC); Catherine Condon, of King's Cove, 1816 (Nfld. Archives KCRC); Patrick, of Carbonear, 1819 (D'Alberti 29); Catherine, of Tickle Cove (Bonavista B.), 1822 (Nfld. Archives KCRC); Patrick, of Ferryland district, 1838 (*Newfoundlander* 25 Oct 1838); Robert, of Aquaforte, 1841 (*Newfoundlander* 4 Feb 1841); Catherine, of Black Island (Bonavista B.), 1845 (Nfld. Archives KCRC); Samuel Condin, of Leading Tickles, 1854 (DPHW 86); Aaron, fisherman of Bay of Islands, 1871 (Lovell); Thomas, fisherman of Caplin Bay (now Calvert), 1871 (Lovell); Thomas, fisherman of Torbay, 1871 (Lovell).

Modern status: Scattered, especially in the Ferryland district.

Place name: Condon Brook 48-57 57-58.

CONGDON, a surname of England from the English place name Congdon (Cornwall). (E.C. Smith).

Traced by Guppy in Cornwall and by Matthews in Devon.

In Newfoundland:

Early instances: John, agent of St. John's, 1794–5, "33 years in Newfoundland," that is, 1761–2 (Census 1794–5); Thomas, merchant of Fermeuse and Renews, 1812 (D'Alberti 22); Mary, of Harbour Grace Parish, 1816 (Nfld. Archives HGRC); Thomas, of Tilton Harbour (now Tilting), 1823 (Nfld. Archives KCRC).

Modern status: Rare, at St. John's.

CONLON, a surname of Ireland, an abbreviated form of (O)Connellan, *Ó Conalláin, Ó Coinghiolláin* in Connacht, *Ó Caoindealbháin* in Munster and Leinster. See QUINLAN. (MacLysaght).

Widespread, especially in Connacht.

In Newfoundland:

Modern status: Rare, at St. John's.

CONNELL. *See* O'CONNELL

CONNOCK, a surname of England, ? from the English place names Conock (Wiltshire) or Cannock (Staffordshire). (Ekwall). ·

In Newfoundland:

Family tradition: The father of Frank Connock came to Seal Cove (Fortune B.), from Somerset, at the age of 14, in 1896 (MUN Hist.).

Modern status: Connock, at Spruce Brook (St. George's district) (*Electors* 1955); Cannock (Connocks in (*Electors* 1955) at Seal Cove (Fortune B.).

Place name: Connock Cove (Labrador) 54-14 57-59.

CONNOLLY, a surname of Ireland, *Ó Conghaile* (Connacht, Monaghan), *Ó Coingheallaigh* (Munster). Connelly is the spelling in Co. Galway. (MacLysaght).

MacLysaght found Connolly widespread.

In Newfoundland:

Family traditions: —— Connolly, from Ireland, settled at North River (Conception B.), about 1780 (MUN Folklore). —— Connally, from Co. Wicklow, settled in Newfoundland, about 1830 (MUN Folklore).

Early instances: Thomas Conely, servant of Harbour Main, 1755 (MUN Hist.); Michael Connelly, of Cupids, 1771 (CO 199.18); Thomas, tailor of St. John's, 1794–5, "11 years in Newfoundland," that is, 1783–4 (Census 1794–5); James, of Placentia, 1794 (D'Alberti 5); Elizabeth, of Ferryland, 1799 (Nfld. Archives BRC); Thomas, from Kilnenall Parish, Cashel (Co. Tipperary), married at St. John's, 1805 (Nfld. Archives BRC); Mary Conelly, of Harbour Grace Parish, 1811 (Nfld. Archives HGRC); Michael Connally, from Co. Waterford, of Careless (now Kerley's) Harbour, 1821 (Nfld. Archives KCRC); Edward Connelly, of Kings Cove, 1824 (Nfld. Archives KCRC); Michael Connally, of Trinity, 1828 (Nfld. Archives KCRC); George Connelly, of Greenspond, 1833 (Nfld. Archives KCRC); Ellen, of Tickle Harbour, 1855 (Nfld. Archives KCRC); —— Conolly, of Port de Grave, 1834 (*Newfoundlander* 23 Jun 1834); Daniel Connelly, planter of Caplin Bay and Rip Raps (Cupids), 1871 (Lovell); Nicholas Conelly, fisherman of Toads (now Tors) Cove, 1871 (Lovell).

Modern status: Connolly (formerly sometimes Connelly in *Electors* 1955) scattered, especially at St. John's.

Place name: Connolly's Cove 48-12 53-33.

CONNORS, O'CONNOR, surnames of Ireland, *Ó Conchobhair*. MacLysaght comments that in Ireland, "the prefix O, formerly widely discarded, has been generally resumed. Similarly the variant Connors has become O'Connor again."

Widespread in Ireland, especially in Co. Kerry.

In Newfoundland:

Family traditions: Patrick Connors, from Co. Kerry, settled at Conception Harbour about ? 1815 (MUN Folklore). —— Connors, from Co. Cork, settled at Grandys Point in the early 19th century, and subsequently at Clattice Harbour and St. Kyran's (MUN Folklore).

Early instances: Thomas Connor, of Little Placentia (now Argentia), about 1730–35 (CO 194.9); Maurice Conners, shoreman of St. John's, 1794–5, "32 years in Newfoundland," that is, 1762–3 (Census 1794–5); Maurice Conors, of Trinity Bay, 1775 (DPHW 64); Dennis Conner, formerly of Waterford, late of Trepassey, deceased 1775 (*Waterford Arch. and Hist. Soc. J.* per Kirwin); Dennis Connor, of Cats Cove (now Conception Harbour), 1779 (CO 199.18); James Connors, of Harbour Main, 1779 (MUN Hist.); Andrew, planter of Fogo, 1780 (D'Alberti 6); Thomas Conner, of Harbour of Quirpon (Island of Jack), 1787 (CO 194.21); Thomas Conners, of Petty Harbour, 1794–5, "10 years in Newfoundland," that is, 1784–5 (Census 1794–5); Timothy, of Dublin, Irish convict landed at Petty Harbour or Bay Bulls, 1789 (CO 194.38); Daniel Connors, from Waterford, lessee of land at Port de Grave, 1799, died 1816 (*Nfld. Mercantile Journal* 11 Sep 1816, CO 199.18); Patrick, from Kilworth, Diocese of Cloyne (Co. Cork), married at St. John's, 1801 (Nfld. Archives BRC); David Connor, of Youghal (Co. Cork), married at St. John's, 1802 (Nfld. Archives BRC); Robert O'Connor, of Harbour Grace Parish, 1807 (Nfld. Archives HGRC); Lawrence Connors, from Kill St. Nicholas (Co. Waterford), fisherman of Burin, deceased 1813 (*Royal Gazette* 17 Jun 1813); James, of Kings Cove, 1816 (Nfld. Archives KCRC); Thomas Pierce Connor, schoolmaster of Carbonear, 1817 (D'Alberti 27); Patrick Connors, of Trinity, 1820 (Nfld. Archives KCRC); John, of Catalina, 1822 (Nfld. Archives KCRC); James, of Keels, 1827 (Nfld. Archives KCRC); Ann, of Adams Cove, 1828 (Nfld. Archives HGRC); Michael, of Riders Harbour, 1829 (Nfld. Archives KCRC); Michael, of Harbour Grace, 1830 (Nfld. Archives HGRC); Dennis, of Greenspond, 1831 (Nfld. Archives KCRC); Catherine O'Connors, of New Harbour (Trinity B.), 1832 (Nfld. Archives KCRC); Mary Connors, of Bay Bulls, 1841 (DPHW 26D); Michael, of Bell Island, 1842 (DPHW 26D); Timothy, of Tickle Cove (Bonavista B.), 1856 (Nfld. Archives KCRC); Joseph, planter of Lawn, 1857 (*Newfoundlander* 16 Nov 1857); James, of Logy Bay, 1858 (*Newfoundlander* 1 Apr 1858); John, of Gooseberry Island (Bonavista B.), 1859 (Nfld. Archives KCRC); Timothy, of Haywards Cove (Bonavista B.), 1859, of Dog Cove, 1861 (Nfld. Archives KCRC); ——, drowned at Twillingate, 1866 (Devine and O'Mara); Tom, of Cottels Island, 1867 (Nfld. Archives KCRC); Mrs. Connors, of Georgetown, died 1870, aged 103 years (Devine and O'Mara); Connors, scattered, Conners, O'Connor and O'Conner, rare, in Lovell 1871.

Modern status: Connors, scattered, especially in the St. John's and Placentia East districts; O'Connor, rare, at St. John's and Stephenville.

Place names (not necessarily from the surname): Connor Island 48-11 53-31; —— Rock 47-37 58-39, 47-39 58-01; —— Cove Point 47-19 55-55; Conners Brook 48-49 57-33; —— Rock 48-41 52-57; —— Rocks (Labrador) 53-08 55-44.

CONRAN, a surname of Ireland, also occurring in the form (O)Condron, *Ó Conaráin*. (MacLysaght).

Traced by MacLysaght especially in Leinster.

In Newfoundland:

Family tradition: —— Conran, from Co. Wexford, settled in or near Harbour Main, in the early 19th century (MUN Folklore).

Early instances: Michael, of Harbour Grace Parish, 1827 (Nfld. Archives HGRC); Joseph, Michael and Nicholas, farmers of Chapel's Cove (Conception B.), 1871 (Lovell).

Modern status: Rare, at Harbour Main (*Electors* 1955) and St. John's.

CONROY, a surname of Ireland, virtually indistinguishable from Conree, Conary and Conry. They represent four Gaelic originals, *Mac Conraoi* (Galway, Clare), *Ó Conraoi* (Galway), *Ó Conaire* (Munster) and *Ó Maolchonaire* (Roscommon). (MacLysaght).

Traced by MacLysaght, especially in Co. Galway.

In Newfoundland:

Early instances: Garrett, of St. John's, 1803 (Nfld. Archives BRC); John, of Harbour Grace Parish, 1806 (Nfld. Archives HGRC); Joseph, of Dumfries, Scotland, late of St. John's, 1857 (*Newfoundlander* 31 Dec 1857); Charles O'Neill, born in Dublin, 1871, came to Newfoundland, aged 18 months, and later established a law practice (*Nfld. Quarterly* June 1903).

Modern status: Rare, at St. John's.

CONSTANTINE, a surname of England and Scotland, Old French *Consta(n)tin* from Latin *Constantinus* – steadfast, the name of the first Christian emperor of Rome; or from the English place name Constantine

(Cornwall), named after a King of Devon and Cornwall of the 6th century who after his conversion to Christianity became a monk in Ireland and subsequently suffered martyrdom in Scotland; or from the French place name, the Cotentin peninsula (La Manche). (Reaney, Black).

Traced by Spiegelhalter in Devon.

In Newfoundland:

Early instances: Jonathan, married at St. John's, 1780, of Petty Harbour, 1782 (DPHW 26C, 26D); Jonathan, of Petty Harbour, 1808 (Nfld. Archives BRC); James and John, fishermen of St. John's, 1871 (Lovell).

Modern status: At St. John's.

CONWAY, a surname of England and Ireland; in England from the Welsh place name Conway, "one of the few Welsh towns that have originated a surname" (Bardsley); in Ireland, the anglicized form of several Gaelic surnames, *Mac Connmhaigh*, Ir. *condmach* – head smashing, *Mac Conmidhe* – hound of Meath, *Ó Conbhuidhe*, Ir. *con* – hound and *buidhe* – yellow, and *Ó Connmhacháin*. (Bardsley, Cottle, MacLysaght).

Traced by MacLysaght in Cos. Clare, Tyrone, Sligo and Mayo.

In Newfoundland:

Early instances: Patrick, of Placentia ? district, 1744 (CO 194.24); Bridget, of Bay Bulls, 1797 (Nfld. Archives BRC); Thomas (and others), of the Cape Shore, 1803 (Mannion); James, of St. John's, hanged 1805 (Dispatches 1803–13); Mary, of Harbour Grace Parish, 1809 (Nfld. Archives HGRC); Judith, from Windgap (Co. Kilkenny), married at St. John's, 1815 (Nfld. Archives BRC); John, of Bonavista, 1822 (Nfld. Archives KCRC); John, from Co. Cork, of Heart's Content, 1825 (Nfld. Archives KCRC); Catherine, of Bay de Verde, 1828 (Nfld. Archives BRC); John, from Co. Cork, of Turks Cove, 1829 (Nfld. Archives KCRC); William and James, of Labrador, 1832 (*Newfoundlander* 8 Nov 1832); William, from Killahy (unidentified) (Co. Kilkenny), planter of St. John's, died 1837 (*Star* 8 Feb 1837); Martin, ? of Ferryland, 1838 (*Newfoundlander* 25 Oct 1838); Catherine, married at Renews, 1841 (Dillon); Thomas, fisherman of Bay of Islands, 1871 (Lovell); Dennis (and others), of Colliers, 1871 (Lovell); Thomas, fisherman of Long Pond (Conception B.), 1871 (Lovell); Michael, fisherman of Mobile, 1871 (Lovell); John, miner of Tilt Cove, 1871 (Lovell).

Modern status: Widespread, especially at St. John's, St. Bride's and Colliers.

Place names: Conway Brook 47-31 52-58, 48-57 58-00; —— Cove 47-22 53-54, 47-26 53-48; Conway's Brook 49-11 58-03.

COOK(E), surnames of England, Scotland and Ireland, Cook of the Channel Islands, from Old English *cōc* – cook, or seller of cooked meats; also in Ireland, (Mac)Cooke may be for Scots MacCook or MacCuagh in Ulster and for *MacDhabhoc* in Connacht. *See* COKE, COX. (Reaney, Cottle, MacLysaght, Turk).

Guppy found Cook(e) widespread in England; MacLysaght found (Mac)Cooke in Leinster, Ulster and Connacht.

In Newfoundland:

Family tradition: Thomas Rex, of Devon, deserted his ship, settled at Sugarloaf (St. John's) and changed his name to Cook, about 1847 (MUN Folklore).

Early instances: Christopher Cooke, of Barrow Harbour, 1675 (CO 1); Thomas, of Old Perlican, 1676 (CO 1); Robert, of St. John's, 1705 (CO 194.3); Robert Cook, of Torbay, 1708–09 (CO 194.4); Richard, of Trinity Bay, 1767 (DPHW 64); Sansom, of Fogo, 1771 (CO 194.30); Joseph, of Petty Harbour, 1794–5, "20 years in Newfoundland," that is, 1774–5 (Census 1794–5); Jane, of Musketta (now Bristol's Hope), 1779 (CO 199.18); Charles, of Placentia, 1794 (D'Alberti 5); George, of Trinity (Trinity B.), 1797 (DPHW 64); Charles Cooke, of Bay Bulls, 1802 (USPG); Richard Cook, of Ship Cove (now part of Port Rexton), 1805 (DPHW 64); Richard Cooke, from Callan (Co. Kilkenny), married at St. John's, 1808 (Nfld. Archives BRC); Margaret Cook, of Joe Batts Arm, 1815 (Nfld. Archives KCRC); Mary, of Harbour Grace Parish, 1815 (Nfld. Archives HGRC); Lawrence, of Bonavista, 1816 (Nfld. Archives KCRC); George Cooke, of Bally Hally Farm (St. John's), 1823 (DPHW 26B); Margaret Cook, of Fortune Harbour, 1830 (Nfld. Archives KCRC); William Cooke, from Biddestone (Wilts.), of Red Cove (Placentia B.), 1835 (Wix); John Cook, cooper of Carbonear, 1857 (DPHW 48); William, fisherman of Bay Roberts, 1838 (DPHW 39); Noah, of Heart's Content, 1854 (DPHW 64B); Thomas, cooper of Catalina, 1854 (DPHW 72); Cook and Cooke, scattered in Lovell 1871.

Modern status: Cook, widespread, especially at St. John's; Cooke, rare.

Place names: Cook Bank 50-37 57-15; Cook(s) Cove 48-58 58-04; —— Harbour 51-37 55-53; —— Hill 47-40 56-11; —— Rock 49-33 55-17; Cooks Brook 48-54 58-03, 48-58 58-04; —— Cove 48-06

53-00; —— Harbour 51-36 55-52, 51-36 55-51;
—— Point 51-37 55-51; —— Pond 47-52 58-10,
48-06 52-59, 48-57 54-09; Cook Stone 47-41 59-17;
Captain Cook Ponds 49-31 55-17; New —— Island
(Labrador) 53-43 59-59.

COOL(E), surnames of England and Ireland, in
England Coole from Manx *MacCumhail, comhal* –
courageous, or ? from the English place name Coole
(Cheshire); in Ireland (Mac)Cool for *Mac Giolla
Comhghaill* – devotee of St. Comhghal, *Mac
Comhghaill.* "In Scotland MacCool a variant of
MacDougall" (MacLysaght). *See* COLE(S). (Reaney,
MacLysaght). Traced by MacLysaght in Co.
Donegal

Early instances: John Coule, of Bonavista, 1830
(DPHW 70); John Coole, of Harbour Grace Parish,
1838 (Nfld. Archives HGRC); John, ? of Northern
Bay 1842 (DPHW 54); Samuel, of Newman's Cove,
1846 (DPHW 70).

Modern status: Coole, especially at Newman's
Cove; Cool, rare.

COOMB(E)S, surnames of England, from one of the
many places named Co(o)mb(e), 9 in Somerset, 6 in
Devon and elsewhere, or from Old English *comb* –
(dweller in a) small valley. (Reaney, Cottle).

Guppy traced Coomb(e)s in Dorset, Hampshire,
Somerset and Wiltshire, Combes also in Wiltshire,
and Coombe in Devon.

In Newfoundland:

Family traditions: Alexander Coombs, from Kent,
settled at Upper Island Cove in the early 19th
century (MUN Folklore). Bill (1830–1902), born at
Shaftesbury (Dorset), settled at Belleoram about
1850 and at Terrenceville in 1854 (MUN Geog.).
William, was one of the first settlers at Black Duck
Cove (St. Barbe district) in the early 19th century
(MUN Hist.).

Early instances: Richard Coons, of Brigus
(unspecified), 1676 (CO 1); —— Come, of Quidi
Vidi, 1703 (CO 194.3); Peter, of St. John's, 1706 (CO
194.22); Ann Combs, of Trinity (Trinity B.), 1773
(DPHW 64); John Coombes, of Upper Island Cove,
1781 (CO 199.18); Thomas Coomb, of Bonavista,
1791 (USPG); Elias Coombs, of Bay Bulls, 1793
(USPG); George Coombes, of Port de Grave, 1800
(CO 199.18); Robert Coomb(e)s, of Fogo, 1803
(D'Alberti 13); William Coombs, enlisted at
Greenspond, 1806–07 (CO 194.46); Robert, cooper
of Burnt Head (Carbonear), 1827 (DPHW 48); John
Coombes, of Pool's Harbour (Burin), 1829 (DPHW

109); Charles, of Furby's Cove, 1834 (DPHW 109);
John Coombs, Combs or Comes, of Kings Cove
Parish, 1835 (Nfld. Archives KCRC); John Coomb, of
Harbour Grace Parish, 1841 (Nfld. Archives HGRC);
John Combs, of Round Harbour, 1846 (DPHW 86);
Edward Coombs, fisherman of Picaria (now
Piccaire), 1854 (DPHW 101); Jane Coombes, of
Fortune, 1855 (DPHW 106); Shadrach Coombs, of
Upper Burgeo, 1855 (DPHW 101); Maria, of Harbour
Grace, 1867 (Nfld. Archives HGRC); David,
fisherman of Burin, 1871 (Lovell); George, of
Cupids, 1871 (Lovell); John Combs, fisherman of
Heart's Desire, 1871 (Lovell); Stephen Coombs,
fisherman of Crocker's Cove (Carbonear), 1871
(Lovell); S. Coomes, fisherman of La Plante
(Burgeo), 1871 (Lovell).

Modern status: Coombes, rare, at St. John's;
Coombs, widespread, especially at Upper Island
Cove, Shoal Cove West, Portugal Cove South, St.
John's, Heart's Desire and Terrenceville.

Place names: Coombe Rock 50-47 57-18;
Coombes Head, —— Islands 47-37 57-40; ——
Rock 47-43 54-02; Coomb's Cove 47-27 55-37.

COONEY, a surname of Ireland, *Ó Cuana*, ? Ir. *cuan*
– elegant. (MacLysaght).

MacLysaght found Cooney "fairly numerous in
all the provinces except Ulster."

In Newfoundland:

Early instances: John, of Bonavista, 1792 (USPG);
Edward, of Musketta (now Bristol's Hope), 1795 (CO
199.18); Patrick, from Cashel (Co. Tipperary),
married at St. John's, 1805 (Nfld. Archives BRC);
Mary Co(o)ney, of Harbour Grace Parish, 1816
(Nfld. Archives HGRC); James Cooney, of Harbour
Grace, 1830 (Nfld. Archives HGRC); Thomas, of
Croque Harbour, 1834 (*Newfoundlander* 27 Nov
1834); Peter, of Outer Cove (St. John's), 1838 (Nfld.
Archives BRC).

Modern status: Scattered, especially at St. John's
and Harbour Grace.

COOPER, a surname of England, Ireland, Scotland,
and the Channel Islands, from Middle English *couper*
– maker or repairer of wooden casks, buckets or tubs.
(Reaney, Turk).

Found widespread in England and Scotland by
Guppy and Black, and by MacLysaght particularly in
Co. Sligo.

In Newfoundland:

Family traditions: Charles, son of a West Country
merchant, settled at Grates Cove about 1705 (MUN
Folklore). ——, moved from Lower Island Cove to

Cooper's Point, Grates Cove, about 1790 (MUN Hist.). John, ? from England, married and settled at Norman's Cove in the early 19th century (MUN Hist.). ——, from Cornwall to Twillingate about 1847, later settled at Point Leamington (MUN Folklore). ——, from ? Hanson (unidentified), England, settled at Ireland's Eye about 1847 (MUN Folklore). ——, settled at Pushthrough about 1850 (MUN Folklore).

Early instances: William, planter of St. John's, 1706 (CO 194.4); William, of Spear Island, 1708–09 (CO 194.4); John and Richard, ? servants of Oderin, about 1730–35 (CO 194.9); Thomas, of Lower Island Cove, 1781 (CO 199.18); Edward, of Great Belle Isle (now Bell Island), 1797 (D'Alberti 7); George and son, proprietors and occupiers of fishing room at Grates Cove, Winter 1800–01 (Census Trinity B.); John, planter of Fogo, 1808 (MUN Hist.); Edward, of Ireland's Eye, 1814 (DPHW 64); Thomas Cooper(s), of Harbour Grace Parish, 1815 (Nfld. Archives HGRC); Tom Cooper, planter of Catalina, 1818 (DPHW 72); Eleanor, of Twillingate, 1820 (USPG); John, of Trinity (Trinity B.), 1821 (DPHW 64); John, of New Harbour (Trinity B.), 1823 (DPHW 64); Edward, pioneer of Lance Cove (Bell Island), died 1825, aged 61 years (MUN Hist.); Patrick K., of Harbour Grace, 1831 (Nfld. Archives HGRC); William, of Blackhead (Conception B.), 1831 (DPHW 52A); James, of Kings Cove Parish, 1839 (Nfld. Archives KCRC); George, planter of Western Bay, 1839 (DPHW 52A); John, of Old Perlican, 1840 (DPHW 58); Henry, of Burgeo, 1846 (DPHW 26D); Henry, of Petty Harbour, 1847 (DPHW 31); John, of Scilly Cove (now Winterton), 1857, of Norman's Cove, 1858 (DPHW 59A); Michael T., cooper of Carbonear, 1871 (Lovell); John (and others), of Chapel Arm, 1871 (Lovell); Samuel, of Green's Harbour, 1871 (Lovell); James, of Mouse Island, 1871 (Lovell); Absolom and John, of Random Sound, 1871 (Lovell); James, of Three Arms, Twillingate, 1871 (Lovell).

Modern status: Widespread, especially in the Trinity North and South districts.

Place names: Cooper Bank 46-59 55-04; —— Brook 48-42 55-13; —— Cove 47-18 53-59, 47-35 54-13, 47-37 56-46, 47-39 54-08; —— Head 47-20 53-54 (Labrador) 52-57 55-47; —— Island 51-20 56-42 (Labrador) 52-55 55-48, (Labrador) 53-35 57-18; —— Pond 48-46 55-13; Coopers Block (Labrador) 52-54 55-47; —— Cove 47-35 54-12, (Labrador) 54-06 58-32; —— Head 47-38 53-13; —— Island (Labrador) 57-40 61-42; —— Pond 47-39 53-29.

COOZE, ? a variant of the surname of England Cuss(e), a pet-form of the female baptismal names Custance or Constance from Latin *constantia* – constancy. *See also* COSE.

Guppy traced Cuss(e) in Wiltshire.

In Newfoundland:

Early instances: William Coos or Cooze, of Greenspond, 1839, of Pouch Island, 1841 (DPHW 76).

Modern status: Scattered, especially in the Bonavista North district.

CORBETT, a surname of England, Ireland, Scotland, with Corbet(t) of the Channel Islands, from Old French *corbet* – raven, "probably a nickname for one with dark hair or complexion" (Reaney), or also for one with a raucous voice (Cottle), or from Old French *corbet*, Latin *curvatus* – bent, crooked (Spiegelhalter); in Ireland it is usually for *Ó Corbáin* (Munster) or *Ó Coirbín* (Connacht), ? Ir. *corb* – chariot. *See* CORBIN. (Reaney, Cottle, MacLysaght, Turk).

Traced by Guppy in Gloucestershire, Herefordshire, Shropshire, Warwickshire and Worcestershire, by Spiegelhalter in Devon, and by MacLysaght in Munster and Connacht.

In Newfoundland:

Early instances: John Corbet, married at St. John's, 1764 (DPHW 26D); Edward Corbitt, of Broad Cove (Bay de Verde district), 1776 (CO 199.18); Thomas Corbett, of Chapels Cove, 1796 (CO 199.18); Ann Corbit, of St. John's, 1805 (Nfld. Archives BRC); Mary Corbit or Corbett, of Harbour Grace Parish, 1813 (Nfld. Archives HGRC); John Corbitt, from Fethard (Co. Tipperary), planter of Broad Cove (unspecified), deceased, 1814 (*Royal Gazette* 17 Feb 1814); Daniel Corbet, from Dungarvan (Co. Waterford), married at St. John's, 1815 (Nfld. Archives BRC).

Modern status: Scattered, especially at St. John's, Chapels Cove, Otterbury (Port de Grave) and Holyrood.

Place names: Corbet Harbour (Labrador) 53-16 55-42; —— Island (Labrador) 53-16 55-44; Corbett Cove 49-06 58-23; Mount Corbett 49-33 56-53.

CORBIN, a surname of England, France and Guernsey (Channel Islands), from Old French *corbin* from *corb* – raven, or from the French place name Corbon (Calvados, Orne), or ? by confusion with the Irish surname (O)Corban(e), a synonym of CORBETT. Occasionally used as a baptismal name in Newfoundland. (Reaney, Dauzat).

Traced in Dorset and Guernsey.

In Newfoundland:

Family tradition: Thomas, from Poole (Dorset) settled at Carbonear (MUN Folklore).

Early instances: John Corban, of Old Perlican, 1675, Corbon in 1677, Corbett in 1681 (CO 1); Henry and John Corbin, of Old Perlican, 1708–09 (CO 194.4); Bartholomew Corban, of Port de Grave, 1770, 1785 (Nfld. Archives T22, CO 199.18); Benjamin Corbin, of Fogo, Twillingate or Tilton (now Tilting), 1771 (CO 194.30); John and Daniel, boatkeepers of Little Placentia (now Argentia), 1776 (D'Alberti 6); John Corbin or Corban, of Harbour Grace Parish, 1807 (Nfld. Archives HGRC); George Allen, from Blandford (Dorset), married at St. John's, 1832 (DPHW 26D); James, fisherman of Freshwater (Carbonear), 1849 (DPHW 49); —— Corben, on the *Caroline* in the seal fishery out of Harbour Grace, 1853 (*Newfoundlander* 28 Mar 1853); William Corbin, fisherman of Great Burin, 1871 (Lovell); William, farmer of Placentia, 1871 (Lovell); John, farmer of Point Verde, 1871 (Lovell); Richard, fisherman of Spaniard's Bay, 1871 (Lovell).

Modern status: Scattered.

Place names: Corbin 46-58 55-14, 47-35 55-25; —— Bay 47-36 55-25; Cape —— 50-02 55-54; —— Cape 51-23 55-30; —— Harbour 46-57 55-14; —— Head 47-29 53-56, 47-37 55-24; —— Island 46-58 55-13; —— Head Promontory 47-36 55-26; —— —— Shoal 47-28 53-57.

CORCORAN, a surname of Ireland, *Mac Corcráin, Ó Corcráin*, Ir. *corcair* – purple ? (-faced). (MacLysaght).

MacLysaght traced (Mac)Corcoran in Co. Offaly, (O)Corcoran in Co. Fermanagh.

In Newfoundland:

Early instances: [baptized] Joannem [daughter of] Jacobi Corcoran and Honora Welsh de Terra Nova, 1776 (St. Patrick's Parish Records, Waterford per Kirwin); John, ? labourer of St. John's, 1779 (CO 194.34); William, of Harbour Grace Parish, 1811 (Nfld. Archives HGRC); Alice, from Ross (unidentified), married at St. John's, 1814 (Nfld. Archives BRC); Andrew, of Greenspond, 1817 (Nfld. Archives KCRC); Anne, from Co. Kilkenny, married at Tilton Harbour (now Tilting), 1817 (Nfld. Archives KCRC); Michael, of Joe Batts Arm, 1822 (Nfld. Archives KCRC); Michael, ? of Harbour Grace, 1845 (*Newfoundlander* 16 Jan 1845); Francis, of Fox Cove (Burin), 1871 (Lovell); Patrick, servant of Mortier, 1871 (Lovell); Maurice (and others), of St. Mary's, 1871 (Lovell); Michael, from Kilkenny,

fisherman of Trepassey, 1871, died 1891 (Lovell, Dillon).

Modern status: Scattered, especially in the St. Mary's district.

CORMACK, a surname of Scotland, MacCormack of Ireland, from the Gaelic personal name *Cormac*, early Celtic *corb-mac* – chariot-lad, charioteer. (Black, MacLysaght). *See* MacCORMAC.

MacLysaght found MacCormack numerous throughout Ireland, with the spelling MacCormick more usual in Ulster.

In Newfoundland:

Early instances: Nathaniel Cormick, of St. John's, 1780 (D'Alberti 6); Alexander Cormack, merchant of St. John's, 1794–5, "12 years in Newfoundland," that is, 1782–3 (Census 1794–5); William Eppes (1796–1868), born at St. John's, the first white man to cross Newfoundland (Devine and O'Mara); Richard Cormick, of Harbour Grace Parish, 1825 (Nfld. Archives HGRC); Matthew, from Rose (unidentified) (Co. Kilkenny), married at St. John's, 1829 (Nfld. Archives BRC); Joanna Cormack, of Kings Cove, 1830 (Nfld. Archives KCRC); Margaret Cormick, from Co. Kilkenny, married at Ragged Harbour (now Melrose), 1830 (Nfld. Archives KCRC); James Cormack, of Bay Roberts, 1838 (*Newfoundlander* 6 Dec 1838); James and Richard, from Co. Tipperary, of Port de Grave, 1844 (*Indicator* 24 Aug 1844); Michael Cormick, ? of Harbour Grace, 1845 (*Newfoundlander* 9 Jan 1845); Michael, of Mosquito (now Bristol's Hope), 1871 (Lovell); Patrick Cormack, farmer and planter of Salmonier, 1871 (Lovell); John, of Plate Cove (Bonavista B.), 1871 (Nfld. Archives KCRC).

Modern status: Rare, at St. John's (*Electors* 1955).

Place names: Cormack 49-18 57-23; Mount —— 48-24 55-57; Cormack's Lake 48-16 57-53.

CORMEY, a Newfoundland variant of the surname of France CORMIER.

In Newfoundland:

Modern status: Formerly in the Codroy Valley district, now rare, in St. John's.

CORMIER, a surname of France, from French *cormier* – service tree, which bears the service apple or berry. It is the name of numerous hamlets in the centre and west of France. (Dauzat). *See also* CORMEY.

In Newfoundland:

Family tradition: Captain Firmin Cormier, of

Margaree, N.S., after several years in the Magdalen Islands, went to Piccadilly, Port au Port Peninsula, in 1849 and shortly moved to Sandy Point. His descendants are now found mainly in the Stephenville-St. George's area and also at Cape St. George and Degras. (G.R. Thomas). A Cormier family from St. Pierre, settled at Stephenville about 1907 (MUN Folklore).

Modern status: In the West Coast districts, especially at Noel's Pond, St. Theresa's and Stephenville.

Place name: Cormier Lake (Labrador) 55-16 66-43.

CORNECT, ? Newfoundland variant of a surname of France in its Breton form Cornec, a derivative of *cornec* – horn, hence cuckold. (Dauzat).

In Newfoundland:

Family tradition: In the form Cornic derived from Lecornic; the first Cornect was a Breton deserter from the French fishery (Thomas, "French Fam. Names"). The Cornack [sic] family arrived in Newfoundland and settled at Cape St. George in 1900 (MUN Geog.). Some French and English speakers currently use the pronunciation Cornack (Thomas, "French Fam. Names").

Modern status: Especially at Cape St. George.

CORNELL, a surname of England, from one of the places named Cornwall, Cornhill (Northumberland, Middlesex) or Cornwell (Oxfordshire), or from French *corneille* – rook, crow, hence a chatterer, or for the French and Irish surname Corneille, or, in Newfoundland, ? by confusion with CARNELL. (Reaney, MacLysaght, Dauzat).

Spiegelhalter traced Cornell in Devon.

In Newfoundland:

Family tradition: John Carnell or ? Cornell, of Catalina, one of the first settlers at Flower's Cove, 1850 (MUN Hist.).

Early instances: John, of Harbour Grace Parish, 1824 (Nfld. Archives HGRC); John, ? of Northern Bay, 1844 (DPHW 54); Charles, fisherman of Bonne Bay, 1871 (Lovell); Patrick, fisherman of St. John's, 1871 (Lovell).

Modern status: Unique, at St. John's.

CORNICK, a surname of England, apparently not recorded elsewhere, ? a variant of Kornick, from the place name Kernick (Cornwall), or ? a variant of CORNISH.

Traced in Yorkshire and Dorset, and by Spiegelhalter in Devon.

In Newfoundland:

Family traditions: Fred, John and Alice, from Toller Porcorum, near Bridport (Dorset), settled at St. John's about 1853 (Kirwin). Audrey, from Yorkshire, settled at Big Pond (unidentified) about 1877 (MUN Folklore).

Early instances: Richard, of Placentia, 1794 (D'Alberti 5); Michael, of Moretons Harbour, 1850 (DPHW 86); James Cornix, fisherman of Burin, 1860 (DPHW 100); Edward (and others) Cornick, of St. John's, 1871 (Lovell).

Modern status: Scattered, especially at St. John's and in the St. Barbe district.

CORNISH, a surname of England and Jersey (Channel Islands), from the English county – (the man from) Cornwall. *See also* CORNICK. (Reaney, Turk).

Traced by Guppy in Berkshire, Devon and Somerset.

In Newfoundland:

Early instances: Henry Cormish, of Fermeuse, 1677 (CO 1); John Cornish, of St. John's, 1751 (CO 194.13); Richard, of Ochre Pit Cove, 1776 (CO 199.18); Richard, ? of Teignmouth (Devon), lessee of land at Harbour Grace, 1799, 1806 (CO 199.18, Nfld. Archives T98); John, of Harbour Grace Parish, 1831 (Nfld. Archives HGRC).

Modern status: Scattered.

CORRIGAN. *See* CARRIGAN

COSE, ? a surname of England, apparently not recorded elsewhere, ? a variant of COOZE.

In Newfoundland:

Early instances: Thomas Coase, of St. John's, ? 1753 (CO 194.13); John ? Cose, of Bonavista, 1820 (DPHW 72); James and Samuel, of Aquaforte, 1871 (Lovell).

Modern status: At Aquaforte (*Electors* 1955).

COSSAR, a surname of England and Scotland, from Middle English *cosser* – dealer, broker, horse-corser. (Reaney, Black).

Spiegelhalter traced ? the variant Corser in Devon.

In Newfoundland:

Early instances: Thomas Corsor, ? of St. John's, 1772 (DPHW 26C); Lot Cossar, of Lower Burgeo, 1846 (DPHW 101); Lot Cosser, of Red Island (Burgeo district), 1871 (Lovell).

Modern status: In the Burgeo-La Poile district.

COSSETT, a Newfoundland variant of the surname of France, Cosset, from *cosse* – pod, husk, a nickname for a seller of peas, beans, etc. (Dauzat).

In Newfoundland:
Modern status: At Corner Brook.

COSTARD, a surname of France – ? a dweller by the coast (in a pejorative sense). (Dauzat). *See* LA COSTA, LE CASTA, of which Costard is due to English influence (Thomas, "French Fam. Names").
In Newfoundland:
Modern status: At Loretto (*Electors* 1955).

COSTELLO, a surname of Ireland, *Mac Oisdeal-bhaigh*. "*Oisdealb* was the name of one of the sons of Gilbert de Nangle, and this is the first example of a Norman family assuming a Mac name. The use of the prefix O is erroneous, though it does occasionally occur in seventeenth century records" (MacLysaght). Cottle suggests that Costello is probably "son of Jocelyn" in an Irish form. *See* NANGLE. (MacLysaght, Cottle).
Traced by MacLysaght in Co. Mayo, and formerly as Costellow in Sussex by Guppy.
In Newfoundland:
Early instances: Darby, of Harbour Main, 1755 (Devine and O'Mara); Thomas, fisherman of St. John's, 1794–5, "30 years in Newfoundland," that is, 1764–5 (Census 1794–5); D. Costelloe, of Kitchuses, 1770 (CO 199.18); Pearce Costello, of Chapels Cove, 1785 (CO 199.18); James, boatkeeper of Quidi Vidi, 1794–5, "born in Newfoundland" (Census 1794–5); P., ? fisherman of Port de Grave, 1797 (Nfld. Archives T22); James, from Rosbericome (unidentified) (Co. Kilkenny), married at St. John's, 1806 (Nfld. Archives BRC); David, of Harbour Grace Parish, 1806 (Nfld. Archives HGRC); Ellen, from Co. Tipperary, of Ragged Harbour (now Melrose), 1821 (Nfld. Archives KCRC); Michael, from Co. Kilkenny, of Kings Cove, 1826 (Nfld. Archives KCRC); Michael Costello or Costilo, of Keels, 1829 (Nfld. Archives KCRC); Thomas Costelloe, of Ferryland, 1830 (Nfld. Archives BRC); Valentine Costolo, of Carbonear, 1837 (Nfld. Archives BRC); William Costello, of Petty Harbour, 1837 (*Newfoundlander* 6 Apr 1837); Martin Costolo, of Indian Arm, 1861 (Nfld. Archives KCRC); Mary Costilo, of Broad Cove (now Duntara), 1864 (Nfld. Archives KCRC); Elizabeth Costello, of Harbour Grace, 1867 (Nfld. Archives HGRC); David Costeloe (and others), of Cats Cove (now Conception Harbour), 1871 (Lovell); Richard, fisherman of Oderin, 1871 (Lovell); Martin, of Spaniard's Bay, 1871 (Lovell); Joseph (and others), of Salmon Cove (now Avondale) and Gasters, 1871 (Lovell).
Modern status: Especially in the Harbour Main and Ferryland districts.

COSTIGAN, a surname of Ireland, *Mac Oistigín* "and corruptly *Mac Costagáin*. Woulfe says *Oistigín* comes from the English name Roger, pet form Hodgkin" (MacLysaght, Withycombe). *See* HODGE.
Traced by MacLysaght in Co. Leix.
In Newfoundland:
Early instances: John, of Torbay, 1794–5, "18 years in Newfoundland," that is, 1776–7 (Census 1794–5); Pat, fisherman of St. John's, 1794–5, "15 years in Newfoundland," that is, since 1777–8 (Census 1794–5); Vincent, of Harbour Grace Parish, 1812 (Nfld. Archives HGRC); Michael, from Callan (Co. Kilkenny), married at Harbour Grace, 1829 (Nfld. Archives BRC); Vincent, of Harbour Main, 1838, of Cat's Cove (now Conception Harbour), 1843 (*Newfoundlander* 27 Sep 1838, 6 Apr 1843); Michael, fisherman of Carbonear, 1871 (Lovell); John and William, of Colliers, 1871 (Lovell).
Modern status: Scattered, especially at Logy Bay and Harbour Main.
Place name: Costigan Lake 48-30 57-05.

COTTER, a surname of England and Ireland; in England from Old French *cotier* – "a villein who held a cot[tage] by labour-service" (Reaney); in Ireland (Mac) Cotter, *Mac Coitir*, "an old Gaelic-Irish family though their name is formed from a Norse personal name" (MacLysaght), which Cottle translates as "son of Terrible Army." (Reaney, Cottle, MacLysaght).
Traced by Spiegelhalter in Devon and by MacLysaght in Co. Cork.
In Newfoundland:
Early instances: James, of Bay de Verde, 1783 (CO 199.18); John, of Cork city, married at St. John's, 1803 (Nfld. Archives BRC); Mary, of Harbour Grace Parish, 1807 (Nfld. Archives HGRC); John, of Ragged Harbour (now Melrose), 1813 (Nfld. Archives BRC); Michael Cottor, of St. John's, 1817 (CO 194.59); Garrett Cotter, of New Perlican, 1818 (DPHW 64); Mary, of Catalina, 1822 (Nfld. Archives KCRC); John, of Twillingate, 1822 (Nfld. Archives KCRC); Joanna, of Trinity, 1825 (Nfld. Archives KCRC); Garrett, of Hearts Content, 1825, of Turks Cove, 1829 (Nfld. Archives KCRC); Ellen, of Bay de Verde, 1828 (Nfld. Archives BRC); John, of Quidi Vidi, 1828 (DPHW 26D); Edmund, of Joe Batts Arm, 1829 (Nfld. Archives KCRC); Johanna, of Riders Harbour, 1832 (Nfld. Archives KCRC); James, ? of Northern Bay, 1838 (DPHW 54); Anne, of the French Shore, 1839 (Nfld. Archives BRC); ——, captain of the *Phoenix* in the seal fishery out of Brigus, 1857 (*Newfoundlander* 16 Mar 1857).
Modern status: Scattered, especially at New Perlican and Melrose.

Place name: Cotter's Point (Labrador) 53-35 60-16.

COTTON, a surname of England and Ireland, from Old English *æt cotum* – (dweller) at the cottages, or from the English place names, with the same meaning, Coton (Cambridgeshire), Cotton (Devon, Cheshire), Coatham (Durham, Yorkshire NR), Cotham (Nottinghamshire) and Cottam (Nottinghamshire, Yorkshire ER). (Reaney).

Found widespread in the Midlands by Reaney, in Devon by Spiegelhalter, and in Dublin and southeast Leinster since the 17th century by MacLysaght.

In Newfoundland:

Early instances: Henry, of Renews, 1675 (CO 1); Kearn Cotten, of Harbour Grace Parish, 1816 (Nfld. Archives HGRC).

Modern status: Rare, at Witless Bay (*Electors* 1955) and St. John's.

COUCH(E), surnames of England, from Cornish and Welsh *coch* – red (of hair or complexion), or from Old French *couch* – (maker of) couches, upholstery. (Reaney).

Traced by Spiegelhalter in Devon and by Guppy in Cornwall.

In Newfoundland:

Early instances: John Couch, of Placentia, 1794 (D'Alberti 6); ——, on the *Leo*, 1853 (*Newfoundlander* 31 Oct 1853)

Modern status: Couch, rare, at St. John's (*Electors* 1955); Couche, at Goose Cove (White Bay) (*Electors* 1955).

COUGHLAN, a surname of Ireland *Mac Cochláin, Ó Cochláin*, ? Ir. *cochal* – cape, hood (Woulfe). The prefixes Mac and Ó "have been almost entirely dropped" (MacLysaght).

MacLysaght traced (Mac)Coughlan in Co. Offaly and (O)Coughlan in Co. Cork.

In Newfoundland:

Early instances: Jeremiah Co(u)ghlan, of Twillingate, 1768 (CO 194.28); William Coghlan, of Bryant's Cove, 1785 (CO 199.18); John Coughlen, ? of St. John's, 1796 (DPHW 26D); James Coughlin, of Harbour Grace Parish, 1807 (Nfld. Archives HGRC); Anne Coughlan, from Carrick-on-Suir (Co. Tipperary), married at St. John's, 1808 (Nfld. Archives BRC); Mary Coughlen, of Harbour Grace, 1813 (Nfld. Archives BRC); James Coughlan, from Co. Cork, of Bonavista, 1826 (Nfld. Archives KCRC); Bridget, of Hearts Content, 1829 (Nfld. Archives KCRC); James, of Harbour Grace, 1830 (Nfld.

Archives HGRC); Patrick Coughlin, of Portugal Cove, 1840 (*Newfoundlander* 16 Jul 1840).

Modern status: At St. John's.

COULTAS, a surname of England – (worker at the) colt-house, colt-keeper. (Reaney).

Traced in Cornwall.

In Newfoundland:

Family tradition: ——, from Cornwall, settled in Conception Bay (? at Carbonear), in the 19th century (MUN Folklore).

Early instances: Joseph, surgeon of Adam's Cove, 1848, of Lower Island Cove, 1857, of Hants Harbour, 1858 (DPHW 52A, 55, 59A); ——, widow of Joseph, of Carbonear, 1871 (Lovell).

Modern status: At St. John's.

COUNSEL, a surname of England, from Old French *conseil, cunseil* – consultation, deliberation. (Reaney).

Traced by Guppy in Somerset.

In Newfoundland:

Early instance: Edward Councille, of Red Island (Placentia B.), 1871 (Lovell).

Modern status: Counsel, rare, at Red Island (Placentia B.), and South Brook (Humber East district).

COURAGE, a surname of England, with **COURISH**, ? a Newfoundland variant, from Old French *corage, curage*, Middle English *corage* – spirit, mind, bravery; or from the English place name Courage (Berkshire); or from Cowridge End (Bedfordshire) "which came to be pronounced *Courage* and is now pronounced *Scourge End*" (Reaney); or a variant of Kerrich, Kerridge from the Old English personal name *Cyneric* – family ruler, or from the English place name Kerridge (Cheshire, Devon). (Reaney).

Traced in Dorset.

In Newfoundland:

Family tradition: John Roland Courage (1852–1938), born at Sturminster Newton (Dorset), came to Newfoundland at the age of 14 years, and died at Garnish (MUN Folklore).

Early instances: John Courage, of Harbour Grace, 1780, of Gasters, 1790 (CO 199.18); Robert, ? of St. John's, 1801 (DPHW 26B); Garland, of Lower Island Cove, 1806, of Catalina, 1823 (CO 199.18, DPHW 72); John, planter of Sheep's Head (Harbour Grace), 1829 (DPHW 43); John and Joseph, fishermen of Riverhead (Harbour Grace), 1871 (Lovell).

Modern status: Courage, scattered, especially at St. John's and Catalina; Courish, at St. John's.

Place names: Courage's Beach 47-41 53-14; ——
Point 48-30 53-05.

COURTENAY, COURTNEY, surnames of England,
Courtney in Ireland, from the French place name
Courtenay (Loiset, Isère) (Reaney) or from French
court nez – short nose (Cottle). In Ireland, Courtney
may also be an anglicized form of (O)Curnane or
MacCourt. (Reaney, Cottle, MacLysaght).

Traced by Spiegelhalter in Devon and by
MacLysaght in Co. Kerry.

In Newfoundland:

Early instances: Margaret Courtney, of St. John's,
1816 (Dispatches 1816–17); Thomas, planter of
Salmon Cove (now Champneys), 1825 (DPHW 64B);
Charles Courtenay, of Mosquito (Hermitage B.),
1835 (DPHW 30); Robert Courtney, of Grand Bank,
1851 (DPHW 106); William, of Petites, 1857 (DPHW
98); Charles, of Frenchman's Cove (Burgeo district),
1860 (DPHW 99); William, of Burnt Island (Burgeo
district), 1871 (Lovell); Charles, planter of Cinq Cerf
(Burgeo district), 1871 (Lovell).

Modern status: Courtenay, at Pushthrough
(*Electors* 1955) and St. John's; Courtney, especially
in the Burgeo-La Poile district and at Bay Bulls
Road (St. John's).

COUSENS, COUSINS, surnames of England, Cousins
of Ireland, from Old French *cosin, cusin* – in Middle
English kinsman, kinswoman, cousin; or a variant of
the English and Irish surname Cussen; or from Old
French *cocine, cuisine* – (worker in the) kitchen.
(Spiegelhalter, Reaney). *See also* CUZA.

Traced, in several variants, by Guppy in
Berkshire, Dorset, Essex, Hampshire, Somerset and
Yorkshire and by Spiegelhalter in Devon.

In Newfoundland:

Early instances: Charles Cuszens or Cozens, from
Blandford (Dorset), of Brigus, 1811 (MUN Hist.,
DPHW 34); John Cousins, from New Ross (Co.
Wexford), married at St. John's, 1817 (Nfld.
Archives BRC); John, from Teignmouth (Devon), of
St. John's, 1833 (DPHW 26D); John Cozens, of
Barren Island (now Bar Haven), 1835 (Wix);
George, of Channel, 1871 (Lovell); James (and
others), of Drogheda (near Clarke's Beach), 1871
(Lovell); John (and others), of Lamaline, 1871
(Lovell); Lavy, fisherman of Lower Gully (now
Riverdale), 1871 (Lovell).

Modern status: Cousens, at Makinsons and St.
John's; Cousins, scattered, especially in the Burin
district.

Place name: Cousin Head 46-55 55-58.

COVE, a surname of England from the English place
names North and South Cove (Suffolk) or Cove
(Devon, Hampshire). (Bardsley, Ekwall).

Traced by Bardsley in Suffolk and by
Spiegelhalter in Devon.

In Newfoundland:

Family tradition: The Cove family came from the
north of England to Petty Harbour in the mid-17th
century (MUN Folklore).

Early instances: Rober[t], ? of St. John's, 1796
(DPHW 26B); Robert, of St. John's, 1821 (Nfld.
Archives BRC); Thomas, of Petty Harbour, 1871
(Lovell).

Modern status: At Petty Harbour.

COVEYDUCK, ? a Newfoundland variant, apparently
not recorded elsewhere, ? of the surname of England
Cobbledick, Cobledick, ? associated with the surname
Cobbold, from the Old English personal name
Cuthbeald which contains the elements *famous* and
bold. (Bardsley, Reaney).

Guppy traced Cobbledick and Cobeldick in
Cornwall.

In Newfoundland:

Early instances: John Cabbaduck or Capbaduck,
of Bay de Verde, 1708–09 (CO 194.4); John Cove-
duck, of Port de Grave, 1760 (CO 199.18); William,
of Cupids, 1783 (CO 199.18); John Cobbydock or
Coveduck, of Broad Cove (? St. Philips), 1816 (DPHW
26B); William Coveyduck, of Change Islands, 1842
(DPHW 83); John Coverduck, of Salmon Cove (now
part of South River), 1848 (DPHW 34); Charles
Cobbaduc, of Seal Cove and Indian Pond (Harbour
Main district), 1871 (Lovell); John Cobbiduck, of
Caplin Cove and Rip Raps (near Cupids), 1871
(Lovell).

Modern status: In the St. John's and Port de
Grave districts.

COWAN, a surname of England, Scotland and Ireland,
usually for Gaelic MacOwen – son of Ewan or Owen,
though other derivations from Scots and Irish names
are suggested by Black and MacLysaght. (Reaney,
Cottle).

Traced by Guppy in Northumberland and south
of the Forth and Clyde and by MacLysaght in Ulster.

In Newfoundland:

Early instances: Francis Cowen, married at St.
John's, 1772 (DPHW 26D); James Cowan, of Harbour
Grace, 1775 (CO 199.18); John, from Argyll,
Scotland, storekeeper of St. John's, died 1820 (Nfld.
Mercantile Journal 3 Aug 1820); William, of Moffat
(Dumfriesshire), died at St. John's, 1843 (Star 9 Nov

1843); Matthew Cowen, miner of La Manche (Placentia B.), 1871 (Lovell).

Modern status: At St. John's.

Place names: Cowan Avenue and Heights (St. John's).

COWARD, a surname of England, from Old English *cūhyrde* – cow-herd. (Reaney).

Traced by Guppy in Lancashire and by Spiegelhalter in Devon.

In Newfoundland:

Early instances: William, of Battle Harbour (Labrador), 1795 (MUN Hist.); Elizabeth, baptized at Greenspond, 1830, aged 46 years (DPHW 76); Henery, of Herring Neck, 1859 (DPHW 85).

Modern status: At Greenspond.

Place name: Cowards Island 48-49 53-39.

COWLEY, a surname of England and Ireland, from the English place name Cowley in eight counties including Devon, and in Ireland also as a variant of Cooley, and, as Mac Cowley, a variant of Mac Auley. (Reaney, MacLysaght).

Traced by Guppy in Derbyshire, Northamptonshire, Sussex and Worcestershire and by Spiegelhalter in Devon.

In Newfoundland:

Early instances: Thomas, enlisted in the Nova Scotia Regiment of Fencible Infantry at St. John's, 1806–7 (CO 194.46); Henry, of Bath (Somerset), married at St. John's, 1861 (DPHW 26D).

Modern status: At St. John's.

COX, a surname of England and Ireland – son of Cock. Reaney writes: "(i)... *Cock*, a common personal name still in use about 1500, may partly be from O[ld] E[nglish] *Cocc* or *Cocca*, found in place-names, although not on independent record. But as *cock* became a common term for a boy, it may also have been used affectionately as a personal name ... (ii) ... O[ld] E[nglish] *cocc* – cock, a nickname for one who strutted like a cock. This became a common term for a pert boy and was used of scullions, apprentices, servants, etc., and came to be attached to christian names as a pet diminutive (*Simcock, Wilcock*, etc.). [Middle English] *cok* is ambiguous and may be for *Cook*. The surname may also mean 'watchman, leader' and, according to Welsh writers, may also be from Welsh, Cornish *coch* – red. (iii)... 'Dweller by the hill,' O[ld] E[nglish] *cocc* 'haycock, heap, hillock.' In London it probably derived from the sign of a house or inn. Occasionally we may have a M[iddle] E[nglish] *cock* – 'a small ship's boat' ... a

name for a boatman." Cottle also suggests "A surname in which many possibilities meet, mostly jests" (one of them ? obscene). MacLysaght notes that Mac Quilly, *Mac an Choiligh*, and Mac Gilly and Magilly, *Mac Coiligh*, ? Ir. *coileach* – cock, "have been extensively changed to the English name Cox." *See also* COOK, COKE, COXON. (Reaney, Cottle, MacLysaght).

Guppy found Cox widespread throughout the South and Midlands of England. MacLysaght found it in Cos. Roscommon and Monaghan.

In Newfoundland:

Family traditions: Elizabeth (1737–1827), of Grand Bank (MUN Hist.). Daniel Farthing, from England, settled at Grand Bank and changed his name to Cox, in the 19th century (MUN Hist.).

Early instances: Christopher, of Salvage, 1675 (CO 1); Richard, of Placentia, 1724–5 (CO 194.8); David, witness at St. John's, ? 1752 (CO 194. 13); Thomas, of Torbay, 1794–5, "40 years in Newfoundland," that is, 1754–5 (Census 1794–5); John, publican of St. John's, 1794–5, "30 years in Newfoundland," that is, 1764–5 (Census 1794–5); John, merchant of Harbour Grace, 1771 (Nfld. Archives L118); John, of Musketta (now Bristol's Hope), 1782 (CO 199.18); James, servant of Bay Bulls, 1786 (CO 194.36); George, apprentice of Battle Harbour (Labrador), 1795 (MUN Hist.); Cox and Bound, operators of salmon fishery at Round Harbour, 1804 (CO 194. 45); Joshua, of Bonavista, 1806 (DPHW 70); John, of Pouch Cove, 1814 (DPHW 26B); Joseph, of Old Perlican, 1820 (DPHW 58); John, mason of Carbonear, 1828 (DPHW 48); ——, of Greenspond, 1830 (*Newfoundlander* 7 Oct 1830); Benjamin, of Western Bay, 1830 (DPHW 52A); John, of Bay de l'Eau, 1835 (DPHW 30); James, from Bristol, of St. John's, died 1836, aged 32 (*Times* 23 Nov 1836); Elizabeth, of Kings Cove Parish, 1841 (Nfld. Archives KCRC); Frederick, of Upper Burgeo, 1842 (DPHW 101); John, of Leading Tickles, 1843 (DPHW 86); John R., of Burgeo Islands, 1843 (*Newfoundlander* 31 Aug 1843); John, of New Bay Head (Twillingate), 1845 (DPHW 86); William, of Gaultois, 1850 (DPHW 101); William, of Wreck Cove, 1855 (DPHW 104); John, of La Poile, 1860 (DPHW 99); widespread in Lovell 1871.

Modern status: Scattered, especially at Wreck Cove, Terrenceville and Bay Bulls Road (St. John's.).

Place names: Cox(es) Cove (Labrador) 52-59 55-47; Cox Head (Labrador) 53-09 55-45; —— Hill (Labrador) 51-43 56-25, —— Island (Labrador) 53-08 55-44, —— Point 47-08 53-29; Cox(es) Cove Pond 52-59 55-48; Coxhill Cove and Point 47-18

53-55; Cox's Cove, —— Brook, —— Rock 47-07 58-04, —— Cove 49-07 58-05, —— Point 49-08 58-05.

COXON, a surname of England – son of Cock. *See* COX.

Traced by Guppy in Derbyshire, Durham, Northumberland and Staffordshire, and by Spiegelhalter in Devon.

In Newfoundland:

Early instance: Mark Cox(s)on or Coxon, from Birmingham, of St. John's, 1800, died 1844, aged 76 (DPHW 26B, *Newfoundlander* 26 Dec 1844, *Royal Gazette* 31 Dec 1844).

Modern status: At Come by Chance (*Electors* 1955).

COXWORTHY, a surname of England, apparently not recorded elsewhere, ? from the English place name Cogworthy (Devon); ? from an unidentified English place name containing the elements Old English *cocc* – wild bird, heap, hill or the unrecorded personal name *Cocc(a)* and *worthig* – enclosure. Ekwall notes of place names that "In modern times *worthy* is especially common in the South-West."

In Newfoundland:

Modern status: Rare, at St. John's, formerly of Grand Bank.

COYLE, a surname of Ireland *Mac Giolla Chomhgaill* – devotee of St. Comgal. "Coyle is also confused with MacCool" (MacLysaght). *See also* HOYLES.

Traced by MacLysaght in Cos. Donegal and Monaghan.

In Newfoundland:

Early instances: John, of Dublin, Irish convict landed at Petty Harbour or Bay Bulls, 1789 (CO 194.38); Richard Coyles, of St. John's, 1806 (CO 194.45); James Coyle, from Glanbryan Parish (unidentified) (Co. Wexford), married at St. John's, 1808 (Nfld. Archives BRC); John Coil, of Garia, 1871 (Lovell).

Modern status: Rare, at St. John's.

CRABBE, a surname of England and France, from Old English *crabba* – (one who walks like a) crab, or Middle English *crabbe* – wild, sour apple, used to denote a sour-tempered person; or, from the French surname Crabe – goat, crab.

(Reaney, Dauzat). Traced by Spiegelhalter in Devon.

In Newfoundland:

Early instances: Richard Crabb, proprietor and occupier of fishing room at Trinity (Trinity B.), Winter 1800–01 (Census Trinity B.); William Crab, of Bonavista, 1824 (DPHW 70); William Crabbe, of Harbour Grace Parish, 1831 (Nfld. Archives HGRC); Charles Crab(b), planter of Broad Cove (Bay de Verde), 1838 (DPHW 52A); Arthur Crabb(e) or Crabble, of Moreton's Harbour, 1842 (DPHW 86); William Crabbe, of Plate Cove, 1845 (DPHW 73); William Crabb, fisherman of Quirpon, 1871 (Lovell).

Modern status: Unique, at St. Andrews (*Electors* 1955).

Place names: Crabb Point 49-14 58-12, Crabbe Cove 47-40 54-07, Crabbes Brook or River, —— Head 48-13 58-52, —— Hill 48-12 58-52, —— River Park 48-11 58-47.

CRAIG, a surname of England, Scotland and Ireland, from Middle English *crag* – (dweller by the) steep or precipitous rugged rock(s); also in Scotland a place name in Forfarshire (now Angus) and Perthshire; the Scots form of Cragg. (Reaney).

Traced by Guppy in Northumberland and south of the Forth and Clyde, and by MacLysaght in Cos. Antrim, Derry and Tyrone.

In Newfoundland:

Early instances: J.G., ordained by Bishop Feild, 1870, of Pinchard's Island, 1871 (Devine and O'Mara, Lovell); Charles and William, of St. John's, 1871 (Lovell); John, from Dundee, chief (? engineer), of S.S. *Eagle*, died 1874, aged 27 (General Protestant Cemetery, St. John's).

Modern status: At Bell Island and St. John's.

CRAMM, a surname of Scotland, a shortened form of Crambie, from the Scots place name Crambeth now Crombie (Fife). (Black).

Traced by Black in Perthshire and vicinity.

In Newfoundland:

Family tradition: ? The name was changed from Palmer to Cramm (MUN Folklore).

Early instances: Thomas Cramm, J.P. for Trinity district, 1750 (CO 194.12); Thomas Cram, of Harbour Grace, 1791 (USPG); William, proprietor and occupier of fishing room at Old Perlican, Winter 1800–01 (Census Trinity B.); James, juror of Greenspond, 1804 (D'Alberti 14); Philip, planter of Hants Harbour, 1820 (DPHW 58); Charles Cramm, of Broad Cove (Bay de Verde district), 1846, of Adam's Cove, 1847, of Small Point (now either Lower Small Point or Kingston), 1853 (DPHW 52A, 52B); —— Cram, captain of the *Rosalie* in the seal fishery out of

Carbonear, 1858 (*Newfoundlander* 5 Apr 1858);
John, fisherman of Mulley's Cove, 1871 (Lovell).

Modern status: Cram, rare, in Green's Harbour
(*Electors* 1955); Cramm, scattered, especially at St.
John's.

CRANE, CRANN, surnames of England and Scotland,
CRANE of Ireland, from Old English *cran* – crane,
? for a long-legged man; also in Ireland as a variant
of Crean and Curran. (Reaney, Black, MacLysaght).

Traced by Spiegelhalter in Devon and by
MacLysaght in Co. Kerry.

In Newfoundland:

Early instances: John Crane, of (Upper) Island
Cove, 1761, "property in possession of the Family
for 62 years," that is, 1699 (CO 199.18); Henry, of
Bay Roberts, 1785, property "possess'd by the
Family for 45 years," that is, 1740 (CO 199.18);
Patrick, from Taghmon (Co. Wexford), married at
St. John's, 1808 (Nfld. Archives BRC); Catherine,
from New Ross (Co. Wexford), married at St.
John's, 1810 (Nfld. Archives BRC); George, of
Harbour Grace Parish, 1812 (Nfld. Archives HGRC);
Patrick, of St. John's, 1816 (CO 194.66); Maria, of
Harbour Grace, 1868 (Nfld. Archives HGRC);
Patrick, fisherman of Cape Broyle, 1871 (Lovell);
Christopher (and others), of Spaniard's Bay, 1871
(Lovell); Henry Cran and John Crann, of Flat Islands
(now Port Elizabeth), 1871 (Lovell); James Crann,
fisherman of Heart's Content, 1871 (Lovell).

Modern status: Crane, scattered, especially at St.
John's, Upper Island Cove and Tilton; Crann,
especially at Fairhaven and Bell Island.

Place name (not necessarily from the surname):
Crane Island 47-31 54-18.

CRAN(I)FORD, surnames of England from the
English place names Cranford (Essex, Northamp-
tonshire, Devon) or Craniford (Devon) or Crandford
(Devon) – ford of the cranes. (Cottle, Ekwall,
Spiegelhalter).

Traced in Kent and by Spiegelhalter in Devon.

In Newfoundland:

Family traditions: George W. Cranford
(1798–1877), from Dartmouth (Devon), first settled
at Bay Roberts; he moved to New Harbour (Trinity
B.), in the 1850s, thence to Normans Cove (MUN
Folklore). Three Cranford brothers from Kent,
England, settled at New Harbour (Trinity B.) in the
18th century; their descendants were some of the
earliest settlers of Grand Falls (MUN Folklore).

Early instances: Robert Cranford, of Bay Roberts,
1814 (Surrogate Court Records of Harbour Grace.

Case: Edward French vs Robert Cranford, of June 1,
1815; and case: Corbon vs Blackler & Cranford, Nov.
21, 1814). (G.J. Cranford); W. Cranford, of Bay
Roberts, 1817 (Nfld. Archives L165); Nicholas
Craniford, of St. John's, 1853 (DPHW 26D); Henry
Cranford, of Broadhempston (Devon), married at St.
John's, 1854 (*Newfoundlander* 26 Jun 1854);
Thomas, of New Harbour, 1862 (DPHW 62).

Modern status: Cranford, scattered, especially at
New Harbour (Trinity B.); Craniford, at St. John's.

Place name: Cranford Head (Labrador) 54-13 57-
57.

CRANN. *See* CRANE

CRANSHAW, a surname of England, from the English
place name Cronkshaw (Lancashire). (Reaney).

In Newfoundland:

Family tradition: From England *via* Pennsylvania
? in the early 20th century.

Modern status: Rare, at St. John's.

CRANT, ? a surname of England, unidentified, formerly ? Craint.

In Newfoundland:

Early instances: Robert Crant, of Wreck Cove,
1835 (DPHW 30); Robert Craint, fisherman of Wreck
Cove, 1851 (DPHW 104); Charles (and others) Crant,
of Gaultois, 1871 (Lovell); Robert, fisherman of
Great Jervis, 1871 (Lovell); John, fisherman of Red
Island (Burgeo-La Poile district), 1871 (Lovell);
Thomas, fisherman of Swoir Cove (Burgeo-La Poile
district), 1871 (Lovell).

Modern status: Especially in the Fortune Bay-
Hermitage district.

Place name: Craint's Cove (South Coast), 1863
(MUN Hist.).

CRAWFORD, a surname of England, Scotland and
Ireland, from the Scots place name Crawford
(Lanarkshire), or from the English place names
Creyford (Devon), Crawford (Lancashire, Dorset).
(Reaney, Spiegelhalter, Cottle).

Traced by Guppy in Lincolnshire,
Nottinghamshire, Northumberland and in southwest
Scotland, by Spiegelhalter in Devon, and by
MacLysaght in Co. Donegal.

In Newfoundland:

Family tradition: ——, from Airth (Stirlingshire),
to Nova Scotia about 1907, thence to St. John's (MUN
Folklore).

Early instances: W., of Placentia, 1724 (CO
194.8); ——, of St. John's, 1779 (DPHW 26C); ——,
from Waterford City, married at St. John's, 1815

(Nfld. Archives BRC); Robert, fisherman of Bay Roberts, 1837 (DPHW 39); David, of Petty Harbour, 1867 (Nfld. Archives HGRC); John, of Harbour Grace Parish, 1870 (Nfld. Archives HGRC); George and Thomas, fishermen of New Harbour, 1871 (Lovell); James (1893–), from Barrow-in-Furness (Lancashire), settled at St. John's, in the early 1900s (*Nfld. Who's Who* 1930).

Modern status: Scattered, especially at Carbonear and St. John's.

CRAWLEY, a surname of England and Ireland, from the English place name Crawley in nine counties (Cottle) including Devon; in Ireland either for *Mac Raghallaigh* or as a variant of CROWLEY. (Cottle, MacLysaght).

Traced by Guppy in Bedfordshire and Northamptonshire and by MacLysaght in Cos. Armagh and Monaghan and vicinity.

In Newfoundland:

Early instances: James, of Placentia ? district, 1744 (CO 194.24); William, of St. John's, 1783 (DPHW 26C); John, of Western Bay, 1784 (CO 199.18); Humphrey, of Chapel's Cove, 1800 (CO 199.18); James, of Harbour Grace, 1803 (D'Alberti 13).

Modern status: Scattered, especially at Holyrood.

Place name: Crawley Island 47-26 53-52.

CREIGHTON, a surname of England, Scotland and Ireland, from the English place name Creighton (Staffordshire), or a variant of CRICHTON, from the Scots place name Crichton (Midlothian), or in Ireland "also sometimes used as a synonym of Creaghan and Crehan" (MacLysaght). Ekwall derives Creighton from Old Welsh *creic* – rock and Old English *tun* – farm, homestead etc. – the farm on the ridge. (Reaney, MacLysaght, Cottle, Ekwall).

Guppy found Crichton "scattered over Scotland, but rare in the North."

In Newfoundland:

Early instance: Abraham Cricheton or Crickington, of Marldon (Devon), married at St. John's, 1830, 1836 (DPHW 26D).

Modern status: Creighton, unique, at Foxtrap; Crichton, unique, at St. John's.

CREWE, a surname of England, from the English place names Crewe (Cheshire) or Crew (Cumberland), Celtic *cryw* – ford, or possibly confused with CREW(E)S and CAREW. (Cottle).

Traced by Spiegelhalter in Devon.

In Newfoundland:

Early instances: Thomas Crews, of Bonavista, 1675 (Crew in 1676) (CO 1); John Crew, prisoner in the gaol at St. John's, 1780 (D'Alberti 6); William, occupier of fishing room at Scilly Cove (now Winterton), Winter 1800–01 (Census Trinity B.); George, from Dorset, of Bonavista, 1808, of Bird Island Cove (now Elliston), 1814, 1817 (DPHW 70, 72, Murray); Samuel, of Connaigre, 1854 (DPHW 102); Samuel, planter of Dawson's Cove (now Sandyville), 1871 (Lovell); William H., fisherman of Fortune, 1871 (Lovell); Joseph, fisherman of Indian Arm, 1871 (Lovell).

Modern status: Crewe, scattered, especially at Elliston, Sandyville and Ramea.

Place names: Crew Cove 47-38 56-23, ⸺ Point 46-51 55-48, ⸺ ⸺ Shoal 46-54 56-00; Point Crew 46-55 55-59; Sam ⸺ Shoal 47-38 57-55.

CREWS, a surname of England, a variant of Cruse, from Middle English *crus(e)* – bold, or ? from the French place name Cruys-Straële (Nord), or possibly confused with CREWE. (Reaney).

Guppy traced Cruse, Cruwys, "sometimes modernised as Crews," in Ashburton (Devon); Matthews traced Cruse, Crew(s)(e) especially in Devon.

In Newfoundland:

Early instances: John, merchant of St. John's, 1803 (D'Alberti 13); James and William, fishermen of Lamaline, 1871 (Lovell).

Modern status: Rare, especially at Point Crewes (Burin district) (*Electors* 1955).

CRIBB, a surname of England, from Old English *crib(b)* – originally a barred receptacle for fodder in cow-sheds (used of the manger of Christ about 1000), a stall or cabin of an ox, cattle-fold, hence a cow-man. (Reaney).

Traced by Matthews in Dorset.

In Newfoundland:

Family traditions: ⸺ Cribbe, from Sussex, England, settled at Grole; the spelling of the surname was later changed to Cribb (MUN Folklore). ⸺, from Christchurch (Hampshire), settled in Fortune Bay about 1828 (Feild per Kirwin).

Early instances: Thompson, fisherman of Grole, 1847 (DPHW 102); Thomas, fisherman of Cat Harbour (now Lumsden), 1871 (Lovell).

Modern status: At Grole and Head of Bay D'Espoir.

Place names: Cribb Cove 47-57 55-46; Crib Nose (hill) 47-38 56-13.

CRICHTON. *See* CREIGHTON

CRICKARD, a surname of Ireland, a Co. Down form of Mac Rickard, the name of a branch of the BUTLER and possibly also of the KAVANAGH families. (Mac-Lysaght 73).

In Newfoundland:

Modern status: At St. John's.

CRIMP, a surname of England, ? from Old English *crympan* – to curl hair (Spiegelhalter), ? or for the English surname Crump, Old English *crump* – bent, stooping. (Reaney, Spiegelhalter).

Traced by Guppy and Spiegelhalter in Devon.

In Newfoundland:

Early instances: Joseph Criump or Crimp, married at St. John's, 1777 (DPHW 26D, 26C); Joseph Crump, of Broad Cove (Bay de Verde district), 1796 (CO 199.18); William Croump, of Shoe Cove (Twillingate district), 1842 (DPHW 86); Robert and William Crimp, of St. John's, 1871 (Lovell); Richard Crump, of Outer Cove, 1871 (Lovell).

Modern status: At St. John's (*Electors* 1955).

CRISBY, a surname of Newfoundland, ? a variant of the English surname Grisby (1 in London Telephone Directory), ? from the English place name Girsby (Lincolnshire), Old Norse *gríss* – young pig, *by* – farm – the farm where pigs were reared. *See* MARTIN. (Ekwall).

In Newfoundland:

Family tradition: ———, from England, a settler at Salvage Bay (now Eastport), changed his name to Martin to avoid detection; the family reassumed Crisby about 1957 (MUN Folklore).

Early instances: James, from Devon, married at St. John's, 1816 (Nfld. Archives BRC); James, cooper of St. John's, 1820 (D'Alberti 30); Joseph, fisherman of Salvage, 1865 (DPHW 81).

Modern status: At Eastport and St. John's.

CRITCH, a variant of the surname of England Crutch – (dweller by the) cross. *See also* CROUCHER, CROSSMAN. (Reaney).

In Newfoundland:

Family tradition: Catherine Ann Critch (1730–1790), born at Lower Island Cove (MUN Geog.).

Early instances: Nathan(iel) Crutch or Critch, of Bay de Verde, 1794 (CO 199.18, DPHW 64); Hanaugh [sic] Critch, of Harbour Grace Parish, 1818 (Nfld. Archives HGRC); George Crutch, fisherman of Hants Harbour, about 1821 (DPHW 58); William Critch, of Brigus, 1826 (DPHW 34); George, of Hants Harbour, 1827 (DPHW 59); Samuel Crutch, planter of Trouty, 1828 (DPHW 64B); James Critch, planter of Deer Harbour, 1842 (DPHW 59A); Clarinda, of Old Perlican, 1858 (DPHW 58); Nathaniel, of Lower Island Cove, 1860 (DPHW 55); John, of Burin, 1871 (Lovell); John (and others), of Gaskiers, 1871 (Lovell); John and Thomas, of Shoal Harbour, 1871 (Lovell); Ambrose, of St. John's, 1871 (Lovell).

Modern status: Widespread, especially at Gaskiers, Hants Harbour, Cavendish and St. John's.

CRITCHELL, a surname of England, from the English place name Crichel (Dorset). (Ekwall).

Traced by Matthews, as captains, at Poole (Dorset).

In Newfoundland:

Early instance: Matthew, fisherman of Belleoram Barrisway, 1879 (DPHW 103).

Modern status: Rare, at Belleoram (*Electors* 1955), Ramea and Corner Brook.

CRITCHLEY, a surname of England, from an unidentified place name in ? Lancashire (Bardsley).

Traced by Guppy in Lancashire.

In Newfoundland:

Early instance: James, of Greenspond, 1841 (DPHW 76).

Modern status: Scattered, especially in the Bonavista North district.

CROCKER, a surname of England, from Old English *croc(c)(a)* – (a maker of) earthen pot(s), hence a potter; in Ireland as Croker. (Reaney, MacLysaght).

Guppy traced Crocker in Devon, Dorset and Somerset.

In Newfoundland:

Early instances: Henry, of St. John's, about 1758 or 1759, then between 70 and 80 years of age (D'Alberti 14); George, of Bonavista, 1792 (USPG); William, of Bradley's Cove, 1796 (CO 199.18); William, of Adam's Cove, 1796 (CO 199.18); Charles, of Scilly Cove (now Winterton), 1798 (DPHW 64); William, of Pond (Greenspond), 1802, owner of fishing room at Little ? Groats Island, 1802 (Bonavista Register 1806); John, of Trinity (Trinity B.), 1808 (DPHW 64); Charles, planter of Heart's Delight, 1823 (DPHW 64B); Jane, of Harbour Grace Parish, 1827 (Nfld. Archives HGRC); Nicodemus, of Fortune, 1835 (DPHW 106); William, planter of Western Bay, 1840 (DPHW 52A); ———, from Dorset, first settler of Trout River, 1849 (Feild); Andrew, of Crocker's Cove (Carbonear), 1851 (DPHW 52A);

Joseph, of Catalina, 1856 (DPHW 67); Alexander, of Barrow Harbour, 1865 (DPHW 81); widespread in Lovell 1871.

Modern status: Widespread, especially at St. John's, Trout River, Heart's Delight, Green's Harbour and Swift Current.

Place names: Crocker Island 47-35 57-37; Crocker's Cove, —— Point 47-44 53-12, —— Gully 47-47 53-15.

CROCKWELL, a surname of England, from the English place name Crockernwell (Devon). (Spiegelhalter).

Traced by Spiegelhalter in Devon.

In Newfoundland:

Family tradition: Henry, a sea-captain, and William, his nephew, of ? Heavitree Hill (Exeter, Devon), settled at Bay Bulls in the latter half of the 18th century (MUN Folklore).

Early instances: Joanne, from Teignmouth (Devon), married at St. John's, 1834 (DPHW 26D); Thomas Row, J.P. for the Labrador district, 1857 (*Nfld. Almanac*); James and William, of Bay Bulls, 1871 (Lovell).

Modern status: Rare, in the Ferryland district, including Bay Bulls.

CROFT, a surname of England and Scotland, Crofts in England and Ireland, with a variant Craft; from the English place name Croft (Devon, Herefordshire, Lincolnshire, Yorkshire NR), or (dweller by the) croft, small field, enclosure. (Reaney).

Croft traced by Spiegelhalter in Devon, by Guppy in Lancashire, Lincolnshire, Warwickshire, Yorkshire NR and ER; Crofts traced by MacLysaght in Co. Cork since the late 16th century.

In Newfoundland:

Early instances: Thomas, married at Mary's Cove (Labrador), 1859 (DPHW 114); James (and others) Craft, fisherman of Aquaforte, 1871 (Lovell).

Modern status: Rare, especially at Aquaforte.

CROKE, a surname of Ireland, *Croc,* "In Co. Kilkenny since the early 14th century." (MacLysaght).

In Newfoundland:

Early instances: Richard, from Ross Parish (unspecified), married at St. John's, 1804 (Nfld. Archives BRC); Lawrence Croak, of Harbour Grace Parish, 1813 (Nfld. Archives HGRC); Nicholas Croke, of St. John's, 1821 (CO 194.64); James Croak or Croke, of Fogo, 1822 (Nfld. Archives KCRC); William Croke, of Harbour Grace, 1868 (Nfld. Archives HGRC); Michael, of Gooseberry Island

(Bonavista B.), 1869 (Nfld. Archives KCRC); Patrick, of Cuckold's Cove (now Dunfield), 1871 (Lovell); Patrick, farmer of Fermeuse, 1871 (Lovell); Thomas, farmer of Logy Bay, 1871 (Lovell); William, farmer of Outer Cove (St. John's district), 1871 (Lovell); Edmund, farmer of Turk's Gut (now Marysvale), 1871 (Lovell); Thomas, fisherman of Fortune Harbour, 1871 (Lovell).

Modern status: Scattered, especially at St. John's and St. Brendans.

CROMWELL, CRUMMELL, surnames of England and Ireland (Grummell in MacLysaght), from the English place name Cromwell (Nottinghamshire, Yorkshire WR), or (dweller by the) winding stream. MacLysaght comments: "This English toponymic in either variant is now very rare in Ireland; it was prominent in the city of Limerick for two centuries before the time of Oliver Cromwell." *See* CRUMMEY. (Cottle, MacLysaght).

Traced by Guppy in Nottinghamshire.

In Newfoundland:

Early instances: J. Crowmwell, of St. John's, 1704 (CO 194.3); Joseph Cromwell, of Western Bay, 1798 (DPHW 48).

Modern status: Cromwell and Crummell at St. John's.

CRON, a surname of Scotland, Crone of Ireland, from the Irish *crón* – brown, swarthy. (Black, MacLysaght).

MacLysaght states that Crone "is not closely associated with any particular area."

In Newfoundland:

Modern status: At Harbour Grace.

CRONIN, a surname of England and Ireland, with variants (O)Cronan in Ireland and Cronan in Scotland, from Ir. *crón* – brown, swarthy. (Spiegelhalter, MacLysaght, Black).

Spiegelhalter traced Cronin in Devon; MacLysaght traced (O)Cronan mainly in Co. Tipperary and (O)Cronin in Cos. Cork and Kerry.

In Newfoundland:

Early instances: Darby, of St. John's, 1780 (DPHW 26C); John Cronan or Cronin, of Harbour Grace Parish, 1821 (Nfld. Archives HGRC); Richard Cronin, from Co. Cork, married at Tilton Harbour (now Tilting), 1822 (Nfld. Archives KCRC); Jeremiah Cronan, from Goolan (unidentified) (Co. Tipperary), married at St. John's, 1827 (Nfld. Archives BRC); Timothy, of Harbour Grace, 1845 (*Newfoundlander* 9 Jan 1845); James Cronin, fisherman of Sandy Point

(St. George's district), 1871 (Lovell); Michael Cronam, miner of Tilt Cove, 1871 (Lovell); Jeremiah, fisherman of Trepassey, 1871 (Lovell); William Cronan, planter of Carbonear, 1877 (Lovell).

Modern status: At St. John's and Kelligrews.

CROSBIE, CROSBY, surnames of England, Crosbie of Scotland and Ireland from the English place name Crosby (Cumberland, Lancashire, Lincolnshire, Westmorland, Yorkshire WR) or the Scots place name Crosbie or Corsbie (Ayrshire, Kirkcudbrightshire, Berwick). (Cottle, MacLysaght, Black).

Guppy found Crosbie especially in Liverpool (Lancashire); Spiegelhalter traced Crosby in Devon; MacLysaght traced Crosbie in Co. Kerry in the 17th century; Black traced Crosbie in Wigtownshire and Dumfriesshire.

In Newfoundland:

Early instances: Sgt. —— Crosby, of St. John's, 1764 (DPHW 26C); Anne Crosby, from Aglus Parish (unidentified) (Co. Waterford), married at St. John's, 1811 (Nfld. Archives BRC); Marshall Crosbie, American fisherman in the service of Messrs. Doyle and Walsh, Fortune Bay, 1818, to assist and instruct them in the art of taking small whales (D'Alberti 28); Robert Crosbie, charged with complicity in grand larceny but released from gaol on turning crown witness, 1823 (D'Alberti 33); James Crosby, fisherman of Twillingate, 1871 (Lovell); George Graham, from Dumfries, Scotland, of Brigus, 1876 (Nfld. Who's Who 1927).

Modern status: Crosbie, rare, especially at St. John's; Crosby, rare, at St. John's.

Place name: Crosby Point (Labrador) 57-45 61-54.

CROSS, a surname of England, Scotland, Ireland and the Channel Islands, from the English place name Cross (9 in Devon), or (dweller by the) market-cross, wayside cross or ? crossroads; in Ireland "sometimes used as a synonym of MacCrossan" (MacLysaght), and ? Cruise (Woulfe). (Reaney, Cottle, Turk).

"A strongly Midland and East Anglian surname" (Cottle), and traced by Spiegelhalter in Devon.

In Newfoundland:

Early instances: Robert, of Bonavista, 1792 (USPG); Richard, murdered ? at St. John's, 1809 (CO 194. 48); Samuel, from Devon, married at St. John's, 1828 (Nfld. Archives BRC); Sarah, of St. John's, died at Lowton (Lancashire), 1828 (Newfoundlander 2 Apr 1828); Thomas, of Gooseberry Island (Bonavista B.), 1830 (DPHW 76); Eliza, of King's Cove

Parish, 1840 (Nfld. Archives KCRC); John, of Tickle Cove (Bonavista South district), 1848 (DPHW 73); Thomas, of Pushthrough, 1852 (DPHW 102); John, of Coomb's Cove, 1854 (DPHW 104); John, of English Harbour (Fortune B.), 1856 (DPHW 104); William, of Trinity (Trinity B.), 1856 (Newfoundlander 7 Jan 1856); John, planter of Doctor's Harbour (Fortune B.), 1871 (Lovell); William, fisherman of Hare Bay, 1871 (Lovell); James and Samuel, fishermen of Ship Island (Bonavista B.), 1871 (Lovell); Thomas, fisherman of Swain's Island, 1871 (Lovell); David, (1891), born in Minsk Province, Russia, immigrated to New York in 1909, thence to Newfoundland in 1910 and settled at Badger (Nfld. Who's Who, 1937).

Modern status: Scattered.

Place names (not necessarily from the surname): Cross Brook 47-31 52-58, 47-51 56-11; —— Cove 49-35 54-32; —— Gulch 47-48 58-05; —— Island 49-37 55-41, (Labrador) 53-47 56-26, (Labrador) 55-23 60-00; —— Lake (Labrador) 54-20 66-55; —— Point 46-56 54-11, 47-05 55-50, 47-09 53-28, 47-14 53-59, 47-24 54-21; —— Pond 47-25 53-19, 47-38 53-29, 48-19 53-36, 48-22 58-03; —— Rocks 47-37 54-20, 47-38 57-31; The Cross 49-40 55-46; —— (Grass) Island 47-21 54-50; —— Point Shoal 47-23 54-22; —— Pond Brook 48-21 58-08.

CROSSLEY, a surname of England, from the English place name Crossley (Yorkshire WR), or ? (dweller by the) clearing or glade with a cross. (Bardsley).

Traced by Guppy in Lancashire and Yorkshire WR.

In Newfoundland:

Early instance: Hunter and Crossley, evangelists, arrived St. John's, 1899 (Devine and O'Mara).

Modern status: At Hatchet Harbour (Twillingate district) (Electors 1955), St. John's and Corner Brook.

CROSSMAN, a surname of England, dweller by the cross. See also CROUCHER. (Reaney).

Traced by Guppy in Somerset, by Spiegelhalter in Devon and by Matthews in Dorset.

In Newfoundland:

Early instances: ——, sexton of St. John's, 1811 (D'Alberti 21); Aaron, of Devon, married at St. John's, 1840 (DPHW 26D); John, of Bonavista, 1843 (DPHW 70); John, fisherman of Wiseman's Cove (White B.), 1871 (Lovell).

Modern status: Rare, at St. John's.

CROTTY, a surname of Ireland, Ó Crotaigh. (MacLysaght).

Traced by MacLysaght in Co. Waterford.

In Newfoundland:

Early instances: C. ? Crotty, one of 72 impressed men who sailed from Ireland to Newfoundland, ? 1811 (CO 194.51); Paul, of Kings Cove, 1815 (Nfld. Archives KCRC); David, married at St. John's, 1831 (Nfld. Archives BRC); David, of Harbour Grace Parish, 1832 (Nfld. Archives HGRC); James, of St. John's, deceased 1851 (*Newfoundlander* 30 Oct 1851).

Modern status: At St. John's.

CROUCHER, a surname of England, – dweller by the cross. *See also* CROSSMAN. (Reaney).

Traced by Matthews in Dorset.

In Newfoundland:

Early instances: John, fisherman of Trinity (Trinity B.), 1759 (DPHW 64); George, from Poole (Dorset), fisherman of St. John's, 1794–5, "9 years in Newfoundland," that is, 1785–6, deceased, 1816 (Census 1794–5, *Nfld. Mercantile Journal* 11 Sep 1816); George, of Bonavista, 1791 (DPHW 70); ? Jos. and son, proprietors and occupiers of fishing room at Old Perlican, Winter 1800–01 (Census Trinity B.); James, of Ward's Harbour (now Beaumont North), 1845, of Southern Head (Twillingate district), 1851 (DPHW 86, 87); James Crowcher, merchant of Burin, 1853 (*Newfoundlander* 12 Sep 1853); Amos Croucher, of Placentia, 1871 (Lovell); James E., of Point Verde, 1871 (Lovell).

Modern status: Scattered, especially at Beaumont and Burnt Island (Burgeo-La Poile).

Place names: Croucher Cove 49-35 55-37; —— Island 49-35 55-36; Croucher's Gulch 49-26 57-54.

CROWDELL, a surname of England, ? from the English place name Crowdhill (Hampshire).

In Newfoundland:

Modern status: Rare, at St. John's.

CROWDY, a surname of England, from the English place name Crowdy Mill (Devon). Crowdy from the Cornish *croudy* – stable. (Spiegelhalter). Crowdy has possibly been confused with CROWLEY in Newfoundland.

Traced by Spiegelhalter in Devon.

In Newfoundland:

Family tradition: Some Crowdys moved from the North Shore of Conception Bay to Pouch Cove between 1820 and 1835 (MUN Hist.).

Early instances: James, from Bristol, colonial secretary at St. John's, 1831 (*Newfoundlander* 15 Sep 1831); Ambrose, fisherman of Pouch Cove, 1871 (Lovell).

Modern status: Rare, at St. John's.

CROWE, a surname of England and Ireland, from Old English *crāwe* – crow; in Ireland also for Mac Enchroe, *Mac Conchradha*. (Reaney, MacLysaght). *See also* McCROWE.

Traced by Spiegelhalter in Devon and by Guppy, as Crow(e), in Cambridgeshire, Durham, Lincolnshire and Norfolk.

MacLysaght, under Mac Enchroe, comments: "Now generally Crowe (which is also an English name). All Crowes in their homeland, Thomond ["Most of Co. Clare with adjacent parts of Cos. Limerick and Tipperary"], are of native Irish stock. In Ulster they are mainly of English origin."

In Newfoundland:

Early instances: John Crow, from Ireland, labourer, banished from Newfoundland to the West Indies, 1780 (D'Alberti 6); Daniel, tailor of Trinity (Trinity B.), 1780 (D'Alberti 6); Thomas, of St. John's, 1803 (Nfld. Archives BRC); Margaret, from Limolin (unidentified) (Co. Carlow), married at St. John's, 1804 (Nfld. Archives BRC); Margaret, of Harbour Grace Parish, 1806 (Nfld. Archives HGRC); James, from Co. Kilkenny, "an old offender," married at St. John's, 1811 (Nfld. Archives BRC); John, of Kings Cove, 1816 (Nfld. Archives KCRC); James, of Torbay, 1839 (Nfld. Archives BRC); Andrew, ? of Northern Bay, 1843 (DPHW 54).

Modern status: At St. John's and Torbay.

Place name: Crowe Lake 48-45 55-22.

CROWELL, a surname of England, from the English place name Crowell (Oxfordshire). (Bardsley, Cottle).

In Newfoundland:

Early instance: —— Crowel, ? captain in the seal fishery, of St. John's, 1847 (*Newfoundlander* 8 Apr 1847).

Modern status: Rare, in the Green Bay district, St. John's (*Electors* 1955) and Glenwood.

CROWLEY, a surname of England, Scotland and Ireland; in England and Scotland from the English place name Crowley (Cheshire, Lancashire), or (dweller in the) wood or clearing with crows; in Ireland (O)Crowley, *Ó Cruadhlaoich*, Ir. *cruadh* – hard and *laoch* – hero. *See* CRAWLEY. (Cottle, MacLysaght).

Traced by MacLysaght in Co. Cork.

In Newfoundland:

Early instances: Cornelius, of St. John's, 1756 (DPHW 26C); William, planter of Western Bay, 1825 (DPHW 52A); John Crowly, of Harbour Grace Parish,

1827 (Nfld. Archives HGRC); Miss Crowley, from Co. Wexford, of Harbour Grace, 1844 (*Indicator* 27 Jul 1844); Francis, fisherman of Goose Cove (White B.), 1871 (Lovell); Patrick, fisherman of Port de Grave, 1871 (Lovell); Charles, fisherman of St. Kyran's, 1871 (Lovell).

Modern status: Scattered, at St. John's, Western Bay and Grand Bank.

Place name: Crowley Lake (Labrador)

CROWTHER, a surname of England from Middle English *crouth* – fiddle, a fiddler. (Reaney).

Traced by Guppy in Lancashire and Yorkshire WR, by Spiegelhalter in Devon.

In Newfoundland:

Early instance: Edwin, born at Carlisle (Cumberland), settled at St. John's in 1910 (MUN Folklore).

Modern status: Rare, at St. John's.

CRUDEN, a surname of Scotland, from the Scots place name Cruden (Aberdeenshire). (Black).

In Newfoundland:

Early instance: James, from Greenock, died at St. John's, 1837 (*Newfoundlander* 26 Jan 1837).

Modern status: At Jackson's Cove (*Electors* 1955).

CRUMMELL. *See* CROMWELL

CRUMMEY, a surname of England and Ireland, from the Scots place name Crombie (Aberdeenshire) "in which the *b* is not pronounced" (Reaney); also in Ireland, Cromie or Crummy, *Ó Cromtha* , Ir. *crom* – bent, crooked. *See also* CROMWELL from which a Newfoundland tradition would derive Crummey. (Reaney, MacLysaght).

MacLysaght states: "This name is peculiar to Co. Armagh, south Down and adjacent areas. Cromie is a Scottish toponymic but families called O'Cromy were in Co. Armagh in the seventeenth century, so the Irish form ... can also be accepted."

In Newfoundland:

Early instances: Joseph Crummy, of Western Bay, 1790 (CO 199.18); Jane, of Harbour Grace Parish, 1812 (Nfld. Archives HGRC); Edward Crummey, planter of Ochre Pit Cove, 1840 (DPHW 52A); William Crummy, of Muddy Hole (now Maberly), 1862 (DPHW 77); William Crummey, fisherman of Brooklyn, 1871 (Lovell).

Modern status: Scattered, especially at Western Bay and St. John's.

CUFF, a surname of England, Cuffe of Ireland, from the Old English personal name *Cuffa*; also in Ireland for Scots Mac Duff, *Mac Dhuibh*, Gaelic *dubh* – black, and Durnin, *Ó Duirnín* ? Ir. *dorn* – fist. (Weekley *Romance*, MacLysaght). *See also* MATCHEM.

Traced by MacLysaght in Co. Kilkenny.

In Newfoundland:

Early instances: David Cuf, of St. John's, 1764 (DPHW 26C); John Cuff, of Bonavista, 1802 (DPHW 70).

Modern status: Scattered, especially at Bonavista, Doting Cove and Carmanville.

Place names (not necessarily from the surname): Cuff Harbour, —— Island, —— Islands (Labrador) 54-11 57-28; —— Head, —— Rocks 47-33 54-54.

CULL, a surname of England and Ireland, in England from the Old English personal name *Cula*, in Ireland a variant of Coll, *Col*. (Spiegelhalter, MacLysaght).

Traced by Spiegelhalter in Devon and by MacLysaght in Co. Limerick.

In Newfoundland:

Early instances: William, of Gander Bay, 1803, of Fogo, 1810, employed by Governor Holloway to obtain information about the native Indians of Newfoundland (D'Alberti 13, 20); Jane, of Greenspond, 1803 (Nfld. Archives KCRC); John, trustee in bankruptcy, 1811 (CO 194.50); John, of Barr'd Islands, 1821 (USPG); John, baptized at Cape Cove, 1830, aged 41 years (DPHW 76); John, of Indian Island, 1862 (DPHW 84); George, planter of Caplin Cove (Bay de Verde), 1871 (Lovell).

Modern status: Scattered, especially at Caplin Cove (Bay de Verde district), Shoal Bay (Fogo district) and Great Brehat (White B.).

Place names: Cull Island 49-30 55-28, 49-21 54-51.

CULLEN, a surname of England, Scotland and Ireland, in England from the German place name Köln – (the man from) Cologne; in Scotland from the Scots place name Cullen (Banffshire) and in Ayrshire and Galloway; ? also for the surnames of Ireland (Mac)Cullen, *MacCuilinn* and (O)Cullen, *Ó Cuilinn*, Ir. *cuileann* – holly, both variants of "other somewhat similar names" (MacLysaght). (Reaney, Black, MacLysaght).

Traced by Guppy in Nottinghamshire and Somerset, by Spiegelhalter in Devon; by Black in Ayrshire and Galloway and other parts of Scotland; by MacLysaght: (Mac)Cullen in Co. Monaghan, (O)Cullen in Co. Kildare.

In Newfoundland:

Early instances: William, property-owner of St. John's, 1794–5, "17 years in Newfoundland," that is, 1777–8 (Census 1794–5); Mary Cullin, of Colliers, 1778 (CO 199.18); Margaret Cullen, from Ross Parish (unspecified), married at St. John's, 1809 (Nfld. Archives BRC); Anne, from Sutton's Parish (Co. Wexford), married at St. John's, 1809 (Nfld. Archives BRC); Nicholas, of Harbour Grace Parish, 1810 (Nfld. Archives HGRC); Thomas, of Torbay, 1829 (*Newfoundlander* 21 May 1829); Julius F. Cullam, of Harbour Breton, 1851 (DPHW 104); Catherine Cullen, of Catalina, 1856 (Nfld. Archives KCRC); Rev. John, of Burin, 1858 (*Newfoundlander* 14 Jan 1858); Thomas, of Harbour Grace, 1866 (Nfld. Archives HGRC).

Modern status: Scattered, especially at Torbay and St. John's.

Place names: Cullen Cove and Point 47-26 53-51.

CULLETON, CULLITON, surnames of Ireland, recorded by MacLysaght as (Mac) Culleton, Colleton, *Mac Codlatáin* – sleeper. "The prefix O is sometimes substituted for Mac." (MacLysaght).

Traced by MacLysaght predominantly in Co. Wexford, but also in Cos. Carlow and Kilkenny.

In Newfoundland:

Family traditions: —— Culleton was the first settler at Clattice Harbour, ? in the late 18th century (MUN Hist.). Culletons from Co. Wexford settled at St. John's, about 1847 (MUN Folklore). Billy Culleton (1820–85), from Ireland, settled in Western Cove, Barren Island (now Bar Haven) (MUN Geog.).

Early instances: Edward Culliton, of Bay de Verde, 1788 (CO 199.18); Bridget Culloton, from Suttons Parish (Co. Wexford), married at St. John's, 1793 (Nfld. Archives BRC); Judith, from Adamstown (Co. Wexford), married at St. John's, 1808 (Nfld. Archives BRC); Moses Culletin or Culliton, of Tickle Cove (Bonavista B.), 1821 (Nfld. Archives KCRC); Moses Culletin, from Co. Wexford, of Kings Cove, 1822 (Nfld. Archives KCRC); Thomas Culleton, late of St. John's, 1830 (*Newfoundlander* 11 Feb 1830); Michael, of Harbour Grace Parish, 1831 (Nfld. Archives HGRC); Michael, from Co. Kilkenny, of Port de Grave, 1844 (*Indicator* 24 Aug 1844); Margaret Culliton, of Open Hole (now Open Hall), 1857 (Nfld. Archives KCRC); Margaret, of Burn Island (Bonavista B.), 1862 (Nfld. Archives KCRC); Margaret Culleton, of Indian Arm, 1862 (Nfld. Archives KCRC); Martha, of Keels, 1862, of Gooseberry Island (Bonavista B.), 1863 (Nfld. Archives KCRC); Sarah, of Plate Cove (Bonavista B.), 1865 (Nfld. Archives KCRC); John, fisherman, and William, planter of Barren Island (now Bar Haven), 1871 (Lovell); James, hotel-keeper of Bay Roberts, 1871 (Lovell); Martin, fisherman of Ferryland, 1871 (Lovell); Michael, farmer of Flatrock (St. John's), 1871 (Lovell).

Modern status: Rare, Culleton, at St. John's, Cuslett and Markland; Culliton, at Bar Haven (*Electors* 1955).

Place name: Culleton Head 47-31 54-26.

CULLIHALL, ? a Newfoundland variant, apparently not recorded elsewhere, of the surname of England Collihole, from the English place name Collihole (Devon). (Spiegelhalter).

Spiegelhalter traced Collihole in Devon.

In Newfoundland:

Family tradition: Elizabeth Cullihal (1871–1937), of Curzon Village (MUN Geog.).

Early instances: —— Culliall, on the *Dove* in the seal fishery out of Harbour Grace, 1853 (*Newfoundlander* Mar 1853).

Modern status: Rare, especially at Rocky Harbour and Cormack.

CULLIMORE, a surname of England of unknown origin, probably a place name. Traced by Guppy in Gloucestershire.

In Newfoundland:

Early instances: William, proprietor and occupier of fishing room at Old Perlican, Winter 1800–01 (Census Trinity B.); Mary, of Harbour Grace Parish, 1836 (Nfld. Archives HGRC); John, planter of Little Catalina, 1844 (DPHW 72); Mary Cullymore, of Tilton, died 1890, aged 115 years (Devine and O'Mara).

Modern status: Rare, especially at Little Catalina.

CULLITON. *See* CULLETON

CUMBIE, CUMBY. *See* COMBY

CUMMINGS, a surname with several variants, of England, Scotland and Ireland; in England and Scotland from a personal name probably of Breton origin ? *Cu(n)min*; in Ireland "(O)Commane, Commons, *Ó Comáin* (in Munster) and *Ó Cuimín* (in Connacht). Usually called Commons in Co. Wexford and Cummins in Co. Cork. *Ó Comáin* has become Hurley in some parts of Cos. Clare and Cork, due to the mistaken belief that it derives from *camán*, a hurley [the stick used in the Irish game of hurling]. Woulfe says it is from *cam*, crooked, which is equally doubtful." (MacLysaght). (Reaney, Black, MacLysaght).

Guppy traced Cuming, Spiegelhalter Cuming, Cummings and Comins in Devon; Guppy traced Cumming in Inverness-shire and adjacent counties; MacLysaght traced Cummins in Co. Cork.

In Newfoundland:

Early instances: Archibald Cuming, of St. John's Harbour, 1703 (CO 194.3); John Cummins, of Western Bay, 1770 (CO 199.18); P., fisherman of Port de Grave, 1791 (Nfld. Archives T22); James, of Ferryland, 1791 (USPG); John Cummens, of Bonavista, 1792 (USPG); John Cummins, of Northern Bay, 1796 (CO 199.18); Sam Cuming, of Bay Bulls, 1802 (USPG); Bridget Cummins, from Glanmore Parish (? for Glenmore) (Co. Kilkenny), married at St. John's, 1802 (Nfld. Archives BRC); Sam Cuming, of Placentia, 1803 (D'Alberti 13); John Commins, of Harbour Grace Parish, 1806 (Nfld. Archives HGRC); Maurice Cummins, from Co. Carlow, of St. John's, 1814 (Nfld. Archives BRC); John Cummings or Cummins, of Ragged Harbour (now Melrose), 1823 (Nfld. Archives KCRC); William Cummings, of King's Cove, 1829 (*Newfoundlander* 17 Sep 1829); Catherine Cummins, of Grand Bank, 1830 (DPHW 106); John Commins, of Tilton Harbour (now Tilting), 1832 (Nfld. Archives KCRC); Charles Cumins, of Petty Harbour, 1837 (Nfld. Archives BRC); Thomas Coming, planter of Newman's Cove, 1849 (DPHW 72); Peter Cummins, of Lower Island Cove, 1851 (DPHW 55); William, of Canvas Town (Lower Island Cove district), 1860 (DPHW 55); Patrick Commins, of Harbour Grace, 1866 (Nfld. Archives HGRC); Anthony (and others) Cummins, of Bell Island, 1871 (Lovell); Richard, of Distress (now St. Bride's), 1871 (Lovell); John Cumins, of Englee Harbour, 1871 (Lovell); Thomas Cummins, farmer of St. Mary's, 1871 (Lovell); George and Peter Cummings, of Whalesbrook, 1871 (Lovell).

Modern status: Scattered, especially at St. John's and North River.

CUNARD, a surname of England from the Old English personal name *Cyneheard* containing the elements *royal* and *hard*, or ? a French variant, ? not recorded elsewhere, of the surname of Germany Kunhardt or Cunard(t). (E.C. Smith, Heintze-Cascorbi).

In Newfoundland:

Family tradition: ——, from France, deserted from a French ship off Bonne Bay and settled in the St. Barbe district (MUN Folklore).

Modern status: At Brig Bay (St. Barbe district).

CUNDALL, a surname of England from the English place name Cundall (Yorkshire NR), or (dweller in the) valley. "The O[ld] E[nglish] [place] name was probably *Cumb* – [valley], to which Scandinavians added an explanatory *dalr* – valley" (Ekwall). (Cottle).

Guppy traced Cundall, Cundell, Cundill in Yorkshire, with Cundall "more characteristic of the West Riding."

In Newfoundland:

Early instance: Azariah Cundell, of Petty Harbour, 1703 (CO 194.3).

Modern status: Unique, at Stephenville.

CUNNING, a surname of Ireland, "an Ulster variant of Gunning," a surname of England from an Old German personal name *Gund(e)win* – battle-friend. (Reaney, MacLysaght).

In Newfoundland:

Modern status: At Curling.

CUNNINGHAM, a surname of Scotland and Ireland, with many variants, from the Scots place name Cunningham (Ayrshire). In Ireland: "The name of Scottish settlers, widely adopted as the modern form of Irish surnames. Matheson in his report on synonyms in birth registrations gives no less than 20 for Cunningham" (MacLysaght). (Reaney, Black, MacLysaght).

Guppy found Cunningham "dispersed over a large part of Scotland, but most frequent in Ayrshire."

In Newfoundland:

Family traditions: John, from Ireland, settled at Little Placentia (now Argentia) about 1820 (MUN Folklore). Rev. John, from Stepney, London, settled at Brigus about 1840 and later at Burgeo (MUN Folklore).

Early instances: Richard Conningham or Cuningham, of St. John's, 1730 (CO 194.9); James Cunningham, of Trinity (Trinity B.), 1786 (DPHW 64); William, of Bay de Verde, 1789 (CO 199.18); Ed, proprietor and occupier of fishing room at Old Perlican, Winter 1800–01 (Census Trinity B.); John, of Harbour Grace Parish, 1812 (Nfld. Archives HGRC); Anty [sic] from Inistioge (Co. Kilkenny), married at St. John's, 1820 (Nfld. Archives BRC); John Cullingham, joiner of Carbonear, 1833 (DPHW 48); James Cunningham, ? of Northern Bay, 1838 (DPHW 54); Charles, planter of Ochre Pit Cove, 1844 (DPHW 52A); John, fisherman of Lower Burgeo, 1849 (DPHW 101); James, of Frenchman's Cove (Fortune B.), 1871 (Lovell); Rev. J., of Lower Burgeo, 1871 (Lovell); Thomas, born at Carrick-on-Suir (Co. Tipperary), died at Tors Cove, 1903, aged 78 years (Dillon).

Modern status: Scattered.

Place names: Cunningham Bight 54-13 58-15; ——— Lake (Labrador) 54-45 66-03.

CURLEW, a surname of England, after the bird. *See* CURLEY. Possibly confused with CURNEW in Newfoundland.

In Newfoundland:

Early instances: John, of Bareneed, 1860 (DPHW 38); Jacob, fisherman of Beachy Cove (Port de Grave district), 1860 (DPHW 38); William, fisherman of Gullys (Brigus district), 1871 (Lovell); William Curlen, fisherman of Brehat, 1871 (Lovell).

Modern status: Rare and scattered, especially at Botwood.

Place names (most likely after the bird): Curlew Harbour (Labrador) 53-45 56-33: ——— Head (Labrador) 53-46 56-33; ——— Hill (Labrador) 53-43 57-01; ——— Island (Labrador) 52-44 55-58, 53-46 56-34; ——— Point 51-35 55-36; ——— ——— (Labrador) 53-43 57-01.

CURLEY, a surname of England and (Mac)CURLEY of Ireland; in England "a bird nickname, the curlew ... found more rarely as *Kirlew*" (Weekley), *see* CURLEW; in Ireland (Mac)Curley, *Mac Thoirdealbhaigh*, "a variant of the Ulster Turley, mainly found in Galway and Roscommon" (MacLysaght). (Weekley *Surnames*, MacLysaght). *See also* CURNEW.

In Newfoundland:

Modern status: Rare, at Corner Brook.

Place name: Curley Cove 47-43 55-53.

CURNELL, ? an unrecorded variant of CURNEW.

In Newfoundland:

Modern status: Unique, at Corner Brook.

CURNEW or Curnow, a surname of England, from the Cornish *Curnow* – a Cornishman, ? especially for one who could speak only the old Cornish language (Weekley). *See also* CURLEW, CURLEY

Guppy traced Curnow especially in Penzance (Cornwall).

In Newfoundland:

Early instances: John, of Port de Grave, 1784 (CO 199.18); William Curnow, enlisted in the Nova Scotia Regiment at St. John's, 1806–07 (CO 194.46); John Carnew, of Freshwater (Carbonear), 1809 (DPHW 48); Philip Curnew, planter of Carbonear, 1840 (DPHW 48).

Modern status: Scattered, especially at Stephenville Crossing and Brigus.

CURRAN, a surname of Ireland, Currane in Co. Kerry, *Ó Corráin*, but also for (Mac)Curreen, Curren, *Mac Corraidhín* and (O)Curreen, Currin, *Ó Cuirín*. (MacLysaght). *See also* CAREEN.

MacLysaght found (O)Curran "now numerous in all the provinces."

In Newfoundland:

Family traditions: Martin, from Galway settled at Conception Harbour in the late 18th century (MUN Hist.). ———, from Cork settled at Sunny Hill, Ferryland (MUN Folklore).

Early instances: Michael, farmer of Quidi Vidi, 1794–5, "18 years in Newfoundland," that is, 1776–7 (Census 1794–5); Richard, property-owner and shoreman of St. John's, 1794–5, "18 years in Newfoundland," that is, 1776–7 (Census 1794–5); Thomas ? Curreen, of Holyrood, 1786 (CO 199.18); Martin Currin, of Northern Arm, Salmon Cove (now Avondale), 1805 (CO 199.18); Patrick Curreen, from Dungarvan Parish (Co. Waterford), married at St. John's, 1806 (Nfld. Archives BRC); Martin Currin, of Harbour Grace Parish, 1813 (Nfld. Archives HGRC); Thomas Curreen, from Co. Waterford, planter of Holyrood, deceased 1814 (*Royal Gazette* 29 Dec 1814); Edward Curran, of Riders Harbour (Trinity B.), 1817 (Nfld. Archives KCRC); William, of Kings Cove, 1825 (Nfld. Archives KCRC); William, from Co. Waterford, of Tickle Cove (Bonavista B.), 1828 (Nfld. Archives KCRC); Catherine Currin, Curren or Curran, of Greenspond, 1831 (Nfld. Archives KCRC); James Curran, of Cape Freels, 1861 (Nfld. Archives KCRC); Patrick Curren, of Indian Arm, 1861 (Nfld. Archives KCRC); James Curran, of Pinchers (for Pinchards) Island, 1861 (Nfld. Archives KCRC); Thomas, of Cat Harbour (now Lumsden), 1861 (Nfld. Archives KCRC); Michael, of Harbour Grace, 1870 (Nfld. Archives HGRC); James Curren, of Goulds Road (Brigus), 1871 (Lovell).

Modern status: Scattered, especially at St. John's and in the Ferryland district.

Place name: Curren's Pond 47-16 53-23.

CURRIE, CURRY, surnames of England, Scotland and Ireland; in England from the English place name Curry (Somerset) or Cory or Corrie Farm (Devon), or from Old French *curie* – (worker in the) kitchen; in Scotland from the Scots place names Corrie (Dumfriesshire) or ? Currie (Midlothian), or a modification of MacVurich – son of Murdoch; in Ireland (O)Curry, *Ó Comhraidhe*, or a variant of (O)Corry. (Reaney, Cottle, Black, MacLysaght).

Guppy traced Curry in Durham and Somerset and Currie south of the Forth and Clyde, especially in

Ayrshire; Spiegelhalter traced Cory, Curr(e)y, Currie in Devon; MacLysaght traced (O)Curry in Cos. Clare and Westmeath.

In Newfoundland:

Family traditions: Pierce Currie, born at Llanberis (Carnarvonshire, Wales) in 1831, came to Britannia to work in the slate quarry there (MUN Hist.). Mrs., of Small's Island (Burgeo), 1800 (MUN Hist.). Caroline Curry (1838–1904), born at Rose Blanche, died at Rocky Harbour (MUN Geog.). Samuel Currie, buried at Channel-Port aux Basques, 1854, aged 34 years (MUN Hist.).

Early instances: Thomas Curry, of St. John's, 1790 (DPHW 26C); John Currie, merchant of Western Bay, 1817 (DPHW 52A); John Currie or Curry, of Harbour Grace, 1821 (D'Alberti 31, DPHW 43); James Manson Currie, of Dunoon (Argyleshire), died at St. John's, 1829 (*Newfoundlander* 4 Jun 1829); William Curry, of Great Burgeo Island, 1830 (DPHW 30); Pat, from Waterford, Ireland, married at St. John's, 1837 (Nfld. Archives BRC); John Currie, of Lower Burgeo, 1844 (DPHW 101); John, of Llanberis (Carnarvonshire, Wales), resident of Harbour Grace, married at St. John's, 1849 (DPHW 23, *Weekly Herald* 26 Dec 1849); William Curry, of Fox Roost, 1871 (Lovell); John, fisherman of Isle aux Morts, 1871 (Lovell).

Modern status: Currie, scattered, especially at Rose Blanche and Britannia; Curry, unique, at Stephenville.

Place name: Curry Cove 54-03 58-35.

CURTIN, a surname of England and Ireland; in England a diminutive of Old French *curt* – short, or ? a variant of Curtain, from dialect *cortain* – straw-yard, courtyard; in Ireland (Mac)Curtin, formerly *Mac Cruitín* now *Mac Cuirtín*, Ir. *cruitín* – hunchback. (Reaney, Spiegelhalter, MacLysaght). Spiegelhalter traced Curtain in Devon; in Ireland "Now found chiefly in Co. Cork" (MacLysaght).

In Newfoundland:

Early instances: Thomas, of St. John's, 1817 (CO 194.59); John, from Co. Cork, married at St. John's, 1825 (Nfld. Archives BRC); Timothy Curtain, of Harbour Grace Parish, 1837 (Nfld. Archives HGRC); Benjamin Curtin, of Moreton's Harbour, about 1840–60 (MUN Hist.).

Modern status: Rare, at St. John's and Corner Brook (*Electors* 1955).

CURTIS, a surname of England and Ireland, from Old French *corteis* etc. – courteous, "in feudal society denoting a man of good education. Used also as a personal name." (Reaney, MacLysaght, Cottle).

Guppy found Curtis widespread, especially in Buckinghamshire and Nottinghamshire; MacLysaght mainly in east Leinster.

In Newfoundland:

Early instances: John Curtis(s), of Bonavista, 1675, 1677 (CO 1); John, constable of St. John's district, ? 1730 (CO 194.9); James, of Western Bay, 1789 (CO 199.18); Mortimer, from Rath Parish (Co. Clare), married at St. John's, 1811 (Nfld. Archives BRC); John, from Devon, of Portugal Cove, 1820, later of Blackhead (D'Alberti 31, *Nfld. Government Bulletin* Feb 1970); Benjamin, planter of Twillingate, 1820 (USPG); Mary, from Adamstown (Co. Wexford), married at St. John's, 1821 (Nfld. Archives BRC); George, planter of Bonaventure (unspecified), 1822 (DPHW 64); Joshua, planter of Brigus, 1825 (DPHW 34); William, of Trepassey, 1828 (Nfld. Archives BRC); Elizabeth, born at Pinchard's Island, 1828 (DPHW 76); James, of King's Cove, 1838 (DPHW 73A); Garritt, of Renews, 1839 (*Newfoundlander* 5 Dec 1839); George, planter of Northern Bay, 1840 (DPHW 52A); John, of Tizzard's Harbour, 1842 (DPHW 86); John, teacher of Ochre Pit Cove, 1845 (DPHW 52A); Harriet, of Trinity (Trinity B.), 1846 (DPHW 64); Francis, of Exploits Burnt Island, 1850 (DPHW 86); ? Apollos, fisherman of Blackhead (Bay de Verde district), 1853, of Broad Cove, 1856 (DPHW 52B); Martha, of Little Bay Islands, 1860 (DPHW 92); widespread in Lovell 1871.

Modern status: Widespread, especially at St. John's and Trepassey.

Place names: Curtis Point 49-38 55-49; Curtis's Rock 47-06 55-04.

CUSACK, CUSICK, surnames of Ireland. "In Ireland this name [Cusack] dates back to the Anglo-Norman invasion of 1171. The family became fully hibernicized. First called de Cussac it became *Ciomhsóg* in Irish. Cusack in Co. Clare is of different origin, viz. *Mac Íosóg*, first anglicized MacIsock and later MacCusack. MacIsaac is the corresponding Scottish name" (MacLysaght). *See* MacISAAC.

In Newfoundland:

Early instances: John Cussick, married at St. John's, 1781 (DPHW 26D); John Cusack, merchant of St. John's, 1827 (*Newfoundlander* 19 Sep 1827); John Cusick, of Harbour Grace Parish, 1827 (Nfld. Archives HGRC); John (and others) Cusack, of Great St. Lawrence, 1871 (Lovell).

Modern status: Cusack, rare, at Allan's Island (Burin district) (*Electors* 1955); Cusick, at St. Lawrence.

CUTLER, a surname of England and Scotland, from Old French *coutelier* – cutler, a maker, repairer or seller of knives. (Reaney, Black). Traced by Spiegelhalter in Devon, by Matthews in Dorset and Hampshire and by Black in Galloway.

In Newfoundland:

Early instances: George, of Trinity (Trinity B.), 1786 (DPHW 64); John, of Bonavista, 1791 (USPG); John, planter of New Perlican, 1823 (DPHW 64B); Elizabeth, baptized at Fair Island, 1830, aged 26 years (DPHW 76); John, planter of Salmon Cove (now Champneys), 1830 (DPHW 64); James, of Pouch Cove, 1836 (Nfld. Archives BRC); Henry, of Lower Burgeo, 1849 (DPHW 101); Henry, of Fox Island, 1871 (Lovell); Jacob, seaman of Harbour Grace, 1871 (Lovell); Amos, planter of West Point (La Poile B.), 1871 (Lovell).

Modern status: Scattered, especially at Ramea, Shallop Cove (St. George's district), Fair Island and Pike's Arm.

Place names: Cutler Harbour and Head 48-31 53-36; Cutler's Rock (Labrador) 52-19 55-45.

CUTTS, a surname of England, a pet-form of the baptismal name Cuthbert. (Reaney, Cottle, Withycombe).

Traced by Guppy in Derbyshire.

In Newfoundland:

Modern status: Rare, at St. John's.

CUZA, ? a Newfoundland variant of the surname of France Cuzin, a southern form of Cousin (*See* COUSENS), or a French place name (Dauzat).

In Newfoundland:

Modern status: Rare, at St. Lawrence and Mick's Cove (Burin district).

D

DAKIN, a surname of England – little David. (Reaney). *See* DAVEY and also DAVIDGE, DAVIDSON.

Traced by Guppy especially in Derbyshire and also in Cheshire, Staffordshire and Suffolk.

In Newfoundland:

Early instances: John Dakins, ? of St. John's, 1855 (*Newfoundlander* 19 Nov 1855); John Dakin, planter of Salmonier, 1871 (Lovell).

Modern status: Rare, at Freshwater (Placentia), Mitchell's Brook (St. Mary's district) (*Electors* 1955), and St. John's.

DALE, a surname of England, Scotland and Ireland, from Old English *dāl* – (dweller in the) dale, or in Ireland also from Irish *dall* – blind, "occasionally found with the prefix Mac." (Reaney, Black, MacLysaght).

Guppy found Dale widespread, especially in Herefordshire.

In Newfoundland:

Early instances: John, of Bay Bulls, 1675 (CO 1); Henry, of Battle Harbour (Labrador), 1787 (MUN Hist.); William, planter of Old Perlican, 1838 (DPHW 58); Thomas, planter of Northern Bay, 1850 (DPHW 55).

Modern status: Scattered, especially in the Port de Grave district.

DAL(E)Y, surnames of England and Ireland, in England a variant of DALLEY, in Ireland, (O)Daly, *Ó Dálaigh*, Ir. *dálach*, from *dáil* – assembly, or a variant of (O)Dealey or ? (O)Deeley. (MacLysaght).

Daly was traced by Spiegelhalter in Devon; (O)Daly, Dawley by MacLysaght originally in Co. Westmeath but later in Cos. Clare, Cork and Galway; and Dailey, Dealley in Devon and Enniscorthy (Co. Wexford) by Matthews.

In Newfoundland:

Family tradition: —— Daly, from Waterford, settled at Riverhead (St. Mary's B.), about 1847 (MUN Folklore).

Early instances: Timothy Dawley, fisherman of St. John's, 1794–5, "20 years in Newfoundland," that is, 1774–5 (Census 1794–5); James Daly, carpenter of St. John's, "8 years in Newfoundland," that is, 1786–7 (Census 1794–5); Pat Daley, of Broad Cove (Bay de Verde district), 1795 (CO

199.18); Matthew Dealy, of Bay de Verde, 1797 (CO 199.18); John Dawley and sons, occupiers of fishing room at Rider's Harbour, Winter 1800–01 (Census Trinity B.); Daniel Daly, of Harbour Grace Parish, 1806 (Nfld. Archives HGRC); James Dawley, of Trinity Bay, 1806 (DPHW 64); Daniel Daily, one of 72 impressed men who sailed from Ireland to Newfoundland, ? 1811 (CO 194.51); Michael Daly, from the city of Cork, married at St. John's, 1813 (Nfld. Archives BRC); Margaret Dawley, married in the northern district, 1814 (Nfld. Archives BRC); Honora Daly or Dayly, of Kings Cove, 1820 (Nfld. Archives KCRC); Honora Daly, of Catalina, 1821 (Nfld. Archives KCRC); Dennis Dealy, from Mothel Parish (unidentified) (Co. Waterford), married at Tilton Harbour (now Tilting), 1821 (Nfld. Archives KCRC); Honora Daly, of Broad Cove (now Duntara), 1822 (Nfld. Archives KCRC); Michael Dawley, from Ballymacoda (Co. Cork), married at St. John's, 1822 (Nfld. Archives BRC); Betsy Dealy, of Ragged Harbour (now Melrose), 1825 (Nfld. Archives KCRC); James Dawlay, of Plate Cove (Bonavista B.), 1829 (Nfld. Archives KCRC); Daniel Daly, tailor of Harbour Grace, 1831 (DPHW 43); Timothy Daley, of Gooseberry Island (Bonavista B.), 1853 (DPHW 76); Patrick Daly, of Topsail, 1855 (*Newfoundlander* 29 Nov 1855); Honora Dawley, of Trinity, 1856 (Nfld. Archives KCRC); James and Patrick Daley, fishermen of Mall Bay, Mother Ixxes (now Regina) and Mosquito area (St. Mary's B.), 1871 (Lovell); Daniel and Dennis, fishermen of Salmonier (St. Mary's B.), 1871 (Lovell); James Daly, storekeeper of Brigus, 1871 (Lovell); John Dawley, planter of Carbonear, 1877 (Lovell).

Modern status: Daley, especially at St. Joseph's (St. Mary's B.); Daly, especially at Riverhead and Mall Bay (St. Mary's B.).

Place names: Cape Daly (Labrador) 59-12 63-21; Dawley Bank (Labrador) 53-07 55-44.

DALL(E)Y, surnames of England, from the English place name Delley (Devon). *See also* DAL(E)Y. (Spiegelhalter).

Traced by Spiegelhalter in Devon.

In Newfoundland:

Early instances: Elias Dally, of Herring Neck, 1820 (USPG); Thomas Dalley, of Clark's Cove

(Twillingate district), 1855 (DPHW 85); Timothy, fisherman of Bloody Bay (later Alexander Bay, now part of Glovertown), 1871 (Lovell); Elias (and others) Dally, of Twillingate, 1871 (Lovell).

Modern status: Dailey, scattered, especially at Durrell's Arm; Dally, rare, at St. John's and Change Islands (*Electors* 1955).

DALTON, a surname of England, Scotland and Ireland, in England from the English place name Dalton (Durham, Lancashire, Northumberland, Westmorland and Yorkshire), or (dweller or worker at the) farm in the dale; in Scotland probably from Dalton (Northumberland); in Ireland it was formerly D'Alton, *de Dalatún*, an Anglo-Norman family, or a variant of Daton, Daughton, that is, d'Auton, also of Anglo-Norman origin. (Reaney, Cottle, MacLysaght).

Traced by Guppy in Buckinghamshire, Derbyshire and Lincolnshire; by Matthews in Hampshire, Devon and Cork; and by MacLysaght in Cos. Clare, Westmeath and Kilkenny.

In Newfoundland:

Family traditions: ——, of French ancestry, from Ireland, settled at Harbour Grace about ? 1817, later at Colinet Island (MUN Folklore). ——, from near Dublin, settled at Western Bay about ? 1847; the family later moved to Little Catalina (MUN Folklore). ——, from England, settled at Conception Harbour in the early 19th century (MUN Folklore).

Early instances: ——, constable of Ferryland district, ? 1730 (CO 194.9); William, ? of Salmon Cove, ? 1752 (CO 194.13); Lawrence, fisherman of Quidi Vidi, 1794–5, "25 years in Newfoundland," that is, 1769–70 (Census 1794–5); Patrick, in the fishery at Petty Harbour, 1794–5, "20 years in Newfoundland," that is, 1774–5 (Census 1794–5); Lawrence, from Ireland, labourer of St. John's, 1776 (CO 194.33); Mary, of Broad Cove (Bay de Verde district), 1777 (CO 199.18); Matthew, ? of Northern Bay, ? after 1777 (CO 194.45); Mary, of Western Bay, 1784 (CO 199.18); John, of Adam's Cove, 1791 (CO 199.18); Edward, of Northern Arm, Salmon Cove (now Avondale), 1797 (CO 199.18); William Dalton or Daulton, of Harbour Grace Parish, 1806 (Nfld. Archives HGRC); Patrick Dalton, from Ballyneal Parish (unidentified) (Co: Kilkenny), married at St. John's, 1816 (Nfld. Archives BRC); Thomas, of Harbour Grace, 1821 (D'Alberti 31); W., of Carbonear, 1832 (*Newfoundlander* 4 Oct 1832); John, of Kings Cove Parish, 1837 (Nfld. Archives KCRC); Matthew, fisherman of Exploits Burnt Island, 1841 (DPHW 88); James, planter of Little Catalina, 1841

(DPHW 72); Peter, of Greenspond, 1858 (Nfld. Archives KCRC); John Alexander, of Pool's Island, 1862 (DPHW 77); John, farmer of Clarke's Beach, 1871 (Lovell); John, farmer of Harbour Main, 1871 (Lovell); James (and others), of Mall Bay, Mother Ixxes (now Regina) and Mosquito (St. Mary's Bay area), 1871 (Lovell).

Modern status: Widespread, especially at Little Catalina, Conception Harbour, Harbour Main, Cape Broyle and St. John's.

Place names: Dalton Point 47-01 53-41; —— Pond 48-19 53-43; Daltons Head 48-12 53-49; —— Pond 47-16 53-04.

DALY. *See* DALEY

DAMPIER, a surname of England, from the French place name Dampierre, "the name of numerous places in France, two of which are in Normandy" (Reaney), all from Latin *dominus* in the sense of 'saint' and *Pierre* – Peter. (Reaney, Cottle, Dauzat).

Traced by Guppy in Somerset and by Matthews in Dorset.

In Newfoundland:

Early instances: John and Thomas, from Sherborne (Dorset), apprentices in Newfoundland, 1741 (Dorset County Record Office per Kirwin); Thomas, proprietor and occupier of fishing room at Trinity (Trinity B.), Winter 1800–01 (Census Trinity B.); John, fisherman of Goose Cove (Trinity North district), 1854 (DPHW 64).

Modern status: Rare, at Musgravetown.

DANCEY, a surname of England and Ireland, from the French place name Anisy (Calvados), or ? from the English place name Dauntsey (Wiltshire). (Reaney, Spiegelhalter, MacLysaght).

Traced by Spiegelhalter in Devon and by MacLysaght in Co. Cavan.

In Newfoundland:

Early instances: F.J., of Harbour Grace, 1845 (*Newfoundlander* 8 Dec 1845); Thomas Dancy, of Burin, 1871 (Lovell).

Modern status: Rare, at Burin (*Electors* 1955), Windsor and St. John's.

DANIELS, a surname of England (with Daniel a baptismal name and surname, of England and Scotland, and Mac Daniell a surname of Scotland and Ireland), from Hebrew *Daniel* – God has judged, though in Ireland Mac Daniell was formerly a widespread synonym of Mac Donnel, and Mac Daniel in Co. Kerry "was the Gaelic patronymic assumed by a family of Welsh origin settled there in the thirteenth century." (MacLysaght, Reaney, Black, Withycombe).

Guppy traced Daniel and Daniels in Bedfordshire, Gloucestershire and South Wales, Daniel also in Cornwall, Devon and Worcestershire, and Daniels also in Kent and Norfolk; Spiegelhalter traced Daniel(s) in Devon; MacLysaght traced MacDaniel in Co. Kerry.

In Newfoundland:

Early instances: Thomas Daniel, fisherman of St. John's, 1794–5, "10 years in Newfoundland," that is, 1784–5 (Census 1794–5); William, of Greenspond, 1830 (DPHW 76); John, of Harbour Grace Parish, 1831 (Nfld. Archives HGRC); John, from Co. Kilkenny, of Harbour Grace, 1844 (*Indicator* 27 Jul 1844); John, from England, drowned at Renews, 1846 (*Mercury* 17 Sep 1846); Stephen J., from Clonmel (Co. Tipperary), late of St. John's, 1852 (*Newfoundlander* 26 Aug 1852); Michael, from Syria, of Harbour Grace Parish, 1898 (Nfld. Archives HGRC).

Modern status: At Bishops Falls, Corner Brook and St. John's.

Place names (not necessarily from the surname): Daniel Island 47-38 56-13; —— Point 46-45 53-23; —— Rattle (Labrador) 55-55 61-05; Daniels Brook 47-22 53-10; —— Cove 48-08 52-58, 50-15 57-35; —— Harbour 50-14 57-35; —— Lookout 51-22 55-47: —— Point 46-45 53-23.

DARBY, a surname of England, Ireland and Jersey (Channel Islands), from the English place name Derby (pronounced Darby); in Ireland also for (O)Darmody, Dermody, *Ó Diarmada*. "The forename *Diarmaid* is anglicized Darby as well as Dermot" (MacLysaght). (Withycombe, Cottle, MacLysaght, Turk).

Traced by Guppy in Essex, Somerset, Worcestershire; by Spiegelhalter in Devon and by Matthews also in Dorset; and by MacLysaght in Cos. Leix, Tipperary and adjacent Leinster counties.

In Newfoundland:

Early instance: Samuel, of Burin, 1805 (D'Alberti 15).

Modern status: At Collins Cove (Burin district), Corner Brook and St. John's.

Place names (not necessarily from the surname): Darby Cove 47-53 54-13, —— Creek 47-53 54-10; —— Harbour 47-28 54-12; —— Ledge 48-09 53-30; Darbys Harbour 47-28 54-32.

DARCY, a baptismal name and surname of England and Ireland, from the French place name Arcy (La Manche), and in Ireland also for *Ó Dorchaidhe*, Ir. *dorchadh* – dark. (Withycombe, Reaney, MacLysaght).

Traced by MacLysaght in Cos. Mayo, Galway and Wexford.

In Newfoundland:

Family tradition: ——, of French origin, settled at St. John's (MUN Folklore).

Early instances: George, property owner and publican of St. John's, 1794–5, "20 years in Newfoundland," that is, 1774–5 (Census 1794–5); Michael Darcey, from Bally Neale (unidentified) (Co. Tipperary), married at St. John's, 1824 (Nfld. Archives BRC); Margaret, of Harbour Grace Parish, 1824 (Nfld. Archives HGRC).

Modern status: At St. John's.

DARRIGAN, a ? Newfoundland variant of the surnames of Ireland (O)Dargan (Leinster), Dargan (Co. Cork), *Ó Deargáin*, Ir. *dearg* – red. (MacLysaght).

In Newfoundland:

Family tradition: Maurice Derigan (1820–70), born in Ireland, came to Newfoundland as a Roman Catholic missionary in 1850, but met and married —— James (1825–75), and was baptized in the Church of England in which he became a layreader. Subsequently Derigan was changed to Darrigan, in the belief that the latter form was less Irish-sounding and therefore less offensive to their neighbours in the communities of John's Beach and Lark Harbour, which were predominantly of English and Church of England stock (MUN Folklore).

Early instances: Michael Darrigan, from Ireland, sentenced to death at St. John's, 1780 (D'Alberti 6); John Dargan, from Dingle (Co. Kerry), married at St. John's, 1835 (Nfld. Archives BRC); Thomas Dargen, of Bay of Islands, before 1849 (Feild); Patrick Darigan, from Killenaule (Co. Tipperary), married at St. John's, 1851 (Nfld. Archives KCRC); Maurice Dargan, fisherman of Bay of Islands, 1871 (Lovell).

Modern status: In the Humber West district, including Batteau Cove and Lark Harbour.

DART, a surname of England, from the English place name Dart Raffe (Devon), or the river Dart. (Cottle, Spiegelhalter).

Traced by Guppy in Devon.

In Newfoundland:

Early instances: Walter, fisherman of St. John's

or Petty Harbour, about 1739–43 (CO 194.11, 24); Robert, planter of Twillingate, 1823 (USPG); Samuel Darth, of Merritts Harbour, 1845 (DPHW 86); Elizabeth Dart, of Herring Neck, 1851 (DPHW 85); Robert, of Exploits Burnt Island, 1858 (DPHW 92).

Modern status: Rare, at Exploits, Badger (*Electors* 1955) and Gander.

DAVEY, a surname of England and Ireland, Davy of Guernsey (Channel Islands), with variants Davie, Davy in England, Scotland and Ireland, a diminutive of the baptismal name David from the Hebrew "originally a lullaby word meaning 'darling', then 'friend' generally" (Withycombe). "In Ireland, Dav(e)y are used occasionally as synonyms of Mac Davitt and even David" (MacLysaght). (Withycombe, Reaney, Cottle, MacLysaght, Turk). *See also* DAKIN, DAVIDGE, DAVIDSON, DEWEY.

Guppy traced Dav(e)y in Cornwall, Devon, Essex, Lincolnshire, Norfolk, Somerset and Suffolk.

In Newfoundland:

Early instances: W. Francis ? Davy, ? of St. John's, 1759 (DPHW 26C); Robert Davey, of Portugal Cove, 1818 (DPHW 26D); William Dav(e)y, of Twillingate, 1818 (USPG); John Davey, of Fogo, 1842 (DPHW 83); Jonathan, fisherman of Channel, 1871 (Lovell).

Modern status: At St. John's (*Electors* 1955).

DAVIDGE, a surname of England – David's (son), "a perverse misspelling of *Davids*" (Cottle). *See* DAVEY and also DAKIN, DAVIDSON.

In Newfoundland:

Early instances: John, of Lower Burgeo, 1848 (DPHW 101); Thomas, planter of Mose Ambrose, 1858 (DPHW 104); Thomas Davage, planter of Bay du Nord, 1871 (Lovell).

Modern status: At Bay du Nord.

DAVIDSON, a surname of England, Scotland and Ireland – son of David. *See* DAVEY and *also* DAVIDGE, DAKIN.

Traced by Guppy especially in the northern counties of England and over a large part of Scotland, but rare in the north. Davison is the commoner form in Durham. MacLysaght found Davidson numerous in northeast Ulster.

In Newfoundland:

Early instances: John Davison, soldier of St. John's, 1756 (DPHW 26C); William, merchant or agent of Conception Bay, 1784 (D'Alberti 6); John Davidson, of St. John's, 1790 (DPHW 26C); William H. (1843–), born at Aberdeen, came to St. John's in

1864 (Mott); Robert, fisherman of Greenspond, 1871 (Lovell).

Modern status: Rare, at St. John's.

Place name: Davidson Rock (Labrador) 59-22 63-12.

DAVIES, a surname of England, Wales and Ireland – son of Davy, David. *See* DAVEY, DAVIS.

Guppy found that Davies, as opposed to Davis, is essentially the Welsh form and that of the counties immediately bordering Wales, and in England and Wales much the more frequent form. The two forms may have been confused in Newfoundland.

In Newfoundland:

Family tradition: Joseph Davies (1861–1947), born at Cardiff, Wales, settled on Pool's Island in the 1870s and at Valleyfield in 1910. At some time his name was changed to DAVIS (MUN Folklore).

Early instances: William Davis (Davies in 1677), of Musketa Cove (now Bristols Hope), 1675 (CO 1); Charles Davies (Davis in 1681), of Carbonear, 1677 (CO 1); George, of Carbonear, 1702, of St. John's, 1706 (CO 194.2,3); Nicholas, of St. John's, 1807 (Nfld. Archives BRC).

Modern status: Rare, at St. John's.

Place names: Davi(e)s Brook 49-30 56-06; ——— Pond 49-33 56-04; Davies Head 47-34 53-16.

DAVIS, a surname of England and Ireland – son of Davy, David. *See* DAVEY, DAVIES.

Guppy found Davis widespread in the Midlands and south of England.

In Newfoundland:

Early instances: William Davis (Davies in 1677), of Musketto Cove (now Bristol's Hope), 1675 (CO 1); Charles Davies (Davis in 1681), of Carbonear, 1677 (CO 1); Davy Davis, of Renews, 1675 (CO 1); John, of Port de Grave, 1708–09 (CO 194.4); John, of Trinity (Trinity B.), 1708–09 (CO 194.4); George, of Clown's Cove (Carbonear), 1803, property "in possession of the Family for upwards of 90 years," that is, before 1713 (CO 199.18); John, of St. John's, 1732 (D'Alberti 22); Thomas, of Placentia ? district, 1744 (CO 194.24); James, of Western Bay, 1746 (CO 199.18); George, of Harbour Grace, 1771 (Nfld. Archives L118); William, in possession of property and shoreman of Quidi Vidi, 1794–5, "20 years in Newfoundland," that is, 1774–5 (Census 1794–5); George, of Chapel's Cove, 1775 (CO 199.18); Benjamin, of Bonavista, 1792 (USPG); Samuel, of Twillingate, 1818 (USPG); Henery [sic], of Crocker's Cove (Carbonear), 1819 (DPHW 48); Robert, of Broad Cove (Bay de Verde district), 1824 (DPHW

52A); William, from Exeter, married at St. John's, 1824 (Nfld. Archives BRC); George, planter of Freshwater (Carbonear), 1826 (DPHW 48); John, from Poole (Dorset), late of Colinet, 1827 (*Ledger* VI, 578); Mary, from Waterford, married at St. John's, 1830 (Nfld. Archives BRC); Abraham, baptized at Pinchard's Island, 1830, aged 13 years (DPHW 76); Catherine, of Fortune Harbour, 1831 (Nfld. Archives KCRC); John, of Riders Harbour (Trinity B.), 1832 (Nfld. Archives KCRC); William, of Cape Island (Bonavista B.), 1833 (DPHW 76); William Mudge, from Dawlish (Devon), married at St. John's, 1833 (DPHW 26D); ———, on the *Dolphin* in the seal fishery out of Bay Roberts, 1838 (*Newfoundlander* 29 Mar 1838); James, married on the French Shore, 1839 (Nfld. Archives BRC); William, ? of Northern Bay, 1852 (DPHW 54); Isaac, of Pool's Island, 1862 (DPHW 77); widespread in Lovell 1871.

Modern status: Widespread, especially in the Bonavista North district, at Grand Falls, Gander, St. John's, Carbonear, and Freshwater (Carbonear).

Place names: Davi(e)s Brook 49-30 56-06; ——— Pond 49-33 56-04; Davis Cove 47-37 54-22, 47-38 54-20, 48-59 58-00, 49-16 58-14; ——— Inlet (Labrador) 55-52 60-52; ——— Island 47-16 54-55; ——— Point 47-13 53-34; ——— House (Labrador) 51-28 56-53; ——— Long Rock 49-12 53-29.

DAWE, a surname of England, either a diminutive of the baptismal name David (*See* DAVEY), or from Old English **dawe*, Middle English *dawe* – jackdaw, ? a nickname for a petty thief. (Reaney, Cottle).

Traced by Guppy in Cornwall, Devon, Dorset, Gloucestershire and Herefordshire.

In Newfoundland:

Early instances: George, of Port de Grave, 1755, "property in possession of the Family" since 1595 (CO 199.18); Stephen, planter of St. John's, 1706 (CO 194.4); James Daw, from Ashburton (Devon), married at St. John's, 1759 (DPHW 26D); Sara Daw(e), of Harbour Grace Parish, 1807 (Nfld. Archives HGRC); Abraham Dawe, of Kelligrews, 1824 (DPHW 26B); George, planter of Cupids, 1827 (DPHW 34); John Daw, of Lower Gully (now Riverdale), 1832 (DPHW 30); Samuel Dawe, of Long Pond, 1836 (DPHW 26D); Samuel, of Lamaline, 1838 (DPHW 109); Job, of Greenspond, 1838 (DPHW 26D); Amy Daw, of Foxtrap, 1839 (DPHW 30); Eli Dawe, born at Bay Roberts, 1843 (Mott); Moses Daw, fisherman of Ship Cove (Port de Grave), 1849 (DPHW 39); Edward, of Southern Gut (now South River), 1849 (DPHW 34); Nicholas, of Burnt Head (Cupids), 1850

(DPHW 34); Robert Hunt Dawe, merchant of Burgeo, 1851 (DPHW 101); Nathaniel Daw, of Seldom Come By, 1855 (DPHW 26D); Carl, of Harbour Grace, 1869 (Nfld. Archives HGRC); widespread in Lovell 1871.

Modern status: Widespread, especially on the Avalon Peninsula.

Place names: Dawes Brook 49-05 56-11; ——— Cove (or Sam Dawes Cove) (Labrador) 55-09 59-04; ——— Harbour (Labrador) 57-15 61-29; ——— Island (Labrador) 57-16 61-30; ——— Islands (Labrador) 56-36 60-52; ——— Pond 49-07 56-12.

DAWSON, a surname of England, Ireland and Scotland – son of Dawe or David (*See* DAVEY).

Traced by Guppy mostly in Cumberland and Westmorland, Durham and Yorkshire, and in Stirlingshire; by MacLysaght in Cos. Monaghan and Tipperary since the mid-17th century.

In Newfoundland:

Family tradition: James, (1797–1856), born at Callan (Co. Kilkenny), carpenter ? of Bay Roberts or Spaniards Bay (MUN Geog.).

Early instances: Thomas, merchant of Harbour Grace, 1771 (Nfld. Archives L118); ? Michael, fiddler of St. John's, 1794–5, "18 years in Newfoundland," that is, 1776–7 (Census 1794–5); Patrick, of Petty Harbour, 1780 (D'Alberti 6); Catherine, from Co. Kilkenny, married at St. John's, 1824 (Nfld. Archives BRC); James, from Co. Kilkenny, of Port de Grave, 1844 (*Indicator* 24 Aug 1844); William, of Bay Roberts, 1866 (Nfld. Archives HGRC).

Modern status: Scattered, especially at Bay Roberts.

Place names: Dawson Passage 47-46 55-51; ——— Point 47-39 56-09, 47-46 55-51, 47-55 55-46; ——— Shoal 47-39 56-09; Dawson's Cove 47-32 55-56, 48-37 53-11.

DAY, a surname of England, Scotland and Ireland, in England from Old English *dæge*, Middle English *day(e)* – (loaf-) kneader, breadmaker, later – dairymaid, servant; or in England and Scotland, a diminutive of David (*See* DAVEY); in Ireland synonymous with O'DEA. (Reaney, Cottle, Black, MacLysaght).

Guppy found Day widespread in the southern parts of England, especially in Cambridgeshire, Huntingdonshire, Kent, and Somerset; Black in Banffshire.

In Newfoundland:

Family tradition: John Day, of Old Perlican, was one of the first settlers at Greens Harbour in 1836 (MUN Hist.).

Early instances: McErand, storekeeper of St. John's, 1756 (DPHW 26C); John, of Trinity Bay, 1765, of Salmon Cove (now Champneys), 1772 (DPHW 64); Thomas, of Cupids, 1780 (CO 199.18); Michael, of St. Mary's Bay, 1804 (D'Alberti 14); James, of Old Perlican, 1813 (D'Alberti 23); John, from Mullinahone (Co. Tipperary), married at St. John's, 1813 (Nfld. Archives BRC); Mary, of Harbour Grace Parish, 1830 (Nfld. Archives HGRC); Joseph, servant of Ship Cove (now part of Port Rexton), 1836 (DPHW 64B); Patrick, ? of Ferryland, 1838 (*Newfoundlander* 25 Oct 1838); Joseph, of Robin Hood (now part of Port Rexton), 1839 (DPHW 64B); James, fisherman of Grole, 1845 (DPHW 102); George, fisherman of Gander Bay, 1850 (DPHW 83); Sarah, of Hants Harbour, 1850 (DPHW 59); John, of Rocky Bay (Fogo district), 1855 (DPHW 83); William, of Catalina, 1856 (DPHW 67); Charles, of Old Shop, died 1857 (*Newfoundlander* 12 Mar 1857); John, of Green's Harbour, 1858 (DPHW 59A); Patrick, of Harbour Grace, 1866 (Nfld. Archives HGRC); Nathaniel, planter of Burin, 1871 (Lovell); Francis (and others), of Fortune Harbour, 1871 (Lovell); James and Job, of Harbour Le Cou, 1871 (Lovell); James, fisherman of Sagona Island, 1871 (Lovell); Francis, of Sandy Point (St. George's), 1871 (Lovell).

Modern status: Widespread, especially at Harbour Breton and Old Shop.

Place names: Day Cove, —— Point, —— —— Cove 47-41 55-55; Jim Day Island 49-31 55-14; Michael —— Cove 47-28 55-44.

(O)DEADY, surnames of Ireland, *Ó Déadaigh.* "Its variant *Ó Daoda* is anglicized Dady which is the local pronunciation of Deady also." (MacLysaght).

Traced by MacLysaght in Cos. Kerry and Limerick.

In Newfoundland:

Early instances: John Deady, of St. John's, 1755 (DPHW 26C); Thomas, from Ireland, of Kings Cove, 1817 (*Royal Gazette* 27 May 1817); John, of Harbour Grace Parish, 1818 (Nfld. Archives HGRC); Eugene, of Lance au Loup (Labrador), 1818 (D'Alberti 30); Thomas, ? of Harbour Grace, 1845 (*Newfoundlander* 25 Jun 1845); Michael, of Harbour Grace, 1867 (Nfld. Archives HGRC); John, of Holyrood, 1871 (Lovell); Thomas, trader of Joe Batt's Arm, 1871 (Lovell).

Modern status: Deady and O'Deady, each unique, at St. John's (*Electors* 1955).

DEAGEN, DEAGON, ? Newfoundland variants of the surname of Ireland (O)Deegan, *Ó Duibhginn*, Ir. *dubh* – black, *ceann* – head. (MacLysaght).

Traced by MacLysaght in Co. Leix.

In Newfoundland:

Early instances: Patrick Deegan, from Thomastown (? Co. Kilkenny), married at St. John's, 1820 (Nfld. Archives BRC); Thomas, from Killea (unidentified) (Co. Waterford), of St. John's, 1837 (Nfld. Archives BRC); Lawrence De(e)gan or Deagan, from Thomastown (Co. Kilkenny), of Harbour Grace, 1824, 1832, 1844 (Nfld. Archives HGRC, *Indicator* 27 Jul 1844); John Deegan, from Thomastown (Co. Kilkenny), ? of Renews, died 1854, aged 77 years (Dillon); Michael Deagin, of Bay Bulls, 1871 (Lovell); Patrick Deegan, of St. John's, 1871 (Lovell).

Modern status: Deagen, at Bay Bulls (*Electors* 1955); Deagon, at Bay Bulls Road (St. John's) (*Electors* 1955).

DEAN, a surname of England and Scotland, Deane of Ireland; in England from several English place names containing the element Dean, or from Old English *denu* – (dweller in or near a) valley, or from Latin *decanus*, Middle English *deen*, etc., – (member of or servant in the) dean('s) service or household; in Scotland from the place names Den (Aberdeenshire), Dean (Ayrshire); Deane in Ireland for *le Den*, *de Denne*, *Ó Déaghain*, or *Mac an Deagánaigh*. (Reaney, Cottle, Black, MacLysaght).

Guppy found Dean(e) in Cheshire, Staffordshire and adjacent counties and in Wiltshire and adjacent counties, with Deane "a comparatively rare form, found mostly in the south of England, in Dorsetshire, Wiltshire and Oxfordshire." MacLysaght found Deane in Cos. Tipperary, Donegal and elsewhere.

In Newfoundland:

Family tradition: John Dean, of Dean's Cove (Random Island), died at Passenger Cove, Northwest Arm, Random Sound in the 19th century (MUN Hist.).

Early instances: Richard Deane, of Blackhead (Bay de Verde), 1708–09 (CO 194.4); Richard (and others) Dean, of Crocker's Cove (Carbonear), 1782 (CO 199.18); James, from Winkton, Christchurch (Hampshire), planter of Old Perlican, 1780, 1787 (Nfld. Archives T18); William, of Bonavista, 1797 (DPHW 70); William, merchant of St. John's, 1801 (D'Alberti 12); Jehu, of Carbonear, 1810 (DPHW 48); Ann Deen, of Hants Harbour, 1823 (DPHW 58); Abraham Deane, of Harbour Grace Parish, 1831

(Nfld. Archives HGRC); Richard Dean, planter of Salmon Cove (Carbonear), 1840 (DPHW 48); Jane Deans, from Roxburghshire, Scotland, married in Newfoundland, 1844 (*Royal Gazette* 27 Aug 1844); —— Dean, on the *Harp* in the seal fishery out of Harbour Grace, 1853 (*Newfoundlander* 28 Mar 1853); Thomas, planter of Western Bay, 1856 (DPHW 52B); Henry Deane, fisherman of Freshwater (Carbonear), 1856 (DPHW 49); Isaac Dean, of Seldom Come By, 1860 (DPHW 84); John, fisherman of Bay de Verde, 1871 (Lovell); Thomas, fisherman of Burin, 1871 (Lovell); William Dean, fisherman of Fox Harbour, 1871 (Lovell); Albert and John, fisher-men of Lobster Harbour (White B.), 1871 (Lovell); Henry, fisherman of Turk's Cove, 1871 (Lovell); Richard, fisherman of Victoria, 1871 (Lovell).

Modern status: Scattered, especially at Victoria.

Place names: Dean Cove 47-40 54-20; Deane Islands (Labrador) 56-36 60-54; Dean's Pond 49-25 57-39.

DEARE, DEER, surnames of England, Deer of Scotland; in England ? from the Old English personal name *Deora*, or from Old English *dēore* – beloved, *dēor* – brave, *dēor* – deer, wild animal, as in DEARING; in Scotland from the place name (Old and New) Deer (Aberdeenshire). (Reaney, Black).

Spiegelhalter traced Deere in Devon.

In Newfoundland:

Early instances: John Dear, of Hearts Content, 1681 (CO 1); John Deer, of St. John's, 1782 (DPHW 26C); George, of Ragged Harbour (now Melrose), 1834 (DPHW 70); William, fisherman of Freshwater (Carbonear), 1837 (DPHW 48); William, fisherman of Bunkers Head (Carbonear), 1842 (DPHW 48); William Dear, planter of Flatrock (Carbonear), 1845 (DPHW 48); John Deer, of Moreton's Harbour, 1848 (DPHW 86); Frances Dear, of Harbour Grace, 1852 (DPHW 26D); Samuel Deer, of Grand Bank, 1871 (Lovell); James, of Otterbury (Carbonear), 1871 (Lovell); John, of Pearce's Harbour, 1871 (Lovell); John Dear, farmer of Burin, 1871 (Lovell); Henry and William, fishermen of Burnt Island (now Port Anne), 1871 (Lovell).

Modern status: Deare, rare, at Chamberlains (*Electors* 1955); Deer, rare, especially at Port Anne (*Electors* 1955).

Place names: The many place names containing the specific Deer doubtless refer to the animal.

DEARIN(G), DEERING, surnames of England, Deering of Ireland, from the Old English personal names *Dēoring, Dȳring*, containing the elements *dēore* –

beloved, *dēor* – brave, or *dēor* – deer (or other wild animal), the last as a nickname for a swift runner or hunter. (Reaney, Cottle, MacLysaght). *See* DEARE.

Traced by MacLysaght as a Kentish name; a branch of the family settled in Co. Leix in the 16th century, though the name is now "mainly found in south-east Leinster."

In Newfoundland:

Early instances: William Dearan, from Bovey Tracy (Devon), married at St. John's, 1813 (Nfld. Archives BRC); William Dearin, of St. John's, ? 1821 (CO 194.64); John J., druggist of Harbour Grace, 1871 (Lovell).

Modern status: Dearin, unique, at St. John's; Dearing, at Moreton's Harbour; Deering, scattered, especially at Victoria and Shearstown.

DEBOURKE. *See* BURKE

DECKER(S), DICKER, surnames of England, from Old English *dīcere* – a maker of ditches, or dweller by the ditch or dyke; with Dicker also from the place name Dicker (Sussex) from Middle English *dyker* – dicker, a number of ten, "perhaps in allusion to a rent of a dicker of iron," that is, a bundle of ten iron rods, from iron mined in the area. (Reaney, Cottle, Ekwall).

Guppy traced Dicker, Spiegelhalter Dicker(s) in Devon.

In Newfoundland:

Family tradition: Henry Dicker, from England was a servant on Flat Island (Bonavista B.), in the mid-19th century (MUN Socio.).

Early instances: Richard Deckers, of Quidi Vidi, 1778 (DPHW 26C); James Dickers, of St. John's, 1782 (DPHW 26C); Daniel Dicker, of Caribou Tickle (Labrador), 1787 (MUN Hist.); James Dickers, of Broad Cove (Bay de Verde district), 1803 (CO 199.18); Ann Decker, of Harbour Grace Parish, 1813 (Nfld. Archives HGRC); Jane Dickers, of Portugal Cove, 1820 (Nfld. Archives BRC); Elizabeth Deker, of Joe Batt's Arm, 1821 (USPG); William Dicker, from Whitechurch (Dorset), deserted service at Harbour Grace, aged 18 (*Weekly Jour. and Conception Bay General Advertiser* 30 Apr 1829); Jesse Decker, of Bonne Bay, 1856 (DPHW 93); William Jr. and Sr. Deckers, of Noddy Bay, 1871 (Lovell); George and Israel Decker, miners of Tilt Cove, 1871 (Lovell).

Modern status: Decker, scattered, especially at Joe Batt's Arm; Deckers, rare, at Grand Falls (*Electors* 1955); Dicker, at Flat Island (Bonavista B.) (*Electors* 1955) and St. John's.

Place name: Decker's Cove 49-31 57-53.

DEER. *See* DEARE

DEERING. *See* DEARING

DE GRUCHY. *See* GROUCHY

DE HANN, ? a variant of the surname of Ireland (O)Deehan, *Ó Díochon.* "Woulfe gives the derivation as great hound, but this is not generally accepted" (MacLysaght).

MacLysaght found Deehan scattered, "mainly in Co. Derry."

In Newfoundland:

Early instance: Lawrence Deehan, of Harbour Grace Parish, 1828 (Nfld. Archives HGRC).

Modern status: Rare, at St. John's and Foxtrap.

DELACEY. *See* LACEY

DELAHUNTY, a surname of Ireland (O)Delahunt(y), *Ó Dulchaointigh,* Ir. *dulchaointeach* – plaintive, satirist. (MacLysaght).

Traced by MacLysaght in Co. Offaly.

In Newfoundland:

Family tradition: ——— Delahunty was an early Irish settler on Bell Island (MUN Hist.).

Early instances: Richard, fisherman of St. John's, 1794–5, "30 years in Newfoundland," that is, 1764–5 (Census 1794–5); Michael, of Trepassey, 1803 (D'Alberti 12); Ellen, from Carrick-on-Suir (Co. Tipperary), married at St. John's, 1812 (Nfld. Archives BRC); Anastasia Delehunty, of Harbour Grace, 1828 (Nfld. Archives BRC); Richard, of Ragged Harbour (now Melrose), 1834 (Nfld. Archives KCRC); Daniel Delahunty, of Burin, 1871 (Lovell); Patrick (and others), of Ferryland, 1871 (Lovell); John, farmer of Goulds Road (St. John's), 1871 (Lovell); Lawrence, of Holyrood, 1871 (Lovell).

Modern status: Rare, at St. John's, Bell Island and Calvert.

DELANEY, a surname of Ireland (O)Delaney, *Ó Dubhshláinne,* Ir. *dubh* – black, *Sláine* – ? the river Slaney. "The prefix O has been almost completely discarded in the anglicized form of the name" (MacLysaght).

Traced by MacLysaght in Cos. Leix and Kilkenny.

In Newfoundland:

Family tradition: A French family name on the west coast (MUN Hist.); Joseph, of Margaree, N.S., son of Michael of Tipperary and Marguerite Ryan of Margaree, married Suzanne Aucoin of Margaree in 1847 when he was 25, and in the same year settled at St. George's. (G.R. Thomas).

Early instances: Grace, of Western Bay, 1740 (CO 199.18); D., surgeon of Petty Harbour, 1794–5, "24 years in Newfoundland," that is, 1770–1 (Census 1794–5); Thomas Delaney, of Trinity Bay, 1772 (DPHW 64); Martin, surgeon of St. John's, 1775 (DPHW 26C); John, shopkeeper of Harbour Grace, 1786 (CO 194.36); Michael, from Ballymore Eustace (Co. Wicklow), Irish convict landed at Petty Harbour or Bay Bulls, 1789 (CO 194.38); L., ? of Port de Grave, 1795 (Nfld. Archives T22); Marcus, of Bay Roberts, 1800 (CO 199.18); Morty Deleany, from Ballivogue Parish (unidentified) (Co. Wexford), married in Bay Bulls district, 1805 (Nfld. Archives BRC); Patrick Delany, from Inistioge (Co. Kilkenny), married at St. John's, 1805 (Nfld. Archives BRC); Elizabeth Delany alias Kenedy, of Harbour Main, 1811 (Nfld. Archives BRC); Honora Delany, of Trinity Bay, 1819 (Nfld. Archives KCRC); Moses Delaney, of Torbay, 1821 (D'Alberti 31); John, of Careless (now Kerleys) Harbour, 1826 (Nfld. Archives KCRC); John, of New Perlican, 1827 (Nfld. Archives KCRC); Grace, of Foxtrap, 1838 (DPHW 2.6D); William, planter of Broad Cove (Bay de Verde district), 1839 (DPHW 52A); Michael, of Middle Cove (St. John's district), 1840 (*Newfoundlander* 16 Jan 1840); Joseph, planter of Little Catalina, 1841 (DPHW 72); John, ? of Northern Bay, 1854 (DPHW 54); Thomas Deleny, of Cat Harbour (now Lumsden), 1859 (Nfld. Archives KCRC); widespread in Lovell 1871.

Modern status: Widespread, especially at Bay de Verde district.

Place names: Delaney Cove (Labrador) 52-38 55-49, 52-55 55-48; ——— Rock 46-47 54-05.

DELGADO, a surname of Spain and ? Portugal; Portuguese, Spanish *delgado* – slender, thin.

In Newfoundland:

Early instance: A.A., businessman of St. John's, 1879 (Devine and O'Mara).

Modern status: Rare, at St. John's.

DELOUCHE, a surname of France and the Channel Islands, Fr. *de l'ouche* – (dweller at a house characterized by an) enclosed garden. (Dauzat).

In Newfoundland:

Early instance: Joseph Deluce, fisherman of Indian Head (St. George's), 1871 (Lovell).

Modern status: Rare, at Port au Port.

DELUNEY, ? a Newfoundland variant of the surname of France, Delaunay, from various French place names Aunou (Orne), Aunay (Calvados etc.), Lauene (La Manche), or (dweller by the) alder grove. (Dauzat).

In Newfoundland:

Modern status: Rare, at Frenchman's Cove, Innismara (Humber West district) (*Electors* 1955) and Benoits Cove.

DELUREY, a variant of the surname of Ireland Deloughery, *Ó Dubhluachra*, Ir. *dubh* – black, with a place name (MacLysaght).

MacLysaght traced Deloughery in Co. Cork, "where it is found under nine different spellings such as Deloorey and Dilloughery, as well as its synonym Dilworth."

In Newfoundland:

Early instances: Richard Deloughley, from Thomastown (Co. Kilkenny), married at St. John's, 1803 (Nfld. Archives BRC); Thomas Deloorhy, married at St. John's, 1833 (Nfld. Archives BRC).

Modern status: Rare, at Riverhead (St. Mary's) and St. John's.

DEMPSEY, a surname of Ireland, *Ó Díomasaigh*, Ir. *díomasach* – proud. (MacLysaght).

MacLysaght found the name "now numerous in all the provinces."

In Newfoundland:

Early instances: Matthew Dempsay, of St. John's, 1782 (DPHW 26C); James Demsy, of Torbay, 1794–5, "11 years in Newfoundland," that is, 1783–4 (Census 1794–5); Matthew Dem(p)sey, from Clouslee (King's Co. now Offaly), ribbon-weaver, Irish convict landed at Petty Harbour, 1789 (CO 194.38, 41); Ellen Dempsey, from Ballimitty (unidentified) (Co. Wexford), married at St. John's, 1814 (Nfld. Archives BRC); John Dempsy, of Kings Cove, 1817 (Nfld. Archives KCRC); John Dempsey, of Harbour Grace Parish, 1818 (Nfld. Archives HGRC); Mary, of Carbonear, 1829 (Nfld. Archives BRC); Joseph, ? of Harbour Grace, 1845 (*Newfoundlander* 9 Jan 1845).

Modern status: Rare, especially at Canada Harbour, and elsewhere in the White Bay North district (*Electors* 1955).

DEMPSTER, a surname of England, Scotland and Ireland, the feminine form of Deemer, used of men, – judge. In Scotland, "The origin of this surname is found in the office of 'judex' or 'dempster' to the Parliament, shire, or baron-bailie. Until the year 1747

every laird whose land had been erected into a barony was empowered to hold courts for the trial and punishment of certain offenders within his barony; and the dempster was part of his retinue." (Black). In Ireland also for DEMPSEY. (Reaney, MacLysaght).

In Newfoundland:

Family tradition: John, from England, worked and married in Labrador and subsequently became the first settler at Lower Flowers Cove (MUN Hist.).

Early instances: George, of Hawke Bay (Labrador), 1787, at Battle Harbour (Labrador), 1795 (MUN Hist.); John, of Harbour Grace Parish, 1817 (Nfld. Archives HGRC); John, fisherman of Flowers Cove, 1871 (Lovell).

Modern status: Rare, at Nameless Cove (St. Barbe district) and St. John's.

DENIEF, a variant of the surname of Ireland Denieffe. "A rare Co. Kilkenny name, sometimes abbreviated there to Neef. Reaney says it is derived from an Old-English personal name" (MacLysaght), "*Denegifu* (feminine), unrecorded, but found in [the English place name] Dennington (Suffolk)" (Reaney *Origin*, 115). (MacLysaght, Reaney *Origin*, Ekwall).

In Newfoundland:

Family tradition: Honora (born 1794), from Co. Cork, married and settled at St. Anne's (Placentia B.) (MUN Geog.).

Early instances: Thomas Deneef, of Harbour Grace Parish, 1812 (Nfld. Archives HGRC); Thomas Denief, of St. John's, died 1828 (*Newfoundlander* 28 Feb 1829); Alice Dineife or Deneef, of Joe Batts Arm, 1829 (Nfld. Archives KCRC); Ellen Denief (born ? 1822), from Thomastown (Co. Kilkenny), married in 1840 and settled at King's Cove (Lawton and Devine).

Modern status: At St. John's.

DENINE, a variant of the surname of Ireland (O)Dinneen, *Ó Duinnín*, from a personal name *Donn* from Ir. *donn* – brown. (MacLysaght).

Traced by MacLysaght in Co. Cork.

In Newfoundland:

Early instances: Jane Dinan, from Lismore (Co. Waterford), married at St. John's, 1804 (Nfld. Archives BRC); William Denian, of Tors Cove, 1812 (Nfld. Archives BRC); John Dinan, of Harbour Grace Parish, 1816 (Nfld. Archives HGRC); Honora Dineen, from Lismore (Co. Waterford), of St. John's, 1824 (Nfld. Archives BRC); Mary Deneen, of Harbour Grace Parish, 1825 (Nfld. Archives HGRC); Michael, ? of Harbour Grace, 1845 (*Newfoundlander* 9 Jan 1845).

Modern status: At St. John's.

DENN(E)Y, surnames of England, Scotland and Ireland, diminutives of the baptismal name DENNIS (also a surname), or from the French pronunciation of Denis, or ? from the English place name Denny (Cambridgeshire); in Scotland from the Scots place name Denny (Stirlingshire); in Co. Kerry also as a variant of the Irish surname Dennehy. *See also* DINNEY. (Spiegelhalter, MacLysaght, Black, Ekwall).

Denny traced by Guppy in Norfolk and Suffolk, by Spiegelhalter in Devon, and by MacLysaght in Cos. Derry and Kerry.

In Newfoundland:

Early instances: George Denny, of St. John's, 1766 (DPHW 26C); Timothy, of Harbour Grace Parish, 1806 (Nfld. Archives HGRC); William, planter of Change Islands, 1821 (USPG); Joseph (and others) Deney, fishermen of Greenspond, 1871 (Lovell); John Denie, fisherman of Cape Broyle, 1871 (Lovell); Thomas Denney, of Englee, 1879 (MUN Hist.).

Modern status: Denney, rare, at Englee; Denny, rare, at St. John's.

Place name: Denny Island 47-37 57-10.

DENNIS, a surname of England, Scotland, Ireland and Guernsey (Channel Islands), and as Denis of France, from the baptismal name Denis, from the Greek and Latin – of *Dionysos*, the name of a convert of St. Paul and of several saints including the patron saint of France; also from Middle English *danais*, Old French *daneis* – Danish, the Dane; also in Ireland as a semi-translation of MacDonagh or for the rare surname *Ó Donnghusa*. (Withycombe, Reaney, Cottle, MacLysaght, Black, Turk). *See also* DENNEY, DINN, DYETT.

Guppy found Dennis widespread in Devon, Essex and Yorkshire, MacLysaght in Dublin and Cork.

In Newfoundland:

Early instances: Ralph, of St. John's, 1703 (CO 194.3); John, of Placentia ? district, 1744 (CO 194.24); John, salmon fisherman of Southeast Brook (St. George's B.), 1786 (CO 194.36); Thomas, of Codroy Islands, 1835 (DPHW 30); Thomas, of Channel, 1845 (DPHW 101); Daniel, of Little Barachoix, 1870 (DPHW 96); William, fisherman of Sandy Point (St. George's B.), 1871 (Lovell).

Modern status: Scattered, on the West Coast, especially at Three Rock Cove and John's Beach (*Electors* 1955).

Place names (from the surname or baptismal name): Dennis Arm 47-40 56-20; —— Brook 48-36 55-09; —— Point 47-17 52-50; —— Pond 48-24 58-10; —— Shoal 47-29 55-23.

DENNY. *See* DENNEY

DENSMORE, a surname of England, ? from the English place name Dinmore (Herefordshire), from the Welsh *din mawr* – great hill, or ? a variant of the surname of Ireland Dinsmore from the Scots place name Dunsmore (Fife). (Ekwall, MacLysaght 73).

In Newfoundland:

Family tradition: Frank (1845–98), of England, was shipwrecked off Newfoundland at the age of 13 years, and settled in the Kilbride area as a farm worker (MUN Geog.).

Modern status: At St. John's.

DENTY, a variant of the English surname Dainty, from Middle English *deinte* – fine, handsome; pleasure, tit-bit (Reaney), or ? from the English place name Daventry (Northamptonshire), pronounced daintree, a conjecture supported perhaps, despite the loss of the medial *r*, by the presence of Dainty as a surname in that county. (Reaney, Bardsley, Guppy).

Guppy traced Dainty in Northamptonshire.

In Newfoundland:

Early instances: Heber Dinty, of Bonavista, 1802 (DPHW 70); James Denty, of Salvage, 1871 (Lovell).

Modern status: In the Bonavista North and Placentia West districts, especially at Boat Harbour (*Electors* 1955).

DERMODY, a surname of Ireland, *Ó Diarmada*. (MacLysaght). *See also* DORMODY.

MacLysaght found Dermody "A fairly numerous but scattered name mainly in Cos. Cavan, Westmeath, Kilkenny and Galway."

In Newfoundland:

Early instances: Dorothy, of Harbour Grace Parish, 1827 (Nfld. Archives HGRC); John, tavern-keeper of Brigus, 1871 (Lovell); John, of Springfield (near Brigus), 1871 (Lovell); James (and others) Dermondy, of Little Placentia (now Argentia), 1871 (Lovell).

Modern status: Unique, at Makinsons (*Electors* 1955).

DESBARATS, ? a surname of France, not recorded by Dauzat, ? a variant of Barat, from a nickname – ruse, deception, which is also the name of many farms and hamlets in the Midi, though these have taken their name from the personal name. (Dauzat).

In Newfoundland:

Modern status: At Mount Pearl since about 1950, from Quebec where the family has lived for some eight generations after emigrating from the Basque area of the south of France.

DESSARD, a variant of the surname of France Dessart, from Fr. *essart* – (dweller in a house which stands in) cleared land, or from various place names containing the element Les Essards. (Dauzat).

In Newfoundland:

Family tradition: Of Irish descent (Family).

Modern status: Rare, at St. John's.

DEUTSCH, a surname of Germany, from German *deutsch* – German.

In Newfoundland:

Modern status: Rare, at St. John's.

DEVERE(A)UX, surnames of England and Ireland, from the French place name Evreux (Eure). (Reaney, Cottle).

Traced by MacLysaght in Co. Wexford and as Devery and Deverill in Cos. Leix and Offaly.

In Newfoundland:

Family tradition: First settlers, ? from France, of Spanish Room (Mortier B.) in 1837.

Early instances: John Devereaux, of Harbour Main, 1755 (MUN Hist.); Anastasia Deverix alias Walsh, from Waterford, married at St. John's, 1793 (Nfld. Archives BRC); M. Devereux, of Portugal Cove, 1794–5 (Census 1794–5); Nicholas Deverix, of St. John's, 1804 (Nfld. Archives BRC); John Devereux, of Harbour Grace Parish, 1812 (Nfld. Archives HGRC); John Devereaux, of Gasters (Conception B.), 1818 (D'Alberti 28); Henry Devereux, of Keels, 1828 (Nfld. Archives KCRC); James, of Trinity, 1830 (Nfld. Archives KCRC); Patrick, of Harbour Grace, 1831 (Nfld. Archives HGRC); Nicholas, of Riders Harbour (Trinity B.), 1833 (Nfld. Archives KCRC); John, of Trepassey, deceased 1838 (*Newfoundlander* 27 Dec 1838); Michael, of Ferryland, 1840 (*Newfoundlander* 27 Feb 1840); Pierce, from Co. Kilkenny, of Brigus, 1844 (*Indicator* 24 Aug 1844); Rev. Nicholas, from Co. Wexford, of Kings Cove, deceased 1845 (*Royal Gazette* 13 May 1845); Andrew Devereaux, of Logy Bay, 1871 (Lovell).

Modern status: Scattered, especially at Logy Bay, Trepassey and Avondale.

DEVINE, a surname of England and Ireland, in England from Old French *devin* – divine, used of persons "of more than ordinary excellence" (*OED* quoted by Reaney); in Ireland, *Ó Daimhín*, Ir. *damh* – ox or stag, not, according to MacLysaght, from Ir. *dámh* – poet. In Co. Tipperary Devin is a synonym of Davin with which Devine is often confused. (Reaney, Cottle, MacLysaght).

Traced by Matheson in Cos. Tyrone, Dublin and Roscommon, and by MacLysaght in Co. Tipperary and, as Devin, in Co. Louth.

In Newfoundland:

Family tradition: Maurice Devine, from Dingle (Co. Kerry), settled at King's Cove in the early 19th century (P.K. Devine, *Old King's Cove*).

Early instances: Patrick and William Divine, of Placentia, 1794 (D'Alberti 5); Matthew Devine, of Trinity (Trinity B.), 1796 (DPHW 64); John Divine, from Taglish Parish (unidentified), Ireland, married at St. John's, 1804 (Nfld. Archives BRC); Catherine, of Harbour Grace Parish, 1818 (Nfld. Archives HGRC); Maurice, from Co. Cork, married at Kings Cove, 1820 (Nfld. Archives KCRC); Maurice Devine, of Keels, 1867 (Nfld. Archives KCRC); Maurice, of Broad Cove (now Duntara), 1868 (Nfld. Archives KCRC); Micahel, of Stock Cove (Bonavista B.), 1869 (Nfld. Archives KCRC); Patrick, of Renews, 1871 (Lovell); John, planter of St. Mary's, 1871 (Lovell).

Modern status: Scattered, especially at St. John's and Renews.

DEVLIN, a surname of Ireland, *Ó Doibhilin*. "Devlin is the name of eight townlands in Cos. Donegal, Mayo and Monaghan." (MacLysaght, Joyce).

Traced by MacLysaght generally in Ulster and especially in Co. Tyrone.

In Newfoundland:

Early instances: John Develin, of Harbour Grace Parish, 1823 (Nfld. Archives HGRC); Henry Devilin or Develin, soldier of St. John's, 1824 (DPHW 26B); James Devlin, manager of St. John's, 1871 (Lovell).

Modern status: Rare, at Bell Island (*Electors* 1955) and St. John's.

DEVOE, ? a Newfoundland variant of the surname of France Devau or Deval – (inhabitant) of the valley. (Dauzat).

In Newfoundland:

Modern status: At Doyles (St. George's district), and Harbour Grace (*Electors* 1955); as Deveau (the usual Acadian spelling) in the Codroy Valley. (G.R. Thomas).

DEWEY, a surname of England, from the Cornish baptismal name *Dewi* – David (See DAVEY). (Spiegelhalter). Traced by Spiegelhalter in Devon.

In Newfoundland:

Early instances: John, of Trinity Bay, 1777 (DPHW 64); Jane Dewy, baptized at Greenspond, 1830, aged 33 years (DPHW 76); ——, ? occupier of Dewy's Room, Bonavista, before 1805 (Bonavista Register 1806); Joseph Dewey, fisherman of Trinity (Trinity B.), 1848 (DPHW 64B); Joseph Dew(a)y, of Trouty, 1853 (DPHW 64B).

Modern status: Rare, at Glovertown (*Electors* 1955), Deer Lake and St. John's.

DEWLAND, a surname of England, ? from the Welsh place name Dew(i)sland (Pembrokeshire).

Matthews traced Dewland in Somerset.

In Newfoundland:

Early instance: Thomas, of Trinity (Trinity B.), 1809 (DPHW 64).

Modern status: At Gaultois (*Electors* 1955).

DEWLING, a surname of England of unknown origin, ? a variant of DEWLAND or DEWEY.

In Newfoundland:

Early instance: Richard, fisherman of Trouty, 1851 (DPHW 64B).

Modern status: At Corner Brook, St. John's and in the Trinity North district, especially at Trouty.

DIAMOND, DYMOND, surnames of England, (O)Diamond and Dimond of Ireland; in England from the Old English personal name *Dægmund* or ? from DAY; in Ireland from the Irish surname *Ó Diamáin*. (Spiegelhalter, MacLysaght).

Guppy traced Dimond and Dymond in Devon, Diment and Dyment in Somerset; Spiegelhalter traced Dayman, Dayment, Daymond, Dimond and Diamond in Devon; MacLysaght traced (O)Diamond and Dimond in Cos. Derry, Donegal and Connacht.

In Newfoundland:

Early instances: Wm. Dimond and Co., of Adam's Cove, 1773 (CO 199.18); Mrs. Diamond, of Carbonear, 1782 (D'Alberti 2); Joseph, of (? Lower) Island Cove, 1798 (DPHW 48); George Dimond, of Lower Island Cove, 1803 (CO 199.18); John Daymond, from Devon, of St. John's, 1818 (*Nfld. Mercantile Journal* 19 Jun 1818); Nathaniel Dimond, planter of Catalina, 1820 (DPHW 72); Ann Dymond, of Harbour Grace Parish, 1833 (Nfld. Archives HGRC); James Diamond, fisherman of Russell's Cove (now New Melbourne), 1853 (DPHW 59A); John, of Change Islands, 1862 (DPHW 84); Abijah, fisherman of Flower's Cove, 1871 (Lovell); Jonathan and William, of Musgravetown, 1871 (Lovell); James and John, of Pouch Cove, 1871 (Lovell).

Modern status: Diamond, widespread, especially at Change Islands; Dymond, at St. John's.

Place names (not necessarily from the surname): Diamond Cove 47-37 58-42; —— Island 49-40 54-25; —— Lake 48-10 55-06; —— Point 47-46 55-52; —— Pond 48-33 53-51, 48-50 57-54; Diamonds Point 48-22 53-51; —— Pond 48-30 53-05.

DIBBON, a surname of England, a variant of Dibben or Dibbin, from *Dib*, a diminutive of the baptismal name Theobald, containing the elements *folk*, *people* and *bold*, or ? a form of Robin, a diminutive of Robert (*See* ROBERTS). (Spiegelhalter, Withycombe).

Guppy traced Dibben in Dorset and Wiltshire; Spiegelhalter traced Dibben in Devon.

In Newfoundland:

Early instances: Henry Dibbin, of Port au Bras, 1860 (DPHW 100); Henry, fisherman of Burgoyne's Cove, Random Sound, 1871 (Lovell); Charles (and others), fishermen of Burin, 1871 (Lovell); Richard, fisherman of Flat Island (now Port Elizabeth), 1871 (Lovell).

Modern status: Rare, in the Burin district.

DICK(S), surnames of England, Dick of Scotland and Ireland, a pet-form of Richard (*See* RICHARDS). (Reaney, MacLysaght, Black).

Guppy traced Dick in Ayrshire and Glasgow, Dicks in Somerset and Dix in Norfolk; MacLysaght traced Dick in Cos. Antrim and Down, "introduced from Scotland in the seventeenth century."

In Newfoundland:

Early instances: Robert Dick, of Heart's Content, 1682 (CO 1); John Dicks, of St. John's, 1755 (DPHW 26C); Mary Dick, of Bonavista, 1797 (DPHW 70); William, of King's Cove, 1802 (Bonavista Register 1806); John, of Pouch Island, 1803 (Bonavista Register 1806); George, of Greenspond, 1804 (D'Alberti 14); William, of Salvage, 1806 (Bonavista Register 1806); George Dix, planter of Twillingate, 1820 (USPG); Samuel Dick, of Swain's Island (Bonavista B.), 1822 (DPHW 76); George Dicks, of Belleoram, 1830 (DPHW 106); Elias, of Shoe Cove (Twillingate district), 1846, of Indian Bight, 1852 (DPHW 86); Edward, of Lower Burgeo, 1857 (DPHW 101); Henry (and others), of Channel, 1871 (Lovell); Joseph, fisherman of Great Barrisway (Burgeo-La Poile district), 1871 (Lovell); Christopher (and others) fishermen of Harbour Buffet, 1871 (Lovell); George (and others), planters of Isle aux Morts, 1871 (Lovell); Henry, miner of La Manche (Placentia B.), 1871 (Lovell); Samuel (and others) Dick, of Pool's Island (Bonavista B.), 1871 (Lovell); George Dicks, fisherman of Upper Burgeo, 1871 (Lovell).

Modern status: Dick, rare, at St. John's; Dicks, widespread, especially at Harbour Buffett (*Electors* 1955).

Place names (not necessarily from the surname): Dick Head 49-39 55-56; —— Hill (Labrador) 56-28 61-36; —— Rock 47-39 57-58; Dick's Cove 48-27 53-48,

49-28 57-43; —— Island 47-31 54-04 —— Point 47-27 54-18, 49-28 57-44; —— Rock 47-26 53-59.

DICKER. *See* DECKER

DICKINSON, DICKSON, DIXON, surnames of England, Dickson especially of Scotland, and Dickson and Dixon of Ireland and of Jersey (Channel Islands), diminutives of Dick, a pet-form of Richard (*See* RICHARDS). (Reaney, Cottle, Black, MacLysaght).

Guppy found Dickenson, Dickinson and Dixon widespread, with Dickinson and Dickenson especially in Northumberland, and Dickson in southern and central Scotland. MacLysaght found Dickson and Dixon among "the more numerous English names in Ireland."

In Newfoundland:

Family tradition: —— Dixon, from Jersey (Channel Islands) settled at Harbour Breton about 1850; he subsequently moved to Fortune (MUN Folklore).

Early instances: William Dixon, merchant of St. John's, 1794–5, "9 years in Newfoundland," that is, 1785–6 (Census 1794–5); William Dix(s)on or Dickson, of Kings Cove, 1820 (Nfld. Archives KCRC); William Dixon, of Harbour Grace Parish, 1835 (Nfld. Archives HGRC); Widow, from Carrick-on-Suir (Co. Tipperary), of Harbour Grace, 1844 (*Indicator* 27 Jul 1844); Thomas, fisherman of Clarkes Beach, 1847 (DPHW 39); John Phillip, son of William and Jane of Jersey (Channel Islands), married Emma Celestine Hardy at Jersey Harbour, 1870, aged 28, to Fortune 1873 (Harbour Breton Anglican Church Records per D.A. Macdonald; Grand Bank Methodist baptisms per P.E.L. Smith); William Dickenson, telegraph operator of Heart's Content, 1871 (Lovell); Thomas Dixon, farmer of Drogheda (Brigus district), 1871 (Lovell).

Modern status: Dickinson, rare, at St. John's; Dickson, rare, at St. John's and Corner Brook; Dixon, scattered, especially at Fortune.

Place name: Dixon Hill 47-14 53-57.

DICKS. *See* DICK

DICKSON. *See* DICKINSON

DIDHAM, a surname of England, from the English place name Didham (Devon). (Spiegelhalter).

Traced by Spiegelhalter in Devon.

In Newfoundland:

Early instances: Samuel, of Trinity (Trinity B.), 1796 (DPHW 64); Samuel, carpenter of St. John's, 1871 (Lovell).

Modern status: Rare, at Whitbourne and Colinet.

DILLON, a surname of Ireland, *Diolún*, "German *Dillo*, ? connected with word for 'destroy', normanized and taken to Ireland in the 12th century." (Cottle).

Traced by MacLysaght in Cos. Meath, Westmeath and Roscommon.

In Newfoundland:

Early instances: William, of St. John's, 1796 (CO 194.39); Eleanor, from Enniscorthy (Co. Wexford), married at St. John's, 1808 (Nfld. Archives BRC); John Dillan, from Windgap Parish (Co. Kilkenny), married at St. John's, 1814 (Nfld. Archives BRC); Moses Dillon, of Harbour Grace Parish, 1814 (Nfld. Archives HGRC); James, of Bonavista, 1821 (Nfld. Archives KCRC); Morgan, of Joe Batts Arm, 1823 (Nfld. Archives KCRC); Morgan, of Tilting Harbour (now Tilting), 1823 (Nfld. Archives KCRC); Philip, of Keels, 1824 (Nfld. Archives KCRC); Judith, from Co. Tipperary, married at Catalina, 1830 (Nfld. Archives KCRC); Stephen, of Ship Island, later of Mobile, about 1830–40 (Dillon); John, member of the General Assembly for Placentia-St. Mary's district, 1844 (*Nfld. Almanac*); ——, of Harbour Grace, 1858 (*Newfoundlander* 22 Apr 1858); Martin, fisherman of Lower Fogo Islands, 1871 (Lovell).

Modern status: Scattered, especially at St. John's.

DIMMER (OR DISMORE), a surname of England, from Old French *dix mars* – ten marks, one of "a certain number of surnames derived from coins" (Reaney, Weekley *Surnames*).

In Newfoundland:

Early instance: Henry, fisherman of Fox Cove (Placentia B.), 1871 (Lovell).

Modern status: At Fox Cove.

Place name: Tom Dimmer's Rock 47-05 55-04.

DINES, a surname of England, one of several variants of Dain, from Middle English *digne, deyn(e)*, etc. – worthy, honourable, or from Middle

English *dain(e)*, etc. – haughty, reserved, or from Old French *d(e)ien*, Modern French *doyen* – dean. *See also* DEAN. "The forms are inextricably confused." (Reaney).

In Newfoundland:

Early instance: James Dine, planter of Belleoram, 1871 (Lovell).

Modern status: Rare, at St. John's.

DING, a surname of China – soldier; adult male; person; to enjoin.

In Newfoundland:

Modern status: At St. John's.

DINGLE, a surname of England, from Middle English *dingle* – (dweller in the) deep dell or hollow, or from the English place name Dingle (Lancashire, Warwickshire), or from the Old English personal name *Dingwulf* or *Dingolf* containing the element *thing* – assembly. (Reaney, Weekley *Surnames*, Cottle).

Traced by Guppy in Cornwall and by Spiegelhalter in Devon.

In Newfoundland:

Early instances: John, of Bay Bulls, 1779 (CO 194.34, D'Alberti 2); Donald, of Channel, 1871 (Lovell).

Modern status: Rare, at St. John's.

DINGWALL, DINGWELL, surnames of England and Scotland, from the Scots place name Dingwall (Ross and Cromarty). (Bardsley, Black).

In Newfoundland:

Family tradition: —— Dingwall, born at Baddeck, N.S., of parents from Ayr (Ayrshire), settled at Port aux Basques about 1852, aged 26 years (MUN Folklore).

Early instance: Donald Dingwall, of Channel, 1863 (DPHW 96).

Modern status: Dingwall, rare, at St. John's; Dingwell, scattered, especially at Corner Brook and Port aux Basques-Channel.

Place name: Dingwall Point 47-34 59-08.

DINHAM, a surname of England, from the English place name Dinham (Monmouthshire), or the French place name Dinan (Côtes-du-Nord). (Bardsley, Spiegelhalter).

Traced by Spiegelhalter in Devon.

In Newfoundland:

Family tradition: —— Dinham, inhabitant of the Stone's Cove (Fortune B.) area between ? 1856 and 1884 (MUN Hist.).

Modern status: Rare, at St. John's and Stone's Cove.

DINN, a surname of England, Din of Scotland, and Denn of Ireland. In England and Scotland a pet-form of Dinis (Denis) (*See* DENNIS); in Ireland from *de Denne*. (Reaney, MacLysaght).

MacLysaght traced Denn in Cos. Waterford and Kilkenny.

In Newfoundland:

Early instances: Richard Den, of St. John's, 1780 (D'Alberti 1); John Dinn, from Co. Waterford, married at St. John's, 1802 (Nfld. Archives BRC); Maurice, of Witless Bay, 1803 (Nfld. Archives BRC); John, from Kilcash (Co. Tipperary), married at St. John's, 1812 (Nfld. Archives BRC); James, of Harbour Grace Parish, 1813 (Nfld. Archives HGRC); William, of Renews, 1828 (Nfld. Archives BRC); Morris Denn, ? of Ferryland, 1838 (*Newfoundlander* 25 Oct 1838); Thomas Dinn, ? of Northern Bay, 1840 (DPHW 54); W. Denn, of Bay Bulls, 1844 (*Nfld. Almanac*); John Dinn, of Goulds (St. John's district), 1871 (Lovell); James (and others), of Salmonier (St. Mary's), 1871 (Lovell).

Modern status: Scattered, especially at St. John's, Goulds and Witless Bay.

DINNEY, a surname of England, ? a pet-form of Dinis (Denis), or a variant of DENN(E)Y (*See* DENNIS); or from Old English *denu* and *īeg* – (dweller by the) low-lying land in the valley. (Reaney Notes).

In Newfoundland:

Early instances: John, of Herring Neck, 1850 (DPHW 85); Patrick Denni, of King's Cove, 1858 (Nfld. Archives KCRC); George Diney, of Change Islands, 1859 (DPHW 85); William Dinny, of Little Bay Islands, 1860 (DPHW 92).

Modern status: Rare, at Deer Lake.

Place name (not necessarily from the surname): Dinnys Pond 47-39 53-25.

DIXON. *See* DICKINSON

DOBBIN, a surname of England and Ireland, a diminutive of Dobb, itself a diminutive of the baptismal name Robert, as also in Rob and Robin. *See* ROBERTS *and also* DOBSON. (Reaney, Bardsley, Cottle, MacLysaght).

Of its occurrence in Ireland, MacLysaght comments: "Families of the name were associated with Co. Kilkenny and the city of Waterford from the fourteenth century. The name has also been continuously in Co. Antrim, the families in question being unrelated. It is now much more numerous in Ulster than in the south."

In Newfoundland:

Family traditions: ——, from Limerick settled at Coachman's Cove, thence to St. John's (MUN Folklore). ——, from Ireland settled near the Straits of Belle Isle; his descendants later moved to St. Mary's Bay and other parts of the Avalon Peninsula (MUN Folklore).

Early instances: J[ohn], of St. John's, 1705 (CO 194.22); Nicholas, of Spoon Cove (Conception B.), 1770 (CO 199.18); Thomas Davin alias Dobbin, native of Ireland, labourer of Bonavista, 1774 (CO 194.32); Thomas Dobbin, of Harbour Main, 1801 (CO 199.18); Anne, of Bay Bulls district, 1804 (Nfld. Archives BRC); Patrick Dobbyn, from Tramore Parish (Co. Waterford), married at St. John's, 1806 (Nfld. Archives BRC); Mary Dobbin, of Harbour Grace Parish, 1808 (Nfld. Archives HGRC); John, of Upper Island Cove, 1828 (Nfld. Archives HGRC); Catherine, from Thomastown (Co. Kilkenny), married at St. John's, 1830 (Nfld. Archives BRC); Catherine Dobbin(s), of Greenspond, 1832 (Nfld. Archives KCRC); Catherine Dobbin, of Middle Bill Cove (Bonavista B.), 1833 (Nfld. Archives KCRC); Nicholas Dobin, of Harbour Grace, 1867 (Nfld. Archives HGRC); James (and others) Dobbin, fishermen of Gaskiers (St. Mary's B.), 1871 (Lovell); Peter, of Isle Valen, 1871 (Lovell); James and Richard, of Mall Bay, Mosquito and Mother Ixxes (now Regina) area, 1871 (Lovell); David (and others), of St. Mary's, 1871 (Lovell); David, miner of Tilt Cove, 1871 (Lovell).

Modern status: Scattered, especially in the St. Mary's district at Gaskiers.

DOBER, a surname of England, from the occupation of daubing, that is, filling the interstices of walls made of wattles with earth or clay. (Reaney *Origin*).

Traced in Dorset.

In Newfoundland:

Family traditions: John (about 1771–1856), from Dorset, of Spanish Room (Placentia B.) (MUN Hist). George (about 1796–1882), from Dorset, was the first settler of Beau Bois (Placentia B.) (MUN Hist.).

Early instance: Richard ? Dober, of St. John's, 1706 (CO 194.22).

Modern status: In the Placentia West district, especially at Spanish Room.

DOBSON, a surname of England, Scotland and Ireland – son of Dobb. *See* ROBERTS and also DOBBIN.

Traced by Guppy especially in Durham, Lancashire and Yorkshire, and by MacLysaght in Co. Leitrim.

In Newfoundland:

Early instances: Samuel, of Harbour Grace Parish, 1823 (Nfld. Archives HGRC); Samuel, of Hants Harbour, 1828 (DPHW 59).

Modern status: Rare, at St. John's.

DODD, a surname of England, Scotland and Ireland, from the Old English personal name *Dodd(a)*, from a German root meaning rounded, used of someone lumpish, stupid, dishonest, or close-cropped, hairless. (Reaney, Cottle, Black, MacLysaght).

Traced by Guppy especially in Berkshire, Cheshire, Northumberland, Oxfordshire, Shropshire and Staffordshire, by Spiegelhalter in Devon, and by MacLysaght in Co. Sligo in the late 16th century (from Shropshire), but now scattered and mainly in Cos. Armagh and Down. Guppy traced Dod(d)s south of the Forth and Clyde.

In Newfoundland:

Early instances: William, in possession of property and fisherman of Torbay, 1794–5, "25 years in Newfoundland," that is, 1769–70 (Census 1794–5); Elizabeth Dad or Dod, from Ross (unspecified) (Co. Wexford), married at St. John's, 1821 (Nfld. Archives BRC); William Dodd, from Broadhempston (Devon), married at St. John's, 1836 (DPHW 26D).

Modern status: At St. John's and Torbay.

DODGE, a surname of England, "A pet-name for Roger, rhymed on Rodge and Hodge." Compare Dob for Robert and Dick for Richard. (Reaney, Spiegelhalter). *See* RO(D)GERS.

Traced by Spiegelhalter in Devon.

In Newfoundland:

Family tradition: ——, from Devon, married at Rock Harbour (Placentia B.), 1841 (MUN Hist.).

Early instances: George, of English Harbour (Fortune B.), 1835 (DPHW 30); John, of Fox Harbour (now Southport) (Trinity B.), 1858 (DPHW 59); William, planter of Conne (Fortune B.), 1871 (Lovell); John (and others), of [Little] Heart's Ease, 1871 (Lovell).

Modern status: Scattered, especially at Little Heart's Ease and in the Fortune Bay-Hermitage district.

DOHENEY, a variant of the surname of Ireland (O)Doheny, *Ó Dubhchonna*, Ir. *dubh* – black. (MacLysaght).

Traced by MacLysaght in Co. Cork.

In Newfoundland:

Early instances: James Dohoney, shoreman of Quidi Vidi, 1794–5, "20 years in Newfoundland," that is, 1774–5 (Census 1794–5); James Dohonay, of St. John's, 1803 (Nfld. Archives BRC); Timothy Doheney, of Harbour Grace Parish, 1826 (Nfld. Archives HGRC); —— Dohany, from Tollorone Parish (unidentified) (Co. Kilkenny), married at St. John's, 1813 (Nfld. Archives BRC); Catherine Dohoney or Dauhiny, of Bonavista, 1832 (Nfld. Archives KCRC); Timothy Dohony, of Harbour Grace, 1866 (Nfld. Archives HGRC).

Modern status: Rare, at St. John's.

DOHERTY, a surname of Ireland (O)Doherty, or Dougherty, *Ó Dochartaigh*, Ir. *dochartach* – hurtful. (MacLysaght).

Numerous in Ireland, especially in Ulster (MacLysaght).

In Newfoundland:

Early instances: John Dougherty, of St. John's, 1794–5, "35 years in Newfoundland," that is, 1759–60 (Census 1794–5); John Dahorty, of Trinity (Trinity B.), 1794 (DPHW 64); George Doherty, from Sutton's Parish (Co. Wexford), married at St. John's, 1797 (Nfld. Archives BRC); Richard Dogherly, of Harbour Grace Parish, 1811 (Nfld. Archives HGRC); —— Doherty, on the *Dart* in the seal fishery out of Harbour Grace and Carbonear, 1849 (*Newfoundlander* 22 May 1849); William, of Barrow Harbour (Bonavista B.), 1863 (Nfld. Archives KCRC); Catherine, of Harbour Grace, 1869 (Nfld. Archives HGRC); Dennis, farmer of Burin, 1871 (Lovell).

Modern status: At Dunfield (Trinity B.) (*Electors* 1955), Bell Island and St. John's.

DOHEY, a variant of surnames of Ireland (O)Dooey, Doey, in turn variants of DUFFY in northeast Ulster. (MacLysaght). *See also* DUFF.

In Newfoundland:

Early instances: James (and others) Dohea, of Distress (now St. Bride's), 1871 (Lovell).

Modern status: At St. Bride's.

DOLAN, a surname of Ireland (O)Dolan, *Ó Dubhláin*, Ir. *dubh* – black, *shlán* – challenge. (MacLysaght).

Traced by MacLysaght "throughout east Connacht and adjacent Ulster counties."

In Newfoundland:

Early instance: Thomas, of Harbour Grace Parish, 1833 (Nfld. Archives HGRC).

Modern status: Rare, at O'Regans.

DOLIMO(U)NT, DOLL(I)MO(U)NT, DOLOMO(U)NT, ? variants of the surname of France Lamon(t), from place names in Saône-et-Loire, Haute-Vienne, etc., or (the man from) *l'amont* – the upper reaches, head waters of a river. (Dauzat).

In Newfoundland:

Family tradition: From Guernsey.

Early instances: Levi Doramount, of Eastern Cul de Sac, 1835 (DPHW 30); George Dolemount, fisherman of West Cul de Sac, 1849 (DPHW 102); George Dolomount, of Bonne Bay, 1866 (DPHW 93); George Dollimount, of Coomb's Cove (Fortune B.), 1871 (Lovell); Joseph (and others) Doloment, of English Harbour West, 1871 (Lovell); John Dollimount, of Fortune, 1871 (Lovell); Levi (and others), of François, 1871 (Lovell); James Dolmiount (sic], planter of Rose Blanche, 1871 (Lovell).

Modern status: Essentially South Coast names.

DOLLAND, a surname of England, borne by a family of opticians in the 18th and 19th centuries of Huguenot extraction, hence ? an anglicization of the French surname (de) Hollande – (the man) from Holland. (*DNB*, Dauzat).

In Newfoundland:

Modern status: Rare, At Nipper's Harbour (*Electors* 1955) and Stephenville.

Place names: Dolland Arm 49-40 55-57, —— Bight 47-42 56-33, 47-43 56-34, 47-44 55-50; —— Brook 47-44 56-35; —— Arm Head 47-40 55-58.

DOLLARD, a surname of Ireland of English origin – dullard, obtuse, stupid. "A descriptive name in Co. Dublin since the thirteenth century." (MacLysaght).

In Newfoundland:

Early instances: Richard Dollard or Dallard, of St. John's, 1771 (DPHW 26C); Thomas Dollard, from Grange Parish (unidentified) (Co. Kilkenny), married at St. John's, 1806 (Nfld. Archives BRC); Andrew, of Harbour Grace Parish, 1837 (Nfld. Archives HGRC); Edward, from Co. Kilkenny, of Brigus, 1844 (*Indicator* 24 Aug 1844).

Modern status: At Stephenville.

DOLL(I)MO(U)NT, DOLOMO(U)NT. *See* DOLIMO(U)NT

DOMALAIN, a surname of France (of a Breton family), the name of the place Domalain (Ille-et-Vilaine) where the family originated. (Dauzat).

In Newfoundland:

Modern status: At Baie Verte and Brent's Cove (White B. South district).

DOMAN, a surname of England, from Old English *dōm* and *mann* – doom-man, judge. (Reaney).

In Newfoundland:

Early instance: Thomas, of Round Harbour (Twillingate, 1853 (DPHW 86).

Modern status: At Petries (Humber West district).

DOMINAS, a surname of Lithuania.

In Newfoundland:

Family tradition: John Dominas, born in Lithuania in 1892, settled on Bell Island about 1927 (MUN Folklore).

Modern status: At Bell Island (*Electors* 1955) .

DOMIN(E)AUX, DOMINO, variants of the surname of France Domino, taken from the opening words of Psalm cx (Vulgate cix), "Dixit Dominus *Domino meo*," a nickname for a chanter, chorister. (Dauzat). Confusion with DOMIN(E)Y etc. is possible.

In Newfoundland:

Early instance: James Domino, of Deer Island (Burgeo-La Poile), 1849 (DPHW 101).

Modern status: Domin(e)aux, in the Fortune Bay-Hermitage district, especially at Anderson's Cove (*Electors* 1955); Domino, rare, at St. John's.

Place names (? from the surname): Domino (Labrador), —— Harbour 53-28 55-47; —— Point 53-28 55-45; —— Run 53-29 55-48.

DOMIN(E)Y, DOMINIC(K), DOMINIE, DOMINIX, variants of a surname of England from the baptismal name Dominic(k), of which Dominey was a pet-form. "The name may have been given originally to children born on a Sunday (*dies dominica*)...but did not come into use as an ordinary Christian name until the 13th c[entury], in honour of St. Dominic (1170–1221), founder of the Order of Preachers." (Withycombe). Confusion with DOMIN(E)AUX etc. is possible.

Guppy traced Dominy in Dorset.

In Newfoundland:

Family tradition: William Dominey, from Ireland, settled at ? Bonavista in the 1830s (MUN Folklore).

Early instances: John Dominee, from Dorset, fisherman of Kelligrews, deceased 1811 (*Royal Gazette* 17 Oct 1811); John Domoney, of Bonavista, 1826 (DPHW 70); Daniel Dominques, of Long Island (near Belleoram), 1835 (DPHW 30); Eleanor Dominey, of Jersey Harbour, 1836 (DPHW 106); John Dominy, fisherman of Cape La Hune, 1842 (DPHW 101); John

Dominie, of Greenspond, 1950 (DPHW 76); John Domoney, of Musgravetown, 1871 (Lovell).

Modern status: Domin(e)y, in the Burgeo-La Poile district; Dominic, scattered; Dominick at Belleoram (*Electors* 1955); Dominie, especially at Little Bay (Fortune B.) (*Electors* 1955); Dominix, especially at Belleoram.

Place name: Dominie Rock 47-13 56-01.

DOMINO. *See* DOMIN(E)AUX

DONAHUE, a variant of the surnames of Ireland O'Donoghue, Donohoe, *Ó Donnchadha.* (MacLysaght).

Traced by MacLysaght originally in Co. Cork, later in Cos. Kerry, Galway and Cavan.

In Newfoundland:

Family tradition: ——, from Ireland settled at Joe Batt's Arm between 1811 and 1816 (MUN Hist.).

Early instances: Christopher ? Donahue, of St. John's, 1816 (CO 194.60); Mary Donoghue, of Harbour Grace Parish, 1822 (Nfld. Archives HGRC); Catherine Donohogue, from Hook (unidentified) (Co. Wexford), married at St. John's, 1829 (Nfld. Archives BRC); Jeremiah Donaheo, ? of Northern Bay, 1840 (DPHW 54); Michael Donaghoo, of Harbour Grace, 1870 (Nfld. Archives HGRC); Michael Donohue, planter of Joe Batt's Arm, 1871 (Lovell); Jeremiah and Michael, miners of Tilt Cove, 1871 (Lovell); Daniel Donahoe, farmer of Turk's Gut (now Marysvale), 1871 (Lovell).

Modern status: Scattered, especially at Joe Batt's Arm.

DONNELLY, a variant of the surname of Ireland (O)Donnelly, *Ó Donnghaile,* Ir. *donn* – brown, *gal* – valour. (MacLysaght).

Traced by MacLysaght in Co. Tyrone.

In Newfoundland:

Early instances: Martin Domilly, servant of Harbour Main, 1755 (MUN Hist.); Thomas Donnelly, ? labourer of St. John's, 1779 (CO 194.34); Timothy Donnolly, of St. Mary's Bay, 1804 (D'Alberti 14); Pat Donnelly, of Harbour Grace Parish, 1807 (Nfld. Archives HGRC); James, from Piltown (Co. Kilkenny), married at St. John's, 1830 (Nfld. Archives BRC); John Donnelly, captain of the *Earl Grey,* Spaniard's Bay, 1837 (*Newfoundlander* 2 Feb 1837); William, of Harbour Grace, 1857 (*Newfoundlander* 18 Jun 1857); John, master mariner of Carbonear, 1871 (Lovell).

Modern status: Scattered, especially at St. John's.

DONOVAN, a surname of Ireland (O)Donovan, *Ó Donnabháin*. (MacLysaght).

Traced by MacLysaght originally in Co. Limerick, later in Cos. Cork and Kilkenny.

In Newfoundland:

Early instances: Cornelius, of Harbour Main, 1756 (CO 199.18); Darby, fisherman of Quidi Vidi, 1794–5, "24 years in Newfoundland," that is, 1770–1 (Census 1794–5); David Donavon, of St. John's, 1780 (DPHW 26D); Daniel Donnovan, of Carbonear, 1800 (CO 199.18); Mary Donevan, from Cashel Parish (Co. Tipperary), married at St. John's, 1802 (Nfld. Archives BRC); Mary Donnevan, of Harbour Grace Parish, 1812 (Nfld. Archives HGRC); John Donnovan, from Ross (unspecified), Ireland, tin-man of St. John's, deceased 1814 (*Royal Gazette* 24 Mar 1814); Michael Donnovan, Dunevan or Durinivan, of Ragged Harbour (now Melrose), 1819 (Nfld. Archives KCRC); Michael Donnivan, of Joe Batts Arm, 1825 (Nfld. Archives KCRC); Michael, of New Harbour (Trinity B.), 1825 (Nfld. Archives KCRC); Andrew Donnivan or Dunivan, of Greenspond, 1826 (Nfld. Archives KCRC); Michael Donnivan, of Catalina, 1826 (Nfld. Archives KCRC); Andrew, from Cloyne (Co. Cork), married at Kings Cove, 1828 (Nfld. Archives KCRC); Daniel Donovan, of Harbour Grace, 1830 (Nfld. Archives HGRC); James, of Torbay, 1836 (Nfld. Archives BRC); Patrick, of Long Pond, 1843 (*Newfoundlander* 22 Jun 1843); Mrs., from Co. Cork, of Port de Grave, 1844 (*Indicator* 24 Aug 1844); Patrick, of Brigus, 1844 (*Indicator* 24 Aug 1844); Terence, of Broad Cove (now Duntara), 1857 (Nfld. Archives KCRC); Ellen, of Burnt Island (Bonavista B.), 1857 (Nfld. Archives KCRC); James, farmer of Cat's Cove (now Conception Harbour), 1871 (Lovell); Michael (and others), of Petty Harbour, 1871 (Lovell).

Modern status: Scattered, especially at Melrose and Petty Harbour Road.

Place name: Donovans 47-32 52-50.

DOODY, a synonym in Co. Kerry, of the surname of Ireland O'Down, *Ó Dubhda*, Ir. *dubh* – black. (MacLysaght).

In Newfoundland:

Family tradition: ——, from Ireland settled at Mosquito (Colinet Island), in the mid-19th century (MUN Folklore).

Early instances: James, of St. John's, 1804 (Nfld. Archives BRC); Thomas, of Harbour Grace Parish, 1809 (Nfld. Archives HGRC); Thomas, of Kings Cove, 1815 (Nfld. Archives KCRC); Catherine, married at Ragged Harbour (now Melrose), 1815 (Nfld. Archives KCRC); Michael, of Bonavista, 1820 (Nfld. Archives KCRC); Thomas, of Catalina, 1826 (Nfld. Archives KCRC); William, from Bay de Verde, married at Trinity (Trinity B.), 1826 (Nfld. Archives KCRC); John Doodey, fisherman of Bay of Islands, 1871 (Lovell); Thomas Doody, planter of Mall Bay, Mosquito and Mother Ixxes (now Regina) area, 1871 (Lovell); Michael, fisherman of Placentia, 1871 (Lovell); John, fisherman of Red Island (Placentia B.), 1871 (Lovell); David, farmer of Torbay, 1871 (Lovell).

Modern status: Scattered, especially at Mosquito (St. Mary's).

Place names: Doody Creek (Labrador) 53-49 57-34; —— Lake 53-50 57-40.

DOOLEY, a surname of England and Ireland; in England ? a variant of D'Oyley from the French place name Ouilly (Calvados); in Ireland (O)Dooley, *Ó Dubhlaoich*, Ir. *dubh* – black, *laoch* – hero, champion. (MacLysaght). *See also* DULEY.

Traced by Guppy in Cheshire, and by MacLysaght originally in Co. Westmeath, later in Co. Offaly.

In Newfoundland:

Early instances: John, carpenter of St. John's, 1794–5, "20 years in Newfoundland," that is, 1774–5 (Census 1794–5); Thomas Dooly, of Western Bay, 1781 (CO 199.18); John Dooley, of Carbonear, 1803 (CO 199.18); Ellena Dooly, of Harbour Grace Parish, 1809 (Nfld. Archives HGRC); Catherine, from Clogheen Parish (Co. Tipperary), married at St. John's, 1813 (Nfld. Archives BRC); Garret, of Harbour Grace, 1813 (Nfld. Archives BRC); Bridget, of Portugal Cove, 1816 (Nfld. Archives BRC); Margaret Dooley, of Catalina, 1822 (Nfld. Archives KCRC); James, of Ragged Harbour (now Melrose), 1823, of King's Cove, 1826, of Plate Cove (Bonavista B.), 1828, of Tickle Cove (Bonavista B.), 1830 (Nfld. Archives KCRC); John Dooly, of Sholes Cove (Bonavista B.), 1855 (Nfld. Archives KCRC); John Dooley, of Hayward's Cove (Bonavista B.), 1857 (Nfld. Archives KCRC); John, of Cottels Island (Bonavista B.), 1858, of Gooseberry Island (Bonavista B.), 1861 (Nfld. Archives KCRC); Patrick Dool(e)y, of Labrador, 1870 (Nfld. Archives HGRC); Patrick Dooley, farmer of Flatrock (St. John's), 1871 (Lovell); Mary, schoolteacher of Joe Batt's Arm, 1871 (Lovell).

Modern status: Scattered, especially at St. John's, Plate Cove and Sweet Bay.

·Place name: Dooley Ledge (Labrador) 53-32 55-44.

DOOLING, a surname of Ireland, the Munster variant of (O)Dowling, *Ó Dúnlaing*. (MacLysaght).

In Newfoundland:

Early instances: Robert, of St. John's, 1796 (CO 194.39); Robert, from Ross (unspecified) (Co. Wexford), married at St. John's, 1801 (Nfld. Archives BRC); Timothy Doolan, of Bay de Verde, 1804 (CO 199.18); Timothy Dooling, of Harbour Grace Parish, 1807 (Nfld. Archives HGRC); Thomas, from Crawkham (Somerset), fisherman of Trinity, deceased 1813 (*Royal Gazette* 17 Jun 1813); Elinor, of New Harbour (Trinity B.), 1817 (Nfld. Archives KCRC); Michael, of Harbour Grace, 1830 (Nfld. Archives HGRC); Mrs., of Forest Pond Gully (unidentified), 1831 (*Newfoundlander* 9 Jun 1831); Richard, planter of Cuckold's Cove (now Dunfield), 1832 (DPHW 64B); F. Doolan, merchant of Greenspond, deceased 1857 (*Newfoundlander* 9 Jul 1857); William Dooling, planter of Salmon Cove (now Champneys), 1871 (Lovell).

Modern status: Rare, in the St. John's districts.

Place names: Doolan Folly, —— —— Ground 49-35 55-35.

DORAN, a surname of Ireland (O)Dor(r)an, *Ó Deoráin*, earlier *Ó Deoradháin* – exile. (MacLysaght).

Traced by MacLysaght in Cos. Leix and Westmeath.

In Newfoundland:

Early instances: William, of Blackhead (St. John's), 1777 (DPHW 26C); Hugh, tailor of St. John's, 1794–5, "10 years in Newfoundland," that is, 1784–5 (Census 1794–5); Hugh, from Thomastown (Co. Kilkenny), married at St. John's, 1798 (Nfld. Archives BRC); Peter, of Harbour Grace Parish, 1824 (Nfld. Archives HGRC); Nicholas, of Kings Cove Parish, 1836 (Nfld. Archives KCRC); John, ? of Harbour Grace, 1845 (*Newfoundlander* 9 Jan 1845); Thomas, of Cape Pine, 1871 (Lovell); Thomas, of St. Mary's Bay, 1871 (Lovell); John and William, farmers of Outer Cove, 1871 (Lovell); Nicholas, fisherman of Ragged Harbour (now Melrose), 1871 (Lovell).

Modern status: Scattered.

DOREY, a surname of England and the Channel Islands, believed by Bardsley to be derived from an unidentified place name, or ? for the French surname Doré, a nickname for a goldsmith, or ? for one with golden hair. (Bardsley, Weekley *Surnames*, Dauzat, Turk). *See also* DOWER.

Traced by Guppy in Dorset.

In Newfoundland:

Early instances: John, of Black Island (Twillingate district), 1839 (DPHW 86); Lawrence, of Moreton's Harbour, 1842, of Black Island (Twillingate district), 1848 (DPHW 86); John, of Keels, 1856 (Nfld. Archives KCRC).

Modern status: Rare, especially at Kyer's Cove (Twillingate district) (*Electors* 1955).

DORMODY, a variant of the surnames of Ireland (O)DERMODY, Darmody, *Ó Diarmada*. (MacLysaght).

"A fairly numerous but scattered name mainly in Cos. Cavan, Westmeath, Kilkenny and Galway" (MacLysaght).

In Newfoundland:

Early instances: Richard Darmidy, from Balbarcken [sic] Parish (unidentified) (Co. Waterford), married at St. John's, 1812 (Nfld. Archives BRC); John Darmody, of Harbour Grace Parish, 1814 (Nfld. Archives HGRC); Michael Dormody, from Co. Kilkenny, married at Renews, 1841 (Dillon); Ellen Dormidy, of Cat Harbour (now Lumsden), 1850 (Nfld. Archives KCRC); John Darmody, of Harbour Grace, 1867 (Nfld. Archives HGRC).

Modern status: Rare and scattered.

DORSEY, a surname of England from the French place name Orsay (Seine-et-Oise), or ? a variant of the surname of Ireland (O)Dorcey, an alternative form of DARCY. (MacLysaght).

In Newfoundland:

Early instances: Patrick Dorcey, of Harbour Grace Parish, 1816 (Nfld. Archives HGRC); John Michael Dorsey, from Barat's Town (unidentified) (Co. Tipperary), late of St. John's, 1848 (*Newfoundlander* 16 Mar 1848).

Modern status: Rare, at Kilbride.

DOUCET, with a variant DOUCETTE, the usual Acadian spelling reflecting the Acadian pronunciation of the final consonant, surnames of France, diminutives of *doux, douce* – sweet (natured), or for *gousse, cosse* – pod, husk. (Dauzat).

In Newfoundland:

Family tradition: Gabriel Doucette, from Acadia, settled at Man o' War's Cove (Port-au-Port Peninsula), 1870 (MUN Folklore).

Early instance: Peter Doucette, fisherman of Indian Head (St. George's B.), 1871 (Lovell), same as Pierre Doucet of Margaree from whom all the Doucettes in the Port-au-Port area are descended. (G.R. Thomas).

Modern status: Doucet, rare; Doucette, scattered on the West Coast, especially in the Port-au-Port district.

DOUGLAS, a surname of England, Scotland and Ireland, from the Scots place name Douglas (Lanarkshire), Gaelic *dubh* – black, *glas* – water.

Traced by Guppy in Northumberland, Durham, Northamptonshire, and the Border counties; by MacLysaght in Ulster.

In Newfoundland:

Early instances: Pat Duglas, of St. John's, 1805 (Nfld. Archives BRC); Patrick Douglas, butcher of St. John's, 1806 (CO 194.45); Thomas, of Brunet Island, 1835 (DPHW 30); ——, of Savage Harbour, 1846 (*Newfoundlander* 26 Nov 1846); James, from Dumfriesshire, of St. John's, deceased 1854 (*Newfoundlander* 2 Nov 1854).

Modern status: At Brunette (*Electors* 1955), and in the Burin district.

Place names (not necessarily from the surname): Lake Douglas 48-28 56-41; The Douglas (Rock) 47-36 57-38; Douglas's Shoal 46-58 55-13.

DOVE, a surname of England, Scotland and Ireland; in England from an Old English personal name **Dūfe*, from *dūfe* – dove, for one gentle as a dove; in Scotland and Ireland, with Dow(e), from Gaelic *dubh* – black, or an anglicization of the surname MacCalman (*colm* – dove), or ? a variant of Daw, a diminutive of David. (Reaney, Black, MacLysaght). *See* DAVEY, DAWE.

Traced by Matthews in Devon and Dorset, and by MacLysaght in Ulster.

In Newfoundland:

Early instances: Charles Doves, of Harbour Grace, 1801 (USPG); William Dow, doctor of Harbour Grace, 1838 (DPHW 43); Howard Dove, fisherman of Salmon Cove (now Champneys), 1847 (DPHW 64B); James (1827–1908), from Darlington, England, for 52 years a Methodist minister in Newfoundland, that is, since 1856, of St. John's, 1857, died there 1908 (*Nfld. Almanac* 1857, General Protestant Cemetery, St. John's); James, of Lower Island Cove, 1860 (DPHW 55); William Dow, farmer of Flatrock (St. John's), 1871 (Lovell); Michael and Robert Dove, fishermen of Twillingate, 1871 (Lovell).

Modern status: Scattered, especially at Twillingate.

Place names (not necessarily from the surname): Dove Brook (Labrador), —— Point (Labrador) 53-39 57-26.

DOVER, a surname of England, from the English place name Dover (Kent).

Traced by Guppy in Buckinghamshire.

In Newfoundland:

Modern status: Rare, at St. John's.

Place name (not necessarily from the surname): Dover (formerly Wellington) 48-53 53-58.

DOWDEN, a surname of England and Ireland, ? from an unidentified place name, or ? a variant of DOWDING.

Traced in Hampshire.

In Newfoundland:

Early instances: Moses, of Bonavista, 1789 (DPHW 70); Moses, soldier of St. John's, 1798 (DPHW 26B); Thomas, cooper of Carbonear, 1831 (DPHW 48); John, of Greenspond, 1838 (DPHW 76); Thomas, of Brunette, 1839, of Jersey Harbour, 1851 (DPHW 109, 106); Jane, of Grand Bank, 1858 (DPHW 106); Thomas, fisherman of Chamberlains, 1871 (Lovell); Henry, fisherman of Pinchard's Island, 1871 (Lovell); William Sr. and Jr., fishermen of Seal Cove and Indian Pond (Harbour Main district), 1871 (Lovell).

Modern status: Scattered, especially at Seal Cove and St. John's.

Place name: Dowden Hole 47-34 54-51.

DOWDING, a surname of England, ? a diminutive of the baptismal name David (*See* DAVEY). (Weekley *Surnames*).

Traced by Guppy in Gloucestershire, Dorset, Wiltshire and Somerset.

In Newfoundland:

Family tradition: John, from ? Devon, settled at Gaultois, as an employee of Newman and Co. before 1848 (MUN Folklore).

Early instances: Josiah, of Harbour Breton, 1851 (DPHW 104); John, fisherman of Hermitage, 1856 (DPHW 102); Esau, fisherman of Isle Valen, 1871 (Lovell); Thomas, of Jersey Harbour, 1871 (Lovell).

Modern status: Scattered.

DOWER, a surname of Ireland, a variant of O'Dore, *Ó Doghair* or *de Hóir* (of Norman origin) in Co. Limerick, elsewhere ? from French Doré. *See* DOREY. (MacLysaght).

Traced by MacLysaght in Cos. Limerick, Kerry and Tipperary.

In Newfoundland:

Family traditions: ——, from Waterford, to Conception Bay and thence to Conche, 1830–40

(MUN Hist.). James (? 1780–1840), ? first settler at Conche (Casey).

Early instances: Michael, in possession of property and fisherman of St. John's, 1794–5, "32 years in Newfoundland," that is, 1762–3 (Census 1794–5); Edmund, of Fogo, 1782 (D'Alberti 2); Thomas, from Carrick-on-Suir (Co. Tipperary), married at St. John's, 1799 (Nfld. Archives BRC); William, one of 72 impressed men who sailed from Ireland to Newfoundland, ? 1811 (CO 194.51); Richard, of Harbour Grace Parish, 1816 (Nfld. Archives HGRC); Catherine, married on the French Shore, 1839 (Nfld. Archives BRC); Peter O'Dower, of Harbour Grace, 1866 (Nfld. Archives HGRC).

Modern status: Rare, especially at Conche.

Place name: Dowers Harbour 50-51 56-08.

DOWLAND, a surname of England and Ireland, from the English place name Dowland (Devon). (Bardsley, Ekwall).

Traced by Matthews as the name of a captain of Poole (Dorset), and by MacLysaght in Co. Limerick early in the 18th century.

In Newfoundland:

Early instances: John Dowlan, of Harbour Grace Parish, 1832 (Nfld. Archives HGRC); Samuel Dowland, house servant of Carbonear, 1837 (DPHW 48); Joseph, fisherman of Little Harbour (Twillingate), 1841 (DPHW 88).

Modern status: At Northern Arm (Gander district) (*Electors* 1955).

DOWN, DOWNS, surnames of England, Ireland and Scotland; in England from Old English *dūn* – (dweller by the) down(s), or from a personal name *Dūn*; in Scotland, Down ? from the Scots place name Doune (Perthshire); in Ireland, Downs ? from the Irish surname *Ó Dubháin*, from *dubh* – black. (Reaney, Black, MacLysaght).

Guppy traced Down in Devon and Somerset, Downs and Downes in Cheshire, Derbyshire, Shropshire and Yorkshire WR, remarking that Downes "is mostly found in Cheshire and Shropshire." MacLysaght traced Downes in Cos. Clare and Limerick.

In Newfoundland:

Early instances: William Downe, of Bonavista, 1681 (CO 1); John Down, of St. John's, 1759 (DPHW 26D); John Downs, ? of Placentia, 1795 (D'Alberti 5); Thomas, from Tintern (Co. Wexford), married at St. John's, 1809 (Nfld. Archives BRC); Thomas, of Kings Cove Parish, 1846 (Nfld. Archives KCRC); Charles, from London, England, preacher and

teacher of Sound Island (Placentia B.), of Sound Island, 1857, died at St. John's, 1888, aged 86 (*Nfld. Almanac* 1857, General Protestant Cemetery, St. John's); Thomas, of Torbay, 1871 (Lovell).

Modern status: Down, at St. John's and Grand Falls; Downs, at St. John's and St. Lawrence.

Place names: Downes Point 49-56 57-47; Downs Point 47-36 55-44.

DOWNER, a surname of England – dweller by the down. (Reaney).

In Newfoundland:

Family tradition: ――, from Aberdeen, settled at Fogo in the late 18th century (MUN Folklore).

Early instances: David, of Fogo, 1841 (DPHW 83); Moses, fisherman of Hare Bay (now Deep Bay) (Fogo district), 1871 (Lovell) .

Modern status: Scattered, especially in the Fogo district.

DOWNEY, a surname of Ireland, (O)Downey, *Ó Dūnadhaigh*, Ir. *dūn* – fort, or an abbreviated form of Muldowney and MacEldowney. (MacLysaght).

Traced by MacLysaght in Cos. Galway and Kerry.

In Newfoundland:

Early instances: Thomas Downy, ? labourer of St. John's, 1779 (CO 194.34); Margaret Downey, occupier of fishing room at Scilly Cove (now Winterton), Winter 1800–01 (Census Trinity B.); John Downy, from Knockaragashill [sic] (unidentified) (Co. Kerry), married at St. John's, 1810 (Nfld. Archives BRC); Margaret Down(e)y or Dounay, of Bonavista, 1816 (Nfld. Archives KCRC); John Downey, of Harbour Grace Parish, 1817 (Nfld. Archives HGRC); Ann, of Ragged Harbour (now Melrose), 1823 (Nfld. Archives KCRC); Ann Downy, of Catalina, 1829 (Nfld. Archives KCRC); Daniel Downey, of Tickle Cove (Bonavista B.), 1830 (Nfld. Archives KCRC); Edward Downy, of Turks Cove (Trinity B.), 1830 (Nfld. Archives KCRC); Ellen, of Burn Island (Bonavista B.), 1863 (Nfld. Archives KCRC); Daniel (and others) Downey, fishermen of Coachman's Cove, 1871 (Lovell); James (and others), of Codroy and Rivers, 1871 (Lovell).

Modern status: Widespread, especially at Coachman's Cove, Baie Verte, Winterton, St. John's, Great Codroy and other parts of the St. George's district.

Place name: Downey's Cove 49-59 56-22.

DOWNING, a surname of England and Ireland, in England from the Old English personal name

Dūning – son of *Dūn*, later confused with Dunning; in Ireland also a Co. Kerry variant of *Ó Duinnín*. (Reaney, MacLysaght).

Traced by Guppy in Suffolk and Cornwall, and by MacLysaght in Co. Kerry.

In Newfoundland:

Family tradition: Samuel, from Devon, settled at Harbour Grace, ? about 1813 (MUN Geog.).

Early instances: John, of St. John's, 1675, "30 years an inhabitant in 1680," that is, since 1650 (CO 1); Edward, of Silly Cove (now Winterton), 1830 (Nfld. Archives KCRC); Joseph, of Bonavista, 1833 (Nfld. Archives KCRC); Samuel, planter of Harbour Grace, 1837 (DPHW 43).

Modern status: At Corner Brook and St. John's.

Place names: Virginia Lake (St. John's) 47-37 52-42 formerly Downing's Pond (D.W. Prowse); Downings (cove in St. John's Harbour) (Visscher c. 1680).

DOWNS. *See* DOWN

DOWNTON, from the English place names Downton (Herefordshire, Shropshire, Wiltshire) or Dunton (Bedfordshire, Berkshire, Essex), or from Old English *dūn* and *tūn* – hill farm. (Reaney, Cottle).

Traced by Matthews as the name of a captain at Weymouth (Dorset).

In Newfoundland:

Family tradition: Edward, from England, settled as a teacher at Northern Harbour (Notre Dame B.) (MUN Folklore).

Early instances: Edward, of Change Islands, 1832 (DPHW 30); Edward, of Exploits Burnt Island, 1842 (DPHW 86).

Modern status: Scattered, especially in the Grand Falls, Gander and St. John's districts.

DOYLE, a surname of Ireland, (O)Doyle, *Ó Dubh-ghaill*, Ir. *dubh* – black, *gall* – foreigner, of Norse origin. (Reaney, MacLysaght).

MacLysaght describes (O)Doyle as one of the most numerous names in Leinster, especially in Co. Wexford.

In Newfoundland:

Early instances: William, inhabitant of Newfoundland, ? 1706 (CO 194.24); Richard, of St. John's, ? 1752 (CO 194.13); Martin, planter of Bay Bulls, 1753 (CO 194.13); John, in possession of property and shoreman of Torbay, 1794–5, "30 years in Newfoundland," that is, 1764–5 (Census 1794–5); Thomas, from Enniscorthy (Co. Wexford), married at St. John's, 1798 (Nfld. Archives BRC); Martin,

constable of St. Mary's Harbour, 1802 (D'Alberti 12); Thomas, of Carbonear, 1803 (CO 199.18); Philip, ? of Harbour Grace, 1806–7 (CO 194.46); Morgan, of Harbour Grace Parish, 1806 (Nfld. Archives HGRC); Anne, of Brigus, 1811 (Nfld. Archives BRC); James, of Trinity, 1816 (Nfld. Archives KCRC); ——, of Fortune Bay, 1818 (D'Alberti 28); Michael, of Hearts Content, 1819 (Nfld. Archives KCRC); William, of Ferryland, married at Tilton Harbour, (now Tilting), 1820 (Nfld. Archives KCRC); Patrick, native of Co. Wexford, of Portugal Cove, 1820 (*Nfld. Mercantile Journal* 4 May 1820); Thomas, of Kings Cove, 1821 (Nfld. Archives KCRC); Michael, of Ragged Harbour (now Melrose), 1824 (Nfld. Archives KCRC); Mary, of Grates Cove, 1828 (Nfld. Archives BRC); Sylvester, of Bonavista, 1828 (Nfld. Archives KCRC); Sylvester, of Fogo, 1829, of Herring Neck, 1829, of Twillingate, 1829, of Catalina, 1829, of Careless (now Kerleys) Harbour, 1829 (Nfld. Archives KCRC); Bridget, from Co. Kilkenny, married at Fortune Harbour, 1830 (Nfld. Archives KCRC); James, of Greenspond, 1831 (Nfld. Archives KCRC); James, of Coblers Island (Bonavista B.), 1832 (Nfld. Archives KCRC); James, of Placentia Bay, 1837 (Nfld. Archives BRC); Michael, ? of Northern Bay, 1838 (DPHW 54); Capt., from Co. Waterford, of Harbour Grace, 1844 (*Indicator* 27 Jul 1844); ——, of Turk's Cove (Trinity B.), 1845 (*Nfld. Quarterly* Dec 1911); E., of Petty Harbour, 1855 (*Newfoundlander* 29 Nov 1855); Catherine, of Knights Cove, 1870 (Nfld. Archives KCRC); widespread in Lovell 1871.

Modern status: Widespread, especially at Gull Island (Bay de Verde district), Avondale and St. John's.

Place names: Doyles 47-50 59-12, 47-27 52-46; —— Brook 47-42 53-12; —— Pond 47-25 53-10.

DRADDY, DREADDY, surnames of Ireland, the latter not in MacLysaght, (O)Draddy, *Ó Dreada*. (MacLysaght).

"Almost exclusively a Co. Cork name, but occasionally a synonym of Drudy, *Ó Draoda*, in Connacht." (MacLysaght).

In Newfoundland:

Family tradition: —— Dreaddy, from Ireland, settled at Fox Harbour (Placentia B.) about 1806 (MUN Hist.).

Early instance: Morris Dready, of Harbour Grace Parish, 1832 (Nfld. Archives HGRC).

Modern status: Draddy, at Windsor (*Electors* 1955); Dreaddy, at Fox Harbour.

DRAKE(S), surnames of England and Ireland, from Old English *draca* – dragon, serpent, water-monster, standard (bearer), or (one who lives at the sign of the) Dragon (inn), or, ? rarely, male duck. (Reaney, Cottle).

Guppy traced Drake in Devon, Dorset, Norfolk and Yorkshire WR, Drakes in Lincolnshire; MacLysaght traced Drake in Cos. Wexford and Meath.

In Newfoundland:

Early instances: Francis William Drake, of St. John's, 1750 (D'Alberti 10); Francis, of Carbonear, 1800 (CO 199.18); Thomas, fisherman of Twillingate, 1821 (USPG); Thomas, of Catalina, 1822 (DPHW 70); Thomas, of Harbour Grace Parish, 1831 (Nfld. Archives HGRC); John, of Long Island (Placentia B.), 1835 (DPHW 30); William, of Harbour Buffet, 1836 (DPHW 30); John, fisherman of Trouty, 1845 (DPHW 64B); ——, captain of the *Kingfisher* in the seal fishery out of Brigus, 1857 (*Newfoundlander* 16 Mar 1857); William, planter of Little Bay (Burin district), 1857 (DPHW 104); John, planter of Lally Cove, 1859 (DPHW 104); John, of Bay of Islands, 1871 (Lovell); Michael and Thomas, of Great St. Lawrence (now St. Lawrence), 1871 (Lovell); Thomas and William, of Haystack, 1871 (Lovell); Joseph, of Lamaline, 1871 (Lovell); Michael (and others), of Oderin, 1871 (Lovell); Josiah and Thomas Drakes, of Sagona, 1871 (Lovell); George, of St. Jacques, 1871 (Lovell).

Modern status: Drake, widespread on the South Coast; Drakes, scattered, especially in the Fortune Bay-Hermitage district.

Place names: Drake Cove 48-57 53-52; —— Island 47-39 56-13, 48-58 53-51; Drake's Island (Labrador) 54-11 57-22; —— Pond 47-32 53-12.

DRAY, a surname of England from ? Middle English *dreg, dregh, dr(e)y* – enduring, patient, doughty, fierce, or ? Old English *dryȳge* – thirsty (a nickname); or a variant of the surname of Ireland *Ó Draoi* (*See* DREA, DREW). (Reaney Notes, MacLysaght).

In Newfoundland:

Early instance: James Drey, of Little Bonah (Placentia B.), 1871 (Lovell).

Modern status: At Little Paradise, Oderin (*Electors* 1955) and St. John's.

DRAYTON, a surname of England, from the English place name Drayton widespread in the Midland and southern counties, or (dweller or worker at the) farm distinguished by a portage, slipway, sled-track or steep hill. (Cottle, Ekwall).

In Newfoundland:

Modern status: Unique, at St. John's.

DREA, a surname of Ireland (O)Drea which, with DREW, is an anglicized form of *Ó Draoi*, Ir. *draoi* – druid, if not of English origin. *See* DRAY, DREW. (MacLysaght).

In Newfoundland:

Early instance: James Drey, of Little Bonah (Placentia B.), 1871 (Lovell).

Modern status: At Gander (*Electors* 1955).

DREADDY. *See* DRADDY

DREDGE, DRODGE, DRUDGE, surnames of England – (a grower of) dredge, a mixture of various kinds of grain, especially of oats and barley, sown together. (Weekley *Surnames*, OED, EDD).

Dredge, the commonest form of the name is found throughout the southern and western counties; Guppy traced Drage in Northamptonshire and Drudge in Hampshire; Drodge is found in Wiltshire.

In Newfoundland:

Family tradition: William, or ? George Dredge was one of the first settlers at Black Duck Cove (St. Barbe district), before 1850 (MUN Hist.).

Early instances: John Drodge, of Bonavista, 1792 (USPG); John, of Grates Cove, 1832 (DPHW 58); George and Solomon, of Random Sound, 1871 (Lovell); William Drudge, of Black Duck Cove, 1873 (MUN Hist.).

Modern status: Dredge, at Black Duck Cove; Drodge, especially at Little Heart's Ease and St. John's; Drudge, at Grandes Oies (White Bay North district) (*Electors* 1955).

DREW, a surname of England, Ireland and Jersey (Channel Islands), and of the Micmacs of Newfoundland, from an Old German personal name *Drogo*, which became in Old French *Dreus, Drues* etc., ? from Old Saxon *(gi)drog* – ghost, phantom; or a diminutive of Andrew; or from Old French *dru* – sturdy, later lover, sweetheart. In Ireland, with (O)Drea, it is also an anglicization of the Irish surname *Ó Draoi*, Ir. *draoi* – druid. (Reaney, Cottle, MacLysaght, Turk). *See* DRAY.

Guppy traced Drew in Cornwall, Devon and Gloucestershire; MacLysaght in Co. Clare (and ? elsewhere).

In Newfoundland:

Early instances: Thomas Drue, boatkeeper of St. John's Harbour, 1682 (CO 1); John Drew, of St. John's Harbour, 1703 (CO 194.3); Mary, of Bay Bulls district, 1805 (Nfld. Archives BRC); Anne, of Pinchard's Island, 1813 (DPHW 76); Thomas, of Harbour Grace Parish, 1822 (Nfld. Archives HGRC);

James, of Bay Bulls, 1829 (Nfld. Archives BRC); John, from Berry Pomeroy (Devon), of St. John's, deceased 1832 (*Royal Gazette* 30 Oct 1832); Robert, of Cupids, 1871 (Lovell); Moses, of Goulds Road (Brigus district), 1871 (Lovell); William, Micmac of Conne River, 1872 (MacGregor).

Modern status: At Bay Bulls and Conne River.

Place name: Drew Rock 47-39 54-59.

(O)DRISCOLL, surnames of Ireland, *Ó hEidersceoil*, Ir. *eidirsceol* – intermediary, interpreter, later *Ó Drisceoil*. (MacLysaght, Cottle).

"The name is very numerous in Co. Cork but not elsewhere." (MacLysaght).

In Newfoundland:

Early instances: John Driscoll, fisherman of St. John's, 1794–5, "born in Newfoundland" (Census 1794–5); James, of Carbonear, 1800 (CO 199.18); Cornelius Driscol, of Harbour Main, 1801 (Nfld. Archives BRC); Daniel, of Toads (now Tors) Cove, 1805 (Nfld. Archives BRC); Elizabeth, of Harbour Grace Parish, 1806 (Nfld. Archives HGRC); Mary Driscol alias Byrne, from Co. Carlow, married at St. John's, 1808 (Nfld. Archives BRC); Lawrence Driscill, of Bay Bulls, 1814 (D'Alberti 24); Michael Driscoll, from Carrick (unspecified), Ireland, of Bonavista, 1817 (Nfld. Archives KCRC); Catherine, of Ragged Harbour (now Melrose), 1823 (Nfld. Archives KCRC); Michael, of Kings Cove, 1825 (Nfld. Archives KCRC); Michael, in possession of land at Bird Island Cove (now Elliston) before 1826 (Nfld. Archives Z66); Elizabeth, of Quidi Vidi, 1828 (Nfld. Archives BRC); Michael, of Plate Cove (Bonavista B.), 1828, of Open Hole (now Open Hall), 1830 (Nfld. Archives KCRC); Cornelius, of Bacon Cove (Conception B.), 1829 (Nfld. Archives BRC); Michael Driscol, ? of Northern Bay, 1838 (DPHW 54); William Driscoll, of Lower Island Cove, 1853 (DPHW 55); Jeremiah, of Harbour Grace, 1869 (Nfld. Archives HGRC); Michael, of Mobile, 1871 (Lovell); Robert Driscoll, of Russell's Cove (now New Melbourne), 1871 (Lovell).

Modern status: Driscoll, scattered, especially at St. John's and New Melbourne; O'Driscoll, scattered, especially at Tors Cove and Bay Bulls.

DRODGE. *See* DREDGE

DROHAN, a surname of Ireland (O)Dro(g)han, *Ó Druacháin*. (MacLysaght).

Traced by MacLysaght originally in Co. Cork, later in Cos. Waterford, Kilkenny and Wexford.

In Newfoundland:

Early instances: Michael, of Harbour Main, 1750 (CO 199.18); John Drohen, of Portugal Cove, 1794–5 (Census 1794–5); Ellen Drohan Hide, of Bay Bulls district, 1806 (Nfld. Archives BRC); John Druhan, of Harbour Grace Parish, 1813 (Nfld. Archives HGRC); Mary Drohan, from Gregg (unidentified) (Co. Kilkenny), married at St. John's, 1821 (Nfld. Archives BRC); Betsy, married at Tilton Harbour (now Tilting), 1823 (Nfld. Archives KCRC); Eliza Druhan, of Kings Cove Parish, 1837 (Nfld. Archives KCRC); Michael, fisherman of St. Mary's, 1871 (Lovell).

Modern status: In the St. Mary's district (*Electors* 1955).

DROVER, a surname of England, – a drover. (Reaney).

Traced by Matthews in Hampshire.

In Newfoundland:

Family tradition: William (1840–), born at Random Island, moved to Blaketown about 1865 (MUN Folklore).

Early instances: William, of [Upper] Island Cove, 1763 (CO 199.18); Thomas, of Harbour Grace Parish, 1822 (Nfld. Archives HGRC); Joseph, of Freshwater (Carbonear), 1854 (DPHW 49); Maria, of Harbour Grace, 1866 (Nfld. Archives HGRC); James, of Bishop's Cove (Conception B.), 1871 (Lovell).

Modern status: Widespread, especially at Upper Island Cove.

Place name: Drover's Gulch 49-43 54-16.

DROWN(S), surnames of England, from Middle English *droun* – drone (a nickname). (Spiegelhalter).

Spiegelhalter traced Drown(e) in Devon.

In Newfoundland:

Modern status: Drown, unique, at St. John's; Drowns, rare, at Bell Island.

DRUDGE. *See* DREDGE

DRUGGETT, ? an anglicization of the surname of France Droguet, from Fr. *drogue* – (seller of) drug(s), nostrum(s), or from the German personal name *Drogo* (*See* DREW). (Dauzat).

In Newfoundland:

Early instance: James Drugart, of Bonne Bay, 1862 (DPHW 93).

Modern status: At Lark Harbour (Humber West district) and St. John's.

DRUKEN, a variant of the surnames of Ireland (O)Droogan, Drugan, *Ó Druagáin*. (MacLysaght).

"An ancient Co. Armagh family...It is found as far west as Co. Leitrim but is nowhere numerous." (MacLysaght).

In Newfoundland:

Early instance: John Drogan, of Horse Cove (now St. Thomas), 1871 (Lovell).

Modern status: In St. John's and district, especially at St. Thomas.

DRYSDALE, a surname of Scotland, from the Scots place name Dryfesdale (Dumfriesshire), "popularly pronounced Drysdale." (Black).

Traced by Guppy in Fife, Stirlingshire and other central counties.

In Newfoundland:

Early instances: Andrew, of Harbour Grace, 1818 (*Nfld. Almanac* 1844); John, of St. John's, 1831 (DPHW 26D).

Modern status: Rare, at St. John's.

DUBIE, ? a variant of the surnames of France, Dub, Duba, Dube, an old Breton nickname – feather-legged pigeon. (Dauzat).

In Newfoundland:

The current pronunciation is Dubé.

Family tradition: The first settler came from Brittany (Thomas, "French Fam. Names").

Modern status: Rare, at Mainland (Port-au-Port district) (*Electors* 1955).

DUBOURDIEU, a surname of France, from a common French place name Bourdieu (Gironde, Haute-Vienne), *bourg [de] Dieu,* named after a religious house, or from *bourdieu, bordie,* from *borde* – farm. (Dauzat).

In Newfoundland:

Tradition: Summerest, of Freshwater, Conception Bay, settled at Port-au-Port as customs officer at the turn of the century. (G.R. Thomas).

Modern status: Rare, at Port-au-Port.

DUCEY, a surname of Ireland (O)Ducey, Doocey, *Ó Dubhghusa,* Ir. *dubh* – black, *gus* – action. (MacLysaght).

"An east Munster name." (MacLysaght).

In Newfoundland:

Early instances: Patrick, of Gooseberry Islands (Bonavista B.), 1774 (DPHW 64); John, of King's Cove, 1815, of Keels, 1823 (Nfld. Archives KCRC); Mary Ducy, of Open Hall, 1859 (Nfld. Archives KCRC).

Modern status: Scattered, especially at Marystown and Keels.

Place name: Ducie Rock 47-36 55-23.

DUDER, a surname of England, of unknown origin, ? from the Old English personal name *Dud(d)a.*

Traced in Kingskerswell (Devon). (Family).

In Newfoundland:

Family tradition: The Duder family, from Kingskerswell (Devon), settled in St. John's and operated a business in partnership with Muir at St. John's, Fogo and Twillingate about 1850 (MUN Hist.).

Early instances: ———, of St. John's, 1839 (*Newfoundlander* 18 Apr 1839); Edwin, of Greenspond, 1851 (DPHW 76); Thomas (about 1786–1855), from Kingskerswell (Devon), died at St. John's, 1855, aged 69 (General Protestant Cemetery, St. John's); John, of Twillingate, 1861 (DPHW 88); Charles (about 1819–1879), from St. Mary Church (Devon), died at St. John's, 1879, aged 60 (General Protestant Cemetery, St. John's).

Modern status: Rare, at St. John's and Grand Falls.

Place name: Duder Lake 49-18 54-41.

DUFF, a surname of Scotland and Ireland, Gaelic – Ir. *dubh* – black; and also in Ireland as a shortened form of Duffin in Co. Wexford, MacElduff in Co. Tyrone, and of DUFFY in several counties. (Black, MacLysaght).

Guppy found Duff widespread in Scotland, especially in Perthshire.

In Newfoundland:

Early instances: Archibald McDuff, of St. John's, 1799 (DPHW 26C); Mary Duff alias Doyle, from Island Parish (Co. Wexford), married at St. John's, 1810 (Nfld. Archives BRC); Arthur Duff, of Harbour Grace Parish, 1826 (Nfld. Archives HGRC); William (1842–), born at Bothkenna (Stirlingshire), of Harbour Grace and Carbonear, to Newfoundland before 1866 (Mott); Edward, from Co. Wexford, late of St. John's, 1858 (*Newfoundlander* 18 Jan 1858); John and Matthew, of North Arm, Holyrood, 1871 (Lovell).

Modern status: Especially at St. John's and district.

Place name: Duffs 47-27 53-07.

DUFFENAIS, DUFFNEY, surnames of Newfoundland, ? from the French surnames Dufresne, Dufresnoy etc., with loss of medial *r.* – (dweller in the) ashgrove, or from the many place names containing the element Fresne(s), Fresnay, Fresnois. (Dauzat).

In Newfoundland:

Early instances: Angus Dufney, of Redbrook (St. George's district), 1869 (DPHW 96); Frederick Duffney, of Flat Bay (St. George's district), 1871 (Lovell).

Modern status: Duffenais, at Winterhouse, Stephenville and West Bay (Port-au-Port); Duffney, especially at West Bay and Cormack.

DUFFETT, DUFFIT(T), surnames of England, from a nickname dove-head or dove-foot. (Reaney).

Traced in Dorset. (Family).

In Newfoundland:

Family tradition: ——, from Dorset, settled at Port de Grave about 1832 (MUN Folklore).

Early instances: Robert Duffett, ? servant of Oderin, about 1730–5 (CO 194.5); Hugh Duffet, of Trinity Bay, 1769 (DPHW 64); Thomas Duffit, of Bay de Verde, 1798 (DPHW 64); Mary Duffit or Duffet, of Harbour Grace Parish, 1810 (Nfld. Archives HGRC); Charles Duffet, of Catalina, 1811 (DPHW 64); Thomas, of Kings Cove Parish, 1847 (Nfld. Archives KCRC); —— Duffett, captain of the *Trial* in the seal fishery out of Harbour Grace, 1857 (*Newfoundlander* 19 Mar 1857); William Dufeet, of Ochre Pit Cove, 1871 (Lovell); Charles Duffett, of St. John's, 1871 (Lovell).

Modern status: Duffett, especially at St. John's and Britannia; Duffit, at Catalina; Duffitt, in the Trinity North district.

DUFFNEY. *See* DUFFENAIS

DUFFY, a surname of Ireland and Scotland, in Ireland (O)Duffy, *Ó Dubhthaigh*, Ir. *dubh* – black, in Scotland a variant of MacFee, of the same origin. (MacLysaght, Black). *See also* DOHEY and DUFF.

MacLysaght found (O)Duffy numerous in all provinces except Munster and the most numerous name in Co. Monaghan.

In Newfoundland:

Family tradition: A French pirate, Dupré, changed his name to Duffy to avoid a charge of murder and fled to Newfoundland; his descendants settled at Abrahams Cove (Port-au-Port district) (MUN Folklore).

Early instances: Philip, of Harbour Grace Parish, 1827 (Nfld. Archives HGRC); Thomas Duffey, of St. John's, 1829 (*Newfoundlander* 17 Sep 1829); Andrew Duffy, of Trinity Bay, 1835 (Nfld. Archives BRC); Margaret, of Kings Cove Parish, 1836 (Nfld. Archives KCRC); J., road commissioner for Distress (now St. Bride's), 1848 (*Nfld. Almanac*); Jacob, of

Harbour Grace, 1866 (Nfld. Archives HGRC); John, fisherman of Port-au-Port, 1871 (Lovell).

Modern status: Scattered, especially on the West Coast.

DUGGAN, a surname of Ireland and Scotland, in Ireland (O)Dug(g)an, *Ó Dubhagáin*, Ir. *dubh* – black, in Scotland Dugan or Dougan, of the same origin. (MacLysaght, Black).

Traced by MacLysaght in Cos. Cork, Galway and Mayo.

In Newfoundland:

Early instances: David, doctor of St. John's, 1794–5, "14 years in Newfoundland," that is, 1780–1 (Census 1794–5); Darby and Michael Duggin, of Harbour Grace, 1792 (CO 199.18); Daniel Duggan, proprietor and occupier of fishing room at Hants Harbour, Winter 1800–01 (Census Trinity B.); John, of Greenspond, 1805 (Bonavista Register 1806); Patrick Duggin, from Grange Parish (Co. Waterford), married at St. John's, 1806 (Nfld. Archives BRC); Anne Duggan alias Lean, married in the Northern District, 1814 (Nfld. Archives BRC); Patrick Duggan, of Ragged Harbour (now Melrose), 1815 (Nfld. Archives KCRC); William, of Hearts Content, 1819 (Nfld. Archives KCRC); John, of Riders Harbour, 1819 (Nfld. Archives KCRC); John, of Catalina, 1822 (Nfld. Archives KCRC); Pat Dugan, of Brigus, 1831 (Nfld. Archives BRC); William Duggin, of Hearts Desire, 1832 (Nfld. Archives KCRC); Catherine Duggan alias Aylward, of Ferryland, 1830 (Nfld. Archives BRC); John, ? of Northern Bay, 1842 (DPHW 54); John Duggan, of Bloody Bay (Bonavista B.), 1869 (Nfld. Archives KCRC); Patrick, of Bay of Islands, 1871 (Lovell); Thomas, of Chapels Cove, 1871 (Lovell); James, of Fermeuse, 1871 (Lovell); Daniel, of Grates Cove, 1871 (Lovell); Patrick and Thomas, of North Arm, Holyrood, 1871 (Lovell); Daniel, of La Scie, 1871 (Lovell).

Modern status: Scattered, especially at St. John's, Cape Broyle and St. Joseph's (St. Mary's district).

Place names: Duggan's Cove 50-23 56-25, Duggin's Tilt Cove 50-00 55-32.

DUHART, a surname of France, from the French place name Uhart (Basses-Pyrénées) – (one) from Uhart. (Dauzat).

In Newfoundland:

Modern status: At Corner Brook.

DUKE, a surname of England, Ireland and Scotland, from Middle English, Old French *duc* – leader, captain, often a nickname for one who was arrogant or served in a ducal household, sometimes, in Yorkshire, a shortened form of the baptismal name Marmaduke; in Scotland ? from an Old Danish or Old Norse personal name *Duk(r)*. (Reaney, Cottle, MacLysaght, Black).

Guppy found Duke widespread in southern England, especially in Sussex and Dorset, Spiegelhalter in Devon. MacLysaght found it mainly in northeast Ulster and to some extent in north Connacht.

In Newfoundland:

Family tradition: —— Duke, settled at Fox Harbour (Placentia B.) between 1836 and 1857 (MUN Hist.).

Early instances: Rev. J.A., of Burin, 1871 (Lovell); Rev. James, of Old Perlican, 1871 (Lovell); John, of Ram's Islands (Placentia B.), 1871 (Lovell).

Modern status: Scattered, especially at Fox Harbour.

DULEY, a surname of England and ? a Newfoundland variant of the surname of Ireland DOOLEY; in England from French *del, du* – from, and Old English *lēah* – clearing, – (the man) from the clearing. (Reaney).

In Newfoundland:

Early instance: Patrick Duly, of Harbour Grace Parish, 1843 (Nfld. Archives HGRC).

Modern status: At St. John's.

DUNCAN, a baptismal name and surname of Scotland, Ireland and England, from the Scots and Irish Gaelic personal name *Donnchadh* – brown warrior; in Ireland also a variant of (O)Donegan. (Reaney, Cottle, Black, MacLysaght, Withycombe).

Traced in the north of England and Somerset by Reaney and Cottle, in Devon by Spiegelhalter and mostly north of the Forth and Clyde by Guppy.

In Newfoundland:

Family tradition: Between 1785 and 1800, Lieut. Alexander Duncan, R.N. deserted his ship at Anchor Point (St. Barbe district) to marry Mary Watts and assumed his mother's maiden name GOULD to avoid detection (MUN Hist.).

Early instances: Thomas, from Kilcock (Co. Meath), Irish convict landed at Petty Harbour or Bay Bulls, 1789 (CO 194.38); James, of Catalina, 1832 (Nfld. Archives KCRC); James, of Ragged Harbour (now Melrose), 1834 (Nfld. Archives KCRC); John (1843–1914), son of John Duncan, shipbuilder from Kingston (Morayshire), Scotland, died at St. John's, 1914 (General Protestant Cemetery, St. John's).

Modern status: Rare, at St. John's.

Place names (not necessarily from the surname): Duncan Brook Point 48-57 57-52; —— Point (Labrador) 58-51 62-59; Duncan's Rock 48-57 57-52.

DUNFIELD, a surname of England, from the French place name Donville (Calvados). (Reaney).

In Newfoundland:

Modern status: Rare, at St. John's.

Place name: Dunfield (formerly Cuckold's Cove) 48-21 53-23.

DUNFORD, a surname of England and Ireland; in England ? from the English place names Dunsford (Devon) or Dunsforth (Yorkshire WR) or Durnford (Wiltshire, Somerset), whence DURNFORD with which confusion is possible; in Ireland a synonym of the surname (O)Donarty in Co. Wexford. (Ekwall, MacLysaght).

Dunford traced by Guppy in Dorset and by MacLysaght in Co. Waterford, Dunsford by Spiegelhalter in Devon.

In Newfoundland:

Family tradition: ——, ? from the north of England settled at Grand Bank (MUN Folklore).

Early instances: John, of Battle Harbour (Labrador), 1795 (MUN Hist.); Philip, from Ballyduff (Co. Waterford), married at St. John's, 1813 (Nfld. Archives BRC); Alice, of Harbour Grace Parish, 1822 (Nfld. Archives HGRC); Thomas, of Harbour Grace, 1828 (Nfld. Archives BRC); Robert, of Grand Bank, 1828 (DPHW 109); Thomas, of Rencontre, 1835 (DPHW 30); Robert, of Eastern Cul de Sac, 1835 (DPHW 30); Samuel, of Mosquito (Hermitage B.), 1835 (DPHW 30); Thomas, from Waterford, died at Harbour Grace, 1851, aged 60 years (*Weekly Herald* 4 Jun 1851); Herbert, fisherman of Burin, 1871 (Lovell).

Modern status: In the Burin district and St. John's.

DUNN(E), a surname of England, Ireland and Scotland; in England from an Old English personal name *Dun*, Old English *dunn* – dull brown, dark, swarthy; in Ireland (O)Dunne, *Ó Duinn* or *Ó Doinn*, Ir. *donn* – brown, "usually spelt with the final e"; in Scotland originally from Celtic *donn* – brown or from a Scots place name ? Dun (Angus). (Reaney, Cottle, MacLysaght, Black).

Guppy traced Dunn in ten counties, including especially Yorkshire, Durham, Northumberland, Warwickshire, Devon and Dorset and found it widespread south of the Forth and Clyde.

MacLysaght found (O)Dunn(e) "one of the most numerous names in the midland counties."

In Newfoundland:

Family traditions: —— Dunne from Co. Kilkenny settled at Renews (MUN Folklore). Denis, of Irish descent, born at Broad Cove (Conception B.) about 1857, settled at Fortune Harbour about 1880 (MUN Geog.). Joseph, was among the first permanent settlers at Hollett's Tickle (now part of Burnside) about 1895 (MUN Geog.).

Early instances: Stephen Dunn, inhabitant of Newfoundland 1704 (CO 194.3); Thomas, ? of Salmon Cove (Conception B.), ? 1752 (CO 194.13); William, of Bay Bulls, ? 1753 (CO 194.13); William, fisherman of St. John's, 1794–5, "20 years in Newfoundland," that is, 1774–5 (Census 1794–5); Dennis, of Broad Cove (Conception B.), 1776 (CO 199.18); Michael, in possession of property and cooper of Torbay, 1794–5, "10 years in Newfoundland," that is, 1784–5 (Census 1794–5); Thomas, of Cupids, 1791 (CO 199.18); Margaret, of Toads (now Tors) Cove, 1793 (Nfld. Archives BRC); Samuel, of Bonavista, 1801 (DPHW 70); Margaret, of Witless Bay, 1805 (Nfld. Archives BRC); Dennis, of Harbour Grace Parish, 1806 (Nfld. Archives HGRC); John, from Bahnakell Parish (Queens Co. now Co. Leix), married at St. John's, 1808 (Nfld. Archives BRC); Lawrence, one of 72 impressed men who sailed from Ireland to Newfoundland, ? 1811 (CO 194.51); Patrick, of Broad Cove (unspecified), 1820 (Nfld. Archives BRC); John, from Shangany (unidentified) (Co. Cork), married at Harbour Grace, 1829 (Nfld. Archives BRC); Edmund, from Waterford, married at Brigus, 1829 (Nfld. Archives BRC); Margaret, of Kings Cove Parish, 1837 (Nfld. Archives KCRC); Bryan, ? of Ferryland, 1838 (Newfoundlander 25 Oct 1838); Thomas, ? of Northern Bay, 1842 (DPHW 54); George, of Bears Cove (Harbour Grace), 1855 (DPHW 43); Michael, of Cats Cove (now Conception Harbour), 1871 (Lovell); Andrew, of Coachman's Cove, 1871 (Lovell); James, planter of Englee, 1871 (Lovell); Joseph, fisherman of Salvage, 1871 (Lovell); Andrew, miner of Tilt Cove, 1871 (Lovell).

Modern status: Dunn, scattered; Dunne, scattered, especially at St. John's.

Place names: Dunn Cove 47-40 54-20; —— Harbour, Island 55-13 58-58; —— Point 47-25 54-21; Dunns Brook 47-44 54-33; —— Pond 47-45 54-35.

DUNPHY, a surname of Ireland (O)Dunphy, Dunfy, Ó Donnchaidh. (MacLysaght).

Traced by MacLysaght in Co. Kilkenny.

In Newfoundland:

Early instances: John Dunfee, of St. John's, 1757 (DPHW 26C); John Dunphy, from Waterford, of Renews, 1775 (Waterford Arch. and Hist. Society J. per Kirwin); Andrew, cooper of St. John's, 1794–5, "10 years in Newfoundland," that is, 1784–5 (Census 1794–5); Mary, of Northern Bay, 1790 (CO 199.18); Edmund Dumphy, of Placentia, 1794 (D'Alberti 5); John Dunphy, of Trepassey, 1809 (Nfld. Archives BRC); Catherine, from St. Mary's Parish (Co. Tipperary), married at St. John's, 1810 (Nfld. Archives BRC); Darby, from Co. Kerry, of St. John's, deceased, 1810 (Royal Gazette 22 Nov 1810); James Dunf(e)y, of Harbour Grace Parish, 1810 (Nfld. Archives HGRC); John Dunphy, one of 72 impressed men who sailed from Ireland to Newfoundland, ? 1811 (CO 194.51); Martin Dunfy, of Bay Bulls, 1822 (D'Alberti 32); Philip Dunphy, of Ragged Harbour (now Melrose), 1825 (Nfld. Archives KCRC); Thomas, of Bonavista, 1828 (Nfld. Archives KCRC); Martin, of Catalina, 1830 (Nfld. Archives KCRC); Catherine, of Brigus, 1838 (Nfld. Archives BRC); Pierce, from Co. Kilkenny, of Harbour Grace, 1844 (Indicator 27 Jul 1844); John, of Mosquito (now Bristol's Hope), drowned 1857 (MUN Hist.); John, of Coachmans Cove, 1871 (Lovell); Michael, of Heart's Content, 1871 (Lovell); John, of Red Island (Placentia B.), 1871 (Lovell); Martin and William, of Salmonier (Placentia B.), 1871 (Lovell); James, of Southeast Bight (Placentia B.), 1871 (Lovell); Edmond (and others), of Torbay, 1871 (Lovell).

Modern status: Widespread, especially at St. John's.

Place names: Dunphy Head 47-30 55-46; Dunphy's Pond 48-28 54-07.

DURANT, a surname of England and Jersey (Channel Islands), Durand of Guernsey and commonly of France, from an Old French personal name Durant – obstinate, enduring. Cottle suggests that the name is of Huguenot or mediaeval stock. (Reaney, Cottle, Dauzat, Turk).

Guppy traced Durrant in Buckinghamshire, Dorset, Norfolk, Suffolk and Sussex; Spiegelhalter traced Durant in Devon.

In Newfoundland:

Early instances: J. Dur(r)and or Durant, planter of Grand Bank and Connaigre, 1710–15 (CO 194.5); William Durant, of Perlican (unspecified), 1811 (Nfld. Archives BRC); William, of King's Cove, 1815 (Nfld. Archives KCRC).

Modern status: Rare, at Clarenville (Electors 1955) and St. John's.

Place name: Durant Island 47-34 59-12.

DURDLE, a surname of England ? from the English place name Durdle Bay (Dorset), or ? a variant of TURTLE, by a not uncommon change of initial T to D as in such surnames as Turberville which becomes Durbyfield, Tunstall which becomes Dunstall, Theobald which becomes Dibble.

In Newfoundland:

Family tradition: Elias (about 1806–1894), ? from Devon, settled at Bonavista in 1829 (MUN Geog.).

Early instances: Joseph, of Trinity Bay, 1772 (DPHW 64); Robert Durdell, of Western Bay, 1796 (CO 199.18); Thomas Durdle, of Bonavista, 1796 (DPHW 70); John, of St. John's, 1802 (DPHW 26B); Samuel, fisherman of Carbonear, 1837 (DPHW 48); James, of Salvage, 1838 (DPHW 76).

Modern status: Especially at Bonavista.

Place name: Durdle Island 47-15 54-57.

DURNFORD, a surname of England, from the English place name Durnford (Wiltshire, Somerset). (Reaney, Spiegelhalter). *See also* DUNFORD.

Traced by Spiegelhalter in Devon.

In Newfoundland:

Family tradition: ——, from Devon settled at François about 1860–70 (MUN Hist.).

Early instances: Philip, of St. John's, 1817 (CO 194.59); Robert, fisherman of Transway [Fransway] (Fortune B.-Burin district), 1850 (DPHW 102); Richard and Robert, of François, 1871 (Lovell); Thomas Jr. and Sr., planters of Rencontre, 1871 (Lovell).

Modern status: In the Burgeo-La Poile district, especially at Francois.

DUSTAN, a surname of Scotland, not recorded by Black, ? a variant of the English surname Thurstan – Thor's stone, of Scandinavian origin.

In Newfoundland:

Family tradition: From Queen's Cottage, near Glasgow to Nova Scotia, thence to St. John's in 1948.

Modern status: Rare, at St. John's.

DUTOT, a surname of France, from the name of several hamlets in Normandy – (the man) from Tot, Scandinavian *toft* – hovel. (Dauzat).

In Newfoundland:

Modern status: Rare, at Channel-Port aux Basques and St. John's.

DUTREY, a variant of the surname of France Dutreil, Dutreuil – (the worker) of the winch of a wine or cider press. (Dauzat).

In Newfoundland:

Modern status: Rare, at Felix Cove (Port-au-Port district) (*Electors* 1955).

DUTTON, a surname of England from the English place names Dutton (Cheshire, Lancashire) or Dotton Farm (Devon). (Ekwall, Spiegelhalter).

Traced by Guppy in Cheshire and by Spiegelhalter in Devon.

In Newfoundland:

Early instances: Michael, in possession of land at Renews, 1779–1797 (D'Alberti 7); Nathaniel, of Ferryland, 1791 (USPG); Michael, of Ragged Harbour (now Melrose), 1825 (Nfld. Archives KCRC); Charles, of Trepassey, 1827 (Nfld. Archives BRC); Charles, of St. John's, 1857 (*Newfoundlander* 12 Feb 1857).

Modern status: Rare, at St. John's and Renews.

DUVAL, a surname of France and Guernsey (Channel Islands) – (the man) from the valley. (Dauzat, Turk).

Dauzat found Duval widespread; Matthews in the Channel Islands.

In Newfoundland:

Early instance: Charles, fisherman of Sandy Point (St. George's district), 1871 (Lovell).

Modern status: At Trout River (*Electors* 1955), Stephenville Crossing, and St. George's (Thomas, "French Fam. Names").

(O)DWYER, surnames of Ireland, *Ó Duibhir,* Ir. *dubh* and *odhar* (genitive *uidhir*) – dark or dun-coloured. (MacLysaght).

Traced by MacLysaght in Co. Tipperary.

In Newfoundland:

Family traditions: Some of the Dwyers of Tilting used to be called O'Dwyer (Widdowson). Alexander, of Cupids, ? 1833 (MUN Folklore).

Early instances: John Dwyer, of St. John's, 1759 (DPHW 26C); Martin, of Bell Island, 1794–5, "31 years in Newfoundland," that is, 1763–4 (Census 1794–5); John, of Trinity Bay, 1766 (DPHW 64); Michael, of Western Bay, 1771 (CO 199.18); Denis, fisherman of Quidi Vidi, 1794–5, "20 years in Newfoundland," that is, 1774–5 (Census 1794–5); John, agent of Renews, 1780 (D'Alberti 6); Patience, of Port de Grave, 1798 (CO 199.18); John, of Trinity (Trinity B.), Winter 1800–01 (Census Trinity B.); Philip and Co., of Kelligrews, 1801 (CO 199.18); Michael, from the parish of Patrick Street (Co. Kilkenny), married at St. John's, 1806 (Nfld. Archives BRC); Winny, of Harbour Grace Parish,

1807 (Nfld. Archives HGRC); John Dwire, of Tilting Harbour (now Tilting), 1812 (Nfld. Archives BRC); Timothy Dwyer, of Fogo, 1815 (Nfld. Archives KCRC); Thomas, of Bonavista, 1816 (Nfld. Archives KCRC); James, of Greenspond, 1823 (Nfld. Archives KCRC); Justin, of Harbour Grace, 1830 (Nfld. Archives HGRC); Jane Dwire, of Moreton's Harbour, 1830 (Nfld. Archives KCRC); Thomas Dwyer, of Catalina, 1833 (Nfld. Archives KCRC); O'Dwyer and Co., of St. John's, 1837 (*Newfoundlander* 9 Nov 1837); Michael Dwyer, planter of Broad Cove (Bay de Verde district), 1839 (DPHW 52A); James, ? of Northern Bay, 1839 (DPHW 54); John Dwire, fisherman of Otterbury (Carbonear), 1848 (DPHW 48); Patrick Dwyer, of Herring Neck, 1851 (DPHW 85); John Dwyre, of Broad Cove (now Duntara), 1863 (Nfld. Archives KCRC); Dwyer, widespread in Lovell 1871; John (and others) O'Dwyer, of St. John's, 1871 (Lovell).

Modern status: Dwyer, widespread, especially at Bell Island (*Electors* 1955), Tilting and St. John's; O'Dwyer, rare, at St. John's.

Place names: Dwyer Hole 47-47 55-48; The O'Dwyer (Hill) 49-07 58-23.

DYER, a surname of England, Ireland, Scotland and of Guernsey (Channel Islands); in all four from Old English *dēagere* – dyer, in Ireland also for Mac D(w)yer, *Mac Duibhir*, cognate with Diver. (Reaney, MacLysaght, Black, Turk).

Traced by Guppy in Cornwall, Devon, Somerset and Suffolk; by MacLysaght in Cos. Sligo and Roscommon.

In Newfoundland:

Early instances: Philip, of St. John's, 1705 (CO 194.22); John, of Torbay, 1708–09 (CO 194.4); John, of Colliers, 1798 (CO 199.18); Michael, from Inistioge (Co. Kilkenny), married at St. John's, 1813 (Nfld. Archives BRC); Mary, of Vere (now Fair) Island, 1812 (DPHW 76); William, of Harbour Grace, 1828 (Nfld. Archives BRC); William, ? of Bonavista,

1844 (*Nfld. Almanac*); Robert William, of Greenspond, 1846 (DPHW 76); Michael (and others), of Logy Bay, 1871 (Lovell); Mary Ann, of King's Cove, 1878 (Nfld. Archives KCRC).

Modern status: Scattered, in the St. John's and White Bay South districts.

DYETT, a surname of England, a diminutive of Dye, a pet-form of the baptismal name *Dionysia* later Denise. *See* DENNIS. (Reaney, Withycombe).

Spiegelhalter traced Dyte (? a variant of Dyett) in Devon.

In Newfoundland:

Modern status: Rare, at St. Jacques (*Electors* 1955) and St. John's.

DYKE, a surname of England, Dykes of Scotland – (dweller by the) ditch or dyke.

Dyke traced by Guppy in Somerset and South Wales, Dykes in Lanarkshire.

In Newfoundland:

Family tradition: Edward, from Poole (Dorset) settled at Pool's Island about 1827; the family moved later to Badger's Quay (MUN Folklore).

Early instances: George, of Greenspond, born ? 1767 (DPHW 76); Richard, of Bonavista, 1791 (DPHW 70); Richard, of St. John's, 1811 (D'Alberti 21); James, of Cape Cove (Bonavista B.), 1816 (DPHW 76); John, of Salvage, 1830 (DPHW 76); Philip, of Isle aux Morts, 1840 (DPHW 101); Charles, of Red Cliff (Bonavista B.), 1841 (DPHW 73A); Tabitha, of Pouch Island (Bonavista B.), 1863 (DPHW 79).

Modern status: Widespread, especially in the Bonavista North and South districts with a large concentration at Eastport and at St. John's.

Place names: Dyke Lake (Labrador) 54-30 66-18; Dykes River (Labrador) 53-38 57-04; —— Island 49-07 53-35.

DYMOND. *See* DIAMOND

E

EADIE, a surname of Scotland and Ireland, one of several diminutives of the baptismal name Adam. *See* ADAMS, EDDY (Black, MacLysaght).

In Newfoundland:

Early instance: James, of Braco (Perthshire), married at St. John's, 1854 (*Newfoundlander* 20 Jul 1854).

Modern status: Unique, at St. John's (*Electors* 1955).

EADY, a surname of England, a pet-form of such Old English personal names as *Ēadgȳth*, *Ēadwīg* etc. (Spiegelhalter). *See also* ADE, ADEY, EDDY, EDISON.

Traced by Spiegelhalter in Devon.

In Newfoundland:

Early instances: Isaac Eadey, planter of Hants Harbour, 1830 (DPHW 59A); John Eady, of Catalina, 1848 (DPHW 67); William, fisherman of Bay de Verde, 1871 (Lovell).

Modern status: Rare, at St. John's and Bay de Verde.

E(A)GAN, variants of the surname of Ireland (Mac) Egan, *Mac Aodhagáin* – son of Egan. "The prefix Mac is now seldom retained with this name." (MacLysaght).

Traced by MacLysaght in Cos. Galway and Tipperary.

In Newfoundland:

Early instances: E. and D. Eagan, proprietors and occupiers of fishing room at Hants Harbour, Winter 1800–01 (Census Trinity B.); Edward, proprietor of fishing room at Grates Cove, Winter 1800–01 (Census Trinity B.); Denis Egan or Egen, of Harbour Grace Parish, 1808 (Nfld. Archives HGRC); Dennis Eagan, of Trinity (Trinity B.), 1812 (DPHW 64); Michael, ? of St. John's, 1816 (CO 194.66); Mary Egan, from Waterford City, married at St. John's, 1817 (Nfld. Archives BRC); Eleaner, of Hearts Content, 1819 (Nfld. Archives BRC); Edward, of Twillingate, 1822 (Nfld. Archives KCRC); Allice, of Keels, 1831 (Nfld. Archives KCRC); William Eagan, from Co. Tipperary, of Brigus, 1844 (*Indicator* 24 Aug 1844); James Eagen, of Tickle Cove (Bonavista B.), 1854 (Nfld. Archives KCRC); Catherine, of Broad Cove (now Duntara), 1856 (Nfld. Archives KCRC); James Egan, ? of King's Cove, 1857 (*Nfld.*

Almanac); James, of Plate Cove (Bonavista B.), 1867 (Nfld. Archives KCRC); Patrick Eagen, of Great Paradise, 1871 (Lovell).

Modern status: Eagan, at Trinity (*Electors* 1955) and St. John's; Egan, unique, at St. John's (*Electors* 1955).

EAGAR, a surname of England and Ireland, from the Old English personal name *Ēadgār* – prosperity-spear, a variant of EDGAR.

Spiegelhalter traced Eager, Eagger in Devon; MacLysaght traced Eagar in Co. Kerry, Eager in Cos. Louth and Down, Agar in Co. Kilkenny.

In Newfoundland:

Early instance: William, of St. John's, 1819 (DPHW 26D).

Modern status: At St. John's.

EALES, ? a variant of the surname ELLIS.

Traced by Matthews in Devon.

In Newfoundland:

Early instances: John, of St. John's, 1752 (DPHW 26C); Diana Eels, of Western Bay, 1788 (CO 199.18); John Eales, of Adam's Cove, 1829 (DPHW 52A); John, tailor of Carbonear, 1830 (DPHW 48); John, from St. Mary Church (Devon), died 1877, aged 84 (General Protestant Cemetery, St. John's).

Modern status: At St. John's.

EARL(E), EARLES, surnames of England and Ireland, from Old English *eorl* – earl (the only rank in the peerage from an Old English word), from service in an earl's household, or from playing the part in a pageant, or as a nickname for one who bore himself proudly like an earl. (Reaney, Cottle).

Guppy traced Earl(e) in Devon; MacLysaght traced Earls in Co. Galway since the 13th century, Earle, of much later introduction, is not closely associated with any particular area.

In Newfoundland:

Early instances: William Earl, of Juggler's Cove (Bay Roberts), 1782, property "in possession of the Family for upwards of 120 years," that is, before 1662 (CO 199.18); William, of Ferryland, 1676 (CO 1); Phillip Earles, of Fermeuse, 1681 (CO 1); John Earle, of Little Bell Island, defended his property against the French in 1696–7 (D.W. Prowse); John, planter of St. John's, 1701 (CO 194.2); John, of Portugal Cove, 1708–9 (CO 194.4); Abigail Earl(e) or Erl, of Harbour Grace Parish, 1809 (Nfld. Archives HGRC); Elias Earl, of Carbonear, 1810 (DPHW 48); Elenor, from Taghmon Parish (Co. Wexford), married at St. John's, 1824 (Nfld. Archives BRC); Elias Earle, of Cat Harbour (now Lumsden), 1833, of Moreton's Harbour, 1840 (DPHW 76, 86); William, of Petty Harbour, 1845 (DPHW 31); John Earl(e), of New Bay Head (Twillingate), 1848 (DPHW 86); William H. Earle, of Spaniards Bay, 1855 (*Newfoundlander* 16 Jan 1855); John, of Leading Tickles, 1856 (DPHW 86); Richard, of Cupids, 1871 (Lovell); Samuel, of Heart's Content, 1871 (Lovell); Solomon, of Port de Grave, 1871 (Lovell); Alonzo, of Trinity (Trinity B.), 1871 (Lovell); Elias (and others), of Twillingate, 1871 (Lovell).

Modern status: Earl, scattered, in the Humber West district (*Electors* 1955); Earle, widespread, especially at St. John's, Carbonear and Shearstown; Earles, at St. John's.

Place name: Earl Island (Labrador) 53-41 57-07.

EARLY, a surname of England and Ireland; in England from the English place names Earley (Oxfordshire, Berkshire), Arley (Cheshire, Lancashire, Warwickshire, Worcestershire), Early (Sussex), or (dweller in or by the) eagle-wood or ploughing-field, or occasionally from Old English *eorlīc* – manly; in Ireland, an anglicization of *Ó Maolmhoicheirge*, Ir. *mocheirghe* – early rising, or a synonym of Loughran. (Reaney, Cottle, Spiegelhalter, MacLysaght).

Spiegelhalter traced Earley in Devon; MacLysaght traced Early in Cos. Cavan and Leitrim.

In Newfoundland:
Early instances: William, planter of Trinity (Trinity B.), 1821, of Trouty, 1825 (DPHW 64, 64B); Catherine, of Kings Cove Parish, 1836 (Nfld. Archives KCRC); Thomas, of British Harbour, 1871 (Lovell); George (and others), of Herring Neck, 1871 (Lovell).

Modern status: Rare, at St. John's (*Electors* 1955).

EASON, a surname of England, Scotland and Ireland; in England ? a variant of EASTON; in Scotland – son of Adam (*See* ADAMS); in Ireland, of Scots origin or an anglicization of *Mac Aoidh*. (Spiegelhalter, Reaney, Black, MacLysaght).

Traced by Spiegelhalter in Devon and by Black in Angus.

In Newfoundland:
Family tradition: The Easons of Long Pond and Manuels are believed to have come to Newfoundland from Norway (MUN Folklore).

Early instances: William, of Long Pond, 1832 (DPHW 30); Thomas, of Ragged Harbour (now Pinsent) (Fogo district), 1840 (DPHW 83); William, of Hare (now Deep) Bay (Fogo), 1871 (Lovell).

Modern status: Scattered, especially at Long Pond and Manuels.

EASTERBROOK, a surname of England – (one who lives to the) east of the brook, or from the English place names Eastbrook and Easterbrook (Devon). (Reaney, Spiegelhalter, Gover).

Guppy traced Easterbrook, E(a)stabrook in Devon.

In Newfoundland:
Family tradition: John, blacksmith of Petty Harbour, settled at Pouch Cove in 1860 (MUN Hist.).

Early instances: Francis Esterbrook, ? of St. John's, 1730 (CO 194.9); James Easterbrook, from Devon, married at Petty Harbour, 1834 (DPHW 31).

Modern status: At Pouch Cove and St. John's.

EASTMAN, a surname of England from the Old English personal name *Ēastmund* – a compound of *e(a)st* – grace, beauty, favour and *mund* – protection, whence the baptismal name Esmond. (Reaney, Withycombe, Cottle).

Spiegelhalter traced Eastman and Eastmond in Devon.

In Newfoundland:
Early instances: Robert, from Yeovil (Somerset), settled at Harbour Breton, about 1822 and was resident of Grandys Passage in 1849 (Feild); Robert Eastmont, of Burnt Island (Burgeo-La Poile district), 1842 (DPHW 101); George Eastman, of Thoroughfare, 1852, of Ireland's Eye, 1855 (DPHW 64B); Richard Eastmont, of Pinchard's Island, 1856, of Cat Harbour (now Lumsden), 1859 (DPHW 75, 76); Francis, of Port au Choix, 1871 (Lovell); Michael, seaman of St. John's, 1871 (Lovell).

Modern status: Scattered.

EASTON, a surname of England and Scotland; in England from the English place name Easton in several counties, or (dweller at the) eastern farm or on or to the east of the village, or from an Old English personal name *Ēadstān* – prosperity-stone; in Scotland ? from the Scots place name Easton (Peeblesshire, West Lothian). (Reaney, Cottle, Ekwall, Black).

Traced by Spiegelhalter in Devon.

In Newfoundland:

Early instances: J., of Twillingate, 1768 (MUN Hist.); William, of St. John's, about 1780–84 (CO 194.35); Thomas Eas(t)on, of Barr'd Islands, 1821 (USPG); John Easton, of Bonavista, 1833 (DPHW 70); Thomas, of Brooklyn, 1871 (Lovell).

Modern status: Scattered.

EATON, a surname of England and Ireland from a common English place name, "around thirty in fifteen counties" (Cottle), "about forty ... but none in Devon" (Spiegelhalter), mainly from either Old English *Ēa-tūn* – farm on a river or *Ēg-tūn* – farm on an island or on land by a river. (Cottle, Spiegelhalter, Ekwall).

Traced by Guppy in Cheshire, Derbyshire, Leicestershire, Rutlandshire and Worcestershire and by Spiegelhalter in Devon, and by MacLysaght in Ulster and Leinster.

In Newfoundland:

Family tradition: ——, from Dorset, settled at St. John's (MUN Folklore).

Early instances: Nicholas Eton, fisherman of Bay of Exploits, ? 1797 (CO 194.39); William, fisherman of Cape Fogo, 1871 (Lovell).

Modern status: At Fogo (*Electors* 1955) and St. John's.

Place name: Eaton Point 49-26 56-08.

EAVIS, a surname of England, from Old English *efes* – (dweller by the) border or edge (of a wood or hill). *See also* REEVES. (Reaney).

Guppy traced Eaves in Lancashire.

In Newfoundland:

Modern status: At Ramea and St. John's.

EBBS, ? with a variant Epps, surnames of England, pet-forms of the baptismal names Isabel and Herbert. (Withycombe, Reaney, Bardsley).

Matthews traced Eppes in Dorset.

In Newfoundland:

Early instances: William Isham Eppes, merchant of St. John's, 1793 (D'Alberti 6); Thomas Ebbs, of Chamberlains, 1827 (DPHW 268); Margaret, of Torbay, 1844 (DPHW 32).

Modern status: Ebbs, rare, at Topsail and St. John's.

EBSARY, a surname of England, from the English place name Ebsworthy (Devon).

Traced by Spiegelhalter in Devon.

In Newfoundland:

Early instance: John, of St. John's, 1826 (Dispatches 1825–26).

Modern status: At St. John's and Long Pond (Manuels).

EDDY, a surname of England and Scotland, in England from the Old English personal name *Ēadwīg* – prosperity-war, in Scotland a variant of EADIE. *See also* EADY, ADAMS, ADE, ADEY. (Reaney, Black).

Traced by Guppy in Cornwall and by Spiegelhalter in Devon.

In Newfoundland:

Family tradition: —— Adey, from Bristol settled first at Hants Harbour, then at Hickman's Harbour; the surname changed from Adey to Eddy (MUN Folklore, MUN Hist.).

Early instances: Martin, of Trinity (Trinity B.), 1757 (DPHW 64); Stephen, of Bay de Verde, 1782 (CO 199.18); Anne, of Harbour Grace Parish, 1808 (Nfld. Archives HGRC); Isaac Edey, planter of Hants Harbour, 1823 (DPHW 58); Samuel Eddy, of Sound Island, 1851 (DPHW 105); Reuben, of Shoal Harbour, 1856, of Random Arm, Holyrood, 1871 (Lovell).

Modern status: Scattered, especially at Little Catalina, North Harbour (Placentia B.) and Sibleys Cove.

Place names (not necessarily from the surname): Eddies or Eddys Cove 51-25 56-27; Eddies Cove 50-45 57-11; —— —— West 50-45 57-10; Eddy Cliff (Labrador) 56-55 61-31; —— Point 47-20 54-35.

EDENS, a surname of England from the Old English personal name *Ēadhūn* or from the English place names Castle Eden or Eden Burn (Durham). (Reaney).

Guppy traced Eden in Cheshire.

In Newfoundland:

Early instances: Thomas, son of John, merchant of Northampton, of St. John's, 1817, deceased 1829 (DPHW 26D, *Newfoundlander* 5 Mar 1829, *Royal Gazette* 3 Mar 1829); Mrs., ? of Trepassey, 1856 (*Newfoundlander* 29 Sep 1856).

Modern status: Rare, at Corner Brook.

EDGAR, a surname of England, Scotland and Ireland from the Old English personal name *Ēadgār* – prosperity-spear. (Reaney). *See* EAGAR.

Traced by Spiegelhalter in Devon, by Guppy in Dumfriesshire, and by MacLysaght in Ulster.

In Newfoundland:

Early instances: John, magistrate of Greenspond, 1810 (D'Alberti 20); Joseph, clerk of St. John's, 1871 (Lovell).

Modern status: At Canada Harbour (*Electors* 1955).

EDGECOMBE, a surname of England from the English place name Edgcumbe (Devon). (Spiegelhalter).

Traced by Guppy in Cornwall and Devon.

In Newfoundland:

Early instances: John, of Ochre Pit Cove, died 1821 (Devine and O'Mara); Thomas Edgecomb, planter of Bradleys Cove, 1837 (DPHW 52A); John, of Catalina, 1865 (DPHW 66); Elie, of Harbour Grace, 1871 (Lovell).

Modern status: At Ochre Pit Cove (*Electors* 1955), Little Catalina, St. John's and Port Union.

EDISON, a surname of England, – son of *Ead* or *Edd*. (Reaney). *See* EADY, HEDDERSON.

Guppy traced Eddison in Nottinghamshire.

In Newfoundland:

Family tradition: ——, of Cupids, inhabitant of Hay Cove, 1876; the family later moved to Northern Arm, Botwood; the family traces a name change from Heddrison to Heddison to Eddison to Edison (MUN Folklore).

Early instance: George, sailor of Harbour Grace, 1871 (Lovell).

Modern status: Especially at Botwood and in the White Bay North district.

EDMONDS, EDMUNDS, surnames of England and Wales, Edmonds of Guernsey (Channel Islands), from the Old English personal name *Ēadmund* – prosperity-protector. Edmund gained early currency as a baptismal name after three kings and two saints. (Reaney, Cottle, Turk).

Guppy traced Edmunds and Edmonds in Buckinghamshire, Devon, Gloucestershire, South Wales and Monmouthshire, Norfolk, Northamptonshire, Oxfordshire and Worcestershire, noting that Edmunds is the common form in South Wales and Monmouthshire.

In Newfoundland:

Early instances: Harry Edmonds, of Bonavista, 1786 (DPHW 70); Nicholas Edmund, from Co. Wexford, married at St. John's, 1824 (Nfld. Archives BRC); James Edmunds, born at Petty Harbour, 1843 (DPHW 113); Charles Edmonds, from Lymington (Hampshire), married at Twillingate, 1846 (*Newfoundlander* 21 May 1846); William Edmonds, married at Fortune, 1848 (DPHW 106, P.E.L. Smith); Emily Edmunds, of Catalina, 1856 (DPHW 67); Thomas, of Eastern Point (Burgeo-La

Poile district), 1860 (DPHW 99); John and Richard Edmonds, of Newman's Cove (Bonavista B.), 1871 (Lovell); William Edmunds, of La Plante (Burgeo-La Poile district), 1871 (Lovell).

Modern status: Edmonds, especially at Newman's Cove (*Electors* 1955); Edmunds, scattered.

EDNEY, a surname of England from the female baptismal name Idonea on which Withycombe comments: "this is a puzzling name, but it seems that it is related to the Old Norse *Idhuna*, the name of a goddess of spring, derived from the Old Norse *idh* – work, labour. It can scarcely be (what it looks like) the Latin adjective *idonea* from *idoneus* – suitable ..." (Withycombe, Reaney at Iddon).

Traced by Guppy in Hampshire.

In Newfoundland:

Early instance: Samuel, mason of St. John's, 1871 (Lovell).

Modern status: At St. John's and Goulds (St. John's).

EDSTROM, a surname of Norway and Sweden – (dweller by the) heath stream. (E.C. Smith).

In Newfoundland:

Family tradition: ——, from Norway settled at Cape Race about 1850; thence to Blackhead, Renews and St. John's (MUN Folklore).

Early instances: Henry, of St. John's, 1832 (DPHW 26D); Henry Eadstrom (and others), of Blackhead (St. John's), 1871 (Lovell).

Modern status: At St. John's.

EDWARDS, a surname of England, Scotland, Ireland and Wales, from the Old English personal name *Ēadweard* – prosperity-guard. (Withycombe, Reaney, Cottle).

Traced by Guppy especially in North and South Wales, Monmouthshire, Shropshire and Herefordshire, Edward(s) north of the Forth and Clyde; and by MacLysaght in Co. Kilkenny.

In Newfoundland:

Early instances: John, of Carbonear, 1675 (CO 1); Henery, of Harbour Grace, 1708–9 (CO 194.4); John, of Greenspond, 1776 (CO 194.33); Maurice, of St. John's, 1780 (D'Alberti 6); Francis, of Placentia, 1803 (D'Alberti 13); George, planter of Change Islands, 1821 (USPG); William, planter of Santamorant (Carbonear district), 1821 (DPHW 48); Benjamin Edward, of Western Bay, 1829 (DPHW 52A); John Edwards, of Lamaline, 1829 (DPHW 109); Charlotte Edward, of Trinity, 1832 (Nfld. Archives KCRC); John Edward(s), planter of Cupids, 1835 (DPHW 34); James, of Logy Bay, 1849 (*Newfoundlander* 15 Feb 1849); John, planter of Crocker's Cove (Carbonear), 1852 (DPHW 49); John, of Gander Bay, 1854 (DPHW 83); Samuel, of Catalina, 1858 (DPHW 67); John, of Rose Blanche, 1860 (DPHW 99); James, of Goulds Road (Brigus district), 1871 (Lovell); Charles (and others), of Lawn, 1871 (Lovell).

Modern status: Scattered, especially at Lawn and St. Lawrence.

Place names (not necessarily from the surname): Edward Islands (Labrador) 53-40 60-03; Edwards or Sam Edwards Cove (Labrador) 55-07 59-09; —— Harbour (Labrador) 54-28 57-15.

EFFORD, a surname of England and the Channel Islands, also HEFFORD with intrusive initial *h*, from the English place name Efford (Cornwall, Devon, Hampshire) – ford that can be used at ebb tide. (Ekwall, Cottle, Turk).

Traced by Spiegelhalter in Devon.

In Newfoundland:

Early instances: William, of New Perlican, 1682 (CO 1); John Eferd, of St. John's, 1705 (CO 194.3); William, of Port de Grave, 1836 (DPHW 39).

Modern status: Especially in the Port de Grave district.

EGAN. *See* EAGAN

EHLERS, a surname of Germany and Denmark, from the Old German personal names *Adalhard* containing the elements *noble* and *brave* or *Adalhari* containing the elements *noble* and *army*. (E.C. Smith).

In Newfoundland:

Early instances: Gustav, son of Ernst, of Hamburg, born 1829, resident of St. John's, 1856 (Nfld. Archives T14, *Newfoundlander* 15 Jan 1857); George Elhers, from Denmark, of St. John's, 1927 (*Nfld. Who's Who* 1927).

Modern status: At St. John's.

EISAN, a surname of German origin, Ger. *Eisen* – (worker with) iron.

In Newfoundland:

Early instance: Michael, of Bonne Bay, 1865 (DPHW 93).

Modern status: Rare, at Gander.

EISENHAUER, a surname of German origin, a variant of the American surname Eisenhower, – worker with iron.

In Newfoundland:

Modern status: Rare, at Grand Falls and St. John's.

ELDRIDGE. *See* ALDRICH

Traced by Guppy in Northamptonshire and Sussex, and by Spiegelhalter in Devon.

In Newfoundland:

Early instance: William E(l)dridge or Edderidge, of Joe Batts Arm, 1817 (Nfld. Archives KCRC).

Modern status: In the Humber West district (*Electors* 1955) and at St. John's.

ELFORD, a surname of England, from the English place name Elford (Northumberland, Staffordshire) or Elfordtown (Devon) now called Yelverton, a "dialectal form adopted by the G[reat] W[estern] R[ailway] when the station was built in 1859." (Spiegelhalter, Ekwall, Gover).

Traced by Guppy in Dorset and by Spiegelhalter in Devon.

In Newfoundland:

Early instances: ——, constable of Ferryland district, ? 1730 (CO 194.9); James, of St. John's, 1757 (DPHW 26C); Wills Terry, of Petty Harbour, 1790 (DPHW 26D); Charles, planter of Dildo Cove, 1824, of New Harbour, 1836 (DPHW 64B); James E., married Sarah Lake, Fortune 1845 (Grand Bank Methodist marriages, per P.E.L. Smith); James, of Fortune, 1860 (DPHW 106); Morgan, from Chard (Somerset), married Sarah Tuck, Fortune, 1846; 1871 (Lovell, MUN Folklore, per P.E.L. Smith).

Modern status: Scattered.

ELGAR, a surname of England from several Old English personal names, *Ethelgār* – noble spear, *Elfgār* – elf spear, *Ealdgār* – old spear, or from Old Norse. (Reaney, Cottle).

Traced by Spiegelhalter in Devon.

In Newfoundland:

Early instances: Joseph, a clerk and John Elger, a sailor of St. John's, 1871 (Lovell).

Modern status: At Great Harbour Deep (*Electors* 1955) and St. John's.

ELKINS, a surname of England, a diminutive of *Elie* (Elias) or of *Ela* (Ellen). (Reaney). *See* ELLIOTT, ELLIS.

In Newfoundland:

Early instances: William, of Greenspond, 1849 (DPHW 76); William, of Shambler's Cove, 1871 (Lovell).

Modern status: At Corner Brook and Hare Bay.

ELLARD, a surname of England and Ireland, in England from the Old English personal name *Ethelheard* – noble-hard, or from an Old German name *Adelard* or *Agilard*; in Ireland a variant of AYLWARD mainly in Cos. Cork and Wexford. (Reaney, MacLysaght).

In Newfoundland:

Early instances: Edward Elliard, of St. John's, 1857 (*Nfld. Almanac*); Michael Ellard, of Lower Gully (now Riverdale), 1871 (Lovell); John (and others) Ellerd, farmers of Torbay, 1871 (Lovell).

Modern status: Rare, at St. John's and Torbay.

ELLIOTT, a surname of England, Scotland and Ireland; in England and Ireland a diminutive of the baptismal name Elias (*see* ELLIS), from Old French *Elie* and the diminutive suffix *-ot*, or from the Old English personal names *Æthelgēat* and *Æthelgȳth*; in Scotland from Old English *Elfweald* – elf-ruler. (Withycombe, Reaney, Black, Cottle).

Guppy found Elliot(t) widespread in England and in the Border counties especially Roxburghshire. MacLysaght found Elliott "mainly, though by no means exclusively, associated with Cos. Cavan and Fermanagh, but in the nineteenth century it was numerous in Co. Leitrim also."

In Newfoundland:

Family tradition: Elliotts of Newman's Cove originally from Scotland to Bonavista (MUN Folklore).

Early instances: John Ellet(t) or Elliott, of Old Perlican, 1675 (CO 1); Edward Ellett, of Old Perlican, 1682 (CO 1); J. Elliot, of Petty Harbour, 1703 (CO 194.3); John Elliott, of St. John's, 1705 (CO 194.22); John Ellett, of Quidi Vidi, 1708 (CO 194.4); J. and S. Elliott, of Placentia, 1724 (CO 194.7); John, of Change Islands, 1787, of Wester Head, 1789 (MUN Hist.); Thomas, of Bonavista, 1800 (DPHW 70); Charles, owner of fishing room at Keels, built by the family before 1805 (Bonavista Register 1806); William, ? of Harbour Grace, 1806–07 (CO 194.46); John Elledd, Ellett or Elliott, planter of Hants Harbour, 1812 (DPHW 58); Edmund Elliott, planter of Fogo, 1816 (MUN Hist.); John, planter of Twillingate, 1820 (USPG); Martha Elliot, of King's Cove, 1824 (Nfld. Archives KCRC); John, of Caplin Cove (Trinity B.), 1829 (DPHW 59A); John Elliott, of Tickle Cove (Bonavista B.), 1835 (DPHW 73A); William, of Long Island (Bonavista B.), 1849 (DPHW 73); Louisa Elliot, of Crocker's Cove (Carbonear), 1853 (DPHW 49); John, of Indian Islands (Fogo district), 1858 (DPHW 83); James Elliott, of Burin Bay, 1860 (DPHW 108); William Elliot, of Herring Neck, 1860 (DPHW 85); Jacob, of

Ward's Harbour (now Beaumont North), 1861 (DPHW 88); Thomas Elliott, of Muddy Hole (now Maberley), 1862 (DPHW 77); James (and others), of Brooklyn, 1871 (Lovell).

Modern status: Widespread, especially at Newmans Cove (Bonavista B.), Twillingate, Botwood, Cook's Harbour (White B.) and St. John's.

Place names: Eliot Brook 49-32 56-53; Mount Eliot (Labrador) 59-11 63-48; Elliot(t) Cove, —— —— Pond 48-09 53-54.

ELLIS, a surname of England, Scotland and Ireland, from Middle English *Elis* – Elias (Reaney), the Greek form of the Hebrew Elijah. *See also* ELLIOTT.

Guppy found Ellis most numerous in Devon, Cambridgeshire, Essex, Kent and Yorkshire WR; MacLysaght "mainly in Dublin and many parts of Ulster."

In Newfoundland:

Early instances: Oliver, of Fermeuse, 1677 (CO 1); Nathaniel, of St. John's Harbour, 1703 (CO 194.3); Samuel, from Fullow (Co. Carlow), Irish convict landed at Petty Harbour or Bay Bulls, 1789 (CO 194.38); Rev. William (?1781–1837), from Co. Down, Methodist minister in Newfoundland from 1808, after whom Bird Island Cove was renamed Elliston (*The Times*, St. John's, 27 Sep 1837, Lench); Robert, one of 72 impressed men who sailed from Ireland to Newfoundland, ? 1811 (CO 194.51); Mary, from St. Nicholas Parish (Co. Tipperary), married at St. John's, 1813 (Nfld. Archives BRC); Joanna, of Ferryland, 1816 (Nfld. Archives BRC); Joanna, of Harbour Grace Parish, 1817 (Nfld. Archives HGRC); Thomas, planter of Scilly Cove (now Winterton), 1825, of Caplin Cove, 1830 (DPHW 64B, 59A); John, planter of Hants Harbour, 1827 (DPHW 58); Andrew, agent of Harbour Breton, 1843 (DPHW 101); William Henry, from the Isle of Wight, late of St. John's, 1858 (*Newfoundlander* 29 Mar 1858); William, fisherman of Codroy and Rivers, 1871 (Lovell); Edward, fisherman of Heart's Delight, 1871 (Lovell).

Modern status: Scattered, especially at St. John's, Hants Harbour and Bishop's Falls.

Place names: Elliston, —— Cove 48-38 53-03; —— Point 48-38 53-01.

EL(L)SWORTH, surnames of England, from the English place name Elsworth (Cambridgeshire). (Ekwall, Bardsley).

In Newfoundland:

Family tradition: Charles Ellsworth (1869–1951), of Rocky Harbour (Bonne B.) (MUN Geog.).

Early instances: Benjamin Elsworth, of Goose Cove (Labrador) 1787, of Matthews Cove (Labrador), 1789 (MUN Hist.); Benjamin, planter of Durrell's Cove (Trinity North district), 1823 (DPHW 64B); Thomas, planter of Western Bay, 1835 (DPHW 52A); Thomas, planter of Little Catalina, 1840, of Seldom-Come-By, 1849 (DPHW 72, 83); William, of Cann Island (Fogo-Twillingate district), 1871 (Lovell); George Ellsworth, of Petites, 1871 (Lovell).

Modern status: Ellsworth, scattered, especially at Rocky Harbour, Carmanville and Englee; Elsworth, rare, at Corner Brook and St. John's.

ELMORE, a surname of England and Ireland, from the English place name Elmore (Gloucestershire) – shore where elms grew, or a variant of Aylmer, a baptismal name and surname from the Old English personal name *Æthelmær* – noble, famous. In Ireland Elmore is also a synonym of Gilmore. (Ekwall, Cottle, Withycombe, MacLysaght).

Withycombe notes: Aylmer "gave rise to several surnames, including that of Elmer ... which has gained independent currency as a christian name in the USA, being the surname of two New Jersey brothers who played an active part in the American Revolution," adding, however, under Elmer, "But as late as 1655 Lyford gives *Elmer* as a christian name from *Ethelmer*, and it is possible that the American use may also represent a survival of this."

Matthews traced Elmore in Dorset; MacLysaght traced Elmore and Elmer in Co. Louth.

In Newfoundland:

Early instances: Edward, ? of Northern Bay, 1846 (DPHW 54); Edward, fisherman of Grates Cove, 1871 (Lovell).

Modern status: Unique, at Grates Cove (*Electors* 1955).

ELMS, a surname of England, from the English place name Elm (Cambridgeshire, Somerset), or from Old English *elm* – (dweller by the) elm(s). (Reaney, Ekwall, Cottle).

Matthews traced Elmes especially in Dorset, Devon and Hampshire.

In Newfoundland:

Family tradition: ——, from Plymouth (Devon), settled in Newfoundland in the 1830s (MUN Folklore).

Early instances: William Elmes, of Newfoundland, ? 1706 (CO 194.24); Henry, shoreman of St. John's, 1794–5, "30 years in Newfoundland," that is, 1764–5 (Census 1794–5); William Elm(e)s, of Bay

Roberts, 1797 (CO 199.18); Joseph Elms, fisherman of Griquet, 1871 (Lovell).

Modern status: Scattered.

ELSON, a surname of England from the English place names Elson (Hampshire, Shropshire) or Elston (Devon, Lancashire, Nottinghamshire, Wiltshire). (Ekwall).

Guppy traced Elston, Spiegelhalter Elson, Elston(e) in Devon.

In Newfoundland:

Early instances: Henry, merchant of Trepassey, 1797 (D'Alberti 7); John, of Harbour Grace Parish, 1809 (Nfld. Archives HGRC); John, from Exmouth (Devon), merchant of Carbonear, 1814, died 1840 (*The Times*, St. John's 4 Mar 1840, D'Alberti 24); ——, of St. John's, 1838 (Devine and O'Mara); John, fisherman of Freshwater (Carbonear), 1848 (DPHW 48).

Modern status: Especially at Botwood.

ELSWORTH. *See* ELLSWORTH

ELTON, a surname of England, from the English place name in eight counties.

Traced by Matthews in Bristol (Gloucestershire).

In Newfoundland:

Modern status: At St. John's.

EMBERLEY, a surname of England, from ? the English place name Embley (Hampshire), or a variant of the surnames Embery, Hembury, etc. from the place names Emborough (Somerset), Hembury (Devon) or Henbury (Dorset), or of Amery. *See* EMERSON. (Bardsley, Reaney).

Reaney traced Embery etc. in Somerset, Guppy traced Embrey in Herefordshire.

In Newfoundland:

Family traditions: ——, ? of French origin, settled at Bay de Verde in the 19th century (MUN Folklore). ——, from Ireland, settled at Joe Batts Arm between 1811–16 (MUN Hist.).

Early instances: Stephen, of Bay de Verde, 1781 (CO 199.18); Stephen Embelly, of St. John's, 1782 (DPHW 26C); Joseph Emberley, of Burin, 1805 (D'Alberti 15); John Emberly, of Harbour Grace Parish, 1808 (Nfld. Archives HGRC); Joanna, of Joe Batts Arm, 1812 (Nfld. Archives BRC); John, of Fogo, 1815 (Nfld. Archives KCRC); Samuel Embesley, bookkeeper of Carbonear, 1836 (DPHW 48); Richard Emberly, of Barren Island (now Bar Haven), 1871 (Lovell); John (and others), of Brule, 1871 (Lovell); Samuel Emberley, of Grand Bank,

1871 (Lovell); John Emberly, of Little Placentia (now Argentia), 1871 (Lovell); Patrick, of North Harbour (Placentia B.), 1871 (Lovell); Samuel, of Petit Forte, 1871 (Lovell).

Modern status: Scattered, especially at Bay de Verde.

Place names: Emberley's Island 47-18 54-47; Emberly Point 47-49 54-04; —— Rock 46-58 55-11.

EMERSON, a surname of England and Ireland – son of Amery, a variant of Almeric, from the Old German personal name *Amalricus* containing the elements *work* and *ruler*. Reaney records a variant Emberson. (Withycombe, Reaney).

Guppy traced Em(m)erson in Durham, Essex, Lincolnshire, Northumberland, Nottinghamshire and Yorkshire; MacLysaght traced Emerson in Ulster.

In Newfoundland:

Early instances: Robert, indicted at assizes in St. John's for crime against Sarah (Emerson), 1807 (CO 194.40); Hugh Alexander, from Windsor, N.S., barrister of St. John's, 1829 (DPHW 26B, *Newfoundlander* 30 Dec 1829); Lewis, clerk of the peace, of Harbour Grace, 1852 (*Newfoundlander* 7 Oct 1852).

Modern status: Rare, at Carbonear and St. John's.

EMIRY, ? a variant of the surnames of England and Ireland, Amery, Emery, Amory, etc. *See* EMERSON.

Guppy traced Emery in Norfolk, Northamptonshire and Staffordshire; Spiegelhalter traced Emary, Embery, Emiry in Devon.

In Newfoundland:

Early instance: Moses, fisherman of Trinity (Trinity B.), 1760 (DPHW 64).

Modern status: Rare, at Trinity (*Electors* 1955).

EMSLEY, a surname of England, ? from the English place name Emley (Yorkshire WR), from Old English *elm* – elm and *lēah* – wood.

Traced in Yorkshire WR.

In Newfoundland:

Early instance: George Elmsley, of St. John's, 1871 (Lovell).

Modern status: Rare, at St. John's (*Electors* 1955).

ENDER. *See* INDER

ENDICOTT, a surname of England, from the English place names Endicott, Indicott, Incott, Yendacott, Yondercott, Youngcott (Devon), or (dweller at the) end of the cottage(s). (Spiegelhalter).

Guppy traced Endacott, Spiegelhalter also Endicott in Devon.

In Newfoundland:

Early instance: Daniel Endacott, of Greenspond, 1847 (DPHW 76).

Modern status: Rare, at Sally's Cove and Corner Brook.

ENGELBRECHT, a surname of Germany (in English, Inglebright or Engelbert), from a personal name in Old German Engelbert, Ingelbert, in Old French Engilbert, Englebert, containing the elements *Angle* and *glorious*. (Reaney).

In Newfoundland:

Modern status: Unique, at St. John's.

ENGLAND, a surname of England and Ireland. Reaney comments: "There is no authority for the *ing-land* – meadowland of Bardsley and Weekley. The reference must be to the name of the country, a surname which appears curiously out-of-place in England." Spiegelhalter, however, suggests that the name does not come from the country, rather from Old English *enge land* – narrow land, the name of places in Essex, Lincolnshire and Somerset. Of the name of the country, Ekwall states that it was originally "the land of the Angles," the people from Angel in Sleswig, later "the land of the English." In Ireland, England is a synonym of ENGLISH or of Anglin, with Angland a variant in Co. Cork. (Reaney, Spiegelhalter, Cottle, Ekwall, MacLysaght).

Traced by Guppy in Huntingdonshire, Somerset and Yorkshire WR, and by Spiegelhalter in Devon.

In Newfoundland:

Early instances: Richard, of St. John's, 1675, "7 years an inhabitant in 1680," that is, since 1673 (CO 1); Richard, of Quidi Vidi, 1676 (CO 1); Mary Thomas, from Cornwall, ? of St. John's, died 1834, aged 40 (*Royal Gazette* 22 Apr 1834); Rev. James, Wesleyan minister of Blackhead (Bay de Verde district), 1844 (DPHW 52A); William, of Shoe Cove (Twillingate), 1849 (DPHW 86); George, from Dorset, married at Torbay, 1851 (DPHW 32); William, fisherman of Grand Bruit, 1871 (Lovell); Joseph, of Harbour Grace, 1871 (Lovell); William, of King's Cove (Fogo district), 1871 (Lovell).

Modern status: Scattered, especially at Harry's Harbour (Green B.).

Place name: England's Brook 49-54 56-05.

ENGLISH, a surname of England and the Channel Islands, also Scotland and Ireland, from Old English

Englisc – English, "formerly referring to Angles (*see* ENGLAND) as opposed to Saxons, but by surname times denoting an Englishman living among Borderers (Welsh, Strathclyde Welsh, Scots), or in the old Scandinavian areas of the north, or in intensely normanized districts; or one who had returned from being so nicknamed in France or elsewhere" (Cottle). (Reaney, Cottle, Turk).

Traced by Guppy in Durham, Lincolnshire, Norfolk and Northumberland; and by MacLysaght in Co. Limerick since the 13th century "and completely hibernicized."

In Newfoundland:

Early instances: John, of St. John's, 1757 (DPHW 26C); Allen, boatkeeper of Harbour Main, 1779 (MUN Hist.); John (and others), of Devil's (now Job's) Cove, 1796 (CO 199.18); Michael, from Wind Gap Parish (Co. Kilkenny), married at St. John's, 1805 (Nfld. Archives BRC); James, of Harbour Grace Parish, 1806 (Nfld. Archives HGRC); Samuel, of Northern Cove (Spaniards B.), 1814 (DPHW 48); John, of Harbour Grace, 1831 (Nfld. Archives HGRC); William, ? of Northern Bay, 1838 (DPHW 54); John W. (and others), of Branch, 1871 (Lovell); John, fisherman of Gull Island (Bay de Verde district), 1871 (Lovell); Samuel (and others), of Ochre Pit Cove, 1871 (Lovell).

Modern status: Scattered, especially at Branch, Job's Cove and St. John's.

Place names (not necessarily from the surname): English Bank 50-44 57-22; —— Bay 48-22 53-17; Cape —— 46-47 53-40; —— Cove 47-29 53-13; —— Harbour 48-22 53-16, 47-38 54-53, 49-04 53-35; —— Head 48-22 53-16; —— Island 51-10 55-43; —— Point (Labrador) 51-29 56-56, 50-48 57-15; —— River (Labrador) 53-54 58-52; —— Harbour Island, —— —— Back Cove, —— —— West 47-27 55-30; —— —— East 47-38 54-54; —— Houses 51-06 55-45; —— River Island (Labrador) 54-57 59-43.

ENGRAM. *See* INGRAHAM

ENNIS, a surname of England and Ireland; in England from various place names Ennis, Ennys, Innis, Enys, Ince (Cornwall), or from Cornish *enys*, Welsh *ynys* – (dweller on the) island or water-meadow; in Ireland for *Ó hAonghuis* – descendant of Angus or for the Scots surname Innes. (Ekwall, Spiegelhalter, MacLysaght). *See* INNIS.

Traced in Devon by Spiegelhalter.

In Newfoundland:

Early instances: James, soldier of St. John's, 1767

(DPHW 26C); Susana, of Harbour Grace Parish, 1817 (Nfld. Archives HGRC); Richard Sr. and Jr., of Harbour Breton, 1871 (Lovell); James (and others) Enniss, of Merasheen, 1871 (Lovell).

Modern status: Scattered, especially at Merasheen (*Electors* 1955) and St. John's.

ENON, ? a variant of the surname of England Eno, a pet-form of the German personal name *Eginhard* containing the elements *awe* and *hard*, or of the surnames of Ireland Ennos, Enos, etc., earlier forms of ENNIS. (E.C. Smith).

In Newfoundland:

Early instance: Philip Eno(e) or Enough, of Harbour Main, 1750 (CO 194.12, 199.18).

Modern status: Unique, at Chamberlains (*Electors* 1955).

ENRIGHT, a surname of Ireland, (Mac) Enright, Enraghty, *Mac Ionnrachtaigh*, Ir. *inreachtach* – lawful or ? Ir. *indrecht* – attack. (MacLysaght).

Traced by MacLysaght in Cos. Limerick and Clare.

In Newfoundland:

Early instance: Edward, corporal in the Royal Newfoundland Regiment, 1797 (D'Alberti 6).

Modern status: Unique, at St. Joseph's (St. Mary's district) (*Electors* 1955).

ENWOOD,? a variant of the surname of England Inwood – (dweller by the) in-wood, home-wood "as opposed to the out-wood" (Reaney).

In Newfoundland:

Modern status: At Burnt Island (Burgeo-La Poile district).

EPSTEIN, a Jewish surname of Germany from the German place name Epstein, a mountain range in Hesse-Nassau and Hesse-Darmstadt. (Unbegaun).

In Newfoundland:

Early instance: Edward (1900–), born at Nackel, Germany, came to St. John's in 1924 and later settled at Corner Brook (*Nfld. Who's Who* 1930).

Modern status: At St. John's and Bishop's Falls.

EREAUT, a surname of the Channel Islands, a variant of the family name of France Eraut, a southern form of Héraud – herald, or ? of the surname of Ireland Erraught, the Co. Kerry form of ENRIGHT. (Dauzat, MacLysaght).

In Newfoundland:

Modern status: At Burgeo and Corner Brook.

ERIKSEN, a surname of Norway – Eric's son.

In Newfoundland:

Family tradition: Albert, from Norway, in the whaling industry, settled at Trinity (Trinity B.) in 1904 (Family).

Modern status: Rare, at Trinity (*Electors* 1955) and St. John's.

ERSH(E)LER, ? an anglicization of the surname of Germany Oechsle – one who plows with oxen or cowherd.

In Newfoundland:

Modern status: Ersheler, Ershler, both unique, at St. John's.

ESCOTT, a surname of England, from various place names: Escot, Arscott (Devon), Eastcott (Middlesex, Wiltshire), Eastcotts (Bedfordshire), Eastcourt (Wiltshire, Sussex), or (dweller at the) eastern cottage. (Reaney, Cottle, Spiegelhalter).

Traced by Spiegelhalter in Devon.

In Newfoundland:

Early instances: James, of St. John's, 1751 (CO 194.13); James Eastcock, of Portugal Cove, 1775 (DPHW 26C); Richard, of Catalina, 1823 (DPHW 72); James Eascott, of Quidi Vidi, 1856 (DPHW 29).

Modern status: At St. John's.

ETCHEGARY, a variant of the surname of France Etchegaray from the Basque *etche* – house and *garay* – high – (dweller in the) high house. (Dauzat)

In Newfoundland:

Family tradition: Michael, ? of Basque origin, went from France to St. Pierre and later settled at St. Lawrence in the 1890s (MUN Folklore).

Modern status: At St. Lawrence and St. John's.

ETH(E)RIDGE, surnames of England from the Old English personal name *Æthelrīc* – noble rule, a variant of ALDRICH.

Traced by Guppy in Sussex and by Spiegelhalter in Devon.

In Newfoundland:

Early instances: John Ethrage, of Salmon Cove (now Champneys), 1758 (DPHW 64); James Etheridge, of Trinity (Trinity B.), 1787 (DPHW 64); Peter, of Greenspond, 1804 (D'Alberti 14); John, of Back Cove (Fogo), 1871 (Lovell); Thomas, of Joe Batt's Arm, 1871 (Lovell); George Ethirage, of New Perlican, 1871 (Lovell).

Modern status: Etheridge, Ethridge, scattered.

ETSELL, ? a surname of Scotland, not recorded by Black, from the Scots place name Edzell (Forfarshire now Angus).

In Newfoundland:

Early instance: William Edsel or Etsell, of Bonavista, 1792 (USPG, DPHW 70).

Modern status: At Twillingate (*Electors* 1955) and Bonavista.

EUSTACE, a baptismal name and surname of England and Ireland, from a Roman personal name, *Eustachius*, from the Greek meaning ? fruitful, borne by two saints. (Withycombe, Reaney, Cottle).

Traced by Spiegelhalter in Devon and by MacLysaght in Co. Kildare.

In Newfoundland:

Early instances: Robert, from Waterford, merchant of Renews, 1777 (CO 194.33, D'Alberti 6); James, of Torbay, 1779 (DPHW 26C); Bridget Enstace, of St. John's, 1804 (Nfld. Archives BRC); Bridget Eustace, from New Ross (Co. Wexford), married at St. John's, 1810 (Nfld. Archives BRC); Mary Huestice or Eustace, of Harbour Grace Parish, 1820, 1825 (Nfld. Archives HGRC).

Modern status: At St. John's and Torbay.

EVANS, a surname of Wales, England and Ireland, from one of the Welsh forms of John – son of John, or sometimes from the Romano-British personal name *Eugenius* – well-born; in Ireland also an anglicized form of the rare *Ó h Éimhin*, in Ormond, derived from a word meaning swift. (Withycombe, Reaney, Cottle, MacLysaght).

Guppy found Evans widespread especially in Wales and the adjoining counties; MacLysaght in Ormond ("much of Co. Kilkenny and north Tipperary").

In Newfoundland:

Early instances: James Ewen, of St. John's Harbour, 1675, "17 years an inhabitant in 1681," that is, since 1664 (spelt Evans in 1681, 2) (CO 1); Edward Evans, of Port de Grave, 1751 (CO 194.13); John, of Western Bay, 1771 (CO 199.18); Robert, of Adam's Cove, 1786 (CO 199.18); John, J.P. of Placentia, 1791 (D'Alberti 4); ——, merchant of Grand Bank, 1802 (D'Alberti 12); John, of Carbonear, 1802 (CO 199.18); Andrew Evans or Evens, of Harbour Grace Parish, 1807 (Nfld. Archives HGRC); James Evans, of Ochre Pit Cove, 1816 (DPHW 52A); Andrew, of Fogo, 1817 (Nfld. Archives KCRC); Elizabeth, born at Cape St. Francis, 1819 (DPHW 52A); Andrew, of Kings Cove, 1820 (Nfld. Archives KCRC); James, of Hants Harbour,

1823 (DPHW 58); Robert, planter of Renews, 1825 (DPHW 31); Andrew, from Lismore (Co. Waterford), of Trinity, 1827 (Nfld. Archives KCRC); Andrew, of Turks Cove (Trinity B.), 1829 (Nfld. Archives KCRC); Robert, planter of Scilly Cove (now Winterton), 1834 (DPHW 48); Thomas, of Brunette Island, 1835 (DPHW 30); Eleanor, of Fortune, 1838 (DPHW 106); William Evins, of Pouch Cove, 1839 (Nfld. Archives BRC); Edward Evans, of Exploits Burnt Island, 1843 (DPHW 86): William, of Bay Roberts, 1848 (DPHW 39); Philip, of Mose Ambrose, 1853 (DPHW 104); John, of Fox Harbour (Trinity B.), 1855 (DPHW 59A); George, of Channel, 1858 (DPHW 98); widespread in Lovell 1871.

Modern status: Widespread, especially at English Harbour West, Femme (Fortune B.) (*Electors* 1955), St. John's and Pouch Cove.

Place names: Evans Bight (Labrador) 59-18 63-32; —— Head 47-04 55-47; —— Lake (Labrador) 54-29 66-11; —— Point 49-09 55-23; —— Ridge 47-11 56-06.

EVELEIGH, EVELLEY, EVEL(L)Y, surnames of England from the English place name Eveleigh (Devon, now lost). (Bardsley, Spiegelhalter, Gover).

Traced by Guppy in Devon.

In Newfoundland:

Early instances: George Evely, of Trinity (Trinity B.), 1784, 1800–01 (DPHW 64, Census Trinity B.); George, of Ragged Harbour (now Melrose), 1810 (DPHW 64); William, of Deadman's Bay (Bonavista North district), 1832 (DPHW 76); George Evelly, planter of Gooseberry Cove (Carbonear), 1834 (DPHW 48); Matthew Eveleigh, fisherman of Change Islands, 1845 (DPHW 83); George Evely, planter of Blowmedown (Carbonear), 1849 (DPHW 49); Ananias Evelly, of Freshwater (Trinity district), 1856 (DPHW 64B); John Eveleigh, of Pease Cove (Trinity North), 1870 (DPHW 65); John, of Ship Cove (now part of Port Rexton), 1870 (DPHW 65); William Evely, of Deer Harbour (Trinity B.), 1871 (Lovell); George (and others) Everly, of Flatrock (Carbonear), 1871 (Lovell); William Eveleigh, of Wild Cove (Fogo district), 1871 (Lovell).

Modern status: Eveleigh, scattered, especially at Comfort Cove and Hampden; Evelley, at Trinity; Evelly, rare, at Long Pond (Manuels) (*Electors* 1955) and St. John's; Evely, in the Carbonear district (*Electors* 1955).

EVERARD, a baptismal name and surname of England and Ireland, from the Old German personal name *Eburhard* (cognate with the Old English name *Eoforheard*) – *boar hard*, introduced into England by the Normans in the French form Everard, giving rise also to the surname Everett. (Withycombe, Reaney, Cottle).

Everard, was traced by Spiegelhalter in Devon and by MacLysaght in Co. Tipperary. Guppy traced Evered in Somerset, and Everett, Everitt in Cambridgeshire, Essex, Lincolnshire, Norfolk and Suffolk.

In Newfoundland:

Early instances: Richard Everarad, of St. John's, 1804 (Nfld. Archives BRC); William Everet, of Carbonear, 1816 (DPHW 48); James Everett, of Petty Harbour, 1844 (DPHW 31); Edward (and others) Everard, of Petty Harbour, 1871 (Lovell).

Modern status: At St. John's and Petty Harbour.

EVERSON, a surname of England – son of Evot, and ? of Norway, ? a variant of Evensen – son of John.

Guppy traced Evison in Lincolnshire.

In Newfoundland:

Family tradition: Edward Everson from Norway, settled at Flatrock (St. John's) in ? the mid-nineteenth century (MUN Folklore).

Modern status: At Flatrock (St. John's).

EVOY, a surname of Ireland, usually with the prefix Mac except in Co. Wexford, *Mac Fhíodhbhuidhe*, Ir. ? *fiodhbhadach* – woodman. (MacLysaght). *See also* McEVOY.

In Newfoundland:

Early instances: Mary, of Harbour Grace Parish, 1828 (Nfld. Archives HGRC); Mary, of St. John's, married at Lower Island Cove, 1828 (Nfld. Archives BRC); John, of Caplin Bay (unspecified), 1829 (Nfld. Archives BRC); P., of St.John's, 1832 (*Newfoundlander* 20 Sep 1832); Bridget, of Kings Cove, 1890 (Nfld. Archives KCRC).

Modern status: At Harricot, Benoits Cove and St. John's.

EWERS, a surname of England, from Old French *ewer* – servant who supplied guests at table with water to wash their hands. (Reaney).

Guppy traced Ewer in Middlesex; Spiegelhalter traced Ewers in Devon.

In Newfoundland:

Early instance: Rev. Thomas Ewer (?1756–1833), from Dublin, of Harbour Grace, 1810 (CO 194.49, *Carbonear Star* 13 Feb 1833).

Modern status: Rare, at St. John's.

EWING, a surname of England, Scotland and Ireland; in Scotland an anglicized form of Ewan or

Ewen; in Ireland for *Mac Eoghain*, Ir. *eoghan*, all ultimately from the Greek, as in the baptismal name Eugene – noble, well-born. (Withycombe, Reaney, Black, MacLysaght, Cottle).

Spiegelhalter traced Ewen, Ewin, Ewings in Devon. Guppy traced Ewing "over a large part of Scotland, but rare in the north," and MacLysaght "quite numerous throughout Ulster."

In Newfoundland:

Early instances: James, from Greenock, merchant of Aquaforte, 1824, of Bay Bulls, 1827, of St. John's, 1853 (DPHW 26B, 31, *Newfoundlander* 11 Jul 1853); James, of Isle Valen, 1871 (Lovell).

Modern status: At St. John's and Corner Brook.

EZEKIEL, a baptismal name and surname of England, from the Hebrew – May God strengthen, the name of one of the major prophets. The surname was borne by a Jewish family of Devon, the best-known members of which were Abraham (1757–1806) miniature-painter and scientific optician, and Solomon (1781–1867), writer. (Withycombe, *DNB*).

In Newfoundland:

Family tradition: ——, from Exeter, settled at Harbour Main in the late 18th century (MUN Folklore).

Early instances: Peter, of Harbour Main, 1794 (CO 199.18); Thomas Ezechiel, of Harbour Grace Parish, 1806 (Nfld. Archives HGRC); Thomas Ezekiel, of Holyrood, 1871 (Lovell).

Modern status: Scattered, especially at Harbour Main and Corner Brook.

Place name: Ezekiel's Cove 47-26 53-11.

F

FACEY, one of twenty-eight variants noted by Reaney of a surname of England from Anglo-French *enveisé* – playful. Other forms are Vaisey, VOISEY, Feasey, Fheazey. Spiegelhalter, however, sees Facey as a short form of the baptismal name Boniface, adopted by several popes. (Withycombe, Reaney, Spiegelhalter).

Spiegelhalter traced Facey in Devon.

In Newfoundland:

Early instances: John, of Trinity (Trinity B.), 1804; (DPHW 64); George, of St. John's, 1822 (DPHW 26D); Robert, planter of New Perlican, 1823 (DPHW 64B); William, of Chamberlains, 1832 (DPHW 30); William, of Exploits Burnt Island, 1842 (DPHW 86); John Sandy, born at Bonavista, 1848 (DPHW 70); Henry, of Catalina, 1859 (DPHW 67).

Modern status: At St. John's and Twillingate.

FAGAN, a surname of Ireland, either of Norman origin as in the French surnames Payen and Pagan, from Latin *paganus* – peasant, rustic, in Cos. Dublin and Meath, or sometimes *Ó Faodhagáin* in Co. Louth, though it is usually anglicized Fegan there. (MacLysaght).

In Newfoundland:

Family tradition: Sally (1808–68), born at Kelligrews (MUN Geog.).

Early instances: Michael and Joseph Feagan, of Upper Foxtrap, 1801 (CO 199.18); John, of St. Mary's, married at St. John's, 1838 (Nfld. Archives BRC); James and Michael Fagan, ? of St. Mary's, 1844 (*Nfld. Almanac*); Michael, from Co. Tipperary, of Port de Grave, 1844 (*Indicator* 24 Aug 1844); James Fagin, farmer of Red Island (Placentia B.), 1871 (Lovell); Peter and John Fagan, of St. John's, 1871 (Lovell); Augustus (and others) Feagan, of Foxtrap, 1871 (Lovell).

Modern status: Scattered, especially at St. John's and in the Harbour Main district.

Place name: Fagan's Pond 48-89 53-49.

FAGNER, ? a surname of England, of unknown origin, apparently not recorded elsewhere.

In Newfoundland:

Early instances: Jasper Faugner of Bonavista, 1791 (DPHW 70); Susanna F(a)gner, of Carbonear, 1794 (CO 199.18); John Fagner, of Lower Island Cove, 1797 (CO 199.18); John Fagnor, planter of Bonavista, 1850 (DPHW 72).

Modern status: At Caplin Cove (Carbonear-Bay de Verde district).

FAHEY, a variant of the surnames of Ireland (O)Fahy, Faghy, *Ó Fathaigh*, Ir. *fothadh* – foundation. (MacLysaght).

Traced by MacLysaght in Co. Galway.

In Newfoundland:

Early instances: Patrick, of Harbour Main, 1779 (MUN Hist.); Thomas, of Western Bay, 1784 (CO 199.18); Edward, of Chapel's Cove, 1789 (CO 199.18); Roger, sergeant of the Royal Newfoundland Regiment, 1797 (D'Alberti 6); Thomas, of Harbour Grace Parish, 1811 (Nfld. Archives HGRC); Jeremiah Fahy, from Castle Hyde (Co. Cork), married at St. John's, 1819 (Nfld. Archives BRC); Judith ? Fahey, from Co. Waterford, married at Kings Cove, 1829 (Nfld. Archives KCRC); Honora, from Clonmel (Co. Tipperary), married at Tickle Cove (Bonavista B.), 1830 (Nfld. Archives KCRC); John, ? of Northern Bay, 1838 (DPHW 54); David, teacher of Torbay, 1839 (*Newfoundlander* 1 Aug 1839); Michael Faity, from Fethard (Co. Tipperary), of Brigus, 1844 (*Indicator* 24 Aug 1844); James Fahey, of Trinity, 1856 (Nfld. Archives KCRC); Helena, of Harbour Grace, 1866 (Nfld. Archives HGRC); Dennis (and others), of Fermeuse, 1871 (Lovell); James, planter of Goulds Road (Brigus district), 1871 (Lovell); Lawrence Fahy, of St. John's, 1871 (Lovell); Patrick Fahey, of St. Mary's, 1871 (Lovell); Edward, of Upper Small Point (now Kingston), 1871 (Lovell).

Modern status: Scattered, especially in the east coast districts.

Place name: Fahey Point 48-25 53-37.

FALK, a surname of England and France, in England a variant of Fawke etc., both from an Old French personal name *Fauque* – falcon. (Reaney, Dauzat).

In Newfoundland:

Family tradition: Enoch Falk (from Norwegian Falch), a sealing captain, came to Newfoundland in the early 1900s (Natalie Falk).

Modern status: Rare, at St. John's and Gander.

FALLE, a surname of England and of Jersey (Channel Islands), in England from Middle English *falle* – (dweller by the water) fall or slope; in Jersey, ? a variant of the French surname Fale which in the northwest may mean *jabot*, used of one who struts or is a glutton. (Reaney, Dauzat, Turk).

In Newfoundland:

Early instances: E., of Burin, 1832 (*Newfoundlander* 26 Jan 1832); Richard, of Jersey Harbour, 1836, of Great Harbour, 1845 (DPHW 101, 106); John, labourer of St. John's, 1846 (DPHW 26B); John, carpenter of La Poile, 1860 (DPHW 99).

Modern status: Rare, in St. George's district.

FALLON, a surname of Ireland (O)Fallon, Falloon, *Ó Fallamhain*. (MacLysaght).

MacLysaght traced (O)Fallon in Cos. Offaly and Roscommon, Falloon in Cos. Armagh and Down.

In Newfoundland:

Early instances: Luke, of St. John's, 1850 (DPHW 23); Luke, of Harbour Grace, 1866, high constable there, 1871 (Nfld. Archives HGRC, Lovell).

Modern status: Rare, at St. John's, Harbour Grace and Gander.

FANC(E)Y, surnames of England, ? from the shortened form of fantasy, used of an imaginative, whimsical person, or ? from the French place name Vancé (Sarthe). (Charnock).

In Newfoundland:

Early instances: John Fanc(e)y, of Bell Island, 1708–09 (CO 194.4); George Fancy, of Heart's Content, 1772 (DPHW 64); G. J. and T., occupiers, and George Fancey, proprietor of fishing room at New Harbour (Trinity B.), Winter 1800–01 (Census Trinity B.); Stephen Fancy, fisherman of Change Islands, 1850 (DPHW 83).

Modern status: Fancey, especially at Glenwood and Wings Point; Fancy, at Deer Lake, Bishops Falls and Change Islands.

FANE, a surname of England, from Middle English *fein* etc. – glad, well-disposed, "proverbially opposed to fools" (Reaney).

Traced by Guppy in Bedfordshire.

In Newfoundland:

Modern status: Rare, at Corner Brook.

Place name: Fane Island 50-53 56-10.

FANNING, a surname of England and Ireland; in England a variant of Fenning – dweller by the fen; in Ireland, with a variant Fannon, for *Fainin*, "a name of Norman origin." (Spiegelhalter, MacLysaght).

Traced by Spiegelhalter in Devon and by MacLysaght in Co. Limerick.

In Newfoundland:

Early instances: John, of Bonavista, 1767 (DPHW 64); Edward, of St. John's, 1775 (DPHW 26C); William Fan(n)ing, of Harbour Grace Parish, 1822 (Nfld. Archives HGRC); P. Fanning, of Harbour Grace, 1832 (*Newfoundlander* 23 Aug 1832); Mary, of Kings Cove Parish, 1841 (Nfld. Archives KCRC); George, of Exploits Burnt Island, 1844 (DPHW 86); Edward, of Carbonear, 1856 (*Newfoundlander* 7 Jul 1856).

Modern status: At St. John's.

FAOUR, a surname of Lebanon-Syria, ? a variant of the Turkish name *Fawrī*, of Arabic origin with the meanings ? boiling; ? immediate, instant. (Bubenik).

In Newfoundland:

Family tradition: ——, from Lebanon, settled at St. John's in the early 20th century.

Modern status: Rare, at Corner Brook.

FARDY, a surname of Ireland, ? a variant of the English surname Faraday, of unknown origin. (MacLysaght).

Traced by MacLysaght in Co. Wexford.

In Newfoundland:

Early instances: Martin, of Belle Isle (now Bell Island), 1805 (Nfld. Archives BRC); Constantine, of Harbour Grace Parish, 1815 (Nfld. Archives HGRC); Martin, from Rosegarland Parish (unidentified) (Co. Wexford), married at St. John's, 1817 (Nfld. Archives BRC); Michael, of Twillingate, 1829 (Nfld. Archives KCRC); Michael, of Fortune Harbour, 1831 (Nfld. Archives KCRC); P., of St. John's, 1832 (*Newfoundlander* 20 Sep 1832); Patrick, carpenter of Brigus, 1871 (Lovell); Lawrence (and 1 other), of Chapel's Cove, 1871 (Lovell).

Modern status: Especially at St. John's.

Place name: Fardy's Cove 50-42 56-08.

FAR(E)WELL, surnames of England from the English place names Farewell (Staffordshire, Yorkshire) or Farwell (Farm) (Devon). (Reaney, Spiegelhalter, Ekwall). *See also* FARRELL.

Traced by Spiegelhalter in Devon.

In Newfoundland:

Early instances: Robert Farwell, of Newfoundland, 1730 (CO 194.23); John, planter of Fogo, 1808 (MUN Hist.); John Farewell, planter of Twillingate, 1818 (USPG); Thomas, of Gooseberry Island (Bonavista North district), 1844 (DPHW 76); Richard Farwell, of Newell's Island, 1857 (DPHW 76); John, fisherman of Burin, 1860 (DPHW 100).

Modern status: Farewell, scattered, especially at Creston South; Farwell, rare, at Fogo and Port aux Choix.

Place names (not necessarily from the surname): Farewell Harbour, —— Head, —— Gull Island 49-33 54-28; —— Duck Islands 49-35 54-28.

FARNELL, a surname of England from English place names Farnell, Farnhill, Fernhill in several counties, or (dweller by the) fern-covered hill. (Reaney, Cottle).

In Newfoundland:

Family tradition: Charles Pace (1840–1925) born in Nova Scotia, died at Corner Brook (MUN Folklore).

Early instance: John A., of Bay of Islands district, 1876 (DPHW 96).

Modern status: Rare, at St. John's and Corner Brook (*Electors* 1955).

FARNHAM, a surname of England and the Channel Islands, from the English place name Farnham in several counties, or, usually (dweller by the) homestead or meadow where ferns grew. (Reaney, Cottle, Ekwall, Turk).

Traced by Spiegelhalter in Devon.

In Newfoundland:

Early instance: John, of Trinity (Trinity B.), 1802 (DPHW 64).

Modern status: Rare, at Heart's Content (*Electors* 1955) and St. John's.

FARR, a surname of England, a nickname from Old English *fearr* – bull. (Reaney).

Traced by Guppy chiefly in Herefordshire and Hertfordshire and by Spiegelhalter in Devon.

In Newfoundland:

Early instance: George, fisherman of Tizzard's Harbour, 1871 (Lovell).

Modern status: Scattered, in the Twillingate and Grand Falls districts.

FARRAR, a surname of England and Scotland, from Old French *ferreor, ferour* – smith, worker in iron, farrier, though Black maintains that its origin is uncertain. (Reaney, Cottle, Black).

Guppy traced Farrar, Farrer in Bedfordshire, Cumberland, Westmorland and Yorkshire WR.

In Newfoundland:

Modern status: Rare, at Bell Island.

FARRELL, a surname of England and Ireland, in England a variant of FAR(E)WELL; in Ireland

(O)Farrell, Ferrall, *Ó Fearghail* – man of valour. (Spiegelhalter, MacLysaght).

Guppy traced Farrall in Staffordshire, Spiegelhalter traced Farrell in Devon, and MacLysaght found (O)Farrell, Ferrall widespread.

In Newfoundland:

Family traditions: ——, from ? Knocklofty Bridge (Co. Tipperary), settled in Newfoundland in the ? late 19th century (MUN Folklore). James, of Beau Bois, died 1852, aged 59 years (MUN Hist.).

Early instances: John, from Waterford, servant of Quidi Vidi about 1730–35 (CO 194.9); John Farrel, soldier of St. John's, 1774 (DPHW 26C); Michael Farrol, boatkeeper of Bay Bulls, 1786 (CO 194.36); Richard Farrell, of Adam's Cove, 1788 (CO 199.18); John, from Dublin, Irish convict landed at Petty Harbour or Bay Bulls, 1789 (CO 194.38); Michael, from Thomastown (Co. Tipperary), married at St. John's, 1798 (Nfld. Archives BRC); John Farril, of Harbour Grace Parish, 1812 (Nfld. Archives HGRC); Mary Farrel, of Renews, 1813 (Nfld. Archives BRC); Michael, of Mint Cove (Spaniards Bay), 1813 (D'Alberti 23); Martin Farrell, of Fogo, 1815 (Nfld. Archives KCRC); John O'Farrell, soldier of St. John's, 1817 (DPHW 26D); Morgan Farrel, of Carbonear, 1828 (Nfld. Archives BRC); Edward Farrell, of Harbour Grace, 1829 (Nfld. Archives BRC); John, of Kings Cove, 1832 (Nfld. Archives KCRC); John Farral or Farrel, fisherman of Port de Grave, 1838, of Northern Gut (now North River), 1849 (DPHW 39); —— Farrell, fisherman of La Poile, 1841 (DPHW 101); Edward, fisherman of Dolman's Cove (Burgeo-La Poile), 1860 (DPHW 99); Martin, of Little Hearts Ease, 1870 (Nfld. Archives KCRC); widespread in Lovell 1871.

Modern status: Widespread, especially at Little Bay (Placentia West district).

Place name: Farrel's Island (Labrador) 53-51 56-54.

FARTHING, a surname of England, from an Old English personal name *Farthegn* – traveller, or the English place name Farthing (Devon, Essex, Sussex, Surrey), or the owner or lessee of a *fēorthing* – a fourth part (of an estate or the like), or one whose rent or assessment was one farthing. (Reaney, Cottle, A.H. Smith).

Traced by Guppy in Somerset and by Spiegelhalter in Devon.

In Newfoundland:

Early instance: Cyrus (and others), of Herring Neck, 1871 (Lovell).

Modern status: Especially at Salt Harbour Island (Twillingate district).

FARWELL. *See* FAREWELL

FAULKNER, a surname of England and Ireland, from Old French *fau(l)connier* – a hunter with falcons, keeper or trainer of hawks, one whose rent was a falcon or falcon's gear; or a worker with a *faucon*, a kind of crane or windlass. Cottle traced nine variants. (Reaney, Cottle, MacLysaght).

Traced by Guppy in Buckinghamshire, Cheshire, Lincolnshire, Oxfordshire and Staffordshire; by Spiegelhalter in Devon; and by MacLysaght in Ulster.

In Newfoundland:

Early instances: Rev. William , of St. John's, 1838, of Carbonear, 1841 (*Newfoundlander* 20 Sep 1838, 3 Jun 1841); John, of (Lower) Island Cove, 1854 (*Newfoundlander* 19 Jan 1854); Hugh and William Falkner, fishermen of Bonavista, 1871 (Lovell).

Modern status: Scattered, especially at Bonavista and Lower Island Cove.

FAWCETT, a surname of England and Ireland, from various place names in England and Scotland, Fawsyde (East Lothian), Fawcett (Westmorland), Facit (Lancashire), Forcett (Yorkshire NR), or (dweller by the) varicoloured hillside. (Reaney, Cottle).

Traced by Guppy in Yorkshire, Cambridgeshire and Westmorland and found by MacLysaght in all the provinces.

In Newfoundland:

Early instance: Col. Morris J. Fawcett, retired British Army officer, head of the Newfoundland Constabulary, 1885–94 (Fox, Mott).

Modern status: Rare, at Goulds Road and Hallstown (Port de Grave district).

FEARN, a surname of England and Scotland; in England from Old English *fearn* – (dweller among the) fern(s); in Scotland, from the Scots place names Fearn (Ross-shire), Fearn or Fern (Angus). (Reaney, Black).

Guppy traced Fearn in Derbyshire and Fern in Staffordshire.

In Newfoundland:

Family tradition: G. L. Fern, from England, settled at Harbour Buffett about 1890 (MUN Hist.).

Early instance: Josiah Fern, convicted at St. John's for stealing wearing apparel, 1804 (D'Alberti 14).

Modern status: Rare, at St. John's.

FE(A)VER, LEFEUVRE, variants of a surname of England, France and the Channel Islands, Fè(b)vre, Lefè(b)vre, from Latin *faber*, Old French *fev(e)re* – smith. (Reaney, Dauzat, Turk).

In Newfoundland:

Early instances: —— Le Feuvre, of Burin, 1789 (D'Alberti 4); Mary Ann Feaver, of St. John's, 1845 (DPHW 26D).

Modern status: Feaver, at St. John's and Corner Brook; Fever, at Deer Lake; LeFeuvre, at St. John's and Bulls Cove (Burin district).

Place name: Lefevre Shoal 51-20 56-05.

FEEHAN, a surname of Ireland, (O)Feehan, *Ó Fiacháin*, Ir. *fiach* – raven or *fiadhach* – hunt. (MacLysaght).

Traced by MacLysaght in Cos. Tipperary and Kilkenny.

In Newfoundland:

Early instances: William, from Oonan Parish (unidentified) (Co. Kilkenny), married at St. John's, 1809 (Nfld. Archives BRC); William, from Oonan (Co. Kilkenny), tailor of St. John's, deceased, 1814 (*Royal Gazette* 6 Oct 1814); John, of Ragged Harbour (now Melrose), 1815 (Nfld. Archives KCRC); Anne, of Catalina, 1822 (Nfld. Archives KCRC); Timothy Feehee, of Greenspond, 1823 (Nfld. Archives KCRC); Michael Feen, of Fogo, 1833 (Nfld. Archives KCRC).

Modern status: At Melrose (Trinity B.) and St. John's.

FEENER, ? a variant of the surname of England Finer, from Old French *fineur* – refiner of gold, silver, etc. (Reaney).

In Newfoundland:

Modern status: At Bishop's Falls, Grand Falls and Point Leamington.

FEILD, FIELD, surnames of England, Field(s) of Ireland; in England and Ireland – (dweller by the) cultivated land or open fields, in Ireland also for (O)Fehilly, *Ó Fithcheallaigh* – chess player, and for Maghery, *An Mhachaire* – of the field. (Reaney, MacLysaght).

Guppy traced Field chiefly in the south Midlands and Sussex, Spiegelhalter in Devon, and MacLysaght (for Maghery) in Co. Armagh.

In Newfoundland:

Family tradition: —— Field, from England to Trinity Bay in ? the early 19th century, thence to Griguet and Cook's Harbour (MUN Folklore).

Early instances: James Feild, of Bonaventure, 1675 (CO 1); John Field, of Petty Harbour, 1677 (CO 1); John Feild, of St. John's Harbour, 1680 (CO 1);

Richard, from Ipplepen (Devon), married at St. John's, 1772 (DPHW 26D); Thomas, of Heart's Content, 1833 (Nfld. Archives KCRC); Will, of Trinity, 1846 (Nfld. Archives KCRC); John, from East Ogwell (Devon), master mariner of St. John's, deceased, 1847 (*Royal Gazette* 29 Jun 1847); James and William, of Gullies (Brigus district), 1871 (Lovell); George, teacher of New Bonaventure, 1871 (Lovell).

Modern status: Feild, rare, at St. John's; Field, scattered, especially at St. John's and Torbay.

Place names (? from the surname): Field Harbour 48-32 53-49; —— —— Pond 48-32 53-47; The Field 49-33 53-03.

FELIX, a baptismal name and surname of England, Felix of France, from the Latin *felix* – happy, "the name of four popes and several saints." (Withycombe, Reaney, Cottle).

In Newfoundland:

Family tradition: ——, from France or St. Pierre, settled at the Maison d'Hiver (Winterhouse), L'Anse au Canard between 1890 and 1910 (MUN Geog.).

Early instances: Amédée Buisson, arrived in L'Anse au Canard from France in 1844, married Christine Felix; Louis Felix, born 1860, moved to Maison d'Hiver from Campbell's Creek between 1880–84 (Thomas, "French Fam. Names"). Alicia, of West St. Modeste, 1909 (Nfld. Archives HGRC).

Modern status: Especially at Felix Cove and elsewhere in the Port au Port district.

Place name: Felix Cove 48-32 58-47.

FELTHAM, a surname of England from the English place name Feltham (Somerset, Middlesex), or (dweller near the) hay meadow. (Cottle, Ekwall).

In Newfoundland:

Early instances: John, of Greenspond, in joint possession of fishing room at Pig Island (Greenspond), 1803 (Bonavista Register 1806); Thomas and Abel, of Deer Island (Bonavista B.), baptized 1830, aged 2 1/2 years (DPHW 76); Sarah, baptized at Pool's Island, 1830, aged 26 years (DPHW 76); Charles, ? from Devon or London, road commissioner for the Deer Island district, 1847 (*Nfld. Almanac*, MUN Folklore); John, of Fair Island (Bonavista B.), 1849 (DPHW 76); Samuel, planter of Silver Hare (now Silver Fox) Island, 1871 (Lovell).

Modern status: Widespread, especially at Glovertown and elsewhere in the Bonavista North district.

FENNELL, a surname of England and Ireland – (a grower of) fennel, or a development of the surname FitzNeal; in Ireland also (O)Fennell, *Ó Fionnghail* – fair valour, or confused with FENNELLY. (Reaney, MacLysaght).

Traced by Spiegelhalter in Devon and by MacLysaght in Cos. Clare, Dublin, Kilkenny and Tipperary.

In Newfoundland:

Family tradition: ——, from Scotland, was one of the first settlers at Plate Cove West (MUN Folklore).

Early instances: Mary Fennel, of Keels, 1813 (Nfld. Archives BRC); Richard Fennell, of Bonavista, 1818 (Nfld. Archives KCRC); ——, guide of Holyrood, 1822 (D'Alberti 32); John Fennell or Fennill, of Harbour Grace, 1836 (Nfld. Archives HGRC); John Fennell, from Waterford, of Harbour Grace, 1844 (*Indicator* 27 Jul 1844); Thomas Fennele or Fennile, of Plate Cove (Bonavista B.), 1845 (Nfld. Archives KCRC); John Fennell, of Birchy Cove (Bonavista B.), 1850 (Nfld. Archives KCRC); Richard, of Numins (for Newman's) Cove, 1850 (Nfld. Archives KCRC); Richard, of St. John's, 1850 (DPHW 23).

Modern status: Especially at Plate Cove West.

FENNELLY, a surname of Ireland (O)Fennelly, *Ó Fionnghalaigh* – fair valour, with which FENNELL is confused. (MacLysaght). *See also* FINLAY.

Traced by MacLysaght in Cos. Kilkenny, Leix and Offaly.

In Newfoundland:

Early instances: James Fenly, of St. John's, 1805 (Nfld. Archives BRC); Margaret Fenly alias Ryan, of Placentia, 1808 (Nfld. Archives BRC); Thomas Fennelly, from Burnt Church (unidentified) (Co. Kilkenny), planter of Trepassey, deceased 1815 (*Royal Gazette* 20 Apr 1815); Margaret Fenly, of Harbour Grace Parish, 1824 (Nfld. Archives HGRC); John and Thomas Fennelly, fishermen of Fermeuse, 1871 (Lovell); Patrick and Thomas, of St. Shotts, 1871 (Lovell).

Modern status: In the Ferryland district.

FENNESSEY, a variant of the surnames of Ireland (O)Fennessy, Finnessy, *Ó Fionnghusa* – fair vigour or action. (MacLysaght).

"Mainly of Co. Waterford" (MacLysaght).

In Newfoundland:

Early instances: James Fennessy, from Carrickbeg (Co. Waterford), married at St. John's, 1809 (Nfld. Archives BRC); James Fenesy, given possession of ground for fishing room on Kelly's Island, 1818 (D'Alberti 28); Silvester Finnesy, of Harbour Grace Parish, 1827 (Nfld. Archives HGRC);

Michael Fennessey, planter of Middle Cove (St. John's district), 1871 (Lovell); William Fennessy, miner of Tilt Cove, 1871 (Lovell); Thomas Finnesey, fisherman of Little Placentia (now Argentia), 1871 (Lovell); James and Nicholas, of Marquise, 1871 (Lovell).

Modern status: In the St. John's district.

FENNIMORE, a variant of the surname of England, Finnemore, from Old French *fin amour* – dear love, or from the English place names Finmere (Oxfordshire) or Fennymere (Shropshire). (Reaney, Spiegelhalter). *See also* FILLMORE.

Guppy traced Fenemore in Buckinghamshire and Oxfordshire; Spiegelhalter traced Fennamore, Finnamore in Devon.

In Newfoundland:

Early instance: Henry Finnemore or Fenemore, fisherman of Barr'd Islands, 1846 (DPHW 83).

Modern status: Rare, at Barr'd Islands, Grand Falls (*Electors* 1955) and St. Anthony.

FERGUSON, a surname of England, Scotland and Ireland, an anglicization of the surname of Scotland MacFergus, Gaelic *MacFe(a)rgus*, Old Irish *Fergus*, *fear* – man, *gus* – vigour. "It is used as a synonym of Fergus in Co. Leitrim." (MacLysaght, Black).

Traced by Guppy in Cumberland, Westmorland and Northumberland, widespread in Scotland; and found numerous in Ulster and in Co. Leitrim by MacLysaght.

In Newfoundland:

Early instance: John, of St. John's, 1776 (DPHW 26C).

Modern status: Rare, at St. John's and Corner Brook.

Place name: Ferguson or Dan Ferguson Bay (Labrador) 52-58 66-15.

FERMAN, an anglicization of the Russian Jewish surname Fúrman(ov), (German Fuhrmann) – driver, coachman. (Unbegaun).

In Newfoundland:

Modern status: Rare, at St. John's.

FERRIE, FERRY, surnames of England, FERRY of Ireland, France and Jersey (Channel Islands); in England from the English place name Ferrybridge (Yorkshire WR) or (dweller near or worker at the) ferry; in Ireland, (O)Fairy, Ferry, *Ó Fearadhaigh*; in France, Ferry, Féry, popular forms of the baptismal name Frédéric. (Reaney, MacLysaght, Dauzat, Turk).

Matthews traced Ferry in Devon and Dorset; MacLysaght traced Farry in Co. Sligo.

In Newfoundland:

Early instances: Patrick Ferry, of Bonavista, 1830 (Nfld. Archives KCRC); Michael, of Birchy Cove (Bonavista B.), 1850 (Nfld. Archives KCRC).

Modern status: Ferrie, rare, at St. Lawrence; Ferry, rare, at Lord's Cove (*Electors* 1955) and St. John's.

FEWER, a surname of Ireland (O)Fewer, *Ó Fiodhabhair* – bushy eyebrow, a variant of Feore in Cos. Kilkenny and Waterford. *See also* FUREY. (MacLysaght).

In Newfoundland:

Early instances: Mary, of St. Mary's, married at St. John's, 1808 (Nfld. Archives BRC); Edmond, of Harbour Grace Parish, 1809 (Nfld. Archives HGRC); Anne, from Mooncoin (Co. Kilkenny), married at St. John's, 1828 (Nfld. Archives BRC); Catherine, of Holyrood, 1839 (Nfld. Archives BRC); Dennis (and others), of Chapel's Cove (Conception B.), 1871 (Lovell); Peter, fisherman of Lawn, 1871 (Lovell); John, farmer of Lear's Cove (St. Mary's district), 1871 (Lovell); Edward, of Rushoon, 1871 (Lovell); Richard and William, of Salmonier (St. Mary's B.), 1871 (Lovell); John, of Trepassey, 1871 (Lovell).

Modern status: Scattered, especially at Chapel's Cove and St. Bernard's.

FIANDER, ? a variant of the surname of England Viant from Old French *viande* – (seller of) meat, food. Reaney Notes traced John Vyander of Sampford Peverell (Devon) in 1524.

In Newfoundland:

Family tradition: ——, from ? Aberporth, Wales, settled at English Harbour West (MUN Folklore).

Early instances: James, of English Harbour (Bay de l'Eau), 1835 (DPHW 30); Mary, of Fortune, 1838 (DPHW 106); Stephen, fisherman of Coomb's Cove (Burin district), 1851 (DPHW 104); Thomas, planter of Belleoram, 1871 (Lovell); William Fyander, of Codroy and Rivers, 1871 (Lovell); James and William Fiander, of St. Jacques, 1871 (Lovell).

Modern status: Scattered, especially at English Harbour West.

FIELD. *See* FEILD

FIFIELD, a surname of England from the English place names Fifield (Oxfordshire, Wiltshire) or Fyfield (Berkshire, Essex, Gloucestershire, Hampshire, Wiltshire) – (owner of or dweller on) five hides of land, a hide being "an amount of land for the support of one free family and its dependants," about 120 acres, but varying in different parts of the country. (Reaney, A. H. Smith).

Guppy traced a variant Fifett in Dorset.

In Newfoundland:

Early instances: Thomas, of Trinity (Trinity B.), 1778 (DPHW 64); James, of Bonavista, 1800 (DPHW 70); John, of Twillingate, 1811 (D'Alberti 22); John, fisherman of Pease Cove (Trinity B.), 1858 (DPHW 64B); Joseph, of Musgravetown, 1871 (Lovell); Giles, of Salmon Cove (now Champneys), 1871 (Lovell); Thomas, of Swain's Island, 1871 (Lovell).

Modern status: Widespread, especially at Bonavista.

FIGARY, ? an anglicization of the surname of France Figuier – (dweller by the) fig-tree, or ? a variant of the surnames of England and Ireland Vicary, Vickery, from Latin *vicarius* – vicar.

Guppy traced Vicary, Vickery in Devon, Vickery in Somerset. MacLysaght traced Vickery especially in Co. Cork.

In Newfoundland:

Modern status: Rare, at Channel.

FILLATRE, a surname of France and Jersey (Channel Islands), Fillâtre – son-in-law. (Dauzat, Turk).

Traced by Dauzat in the area of Lyons.

In Newfoundland:

Early instances: Francis Lafillartre, of St. George's Harbour (St. George's B.), 1830 (DPHW 30), alternatively, Francis LaFillatre, native of France (Thomas, "French Fam. Names"); Francis Fillatre, of Little Barachoix (St. George's district), 1870 (DPHW 96); Samuel Fillatre or Le Filatre, of Sandy Point (St. George's district), 1871 (DPHW 96, Lovell).

Modern status: Scattered, on the West Coast, especially in the St. George's district.

FILLIER, a Newfoundland variant of FILLEUL, a surname of the Channel Islands, in France also Filhoh, Fr. *filleul* – godchild.

Traced by LeMessurier and Turk in the Channel Islands.

In Newfoundland:

Family tradition: Derives Fillier from an English surname Phillyard. —— from the west of England to St. John's in the 1830s, to Englee in the 1860s (Family).

Early instances: Elias Filleul, of Port de Grave, 1790, property "in possession of the Family for upwards of 120 years," that is, before 1670 (CO 199.18); Ann Feller or Fillier, of Port de Grave, 1816 (DPHW 31, 58); Isaac Philiar, of the Goulds (Brigus), 1840 (DPHW 34); John Filyer, fisherman of Clarkes Beach, 1842 (DPHW 39); Elias Fillier, of Salmon Cove Beach (now part of South River), 1851 (DPHW 34); John, fisherman of Northern River (now North River), 1860 (DPHW 38); John Filliar, of Bareneed, 1871 (Lovell).

Modern status: Fillier, scattered, especially in the Port de Grave district and at Englee and Roddickton; Filleul, unique, at Burgeo (*Electors* 1955).

FILLMORE, a surname of England, ? a variant of Fil(l)imore or Filmer from ? German personal names such as *Filimar* or *Filomor* – very famous, or ? from the English place name Filmore Hill (Hampshire), or ? a variant of FENNIMORE. (E.C. Smith, Reaney Notes, Bardsley).

Guppy traced Phillimore in Gloucestershire; Matthews traced Filmore in Devon.

In Newfoundland:

Early instances: Thomas Filmore, of Ferryland, 1681 (CO 1); —— Fillmore, on the *New Era*, 1853 (*Newfoundlander* 29 Aug 1853); Mrs. E. Filmore, of St. John's, 1871 (Lovell).

Modern status: Rare, at Corner Brook.

FINCH, a surname of England and Ireland, from Old English *fink* – finch, ? used as a nickname for a simpleton. (Reaney, Cottle, MacLysaght).

Traced by Guppy in Hertfordshire, Gloucestershire and Worcestershire, by Spiegelhalter in Devon, and by MacLysaght first in Munster but now mainly in Ulster.

In Newfoundland:

Early instances: Samuel Thomas, of Trinity (Trinity B.), 1798 (DPHW 64); James, of Harbour Grace Parish, 1810 (Nfld. Archives HGRC); Elizabeth, of Brigus, 1829 (*Newfoundlander* 9 Jul 1829).

Modern status: At St. John's.

FINDLATER, a surname of Scotland, from the Scots place name Findlater (Banffshire).

In Newfoundland:

Early instances: ——, of Bunting, Findlater and Co., of St. John's, 1838 (*Newfoundlander* 11 Jan 1838); Henry, physician of Fogo, 1857 (*Nfld. Almanac*, DPHW 83).

Modern status: Rare, at St. John's (*Electors* 1955).

FINLAY, a surname of Scotland and Ireland, with a number of variants such as Findlay, Fin(d)ley, an anglicization of the Gaelic name *Fionnlagh* – fair hero; in Ireland also as a synonym of FENNELLY in Cos. Leix and Offaly. (Black, MacLysaght).

Traced by Guppy in Ayrshire and by MacLysaght in Cos. Leix and Offaly and presumably also elsewhere.

In Newfoundland:

Early instances: James Finley, of Halifax, N.S., married at St. John's, 1814 (DPHW 26D); Mary Finly, of St. John's, 1819 (Nfld. Archives BRC); Margaret Finlay, of Harbour Grace Parish, 1825 (Nfld. Archives HGRC); John Finnley, of Riders Harbour (Trinity B.), 1832 (Nfld. Archives KCRC); Daniel, fisherman of Codroy and Rivers, 1871 (Lovell); —— Finlay, from Waterford, of St. Shotts, died 1891, aged 76 years (Dillon).

Modern status: Scattered, especially at St. Shotts.

FINN, a surname of England, Scotland and Ireland; in England and Scotland from an Old English and Old Scandinavian personal name *Fin(n)(r)* – the Finn; in Ireland (O)Finn, *Ó Finn*, Ir. *fionn* – fair. (Reaney, Black, MacLysaght).

Traced by Guppy in Kent and by MacLysaght in Cos. Monaghan, Sligo and Cork.

In Newfoundland:

Early instances: Robert, of Harbour Main, 1755 (MUN Hist.); Alexander, of St. John's, 1765 (DPHW 26C); James, from Odennahaugh (Co. Armagh), Irish convict landed at Petty Harbour or Bay Bulls, 1789 (CO 194.38); John, fisherman of Torbay, 1794–5, "born in Newfoundland" (Census 1794–5); Eleanor Fynn, of Trepassey, 1808 (Nfld. Archives BRC); Alice Finn, from St. Mullins (Co. Carlow), married at St. John's, 1813 (Nfld. Archives BRC); Patrick, of Harbour Grace Parish, 1821 (Nfld. Archives HGRC); Thomas, of Carbonear, 1829 (Nfld. Archives BRC); Edward, from Co. Tipperary, of Harbour Grace, 1844 (*Indicator* 27 Jul 1844); Thomas, from Co. Wexford, of Carbonear, died 1880, aged 84 years (R.C. Cemetery, Carbonear); Patrick, planter of Fermeuse, 1871 (Lovell); James, farmer of Goulds Road (Brigus district), 1871 (Lovell); Patrick, fisherman of Shoal Bay (Ferryland district), 1871 (Lovell); John and Richard, of Spaniards Bay, 1871 (Lovell).

Modern status: Scattered, especially at St. John's and Carbonear.

FINNEY, a surname of England, Scotland and Ireland; in England ? from the English place name Fenny (Worcestershire); in Scotland and Ireland (Ulster), a variant of (O)Feeney, *Ó Fidhne*, *Ó*

Fiannaidhe – soldier. (A. H. Smith, Black, MacLysaght).

Traced by Guppy in Derbyshire, Staffordshire and Worcestershire and by MacLysaght in Ulster.

In Newfoundland:

Early instances: John Finne, planter of Western Bay, 1834 (DPHW 52A); Rev. John Phinney, of Grand Bank, 1866 (MUN Hist.); John Finnie, of St. John's, 1871 (Lovell); James Finny, of Renews-Cape Race district, 1871 (Lovell).

Modern status: Rare, at St. John's.

Place name: Finnies Pond 47-22 53-04.

FIRMAGE, a surname of England (Reaney). *See also* FORMANGER.

In Newfoundland:

Early instances: —— Fermage, of Fortune Bay, 1789 (D'Alberti 4); Samuel Furmidge or Firmage, of Fair Islands, 1850 (DPHW 76).

Modern status: Firmage, at Wareham (Bonavista B.).

Place names: Firmage's Cove, —— Head, —— Island 47-39 58-34.

FIRTH, a surname of England and Scotland, in England from Old English *firhthe* etc. – frith, wood (land); in Scotland from the place name Firth (Roxburghshire, Orkney). (Reaney, Cottle, Black).

Traced by Guppy in Yorkshire WR and by Black in Orkney.

In Newfoundland:

Early instances: Gideon, of Harbour Grace, 1771 (Nfld. Archives L118); George Robert, born at Gosport (Hampshire), baptized at St. John's, 1821 (DPHW 26B).

Modern status: Rare, at St. John's.

FISHER, a surname of England, Scotland, Ireland and the Channel Islands, from Old English *fiscere* – fisherman, or occasionally (dweller by the) fishery, enclosure for catching fish; in Ireland also a synonym of Salmon and an anglicized form of the Scots surname MacInesker. (Reaney, Cottle, Black, MacLysaght, Turk).

Found widespread by Guppy especially in Cumberland and Westmorland, and scattered in Scotland, and by Spiegelhalter in Devon.

In Newfoundland:

Early instances: William, of Trinity Bay, 1769 (DPHW 64); Robert, from Dublin, Irish convict landed at Petty Harbour or Bay Bulls, 1789 (CO 194.38); John, of Bonavista, 1792 (USPG); William, proprietor and occupier of fishing room at New

Perlican, Winter 1800–01 (Census Trinity B.); Michael, of St. John's, 1814 (CO 194.55); James, of Bird Island Cove (now Elliston), 1823 (DPHW 70); Robert, of Port de Grave, 1847 (DPHW 39); John, of Harbour Grace, 1858 (*Newfoundlander* 22 Apr 1858); Christopher, from Musqodokit, Nova Scotia, a descendant of United Empire Loyalists, settled at Corner Brook in 1871 (*Nfld. Who's Who* 1930).

Modern status: Scattered, especially at Bonavista.

Place names (not necessarily from the surname): Fisher Cove 48-22 53-22; —— Island (Labrador) 57-56 62-02; Fishers Point 46-40 53-04.

FITZGERALD, a surname of England and Ireland, in Irish *MacGerailt* – son of Gerald. (Reaney, MacLysaght).

Traced by Spiegelhalter in Devon and found "very numerous" by MacLysaght.

In Newfoundland:

Early instances: Dennis, fisherman of St. John's, 1794–5, "46 years in Newfoundland," that is, 1748–9 (Census 17945); Maurice, of Western Bay, 1771 (CO 199.18); John, in possession of property in the fishery at Torbay, 1794–5, "8 years in Newfoundland," that is, 1786–7 (Census 1794–5); Martin, from Stradbally (Co. Kerry), married at St. John's, 1801 (Nfld. Archives BRC); Elizabeth, of Bonavista, 1803 (Nfld. Archives BRC); Edward, in possession of fishing room at Keels, built by the family before 1805 (Bonavista Register 1806); Thomas, of Harbour Grace Parish, 1806 (Nfld. Archives HGRC); John, from Waterford, of the Isle of Spear, deceased, 1810 (*Royal Gazette* 30 Jun 1810); John, one of 72 impressed men who sailed from Ireland to Newfoundland, ? 1811 (CO 194.51); Patrick, from Middleton (Co. Cork), labourer of Harbour Grace, deceased, 1814 (*Royal Gazette* 1814); William, of King's Cove, 1816 (Nfld. Archives KCRC); Patrick, of Trinity, 1826 (Nfld. Archives KCRC); John, of Joe Batts Arm, 1831 (Nfld. Archives KCRC); James, from Wexford, of Fogo, 1837 (*Nfld. Patriot* 21 Oct 1837); Thomas, ? of Northern Bay, 1838 (DPHW 54); Eleanor, of Riders Harbour (Trinity B.), 1838 (Nfld. Archives KCRC); Edward, of Open Hall, 1841 (DPHW 73A); James, from Co. Cork, of Port de Grave, 1844 (*Indicator* 24 Aug 1844); Hanah, of Indian Arm, 1858 (Nfld. Archives KCRC); Joseph, of Broad Cove (now Duntara), 1858 (Nfld. Archives KCRC); Mary, of Haywards Cove (Bonavista B.), 1866 (Nfld. Archives KCRC); widespread in 1871.

Modern status: Widespread, especially at St. John's and Keels.

Place name: Fitzgerald's Cove (Labrador) 55-10 59-08.

FITZGIBBON, a surname of Ireland, in Irish *Mac Giobúin* – son of *Gibb-un*, a diminutive of *Gibb* (Gilbert). (MacLysaght, Reaney). *See* GILBERT.

Traced by MacLysaght especially in Co. Limerick.

In Newfoundland:

Early instances: Catherine Fitzgibbon alias Costelloe, of St. John's, 1804 (Nfld. Archives BRC); Conrad Fitzgibbons, of Harbour Grace Parish, 1816 (Nfld. Archives HGRC); William Fitzgibbon, of Harbour Grace, 1869 (Nfld. Archives HGRC); Jeremiah, fisherman of Bay de Verde, 1871 (Lovell); Edward (and others), of St. John's, 1871 (Lovell).

Modern status: Fitzgibbon, rare, at St. John's; Fitzgibbons, unique, at Bay de Verde.

FITZPATRICK, a surname of England and Ireland, *Mac Giolla Phádraig* – devotee of St. Patrick, "The only Fitz name of Gaelic-Irish origin," the others being of Norman origin. (MacLysaght). *See* PATRICK.

Traced by Spiegelhalter in Devon and by MacLysaght in Cos. Kilkenny, Fermanagh and Leix.

In Newfoundland:

Family traditions: Peter and Catherine, born On St. Pierre, moved to Lamaline in 1880 (MUN Folklore). Susan, of St. Lawrence, 1863 (MUN Geog.).

Early instances: Patrick, of St. John's, 1753 (DPHW 26C); John, of Placentia, 1794 (D'Alberti 5); Michael, from Golmoy (unidentified) (Co. Kilkenny), married at St. John's, 1803 (Nfld. Archives BRC); Patrick, from Mullinvat (Co. Kilkenny), of Bay Roberts, 1803, deceased, 1817 (CO 199.18, *Royal Gazette* 10 Jun 1817); Mary, of Ragged Harbour (now Melrose), 1817 (Nfld. Archives KCRC); John, of Harbour Grace Parish, 1819 (Nfld. Archives HGRC); Frederic, of Little Placentia (now Argentia), 1821 (Nfld. Archives BRC); William, of Trepassey, 1823 (Nfld. Archives BRC); Thomas, of Harbour Grace, 1828 (Nfld. Archives BRC); widespread in Lovell 1871.

Modern status: Widespread, especially at Marystown, St. Lawrence, Lord's Cove and St. John's.

FIZZARD, a surname of England, a variant of Wishart, Vizard etc., from a personal name, Old Norman French *Wise(h)ard*, Old French *Guisc(h)ard*, *Guiscart* from Old Norse *vizkr* – wise and the French suffix *-(h)ard*. (Reaney).

Traced by Matthews in Dorset.

In Newfoundland:

Early instance: William, servant of Muddy Hole (Burin), 1871 (Lovell).

Modern status: Scattered, especially at Creston North.

(O)FLAHERTY, surnames of Ireland, *Ó Flaithbheartaigh* – bright ruler. (MacLysaght).

Traced by MacLysaght in Cos. Kerry and Galway.

In Newfoundland:

Early instances: John Flaherty, fisherman of St. John's, 1794–5, "43 years in Newfoundland," that is, 1751–2 (Census 1974–5); Bryant Flaharty, of Long Harbour, 1765 (CO 194.16); Mary Anne, of Harbour Grace Parish, 1813 (Nfld. Archives HGRC); E. Flaherty, from Carrick-on-Suir (Co. Tipperary), married at St. John's, 1813 (Nfld. Archives BRC); Mary Flaharty, of Perlican (unspecified), 1815 (Nfld. Archives KCRC); Edward O'Flaherty, of St. John's, 1856 (*Newfoundlander* 11 Dec 1856); Edward Flaherty, of Gasters, 1859 (Nfld. Archives T14); Edward, fisherman of Fermeuse, 1871 (Lovell); James and Patrick, farmers of Turk's Gut (now Marysvale), 1871 (Lovell).

Modern status: Flaherty, at Avondale; O'Flaherty, scattered.

Place names: Flaherty Hill 46-58 55-41; —— Island 47-48 54-56.

FLAN(N)IGAN, for the surname of Ireland (O)Flanagan, *Ó Flannagáin*, Ir. *flann* – red, ruddy. (MacLysaght).

Traced by MacLysaght in Cos. Fermanagh, Offaly and Roscommon.

In Newfoundland:

Early instances: James Flanagan, from Waterford, carpenter ? of St. John's, 1777 (CO 194.33); Thomas Flannagan, of Bay de Verde, 1789 (CO 199.18); John Flanagan, of Gasters, 1790 (CO 199.18); Pierce, of Harbour Grace Parish, 1813 (Nfld. Archives HGRC); —— O'Flanagan, married at St. John's, 1833 (Nfld. Archives BRC); Peter Flanigan, farmer of Holyrood, 1871 (Lovell); Martin, of Maddox Cove (St. John's), 1871 (Lovell); James and Michael Flannigan, farmers of Logy Bay, 1871 (Lovell).

Modern status: Flanigan, rare, at Avondale; Flannigan, scattered.

Place name: Flannagan Island 47-37 57-42.

FLEET, a surname of England from the English place name Fleet (Devon, Lincolnshire), or (dweller by the) estuary or stream. (Reaney, Spiegelhalter).

Traced by Spiegelhalter in Devon.

In Newfoundland:

Early instances: George, soldier of St. John's, 1815 (DPHW 26B); Alexander, born at Cuckold's Cove (now Dunfield), 1826 (DPHW 64B); Mary, servant of Trinity (Trinity B.), 1829 (DPHW 64B); Rev. B., of Middle Bight (now Codner), 1871 (Lovell).

Modern status: Scattered, especially at St. John's.

FLEM(M)ING(S), surnames of England, Scotland and Ireland – the Fleming, the man from Flanders. (Reaney, Cottle, Black, MacLysaght).

Guppy traced Fleming in Cumberland and Westmorland and found it widespread in Scotland except in the north; Spiegelhalter traced Flemen, Fleming and Flamank in Devon; Cottle traced Fleming in Kent and Pembrokeshire; and MacLysaght found it "very numerous in all the four provinces."

In Newfoundland:

Family tradition: —— Fleming, from Ireland, settled at Burin in the early 19th century (MUN Folklore).

Early instances: John Fleming, of Newfoundland, ? 1706 (CO 194.24); Mary Flemming, baptized at St. John's, 1765 (DPHW 26C); Michael, from Ross (unspecified), Ireland, married at St. John's, 1805 (Nfld. Archives BRC); Matthew Flem(m)ing, of Harbour Grace Parish, 1807 (Nfld. Archives HGRC); Michael Fleming, from Waterford, married in the Northern District, 1812 (Nfld. Archives BRC); Richard, from Ballynabogue, Parish of Ballylalen (unidentified) (Co. Waterford), fisherman of Marystown, deceased, 1813 (*Royal Gazette* 10 Jun 1813); James, from Ballicloheen, Windgap Parish (Co. Waterford), fisherman of St. John's, deceased, 1813 (*Royal Gazette* 2 Dec 1813); Patrick, of Bonavista, 1815 (Nfld. Archives KCRC); Elinor, of Trinity, 1816 (Nfld. Archives KCRC); William, of Bareneed, 1816 (Nfld. Archives L165); John Flemming, of Renews, 1830 (Nfld. Archives BRC); Patrick Fleming, of Torbay, 1835 (Nfld. Archives BRC); Michael, ? of Northern Bay, 1838 (DPHW 54); Edward, from Co. Waterford, of Harbour Grace, 1844 (*Indicator* 27 Jul 1844); Thomas Flemming, planter of Spillers Cove (Bonavista district), 1849 (DPHW 72); widespread in Lovell 1871.

Modern status: Fleming, widespread, especially at Spillers Cove and St. John's; Flemming, scattered, especially at St. John's; Flemmings, rare, at Middle Arm (Green B.).

Place names: Fleming Lake (Labrador) 54-50 67-07; Mount —— 49-33 56-50; —— Point 49-07 58-21; Flemming Rock (Labrador) 53-54 56-55.

FLETCHER, a surname of England, Scotland and Ireland from Old French *flech(i)er* – maker or seller of arrows, but originally "apparently one who attached the *flèches* or feathers to the arrowshaft" (Black); or for the surname Flesher – butcher. (Reaney, Black, Spiegelhalter, MacLysaght).

Found widespread by Guppy especially in Derbyshire and Nottinghamshire, by Spiegelhalter in Devon; and by MacLysaght ? in Ulster.

In Newfoundland:

Early instances: J., of St. John's Harbour, 1703 (CO 194.3); John, of Ferryland, 1708–09 (CO 194.4); John, in possession of land in Northern Bay before 1775 (CO 194.45); Benjamin, of Hermitage Cove (Burin district), 1834 (DPHW 109); Daniel, cooper of Harbour Grace, 1871 (Lovell).

Modern status: Rare, at Lark Harbour, Grand Falls (*Electors* 1955) and St. John's.

Place names: Fletcher Lake (Labrador) 54-20 66-01; —— Point (Labrador) 56-56 61-21.

FLIGHT, a surname of England, ? an archer who used the longbow. (E.C. Smith).

In Newfoundland:

Family tradition: ——, from "somewhere around Plymouth," settled at Small Point (Conception B.) in the late 18th century (MUN Folklore).

Early instances: James, of Small Point (Conception B.), 1796 (CO 199.18); James, fisherman of Mulley's Cove, 1828 (DPHW 52A); Richard, fisherman of Blackhead (Bay de Verde district), 1854 (DPHW 52B); Alfred, fisherman of Moreton's Harbour, 1871 (Lovell); Job, farmer of Pouch Cove, 1871 (Lovell).

Modern status: Scattered, especially at Small Point.

Place name: Flights Brook 49-21 57-00.

FLOOD, a surname of England and Ireland; in England from Old English *flōd* or *flōde* – (dweller by the) stream or by the channel, gutter; in Ireland also for *Ó Maoltuile* or *Mac Tuile*, Ir. *tuile* – flood or *toil(e)* – will (of God), and in parts of Ulster for the Welsh surname Floyd, Welsh *llwyd* – grey. (Reaney, MacLysaght).

Traced by Spiegelhalter in Devon.

In Newfoundland:

Early instances: John, from Inistioge (Co. Kilkenny), resident of St. John's since 1782, died in 1840, aged 74 years (Census 1794–5, *Times* 26 Feb 1840); Thomas, of Harbour Grace Parish, 1810 (Nfld. Archives HGRC); Henry, of Bonavista, 1815 (Nfld. Archives KCRC); James, of Kings Cove, 1826

(Nfld. Archives KCRC); ? John, of Holyrood, 1839 (Nfld. Archives BRC); James, of Ferryland, 1840 (DPHW 31); Charles, of Bonavista, 1845 (DPHW 70); Charles, of Catalina, 1871 (Lovell).

Modern status: At St. John's and Grand Falls.

Place name: Flood's Pond 48-32 53-04.

FLORENCE, a baptismal name (both masculine and feminine) and surname of England and Scotland, from the Latin personal names *Florentius, Florentia*, Lat. *florens* – blooming, or (the man from) Florence, Italy. (Withycombe, Reaney, Black).

Traced by Black in Aberdeenshire.

In Newfoundland:

Early instances: John, carpenter of Carbonear, 1836 (DPHW 48); George, fisherman of Herring Neck, 1871 (Lovell).

Modern status: Unique, at Main Brook (White B.).

Place name: Florence Lake (Labrador) 56-53 61-32.

(O)FLYNN, surnames of Ireland, also Flinn, Flyng, *Ó Floinn*, Ir. *flann* – ruddy. (MacLysaght).

MacLysaght found the names "numerous and widespread."

In Newfoundland:

Family traditions: Nicholas Flynn (?1857–?1927), from Harbour Main, settled at West Bay (Port-au-Port district) about 1887 (MUN Geog.).

——, from Ireland, settled at Ann's Cove (Placentia B.) in 1837 (MUN Folklore).

Early instances: Edward Fling, of St. John's, 1759 (DPHW 26C); Michael Flynn, from Cork (Co. Cork), Irish convict landed at Petty Harbour or Bay Bulls in 1789 (CO 194.38); John Flinn, of Bonavista, 1790 (DPHW 70); Dominic Flynn, of Bay de Verde, 1797 (CO 199.18); James Flyn, from Ferron Parish (unidentified) (Co. Waterford), married at St. John's, 1798 (Nfld. Archives BRC); Robert Fling, of Colliers, 1802 (CO 199.18); Thomas Flynn, of Harbour Grace Parish, 1806 (Nfld. Archives HGRC); James Flinn, from Co. Cork, married in the Northern District, 1812 (Nfld. Archives BRC); Patrick, from Carrick-on-Suir (Co. Tipperary), shoreman of Harbour Grace, deceased, 1814 (*Royal Gazette* 13 Oct 1814); James Flynn, of Kings Cove, 1815 (Nfld. Archives KCRC); Samuel ? Fling, of Bareneed, 1816 (Nfld. Archives L165); John Flynn, of Bonavista, 1817 (Nfld. Archives KCRC); Patrick, of Tilton Harbour (now Tilting), 1822 (Nfld. Archives KCRC); Michael, of Trinity, 1822 (Nfld. Archives KCRC); Thomas, of Bird Island Cove (now Elliston), 1822 (DPHW 70); William, of Cats Cove (now Conception

Harbour), 1828 (Nfld. Archives BRC); Bridget Flynn or Fling, of Herring Neck, 1829 (Nfld. Archives KCRC); James Flynn, of Fortune Harbour, 1832 (Nfld. Archives KCRC); John, ? of Northern Bay, 1838 (DPHW 54); John Flinn, of Harbour Main, 1839 (Nfld. Archives BRC); David, from Co. Waterford, of Brigus, 1844 (*Indicator* 24 Aug 1844); Michael, ? from Cloyne (Co. Cork), of Port de Grave, 1844 (*Indicator* 24 Aug 1844); Thomas, of Keels, 1856 (Nfld. Archives KCRC); Michael Flynn, from Cloyne (Co. Cork), of Bay Roberts, 1856 (*Newfoundlander* 7 Aug 1856); James Flinn, of Muddy Hole (now Maberly), 1858 (DPHW 83); James, of Open Hall, 1859 (Nfld. Archives KCRC); Michael, of Cottels Island (Bonavista B.), 1868 (Nfld. Archives KCRC); Michael, of Stock Cove (Bonavista B.), 1870 (Nfld. Archives KCRC); widespread in Lovell 1871.

Modern status: Flynn, widespread, especially at West Bay, Conche and St. John's; O'Flynn, rare, at Placentia (*Electors* 1955).

Place names: Fling Bank (Labrador) 52-28 55-40; —— Islands (Labrador) 53-12 55-44; Fling's Big Pond, —— Long Pond 47-44 53-18; Little —— Pond 47-43 53-18; Flinn River 47-10 53-39.

FOGARTY, a surname of Ireland (O)Fogarty, *Ó Fógartaigh*, Ir. *fógartach* – expelling. (MacLysaght).

Traced by MacLysaght in Co. Tipperary.

In Newfoundland:

Family tradition: —— Fogarthy, of Joe Batts Arm, 1811–16 (MUN Hist.).

Early instances: Timothy Fogerty, in possession of property and shoreman of Torbay, 1794–5, "29 years in Newfoundland," that is, 1765–6 (Census 1794–5); Thomas Fogarty, of Northern Bay, 1796 (CO 199.18); Martin Fogerty, of St. John's, 1796 (CO 194.39); Margaret Fogarty, from Thurles (Co. Tipperary), married at Fogo, 1803 (Nfld. Archives BRC); Bartholomew Fogerty, married at Harbour Grace Parish, 1806 (Nfld. Archives HGRC); Peggy, from Tramore (Co. Waterford), married at St. John's, 1812 (Nfld. Archives BRC); Patricia, of Ochre Pit Cove, 1813 (Nfld. Archives BRC); Michael Fogarty, of Catalina, 1821 (Nfld. Archives KCRC); Judith, from Thurles (Co. Tipperary), of Harbour Grace, 1844 (*Indicator* 27 Jul 1844).

Modern status: Rare, at St. John's.

FOGWILL, a surname of England from the English place name Vogwell (Devon). (Spiegelhalter, Gover).

Traced by Spiegelhalter in Devon.

In Newfoundland:

Early instance: Samuel, storekeeper of Carbonear, 1871 (Lovell).

Modern status: Scattered, especially at St. John's and Millertown.

FOLEY, a surname of England, Ireland and Guernsey (Channel Islands); in England and Guernsey, ? a variant of FOLLETT; in Ireland (O)Foley, *Ó Foghladha*, Ir. *foghlaidhe* – plunderer, though in Co. Roscommon a synonym of Mac Sharry, *Mac Searraigh*, from *searrach* – foal. MacLysaght states that "The distinguished English family of Foley is said to be of Irish origin," but Cottle suggests that the Worcestershire family has probably another origin. (MacLysaght, Cottle, Bardsley, Turk). *See also* FOWLER.

Traced by MacLysaght in south Munster and Co. Roscommon, by Cottle and Bardsley in Worcestershire and neighbouring counties, and by Spiegelhalter in Devon.

In Newfoundland:

Family tradition: Mike (1796–1879), came to Newfoundland from Ireland in 1815 and settled at Fox Harbour (MUN Geog.).

Early instances: Patrick, fisherman of Torbay, 1794–5, "20 years in Newfoundland," that is, 1774–5 (Census 1794–5); John, from Dublin, Irish convict landed at Petty Harbour or Bay Bulls, 1789 (CO 194.38); Martin Foaley, of Placentia, 1794 (D'Alberti 5); William Foley, from Cashel Parish (Co. Tipperary), married at St. John's, 1804 (Nfld. Archives BRC); Thomas, of Harbour Grace, 1808 (D'Alberti 18); Bridget, of Tilting Harbour (now Tilting), 1812 (Nfld. Archives BRC); David, of Bonavista, 1818 (Nfld. Archives KCRC); Catherine, of King's Cove, 1829 (Nfld. Archives KCRC); Elenor Foly, of Joe Batts Arm, 1830 (Nfld. Archives KCRC); James Foley, of Burin, 1837 (Nfld. Archives BRC); Thomas, of Carbonear, 1837 (*Newfoundlander* 18 May 1837); Thomas, from Co. Waterford, of Brigus, 1844 (*Indicator* 24 Aug 1844); William, of Cat Harbour (now Lumsden), 1870 (Nfld. Archives KCRC); widespread in Lovell 1871.

Modern status: Widespread, especially at Tilting and Little Barrasway (Placentia B.).

Place names: Foley Cove 47-53 55-48; —— Gulch 48-04 59-09; Foley's Hill 47-32 53-15.

FOLK(E)S, FOOKES, surnames of England, (of 27 variants recorded by Reaney), from the Old French personal names *Fulco, Fouques* or Old German *Folco, Folco* – people. (Reaney).

Spiegelhalter traced ffoulkes, Fookes, Fowke(s) in Devon; Guppy traced Fooks in Dorset, Foulke and Fowke in Derbyshire, and Foulkes in North Wales.

In Newfoundland:

Early instances: Thomas Fooke, Fooks or Foolk, of Fogo, 1849 (DPHW 83); Thomas Fooks, of Island Harbour (Twillingate), 1871 (Lovell).

Modern status: Folkes, rare, at St. John's and Grand Falls; Folks, unique, at St. John's; Fookes, unique, at Twillingate (*Electors* 1955).

FOLLETT, a surname of England and the Channel Islands, from Old French *folet* – little fool or jester (Reaney, Spiegelhalter, Turk). *See also* FOLEY.

Traced by Guppy in Hampshire and Somerset and by Spiegelhalter in Devon.

In Newfoundland:

Family tradition: John (b. about 1780), at Scilly Cove (now Winterton), of French ancestry (MUN Folklore).

Early instances: Robert, J.P. of Trepassey, 1750 (CO 194.12); Joseph, of Western Bay, 1799 (CO 199.18); John, of St. John's, 1816 (DPHW 26D); Gaius, of Scilly Cove (now Winterton), 1823 (DPHW 64B); Mary, of Greenspond, 1830 (DPHW 76); Michael, planter of Cape St. Francis, 1838 (DPHW 52A); Mary Gassard Follet, of (Little) Heart's Ease, 1855 (Nfld. Archives KCRC); George and William Follett, of Clattice Harbour, 1871 (Lovell).

Modern status: Widespread, especially at Grand Beach (Burin district).

FONG, a Chinese name with a variety of meanings: square, place, method, compass directions, art, righteousness, justice.

In Newfoundland:

Family tradition: Jim, from Canton, China, settled at Baie Verte (MUN Folklore).

Modern status: At Botwood, St. John's and Carbonear.

FONTAINE, a surname of England, France and Jersey (Channel Islands), from Old French *fontaine*, Middle English *fontayne* – (dweller near the) spring, or from a French place name (La) Fontaine commonly found in combination with a determinative name. (Reaney, Dauzat, (Turk).

Guppy traced Fountain(e) in Buckinghamshire.

In Newfoundland:

Early instance: Thomas Fountin, of Western Bay, 1777 (CO 199.18).

Modern status: At Cape Bauld (*Electors* 1955).

FOOKES. *See* FOLKES

FOOTE, a surname of England and Ireland, from the Old Norse nickname *Fótr* or Old English *fōt* – (one with some deformity or oddity of the) foot; in Ireland, with LEGGE, an anglicized form of *Mac Coise*, Ir. *cos* – foot, leg. (Reaney, Cottle, MacLysaght).

Foot was traced by Guppy in Dorset, by Spiegelhalter in Devon, and by MacLysaght ? in Ulster.

In Newfoundland:

Family tradition: Thomas, was the first Foote to settle at Grand Bank, in the early 19th century (MUN Hist.).

Early instances: John Foots, of St. John's, about 1795 (Exeter Public Library Archives per Kirwin); Andrew Foote, of Battle Harbour, 1795 (MUN Hist.); Nicholas Foot, occupier of fishing room at Old Perlican, Winter 1800–01 (Census Trinity B.); Thomas, of Burin, 1805 (D'Alberti 15); William ? Foot, from Melvin Porlin (? Milborne Port) (Somerset), married at St. John's, 1806 (Nfld. Archives BRC); John, of Trinity (Trinity B.), 1811 (DPHW 64); William, of Harbour Grace Parish, 1818 (Nfld. Archives HGRC); Thomas Foote, of Grand Bank, 1826 (DPHW 106); John Foot, from Wincanton (Somerset), sailmaker of Carbonear, 1833 (DPHW 48, *Carbonear Star* 10 Apr 1833); Henry, of Long Island (Placentia B.), 1835 (DPHW 30); John Foote, of Exploits Burnt Island, 1842 (DPHW 86); Michael, planter of Western Bay, 1846 (DPHW 52A); John, fisherman of Seal Rocks (Burin district), 1847 (DPHW 102); John, merchant of Twillingate, 1852 (*Newfoundlander* 13 May 1852); Henry, of Red Island, 1856 (DPHW 101); William, of Pardy's Island, 1860 (DPHW 108); William, of Peter's Arm, 1860 (DPHW 92); Richard Foot, of Cinq Cerf, 1861 (DPHW 99); Joseph, fisherman of Foot's Cove (Burin district), 1861 (DPHW 108); Emmanuel Foot, son of John and Maria of Sturminster Newton (Dorset), servant of Newman and Co., Harbour Breton, married there 1863 (Harbour Breton Anglican Church Records per D.A. Macdonald); he later became a skipper; widespread in Lovell 1871.

Modern status: Widespread, especially at Burin and Lamaline.

Place names: Foot's Cape 47-14 54-51; —— Cove 47-33 56-52; —— Point 47-17 54-54.

FORAN, a surname of Ireland (O)Foran, *Ó Fuaráin*. (O)Forhane, Forahan, *Ó Fuartháin*, are "older forms of Foran used in Cos. Kerry and West Cork." (MacLysaght).

"Mainly found in Cos. Limerick and Waterford; also often changed to FORD." (MacLysaght).

In Newfoundland:

Early instances: Patrick For(e)han, merchant of St. John's, 1770 (CO 194.19, 29); Edward Foran, of Bell Isle (now Bell Island), 1812 (Nfld. Archives BRC); Michael, of Ferryland, 1813 (Nfld. Archives BRC); Thomas Forhan, ofHarbour Grace Parish, 1814 (Nfld. Archives HGRC); Anastasia Foran, from Waterford City, married at St. John's, 1816 (Nfld. Archives BRC); John W., born at Placentia, 1841 (Mott); James, fisherman of Bay of Islands, 1871 (Lovell).

Modern status: At St. John's.

FORBES, a surname of Scotland and Ireland from the Scots place name Forbes (Aberdeenshire); also in Ireland for Mac Firbis, *Mac Firbhisigh* – ? man of property. The name was pronounced until recently with two syllables. (Black, Cottle, MacLysaght).

Traced by Guppy especially in Aberdeenshire and Perthshire, and by MacLysaght in Co. Longford and in Connacht.

In Newfoundland:

Early instances: John Forbus, of St. John's, 1794–5 (Census 1794–5); Thomas Forbes, of St. John's, 1805 (Nfld. Archives BRC); Pat, of Harbour Grace Parish, 1843 (Nfld. Archives HGRC); Robert (1842–1901), from Downe (Perthshire), Scotland, died at St. John's, 1901 (General Protestant Cemetery, St. John's).

Modern status: At St. John's and Gander.

FORCEY, FORSEY, surnames of England and Guernsey (Channel Islands), ? a variant of Fossey from Old English **foss* – ditch, *ēg* – island, low-lying land – (dweller on or by the) low-lying land near, or surrounded by, a ditch or dike. The relationship between Forsey and Fossey may be similar to that between Forster and FOSTER, and between FORSE and FOSS. (Reaney, A. H. Smith).

Matthews traced Forsey and Fossey as planters in Devon and Dorset.

In Newfoundland:

Family tradition: George Forsey, from the Channel Islands settled at Grand Bank about 1763; his son Samuel, was the first Forsey to settle at Fortune (MUN Hist.).

Early instances: Samuel Forsey, planter of Fortune, 1811 (Surrogate Court, Fortune Bay 1802–19, 1821, pp. 73–152, PANL GN5/1/C/1 per P.E.L. Smith); George Forsey, planter of Grand Bank, 1818 (DPHW 109); John, of Fortune, 1823 (DPHW 106); Samuel Forsay, of Fogo, 1841 (DPHW 83); Aaron Forcey, fisherman of Channel, 1841 (DPHW 101).

Modern status: Forcey, rare, at Dark Cove East (Bonavista North district); Forsey, scattered, especially at Grand Bank, Seal Cove (Fortune B.) and Burin.

FORD, a surname of England and Ireland – (dweller by the) ford or from the English place name Ford (Somerset, Devon etc.); also in Ireland Ford(e), a synonym of several Irish surnames including FORAN. (Reaney, Spiegelhalter, MacLysaght).

Guppy found Ford widespread, especially in the southern and western counties.

In Newfoundland:

Family traditions: John, from Ireland settled at Fogo in the early 19th century, thence to Wesleyville (MUN Folklore). ——, from St. Malo, settled at Port aux Basques, about 1825 (MUN Folklore).

Early instances: William, of New Perlican, 1676 (CO 1); Thomas, of Petty Harbour, 1703 (CO 194.3); Thomas, of St. John's, 1705 (CO 194.3); Thomas, of Cupids, 1785 (CO 199.18); William, of Fogo, 1787 (MUN Hist.); Ger(r)ard or Gerald, of Bonavista, 1790 (D'Alberti 4); Sarah, of Tilton Harbour (now Tilting), 1808 (Nfld. Archives BRC); Stephen, of Brigus, 1810 (DPHW 34); William, of Port de Grave, 1816 (DPHW 58); James, of Harbour Grace Parish, 1818 (Nfld. Archives HGRC); Jerry Foard, from Waterford, Ireland, married at St. John's, 1821 (Nfld. Archives BRC); John ? Forde, from Bristol, England, married at St. John's, 1829 (Nfld. Archives BRC); John Ford, of Smart's Island (Bonavista North district), 1832 (DPHW 76); James, of Miller's Passage, 1835 (DPHW 30); John, of Red Island (Burgeo-La Poile district), 1841 (DPHW 101); Jeremiah, ? of Northern Bay, 1842 (DPHW 54); James, planter of Salmon Cove (now Champneys), 1843 (DPHW 64B); Enos, of Pushthrough, 1849 (DPHW 102); George, of English Harbour (Trinity B.), 1853 (DPHW 64B); James, of Parry's Cove (Random), 1858 (DPHW 64B); Walter, of Lower Burgeo, 1859 (DPHW 101); Thomas, of Channel, 1864 (DPHW 97); Edward, of Harbour Grace, (Nfld. Archives HGRC); widespread in Lovell 1871.

Modern status: Widespread, especially at Amherst Cove (Bonavista district) and Jackson's Arm.

Place names (not necessarily from the surname): Ford (Labrador) 56-28 61-12; —— Island 49-04 53-36; Mount —— (Labrador) 59-07 63-50; —— Point 49-52 56-47; Ford's Bight (Labrador) 55-06 59-05; —— Island 47-35 59-08, 49-08 53-33; —— Point

50-07 56-08; ―― Rock 47-18 54-46; ―― Bight
Point (Labrador) 55-08 59-07.

FORDHAM, a surname of England – (dweller at the)
homestead by the ford, or from the English place
name Fordham (Essex, Norfolk, Cambridgeshire).
(Bardsley, Cottle).
   Traced by Spiegelhalter in Devon.
   In Newfoundland:
   Modern status: Rare, at St. John's.

FORMANGER, a surname of France, Formage,
Fromage(r), from French *fromage* – (maker or seller
of) cheese. (Dauzat). *See also* FIRMAGE, CHEESEMAN.
   In Newfoundland:
   Family tradition: ―― Fromanger, from France
or St. Pierre, settled at Maison d'Hiver
(Winterhouse), at La Barre or L'Anse au Canard
between 1890 and 1910 (MUN Geog.).
   Modern status: At Long Point (Port-au-Port dis-
trict), Port Saunders (*Electors* 1955) and Aguathuna.

FORRESTAL, FORRISTAL(L), surnames of England
and Ireland, according to Weekley *Surnames*, from a
dialect word fore-stall, a paddock or way in front of
a farmhouse, used in Kent and Sussex, or from the
English place name Forstall (Sussex). (Reaney, A. H.
Smith).
   Traced by Weekley as a mediaeval surname in
Kent and Sussex, and by MacLysaght in Co.
Kilkenny.
   In Newfoundland:
   Early instances: Isaac Forristal, soldier of St.
John's, 1760 (DPHW 26C) Mary, of Harbour Grace,
1797 (Nfld. Archives BRC); Pierce Forestall, from
Co. Wexford, surgeon of St. Lawrence, 1797,
deceased 1814 (D'Alberti 7, *Royal Gazette* 14 Apr
1814); Richard Furstall, boatkeeper of Placentia,
1800 (D'Alberti 11); Mary Forestal, from Govan
Parish (? for Gowran, Co. Kilkenny), married at St.
John's, 1805 (Nfld. Archives BRC); Lawrence
Forrestall, from Middle Quarter (Co. Kilkenny),
fisherman of St. John's, 1815 (*Royal Gazette* 26 Oct
1815); Gregory Foristal, of Northern Bay, 1843
(DPHW 54); Thomas Forrestal, planter of Bareneed,
1871 (Lovell); Martin (and others) Forrestall, of
Pussett's Cove (Twillingate district), 1871 (Lovell);
Elizabeth Forristal, from Co. Wexford, died at
Ferryland, 1894, aged 80 (Dillon).
   Modern status: Forrestal, unique, at St. John's;
Forristal(l), rare, at St. John's.

FORSE. *See* FURZE

FORSEY. *See* FORCEY

FORSYTHE, a surname of England and Ireland,
Forsyth of Scotland, from ? an unidentified Scots
place name or from ? an Old German personal name
Fearsithe – man of peace. (Black, MacLysaght).
   Forsyth was traced by Guppy south of the Forth
and Clyde, Forsythe by MacLysaght in Cos. Antrim
and Down.
   In Newfoundland:
   Early instances: Robert Forsyth, J.P. of Fogo,
1782 (D'Alberti 2); Joseph Foresyte or Foresight, of
Tilton Harbour (now Tilting), 1820 (Nfld. Archives
KCRC); Robert Forsyth, fisherman of Sandy Cove
(Fogo district), 1871 (Lovell).
   Modern status: Rare, at St. John's (*Electors* 1955).

FORTUNE, a surname of England, Ireland and
Scotland, in England from the English place name
Fordton (Devon), in Ireland as (O)Fortune, Forty, *Ó
Foirtcheirn* – overlord, in Scotland from the Scots
place name Fortune (now East and West Fortune)
(East Lothian). (Spiegelhalter, MacLysaght, Black).
   Traced by Spiegelhalter in Devon, by MacLy-
saght in Co. Wexford, and by Black in the Lothians
and Fife.
   In Newfoundland:
   Early instances: Thomas, of Harbour Main, 1675
(CO 1); William, shoreman of St. John's, 1794–5,
"30 years in Newfoundland," that is, 1764–5 (Cen-
sus 1794–5); John, from Adamstown (Co. Wex-
ford), of St. John's, 1809 (Nfld. Archives BRC);
Ellen, of Harbour Grace Parish, 1822 (Nfld.
Archives HGRC); Andrew, of Crabbe's, 1869 (DPHW
96); Matthew, fisherman of Carbonear, 1871
(Lovell); Patrick (and others), of Toad's (now Tors)
Cove, 1871 (Lovell).
   Modern status: Scattered, especially at Jeffrey's.
   Place names (not necessarily from the surname):
Fortune, ―― Barasway, ―― Gut 47-04 55-50;
―― Arm (Labrador) 52-50 55-55; ―― Bay 47-15
55-30; ―― Harbour 49-31 55-15; ―― Head 47-05
55-51; ―― Hill 47-02 55-50; 49-32 55-15; ――
Rock 47-33 57-39; ―― Tolt 47-02 55-50.

FORWARD, a surname of England from Old English
fōr – pig, hog and *weard* – guard – swineherd
(Reaney), though Spiegelhalter suggests a derivation
from Old English *forthweard* – pilot. (Reaney,
Cottle, Spiegelhalter).
   Traced by Spiegelhalter in Devon.
   In Newfoundland:
   Family tradition: Frances (1778–1842), wife of

Ambrose Forward of Grand Bank (MUN Hist.). ——, from Corfe Mullen (Dorset) settled at Carbonear before 1850 (MUN Folklore).

Early instances: James, of Carbonear, 1811 (DPHW 48); George and Co., of Harbour Grace, 1817 (D'Alberti 27); Elizabeth, of Grand Bank, 1819 (DPHW 106); John, planter of Tizzard's Harbour, 1821 (USPG); George, of Harbour Grace Parish, 1824 (Nfld. Archives HGRC); George, from Somerset, England, married at St. John's, 1825 (Nfld. Archives BRC); G., of St. John's, 1831 (*Newfoundlander* 29 Dec 1831); Mary Teresa, baptized at Northern Bay, 1856 (DPHW 54); O.H., trader of Port de Grave, 1871 (Lovell); Lambert Jr. and Sr., of Upper Burgeo, 1871 (Lovell).

Modern status: Scattered, especially at Carbonear.

FOSS, a surname of England, from Old English **foss* – (dweller by the) ditch or dike or (by the Roman road called the) Fosse Way, or from various place names, Foss(e) (Norfolk, Warwickshire, Wiltshire, Lincolnshire), Vos (Devon), and Fos(se), France. *See also* FORSE, FOST. (Reaney, Ekwall, Cottle, Spiegelhalter, Dauzat).

Traced by Guppy in Devon and by Cottle also in Dorset.

In Newfoundland:

Early instances: William, servant of Battle Harbour, 1795 (MUN Hist.); John, of Round Harbour (Twillingate district), 1854 (DPHW 86); Richard, of Aquaforte, 1871 (Lovell); James and William, of Snook's Arm (Fogo district), 1871 (Lovell).

Modern status: Scattered, especially at Salt Pond (Gander district) (*Electors* 1955).

FOST, a surname of England, ? a variant of FOSS with an epithetic or additional final consonant.

In Newfoundland:

Early instances: Henry, of St. John's Harbour, 1680 (CO 1); Mary, married at Herring Neck, 1831 (Nfld. Archives KCRC); Henry, of Heart's Delight, 1880 (DPHW 61).

Modern status: At Heart's Delight, Corner Brook, Milltown and St. John's.

FOSTER, a surname of England, Ireland and Scotland, from Middle English *foster* – foster-parent, nurse, or a development of For(e)ster – forester, or from Forseter – shearer, cutter, or a variant of Fewster – saddle-tree maker. (Reaney, Cottle).

Found widespread by Guppy especially in Nottinghamshire, by Spiegelhalter in Devon and by MacLysaght in Ulster.

In Newfoundland:

Family tradition: John, from England, settled at Shoe Cove (Green Bay district) in the late 18th century, thence to La Scie (MUN Folklore).

Early instances: William Forrester, of St. John's, about 1730–5 (CO 194.9); Joseph Foster, of Trinity Bay, 1766 (DPHW 64); John, married at St. John's, 1772 (DPHW 26D); Joseph, of Northern Cove (Spaniard's Bay), 1804 (CO 199.18); Joseph, of Harbour Grace Parish, 1810 (Nfld. Archives HGRC); James Fo(r)ster, of Fogo, 1810, 1816 (D'Alberti 20, MUN Hist.); Sera [sic] Foster, of Trinity, 1817, of Careless (now Kerley's) Harbour, 1821 (Nfld. Archives KCRC); Jane, of Barr'd Islands, 1821 (USPG); Mary, of Riders Harbour (Trinity B.), 1822 (Nfld. Archives KCRC); Mary, of Ship Cove (unspecified), 1830 (Nfld. Archives KCRC); John, planter of Western Bay, 1842 (DPHW 52A); James, of Shoe Cove, 1850 (DPHW 86); Helena, of Harbour Grace, 1869 (Nfld. Archives HGRC); Edward, fisherman of Chamberlains, 1871 (Lovell); Joseph Forster, fisherman of Shoal Bay (now Dover), 1871 (Lovell); Alexander M. Foster (1891–), from Glasgow, Scotland, butcher and victualler, came to St. John's in 1914 (*Nfld. Who's Who* 1930).

Modern status: Scattered, especially at La Scie and in the Green Bay district.

Place names: Forresters or Foster Point 51-11 56-49; Forrest's Point 51-11 56-48; Forster or Fosters Point 48-07 53-53; Forster or Fosters Rock 48-07 53-54; Fosters Point 48-11 53-51; —— Pond 49-43 54-17.

FOWLER, a surname of England and Ireland, in England from Old English *fugelere* – hunter of wild birds, fowler, in Ireland for Fowloo, a variant of FOLEY. *See also* FOWLOW. (Reaney, MacLysaght).

Found widespread by Guppy especially in Gloucestershire and Dorset, and by Spiegelhalter in Devon.

In Newfoundland:

Early instances: Patrick Fouler, of Newfoundland, 1730 (CO 194.3); Patrick Fowler or Fowlow, fisherman of Trinity (Trinity B.), 1758, 1764 (DPHW 64); William Fowler, of St. John's, 1760 (DPHW 26C); William, of Baccalieu Island, 1803 (D'Alberti 13); James, of Harbour Grace Parish, 1806 (Nfld. Archives HGRC); Philip, from Cushonstown (unidentified) (Co. Wexford), married at St. John's, 1815 (Nfld. Archives BRC); Lawrence, of Renews, 1834 (Nfld. Archives BRC); Daniel, from Bridport (Dorset), of St. John's, 1834 (*Newfoundlander* 31 Jul 1834, 23 Feb 1837); scattered, in Lovell 1871.

Modern status: Widespread, especially at Chamberlains and St. John's.

Place name: Fowler's Brook 47-32 52-57.

FOWLOW, ? a variant of the surnames of Ireland, Fowloo and FOLEY, or ? a surname of England, ? from the English place name Foolow (Derbyshire). *See also* FOWLER.

In Newfoundland:

Family tradition: ——, from Ireland, settled at Port Anson in the late 17th or early 18th century (MUN Folklore).

Early instances: John Fouleau, of St. John's, 1794–5, "40 years in Newfoundland," that is, 1754–5 (Census 1794–5); Patrick Fowlow or Fowler, of Trinity (Trinity B.), 1758, 1764 (DPHW 64); Lawrence Fowlow, of Cupids, 1785 (CO 199.18); Michael, of Western Bay, 1789 (CO 199.18); Thomas, of English Harbour (Trinity B.), 1789 (DPHW 64); J. Fowloe, occupier of fishing room at Bonaventure (unspecified), Winter 1800–01 (Census Trinity B.); P. Fowlue, of Fogo Island, 1805 (D'Alberti 15); Anne Fowlow, of Harbour Grace Parish, 1806 (Nfld. Archives HGRC); William, of Northern Bay, 1806 (CO 199.18); Mary, of Riders Harbour, 1826 (Nfld. Archives KCRC); George, fisherman of Pease Cove (Trinity B.), 1856 (DPHW 64B); William, of Cat Harbour (now Lumsden), 1863 (Nfld. Archives KCRC); Matthew Fowloo, of Placentia, 1871 (Lovell).

Modern status: Scattered, especially at Trinity (Trinity B.).

FOX, a surname of England and Ireland a nickname from slyness or other attributes, or ? for Fowkes (*see* FOLKES) or Fawkes; in Ireland also a synonym of KEARNEY and other Irish surnames. (Reaney, Cottle, Spiegelhalter, MacLysaght).

Found widespread by Guppy especially in Derbyshire, Nottinghamshire and Oxfordshire and by Spiegelhalter in Devon; found widespread also by MacLysaght especially in Cos. Dublin, Longford, Tyrone, Leitrim and Limerick.

In Newfoundland:

Family tradition: Kitty (1815–1900), from Ireland, of Patrick's Cove (Mannion).

Early instances: James, of Newfoundland, ? 1706 (CO 194.24); Fox and Stigings, merchants of St. John's, 1802 (D'Alberti 12); George, of St. John's, 1814 (DPHW 26D); James, of Harbour Grace Parish, 1817 (Nfld. Archives HGRC); Thomas, of Kings Cove, 1826 (Nfld. Archives KCRC); Benjamin, planter of Western Bay, 1828 (DPHW 52A); Alice,

died at Harbour Grace, 1829 (*Newfoundlander* 16 Apr 1829); Thomas, schoolmaster and catechist of Cupids, 1835 (DPHW 34); Robert, of Carbonear, 1837 (*Newfoundlander* 8 Jun 1837); Mary, of Black Island (Bonavista B.), 1845 (Nfld. Archives KCRC); Rev. Thomas, of Grand Bank, 1849 (MUN Hist.); Matthews [sic], of Outer Cove, 1858 (*Newfoundlander* 1 Apr 1858); Patrick, of Bay de Verde, 1871 (Lovell); John and Samuel, of Twillingate, 1871 (Lovell).

Modern status: At Gander, Grand Bank and St. John's.

Place names: More than ninety place names contain the specific Fox, but most of them are doubtless derived from the animal.

FRADSHAM, a surname of England, ? from the English place name Frodsham (Cheshire).

In Newfoundland:

Early instances: P., from Bristol, of Harbour Grace, before 1843 (*Sentinel* 12 Sep 1843); Henry (and others), of Coley's Point, 1871 (Lovell).

Modern status: Scattered.

FRAIZE, a variant of the surnames of England, Frais, Frose, from Old French *freis, fresche* – vigorous, active, blooming, youthful. (Reaney).

In Newfoundland:

Early instances: Joseph Frayse, of Musquito (now Bristol's Hope), 1800 (CO 199.18); Thomas Frase or Fraize or Fraze, planter of Carbonear, 1820 (DPHW 48); Joseph William Fraze, of Savage Cove (St. Barbe district), 1874 (DPHW 95).

Modern status: Rare, at St. John's and Carbonear.

FRALIC, FRELICH, anglicizations of the surname of Germany, Froelich – merry, cheerful.

In Newfoundland:

Modern status: Fralic, unique, at St. John's; Frelich, rare, at St. John's.

FRAMP, a surname of England, ? from an Old English personal name *Frēola* or *Fram*. (Ekwall).

In Newfoundland:

Early instances: Elinor, of Great Harbour (Fortune B.), 1853 (DPHW 104); James, planter of Burnt Island (Burgeo-La Poile), 1871 (Lovell).

Modern status: In the Fortune Bay-Hermitage district.

FRAMPTON, a surname of England, from the English place name Frampton (Dorset, Gloucestershire, Lincolnshire). (Cottle).

Traced by Guppy in Berkshire, Dorset, Oxfordshire and Somerset, and by Spiegelhalter in Devon.

In Newfoundland:

Early instances: Joseph Framton, of Trinity (Trinity B.), 1760 (DPHW 64); —— Frampton, of St. Mary's, 1779 (CO 194.34); Thomas, of Bonavista, 1792 (DPHW 70); George, of Battle Harbour, 1795 (MUN Hist.); Robert, of Trouty, 1809, of Old Bonaventure, 1814 (DPHW 64); William, of Tilton Harbour (now Tilting), 1829 (Nfld. Archives KCRC); ——, of Greenspond, 1830 (*Newfoundlander* 7 Oct 1830); William, of Catalina, 1839 (DPHW 67); Leonard, of Channel, 1842 (DPHW 101); Henry, of Exploits Burnt Island, 1843 (DPHW 86); William, planter of British Harbour, 1844 (DPHW 64B); William, of Ferryland, 1854 (DPHW 31); Robert, of Seldom-Come-By, 1856 (DPHW 67); John, of Burin, 1871 (Lovell); Alfred and William, of Indian Islands (Twillingate), 1871 (Lovell).

Modern status: Scattered, especially at Port Elizabeth (*Electors* 1955).

Place name: Frampton's Cove 49-28 55-02.

FRANCIS, a baptismal name and surname of England, Ireland and Guernsey (Channel Islands), from Old French *Franceis* – Frenchman, though after 1220 AD after Saint Francis of Assisi. (Withy-combe, Reaney, Cottle, MacLysaght, Turk).

Traced by Guppy especially in the southwest of England and in South Wales, by Spiegelhalter in Devon, and by MacLysaght in Galway and Belfast.

In Newfoundland:

Family tradition: Charles, a Micmac of Gander Bay in the early 19th century (MUN Hist.).

Early instances: John, of Newfoundland, 1730 (CO 194.23); Francis, of St. John's, 1785 (DPHW 26D); Edward, of Fogo, 1787 (MUN Hist.); Owen, of Harbour Grace Parish, 1807 (Nfld. Archives HGRC); John, of Grand Bank, 1817 (DPHW 109); George, of Broad Cove (Bay de Verde), 1829 (DPHW 52A); Joseph, planter of Seal Cove (now New Chelsea), 1833, of Little Islands (Trinity B.), 1838 (DPHW 59A); William, of Upper Burgeo, 1842 (DPHW 101); Will, of King's Cove Parish, 1854 (Nfld. Archives KCRC); John Frances, planter of Long Harbour (Burin district), 1858 (DPHW 104); Aquilla Francis, trader of Hermitage Cove, 1858 (DPHW 102); Ann, of Hants Harbour, 1860 (DPHW 59A); John, of La Plant (Burgeo-La Poile), 1860 (DPHW 99); scattered in Lovell 1871.

Modern status: Widespread, especially at Clarke's Head (Fogo district).

Place names: Frances Bay (Labrador) 56-58 61-21; —— Island 49-41 54-24; Francis Harbour (Labrador) 52-33 55-43; —— Reef 49-33 56-50..

FRANEY, a surname of England, Freeney also in England and Ireland, from Old French *fraisnaie, fresnay* – (dweller near the) ashwood, or from one of the many French place names containing the element Fraisnes, Fresne(s), etc. In Ireland, Freeney is a late popular variant of de Freyne, *de Fréine*. (Reaney, MacLysaght, Dauzat).

MacLysaght traced Freeney in Waterford and adjacent counties, de Freyne in Co. Kilkenny.

In Newfoundland:

Family tradition: Peter, from Co. Down, ? landowner of Spaniards Bay, 1775 (MUN Geog.).

Early instances: Thomas Freany, from Co. Wexford, married at St. John's, 1813 (Nfld. Archives BRC); Matthew Franey, of Bonavista, 1824 (Nfld. Archives KCRC); James Freany, of Harbour Grace Parish, 1824 (Nfld. Archives HGRC); Matthew Fran(a)y or Frenay, of King's Cove, 1829 (Nfld. Archives KCRC); Richard Frane and Matthew Frayne, of Spaniards Bay, 1871 (Lovell).

Modern status: In the Harbour Grace district.

Place name: Franey's Pond 48-35 53-21.

FRANKLIN, a surname of England and Ireland, from Middle English *frankeleyn* – freeman, landowner of free but not noble birth. (Reaney, MacLysaght).

Traced by Guppy in the south Midland counties, especially Oxfordshire, and by MacLysaght in Cos. Limerick and Tipperary.

In Newfoundland:

Early instances: Francis Francklyn, inhabitant of Newfoundland, ? 1706 (CO 194.24); William Franklin, of Dublin, Irish convict landed at Petty Harbour or Bay Bulls, 1789 (CO 194.38).

Modern status: Unique, at Corner Brook (*Electors* 1955).

FRASER, FRAZER, surnames of Scotland and Ireland. "The name was originally de Frisselle, de Fres-liere, or de Fresel ['as if from a place in France'] and Frisale or Frisell [*see* FRIZZELL] is still the common pronunciation in Tweeddale – the first Scots home of the family – and in Lothian. The name then be-came Fraissier or strawberry bearer, probably from adoption of the flower of the *fraisse*, strawberry, as part of the armorial bearings ..." (Black, Cottle).

Guppy found Fraser "generally distributed" in Scotland; MacLysaght found it "numerous in Ulster."

In Newfoundland:

Early instances: Elizabeth Frazer, of St. John's, 1805 (Nfld. Archives BRC); James Fraser, from Co. Kilkenny, of Bonavista, deceased 1816 (*Royal Gazette* 30 Jul 1816); Edward Frazer, of Harbour Grace Parish, 1824 (Nfld. Archives HGRC); Major R.A. Fraser, of St. John's, 1839 (*Newfoundlander* 17 Jan 1839); James Oliphant, born at St. John (New Brunswick), 1826, of St. John's, 1841 (Mott); Rev. Donald Allan (1793–1845), born at Torosway (Isle of Mull), Scotland, first Presbyterian minister in Newfoundland (MUN Folklore).

Modern status: Fraser, especially at St. John's; Frazer, rare, at Botwood; Frazier, unique at Renews.

Place names: Fraser Lake (Labrador) 54-24 63-40; —— River (Labrador) 56-39 63-10; Frazer Point 47-08 53-30.

FREAKE, a surname of England, a variant of FIRTH, or from Middle English *freke* – man, warrior, hero, or *frech* – bold, brave, zealous. (Reaney, Cottle).

Traced by Spiegelhalter in Devon.

In Newfoundland:

Early instances: John Frake or Freke, planter of Joe Batt's Arm, 1821 (USPG); John Freke, Sr., of Fogo, 1844 (*Nfld. Almanac*); George, of Barr'd Island, 1871 (Lovell); William Freak, of Griquet, 1871 (Lovell).

Modern status: Scattered, especially at Joe Batt's Arm and Boyd's Cove.

Place name: Freak Island 49-16 55-01.

FRECKER, ? a variant of the surname of England, Fricker, from the Old English personal name *Frithugar*, containing the elements *peace* and *spear*. (Weekley *Surnames*).

In Newfoundland:

Early instances: M. Freker, Frehen or Freken, planter of St. John's, 1701 (CO 194.2); John E. Frecker, ? of St. John's, 1704 (CO 194.3); Frederic Fricker, of Shoe Cove (Green Bay district), 1846 (DPHW 86); John P. Frecker, agent of St. Pierre, married ? at Fortune Bay, 1855 (*Newfoundlander* 9 Aug 1855).

Modern status: Rare, at St. John's and Rattling Brook (Green B.).

FREEBAIRN, a surname of England and Scotland, from Old English *frēo* – free, *bearn* – child. (Reaney, Black).

In Newfoundland:

Early instance: R. Jardine, M.B.C.M., from Bonhill (Dumbartonshire), died (at St. John's),

1834, aged 71 (General Protestant Cemetery, St. John's).

Modern status: Unique, at Ferryland (*Electors* 1955).

FREEBORN(E), surnames of England and Ireland, from the Old English personal name *Frēobeorn* – free-man, or from Old English *frēo* – free, *boren* – born, one born free, inheriting liberty. (Reaney, MacLysaght).

Traced by Bardsley in Essex and Suffolk, by MacLysaght formerly in Co. Wexford, later mainly in Co. Donegal.

In Newfoundland:

Modern status: Freeborne, at Harbour Mille (Fortune B.); Freeborn, rare, at St. John's.

FREEMAN, a surname of England, Ireland and Guernsey (Channel Islands), from the Old English *frēomann* – free (born) man, "used also as a personal name"; in Ireland also as the anglicized form of Mac Ateer, *Mae an tSaoir*, Ir. *saor* – craftsman. (Reaney, MacLysaght, Turk).

Guppy found Freeman "confined to the centre of England and to the adjoining eastern and western counties" and especially in Suffolk and Worcestershire. Spiegelhalter traced it in Devon and MacLysaght in all the provinces of Ireland.

In Newfoundland:

Early instances: Edward, of St. John's, 1705 (CO 194.22); John, of Conception Bay, [1706] (CO 194.4); Michael, of St. John's, 1804 (Nfld. Archives BRC); Mary, from New Ross (Co. Wexford), married at St. John's, 1814 (Nfld. Archives BRC); Thomas, from Old Ross (Co. Wexford), fisherman of Witless Bay, deceased 1814 (*Royal Gazette* 15 Dec 1814); Michael, of Harbour Grace Parish, 1823 (Nfld. Archives HGRC); George, of Salmon Cove (now Champneys), 1824 (DPHW 64B); William Freemen, of Trinity (Trinity B.), 1850 (DPHW 26D); Thomas Freeman, of Little Placentia (now Argentia), 1857 (*Newfoundlander* 28 May 1857); Michael, of Brigus, 1871 (Lovell); Robert, of Fogo, 1871 (Lovell); Thomas, of Sandy Cove (Placentia B.), 1871 (Lovell); John, of Twillingate, 1871 (Lovell).

Modern status: Scattered, especially at Champneys.

Place names: Freeman Lake (Labrador) 54-44 66-32; Freeman's Pond 49-43 54-16.

FREID, a variant of the surname of Germany Freud, Ger. *Freude* – joy.

In Newfoundland: ——, from Nova Scotia, settled at St. John's in 1945–6 (Family).

Modern status: Rare, at St. John's.

FRELICH. *See* FRALIC

FRENCH, a surname of England and Ireland from Old English *frenisc*, Middle English *frenche* – French(man); also in Ireland from the French *frêne* – (dweller by the) ash tree, as in FRANEY. (Reaney, MacLysaght).

Guppy found French scattered, especially in Devon, Essex and Oxfordshire; MacLysaght in Co. Galway.

In Newfoundland:

Early instances: Edward, of Bay Roberts, 1764, property "possess'd by his Ancestors for upwards of 130 years," that is, before 1634 (CO 199.18); Edward, of Torbay, 1681 (CO 1); John, of Harbour Grace, 1770, property "in Possession of the Family for upwards of 60 years," that is, before 1710 (CO 199.18); John, of Trinity (Trinity B.), 1779 (DPHW 64); Arthur, from Dartmouth (Devon), merchant of St. John's, 1780 (Exeter Public Library Archives per Kirwin, CO 194.36); John, of Carbonear, 1784 (CO 199.18); James, in fishery at Petty Harbour, 1794–5, born in Newfoundland (Census 1794–5); Edward, of Port de Grave, 1797 (CO 199.18); Thomas, of Holyrood, 1802 (CO 199.18); John, from Co. Wexford, married at St. John's, 1813 (Nfld. Archives BRC); John, planter of Turk's Cove (Trinity B.), 1825 (DPHW 64B); Benjamin, of Brigus, 1834 (DPHW 34); John, of Moreton's Harbour, 1839 (DPHW 86); William, of Bareneed, 1842 (DPHW 39); Solomon, of Snow's Cove (Port de Grave district), 1851 (DPHW 39); Amelia, of Scilly Cove (now Winterton), 1855 (DPHW 59); John, from England, married at Grand Bank, 1857 (DPHW 106); scattered in Lovell 1871.

Modern status: Widespread, especially in the Port de Grave district.

Place names: Fourteen place names have the specific French, but probably only French('s) Cove (Bay Roberts) 47-37 53-13 derives from the surname.

FREW, a surname of Scotland and Ireland from the Scots place name Ford(s) of Frew (Perthshire), or also in Ireland from the Old English personal name *Frēowine* – noble lord. (Black, MacLysaght).

Traced by Black in Perthshire and by Mac-Lysaght in northeast Ulster.

In Newfoundland:

Early instance: William, (? 1843–1924), from Saltcoats (Ayrshire) came to St. John's in 1869. (Mott, General Protestant Cemetery, St. John's).

Modern status: Rare, at St. John's.

FRIZZELL, a surname of Scotland and Ireland, a variant of Frizell(e), Frissell, "Old forms of FRASER which have become independent surnames" (Black).

MacLysaght found Frizell scattered.

In Newfoundland:

Early instances: John Frizzle or Frissell, ? of St. John's, 1844 (DPHW 29); Richard Frizell, of Big Pond (St. John's South district), 1859 (DPHW 26D); Richard and William Frizel, of Shoal Bay (Ferryland district), 1871 (Lovell).

Modern status: Rare, especially at Lower Goulds (St. John's district).

FROST, a surname of England and Ireland, the Old English personal names *Forst*, *Frost* from Old English *forst*, *frost* – frost, with a variety of implications associated with frost, such as white-haired, white-bearded, cold in demeanour, born in a notoriously cold spell, similar in usage to SNOW; or from the English place name Frost (Devon). (Reaney, Cottle, Spiegelhalter).

Traced by Guppy especially in Derbyshire and Somerset, by Spiegelhalter in Devon, and by MacLysaght in Co. Clare.

In Newfoundland:

Early instances: Richard, of St. John's, 1752 (DPHW 26C); ——, planter of Fogo, 1792 (MUN Hist.); James, of Bay de Verde, 1802 (CO 199.18); William, of Trinity (Trinity B.), 1813 (DPHW 64B); William, of Harbour Grace Parish, 1818 (Nfld. Archives HGRC); James, of Grates Cove, 1833 (DPHW 58); William, of North(ern) River, 1860 (DPHW 38); Thomas, of Heart's Delight, 1871 (Lovell).

Modern status: Scattered.

Place name (not necessarily from the surname): Frost Pond 48-05 54-10.

FROUDE, a surname of England, from the Old English personal name *Froda*, from Old English *frōd* – wise, old. (Spiegelhalter).

Traced by Spiegelhalter in Devon.

In Newfoundland:

Early instances: William Frowd, of Trinity Bay, 1766, of Bay de Verde, 1770 (DPHW 64); John Froud, occupier of fishing room at Old Perlican, Winter 1800–01 (Census Trinity B.); Stephen, of Harbour Grace Parish, 1836 (Nfld. Archives HGRC); Henry (and others) Frowd, of Old Man's Bay (Burgeo district), 1871 (Lovell); James Froud, of Twillingate, 1871 (Lovell).

Modern status: Scattered, especially in the Twillingate district, and at Windsor.

FRY(E), surnames of England, Fry of Ireland, from Old English *frīg* – free (born), noble, generous, or sometimes ? little person, child, offspring, as in the *fry* of fish; in Ireland an occasional synonym of Ferris in west Ulster. (Reaney, Cottle, MacLysaght 73).

Guppy traced Fry in Devon, Dorset, Somerset, Surrey and especially in Wiltshire.

In Newfoundland:

Early instances: Francis Fry, married at St. John's, 1777, of Portugal Cove, 1779 (DPHW 23D, 26C); Richard, from England, married at Kings Cove, 1820 (Nfld. Archives KCRC); Charles, planter of Brigus, 1829, of English Cove (Conception B.), 1834 (DPHW 34); Richard, of Tickle Cove (Bonavista South district), 1837, of Indian Arm, 1841 (DPHW 73A); John, from Exeter (Devon), late of St. John's, died 1842, aged 70 years (*Times* 2 Feb 1842); Jane, of Burned (? for Burnt) Islands (Bonavista B.), 1855 (Nfld. Archives KCRC).

Modern status: Fry, scattered, especially at Brigus, Charleston and Summerville; Frye, scattered.

Place names: Fry's Cove (Labrador) 51-46 56-17; —— Point 48-24 53-39; —— Pond 48-20 53-33.

FUDGE, a surname of England with a variant Fuge found also in Ireland, pet-forms of the personal names *Fu(l)cher*, from Old German *Fulchar*, *Fulcher*, Old French *Foucher*, *Fouquier*, containing the elements *people* and *army*; or from the English place names Fuge or Fuidge (Devon). (Reaney, Spiegelhalter).

Traced by Spiegelhalter in Devon. MacLysaght traced Fuge in Cos. Waterford and Cork, and Fudge in Co. Tipperary in 1664.

In Newfoundland:

Family tradition: Edward, of Belleoram, 1780 (MUN Hist.).

Early instances: John, servant of Battle Harbour, 1795 (MUN Hist.); John, of Fogo, 1803 (D'Alberti 13); Job, of Fortune Bay, 1815 (D'Alberti 25); Emmanuel, of Western Bay, 1817 (DPHW 52A); George, planter of Little Harbour (Twillingate district), 1820 (USPG); Samuel, planter of Herring Neck, 1822 (USPG); John, of Little Bay (Bay de l'Eau), 1835 (DPHW 30); John, of Lower Burgeo, 1842 (DPHW 101); Jeremiah, of Pass Island (Fortune B.), 1843 (DPHW 102); Charles, of Round Harbour (Twillingate district), 1847 (DPHW 86); Samuel, of Donier Harbour (Twillingate district), 1848 (DPHW

86); John, planter of Blackhead (Bay de Verde district), 1854 (DPHW 52B); Jeremiah, of Moonsface (Burgeo-La Poile district), 1857 (DPHW 98); John, of Pike's Arm (Twillingate), 1859 (DPHW 85); scattered in the Twillingate and Burgeo-La Poile districts, 1871 (Lovell).

Modern status: Widespread, especially at Brighton (Green B.).

Place name: Fudge Ground 49-42 54-43.

FULFORD, a surname of England, – (dweller by the) foul, dirty ford, or from the English place names Fulford (Devon, Somerset, Yorkshire ER) or Fullaford (Devon). (E.C. Smith).

Traced by Guppy in Devon and Wiltshire.

In Newfoundland:

Early instances: Robert, inhabitant of Newfoundland, ? 1706 (CO 194.24); William, fisherman of Petty Harbour, 1794–5, "6 years in Newfoundland," that is, 1788–9 (Census 1794–5).

Modern status: Rare, especially at Merasheen (*Electors* 1955).

FULLER, a surname of England, Ireland and Guernsey (Channel Islands), from Old English *fullere*, Old French *fouleor* – fuller of cloth. "The raw cloth had to be *fulled*, ie. scoured and thickened by beating it in water, a process known as *walking* because originally done by men trampling upon it in a trough. Hence WALKER, by the side of Fuller and TUCKER from Old English *tucian*, originally 'to torment,' later 'to tuck,' 'to full.'" (Reaney). In Ireland, according to Woulfe, Fuller is used as the modern anglicized form of the obsolete surname MacEnookery, *Mac an Úcaire* – son of the fuller. (MacLysaght, Turk).

Traced by Guppy in Buckinghamshire, Kent, Norfolk, Oxfordshire and Sussex, by Spiegelhalter in Devon (though he notes that the usual Devon word is Tucker), and by MacLysaght in Co. Down.

In Newfoundland:

Early instance: John E., from Sydney, N.S. to St. John's, 1857 (*Newfoundlander* 6 Aug 1857).

Modern status: Rare, at St. John's.

FUREY, a surname of Ireland (O)Furey, *Ó Foirreith*, *Ó Furreidh*, ? *Ó Fíodhabhra*, *Ó Fiura*, or for the French surname Furet, Fr. *furet* – ferret, hence one who is inquisitive, a Nosy Parker, Paul Pry. (MacLysaght, Mansion, Dauzat).

Traced by MacLysaght in Co. Westmeath.

In Newfoundland:

Family traditions: ——, from Jersey (Channel

Islands), settled at Harbour Main in 1750 (MUN Hist.). ——, from Ireland, settled at Harbour Main about 1700 (MUN Folklore).

Early instances: Richard Fure, of Chapel's Cove (Conception B.), 1772 (CO 199.18); William Furys, of St. John's, 1781 (DPHW 26C); William Fury, of Harbour Main, 1784 (CO 199.18); George, of Harbour Grace Parish, 1814 (Nfld. Archives HGRC); Richard Furye, from Wilton (? Somerset), married at St. John's, 1835 (DPHW 26D); Nicholas Furey, farmer of Cat's Cove (now Conception Harbour), 1871 (Lovell); John Fury, farmer of Salmon Cove and Gasters (now Avondale), 1871 (Lovell).

Modern status: Scattered, especially in the Harbour Main district.

FURLONG, a surname of England and Ireland, from Old English *furhlang* – furrow-long, eventually meaning furlong, eighth of a mile, square furlong (about ten acres) and as a surname ? speed at foot-racing; or from the English place name Furlong (Devon). (Reaney, Cottle, Spiegelhalter).

Traced by Spiegelhalter in Devon and by MacLysaght in Co. Wexford).

In Newfoundland:

Early instances: J., of St. John's Harbour, 1703 (CO 194.3); John, of Gull Island (Conception B.), 1798 (CO 199.18); John, of Harbour Grace Parish, 1806 (Nfld. Archives HGRC); Richard, from Tipperary, of Cape Broyle, about 1813 (Dillon); James, of Trinity, 1825 (Nfld. Archives KCRC); John, of Joe Batts Arm, 1826 (Nfld. Archives KCRC); John, of Pouch Cove, 1835 (Nfld. Archives BRC); Patrick, of Ferryland, 1837 (Nfld. Archives BRC); Richard, ? of Bay Bulls, 1838 (*Newfoundlander* 25 Oct 1838); James, of Placentia, 1844 (*Nfld. Almanac*); Thomas, of Carbonear, 1845 (*Newfoundlander* 15 May 1845); Patrick, of Plate Cove (Bonavista B.), 1853 (Nfld. Archives KCRC); Martin W., born at Oderin, 1864 (*Nfld. Quarterly* Jun 1903); Helena, of Harbour Grace, 1867 (Nfld. Archives HGRC); scattered, in Lovell 1871.

Modern status: Scattered, especially at Plate Cove West, Shalloway Cove (Bonavista B.) and St. John's.

FURNEAUX, a surname of England from the French place name Fourneaux (Calvados, La Manche) –

furnaces, especially intended for the use of charcoal. (Reaney, Dauzat).

Traced by Guppy in Devon.

In Newfoundland:

Early instances: William, of St. John's, 1751 (CO 194.13); Joseph, lessee of land at Port de Grave, 1765 (CO 199.18); John Furneau, trader of Burgeo, 1855 (DPHW 102); John Furneaux, merchant of Channel, 1871 (Lovell).

Modern status: At St. John's.

FURZE, a surname of England, ? with a variant FORSE though this may also be a variant of FOSS, from Old English *fyrs* – (dweller by the) furze (-covered land), or from a common place name Furze (Devon). (Reaney, Spiegelhalter).

Guppy traced Furse, Furze in Devon.

In Newfoundland:

Early instance: William Forse or Furse, of St. John's, 1703, 1709 (CO 194.3, 4)

Modern status: Furze, unique, at Botwood (*Electors* 1955); Forse, rare, at St. John's (*Electors* 1955).

FUSHELL, ? an anglicization of the surname of France, Fusil – (seller of the) steel for striking the flint in a gun. (Dauzat).

In Newfoundland:

Family tradition: At St. John's from St. Pierre since about 1945 (Family).

Early instance: Allain Le Faucheur, of Point Crew (now Point May) married Elizabeth Thornhill, Fortune, 1897; later pronounced Fushell (Fortune Methodist marriages, per P.E.L. Smith).

Modern status: Rare, at St. John's.

Place names: Fischells 48-19 58-42; —— Brook 48-19 58-43.

FYME, a surname of Holland, of unknown origin.

In Newfoundland:

Early instance: Rev. Anthony G. Fyme (1879–1964), born at Amsterdam, priest in Newfoundland from 1903–04.

Modern status: Unique, at Merasheen (*Electors* 1955).

G

GABRIEL, a baptismal name and surname of England, Scotland and France and of the Micmacs of Newfoundland, Hebrew – "God is a strong man" or "strong man of God." (Withycombe, Reaney, Dauzat).

Traced by Spiegelhalter in Devon and by Black in Aberdeenshire.

In Newfoundland:

Tradition: Louis and André Teesh Gabriel, Micmacs of the St. George's area. (G.R. Thomas).

Early instances: Thomas Gabriell, of Trinity Harbour, 1675, of Hearts Content, 1681 (CO 1); Andrew Gabriel, of Codroy and Rivers, 1871 (Lovell); Alfred E., school teacher of Lamaline, 1871 (Lovell).

Modern status: In the West Coast districts, especially at Kippens.

GADEN, a surname of England, ? a variant of Gayden from the English place name Gayden (Warwickshire). (Ekwall).

Traced by Matthews in Dorset.

In Newfoundland:

Early instances: Thomas, of Placentia ? district, 1744 (CO 194.24); William Gadden or Gaden, of St. John's, 1762 (CO 194.15, 16); William Gaden, of Greenspond, 1776 (MUN Hist.); George T., of Little St. Lawrence, 1829 (*Newfoundlander* 4 Jun 1829); Thomas Eppes, of Harbour Breton, 1831 (DPHW 26B); Emma, of Harbour Grace, 1842 (Nfld. Archives T98); George T., of White Bear Bay (1871 (Lovell).

Modern status: Rare, at St. John's (*Electors* 1955).

GAGNON, a surname of France from Old French *ganhon* – (raiser of) little pig(s). (Dauzat).

In Newfoundland:

Modern status: Rare, at Corner Brook.

GALE, a surname of England, the Channel Islands and Ireland; in England and the Channel Islands from Old English *gāl* – pleasant, merry, or from a French form of Old German *Walo* which has also given the surname Wale(s), or from Old Norman French *gaiole* etc. – (keeper of the) gaol, hence jailer in which *gaol* retains the Norman spelling, *jail* the Old French pronunciation, or from the place name Gale (Devon); in Ireland in Leinster for Gaule, *Mac an Ghaill*, Ir. *gall* – foreigner. (Reaney, Cottle, Spiegelhalter, MacLysaght, Turk).

Traced by Guppy in Devon, Dorset, Hampshire, Northamptonshire, Oxfordshire and Wiltshire, and especially in Monmouthshire, and by MacLysaght in Leinster.

In Newfoundland:

Family traditions: Three brothers from Wales came to Newfoundland in the late 17th or early 18th century, one to settle on the west coast, the second in White Bay and the third in Notre Dame Bay (MUN Folklore). Sarah, of Grand River, 1854 (MUN Hist.).

Early instances: Robert, of Newfoundland, ? 1706 (CO 194.24); Gregory, of Quidi Vidi, 1708 (CO 194.4); John, merchant of St. John's, ? 1765 (CO 194.16); John, of Bay Bulls, about 1772–5 (USPG); James, of Battle Harbour, 1795 (MUN Hist.); Anne, of Bonavista, 1803 (Nfld. Archives BRC); William Gall, of Harbour Grace Parish, 1808 (Nfld. Archives HGRC); Richard and William, planters of Fogo, 1808 (MUN Hist.); John, from Thomastown (Co. Kilkenny), married at St. John's, 1814 (Nfld. Archives BRC); William Gale, of Kings Cove, 1815, of Tickle Cove (Bonavista B.), 1825 (Nfld. Archives KCRC); John and Mark, fur-trappers of Moreton's Harbour, 1819 (D'Alberti 29); John, fisherman of White Bay, 1823 (USPG); Patrick Gall, from Inistioge (Co. Kilkenny), married at Brigus, 1829 (Nfld. Archives BRC); William Gale, of Great Codroy River, 1835 (DPHW 30); Jeremiah, of Barrisways (St. George's B.), 1835 (DPHW 30); T., from ? Glockenglow (Devon), of St. John's, 1856 (*Newfoundlander* 3 Jul 1856); Luke, of Riverhead (White B.), 1864 (DPHW 94); Abram, of Sop's Island (White B.), 1864 (DPHW 94); William, of Cape Ray, 1871 (Lovell); Edward (and others), of Codroy and Rivers, 1871 (Lovell); Charles, of Robinson's Head, 1871 (Lovell); Joseph, skipper, born at Jersey Harbour, died there 1876, aged 63 (D.A. Macdonald).

Modern status: Widespread, especially in the St. George's and White Bay districts with large concentrations at Millville and Sop's Island.

Place names: Gales Brook 49-31 57-05; Galeville 49-33 56-51.

GALGAY, a surname of Ireland, not recorded by MacLysaght, ? a variant of GALWAY with which it is sometimes confused in Newfoundland, or ? of GALLAGHER of which MacLysaght has noted at least 23 variant spellings.

Galgey traced uniquely in Waterford (*Telephone Directory*).

In Newfoundland:

Early instances: Nicholas and William, of St. John's, 1871 (Lovell).

Modern status: Rare, at St. John's.

GALLAGHER, a surname of Ireland and Scotland, (O)Gallagher, *Ó Gallchobhair*, Ir. *gallchobhar* – foreign help. (MacLysaght). *See also* GALLAHUE.

Traced by MacLysaght in Co. Donegal, and by Black as a "recent introduction" in Scotland.

In Newfoundland:

Early instances: Antony, of Harbour Grace Parish, 1811 (Nfld. Archives HGRC); Elenor Galahar, of Kings Cove, 1812 (Nfld. Archives BRC); Patrick Gallagher, soldier of St. John's, 1823 (DPHW 26D); James Gallaho(r), of Knights Cove (Bonavista B.), 1857 (Nfld. Archives KCRC); Ellen Gallahor, of Tickle Cove (Bonavista B.), 1859 (Nfld. Archives KCRC); Thomas Galla(g)her, of Harbour Grace, 1868 (Nfld. Archives HGRC); James and Thomas Galleher, of Stock Cove (Bonavista B.), 1871 (Lovell).

Modern status: At St. John's.

GALLAHUE, a surname of Ireland, (O)Gallahue, *Ó Gallchú*, a shortened form of GALLAGHER, and in east Co. Cork confused with DONAHUE. (MacLysaght).

In Newfoundland:

Early instances: Jane Gollihoo, of Harbour Grace Parish, 1824 (Nfld. Archives HGRC); James Gallaho, of Stock Cove (Bonavista B.), 1856 (Nfld. Archives KCRC); Elizabeth Gallaho(o), Gallahue or Gollohue, married at Kings Cove, 1865 (Nfld. Archives KCRC); William Gollahow, of Tickle Cove (Bonavista B.), 1872 (Nfld. Archives KCRC); Mary Golohue, of Cat Harbour (now Lumsden), 1873 (Nfld. Archives KCRC); Michael Gallahue, of Sweet Bay (Bonavista B.), 1907 (Nfld. Archives KCRC).

Modern status: At Stock Cove (Bonavista South district) (*Electors* 1955)

GALLANT, a surname of England and France, and of the Micmacs of Newfoundland, from an Old French personal name *Galand, Galant* or Old German *Wa-land*, or from Old French, Middle English *galant* – dashing, spirited, bold. Dauzat notes that the sense, "one who dances attention on the ladies," was taken from Italian usage in the 16th century. (Reaney, Dauzat).

In Newfoundland:

Tradition: Felix of Margaree, N.S., an Acadian, the first Gallant to settle at Stephenville, in 1846. (G.R. Thomas).

Early instance: John, of Newfoundland, ? 1706 (CO 194.24).

Modern status: Scattered, especially at Stephenville.

Place name: Gallants 48-42 58-14.

GALLIOTT, a surname of England, Galliot of France, from Old French *galiot* – sailor in a galley, galley-slave, pirate, "Noted in the sea-board counties of Essex, Kent, Sussex and Suffolk (1296–1327)" by Reaney and also as a maritime name by Dauzat who adds, however, that in inland parts of France it is explained as a pet-form of Galier – the light-hearted man, as in the first meaning of GALE. (Reaney, Dauzat).

In Newfoundland:

Early instance: William, fisherman of Rose Blanche, 1860 (DPHW 99).

Modern status: Rare, especially in the Humber West district.

GALLIVAN, a surname of Ireland, a Co. Kerry variant of (O)Galvin, *Ó Gealbháin*, Ir. *geal* – bright, *bán* – white. (MacLysaght).

In Newfoundland:

Early instances: John Gallavan, fisherman of Quidi Vidi, 1794–5, "18 years in Newfoundland," that is, 1776–7 (Census 1794–5); Danniel [sic] Galavan, from Waterford City, Ireland, married at St. John's, 1806 (Nfld. Archives BRC); Michael Gallivan, of St. John's, 1819 (D'Alberti 29); Thomas Galavan or Gallivan, of Harbour Grace Parish, 1823 (Nfld. Archives HGRC); Kitty Galavan or Galvin, from Co. Kilkenny, of Ragged Harbour (now Melrose), 1828 (Nfld. Archives KCRC); John, of Trinity, 1830 (Nfld. Archives KCRC); Richard Gallivan, of Bay of Islands, 1871 (Lovell).

Modern status: At St. John's.

Place name: Gallivan Hill 47-26 54-16.

GALLOP, GOLLOP, surnames of England, ? from the English place name Nether Wallop (Hampshire) (Spiegelhalter), but possibly confused with GALPIN.

Traced by Spiegelhalter in Devon; and found also in Dorset (Will of William Gallop, of Bere Regis).

In Newfoundland:

Early instances: Amelia, married at Grand Bank, 1823 (MUN Hist.); William, of Codroy Island, 1835 (DPHW 30); Susannah Gallope, of Fortune, 1835

(DPHW 106); ——, agent for Newman and Co., Gaultois (Wix 1836, D.A. Macdonald); Mary Gollop, of Old Perlican, 1836 (DPHW 58); William Gallop, merchant of Harbour Breton, 1871 (Lovell).

Modern status: Gallop, at Mouse Island (Burgeo-La Poile district) and Codroy (*Electors* 1955); Gollop, at St. John's.

Place name: Gallop Shoals 47-12 56-03.

GALPIN, a surname of England, from Old French *galopin* – galloper, messenger, errand-boy; turnspit, scullion in a monastery. (Reaney, Cottle). *See also* GALLOP with which confusion is possible.

Traced by Guppy in Dorset.

In Newfoundland:

Early instances: Robert, occupier of fishing room at Scilly Cove (now Winterton), Winter 1800–01 (Census Trinity B.); Joseph Galpin or Gallop, married at Grand Bank, 1831 (MUN Hist.); Joseph Galpin, of Fortune, 1841, of Lower Burgeo, 1844 (DPHW 109, 101); George, of Codroy and Rivers, 1871 (Lovell).

Modern status: Rare, at Woodville (*Electors* 1955), and Shallop Cove (St. George's district).

GALWAY, a variant of the surname of Ireland, Gal(l)way, *de Gallaidhe,* in Ulster from the Scots place name Galloway, a district in southwest Scotland including Wigtownshire and Kirkcudbrightshire, in the south from the Irish place name Galway (Co. Galway). (MacLysaght). *See also* GALGAY.

Traced by MacLysaght especially in Ulster and Co. Cork.

In Newfoundland:

Early instances: Mary Galloway, of Harbour Grace Parish, 1809 (Nfld. Archives HGRC); John, ? of St. John's, 1810 (CO 194.50); John, of Carbonear, 1812 (DPHW 48); Anthony, of Harbour Grace, 1866 (Nfld. Archives HGRC); John and William Galway, of (Upper) Island Cove, 1871 (Lovell).

Modern status: Scattered, especially in the Harbour Grace district and at St. John's.

Place name: Galway Bay (Labrador) 53-06 66-13.

GAMBERG, a surname ? of England or of Germany, ? from an unidentified place name.

In Newfoundland:

Early instance: Charles, painter of St. John's, 1871 (Lovell).

Modern status: Rare, at St. John's and Corner Brook.

GAMBIN, a variant of the surname of Ireland (Mac) Gammon, Gambon in Co. Waterford, from the French surnames Gambin, Gambon, Fr. *gambon* – little leg. (MacLysaght, Dauzat).

Traced by MacLysaght in Co. Waterford.

In Newfoundland:

Early instances: Frances Gambon, of Harbour Grace Parish, 1809 (Nfld. Archives HGRC); Edward Gambin, of Grates Cove, 1871 (Lovell).

Modern status: Scattered, in the Placentia West district.

GAMBLE, a surname of England and Ireland, from Old Norse *Gamall,* Old Danish, Old Swedish *Gamal* – old. (Reaney, MacLysaght).

Traced by Guppy in Norfolk and by MacLysaght in Ulster and Co. Cork.

In Newfoundland:

Early instances: Thomas, of Carbonear, 1832 (*Newfoundlander* 8 Nov 1832); Robert Gambol, from Co. Waterford, of Fogo, 1818 (Nfld. Archives KCRC); Thomas Gamble, of Harbour Grace Parish, 1834 (Nfld. Archives HGRC); Sarah, from Newry (Co. Down), married at St. John's, 1850 (DPHW 26D); John, of Lion's Den (Twillingate district), 1871 (Lovell).

Modern status: Rare, at Boyd's Cove (Twillingate district) and Badger (*Electors* 1955).

Place name: Gamble's Tickle (Labrador) 52-49 55-51.

GARCIN, a surname of France, an old pet-form of western France – little fellow. (Dauzat).

In Newfoundland:

Modern status: At Corner Brook.

GARD, a surname of England, Garde of Ireland, from Old French *garde* – guard, watchman, warden. (Reaney, Spiegelhalter).

Spiegelhalter traced G(u)ard in Devon; MacLysaght traced Garde in east Cork from Kent in the 17th century.

In Newfoundland:

Early instances: George, of Witless Bay, 1808 (Nfld. Archives BRC); Charles, from Somerset, of Fogo, 1856 (DPHW 83, MUN Hist.).

Modern status: Rare, at St. John's and Fogo.

GARD(I)NER, surnames of England, Scotland and Ireland, from Old Norman French *gardinier* – gardener. (Reaney, Cottle).

Guppy found Gardiner and Gardner widespread, with Gardner the most common form, Gardiner more characteristic of Norfolk, Essex, Cheshire and Gloucestershire, and Gardener rare, mostly in Northamptonshire. He found Gardner and Gardiner dispersed over a large part of Scotland, especially in Perthshire. MacLysaght found Gardiner in Ulster.

In Newfoundland:

Early instances: Luke Gardner, shoreman of St. John's, 1794–5, "26 years in Newfoundland," that is, 1758–9 (Census 1794–5); Alan Hyde Gardener, J.P. of Ferryland district, 1792 (D'Alberti 4); John Gard(e)ner or Gardiner (1795–1879), from Haselbury (Somerset), of British Harbour, 1815 (MUN Folklore, DPHW 64); Catherine Gardiner, from Old Ross (Co. Wexford), married at St. John's, 1815 (Nfld. Archives BRC); William Gardner, of Tilton Harbour (now Tilting), 1815 (Nfld. Archives KCRC); John, of Harbour Grace Parish, 1820 (Nfld. Archives HGRC); William, of Fogo, 1824 (Nfld. Archives KCRC); Catherine, of Renews, 1828 (Nfld. Archives BRC); William Gard(i)ner or Gardaner, of Herring Neck, 1829 (Nfld. Archives KCRC); Mary Gardner, of Fortune Harbour, 1832 (Nfld. Archives KCRC); Richard Gardener, from Devon, died (at St. John's), 1849, aged 47 (*Royal Gazette* 11 Dec 1849); George Gardiner, of Bareneed, 1860 (DPHW 38); John, of North(ern) River, 1860 (DPHW 38); Christopher Gard(e)ner, of Harbour Grace, 1868 (Nfld. Archives HGRC); Benjamin Gardner, telegraph operator of Brigus, 1871 (Lovell); Thomas, of Merasheen, 1871 (Lovell); James and Rev. George, of Heart's Content, 1871 (Lovell).

Modern status: Gardiner, scattered, especially at Groais Islands (White B.) (*Electors* 1955); Gardner, scattered, especially at British Harbour (*Electors* 1955)

Place name: Gardner Brook 48-22 55-42.

GARF, a surname of Sweden.
In Newfoundland:
Modern status: At St. John's.

GARLAND, a surname of England, Scotland and Ireland; in England and Scotland – (a maker or seller of metal) garland(s) or chaplets, or from Old English *gāra* – (dweller by the) gore, triangular piece of land, or from the English place name Garland (Devon), or from an inn sign, or from Old French *grailler* – to bark; in Ireland for the surname Gernon, *Gearnún*, which it has "almost entirely superseded." (Reaney, Cottle, Black, MacLysaght).

Traced by Spiegelhalter in Devon and by MacLysaght in Cos. Meath and Louth.

In Newfoundland:

Early instances: ? Jon, of Musketa Cove (now Bristol's Hope), 1675 (CO 1); Emelin, of Harbour Grace, 1675 (CO 1); John, of Little Bell Island, 1708–09 (CO 194.4); Moses, of Placentia, 1725 (CO 194.8); ——, Justice of Carbonear district, ? 1730 (CO 194.9); George, Justice of St. John's district, ? 1730–32 (CO 194.9); Charles, in possession of property at various localities in Conception Bay, from Manuels to Lower Island Cove, from 1757 to 1810 (Nfld. Archives L118, T3, CO 199.18); Henry, of Lower Island Cove, 1790 (CO 199.18); George, operator of salmon fishery at Trouty and New Harbour, 1804, at Indian Bay, Freshwater Bay, Dog Creek and Indian Arm, 1808 (CO 194.45, 48); James P., Magistrate of Trinity district, 1816 (D'Alberti 26); George, of ? Bonavista, 1821 (CO 194.64); ——, of Greenspond, 1830 (*Newfoundlander* 7 Oct 1830); John, of Freshwater (Carbonear), 1840 (DPHW 48); John, of Pushthrough, 1845 (DPHW 102); Ebenezer, merchant of Brigus, 1852 (DPHW 34); Henry, of Seal Cove (now Champneys), 1869 (DPHW 59); scattered in Lovell 1871.

Modern status: Scattered, especially at St. John's, Carbonear and Lower Island Cove.

Place names: Garland Bight (Labrador) 56-13 61-46; —— Cove 47-50 56-10; Garland's Pond 48-37 54-00.

GARNER, a surname of England, from the Old French personal name *Garnier*, or Old French *gern(i)er* – (keeper of the) granary, or a late form of GARDNER, or a dialect form of Warner. (Reaney, Spiegelhalter).

Traced by Guppy in Cheshire, Leicestershire and Rutlandshire, and by Spiegelhalter in Devon.

In Newfoundland:

Early instances: Luke, of St. John's, 1804 (Nfld. Archives BRC); James and William, planters of Belle Isle South (White B.), 1871 (Lovell); Edward, of Harbour Grace Parish, 1880 (Nfld. Archives HGRC).

Modern status: Rare, at St. John's.

GARNIER, a surname of England, France and Jersey (Channel Islands); in England a variant of GARNER; in France from an old baptismal name of German origin containing the elements *govern* or *protect* and *army*. (Dauzat, Turk).

In Newfoundland:

Early instance: Constant, planter of Sandy Point (St. George's district), 1871 (Lovell).

Modern status: At Bishops Falls, Corner Brook and in the St. George's district.

GARREAUX, a variant of the surnames of France, Garel, Gar(r)eau, from Fr. *garer* – sheep fold, park for animals, or of Garret, the Norman-Picard form of *jarret* – ? a nickname for one strong on his legs. (Dauzat).

In Newfoundland:

Early instance: Louis Garrow, of Brig Bay, 1873 (MUN Hist.).

Modern status: Unique, at Corner Brook.

GARRETT, a surname of England and Ireland, one of several variants including JERRETT, of the personal names Gerald and Gerard; also in Ireland a synonym of FITZGERALD. (Reaney, MacLysaght).

Guppy found Garratt, Garrett widespread with the two forms often associated, but with Garratt especially in Derbyshire and Garrett in Suffolk; Spiegelhalter traced Garrard, Garratt, Garrett in Devon; MacLysaght traced Garrett especially in northeast Ulster.

In Newfoundland:

Early instances: Thomas Garrett, of Bay de Verde, 1681 (CO 1); Thomas ? Garrott, of Newfoundland, 1706 (CO 194.24); Abram ? Garratt, of Quidi Vidi, 1708 (CO 194.4); William Garrett, married at St. John's, 1796 (DPHW 26D); Bridget Garret, married at Harbour Grace Parish, 1829 (Nfld. Archives HGRC); Henry Garrot, of Salvage, 1854 (DPHW 73A); Thomas Garrett, of Baker's Tickle (Burgeo-La Poile district), 1871 (Lovell); Lewis, of Flowers Cove to Point Ferolle area, 1871 (Lovell); Mark, of Middle Bill Cove, 1871 (Lovell).

Modern status: Scattered, especially in the Bonavista South district.

GASH, one of several variants, including GAZE, WASS, WAYSON, of a surname from Old French *Gace*, a diminutive of Old German names in *Wad-* or *Warin*. (Reaney).

Matthews traced Gash and Spiegelhalter Gass, Gaze in Devon.

In Newfoundland:

Early instances: Thomas, of Broad Cove (now Duntara), 1827 (Nfld. Archives KCRC); Thomas, of Kings Cove, 1829 (Nfld. Archives KCRC); Thomas, of Keels, 1858 (Nfld. Archives KCRC).

Modern status: At Corner Brook and Curling.

GASLARD, for the surname of France, Gouslard, from an old baptismal name of German origin *Godal-hard* containing the elements *god* – god and *hard* – hard, strong.

In Newfoundland:

Modern status: At Port au Choix.

GATEHOUSE, a surname of England, (dweller at the) house at the entrance of a monastery, castle, etc. (Cottle).

Traced by Guppy in Dorset.

In Newfoundland:

Early instances: Stephen, of Bonavista, 1828 (DPHW 70); Thomas, of Moreton's Harbour, 1871 (Lovell).

Modern status: At Seldom (*Electors* 1955), Bishop's Falls and Botwood.

GATES, a surname of England and Scotland, from Old English *gatu* – (dweller by the) gates, or in areas of Scandinavian settlement from Old Norse *gata* – (dweller by the) road(s), or from the English place names Yate, Yeat (Devon), or a variant of the surname Wait(e) etc., from Old Norman French *waite*, Old French *g(u)aite* – watchman. (Reaney, Cottle, Black, Spiegelhalter).

Guppy traced Gates in Sussex; Spiegelhalter traced Gate in Devon.

In Newfoundland:

Early instances: James, soldier of St. John's, 1778 (DPHW 26C); Benjamin, of Fogo, 1787 (MUN Hist.); Michael Gate, of Harbour Grace Parish, 1838 (Nfld. Archives HGRC); John and Josiah Gates, of Tizzard's Harbour, 1871 (Lovell).

Modern status: In the Green Bay district (*Electors* 1955), St. John's and Summerford (Twillingate district).

Place names: Gateville or Galeville 49-33 56-51; Lake Gates (Labrador) 54-58 63-23.

GATHERALL, a surname of England, ? from the English place name Catterall (Lancashire) or an unidentified place in Hampshire, or a nickname. (Reaney, Weekley).

Matthews traced Gattrell in Hampshire.

In Newfoundland:

Early instances: —— Gattrell, of Carbonear, 1702 (CO 194.2); Richard Gatrell, of Newfoundland, 1704 (CO 194.3); Richard Gatrell, of Newfoundland, 1704 (CO 194.3); Stephen Getherell, of Bay Bulls, 1793 (USPG); Esther Gatherale, of Bauline, 1812 (Nfld. Archives BRC); Stephen Gathoril, of St. John's, 1823 (Nfld. Archives BRC); Thomas Gatherall, of Caplin Bay (now Calvert), 1871 (Lovell); William, of Renews, 1871 (Lovell).

Modern status: At St. John's, Bauline (Ferryland district) and Bay Bulls.

GAUCI, a surname of Malta, of unascertained origin.

In Newfoundland: From Malta to Bell Island in 1941, thereafter in St. John's.

Modern status: Unique, at St. John's (*Electors* 1955).

GAUDET, GAUDON, GAUTHIER, GAUTREAUX, surnames of France from an old baptismal name derived from the Old German personal name *Waldo*. (Dauzat). *See also* VOUTIER.

In Newfoundland:

Tradition: Ignace Gaudet, from Margaree, N.S., settled at Stephenville about 1855. (G.R. Thomas).

Modern status: Gaudet, especially at Kippens; Gaudon, especially at Stephenville; Gauthier, at St. John's and St. Lawrence (*Electors* 1955); Gautreau, unique, at Harmon Field (*Electors* 1955); and Gautreaux, unique, at St. John's.

Place names: Gauthier Lake (Labrador) 54-55 65-53; Gautier Lake (Labrador) 53-53 65-24.

GAUL, a surname of England and Scotland, Gaule, *Mac an Ghaill*, of Ireland, from Celtic *gall* – foreigner, stranger. In Scotland, in Perthshire and Aberdeen, it was used of Lowlanders. (Reaney, Black, MacLysaght).

In Newfoundland:

Early instances: Mary, from Ross Parish (unspecified), Ireland, married at St. John's, 1804 (Nfld. Archives BRC); Patrick, tailor of St. John's, 1806 (CO 194.45); Mary Gaul or Gawl, of Harbour Grace Parish, 1816 (Nfld. Archives HGRC).

Modern status: Unique, at St. John's.

Place name: Kitty Gaul's Brook 47-32 52-45.

GAULTOIS, ? a variant, not recorded by Dauzat, of the surnames of France, Gaud, Gault, Gaudez, etc., from an Old baptismal name derived from the Old German personal name *Waldo*, or from Old French *gaud* – wood, small forest, common in many place names. (Dauzat).

In Newfoundland:

Family tradition: The name seems to have been given arbitrarily to a Maronite family (*see* Introduction) whose original name, presumably of Arabic origin, was unintelligible to some official or other (Family).

Modern status: Rare, especially at Stephenville Crossing.

Place name: Gaultois 47-36 55-54.

GAULTON, a variant of the surname of England, Galton, from the English place name Galton (Dorset) – (dweller at the) ? taxed or rented farm, or ? farm where bog myrtle or sweet gale grew. (Cottle, Ekwall).

Matthews traced Gaulton in Dorset.

In Newfoundland:

Early instances: John Galton, of Trinity Bay, 1767 (DPHW 64); John Gaulton, of Trinity (Trinity B.), 1832 (DPHW 64B); Joseph Galtin, of Grand Bank, 1832 (DPHW 109); John Gaulton, sailmaker of St. John's, 1843 (DPHW 26B); John Galton, of Port aux Basques, 1848 (*Nfld. Almanac*); Alfred, of Cold Harbour (Bonavista North district), 1854 (DPHW 76); Mary Gaulton, of Cape Freels, 1863 (DPHW 79); James Galton, of Brunet(te), 1871 (Lovell); John, of Cape Ray, 1871 (Lovell); James and Patrick Gaulton, of Burin, 1871 (Lovell); John and Martin, of Isle Valen, 1871 (Lovell); John, of Little Bay (Burin district), 1871 (Lovell); Alfred, of Middle Bill Cove, 1871 (Lovell); George (and others), of Savage Cove, 1871 (Lovell).

Modern status: Scattered, especially in the Placentia West and St. Barbe districts, and at St. John's.

Place names: Galton Island 47-33 54-16; —— Point 47-14 55-03.

GAUTHIER, GAUTREAUX. *See* GAUDET

GAVIN, a baptismal name and surname of Scotland, and a surname of Ireland, (O)Gavan, Gavin, *Ó Gábháin, Ó Gaibhín*; in Scotland for the Old French and Middle English personal name *Gavain* – hawk of battle, hawk of the plain, in Ireland ? from Ir. *gábhadh* – want. (Reaney, Cottle, Black, MacLysaght).

In Newfoundland:

Early instances: Maurice Gavan, soldier of St. John's, 1778 (DPHW 26C); Michael Gavin, of Harbour Grace Parish, 1838 (Nfld. Archives HGRC); Thomas, labourer of St. John's, 1840 (DPHW 26B).

Modern status: At Curling and in the White Bay South district.

GAY, a surname of England, Scotland and Ireland, from Middle English *gai(e)*, Old French *gai* – full of joy, light-hearted, or from the English place name Gay (Shropshire), or ? from the French place name Gaye (La Manche), or, in Ireland, occasionally for the Irish surname Gildea, *Mac Giolla Dhé* – devotee of God. (Reaney, Spiegelhalter, Cottle, MacLysaght).

Traced by Guppy in Cornwall, Devon, Essex, Hampshire and especially in Wiltshire.

In Newfoundland:
Early instances: William, married at St. John's, 1801 (DPHW 26D); Ambrose, planter of Lower Burgeo, 1871 (Lovell).
Modern status: Rare, at Corner Brook (*Electors* 1955), Bishop's Falls and St. John's.
Place name: Gay Side (P.O.) 49-20 54-46.

GAZE. *See* GASH
In Newfoundland:
Modern status: At St. John's (*Electors* 1955).
Place name (not necessarily from the surname): Gaze Point 47-53 55-43.

GEANGE. *See* GENGE

GEAR, a surname of England and Scotland; in England from Middle English *gere* – sudden fit of passion, wild or changeful mood, or from the place name Gear (Cornwall); in Scotland from Gaelic *gearr* – short. (Reaney, Cottle, Spiegelhalter, Black).
Traced by Spiegelhalter in Devon and by Black in Ross and Sutherland and in the Shetland Islands.
In Newfoundland:
Early instances: William, fisherman of Trinity (Trinity B.), 1757 (DPHW 64); Alexander, of Harbour Grace Parish, 1830 (Nfld. Archives HGRC); William, of Kings Cove, 1825 (Nfld. Archives KCRC); Robert Geare, from East Coker (Somerset), married at St. John's, 1836 (DPHW 26D); George Gear, from Bridport (Dorset), settled at St. John's, 1846 (Mott, *Newfoundlander* 2 Nov 1848); Edward, ? of Northern Bay, 1860 (DPHW 54); Richard, of Harbour Grace, 1866 (Nfld. Archives HGRC); Alexander (and others), of Perry's Cove, 1871 (Lovell).
Modern status: Scattered.
Place name: Gear Pond 47-27 52-54.

GEARIN, a variant of the surnames of Ireland (O)Geran, Gerin, Guerin, ? *Ó Gearáin.* (MacLysaght).
Gearin is probably the Co. Kerry form of the name.
In Newfoundland:
Early instance: Thomas Gearan, of Renews, 1837 (Nfld. Archives BRC).
Modern status: Rare, at Renews.

GEARY, a surname of England, Ireland and the Channel Islands, in England from the Old French and Old German personal names *Geri, Geric,* or from the French place names Géry (Meuse), Giry (Nièvre), or from Middle English *ge(e)ry* – changeable, giddy; in Ireland, (O)Geary, *Ó Gadhra, Mac Gadhra.* (Reaney, Spiegelhalter, Cottle, Dauzat, MacLysaght).
Traced by Guppy in Leicestershire and Rutlandshire, by Spiegelhalter in Devon, by MacLysaght in Cos. Cork and Roscommon; and in Jersey (Channel Islands).
In Newfoundland:
Family tradition: ——, from Channel Islands, settled at Carbonear ? in the early nineteenth century (Family).
Early instances: James, of Carbonear, 1785 (CO 199.18); Martin, of Harbour Grace Parish, 1807 (Nfld. Archives HGRC); Martin, ? of St. John's, 1810 (CO 194.50); John, of Tilton Harbour (now Tilting), 1815 (Nfld. Archives KCRC); Catherine, from Middleton (Co. Cork), married at St. John's, 1824 (Nfld. Archives BRC); Michael, of Witless Bay, 1825 (Nfld. Archives BRC); Margaret, of Joe Batts Arm, 1833 (Nfld. Archives KCRC); Ridman, of Grates Cove, 1842 (DPHW 58); Francis, gaoler of Ferryland district, 1844 (*Nfld. Almanac*, DPHW 31); Patrick, from Waterford City, of Harbour Grace, 1844 (*Indicator* 27 Jul 1844); Henry, of Cat Harbour (now Lumsden), 1850 (Nfld. Archives KCRC).
Modern status: Unique, at St. John's.

GEDDES, a surname of Scotland and Ireland, from the Scots place name Geddes (Nairnshire). (Black).
Traced by Guppy in northern Scotland and by MacLysaght in Ulster.
In Newfoundland:
Early instances: John, of St. John's, 1843 (DPHW 26D); George, from Scotland, clerk of St. John's, 1871, died at St. John's in the 1880s (Lovell, General Protestant Cemetery, St. John's).
Modern status: Unique, at St. John's.

GEEHAN, a surname of Ireland, (O)Geehan, a variant of the Co. Wicklow name (O)Gahan, *Ó Gaoithín,* Ir. *gaoth* – wind. (MacLysaght).
MacLysaght traced (O)Gahan in Cos. Wexford and Wicklow.
In Newfoundland:
Family tradition: ——, from Harbour Grace settled at Topsail, about 1822 (MUN Hist.).
Early instances: Nicholas Gehan, married at St. John's, 1808 (Nfld. Archives BRC); William Geehan, ? of Harbour Grace, 1845 (*Newfoundlander* 16 Jan 1845); John and Richard, farmers of Topsail, 1871 (Lovell).
Modern status: At Topsail.

GELLATELY, a surname of England and Scotland, one of several variants of Golightly – a nickname for a messenger or runner. (Reaney, Cottle, Black).

Traced by Black in Perth, Carse of Gowrie and Dundee.

In Newfoundland:

Modern status: At St. John's.

GENDREAU, a surname of France, a name of relationship used when a son-in-law, *gendre*, inherited the house of his father-in-law. (Dauzat).

In Newfoundland:

Modern status: Rare, at Bell Island.

GENGE, GEANGE, a surname of England, ? from the English place names East and West Ginge, Ginge Brook (Berkshire) or ? from Old English *genge* – agreeable.

Traced by Guppy in Dorset.

In Newfoundland:

Family tradition: Geange was mistakenly written in a birth certificate (Natalie Geange Falk).

Early instances: John Gainge (Genge in 1682), of Old Perlican, 1675 (CO 1); Edward Genge, of Petty Harbour, 1708 (CO 194.4); Elizabeth Geng, of Harbour Grace Parish, 1808 (Nfld. Archives HGRC); Edward Genge, of Grand Bank, 1839, of Channel, 1844 (DPHW 101, 106); George, of Greenspond, 1853 (DPHW 76); John William, son of John and Sarah, of Harrington, Yeovil (Somerset), servant of Newman and Co., Harbour Breton, married in 1870, aged 30 (Harbour Breton Anglican Church Records per D.A. Macdonald); Thomas and William Gange, of Flowers Cove to Point Ferolle area, 1871 (Lovell).

Modern status: Scattered, especially in the St. Barbe district with a large concentration at Anchor Point; Geange in Gander and Foxtrap.

Place names: Genge Cove 47-54 55-46, —— Point 51-15 56-48, Gengeville or Deadman's Cove 51-15 56-47.

GENNEAUX, GENOE, GIANNOU, ? variants of the surnames of France, Génau(d), from the Old German personal name *Genwald* – ruler of the race, or of Gueneau, from an Old German personal name containing the element *wan* – hope. (Dauzat).

In Newfoundland:

Modern status: Genneaux, unique, at Port au Choix (*Electors* 1955); Genoe, unique, at St. John's; Giannou, at St. John's.

GENT, GHENT, surnames of England, from Old French *gent*, Middle English *gente* – well-born, noble (in conduct), courteous. (Reaney). The spelling Gh indicates the pronunciation as in *gag*. Gent was traced by Guppy in Derbyshire and by Spiegelhalter in Devon.

In Newfoundland:

Early instances: Samuel Augustus Gent, of Trinity (Trinity B.), 1810 (DPHW 64); Charles, cooper of St. John's, 1871 (Lovell).

Modern status: Gent, at Windsor (*Electors* 1955); Ghent, at New Perlican.

GENTRY, a surname of England – (one of) high rank and good breeding. (Weekley).

In Newfoundland:

Modern status: Unique, at St. John's.

GEORGE, a baptismal name and surname of England, Ireland and Scotland, from the Greek – farmer, tiller of the soil. St. George was a Roman military tribune martyred in A.D. 303, whose cult was brought to England from the East by returning Crusaders. (Withycombe, Reaney, Cottle, MacLysaght 73).

Traced by Guppy in eleven English counties and south Wales, especially in Monmouthshire, and by MacLysaght mainly in Ulster since the seventeenth century "where it is of Scottish origin."

In Newfoundland:

Early instances: Robert, of Heart's Content, 1708–09 (CO 194.4); Thomas, of Trinity Bay, 1769 (DPHW 64); Henry, soldier of St. John's, 1774 (DPHW 26C); Martin, of Crocker's Cove (Carbonear), 1785 (CO 199.18); Jordan, of Scilly Cove (now Winterton), 1779 (DPHW 64); Thomas, proprietor and occupier of fishing room at ? New Harbour (Trinity B.), Winter 1800–01 (Census Trinity B.); Robert, fisherman of Trinity (Trinity B.), 1811 (Nfld. Archives Z30); Matthew, of Harbour Grace Parish, 1813 (Nfld. Archives HGRC); Robert, planter of Carbonear, 1822 (DPHW 48); Thomas, of Heart's Desire, 1825 (Nfld. Archives KCRC); Robert, of Trouty, 1830, of Heart's Ease, 1839 (DPHW 64B); Thomas, of New Harbour (Trinity B.), 1836 (DPHW 30); Edward, of Grand Bank, 1841 (DPHW 104); Richard, of Delby's Cove (Trinity B.), 1856, of Ireland's Eye, 1858 (DPHW 64B); Stephen, of Bay of Islands, 1871 (Lovell); John, of New Perlican, 1871 (Lovell).

Modern status: Widespread, especially in the Trinity South, Humber East and West districts.

Place names: 39 place names contain the specific George(s), not all necessarily from the surname.

GHANEY, a Newfoundland variant of the surname of Ireland, (O)Geaney, *Ó Géibheannaigh,* Ir. *géibheannach* – fettered. (MacLysaght).

Traced by MacLysaght in Co. Cork.

In Newfoundland:

Early instances: Patrick Gan(e)y, merchant of St. John's, 1787 (CO 194.37); Benjamin (and others) Gahany, farmers of Colliers, 1871 (Lovell); Thomas Geaney, of Tilton Harbour (now Tilting), 1871 (Lovell).

Modern status: Scattered, especially at Colliers.

GHENT. *See* GENT

GIANNOU. *See* GENNEAUX

GIBBONS, a surname of England and Ireland, a diminutive of Gibb, itself a diminutive of the baptismal name Gilbert; in Ireland also for *Mac Giobúin* and for "those Fitzgibbons who have dropped the Fitz." (Reaney, Cottle, MacLysaght). *See* GILBERT.

Traced by Guppy in Bedfordshire, Lincolnshire, Oxfordshire and Somerset, and by Spiegelhalter in Devon.

In Newfoundland:

Family tradition: Matthew (born 1781 at Southampton), settled at Harbour Grace in 1806; the family thence moved to Cat Harbour (now Lumsden) (MUN Folklore).

Early instances: W. and S., of Placentia, 1724 (CO 194.8); John, married at St. John's, 1767 (DPHW 26D); William Gibbeons, from Dublin, Irish convict landed at Petty Harbour or Bay Bulls, 1789 (CO 194.38); John Gibbons, of Harbour Grace Parish, 1813 (Nfld. Archives HGRC); Edward, of Greenspond, 1820 (DPHW 76); John, born at Vere (now Fair) Island, 1823 (DPHW 76); Edward, of Swain's Island (now Wesleyville), 1827 (DPHW 76); Elizabeth Gibbins, of Cat Harbour (now Lumsden), 1829 (Nfld. Archives KCRC); John Gibbons, of Portugal Cove, 1830 (MUN Hist.); Patrick, of Harbour Grace, 1844 (*Indicator* 27 Jul 1844); John, ? of Northern Bay, 1844 (DPHW 54); John, of Exploits Burnt Island, 1851 (DPHW 86); scattered in Lovell 1871.

Modern status: Scattered, especially at St. Vincent's (St. Mary's B.), and Current Island (St. Barbe district).

GIBBS, a surname of England, Gibb of Scotland and Ireland, from *Gibb,* a diminutive of Gilbert. (Reaney, Cottle). *See* GILBERT.

Traced by Guppy in the West Midlands, especially in Gloucestershire and Warwickshire and by Spiegelhalter in Devon.

In Newfoundland:

Early instances: Michael, ? of Port de Grave, 1783 (Nfld. Archives T22); Benjamin, of St. John's, 1790 (DPHW 26C); George, of Ferryland, 1791 (USPG); John, from Faha (unidentified), Waterford City, married at St. John's, 1799 (Nfld. Archives BRC); Nathaniel, of Brigus, 1802 (CO 199.18); Edmund, of Harbour Grace Parish, 1815 (Nfld. Archives HGRC); Esau, of Bonavista, 1827 (DPHW 70); William, from Plymouth, married at Harbour Grace, 1837 (*Star and Conception B.J.* 13 Sep 1837); Joseph, of Catalina, 1857 (DPHW 67); John, of Twillingate, 1871 (Lovell).

Modern status: Scattered, especial at Mockbeggar (Bonavista B.).

GIBSON, a surname of England, Scotland and Ireland – son of Gib(b), diminutive of Gilbert. *See* GILBERT.

Traced by Guppy in the north of England, especially in Durham and Northumberland, and south of the Forth and Clyde; by MacLysaght especially in the Belfast area.

In Newfoundland:

Early instances: Thomas, of Tilton Harbour (now Tilting), 1823 (Nfld. Archives KCRC); James, from Lanark, married at St. John's, 1833 (DPHW 26D); ? Lewis, of Harbour Grace Parish, 1843 (Nfld. Archives HGRC).

Modern status: Rare, at St. John's (*Electors* 1955).

Place name: Gibson Shoal 50-58 57-10.

GIDGE, a variant of the surnames of England, Gedge, Gigg, from Middle English *gegge,* a contemptuous term applied to both men and women, – wench, bloke. (Reaney, Cottle).

Guppy traced Gedge in Norfolk.

In Newfoundland:

Early instances: Thomas Gidge or Gedge, of Twillingate, 1818 (USPG); Thomas and William Geage, of Dildo Cove, 1871 (Lovell).

Modern status: Scattered, especially in the Twillingate district.

GIFFIN, a surname of England, (Mac) Giffen, *Mac Dhuibhfinn* in Ireland, Giffen of Scotland; in England from the personal name Giff, an abbreviation of Geoffrey, in Ireland from ? *dubh* – black and a personal name *Fionn* – fair, and in

Scotland from the Scots place name Giffen (Ayrshire). (Withycombe, Reaney, MacLysaght, Black).

Traced by MacLysaght in Cos. Antrim, Derry and Tyrone.

In Newfoundland:

Modern status: Rare, at Corner Brook.

GIFFORD, a surname of England, Scotland and Ireland, from an Old German personal name *Gifard*, or Old French *giffard* – chubby-cheeked, bloated. (Reaney). *See also* JEFFORD.

Traced by Guppy in Cambridgeshire, Dorset, Huntingdonshire and Somerset, by Spiegelhalter in Devon, and by MacLysaght in Co. Down.

In Newfoundland:

Early instances: John, of Brigus, 1675, 1677 (CO 1); William, of New Perlican, 1677 (CO 1); Benjamin Giffard, of Bay de Verde, 1730 (CO 194.23); William Gifford, married at St. John's, 1796 (DPHW 26D); Francis, of Freshwater (Carbonear), 1820 (DPHW 48); William, of Port de Grave, 1848 (DPHW 39); Elias, of St. Paul's Bay, 1873 (MUN Hist.).

Modern status: At Port de Grave and Coleys Point.

GIGUERE, ? a variant, not recorded by Dauzat, of a surname of France such as Giger or Giguet.

In Newfoundland:

Modern status: Rare, at Wabana (*Electors* 1955) and St. John's.

GILBERT, a baptismal name and surname of England, Ireland, Scotland and France, G(u)ilbert of Guernsey (Channel Islands), from an Old German personal name *Gisilbert* or *Gislebert*, containing the elements *pledge* or *hostage* and *bright*, Old French *Gislebert, Gil(l)ebert, Guilbert*; in Scotland also for the unrelated name Gilbride. (Withycombe, Reaney, Dauzat, Black, Turk). *See also* GIBBONS, GIBBS, GIBSON.

Found widespread by Guppy in the Midlands and south of England, and by MacLysaght in Leinster.

In Newfoundland:

Family traditions: ——, from Devon, settled at Haystack (Placentia B.), in the early 19th century (MUN Folklore). Mary (1836–1900), of Come-by-Chance (MUN Geog.).

Early instances: John, of St. John's, 1751 (CO 194.13); John, of Sound Island, 1861 (DPHW 105); Gabriel, of Black River (Placentia B.), 1871 (Lovell); John, of Mussell Harbour (Placentia B.), 1871 (Lovell); Samuel and Thomas, of Haystack, 1871 (Lovell).

Modern status: Scattered.

Place names (not necessarily from the surname): Gilbert Lake (Labrador) 52-41 56-14; —— Bay (Labrador) 52-38 56-00; —— River (Labrador) 52-39 56-06; Gilbert's Cove 47-25 54-35; —— Point 47-50 54-08.

GILES, a baptismal name and surname of England, Scotland, Ireland and the Channel Islands, from the Latin personal name *Aegidius*, a derivative of the Greek – kid. St. Aegidius is described as a 6th century Athenian miracle-worker who fled to France; he is the patron saint of cripples and beggars. In Ireland, in Co. Louth, Giles is often for *Ó Glaisne*, in Co. Galway ? for *Mac Goill*. (Withycombe, Reaney, Cottle, MacLysaght, Black, Turk).

Traced by Guppy in Cornwall, Devon, Northamptonshire, Somerset and especially Wiltshire; by MacLysaght in Youghal (Co. Cork) and elsewhere.

In Newfoundland:

Family tradition: William, son of ——, from Poole (Dorset), was born at Carbonear, 1831 (MUN Folklore).

Early instances: Michael Gile, ? of St. John's, ? 1771–89 (CO 194.41); John, of Torbay, 1801 (DPHW 26B); William Giles, planter of Carbonear, 1823 (DPHW 48); ——, on the *Samuel* in the seal fishery out of Bay Roberts, 1838 (*Newfoundlander* 29 Mar 1838); Isaac, of Indian Burying Place, 1843 (DPHW 86); Solomon, of Nipper's Harbour, 1850, of Rogues Harbour, 1854 (DPHW 86); George, of Transway [Fransway], 1852 (DPHW 102); John Gile, schoolmaster of Pushthrough, 1853 (DPHW 102); Joseph Giles, of Bay of Islands, 1871 (Lovell); Samuel, of Ramea Islands, 1871 (Lovell); George, of Rose Blanche, 1871 (Lovell); Thomas, of Sound Island, 1871 (Lovell) .

Modern status: Scattered.

Place names (not necessarily from the surname): Giles Cove 49-45 56-55; —— Island 49-37 55-40; Point 48-58 58-03; —— Pond 47-39 53-27.

GILL, a surname of England, Scotland, Ireland and the Channel Islands, from Old Irish **Gilla*, Old Norse *Gilli* – servant, or from Middle English *gille*, Old Norse *gil* – (dweller in the) ravine, or a pet-form of Gillian, Julian; in Ireland also for Mac Gill, *Mac an Ghaill*, Ir. *gall* – foreigner, or as an abbreviation of one of the many names beginning with *Mac Giolla* – devotee of. (Reaney, Cottle, Black, MacLysaght, Turk).

Guppy found Gill widespread, especially in

Yorkshire WR; Black found it "of great antiquity on both sides of the Border."

In Newfoundland:

Early instances: Patrick, ? servant of Little Placentia (now Argentia), about 1730–35 (CO 194.9); Michael, from Charlestown (New England), merchant of St. John's, 1730 (CO 194-24, Prowse); Michael, of Quidi Vidi Cove, 1771 (CO 194.18, 30); John, from Wimborne (Dorset), apprentice at Carbonear, 1777 (Dorset County Record office per Kirwin); Owen, of Torbay, 1780 (D'Alberti 14); William, of Cupids, 1799 (CO 199.18); William, of Adam's Cove, 1800 (CO 199.18); Thomas, of Brigus, 1803 (CO 199.18); Anne, of Harbour Grace Parish, 1823 (Nfld. Archives HGRC); John, of Ochre Pit Cove, 1829 (Nfld. Archives BRC); George, baptized at Pinchard's Island, 1830, aged 33 years (DPHW 76); Joseph, of Cape Island (Bonavista B.), 1834 (DPHW 76); Patrick, planter of Harbour Grace, 1838 (DPHW 43); Henry, of Salmon Cove (unspecified), 1840 (*Newfoundlander* 13 Feb 1840); William, surgeon of Trinity (Trinity B.), 1842 (DPHW 64B); Thomas, of Black Island (Twillingate district), 1842 (DPHW 86); James, of Exploits Burnt Island, 1842 (DPHW 86); Thomas, of White Bay, 1855 (DPHW 85); Joseph, of Indian Islands, 1858 (DPHW 83); Charles, of Peter's Arm, 1860 (DPHW 92); John, of Robinson's Head, 1870 (DPHW 96); Leander, miner of Tilt Cove, 1871 (Lovell); John and Thomas Gills, of Charles Brook, 1871 (Lovell); William, of Wiseman's Cove, 1871 (Lovell).

Modern status: Scattered, especially at Botwood and Newtown.

Place names: Gill Lake (Labrador) 54-42 65-34; Gills Cove 49-46 56-49; —— Point 49-07 55-18.

GILLAM, GILLIAM, surnames of England, English forms of the French baptismal name and the surname of Jersey (Channel Islands) Guillaume (William). (Reaney, Dauzat, Turk).

Spiegelhalter traced Gillam, Gillham, Gilliam, Gillum, Gilhome in Devon.

In Newfoundland:

Early instances: Joseph and Michael Gillam, of St. John's, 1816 (CO 194.60); William Gillham, of Cupids, 1828 (DPHW 34); —— Gillam, of Channel, about 1829 (Feild); Joseph Gillham, from Bristol, late of Harbour Grace, 1830 (*Newfoundlander* 25 Feb 1830); Charles Guillam, of Port aux Basques, 1830 (DPHW 30); Michael, of Burnt Island (Burgeo-La Poile district), 1841 (DPHW 101); Robert Gillam, of Greenspond, 1845 (DPHW 76); William Gilham, of Gander Bay, 1850 (DPHW 83); George, of Ochre Pit

Cove, 1854 (DPHW 52B); Robert Gillham, of Exploits Burnt Island, 1861 (DPHW 92); Thomas, of Seal Cove (White B.), 1864 (DPHW 94); George Gillam, of Middle Barachoix (St. George's district), 1870 (DPHW 96); John Gilham, of Robinson's Head, 1871 (DPHW 96); Philip Gillam, of Cape Ray, 1871 (Lovell); Benjamin (and others), of Hiscock's Point, 1871 (Lovell); James Gillham, of Round Harbour (Fogo district), 1871 (Lovell).

Modern status: Gillam, scattered, especially at McKays; Gilliam, rare, in the Humber West and St. George's districts.

Place names: Gilham Cove, —— Head 47-38 54-42; Gillam(s) Rock 47-34 59-09; Gillams, —— Brook 49-01 58-04; ——Cove 49-01 58-05.

GILLARD, a surname of England, pronounced with G as in *gag* from the Old French *Guilard*, with G as in *gem*, a derivative of French *Gillard*, a diminutive of Gille (GILES). (Reaney, Cottle).

Traced by Guppy in Devon.

In Newfoundland:

Family traditions: ——, from England, settled at Englee in the late 1840s (MUN Hist.). Henry (1810–), born at Twillingate (MUN Folklore).

Early instances: Bridget, of Twillingate, 1829 (Nfld. Archives KCRC); Daniel, fisherman of Western Bay, 1831 (DPHW 52A); William Gilliard, of Fortune, 1839 (DPHW 106); John P. and Nathaniel Jillard, of Harbour Grace, 1871 (Lovell); John, of St. John's, 1871 (Lovell); George Gillard, of Broad Cove (now St. Philips), 1871 (Lovell); Henry and Robert, of Englee Harbour, 1871 (Lovell).

Modern status: Scattered, especially at Gillard's Cove (Twillingate district).

Place names: Gillard Pond 49-59 56-05; Gillard's Bight (Labrador) 53-32 59-46; —— Cove 49-37 54-45; —— Lake 49-24 56-37.

GILLESPIE, a surname of Scotland, and as (Mac) Gillespie of Ireland, Scots Gaelic *Gilleasbuig*, Ir. *Mao Giolla Easpaig*, Ir. *easpog* (Latin *episcopus*) – servant of the bishop. MacLysaght notes that "Synonyms of the name are Clusby and Glashby in Co. Louth, Clasby in Co. Galway, and also, by translation, BISHOP." (Black, MacLysaght).

Traced by Guppy south of the Forth and Clyde, by MacLysaght in Co. Donegal.

In Newfoundland:

Early instances: William, Samuel and John Glasby, of Carbonear, 1785, property "possessed by the Family for upwards of 90 years," that is, before 1695 (CO 199.18); Mary Gelasby or Gillasby, of

Harbour Grace Parish, 1814 (Nfld. Archives HGRC); Alexander Gilespy, of Harbour Grace, 1821 (DPHW 52A); Julia Gelaspy, of Riverhead, married at Harbour Grace, 1829 (Nfld. Archives BRC); Mary Gilasby, of Fortune Harbour, 1830 (Nfld. Archives KCRC); William Gillespie, of St. John's, 1848 (DPHW 23); Thomas, from Greenock, Scotland, married at St. John's, 1849 (*Royal Gazette* 13 Feb 1849).

Modern status: Rare, at Fortune Harbour (*Electors* 1955) and Carbonear.

Place name: Gillespie Island 49-31 55-15.

GILLETT, JILLETT, surnames of England, with G as in *gag*, from French Guillot, a pet-form of Guillaume (William), or from Old Norse *gil* – (dweller at the) head of the ravine, or with G as in *gem* or J diminutives of Gille (GILES), or late forms of GILLARD. (Reaney, Cottle).

Guppy traced Gillett in Kent and Somerset and especially in Oxfordshire, Spiegelhalter in Devon.

In Newfoundland:

Early instances: —— Gillett, constable of Trinity district, ? 1730 (CO 194.9); Richard Gillet, of Trinity (Trinity B.), 1757 (DPHW 64); John Gellet, of Bonavista, 1792 (USPG); John, shoreman of St. John's, 1794–5, "born in Newfoundland" (Census 1794–5; Robert Gillet, of Carbonear, 1795 (CO 199.18); John Gillitt, from Christchurch (Hampshire), blacksmith of Trinity, deceased 1813 (*Royal Gazette* 2 Dec 1813); John Gillet, blacksmith of Twillingate, 1817 (USPG); William Gillit or Gillett, of Herring Neck, 1845, of Canister Cove, 1853 (DPHW 86); George Gillett, of Exploits Burnt Island, 1871 (Lovell).

Modern status: Gillett, scattered, especially in the Twillingate and Grand Falls districts; Jillett, rare, at Clarenville (*Electors* 1955) and Carbonear.

Place name: Gillet Island 49-15 55-12.

GILLEY, a surname of England, ? from Cornish *gilly* – (dweller in or by the) grove. (Ewen).

In Newfoundland:

Early instances: Lewis W., from Maine, U.S.A., married at St. John's, 1836 (DPHW 26D); John Gilly, of Broom Point (St. Barbe district), 1873 (MUN Hist.).

Modern status: At Deer Lake, Curling and in the St. Barbe district.

GILLIAM. *See* GILLAM

GILLIES, GILLIS, surnames of Scotland and Ireland, Scots Gaelic *Gille Iosa* – servant of Jesus, "sometimes used for Mac Aleese [of the same

significance] in Ireland." (Black, MacLysaght). Traced by Black in the Hebrides.

In Newfoundland:

Family tradition: Ian Gillis, from Scotland, settled at Judique (Cape Breton Island) in 1830; later, his sons, en route to Boston, were shipwrecked and rescued by a vessel which was driven into Bay St. George and they settled there (MUN Folklore).

Early instances: James Gillies, from Scotland, master-builder of Harbour Grace, 1845 (*Times* 1 Mar 1845); Daniel and John Gillis, of Codroy and Rivers, 1871 (Lovell); Rev. Donald, of Sandy Point (St. George's district), 1871 (Lovell).

Modern status: Gillies, at St. John's Gillis, scattered, especially at Highlands.

Place name: ? Gillesport 49-40 54-45.

GILLINGHAM, a surname of England, from the English place name Gillingham (Norfolk, Dorset, Kent). (Bardsley). Traced by Guppy in Dorset.

In Newfoundland:

Family traditions: George Freeman, from Gillingham (Dorset or Kent) settled at Lower Island Cove about 1800 (Family per Kirwin). Eliza (1836–1926), of Clarke's Head (Gander B.) (MUN Geog.).

Early instances: ——, proprietor and occupier of fishing room at Trinity (Trinity B.), Winter 1800–01 (Census Trinity B.); William, of Greenspond, 1816 (DPHW 76); Thomas, planter of Kelligrews, 1817 (D'Alberti 27); James, baptized at Pool's Island, 1830, aged 35 years (DPHW 76); Charles, planter of Ochre Pit Cove, 1834 (DPHW 52A); Thomas, of Change Islands, 1841 (DPHW 83); Charles, planter of Lower Island Cove, 1851 (DPHW 55); Robert, of Carbonear, 1851 (DPHW 49); Robert, of Gander Bay, 1851 (DPHW 83); Margaret, of Herring Neck, 1854 (DPHW 85); William, of Exploits Burnt Island, 1859 (DPHW 92); Henry, of Gut Arm (Twillingate district), 1860 (DPHW 85); Reuben, of Burnt Island (Burgeo-La Poile district), 1871 (Lovell).

Modern status: Widespread, especially at Ochre Pit Cove, Clarke's Head and Noggin Cove (Fogo district).

GILLIS. *See* GILLIES

GINN, a surname of England, from Middle English *gin(ne)*, Old French *engin* – skill, ingenuity, snare, trap; but in Newfoundland also for the surname of Ireland Mac Ginn, *Mag Fhinn*, Ir. *fionn* – fair. (Reaney). MacLysaght traced MacGinn in Co. Tyrone.

In Newfoundland:

Family tradition: Thomas Ginn or McGinn from England, settled in Newfoundland in 1840 (MUN Folklore).

Early instances: Mary, of Harbour Grace Parish, 1819 (Nfld. Archives HGRC);

John, of Change Islands, 1832 (DPHW 30).

Modern status: Scattered, especially at Horwood (Fogo district).

GIOVANNETTI, a surname of Italy, a diminutive of the baptismal name Giovanni – John. *See* JOHN.

In Newfoundland:

Modern status: At Bell Island (*Electors* 1955) and St. John's.

GIOVANNINI, a surname of Italy, a diminutive of the baptismal name Giovanni – John. *See* JOHN.

In Newfoundland:

Family tradition: Celestine Guglielmo, born at Lucca or Florence, Italy, came to Newfoundland about 1850, subsequently settled at St. Lawrence; Henry, his brother, settled at Fortune (MUN Folklore).

Modern status: At St. Lawrence, Rencontre East and St. John's.

GLADNEY, a surname of England and ? Scotland and ? Ireland; from the Scots place name Gla(i)dney (Fifeshire) or ? (dweller by or in the) small, enclosed or fenced yard (E.C. Smith) or ? for gledney = gladwyn, a kind of iris, untraced. (W.J. Kirwin). *See also* CLATNEY.

In Newfoundland:

Family traditions: ——, from England to Waterford; his brother ——, settled at Topsail and subsequently at Portugal Cove Road (St. John's) (MUN Folklore). Edward (1827–), born in Ireland, came to St. John's in 1857 (MUN Folklore). John, involved in a religious dispute at Portugal Cove, 1850 (MUN Hist.).

Early instances: Patrick Gladney, from St. Mollens (? for St. Mullins) Parish (Co. Carlow), married at St. John's, 1816 (Nfld. Archives BRC); three brothers Gladney drowned in Windsor Lake 1830 (*Newfoundlander* 21 Jan 1830); John Gladny, of Kings Cove Parish, ? 1840 (Nfld. Archives KCRC).

Modern status: Especially at St. John's.

Place name: Gladney's Arm 47-36 52-48.

GLASCO, a surname of Ireland, a variant of the surname of England, Glasscock, from the English place name Glascote (Warwickshire) (MacLysaght); but possibly confused with GLASGOW.

MacLysaght traced Glasscock as an "English toponymic formerly numerous in Co. Kildare. Glascoe is a synonym of Glasscock not of Glasgow."

In Newfoundland:

Early instances: John Glascol, of St. John's, 1790 (DPHW 26C); W.N. Glascock, surrogate, 1818–19 (CO 194.62); Alice Glasco, married at St. John's, 1837 (Nfld. Archives BRC).

Modern status: Rare, at St. John's.

GLASGOW, a surname of Scotland and Ireland, from the Scots place name Glasgow; also in Ireland (Mac) Glasgow, a variant of Mac Gloskey. *See* GLASCO.

MacLysaght traced (Mac) Glasgow in Co. Tyrone and other parts of Ulster.

In Newfoundland:

Early instances: Peter Glasgow, Glascow or Glasco, of St. John's, 1833, 1834, 1847 (*Newfoundlander* 14 Feb 1833, 3 Apr 1834, 25 Feb 1847); John Glasgow, butcher of St. John's, 1871 (Lovell).

Modern status: At St. John's (*Electors* 1955).

GLAVINE, a variant of the surname of Ireland, (O)Glavin, *Ó Gláimhín*, a diminutive of Ir. *glám* – satirist, rather than of (Mac) Glavin, *Mag Láimhín* formerly *Mag Fhlaithimhín*, Ir. *flaitheamh* – ruler. (MacLysaght).

MacLysaght traced (O)Glavin in Cos. Cork and Kerry, (Mac) Glavin, rare, in Ulster.

In Newfoundland:

Family traditions: David, born in Co. Cork in the early 19th century, settled in Newfoundland, at the age of 18 years (MUN Folklore).

Early instances: John Glavin & Co., of Kettle Cove (North Shore, Conception B.), 1804 (CO 199.18); James, of Harbour Grace, 1805 (CO 199.18); Margaret, of Ferryland, 1805 (Nfld. Archives BRC); James Glaveen, servant of Conche Harbour, died 1821 (D'Alberti 31); David Glavine or Glaveen, of Twillingate, 1822, of Tilting Harbour (now Tilting), 1829 (Nfld. Archives KCRC); Anty [sic] Glavene, of Fortune Harbour, 1830 (Nfld. Archives KCRC); James Glaven, master mariner of St. John's, 1871 (Lovell).

Modern status: Scattered, especially at Bishop's Falls.

GLEASON, a variant of the surnames of Ireland, (O)GLEESON, *Ó Glasáin* or *Ó Gliasáin*. (MacLysaght).

MacLysaght traced (O)Gleeson in Co. Tipperary.

In Newfoundland:

Early instances: James Gleeson, fisherman of St. John's, 1794–5, "20 years in Newfoundland," that is, 1774–5 (Census 1794–5); Margaret, from Monchine (? for Mooncoin) Parish (Co. Kilkenny), married at St. John's, 1803 (Nfld. Archives BRC); Thomas Gleason or Gleeson, of Harbour Grace Parish, 1809 (Nfld. Archives HGRC); Ellen Gleeson, of Harbour Grace, 1816 (Nfld. Archives BRC); Thomas, of Kings Cove, 1820 (Nfld. Archives KCRC); Rev. J. P., of Carbonear, 1848 (*Newfoundlander* 10 Feb 1848); Philip, from Loughmore (Co. Tipperary), died at St. John's, 1852, aged 30 years (*Weekly Herald* 30 Jun 1852); Henry, of Harbour Buffett, 1871 (Lovell); Timothy, of Topsail, 1871 (Lovell); Nicholas, of Twillingate, 1871 (Lovell).

Modern status: Gleason, in the Twillingate district and at St. John's; Gleeson, at Topsail.

GLENN, a surname of England, Ireland and Scotland; in England from the place names, Glen (Leicestershire), Glyn (Cornwall), or from Cornish *glen, glyn* – (dweller in the) river valley; in Ireland, with variants Glann(y), Glenny, Ir. *an Ghlenna* – of the glen, one of the few Irish locative surnames; in Scotland from the Scots place name Glen (Peeblesshire); confused with GLYNN. (Cottle, Spiegelhalter, MacLysaght).

Traced by Spiegelhalter in Devon, and as Glen, found scattered by Guppy in Scotland.

In Newfoundland:

Early instances: Mary Glinn, of Bay Bulls, 1805 (Nfld. Archives BRC); James Glen, of Bay Bulls, 1822 (D'Alberti 32); Mary Glin, of St. John's, 1828 (Nfld. Archives BRC); Thomas Glen, son of Alexander of Glasgow, Scotland, of St. John's, 1846 (*Newfoundlander* 7 May 1846); Ellen, of Kings Cove, 1859 (Nfld. Archives KCRC); Thomas, from Greenock, Scotland, died 1887, aged 91 (General Protestant Cemetery, St. John's).

Modern status: Unique, at Bell Island (*Electors* 1955).

GLODE, a surname of the Micmacs of Newfoundland, ? a variant of the surname of France Glodeau, from the old pronunciation of the baptismal name Claude. (Dauzat).

In Newfoundland:

Early instance: Joseph, of Gambo, 1885 (Nfld. Archives KCRC).

Modern status: Rare, at Corner Brook (*Electors* 1955) and Deer Lake.

Place names: (Joe) Glode's Brook 48-52 56-27; —— —— Pond or Little —— —— —— 49-00 56-21.

GLOVER, a surname of England, Scotland and Ireland, from Old English *glōf* – (maker or seller of) glove(s).

Traced by Guppy in Cheshire, Lancashire, Leicestershire and Rutlandshire, Staffordshire and Warwickshire, by Spiegelhalter in Devon, and by MacLysaght in Ulster.

In Newfoundland:

Early instances: Matthew and George, of Placentia ? district, 1744 (CO 194.24); John, of St. John's, 1765 (DPHW 26C); George, of Swain's Island, 1835 (DPHW 76); George Glower, of Bragg's Island, 1871 (Lovell).

Modern status: Scattered, especially at Brigg's Island (*Electors* 1955).

Place names: Glover or Sir John Glover Island 48-46 57-43; Glover's Harbour 49-27 55-30, 49-28 55-29; —— Point 49-27 55-28; Glovertown 48-41 54-02; Glovertown South 48-40 54-01.

GLYNN, a surname of England and Ireland, a variant of, or confused with, GLENN, or in Ireland (Mac) Glynn, *Mac Fhloinn*, Ir. *flann* – ruddy. (Cottle, Spiegelhalter, MacLysaght).

Traced by Spiegelhalter in Devon and by MacLysaght in Connacht and Co. Clare.

In Newfoundland:

Family tradition: William (1805–68), from Ulster, settled at Bay Bulls, about 1830 (MUN Geog.).

Early instances: James Glyn, of Bay Bulls, ? 1753 (CO 194.13); John Glynn, of Bay Bulls, 1810 (Nfld. Archives BRC); Michael M., of St. John's, 1814 (D'Alberti 24); Thomas, J.P. for Southern Districts (Ferryland), 1834, member of the General Assembly for Ferryland district, 1842 (*Newfoundlander* 10 Jul 1834, *Nfld. Almanac* 1844); Edmund, gaoler of Burin district, 1844 (*Nfld. Almanac*); Mrs., teacher of Green Bay, 1857 (*Nfld. Almanac*).

Modern status: At Bay Bulls and St. John's.

GODDEN, a surname of England and Jersey (Channel Islands), from the Anglo-French form *Godin* of the Old English personal name *Godwine* containing the elements *God* and *wine* – friend. (Withycombe, Turk). *See also* GODWIN. Traced by Guppy in Kent.

In Newfoundland:

Early instances: Joseph ? Godden, of Bonavista, 1792 (USPG); William, of Barr'd Islands, 1821 (USPG); Thomas, tailor of Carbonear, 1825 (DPHW 48); Thomas, of St. John's, 1831 (*Newfoundlander* 7 Jul 1831); T., of Harbour Grace, 1832 (*Newfound-*

lander 11 Oct 1832); John, planter of Seal Cove (now New Chelsea), 1832 (DPHW 59A).

Modern status: Scattered, especially at St. John's.

Place names: Godden's Pond 47-48 53-14; Goddenville 47-36 53-21.

GODFREY, a surname of England, Ireland and the Channel Islands, from the Old German personal name *Godefrid*, containing the elements *god* and *peace*; in Old French *Godefroi(s)*; also in Ireland for *Mac Gothraidh*. (Reaney, MacLysaght, Turk).

Guppy found Godfrey widespread in the Midlands, Spiegelhalter in Devon.

In Newfoundland:

Early instances: William, of Petty Harbour, 1675, (Godfry in 1677) (CO 1); John, of St. John's, 1799 (DPHW 26B); Michael, of Bay de Verde, 1803 (CO 199.18); Mary, of Harbour Grace Parish, 1809 (Nfld. Archives HGRC); Hannah Godfrey or Godfree, of Catalina, 1832, of Ragged Harbour (now Melrose), 1834 (Nfld. Archives KCRC).

Modern status: Rare, at St. John's (*Electors* 1955).

GODSELL, a surname of England and Ireland, from the English place names Gadshill (Kent), or Godshill (IOW, Hampshire), or Godsell Farm (Wiltshire) – god's hill, or by confusion with Godsal(l) – good soul, honest fellow. (Reaney).

Traced by Guppy (with Godsall) in Herefordshire, and by MacLysaght in Cos. Cork and Limerick.

In Newfoundland:

Early instances: Michael Godsil, of Harbour Grace Parish, 1816 (Nfld. Archives HGRC); William Godsell, of Tilton Harbour (now Tilting), 1818 (Nfld. Archives KCRC); Thomas, of Harbour Grace, 1831 (*Newfoundlander* 10 Mar 1831); ——, from Co. Cork, married at St. John's, 1831 (Nfld. Archives BRC); Maria, of Spaniard's Bay, 1866 (Nfld. Archives HGRC).

Modern status: Rare, at Spaniard's Bay (*Electors* 1955) and St. John's.

GODWIN, a surname of England and Ireland, from the Old English personal name *Godwine*, containing the elements *God* and *wine* – friend. *See also* GODDEN, and GOODWIN with which confusion occurs. In Ireland, Connacht, Godwin is a synonym of O'DEA.

Traced by Guppy in Berkshire, Hampshire, Oxfordshire and especially Wiltshire, by Spiegelhalter in Devon, and by MacLysaght in Connacht.

In Newfoundland:

Early instances: Eleanor, from Ballymany (? for Ballymoney) Parish (Co. Wexford), married at St. John's, 1815 (Nfld. Archives BRC); George, of Barr'd Island, 1847 (DPHW 83).

Modern status: Rare, especially at Barr'd Island (*Electors* 1955).

GOFF, a surname of England and Ireland, from Irish, Gaelic *gobha*, Welsh, Breton *gof*, Cornish *gov* – smith; confused with GOUGH. (Reaney, Cottle, MacLysaght).

Traced by Guppy in Northamptonshire.

In Newfoundland:

Early instances: William, of Torbay, 1775 (DPHW 26C); George, of Bonavista, 1792 (USPG); George, of St. John's, 1802 (DPHW 26B); Patrick ? Goff, one of 72 impressed men who sailed from Ireland to Newfoundland, ? 1811 (CO 194.51); John Goffe, from Co. Waterford, married at St. John's, 1814 (Nfld. Archives BRC); George Goff (? 1759–1834), from Hampshire to Newfoundland about 1774, High Constable of Portugal Cove, 1815 (*Star and Conception B.J.* 7 Jan 1835, D'Alberti 25); William, merchant of Ferryland, 1822 (CO 194.65); John, of Kings Cove, 1829 (Nfld. Archives KCRC); Edward, of Harbour Grace Parish, 1832 (Nfld. Archives HGRC); David, from Waterford City, of Harbour Grace, 1844 (*Indicator* 27 Jul 1844); William, ? from Tottenham Green (Co. Wexford), of St. John's, 1846 (*Newfoundlander* 30 Apr 1846); William, of Bird Island Cove (now Elliston), 1871 (Lovell); James and Thomas, tailors of Carbonear, 1871 (Lovell); Michael, of Flatrock (St. John's), 1871 (Lovell); Richard, of Salmonier (St. Mary's), 1871 (Lovell).

Modern status: Rare, at Carbonear and St. John's.

GOLDEN, a surname of England and Ireland, from Old English *gylden* – golden-haired; also in Ireland an anglicized form of *Ó Góillín, Ó Goilín, Mag Ualghairg*; also a variant of GOULDING. (Reaney, MacLysaght).

Traced by Guppy in Cambridgeshire and Norfolk, by Spiegelhalter in Devon, and by MacLysaght in Co. Cork.

In Newfoundland:

Early instances: Samuel Goulden, in possession of property at Petty Harbour, 1794-5 (Census 1794-5); Jacob Golden(s), of Greenspond, 1841 (DPHW 76).

Modern status: Rare, at Whiteway (Trinity B.), and St. John's.

Place names (not necessarily from the surname): Golden Bay 46-49 54-09; —— Bay or Branch Cove 46-52 53-56; Golden Gullies 47-25 53-22.

GOLDSMITH, a surname of England and Ireland, from Old English *goldsmith* – goldsmith. (Reaney).

Traced by Guppy in Suffolk and Sussex and by MacLysaght formerly in Dublin and elsewhere, now in the Belfast area.

In Newfoundland:

Early instance: James, of St. John's, 1825 (DPHW 26B).

Modern status: Rare, at Corner Brook (*Electors* 1955).

GOLDSTEIN, a Jewish name from the German – gold stone, chrysolite, or a touchstone to test gold, or "for the dweller at the sign of the Gollstein, a topaz emblematic of the goldsmith's shop," or from a place name. (E.C. Smith). *See* GOLDSTONE.

In Newfoundland:

Modern status: Rare, at St. John's.

GOLDSTONE, an English version of GOLDSTEIN, or from the English place name Goldstone (Kent, Shropshire). (Reaney).

In Newfoundland:

Modern status: Rare, at St. John's (*Electors* 1955).

GOLDSWORTHY, a surname of England, a variant of Galsworthy, from the English place name Galsworthy (Devon) or from Goldworthy (Devon). (Spiegelhalter).

Traced by Guppy in Cornwall.

In Newfoundland:

Early instances: James Goldworthy or Goldwythy, of Trinity Bay, 1769, of Salmon Cove (now Champneys), 1772, of Trinity (Trinity B.), 1781 (DPHW 64); Benjamin Goldsworthy, of St. John's, 1806–07 (CO 194.46); Henry Goldworthy, of Keels, 1822 (DPHW 70); Catherine Goldworthy, G(o)uldwardy or Goulwoddy, of Kings Cove, 1828 (Nfld. Archives KCRC); Joseph Goldsworthy, member of the Board of Road Commissioners, Great to Little Paradise (Placentia B.), 1844 (*Nfld. Almanac*); Ephraim Goleworthy, of Burnt Island (now Port Anne), 1871 (Lovell).

Modern status: Scattered, especially at Champneys West.

GOLLOP. *See* GALLOP

GOOBIE, a surname of England, ? from the English place name Guppy (Dorset). *See* GUPPY.

Matthews traced Go(o)by in Dorset.

In Newfoundland:

Family tradition: James Goby (–1812), from Christchurch (Hampshire) pastor at Old Perlican from about 1785; the surname later changed to Gooby and Goobie (MUN Hist.).

Early instances: Henry Goobie(s), of Carbonear, 1702 (CO 194.2); James Gooby, of Trinity Bay, 1773 (DPHW 64); Charles, of Burnt Point (Conception B.), 1797 (CO 199.18); James Gooby and Son, proprietor and occupier of fishing room at Old Perlican, Winter 1800–01 (Census Trinity B.); Ellena, of Harbour Grace Parish, 1809 (Nfld. Archives HGRC); James, of Hants Harbour, 1832 (DPHW 59); John, planter of Caplin Cove (Trinity B.), 1842 (DPHW 59A); Richard, planter of Lower Island Cove, 1852 (DPHW 58); James Gobey and Barnett Goby, of St. John's, 1871 (Lovell).

Modern status: Scattered, especially at St. John's and Queen's Cove (Trinity B.).

Place name: Goobies 47-56 53-58.

GOOD(E), GOODS, surnames of England, Scotland and Ireland, from the Old English personal names *Goda*, *Gode*, or the first element of a name like Goodman, Goodwin, or a nickname from Old English *gōd* – good. (Reaney, Cottle, Black).

Guppy traced Goode in Northamptonshire, Spiegelhalter traced Good(e) in Devon, and MacLysaght found Good "fairly numerous in Ireland especially Co. Cork, first settled in Co. Leix in the sixteenth century."

In Newfoundland:

Early instances: John Good, of Caplin Bay (now Calvert), 1675 (CO 1); William, of Freshwater (Carbonear), 1871 (Lovell); James and William, of Upper Island Cove, 1871 (Lovell).

Modern status: Good, at St. John's and Little Bay East (Fortune B.); Goode, rare, at St. John's; Goods, rare, at Hermitage.

Place names (not necessarily from the surname): Good Bay 50-49 57-12; —— Cove 51-33 55-28; (Labrador) 52-39 55-45; —— Harbour or Venison Cove 47-21 55-18; —— Point 50-47 56-10; —— Rock 47-30 57-21.

GOODENOUGH, a surname of England, a nickname ? for one easily satisfied, or from a nickname *Goodknave* – good boy or servant. (Reaney, Cottle).

In Newfoundland:

Early instance: William, born in Labrador, 1829, baptized at St. John's, 1831, married at Battle Harbour, 1850 (DPHW 26B, 114).

Modern status: Unique, at Curling.

GOODLAND, a surname of England, – (dweller by the) good land. (Reaney).

In Newfoundland:

Family tradition: ——, from the Devon-Somerset border, settled in Newfoundland (Family).

Early instances: William, of Bonavista, 1792, of Trinity Bay, 1796 (DPHW 70, 64); William, of St. John's, 1829 (*Newfoundlander* 23 Jul 1829); Mary Goodlin, of Catalina, 1830 (Nfld. Archives KCRC); James Goodland, baptized at Greenspond, 1830, aged 5 years (DPHW 76); John, planter of Seal Cove (now New Chelsea), 1840 (DPHW 59A); Henry, fisherman of Russell's Cove (now New Melbourne), 1853 (DPHW 59); Azarias (and others), of Bird Island Cove (now Elliston), 1871 (Lovell).

Modern status: Scattered, especially at St. John's and Maberly.

Place name: Goodland Point 48-31 53-04.

GOODRIDGE, a surname of England, from the Old English personal name *Godrīc*, containing the elements *good* or *god* and *ruler*, or ? from the English place name Goodrick (Herefordshire). (Reaney, Cottle).

Guppy traced Goodrich in Suffolk and South Wales, Goodridge in Devon and South Wales.

In Newfoundland:

Family tradition: ——, from Paignton (Devon), settled in Newfoundland (Family).

Early instances: James, of English Harbour (Trinity B.), 1708–09 (CO 194.4); Alan, from Paignton, of Renews, 1833 (DPHW 26B); Allan (and others), of St. John's, 1871 (Lovell).

Modern status: At Renews (*Electors* 1955), Lewins Cove (Burin district), Corner Brook and St. John's.

GOODS. *See* GOOD(E)

GOODWIN, a surname of England, Scotland and Ireland, from the Old English personal name *Godwine*, containing the elements *gōd* – good and *wine* – friend. *See also* GODDEN, and GODWIN with which confusion occurs. In Ireland, Goodwin may be for MacGoldrick in Co. Tyrone, for MacGuigan in Cos. Derry and Tyrone, and for *Ó Goidín* in Co. Mayo. (Reaney, Cottle, MacLysaght).

Guppy found Goodwin widespread in the Midlands and South of England, Spiegelhalter in Devon, MacLysaght as above, and Black in Ayrshire, Lanarkshire and Stirlingshire.

In Newfoundland:

Early instances: Abraham, of Grand Bank, 1765 (CO 194.16); John, of Cat Harbour (now Lumsden), 1831 (DPHW 76); Abraham, trader of Richard's Harbour (Fortune B.), 1849 (DPHW 102); William Gooden, of Russell's Cove (now New Melbourne), 1853 (DPHW 59); Henry, of Indian Point (Trinity B.), 1853, of Russell's Cove, 1860 (DPHW 59, 59A); Whitman Smith Goodwin, born 1868 at Baie Verte (New Brunswick), of Harbour Grace, 1900 (*Nfld. Who's Who* 1930) .

Modern status: Scattered, including New Melbourne and Harbour Grace.

Place name: Goodwin Cove 47-48 55-49.

GOODYEAR, a surname of England, ? a nickname for one who gave "Good Year!" as a New Year's greeting. (Reaney, Cottle).

Traced by Guppy in Lincolnshire and by Matthews in Devon.

In Newfoundland:

Family tradition: Thomas, from Cornwall, settled at Harbour Grace in the late 18th century; his son, Thomas Jr., settled at Ladle Cove; Josiah, son of Thomas Jr., settled at Grand Falls in 1906 (MUN Hist.). John (1819–94), of Catalina (MUN Geog.).

Early instances: Sarah, of St. John's, 1850 (DPHW 24D); James, of Carbonear, 1855 (DPHW 49).

Modern status: Widespread, especially at Lumsden, Carmanville, Deadman's Bay and St. John's.

Place name: Goodyear or Coal Brook 49-09 57-32.

GOOSNEY, GOSNEY, surnames of England, ? from an unidentified place name from Old English *gōs* – goose and *ēg* – island.

In Newfoundland:

Family tradition: ——, from Guernsey settled at ? Coleys Point between 1790 and 1810 (MUN Folklore).

Early instances: —— Goozeney, of the *Dispatch* in the seal fishery out of Bay Roberts, 1838 (*Newfoundlander* 29 Mar 1838); Robert Goosney, of Coleys Point, 1871 (Lovell); Alfred Gosney, of Black River (Placentia B.), 1871 (Lovell).

Modern status: Goosney, scattered; Gosney, rare, at Swift Current (*Electors* 1955).

GORDON, a surname of England, Scotland and Ireland, from the Scots place name Gordon (Berwickshire, Kincardineshire) or the French place name Gourdon (Saône-et-Loire, etc.), or from a French personal name Gourdon, from a diminutive of Old French *gourd* – dull, stupid, boorish; in Ireland also a synonym of Magournahan, *Mag Mhuirneacháin*. (Reaney, Black, Dauzat, MacLysaght).

Traced by Guppy especially north of the Forth and Clyde, by Spiegelhalter in Devon, and by MacLysaght in Ulster.

In Newfoundland:

Early instances: Mother, of St. John's, 1669–70 (CO 194.2); Nicholas Gorden, of New Perlican, 1708–09 (CO 194.4); Samuel Gordon, of Mosquito (now Bristols Hope), 1800 (CO 199.18); Thomas, of Witless Bay, 1804 (Nfld. Archives BRC); Marks, of Harbour Grace Parish, 1810 (Nfld. Archives HGRC); John, of Bay Bulls, 1822 (D'Alberti 32); James, from Saltcoats (Ayrshire), to St. John's, 1857 (Mott); George, of Brehat, 1871 (Lovell); George (and others), of Harbour Grace, 1871 (Lovell).

Modern status: Scattered, especially at St. John's.

Place names: Mount Gordon 49-06 58-23; —— Point (Labrador) 60-03 64-19.

GORMAN, a surname of England and Ireland, in England ? from the Old English personal name *Garmund*, or dweller by the gore (a triangular piece of land) as in the place names Gore Court (Kent) and Gore (Wiltshire); in Ireland for (Mac) Gorman, (O)GORMAN, *Mac Gormáin*. MacLysaght remarks that the prefix O has been widely substituted for Mac. (Reaney, Spiegelhalter, MacLysaght).

Traced by Spiegelhalter in Devon and by MacLysaght in Cos. Clare and Monaghan.

In Newfoundland:

Family tradition: Thomas, of Daniel's Cove, 1836 (MUN Hist.).

Early instances: Richard, fisherman of St. John's, 1794–5, "24 years in Newfoundland," that is, 1770–1 (Census 1794–5); Simon, of Harbour Main, 1781 (CO 199-18); John, of Placentia, 1794 (D'Alberti 5); Michael, of Harbour Grace Parish, 1807 (Nfld. Archives HGRC); Thomas, from Co. Kilkenny, married at St. John's, 1810 (Nfld. Archives BRC); Edward, of Ragged Harbour (now Melrose), 1820 (Nfld. Archives KCRC); Elizabeth, of Kelligrews, 1820 (Nfld. Archives BRC); Richard, clerk of the peace, Ferryland district, 1821 (D'Alberti 31); Margaret, of Ferryland, 1824 (Nfld. Archives BRC); William, from Co. Kilkenny, of Keels, 1827 (Nfld. Archives KCRC); Bridget, of

Careless (now Kerleys) Harbour, 1829, of Tickle Cove (Bonavista B.), 1829, of Kings Cove, 1832 (Nfld. Archives KCRC); Eleanor Gormon, of Grand Bank, 1844 (DPHW 106); John, of Harbour Grace, 1866 (Nfld. Archives HGRC); Michael and Thomas Gorman, traders of Burin, 1871 (Lovell); William, of Upper Island Cove, 1871 (Lovell); Joseph, merchant of Miller's Passage, 1871 (Lovell); Michael, farmer of Salmon Cove and Gasters (now Avondale), 1871 (Lovell).

Modern status: Gorman, scattered, especially at St. John's; O'Gorman, rare, at Stephenville, Lourdes and Searston.

GOSINE, a surname of Syria-Lebanon, from the Arabic *ġusn* – small branch, twig. *See* Introduction (IV.7).

In Newfoundland:

Modern status: At Bell Island, Portugal Cove and St. John's.

GOSLING, a surname of England and Ireland, from Middle English *geslyng* – gosling, or from the personal name Goslin (Jocelyn). (Reaney).

Traced by Guppy in Berkshire, Hampshire, Lincolnshire, Suffolk, by Spiegelhalter in Devon, and by MacLysaght in east Leinster.

In Newfoundland:

Early instances: Edward, of Bonavista, 1790 (DPHW 70); William Gilbert (1863–1930), born in Bermuda, came to Newfoundland in 1881 (*Nfld. Who's Who* 1927); John, of Burin, 1871 (Lovell); Richard Goslin(g), of Flat Island (now Port Elizabeth), 1871 (Lovell, DPHW 105).

Modern status: Scattered.

Place names (not necessarily from the surname): Gosling Brook (Labrador) 53-24 60-20; —— Island (Labrador) 60-03 64-10; —— Lake (Labrador) 53-25 60-23.

GOSNEY. *See* GOOSNEY

GOSS(E), surnames of England, Gosse of Guernsey (Channel Islands), from Old French personal names *Jo(s)ce*, *Gosse*, or a pet-form of *Gocelin*. *See also* GOSLING. (Reaney, Turk).

Guppy traced Goss in Buckinghamshire and Devon; Matthews traced Gosse in Dorset and Hampshire.

In Newfoundland:

Family tradition: —— ? Le Gross or some such name, ? from Guernsey settled at Spaniard's Bay about 1800; some descendants later moved to Champneys (MUN Folklore).

Early instances: Giles Goss, of St. John's Harbour, 1703 (CO 194.3); Solomon, of Torbay, 1756 (DPHW 26C); Richard Gosse, of Bread and Cheese Cove (now Bishop's Cove), before 1775 (CO 199.18); James Goss, of Greenspond, 1776 (MUN Hist.); John Gosse, of Carbonear, 1790, died at Poole (Dorset), 1834, aged 70 years (CO 199.18, *Star and Conception B.J.* 6 Aug 1834); William, of Bryant's Cove, 1799 (CO 199.18); John, of Broad Cove (Bay de Verde district), 1800 (CO 199.18); John, of Bay Roberts, 1803 (CO 199.18); Rachel, of Harbour Grace Parish, 1812 (Nfld. Archives HGRC); Jeffry [sic] Goss, from Ventry (Co. Kerry), married at St. John's, 1817 (Nfld. Archives BRC); Soloman Gosse, of Flatrock (St. John's), 1821 (DPHW 26B); Solomon Goss, of Spaniard's Bay, 1832 (DPHW 30); Richard, of Harbour Grace, 1866 (Nfld. Archives HGRC); John, planter and trader of Salmon Cove (now Champneys), 1871 (Lovell); John, miner of Tilt Cove, 1871 (Lovell).

Modern status: Goss, rare, at St. John's; Gosse, widespread, especially at Spaniards Bay, Torbay and St. John's.

Place names: Goss Island (Labrador) 53-18 55-46; —— Pond 49-54 55-38.

GOUDIE, a surname of Scotland, a Scots variant of Goldie, a diminutive of Gold, GOULD. (Reaney, Black).

In Newfoundland:

Family tradition: —— was an early settler of Lower Island Cove; the family later moved to Boston (Mass.) (MUN Hist.).

Early instances: Elias Goudy, of Lower Island Cove, 1854 (DPHW 55); Elizabeth Goudie, of St. John's, 1855 (*Newfoundlander* 15 Nov 1855); Thomas, fisherman of Stocking Harbour, 1871 (Lovell).

Modern status: Scattered, especially in the Green Bay district.

Place names: Goudies Cove 49-35 55-56, (Labrador) 54-15 58-25.

GOUGH, a surname of England and Ireland, from the Welsh *coch, goch* – red, for one with red hair or complexion; confused with GOFF, both having the same pronunciation. (Cottle, MacLysaght).

Traced by Guppy in Buckinghamshire, Herefordshire, Shropshire and Wiltshire, by Spiegelhalter in Devon, and by MacLysaght in Cos. Waterford and Dublin.

In Newfoundland:

Early instances: John, shoreman of Torbay,

1794–5, "20 years in Newfoundland," that is, 1774–5 (Census 1794–5); George, fisherman of St. John's, 1794–5, "16 years in Newfoundland," that is, 1778–9 (Census 1794–5); John, ? from Devon, fisherman of Bird Island Cove (now Elliston), 1825 (DPHW 72, MUN Folklore); David, ? of Harbour Grace, 1845 (*Newfoundlander* 9 Jan 1845); James, fisherman of Bonavista, 1857 (DPHW 72).

Modern status: Scattered.

GOULD, a surname of England and Ireland, from the Old English personal names *Golda, Golde*, or for one with golden hair, or for one who is rich. (Reaney). Traced by Guppy in the west Midlands and southwest, and by MacLysaght in Co. Cork.

In Newfoundland:

Family traditions: Lieut. Alexander Duncan, R.N. deserted his ship between 1785 and 1800 to marry Mary Watts of Anchor Point (St. Barbe district) and assumed the name of Gould, his mother's maiden name, to avoid detection (MUN Hist.). George, from Somerset to Pouch Cove in 1825 (MUN Hist.).

Early instances: Michael, of St. John's, 1682 (CO 1); John Golds, of Port de Grave, 1751 (CO 194.13); John Gould, of Conche, 1787, of Wester Head, 1789, and servant of Battle Harbour, 1795 (MUN Hist.); John, of Bonavista, 1789 (DPHW 70) ; John and Luke, of Open Hole (now Open Hall), 1806 (Bonavista Register 1806); William, of Bay de Verde, 1807 (DPHW 64); William Goold, of Catalina, 1815 (DPHW 26B); Thomas Gould, shopkeeper of Carbonear, 1819 (DPHW 48); James, of Harbour Grace Parish, 1829 (Nfld. Archives HGRC); William, baptized at Pool's Island, 1830, aged 28 years (DPHW 76); Amy, baptized at Gooseberry Island, 1830, aged 10 years (DPHW 76); James, from Coyne (Co. Cork), died at Carbonear, 1831, aged 63 years (Carbonear R.C. Cemetery); Philip, of Belleoram, 1835 (DPHW 30); George, of Pouch Cove, 1837 (DPHW 30); Jacob, of Harbour Grace, 1869 (Nfld. Archives HGRC); John, of Flowers Cove, 1871 (Lovell); Alexander and James, of Flowers Cove to Point Ferolle area, 1871 (Lovell); Christopher, of Southern Bay (now ? Charleston), 1871 (Lovell).

Modern status: Scattered, especially in the St. Barbe district and at Charleston.

Place names (not necessarily from the surname): Gould Cove, —— Head 47-10 55-04; Goulds 47-29 52-46, 47-31 53-17; —— Brook 47-31 53-18; —— Pond 47-25 53-23; —— Big Pond 47-25 53-21; —— Grave River 47-10 55-07; —— Road 47-30 53-19.

GOULDING, a surname of England and Ireland, from the Late Old English personal name *Golding*. *See also* GOLDEN. (Reaney, MacLysaght).

Guppy traced Golding in Norfolk and Wiltshire, Goulding in Gloucestershire; Spiegelhalter traced Go(u)lding in Devon; and MacLysaght traced Golden, Goulding in Co. Cork.

In Newfoundland:

Early instances: Jacob Golding, of Greenspond, 1822 (DPHW 76); Thomas Go(u)lding, of Flatrock (Carbonear), 1840, of Blow me Down (Carbonear), 1846, of Otterbury (Carbonear), 1855 (DPHW 48).

Modern status: Scattered, especially at Dark Cove (Bonavista B.).

GOUNDREY, a surname of England, a variant of Gundr(e)y, from the Old German personal name *Gundric*, Old French *Gondri*, containing the elements *battle* and *ruler*. (Reaney).

In Newfoundland:

Modern status: At St. John's since 1954 from Western Canada.

GOURLEY, a surname of England and Ireland, Gourlay, Gourlie of Scotland, in England and ? Scotland from the English place name Gorley (Hampshire); in Ireland (Mac) Gourley, *Mag Thoirdhealbhaigh*, a variant of MacTurley.

Spiegelhalter traced Go(u)rley in Devon; MacLysaght traced (Mac) Gourley in Cos. Tyrone and Antrim.

In Newfoundland:

Modern status: Rare, at St. John's, from Edinburgh via Toronto.

GOVER, a surname of England from the English place name Gover (Cornwall), Cornish *gover* – (dweller by the) rivulet, or for "Go fairly," probably meaning one who used gentle means; or confused with GOWER. (Spiegelhalter, Reaney).

Traced by Spiegelhalter in Devon.

In Newfoundland:

Family tradition: John, from Somerset, settled at Greenspond, thence to Trinity (MUN Folklore).

Early instances: John, schoolmaster of Trouty, 1854 (DPHW 64B); John, of Greenspond, 1858 (DPHW 75); James and Thomas, of Trinity (Trinity B.), 1871 (Lovell).

Modern status: Somewhat rare and scattered.

Place names: Govers Harbour 49-19 55-15; —— Point 49-19 55-14.

GOWER, a surname of England, from Old French

Go(h)ier, Old German *Godehar*, personal names containing the elements *good* and *army*; or for French Gohier, an inhabitant of the Goelle, the country north of Paris; or for one from Gouy (Aisne, Seine-Maritime); or one from Gower (Glamorgan, Wales). (Reaney). *See also* GOVER.

Traced by Guppy in Kent.

In Newfoundland:

Early instance: John, of Greenspond, 1871 (Lovell).

Modern status: Rare, at Goose Cove and Trinity (Trinity B.) (*Electors* 1955) and St. John's.

GRACE, a surname of England and Ireland, from Old French *gras* – fat, or from Old French, Middle English *grace* – a pleasing quality, hence attractive, charming, or from Old English *græs* – grass, pasture, hence a grazier, or from a personal name from Old German *grisja* – grey, latinized as *Gratia* and associated with Old French *grace*. (Reaney, Cottle).

Traced by Guppy in Buckinghamshire and Lancashire, by Spiegelhalter in Devon, and by MacLysaght in Co. Kilkenny.

In Newfoundland:

Early instances: Martin, servant of St. John's, 1803 (D'Alberti 13); Oliver, from St. Mullins Parish (Co. Carlow), married at St. John's, 1810 (Nfld. Archives BRC); Patrick, of Harbour Grace Parish 1815 (Nfld. Archives HGRC); Richard, planter of Crocker's Cove (Carbonear), 1818 (DPHW 48); Robert, drowned at Soldier's Hole in Brine's River (unidentified), 1829 (*Newfoundlander* 30 Jul 1829); Lawrence, of Kings Cove, 1829 (Nfld. Archives KCRC); John, of Riders Harbour (Trinity B.), 1829 (Nfld. Archives KCRC); Mary, of Torbay, 1830 (Nfld. Archives BRC); John, of Harbour Grace, 1830 (*Newfoundlander* 4 Mar 1830); Henry, of Bonavista, 1831 (DPHW 72); John, of Pouch Cove, 1835 (Nfld. Archives BRC); Patrick, ? of Northern Bay, 1838 (DPHW 54); Thomas, from Co. Tipperary, of Port de Grave, 1844 (*Indicator* 24 Aug 1844).

Modern status: Scattered, especially at Mount Carmel (*Electors* 1955) and St. John's.

Place names: Grace Lake (Labrador) 52-13 65-37; Graces Gully 47-25 53-16.

GRAHAM, a surname of England, Scotland, Ireland and Jersey (Channel Islands), from the English place name Grantham (Lincolnshire), in Scotland since the 12th century. In Ireland it is also used as an anglicization of the Irish surnames Gormely and Grehan. (Reaney, Cottle, Black, MacLysaght, Turk).

Traced by Guppy in Berkshire, Cumberland,

Westmorland, Durham, Northumberland and Yorkshire, and in central and southern Scotland, and by MacLysaght in Ulster.

In Newfoundland:

Early instances: Aaron, judge of the Court of Common Pleas, St. John's, 1789 (D'Alberti 4); William, from Edinburgh, Scotland, married at St. John's, 1813 (Nfld. Archives BRC); James, from Killinall (? for Killenaule) (Co. Tipperary), married at St. John's, 1817 (Nfld. Archives BRC); Catherine, of Harbour Grace Parish, 1817 (Nfld. Archives HGRC); Archibald, cooper of Trinity (Trinity B.), 1823 (DPHW 64B); Archibald, planter of New Harbour, 1826 (DPHW 58); Mary, of King's Cove Parish, 1842 (Nfld. Archives KCRC); Arthur, of Harbour Grace, 1847 (DPHW 26D); John, of Aquaforte, 1857 (DPHW 31).

Modern status: Scattered.

Place name: Graham Lake (Labrador) 54-06 65-43.

GRANDY, a surname of England, Ireland and the Channel Islands, and as Grandin of Jersey (Channel Islands), from the French surname Grandin – the little big one. (Dauzat, E.C. Smith, Turk).

In Newfoundland:

Family tradition: The Grandys moved from St. Pierre to Garnish and elsewhere on the Burin Peninsula after the Treaty of Paris 1763 (MUN Hist.).

Early instances: James, of Broad Cove (Bay de Verde district), 1791 (CO 199.18); William, of Garnish, 1826 (DPHW 109); Margaret, ? of St. John's, daughter of Richard, of Duncannon (Co. Wexford), 1830 (*Newfoundlander* 10 Jun 1830); John, of Belleoram, 1835 (DPHW 30); John, of Frenchman's Cove (Burin), 1871 (Lovell); Thomas, of Grand Bank, 1871 (Lovell).

Modern status: Scattered, especially at Garnish.

Place names: Grandy Brook 47-38 57-42; Passage 47-36 58-51; —— Point 47-27 54-24, 47-45 57-19; —— Rock 47-32 55-24; —— Rocks 47-43 56-02; —— Sound 47-36 58-50; Grandys (Sound) Brook 47-37 58-51, (or Northwest Brook) 47-42 58-34; —— Lake 47-52 58-44.

GRANGER, a surname of England and Ireland, from Old French *grangier* – one in charge of, or who works at, a grange, granary, barn, a farm bailiff. (Reaney, Cottle).

Guppy traced Grainger in Yorkshire NR and ER, Granger in Worcestershire; Spiegelhalter traced Gra(i)nger in Devon; MacLysaght found Grainger "quite numerous in Co. Antrim ... but ... not confined to Ulster."

In Newfoundland:

Early instances: Charles, servant of Trinity (Trinity B.), 1628 (DPHW 64B); Daniel, of St. John's, 1840 (DPHW 23); Charles, of Catalina, 1871 (Lovell).

Modern status: Rare, at St. John's.

GRANT, a surname of England, Scotland and Ireland, from Old French *grand, grant* – big, tall; elder, senior, or from the Old English personal names *Grante, Grente* – grinner, snarler, grumbler, which occurs in a number of place names, such as Grantham. *See* GRAHAM. In Ireland also an occasional synonym of Granny, *Mag Raighne*. (Reaney, Cottle, MacLysaght, Black).

Traced by Guppy in Devon, Dorset, Lincolnshire and Warwickshire, and north of the Forth and Clyde especially in Inverness-shire; and found by MacLysaght numerous in all provinces except Connacht.

In Newfoundland:

Family tradition: John (1822–1900), from England, settled at Grand Bank (MUN Hist.).

Early instances: John, of St. John's, 1751 (CO 194.13); P., fisherman of Torbay, 1794–5, "30 years in Newfoundland," that is, 1764–5 (Census 1794–5); James, from Dublin, Irish convict landed at Petty Harbour or Bay Bulls, 1789 (CO 194.38); John, of Mosquito (now Bristol's Hope), 1790 (CO 199.18); Thomas, of Placentia, 1794 (D'Alberti 5); William, of Trinity (Trinity B.), 1801 (DPHW 64); Thomas, of Freshwater (Carbonear), 1802 (CO 199.18); John, of Harbour Grace Parish, 1807 (Nfld. Archives HGRC); Catherine, ? of Cape Broyle, 1810 (Dillon); Bridget, from Rossbugon Parish (unidentified) (Co. Kilkenny), married at St. John's, 1811 (Nfld. Archives BRC); Edward, of Bonavista, 1816 (Nfld. Archives KCRC); William, of Island Cove (unspecified), 1824 (Nfld. Archives BRC); Mary, of Catalina, 1827 (Nfld. Archives KCRC); T., of Harbour Grace, 1832 (*Newfoundlander* 23 Aug 1832); William, ? of Northern Bay, 1839 (DPHW 54); John, from England, of Grand Bank, 1846 (DPHW 106); Robert, fisherman of Jersey Harbour, 1852 (DPHW 106); Bridget, of Broad Cove (now Duntara), 1867 (Nfld. Archives KCRC); scattered in Lovell 1871.

Modern status: Scattered, especially at St. John's.

Place names: Grant Cove 47-35 55-07; —— Falls 48-35 54-06; Grant's Lake 49-05 55-11.

GRANTER, a surname ? of England, ? from Anglo-French *grantor* – one who makes a conveyance in legal form. (*OED*).

In Newfoundland:
Modern status: Scattered, especially in the Bonavista North district.

GRANVILLE, a surname of England and Ireland, from the French place name Grainville-la-Teinturière (Seine-Maritime). (Reaney *Origin*).

Spiegelhalter traced Granville, Grenville, Grandfield in Devon. MacLysaght traced Gran(d)field in Co. Kerry.

In Newfoundland:
Early instances: William, of Quidi Vidi, 1810 (Nfld. Archives BRC); Christopher Grenville, from Co. Kerry, married at St. John's, 1811 (marriage annulled) (Nfld. Archives BRC); Christopher Granville, of Broad Cove (Bay de Verde district), 1816 (D'Alberti 26); John Grenville, of St. John's, 1820 (DPHW 26D); Robert Grandfield, of Harbour Grace Parish, 1833 (Nfld. Archives HGRC); Arthur Granville, ? of Harbour Grace, 1845 (*Newfoundlander* 9 Jan 1845).

Modern status: Rare and scattered.

GRAY, GREY, surnames of England, Scotland, Ireland and the Channel Islands, from Old English *græg* – grey (-haired), or from the French place name *Graye* (Calvados). In Ireland, Connacht and Co. Longford, Gray is also for Culreavy. (Reaney, Cottle, MacLysaght, Turk).

Guppy found Gray widespread in England and in southern Scotland, Grey in Durham and Northumberland. Spiegelhalter traced Gray in Devon.

In Newfoundland:
Early instances: Nicholas and Thomas Gray, of Carbonear, 1676 (CO 1); Henry, of St. John's Harbour, 1703 (CO 194.3); Patrick, of Trinity Bay, 1767 (DPHW 64); John Grey, of Great Belle Isle (now Bell Island), 1770 (DPHW 26C); Robert Gray, merchant of Harbour Grace, 1771 (Nfld. Archives L118); —— Grey, of Flat Island (Bonavista B.), 1806 (Bonavista Register 1806); Patrick Gray, one of 72 impressed men who sailed from Ireland to Newfoundland, ? 1811 (CO 194.51); Mary Grea or Grey, of Bonavista, 1815 (Nfld. Archives KCRC); Francis Grey, from Hampshire, married at ? Bareneed, 1837 (*Star and Conception B.J.* 20 Dec 1837); Henry Gray, from Ireland, married at St. John's, 1838 (Nfld. Archives BRC); James, of Shoe Cove (Twillingate district), 1842 (DPHW 86); Thomas Grey, fisherman of Bonne Bay (Fortune B.), 1853 (DPHW 102); William, of Southside Trinity (Trinity B.), 1854 (DPHW 64B); scattered in Lovell 1871.

Modern status: Gray, scattered, especially at Shoe Cove, Lumsden and St. John's; Grey, rare (*Electors* 1955), now mostly Gray.

Place names: Gray 4, Grey 12, are unlikely to be from the surname.

GREAVES, a surname of England and Ireland, from Old English *græfe* – (dweller by the) thicket, grove, or from the English place name Greaves (Lancashire), or from confusion with the surnames Grave(s), GRIEVE(S). (Reaney, MacLysaght 73).

Found widespread by Guppy in the Midlands, especially in Worcestershire, and by Spiegelhalter in Devon, and as Greaves by MacLysaght in Ulster.

In Newfoundland:
Modern status: Rare, at St. John's.

GREELEY, a surname of England with many variants, Le Gresley of the Channel Islands, Greally of Ireland; in England and the Channel Islands from Old French *greslet* – marked as by hail, pitted, pockmarked; in Ireland, (Mac)Greally, *Mag Raoghallaigh*. (Reaney, MacLysaght, Turk).

MacLysaght traced Greally in Cos. Galway and Mayo.

In Newfoundland:
Family tradition: Joseph Le Grizzly, from the Channel Islands, settled at Ladle Cove, drowned 1887 (MUN Hist.).

Early instances: John Grealy, of Hibb's Hole, 1783 (CO 199.18); Elias Graley, in possession of property in fishery at Portugal Cove, 1794–5 (Census 1794–5); Edward Grealy, of Port de Grave, 1829 (*Newfoundlander* 5 Nov 1829); Jane Grealey, of St. John's, 1847 (DPHW 26D); Jacob, of Foxtrap, 1871 (Lovell); Edward (and others) Greley, of Upper Island Cove, 1871 (Lovell).

Modern status: Scattered, especially at Greeleytown.

Place name: Greeleytown (Harbour Main district).

GREEN, a surname of England, Scotland and Guernsey (Channel Islands), GREENE of England and Ireland – (dweller near the village) green, or young, immature as in slang "green," or a personal name; in Ireland also for a number of Irish names, including FAHEY. (Reaney, Cottle, Black, MacLysaght, Turk).

Guppy found Green widespread, especially in Worcestershire; Spiegelhalter traced Green(e) in Devon.

In Newfoundland:

Family traditions: John Green, of Point Verde (Placentia district) before 1829 (Mannion). James, from Old Perlican, was an early settler of Greens Harbour in 1835 (MUN Hist.). Michael Greene (1793–1857), from Carrick-on-Suir (Co. Tipperary), settled at Tilton Harbour (now Tilting), about 1815 (MUN Hist., MUN Folklore).

Early instances: William Green, of Old Perlican, 1675, 1682 (CO 1); Edward, of Harbour Grace, 1677 (CO 1); Alexander, of Torbay or Portugal Cove, 1708 (CO 194.4); Robert, of Placentia ? district, 1744 (CO 194.24); William, of Trinity (Trinity B.), 1753 (CO 194.13); William, of St. John's, 1755 (DPHW 26C); Humber, of Bonavista, 1789 (DPHW 70); Joseph, of Quidi Vidi, 1794–5 (Census 1794–5); James, fisherman of Bay of Exploits, ? 1797 (CO 194.39); John, occupier of fishing room at New Harbour (Trinity B.) and Heart's Content, Winter 1800–01 (Census Trinity B.); William, occupier of fishing room at Scilly Cove (now Winterton), Winter 1800–01 (Census Trinity B.); Benjamin, of Bay Bulls, 1802 (USPG); Thomas, of Pond, owner of fishing room at Ship Island (Greenspond), 1803 (Bonavista Register 1806); John, of Fogo, 1803 (D'Alberti 13); Mary, of Witless Bay, 1804 (Nfld. Archives BRC); Edward, of King's Cove, 1804 (Bonavista Register 1806); Benjamin, of Burin, 1805 (D'Alberti 15); Catherine, from Carrick-on-Suir (Co. Tipperary), married at St. John's, 1806 (Nfld. Archives BRC); Michael, of Fortune Bay, 1811 (Nfld. Archives BRC); John, of Greenspond, 1816 (DPHW 76); Michael Greene, from Carrick-on-Suir (Co. Tipperary), married at Tilton Harbour (now Tilting), 1818 (Nfld. Archives KCRC); John Green, planter of Hants Harbour, 1821 (DPHW 58); William, merchant of Brigus, 1824 (DPHW 34); William, of Hermitage Cove, 1825 (DPHW 109); John, of Ship Island (Bonavista district), 1826 (DPHW 76); William, schoolmaster of Cupids, 1831 (DPHW 34); William, planter of Western Bay, 1831 (DPHW 52A); Joshua, of Port de Grave, 1834 (DPHW 26D); John, of Brigus by South, 1836 (Nfld. Archives BRC); William, of Grand Bank, 1836 (DPHW 106); Walter Green(e), ? of Northern Bay, 1838 (DPHW 54); William Green, of Brunette, 1855 (DPHW 104); Jonathan, of English Harbour (Fortune Bay district), 1857 (DPHW 104); George, of New Harbour (Fortune Bay district), 1858 (DPHW 102); Benjamin, of Hunt's Island (Burgeo-La Poile district), 1858 (DPHW 101); Henry, of Inkpen Point (Burin district), 1860 (DPHW 108); Samuel Greene, of Pinchard's Island, 1862 (DPHW 79); widespread in Lovell 1871.

Modern status: Green, widespread, especially at Winterton and St. John's; Greene, widespread, especially at Point Verde (Placentia B.).

Place names: 162 place names contain the element Green, rarely from the surname.

Green's Bight 48-12 53-45; —— Gully 47-44 53-20; —— Harbour 47-39 53-30; —— Hill 47-42 53-14; —— Island 47-36 54-16, (Labrador) 53-05 55-46; Greenspond, —— Harbour 49-04 53-34; —— Island 49-05 53-35; John Green Shoal 47-28 55-39.

GREENHAM, a surname of England, from the English place name Greenham (Somerset, Berkshire). (Reaney, Cottle).

In Newfoundland:

Early instances: Joseph Greenan, of Bonavista, 1796 (DPHW 70); Henry and Richard Greenham, of St. John's, 1871 (Lovell); Alfred Grennan, of Brandy Island (St. Barbe district), 1873 (DPHW 95).

Modern status: Scattered, especially in the Twillingate and White Bay South districts.

Place names: Greenham Bight 51-57 55-19.

GREENING, a surname of England, – ? (dweller by the) green meadow. (Weekley Surnames).

In Newfoundland:

Early instances: Joseph, of Tickle Cove (Bonavista B.), 1836 (DPHW 73); Joseph (and others), of Indian Arm (Bonavista B.), 1871 (Lovell); John (and others), of Musgravetown, 1871 (Lovell).

Modern status: Scattered, especially at Musgravetown and Port Blandford.

GREENLAND, a surname of England – (dweller near the) green meadow or stretch of open country or from the English and Scots place name Greenland (Cornwall, Yorkshire WR, Caithness). (Weekley Surnames).

In Newfoundland:

Family tradition: George, from Chard (Somerset) settled at Coleys Point in 1826 (MUN Hist.).

Early instances: John, of Quidi Vidi, 1708–09 (CO 194.4); George Greenlan, fisherman of Coleys Point, 1841 (DPHW 39).

Modern status: At Corner Brook, St. John's and in the Port de Grave district especially at Coleys Point.

Place name: Greenland 47-34 53-11.

GREENLEY, a surname of England, from the English place names Little Gringley (Nottinghamshire) or Grindley (Staffordshire), or (dweller near a) green clearing. (Reaney).

In Newfoundland:

Modern status: Rare, at Harbour Grace (*Electors* 1955).

GREENSLADE, a surname of England and Guernsey (Channel Islands), from the English place name Greenslade (Devon), or (dweller by or in the) green valley. (Spiegelhalter, Turk).

Traced by Guppy in Devon and Somerset.

In Newfoundland:

Early instances: Matthew, of St. John's, 1753 (DPHW 26C); Matthew, of Long Pond (South Shore Conception B.), 1825 (DPHW 26B); William Grinslate, of Kelligrews, 1837 (Nfld. Archives BRC).

Modern status: In the Harbour Main district, especially at Long Pond.

GREENWOOD, a surname of England – (dweller by the) green wood.

Traced by Guppy in Berkshire, Cornwall, Lancashire, Norfolk and Yorkshire WR, and by Spiegelhalter in Devon.

In Newfoundland:

Modern status: Unique, at St. John's.

GREGORY, a baptismal name and surname of England, Scotland and Ireland, ultimately from the Greek – watchful, though at times confused with Latin *gregarius* from *grex* – flock; the name of at least three saints and of sixteen Popes including St. Gregory the Great. (Withycombe, Reaney, Cottle).

Traced by Guppy in the Midlands and Somerset and Wiltshire, by Spiegelhalter in Devon, and by MacLysaght in Kerry in the 17th century and later in Co. Galway.

In Newfoundland:

Early instances: Andrew (Grigory in 1677), of Port de Grave, 1675 (CO 1); John Gregry, of Newfoundland, ? 1706 (CO 194.24); Joseph Gregory, soldier of St. John's, 1756 (DPHW 26D); William, of Brigus, 1769 (DPHW 26C); John, planter of Old Perlican, 1828 (DPHW 58); Benjamin, clerk of Trinity (Trinity B.), 1831 (DPHW 64B); James, from Devon, of St. John's, died 1836, aged 66 years (*Times* 14 Dec 1836); Martha, of Harbour Grace Parish, 1837 (Nfld. Archives HGRC); William, ? of Ferryland, 1838 (*Newfoundlander* 25 Oct 1838); William, of Brigus by South, 1838 (Nfld. Archives BRC); Christianna, of Hants Harbour, 1844 (DPHW 59); scattered in Lovell 1871.

Modern status: Scattered.

Place names (not necessarily from the surname): Gregory Island 49-17 58-18; —— River 49-22 58-14; —— Rock 47-02 55-08.

GREY. *See* GRAY

GRIEVE, a surname of England, Ireland and Scotland, from Scots and Northern English *grieve* – originally governor of a province, later overseer, manager, farm-bailiff, but confused with Grave(s), GREAVES. (Reaney, Cottle, MacLysaght 73).

Traced by Guppy over a large part of Scotland, especially in Roxburghshire, and by Cottle also in the north of England.

In Newfoundland:

Early instance: William, of St. John's, 1812 (D'Alberti 32).

Modern status: Rare, at St. John's.

GRIFFIN, a surname of Wales, England and Ireland, a pet-form of the Middle Welsh baptismal name *Gruffudd*, "in the Welsh border counties introduced direct from Wales, in the eastern counties by the Bretons who came over with the Conqueror and were numerous there." Also in Ireland (O)Griffin, *Ó Gríobhtha*, Ir. *gríobhtha* – griffin-like. (Reaney, MacLysaght). *See* GRIFFITHS.

Traced by Guppy in the Midlands and West, especially in Buckinghamshire and Warwickshire, and by MacLysaght in Co. Clare.

In Newfoundland:

Family tradition: Thomas, from Northern Ireland settled at Upper Island Cove in the late 18th century (MUN Folklore).

Early instances: R., of Upper Bacon Cove (Conception B.), 1794 (CO 199.18); Patrick, of St. John's, 1796 (CO 194.39); Terry, of Harbour Grace Parish, 1807 (Nfld. Archives HGRC); James, from Co. Kilkenny, of Harbour Grace, deceased 1811 (*Royal Gazette* 7 Feb 1811); John, from Brixham (Devon), planter of Renews, deceased 1814 (*Royal Gazette* 28 Apr 1814); Catherine, of Bonavista, 1820 (Nfld. Archives KCRC); Daniel, from Co. Dublin, married at St. John's, 1822 (Nfld. Archives BRC); John, from Co. Waterford, of Trinity, 1825 (Nfld. Archives KCRC); Catherine, from Co. Kilkenny, married at Ragged Harbour (now Melrose), 1827 (Nfld. Archives KCRC); Patrick, from Co. Waterford, married at Kings Cove, 1829 (Nfld. Archives KCRC); Patrick, of Broad Cove (now Duntara), 1830 (Nfld. Archives KCRC); Susanna, baptized at Greenspond, 1830, aged 17 years (DPHW 76); Mary Griffen, of Tickle Cove (Bonavista B.), 1852 (Nfld. Archives

KCRC); Margaret Griffin, of Indian Arm, 1858 (Nfld. Archives KCRC); Thomas, of Keels, 1867 (Nfld. Archives KCRC); John, policeman of Carbonear, 1871 (Lovell); John (and others), of Cat's Cove (now Conception Harbour), 1871 (Lovell); John, of Colliers, 1871 (Lovell); Thomas, of Kelligrews, 1871 (Lovell); Daniel, of Outer Cove, 1871 (Lovell); James, of Ram's Islands (Placentia B.), 1871 (Lovell).

Modern status: Widespread, especially at Grand Falls and in the Humber West and Placentia East districts.

Place names: Griffin Harbour (Labrador) 53-32 55-48; —— Point 48-30 58-21.

GRIFFITHS, a surname of Wales, England and Ireland, from Old Welsh *Griph-iud*, Middle Welsh *Gruffudd*, containing the elements *iud*, *udd* – chief, lord. (Reaney, Cottle). *See also* GRIFFIN.

Griffith(s) traced by Guppy in the West Midlands and especially in North and South Wales; Griffith, used synonymously with Griffin, by MacLysaght in Co. Kilkenny.

In Newfoundland:

Early instances: Henry Griffith, of St. John's Harbour, 1703 (CO 194.3); Honora, of Trinity, 1827 (Nfld. Archives KCRC); William Griffiths, of Keels, 1831 (DPHW 70); Patrick Griffith, of Bonavista, 1833 (Nfld. Archives KCRC); John, of Harbour Grace Parish, 1839 (Nfld. Archives HGRC); Griffith Griffiths, slate quarrier of Burnt Head, Cupids, 1850 (DPHW 34); Patrick and Thomas, of Long Harbour (Placentia B.), 1871 (Lovell).

Modern status: Scattered, especially at Ship Harbour (Placentia B.) and St. John's.

GRIMES, a surname of England and Ireland, from an Old Norse personal name *Grímr* – mask, helmet, or from Old English *grim* – grim, fierce; spectre, goblin; in Ireland also for Grehan and Gormley. (Cottle, Reaney, MacLysaght). *See* GRIMM.

Traced by Guppy in Warwickshire and by MacLysaght in Ulster.

In Newfoundland:

Family tradition: George, from Herring Neck, settled at Little Bay Islands (Green B.), in 1854 (MUN Hist.).

Early instances: Catherine, of Harbour Grace Parish, 1816 (Nfld. Archives HGRC); William, of St. John's, 1817 (DPHW 26B); George, of Herring Neck, 1850, of Green Cove (Twillingate district), 1852 (DPHW 85); Timothy, of Stone Harbour (Twillingate district), 1856 (DPHW 85).

Modern status: Scattered, especially at Little Bay Islands.

GRIMM, a surname of England and Germany, associated with, and having the same meaning as, GRIMES.

In Newfoundland:

Early instances: Daniel Grim, of Harbour Grace Parish, 1839 (Nfld. Archives HGRC); Fritz Grimm, cooper of Harbour Grace, 1871 (Lovell).

Modern status: Unique, at Harbour Grace (*Electors* 1955).

GROUCHY, (DE)GRUCHY, surnames of the Channel Islands, variants of the surnames of France, Grouchy and Gruchey, from the French place names Grouchy (La Manche), Gruchy (Calvados). (Turk).

In Newfoundland:

Family tradition: William (de) Gruchy was one of the earliest settlers at Pouch Cove in the early 19th century (MUN Hist.).

Early instances: Thomas Grecy or Gruchy, of St. John's Harbour, 1703–04 (CO 194.3); Thomas Degrish, shoemaker of Trinity (Trinity B.), 1758 (DPHW 64); M. ? Grucey, proprietor of fishing room at Grates Cove, Winter 1800–01 (Census Trinity B.); John Grishy, of Pouch Cove, 1815 (DPHW 26B); Thomas (de)Gruchy, from Jersey, of Fortune, 1848 (MUN Hist., DPHW 106); Elizabeth Grouchy, of Portugal Cove, 1853 (DPHW 26D); Philip de Gruchy, cooper of Jersey Harbour, 1856 (DPHW 104).

Modern status: Grouchy, scattered, especially at St. John's; Gruchy, especially at Pouch Cove; de Gruchy, at Rencontre West (*Electors* 1955).

Place name: Degrouchy Point 48-57 57-58.

GROVES, a surname of England – (dweller by the) grove(s), or from the place name Grove (Devon).

Traced by Guppy especially in Dorset and by Spiegelhalter in Devon.

In Newfoundland:

Early instances: Henry, of Bonavista, 1793 (DPHW 70); Joseph Grove, of St. John's, 1807 (D'Alberti 17); John Groves, of Trinity (Trinity B.), 1811 (DPHW 64); John, of Harbour Grace Parish, 1834 (Nfld. Archives HGRC); George, of Cinq Cerf, 1860 (DPHW 99); Nicholas, of Heart's Desire, 1871 (Lovell).

Modern status: Scattered, especially at Bonavista and St. John's.

Place names: Grove Island (Labrador) 52-32 56-10; Groves Point (Labrador) 53-21 60-22.

GRUCHY. *See* GROUCHY

GUEST, a surname of England, from Old Norse *gestr* – stranger, guest, traveller. (Reaney, Cottle).

Traced by Guppy in Kent and Worcestershire and by Spiegelhalter in Devon.

In Newfoundland:

Early instance: John, shopkeeper of St. John's, 1811 (CO 194.50).

Modern status: At St. John's.

GUILFOYLE, a variant of the surname of Ireland (Mac) Gilfoyle, *Mac Giolla Phóil* – devotee of St. Paul. (MacLysaght). *See* KILFOY.

Traced by MacLysaght in Co. Offaly.

In Newfoundland:

Early instances: Anastasia Gilfoy, of Harbour Grace Parish, 1810 (Nfld. Archives HGRC); John, from Callan (Co. Kilkenny), married at St. John's, 1834 (Nfld. Archives BRC).

Modern status: Rare, at Riverhead (Harbour Grace) (*Electors* 1955) and St. John's.

GUINCHARD, ? a variant, noted by Dauzat, of the surname of France, Guichard, of German origin, containing the elements *wig* – battle and *hard* – strong, hence strong in battle. (Dauzat).

In Newfoundland:

Family tradition: James, from St. Malo, settled at Flowers Cove in the mid 1850s, thence to Daniel's Harbour (MUN Folklore).

Early instance: Mr. Guichard, of Daniel's Harbour, 1873 (MUN Hist.).

Modern status: Rare, at Nicholsville (Humber East district) and in the St. Barbe district, including Daniel's Harbour.

GUINEY, a surname of Ireland, (O)Guiney, *Ó Guinidhe*. (MacLysaght).

Traced by MacLysaght mainly in Cos. Kerry and Cork.

In Newfoundland:

Early instance: Samuel ? Guaney, of Colliers, 1800 (CO 199.18).

Modern status: In the Ferryland district.

GULLAGE, a variant of the surname of England, Gullidge, ? from an unidentified place name.

Gullidge traced in Devon (*Tel. Dir.*).

In Newfoundland:

Early instance: Joseph Gulledge or Gullidge, of Catalina, 1822 (DPHW 70).

Modern status: Scattered.

GULLIFORD, a surname of England, from the Old French *goulafre* – glutton, or from the English place name Gulliford (Devon). (Reaney, Spiegelhalter). *See* GULLIVER, with which Gulliford is interchangeable.

Traced by Spiegelhalter in Devon.

In Newfoundland:

Early instances: William, of Hants Harbour, 1821 (DPHW 58); William, of Bald Nap (Trinity North district), 1883 (DPHW 68).

Modern status: Scattered, especially at Hants Harbour.

GULLIVER, a variant of GULLIFORD.

Traced by Guppy in Northamptonshire and by Bardsley in Somerset.

In Newfoundland:

Early instances: William, planter of Hants Harbour, 1822 (DPHW 58); James, from Ansford (Somerset), married at St. John's, 1855 (DPHW 26D).

Modern status: At St. John's.

GUNN, a surname of England, Scotland and Ireland, from the Old Norse personal name *Gunnr*, or from *Gunne*, a pet-form of *Gunnhildr*, containing the element *battle*; in Ireland also as an abbreviation of Gilgunn and MacElgun, *Mac Giolla Dhuinn*, Ir. *donn* – brown. (Reaney, MacLysaght).

Traced by Guppy in Nottinghamshire and by Spiegelhalter in Devon.

In Newfoundland:

Early instances: Richard, married at St. John's, 1782 (DPHW 26D); Michael Guin, of Tilton (now Tilting Harbour), 1832 (Nfld. Archives KCRC); Thomas Gunn, fisherman of Back Cove (Fogo), 1871 (Lovell).

Modern status: Scattered.

GUNSON, a surname of England, – son of *Gunnhildr*. *See* GUNN.

In Newfoundland:

Modern status: Rare, at St. John's.

GUPPY, a surname of England, from the English place name Guppy (Dorset). *See also* GOOBIE. (Spiegelhalter).

Traced by Spiegelhalter in Devon.

In Newfoundland:

Early instances: John, planter of Ship Cove (now part of Port Rexton), 1822 (DPHW 64); R., of Harbour Grace, died 1831 (*Newfoundlander* 22 Dec 1831).

Modern status: Rare, at Port Blandford, Port Rexton (*Electors* 1955) and Gander.

GUSH, a surname of England, ? from Old English *gyse* – (dweller near the) water-course, as in the place names Gussage All Saints, St. Andrew and St. Michael (Dorset), or ? a variant of the surname Gooch, a variant of GOUGH, from Welsh *coch* – red. (Ekwall, Reaney *Origin*).

In Newfoundland:

Modern status: Rare, at St. John's.

GUSHUE, a Newfoundland variant of the surname of France and Jersey (Channel Islands), Guizot, probably in its Breton form Guiziou, a diminutive of the baptismal name Guy (*see* GUY). (Dauzat).

In Newfoundland:

Early instances: John Gucho, servant of Harbour Main, 1755 (MUN Hist.); John Goushou, of Lower Bacon Cove (Conception B.), 1775 (CO 199.18); James, of Brigus, 1785 (CO 199.18); Denis Guisshou, of St. John's, 1806 (Nfld. Archives BRC); James Goushu, of Harbour Grace Parish, 1806 (Nfld. Archives HGRC); Charles Gishue, ? of St. John's, 1810 (CO 194.50); James Gushue, planter of Cupids, 1834 (DPHW 34); Mrs., of Harbour Grace, 1858 (*Newfoundlander* 22 Apr 1858); Timothy Goshue or Gushue, of Indian Arm, 1867 (Nfld. Archives KCRC); George (and others) Gushue, of Cat's Cove (now Conception Harbour), 1871 (Lovell); James Gershue, farmer of Salmon Cove (now Avondale) and Gasters, 1871 (Lovell).

Modern status: Scattered, especially in the Harbour Main district at Bacon Cove.

Place names: Gushue Rock (Labrador) 53-21 55-44; Gushue's Pond (Park) 47-24 53-17.

GUT, a surname of Germany – ? (an owner of) landed property, of an estate, rather than the adjective good (Dauzat).

In Newfoundland:

Modern status: At St. John's since 1925.

GUY, a baptismal name and surname of England, Ireland and France, from the Old German personal name *Wido*, containing the element ? *witu* – wood, forest, or *wit* – wide, introduced into England by the Normans, or from Old French *gui* – guide. (Withycombe, Reaney, MacLysaght 73, Dauzat). *See also* WYATT, GUSHUE.

Traced by Guppy in Buckinghamshire, Dorset and Yorkshire NR and ER, and by MacLysaght in Ulster since the seventeenth century.

In Newfoundland:

Early instances: Lewis, of Harbour Grace, 1675 (CO 1); John Sr. and Jr., of Carbonear, 1675 (CO 1); Nicholas, of Bay Roberts, 1708–09 (CO 194.4); William, of Trinity (Trinity B.), 1758 (DPHW 64); Hezekiah, of Twillingate, 1768, of Fogo, 1771 (MUN Hist.); John, of St. John's, 1769 (DPHW 26C); Samuel, of Bonavista, 1823 (DPHW 70); William, of Great Burgeo Island, 1830 (DPHW 30); Edmund, of Catalina, 1840 (DPHW 67); William, of Cat Harbour (now Lumsden), 1845 (DPHW 76); Thomas, of Brigus, 1850 (DPHW 34); George, of Coombs Cove, 1851 (DPHW 104); Ambrose and John, of Arnolds Cove, 1871 (Lovell); John, of Lower Burgeo, 1871 (Lovell).

Modern status: Scattered, especially at Arnolds Cove and Musgrave Harbour.

Place name: Guy's Cove 49-30 55-44.

GUZZWELL, a surname of England, ? from the English place name Guzzle Down (Devon), or Goswell (Middlesex), or (dweller by the) goose spring. (Gover, A. H. Smith). Traced by Matthews in Devon.

In Newfoundland:

Early instances: Matthew Guswell, fisherman of St. John's or Petty Harbour, about 1739–43 (CO 194.11, 24); Matthew Gussel, fisherman of St. John's, 1794–5, "40 years in Newfoundland," that is, 1754–5 (Census 1794–5); Matthew Guswell, church warden of Portugal Cove, 1821 (D'Alberti 31).

Modern status: At St. John's.

GYLLAND, a surname of Norway – ? (dweller on the) golden land.

In Newfoundland:

Modern status: Unique, at St. John's.

H

HAAS, a surname of France, from the German *Haas* – hare. (Dauzat).

In Newfoundland:

Modern status: At Brent's Cove and Baie Verte.

HACKETT, HAGGETT, surnames of England, Haggett of Ireland, from an Anglo-Norman diminutive of the Old Norse personal name *Haki*, or a nickname from a kind of fish, or in Ireland also as "a synonym of MacCahey, MacGahey and Gaggy from the sound of the Irish form *Mag Eachaidh*." (Reaney, Cottle, MacLysaght).

Haggett traced by Guppy in Somerset; Hackett and Haggitt by Spiegelhalter in Devon; and Hackett by MacLysaght in Cos. Kilkenny and Kildare.

In Newfoundland:

Family traditions: The Hacketts were early settlers at Joe Batts Arm (about 1811–16) (MUN Hist.). —— Hackett was one of the first settlers of Bird Island Cove (now Elliston); he settled at Northern Cove (Elliston) before 1786 (MUN Hist.).

Early instances: Thomas Hacket, of St. John's, 1753 (DPHW 26C); John Hackett, of Torbay, 1804 (Nfld. Archives BRC); James Hacet, from Waterford, married at St. John's, 1812 (Nfld. Archives BRC); Margaret Hackett, of Tilton Harbour (now Tilting), 1813 (Nfld. Archives BRC); Bartholomew, from Co. Cork, married in the Northern District, 1813 (Nfld. Archives BRC); Bartholomew, of Trinity, 1816 (Nfld. Archives KCRC); Maurice, of Fogo, 1817 (Nfld. Archives KCRC); James Hacet, of Harbour Grace Parish, 1817 (Nfld. Archives HGRC); John Hackett, of Ragged Harbour (now Melrose), 1820 (Nfld. Archives KCRC); Michael, of Joe Batts Arm, 1825 (Nfld. Archives KCRC); Andrew, J.P. for Trinity Bay, 1844 (*Nfld. Almanac*); John, of Leading Tickles, 1844 (DPHW 86); T., of Bay Roberts, 1855 (*Newfoundlander* 4 Jun 1855); Joseph Hackett or Haggett, labourer, later skipper and planter, son of Joseph and Harriet of Hardington Moor (Somerset), arrived in Harbour Breton in 1856, aged 17, baptised on Sagona Island 1861 and married there 1865. ? Same as Joseph Hackett 1871 (Lovell) (D.A. Macdonald); Tobias, of Harbour Grace, 1866 (Nfld. Archives HGRC); George and Robert Haggett, miners of Tilt Cove, 1871 (Lovell); John Haggott, of Leading Tickles, 1871 (Lovell); John (and others) Hacket,

of English Harbour East, 1871 (Lovell); Edward, of Trepassey, 1871 (Lovell).

Modern status: Hackett, especially at English Harbour East and Wood's Island Harbour; Haggett, especially at Leading Tickles.

Place names: Hacket's Head (Labrador) 53-38 56-32; Hackett's Head 51-12 55-59.

HACQUOIL, ? a Jersey (Channel Islands) form ? of the French surnames Hac(qu)ard, containing the German element *hag* – enclosure. (Dauzat, Turk). *See* CLEMENS, HASKELL, HAWCO.

In Newfoundland:

Modern status: At Pool's Cove and Lally Cove (*Electors* 1955).

HADDEN, a surname of England, Ireland and Scotland; in England, from the place names Haddon, Hadden (Derbyshire, Dorset, Northamptonshire, Devon); in Ireland also as a synonym of (O)Hadian; in Scotland, a variant of Howden. (Cottle, Spiegelhalter, MacLysaght, Black).

Haddon traced by Guppy in Northamptonshire and Warwickshire and by Spiegelhalter in Devon; Hadden, Haddon by MacLysaght in Ulster and Co. Louth; and Hadden by Black in Aberdeenshire.

In Newfoundland:

Early instances: James, student of St. John's, 1829 (*Newfoundlander* 24 Dec 1829); John Haddon, of Bonavista, 1851 (DPHW 70); Henry Jabez Haddon, of Fortune, teacher 1863 (Jour. Legis. Council 1864 per P.E.L. Smith); James Norris Haddon, of Fortune, teacher 1867 (Jour. Legis. Council 1868? per P.E.L. Smith); William, of Isle Valen, 1871 (Lovell); John, of Long Pond (Conception B.), 1871 (Lovell).

Modern status: Unique, at St. John's (*Electors* 1955).

HAFEY, ? a variant of the surname of Ireland, (O)Haffey, *Ó hEachaidh*. (MacLysaght).

Traced by MacLysaght in Co. Armagh.

In Newfoundland:

Early instance: Thomas (and others), of St. John's, 1871 (Lovell).

Modern status: At St. John's.

HAGAN, a surname of England and Ireland; in England from an Old German or Scandinavian personal name containing the element *Hag*; in Ireland (O)Hagan, *Ó hÁgáin*, originally *Ó hÓgáin*, Ir. *óg* – young. (Reaney, MacLysaght). *See also* HOGAN.

Traced by MacLysaght in Co. Tyrone.

In Newfoundland:

Early instance: John, ? of Northern Bay, 1839 (DPHW 54).

Modern status: Rare, at Kingmans (*Electors* 1955) and St. John's.

HAGARTY, HAG(G)ERTY, variants of the surnames of Ireland O Hegarty, (O)Haggerty, *Ó hÉigceartaigh*, Ir. *éigceartach* – unjust. (MacLysaght).

Traced by MacLysaght in Co. Derry.

In Newfoundland:

Early instances: Michael Hagerty, fisherman of Quidi Vidi, 1794–5, "9 years in Newfoundland," that is, 1785–6 (Census 1794–5); Dennis, of Harbour Grace Parish, 1813 (Nfld. Archives HGRC); Bartly Hergerty, from Youghal (Co. Cork), married at St. John's, 1818 (Nfld. Archives BRC); James Hegarty, of the White Hills (St. John's), 1838 (Nfld. Archives BRC); Honora Heagerty, of King's Cove Parish, 1838 (Nfld. Archives KCRC); Bartholomew Hagerty, of St. John's, 1856 (*Newfoundlander* 11 Dec 1856); Julian Heagarty, of Harbour Grace, 1866 (Nfld. Archives HGRC); John Hagarty, of St. Juliens, 1871 (Lovell).

Modern status: Hagarty, unique, at St. John's; Hagerty, rare, at St. John's; Haggerty, at St. Albans, Botwood and St. John's.

Place name: Mount Haggarty 49-32 56-53.

HAGGETT. *See* HACKETT

HAIGH, a surname of England, from the English place name Haigh (Lancashire, Yorkshire WR), or from Old English *haga*, Old Norse *hagi* – (dweller by the) enclosure. (Cottle).

Traced by Guppy in Yorkshire WR.

In Newfoundland:

Early instance: John, minister of Blackhead (Bay de Verde district), 1825 (DPHW 52A).

Modern status: Rare, at St. John's.

HAINES, HAYNES, surnames of England, Ireland and the Channel Islands, from the common place name Hayne or Hayes (Devon), or from Old English *(ge)hæg* – (dweller by the) enclosure, or from Middle English *heyne*, *haine*, *hayn* – mean, humble, niggardly; in Ireland, also for HYNES (*see* HINES) in Munster. (Reaney, Cottle, MacLysaght 73, Turk).

Guppy traced Haines in Herefordshire, Oxfordshire and Somerset, Haynes widespread in the Midlands; Spiegelhalter traced Haynes in Devon.

In Newfoundland:

Family tradition: —— Haynes, from Hull (Yorkshire ER), settled at Catalina in the 19th century (MUN Folklore).

Early instances: Edward Hayns, of Trinity Bay, 1782 (DPHW 64); John Haynes, of Bonavista, 1791 (USPG); John Hain, servant of Battle Harbour, 1795 (MUN Hist.); W. Haynes, of St. John's, 1811 (CO 194.52); Charles Haynes or Haines, of Catalina, 1813 (DPHW 64); John Hanes, of Harbour Grace Parish, 1814 (Nfld. Archives HGRC); Thomas Haines, planter of Joe Batt's Arm, 1818 (CO 194.61); Richard Haynes, planter of Twillingate, 1821 (USPG); John Haynes or Haines, planter of Salmon Cove (now Champneys), 1826 (DPHW 64B); George Haynes, of Change Islands, 1840 (DPHW 83); James Haines, of Grand Bank, 1843 (DPHW 109); William, of Triton Harbour, 1853 (DPHW 86); ——, captain in the seal fishery out of Greenspond, 1858 (*Newfoundlander* 1 Apr 1858); Richard, of Indian Island (Fogo district), 1858 (DPHW 83); Henry Hanes, of Exploits Burnt Island, 1859 (DPHW 92); William, of Little Bay Islands, 1860 (DPHW 92); scattered in Lovell 1871.

Modern status: Haines, scattered, especially at Codner; Haynes, scattered, especially at Catalina.

Place names: Haines Island (Labrador) 53-54 58-55; Haynes Lake 48-45 55-28.

HAIRE, a variant of the surname of Ireland, (O)Hare, *Ó hIr*, *Ó hÉir* – the sharp, angry one, Hair, Hare in Scotland; but also a variant of the surname of England, HARE.

MacLysaght traced O'Hare in Co. Armagh; Black traced Hair, Hare in Ayrshire.

In Newfoundland:

Early instances: Alexander, of St. John's, 1802, died 1828 (D'Alberti 12, (*Newfoundlander* 11 Dec 1828); Luke Hear (Hare in 1819), of Harbour Grace Parish, 1813 (Nfld. Archives HGRC); Bonaventure, from ? Rathnure Parish (Co. Wexford), married at St. John's, 1819 (Nfld. Archives BRC); Bridget Haire, of Pouch Cove, 1837 (*Newfoundlander* 3 Aug 1837).

Modern status: Scattered, especially at Harbour Grace.

HALBOT, ? a variant of the surnames of France, Halbout – bold, or Halbert – a nickname for a merchant or porter. (Dauzat).

In Newfoundland:

Early instance: Modeste, fisherman of Sandy Point (St. George's B.), 1871 (Lovell).

Modern status: In the St. George's and Port-au-Port districts.

HALE, a surname of England and Ireland, from Old English *halh* – (dweller in a) recess, nook or remote valley, or from the English place name Hale Farm (Devon). (Reaney, Spiegelhalter, MacLysaght).

Traced by Guppy in Cheshire, Gloucestershire, Hertfordshire, Monmouthshire, Surrey and Wiltshire, by Spiegelhalter in Devon, and by MacLysaght in Ulster.

In Newfoundland:

Early instances: Robert Hales, soldier of St. John's, 1768 (DPHW 26C); William Hale, of Bonavista, 1831 (DPHW 70); George Hales, of Fair Island (Bonavista B.), 1849 (DPHW 76); William Hole, of Change Islands, 1858 (DPHW 85).

Modern status: Rare, in the Fogo and Twillingate districts, especially at Change Islands and Newstead.

HALEY, HAYLEY, surnames of England and Ireland, from the English place name, Hailey (Oxfordshire, Buckinghamshire, Hertfordshire), or (dweller by the) hay field. (O)Haly in Ireland, however, is a variant of HEAL(E)Y or HANLEY. (Spiegelhalter, MacLysaght, E.C. Smith).

Haley traced by Guppy in Yorkshire WR; Hal(e)y by Spiegelhalter in Devon; (O)Haly by MacLysaght formerly in Co. Cork, also in Co. Limerick.

In Newfoundland:

Early instances: William Haley, of St. John's, 1767 (DPHW 26C); Robert, soldier of Great Belle Isle (now Bell Island), 1771 (DPHW 26C); William, of Trinity (Trinity B.), 1788 (DPHW 64); John Hailey, of Bonavista, 1792 (USPG); William Haly, fort major of St. John's, lessee of land near St. John's, 1804 (D'Alberti 14, CO 194.45); Ann Hailey, of Witless Bay, 1822 (Nfld. Archives BRC); Edward Haly, of Ferryland, 1840 (*Newfoundlander* 27 Feb 1840); Peter Hayley, ? of Harbour Grace, 1845 (*Newfoundlander* 16 Jan 1845); Cornelius (and others), of Lamaline, 1871 (Lovell).

Modern status: Haley, scattered, especially at Allan's Island (*Electors* 1955); Hayley, at Bonavista.

Place names: Haley's Pond 48-28 54-02; Bally Haly (St. John's).

HALFYARD, a surname of England, from Old English *healf* – half and *gierd* – yard – (dweller on a) homestead of half a yardland, ? about 15 acres, or

? from the Old English personal name *Ælfheard*. (Reaney, Spiegelhalter).

Traced by Spiegelhalter in Devon.

In Newfoundland:

Family tradition: George (1829–1907), from Ochre Pit Cove settled at Bonne Bay in 1874 (MUN Geog.).

Early instances: Richard, juror ? of St. John's, 1750 (CO 194.12); Richard, from South Bovey (Devon), married at St. John's, 1772 (DPHW 26D); Richard, of Northern Bay, 1764, of Ochre Pit Cove, 1780 (CO 199.18); Ann, of Grates Cove, 1832 (DPHW 58); James, of Bonne Bay, 1874 (DPHW 95); John, of Harbour Grace Parish, 1883 (Nfld. Archives HGRC).

Modern status: Scattered, including Ochre Pit Cove and Curzon Village (Bonne B.).

HALIBURTON, a surname of Scotland, from the Scots place name Haliburton (Berwickshire). (Black).

In Newfoundland:

Modern status: Rare, at St. John's (*Electors* 1955), and Lewisporte.

HALL, a surname of England, Scotland and Ireland, from Old English *heall* – (worker at the) hall, or from the English place name Hall (Devon), or from Old Norse *hallr* – (dweller by the) boulder, rock. (Reaney, Cottle, Spiegelhalter, MacLysaght 73).

Found by Guppy widespread in England and in central and southern Scotland, and by MacLysaght in Ulster and Munster.

In Newfoundland:

Family traditions: Paul and John settled in the Codroy Valley in the 1840s (MUN Folklore). Isaac, deserter from a naval vessel, settled at Hallstown (North River) in the early 19th century (Family). ——, from Greenspond, was one of the first settlers of Newtown formerly Inner Islands in the 1850s (MUN Hist.).

Early instances: William, of Toads (now Tors) Cove, 1681 (CO 1); William, of Witless Bay, 1682 (CO 1); Thomas, soldier of St. John's, 1760 (DPHW 26C); John, of Trinity (Trinity B.), 1790 (DPHW 64); Sarah, baptized at Pinchard's Island, 1830, aged 22 years (DPHW 76); James, of Harbour Grace Parish, 1830 (Nfld. Archives HGRC); John, of Petty Harbour, 1836 (Nfld. Archives BRC); John, of Aquaforte, 1839 (DPHW 26D); James, ? of Harbour Grace, 1845 (*Newfoundlander* 16 Jan 1845); Sarah Jean, of Ferryland, 1854 (DPHW 31); Jacob, of Bare-need, 1871 (Lovell); John, of Bay Bulls, 1871

(Lovell); Edward (and others), of Codroy and Rivers, 1871 (Lovell); John, of Inner Islands (Bonavista B.), 1871 (Lovell); Robert, of Little Bay Island, 1871 (Lovell); John, of Point Mall (Placentia B.), 1871 (Lovell).

Modern status: Widespread, including Hallstown and Newtown (Bonavista B.).

Place names: Hall Hill 49-21 56-04; —— Pond 48-40 55-06; Hall(s) Rock 48-36 53-51; Halls Bay 49-30 56-00; —— Gullies 47-22 53-27, 47-28 53-28; —— Pond 48-36 53-50; Hallstown 47-32 53-20; Hall's Bay Head 49-37 55-50; John —— Long Rock, Roy —— Island 49-21 53-30.

HALLAHAN, a surname of Ireland (O)Hallahan, Hallighan, *Ó hAileacháin.* (MacLysaght), probably confused with HALLERAN.

Traced by MacLysaght in Cos. Cork and Waterford.

In Newfoundland:

Early instances: John, married at St. John's, 1772 (DPHW 26D); Edmond, from Kill Parish (unidentified) (Co. Waterford), married at St. John's, 1816 (Nfld. Archives BRC); James Hallihan, of Middle Bill Cove (Bonavista B.), 1833 (Nfld. Archives KCRC); John Hallahan, planter of Bird Island Cove (now Elliston), 1844 (DPHW 72); John Hallaghan, ? of Northern Bay, 1844 (DPHW 54); Johanna Hallahan, of Harbour Grace, 1866 (Nfld. Archives HGRC); Joseph, of Bay of Islands, 1871 (Lovell); David and William, of Old Perlican, 1871 (Lovell); James and Michael, of Peter's River and Holyrood, 1871 (Lovell); Patrick and Thomas, of Trepassey, 1871 (Lovell).

Modern status: Rare, at St. John's (*Electors* 1955)

HALLERAN, a variant of the surname of Ireland (O)Halloran, *Ó hAllmhuráin,* Ir. *allmhurach* – pirate, stranger from overseas. (MacLysaght). *See* HALLAHAN.

Traced by MacLysaght in Cos. Clare and Galway.

In Newfoundland:

Family tradition: Leo, from St. Vincent's (St. Mary's B.), was an early settler at St. Stephen's (St. Mary's B.) (MUN Hist.).

Early instances: —— Halluran, accused of murder of William Keen, 1750 (CO 194.13, Prowse); Dennis Halloran, from Middleton (unidentified) (Co. Cork), married at St. John's, 1807 (Nfld. Archives BRC); Bridget Hallaran, of Harbour Grace Parish, 1815 (Nfld. Archives HGRC).

Modern status: Scattered, especially at St. Vincent's, and in the Ferryland district.

HALLETT, a surname of England and Jersey (Channel Islands), ? a diminutive of the English personal name *Æthelheard,* containing the elements *noble* and *hard,* or from Old German *Adelard.* (Reaney,

Cottle, Turk).

Traced by Cottle in Dorset, Devon and Somerset.

In Newfoundland:

Early instances: Mary Hallet, of Harbour Grace Parish, 1815 (Nfld. Archives HGRC); Orlando, of Bonavista, 1824 (DPHW 70); John, member of the Board of Road Commissioners for Sound Island (Placentia B.), 1844 (*Nfld. Almanac*); Benjamin Hallett, of Great Burin, 1860 (DPHW 108); Esther, of St. John's, 1860 (DPHW 26D); George, of Burin Bay, 1861 (DPHW 108); Reuben, of Flat Island (Bonavista B.), 1864 (DPHW 81); George (and others) Hallott, of Newman's Cove, 1871 (Lovell); Thomas Hallett, of Twillingate, 1871 (Lovell); Reuben and William, of Pool's Island, 1871 (Lovell).

Modern status: Rare, especially at Flat Island (Bonavista B.).

HALLEY, a surname of Ireland, (O)Hall(e)y, *Ó hAilche* in Cos. Waterford and Tipperary, *Ó hAille* in Co. Clare. (MacLysaght).

In Newfoundland:

Early instances: Mary, of St. John's, 1805 (Nfld. Archives BRC); Mary Hal(l)y, of Harbour Grace Parish, 1808 (Nfld. Archives HGRC); James Hally, from Waterford City, married at St. John's, 1817 (Nfld. Archives BRC); William, of Ferryland, 1831 (Nfld. Archives BRC); John Hally or Holly, of King's Cove Parish, 1835 (Nfld. Archives KCRC); Thomas Halley, of Western Bay, 1854 (DPHW 52B); Michael Hally, of Cape Race, 1871 (Lovell).

Modern status: At St. John's and Topsail.

HALLIDAY, a surname of England, Scotland and Ireland, from Old English *hālidæg* – (one born on a) holy day, festival, as, for example, also CHRISTMAS. (Reaney, Black, MacLysaght).

Traced by Guppy in Dumfriesshire, and by MacLysaght in Ulster.

In Newfoundland:

Early instances: David, tailor of Carbonear, 1826 (DPHW 48); David, from Wamphry (Dumfriesshire), Scotland, tailor of St. John's, deceased 1832 (*Royal Gazette* 3 Jan 1832); John, storekeeper of Harbour Grace, 1834 (DPHW 43); John Hal(l)iday, from Moffat (Dumfriesshire), of St. John's, died 1855, aged 47 (MUN Folklore, *Newfoundlander* 31 Dec 1855, General Protestant Cemetery, St. John's).

Modern status: Scattered, especially at St. John's and Job's Cove.

Place name: Job Halliday Shoal 47-38 58-32.

HALLINGHAM. *See* ALLINGHAM

HAMBLING, HAMLYN, surnames of England, Hamlin of Ireland, diminutives of the Old German personal name *Haimo*. (Reaney, Cottle, MacLysaght 73). *See also* HAMEN, HAMMOND.

Spiegelhalter traced Hamblen, Hamblin(g), Ham(b)lyn in Devon; MacLysaght traced Hamlin in Co. Meath, especially from the thirteenth to the eighteenth century.

In Newfoundland:

Family tradition: Job Hamlyn (1814–1894), from Yorkshire settled at Crow Head (Twillingate) in 1830 (MUN Folklore).

Early instances: Richard Hamline, of Ferryland, 1709 (CO 194.4); Hugh Hamlin, shoreman of St. John's, 1794–5, "24 years in Newfoundland," that is, 1770–1 (Census 1794–5); James of Fortune, 1811 (Surrogate Court, Fortune Bay 1802–19, 1821, pp. 73–152, PANL GN85/1/C/1 per P.E.L. Smith); James, of Ward's Harbour (now Beaumont North), 1855 (DPHW 86); Job Hamelin, planter of Twillingate, 1871 (Lovell); George Hamlin, of Great Burin, 1871 (Lovell).

Modern status: Hamblin, rare, at Bay Roberts (*Electors* 1955); Hamlyn, scattered, especially at Twillingate and St. John's.

HAMEN, ? a variant of the surname of England, France and the Channel Islands, Hamon, from the Old French personal name *Haimon*, Old German *Haimo* – home, "a popular Norman name." (Reaney, Dauzat, Turk). *See also* HAMBLING, HANHAM and HAMMOND.

In Newfoundland:

Early instances: Widow Haman, of St. John's Harbour, 1677 (CO 1); Samuel Hamon, of Conception Bay, [1706] (CO 194.4); Edward Hamman, of Harbour Grace Parish, 1816 (Nfld. Archives HGRC); Elizabeth Haman, of Fox Island (Burgeo-La Poile), 1849 (DPHW 101).

Modern status: Rare, at Creston South (Placentia West district).

HAMILTON, a surname of England, Scotland and Ireland, from the English place names Hamilton (Leicestershire), Hambelton (Lancashire, Rutland-shire, Yorkshire NR), Hambledon (Hampshire, Surrey, Dorset), Hambleden (Buckinghamshire), Hameldon (Lancashire), or Hamel Down (Devon). (Cottle, Spiegelhalter, MacLysaght).

Traced by Guppy in the southern half of Scotland, especially in Lanarkshire, by Spiegelhalter in Devon, and by MacLysaght in Ulster and elsewhere.

In Newfoundland:

Family tradition: —— Hamilton, from Ireland settled at Joe Batt's Arm between 1811 and 1816 (MUN Hist.).

Early instances: J., soldier of St. John's, 1779 (DPHW 26C); Daniel, of Harbour Grace Parish, 1808 (Nfld. Archives HGRC); Andrew Hammilton or Hamlinton, from Co. Kilkenny, married at Fortune Harbour, 1830 (Nfld. Archives KCRC); Charles Hamilton, from Warwickshire, married ? at St. John's, 1834 (*Royal Gazette* 18 Mar 1834); William, commissioner of roads between Burin and Grand Bank, 1834 (*Newfoundlander* 19 Jun 1834); Alexander, of Isle Valen (Placentia B.), 1835 (DPHW 30); James, of Oderin, 1843 (*Newfoundlander* 31 Aug 1843); J., J.P. of Burin district, 1844 (*Nfld. Almanac*); Henry Harris, clergyman of Ferryland, 1850 (DPHW 31); Richard, of Green Bay, 1852 (*Newfoundlander* 9 Sep 1852); Emmanuel, of Petites, 1856 (DPHW 98); Eugene, of Harbour Grace, 1866 (Nfld. Archives HGRC); John (and others), of Black Island, 1871 (Lovell); Matthew, of Joe Batt's Arm, 1871 (Lovell).

Modern status: Scattered.

Place names: Hamilton (now Churchill) Falls (Labrador) 53-36 64-19; —— Inlet (Labrador) 54-00 57-30; —— Island 49-32 55-00, (Labrador) 53-52 56-58; Hamilton or Sir Charles Hamilton Sound 49-30 54-15; —— (or Churchill) River (Labrador) 53-22 60-11.

HAMLYN. *See* HAMBLING

HAMMOND, a surname of England and Ireland from the Old German personal names *Haimo*, *Hamon* or Old French *Hamond*. (Reaney, Cottle, MacLysaght 73).

Traced by Guppy in the east and southeast counties and near the Welsh border, and by Spiegelhalter in Devon.

In Newfoundland:

Early instances: John, in possession of property in fishery, at Portugal Cove, 1794–5 (Census 1794–5); Thomas, of Freshwater (Carbonear), 1795 (CO 199.18); Peter, married at St. John's, 1801 (DPHW 26D); James (and others), of Bell Island, 1871 (Lovell).

Modern status: Scattered, especially at St. John's, Bell Island and Beachy Cove (Portugal Cove).

Place name: Tom Hammond's Pond (Labrador) 52-27 55-47.

HAMPTON, a surname of England and Ireland, from a common English place name found in nine counties in the south and Midlands, or (dweller at the) homestead farm, manor, or place in a river meadow, or high place. (Cottle, Ekwall, MacLysaght 73).

Traced by Guppy in Shropshire, Sussex and Worcestershire, by Spiegelhalter in Devon and by MacLysaght in Co. Down.

In Newfoundland:

Early instances: Robert, grand juror of St. John's, 1811 (CO 194.51); James, planter of Bonavista, 1823 (DPHW 72); William, of Port de Grave Parish, 1829 (*Newfoundlander* 5 Nov 1829); Robert, fisherman of Bareneed, 1846 (DPHW 39); Frederick, of Harbour Grace, 1868 (Nfld. Archives HGRC).

Modern status: Scattered, especially in the Bonavista South district.

Place name: Hampton Bank (Labrador) 52-43 55-47.

HANAM(ES). *See* HANHAM

HANCOCK, a surname of England, a diminutive of the baptismal names John or Henry. (Reaney). *See* HENRY, JOHN and *also* HANCOTT, HANN.

Guppy found Hancock widespread, especially in the west Midlands and southwestern counties, including Devon, with Handcock characteristic of Gloucestershire.

In Newfoundland:

Family tradition: Elizabeth (1837–), born at Englee (MUN Folklore).

Early instances: William Handcock, of St. John's Harbour, 1703 (CO 194.3); Thomas Hencock (Hancock in 1768), of Trinity Bay, 1763 (DPHW 64); Mary Handcock, died at King's Cove, 1784 (Devine); James Hancock, of Trinity (Trinity B.), 1797 (DPHW 64); Thomas, proprietor and occupier of fishing room at English Harbour (Trinity B.), Winter 1800–01 (Census Trinity B.); William Handcock, of Bonavista, 1805 (DPHW 70); Joseph Hancock, planter of Barr'd Islands, 1821 (USPG); Henry, of Greenspond, 1829, of Newell's Island, 1830 (DPHW 76); James, planter of Cuckold's Cove (now Dunfield), 1835 (DPHW 64B); William Handcock, of Knight's Cove, 1839 (DPHW 73); Jacob Esau, of Flatrock (unspecified), 1857 (*Newfoundlander* 22 Jan 1857);

John, of Hooping Harbour, 1864 (DPHW 94); Henry Hancock, of Englee, 1864 (DPHW 94); James Handcock, of Little Harbour (Bonavista B.), 1865 (DPHW 81); Philip, of Musgravetown, 1871 (Lovell); William, of Old Bonaventure, 1871 (Lovell); William, of Salvage, 1871 (Lovell).

Modern status: Widespread, especially at Roddickton, Botwood and Brooklyn.

Place names: Hancock's Pond 48-32 53-49; Hencock Brook 50-41 56-08; —— Pond 50-41 56-09.

HANCOTT, ? a variant of HANCOCK, or ? from an unidentified English place name.

In Newfoundland:

Modern status: At Port Albert, Mann Point (*Electors* 1955) and Frederickton (Fogo district).

HAND, a surname of England and Ireland, ? from an Old English personal name **Hand*, a nickname for one possessing a deformity or unusual dexterity, or a pet-form of Randolf or Randall. In Ireland Hand is used "by pseudo-translation, for Claffey, MacClave, Glavy and Lavan, through confusion with the word *lámh* – hand." (Reaney, Cottle, MacLysaght).

Guppy traced Hand in Derbyshire, Lincolnshire and Staffordshire, Hands in Warwickshire; Spiegelhalter traced Hands in Devon.

In Newfoundland:

Early instances: William, of Greenspond, 1827 (DPHW 76); John, married at St. John's, 1831 (Nfld. Archives BRC); Isaac, of Harbour Buffett, 1835 (DPHW 30); Francis, of Lamaline, 1836 (DPHW 109); John, of Logy Bay, 1840 (*Newfoundlander* 23 Jan 1840); Alexander, planter of Catalina, 1843 (DPHW 72); W. Hands, road commissioner for the area Cape Freels to Cobbler's Island, 1847 (*Nfld. Almanac*); James Hand, of Bay of Islands, 1871 (Lovell); John, of Outer Cove, 1871 (Lovell); William, cooper of St. John's, 1871 (Lovell).

Modern status: At St. John's.

HANDRIGAN, a variant of the surname of Ireland HANRAHAN, not recorded by MacLysaght.

In Newfoundland:

Early instance: Richard Handragan, of Long Harbour (Fortune), 1871 (Lovell).

Modern status: Scattered.

HANFORD, a surname of England, from the English place names Hannaford (Devon), or Hanford (Dorset, Somerset). (Cottle, Spiegelhalter). *See also* HANNAFORD.

Traced by Guppy in Derbyshire. Spiegelhalter traced Handford in Devon.

In Newfoundland:

Early instance: John, from Sunderland, deserted his ship in Newfoundland, 1837 (*Newfoundlander* 15 Jun 1837).

Modern status: Rare, at Isle aux Morts (*Electors* 1955).

HANHAM(S), HANAMES, HANNAM, HANNAN, HANNEM, surnames of England, from the English place name Hanham (Gloucestershire), but possibly confused with HAMEN, HANLON and HANNON. (Spiegelhalter).

Spiegelhalter traced Hanham and Hannam in Devon.

In Newfoundland:

Early instances: James Hanham, planter of Hants Harbour, 1829 (DPHW 59A); —— Hannan, of St. John's, 1832 (*Newfoundlander* 20 Dec 1832); William, of Leading Tickles, 1845 (DPHW 86); John, of Rose Blanche, 1846 (DPHW 101); John, from England, married at Grand Bank, 1846 (DPHW 106); Alfred Hannum, of Brunette, 1851, of Blue Pinion, 1853 (DPHW 104); James Hannan, of Burin, 1860 (DPHW 100); John, of Harbour Le Cou, 1861 (DPHW 99); Edward (and others) Hannin, of Harbour Main, 1871 (Lovell); Thomas Hannan, of Red Head Cove, 1871 (Lovell); Alfred Hannon, of Turnip Cove, 1871 (Lovell); James Hanham, of Jean de Baie, 1871 (Lovell); George Hanan, of Island Cove (now Dunfield), 1871 (Lovell); James Hannan, of Mosquito (now Bristol's Hope), 1871 (Lovell).

Modern status: Hanham, Hannam, Hanam, Hannan, in the Placentia East and West districts; Hannem, at Burin; Hanames, rare, at St. John's.

HANLEY, a surname of England, and (O)HANLEY, surnames of Ireland; in England from the English place names Hanley (Staffordshire, Worcestershire) or Handley (Cheshire, Devon, Derbyshire, Dorset, Northamptonshire); in Ireland (O)Hanley, Handly, *Ó hÁinle,* Ir. *áinle* – beauty. (Cottle, Spiegelhalter, MacLysaght). *See also* HENLEY.

Spiegelhalter traced Handley in Devon; MacLysaght traced (O)Hanley, Handly in Connacht and Co. Cork.

In Newfoundland:

Early instances: Margaret Hanl(e)y, of Harbour Grace Parish, 1811 (Nfld. Archives HGRC); John Hanly, from Berehaven (Co. Cork), fisherman of St. John's, deceased 1815 (*Royal Gazette* 16 Nov 1815).

Modern status: Hanley, rare, at St. John's; O'Hanley, unique, at St. John's (*Electors* 1955).

(O)HANLON, surnames of Ireland, (O)Hanlon, *Ó hAnluain,* ? Ir. *luan* – champion. (MacLysaght). *See also* HANHAM.

Traced by MacLysaght in Ulster and west Munster.

In Newfoundland:

Family tradition: —— Hanlon, from Co. Cork to Port Rexton about 1800 (MUN Folklore).

Early instances: Michael Hanlen, servant of Harbour Main, 1755 (MUN Hist.); Michael Hanlon, butcher of St. John's, 1794–5, "20 years in Newfoundland," that is, 1774–5 (Census 1794–5); Denis, in possession of property in fishery at Portugal Cove, 1794–5 (Census 1794–5); Mary, from Tintern Parish (Co. Wexford), married at St. John's, 1812 (Nfld. Archives BRC); James Hanlon or Hanlen, of Harbour Grace Parish, 1817 (Nfld. Archives HGRC); Michael Hanlon, of Fogo, 1819 (Nfld. Archives KCRC); Anne Hanlan or Handlon, of Trinity, 1832 (Nfld. Archives KCRC); John Handlon, planter of Ship Cove (now part of Port Rexton), 1839 (DPHW 64B); James Handlen, ? of Fortune, 1845 (*Nfld. Almanac*); William Hanlon, of Burnt Island (Bonavista B.), 1859 (Nfld. Archives KCRC); William, of Open Hall, 1865 (Nfld. Archives KCRC); Philip Hanlin and John Hanlon, of Barren Island (now Bar Haven), 1871 (Lovell); Michael Hanlin, of Cape La Hune, 1871 (Lovell); John Hanlon, of St. Mary's, 1871 (Lovell).

Modern status: Hanlon, scattered, especially at O'Donnells and St. John's; O'Hanlon, unique, at St. John's.

HANN, a surname of England, a diminutive of the baptismal names John or Henry. (Reaney). *See* HENRY, JOHN and *also* HANCOCK.

Traced by Guppy in Dorset.

In Newfoundland:

Family tradition: Thomas, from England, settled at Harbour Buffett about 1812 (MUN Hist.).

Early instances: John Han, of Trinity, 1794 (DPHW 64); Charles Hann, from Somerset, married at St. John's, 1830 (Nfld. Archives BRC); John Han, of Pushthrough, 1835 (DPHW 30); Isaiah Hann, of Moreton's Harbour, 1846 (DPHW 86); John, of Hunt's Island, 1848 (DPHW 101); John, of Cape Freels (Bonavista district), 1850 (DPHW 76); Job, of Harbour Breton, 1854 (DPHW 104); George, of Change Islands, 1856 (DPHW 83); David, of Middle Bill Cove, 1857 (DPHW 76); John, of Harbour Le

Cou, 1860 (DPHW 99); James Pitman, of Allan's Island, 1860 (DPHW 107); Solomon, of Exploits Burnt Island, 1861 (DPHW 92); Emma, of Pinchard's Island, 1862 (DPHW 79); scattered in Lovell 1871.

Modern status: Widespread, especially at Channel, Cape Freels and Trout River.

Place name: Hann's Rocks 49-09 53-33.

HANNAFORD, a surname of England, from the English place name Hannaford (Devon). (Cottle, Spiegelhalter). *See also* HANFORD.

Traced by Guppy in Devon.

In Newfoundland:

Early instances: John, of St. John's, 1778 (DPHW 26C); William Hanaford, carpenter of Petty Harbour, 1794–5, "5 years in Newfoundland," that is, 1789–90 (Census 1794–5); John Hanniford, of Burin Bay, 1860 (DPHW 100).

Modern status: Especially at St. John's and Petty Harbour.

HANNAM, HANNAN, HANNEM. *See* HANHAM

HANNIFAN, a variant of the surname of Ireland, (O)Hanafin, *Ó hAinbhthin* now spelt *Ó hAinifin,* Ir. *ainbhioth* – storm. (MacLysaght).

MacLysaght traced (O)Hanafin in Co. Kerry.

In Newfoundland:

Early instances: Cornelius Hanefin, of Harbour Grace Parish, 1821 (Nfld. Archives HGRC); Richard Haniven, married at St. John's, 1833 (Nfld. Archives BRC); John and Michael Hanifin, farmers of Broad Cove (now St. Phillip's), 1871 (Lovell).

Modern status: Rare, at Avondale South.

HANNIHAN, a variant of the surname of Ireland, (O)Hanahan, *Ó hAnnacháin,* "now much changed to HANNON." (MacLysaght).

MacLysaght traced (O)Hanahan in Co. Limerick.

In Newfoundland:

Early instances: Michael Hannahan, of Joe Batts Arm, 1817 (Nfld. Archives KCRC); Pierce Hannahan, of Western Bay, 1843 (DPHW 54, Lovell 1871).

Modern status: Unique, at St. John's (*Electors* 1955.).

HANNON, a surname of Ireland (O)Hannon, *Ó hAnnáin,* or for (O)Hanahan (*see* HANNIHAN), or for (O)Haneen, Hanheen, *Ó hAinchín.* (MacLysaght). *See also* HANHAM.

Traced by MacLysaght in Connacht and Co. Limerick.

In Newfoundland:

Family tradition: Elizabeth, married at Spanish Room (Mortier B.), 1867 (MUN Hist.).

Early instances: Edmond, from Tintern Parish (Co. Wexford), married at St. John's, 1802 (Nfld. Archives BRC); Dennis Hannen, one of 72 impressed men who sailed from Ireland to Newfoundland, ? 1811 (CO 194.51); Edmund Hanan, of Harbour Grace Parish, 1813 (Nfld. Archives HGRC); Michael ? Hannon, of St. John's, 1822 (CO 194.65); John Hannen, of Harbour Grace, 1829 (Nfld. Archives BRC); Michael Hannan, of Kings Cove Parish, 1838 (Nfld. Archives KCRC); Thomas Hannon, ? of Northern Bay, 1849 (DPHW 54).

Modern status: Scattered, especially at Bishop's Falls.

HANRAHAN, with a Newfoundland variant HANDRIGAN, a surname of Ireland (O)Hanrahan, *Ó hAnracháin,* ? a variant of (O)Hourahan or (O)Hourihan(e). (MacLysaght).

Traced by MacLysaght in Co. Clare and, as Handrahan, in Co. Tipperary.

In Newfoundland:

Family tradition: Michael Hanrahan or Handrigan, settled at Little Bay (Placentia B.), between ? 1840 and 1867 (MUN Folklore, MUN Hist.).

Early instances: S., fisherman of St. John's 1794–5, "40 years in Newfoundland," that is, 1754–5 (Census 1794–5); Roger, of Musketta (now Bristol's Hope), 1789 (CO 199.18); Philip, of Bay Bulls, 1793 (USPG); Mary, from Mooncoin Parish (Co. Kilkenny), married at St. John's, 1808 (Nfld. Archives BRC); Alice, of Harbour Grace Parish, 1813 (Nfld. Archives HGRC); Patrick Hanarahan, of Greenspond, 1823 (Nfld. Archives KCRC); Michael Hanrahan, of Ferryland, 1825 (Nfld. Archives BRC); Patrick, of Gooseberry Island (Bonavista B.), 1825 (Nfld. Archives KCRC); John, of Harbour Grace, 1829 (Nfld. Archives BRC); Patrick, of Kings Cove, 1829 (Nfld. Archives KCRC); Martin, of Catalina, 1832 (Nfld. Archives BRC); William, M.D., from New Ross (Co. Wexford), of Carbonear, died in a snowstorm near Carbonear, 1844 (*Sentinel* 23 Jan 1844, (*Royal Gazette* 6 Feb 1844); Thomas, of Bauline (Conception B.), 1871 (Lovell); Peter, of Beau Bois, 1871 (Lovell); Michael, of Grand Bank, 1871 (Lovell); Daniel (and others), of Little Bay (Burin), 1871 (Lovell); Patrick, of Low Point, 1871 (Lovell); Michael, of Spanish Room, 1871 (Lovell).

Modern status: Scattered, especially at Little Bay (Placentia West district).

Place name: Hanrahan Point (Labrador) 53-45 56-38.

HANSEN, a surname of Scandinavia, – son of Hans, that is, John. *See* JOHN *and also* HANSON.

In Newfoundland:

Modern status: Rare, at Corner Brook and St. John's.

HANSFORD, a surname of England, from the English place name Hansford Barton (Devon). (Spiegelhalter). *See also* ANSFORD.

Traced by Guppy in Dorset and by Spiegelhalter in Devon.

In Newfoundland:

Early instance: Charles, of Hants Harbour, 1830 (DPHW 59); William Handsford or Handsforth, born ? 1848 at Sturminster Newton (Dorset), married at Harbour Breton, 1878 (Harbour Breton Anglican Church Records per D.A. Macdonald).

Modern status: At St. John's, and in the Trinity North district.

HANSON, a surname of England, Ireland and Scandinavia; in England – son of Hann or Hand; in Scandinavia as in HANSEN. (Reaney, MacLysaght).

Traced by Guppy in Yorkshire WR, by Mac-Lysaght formerly in Co. Derry, now Hampson.

In Newfoundland:

Early instances: Martha, of Trinity (Trinity B.), 1847 (DPHW 64B); H. C. Hanson (? for Hansen), born 1877 at Govik, Norway, of Grand Falls, 1927 (*Nfld. Who's Who*).

Modern status: At Grand Falls.

HANTON, a surname of England and ? of Ireland, from the English place name, Southampton (Hampshire). (Reaney).

In Newfoundland:

Early instances: John, of Bonavista, 1820 (Nfld. Archives KCRC); Patrick, of Burin, 1871 (Lovell); James, of Outer Cove, 1871 (Lovell).

Modern status: At Path End, Burin (*Electors* 1955) and St. John's.

HAPGOOD, a surname of England, ? containing the Middle English *hap*, *hop* – to cover, wrap up. (Weekley *Surnames*).

In Newfoundland:

Early instances: Charles Habgood, ? from Dorset, apprenticed at Placentia, 1789 (Dorset County Record Office per Kirwin); James Hapgood, of Bonavista, 1791 (DPHW 70); Richard (H)apgood, of Bird Island Cove (now Elliston), 1819 (DPHW 72); James Habgood, of Keels, 1843 (DPHW 73A); Richard Hapgood, of Salvage, 1850, of Broom Close

(Bonavista B.), 1862 (DPHW 73A, 77); William, of Isle Valen, 1871 (Lovell)

Modern status: Scattered, especially at Tacks Beach (*Electors* 1955) and in the Bonavista North district.

HARBIN, a surname of England and Ireland, a diminutive of the baptismal name, Herbert, from the Old German personal name *Hariberct* containing the elements *army* and *bright*. (Withycombe, Reaney, MacLysaght 73).

Traced by MacLysaght in Co. Clare.

In Newfoundland:

Early instances: In the early 1800s two brothers, Henry and William Harbin left Poole (Dorset) for Newfoundland. William settled at Dog Bay (Gander Bay) and Henry at Twillingate as an apprentice of Waterman & Co. of that place. William became the ancestor of all the Harbins now living in the area around Gander Bay (D.V. Harbin); William Harben or Harbin, of Hare Bay (Fogo district), 1841 (DPHW 83); William Harbin, of Fogo, 1851 (DPHW 83); Henry, of Twillingate, 1871 (Lovell).

Modern status: At St. John's and in the Fogo district.

HARDIMAN, a surname of England and Ireland, in England – bold man; in Ireland for O Hargadan, *Ó hArgadáin*, Ir. *argat*, *airgead* – silver, shining, or for HARDY. (Reaney, MacLysaght).

Traced by MacLysaght in Co. Galway.

In Newfoundland:

Early instance: John Hardyman, of Bonavista, 1789 (DPHW 70).

Modern status: In the Burin and Fortune Bay-Hermitage districts.

HARDING, a surname of England and Ireland, from the Old English personal name *Hearding* – hard, brave, warrior, hero, or from the English place name Haredon (Devon). (Reaney, Cottle, Spiegelhalter, MacLysaght).

Found widespread by Guppy, especially in Somerset and Wiltshire, and by MacLysaght in Co. Tipperary and adjoining counties in the 17th century, elsewhere as early as the 19th century.

In Newfoundland:

Family traditions: William (1793–1868), born at Bedford, England, alleged to be a deserter from the battle of Waterloo, settled at Collins Cove (Burin) (MUN Folklore). George, from Lancashire, settled at Burnt Islands; thence to Bonne Bay in 1858 (MUN Hist.).

Early instances: John Hardings, of Trinity, 1758 (DPHW 64); John Harding, of St. John's, 1763 (DPHW 26C); Martin, ? in possession of property at Twillingate, ? 1768 (CO 194.28); E., in possession of property in fishery at Portugal Cove, 1794–5 (Census 1794–5); Nathaniel, of Greenspond, 1817 (DPHW 76); William Harden, of Harbour Grace Parish, 1819 (Nfld. Archives HGRC); Robert Harding, of Harbour Grace Parish, 1819 (Nfld. Archives HGRC); John, of Richard's Harbour, 1835 (DPHW 30); ——, ? of Harbour Grace, 1837 (*Newfoundlander* 5 Jan 1837); George, blacksmith of Collins Cove, 1860 (DPHW 108); William, of Baker's Tickle, 1871 (Lovell); John and William, of Burin, 1871 (Lovell); George, blacksmith of Grand Bank, 1871 (Lovell); Richard, of Little Bay (Burin district), 1871 (Lovell).

Modern status: Scattered, especially at St. John's, Greenspond and Portugal Cove.

Place names: Harding Cove 49-04 53-34; Hardings Head 49-05 53-34.

HARDY, a surname of England, France, Ireland, Scotland and the Channel Islands, in Scotland also Hardie, originally from an Old German verb – to make hard, or a past participle – hardened, Middle English *hardi* – bold, courageous; or in Ireland for *Mac Giolla Deacair*, Ir. *deacair* – hard. (Reaney, Cottle, Black, MacLysaght, Dauzat, Turk). *See also* HARDIMAN.

Found widespread by Guppy, especially in Leicestershire, Rutlandshire and Nottinghamshire, by Spiegelhalter in Devon, and by MacLysaght in Connacht.

In Newfoundland:

Early instances: Edward, juror ? of St. John's, 1750 (CO 194.12); John, of Bonavista, 1792 (USPG); Simeon, of Furby's Cove, 1827 (DPHW 109); John, of Richard's Harbour, 1835 (DPHW 30); David, inspector of pickled fish at Jersey Harbour, 1844 (*Nfld. Almanac*, DPHW 104); Anne, of Broad Cove (now Duntara), 1855 (Nfld. Archives KCRC); Charles, planter of Pointe Enragée, 1858 (DPHW 104); James, storekeeper of Harbour Breton, 1859 (DPHW 104); Richard, of Rose Blanche, 1861 (DPHW 99); John and Thomas, of Corbin, 1871 (Lovell); John, of Freshwater (Placentia), 1871 (Lovell); John, of West Cul de Sac, 1871 (Lovell).

Modern status: A South Coast name, especially at Rose Blanche.

Place names: Hardy Cove 47-36 55-57, 47-38 56-10, 47-38 56-12, 47-38 56-14, 47-47 54-11, 47-48 55-51; —— Harbour 50-01 55-54; —— Point 47-38

56-12; —— Rocks 47-47 54-11; Hardy's Cove 47-40 55-40.

HARE, a surname of England, Scotland and Ireland; in England, from Old English *hara* – hare, a nickname for speed or timidity, or from *hær* – hair, a nickname from the ? colour of the hair, or from Old English *hær* – (dweller on the) stony-ground; in Scotland a variant of Hair, of the same origin as the Irish (O)Hare, *Ó hIr, Ó hÉir. See* HAIRE. (Reaney, Black, MacLysaght).

Traced by Spiegelhalter in Devon, and by Black in Ayrshire. MacLysaght traced (O)Hare in Co. Armagh.

In Newfoundland:

Early instances: Thomas, of St. John's Harbour, 1703 (CO 194.3); William, of Belleoram, 1815 (DPHW 109); ? E(l)isha, planter of Carbonear, 1819 (DPHW 48); John, of Grand Bank, 1828 (DPHW 109); James, of Lower Burgeo, 1847 (DPHW 101).

Modern status: In the Burgeo-La Poile district and at Corner Brook.

Place names: Some 38 place names contain the specific Hare, but few of these are likely to be from the surname.

HARFITT, a surname of England, from Old Norse *harfótr* – hare's foot, or some similar Old English nickname for a swift runner. Compare the forms BARFITT and BAR(E)FOOT. (Reaney, Cottle).

In Newfoundland:

Family tradition: Samuel Harfitt or Horfitt, ? from England, settled at Wandsworth (Burin district) ? in the mid-19th century (Family).

Modern status: Rare, at Lewin's Cove.

HARLICK, HORLICK, surnames of England, from Old English *hār* – grey, hoary and *locc* – lock (of hair). (Reaney).

In Newfoundland:

Early instances: Samuel Harlick, of Fair Island (Bonavista B.), 1846 (DPHW 76); Catherine, of Harbour Grace Parish, 1879 (Nfld. Archives HGRC).

Modern status: Harlick, rare, at St. John's; Horlick, at Fair Island (*Electors* 1955), Middle Brook (Bonavista B.), Trinity (Bonavista B.) and St. John's.

HARMON, a surname of England and Ireland, from the personal names, Old German *Hariman, Her(e)man*, Old French *Herman(t)* – army man, warrior; in Ireland, Harman is occasionally a variant of HARDIMAN. (Reaney, Cottle, MacLysaght).

Spiegelhalter traced Harman, Herman in Devon; MacLysaght traced Harman in Leinster and Harmon mainly in Co. Louth.

In Newfoundland:

Early instance: Thomas, ? of Northern Bay, 1841 (DPHW 54).

Modern status: Rare, at Hawkes Bay (*Electors* 1955).

HARNETT, a surname of England and Ireland; in England a variant of ARNOLD, ARNOT; in Ireland, (O)Hartnett, Harnet, *Ó hAirtnéada*. (Reaney, MacLysaght).

Traced by MacLysaght in Cos. Cork and Limerick.

In Newfoundland:

Family tradition: James (born 1794), from Lismore (Co. Waterford), who came to Newfoundland in 1817, was possibly the first settler on Allan's Island. (MUN Folklore, H.G. Harnett).

Early instances: James Harnett or Harnell, ? of St. John's, died ? 1795 (CO 194.40); William Harnet, of Harbour Grace Parish, 1817 (Nfld. Archives HGRC); James Hornett, fisherman of Exploits, 1821 (USPG); Elizabeth, of Change Islands, 1821 (USPG); John Harnett (1827–92), of Lord's Cove (Lord's Cove Cemetery); William Harnet, of Bonavista, 1832 (Nfld. Archives KCRC); William Harnett, of Seldom Come By, 1843 (DPHW 83); John and Maurice Harnot, of Lord's Cove (Burin district), 1871 (Lovell); Mark Harnet, of Wild Cove (Fogo district), 1871 (Lovell).

Modern status: Scattered, especially at Lord's Cove and Campbellton (Twillingate district).

HARNEY, a surname of Ireland, (O)Harney, *Ó hAthairne*, ? Ir. *athardha* – paternal. (MacLysaght).

Traced by MacLysaght in Connacht and Co. Tipperary.

In Newfoundland:

Early instances: James, from Waterford City, married at St. John's, 1814 (Nfld. Archives BRC); John Harny, of Harbour Grace Parish, 1824 (Nfld. Archives HGRC); Thomas Harney, of St. John's, 1832 (*Newfoundlander* 17 May 1832); James, trader of Burin, 1871 (Lovell).

Modern status: At Bell Island (*Electors* 1955).

HARNUM, a surname of England, from the English place name Harnham (Northumberland, Wiltshire). (Ekwall).

In Newfoundland:

Early instances: William Harnham, proprietor and occupier of fishing room at Heart's Delight, Winter

1800–01 (Census Trinity B.); William Harnum, planter of New Perlican, 1823 (DPHW 64B); James, planter of Hants Harbour, 1832 (DPHW 59A); Christiana, of Scilly Cove (now Winterton), 1856 (DPHW 59A).

Modern status: Scattered, especially in the Trinity South district.

HAROLD, a baptismal name and surname of England and Ireland, from the Old Norse personal name *Haraldr* or Old English *Hereweald* – army-power; in Ireland, also for the surnames Harrell and Hurrell. (Withycombe, Reaney, MacLysaght).

Traced by Reaney in Suffolk, by Spiegelhalter in Devon and by MacLysaght in Cos. Dublin and Limerick.

In Newfoundland:

Early instance: Thomas Harrold, planter of Twillingate, 1821 (USPG).

Modern status: At Corner Brook.

HARPER, a surname of England, Scotland and Ireland, from Old English *hearpere* – harper. (Reaney).

Found widespread by Reaney, especially in Buckinghamshire and Suffolk by Guppy, in Devon by Spiegelhalter; scattered in Scotland by Guppy; as Harper and Harpur in Co. Wexford, and as Harper in Ulster by MacLysaght.

In Newfoundland:

Early instances: Anthony, ? servant of Oderin, about 1730–35 (CO 194.9); N., of St. John's, 1831 (*Newfoundlander* 14 Jul 1831); Patrick, of Harbour Grace Parish, 1840 (Nfld. Archives HGRC); Patrick, ? of Harbour Grace, 1845 (*Newfoundlander* 16 Jan 1845).

Modern status: Rare, at Ship Cove (Burin district), Flat Bay (St. George's district), Stephenville (*Electors* 1955) and St. John's.

Place names: Harper Island (Labrador) 53-06 55-46; —— Ledge 49-42 54-43; Harper's Cove (Labrador) 52-50 55-48.

HARRIET, ? a variant of the surnames of England, Herriot, a diminutive of the baptismal name Henry, or of Heriot, etc. from the English place name Herriard (Hampshire). (Reaney). *See* HENRY and HERRIOTT.

In Newfoundland:

Early instance: Anne Rowley, of St. John's, 1819 (DPHW 26B).

Modern status: Rare, at Isle aux Morts (*Electors* 1955) (? for Herritt as in Tel. Dir. 1970).

HARRIGAN, a surname of Ireland, (O)Harrigan, in South and west Munster usually a variant of Horgan (*see* ORGAN), or for a former Leix sept *Ó hArragáin*. (MacLysaght).

In Newfoundland:

Early instances: Andrew, of Carbonear, 1803 (CO 199-18); Edmond, from Ballybrack Parish (unidentified) (Co. Waterford), married at St. John's, 1805 (Nfld. Archives BRC); Patrick Haragan, of Harbour Grace Parish, 1817 (Nfld. Archives HGRC); Margaret Harragan, of Bell Isle (now Bell Island), 1822 (Nfld. Archives BRC); Edward Horrigan, of Joe Batt's Arm, 1833 (Nfld. Archives KCRC); David Harrigan, of Little Fogo Islands, 1871 (Lovell); Helen, of St. John's, 1871 (Lovell).

Modern status: Rare, at Norris Arm (*Electors* 1955) and at Witless Bay.

Place names: Cape Harrigan or Tagaulik (Labrador), —— —— Harbour (Labrador), —— —— Island (Labrador) 55-51 60-21.

HARRINGTON, a surname of England and Ireland; in England from the English place name Harrington (Cumberland, Lincolnshire, Northamptonshire, Devon); in Ireland for *Ó hIongardail* or *Ó hArrachtáin*. (Cottle, MacLysaght).

Traced by Spiegelhalter in Devon and by MacLysaght in Connacht and Co. Kerry.

In Newfoundland:

Early instances: Mary, of St. John's, 1794–5 (Census 1794–5); Philip, ? Hannington or Harrington, one of 72 impressed men who sailed from Ireland to Newfoundland, ? 1811 (CO 194.51); Ellen Harrington, of Harbour Grace Parish, 1811 (Nfld. Archives HGRC); Joanna, from "Barerstone near Cork" (unidentified), Ireland, 1822 (Nfld. Archives BRC); Thomas, of Oderin, 1829 (*Newfoundlander* 28 Feb 1829); Daniel, ? of Harbour Grace, 1845 (*Newfoundlander* 9 Jan 1845); William, of Fermeuse, 1871 (Lovell); John, of Witless Bay, 1871 (Lovell).

Modern status: At St. John's and Carbonear.

HARRIS, a surname of England and Ireland – son of Harry (Henry); in Ireland also for the surnames Harrihy and Horohoe. (Reaney, Cottle, MacLysaght). *See* HENRY and *also* HARRISON.

Found widespread in England and especially as Harries in South Wales by Guppy; and usually in Ulster, but also in Co. Mayo, by MacLysaght.

In Newfoundland:

Early instances: John, of Bay Roberts, 1681 (CO 1); Henry, of St. John's Harbour, 1701 (CO 194.2);

Thomas, fisherman of St. John's or Petty Harbour, about 1739–43 (CO 194.11, 24); Wilton, of Trinity, 1757 (DPHW 64); Christopher, of Ochre Pit Cove, 1786, of Devil's (now Job's) Cove, 1791 (CO 199.18); John, servant of Battle Harbour, 1795 (MUN Hist.); Robert, of Burnt Point (Conception B.), 1797 (CO 199.18); Christopher, of Northern Bay, 1801, of Kettle Cove (Conception B.), 1804 (CO 199.18); James, of Bonavista, 1810 (DPHW 70); John, of Ragged Harbour (now Melrose), 1813 (DPHW 64); William, of Ferryland, 1818 (D'Alberti 28); Madeline, of Seal Cove (now New Chelsea), 1818 (Nfld. Archives T51); James Niner, of Brigus, 1822 (D'Alberti 32); Charles, of Catalina, 1822 (DPHW 70); Gregory, of Hants Harbour, 1823 (DPHW 58); D., of Carbonear, 1831 (*Newfoundlander* 14 Jul 1831); George, of Lamaline, 1835 (DPHW 109); Roger, of Bonne Bay (Fortune B.), 1835 (DPHW 30); George, of Open Hall, 1839 (DPHW 73A); John B., of Twillingate, 1845 (*Newfoundlander* 19 Jun 1845); Robert, of Upper Burgeo, 1845 (DPHW 101); George, of Hermitage Cove, 1846 (DPHW 102); George, from Shropshire, England, married at St. John's, 1847 (*Royal Gazette* 16 Nov 1847); Benjamin, of Grole, 1848 (DPHW 102); John, of Russell's Cove (now New Melbourne), 1850 (DPHW 59A); Charles, of Muddy Hole (now Maberly), 1851 (MUN Hist.); John, of Gander Bay, 1851 (DPHW 83); Henry, of Freshwater (Carbonear), 1855 (DPHW 49); William, of Mulley's Cove, 1856 (DPHW 52B); John, of Great Harbour (Burin district), 1856 (DPHW 104); Rev. Thomas, of Bird Island Cove (now Elliston), 1856 (MUN Hist.); James, of Ramea, 1858 (DPHW 101); Robert, of Little La Poile, 1860 (DPHW 99); Anna, of Harbour Grace, 1866 (Nfld. Archives HGRC); widespread in Lovell 1871.

Modern status: Widespread, especially at St. John's, New Chelsea, Jacques Fontaine and Bonavista.

Place name: Harris Hill 49-49 56-35.

HARRISON, a surname of England and Ireland – son of Harry (Henry); in Ireland, like HARRIS, also for the surnames Harrihy and Horohoe. (Reaney, Cottle, MacLysaght). *See* HENRY.

Found widespread in England by Guppy, and usually in Ulster, but also in Co. Mayo, by MacLysaght.

In Newfoundland:

Early instances: Samuel, agent at Little Placentia (now Argentia), 1780 (D'Alberti 6); Michael, of St. John's, 1797 (D'Alberti 6); John, of Burin, 1811 (D'Alberti 21); John, from Poole (Dorset), at Mortier, 1813 (H. P. Smith); Thomas, partner in firm of Thomas Ridley and Co. of Harbour Grace, died at Liverpool, 1839 (*Star and Conception B.J.* 1 May 1839); Nicholas, of Cornet (now Colinet) Islands, 1841 (*Newfoundlander* 6 May 1841); Gilbert H., a principal in the firm of Ridley, Harrison & Co., Harbour Grace, died at St. Helier, Jersey, 1849 (*Weekly Herald* 31 Oct 1849).

Modern status: Rare, at St. John's.

Place names: Harrison 48-59 57-47; Cape Harrison (Labrador) 54-57 57-57; —— Cove, —— Point 47-51 55-50.

HARSANT, a surname of England and France, from the Old German personal name *Herisint*, Old French *Hersent*, *Hersant*, containing the elements *army* and *truth*. (Reaney, Dauzat).

In Newfoundland:

Modern status: Rare, at Corner Brook.

HART, a surname of England and the Channel Islands, (O)Hart of Ireland, from Old English *heorot*, Middle English *hert* – hart, stag, or from the English place name Hart (Durham), or in Ireland for *Ó hAirt*, "from the Christian name *Art*." (Reaney, MacLysaght, Turk). *See also* HARTIGAN, HARTSON.

Found widespread, especially in Gloucestershire and Durham, by Guppy; as Hart(e) in Devon by Spiegelhalter; and in Co. Sligo by MacLysaght.

In Newfoundland:

Early instances: Joseph, of Trinity, 1759 (DPHW 64); Robert, of English Harbour (Trinity B.), 1773 (DPHW 64); —— of St. John's, 1778 (DPHW 26C); Patrick, from Dublin, Irish convict landed at Petty Harbour or Bay Bulls, 1789 (CO 194.38); Andrew, boatkeeper of Fermeuse, 1797 (D'Alberti 7); Edmond, of Harbour Grace Parish, 1821 (Nfld. Archives HGRC); Sylvia, from Kilkenny, married at St. John's, 1825 (Nfld. Archives BRC); George, of Hants Harbour, 1825 (DPHW 59); Joseph, planter of Salmon Cove (now Champneys), 1826 (DPHW 64B); Mary, of Ochre Pit Cove, 1829 (Nfld. Archives BRC); David, of Harbour Grace, 1831 (Nfld. Archives HGRC); Catherine, of Riders Harbour (Trinity B.), 1832 (Nfld. Archives KCRC); George, of Fogo, 1841 (DPHW 83); William, of Seal Cove (now New Chelsea), 1857 (DPHW 59); James, of Island Harbour (Fogo district), 1861 (DPHW 82); William, of Catalina, 1865 (DPHW 66); scattered in Lovell 1871.

Modern status: Scattered, especially at St. John's and in the Fogo district with large concentrations at Fogo and Horwood South.

Place names: Hart Head (Labrador) 54-12 58-25; —— Island 48-41 53-41; Hart's Island 49-40 54-46.

HARTERY, a variant of the surname of Ireland, (O)Hartry, *Ó hAirtrí*. (MacLysaght).

Traced by MacLysaght originally in Connacht, now in Cos. Waterford and south Tipperary.

In Newfoundland:

Family tradition: Five brothers of the surname Cartwright or Hartley, from England, settled at various places in Newfoundland: Bonavista Bay, St. John's, Cape Broyle, Portugal Cove South, and changed their name to HARTERY (MUN Folklore).

Early instances: Darby Hartry, of Harbour Grace, 1785 (CO 199.18); Michael Hatery, of Harbour Main, 1788 (CO 199-18); Demetrius Hartery, of St. John's, 1794 (M.F. Howley, *Ecclesiastical History*); William Hartrey, in possession of property in fishery at Portugal Cove, 1794–5 (Census 1794–5); Darby Hartry, from Dungarvan (Co. Waterford), dealer of Harbour Grace, deceased 1814 (*Royal Gazette* 10 Feb 1814); William Hart(e)ry, of Kings Cove, 1815 (Nfld. Archives RC); William Hartry, from Co. Waterford, planter of Portugal Cove, deceased 1815 (*Royal Gazette* 28 Sep 1815); William Hartery, member of the Bonavista South Board of Education, 1844 (*Nfld. Almanac*); Mary, of Keels, 1852 (Nfld. Archives KCRC); Catherine Hartry, of Gooseberry Islands (Bonavista B.), 1858 (Nfld. Archives KCRC); William Hart(e)ry, of Indian Arm (Bonavista B.), 1859 (Nfld. Archives KCRC); Con Hartery, schoolteacher of Cape Broyle, about 1860 (Dillon).

Modern status: Scattered, especially at Portugal Cove South and St. John's.

HARTIGAN, a surname of Ireland, (O)Hartigan, *Ó hArtagáin*, "formed from the Christian name *Art*." (MacLysaght). *See also* HART. Traced by MacLysaght in Cos. Clare and Limerick.

In Newfoundland:

Early instances: Denis, of St. John's, 1804 (Nfld. Archives BRC); Michael, of Placentia, 1871 (Lovell); Patrick and Thomas, of Rencontre (Fortune B.), 1871 (Lovell).

Modern status: Rare, at Placentia.

HARTLEY, a surname of England and Ireland, from the English place name in several counties including Devon and Dorset; in Ireland (O)Hartily, Hartley, usually for *Ó hArtghaile*, Ir. *Art* (baptismal name) and *gal* – valour. (Cottle, Maclysaght). *See also* HARTERY.

Traced by Guppy in Huntingdonshire, Lancashire and especially Yorkshire WR, by Spiegelhalter in Devon, and by MacLysaght in Co. Wexford.

In Newfoundland:

Early instances: John Harley, ? for Hartley, of North Harbour, John's Point, Tickles or Colinet, 1871 (Lovell); Francis, plasterer of St. John's, 1871 (Lovell).

Modern status: Rare, at St. John's and Dunville.

HARTMAN(N), surnames of Germany – strong, hard man.

In Newfoundland:

Modern status: Hartman, rare, at St. John's; Hartmann, unique, at St. John's.

HARTSON, a surname of England, ? son of HART, or ? from the English place names Hartshorn (Northumberland), Hartshoone (Derbyshire), Hardstone (Devon) or Hareston (Devon).

Spiegelhalter traced Harston in Devon.

In Newfoundland:

Early instance: John Hartstone, of Burin, 1871 (Lovell).

Modern status: Rare, in the Burin district and at Colinet.

HARTY, a surname of Ireland, (O)Harty, *Ó hAthartaigh*, modern *Ó hÁrtaigh*, ? Ir. *faghartach* – noisy; not the same as HEARTY. (MacLysaght).

Traced by MacLysaght principally in Cos. Cork and Tipperary.

In Newfoundland:

Early instances: Henry Hartey or Hortey, ? of St. John's, 1730 (CO 194.9); Thomas Harty, from Lismore (Co. Waterford), married at St. John's, 1801 (Nfld. Archives BRC); Edmund, from Temple Bradon (unidentified) (Co. Tipperary), fisherman of Capelin Bay (unspecified), deceased 1814 (*Royal Gazette* 27 Oct 1814); Edward, of Bonavista, 1825 (Nfld. Archives KCRC); Philip, of Heart's Content, 1825 (Nfld. Archives KCRC); William, of Kings Cove, 1828 (Nfld. Archives KCRC); Bartholomew, of Harbour Grace, 1829 (Nfld. Archives BRC); Philip, of Turks Cove, 1830 (Nfld. Archives KCRC); Mary, of Broad Cove (now Duntara), 1830 (Nfld. Archives KCRC); John, ? of Northern Bay, 1848 (DPHW 54); James, of Keels, 1860 (Nfld. Archives KCRC); David, farmer of Ochre Pit Cove, 1871 (Lovell); Thomas, of Western Bay, 1871 (Lovell).

Modern status: At Duntara and Gambo.

HARVEY, a baptismal name and surname of England, Scotland, Ireland and the Channel Islands, from the personal names Old French *Hervé*, Old Breton *Aeruiu, Hærviu* – battle worthy, introduced by the Bretons at the Norman Conquest, or occa-

sionally from Old German *Herewig* – army war; in Ireland also occasionally for *Ó hAirmheadhaigh*, ? Ir. *airmheadhach* – having a herd of cattle, or ? Ir. *airmed* – a measure of grain. (Withycombe, Reaney, Black, Cottle, MacLysaght, Turk). *See* HARVIEW.

Found widespread by Guppy, especially in Cornwall, Hampshire and Kent, and generally distributed (in a variety of forms) in Scotland, and by MacLysaght in Ulster, and Cos. Wexford and Galway.

In Newfoundland:

Family traditions: William and Bridget, from Sussex, England, settled at Cape Broyle in the early 18th century (MUN Folklore). George, from Jersey (Channel Islands), settled at Isle aux Morts (MUN Folklore).

Early instances: John Hervey, of Chapples [sic] Cove, 1681 (CO 1); William Harvey, of Trinity, 1708–09 (CO 194.4); Lawrence, of Petty Harbour, about 1739–43, of St. John's, 1751 (CO 194.11, 13, 24); John, in possession of property in fishery at Portugal Cove, 1794–5 (Census 1794–5); Michael, of Harbour Grace Parish, 1806 (Nfld. Archives HGRC); William Hervy, of Crocker's Cove (Carbonear), 1810 (DPHW 48); Thomas Harvey, from Torquay (Devon), married at St. John's, 1814 (Nfld. Archives BRC); Thomas, of Fortune Bay, 1815 (D'Alberti 25); Thomas, of Isle aux Morts, 1822 (Cormack); James, of Western Point (unidentified), 1823 (DPHW 26B); James, from Blackawton near Dartmouth, England, of St. John's, deceased 1829 (*Royal Gazette* 14 Jul 1829); George, of Point Blanche (Port aux Basques district), 1830 (DPHW 30); William Hervey, of Clown's Cove (Carbonear), 1831 (DPHW 48); William Harvey, planter of Freshwater (Carbonear), 1841 (DPHW 48); John, of Dead Island (Burgeo-La Poile district), 1842 (DPHW 101); William, of Pouch Cove, 1847 (DPHW 32); James, of Middle Bill Cove (Bonavista B.), 1854 (DPHW 76); George, seaman of Burgeo, 1855 (DPHW 101); scattered in Lovell 1871.

Modern status: Widespread, especially at St. John's, Isle aux Morts and Boswarlos.

Place names: Harvey Cove 47-32 55-46; —— Hill 47-33 55-46; —— Rock 49-46 54-17.

HARVIEW, a Newfoundland variant of the surname of France and the Channel Islands, Hervieu(x), itself a variant of Hervé. *See* HARVEY. (Dauzat).

Dauzat traced Hervieu(x) in Normandy and elsewhere.

In Newfoundland:

Early instance: ? Philip Le Arvy, of St. George's Bay, 1819 (Cormack).

Modern status: Rare, at Felix Cove, Winterhouse (Port-au-Port district) (*Electors* 1955) and St. George's.

HASKELL, a surname of England, a variant of Askell from the Old Norse personal name *Áskell* etc., a contracted form of *Ásketill*, or ? from the Old English personal name *Æscwulf*, or of the surname of Jersey (Channel Islands) HACQUOIL. (Reaney, Spiegelhalter, Turk). *See also* ANTLE.

Spiegelhalter traced Haskell and Haskoll in Devon.

In Newfoundland:

Early instances: ——, of Salvage, 1806 (Bonavista Register 1806); John Haskill, of Broad Cove (unspecified), (Conception B.), 1816 (D'Alberti 26); John Moore Haskell, married at St. John's, 1845 (DPHW 23); John Haskiel, of Carbonear, 1871 (Lovell); Henry Haskell, of Lamaline, 1871 (Lovell).

Modern status: Rare, at Lamaline (*Electors 1955*), Foxtrap and St. Lawrence.

HATCH, a surname of England and Ireland, from the English place name Hatch (Bedfordshire, Devon, Hampshire, Somerset and Wiltshire), or from OE *hæcce* – (dweller by the) hatch or gate, "generally one leading to a forest, sometimes a sluice." (Reaney, Spiegelhalter, MacLysaght 73).

Traced by Guppy in Somerset and Surrey, by Spiegelhalter in Devon, and by MacLysaght in Cos. Meath and Louth.

In Newfoundland:

Family tradition: Richard, from southern Ireland, settled at Red Head Cove (Conception B.) after 1850 (MUN Folklore).

Early instances: Obadiah, of St. John's, 1704 (CO 194.3); Richard, from Fanetshire [sic], Gillingham Parish, England, married at St. John's, 1820 (Nfld. Archives BRC); Richard, of Harbour Grace Parish, 1822 (Nfld. Archives HGRC); Edward, of ? Conne (Fortune B.), 1835 (DPHW 30); Richard, of ? Northern Bay, or ? Red Head Cove, 1838 (DPHW 54).

Modern status: Scattered, especially at Red Head Cove.

HATCHER, a surname of England – dweller by the hatch or gate. (Reaney). *See* HATCH.

In Newfoundland:

Early instances: James, of Harbour Grace Parish, 1819 (Nfld. Archives HGRC); Philip, of Hermitage Cove, 1830 (DPHW 109); George, of Furby's Cove, 1835 (DPHW 30); Charles, of Pushthrough, 1835

(DPHW 30); Grace, of Ramea, 1842 (DPHW 101); Benjamin, of Rose Blanche, 1860 (DPHW 99); John, of Eastern Point (Burgeo-La Poile district), 1860 (DPHW 99); George, of Bonne Bay, 1866 (DPHW 93); John, of Baker's Tickle, 1871 (Lovell); Thomas, of Lamaline, 1871 (Lovell); John, of Little Bay (Burgeo-La Poile district), 1871 (Lovell); Emmanuel (and others), of Lower Burgeo, 1871 (Lovell).

Modern status: Scattered, especially in the Burgeo-La Poile district with large concentrations at Rose Blanche and Ramea.

Place names: Hatcher Arm 47-35 55-25; —— Cove 47-27 55-46, 47-40 56-13, 47-43 55-52; —— Shoal 47-37 56-14; Hatcher's Cove 47-39 58-33 (or Hatchet's Cove) 48-02 53-48.

HATFIELD, a surname of England, from the English place name Hatfield (Essex, Herefordshire, Hertfordshire, Nottinghamshire, Worcestershire and Yorkshire), or from Old English *hæthfeld* – (dweller near the) field or open land overgrown with heather or some similar shrub. (Cottle, Ekwall).

Traced by Guppy in Derbyshire and Nottinghamshire.

In Newfoundland:

Early instance: George (and others), of Toad's (now Tors) Cove, 1871 (Lovell).

Modern status: Rare, at Tors Cove (*Electors* 1955), Placentia and St. John's.

HATT, a surname of England, from Old English *hætt* – (maker of) hat(s), or *hætt* – (dweller by the) hill; or from the English place name Hatt (Cornwall, Hampshire, Wiltshire). (Reaney, A. H. Smith).
Traced by Guppy in Oxfordshire.

In Newfoundland:

Modern status: Rare, at Grand Falls.

HATTIE, ? a surname of England, ? a diminutive of HATT.

In Newfoundland:

Modern status: Rare, at Norris Arm.

HATTON, a surname of England, Scotland and Ireland, from the place name Hatton in several counties in England and Scotland, or from Old English *hæthtūn* – place, farm on a heath; or in Scotland and Ireland, a shortened form of MacIlhatton, Gaelic *Mac Gille Chatáin* – devotee of Saint Catan, an obscure saint honoured in Scotland from Bute to Skye. (Cottle, Ekwall, Black, MacLysaght).

Traced by Guppy in Cheshire, Hertfordshire, Leicestershire, Rutlandshire and Suffolk; by

Spiegelhalter in Devon; by Black in Argyllshire; and by MacLysaght in Cos. Antrim and Derry.

In Newfoundland:

Early instances: Giles ? Hatton, of Newfoundland, ? 1706 (CO 194.24); Henry Hatten, of St. John's, 1806 (D'Alberti 16); George Hatton, from Pictou, Nova Scotia, married at St. John's, 1847 (*Royal Gazette* 7 Sep 1847).

Modern status: Unique, at St. John's.

HAWCO, a surname of Newfoundland and ? elsewhere in North America, a variant of the surname of the Channel Islands HACQUOIL, or ? of the surname of France Hautcoeur – (one possessing a) high heart, courageous. (Dauzat, Turk).

In Newfoundland:

Early instances: Thomas Hawko, of Chapel's Cove, 1785, of Harbour Main, 1802 (CO 199.18); Susanna Haco, of Harbour Grace Parish, 1807 (Nfld. Archives HGRC); Michael and Thomas Hawcoe, of Goulds Road (Brigus), 1871 (Lovell); John Hawcock, sailor of St. John's, 1871 (Lovell).

Modern status: Scattered, especially at Chapel's Cove, Holyrood and Mount Carmel.

Place names: Hawco Pond 47-24 53-07; Hawcos Pond 47-18 53-18.

HAWE, HAWSE, surnames of England, Hawe of Ireland, from Old English *haga* or Old Norse *hagi* – (dweller by the) enclosure, or from the English place name Halse (Devon), or a pet-form of a personal name such as *Hafoc* from the diminutive HAWKINS, or from a personal name, Old German *Hadewidio*, Old French *Haueis*, containing the elements *battle* and *wide*; in Ireland also a variant of (O)Haugh. (Reaney, Cottle, MacLysaght).

Hawes traced by Guppy in Buckinghamshire, Cambridgeshire and Suffolk, and by Spiegelhalter in Devon.

In Newfoundland:

Early instances: Pierce Hawe(s), ? of St. John's, 1796 (CO 194.39); Sarah Haw, of Harbour Grace Parish, 1812 (Nfld. Archives HGRC); William Hawe, from Co. Kilkenny, of Harbour Grace, 1844 (*Indicator* 27 Jul 1844); James Haw, farmer of Goulds Road (Brigus), 1871 (Lovell).

Modern status: Hawe, at St. John's and in the Port de Grave district; Hawse, rare, at Lewins Cove and St. Lawrence (Burin district).

HAWKE, a surname of England, from Old English *hafoc* – (keeper, trainer of) hawk(s); or one who paid rent in hawks; or one notorious for rapacity. (Reaney, Cottle).

Traced by Guppy in Cornwall and by Spiegelhalter in Devon.

In Newfoundland:

Early instance: Maria Hawks, of Harbour Grace, 1870 (Nfld. Archives HGRC).

Modern status: Unique, at Joe Batt's Arm (*Electors* 1955).

Place names: Some 12 places appear to bear the specific Hawke(s) from the surname.

HAWKER, a surname of England, from Old English *hafocere* – falconer, hawker.

Traced by Spiegelhalter in Devon.

In Newfoundland:

Early instances: Elinor, of Harbour Grace Parish, 1813 (Nfld. Archives HGRC); Benjamin, planter of Twillingate, 1823 (USPG); William, of Carbonear, 1871 (Lovell); John Hawkers, of Swain's Island (now Wesleyville) (Bonavista B.), 1871 (Lovell).

Modern status: Rare, at Carbonear.

HAWKINS, a surname of England and Ireland, a diminutive of the Old English personal name *Hafoc* or ? a diminutive of Hal (Henry); in Ireland also a variant of Haughan. (Reaney, Cottle, MacLysaght).

Traced by Guppy in the south Midlands and west, especially in Somerset and Gloucestershire.

In Newfoundland:

Early instances: Thomas Hawkin(g)s, of St. John's Harbour, 1701 (CO 194.2); P. Hawkins, of Placentia, 1724 (CO 194.7); Henry, of Greenspond, 1776 (CO 194.33); William, ? of Carbonear, 1810 (DPHW 48); Joanna Hawkins alias Curren, from Clashmore (Co. Waterford), married at St. John's, 1815 (Nfld. Archives BRC); John Hawkins, of Harbour Grace Parish, 1824 (Nfld. Archives HGRC); John, of Grand Bank, 1830 (DPHW 106); Thomas, of Vere (now Fair) Island, 1834 (DPHW 76); John, of Fogo, 1838 (DPHW 83); William, of Harbour Grace, 1851 (DPHW 76); George, of Ward's Harbour (now Beaumont North), 1854 (DPHW 92); John, of Twillingate, 1860 (DPHW 26D); George and John, of Change Islands, 1871 (Lovell).

Modern status: Scattered, especially at St. John's, Stephenville Crossing and in the Twillingate district.

Place name: Hawkins (or Buckle) Point (Labrador) 51-29 56-57.

HAWLEY, a surname of England, from the English place name Hawley (Kent, Hampshire). (Ekwall).

Traced by Guppy in Derbyshire.

In Newfoundland:

Early instances: John, of Corbin (Fortune B.),

1835 (DPHW 30); Catherine, of St. John's, 1871 (Lovell).

Modern status: Rare, at St. John's.

HAY, HAYE, surnames of England and France, Hay of Scotland and Ireland, from Old English *(ge)hæg* – (dweller by the) enclosure, or from the English place names Hay (Devon, Herefordshire), Hayes (Devon, Dorset), or from Old French *haie*, a common element in French place names, or from personal names, or a nickname, containing the Old English adjective *hēah* – high, tall. In Ireland, Hay, Norman *de la Haye*, "in modern times has widely become HAYES." (Reaney, Black, Dauzat, MacLysaght).

Hay was traced by Guppy in Lincolnshire, by Spiegelhalter in Devon, and by MacLysaght in Co. Wexford. Guppy found Hay scattered in Scotland.

In Newfoundland:

Early instances: George T. Haye, of St. John's, 1811, land in possession of family for nearly 50 years, that is, about 1761 (D'Alberti 21); Peter, of Bay Bulls, 1793 (USPG); Adam Alexander Hay, from Blandford (Dorset), married at St. John's, 1858 (DPHW 26D); James (and others), of Bonavista, 1871 (Lovell).

Modern status: Hay, Haye, rare, at St. John's.

Place names: Hay occurs as the specific in 9 place names, but probably not from the surname.

HAYDEN, HAYDON, surnames of England, Hayden or Headon of Ireland; in England from a common English place name Haydon, in Ireland (O)Hayden, *Ó hEideáin.* (Cottle, MacLysaght).

Guppy traced Hayden and Haydon in Devon and Hertfordshire; MacLysaght traced (O)Hayden in Co. Carlow.

In Newfoundland:

Early instances: Dan Haden, servant of Harbour Main, 1755 (MUN Hist.); Daniel Headon, of St. John's, 1765 (DPHW 26C); Mary Headen, from Kilnenall [sic], Cashel (Co. Tipperary), married at St. John's, 1802 (Nfld. Archives BRC); Edmond, of Harbour Grace Parish, 1814 (Nfld. Archives HGRC); Richard Haydon, ? of Broad Cove (now St. Phillip's), 1821 (DPHW 26D); —— Hayden, ? of Harbour Grace, 1837 (*Newfoundlander* 5 Jan 1837); Michael, of Barren Island (now Bar Haven), 1871 (Lovell); Joseph Haydon, planter of Twillingate, 1871 (Lovell); Thomas Headon, of Caplin Bay (now Calvert), 1871 (Lovell); Patrick Headen, of Petit Forte (Placentia B.), 1871 (Lovell); Richard and Timothy, traders of Upper Small Point (now Kingston), 1871 (Lovell).

Modern status: Hayden, scattered, especially at Petit Forte and Cape Broyle; Haydon, unique, at Gander (*Electors* 1955).

Place names: Cappahayden 46-52 52-57; Haydon Island 48-12 53-32; —— Point 48-12 53-33.

HAYE. *See* HAY

HAYES, a surname of England, Ireland and Guernsey (Channel Islands), of the same origin as HAY(E), or from Old English **hæs* – (dweller by the) brushwood, or from the English place names Hayes (Devon, Dorset, Kent, Middlesex), Hays (Sussex); in Ireland, also for (O)Hea, *Ó hAodha.* (Reaney, MacLysaght, Turk).

Traced by Guppy in Cheshire, Derbyshire, Lancashire, Oxfordshire, Somerset, Wiltshire and Worcestershire, by Spiegelhalter in Devon, and by MacLysaght especially in Munster.

In Newfoundland:

Family tradition: Elizabeth Hayes (1819–83), born at Bryant's Cove (MUN Geog.).

Early instances: Timothy Haize, of St. John's, 1756 (DPHW 26C); James Hays, of Brigus, 1790 (CO 199.18); Peter, in possession of property at Petty Harbour, 1794–5 (Census 1794–5); James Hay(e)s, of Salmon Cove (now Avondale), 1798, of Kit Hughes (Kitchuses), 1799 (CO 199.18); James Hay(e)s or Hase, of Harbour Grace Parish, 1806 (Nfld. Archives HGRC); Thomas ? Hays, one of 72 impressed men who sailed from Ireland to Newfoundland, ? 1811 (CO 194.51); Michael Hays, from Co. Wexford, married at St. John's, 1812 (Nfld. Archives BRC); James, from Co. Kilkenny, publican of St. John's, deceased 1815 (*Royal Gazette* 9 Mar 1815); James Hayse, of Tilton Harbour (now Tilting), 1819 (Nfld. Archives KCRC); Thomas, of King's Cove, 1820 (Nfld. Archives KCRC); Mary Hay(e)s or Hayse, of Broad Cove (now Duntara), 1823 (Nfld. Archives KCRC); John Hayse, of Harbour Grace, 1828 (Nfld. Archives BRC); Nicholas Hayes, of Little Placentia (now Argentia), 1828 (*Newfoundlander* 29 May 1828); Patrick, of Ferryland, 1837 (Nfld. Archives BRC); Richard, from Tramore (Co. Waterford), of Port de Grave, 1844 (*Indicator* 24 Aug 1844); Edward, farmer of Placentia Road, 1849 (*Newfoundlander* 25 Oct 1849); Mary Ann, of Bay Roberts, 1857 (DPHW 26D); widespread in Lovell 1871.

Modern status: Widespread, especially at St. John's and Brigus South.

Place names: Hayes Cone (Hill) (Labrador) 56-41 61-10; —— Point (Labrador) 56-42 61-10.

HAYLEY. *See* HAILEY

HAYMAN, a surname of England, from ? Old English *(ge)hæg* – (dweller by the) enclosure, or ? *hēg, hig* – (seller of) hay, or ? *hēah* – high, tall, or a variant of HAMMOND. (Reaney).
Traced by Guppy in Devon.
In Newfoundland:
Early instances: Thomas, boatkeeper of St. John's Harbour, 1682 (CO 1); Samuel, of Bell Island, 1709 (CO 194.4); Benjamin, fisherman of Fox Island (Burgeo-La Poile district), 1840 (DPHW 101); Abraham, planter of Rose Blanche, 1871 (Lovell).
Modern status: At St. Davids (St. George's district) and in the Burgeo-La Poile district including Fox Island.

HAYNES. *See* HAINES

HAYTER, a surname of England from the English place name Hayter (Devon) or dweller on the height or top of the hill. (Reaney).
Traced by Guppy in Dorset.
In Newfoundland:
Early instances: John, of Fogo, Twillingate or Tilton (now Tilting), 1771 (CO 194.30); John Haiter (later Hayter), planter of Trinity, 1830 (DPHW 64B); Charles Hayter, fisherman of Herring Neck, 1850, of Gut Arm, 1851, of Stone Harbour, 1856 (DPHW 85).
Modern status: Scattered, especially at Trinity.

HAYWARD, a surname of England, from Old English *hege-weard* – keeper of the fence or hedge, or *(ge)hægweard* – enclosure-protector, an official who supervised land under crops and controlled straying cattle. (Reaney, Cottle). *See also* HOWARD.
Traced by Guppy in the Midlands and South, especially in Suffolk and Wiltshire.
In Newfoundland:
Early instances: Elizabeth, of Carbonear, 1769, "property in possession of the Family for 61 years," that is, 1708 (CO 199.18); Will (and others), of Bonavista, 1792 (USPG); Francis, merchant of St. Mary's Bay, 1804 (D'Alberti 14); William, of St. John's, 1806 (CO 194.45); Thomas, of Greenspond, 1815 (DPHW 76); Mr. Justice (1819–85), born at Harbour Grace (Mott); Mary, of Kings Cove, 1822 (Nfld. Archives KCRC); Susan, baptized at Gooseberry Island (Bonavista B.), 1830, aged 17 (DPHW 76); William, of Tickle Cove (Bonavista B.), 1835 (DPHW 73A); John Will, planter of Trinity, 1835 (DPHW 64B); James, of Catalina, 1841, of Little

Catalina, 1845 (DPHW 67); John, of Garia, 1857 (DPHW 98); scattered in Lovell 1871.
Modern status: Widespread, especially at Bonavista, St. Vincent's and St. John's.
Place names: Hayward Cove 49-33 54-53; Hayward's Bight 49-31 55-48; —— Cove 48-52 53-39; —— Head 49-31 55-47; —— Gull Island 49-30 55-46.

HAZELTINE, a surname of England, one of 26 variants, from the English place names Heselden (Durham), Haselden (Sussex), Haslingden (Lancashire), Hazledon Farm (Wiltshire), Hazelton (Gloucestershire), or dweller in a hazel valley, or confused with Hazelton. (Reaney, Cottle).
In Newfoundland:
Early instance: Thomas Haslendine or Hasseltine, of Brigus, 1849 (DPHW 35).
Modern status: Rare, at Brigus.

HEAD, HEDD, surnames of England, Head(e) of Ireland, from Old English *hēafod* – head (a nickname), or (dweller by the) promontory, hill, source of a stream, or head of a valley. (Reaney, MacLysaght 73).
Guppy traced Head in Sussex, Spiegelhalter in Devon. MacLysaght traced Head(e) formerly in Cos. Meath, Tipperary, Waterford and Cork and today in east Galway.
In Newfoundland:
Early instances: Stephen Head, proprietor and occupier of fishing room at Grates Cove, Winter 1800–01 (Census Trinity B.); William, married at St. John's, 1806 (DPHW 23); Henry, planter of Fogo, 1808–16 (MUN Hist.); Henry, of Joe Batts Arm, 1817 (Nfld. Archives KCRC); John Heade, of Harbour Grace Parish, 1819 (Nfld. Archives HGRC); John Heads, planter of Bird Island Cove (now Elliston), 1824 (DPHW 72); William Head, planter of New Perlican, 1824 (DPHW 64B); Henry, of Tilting Harbour (now Tilting), 1829 (Nfld. Archives KCRC); Humphrey, of Ragged Harbour (Labrador), 1853 (DPHW 39); James, of Lance Cove (now Brownsdale), 1857 (DPHW 59); Lawrence, of Fortune Harbour, 1871 (Lovell); Henry and James, miners of Tilt Cove, 1871 (Lovell).
Modern status: Head, scattered, especially at Joe Batts Arm and Comfort Cove; Hedd, rare, at Bell Island and St. John's.
Place names (not necessarily from the surname): Head Harbour 49-29 55-41, 48-35 58-55, 49-30 55-41; —— Shoal 47-25 55-41; Head's Pond 49-31 55-43.

HEADGE, HEDGE(S), surnames of England, from Old English *hecg* – (dweller by the) hedge(s) or enclosure(s). (Reaney).

Guppy traced Hedges in Berkshire, Buckinghamshire, Hertfordshire and Oxfordshire.

In Newfoundland:

Early instance: John Hedge, planter of Carbonear, 1846 (DPHW 48).

Modern status: Headge, at Stephenville and Gander; Hedge, rare, at Green Island Cove (St. Barbe district); Hedges, at Grand Falls, Carbonear and St. John's.

HEALE, a surname of England, from the English place names Hele and Heal(e), common in the south and west, especially in Devon, or Middle English *hēle* – (dweller in a) nook, secluded place. (Reaney).

Guppy traced Heal(e) in Devon and Somerset.

In Newfoundland:

Early instances: Edward M. Heal, of St. John's, 1851 (*Newfoundlander* 10 Jul 1851); William Heale, of Quidi Vidi, 1858 (DPHW 29); Henry Heal, of Black Island, 1871 (Lovell).

Modern status: At St. John's.

HEALEY, HEALY, surnames of England, (O)Healy, Hely of Ireland; in England from the English place name Healey (Yorkshire, Lancashire, Northumberland) or Heeley (Yorkshire); in Ireland for *Ó hÉalaighthe* – ingenious, in Munster, or *Ó hÉilidhe* – claimant, in north Connacht. (Ekwall, MacLysaght).

Guppy traced Heal(e)y in Buckinghamshire and Lincolnshire, and also Heley in Buckinghamshire; MacLysaght traced (O)Healy, Hely in Cos. Cork and Sligo.

In Newfoundland:

Family traditions: ——, from Co. Tipperary, settled at Lamaline before 1817 (MUN Folklore). ——, from Ireland, settled at Fox Harbour (Placentia B.), about 1806 (MUN Hist.).

Early instances: Pearce Healy, servant of Harbour Main, 1779 (MUN Hist.); Joseph, of Chapel's Cove, 1781 (CO 199.18); Edmund, from Kilmachae (for Kilmacow) (Co. Kilkenny), married at St. John's, 1793 (Nfld. Archives BRC); William Healey, of Trinity Bay, 1794 (DPHW 64); Peter Healy, of Carbonear, 1797 (CO 199.18); James, of Holyrood Head, 1798 (CO 199.18); Thomas, of Cupids, 1802 (CO 199.18); Mary, of Harbour Grace Parish, 1811 (Nfld. Archives HGRC); Michael Heal(e)y, of Ragged Harbour (now Melrose), 1826, of Catalina, 1829 (Nfld. Archives KCRC); Mary Healy, of Witless Bay,

1828 (Nfld. Archives BRC); Joseph, of Tilting Harbour (now Tilting), 1829 (Nfld. Archives KCRC); Joseph, of Fogo, 1830 (Nfld. Archives KCRC); Jane, of Bonavista, 1834 (Nfld. Archives KCRC); Matthew, of Blackhead Bay, married at St. John's, 1837 (Nfld. Archives BRC); Patrick, of Harbour Grace, 1866 (Nfld. Archives HGRC); scattered in Lovell 1871.

Modern status: Healey, scattered, especially at Holyrood and Fox Harbour; Healy, rare, at St. John's.

Place names: Healey's Pond 47-25 53-15, 47-35 52-51; Healy's Cove 47-24 53-09.

HEANEY, a surname of Ireland, (O)Heaney, Heeney, *Ó hÉanna*. (MacLysaght).

Traced by MacLysaght in Co. Armagh.

In Newfoundland:

Family tradition: ——, was an early Irish settler at Bird Island Cove (now Elliston) (MUN Hist.).

Early instances: Richard Heany, from Co. Waterford, married at St. John's, 1805 (Nfld. Archives BRC); Richard Heaney, publican of St. John's, 1806 (CO 194.45); Pierce Heaney or Heney, of Kings Cove, 1816 (Nfld. Archives KCRC); Mary Heany, of Open Hole (now Open Hall), 1830 (Nfld. Archives KCRC); Thomas Heane, of Harbour Grace Parish, 1831 (Nfld. Archives HGRC); John Heaney, Haney or Hainy, of Plate Cove, 1850 (Nfld. Archives KCRC); Patrick Heany, of Red Cliff Island (Bonavista B.), 1865 (Nfld. Archives KCRC).

Modern status: Rare, at Stock Cove and Plate Cove East (Bonavista B.).

HEARN, a variant of the surname of England, Hern(e) etc., Hearne in Ireland, from the English place names Herne (Kent, Bedfordshire), Hirn (Hampshire), Hearn Farm (Devon), or from Old English *hyrne* – (dweller in the) nook or corner of land or in a bend; in Ireland also a variant of Ahearne in Co. Waterford (*see* AHEARN). (Reaney, Spiegelhalter, MacLysaght).

Guppy traced Hearn in Devon and Essex, Hern(e) in Devon and Norfolk; Matheson traced Hearn(e) mainly in Co. Waterford, but it has also been found in Cos. Wexford, Cork and Tipperary.

In Newfoundland:

Family traditions: James Hearn (formerly Ahearn) (–1855), from Carrick-on-Suir (Co. Tipperary), settled at Harbour Grace in 1798, thence to Brigus (MUN Folklore). —— Heurn, escaped from an Irish prison ship at Ferryland in 1734 and settled at Bay Bulls (MUN Folklore).

Early instances: Timothy Hearne, of St. John's, 1771 (DPHW 26C); Edward, cooper of Quidi Vidi 1794–5, "8 years in Newfoundland," that is, 1786–7 (Census 1794–5); David Hearn, agent at Bay Bulls, 1786 (CO 194.36); Philip, of Placentia, 1794 (D'Alberti 5); Timothy Hearn(e), of Bryant's Cove, 1794 (CO 199.18); James Hearn, of Colliers, 1798 (CO 199.18); John, from Ballyhack (Co. Wexford), married at St. John's, 1803 (Nfld. Archives BRC); Jeremiah, from Waterford, shopkeeper of St. John's, 1805, deceased 1812 (D'Alberti 15, *Royal Gazette* 14 Nov 1811, 22 Oct 1812); John, of Harbour Grace Parish, 1806 (Nfld. Archives HGRC); Patrick, of Ragged Harbour (now Melrose), 1817 (Nfld. Archives KCRC); James, of Ferryland, 1820 (Nfld. Archives BRC); Patrick, of Careless (now Kerleys) Harbour, 1825 (Nfld. Archives KCRC); John, of St. John's, 1830, of St. Mary's Bay, 1843 (Basilica Records, St. John's, A.J. Hearn); Patrick Hearne, from Co. Cork, married at Riders Harbour (Trinity B.), 1830 (Nfld. Archives KCRC); Patrick Hearn, of Harbour Grace, 1830 (Nfld. Archives HGRC); James, from Carrick-on-Suir (Co. Tipperary), of Brigus, 1844 (*Indicator* 24 Aug 1844); Patrick O'Hearn, shoemaker of St. John's, 1871 (Lovell); Hearn, widespread in Lovell 1871.

Modern status: Scattered, especially at St. John's, Petty Harbour, Bay Bulls, Harbour Grace and Colliers.

HEARTY, a surname of Ireland (O)Hearty, *Ó hAghartaigh*, not the same as HARTY. (MacLysaght).

Traced by MacLysaght in Cos. Louth and Monaghan.

In Newfoundland:

Early instances: Matthew, of St. John's, 1780 (D'Alberti 1); Michael and John, planters of Bonavista, 1789 (CO 194.38).

Modern status: Rare, at Turk's Cove (*Electors* 1955) and St. John's.

HEATER, a surname ? of England, ? a variant of Heather – dweller on the heath, or ? of HAYTER.

In Newfoundland:

Early instance: George, planter of Harbour Grace, 1834 (DPHW 43).

Modern status: Unique, at St. John's.

HEATH, a surname of England and Ireland, from Old English *hæth* – (dweller on the) heath, or from the English place name in 10 counties including 12 occurrences in Devon.

Traced by Guppy in 8 counties, especially

Berkshire, Staffordshire and Warwickshire, by Spiegelhalter in Devon, and by MacLysaght in Dublin.

In Newfoundland:

Early instances: Richard, witness at St. John's, ? 1752 (CO 194.3); Thomas, of Fogo, 1803 (D'Alberti 13); Thomas, of Hare Bay (Fogo district), 1840 (DPHW 83); George, fisherman of Port de Grave, 1842 (DPHW 39); Robert, of Tilt Cove, 1871 (Lovell); George and James Hearth, of Ward's Harbour (now Beaumont North), 1871 (Lovell).

Modern status: Scattered, especially at Beaumont.

Place name: Heath Lake (Labrador) 53-02 66-58.

HEBBARD, HIBBARD, surnames of England, for the baptismal name and surname, Herbert, "with loss of the first *r*." (Reaney). *See* HARBIN.

In Newfoundland:

Early instances: John Hebbard, of Bonavista, 1807 (DPHW 70); Charles Hibbert, of Lower Burgeo, 1860 (DPHW 101) .

Modern status: Hebbard, rare, at St. John's; Hibbard, unique, at Stephenville.

HEDD. *See* HEAD

HEDDERSON, a variant, apparently not recorded elsewhere, of ? EDISON.

In Newfoundland:

Early instances: James, of Colliers, 1768 (CO 199.18); James Edderson, of Turk's Gut (now Marysvale), 1796 (CO 199.18); James Hederson, of Brigus, 1816 (DPHW 34); Margaret Hedderson, of Harbour Grace Parish, 1821 (Nfld. Archives HGRC); Henry Hedeson, fisherman of Cupids, 1841 (DPHW 39); John Heddeson, miner of Tilt Cove, 1871 (Lovell).

Modern status: In the White Bay North and South districts and at St. John's.

HEDGE(S). *See* HEADGE

HEFFERAN, HEFFERN, variants of the surnames of Ireland (O)Heffron, Hefferan, *Ó Éimhrín* or *Ó hUidhrín*, sometimes confused with HEFFERNAN. (MacLysaght).

Traced by MacLysaght in Cos. Mayo and Offaly.

In Newfoundland:

Family tradition: Frederick Heffern, originally Heffernan, of Salvage in the late 19th century (MUN Folklore).

Early instances: George Hefferan, of Port de Grave, 1755 (CO 199.18); Denis Hefferna, from

Cashel (Co. Tipperary), married at St. John's, 1806 (Nfld. Archives BRC); John Hefren, from Lismore (Co. Waterford), married at St. John's, 1822 (Nfld. Archives BRC); Mary Hefferen, of Trinity, 1833 (Nfld. Archives KCRC); William Heffer(e)n, planter of Bonavista, 1845, of Barrow Harbour, 1846 (DPHW 72); James Hepfron, of Kings Cove Parish, 1848 (Nfld. Archives KCRC); Thomas Hefferan, of Fermeuse, 1871 (Lovell); Michael Hefferon, of Southeast Bight (Placentia B.), 1871 (Lovell); Thomas Hefferen, of Harbour Grace Parish, 1874 (Nfld. Archives HGRC).

Modern status: Hefferan, scattered; Heffern, in the Bonavista North and South districts.

Place names: Heffern's Cove 48-34 53-54; —— —— Pond 48-33 53-55.

HEFFERMAN, a surname of England, apparently not recorded elsewhere, – ? keeper of the heifers, young cows (Compare Bestman – herdsman, Bullman – bullherd, Coltman – keeper of colts, Palfreyman – keeper of the palfreys, saddle-horses); or ? a Newfoundland variant of HEFFERAN and HEFFERNAN.

In Newfoundland:

Early instances: Michael, of Maddox Cove (St. John's district), 1871 (Lovell); Henry, from England, of Bloom Cove (Bonavista South district), 1882, of Port Blandford, 1889 (DPHW 80, MUN Hist.).

Modern status: Scattered, especially in the St. John's South district.

HEFFERN. *See* HEFFERAN

HEFFERNAN, a surname of Ireland, (O)Heffernan, *Ó hIfearnáin.* (MacLysaght). *See also* HEFFERMAN, HEFFERAN.

Traced by MacLysaght on the Limerick-Tipperary border.

In Newfoundland:

Family tradition: Frederick Heffern, originally Heffernan, of Salvage in the late 19th century (MUN Folklore).

Early instances: John, of Harbour Grace, 1792 (USPG); John, of Harbour Main, 1797 (CO 199.18); William, from Co. Tipperary, married at St. John's, 1799 (Nfld. Archives BRC); John, one of 72 impressed men who sailed from Ireland to Newfoundland, ? 1811 (CO 194.51); Maria, of Harbour Grace Parish, 1812 (Nfld. Archives HGRC); John, of Trinity, 1820 (Nfld. Archives KCRC); Mary, of Petty Harbour, 1828 (Nfld. Archives BRC); T., of St. John's, 1832 (*Newfoundlander* 20 Sep 1832); John (and others), of Shoal Bay (Ferryland), 1871 (Lovell).

Modern status: At St. John's.

HEFFERTON, ? a surname of England, ? from the English place name Heatherton (Somerset), or ? from an unidentified English place name – the place where heifers were bred or raised.

In Newfoundland:

Family tradition: Robert, from Devon, settled at Bonavista in 1820 (MUN Folklore).

Early instances: James, of Greenspond, 1818 (DPHW 76); Edward, of Pinchard's Island (Bonavista B.), 1862 (DPHW 79); Edward and John Efferton, planters of Inner Islands (now Newtown), (Bonavista B.), 1871 (Lovell).

Modern status: At Newtown and St. John's.

HEFFORD. *See* EFFORD

In Newfoundland:

Early instances: William Heyford (spelt Hettford in 1681), of New Perlican, 1675 (CO 1); John Hayford or Heyfords, of St. John's, 1704–08 (CO 194.3, 4); William Hefford, of Trinity Bay, 1773 (DPHW 64); John, of Port de Grave, 1797 (DPHW 48); E. Heffard, proprietor and occupier of fishing room at New Perlican, Winter 1800–01 (Census Trinity B.); ——, proprietor and occupier of fishing room, New Harbour, Winter 1800–01 (Census Trinity B.); John, fisherman of Trinity, 1842 (DPHW 64B).

Modern status: Scattered, especially at New Harbour.

HELLIER, HELLYER, HILLIER, HILLYER, surnames of England and the Channel Islands, in England from Old English *helian* – to cover, roof, hence a slater, tiler, ? thatcher; in the Channel Islands, and as Helier, Hellier in France, from St. Hilarius, bishop of Poitiers. (Reaney, Cottle, Dauzat, Turk).

Guppy traced Hellier and Hellyer in Cornwall, Devon, Dorset and Somerset, Hellyer in Cornwall, Hillier in Hampshire, Monmouthshire and Wiltshire.

In Newfoundland:

Family tradition: The Hills of Griquet now known as Hilliers (MUN Folklore).

Early instances: Richard Hellier, fisherman of St. John's, 1794–5, "31 years in Newfoundland" that is, 1763–4 (Census 1794–5); James Halyer, of New Harbour (Trinity B.), 1774 (DPHW 64); Edward Hellyer or Hellier, of Battle Harbour (Labrador), 1787, of Caribou Tickle, 1789–95 (MUN Hist.); James Hillier, of Trinity, 1788 (DPHW 64); John, of Bonavista, 1792 (USPG); C. Hillyer, ? of Port de Grave, 1797 (Nfld. Archives T22); James Hillier, proprietor and occupier of fishing room at New

Harbour (Trinity B.), Winter 1800–01 (Census Trinity B.); John or George Hellyar or Hellier, from Buckland Newton (Dorset), apprenticed to John King of Bradley's Cove (Conception B.), 1812 (Dorset County Record Office per Kirwin); Edward Hilliar, of Twillingate, 1823 (USPG); Charles Hillier, of Lamaline, 1825 (DPHW 109); Anne Hillyer, baptized at Greenspond, 1830, aged 86 years (DPHW 76); George Hellyear, planter of Crocker's Cove (Carbonear), 1831 (DPHW 48); Giles Hilliar or Hilier, of Hants Harbour, 1841, 1848 (DPHW 58, 59A); Edward Hillier, of Fortune, 1850 (DPHW 106); Thomas Hellier or Hillyer, of Brunette, 1855 (DPHW 104); Henry Hilyear or Hil(l)yard, fisherman of Freshwater (Carbonear), 1855 (DPHW 49); Manuel Hillier, ? from France, of Point aux Gauls, 1860 (DPHW 107, MUN Folklore); Charles, of Church Side (Burin district), 1860 (DPHW 107); James Hillier and Thomas Hellier, of Griquet, 1871 (Lovell); Charles (and others) Hillier, of Muddy Hole (Fogo district), 1871 (Lovell).

Modern status: Hellier, rare; Hellyer, rare, at St. John's; Hillier, widespread, especially at St. John's, Point aux Gaul, Lamaline, Campbellton and Griquet.

Place names: Hillier Rock 46-51 55-42; Hillier's Harbour 54-47 56-02.

HELLINGS, a surname of England, from the English place name Healing (Lincolnshire), or a variant of Elion, Helin, etc. from the French place name Helléan (Morbihan). (Reaney).

Traced by Reaney in Somerset.

In Newfoundland:

Early instances: William Helling, of Temple Bay, 1782 (D'Alberti 2); Charles Hellings, of Fogo, 1803 (D'Alberti 13); Robert, of Eastern Tickle, Fogo, 1857 (DPHW 83).

Modern status: Unique, at Fogo (*Electors* 1955).

HELLYER. *See* HELLIER

HELPARD, HELPERT, variants of the baptismal name and surname of England ALBERT, from the Old German personal name *Adalbert,* containing the elements *noble* and *bright.* Withycombe found Halbert common on the Scottish borders.

In Newfoundland:

Modern status: Helpard, rare, at St. John's; Helpert, in the Placentia West district (*Electors* 1955), at Freshwater (Placentia) and St. John's.

HEMEON, ? a surname of Syria-Lebanon, of unknown origin.

In Newfoundland:

Modern status: At Botwood.

HEMMENS, a surname of England, a variant of Hemans (as in Mrs. F. D. Hemans, author of "The Boy Stood on the Burning Deck"), ? from an obsolete baptismal name, *Emayn* or *Imania.* (Bardsley).

Traced by Bardsley in Yorkshire.

In Newfoundland:

Modern status: At St. John's.

HENDER, a surname of England, from the English place name Hendra (Cornwall) – old farm, which occurs in 27 localities in that county. (Spiegelhalter). *See* INDER.

Traced by Spiegelhalter in Devon.

In Newfoundland:

Modern status: At Middle Brook (Bonavista North district).

HENDERSON, a surname of England, Scotland and Ireland – son of Henry, with an intrusive *d* as in the surname HENDRY. (Cottle, MacLysaght). *See* HENRY.

Traced by Guppy in Northumberland, Durham, Cumberland and Westmorland, and found widespread in Scotland, especially in the south. Found by MacLysaght in Ulster.

In Newfoundland:

Early instances: William, ? of Port de Grave, 1784 (D'Alberti 1, Nfld. Archives T22); James, of St. John's, 1797 (DPHW 26D); William, of Harbour Grace, 1797 (CO 199.18); Peter (–1829), merchant of St. John's, died at Rosebank (Stirlingshire) (*Newfoundlander* 29 Oct 1829); John, of Grandy's Brook, 1871 (Lovell).

Modern status: At The Reach (Burgeo-La Poile district), Corner Brook and St. John's.

HENDRICK, a variant of the surnames of Ireland (O)Henrick, Han(d)rick, *Mac Annraic,* "from a Norse personal name cognate with Henry." (MacLysaght).

Traced by MacLysaght in Co. Wexford.

In Newfoundland:

Early instances: James Hanrick, from Ireland to Newfoundland, 1809 (*Royal Gazette* 30 Jul 1812); Patrick Henrick, from Ireland to Newfoundland, 1811 (*Royal Gazette* 2 Jul 1812); Patrick Henrihik [sic], of Harbour Grace Parish, 1819 (Nfld. Archives HGRC); Margaret Henrick, married at St. John's, 1832 (Nfld. Archives BRC); Thomas Hanrick, of St. John's, 1858 (*Newfoundlander* 29 Mar 1858); James, fisherman of Placentia, 1871 (Lovell).

Modern status: Hendrick, unique, at Placentia (*Electors* 1955) and Hendricks, unique, at St. John's.

HENDRY, a surname of Scotland and Ireland, from Old French *Henri* – Henry, with an intrusive *d*. (Reaney, Black). *See* HENRY.

Traced by Black especially in Ayrshire and Fifeshire, and by MacLysaght in Co. Armagh.

In Newfoundland:

Early instance: William, ? labourer of St. John's, 1779 (CO 194.34).

Modern status: At St. John's.

HENLEY, a surname of England and Ireland; in England from the English place name Henley (Somerset, Dorset, Oxfordshire etc.); in Ireland for Hennelly and occasionally for HANLEY. (Ekwall, Cottle, Spiegelhalter, MacLysaght).

Traced by Guppy in Wiltshire and by Spiegelhalter in Devon.

In Newfoundland:

Early instances: Samuel Henl(e)y, of Island of Spear, 1708, of Bay Bulls, 1708 (CO 194.4); Bartholomew Henly, of St. John's, 1759 (DPHW 26D); Samuel, of Greenspond, 1776 (MUN Hist.); ––––– Henley, fish merchant of Ferryland, 1818 (D'Alberti 28); Samuel, from Devon, merchant of St. John's, deceased before 1843 (*Royal Gazette* 3 Oct 1843); Marion, from London, married at Bay Roberts, 1857 (*Conception Bay Man* 13 May 1857).

Modern status: At St. John's.

Place names: Henley Harbour (Labrador); ––––– Island (Labrador) 51-59 55-51.

HENNEBURY, a surname of England, from the English place names Henbury (Dorset, Gloucestershire, Cheshire) or ? Hanbury (Staffordshire, Worcestershire); Henebry, of Ireland, formerly de Hindeberg and gaelicized *de Hionburgha*. (Ekwall, MacLysaght).

Traced by MacLysaght in Cos. Kilkenny and Waterford.

In Newfoundland:

Early instances: William Hanbury, planter of St. John's, 1701 (CO 194.2); John Henebury, of Quidi Vidi, 1790 (DPHW 26D); Anty [sic] Hanebury, from Carrickbeg (Co. Waterford), married at St. John's, 1812 (Nfld. Archives BRC); Marks Haneberry, of Harbour Grace Parish, 1821 (Nfld. Archives HGRC); John Heneberry, of Kings Cove, 1830 (Nfld. Archives KCRC); ––––– Hennebry, of Port de Grave, 1834 (*Newfoundlander* 23 Jan 1834); Mark Hen(n)eb(e)ry, from Co. Cork, of Port de Grave, 1839 (Nfld.

Archives BRC, *Indicator* 24 Aug 1844); R. Henebury, Carbonear, 1856 (*Newfoundlander* 3 Jan 1856); Marcus Hannhabery, of Harbour Grace, 1868 (Nfld. Archives HGRC); Robert and Richard Henneberry, of Fox Cove (Burin), 1871 (Lovell); Rev. Thomas R. Hennebery, of Trepassey, 1871 (Lovell); Mark and Richard Henebery, of Bareneed, 1871 (Lovell).

Modern status: Scattered, especially in the Burin district and at St. John's.

HENNESSEY, a surname of Ireland, (O)Hennessy, *Ó hAonghusa* – descendant of Angus. (MacLysaght). *See* HINCHEY.

Traced by MacLysaght in Munster.

In Newfoundland:

Early instances: Michael Henesee or Hennesey, from Fethard (Co. Tipperary), of St. John's, 1765, died 1812 (*Royal Gazette* 23 Jul 1812, DPHW 26D); Michael Hennecy or Hennisey, of Harbour Grace Parish, 1806 (Nfld. Archives HGRC); Mary Henessy, of Ferryland, 1809 (Nfld. Archives BRC); David ? Henesey, of Broad Cove (unspecified) (Conception B.), 1813 (Nfld. Archives BRC); Philip Hennessey, from Thomastown (Co. Kilkenny), planter of Placentia, deceased 1814 (*Royal Gazette* 26 May 1814); John Henesy, of Joe Batts Arm, 1823 (Nfld. Archives KCRC); Ellen Hennesey, Henesy or Hynesi, of Trinity, 1832 (Nfld. Archives KCRC); Michael Hennissy or Hennessy, of ? Northern Bay, 1838 (DPHW 54); Capt. John Hennessey, born at Harbour Grace, 1840 (Mott); Michael Hennesy, from Co. Tipperary, of Harbour Grace, 1844 (*Indicator* 27 Jul 1844); Thomas Hennessy, of Plate Cove (Bonavista B.), 1850 (Nfld. Archives KCRC); J. Henesy, of Merasheen, 1855 (*Newfoundlander* 29 Nov 1855); J. J. Hennessy, of Kelligrews, 1871 (Lovell); John and Patrick, of Low Point (Conception B.), 1871 (Lovell).

Modern status: Scattered, especially at St. John's and in the Harbour Main district.

Place names: Hennessey Island 49-42 55-53; ––––– Rock 47-21 54-17; Hennessey's Pond 47-26 52-57; Hennesy Cove 47-36 54-06.

HENNIFANT, HENNIFENT, ? variants of the surname of Ireland (O)Hannavan, *Ó hAinbheáin*. (MacLysaght).

Traced by MacLysaght in Co. Monaghan.

In Newfoundland:

Modern status: Hennifant, at Kyer's Cove and Black Island (Twillingate district) (*Electors* 1955); Hennifent, rare, at Norris Arm.

HENRY, a baptismal name and surname of England, Scotland, Ireland and the Channel Islands, from Old German *Haimric, Henric,* Old French *Henri,* containing the elements *home* and *rule*; in Ireland for (Mac) Henry, *Mac Éinrí* or *Mac Einri,* or a variant of MacEniry, or for (O)Henry, *Ó hInneirghe.* (Withycombe, Reaney, Spiegelhalter, MacLysaght, Turk). *See also* HENDERSON, HENDRY, HARRIS.

Traced by Cottle from Shetland to Cornwall, by Spiegelhalter in Devon. MacLysaght traced (Mac) Henry in Co. Galway, Mac Henry mainly in southeast Ulster, and (O)Henry in Cos. Derry and Tyrone.

In Newfoundland:

Early instances: William, of St. John's, 1821 (CO 194.64); Elinor, of Greenspond, 1829 (Nfld. Archives KCRC); Francis, of Rose Blanche, 1871 (Lovell); John, of Bay of Islands, 1875 (DPHW 95).

Modern status: Rare, at St. John's.

Place names (not necessarily from the surname): Henry Island 51-19 55-36, (Labrador) 56-40 61-15, 56-58 61-20; —— Peninsula (Labrador) 59-49 64-02; Henry Street (St. John's).

HENSTRIDGE, a surname of England, from the English place name Henstridge (Somerset) – the ridge where stallions were kept. (Ekwall, Cottle). *See also* HINKS.

In Newfoundland:

Family tradition: William, from Poole (Dorset), settled at ? Twillingate (MUN Folklore).

Early instances: William Henstritch, of Donier (Twillingate district), 1854 (DPHW 86); William Henstreet, of Troy Town (now Triton), 1871 (Lovell).

Modern status: Rare, at Triton West and Badger.

HEPDITCH, HIPDITCH, surnames of England, from ? an unidentified English place name, or (dweller by the) ditch where wild roses or brambles grow. (A.H. Smith).

Guppy traced Hebditch in Somerset.

In Newfoundland:

Early instances: David Hepditch or Hipditch, of Trinity Bay, 1785 (DPHW 64); Hannah Hebditch, of Lamaline, 1829 (DPHW 106); Richard Hipditch, from Shaldon (Devon), late of St. John's, 1851 (*Newfoundlander* 27 Nov 1851); David Hebditch, of Brunette, 1852 (DPHW 104); Richard Hibditch, of Muddy Hole (Burin district), 1860 (DPHW 107); John (and others) Heptidge, of Clattice Harbour, 1871 (Lovell); Richard Hapditch, of Point aux Gaul, 1871 (Lovell).

Modern status: Hepditch, scattered, especially at Point au Mal (Port-au-Port district); Hipditch, rare and scattered, especially at English Harbour West and St. John's.

Place name: Heptige Rock 47-21 54-33.

HERALD, a surname of England, Scotland and Ireland, from the Old Norse personal name *Heraldr* or Old English *Hereweald,* or from Middle English *heraud* etc. – herald; or in Ireland for Harold.

Guppy traced a variant Herrod in Nottinghamshire; MacLysaght traced Herald in Ulster.

In Newfoundland:

Early instances: Rebecca Herrald, of Harbour Grace, 1806 (Nfld. Archives BRC); Richard Herald, of Forteau (Labrador), married at St. John's, 1840 (DPHW 26D); Philip, fisherman of Mosquito (now Bristols Hope), 1871 (Lovell).

Modern status: Rare, at Harbour Grace and St. John's (*Electors* 1955).

HERDER, a surname of England – a herdsman. (Reaney).

In Newfoundland:

Early instances: Lawrence, of Newfoundland, ? 1706 (CO 194.24); —— Hearder, constable of Placentia district, ? 1730 (CO 194.9); Henry, mariner of Carbonear, 1833 (DPHW 48); ——, of St. John's, 1847 (*Newfoundlander* 18 Jan 1847); John He(a)rder, of Old Perlican, 1848 (DPHW 58); Henry, lighthouse keeper at Cape Pine, 1856 (*Newfoundlander* 7 Jul 1856, *Nfld. Almanac* 1857).

Modern status: At St. John's.

Place name: Herder River (Labrador) 53-53 57-31.

HERDMAN, a surname of England, Scotland and Ireland – a herdsman, or ? a retainer. (Reaney, Black). *See also* HERDER, HEFFERMAN.

Traced by Guppy in Northumberland and by MacLysaght in Co. Antrim.

In Newfoundland:

Modern status: Rare, at Corner Brook.

HERLIDAN, a surname of unascertained origin.

In Newfoundland:

Family tradition: John, from Brest, France, settled at Lord's Cove (Burin district), about 1899 (MUN Folklore).

Modern status: Rare, at Lord's Cove.

HERON, a surname of England, Scotland and Ireland, in France (Le) Héron, from Old French *hairon*, Middle English *heiroun* – heron, a nickname for a thin man with long legs, or, except in France, from the English place name Harome (Yorkshire NR); in Ireland more usually for Heffron, HEFFERAN, AHEARN or MacElheron. (Reaney, Dauzat, MacLysaght).

Spiegelhalter traced Herron in Devon.

In Newfoundland:

Early instances: Robert, of St. John's, 1790 (DPHW 26C); Anstace [sic] Herron, from Waterford Diocese, Ireland, married at St. John's, 1810 (Nfld. Archives BRC); James, of Harbour Grace Parish, 1812 (Nfld. Archives HGRC); Mr., of King's Cove, 1828 (Nfld. Archives KCRC); Nicholas Herran, of Renews, 1829 (Nfld. Archives BRC); Michael Heron, of Harbour Grace, 1870 (Nfld. Archives HGRC).

Modern status: At Harbour Le Cou (*Electors* 1955).

Place name (not necessarily from the surname): Heron Rock 49-44 54-20.

HERRICK, a surname of England and Ireland, from the Old Norse personal name *Eirikr*, Old Danish, Old Swedish *Erik* – Eric; "in Ireland it is probably a synonym of Erck(e)," a Co. Tyrone name. (Reaney, MacLysaght).

Traced by Guppy in Nottinghamshire and Leicestershire.

In Newfoundland:

Modern status: Rare, at St. John's.

HERRIDGE, a surname of England, from the English place name Highridge (Devon). (Spiegelhalter).

Traced by Spiegelhalter in Devon.

In Newfoundland:

Early instances: William Herrage, married at St. John's, 1784 (DPHW 26D); William Herridge, fisherman of Indian Harbour (Burgeo-La Poile district), 1860 (DPHW 99); John Herrage, planter of Long Harbour (Fortune B.), 1871 (Lovell).

Modern status: Scattered, in the Fortune Bay-Hermitage district.

HERRIOTT, HERRITT, surnames of England, from the English place name, Herriard (Hampshire). (Reaney). *See also* HARRIET.

In Newfoundland:

Early instances: Henry Herritt, teacher at Windsor Lake, 1839 (*Newfoundlander* 1 Aug 1839); William Herrot(t) or Herriett, of Sagona, 1852, of Harbour Breton, 1854 (DPHW 104); Matthew Herrett, planter of Grandy's Passage, 1871 (Lovell).

Modern status: Herritt, scattered, especially at

Burnt Island (Burgeo-La Poile district); Herriott, rare, at Harbour Breton (*Electors* 1955).

HERRO, ? a surname of Syria-Lebanon, of unknown origin.

In Newfoundland:

Modern status: ? At Burin, and unique, at Bell Island (*Electors* 1955).

HEUDES, a variant of the surname of France, Heude, from the Old German personal name *Hildo*, containing the element *battle*. (Dauzat). Heulin is a diminutive of Heude. *See* HEWLIN.

In Newfoundland:

Modern status: Rare, at Corner Brook.

HEWARDINE, a surname ? of England, ? from an unidentified place name.

In Newfoundland:

Early instance: William, sexton of St. John's, 1846, 1871 (DPHW 29, Lovell).

Modern status: Unique, at St. John's (*Electors* 1955).

HEWITT, a surname of England, Scotland and Ireland, a diminutive of the baptismal name Hugh (*see* HUE), or occasionally from Old English *hūwett* – (dweller in a) clearing where trees had been cut down. (Withycombe, Reaney, Cottle, Black, MacLysaght).

Guppy traced Hewett in Berkshire and Surrey, Hewitt in Cheshire and Nottinghamshire, and both in Norfolk. Spiegelhalter traced both in Devon. MacLysaght states that Hewitt, "though now regarded as of Ulster, practically all the early references to it, beginning in 1295, are to families in Munster or the city of Dublin."

In Newfoundland:

Family tradition: ——, from England, settled at Trepassey in the mid-18th century (MUN Folklore).

Early instances: Amos Hewett, of St. John's, 1704 (CO 194.3); Michael Huet, from St. Mullins (Co. Carlow), married at St. John's, 1810 (Nfld. Archives BRC); Stephen Hewitt, from New Ross (Co. Wexford), of Bonavista, deceased 1816 (*Royal Gazette* 30 Jul 1816); Joseph, of Trinity, 1827 (DPHW 64B); Hezekiah, of Joe Batt's Arm, 1842 (DPHW 83); John Hewnett, of Shoe Cove (Twillingate), 1846 (DPHW 86); Jacob, from England, married at Fortune, 1846, of Petites, 1857 (DPHW 106, 98); Philip, fisherman of Goose Cove (Trinity North district), 1860 (DPHW 63); Hezekiah, planter of Barr'd Island, 1871 (Lovell); George Hewett, of

Cape Pine, 1871 (Lovell); James and Joseph Hewett, Samuel and William Hewitt, of Trepassey, 1871 (Lovell).

Modern status: Scattered, especially at Barr'd Islands, Joe Batt's Arm and Trepassey.

HEWLETT, a surname of England and Ireland, a double diminutive of the baptismal name Hugh. (Withycombe, Reaney). *See* HUE *and also* HOWLETT.

Traced by Guppy in Gloucestershire and Somerset, and by Spiegelhalter in Devon.

In Newfoundland:

Early instances: John Hewlett, from Kilmacow (Co. Kilkenny), married at St. John's, 1805 (Nfld. Archives BRC); Nicholas Hewlet, of Bonavista, 1823 (DPHW 70); Robert Hulett, of Ward's Harbour (now Beaumont North), 1846 (DPHW 86); Hezekiah Hewlit, fisherman of Barr'd Island, 1847 (DPHW 83); Ezekial Ullit, of Joe Batt's Arm, 1853 (DPHW 83); William Ulet, of Nipper's Harbour, 1854 (DPHW 86); Thomas Hewlett, of Petites, 1871 (Lovell); Henry Hewlitt, of Shoe Cove (Fogo), 1871 (Lovell); Henry and Joseph Hewlett, of Sunday Cove Island (now Port Anson), 1871 (Lovell).

Modern status: Scattered, especially in the Green Bay district with a large concentration at Port Anson.

Place name: John Hewlett Rock 49-38 55-38.

HEWLIN, a surname of England, from the Old German personal name *Huglin*, Old French *Hu(g)elin*, diminutives of *Hugo*, Hugh. (Withycombe, Reaney). *See* HEUDES, HUE, HUELIN.

In Newfoundland:

Early instances: Philip Heulan, of Crabbe's, 1869 (DPHW 96); William, of Robinson's Head, 1870 (DPHW 96); James (and others) Henlan (? for Hewlan), of Middle Brook (St. George's B.), 1871 (Lovell).

Modern status: At Stephenville and in the St. Barbe district.

HEWSON, a surname of England and Ireland, – son of Hugh. *See* HUE *and also* HEWLETT, HEWLIN. Traced by Guppy in Lincolnshire.

In Newfoundland:

Modern status: Rare, at St. John's.

HIBBARD. *See* HEBBARD

HIBBS, a surname of England from a pet-form of the baptismal names Isabel (Elizabeth) from the Hebrew – my God (is) satisfaction, or Ilbert from the Old German personal name *Hildeberht* containing

the elements *strife* and *bright*. (Withycombe, Reaney).

In Newfoundland:

Early instances: Joan, of Harbour Grace, 1675 (CO 1); Thomas, of Bryant's Cove, 1676 (CO 1); Henry, of (Upper) Island Cove, 1773 (CO 199.18); William, of Trinity Bay, 1785 (DPHW 64); Henry and James Hibs, in possession of property in fishery at Portugal Cove, 1794–5 (Census 1794–5); Elizabeth, of Little Bay (Burin district), 1855 (DPHW 106); John Hibbs, of Little Bay Islands, 1859 (DPHW 92); James and John, of Kelligrews, 1871 (Lovell); James, of Topsail, 1871 (Lovell); Thomas, of Lower Gully (now Riverdale), 1871 (Lovell).

Modern status: Scattered, especially at Peter's Arm, Portugal Cove and Topsail.

Place name: Hibbs Hole 47-36 53-11.

HICKEY, a surname of Ireland, (O)Hickey, *Ó hÍcidhe*, Ir. *íceadh* – healer. (MacLysaght).

Traced by MacLysaght in Cos. Limerick, Tipperary and Clare.

In Newfoundland:

Family tradition: Michael O'Hickey (later Hickey), from Co. Tipperary, settled at Brigus about 1837, aged 12; he later moved to Harbour Grace and St. John's (MUN Folklore).

Early instances: William, of St. John's, 1755 (DPHW 26C); Michael, of Chapel's Cove (Conception B.), 1782 (CO 199.18); Thomas, of Harbour Main, 1783 (CO 199.18); John, servant of Harbour Grace, 1786 (CO 194.36); Susanna, of Placentia, 1801 (Nfld. Archives BRC); Margaret, of St. Mary's, 1802 (Nfld. Archives BRC); John, from Maglass Parish (unidentified), Thurles (Co. Tipperary), married at St. John's, 1802 (Nfld. Archives BRC); Robert, from Waterford, fisherman of Bay Bulls, deceased, 1813 (*Royal Gazette* 2 Dec 1813); John, of Tickle Harbour (now Bellevue), 1817 (Nfld. Archives KCRC); John, of Riverhead (? Harbour Grace), 1829 (Nfld. Archives BRC); William Hickley, planter of Catalina, 1824 (DPHW 64B); Anne Hickey, of Torbay, 1829 (Nfld. Archives BRC); Patrick, of Bonavista, 1832 (Nfld. Archives KCRC); Ann, of King's Cove Parish, 1835 (Nfld. Archives KCRC); Patrick, from Thurles (Co. Tipperary), of Brigus, 1844 (*Indicator* 24 Aug 1844); Daniel, of Grand Beach, 1864 (MUN Hist.); widespread in Lovell 1871.

Modern status: Widespread, especially in St. John's and district.

Place names: Hickey's Brook 48-43 53-13; —— Pond 47-41 52-49.

HICKMAN, a surname of England and Ireland – servant of Hick, a pet-form of Hick (Richard) (*see* RICHARDS). (Reaney, MacLysaght).

Traced by Guppy in Berkshire and Kent, by Spiegelhalter in Devon, and by MacLysaght in Co. Clare.

In Newfoundland:

Family tradition: Jonathan (1747–1847), born at sea en route from England to Halifax (Nova Scotia), thence to St. Pierre, settled at Grand Bank after the Treaty of Paris, 1763 (MUN Hist.).

Early instances: Thomas, of Fortune, son of Jonathan, 1824 (DPHW 109, MUN Hist.); William, of Channel, 1862 (DPHW 97).

Modern status: Scattered, especially at Grand Bank.

Place names: Hickman Harbour 48-13 53-35; —— Islands 48-13 53-34; Hickman's Harbour 48-06 53-44; —— Brook 48-13 53-36.

HICKS, a surname of England and the Channel Islands, – son of Hick (Richard) (*see* RICHARDS). (Reaney, Turk).

Traced by Guppy in Berkshire, Devon, Durham, Essex, Somerset, Suffolk and Yorkshire, and especially in Cornwall.

In Newfoundland:

Early instances: John, of Harbour Main, 1764, of Chapel's Cove (Conception B.), 1791 (CO 199.18); William, of Bonavista, 1786 (DPHW 70); Edward, of Pinchard's Island (Bonavista B.), 1802 (Bonavista Register 1806); Elisa, of Harbour Grace Parish, 1807 (Nfld. Archives HGRC); Thomas, planter of Bayleys Cove (Bonavista B.), 1818 (DPHW 72); Robert, of Quidi Vidi, 1828 (DPHW 26B); Bernard, of Flat Islands (Bonavista B.), 1845 (DPHW 70); Joseph, fisherman of Merritt's Harbour, 1851 (DPHW 85); John, fisherman of Doubty (for Doting) Cove (Bonavista district), 1852 (DPHW 72); John, of Catalina, 1864 (DPHW 66); scattered, especially in the Bonavista Bay districts, in Lovell 1871.

Modern status: Widespread, especially in Rolling Cove and Doting Cove (Bonavista South district).

Place name: Mother Hicks Cove 47-01 53-40.

HIERLIHY, a variant of the surname of Ireland, (O)Herlihy, *Ó hIarlatha*, Ir. *iarfhlaith* – underlord, sometimes changed to HURLEY. (MacLysaght).

Traced by MacLysaght in Co. Cork.

In Newfoundland:

Early instances: John, of St. John's, 1795 (CO 194.41); J. G., of Bryant's Cove, 1847 (*Newfoundlander* 14 Jan 1847); George W., revenue collector at Bay Roberts, 1858 (*Newfoundlander* 22 Mar 1858).

Modern status: At St. John's, Chamberlains, Bay Roberts and Gander.

HIGDON, a surname of England, a diminutive of Richard (*see* RICHARDS). (Reaney).

In Newfoundland:

Early instances: Benjamin Higdens, of Trinity Bay, 1765 (DPHW 64); Benjamin Higden, occupier of fishing room at Trinity, Winter 1800–01 (Census Trinity B.); Benjamin and Sons, proprietors and occupiers of fishing rooms at English Harbour, Winter 1800–01 (Census Trinity B.); William, of New Harbour (Trinity B.), 1814 (DPHW 64); George, planter of British Harbour (Trinity B.), 1831 (DPHW 64); George, of Catalina, 1843 (DPHW 67); George (and others) Higdon, of Salmon Cove (now Champneys), 1871 (Lovell).

Modern status: Scattered, especially at New Harbour.

HIGGINS, a surname of England and Ireland; in England a diminutive of Higg, that is, Hick (Richard) (*see* RICHARDS); in Ireland (O)Higgins, *Ó hUigín* – "from an old Gaelic word akin to Viking." (Reaney, MacLysaght).

Traced by Guppy in several counties, by Spiegelhalter in Devon, and by MacLysaght in Co. Sligo.

In Newfoundland:

Family tradition: ——, from Ireland to Joe Batt's Arm, about 1811–16 (MUN Hist.).

Early instances: John, ? of St. John's, 1751 (CO 194.13); Elizabeth, of Harbour Grace, 1774 (CO 199.18); William, from Shenren (unidentified) (Co. Kilkenny), married at St. John's, 1815 (Nfld. Archives BRC); George, of Sagona Island, 1823 (D'Alberti 33); Michael, of Fogo, 1824 (Nfld. Archives KCRC); Thomas, of Fortune, 1825 (DPHW 106); Daniel, of Bay de Verde, died 1826 (*Newfoundlander* 28 Feb 1829); Michael, of Tilting Harbour (now Tilting), 1829 (Nfld. Archives KCRC); John, of Harbour Grace, 1832 (*Newfoundlander* 23 Aug 1832); George, from Stratford (Somerset), married at Catalina, 1842 (DPHW 67); James, of Hall's Bay, 1854 (DPHW 86); Jane, of Grand Bank, 1859 (DPHW 106); scattered in Lovell 1871.

Modern status: Scattered, especially at Norris Arm.

Place names: Higgins Island 49-41 54-46, (Labrador) 52-04 55-44; —— Line (St. John's).

HIGHMORE, a surname of England, from the English place name Highmoor (Dorset). (Spiegelhalter).

Traced by Spiegelhalter in Devon.

In Newfoundland:

Early instance: Joseph Bessant, member of the Anglican School Board, Fogo, 1855 (MUN Hist.).

Modern status: Rare, at Bell Island and St. John's.

HILL, a surname of England, Scotland, Ireland and the Channel Islands, from Old English *hyll* – (dweller on the) hill, or from a common English place name, or from a personal name *Hille*, a pet-form of Hilary, or a German name containing the element *Hild* – battle. (Reaney, Cottle, MacLysaght, Turk). *See also* HELLIER.

Found widespread by Guppy, from Yorkshire to Cornwall, especially in Gloucestershire, Somerset and Devon, and by MacLysaght in northeast Ulster and Co. Kerry.

In Newfoundland:

Early instances: Christopher, of Bay de Verde, 1675 (CO 1); Bartholomew, boatkeeper of St. John's Harbour, 1682 (CO 1); Edward, of Petty Harbour and St. John's, 1708 (CO 194.4); William, mariner of St. John's, 1794–5, "20 years in Newfoundland," that is, 1774–5 (Census 1794–5); William, of Trinity Bay, 1780 (DPHW 64); William, of Port de Grave, 1790 (Nfld. Archives T22); Joseph, of Bay Bulls, 1793 (USPG); James, of Bonavista, 1808, of Bird Island Cove (now Elliston), 1817 (DPHW 70, 72); Mary, of Torbay, 1820 (Nfld. Archives BRC); Nathaniel, from Ugborough (Devon), of St. John's, deceased 1829 (*Royal Gazette* 3 Mar 1829); James, baptised at Swain's Island (now Wesleyville), 1830, aged 18 (DPHW 76); William, of Moreton's Harbour, 1841 (DPHW 86); S., from England, of Griquet, 1849 (Feild); John, of Harbour Breton, 1850 (DPHW 104); William, of Greenspond, 1852 (DPHW 76); William, of Black Island (Twillingate district), 1852 (DPHW 86); James, of Little Placentia (now Argentia), 1871 (Lovell).

Modern status: Scattered, especially at St. John's.

Place names: Hill's Harbour (Labrador) 53-14 55-42; —— Rock 47-36 58-38.

HILLIARD, HILLYARD, surnames of England and Ireland, with variants in the Channel Islands, from an Old German personal name *Hildigard*, containing the elements *war* and *stronghold*. (Withycombe, Reaney, MacLysaght, Turk).

Traced by MacLysaght in Co. Kerry, "to Ireland from Yorkshire in the 17th century."

In Newfoundland:

Early instances: Richard Hilliard (Halliard in

1681), of St. John's or Bay Bulls, 1680, "14 years an inhabitant," that is, since 1666 (CO 1); Lawrence Hilliard (Helward in 1681), of Fermeuse, 1676 (CO 1); Philip Halliard, of Harbour Grace Parish, 1807 (Nfld. Archives HGRC); John Hillyard, minister of Burin, 1812 (D'Alberti 22); Mary Hillier or Hilliard, of New Harbour (Trinity B.), 1817 (Nfld. Archives KCRC); John, of Bonavista, 1821 (CO 194.64); John, fisherman of Broad Cove (Bay de Verde district), 1830 (DPHW 52A); George Hilliard, planter of Crocker's Cove (Carbonear), 1833 (DPHW 48); Giles, planter of Green's Harbour, 1844 (DPHW 59A); Harvey Hillyard, planter of Ochre Pit Cove, 1849 (DPHW 52A); Richard Hilliard, of Heart's Content, 1871 (Lovell); Thomas Hillyard, of Hope-all, 1871 (Lovell); Elijah (and others), of New Harbour (Trinity B.), 1871 (Lovell).

Modern status: Hilliard, scattered, especially at Petries; Hillyard, scattered.

HILLIER. *See* HELLIER

HILLYARD. *See* HILLIARD

HILLYER. *See* HELLIER

HINCHEY, a surname of Ireland, (O)Henchy, Hinchy, *Ó hAonghusa* – descendant of Angus, the Co. Clare form of HENNESSEY. (MacLysaght).

In Newfoundland:

Early instances: Morgan Hingey or Hangey, of Broad Cove (Bay de Verde district), 1766 (CO 199.18); Ann Hingey, of Harbour Grace Parish, 1808 (Nfld.

Archives HGRC); Elinor Hingy, of King's Cove, 1815 (Nfld. Archives KCRC); Thomas Hinchy or Hingy, of Broad Cove (now Duntara), 1827 (Nfld. Archives KCRC); Morgan Hinchey, ? of Northern Bay, 1844 (DPHW 54); William Henchy, of St. John's, 1871 (Lovell); John Hingy, of Northern Bay, 1871 (Lovell).

Modern status: Rare, including Northern Bay, St. John's and Gander.

HINDS, a surname of England, from Old English *hind* – (timid as a) female deer, or a variant of HINE(S). (Reaney).

Guppy traced Hind in Leicestershire, Rutland-shire, Lincolnshire and, as Hinde, in Nottingham-shire; Spiegelhalter traced Hind in Devon.

In Newfoundland:

Early instances: Edward and Andrew Hinde (Haine in 1677), of Petty Harbour, 1675, 1682 (CO

1); Cornelius Hind, of Trinity Bay, 1767 (DPHW 64); John Hinds, of Middle Bight (now Codner), 1832 (DPHW 30); Robert, of Foxtrap, 1835 (DPHW 30); John, of St. John's, 1838 (DPHW 26B); Thomas, of Catalina, 1844 (DPHW 67); Jane Hynds, of Grand Bank, 1845 (DPHW 106); Patrick Hinds, ? of Harbour Grace, 1845 (*Newfoundlander* 16 Jan 1845); Thomas, planter of Cupids, 1848 (DPHW 34); William, of Triton Harbour, 1851 (DPHW 86); Thomas, fisherman of Little Bay (Burin district), 1853 (DPHW 104); Thomas, labourer of Brigus, 1853 (DPHW 34); scattered in Lovell 1871.

Modern status: Rare, at Back Harbour (Twillingate district) (*Electors* 1955) and St. John's.

Place names (not necessarily from the surname): Hind's Brook, —— Point 49-05 57-13; —— (or Hyne's) Cove 48-02 59-13; —— Hill 49-00 56-56; —— Lake 48-58 57-00; —— Plains 49-01 56-54.

HINDY, a variant of the surname of England and Ireland, Hendy, from Middle English *hendy* – courteous, kind, gentle, used also as a personal name. (Reaney).

Hendy was traced by Guppy in Cornwall and Devon, and by MacLysaght in Co. Kildare.

In Newfoundland:

Early instances: Josiah Hendy, planter of Scilly Cove (now Winterton), 1825 (DPHW 64B); —— Hindy, on the *Robert and James* in the seal fishery out of Hants Harbour, 1847 (*Newfoundlander* 1 Apr 1847).

Modern status: At Marquise (Placentia B.) (*Electors* 1955), St. John's, Corner Brook and a large concentration at Winterton.

HINES, HYNES, surnames of England and Ireland; in England from Middle English *hīne* – servant; in Ireland for (O)Heyne, *Ó hEidhin*, ? Ir. *eidhean* – ivy. (Reaney, MacLysaght). *See* HINDS.

Hine traced by Guppy in Devon and Staffordshire; Hine(s), Hyne(s) by Spiegelhalter in Devon; and Hynes by MacLysaght in Co. Galway.

In Newfoundland:

Early instances: Philip Hines, of Holyrood Head, 1801 (CO 199.18); William Hyndes or Hines, of Bay Bulls district, 1803 (Nfld. Archives BRC); Pat Hines or Hynes, of Harbour Grace Parish, 1808 (Nfld. Archives HGRC); John Hynes, from Co. Tipperary, married at St. John's, 1809 (Nfld. Archives BRC); Pat ? Hine, merchant of St. John's, 1810 (CO 194.49); John Hynes, of Colliers, 1813 (Nfld. Archives BRC); James Hines, married in the Northern district, 1814 (Nfld. Archives BRC); Alexander Hines or Hinds, of

Brigus, 1815, of Cupids, 1823 (DPHW 34); James Hines, of King's Cove, 1816 (Nfld. Archives KCRC); James, of Bonavista, 1818 (Nfld. Archives KCRC); Thomas, of Joe Batt's Arm, 1819 (Nfld. Archives KCRC); Michael Hynes, of Portugal Cove, 1821 (Nfld. Archives BRC); Betsy Hines, of Twillingate, 1822 (Nfld. Archives KCRC); James Hines or Hynes, of Gooseberry Islands (Bonavista B.), 1825 (Nfld. Archives KCRC); James Hynes, of Fortune, 1833 (DPHW 106); John, planter of Broad Cove (Bay de Verde district), 1835 (DPHW 52A); John Hines, planter of Salmon Cove (now Champneys), 1840 (DPHW 64B); Charles, of Catalina, 1847 (DPHW 67); Joseph Hynes, of the French shore, 1848 (DPHW 113); Thomas Heynes, of King's Cove, 1855 (Nfld. Archives KCRC); Ric[h]ard Hines, of Leading Tickles, 1855 (DPHW 86); Sally Hynes, of Trinity, 1856 (Nfld. Archives KCRC); Catherine, of Keels, 1856 (Nfld. Archives KCRC); John, of Haywards Cove (Bonavista B.), 1857 (Nfld. Archives KCRC); John, of Petites, 1859 (DPHW 98); Charles Hines, of St. Jacques, 1859 (DPHW 104); Reuben Hynes, of Indian Island (Fogo district), 1861 (DPHW 84); Thomas Heynes, of Stock Cove (Bonavista B.), 1862 (Nfld. Archives KCRC); Bridget Hyans, of Harbour Grace, 1866 (Nfld. Archives HGRC); Thomas Hynes, of Round Cove, 1866 (Nfld. Archives KCRC); Elizabeth, of Cottells Island, 1870 (Nfld. Archives KCRC); George, of The Gravel[s] (St. George's district), 1870 (DPHW 96); Hynes, widespread in Lovell 1871.

Modern status: Hines, rare, especially in the St. George's district; Hynes, widespread, especially at Port-au-Port, Jacques Fontaine, Ferryland and St. Brendan's.

Place names: Hine's (or Hyne's or Hind's) Cove, —— (or Hyne's) Gulch 48-02 59-13; Hine's Pond 48-49 58-23; Hyne's Cove 49-32 55-39, 49-38 55-49; Hyne's Point 49-38 55-49; —— Rock 49-33 55-39.

HING, a surname of China, of unascertained meaning.

In Newfoundland:

Modern status: Rare, at St. Lawrence (*Electors* 1955) and Port aux Basques.

HINKS, a surname of England and of the Micmac Indians of Newfoundland, ? from the Old English personal names *Hynca* or *Hengest,* or from *hengest* – stallion. (A. H. Smith, Ekwall, Weekley *Romance*). *See also* HENSTRIDGE.

In Newfoundland:

Early instances: John, of Harbour Grace Parish, 1829 (Nfld. Archives HGRC); Edmund, ? of Harbour Grace, 1845 (*Newfoundlander* 9 Jan 1845); John Hincks, fisherman of Indian Harbour (Burgeo-La Poile district), 1860 (DPHW 99); John Hinks, fisherman of Baker's Tickle, 1871 (Lovell); James, planter of Cape Ray, 1871 (Lovell); John, planter of Channel, 1871 (Lovell); William, fisherman of Fox Island Harbour, 1871 (Lovell); John, Paddy and Johnny Hinx, Indian trappers of the Eastern Partridgeberry Hills, 1900–06 (Millais).

Modern status: Scattered, at Conne River and in the Port-au-Port and Humber East districts.

Place name: Hinck's Rocks 49-11 53-28.

HINTON, a surname of England, from a common English place name in Devon, Dorset, Somerset etc. – the high place or farm, or the monks', nuns' farm. (Ekwall, Cottle).

Traced by Guppy in Shropshire and by Spiegelhalter in Devon.

In Newfoundland:

Early instance: George, juror of St. John's, 1751 (CO 194.13).

Modern status: Rare, at Deer Lake.

HIPDITCH. *See* HEPDITCH

HIPPERN, ? an arbitrary Newfoundland variant of the surnames of England Epper (untraced) or Epperson, from the Old English personal name *Eorphere*, which survives in the place name Epperstone (Nottinghamshire). However, Reuben Hipper (born ?1882 at Heart's Content), who has always known his name thus, has the impression that it is of German origin since Hipper is a not un-common German surname. (Ekwall, Bardsley, E.C. Smith, D. Hippern).

In Newfoundland:

Family tradition: ——, ? from Wales, ? about 1840–50 (Family); Frederick Hippern, from Somerset in the 1850s, settled at Heart's Content. (D. Hippern).

Early instance: Frederick Hepburn [sic], fisherman of Heart's Content, 1871 (Lovell).

Modern status: Rare, at Heart's Content (*Electors* 1955), St. John's and Gander.

HISCOCK, HISCOTT, surnames of England, diminutives of Hitch (Richard) (*see* RICHARDS), or from the English place name Hiscott (Devon). (Reaney, Spiegelhalter). *See* ALCOCK.

Traced by Guppy in Berkshire, Dorset, Somerset and Wiltshire, and by Spiegelhalter in Devon.

In Newfoundland:

Family tradition: John Hiscock (1825–69), from Carbonear, settled at Victoria (MUN Geog.).

Early instances: Joseph Hiscock, of Trinity, 1758 (DPHW 64); William, of Salmon Cove (now Champneys), 1786 (DPHW 64); Edward, of Portugal Cove, 1788 (DPHW 26C); Josiah, of Fox Island (Trinity North district), 1789 (DPHW 64); Francis, of Lower Island Cove, 1791 (CO 199.18); Edward, of St. John's, 1799 (DPHW 26B); Thomas, proprietor and occupier of fishing room at Rider's Harbour, Winter 1800-01 (Census Trinity B.); Josiah, pro-prietor and occupier of fishing room at Scilly Cove (now Winterton), Winter 1800–01 (Census Trinity B.); John, occupier of fishing room at Bonaventure, Winter 1800–01 (Census Trinity B.); Henry Hitch-cock, occupier of fishing room at Old Perlican, Winter 1800–01 (Census Trinity B.); William Hiscock, of Fogo, 1803 (D'Alberti 13); Phillip, of Brigus, 1804 (DPHW 34); Philip Hitchcock, of Crocker's Cove (Carbonear), 1809 (DPHW 48); Edward Hiscock, Iscock, or Hiskcock, of Torbay, 1813 (DPHW 26B); James Hiscock, married in the Northern District, 1814 (Nfld. Archives BRC); John, of Greenspond, 1815 (DPHW 76); George, of Belle Isle (now Bell Island), 1818 (DPHW 26B); Richard, planter of Catalina, 1820 (DPHW 72); James, fisher-man of Port de Grave, 1824 (DPHW 39); Joseph, of Careless (now Kerleys) Harbour, 1825 (Nfld. Ar-chives KCRC); Thomas, planter of Heart's Ease, 1826 (DPHW 64B); Henry, planter of Burnt Head (Carbonear), 1828 (DPHW 43); Richard, of Grates Cove, 1828 (DPHW 58); Edward, of Broad Cove (unspecified), 1831 (DPHW 30); Giles His(s)cock, of Burnt Island (Burgeo-La Poile district), 1841, of Hisscock's Point, 1857 (DPHW 98, 101); Robert, planter of Southside (Trinity North district), 1842 (DPHW 64B); Roger, fisherman of Pouch Cove, 1843 (DPHW 32); Samuel, of Sibley['s] Cove, 1850 (DPHW 58); Harry, of Thoroughfare, 1852 (DPHW 64B); William, of Chamberlains, deceased 1854 (*New-foundlander* 4 Sep 1854); Joshua, of Freshwater (Carbonear), 1855 (DPHW 49); Edward, of Flat Is-land (Bonavista B.), 1865 (DPHW 81); Richard His-cott, of Petty Harbour, 1871 (Lovell); Hiscock, widespread in Lovell 1871.

Modern status: Hiscock, widespread, especially at Winterton, Champneys West and St. John's; Hiscott, rare, at Bell Island.

Place names: Hiscock Islands 47-35 58-55, (Lab-rador) 53-12 55-43; —— Point (or Coney Head) 47-35 58-56; —— Rocks 47-15 54-55; Hiscock's Point 47-36 58-50, —— or Hiscox Point 48-31 53-04.

HITCHENS, a surname of England, a diminutive of Hitch (Richard) (*see* RICHARDS), or from the English place name Hitchin (Hertfordshire). (Reaney).

Guppy traced Hitchen, Hitchin in Cheshire and Lancashire, Hitchin(g)s in Cornwall and Wiltshire.

In Newfoundland:

Modern status: Rare, at St. John's.

HOARE, a surname of England and Ireland, from Old English *hār* – hoary, grey-haired, or in England from the English place names Ore (Sussex), or Rora (Devon), both from Old English *ōra* – (dweller by the) bank, slope. (Reaney, Spiegelhalter, Ekwall, MacLysaght).

Guppy traced Hoar(e) in Cornwall and Devon and especially in Dorset; MacLysaght traced Hoare mainly in Co. Cork and Hore mainly in Co. Wexford.

In Newfoundland:

Early instances: Thomas, boatkeeper of St. John's Harbour, 1682 (CO 1); Edward (Hoan in 1681), of New Perlican, 1682 (CO 1); Edward, thief at Petty Harbour, 1751 (CO 194.13); William, of Battle Harbour (Labrador), 1795 (MUN Hist.); Robert Hoar, from Charmouth (Dorset), late of St. John's, 1830 (*Newfoundlander* 15 Apr 1830); George Hoare, of Sandy Point (St. George's district), 1835 (DPHW 30); Michael Hoar, from Kilmacow (Co. Kilkenny), married at St. John's, 1837 (Nfld. Archives BRC).

Modern status: Rare, at Tide's Cove (Placentia B.) (*Electors* 1955).

HOBBS, a surname of England, from *Hobb,* a pet-form of Robert, rhyming with Rob. (Reaney, Cottle). *See* ROBERTS.

Traced by Guppy in seven south Midland counties especially in Buckinghamshire, Gloucestershire and Wiltshire, and by Spiegelhalter in Devon.

In Newfoundland:

Early instances: William, of Topsham (Devon), in possession of Hunt's plantation, Petty Harbour, before 1765 (Exeter Public Library Archives per Kirwin); Robert, of Bonavista, 1792 (USPG); Abraham, in possession of fishing room at Keels, built by the family before 1805 (Bonavista Register 1806); John, of Bird Island Cove (now Elliston 1823 (DPHW 70); James, planter of Bonaventure (unspecified), 1825 (DPHW 64B); Thomas Hobes or Hobbs, of King's Cove Parish, 1849, of Keels, 1856 (Nfld. Archives KCRC); Samuel, fisherman of Salmon Cove (now Champneys), 1853 (DPHW 64B); Alfred, fisherman of Whale Cove (Burin district),

1860 (DPHW 108); William, from Cerne (Dorset), married at St. John's, 1861 (DPHW 26D); Robert, of Cat Cove (Trinity B.), 1871 (Lovell); Charles, ? from Scotland, of Long Islands (Bonavista B.), 1871 (Lovell); Richard and Samuel, of New Perlican, 1871 (Lovell); Charles, of Red Cliff Island (Bonavista B.), 1871 (Lovell).

Modern status: Widespread, especially at Elliston, Keels and Bunyan's Cove.

Place names: Hobbs Cove 48-37 53-42; —— Hole 48-12 53-32, —— Rock 47-34 59-10.

HOBEN, a variant of the surname of Ireland (O)Hoban (as in *Electors* 1955), *Ó h Úbáin.* (MacLysaght).

Traced by MacLysaght in Cos. Mayo and Kilkenny.

In Newfoundland:

Early instances: Richard Hoban, ? of St. John's, 1810 (CO 194.50); John (and others), of Burin, 1871 (Lovell).

Modern status: At Port Anne (*Electors* 1955), Collins Cove (Burin district) and Burin Bay.

HOBEY, a surname of England, ? from the English place name, Hoby (Leicestershire). (Ekwall).

Guppy traced Hobye in Berkshire.

In Newfoundland:

Early instance: —— Hobby, of Carbonear, 1814 (D'Alberti 24).

Modern status: Rare, at Marystown.

HODDER, a surname of England and Ireland, from Old English *hōd* – (maker of) hood(s). (Reaney, MacLysaght). *See also* HOOD.

Traced by Guppy in Devon, Dorset and Somerset, and by MacLysaght as a rare name in Co. Cork.

In Newfoundland:

Early instances: John, of Trinity Bay, 1780 (DPHW 64); Richard, proprietor and occupier of fishing room at Rider's Harbour, Winter 1800–01 (Census Trinity B.); Charles, proprietor and occupier of fishing room at Ireland's Eye, Winter 1800–01 (Census Trinity B.); John, of Fogo, 1816 (MUN Hist.); William, fisherman of Dog Bay (Fogo district), 1821 (USPG); Richard, of Careless (now Kerleys) Harbour, 1829 (Nfld. Archives KCRC); Richard, of Trinity, 1830 (Nfld. Archives KCRC); John, fisherman of Gander Bay, 1850, of Bonavista, 1854 (DPHW 83, 70); William Wish, of St. John's, 1855 (DPHW 26D); Charles, of Knights Cove (Bonavista B.), 1859 (Nfld. Archives KCRC); John, of Port au Bras, 1860 (DPHW 100); Catherine, of Grates

Cove, 1860 (DPHW 56); James, of Cinq Cerf, 1861 (DPHW 99); David, of Harbour Grace, 1865 (Nfld. Archives HGRC); scattered in Lovell 1871.

Modern status: Widespread, especially at Creston, Mann Point (Fogo district), Rock Harbour (Placentia B.), St. Bernards (Fortune B.) and Ireland's Eye.

Place names: Hodder Rock 48-12 53-28; Hodderville 48-32 53-18; Jim Hodder Shoal 47-39 58-04.

HODDINOTT, a variant of the surname of England, also Hodnett, Hoddnott, from the English place name Hodnet (Shropshire), from Old Welsh *hōth* – pleasant, peaceful, and *nant* – valley, stream. (Cottle, Ekwall). *See* HOLMES.

Guppy traced Hoddinott in Dorset, Hampshire, Somerset, Warwickshire, Wiltshire and Worcestershire, Hoddnott and Hodnett in Worcestershire, and Hodnett in Shropshire; MacLysaght traced Hodnett in Co. Cork as the name of a family which assumed the Gaelic patronymic MacSherry.

In Newfoundland:

Early instances: Gustavus Hoddinott, Hodnot(t), of Swain's Island (now Wesleyville), 1827, of Middle Bill Cove, 1838, of Greenspond, 1844 (DPHW 72, 76); John Hodnett, of Seldom-Come-By, 1828 (DPHW 83); Thomas Hoddinott, of Exploits Burnt Island, 1844 (DPHW 86); James Hodnet, of Indian Islands, 1871 (Lovell).

Modern status: Scattered, especially at Salt Pond (Gander district), Brig Bay (St. Barbe district) and St. John's.

HODGE, a surname of England, a pet-form of the baptismal name, Roger. "The colloquial use of *Hodge* to denote an agricultural labourer is an indication of the former frequency of the name." (Withycombe, Reaney). *See* RO(D)GERS.

Traced by Guppy in Cornwall, Devon and Lancashire.

In Newfoundland:

Early instances: Thomas, of Island of Spear (now Spear Island), 1708 (CO 194.4); John, of St. John's, 1708 (CO 194.4); Caleb, captain of the *William* of Petty Harbour, 1760 (CO 194.15); Jeremiah, of Port de Grave, 1785 (CO 199.18); Caleb, of Ferryland, 1791 (USPG); James, of Kelligrews, 1832 (DPHW 30); Thomas, trader of Fogo, 1871 (Lovell); Richard and Thomas, of Lord's Cove (Burin district), 1871 (Lovell); John, of Savage Cove (St. Barbe district), 1875 (DPHW 95).

Modern status: Scattered, especially at Lord's Cove, Savage Cove and Main Brook (White B.).

Place names: Hodge's Cove, —— —— Island 48-01 53-44; —— Hill 46-54 55-47, 49-04 55-53; Hodgewater Pond 47-27 53-24; —— River (or Rocky River) 47-13 53-35.

HODGSON, a surname of England, – son of Hodge (Roger). *See* HODGE. (Reaney).

Traced by Guppy mainly in the north of England and especially in Durham.

In Newfoundland:

Early instances: David, of St. John's, 1796 (DPHW 26B); John Hodgion, of Heart's Ease, 1827 (DPHW 59A); Frances Margaret Hodgson, from Woodhead (Cumberland), married at St. John's, 1854 (DPHW 26D).

Modern status: Rare, at Shoal Harbour West (*Electors* 1955), and St. John's.

HOFFE, a surname of England, ? from the English place name Hoff (Westmorland), or Old English, Old Norse *hof* – (dweller by the) house, or ? heathen temple; or, if a variant of HOWE, HOUGH, Houf etc., from Old English *hōh* – heel, projecting ridge of land, steep ridge, spur of a hill, slight rise, common in many English place names, including Hough (Cheshire, Derbyshire). (Ekwall, Reaney).

In Newfoundland:

Early instances: Joseph Hoff(e), of Gander Bay, 1851 (DPHW 83); John and Philip Hoffe, fishermen of Change Islands, 1871 (Lovell).

Modern status: Scattered, especially at Change Islands.

HOGAN, a surname of Ireland, (O)Hogan, *Ó hÓgáin*, Ir. *óg* – young. (MacLysaght).

Traced by MacLysaght in Cos. Cork and Tipperary.

In Newfoundland:

Early instances: Patrick Hocgan, servant in fishery at Oderin, about 1730–35 (CO 194.9); Edmund Hogan, of St. John's, 1770 (DPHW 26C); Daniel, from Ireland, labourer of Bonavista, 1774 (CO 194.32); Patrick, of Harbour Main, 1779 (MUN Hist.); William, of Ochre Pit Cove, 1786 (CO 199.18); Timothy, of Burin, 1789 (D'Alberti 4); William, of Northern Bay, 1796 (CO 199.18); Thomas, from Monchaen (? for Mooncoin) (Co. Kilkenny), married at St. John's, 1804 (Nfld. Archives BRC); John, of Broad Cove (now Duntara), 1805 (Bonavista Register 1806); Thomas, of Harbour Grace Parish, 1808 (Nfld. Archives HGRC); Michael, one of 72 impressed men who sailed from Ireland to Newfoundland, ? 1811 (CO 194.51); John, of Broad Cove (unspecified) (Conception B.), 1812 (Nfld. Archives BRC); Edward, of King's Cove, 1815 (Nfld. Archives KCRC); Margaret, from Middleton (Co. Cork), married at Bonavista, 1829 (Nfld. Archives KCRC); James, of Bird Island Cove (now Elliston), 1830 (Nfld. Archives KCRC); Patrick, member of the Roman Catholic School Board, Placentia, 1844 (*Nfld. Almanac*); ——, on the *Science* in the seal fishery out of Harbour Grace, 1847 (*Newfoundlander* 25 Mar 1847); Thomas, from Newton (Co. Waterford), of Carbonear, 1855, died 1866 aged 68 (*Newfoundlander* 29 Nov 1855, R.C. Cemetery, Carbonear); James, of Plate Cove (Bonavista B.), 1857 (Nfld. Archives KCRC); James, of Tickle Cove (Bonavista B.), 1858 (Nfld. Archives KCRC); Ellen, of Round Cove (Bonavista B.), 1866 (Nfld. Archives KCRC); Ellen, of Deer Harbour (Bonavista B.), 1866 (Nfld. Archives KCRC); Catherine, of Dog Cove (Bonavista B.), 1866 (Nfld. Archives KCRC); Edward, of Shoals [sic] Cove (Bonavista B.), 1866 (Nfld. Archives KCRC); Alice, of Knights Cove (Bonavista B.), 1867 (Nfld. Archives KCRC); Edmund, of Cottells Island (Bonavista B.), 1870 (Nfld. Archives KCRC); Michael, of St. Mary's, 1871 (Lovell); Patrick, miner of Tilt Cove, 1871 (Lovell).

Modern status: Scattered, especially at Carbonear, Northern Bay and St. John's.

Place names: Hogan Cove, —— —— Head 47-25 54-14, (Labrador) 52-24 55-41; Hogan's Pond 47-35 52-51.

HOGARTH, a surname of England, from Old English *hogg* and *hierde* – swineherd. (Reaney).

Traced by Guppy in Cumberland, Westmorland, Northumberland and Yorkshire.

In Newfoundland:

Early instances: Isaac, of Trinity, 1787 (DPHW 64); William, of Bonaventure (unspecified), 1806, of Filthy (now British) Harbour, 1812, 1815 (DPHW 64); James, of Pope's Harbour, 1811 (DPHW 64); William, planter of Ireland's Eye, 1846 (DPHW 59A).

Modern status: Rare, at St. John's and Trinity (Trinity B.).

HOLDEN, a surname of England and Ireland, from the English place name Holden (Lancashire, Yorkshire WR) or Old English *holh*, *denu* – (dweller in the) hollow valley; in Ireland also for Howlin, a Breton diminutive of Hugo (*see* HUE). (Reaney, MacLysaght).

Traced by Guppy in Lancashire, Lincolnshire, Suffolk and Yorkshire WR, and by MacLysaght in Cos. Kilkenny and Wexford.

In Newfoundland:

Early instances: William, in fishery at Petty Harbour, 1794–5, "25 years in Newfoundland," that is, 1769–70 (Census 1794–5); Robert, of Harbour Grace, 1780 (CO 199.18); John, from Inistioge (Co. Kilkenny), married at St. John's, 1811 (Nfld. Archives BRC); Thomas, from Birmingham (Warwickshire), married at St. John's, 1812 (Nfld. Archives BRC); Richard, of St. John's, 1813 (DPHW 26B); William, of Brigus, 1855 (*Newfoundlander* 8 Nov 1855); Michael, fisherman of Cupids, 1871 (Lovell); Patrick and William, farmers of Harbour Main, 1871 (Lovell).

Modern status: At St. John's and Come-by-Chance.

HOLLAHAN, HOLLIHAN, HOLLOHAN, HOULAHAN, HOULIHAN, variants of the surname of Ireland, (O)Hoolahan, *Ó hUallacháin*, Ir. *uallach* – proud, of which seventeen variants have been recorded. (MacLysaght).

See also HOLLAND, NOLAN.

MacLysaght traced (O)Hoolahan in Co. Clare and mid-Leinster, Houlihan in Munster, Holohan in Co. Kilkenny, and NOLAN as a frequent synonym in north Connacht.

In Newfoundland:

Early instances: John Houlahan, shoemaker of St. John's, 1794–5, "18 years in Newfoundland," that is, 1776–7 (Census 1794–5); Denis Hollihan, fisherman of St. John's, 1794–5, "8 years in Newfoundland," that is, 1786–7 (Census 1794–5); —— Holahan, of Bay Bulls, 1789 (D'Alberti 4); William Hollanan, of Bonavista, 1806 (DPHW 70); James Hollehen or Holihan, of Harbour Grace Parish, 1811 (Nfld. Archives HGRC); Cornelius Hollihan, one of 72 impressed men who sailed from Ireland to Newfoundland, ? 1811 (CO 194.51); Richard Holaghan, of Trepassey, 1815 (Nfld. Archives BRC); Richard Holahan or Hollohand, of Kings Cove, 1815 (Nfld. Archives KCRC); Patrick Holahan, of Bonavista, 1816 (Nfld. Archives KCRC); —— Hollahan, in fishing partnership at Bareneed, 1821 (CO 194.64); James, of Greenspond, 1823, of Cape Cove (Bonavista B.), 1827 (Nfld. Archives KCRC); John Holahan, of Bird Island Cove (now Elliston), 1830 (Nfld. Archives KCRC); Pat Holohen, of Placentia, 1839 (Nfld. Archives BRC); Margaret Hollahan, of Old Perlican, 1843 (DPHW 58); Patrick Houlahan, from Graguenamara (for Graiguenamanagh) (Co. Kilkenny), of Harbour Grace, 1844 (*Indicator* 27 Jul 1844); Thomas Hollohan, of Cat Harbour (now Lumsden), 1845 (Nfld. Archives KCRC); Thomas, of Tickle Cove (Bonavista B.),

1846 (Nfld. Archives KCRC); —— Houlahan, on the *Caledonia* in the seal fishery out of New Perlican, 1847 (*Newfoundlander* 1 Apr 1847); Lawrence Hollohan, of Gooseberry Island (Bonavista B.), 1856 (Nfld. Archives KCRC); Thomas, of Indian Arm (Bonavista B.), 1857 (Nfld. Archives KCRC); Margaret Hoolahan, of Catalina, 1857 (Nfld. Archives KCRC); Denis Hollohan, of Burn (for Burnt) Island (Bonavista B.), 1858 (Nfld. Archives KCRC); James, of Cape Freels (Bonavista B.), 1859 (Nfld. Archives KCRC); John, of Keels, 1868 (Nfld. Archives KCRC); Richard, of Broad Cove (now Duntara), 1869 (Nfld. Archives KCRC); Michael Holahan, farmer of Flatrock (St. John's), 1871 (Lovell); William Holihan, of Merasheen, 1871 (Lovell); James Hollohn, of Middle Bill Cove (Bonavista B.), 1871 (Lovell); James and William Hulahan, of Little Placentia (now Argentia), 1871 (Lovell); James, of Salmonier (Placentia), 1871 (Lovell).

Modern status: Hollahan, scattered; Hollihan, at St. John's; Hollohan, especially at Summerville; Houlahan, at Grand Falls; Houlihan, scattered.

HOLLAND(S), surnames of England, HOLLAND of Ireland, from the English place name Holland (Essex, Lancashire, Lincolnshire, Devon), rather than from the country; in Ireland also for Mulholland in Co. Limerick, sometimes for Holohan (*see* HOLLAHAN) in Co. Clare, and for (O)Holian, *Ó hOileáin*, in Co. Galway. (Reaney, Cottle, Spiegelhalter, MacLysaght).

Guppy traced Holland in nine counties, especially Cheshire, Spiegelhalter in Devon, and MacLysaght in Ireland as shown above.

In Newfoundland:

Family tradition: C. W. Hollands, from Gravesend (Kent) settled in the Bonne Bay district about ? 1870 (MUN Folklore).

Early instances: Robert Holland, of St. John's, 1708–09 (CO 194.4); Daniel, of Harbour Grace Parish, 1819 (Nfld. Archives HGRC); James, of Greenspond, 1824 (Nfld. Archives KCRC); D., of Harbour Grace, 1832 (*Newfoundlander* 23 Aug 1832); William, fisherman of ? Codroy, 1838 (DPHW 101); James (and others), of Bird Island Cove (now Elliston), 1871 (Lovell); Frederick, of Rose Blanche, 1871 (Lovell).

Modern status: Holland, rare and scattered; Hollands, rare, at St. John's.

Place name: Holland Rock 47-10 55-30.

HOLLETT, a surname of England, ? an unrecorded variant of HALLETT.

In Newfoundland:

Early instances: Thomas Hollitt & Co., and Samuel, of Burin, 1805 (D'Alberti 15); Samuel Hollett, of Adams Cove, 1806 (CO 199.18); Mary Hollet, of Harbour Grace Parish, 1819 (Nfld. Archives HGRC); James Hollett, of Bird Island Cove (now Elliston), 1825 (MUN Hist.); John, planter of Western Bay, 1827 (DPHW 52A); Thomas Hollet(t), of St. John's, 1828 (DPHW 26B); Ed Holet, married at St. John's, 1831 (Nfld. Archives BRC); Joseph Hollett, born at Biscayan Cove, 1834 (DPHW 52A); ——, planter of Sound Island, 1835 (Wix); Thomas, of Blackhead (Bay de Verde district), 1835, of Broad Cove (Bay de Verde district), 1843 (DPHW 52A); Mary, of Seldom-Come-By, 1858 (DPHW 85); Philip and William, of Arnold's Cove, 1871 (Lovell); Isaac, of Flat Island (now Port Elizabeth), 1871 (Lovell); Theodore, of Harbour Breton, 1871 (Lovell); John, of Harbour Buffett, 1871 (Lovell); James, miner of La Manche, 1871 (Lovell); Edward, of Mulley's Cove (Conception B.), 1871 (Lovell).

Modern status: Widespread, especially in the Burin, Placentia West and St. John's districts.

Place names: Hollett Rock 47-18 54-19; Hollett's Cove 47-48 54-03; —— Islands 47-39 54-10; —— Point 47-47 54-11.

HOLLEY, a surname of England, HOLLY of Ireland, from Old English *hol* and *lēah* – (dweller by the) clearing in the hollow, or *hol* and *ēage* – hollow-eye, a nickname; in Ireland for *Mac Cuilinn* by translation (Co. Kerry), and an occasional synonym of MacQuillan in Ulster. (Reaney, MacLysaght).

In Newfoundland:

Early instances: William Holly, fisherman of St. John's, 1794–5, "30 years in Newfoundland," that is, 1764–5 (Census 1794–5); Robert, planter of Renews, about 1788 (D'Alberti 7); William Holley, servant of Battle Harbour (Labrador), 1795 (MUN Hist.); Michael Holey, of Ferryland, 1818 (D'Alberti 24); Anne Holly, of Harbour Grace Parish, 1823 (Nfld. Archives HGRC); Thomas Holly or Hally, of Tilton Harbour (now Tilting), 1824 (Nfld. Archives KCRC); Thomas Holl(e)y or Helley, of Western Bay, 1842 (DPHW 52A); James Holly, fisherman of Harbour Breton, 1854 (DPHW 104); Edward, farmer of Topsail, 1871 (Lovell).

Modern status: At Mockbeggar (Bonavista B.), Point Enragée (*Electors* 1955), Harbour Breton and Corner Brook.

HOLLIHAN, HOLLOHAN. *See* HOLLAHAN

HOLLOWAY, a surname of England and Ireland from Old English *hol, weg* – (dweller by the) hollow, sunken road, or from the place names Holloway (Middlesex) or Holloway Farm and Wood (Devon). (Reaney, Cottle, Spiegelhalter, Guppy, MacLysaght).

Traced by Guppy in Dorset, Gloucestershire, Wiltshire and Worcestershire, by Spiegelhalter in Devon, and by MacLysaght ? in Leinster.

In Newfoundland:

Early instances: Thomas Hollowaye, of St. John's Harbour, 1675 (CO 1); William Holloway, of Battle Harbour (Labrador), 1795 (MUN Hist.); Stephen, of Bonavista, 1808 (DPHW 70); Elizabeth Hol(lo)way, Holliway or Halloway, of King's Cove, 1824 (Nfld. Archives KCRC); Thomas Halloway, of Catalina, 1834 (DPHW 67); James Holloway, of Red Cliff Island (Bonavista B.),1841 (DPHW 73A); William, of Barrow Harbour (Bonavista B.), 1842 (DPHW 73A); John, of Plate Cove (Bonavista B.), 1849, of Open Hall, 1852 (DPHW 73); John, of Stock Cove (Bonavista B.), 1868 (Nfld, Archives KCRC); Kate, of Broad Cove (now Duntara), 1869 (Nfld. Archives KCRC); Samuel (and others), of Musgravetown, 1871 (Lovell); William Hallaway, of Grates Cove, 1871 (Lovell); Charles Helleway, of Pool's Island, 1871 (Lovell).

Modern status: Widespread, especially at Glovertown (Bonavista North district) and in the Bonavista South district with large concentrations at Bloomfield, Lethbridge and Port Blandford.

Place names: Holloway Bight (Labrador) 53-03 55-46; —— Cove 48-23 53-54; —— Passage 47-22 54-48; —— Rock 48-05 53-42.

HOLMAN, a surname of England, from Old English *holh* and *man* – dweller in the hollow. (Reaney).

Traced by Guppy in Cornwall and Sussex and by Spiegelhalter in Devon.

In Newfoundland:

Early instances: Andrew, boatkeeper of St. John's Harbour, 1682 (CO 1); Andrew, of Petty Harbour, 1708 (CO 194.4); Francis, merchant's clerk, of Harbour Breton, 1858 (DPHW 104); Henry S., agent at Gaultois, 1871 (Lovell); Elizabeth, married in Harbour Grace Parish, 1879 (Nfld. Archives HGRC).

Modern status: Unique, at St. John's.

HOLMES, a surname of England, Scotland and Ireland; in England from Old Norse *holmr* – (dweller near a) piece of flat land in a fen or land partly surrounded by streams, or from Middle English *holm* – holly, holm-oak, as in the place names Holne (Devon), Holme (Dorset, Yorkshire WR); in Scotland from places named Holmes; in Ireland from the

Scots surname or in north Connacht for Cavish (MacAvish). (Reaney, Cottle, Black, MacLysaght). *See* HODDINOTT.

Found widespread by Guppy in England and by MacLysaght in Ireland, especially in Ulster.

In Newfoundland:

Family traditions: Thomas Henry, William and James Hoddinott, ? from Kent settled at Seldom-Come-By in the early 19th century and changed their name to Holmes to avoid detection. Later some of the family reassumed the name Hoddinott (MUN Folklore). John Holmes, from Bradford (Yorkshire), settled at Shearstown about 1855 (MUN Folklore).

Early instances: James Homes, of St. John's, 1770 (DPHW 26C); John Holmes, of Adams Cove, 1791 (CO 199.18); Mary Homes, of Harbour Grace Parish, 1815 (Nfld. Archives HGRC); Thomas, of Grand Bank, 1834 (DPHW 106).

Modern status: Scattered, especially at Seldom-Come-By (Fogo district) and Shearstown.

Place name: Holme Point (Labrador) 54-08 58-25.

HOLWELL, a surname of England, – (dweller by the) holy spring, or from the common English place name Holwell (Devon, Dorset). (Spiegelhalter).

Spiegelhalter traced Holwill in Devon.

In Newfoundland:

Early instances: John Hollowell, of St. John's Harbour, 1675 (CO 1); William Holwell, schoolteacher of Tizzard's Harbour, 1871 (Lovell).

Modern status: At Salt Harbour Island (Twillingate district), Corner Brook and St. John's.

HOMER, a surname of England and Guernsey (Channel Islands), from Old English sources – (dweller by the) pool (*mere*) in the hollow, or by a holly-bush, or on flat land near water, or from English place names Holmer (Buckinghamshire, Herefordshire) or Homer (Devon, Shropshire), or from Old French *he(a)umier* – maker of helmets. (Reaney, Cottle, Turk).

Traced by Guppy in Dorset.

In Newfoundland:

Early instances: Robert, servant of Battle Harbour (Labrador) 1795 (MUN Hist.); James, of Freshwater (Carbonear), 1812 (DPHW 48); Roger, cooper of Carbonear, 1826 (DPHW 48).

Modern status: Rare, at Carbonear (*Electors* 1955), Victoria and St. John's.

HONEYCOTE, a surname of England, from the English place names Huncoat (Lancashire) or Huncote (Leicestershire). (Ekwall, E. C. Smith).

In Newfoundland:

Early instance: Henry Honeycot, of Hermitage Cove, 1835 (DPHW 30).

Modern status: Rare, at Harbour Breton (*Electors* 1955).

HONEYGOLD, a surname of England, ? a variant of Hornagold or Hornigold, from the English place name Horninghold (Leicestershire). (Reaney).

In Newfoundland:

Modern status: Rare, at St. John's.

HONG, a surname of China – ease, repose, peace, vigour, health, fragrant.

In Newfoundland:

Modern status: At St. John's and Carbonear.

HOOD, a surname of England, Scotland and Ireland, from a Middle English personal name *Hod, Hudde* etc., or from Old English *hōd* – (maker of) hood(s), or from the place name Hood (Devon); in Ireland also for O'Hood, *Ó hUid,* changed to Mahood (MacHood). (Reaney, Spiegelhalter, MacLysaght). *See also* HODDER.

Traced by Guppy in Dorset and Norfolk, and south of the Forth and Clyde.

In Newfoundland:

Early instances: Richard, of Lewis Bay (Labrador), 1787, of Fogo, 1789, servant of Battle Harbour (Labrador), 1795 (MUN Hist.); Jane, of St. John's, 1806 (Nfld. Archives BRC); Richard, of Harbour Grace Parish, 1822 (Nfld. Archives HGRC); John Dreweatt, from Newcastle-upon-Tyne, married at St. John's, 1855 (*Newfoundlander* 9 Aug 1855); Francis, of Greenspond, 1857 (DPHW 76); Henry, of Herring Neck, 1871 (Lovell); Elizabeth Hoods, of Bay Roberts, 1871 (Lovell).

Modern status: Rare, at St. John's.

HOOKEY, a surname of England, ? a variant of Hockey, ? from an Old English personal name such as *Hocca,* or of Hookway, from the English place name Hookway (Devon). (Spiegelhalter).

Guppy traced Hockey in Somerset and Hookway in Devon.

In Newfoundland:

Early instances: Stephen Hook(e)y, of Trinity Bay, 1772, of Bonaventure (unspecified), 1788 (DPHW 64); Stephen Hookey, of Salmon Cove (now Champneys), 1802 (DPHW 64); Samuel, planter of Bonavista, 1833 (DPHW 64B); Samuel, planter of Old Bonaventure, 1842 (DPHW 64B); Mary, of Trinity, 1852 (DPHW 64B).

Modern status: Scattered, especially at Champneys and St. John's.

HOOPER, a surname of England and Guernsey (Channel Islands), from Old English *hōp* – (maker of) hoop(s), cooper. (Reaney, Cottle, Turk).

Traced by Guppy in Berkshire, Cornwall, Devon, Gloucestershire, Somerset and Wiltshire.

In Newfoundland:

Early instances: John, of Renews, 1676 (CO 1); Moses, of Twillingate, 1768 (MUN Hist.); Stephen, of Bonavista, 1791 (USPG); William, of Placentia, 1794 (D'Alberti 5); William, fisherman of Bay of Exploits, ? 1797 (CO 194.39); William, of Trinity and Mortier, 1813 (H.P. Smith); William, of Burin, 1818 (D'Alberti 28); William, of Lamaline, 1822 (DPHW 109); Thomas, hoopmaker of Bay Despair, 1854 (DPHW 102); Thomas, fisherman of La Plant(e) (Burgeo-La Poile district), 1860 (DPHW 99); Charles, of Rock Harbour (Placentia B.), 1860 (DPHW 100); John, of Sandy Point (St. George's district), 1871 (DPHW 96); William, of Northern Harbour (head of Exploits B.), 1871 (Lovell).

Modern status: Scattered, especially at Rock Harbour and Creston South.

Place names: Hooper Point, —— Rock 47-02 55-10.

HOOPY, ? a Newfoundland variant of the surname of France Houpert, from an Old German personal name *Holdberht* containing the elements *obliging* and *brilliant, illustrious.* (Dauzat).

In Newfoundland:

Tradition: Borne by a French sailor who settled at Fortune. (P.E.L. Smith).

Modern Status: Rare, at Fortune (*Electors* 1955).

HOPEN, ? a variant of the surnames of England, Hoppen, Hopping or Hoppins, from the Old English personal name *Hoppa,* from the diminutive Hob for Robert, or from Old English *hop* – (dweller in or near the) raised land in a fen, or in a small enclosed valley, or from the English place name Hoppen (Northumberland). (Reaney, Cottle, Spiegelhalter, Ekwall).

Spiegelhalter traced Hopping, Hoppins in Devon.

In Newfoundland:

Early instance: Richard Hoppins (Hoppings in 1677), of St. John's, 1675, 1681 (CO 1).

Modern status: Rare, at Burin Bay Arm (*Electors* 1955).

HOPKINS, a surname of England and Ireland, a diminutive of *Hobb* (Robert) (*see* ROBERTS); in Ireland also for *Mac Oibicín* in Connacht and Co. Longford.

Traced by Guppy in Bedfordshire, Cambridgeshire, Dorset, Monmouthshire and South Wales, and by Spiegelhalter in Devon. Hopkin is associated with Hopkins in South Wales and Cambridgeshire.

In Newfoundland:

Family tradition: —— Hopkins, from ? Bideford (Devon), settled at Green's Harbour (Trinity B.) (MUN Hist.).

Early instances: Richard, of Scilly Cove (now Winterton), 1675, 1682 (CO 1); Lady, sister of Sir David Kirke, of Ferryland, 1675 (CO 1); Henry, of Keelegs [sic] (for Keels), north of Bonavista, 1681 (CO 1); Edward, of Trinity Bay, 1768 (DPHW 64); Henry, proprietor and occupier of fishing room at Old Perlican, Winter 1800–01 (Census Trinity B.); Edward, occupier, and Richard and Thomas, proprietors and occupiers of fishing rooms at Heart's Content, Winter 1800–01 (Census Trinity B.); Richard, of Carbonear, 1810 (DPHW 48); Henry, of Petty Harbour, 1813 (DPHW 26B); William, planter of Hants Harbour, 1823 (DPHW 58); ——, on the *Native* in the seal fishery out of New Perlican, 1847 (*Newfoundlander* 1 Apr 1847); ——, on the *Henry* in the seal fishery out of Harbour Grace and Carbonear, 1849 (*Newfoundlander* 22 Mar 1849); ——, on the *Native* in the seal fishery out of St. John's, 1854 (*Newfoundlander* 9 Mar 1854); Charles, of Englee, 1870 (MUN Hist.); David, of Braha (now Brehat), 1871 (Lovell); William, of Green's Harbour, 1871 (Lovell); Robert, of Twillingate, 1871 (Lovell); Thomas, of Whales Brook (Trinity B.), 1871 (Lovell).

Modern status: Scattered, especially at Englee, Whales Brook and Old Perlican.

Place name: Hopkins Island 47-36 58-43.

HOPLEY, a surname of England, from Old English *hop* and *lēah* – (dweller in the) clearing in a valley, or from an unidentified English place name. (Bardsley).

Traced by Guppy in Cheshire.

In Newfoundland:

Early instance: S., of Placentia, 1724 (CO 194.8).

Modern status: Rare, at St. John's.

HORAN, a surname of Ireland, (O)Horan, *Ó hOdhráin*, Ir. *odhar* – dun-coloured, or for Haren and Hourihan. (MacLysaght).

Traced by MacLysaght in Cos. Cork and Mayo.

In Newfoundland:

Early instances: David, of St. John's, 1783 (DPHW 26C); Elenor, from Co. Tipperary, married at St. John's, 1803 (Nfld. Archives BRC).

Modern status: At St. John's.

HORDERN, a surname of England, from the English place name Horden (Lancashire), Horderne (Cheshire), or (dweller at the) storehouse. (Cottle, Bardsley).

Traced by Bardsley in Cheshire.

In Newfoundland:

Modern status: Unique, at St. John's (*Electors* 1955).

HORLICK. *See* HARLICK

HORTON, a surname of England, from the English place name Horton, found in over fourteen counties, usually from Old English *Horh-tūn* or *Horu-tūn* – the farm, village on muddy land, but in Gloucestershire from *heorta-dūn* – hill frequented by stags. (Cottle, Ekwall).

Traced by Guppy in Buckinghamshire, Cheshire, Devon, Shropshire, Warwickshire and Worcestershire.

In Newfoundland:

Early instances: Jarvas, Edward and David, (also Richard in 1682), of Trinity, 1675 (CO 1); Thomas, (also John in 1676), of Harbour Grace, 1675 (CO 1); Richard, (Orton in 1680), of St. John's, 1676, 1682 (CO 1); Robert Hurton, of Bay Bulls district, 1803 (Nfld. Archives BRC).

Modern status: Rare, at St. John's.

Place names: Horton (or Jonathan) Island (Labrador) 56-50 61-13; —— Rocks 47-45 53-11.

HORWOOD, a surname of England – (dweller by the) muddy wood, or from the place name Horwood (Buckinghamshire, Devon). (Reaney, Spiegelhalter).

Traced by Guppy in Buckinghamshire and by Spiegelhalter in Devon.

In Newfoundland:

Early instances: John, in possession of property and fisherman of Quidi Vidi, 1794–5, "45 years in Newfoundland," that is, 1749–50 (Census 1794–5); Richard, fisherman of St. John's, 1794–5, "born in Newfoundland" (Census 1794–5); Robert, of Western Bay, 1799 (CO 199.18); Robert, planter of Harbour Grace, 1832 (DPHW 43); Richard, planter of Carbonear, 1833 (DPHW 48); William, from Chudleigh (Devon), married at St. John's, 1854 (*New-*

foundlander 26 Jan 1854); William, of Brigus, 1855 (DPHW 35); Matthew Harwood, fisherman of Little Bay (Burgeo-La Poile district), 1860 (DPHW 99); John, of Exploits Burnt Island, 1871 (Lovell); John, of Moreton's Harbour, 1871 (Lovell); Henry, of Twillingate, 1871 (Lovell).

Modern status: Scattered, especially at Carbonear, Durrell's Arm (Twillingate district) and St. John's.

Place names: Horwood (formerly Dog Bay) 49-27 54-32; —— (or Dog) Bay 49-30 54-30; —— —— (or Dog Bay) Islands 49-32 54-25.

HOSKINS, a surname of England and Ireland, and of the Micmacs of Newfoundland, from a diminutive of the Old English personal name *Os-*, a shortened form of such names as *Ōsgōd*, *Ōsbeorn*, *Ōsmǣr*, etc. (Reaney).

Guppy traced Hoskin(g) in Cornwall and Devon, Hoskin(g)s in Monmouthshire and Somerset.

In Newfoundland:

Family tradition: John, from Devon, settled at Old Perlican before 1792 (MUN Hist.).

Early instances: William, of Trinity, 1760 (DPHW 64); Richard, of Cat's Cove (now Conception Harbour), 1779 (CO 199.18); William, proprietor and occupier of fishing room at New Harbour (Trinity B.), Winter 1800–01 (Census Trinity B.); John, proprietor and occupier of fishing room at Grates Cove, Winter 1800–01 (Census Trinity B.); John, performer of divine service at Twillingate, 1811 (D'Alberti 21); Martha, of Tickle Harbour (now Bellevue), 1817 (Nfld. Archives KCRC); Henry, of Harbour Grace Parish, 1828 (Nfld. Archives HGRC); Anne, baptized at Cape Cove (Bonavista North district), 1830, aged 23 years (DPHW 76); Henry, ? of Northern Bay, 1840 (DPHW 54); George, trader "lately established at Ship Cove" on the South Coast, about 1851 (*Gisborne's Journal of an Electric Telegraph Survey in Newfoundland, 1851*, by Frederick Newton Gisborne (1824–92), ? same as George Hoskins, Micmac of Conne River about 1872 (Raoul Andersen); Thomas, of Harbour Grace, 1866 (Nfld. Archives HGRC); scattered in Lovell 1871.

Modern status: Scattered, especially at St. Albans and St. John's.

Place names: Hoskins Harbour 49-20 55-11; —— Pond 47-43 53-14; Hoskyn Rock 49-39 55-47.

HOUGH, a surname of England and Ireland; in England a variant of HOFFE, HOWE; in Ireland a variant of (O)Haugh, *Ó hEachach*. (MacLysaght)

Traced by Guppy in Cheshire and Lancashire, and by MacLysaght in Co. Limerick.

In Newfoundland:

Early instance: Thomas ? Hough, merchant of St. John's, 1775 (CO 194.19).

Modern status: Rare, at St. John's (*Electors* 1955).

HOULAHAN, HOULIHAN. *See* HOLLAHAN

HOUNSELL, a surname of England, ? from an unidentified place name.

Traced by Guppy in Dorset.

In Newfoundland:

Family traditions: Varying traditions ascribe the origins of the family to Bedfordshire, Isle of Wight and Bristol (MUN Folklore, MUN Hist.). Richard, ? from Bedfordshire, of Pinchard's Island, in the late 18th century (MUN Hist.).

Early instances: Grace Ownsel [sic], baptized at Greenspond, 1830, aged 25 (DPHW 76); Richard Hounsell, of Pinchard's Island (Bonavista B.), 1833 (DPHW 76); ——, merchant of St. John's, 1844 (*Newfoundlander* 19 Dec 1844); George, of Indian Burying Place, 1847, of Nippers Harbour, 1853 (DPHW 86); George, of Fair Island (Bonavista B.), 1871 (Lovell); George, of Stocking Harbour (Green B.), 1871 (Lovell).

Modern status: Scattered, especially at Pound Cove (Bonavista B.).

Place name: Jimmy Hounsell's Island 49-11 53-32.

HOUSE, HOWSE, surnames of England, from Old English *hūs* – (employee at the) house, monastery, convent, or a variant of HOWE(s) (*see* HOFFE), or from the place name Ovis (Devon). (Reaney, Spiegelhanter).

Guppy traced House in Dorset, Hampshire and Somerset, Howse in Wiltshire. Spiegelhalter traced House, Howse and Howes in Devon.

In Newfoundland:

Early instances: Edward House, of New Perlican, 1675 (CO 1); William, of St. John's or place adjacent, ? 1706 (CO 194.24); George, of Bonavista, 1791 (DPHW 70); John, of Carbonear, 1801 (CO 199.18); John, of Greenspond, 1815 (DPHW 76); John, planter of Catalina, 1818 (DPHW 72); John, of Twillingate, 1822 (USPG); George, of Trinity, 1835 (DPHW 64B); Patrick Howse, of Harbour Grace Parish, 1835 (Nfld. Archives HGRC); Robert House, of New Bay Head (Twillingate district), 1851 (DPHW 86); John, of Gaultois, 1853 (DPHW 104); Robert, of Back Harbour (Twillingate district), 1861 (DPHW 88); Patrick, of Harbour Grace, 1866 (Nfld. Archives HGRC); scattered in Lovell 1871.

Modern status: House, widespread, especially at Bellburns and Gillams; Howse, scattered, especially at St. Albans and Glovertown.

Place names: House Cove 48-01 53-41; —— Harbour (Labrador) 56-14 61-03; —— Island 48-26 53-40; Howse Lake (Labrador) 55-09 66-30.

HOUSTON, a surname of Scotland and Ireland, from the Scots place name Houston (Renfrewshire); also in Ireland for MacQuiston and MacTaghlin. (Cottle, Black, MacLysaght).

Traced by MacLysaght in Ulster and Co. Donegal.

In Newfoundland:

Early instances: John, of St. John's, 1803 (D'Alberti 13); Daniel Houstan, farmer of Outer Cove, 1871 (Lovell).

Modern status: Rare, at Outer Cove (*Electors* 1955) and St. John's.

HOVEN, a surname ? of England, of unknown origin.

In Newfoundland:

Early instance: Lawrence ? Haven, labourer of St. John's, 1871 (Lovell).

Modern status: At Fogo and Baie Verte.

HOWARD, a surname of England and Ireland, from the personal names, Old German *Hugihard,* Old French *Huard,* containing the elements *heart* and *brave;* or from Old German *Howard, Howart* – high or chief warden; or from Old English *ēwe* and *hierde* – ewe-herd; also in Ireland for O'Hare, *Ó hÍomhair.* (Reaney, Cottle, MacLysaght).

Guppy found Howard widespread especially in Lancashire, Norfolk and Nottinghamshire; MacLysaght traced it in Co. Clare.

In Newfoundland:

Family tradition: Patrick, of Daniel's Cove (Bay de Verde district), 1836 (MUN Hist.).

Early instances: Edward, of New Perlican, 1675 (CO 1); Benjamin and Thomas, of Keelegs (for Keels), north of Bonavista, 1681 (CO 1); Richard, of Bayley's Cove (Bonavista B.), 1708–09 (CO 194.4); John, merchant of St. John's, 1787 (CO 194.38); Thomas, of Bonavista, 1794 (DPHW 70); Edward, of Carbonear, 1798 (CO 199.18); Sara, of Harbour Grace Parish, 1806 (Nfld. Archives HGRC); William, from Colleysbiddle (Dorset), married at St. John's, 1809 (Nfld. Archives BRC); David, from Ratheomick [sic], unidentified, ? Ireland, married at Harbour Grace, 1829 (Nfld. Archives BRC); Thomas, baptized at Gooseberry Island (Bonavista B.), 1830, aged 18 years (DPHW 76); James, of Kings Cove Parish, 1841

(Nfld. Archives KCRC); William, of Cat Harbour (now Lumsden), 1868 (Nfld. Archives KCRC).

Modern status: Scattered, especially at Daniel's Cove.

Place name: Howard Lake (Labrador) 59-36 63-53.

HOWE, one of at least sixteen variants of a surname of England and Ireland including HOFFE and HOUGH, from Old English *hōh* – heel, projecting ridge of land, steep ridge, spur of a hill, slight rise, common in many English place names, or from Old Norse *haugr* – mound, hill, as in Howe (Norfolk) and Howe Hill (Yorkshire ER); in Ireland "an occasional synonym of Hoey and of HOUGH." (Reaney, Cottle, MacLysaght).

Traced by Guppy in Bedfordshire, Derbyshire, Huntingdonshire, Northamptonshire and Somerset.

In Newfoundland:

Early instances: Daniel ? How, planter of St. John's, 1706 (CO 194.4); Samuel Howe, in fishery at Petty Harbour, 1794–5, "20 years in Newfoundland," that is, 1774–5 (Census 1794–5); Patrick Howe(s), of Harbour Grace Parish, 1828 (Nfld. Archives HGRC); John Howe, captain of Carbonear, 1828 (DPHW 48); ——, captain of the *Water Lily* in the seal fishery out of Trinity South, 1857 (*Newfoundlander* 19 Mar 1857); Samuel How, agent of Harbour Breton, 1859 (DPHW 104); Thomas Howe, fisherman of Harbour Buffett, 1871 (Lovell); James and Richard, fishermen of Mosquito (now Bristol's Hope), 1871 (Lovell).

Modern status: Scattered, especially at Corner Brook.

Place names: How(e) Harbour 51-21 55-56; How Lake (Labrador) 54-30 66-24; Mother Howe Bank 49-53 55-36.

HOWELL, a surname of England, Wales, Ireland and Guernsey (Channel Islands), from the Old Welsh personal name *Houel,* Old Breton *Houuel* – eminent, in the west of England from Wales, in the east from Brittany; or from the English place name Howell (Lincolnshire); in Ireland also for MacHale. (Reaney, Cottle, MacLysaght, Turk). *See also* POWELL.

Traced by Guppy in North and South Wales and in Norfolk, and by MacLysaght in Co. Mayo.

In Newfoundland:

Early instances: Robert, of Harbour Grace, 1681 (CO 1); James, of Carbonear, 1775, "property in possession of the Family for upwards of 91 years," that is, before 1684 (CO 199.18); John, planter of St.

John's, 1701 (CO 194.2); James, fisherman of Quidi Vidi, 1794–5, "20 years in Newfoundland," that is, 1774–5 (Census 1794–5); Richard, of Western Bay, 1788 (CO 199.18); Henry, of Bonavista, 1792 (USPG); Matthias, ? of Northern Bay, 1842 (DPHW 54); Henry Howel, of Cobbler's Island (Bonavista B.), 1843 (DPHW 76); William Howell, planter of Catalina, 1843 (DPHW 72); Francis, planter of New Perlican, 1845 (DPHW 48); Plemon, planter of Freshwater (Carbonear), 1851 (DPHW 49); Nathaniel, fisherman of Heart's Content, 1856 (DPHW 59A); George, of Old Perlican, 1871 (Lovell); Henry and James, of Pool's Island (Bonavista B.), 1871 (Lovell).

Modern status: Widespread, especially at Carbonear, St. John's and in the Bonavista North district.

Place names: Howell Lake (Labrador) 54-28 66-55; Howell's Lake (Labrador) 55-05 67-25; —— River (Labrador) 54-35 66-40.

HOWLETT, a surname of England, Ireland and the Channel Islands, a variant of HEWLETT, a double diminutive of the personal name Hugh (*see* HUE). (Reaney, MacLysaght, Turk).

Traced by Guppy in Norfolk and Suffolk, and by MacLysaght in Co. Wexford.

In Newfoundland:

Early instances: James, in fishery at Petty Harbour, 1794–5, "30 years in Newfoundland," that is, 1764–5 (Census 1794–5); Michael, shoreman of St. John's, 1794–5, "15 years in Newfoundland," that is, 1779–80 (Census 1794–5); Sara Houlet (or Howlet), of Harbour Grace Parish, 1806 (Nfld. Archives HGRC); Thomas Howelet, from Ross Parish (Co. Wexford), married at St. John's, 1813 (Nfld. Archives BRC); Michael Howlet, of Petty Harbour, 1828 (Nfld. Archives BRC); James, of King's Cove Parish, 1838 (Nfld. Archives KCRC); Catherine Howlett, of Harbour Grace, 1866 (Nfld. Archives HGRC); James Howlet, of Cape Broyle, 1871 (Lovell); James, of Great Paradise (Placentia B.), 1871 (Lovell); James Howlett, of Round Harbour (Fogo district), 1871 (Lovell); William, of Salmonier (St. Mary's), 1871 (Lovell); David (and others), of Toad's (now Tors) Cove, 1871 (Lovell); John, of Witless Bay, 1871 (Lovell).

Modern status: Scattered, especially at St. John's and on the Southern Shore.

Place name: Howlett Point 47-00 52-55.

HOWLEY, a surname of England and Ireland, in England from the English place name Howley (Gloucestershire, Lancashire, Somerset), Howle Hill (Herefordshire) or Howle (Shropshire); in Ireland, (O)Howley, *Ó hUallaigh*, ? Ir. *uallach* – proud. (MacLysaght, E.C. Smith).

Assumed by Bardsley to be a surname of Yorkshire, Lancashire or Cheshire, and traced by MacLysaght in Connacht and Co. Clare.

In Newfoundland:

Early instances: John, from Tipperary, of St. John's since 1815, died at Riverhead (St. John's), 1845, aged 54 years (*Times* 29 Jan 1845); John, from Waterford, married at St. John's, 1822 (Nfld. Archives BRC); Mary Howl(e)y, of Harbour Grace Parish, 1835 (Nfld. Archives HGRC); Michael Howley, of Carbonear, 1837 (*Newfoundlander* 18 May 1837).

Modern status: At St. John's and Corner Brook.

Place names: Howley 49-10 57-07; —— Lake 48-18 57-20; Mount —— 48-16 58-26.

HOWSE. *See* HOUSE

HOYLES, HOYLE, surnames of England, Hoyle of Ireland and Jersey (Channel Islands); in England from Old English *hol(h)* – hole, (dweller in the) hollow, reflecting the South Yorkshire dialectal pronunciation of "hole": in Ireland a variant of (Mac) Coyle, Mac Ilhoyle (*see* COYLE). (Reaney, Cottle, MacLysaght, Turk).

Guppy traced Hoyle in Yorkshire WR and Lancashire, Hoyles in Lincolnshire.

In Newfoundland:

Early instances: Newman, of St. John's, 1810 (D'Alberti 20); William John, clergyman of Brigus, 1849, of Carbonear, 1871 (DPHW 26D, Lovell); Joseph, fisherman of Swain's Island (now Wesleyville), 1871 (Lovell); James and Joseph, of Cupids, 1871 (Lovell); George, of Twillingate, 1871 (Lovell).

Modern status: Scattered, especially at Pool's Island (Bonavista B.) and Cupids.

Place name: Hoylestown (St. John's); Sammy Hoyles Island 49-09 53-34.

HUBBARD, a surname of England and Jersey (Channel Islands), from the baptismal name Hubert, Old German *Hugibert*, containing the elements *mind* and *bright*. (Withycombe, Reaney, Turk).

Traced by Guppy in Leicestershire, Rutlandshire, Norfolk and Suffolk, and by Spiegelhalter in Devon.

In Newfoundland:

Modern status: Rare, at Corner Brook.

Place names: Hubbard Island (Labrador) 57-19 61-19; —— River (Labrador) 59-55 64-10.

HUBLEY, a surname of England from ? the English place name Ubley (Somerset). (Ekwall).

In Newfoundland:

Early instance: Clarence Arthur (born 1877), from St. Margaret's Bay (Nova Scotia), settled at St. John's, 1917 (*Newfoundland Who's Who* 1930).

Modern status: At St. John's.

HUDDY, a surname of England and Ireland; in England a diminutive of *Hudd* (Richard) (*see* RICHARDS), in Ireland (O)Huddy, *O hUada*, "a Munster variant of the Connacht name Foody." (Bardsley, Reaney, MacLysaght).

Traced by Spiegelhalter in Devon and by MacLysaght in Munster.

In Newfoundland:

Modern status: Rare, at Burin and Epworth.

HUDSON, a surname of England and Ireland, son of *Hudd* (Richard), (*see* RICHARDS), or from the English place name Hudson (Devon). (Reaney, Spiegelhalter).

Traced by Guppy throughout the Midlands and north of England, by Spiegelhalter in Devon, and by MacLysaght in Dublin and Ulster.

In Newfoundland:

Family tradition: George, from Guernsey or Jersey (Channel Islands), settled at Adam's Cove (MUN Folklore).

Early instances: Matthew, of St. John's, 1677, of Quidi Vidi, 1680 (CO 1); George, of Adam's Cove, 1766 (CO 199.18); Matthew, of Blackhead (Bay de Verde district), 1803 (CO 199.18); Thomas, from Dunnamore (unidentified) (Co. Wexford), married at St. John's, 1816 (Nfld. Archives BRC); Anne, of Ragged Harbour (now Melrose), 1818 (Nfld. Archives KCRC); Elizabeth, of Harbour Grace Parish, 1822 (Nfld. Archives HGRC); John, planter of Catalina, 1822 (DPHW 72); Clement, fisherman of Biscayan Cove, 1824, of Cape St. Francis, 1826 (DPHW 52A); John, of Broad Cove (Bay de Verde district), 1840 (*Newfoundlander* 13 Feb 1840); ——, on the *Philanthropy* in the seal fishery out of Carbonear, 1847 (*Newfoundlander* 25 Mar 1847); Caroline, of Pouch Cove, 1849 (DPHW 32); Matthew, of Dantzick Cove, 1871 (Lovell).

Modern status: Scattered, especially at Pouch Cove, Adams Cove and St. John's.

Place names: Hudson Cove (Labrador) 52-27 55-46; —— Rock 47-41 53-45.

HUE, a surname of England and France, Huie of Scotland, one of many variants of the baptismal name Hugh, from Old German *Hugo*, Old French *Hue*, containing the elements *heart* and *mind;* in Scotland, Huie is an abridged form of Macilghuie, *Mac Gille dbuih* – son of the black lad. (Withycombe, Reaney, Black). *See also* HEWITT, HEWLETT, HEWLIN, HEWSON, HOWLETT, HUELIN, HUGHES, HULL, HUTCHENS, HUTCHINSON.

Black traced Huie in Argyllshire.

In Newfoundland:

Early instances: Major, Huie & Co., of Port de Grave, 1778 (Nfld. Archives T22); Patrick, from Port Glasgow, Scotland, merchant of St. John's, 1809, died 1842, aged 60 years (*Star and Newfoundland Advocate* 21 Apr 1842, D'Alberti 19).

Modern status: Rare, at St. John's.

HUELIN, HULAN, surnames of England, variants of HEWLIN, from Old German *Hughlin*, Old French *Hu(g)elin*, diminutives of the personal name *Hugo*. HU(E)LIN, surnames of France and of Jersey (Channel Islands) may derive from the hoot of the owl or from the Old German personal name *Hildo*, containing the element *battle*. (Withycombe, Reaney, Dauzat, Turk). *See* HUE.

In Newfoundland:

Early instances: Mrs. Hulan, at Second Barasway River (now McKay's) since before 1762 (Cormack 1822); Joseph Hulin, of St. John's, 1820 (D'Alberti 30); James Hulan, of Harbour Grace Parish, 1828 (Nfld. Archives HGRC); Joseph Huelin, of Little Codroy River, 1835 (DPHW 30); James Huelen, of Crabbes, 1835 (Wix); John Huelin, of Barrisways (St. George's B.), 1835 (DPHW 30); John, fisherman of Isle aux Morts, 1842 (DPHW 101); Moses, of Cape Ray, 1871 (Lovell); Isaac, of Channel, 1871 (Lovell); Joseph, of Fox Roost, 1871 (Lovell); ——, of Cow Head, 1873 (MUN Hist.).

Modern status: Huelin, rare, at Isle aux Morts and Robinson's; Hulan, scattered, especially at McKay's and elsewhere in the St. George's district.

HUGHES, a surname of England, Wales, Ireland and the Channel Islands, from the baptismal name Hugh (*see* HUE); in Ireland often a synonym of HAYES, *Ó hAodha*. (Reaney, MacLysaght, Turk).

Found widespread by Guppy especially in North and South Wales and the Welsh border counties, and by MacLysaght in all provinces except Munster.

In Newfoundland:

Early instances: William Henry, formerly of the East Norfolk Militia, of St. John's, 1812 (D'Alberti 22); Ann, from Ross (unspecified) (Co. Wexford), married at St. John's, 1813 (Nfld. Archives BRC);

Hugh, from Wales, of Joe Batt's Arm, 1818 (Nfld. Archives KCRC); Hugh, of Fogo, 1819 (Nfld. Archives KCRC); John, teacher of Broad Cove (unspecified), 1839 (*Newfoundlander* 1 Aug 1839); Henry, of Flowers Cove to Point Ferolle area, 1871 (Lovell); John, miner of Tilt Cove, 1871 (Lovell).

Modern status: At St. John's and in the St. Barbe district especially at Green Island Brook.

Place names: Hughes Brook, —— Point 47-51 56-09; —— Brook 48-59 57-54; —— Lake 49-04 57-43, (Labrador) 54-30 66-13; ? Hughs Pond 47-36 52-51; Father Hughes Hill 47-39 57-46.

HULAN. *See* HUELIN

HULL, a surname of England and Ireland, from the English place names Hull (Cheshire, Somerset, Worcestershire), rarely after Kingston upon Hull (Yorkshire ER), or Rull (Devon), or from Old English *hyll* – (dweller by the) hill, or a pet-form of the baptismal name Hugh or its diminutives Hulin, Hulot. *See* HUE. (Reaney, Cottle, Spiegelhalter).

Traced by Guppy in Bedfordshire, Dorset, Durham, Hampshire, Lancashire and Wiltshire, by Spiegelhalter in Devon, and by MacLysaght in Ulster.

In Newfoundland:

Early instances: Abraham, of Burin, 1805 (D'Alberti 15); William, ? of Northern Bay, 1842 (DPHW 54); John, of Freshwater (unspecified), married at St. John's, 1853 (DPHW 26D); Robert, of Little Bay Islands, 1859 (DPHW 92); Silas, of Great Jervis (Fortune B.), 1871 (Lovell); Uriah, of Heart's Content, 1871 (Lovell); George, of Twillingate, 1871 (Lovell).

Modern status: Scattered, especially at Twillingate South Side and Corner Brook.

HUMBER, a surname of England, from the English place name Humber (Herefordshire, Devon), or river name, "formerly a common name of streams in England." (Ekwall, Spiegelhalter).

Traced by Spiegelhalter in Devon.

In Newfoundland:

Family tradition: William, from England, settled at Norris Point, about 1833 (MUN Hist.).

Early instances: ——, of Twillingate, 1768 (MUN Hist.); John, married at St. John's, 1772 (DPHW 26D); Jesse, of Cow Harbour (now ? Cow Head), 1871 (Lovell); James, of Bonne Bay, 1871 (Lovell).

Modern status: Scattered, especially at Corner Brook and in the St. Barbe district.

Place names: Humber Arm 49-00 58-05; ——

Canal 49-11 57-22; —— River 48-58 57-54; Humbermouth 48-57 57-57.

HUMBY, a surname of England, from the English place name Humby (Lincolnshire). (Bardsley).

In Newfoundland:

Early instances: John, of Fogo, 1787, of Guy's Cove (Labrador), 1789 (MUN Hist.); William, of Bonavista, 1806 (DPHW 70); Henry, of Tickle Cove (Bonavista B.), 1831 (DPHW 70); William Umby, of King's Cove Parish, 1838 (Nfld. Archives KCRC); Joseph Humby, of Catalina, 1847 (DPHW 67); John, of Indian Arm, 1850 (DPHW 73); Edward, married Jane Lake, Fortune, 1871 (Grand Bank Methodist marriages, 1871 per P.E.L. Smith).

Modern status: Scattered, especially at Summerville (Bonavista B.).

Place names: Humby's Cove (Labrador) 55-07 59-07; —— Island (Labrador) 56-20 61-00.

HUMPHRIES, a surname of England, Wales and Ireland, one of several variants from the baptismal name Humphrey, from the Old German personal names *Humfrid, Hunfrid*, Norman-French *Onfroi*, containing a name *Huni* – ? *giant* and *peace*. (Withycombe, Reaney).

Spiegelhalter traced Humphries (and variants) in Devon. Guppy traced Humphrey and Humphries in Buckinghamshire, Gloucestershire, Herefordshire, Shropshire, Wiltshire, Worcestershire and especially in North Wales. MacLysaght traced Humphries in Ulster.

In Newfoundland:

Early instances: William Humfrey, of St. John's, 1787 (DPHW 26C); John Humphries, of Bonavista, 1789 (DPHW 70); Richard Humpries, of Brigus, 1805 (DPHW 34); William Humphreys, of Bay de Verde, 1806 (CO 199.18); Eliza Humphrie, of Harbour Grace Parish, 1806 (Nfld, Archives HGRC); William Humphreys or Umfries, of Ragged Harbour (now Melrose), 1815 (Nfld. Archives KCRC); Jane Humphries, of Petty Harbour, 1816 (Nfld. Archives BRC); Thomas Humphriss, planter of Fogo, 1821 (USPG); Mary, of Change Islands, 1821 (USPG); R. Humphreys, of Greenspond, 1823 (DPHW 76); Betsy Umfries, of King's Cove, 1830 (Nfld. Archives KCRC); Edward Humphrey, from Dartmouth (Devon), married at Petty Harbour, 1833 (DPHW 31); John Humphreys, from Torquay (Devon), married at St. John's, 1836 (DPHW 26D); James Kerslake Humphrey, from Dartmouth (Devon), married at St. John's, 1840, died 1845, aged 38 (DPHW 26D, *Indicator* 4 Jan 1845, *Times* 4 Jan 1845); James

Humphries, of Cape Freels (Bonavista North district), 1849 (DPHW 76); —— Humphry, on the *Trail* in the seal fishery out of Carbonear, 1853 (*Newfoundlander* 28 Mar 1853); Mary Humphries or Humphress, of Plate Cove (Bonavista B.), 1858 (Nfld, Archives KCRC); Jeremiah Humphry, of Harbour Grace, 1866 (Nfld. Archives HGRC); George and Jonas, of Middle Bill Cove (Bonavista B.), 1871 (Lovell).

Modern status: Scattered, especially in the Gander and Bonavista North districts with a large concentration at Cape Freels.

Place names: Humphrey Island (Labrador) 52-17 55-36; John Humphrey Island 49-13 53-32.

HUNT, a surname of England and Ireland, Old English *hunta* – hunter; in Ireland, except Ulster, also by pseudo-translation for several Irish names such as Feighney, Feighrey and Fey. (Reaney, Cottle, MacLysaght).

Found widespread by Guppy, especially in the south and Midlands, and by MacLysaght in all provinces, least in Ulster and most in Connacht.

In Newfoundland:

Family traditions: George, ? from Ireland, arrived at Harbour Breton in 1866 and settled at Hunt's Point (MUN Geog.). John and Bridget, from Ireland, settled at Holyrood and subsequently at Colliers (MUN Folklore).

Early instances: Nicholas, of Petty Harbour, 1675, 1682 (CO 1); R., of Placentia, 1724 (CO 194.8); John, of Trinity Bay, 1784 (DPHW 64); Charles, of Change Islands, 1787, of Wester Head, 1789 (MUN Hist.); Arthur, of Ferryland, 1791 (USPG); William, of Lower Island Cove, 1791 (CO 199.18); Margaret Hunt alias Walsh, from Waterford, married at St. John's, 1805 (Nfld. Archives BRC); Samuel Hunt, of Bonavista, 1808 (DPHW 70); Hunt, Stabb, Preston & Co., of St. John's, 1810 (CO 194.50); James, of Harbour Grace Parish, 1810 (Nfld. Archives HGRC); Edmund, of Trouty, 1815 (DPHW 64); Anthony, of Greenspond, 1816 (DPHW 76); Jean, of Bonavista, 1817 (Nfld. Archives KCRC); Anne, of King's Cove, 1820 (Nfld. Archives KCRC); William, of Joe Batt's Arm, 1825 (Nfld. Archives KCRC); James, from Dorset, of Catalina, 1830 (Nfld. Archives KCRC); Phillip, of Harbour Grace, 1830 (Nfld. Archives HGRC); Anthony, baptized at Vere (now Fair) Island, 1830 (DPHW 76); George, of Freshwater Bay (Bonavista North district), 1830 (DPHW 76); James, of Ragged Harbour (now Melrose), 1833 (Nfld. Archives KCRC); Alfred, of Grand (? for Great) Jervis, 1835 (DPHW 30); Robert, planter of

Freshwater (Carbonear), 1836 (DPHW 48); Edmund, of Trinity (Trinity B.), 1840 (DPHW 64B); Thomas, from Sherborne (Dorset), married at Catalina, 1843 (DPHW 67); James, of Harbour Breton, 1853 (DPHW 104); George, of Ramea, 1858 (DPHW 101); widespread in Lovell 1871.

Modern status: Widespread, especially at St. John's, Harbour Grace, Harbour Breton and in the Bonavista North district.

Place names: Hunt Bank 49-33 55-50; —— Island 48-28 53-39; —— (or Woody) Island 48-27 53-40; —— River (Labrador) 55-31 60-42; —— Rocks 49-33 55-51; Hunt's Brook 48-54 54-50; —— (or Hunter) Cove 47-47 55-47; Hunt's Cove 48-55 54-50; —— Island 47-36 55-37; —— Ponds 48-49 54-49.

HUNTER, a surname of England, Scotland and Ireland, from Old English *huntian* – to hunt, hence huntsman, "a younger and rarer surname than HUNT." (Reaney, Cottle).

Found by Guppy in the northern counties of England and throughout Scotland, and by MacLysaght in north Ulster.

In Newfoundland:

Early instances: Francis, soldier of St. John's, 1753 (DPHW 26C); Patrick, merchant of Trepassey, 1797 (CO 194.39); John, of King's Cove, 1830 (Nfld. Archives KCRC); George (about 1824–1854), born at Wedderburn Mains, Scotland, drowned at La Poile, aged 30 (General Protestant Cemetery, St. John's); William, fisherman of Salvage, 1866 (DPHW 81).

Modern status: Scattered, especially at Salvage and Burnside.

Place names (not necessarily from the surname): Hunter (or Hunt's) Cove 47-47 55-47; Hunter Point 47-47 55-47; Hunter's Point 50-45 57-13.

HURDLE, a surname of England, ? from an Old English personal name *Hudela*, which survives in the English place name Hurdlecombe (Devon) – Hudel's valley. (Gover).

In Newfoundland:

Early instances: Thomas Hurdell or Hurdle, fisherman of Cuckold's Cove (now Dunfield), 1757, of Trinity (Trinity B.), 1763 (DPHW 64); Jane Hurdle, of Harbour Grace Parish, 1827 (Nfld. Archives HGRC); Charles, planter of English Harbour (Trinity B.), 1827 (DPHW 64B); John Hurdel, planter of Island Cove (now Dunfield) 1842 (DPHW 64B); John Hurdle, of Job's Cove, about 1853 (DPHW 55).

Modern status: At Riverhead (Harbour Grace), Windsor and Dunfield.

HURLEY, a surname of England and Ireland, in England from the English place name Hurley (Berkshire, Warwickshire, Somerset); in Ireland (O)Hurley, *Ó hUrthuile, Ó Muirthile, Ó Murghaile,* the last two also anglicized as MURLEY, and also for (O)Herlihy. *See* HIERLIHY. (Cottle, Spiegelhalter, MacLysaght).

Traced by Guppy in Somerset, by Spiegelhalter in Devon, and by MacLysaght especially in Co. Cork.

In Newfoundland:

Early instances: Maurice, married at St. John's, 1783 (DPHW 26D); John, servant of Bonavista, 1789 (CO 194.38); Michael Hurly, of Small Point (Conception B.), 1793 (CO 199.18); Daniel Hurley, from Youghal (Co. Cork), married at St. John's, 1803 (Nfld. Archives BRC); John, of Carbonear, 1804 (CO 199.18); Daniel, of Harbour Grace Parish, 1806 (Nfld. Archives HGRC); William, planter of Trinity (Trinity B.), 1822, of Trouty, 1827 (DPHW 64, 64B); Michael, of Bay de Verde, 1829 (Nfld. Archives BRC); Catherine, of Harbour Grace, 1829 (Nfld. Archives BRC); Mary, from Kells (Co. Kilkenny), married at Fortune Harbour, 1831 (Nfld. Archives KCRC); James, ? of Port de Grave, 1842 (*Newfoundlander* 13 Jan 1842); William, from Co. Cork, of Harbour Grace, 1844 (*Indicator* 27 Jul 1844); Elizabeth, of Herring Neck, 1855 (DPHW 85); James, of Catalina, 1857 (Nfld. Archives KCRC); George, fisherman of Green Cove (Twillingate district), 1857 (DPHW 85); Patrick, way officer of Salmonier (unspecified), 1857 (*Nfld. Almanac*); Joseph, of Bay of Islands, 1871 (Lovell); James and John, of Salmon Cove (now part of South River), 1871 (Lovell); Lawrence, of Tilton Harbour (now Tilting), 1871 (Lovell); Francis (and others), of Upper Small Point (now Kingston), 1871 (Lovell); Thomas Hirly, of Wiseman's Cove (White B.), 1871 (Lovell).

Modern status: Scattered, especially at Too Good Arm (Twillingate district) and Kingston.

HURRELL, a surname of England and Ireland, Hurrel of Guernsey (Channel Islands), diminutives of Old French *hure* – hair, hence shaggy-haired, or ? from the Old English personal names *Hereweald* or *Hearuwulf;* also in Ireland possibly for Arrell, *Ó hEarghail.* (Reaney, Spiegelhalter, MacLysaght, Turk).

Traced by Guppy in Devon.

In Newfoundland:

Early instances: Philip Herrul, of Back Cove (Port de Grave), 1798 (CO 199.18); Philip Hurrell, bombardier in Royal Artillery, St. John's, 1814 (DPHW 26B); Elizabeth Hurrel, of Green Bay Point, baptized at Greenspond, 1829 (Nfld. Archives KCRC); Richard Hurrell, from Dartmouth (Devon), married at St. John's, 1839 (DPHW 26D).

Modern status: Rare, at Smooth Cove (near Ochre Pit Cove) and St. John's.

HURST, a surname of England and Ireland; in England from Old English *hyrst* – (dweller by the) wood, wooded hill, or from several English place names containing the element Hirst or Hurst, including a lost Hurst (Devon); in Ireland from *de Horsaigh* from the English place name Horsey (Norfolk). (Reaney, Gover, MacLysaght 73).

Guppy traced Hurst in Buckinghamshire and Lancashire, Hirst in Yorkshire WR. Spiegelhalter traced Hurst in Devon.

In Newfoundland:

Early instance: John, tailor of St. John's, 1852 (DPHW 29).

Modern status: Unique, at St. John's.

HUSK, a surname of England, apparently not recorded elsewhere, ? a shortened form of some such name as Hosken, Hoskin(g)(s) etc., Huski(n)son, from Old English *os* and *-kin,* where *Os* is a short form of such names as *Ōsgod, Ōsbeorn, Ōsmǣr,* etc., or ? a shortened, metathesized form of the place names Huxham, Huxbear, Huxford, Huxhill, Huxton (Devon), which contain the Old English personal name *Hoc(c)* or *Hucc,* or ? for the river – (dweller by the Usk). (Reaney, Gover).

In Newfoundland:

Early instance: At St. John's, from Plymouth (Devon) since about 1890. (Family).

Modern status: At St. John's.

HUSSEY, a surname of England, Ireland and ? Wales, in England from Old French *hosed (housé)* – trunk-hosed, booted, or Middle English *hus(e)wyf* – housewife, mistress of a family, or from the French place and family name Houssay; in Ireland (O)Hussey, *Ó hEodhusa,* or a variant of de Hosey. (Reaney, Cottle, Spiegelhalter, MacLysaght).

Traced by Guppy in Somerset and Wiltshire, by Spiegelhalter in Devon, and by MacLysaght from de Hosey in Cos. Kerry and Meath, and from O'Hussey in Cos. Fermanagh and Tyrone.

In Newfoundland:

Early instances: John, of Port de Grave, 1762, property "possessed by the Family for 74 years," that is, since 1688 (CO 199.18); Joseph, of [Upper] Island Cove, 1775, property "in possession of the Family for 65 years," that is, since 1710 (CO 199.18); John Huzsey, merchant of Trinity (Trinity B.), 1759 (DPHW 64); John Hussey, of Salmon Cove (now Champneys), 1786 (DPHW 64); Margaret, from Youghal (Co. Cork), married at St. John's, 1803 (Nfld. Archives BRC); Henry ? Hussey, one of 72 impressed men who sailed from Ireland to Newfoundland, ? 1811 (CO 194.51); Margaret, of Harbour Grace Parish, 1814 (Nfld. Archives HGRC); William Huse, from Clooneen Parish (unidentified) (Co. Kilkenny), married at St. John's, 1817 (Nfld. Archives BRC); Charles Watson Hussey, planter of Salmon Cove (now part of South River), 1848 (DPHW 34); Thomas Hussy, of Burnt Head (Cupids), 1856 (DPHW 35); Patrick Haussey, shipowner of Brigus, 1871 (Lovell); John and Nathaniel Hussey, of Broad Cove (now St. Phillips), 1871 (Lovell); George and John, of Clarke's Beach, 1871 (Lovell); Charles, of Kelligrews, 1871 (Lovell); Thomas, of Spaniard's Bay, 1871 (Lovell).

Modern status: Widespread, especially at St. John's and in the Port de Grave district.

Place names: Hussey(s) Pond 48-43 55-02; Hussey Rock 49-36 54-55; —— Shoal (Labrador) 52-17 55-36; Huzzie Head, —— Hill 48-23 53-17.

HUSTIN(S), surnames, ? of England, of unknown origin.

In Newfoundland:

Early instances: Charles Hustins, of Little Bay Islands, 1859 (DPHW 92); James, of New Bay (Exploits district), 1886 (DPHW 92).

Modern status: Hustin, rare, at South East Arm (Green B.) (*Electors* 1955); Hustins, rare, at St. John's.

HUTCHCRAFT, a surname of England, a variant of Huscroft, from Old English *hūs* – house and *croft* – small enclosed field, hence (dweller at the) house (in the) field. (Bardsley).

In Newfoundland:

Modern status: Rare, at Stephenville, Paradise (Green B.) (*Electors* 1955) and Deer Lake.

HUTCHENS, HUTCHINGS, surnames of England, Hutch(e)on of Scotland, from Old French *Huchon*, a double diminutive of *Hue* (Hugh). *See* HUE. (Reaney, Cottle, Black).

Guppy traced Hutchings in Cornwall, Devon,

Oxfordshire, and with Hutchins in Somerset; Spiegelhalter traced Hutchin(g)s in Devon.

In Newfoundland:

Early instances: Tobias Hutchins, of St. John's, 1682 (CO 1); James Hutchens, J.P. of Ferryland district, ? 1730 (CO 194.9); George Hutchings given an estate at St. John's, 1762 (Prowse); John Hutchins, of Bread and Cheese (now Bishop's) Cove, 1775 (CO 199.18); Richard Hutchings, of Greenspond, 1776 (MUN Hist.); Alex., of Battle Harbour (Labrador), 1787–9 (MUN Hist.); Richard, in possession of property at Petty Harbour, 1794–5 (Census 1794–5); Samuel Hutching, planter of Northern Cove (Harbour Grace), 1820 (DPHW 43); Samuel Hutchings, of Harbour Breton, 1835 (DPHW 30); Thomas, of Bay de Verde, 1843 (*Newfoundlander* 31 Aug 1843); James Hutching, of Exploits Burnt Island, 1844 (DPHW 86); James Hutchings, of Mobile, 1871 (Lovell); John, of Northern Harbour (Twillingate district), 1871 (Lovell); Archibald (and others), of Spaniard's Bay, 1871 (Lovell); William and Walter, of Cowhead, 1873 (MUN Hist.).

Modern status: Hutchens, unique, at St. John's; Hutchings, widespread, especially at Whitbourne, Spaniard's Bay and St. John's.

HUTCHINSON, a surname of England, Scotland and Ireland, – son of *Huchun* (*see* HUTCHENS, HUE), cognate with (Mac) Cutcheon, Ir. *Mac Úistin*, Scots Gaelic *Mac Uisdin*. (Reaney, MacLysaght, Black).

Guppy traced Hutchinson in the northern counties of England, Hutchison "over a large part of Scotland, but rare in the north." Spiegelhalter traced Hutchi(n)son in Devon, and MacLysaght Hutchinson in Ulster.

In Newfoundland:

Early instances: Christopher Hutcheson, from Co. Cork, of Trinity, deceased 1814 (*Royal Gazette* 19 May 1814); Elizabeth Huchisson, from Ross (unspecified) (Co. Wexford), married at St. John's, 1821 (Nfld. Archives BRC); Margaret Hucheson, of Harbour Grace Parish, 1831 (Nfld. Archives HGRC); Rev. George Hutchison, of Topsail, 1871 (Lovell).

Modern status: Rare, at St. John's.

HUTTON, a surname of England and Ireland, from a place name common in the north of England, especially in Yorkshire. (Cottle).

Traced by Guppy in Lincolnshire, and by MacLysaght from Cumberland in Cos. Antrim and Armagh.

In Newfoundland:

Early instances: Dr., of Fermeuse, 1797 (D'Alberti 7); Robert, merchant of St. John's, 1801, and Bay Bulls, 1802 (CO 194.43, D'Alberti 12).

Modern status: At St. John's.

Place name: Hutton Peninsula (Labrador) 60-07 64-24.

HUXTER, a surname of England, from Middle English *hucke* – to bargain, hence a female seller of small goods, pedlar, hawker. (Reaney *Origin*).

In Newfoundland:

Early instances: William, planter of Spaniard's Bay, 1830 (DPHW 64B); William Uxter, of Catalina, 1833 (DPHW 70); Stephen Huxter, of Herring Neck, 1857 (DPHW 85); Joanna, of Catalina, 1859 (DPHW 67); Stephen, of Seldom-Come-By, 1871 (Lovell).

Modern status: At Badger, South Brook (Green B.) and Springdale.

Place name: Huxter Pond 48-26 55-35.

HYDE, a surname of England and Ireland, from *hīd* – (holder of a) hide (about 120 acres) of land, or from a feminine personal name ? *Ida*. (Reaney, Cottle, MacLysaght).

Traced by Guppy in Worcestershire, by Spiegelhalter in Devon, and by MacLysaght especially in Co. Cork.

In Newfoundland:

Family traditions: ——, from Ireland, settled at Bay de Verde in the 1840s, thence to Red Head Cove (MUN Hist.). George (1801–57), of Grand Bank (MUN Hist.).

Early instances: William Hid, of St. John's, 1764 (DPHW 26C); Charles Hide, of Trinity, 1772 (CO 194.30); James Hyde, of Bay Bulls district, 1803 (Nfld. Archives BRC); Jane Hide, of Bay Bulls, 1806 (Nfld. Archives BRC); Michael, of Ragged Harbour (now Melrose), 1825 (Nfld. Archives KCRC); Patrick Hyde, of Broad Cove (unspecified), married at St. John's, 1826 (DPHW 26D); Maurice, of Harbour Grace Parish, 1828 (Nfld. Archives HGRC); George, of Grand Bank, 1833 (DPHW 109); Michael, ? of Northern Bay, 1838 (DPHW 54); James Hide or Hyde(s), planter of Careless (now Kerleys) Harbour, 1839 (DPHW 64B); Lawrence and Patrick Hyde, of Bay de Verde, 1871 (Lovell); Isaac (and others), of George's Cove (Trinity B.), 1871 (Lovell); John, of Job's Cove, 1871 (Lovell); Thomas, of Red Head Cove, 1871 (Lovell).

Modern status: Scattered, especially at Red Head Cove.

Place name: Mount Hyde (Labrador) 53-33 64-12.

HYNES. *See* HINES

HYSLOP, a surname of England and Scotland – (dweller in the) hazel-valley.

Traced by Guppy in Dumfriesshire.

In Newfoundland:

Modern status: Rare, at St. John's.

I

INDER, ENDER, surnames of England. Inder was identified by Bardsley who, however, could make nothing of it. ? An extended form of the surname Ind – (dweller at the) end (of the village), ? a variant of HENDER, from the common Cornish place name Hendra – old farm. (Spiegelhalter).

Traced by Bardsley in Somerset and Hampshire.

In Newfoundland:

Early instances: Peter Inider, a Blue (soldier), of St. John's, 1774 (DPHW 26C); Alfred Inder, of Freshwater Bay (Bonavista district), 1871 (Lovell).

Modern status: Inder, scattered, especially in the Green Bay district; Ender, unique, at St. John's (*Electors* 1955).

INGERMAN, an anglicized form of the surname of Germany, Ingermann – servant of *Ing(w)e,* a Germanic personal name of uncertain meaning. (Heintze-Gascori).

In Newfoundland:

Family tradition: ——, from Germany, settled in Newfoundland in the late 19th century (Family).

Modern status: At St. John's.

INGRAHAM, INGRAM, ENGRAM, surnames of England and Ireland (Ingraham a common North American form) and Engram from the English place name Ingram (Northumberland), or from Old English *angr* – (dweller on or near the) grassland, or a personal name from Old German containing the elements *Angle* or *angel* or *Ingil* (a personal name from *Ing*) and *raven.* (Reaney, Cottle, Bardsley, MacLysaght).

Ingram traced by Guppy in Norfolk, by Spiegelhalter in Devon, and by MacLysaght in Co. Limerick in the 17th century, now mainly in Ulster.

In Newfoundland:

Early instances: Benjamin Ingram, of Bonavista, 1792 (USPG); Pierce, of St. John's, 1796 (CO 194.39); William, of Harbour Grace, 1817 (DPHW 48); William Ingham or Ingraham, of Hermitage Cove (Burin district), 1827 (DPHW 109); Joseph Ingraham, of Pool's Harbour (Burin district), 1829 (DPHW 109); Joseph Ingram, of Bonne Bay (Fortune B.), 1835 (DPHW 30); James, of Lower Burgeo, 1847 (DPHW 101); Robert, of Little Bay (Burin district), 1853 (DPHW 104); Thomas Engram, of Pass Island (Burin district), 1853 (DPHW 102); Susan Ingram, of Harbour Le Cou, 1860 (DPHW 99); Henry, of Brazil's (Burgeo district), 1871 (Lovell); George, of Harbour Buffett, 1871 (Lovell); Robert and William, of Pickaree (now Piccaire), 1871 (Lovell); Morgan, of Pushthrough, 1871 (Lovell).

Modern status: Ingraham, rare, in the Burgeo-La Poile district; Ingram, scattered, especially in the Burgeo-La Poile district and at Kingwell (*Electors* 1955); Engram, in the Fortune Bay-Hermitage Bay district.

Place names: Ingram Cove, —— Point 47-46 55-50.

INGS, a surname of England, from the personal name – son of *Ing,* though according to Weekley, Ing is "A Middle English name for meadow, especially a swampy one, and still in dialect use." (Weekley *Surnames).*

Guppy traced Ing in Buckinghamshire.

In Newfoundland:

Modern status: At Clarenville and in the Twillingate district, especially Virgin Arm.

INKPEN, a surname of England, from the English place name Inkpen (Berkshire), from Old English **ing* – hill and British *Penn,* Welsh *pen* – hill. (Reaney, Ekwall, Cottle).

In Newfoundland:

Early instances: John, of Ochre Pit Cove, 1823 (D'Alberti 33); James, of Great Burin, 1860 (DPHW 108); Benjamin, of Inkpen's Island (Burin district), 1861 (DPHW 108); Benjamin (and others), of Burin (Placentia B.), 1871 (Lovell); George, of English Harbour West, 1879 (MUN Hist.); John and Robert, of Bay d'Est, 1879 (MUN Hist.).

Modern status: Scattered, especially at Ship Cove (Burin district).

INNES, INNIS, surnames of England, Scotland and Ireland, with ? a Newfoundland variant INNISS; in England from Cornish *enys* – island or several place names Ennis, Ennys, Innis, Enys, Ince (Cornwall); in Scotland from the place name Innes (Morayshire); in Ireland (Mac) Innes, *Mac Aonghuis,* "the Scottish form of MacGuinness." *See also* ENNIS of which, in England and Ireland, Innes is a variant. (Spiegelhalter, Black, MacLysaght).

Traced by Spiegelhalter in Devon and by Guppy "mostly in Aberdeenshire, though fairly represented in Roxburghshire."

In Newfoundland:

Early instances: Ann Inis, of Harbour Grace Parish, 1813 (Nfld. Archives HGRC); John Innis, soldier of St. John's, 1828 (DPHW 26B); James Innis, of Jamaica or Barbados, of Fortune, about 1920 (P.E.L. Smith).

Modern status: Innes, Innis, rare, at St. John's; Inniss at Victoria and St. John's.

Place name: ? Innismara 49-06 58-14.

IRELAND, a surname of England and Ireland – (the man from) Ireland. In Ireland "This name is said to have originated in England through early emigrants from Ireland called *de Irlande,* whose descendants returned as strangers." (Cottle, MacLysaght).

Traced by Guppy in Lancashire, Sussex and Yorkshire NR, ER, by Spiegelhalter in Devon, and by MacLysaght in Cos. Armagh and Antrim.

In Newfoundland:

Early instances: Richard, fisherman of St. John's, 1794–5, "9 years in Newfoundland," that is, 1785–6 (Census 1794–5); John, servant of Battle Harbour (Labrador), 1795 (MUN Hist.); William, of St. Anthony, 1854 (DPHW 114); William, planter of Braha (now Brehat), 1871 (Lovell).

Modern status: At Grand Falls, Gander and Bay Bulls Road (St. John's).

Place names (not necessarily from the surname): Ireland Island 47-38 58-22; Ireland's Bight 51-20 55-46; —— Brook 51-21 55-45; —— Point 51-20 55-45; —— Eye 48-13 53-30; —— —— Harbour 48-12 53-30; —— —— Point 48-14 53-29.

IRISH, a surname of England and ? formerly of Ireland, – the man from Ireland. (MacLysaght).

Traced by Guppy in Devon, and by MacLysaght formerly in Co. Kilkenny, though it "now seems to be obsolete."

In Newfoundland:

Early instances: Robert, servant of Battle Harbour (Labrador), 1795 (MUN Hist.); John, of Fogo, 1803–5 (D'Alberti 13, 15).

Modern status: Rare, at Grand Falls and Gander.

Place names (not necessarily from the surname): Irish Bay 51-02 55-48; —— (or Black) Island 51-05 55-44, (Labrador) 53-46 57-07; —— Ledge 46-57 55-12.

ISAACS, a surname of England, Isaac of Wales, (MAC)ISAAC of Scotland, from the baptismal name

Isaac, Hebrew – He (God) may laugh, that is, regard the bearer of the name in a friendly light. "The name was not confined to Jews, and the mediaeval surname was certainly not Jewish." (Withycombe, Reaney, Cottle). *See* MacISAAC.

Guppy traced Isaac(s) in Devon, Isaac in Gloucestershire.

In Newfoundland:

Early instances: Ip, of Trinity (Trinity B.), 1794 (DPHW 64); Isaac Isaacs, English planter of Quirpon, 1820 (D'Alberti 31); William Isaac(s), of Lamaline, 1838, 1871 (DPHW 109, Lovell); Thomas Isaac, of St. John's, 1846 (DPHW 29); Robert (and others), of Burin (Placentia B.), 1871 (Lovell).

Modern status: Especially in the Burin district.

Place names (not necessarily from the surname): Isaac Heads 47-20 53-56; —— Island 47-31 54-04; —— Point 47-19 53-57; —— Rock 47-23 54-22, 57-28 53-58.

IVANY, IVIMEY, surnames of England. Weekley *Surnames* comments: "In City A (The Letter Books (A to F) of the City of London 1275–1377) I find Peter Yvenes *or* Yvemeys, a Spanish immigrant. I do not know the origin of his name, but he looks like the true ancestor of the *Ivimeys*" and, one may add, of the Ivanys.

Matthews traced Ivamy, Ivormy as planters in Dorset.

In Newfoundland:

Early instances: Nicholas Ivany, of St. John's, 1755 (DPHW 26C); George Ivymy, of Trinity (Trinity B.), 1757, of English Harbour (Trinity B.), 1774 (DPHW 64); James Ivamy, of Bonaventure (unspecified), 1788 (DPHW 64); Catherine Iveney, of Trinity Bay, 1823 (Nfld. Archives BRC); George Ivamy, of Ship Cove (now part of Port Rexton), 1825 (DPHW 64B); Joseph, planter of Salmon Cove (now Champneys), 1831 (DPHW 64B); Matthew Ivemy or Ivanny, planter of New Bonaventure, 1841 (DPHW 64B); John Ivany or Ivamy, planter of Cupids, 1848 (DPHW 34); George Ivamy, of Robin Hood (now part of Port Rexton), 1852 (Nfld. Archives, Registry Crown Lands); John Ivany, of Kerley's Harbour, 1853 (DPHW 64B); George Ivanny, of Cuckold's Cove (now Dunfield), 1871 (Lovell); James and Mark Ivamy, of Thoroughfare, 1871 (Lovell).

Modern status: Ivany, widespread, especially at Traytown, Britannia and St. John's; Ivimey, rare, at St. John's and Cupids.

Place names: Ivany Cove 48-02 53-57; Ivanhoe (formerly Old Tilt), (renamed 1917 after the Ivany family) 48-12 53-31.

IVEY, a surname of England, from the French place name Ivoy (Cher), or from the Old French personal name *Ive,* Modern French Yves. (Reaney, Spiegelhalter, Cottle).

Traced by Guppy in Cornwall and by Spiegelhalter in Devon.

In Newfoundland:

Early instances: Benjamin, labourer of St. John's, 1853 (DPHW 29); George and Joseph, of Petites, 1871 (Lovell).

Modern status: At St. John's.

IVIMEY. *See* IVANY

J

JACK, a surname of England, Scotland and Ireland, a diminutive of the baptismal names John or James (French Jacques). *See* JAMES, JOHN. (Withycombe, Reaney, Cottle, Black, MacLysaght 73).

Traced by Spiegelhalter in Devon, by Guppy in Lanarkshire and neighbouring counties, and by Mac-Lysaght formerly in Co. Kilkenny but now in Cos. Donegal and Tyrone and Belfast.

In Newfoundland:

Early instance: William ? Jack, of St. John's, 1796 (CO 194.39).

Modern status: Rare, at St. John's (*Electors* 1955).

Place names: Several place names contain Jack(s) as the specific, or part of the specific, but it is unlikely that these are from the surname.

JACKMAN, a surname of England and Ireland – servant of Jack. *See* JACK.

Traced by Guppy in Devon, and by MacLysaght formerly in Co. Kilkenny, now in Co. Waterford.

In Newfoundland:

Family tradition: The Jackmans, of Exeter (Devon) traded with Newfoundland as early as 1562. Some were shipwrecked, and settled at Renews about 1637 (MUN Folklore).

Early instances: Tobias, cooper of St. John's, 1794–5, "11 years in Newfoundland," that is, 1783–4 (Census 1794–5); Arthur, servant of Renews, 1784 (D'Alberti 2); Thomas, fisherman of Quidi Vidi, 1794–5 (Census 1794–5); Peter, of Portugal Cove, 1805 (Nfld. Archives BRC); John, from Co. Kilkenny, fisherman of Bell Island, died 1810 (MUN Hist., *Royal Gazette* 3 Jan 1811); Patrick, from Duncaman (for Duncannon) (Co. Wexford), married at St. John's, 1819 (Nfld. Archives BRC); Simon Jackman, Chackman or Chatman, from Co. Carlow, of King's Cove, 1829 (Nfld. Archives KCRC); Robert Jackman, of Harbour Grace Parish, 1830 (Nfld. Archives HGRC); Thomas W., from Teignmouth (Devon), of St. John's, died 1832, aged 37 years (*Times* 21 Nov 1832); William, tailor of Carbonear, 1837 (DPHW 48); James, ? of Bay Bulls, 1838 (*Newfoundlander* 25 Oct 1838); Michael, of Fermeuse, 1843 (*Newfoundlander* 4 May 1843); ——, on the *Dartford*, in the seal fishery out of Catalina, 1847 (*Newfoundlander* 1 Apr 1847);

Michael, granted land at Biscay Bay Road, Trepassey, 1853 (Nfld. Archives, Registry Crown Lands); Andrew, of Knights Cove (Bonavista B.), 1870 (Nfld. Archives KCRC); Peter, of Harbour Grace, 1870 (Nfld. Archives HGRC); James, of Renews to Cape Race area, 1871 (Lovell).

Modern status: Scattered, especially at Bell Island, Grand Falls and St. John's.

JACKSON, a surname of England, Scotland, Ireland and the Channel Islands – son of Jack. *See* JACK. (Turk).

Found widespread by Guppy in England, "fairly distributed [in Scotland], but most numerous in Renfrewshire and in the neighbouring counties," and by MacLysaght "numerous, especially in Ulster, since mid-seventeenth century."

In Newfoundland:

Early instances: ——, of Petty Harbour, 1703 (CO 194.3); John, minister of St. John's, 1704 (CO 194.3, 22); William, J.P. of Ferryland district, 1730, 1732, of Trepassey district, 1750 (CO 194.9, 12); Jeremiah, planter of Fogo, 1792 (MUN Hist.); Amelia, of Trepassey, 1822 (Nfld. Archives BRC); Ellen, from Ballyneal (unidentified) (Co. Kilkenny), married at St. John's, 1825 (Nfld. Archives BRC); John, of Harbour Grace, 1844 (DPHW 43); Henry, planter of Lower Island Cove, 1851 (DPHW 55); George, of Green's Harbour (Trinity B.), 1858 (DPHW 59A); George, cooper of Coley's Point, 1871 (Lovell); George, fisherman of Flowers Cove to Point Ferolle area, 1871 (Lovell); George (and others), of Shoal Harbour (Trinity B.), 1871 (Lovell).

Modern status: Scattered, especially at Cavendish (Trinity B.).

Place names: Jackson's Arm 49-52 56-47; —— Cove 49-41 56-00.

JACOBS, a surname of England, Jacob of Ireland, from a Hebrew personal name of disputed meaning, but popularly explained as "he seized the heel" or "he supplanted" (Genesis XXV. 26). Reaney maintains that the mediaeval surname was not Jewish. (Withycombe, Reaney, Cottle).

Guppy traced Jacob(s) in Norfolk and Somerset, and MacLysaght in Cos. Wexford and Leix.

In Newfoundland:

Early instances: Henry, of Bay de Verde, 1788 (CO 199.18); Mary, of St. John's, 1791 (DPHW 26C); David Jacob, servant of Battle Harbour (Labrador), 1795 (MUN Hist.); Margaret Jacobs, occupier of fishing room at Old Perlican, Winter 1800–01 (Census Trinity B.); Samuel, planter of Fogo, 1808 (MUN Hist.); Ruth Jacob(s), of Harbour Grace Parish, 1817, 1827 (Nfld. Archives HGRC); William Jacobs, planter of Twillingate, 1821 (USPG); James, of Joe Batt's Arm, 1821 (USPG); Samuel, planter of Moreton's Harbour, 1822 (USPG); Joseph, planter of Northern Bay, 1828 (DPHW 52A); John, of Port de Grave, 1828 (*Newfoundlander* 18 Dec 1828); Joseph Jacob, of Change Islands, 1849 (DPHW 83); William Jacobs, of Gooseberry Island (Bonavista B.), 1854 (DPHW 76); Thomas, of Bear Cove (White B.), 1864 (DPHW 94); John, of Herring Neck, 1871 (Lovell); James and John, of Random Sound, 1871 (Lovell); Isaac (and others), of Wiseman's Cove (White B.), 1871 (Lovell).

Modern status: Scattered, especially at Little Heart's Ease and Westport (White B.).

Place names (not necessarily from the surname): Jacob Cove 49-31 55-20; Jacobs Cove 48-13 53-29; —— Ground 49-07 53-26; —— Point 49-07 53-35; —— Rock 49-39 55-38.

JACOBSON, a surname of England – son of Jacob (*see* JACOBS) or of James (Latin *Jacobus*). See JAMES. (Cottle).

In Newfoundland:
Modern status: Rare, at St. John's.

JAMES, a surname of England, Wales, Scotland, Ireland and the Channel Islands, the form of Jacob (*see* JACOBS) made popular by the two Apostles. (Withycombe, Reaney, Cottle, Black, MacLysaght, Turk).

Found widespread by Guppy especially in South Wales and the Welsh Border counties, by Black as a recent introduction from England, and by MacLysaght in northeast Ulster as a comparatively recent introduction from England, but also as a shortened form of Macjames and Fitzjames, "now fairly numerous in Cos. Carlow and Wicklow."

In Newfoundland: Sometimes confused with JANES.

Early instances: Henry, of Harbour Grace, 1681 (CO 1); John, inhabitant of Newfoundland, ? 1706 (CO 194.24); William, of Bay de Verde, 1730 (CO 194.23); Samuel, fisherman of Trinity (Trinity B.), 1760 (DPHW 64); Darby, of Carbonear, 1797 (DPHW 48); James, of Brigus, 1818 (DPHW 34); Catherine, of St. John's, 1820 (Nfld. Archives BRC); Charles, of Greenspond, 1821 (DPHW 76); James James or Janes, planter of Heart's Content, 1823 (DPHW 64B); Johanna, born at Spaniard's Bay, 1824 (DPHW 64B); William James, planter of Broad Cove (Bay de Verde district), 1833 (DPHW 52A); John, of New Harbour (east of Chaleur B., Labrador), 1835 (DPHW 30); David, of King's Cove Parish, 1838 (Nfld. Archives KCRC); George, of Lower Burgeo, 1842 (DPHW 101); John, of Sagona, 1850 (DPHW 104); Jacob, of Hall's Bay, 1854 (DPHW 86); Thomas, granted land near Bull Cove (Conception B.), 1863 (Nfld. Archives, Registry Crown Lands); scattered in Lovell 1871.

Modern status: Scattered, especially at St. John's.

Place names (not necessarily from the surname): James Cove 47-29 53-11; —— Gully 47-44 53-22; —— Head 48-27 53-49; —— Island 49-18 55-07, 50-55 57-11; —— Point 47-42 54-13; —— town 48-26 53-48.

JAMIESON, a surname of England and Scotland, also Jameson in England, Scotland and Ireland, – son of James (*see* JAMES).

Guppy traced Jam(i)eson in Durham and over a large part of Scotland except in the North. MacLysaght traced Jameson, from Scotland, in Ireland since the mid-18th century.

In Newfoundland:
Family tradition: Alexander, from Peterhead (Aberdeenshire), settled at Harbour Grace in 1882, thence to Garden Cove (Placentia B.) about 1894 (MUN Folklore).

Early instances: George Jemminson, soldier of St. John's, 1778 (DPHW 26C); Patrick Jamieson, of Harbour Grace Parish, 1825 (Nfld. Archives HGRC); Elizabeth Jamesson, of Grates Cove, 1833 (DPHW 58); John Jamison, of King's Cove Parish, 1839 (Nfld. Archives KCRC); Joseph Jameson, fisherman of Brigus, 1849 (DPHW 34); John, of Trinity (unspecified), 1869 (Nfld. Archives KCRC);

Modern status: At St. John's.
Place name: Jamieson Hills 48-20 56-05.

JANES, a surname of England, a form of JOHNS. See JOHN.

Traced by Guppy in Bedfordshire and Hertfordshire, Jane in Cornwall. Spiegelhalter traced Jane(s) in Devon.

In Newfoundland: Sometimes confused with JAMES and ? JEANS.

Early instances: J., planter of St. John's, 1701 (CO 194.2); John, of Bryant's Cove, 1765 (CO 199.18);

William, of Trinity Bay, 1770 (DPHW 64); Daniel, of Carbonear, 1784 (CO 199.18); Philip & Co., of Broad Cove (Bay de Verde district), 1784 (CO 199.18); John, of Bay de Verde, 1792 (CO 199.18); William, of Trinity (Trinity B.), 1792 (DPHW 64); John (and others), proprietors and occupiers of fishing rooms at Grates Cove, Winter 1800–01 (Census Trinity B.); O.B., of Long Pond Lookout, 1803 (CO 199.18); Elenor, of Harbour Grace Parish, 1807 (Nfld, Archives HGRC); Thomas, of Greenspond, 1821 (DPHW 76); William, planter of Suley's (? Sooley's) Cove (Trinity North district), 1826 (DPHW 64B); Stephen, planter of Catalina, 1829 (DPHW 64B); John, planter of Hants Harbour, 1830 (DPHW 59A); Philip, of Bell Island (unspecified), 1831 (DPHW 30); Nicholas, blacksmith of Brigus, 1833 (DPHW 34); Flora, of King's Cove Parish, 1835 (Nfld. Archives KCRC); Thomas, fisherman of Ramea, 1840 (DPHW 101); John Jeynes, ? of Fogo, 1844 (*Nfld. Almanac*); John, of Pool's Island (Bonavista B.), 1846 (DPHW 76); William Janes, planter of Goose Cove (Trinity North district), 1848 (DPHW 64B); Augustus Demas, fisherman of New (now Parson's) Harbour, 1853 (DPHW 102); Alfred, of Bradley's Cove, 1854 (DPHW 52B); John Jeynes, of Sagona, 1855 (DPHW 104); Aubrey and John Janes, of Spaniard's Bay (now Cove) (Trinity B.), 1871 (Lovell).

Modern status: Widespread, especially at St. John's.

Place names: Janes Creek (Labrador) 53-50 57-37; —— Lake (Labrador) 53-51 57-40; Jeynes Bay (Labrador) 60-19 64-27.

JARDINE, a surname of Scotland, from Old French *jardin* – (dweller near, or worker at the) garden. (Reaney, Black). Traced by Guppy in Dumfriesshire.

In Newfoundland:

Early instance: Mrs. Jardin, of Pokeham Path (now Hamilton Avenue), St. John's, 1852 (*Newfoundlander* 6 May 1852).

Modern status: At Bell Island, Corner Brook and St. John's.

JARVIS, a surname of England and the Channel Islands, and with Jervois of Ireland, from the personal names Old German *Gervas*, Old French *Gervais*, containing the elements *spear* and *servant*, or, especially in Yorkshire, from the English place name Jervaulx (Yorkshire), often pronounced *Jarvis*. (Withycombe under Gervais, Cottle under Jervis, Reaney, Turk).

Guppy traced Jarvis in Devon, Essex, Kent, Shropshire and Sussex, Jervis in Shropshire, Staffordshire and North Wales; MacLysaght traced Jervois in Co. Cork.

In Newfoundland:

Early instances: James Jervis, fisherman of St. John's, 1794–5, "25 years in Newfoundland," that is, 1769–70 (Census 1794–5); Thomas Jarvis, of Ferryland, 1791 (USPG); Robert, of the west side of Placentia Bay, 1817 (D'Alberti 27); William Jervice, from Devon, deserted apprenticeship, 1836 (*Times* 27 Jul 1836); Thomas Jarvis, of Sagona, 1853 (DPHW 104); John Jarves, fisherman of Flat Island (Burin district), 1859 (DPHW 108); James Jervis, of Oderin, 1871 (Lovell).

Modern status: Scattered, especially in the Placentia West and Burin districts.

JEANS, a surname of England, a form of JOHNS (*see* JOHN), or from the Italian place name Genoa – (the man from) Genoa. (Reaney).

Spiegelhalter traced Jean in Devon.

In Newfoundland: ? Sometimes confused with JANES.

Early instances: William Jean(e)s, of Trinity Bay, 1776 (DPHW 64); Thomas Jeans, servant of Battle Harbour (Labrador), 1795 (MUN Hist.); Daniel, of Carbonear, 1810 (DPHW 48); James, of Twillingate, 1818 (D'Alberti 28, USPG); Anne, of Pool's Island (Bonavista B.), 1815 (DPHW 76); James, of Trouty, 1821 (DPHW 64); John, planter of Hants Harbour, 1821 (DPHW 58); Flora Jeans or James, of Careless (now Kerley's) Harbour, 1821 (Nfld. Archives KCRC); William Jeans, of Harbour Grace Parish, 1834 (Nfld. Archives HGRC); John Robert Jeanes, of St. John's, 1841 (DPHW 23); John Jeans, of Change Islands, 1841 (DPHW 83); James, of La Poile, 1842 (DPHW 101); Stephen, of Catalina, 1843 (DPHW 67); John Jeanes, of Sagona, 1850 (DPHW 104); Arthur Jeans, of Ship Cove (now part of Port Rexton), 1858, of Pease Cove (Trinity North district), 1860 (DPHW 64B, 63); James, trader of Cape Ray, 1871 (Lovell); Benjamin (and others), of Rose Blanche, 1871 (Lovell); Joseph, of St. Anthony, 1871 (Lovell).

Modern status: Scattered, especially at St. John's, and in the Gander district.

Place names (not necessarily from the surname): Jean Cove 47-47 54-12; —— Lake (Labrador) 52-54 66-52; Jean's Head 47-55 53-22; —— Point, —— Rock 47-02 55-10; —— Rock 47-19 54-27; Jim Jeans Rock 47-29 57-25; Sam Jeans Cove 49-34 55-49.

JEDDORE, a surname of the Micmacs of Newfoundland, of unknown (? French) origin.

In Newfoundland:

Family tradition: Nicholas, from North Sydney (Nova Scotia), settled at Conne River in the late 19th century (MUN Folklore).

Early instances: Nicholas, Noel and John Denny Jed(d)ore, Micmacs at Conne River, about 1872 (MacGregor).

Modern status: At Glenwood and Conne River.

JEFFERIES, JEFFERS, JEFFERY, three of no less than some 23 variants of a surname of England and Ireland, with Jeffreys of Guernsey (Channel Islands), from Old French *Geoffroi, Geuffroi*, Middle English *Geffrey*, which may represent three Old German personal names in which the second element is *peace*. In Ireland, Jeffers may occasionally be for MacShaffery, *Mac Seafraidh*. (Withycombe, Reaney, Cottle, MacLysaght, Turk).

Guppy traced Jefferies, Jeffreys in Bedfordshire, Berkshire, Gloucestershire, Monmouthshire, Somerset, Suffolk and Wiltshire, noting that Jefferies is the usual form, Jeffreys occurs in Wiltshire and Monmouthshire, Jeffries in Suffolk, and Jefferys "characteristic of Wiltshire." He also traced Jeffery in Cornwall, Derbyshire, Devon, Dorset, Somerset and Wiltshire, noting that Jeffrey is a rare form found mostly in Cornwall, where it is associated with Jeffery. Spiegelhalter traced Jeffery, Jefferiss, Jeffrey, Jeffries in Devon. MacLysaght found Jeffers "formerly mainly in Cos. Cork and Carlow and in Dublin, Jeffares in Co. Waterford. Jeffers is now numerous in Belfast and adjoining Ulster counties."

In Newfoundland:

Early instances: William Jeffory (Jeffery in 1677, Jeoffery in 1681), of Bay de Verde, 1676 (CO 1); William Jefferys, of St. John's, 1708–09 (CO 194.4); —— Jeffers, of Port de Grave, 1765 (CO 199.18); Joseph White Jeffery, a Quaker from Poole (Dorset), of Trinity (Trinity B.), 1796 (DPHW 64, D'Alberti 5); John, proprietor and occupier of fishing rooms at Green's Harbour, Old Perlican and Heart's Content, Winter 1800–01 (Census Trinity B.); Joseph Jeffers, of Freshwater (Carbonear), 1803 (CO 199.18); Henry Jefferies, of La Plante (Burgeo district), 1871 (Lovell); William (and brothers), of Long Pond (Conception B.), 1871 (Lovell).

Modern status: Jefferies, at Deer Lake, Lawrencetown and Botwood; Jeffers, at Kelligrews, Freshwater (Carbonear) and St. John's; Jeffery, rare, at St. John's.

Place names: Jeffrey Cove 47-50 54-10; Jeffreys 48-14 58-51; Jeffries Pond (Labrador) 52-47 56-34.

JEFFORD, a surname of England, a variant of GIFFORD.

Spiegelhalter traced Jefferd, Jefford in Devon.

In Newfoundland:

Early instances: John, of Matthews Cove (Labrador), 1787, of Battle Harbour, 1789 (MUN Hist.); Simon Jeffard, proprietor and occupier of fishing room at Scilly Cove (now Winterton), Winter 1800–01 (Census Trinity B.).

Modern status: At Long Pond, Kelligrews and Manuels.

JENKINS, a surname of England and Wales, a double diminutive of John. *See* JOHN. (Reaney, Cottle).

Found widespread by Guppy in the south and west, especially in Monmouthshire, and South Wales. Spiegelhalter traced Jenkin(s), Jenkyns in Devon.

In Newfoundland:

Family tradition: John Melford, from England, deserted from the Royal Navy in Newfoundland and changed his name to Jenkins (MUN Folklore).

Early instances: Major, ? of St. John's, 1685 (CO 194.41); John, J.P. of Ferryland district, ? 1730, 1732 (CO 194.9); William, of Twillingate, 1768 (MUN Hist.); John, of Trinity Bay, 1785 (DPHW 64); John, proprietor and occupier of fishing room at Trinity (Trinity B.), Winter 1800–01 (Census Trinity B.); Mary, of Fermeuse, 1806 (Nfld. Archives BRC); William, of Brigus, 1812 (DPHW 26B); William, planter of Western Bay, 1827 (DPHW 52A); Mary, of Petty Harbour, 1843 (DPHW 31); William, planter of Ochre Pit Cove, 1843 (DPHW 52A); Thomas, of Harbour Grace, 1855 (DPHM 26D); Moses, of Troytown (now Triton), 1871 (Lovell).

Modern status: Scattered, especially at Durrell's Arm, Burt's Cove and St. John's.

Place name: Jenkins Cove 49-40 54-45.

JENN(I)EX, ? variants of the surname of England Jenness, itself a variant of JEANS – the man from Genoa, or in Newfoundland variants of the surname of France, Chinoux, probably associated with the popular or slang verb *chiner* – to work, to toil and moil. (Dauzat, R. F. Sparkes).

In Newfoundland:

Modern status: Jennex, in the St. Barbe district (*Electors* 1955), and at Corner Brook; Jenniex, rare, at Norris Point (Bonne B.).

JENNINGS, a surname of England and Ireland, a diminutive of John, based on an Old French diminutive *Jeanin*; in Ireland also for *Mac Sheóinín*. (Reaney, Cottle, MacLysaght). *See* JOHN.

Traced by Guppy in Cambridgeshire, Cheshire, Hertfordshire, Somerset, Suffolk, Surrey and Warwickshire, by Spiegelhalter in Devon, and by MacLysaght in Cos. Galway and Mayo and in Ulster.

In Newfoundland:

Family traditions: John, from Okehampton (Devon), settled at Moreton's Harbour ? after 1660 (MUN Folklore). Joshua, from England settled at Portugal Cove about 1805 (MUN Folklore).

Early instances: John, ? of St. John's, 1832 (Exeter Public Library Archives per Kirwin); Susan, of Portugal Cove, 1835 (DPHW 30); John, granted land at Aquaforte, 1837 (Nfld. Archives, Registry Crown Lands); Daniel, ? of Fermeuse, 1857, of Aquaforte, 1871 (*Nfld. Almanac*, Lovell); Elijah, of Moreton's Harbour, 1860 (DPHW 87); Samuel, of Western Head (Twillingate district), 1861 (DPHW 88); J. and Martin, of Twillingate, 1871 (Lovell).

Modern status: Scattered, especially at Moreton's Harbour and Bridgeport (Twillingate district).

Place name: Jennings Cove 49-08 58-06.

JENSEN, a surname of Holland and Scandinavia, – son of Jan. *See* JOHN.

In Newfoundland:

Early instances: Robert Jenson, of Belleoram, 1871 (Lovell); Jonas Jurson, planter of Harbour Breton, 1871 (Lovell); Jens, carpenter or cabinet-maker, ? from Denmark, at Harbour Breton, died 1887, aged 72 (D.A. Macdonald).

Modern status: At St. John's and in the Fortune Bay-Hermitage district especially at Harbour Breton.

Place name: Jensen Inlet (Labrador) 58-04 62-22.

JERRETT, a surname of England, a diminutive of the baptismal names Gerald, Old German *Gairovald,* containing the elements *spear* and *rule*, or Gerard, Old German *Gairhard,* containing the elements *spear* and *hard*. (Withycombe, Reaney, Cottle).

Spiegelhalter traced Jerrard, Jerred and Jerrett in Devon.

In Newfoundland:

Family tradition: ——, from New Jersey, USA, settled at Heart's Delight, about 1855; thence moved to Shoal Harbour (? Shoal Bay now Cavendish) (MUN Hist.).

Early instances: John Jerard, of Newfoundland, ? 1706 (CO 194.24); Richard Jarret(t), of New

Perlican, 1790 (DPHW 64, Census Trinity B.); Anty [sic] Jerrerd "otherwise Walsh," of St. John's, 1819 (Nfld. Archives BRC); Catherine Gerret, of Harbour Grace Parish, 1830 (Nfld. Archives HGRC); James Jerrett, of Little Codroy River, 1835 (DPHW 30); George and William, of Brigus, 1871 (Lovell); Joseph, of Shoal Harbour (? Shoal Bay now Cavendish), 1879 (DPHW 61).

Modern status: Scattered, especially at Cavendish.

Place name: Jerret Point 47-37 59-16.

JESSEAU, JESSO, ? [Newfoundland variants of] CHAISSON. Note: Thomas does not accept Jesseau, Jesso as variants of CHAISSON.

In Newfoundland:

Family tradition: —— Jesseau, from Bras d'Or, N.S., settled at St. George's about 1830 (G.R. Thomas); Alexander (1815–1917), from Cape Breton settled on the Port-au-Port peninsula, ? in the mid-19th century (MUN Geog., MUN Folklore).

Early instances: Daniel and William Jesso, fishermen of Bay of Islands, 1871 (Lovell); Alexander Jesseau, of Indian Head (St. George's B.), 1871 (Lovell); John Jesso, of Henly Harbour (Labrador), 1875 (Nfld. Archives HGRC).

Modern status: Jesseau, rare, at Grand Falls; Jesso, especially in the Port-au-Port district.

JESTICAN, a surname of unknown origin, unless a variant of Jestico which, Weekley comments, "looks like a perversion of Fr[ench] *justaucorps*, corrupted forms of which were common in Scotland ..." *Justaucorps* – (maker or seller of) jerkin(s). (Weekley *Surnames*).

Matthews traced Jestican, Justican, as captains, at Poole (Dorset).

In Newfoundland:

Early instances: Thomas Gestican, of Trinity Bay, 1766 (DPHW 64); William Jestican, of Trinity (Trinity B.), 1803 (DPHW 64); Sarah Jestigan, married at St. John's, 1835 (Nfld. Archives BRC).

Modern status: Rare, at Lockston (Trinity B.), Gander (*Electors* 1955) and Trinity (Trinity B.).

JEWER, ? an unrecorded variant of the surname of Scotland, Dewar (on the analogy of the pronunciation Jewsbury for Dewsbury, recorded by Reaney), Gaelic *deoradh* – pilgrim, custodian of a sacred relic, or from the Scots place name Dewar (Midlothian). (Black, Cottle).

In Newfoundland:

Family tradition: James, born at Moreton's

Harbour about 1795, later of Ship Cove (now Botwood) (MUN Folklore).

Early instances: James Juer, of Harbour Grace, 1770, property "in possession of the Family for upwards of 105 years," that is, before 1665 (CO 199.18); Nicholas, of Bryant's Cove, 1794, of Carbonear, 1804 (CO 199.18); Alice, of St. John's, deceased 1854 (*Newfoundlander* 27 Nov 1854); George Joer or Jewer, of Moreton's Harbour, 1874 (DPHW 89).

Modern status: Scattered, especially in the Gander district with a large concentration at Botwood.

JEWETT, a variant of the surname of England, Jowett, a diminutive of *Jull,* a short form of the baptismal name Juliana. (Withycombe, Reaney, Cottle).

Guppy traced Jowett in Yorkshire WR.

In Newfoundland:

Early instance: Richard Joewitt, married at St. John's, 1786 (DPHW 26D).

Modern status: Rare, at Curling.

JILLETT. *See* GILLET

JIM, a surname of China with the meanings oversee, direct; verbose; excellent.

In Newfoundland:

Modern status: Unique, at St. John's.

JOE, a surname of the Micmacs of Newfoundland, the nickname from the baptismal name and surname, JOSEPH, probably of French origin.

In Newfoundland:

Early instances: Newell, an Indian of King's Cove, 1827 (Nfld. Archives KCRC); John, of Goose Bay (? Bonavista B.), 1870 (Nfld. Archives KCRC); Abraham (and others), of Hall's Bay, 1871 (Lovell); Frank, fisherman of Grandy's Brook (Burgeo district), 1871 (Lovell); Stephen, Micmac of Conne River, about 1872 (MacGregor); Madeleine, of Gambo, 1876 (Nfld. Archives KCRC).

Modern status: At Conne River.

Place names: Joe is the specific, or part of the specific, in some 20 place names, but ? mostly from the baptismal name.

JOHANSEN, a surname of Norway – son of John. *See* JOHN.

In Newfoundland:

Early instance: Christian, engineer of Norwegian whaler, at St. Lawrence, 1905 (Millais).

Modern status: Rare, at St. John's and Milltown (Bay d'Espoir).

JOHN, a baptismal name and surname of England and Wales, and of the Micmacs of Newfoundland (the latter probably from the French baptismal name and surname, Jean), ultimately from the Hebrew *Johanan* – Jehovah (God) has favoured. As a favourite baptismal name, chiefly after St. John the Baptist but also after St. John the Evangelist, and in its feminine forms Joan and Joanna, and with its numerous pet-forms and diminutives, it gave rise to many surnames: JOHN(S), JOHNSON, JONES, JACK(S), JACKMAN, JACKSON, JANES, JEANS, JENKINS, JENNINGS, JENSEN, HANCOCK, HANN, EVANS. (Withycombe, Reaney, Cottle).

Traced by Guppy in Monmouthshire and South Wales, and by Spiegelhalter in Devon.

In Newfoundland:

Early instances: James, "mountaineer Indian" from Labrador, met by Cormack, 1822 (Millais); Peter, of Fogo, 1823 (Nfld. Archives KCRC); Peter, an Indian in pursuit of the Aborigines, 1828 (*Newfoundlander* 13 Feb 1828); Bernard, Louis Sr. and Jr., and Peter, Micmacs of Conne River, about 1872 (MacGregor).

Modern status: At Conne River, Glenwood and Grand Falls.

Place names: John is the specific or part of the specific, in some 24 place names, but ? mostly from the baptismal name.

JOHNS, a surname of England and Wales – son of John. *See* JOHN.

Traced by Guppy in Cornwall, Devon, Monmouthshire and South Wales.

In Newfoundland:

Early instances: Philip, of Newfoundland, ? 1706 (CO 194.24); Francis, of Bryant's Cove, 1871 (Lovell); Captain August F.J. (1848–1909), born at Stettin, Germany, ? of St. John's (General Protestant Cemetery, St. John's).

Modern status: Rare, at St. John's, Gander and Glenwood.

JOHNSON, a surname of England, Scotland, Ireland and Guernsey (Channel Islands) – son of John; in Ireland also for MacShane, *Mac Seáin,* and MacKeo(w)n, *Mac Eoghain, Mac Eoin,* the last two from Irish forms of John. *See* JOHN, and JOHNSTON with which confusion seems to have occurred. (Reaney, Cottle, MacLysaght, Turk).

Found widespread by Guppy in England, and by MacLysaght in Ulster, but much less numerous than JOHNSTON in Ireland.

In Newfoundland:

Family tradition: Olaf Gustav Johnson (1875–), born in Kalla, Sweden, settled at Grand Falls in 1900; thence to Millertown and Lomond (MUN Folklore).

Early instances: Thomas, of St. John's, 1677, "14 years an inhabitant" in 1680, that is, since 1666 (CO 1); Thomas, of Quidi Vidi, 1680 (CO 1); James, of Lower Island Cove, 1768 (CO 199.18); John, of Devil's (now Job's) Cove, 1784 (CO 199.18); John, of Harbour Grace, 1796 (CO 199.18); Benjamin, joint purchaser of fishing room in Pond Island, Greenspond Harbour, 1799 (Bonavista Register 1806); John, of Northern Bay, 1803 (CO 199.18); Robert, of Kettle Cove (North Shore, Conception B.), 1804 (CO 199.18); Thomas, from Greenwich, England, deserter from the brig *Ann* at St. John's, 1810 (*Royal Gazette* 12 Jul 1810); William, of Caplin Bay (now Calvert), 1816 (DPHW 26B); Flora, of Tilton Harbour (now Tilting), 1818 (Nfld. Archives KCRC); John, servant of Trinity (Trinity B.), 1822 (DPHW 64); William, planter of Renews, 1824 (DPHW 31); Robert, fisherman of Seal Cove (now New Chelsea), 1824 (DPHW 59A); Jane, widow of the late Henry, of Dartmouth (Devon), died at St. John's, 1844 (*Nfld. Patriot* 19 Mar 1844); James, granted land at Ferryland, 1847 (Nfld. Archives, Registry Crown Lands); John, fisherman of Little Catalina, 1854 (DPHW 72); William, of Havre de Nieux (unidentified), married at St. John's, 1858 (DPHW 26D); William, of Little Seldom-Come-By, 1871 (Lovell).

Modern status: Widespread, especially at St. John's, Little Catalina, Trouty, Job's Cove and Jacques Fontaine.

Place names: Johnson Point 51-14 55-50; ―― Lookout 49-20 56-11; Johnson's (or Johnston(e)'s) Cove, ―― Gulch 48-04 59-09; ―― Ground 49-08 53-22.

JOHNSTON, a surname of England, Scotland and Ireland; in the south and west of England from the English place names Johnstone (Devon), Johnston (Pembrokeshire), or Johnson Hall (Staffordshire); in the north of England and Scotland from the Scots place names Johnstone (Dumfriesshire) or St. Johnston (now Perth); in Ireland, also erroneously for MacKeo(w)n. *See* JOHNSON. (Reaney, Cottle, Spiegelhalter, Black, MacLysaght).

Traced by Guppy in Cumberland and Westmorland, as Johnston(e), south of the Forth and Clyde, especially in the Border counties and particularly in Dumfriesshire, and by Spiegelhalter in Devon.

In Newfoundland:

Early instances: William, grand juror of St. John's, 1780 (D'Alberti 6); John, from Berwick, Scotland, married at St. John's, 1828 (Nfld. Archives BRC); James, from Burristowness, Scotland, cabinet-maker of St. John's, deceased, 1829 (*Royal Gazette* 25 Aug 1829); William, of Renews, 1830 (DPHW 26B); John Johnstone or Johnson, of Greenspond, 1836 (DPHW 76); Henry Johnston or Johnson, planter of Seal Cove (now New Chelsea), 1842 (DPHW 59A); James Johnston, blacksmith of Ferryland, 1848 (DPHW 31); John Johnstone, planter of Trouty, 1850 (DPHW 64B); James Johnston, granted land at Riders Hill, Trinity (? Trinity B.), 1851 (Nfld. Archives, Registry Crown Lands); George, planter of Bay of Islands, 1871 (Lovell); William, fisherman of Caplin Bay (now Calvert), 1871 (Lovell); Richard, planter of Fox Cove (Fortune B.), 1871 (Lovell); John (and others) Johnstone, of Jacques Fontaine, 1871 (Lovell).

Modern status: Scattered, especially at St. John's and Renews.

Place names: Johnston(e)'s (or Johnson's) Cove 48-04 59-09.

JOLLIFFE, a surname of England, from Old French, Middle English *jolif* – gay, lively. (Reaney, Cottle).

Traced by Guppy in Hampshire and by Spiegelhalter in Devon.

In Newfoundland:

Early instances: Elijah Jollieff, proprietor and occupier of fishing room at Old Perlican, Winter 1800–01 (Census Trinity B.); Peter Jolliff, Jr., merchant of Placentia Bay, 1804 (D'Alberti 14); James, planter of Fogo, 1816 (MUN Hist.); James Joliffe, planter of Joe Batt's Arm, 1821 (USPG); James Jollop, of Barr'd Islands, 1851 (DPHW 83); Virtue Joliffe, of St. John's, 1856 (DPHW 26D).

Modern status: At St. John's and Old Perlican.

JONES, a surname of England, Wales, Ireland and the Channel Islands – son of John, from the form *Ioan* adopted from the Welsh Authorized Version of the Bible. Cottle points out that "Anomalously, there is no *J* in the excellent Welsh alphabet! – but Jones is notoriously the commonest surname in Wales ..." *See* JOHN. (Reaney, Cottle, Turk).

Found widespread by Guppy in England and Wales and by MacLysaght in Ireland.

In Newfoundland:

Early instances: William, of Ferryland, 1676 (CO 1); Rev. Henry, J.P. of Bonavista district, ? 1730–32 (CO 194.9); Stephen, of Trinity (Trinity B.), 1756 (DPHW 64); William, of English Harbour (unspecified), about 1755–65 (Dorset County Record Office per Kirwin); John, in possession of property and minister of St. John's, 1794–5, "29 years in Newfoundland," that is, 1765–6 (Census 1794–5); John and William, of Bay Roberts, 1765 (CO 199.18); Francis, of Upper Island Cove, 1770 (CO 199.18); James, of Grates Cove, 1798 (DPHW 48); Thomas, of Western Bay, 1798 (CO 199.18); Thomas, of Harbour Grace, 1800 (CO 199.18); George, (? from London), of Aquaforte, 1842 (*Royal Gazette* 11 Aug 1835, DPHW 31); James, of Moreton's Harbour, 1842 (DPHW 86); George, of Exploits Burnt Island, 1850 (DPHW 86); John, fisherman of Bull Cove (Conception B.), 1854 (DPHW 35); Edward, of Carbonear, 1856 (*Newfoundlander* 17 Jan 1856); Thomas, fisherman of Little Bay Islands, 1860 (DPHW 92); Silas, of Western Head, Twillingate, 1861 (DPHW 88); widespread in Lovell 1871.

Modern status: Widespread, especially at Upper Island Cove, Trinity (Trinity B.), Little Bay Islands, Whitbourne and St. John's.

Place names: Jones Cove 47-36 52-53; —— Head 47-36 53-14; —— Island 47-39 58-13; —— Pond 47-39 52-42; —— Rock 47-11 55-08; Rupert Jones Shoal 50-56 57-16; St. Jones Harbour 47-55 53-43; —— within 48-03 53-45.

JORDAN, JORDON, surnames of England, JORDAN of Ireland. On Jordan as a baptismal name, Withycombe writes: "Hebrew 'flowing down,' the name of the principal river of Palestine. There was an Old German personal name *Jordanes,* probably from the same root as Old Norse *jördh* 'land.' *Jordan* is found as a Christian name in England from the end of the 12th C, and the probability is that its ultimate source was the Old German *Jordanes,* but that its continued use was due to confusion with the name of the river, which would be familiar to returning Crusaders, who were in the habit of bringing back Jordan water to be used in the baptism of their children." (Reaney, Withycombe).

Jordan was found in nine counties by Guppy, and numerous in all provinces by MacLysaght.

In Newfoundland:

Early instances: John Jorden, juror ? of St. John's, 1750 (CO 194.12); William Jordan, of Quidi Vidi, 1765 (DPHW 26C); William Jorden, of Great Belle Isle (now Bell Island), 1770 (DPHW 26C); Richard Jordan, from Newton Abbot (Devon), boatkeeper of St. John's, 1776 (D'Alberti 6); William, of Harbour Grace, 1799 (CO 199.18); Judith, of Brigus (unspecified) married at St. John's, 1799 (Nfld.

Archives BRC); Mary Jordan alias Globe, of Brigus-By-South, 1813 (Nfld. Archives BRC); Mary Jordon, from Carrick-on-Suir (Co. Tipperary), married at St. John's, 1814 (Nfld. Archives BRC); Catherine Jordan, from Co. Wexford, married at Trinity, 1816 (Nfld. Archives KCRC); Peter, of Heart's Content, 1819 (Nfld. Archives KCRC); Catherine Jurdin, of Ferryland, 1820 (Nfld. Archives BRC); Mary Jourdan, of Bay Bulls, 1822 (Nfld. Archives BRC); ——, schoolmaster of Burgeo, 1849 (Feild); Henry and Thomas Jordan, of Pouch Cove, 1871 (Lovell).

Modern status: Jordan, scattered, especially at Pouch Cove; Jordon, rare, at St. John's and Riverhead (Harbour Grace).

Place name: Jordan's Point (Labrador) 54-13 58-15.

JORGENSEN, a surname of Norway and Denmark – son of Jurgen (George). *See* GEORGE.

In Newfoundland:

Modern status: Rare, at Bulls Cove (Burin district), Burin and St. John's.

JOSEPH, a baptismal name and surname of England, Wales, France and Syria-Lebanon, from Hebrew – "May Jehovah add" or "Jehovah added" (a son or children). *See* JOE. (Withycombe).

Traced by Guppy in South Wales and by Spiegelhalter in Devon.

In Newfoundland: Name adopted by two different Lebanese families since arrival in St. John's about 1911 (Andrews).

Early instances: Thomas, of King's Cove, 1815 (Nfld. Archives KCRC); S. M., of Harbour Grace, 1904 (Nfld. Archives HGRC).

Modern status: At Corner Brook and Deer Lake.

JOSEPHSON, a surname of England – son of Joseph. *See* JOSEPH.

In Newfoundland:

Modern status: Rare, at St. John's.

JOY, a surname of England and Ireland, from the common noun joy, or from the male and female baptismal names *Joie* and *Joia,* or also in Ireland as a variant of JOYCE. (Withycombe, Reaney, MacLysaght).

Traced by Guppy in Essex, by Spiegelhalter in Devon, and by MacLysaght in Connacht and Cos. Kerry and Waterford.

In Newfoundland:

Family tradition: ——, from Harbour Main, settled at Conche about 1850 (MUN Geog.).

Early instances: William, ? of Salmon Cove (unspecified) (Conception B.), about 1752 (CO 194.13); Patrick, of St. John's, 1758 (DPHW 26C); John, of Harbour Main, 1760 (CO 199.18); William, of Torbay, 1763 (DPHW 26C); Hezekiach, of Fogo, Twillingate or Tilton (now Tilting), 1771 (CO 194.30); James, from Granny Ferry (unidentified), married at Bonavista, 1803 (Nfld. Archives KCRC); Sara, of Harbour Grace Parish, 1806 (Nfld. Archives HGRC); Patrick, of Carbonear, 1828 (Nfld. Archives BRC); Honora, of King's Cove, 1832 (Nfld. Archives KCRC); Patrick, of Open Hole (now Open Hall), 1846 (Nfld. Archives KCRC); ——, on the *Troubadour* in the seal fishery out of Catalina, 1853 (*Newfoundlander* 17 Mar 1853); ——, on the *Sea* in the seal fishery out of Brigus, 1857 (*Newfoundlander* 16 Mar 1857); Thomas, of Tickle Cove (Bonavista B.), 1862 (Nfld. Archives KCRC); Margaret, of Harbour Grace, 1866 (Nfld. Archives HGRC); Catherine, of Indian Arm (Bonavista B.), 1870 (Nfld. Archives KCRC); Richard, of Conche, 1871 (Lovell); Ellen, schoolteacher of North Arm, Holyrood, 1871 (Lovell); Henry, of Port-au-Port, 1871 (Lovell).

Modern status: Scattered, especially at Catalina and St. John's.

Place name: Joy's Point 47-24 53-09.

JOYCE, a baptismal name and surname of England and Ireland, from a number of mediaeval personal names such as *Josse, Goce* after a 7th century Breton saint *Jodoc*, whose hermitage was at the place now called St. Josse-sur-Mer (Pas-de-Calais), or from the French place name Jort (Calvados); in Ireland from a family of Welsh origin. (Withycombe, Reaney, MacLysaght).

Traced by Guppy in Bedfordshire, Essex and Somerset, by Spiegelhalter in Devon, and by Mac-Lysaght in Co. Galway.

In Newfoundland:

Family traditions: ——, was an early settler in Conche in the early 19th century (Casey). George Edward, born at St. Helier (Jersey-Channel Islands), in 1801, settled at Carbonear in the 1820s (MUN Folklore).

Early instances: Peter, fisherman of St. John's, 1794–5, "15 years in Newfoundland," that is,

1779–80 (Census 1794–5); Robert Joyce or Joice, of Freshwater (Carbonear), 1799 (DPHW 48); John (and others) Joyce, of Crocker's Cove (Carbonear), 1804 (CO 199.18); William Joyse, planter of Northern Cove (Harbour Grace), 1821 (DPHW 43); Matthew Joyce, from Inistioge (Co. Kilkenny), married at St. John's, 1822 (Nfld. Archives BRC); Nicholas, planter of Scilly Cove (now Winterton), 1823 (DPHW 64B); James, of Fellow Cove (Placentia B.), 1836 (DPHW 30); William Joyse, of Brigus (unspecified), 1836 (Nfld. Archives BRC); John Joyce, of Conche, 1871 (Lovell); Charles (and others), of Flat Island (now Port Elizabeth), 1871 (Lovell); Matthew, farmer of Petty Harbour, 1871 (Lovell); Robert, of Port-au-Port, 1871 (Lovell).

Modern status: Scattered, especially at St. John's and Corner Brook.

Place name: Joyce 48-23 58-36.

JUDGE, a surname of England and Ireland, from Old French *juge* – judge; in Ireland as a translation of (Mac)Breheny, *Mac an Bhreitheamhnaigh.* (Reaney, MacLysaght).

Traced by Guppy in Buckinghamshire and Kent, and by MacLysaght in Co. Sligo.

In Newfoundland:

Early instances: William, from ? Ballagh (Co. Limerick) or ? Ballaghlea (Co. Galway), married at St. John's, 1848 (DPHW 23); Robert and Samuel, of Dark Tickles (now Brighton), 1871 (Lovell); Patrick, of Isle Valen, 1871 (Lovell).

Modern status: Scattered.

JUDSON, a surname of England – son of *Judd* or *Jutt*, ? variants of the baptismal name Jude, from the Hebrew – ? Jehovah leads or ? He will be confessed. (Withycombe, Reaney).

Traced by Guppy in Yorkshire ER, NR.

In Newfoundland:

Early instances: Samuel Jutsham, of St. John's, 1776 (CO 194.33); Joseph Jutson or Judson, planter of Flat Head (? for Flat Rock)(Carbonear), 1827 (DPHW 48).

Modern status: Rare, at St. Lawrence (*Electors* 1955).

K

KANE, a surname of England and Ireland, in England a variant of CAIN or CANE, in Ireland (O)Kane, O Cahan, *Ó Catháin* or a variant of (O)Keane, *Ó Céin*. (Reaney, MacLysaght). *See also* KEAN.

Traced by MacLysaght in Ulster.

In Newfoundland:

Family tradition: Charles (–1925), from Northern Ireland, came to St. John's in the late 1800s, he later settled at Traytown (MUN Folklore).

Early instances: Patrick Kain, married at St. John's, 1765 (DPHW 26D); Marion Kane, of Harbour Grace Parish, 1816 (Nfld. Archives HGRC); Edmund, from Dunmore (Co. Waterford), married at St. John's, 1828 (Nfld. Archives BRC); John W. Kaines, from Manston (Dorset), died at St. John's, 1839 (*Newfoundlander* 10 Jan 1839); W. Kane, road commissioner for the Flowers Island and Pools Island area (Bonavista B.), 1847 (*Nfld. Almanac*); Patrick Kane or Keane, of Burnt Island (Bonavista B.), 1857 (Nfld. Archives KCRC); Patrick Kane, of Hayward's Cove (Bonavista B.), 1859 (Nfld. Archives KCRC); Thomas, of Harbour Grace, 1866 (Nfld. Archives HGRC); Thomas, of Gooseberry Island (Bonavista B.), 1867 (Nfld. Archives KCRC); Anastasia, of Stock Cove (Bonavista B.), 1870 (Nfld. Archives KCRC); George (and others) Kanes, of the Flowers Cove to Point Ferolle area, 1871 (Lovell); Edward (and others) Kane, of Renews, 1871 (Lovell); Michael Kaine, from Co. Waterford, died at Carbonear, 1882, aged 54 (Carbonear R.C. Cemetery).

Modern status: Scattered, especially at St. John's.

Place name: Kane Rock 47-45 53-10.

KARN, a surname of England of unknown origin, ? a variant of the Scots surname Carne from Welsh and Cornish *carn* – cairn, heap of stones, as in such place names as Blencarn (Cumberland) and Carnwinnick, Carnyorth (Cornwall). Reaney Notes cites Andrew Karn 1274. (A. H. Smith, E. C. Smith, Black, Reaney).

Traced by Guppy in Surrey.

In Newfoundland:

Modern status: Rare, at Corner Brook.

KAVANAGH, a surname of Ireland, "said to have been adopted from the first Kavanagh having been fostered by a successor of St. Caomhan." (MacLysaght).

Traced in Co. Wexford by MacLysaght.

In Newfoundland:

Family tradition: ——, from Ireland, settled on Bell Island about 1840 (MUN Folklore).

Early instances: Lawrence, of St. John's, 1757 (DPHW 26C); Morgan Cavanaugh, of Port de Grave, 1783 (CO 199.18); Mary Cavanagh, from Limolin Parish (unidentified) (Co. Carlow), married at St. John's, 1803 (Nfld. Archives BRC); Mary Kavanagh, of Harbour Grace Parish, 1806 (Nfld. Archives HGRC); Elizabeth Kavanagh alias Stokes, of Bay Bulls, 1811 (Nfld. Archives BRC); Michael Kavanagh, one of 72 impressed men who sailed from Ireland to Newfoundland ? 1811 (CO 194.51); Elenor, from Co. Wexford, married in the Northern District, 1813 (Nfld. Archives BRC); Bryan, of Fogo, 1815 (Nfld. Archives KCRC); Alice, of Twillingate, 1829 (Nfld. Archives KCRC); John, of Harbour Grace, 1830 (Nfld. Archives HGRC); Mary, married on the French Shore, 1839 (Nfld. Archives BRC); John, from Waterford, married at St. John's, 1843 (*Newfoundlander* 7 Sep 1843); John, from Co. Wexford, of Harbour Grace, 1844 (*Indicator* 27 Jul 1844); Patrick, granted land on road to Petty Harbour, 1847 (Nfld. Archives, Registry Crown Lands); Patrick, granted land on west side of Caplin B. (Ferryland), 1847 (Nfld. Archives, Registry Crown Lands); Bryan, granted land near Catalina, 1853 (Nfld. Archives, Registry Crown Lands); James, granted land at Northern Gut (now North River), 1855 (Nfld. Archives, Registry Crown Lands); William Cavanagh, of Northern Bay, 1862 (DPHW 57); Edward (and others) Kavannagh, of Bell Island, 1871 (Lovell); Patrick Kavanagh, of Caplin Bay (now Calvert), 1871 (Lovell); Gregory and Patrick, farmers of Flat Rock (St. John's), 1871 (Lovell); Dennis and James, farmers of Logy Bay, 1871 (Lovell); James and Patrick, of Fox Cove (Burin district), 1871 (Lovell); William Kavanah, of Old Perlican, 1871 (Lovell).

Modern status: Scattered, especially at St. John's, Bell Island, Calvert and Flat Rock (St. John's).

Place name: Cavanagh (Labrador) 54-02 66-26.

KAVLI, a surname of unknown, ? Baltic, origin.
In Newfoundland:
Modern status: Rare, at Corner Brook.

KAWAJA, a surname of Syria-Lebanon, probably from the Persian – lord, master, a title of respect used of civic ministers, learned members of the religious classes, distinguished men of letters, etc.
In Newfoundland:
Modern status: At Corner Brook.

KAYS, a surname of England, from the Old Welsh personal name *Cai,* as in Sir Kay in Arthurian legend, from Latin *Caius, Gaius* – rejoicing, used in Wales, the Welsh Border counties and by Bretons; or from Old French *cay, kay,* Middle English *kay(e)* etc. – (dweller near or worker at the) quay or wharf; or from Old Norse *ká,* Middle English *ka(e), kay* – jackdaw; or Middle English *kei* – left-handed, clumsy; or from *keyer* – a maker or bearer of keys. (Withycombe, Reaney, Cottle). *See also* KEY(E)S.
Guppy traced Kay(e) in Durham, Lancashire and Yorkshire, Kay in Ayrshire. Spiegelhalter traced Kay(e) in Devon.
In Newfoundland:
Early instances: Richard, fisherman of St. John's, 1794–5, "11 years in Newfoundland," that is, 1783–4 (Census 1794–5); Lawrence, of Harbour Grace Parish, 1823 (Nfld. Archives HGRC); Joanna Pease, of Harbour Grace, 1870 (Nfld. Archives HGRC); Lawrence and Patrick Kay, fishermen of Bay de Verde, 1871 (Lovell).
Modern status: Rare, at Stephenville.

KEAN. *See* CAIN, CANE, KANE
In Newfoundland:
Early instances: William Keen, of St. John's, 1708 (D.W. Prowse); Wm., merchant of ? Bonavista, about 1719 (CO 194.6); Robert, from Teignmouth (Devon), in possession of Hudsons Cove (St. John's Harbour), 1820, "in possession of the family more than a hundred years," that is, before 1720 (D'Alberti 29); —— Kean, from Great Britain, owner of fishing room at Ship Island (Greenspond Harbour), 1826, built by his family in 1725 (Bonavista Register 1806); Mrs. Keene, widow of —— Keene, from England who came to Ferryland about 1739, of the Grove, Ferryland, 1794 (*Nfld. Jour. of Aaron Thomas*); Marks Kean or Cane, of Bay de Verde, 1802 (CO 199.18); James Keans, of Placentia, 1806 (D'Alberti 16); Thomas Kean(s), of Harbour Grace Parish, 1807 (Nfld. Archives HGRC); Mary Kean, from Co. Tipperary, married at St. John's, 1819

(Nfld. Archives BRC); Anastasia Kean, Kane or Cain, of King's Cove, 1820 (Nfld. Archives KCRC); Thomas Kean, of Bonavista, 1823 (Nfld. Archives KCRC); —— Keane, of Harbour Grace, 1830 (*Newfoundlander* 20 May 1830); William Kean, of Flowers Island (Bonavista B.), 1834 (DPHW 76); William Kean, of Pool's Island (Bonavista B.), 1851 (Nfld. Archives, Registry Crown Lands); Thomas Keane or Kane, of Burn (? for Burnt) Island (Bonavista B.), 1855 (Nfld. Archives KCRC); Isaac Keanes, of Bonne Bay, 1867 (DPHW 93).
Modern status: Scattered, especially at St. John's and in the Bonavista North district with a large concentration at Pound Cove.
Place name: Keans Island 49-08 53-27, 49-11 53-32.

KEARLEY, a surname of England, ? from an unidentified English place name.
In Newfoundland:
Early instances: John, of Bay Roberts, 1765 (CO 199.18); John Kearly, of Trinity Bay, 1777 (DPHW 64); Edward, of English Harbour (Fortune B.), 1857 (DPHW 104); James and Joseph, of Herring Neck, 1871 (Lovell).
Modern status: Scattered, especially in the Fortune Bay and Hermitage district with a large concentration at Head Bay D'Espoir.

KEARNEY, CARNEY, surnames of Ireland, (O)Kearney, *Ó Catharnaigh* – warlike, or *Ó Cearnaigh,* Ir. *cearnach* – victorious. (MacLysaght).
Traced by MacLysaght in Co. Meath where it is now often changed to FOX, in Cos. Mayo and Tipperary, and as Carney in Connacht.
In Newfoundland:
Early instances: Matthew Kerney, of Harbour Grace, 1775 (CO 199.18); Michael Kearney, of St. John's, 1777 (DPHW 26D); John, of Bay Bulls district, 1803 (Nfld. Archives BRC); Michael, operated salmon fishery at Trepassey, 1804, at Biscay Bay, 1810 (CO 194.49); Catherine Kearny, from Waterford, married at St. John's, 1808 (Nfld. Archives BRC); William, of Big Bellisle (now Bell Island), 1808 (Nfld. Archives BRC); Michael Kearney (1811–1885), master shipbuilder, born at Ferryland, died at St. John's (*Evening Telegram* 17 Jun 1965); John Kerney, of Quidi Vidi, 1836 (Nfld. Archives BRC); Pierce Kearney, of Mobile (Ferryland district), 1871 (Lovell); Michael, storekeeper of Carbonear, 1871 (Lovell); W(illiam) Kearny, of St. Mary's, 1871
Modern status: Kearney, scattered; Carney, unique, at Kilbride (St. John's).

Place names: Kearney Head 47-34 54-05; Kearneys Gullies 47-26 53-22; —— Hill 47-17 52-49.

KEARNS, a surname of Ireland, a variant of (O)Kieran, Kerin, *Ó Ciaráin*, *Ó Céirín*, Ir. *ciar* – black or dark brown. (MacLysaght).

Traced by MacLysaght in Cos. Cork and Mayo.

In Newfoundland:

Early instances: William Kearon, from Tallon (Co. Waterford), married at St. John's, 1801 (Nfld. Archives BRC); James Kearns, of King's Cove, 1824 (Nfld. Archives KCRC); ——, of Archibalds and Kearns, St. John's, 1856 (*Newfoundlander* 8 May 1856).

Modern status: Rare, at Manuels.

KEARSEY, a surname of England and Ireland, in England from the English place name Kersey (Suffolk), in Ireland for Keirsey, Kiersey, *Ciarasach* and *de Céarsaigh* from an unidentified Norman place name. (MacLysaght).

Traced by MacLysaght in Co. Waterford since the 13th century.

In Newfoundland:

Family tradition: ——, was an early settler at Conche in the early 1800s (Casey).

Early instances: James Keresy, fisherman of St. John's, 1794–5, "20 years in Newfoundland," that is, 1774–5 (Census 1794–5); Mary Keersey, from Kilkenny, married at St. John's, 1824 (Nfld. Archives BRC); Thomas Keresy, married on the French Shore, 1839 (Nfld. Archives BRC); Maurice Kersey, fisherman of Cape Broyle, 1871 (Lovell); John Kearsey, fisherman of Conche, 1871 (Lovell).

Modern status: At Corner Brook, Grand Falls and St. John's.

KEATING, a surname of Ireland, in Irish *Céitinn*, an Anglo-Norman family name ? from a Welsh personal name Cethyn. (MacLysaght 73).

Traced by MacLysaght in south Leinster.

In Newfoundland:

Family tradition: William, from Co. Wexford, Ireland, settled at Conception Harbour about 1841; later some of the family moved to Burin, the Codroy Valley, St. George's and Port aux Basques area (MUN Folklore).

Early instances: Michael, of Harbour Main, 1750 (CO 199.18); Garret, tailor of St. John's, 1794–5, "25 years in Newfoundland," that is, 1769–70 (Census 1794–5); William, of Brigus, 1784 (CO 199.18); Michael, of Cats Cove (now Conception Harbour)., 1791 (CO 199.18); Margaret, widow of Quidi Vidi,

1794–5 (Census 1794–5); John, of Salmon Cove, Northern Arm (now Avondale), 1799 (CO 199.18); Mary, from Cashel (Co. Tipperary), married at St. John's, 1800 (Nfld. Archives BRC); Michael Keaton, of Harbour Grace Parish, 1806 (Nfld. Archives HGRC); John Keating, from Trinity (Co. Waterford), married at Bonavista, 1821 (Nfld. Archives KCRC); William, constable of Port de Grave, 1821 (CO 194.64); Mary, of Bird Island Cove (now Elliston), 1826 (Nfld. Archives KCRC); Thomas, of Ragged Harbour (now Melrose), 1833 (Nfld. Archives KCRC); ——, on the *Sally* in the seal fishery out of Chapel Cove, 1838 (*Newfoundlander* 29 Mar 1838); John and Luke, from Co. Wexford, of Brigus, 1844 (*Indicator* 24 Aug 1844); John, commissioner for erection of a breakwater at Fortune, 1845 (*Nfld. Almanac*); James, of Broad Cove (now Duntara), 1864 (Nfld. Archives KCRC); Michael (and others), of Burin, 1871 (Lovell); John Keatings, of Channel, 1871 (Lovell); Richard Keating, of Grand Bank, 1871 (Lovell); Michael and Patrick, of Long Harbour (Placentia B.), 1871 (Lovell); Walter, farmer of Renews, 1871 (Lovell).

Modern status: Scattered, especially at Mount Arlington Heights and Renews.

KEATS, a surname of England, from Old English *cȳta*, Middle English *kete*, *kyte* – kite (the bird) from greed or rapacity, or from Old English *cyte* – (worker at the) shed, outhouse for animals, hence herdsman. (Reaney, Cottle).

Traced by Spiegelhalter in Devon.

In Newfoundland:

Early instances: John Keates, Justice of Ferryland district, ? 1730 (CO 194.9); William Keate(s), of Trinity Bay, 1765 (DPHW 64); M. Keates, of St. Mary's, 1782 (D'Alberti 2); Sarah, of Trinity (Trinity B.), 1794 (DPHW 64); Robert Keats, of Bonavista, 1794 (DPHW 70); —— Keat, joint purchaser of fishing room on Pond Island, Greenspond Harbour, 1802 (Bonavista Register 1806); Robert Keates, missionary of Twillingate, 1813 (CO 194.54); James Keat, of St. John's, 1828 (*Newfoundlander* 27 Feb 1828); George Keets, schoolmaster of Ship Cove (now part of Port Rexton), 1843 (DPHW 64B); Samuel Keates, of Castle Cove (Bonavista B.), 1856 (DPHW 73B); Thomas J., granted land at Little Placentia (now Argentia), 1857 (Nfld. Archives, Registry Crown Lands); Ann Kates, of Herring Neck, 1857 (DPHW 85); Robert Kates or Keates, of Grates Cove, 1860, of Caplin Cove (Conception B.), 1871 (DPHW 56, Lovell); Samuel Keats, of Musgravetown, 1871 (Lovell);

Samuel and William, of Newman's Cove, 1871 (Lovell); Theodore Kates, of Cape Norman, 1871 (Lovell).

Modern status: Widespread, especially at Dover, Glovertown and Bunyans Cove.

Place name: Keats Island 48-39 53-39.

(O)KEEFE, variants of the surname of Ireland, (O)Keeffe, *Ó Caoimh*, Ir. *caomh* – gentle. (MacLysaght).

Traced by MacLysaght in south Munster, especially in Co. Cork.

In Newfoundland:

Family traditions: Peter O'Keefe (1797–1862), from west Ireland, settled at Port de Grave in 1832, thence to Coley's Point in 1836; his second son Peter was baptized Anglican and changed his name to Keefe (MUN Geog.); Ellen O'Keefe (about 1827–1902), born at Lance Cove, Upper Gullies (MUN Folklore).

Early instances: Miles Kief, of Bay Bulls, ? 1753 (CO 194.13); Thomas Keef(e), of St. John's, 1757 (DPHW 26C); Mary Keefe, of Carbonear, 1765 (CO 199.18); Michael, of Bay de Verde, 1788 (CO 199.18); ——, ? of Bristol, England, occupier of fishing room in Northern Bay after 1789 (CO 194.45); James, of Chapel Coye, 1793 (CO 199.18); Deniss [sic] Keef, from Thomastown (Co. Kilkenny), married at St. John's, 1793 (Nfld. Archives BRC); Mary, of Toads (now Tors) Cove, 1793 (Nfld. Archives BRC); James, of Trinity (Trinity B.), 1800 (DPHW 64); Bridget Kief, of Tilton Harbour (now Tilting), 1803 (Nfld. Archives BRC); Michael Keefe, of Harbour Grace Parish, 1806 (Nfld. Archives HGRC); James, from Co. Kilkenny, labourer of St. John's, deceased, 1810 (*Royal Gazette* 22 Nov 1810); Michael O'Keef, of Harbour Grace Parish, 1812 (Nfld. Archives HGRC); James, from Rathcormack (Co. Cork), of Carbonear, died 1815, aged 55 (Carbonear R.C. Cemetery); John Keef or Kief, from Ireland, of King's Cove, 1815, 1817 (*Royal Gazette* 27 May 1817, Nfld. Archives KCRC); Richard Keefe, from Kilkenny, aged 30, deserted from service at Torbay, 1820 (*Nfld. Mercantile Journal* 10 Aug 1820); Ellen Keefe, of Trepassey, 1824 (Nfld. Archives BRC); Mary Keefe, of Cape Cove (Bonavista B.), 1826 (Nfld. Archives KCRC); Daniel, of Ragged Harbour (now Melrose), 1827 (Nfld. Archives KCRC); Lawrence Keeffe, of Harbour Grace, 1828 (Nfld. Archives BRC); Michael Keefe, of Crocker's Cove (Carbonear), 1828 (Nfld. Archives BRC); John O'Keefe, of Duckworth Street, St. John's, 1828 (*Newfoundlander* 25 Sep 1828);

Owen Keefe, of Outer Cove, 1836 (Nfld. Archives BRC); Edward, granted land at Caplin Bay (unspecified), 1838 (Nfld. Archives, Registry Crown Lands); ——, on the *John and William* in the seal fishery out of Port de Grave, 1838 (*Newfoundlander* 29 Mar 1838); Thomas, granted land at Harbour Main, 1850 (Nfld. Archives, Registry Crown Lands); Thomas, granted land at Bay Roberts, 1850 (Nfld. Archives, Registry Crown Lands); James, granted land at Cat's Cove (now Conception Harbour), 1861 (Nfld. Archives, Registry Crown Lands); Maria, of Twillingate, 1867 (Nfld. Archives HGRC); widespread in Lovell 1871; Valentine Keefe, from Co. Tipperary, of Ferryland, died 1872, aged 80 (Dillon).

Modern status: Keefe, scattered, especially at Tilting; O'Keefe, widespread especially at Ferryland, Placentia and St. John's.

Place names: Keefe Island (Labrador) 53-16 55-44; Keefes Cove 48-25 53-43; —— Point 50-42 55-34.

KEEL(S), surnames of England, from the English place names Keal (Lincolnshire), Keele (Staffordshire) or Kayle (Cornwall). (Cottle, Spiegelhalter).

Keel was traced by Guppy in Somerset and by Spiegelhalter in Devon.

In Newfoundland:

Early instances: Samuel Keel, fisherman of Trinity (Trinity B.), 1758 (DPHW 64); Moses Keel(s), of Bonavista, 1787, joint lessee of fishing room at Bayley's Cove, 1805 (DPHW 70, Bonavista Register 1806); Moses Keel, of Catalina, 1838 (DPHW 67); Moses, of Little Catalina, 1871 (Lovell).

Modern status: Keel, scattered, especially at Bonavista; Keels, at Bell Island.

Place name: Keels, —— Cove 48-36 53-24.

KEEPING, a variant of the surnames of England Kippin(g), Kippen, and of Scotland, Kippen; in England from the Old English personal name *Cypping*, a nickname used of a fat, round man, in Scotland from the Scots place name Kippen (Stirlingshire). (Reaney, Black).

Spiegelhalter traced Kipping in Devon.

In Newfoundland:

Family tradition: ——, from Scotland, settled at Ramea; the family later moved to Port aux Basques (MUN Folklore).

Early instances: John, of Fortune, 1811 (Surrogate Court, Fortune Bay 1802–19, 1821, pp. 73–152, PANL GN5/1/C/1 per P.E.L. Smith); Grace, of Fortune, 1842 (DPHW 106); Richard, of Grand Bank, 1843 (DPHW 109); James, ? of St. John's,

1844 (*Newfoundlander* 20 Jun 1844); Bethana, of Hare Harbour (Burin district), 1846 (DPHW 106); George, of Sagona (Island), 1851, of Little Bay (Burin district), 1852, of River Head (Burin district), 1854 (DPHW 104); Abraham, of Lower Burgeo, 1851 (DPHW 101); James, of Boxey, 1853 (DPHW 104); John, of Moonsface (Burgeo-La Poile district), 1856 (DPHW 98); George, of Rencontre East, 1856 (DPHW 104); William, planter of Lally Cove (Burin district), 1856 (DPHW 104); John, J.P., Conception Bay, 1857 (*Nfld. Almanac*); John, of Stones Cove, 1858, of Lobster Cove (Fortune B.), 1858 (DPHW 104); Benjamin, of Ramea, 1859 (DPHW 101); William Keepin, of La Plante (Burgeo-La Poile district), 1860 (DPHW 99); scattered in the south coast districts in Lovell 1871.

Modern status: Widespread, especially at Burnt Island (Burgeo-La Poile district), Rencontre East and Ramea.

Place names: Keeping Cove 47-40 55-03; —— Rock 47-27 55-40.

KEHOE, a surname of England and Ireland, with variants KEO(U)GH also of Ireland; in England "from Caieu, a lost town in the vicinity of Boulogne-sur-Mer (Pas-de-Calais)," in Ireland for (Mac)Keogh, *Mac Eochaidh.* (Reaney, MacLysaght).

MacLysaght traced (Mac) Keogh in Cos. Limerick, Tipperary, Roscommon, Wexford, and usually Kehoe in Wicklow. Keough is the Midland form.

In Newfoundland:

Family traditions: Edward Kehoe (1796–1876), born in Co. Wexford, settled at Stone Island, Calvert in 1816 (MUN Geog.). Three Keough brothers, from Ireland, came to Newfoundland and settled at King's Cove, Placentia and Sunny Hill, Ferryland prior to 1815 (MUN Folklore).

Early instances: Thomas Kough, of St. John's, 1774 (DPHW 26D); James Kehoe (about 1778–1864), born at Carbonear, died there aged 86 (Carbonear R.C. Cemetery); John Keough, from Dublin, Irish convict landed at Petty Harbour or Bay Bulls, 1789 (CO 194.38); G. and T. Kough, in possession of property at Torbay, 1794–5 (Census 1794–5); Andrew Kehoe, from Sutton's Parish (Co. Wexford), married at St. John's, 1798 (Nfld. Archives BRC); William Keough, of Harbour Grace Parish, 1809 (Nfld. Archives HGRC); Steve Kehoe, of Placentia, 1814 (*Preliminary Inventory*, Nfld. Archives); Patrick Thehoe [sic], married at Harbour Grace, 1815 (Nfld. Archives HGRC); Andrew Keough or Kehoe, of King's Cove, 1816, of Plate Cove, 1824, of Open Hole (now Open Hall), 1829 (Nfld. Ar-

chives KCRC); Patrick Keough, of Bonavista, 1816 (Nfld. Archives KCRC); Edward, (about 1796–1876), from Co. Wexford, of Ferryland, came to Newfoundland in 1816 (Dillon); James, from Co. Wexford, of Tilting Harbour (now Tilting), 1825 (Nfld. Archives KCRC); Peter, of Careless (now Kerley's) Harbour, 1825 (Nfld. Archives KCRC); Patrick, from the parish of Eathemune [sic], Co. Wexford, of Carbonear, died 1826, aged 42 (Carbonear R.C. Cemetery); John Kehoe, from Old Ross (Co. Wexford), of Harbour Grace, 1829 (Nfld. Archives BRC); Michael, of Fogo, 1830 (Nfld. Archives KCRC); Peter Keough or Kehoe, of Trinity, 1830 (Nfld. Archives KCRC); Andrew Keough, of Broad Cove (now Duntara), 1831 (Nfld. Archives KCRC); John Kehoe, granted land at Brigus, 1834 (Nfld. Archives, Registry Crown Lands); Timothy, of Bell Isle (now Bell Island), 1835 (Nfld. Archives BRC); Mary Keogh, married on the French Shore, 1839 (Nfld. Archives BRC); Sylvester Kough, granted land at "Sun Hill," Ferryland, 1841 (Nfld. Archives, Registry Crown Lands); Valentine Keheo, ? of Northern Bay, 1841 (DPHW 54); Andrew Keogh, of Cottell's Island, 1870 (Nfld. Archives KCRC); widespread in Lovell 1871.

Modern status: Kehoe, scattered; Keough, widespread, especially at Plate Cove East, St. John's and Parsons Pond (St. Barbe district).

Place name: Keogh Island 49-33 55-10.

KEITH, a surname of Scotland from the Scots place name Keith (East Lothian).

Traced by Matthews as captains and traders in Devon, Greenock and Glasgow.

In Newfoundland:

Early instances: John, of St. John's, 1766 (DPHW 26C); Thomas, of Twillingate, 1871 (Lovell).

Modern status: Rare at Grand Falls.

KELLAND, a surname of England from the English place name Kelland Barton (Devon) according to Spiegelhalter, though the place name is not given in Gover.

Traced by Spiegelhalter in Devon.

In Newfoundland:

Family tradition: Mary (1792–1846), of Scilly Cove (now Winterton) (MUN Geog.).

Early instances: John, at Scilly Cove (now Winterton), married Elizabeth Crew(e), 7 Dec 1771 (PANL, Vital Statistics, 64B, per D.E.J. Kelland); ——, co-occupier of fishing room at Shole Harbour (now Cavendish), Winter 1800–01 (Census Trinity B.); Elizabeth, of Shoal Harbour (now Cavendish),

T.B., baptized 27 Aug 1803 (PANL, Births, 64A, Trinity, per D.E.J. Kelland); George, shoemaker of St. John's, 1806 (CO 194.45); John Kelland(s), of Trinity (Trinity B.), 1809 (DPHW 64); Charles (1806–65), of New Perlican, baptized 14 Dec 1817 (PANL, Births, 64A, Trinity, per D.E.J. Kelland); Robert Kelland, fisherman of Port de Grave, 1843 (DPHW 39); John, member of the Board of Road Commissioners of Heart's Content, 1844 (*Nfld. Almanac*); Arianna, of Scilly Cove (now Winterton), 1856 (DPHW 59).

Modern status: Scattered, especially at St. John's.

KELLEHER, a surname of Ireland, (O)Kelleher, *Ó Céileachair* – companion dear. (MacLysaght).

Traced by MacLysaght in Cos. Cork and Kerry.

In Newfoundland:

Early instances: Philip Kellehee or Kileher, of Harbour Grace Parish, 1842, 1844 (Nfld. Archives HGRC); Philip Kelahar, shoemaker of St. John's, 1871 (Lovell).

Modern status: Rare, at Sibleys Cove (*Electors* 1955) and St. John's.

KELLEY. *See* KELLY

KELLIGREW, a surname of England, Killigrew of England and Ireland, from the English place name Killigrew (Cornwall). (Reaney, MacLysaght).

Killigrew was traced by Spiegelhalter in Devon and by MacLysaght in Co. Waterford.

In Newfoundland:

Early instances: William Killigrew, of Port de Grave, 1760 (CO 199.18); —— Kelligrew, ? fish merchant of Ferryland, 1818 (D'Alberti 28); William, of Flat Island (Bonavista B.), 1838 (DPHW 76); Jane Kelligrews, from Paignton (Devon), married at Renews, 1844 (*Times* 14 Feb 1844); John Killigrew granted land at Renews, 1849 (Nfld. Archives, Registry Crown Lands).

Modern status: Rare, at Flat Island (Bonavista B.) (*Electors* 1955) and St. John's.

Place names: Kelligrews, —— Point, —— River 47-30 53-01.

KELLOWAY. *See* CALLOWAY

(O)KELLY, with a rare variant KELLEY, surnames of England, Ireland and Scotland; in England from the English place name Kelly (Devon), Cornish *celli* – wood, grove; in Ireland and Scotland for (Mac) Kelly, *Mac Ceallaigh* or O'KELLY, *Ó Ceallaigh*, ? Ir. *ceallach* – strife; also in Scotland from the Scots

place names Kelly (Angus, Renfrewshire) or Kellie (Fife). (Reaney, MacLysaght, Black).

MacLysaght remarks that MacKelly and O'Kelly are indistinguishable now that the Mac and O have been widely dropped, though he notes that O is being to some extent resumed.

Traced by Guppy in Cornwall and Devon and the Scots Border counties, and by MacLysaght from MacKelly in east Connacht and from O'Kelly throughout Ireland where it is the second commonest name.

In Newfoundland:

Family traditions: Michael Kelly, from Ireland, settled at Daniel's Cove (Trinity B.), about 1810 (MUN Folklore). Edward, (–1816), from Co. Kilkenny, settled at Coley's Point before 1799 (MUN Folklore).

Early instances: John Kelly, of Harbour Main, murdered 1750 (CO 194.12); Patrick, of St. John's, 1751 (CO 194.13); Nicholas, of Harbour Grace, 1787 (CO 199.18); Martin, from Old Court (Co. Wicklow), Thomas, from Rathcoole (Co. Dublin) and John, from Athlone (Co. Roscommon), Irish convicts landed at Petty Harbour or Bay Bulls, 1789 (CO 194.38); James, of Bay de Verde, 1789 (CO 199.18); Edmond Kelley, of St. Mary's, 1797 (D'Alberti 7); —— Kelly, from Ballybrack (unidentified) (Co. Wexford), married at St. John's, 1798 (Nfld. Archives BRC); Morris, of Bonavista, 1803 (Nfld. Archives BRC); John, of Salmon Cove, Northern Arm (now Avondale), 1805 (CO 199.18); James, of Green Head (Spaniards B.), 1805 (CO 199.18); John, of Broad Cove (now Duntara), 1805 (Bonavista Register 1806); Pat and J., of Burin, 1805 (D'Alberti 15); Elenor, of Tilton Harbour (now Tilting), 1808 (Nfld. Archives BRC); Joseph, of Brigus, 1809 (DPHW 34); James, of Great St. Julian's, 1810 (D'Alberti 20); Mary, of Fogo Island, 1812 (Nfld. Archives BRC); Margaret, of Petty Harbour, 1813 (Nfld. Archives BRC); Owen, of Bell Island, 1814 (D'Alberti 24); Maurice, of King's Cove, 1815 (Nfld. Archives KCRC); George, of Cupids, 1816 (Nfld. Archives L165); Robert, from Garuavella (Co. Tipperary), fisherman of St. John's, died 1815 (*Royal Gazette* 15 Jun 1815); Miles, from Co. Wexford, planter of St. John's, died 1817 (*Nfld. Mercantile Jour.* 9 May 1817); Philip, of Heart's Content, 1819 (Nfld. Archives KCRC); Honora, of Plate Cove (Bonavista B.), 1820 (Nfld. Archives KCRC); Mary, of Tickle Cove (Bonavista B.), 1820 (Nfld. Archives KCRC); Bridget, of Bay Bulls, 1820 (Nfld. Archives BRC); Maurice, of Catalina, 1822 (Nfld. Archives KCRC); Mary, of Ragged Harbour (now Melrose), 1824 (Nfld. Archives KCRC); Garrett, of Keels, 1824 (Nfld. Archives KCRC); James, of New Harbour (Trinity B.), 1825 (Nfld. Archives KCRC); Patrick, of Job's Cove, 1828 (Nfld. Archives BRC); Mary, of Open Hole (now Open Hall), 1829 (Nfld. Archives KCRC); Charles, of Greenspond, 1829 (Nfld. Archives KCRC); Nicholas, of Fortune Harbour, 1830 (Nfld. Archives KCRC); Michael, of Turks Cove (Trinity B.), 1830 (Nfld. Archives KCRC); John, of Cape Cove (Bonavista B.), 1831 (Nfld. Archives KCRC); John, of Cobbler's Island (Bonavista B.), 1832 (Nfld. Archives KCRC); Mahala, of Grand Bank, 1834 (DPHW 106); ——, of Bull Cove (Conception B.); 1837 (MUN Hist.); John, granted land at Middle Cove (St. John's district), 1837 (Nfld. Archives, Registry Crown Lands); Patrick, ? of Northern Bay, 1838 (DPHW 54); ——, schoolteacher of Cape Broyle, 1845 (*Nfld. Quarterly* Dec 1911); Margaret, of Pinckers (for Pinchards) Island (Bonavista B.), 1845 (Nfld. Archives KCRC); George, of Rogue's Harbour, 1846 (DPHW 86); George, of Nippers Harbour, 1847 (DPHW 86); James, granted land in Ferryland-Caplin Bay area, 1847 (Nfld. Archives, Registry Crown Lands); William Phillip O'Kelly alias William Francis Naughton, from London, arrested for larceny and counterfeiting in Newfoundland, 1848 (*Royal Gazette* 8 Aug 1848); Philip, of St. John's, 1848 (*Newfoundlander* 3 Aug 1848); David Kelly, of Ireland's Eye, 1851 (DPHW 64B); Thomas, granted land at Great Placentia, 1851 (Nfld. Archives, Registry Crown Lands); John, granted land at Coley's Point, 1855 (Nfld. Archives, Registry Crown Lands); Maurice, of Burn[t] Island (Bonavista B.), 1855 (Nfld. Archives KCRC); Bridget, of Indian Arm (Bonavista B.), 1855 (Nfld. Archives KCRC); Catherine, of Hayward's Cove (Bonavista B.), 1859 (Nfld. Archives KCRC); Samuel Kelley, fisherman, married Jane Lake, Fortune, 1860 (Grand Bank Methodist marriages per P.E.L. Smith); Samuel, of Cat Harbour (now Lumsden), 1861 (Nfld. Archives KCRC); Maurice, of Shoels [sic] Cove (? Bonavista B.), 1863 (Nfld. Archives KCRC); Samuel, of Gooseberry Island (Bonavista B.), 1864 (Nfld. Archives KCRC); Maurice, of Bloody Bay, 1869 (Nfld. Archives KCRC); Kelly, widespread in Lovell 1871.

Modern status: Kelley, scattered; Kelly, widespread, especially at Freshwater (Placentia), Gambo and St. John's; O'Kelly, rare, at Avondale.

Place names: Kelly Brook 47-39 57-33; —— Cove, —— Head 49-29 55-45; —— Point 47-19 53-56; —— Pond 47-25 53-01; Kellys Cove 47-06 55-43; —— Island 47-33 53-01; —— Pond 47-38 53-22, 48-37 53-59.

KELSEY, a surname of England, from the Old English personal name *Cēolsīge* or from the English place name Kelsey (Lincolnshire). (Spiegelhalter).

Traced by Guppy in Surrey, Kent and Lincolnshire and by Spiegelhalter in Devon.

In Newfoundland:

Modern status: At St. John's.

KEMP, a surname of England and Ireland, from Old English *cempa* – warrior, Middle English *kempe* – warrior, athlete, wrestler. (Reaney).

Traced by Guppy mainly in the eastern and southern counties, with the form Kempe also in Cornwall and Devon. MacLysaght comments that Kemp "recurs in Irish records from the fourteenth century till the present day but has never been closely identified with any particular locality." It is now fairly numerous in Dublin and Belfast.

In Newfoundland:

Early instances: John, of Northern Bay, 1764 (CO 199.18); John, in fishery at Petty Harbour, 1794–5, "25 years in Newfoundland," that is, 1769–70 (Census 1794–5); George and James, from Poole (Dorset), in possession of property at Carbonear, 1794, at Brigus, 1797, at Muskette (now Bristol's Hope), 1800, at Freshwater (Carbonear), 1803, at Crocker's Cove (Carbonear), 1804 (CO 199.18); John, of St. John's, ? 1799 (CO 194.42); Joseph, of Harbour Grace Parish, 1809 (Nfld. Archives HGRC); Patrick, from Ireland to Placentia to join the firm of Saunders and Sweetman, 1828. (W.J. Walsh).

Modern status: At St. John's, Jerseyside (Placentia) and Corner Brook.

KENDALL, KENDELL, surnames of England from the English place name Kendal (Westmorland, Warwickshire, Worcestershire, etc.). (Reaney, Spiegelhalter).

Traced by Guppy in the north Midlands and Cornwall, and by Spiegelhalter in Devon.

In Newfoundland:

Family traditions: John Kendall, from Westmorland, settled at Furby's Cove (Hermitage B.), in the early 19th century (MUN Folklore). —— Kendell, from Dorset, settled at Piccaire (MUN Hist.). Louisa, of Channel, 1861 (MUN Geog.).

Early instances: Robert Kendle, of Round Harbour (Burin district), 1827 (DPHW 109); Judith Kembel, of Harbour Grace Parish, 1828 (Nfld. Archives KCRC); —— Kendal, of St. John's, 1832 (*Newfoundlander* 17 May 1832); John Kendle, of Hermitage, 1834 (DPHW 106); Elizabeth, of Furby's Cove, 1835 (DPHW 106); John, of Eastern Cul de

Sac, 1835 (DPHW 30); John, fisherman of Western Point (Burgeo-La Poile district), 1844 (DPHW 101); Robert Kendal(l), fisherman of New (now Parsons) Harbour, 1850 (DPHW 102); Francis Kendall, from ? Marnell Fifed, Dorchester (Dorset), of Grand Bank, 1853 (DPHW 106, MUN Hist.); Sarah, of Burgeo, 1855 (DPHW 101); John (and others), of Ramea, 1871 (Lovell).

Modern status: Scattered, on the south and west coasts: Kendall, especially at Ramea; Kendell, especially at Woodville (St. George's district) and Morrisville (Fortune B.).

KENDRICK, a surname of England and Ireland, in England from the Welsh personal name *Cynwrig* from *cyn* – chief and *(g)wr* – man, hero, or from the Old English personal name *Cyneric*, containing the elements *family* and *ruler*; in Ireland for (Mac) Kendrick, *Mac Eanraic.* (Reaney, MacLysaght).

In Newfoundland:

Early instance: Margaret Kendrick, married at St. John's, 1833 (Nfld. Archives BRC).

Modern status: Rare, at St. John's.

KENEALLY. *See* KENNEALLY

KENEFICK, a surname of Ireland, *Cinipheic,* from a Welsh place name. (MacLysaght).

Traced by MacLysaght in Co. Cork.

In Newfoundland:

Early instances: Edward Kinefick or Kinific, of King's Cove, 1832 (Nfld. Archives KCRC); Margaret Kenefic, of Harbour Grace Parish, 1833 (Nfld. Archives HGRC); Maurice Kenefie, married at St. John's, 1835 (Nfld. Archives BRC); Maurice Kenefic, ? of Harbour Grace, 1845 (*Newfoundlander* 16 Jan 1845); Mary Kinifick, Kinefic or Kennifick, of Broad Cove (now Duntara), 1855 (Nfld. Archives KCRC); Patrick Kennefick, of Harbour Grace, 1870 (Nfld. Archives HGRC).

Modern status: Unique, at Duntara (*Electors* 1955).

KENNARD, a surname of England, a variant of Kenward from the Old English personal names *Cénweard* – bold guardian or *Cyneweard* – royal guardian, or from the English place name Kennard (Somerset). (Reaney).

Guppy traced Kennard in Devon and Kent, and Kenward in Sussex.

In Newfoundland:

Family tradition: A. R., from Worthing (Sussex), settled in St. John's in the 1900s (MUN Folklore).

Modern status: Rare, at St. John's (*Electors* 1955).

Place name: Kennard Island (Labrador) 59-26 63-40.

KEN(N)EALLY, variants of the surname of Ireland, (O)Kinneally, *Ó Cinnfhaolaidh,* Ir. *ceann* – head, *faol* – wolf. (MacLysaght).

MacLysaght traced (O)Kinneally in south Munster.

In Newfoundland:

Early instances: John Ken(n)elly, ? labourer of St. John's, 1779–80 (CO 194.34, D'Alberti 4); James Kennelly, of Placentia, 1794 (D'Alberti 5); Thomas, of Lower Island Cove, 1796 (CO 199.18); John Kenelly, from Waterford City, married at St. John's, 1818 (Nfld. Archives BRC); Thomas Kinnelly, of Harbour Grace Parish, 1822 (Nfld. Archives KCRC); J. Kenealy, of Carbonear, 1856 (*Newfoundlander* 3 Jan 1856); David Kenneally, from Co. Cork, of Carbonear, died 1874, aged 78 (Carbonear R.C. Cemetery).

Modern status: Keneally, unique, at St. John's (*Electors* 1955); Kenneally, rare, at Carbonear.

KENNEDY, a surname of Ireland and Scotland, (O)Kennedy, *Ó Cinnéide,* Ir. *ceann* – head, *éidigh* – ugly, modern Gaelic *Ceannaideach.* "The Scottish Kennedys are by remote origin Irish Gaels." (MacLysaght, Black).

Traced by MacLysaght in Cos. Tipperary and Wexford, and by Guppy especially in Ayrshire, Dumfriesshire, Inverness-shire and Argyleshire.

In Newfoundland:

Early instances: Widow, of Harbour Grace, 1770, property "possessed by the Family for upwards of 90 years," that is, before 1680 (CO 199.18); Edward, of Hibbs Hole, 1800, property "in possession of the Family for upwards of 70 years," that is, before 1730 (CO 199.18); Patrick, shoreman of St. John's, 1794–5, "40 years in Newfoundland," that is, 1754–5 (Census 1794–5); Bartholomew, fisherman of Trinity (Trinity B.), 1757 (DPHW 64); Richard, in fishery at Petty Harbour, 1794–5, "27 years in Newfoundland," that is, 1767–8 (Census 1794–5); John and James, of Harbour Main, 1782 (CO 199.18); Terrence, of Crockers Cove (Carbonear), before 1796 (CO 199.18); Ralph, of Western Bay, 1798 (CO 199.18); William and Co., of Salmon Cove, Northern Arm (now Avondale), 1798 (CO 199.18); William Kenedy, from Waterford City, married at St. John's, 1799 (Nfld. Archives BRC); Anastasia, of Bay Bulls, 1801 (Nfld. Archives BRC);

John Kennedy, of Long Pond Lookout, 1803 (CO 199.18); Edmond, from Cloyne (Co. Cork), married at Fogo, 1803 (Nfld. Archives BRC); Richard, from Passage Parish (unidentified), Diocese of Waterford, married at Greenspond, 1803, of Greenspond, 1805 (Nfld. Archives BRC, Bonavista Register 1806); Cornelius, of Holyrood Head, 1804 (CO 199.18); Edward, operated salmon fishery at Fogo, 1804 (CO 194.45); John, ? fisherman of Port de Grave, 1805 (Nfld. Archives T22); Phillip, one of 72 impressed men who sailed from Ireland to Newfoundland, ? 1811 (CO 194.51); William Kenedy, from Knocpherson (Co. Waterford), fisherman of Trepassey, died 1811 (*Royal Gazette* 28 Nov 1811); William Kennedy, of Lance Cove (Bell Island), 1814 (D'Alberti 24); Patrick, of Bonavista, 1815 (Nfld. Archives KCRC); Elizabeth, of Joe Batts Arm, 1817 (Nfld. Archives KCRC); Michael, of Tilton Harbour (now Tilting), 1819 (Nfld. Archives KCRC); John, from Carrick (unspecified), of Ragged Harbour (now Melrose), 1820 (Nfld. Archives KCRC); Jean, of Catalina, 1821 (Nfld. Archives KCRC); John, of King's Cove, 1826 (Nfld. Archives KCRC); Catherine, of Cape Cove (Bonavista B.), 1827 (Nfld. Archives KCRC); ——, of Bell Isle (now Bell Island), 1827 (Nfld. Archives BRC); Thomas, of Carbonear, 1828 (Nfld. Archives BRC); John Keniddy, of Fortune Harbour, 1830 (Nfld. Archives KCRC); John Kennedy, of Middle Bight (now Codner), 1832 (DPHW 30); David Kenedy, of the White Hills, 1836 (Nfld. Archives BRC); Maurice, from Dingle (Co. Kerry), of Harbour Grace, 1844 (*Indicator* 27 Jul 1844); Jane Kennedy, of Hare Bay (Fogo district), 1847 (DPHW 83); Mary, of Little Catalina, 1850 (DPHW 67); George, of Catalina, 1851 (DPHW 72); Martin Kenedy, of Cats Cove (now Conception Harbour), 1853 (Nfld. Archives, Registry Crown Lands); Thomas Kennedy, of the French Shore, 1868 (Nfld. Archives HGRC); widespread in Lovell 1871.

Modern status: Widespread, especially at Shoal Point (Ferryland district), Long Pond (Manuels) and St. John's.

Place names: Kennedy Bight, —— Head (Labrador) 52-08 55-42; —— Cove (Labrador) 52-39 55-47; —— Island (Labrador) 53-04 55-45; —— Hill 46-53 55-49; —— Lake 49-15 57-52; —— Point 47-41 58-22, 47-49 59-20; Kennedys Brook 47-39 52-42; —— Cove (Labrador) 55-07 59-13; —— Pond 47-21 53-23.

KENNELL, a surname of England, ? from the English place names Kennal Vale (Cornwall), or Kendal

(Westmorland), or Kentwell (Suffolk). (Bardsley, Ewen).

Traced in Devon by Gover in the place name Kennel Wood, "probably to be associated with the family of John Kynewyll" (about 1361), and by Bardsley in Herefordshire and Dorset.

In Newfoundland:

Early instances: John Kennel, fisherman of Western Bay, 1817 (DPHW 52A); Thomas, planter of Bradleys Cove, 1851 (DPHW 52A).

Modern status: Scattered, especially at Western Bay.

Place names: Kennel Brook, —— Head 47-57 59-18.

KENN(E)Y, surnames of England and Ireland; in England ? a variant of KENWAY; in Ireland sometimes of English origin, but usually from MacKenny, an Ulster variant of MACKENNA, or (O)Kenny, *Ó Cionaoith*, ? Ir. *cionaodh* – firesprung, or a synonym of KINNEY or Kilkenny. (MacLysaght).

MacLysaght traced (O)Kenny in Cos. Donegal and Galway.

In Newfoundland:

Early instances: Timothy Kenny, of St. John's, 1759 (DPHW 26C); David, of Kit Hughes (now Kitchuses), 1775 (CO 199.18); Francis, of Torbay, 1798 (Nfld. Archives BRC); James, from Ballinakill (Co. Laois), married at St. John's, 1805 (Nfld. Archives BRC); Bridget, of Harbour Grace Parish, 1813 (Nfld. Archives HGRC); Joanna, of Petty Harbour, 1813 (Nfld. Archives BRC); John, from Co. Kilkenny, fisherman of St. John's, died 1813 (*Royal Gazette* 18 Nov 1813); Patrick, from Carrick-on-Suir (Co. Tipperary), planter of Torbay, died 1814 (*Royal Gazette* 26 May 1814); John, of Twillingate, 1820 (Nfld. Archives KCRC); John, of King's Cove, 1822 (Nfld. Archives KCRC); Catherine Kinney, of Greenspond, 1822 (Nfld. Archives KCRC); Thomas Kenny, of Cape Cove (Bonavista B.), 1829 (Nfld. Archives KCRC); Mary, from Co. Kilkenny, of Ragged Harbour (now Melrose), 1829 (Nfld. Archives KCRC); John Kenney, of Cobblers (now Cape) Island (Bonavista B.), 1830 (Nfld. Archives KCRC); Mary Kenny, from Waterford (unspecified), of Port de Grave, 1844 (*Indicator* 24 Aug 1844); Thomas, J.P. of La Poile, 1844 (*Nfld. Almanac*); Thomas, granted land at Upper Long Pond, 1845 (Nfld. Archives, Registry Crown Lands); Mary, of Twillingate, 1846 (*Newfoundlander* 4 Jun 1846); John, fisherman of Trepassey, died 1852 (*Newfoundlander* 28 Jun 1852); Richard, of South River (Conception B.), 1849 (Nfld. Archives,

Registry Crown Lands); James, of Broad Cove (now Duntara), 1850 (Nfld. Archives KCRC); scattered in Lovell 1871.

Modern status: Kenney, rare, especially at St. John's; Kenny, scattered, especially at Riverhead (Fermeuse), Kitchuses and St. John's.

Place names: Kennys Pond 47-35 52-43; —— Rocks 49-13 53-29.

KENT, a surname of England and Ireland, from the English place name Kent (Devon) or the county, or from Celtic *canto*-, Welsh *cant* – (dweller on the) border, rim, coast. (Spiegelhalter, MacLysaght, Ekwall).

Traced by Guppy in the south and Midlands, by Spiegelhalter in Devon, and by MacLysaght in Co. Cork.

In Newfoundland:

Early instances: John, of Brigus (unspecified), 1676 (CO 1); James and William, in possession of property in fishery at Bell Island, 1794–5, "born in Newfoundland" (Census 1794–5); Michael, from St. James (unidentified) (Co. Wexford), married at St. John's, 1815 (Nfld. Archives BRC); James, of Harbour Grace Parish, 1816 (Nfld. Archives HGRC); Patrick, ? of Ferryland, 1817 (D'Alberti 27); John Kents, of Lance Cove (unspecified), 1818 (Nfld. Archives BRC); George Kent, planter of Small Point (Conception B.), 1818 (DPHW 52A); James, of St. John's, 1828 (*Newfoundlander* 25 Sep 1828); Walter, from Co. Wexford, of Herring Neck, 1829 (Nfld. Archives KCRC); D., of Brigus, 1831 (*Newfoundlander* 24 Nov 1831); John ? Kent, granted land at Southern Gut (now South River), 1850 (Nfld. Archives, Registry Crown Lands); Martin Kent, of Harbour Grace, 1866 (Nfld. Archives HGRC); John (and others), of Cape Broyle, 1871 (Lovell); John, farmer of Clarke's Beach, 1871(Lovell); Job Kents, of Pools Island (Bonavista B.), 1871 (Lovell); Francis and James Kent, of Spaniards Bay, 1871 (Lovell).

Modern status: Scattered, especially at Lance Cove and Wabana (Bell Island).

Place names: Kent Cove 47-40 56-19; —— Point 50-39 57-16; Kents Pond 47-35 52-43.

KENWAY, a surname of England, from the Old English personal names *Cēnwīg* – bold war or *Cynewīg* – royal war. (Reaney). *See also* KENN(E)Y.

In Newfoundland:

Modern status: At Baine Harbour, Port Elizabeth, Gallants (*Electors* 1955), and Winterland (Burin district).

KEOUGH. *See* KEHOE

KEPPIE, a variant of the surname of Scotland, Kippie, from the Scots place name Kippo (Fife). (Black).

Traced by Black in Fife and the Shetland Isles.

In Newfoundland:

Modern status: Unique, at St. John's.

KERFONT, ? a Newfoundland variant of ? a French surname Kerfot (not cited in Dauzat) from the place name Kerfot (Côtes-du-Nord), Breton *ker* – village, later house and ? *feunteum* – spring, fountain. (Dauzat).

In Newfoundland:

Family tradition: The Kerfont family arrived in Newfoundland and settled at Cape St. George in 1900 (MUN Geog.).

Modern status: In the Port-au-Port district especially at Cape St. George (*Electors* 1955).

KERIVAN. *See* CARAVAN

KERR. *See* CARR

KERRIVAN. *See* CARAVAN

KERROTRET, ? a Newfoundland variant of the surname of France, Kérobert, from Breton *ker* – village, later house and Robert.

In Newfoundland:

Modern status: Rare, at Mainland (Port-au-Port) (*Electors* 1955).

KERWIN, KIRWIN, surnames of Ireland, variants of (O)Kirwan, *Ó Ciardhubháin*, Ir. *ciar dubh* – black. (MacLysaght).

Traced by MacLysaght in Co. Galway.

In Newfoundland:

Early instances: John Kerwin, of Harbour Grace Parish, 1815 (Nfld. Archives HGRC); Elizabeth, from Goer's Bridge (unidentified) (Co. Kilkenny), married at St. John's, 1820 (Nfld. Archives BRC); Philip Kirivin, Kervin or Kerravan, of King's Cove, 1831 (Nfld. Archives KCRC); Mother Mary Bernard Kirwan (1797–1857), from Galway, arrived at St. John's, 1833, founded a convent at Admirals Cove (now Port Kirwan) in 1853 (*Carbonear Star* 20 Oct 1833, Dillon); Michael, from Ireland, of Burin, 1839 (*Newfoundlander* 5 Dec 1839); Bridget Kirwen, of Riverhead (St. John's), 1856 (Nfld. Archives, Registry Crown Lands); John Kirwin, of Brule (Placentia B.), 1871 (Lovell); Michael and William, of Salmonier (St. Mary's), 1871 (Lovell); James Kerwin, of Ferryland, 1871 (Lovell); James, of Ward's Harbour (now Beaumont North), 1871 (Lovell); Michael Karwan, blacksmith of St. John's, 1871 (Lovell).

Modern status: Kerwin, rare, at St. John's; Kirwin, unique, at Searston (*Electors* 1955).

Place names: Kerwan Point 47-08 53-29; Port Kirwan 46-58 52-55.

KETTLE, a surname of England, Scotland and Ireland, from an Old Norse personal name *Ketill* – (sacrificial) cauldron, in Irish *Mac Coitil*. (Reaney, MacLysaght).

Traced by Spiegelhalter in Devon, by Black in Fife, and by MacLysaght in Cos. Louth and Dublin since the early 14th century.

In Newfoundland:

Early instances: William, fisherman of Fox Island (Burgeo-La Poile district), 1844 (DPHW 101); William Sr. and Jr., of Channel, 1871 (Lovell).

Modern status: At St. Lawrence and in the Burgeo-La Poile district, especially at Grand Bay.

Place names (not necessarily from the surname): Kettle Bay (Labrador) 54-49 58-17; —— Cove 49-36 54-43, 48-04 52-57, 49-28 55-43; —— Ponds 48-32 53-52; —— Rocks 46-51 55-47; The —— 47-25 52-40; —— Cove Head (Labrador) 53-49 56-58.

KEY(E)S, a surname of England and Ireland, in England a variant of KAYS, in Ireland often of MacKee.

Spiegelhalter traced Key(e)s and Keyse in Devon; Guppy traced Keys in Buckinghamshire.

In Newfoundland:

Early instances: Bartholomew Keys, of Crocker's Cove (Carbonear), 1675 (CO 1); Ellen, of Bay Bulls district, 1803 (Nfld. Archives BRC); John, of Capiland [sic] Cove (unspecified), married at St. John's, 1814 (Nfld. Archives BRC); Patrick, of Harbour Grace Parish, 1816 (Nfld. Archives HGRC); Lawrence Key, ? of Northern Bay, 1838 (DPHW 54); Michael and Thomas Keys, fisherman of Caplin Cove (Fogo district), 1871 (Lovell).

Modern status: Keyes, at St. Michaels (Ferryland district) (*Electors* 1955) and Bay de Verde; Keys, unique, at St. John's (*Electors* 1955).

KEYNES, a surname of England, a variant of CAIN(ES).

Traced by Guppy in Dorset.

In Newfoundland:

Modern status: Rare, at Path End (Burin district) (*Electors* 1955).

Place name: Keynes Rock 47-05 55-04.

KEYS. *See* KEY(E)S

KIDNEY, a surname of England and Ireland, in England ? a variant of Gidney or Gedney from the English place name Gedney (Lincolnshire) or ? of Gidley from the place name Gidleigh (Devon); or ? of Kitley from the place name Ketley (Shropshire), or ? from Kitley (Devon); in Ireland, "a synonym, by pseudo-translation, of Duane." (Bardsley, MacLysaght).

Traced by MacLysaght mainly in Co. Cork. Spiegelhalter traced Gidley in Devon.

In Newfoundland:

Family tradition: Patrick, of Bryant's Cove, 1847 (MUN Geog.).

Early instances: Pat, of Harbour Grace Parish, 1835 (Nfld. Archives HGRC); John, ? of Harbour Grace, 1845 (*Newfoundlander* 16 Jan 1845); Timothy and John, of Upper Island Cove, 1859 (Nfld. Archives, Registry Crown Lands); Daniel, of St. John's, 1871 (Lovell).

Modern status: Rare, at St. John's.

Place names (not necessarily from the surname): Kidney Pond 48-18 57-22, 49-57 56-05.

KIEL(L)(E)Y, variants of the surname of Ireland (O)Kiely, *Ó Cadhla*, Ir. *cadhla* – graceful, "much confused with Keeley and Queally." (MacLysaght).

MacLysaght traced Kiely mainly in Cos. Waterford and Limerick.

In Newfoundland:

Early instances: Lawrence Kiley, in possession of property in fishery at Petty Harbour, 1794–5, "32 years in Newfoundland," that is, 1762–3 (Census 1794–5); Thomas Kieley, planter of Harbour Grace, 1783 (D'Alberti 2); Edmond Kiley, planter of St. Mary's, 1792 (D'Alberti 6); Michael Kiely, from Waterford City, married at St. John's, 1803 (Nfld. Archives BRC); Robert Keily, of Four Mile Water (unidentified), married at St. John's, 1803 (Nfld. Archives BRC); John, one of 72 impressed men who sailed from Ireland to Newfoundland ? 1811 (CO 194.51); Maurice Kiely, from Ireland, planter of Bay Bulls, died 1811 (*Royal Gazette* 17 Oct 1811); William Keiley, from Dungarvan (Co. Waterford), cooper of St. John's, died 1811 (*Royal Gazette* 17 Oct 1811); David Keily, of Ragged Harbour (now Melrose), 1827 (Nfld. Archives KCRC); Reverend Thomas W., of Bonavista, 1832 (Nfld. Archives KCRC); Edward Kielley, granted land at Riverhead (St. John's), 1834 (Nfld. Archives, Registry Crown

Lands); William Keily, of Maggotty Cove (St. John's district), 1835 (Nfld. Archives BRC); Mary Kielley, granted land at Caplin Cove, Salmon Cove (Port de Grave), 1846 (Nfld. Archives, Registry Crown Lands).

Modern status: Kieley, scattered, especially at St. John's and Holyrood; Kielley, rare, at Grand Falls (*Electors* 1955) and St. John's; Kielly, scattered, especially at St. John's and Gaskiers; Kiely, rare, at Gander.

KILFOY, ? a variant of the surname of Ireland, (Mac) Gilfoyle, *Mac Giolla Phóil* – devotee of St. Paul. (MacLysaght).

In Newfoundland:

Early instances: Edward, of Carbonear, 1796 (CO 199.18); Edmond Killjoy, of Harbour Grace Parish, 1807 (Nfld. Archives HGRC); Mary Killfoil, married at St. John's, 1815 (Nfld. Archives BRC); Bridget Kilfoy, from Blackwater (Co. Wexford), married at St. John's, 1820 (Nfld. Archives BRC); James Kilfoyle, of Grates Cove, 1828 (Nfld. Archives BRC); Catherine, of Harbour Grace, 1828 (Nfld. Archives BRC); John, fisherman of Little Bay (Burin district), 1871 (Lovell).

Modern status: At Marystown (*Electors* 1955), Little Bay and St. John's.

KILPATRICK, a surname of Scotland and Ireland, (Mac) Kilpatrick, *Mac Giolla Phádraig* – devotee of St. Patrick, "an older form of Fitzpatrick almost peculiar to Ulster," or from the Scots place name Kilpatrick (Dumfriesshire, Dumbartonshire), or synonymously with Kirkpatrick (*See also* KIRKPATRICK) from the Scots place name Kirkpatrick (Kirkcudbrightshire, Dumfriesshire). (MacLysaght, Black). *See* PATRICK.

In Newfoundland:

Early instances: Maria, of St. John's, 1839 (DPHW 26D).

Modern status: Rare, at St. John's.

KINDEN, ? a variant of the surname of England, Kingdon, from the English place names Kingdon, Kendon, Keynedon (Devon), or ? from the English place names Kinden (? Worcestershire) or Kineton (Gloucestershire, Warwickshire). (Spiegelhalter, Bardsley).

Spiegelhalter traced Kingdon in Devon.

In Newfoundland:

Early instance: Jessie, of Englee, 1872 (MUN Hist.).

Modern status: In the Fogo district, especially at Stag Harbour and Indian Islands, and in the Gander district.

KING, a surname of England, Scotland and Ireland, from Old English *Cyng*, a nickname from *cyn(in)g* – king, or also from *cyn(in)g* – king, a nickname for one of kingly appearance or qualities, or for one who had acted the part of a king in a play or pageant or had been "king" of some festivity, or had seen service in a royal household. In Ireland, King is usually an English name, but it is also widely used as an anglicized form of several names, including CONROY, by pseudo-translation. (Reaney, Cottle, MacLysaght).

Guppy found King widespread in England, especially in Bedfordshire, Buckinghamshire and Wiltshire, and Scotland, except the North.

In Newfoundland:

Family traditions: Jacob, blacksmith from Wales, settled at Harbour Buffett about 1820, later moved to King's Island (MUN Geog.). George, from Compton (Dorset), settled at Greenspond in 1846 (MUN Folklore). Cephus (1816–1893), of Catalina (MUN Geog.). William, of Portugal Cove, 1830 (MUN Hist.).

Early instances: Absalon, of Fermeuse, 1675 (CO 1); Abraham, of Carbonear, 1676 (CO 1); Abraham, of Renews, 1681 (CO 1); William, of Fair Islands (Bonavista B.), 1681 (CO 1); John, boatkeeper of St. John's, 1682 (CO 1); Abraham, of Bay de Verde, 1708–09 (CO 194.4); John, of Green Island (Bonavista B.), 1708–09 (CO 194.4); William, of Bonavista, 1708–09 (CO 194.4); John, in possession of property in fishery at Bell Island, 1794–5, "40 years in Newfoundland," that is, 1754–5 (Census 1794–5); James, of (Upper) Island Cove, 1763 (CO 199.18); Messrs. King, of Twillingate, 1768 (MUN Hist.); Robert, splitter and salter of Trinity Bay, 1772 (CO 194.30); James Sr., of Bradleys Cove (Conception B.), 1773 (CO 199.18); Jane, of Brigus, 1784 (CO 199.18); James and Edward, of Mully's Cove, 1784 (CO 199.18); John, of Perry's Cove, 1791 (CO 199.18); John, of Small Point (Conception B.), 1793 (CO 199.18); M., of Placentia, 1794 (D'Alberti 5); William, in possession of property and fisherman of Torbay, 1794–5, "born in Newfoundland" (Census 1794–5); James, of Broad Cove (Bay de Verde district), 1797 (DPHW 48); Daniel, of Port de Grave, 1799 (CO 199.18); James, of Western Bay, 1800 (CO 199.18); Richard and sons, proprietors and occupiers of fishing room at Old Perlican, Winter 1800–01 (Census Trinity B.); William and

John, of Crocker's Cove (Carbonear), 1802 (CO 199.18); Robert, of Old Bonaventure, 1806 (DPHW 64, 64B); Mary, of Harbour Grace Parish, 1807 (Nfld. Archives HGRC); Michael, from Nochbuie (unidentified) (Co. Waterford), married at St. John's, 1811 (Nfld. Archives BRC); John, of White Point (Trinity North district), 1812 (DPHW 64); Francis, of Quidi Vidi, 1813 (DPHW 26B); Philip, planter of Hants Harbour, 1821 (DPHW 58); John, planter of Fogo, 1823 (USPG); Thomas, sailmaker of Trinity (Trinity B.), 1825 (DPHW 64B); Charles, of Pushthrough, 1830 (DPHW 30); Joana [sic], of Bay Barbes (for Bay Bulls), 1830 (Nfld. Archives BRC); John, of Greenspond, baptized 1830, aged 20 (DPHW 76); Henry, planter of Grates Cove, 1830 (DPHW 38); Nathanial, of Pool's Island, baptized 1830, aged 23 (DPHW 76); George, commissioner of roads between Burin and Grand Bank, 1834, of Burin, 1843 (*Newfoundlander* 19 Jun 1834, 31 Aug 1843); Stephen, of Lamaline, 1834, of Grand Bank, 1835 (DPHW 109); John, from Shaftesbury (Dorset), married at Twillingate, 1837 (*Newfoundlander* 6 Apr 1837); Matthew, fisherman of Burnt Island (Burgeo-La Poile district), 1841 (DPHW 101); John, planter of New Bonaventure, 1842 (DPHW 64B); James, of Nippers Harbour, 1845 (DPHW 86); Zebedee, of Scilly Cove (now Winterton), 1846 (DPHW 59A); John Caleb, from Poole (Dorset), married at Fogo, 1849 (*Nfld. Patriot* 1 Dec 1849); Thomas, of Little Catalina, 1850 (DPHW 72); Richard, planter of Lower Island Cove, 1851 (DPHW 55); Edward, of Blackhead (Bay de Verde district), 1859 (DPHW 58); Thomas, of Muddy Hole (Burin district), 1860 (DPHW 107); John, of Harbour Grace, 1861 (DPHW 43); widespread in Lovell 1871.

Modern status: Widespread, especially at Broad Cove (Bay de Verde district), Perry's Cove, Fox Harbour (Placentia B.), Bauline (St. John's East district), Lamaline, Harry's Harbour (Green B.) and St. John's.

Place names: King Island 47-36 54-12, 47-36 55-59, 47-24 53-58; ―― Cove 47-43 56-03, 49-43 55-54; ―― Rocks (Labrador) 52-15 55-36, 52-58 55-46; Kings Beach 47-40 53-14; ―― Brook 49-03 56-23; ―― Cove 48-34 53-20, 49-42 55-54, 47-36 52-53, 47-37 55-59, 48-34 53-20, (Labrador) 52-34 55-45; ―― Harbour 47-38 57-34; ―― Head 48-08 52-58, 47-38 57-34, 47-59 53-19; ―― Point 48-56 54-53, 49-35 56-11; ―― Pond 47-43 53-24; ―― Ridge 46 53-34; The ―― ―― 49-08 55-22; ―― Cove Head 48-35 53-20; ―― Harbour Brook 47-39 57-35; ―― Head Pond 48-00 53-18; Kingston 47-49 53-07.

KINGMAN, a surname of England, from the Old English personal name *Cynemann* – the king's man or servant. (Reaney, Spiegelhalter). *See also* KINSMAN.

Traced by Spiegelhalter in Devon and by Guppy in Dorset.

In Newfoundland:

Early instance: William, of Merritt's Harbour, 1878 (DPHW 89).

Modern status: Rare, at Campbellton (Twillingate district).

Place name: Kingmans, ―― Cove 46-58 52-57.

KINGSLEY, a surname of England, from the English place name Kingsley (Cheshire, Hampshire, Staffordshire) – king's wood, glade, clearing. (Cottle).

Traced by Guppy in Hertfordshire.

In Newfoundland:

Early instances: William Kinslea, St. Jacques, 1835 (DPHW 30); John Kinsley, fisherman of Clarkes Beach, 1871 (Lovell); John Kinsley and Mrs. Jane Kingsley, of St. John's, 1871 (Lovell).

Modern status: In the Port de Grave district (*Electors* 1955), Corner Brook, Long Pond (Manuels) and St. John's.

KINNEY, a surname of Ireland, (Mac) Kinney, *Mac Coinnigh*. *See also* KENN(E)Y. (MacLysaght).

Traced by MacLysaght in Cos. Tyrone and Fermanagh.

In Newfoundland:

Modern status: Unique, at St. John's (*Electors* 1955).

KINSELLA, a surname of Ireland, *Cinnsealach*, "One of the few Gaelic-Irish surnames without the prefix O and Mac, being taken from the ancient clan name *Ui Ceinnsealaigh* which became a territorial designation covering much of the north of Co. Wexford." (MacLysaght).

Traced by MacLysaght in Cos. Carlow and Wexford.

In Newfoundland:

Early instances: James Kinchelagh, fisherman of St. John's, 1794–5 (Census 1794–5); Mary Kinsela or Kinchela, of Harbour Grace Parish, 1819 (Nfld. Archives HGRC); Thomas Kinsela, of Fogo, 1822 (Nfld. Archives KCRC); Anastasia, of Job's Cove, 1828 (Nfld. Archives BRC); Margaret Kinsella, of Harbour Grace, 1829 (Nfld. Archives BRC); Michael, of Fortune Harbour, 1833 (Nfld. Archives KCRC); Richard Kinchela, Kinsella or Kinchlea, of Ferryland, 1838 (*Newfoundlander* 25 Oct 1838,

Lovell); T. Kinshela, member of Roman Catholic
Board of Education of Fortune Bay, 1845 (*Nfld.
Almanac*); Timothy Kinsella, ? of Northern Bay,
1846 (DPHW 54); Thomas Kinshella, granted land
between Outer and Middle Cove (St. John's district),
1848 (Nfld. Archives, Registry Crown Lands);
Thomas and Sons, granted land at Belleoram, 1860
(Nfld. Archives, Registry Crown Lands); James
Kinsella, of Bareneed, 1871 (Lovell); Rev. John R.,
of Great St. Lawrence, 1871 (Lovell); Philip, of
Middle Cove (St. John's district), 1871 (Lovell);
Patrick Kinsela, farmer of Torbay, 1871 (Lovell).

Modern status: Scattered, especially at Job's
Cove and Ferryland.

KINSLOW, ? a variant of the surname of England,
Kingslow, from the English place name Kingslow
(Shropshire), Old English *cyne-setl* – king's seat.
(Ekwall).

In Newfoundland:

Early instances: William, of Lower Burgeo, 1843
(DPHW 101); John and Owen, of Red Island (Burgeo-
La Poile district), 1871 (Lovell).

Modern status: At English Harbour West, Red
Island (Burgeo-La Poile district) (*Electors* 1955),
and Isle aux Morts.

KINSMAN, a surname of England, ? a variant of
KINGMAN, or a relative by blood or (loosely) by
marriage. (Reaney).

Traced by Spiegelhalter in Devon.

In Newfoundland:

Modern status: Rare, at St. John's.

KIPPENHUCK, ? a Newfoundland variant of the
surname of Germany, Köpenick, from the German
place name Köpenick, a suburb of Berlin.

In Newfoundland:

Early instances: Samuel Kippenock, of William's
Harbour (Labrador), 1850 (DPHW 113); Samuel, of
Battle Harbour (Labrador), 1850 (DPHW 113).

Modern status: Rare, at Springdale, Harbour
Grace (*Electors* 1955) and Carbonear.

KIRBY, a surname of England and Ireland; in
England from the common English place names
Kir(k)by – the village with a church; in Ireland
(O)Kirby, *Ó Ciarmhaic*, Ir. *ciar* – black, dark-brown,
mac – son, or the modern form of Kerribly, *Mac
Geirble* in Co. Mayo. (Reaney, MacLysaght).

Traced by Guppy in several counties, especially
in Yorkshire NR and ER, by Spiegelhalter in Devon,
and by MacLysaght in Cos. Limerick and Mayo.

In Newfoundland:

Family traditions: Patrick and his brother from
Ireland, came to Newfoundland ? before 1825;
Patrick settled at Blow-Me-Down (Carbonear) and
the brother settled in Trinity Bay (MUN Folklore).
William, from Devon, came to Newfoundland in
1854, was ordained Anglican minister in 1859,
served for 50 years in King's Cove (MUN Folklore).
——, from Bristol, settled at Pouch Cove ? before
1831 (MUN Folklore).

Early instances: William Kirbie, soldier of St.
John's, 1757 (DPHW 26C); John Kirby, of Trinity
(Trinity B.), 1801, of Old Shop, 1817 (DPHW 64);
Richard, of Burin, 1805 (D'Alberti 15); John, of
New Harbour (Trinity B.), 1815 (Nfld. Archives
KCRC); Margaret Kerby, of Harbour Grace Parish,
1818 (Nfld. Archives HGRC); Thomas, of Grand
Bank, 1827 (DPHW 109); Isaac Kirby, of Pouch
Cove, 1838 (DPHW 26D); Patrick Curby, Kerby or
Kirby, planter ? of Otterbury (Carbonear), 1852
(DPHW 49); James Kerby, fisherman of Round
Harbour (Fortune B.), 1857 (DPHW 102); Samuel
Kirby, of Harbour Buffett, 1871 (Lovell); Rev.
William, of King's Cove, 1871 (Lovell); Joseph, of
Lawn, 1871 (Lovell); John, of Upper Small Point
(now Kingston), 1871 (Lovell).

Modern status: Scattered, especially at St. John's
and Kirby's Cove (Burin district).

Place name: Kirby's Cove 47-02 55-10.

KIRK, a surname of England, Scotland and Ireland,
from Old Norse *kirkja* – (dweller by the) church; in
Munster also a variant of QUIRK(E). (Reaney,
MacLysaght).

Traced by Guppy in the Midlands and Yorkshire,
south of the Forth and Clyde, and by MacLysaght in
Ulster, Munster and Co. Louth.

In Newfoundland:

Early instances: George (and others) Kirke or
Kerke, of Ferryland, 1675, 1677 (CO 1); Jeremiah
Kirke, of Caplin Bay (now Calvert), 1676 (CO 1);
John, of Renews, 1677 (CO 1); Nicholas Kirk, of
Harbour Grace Parish, 1814 (Nfld. Archives HGRC);
Alexander, clerk of St. John's, 1871 (Lovell).

Modern status: Rare, at Grand Falls (*Electors*
1955).

KIRKLAND, a surname of England and Scotland,
from many places so-called – (dweller on or by the)
churchland.

Traced by Guppy in Derbyshire and Nottinghamshire.

In Newfoundland:

Early instance: Mrs. Ann, of St. John's, 1871 (Lovell).

Modern status: At St. John's.

KIRKPATRICK, a surname of Scotland and Ireland, from the Scots place name Kirkpatrick (Kirkcudbrightshire, Dumfriesshire). *See* KILPATRICK and PATRICK.

Traced by Guppy in Dumfriesshire and by MacLysaght in Ulster.

In Newfoundland:

Modern status: Rare, at St. John's.

KIRWIN. *See* KERWIN

KISS, a rare surname of England, from Old French *cuisse* – (maker of leather) thigh (armour). (Bardsley, Weekley *Romance*, Reaney *Origin*).

In Newfoundland:

Modern status: Rare, at St. John's.

KITCHEN, a surname of England and Ireland, from Old English *cycene* – (worker in a) kitchen; in Ireland also for (Mac) Cutcheon. (Reaney, MacLysaght).

Traced by Guppy in Cumberland, Westmorland, Lancashire, Lincolnshire, Nottinghamshire and Yorkshire NR and ER, and by MacLysaght in Co. Down.

In Newfoundland:

Family tradition: John (1771–1832), from Yorkshire, stonemason of Harbour Grace (MUN Folklore).

Early instances: William, married at St. John's, 1836 (Nfld. Archives BRC); Phil, of Harbour Grace Parish, 1838 (Nfld. Archives HGRC); Mrs., of St. John's, 1841 (*Newfoundlander* 18 Feb 1841).

Modern status: At St. John's, Bell Island and Harbour Grace.

KNAPMAN, a surname of England, from Old English *cnæpp* – (dweller at the) top of the hill, hillock, or from the English place name Knap(p) (Devon). (Reaney).

Traced by Guppy in Devon.

In Newfoundland:

Early instance: William Napman, fisherman of Lower Island Cove, 1871 (Lovell).

Modern status: At St. John's (*Electors* 1955), and Lower Island Cove.

KNEE, a variant of the surname of Ireland, (O)Nee, *Ó Niadh*, Ir. *niadh* – champion. (MacLysaght).

Traced by MacLysaght in Co. Galway.

In Newfoundland:

Early instances: William, born at Pool's Island,

1821 (DPHW 76); ——, captain of the *Ice King*, in the seal fishery out of Greenspond, 1858 (*Newfoundlander* 1 Apr 1858).

Modern status: Scattered, especially at Badgers Quay and St. John's.

KNIGHT, a surname of England, Ireland and the Channel Islands, from the Old English personal name *Cniht*, Old English *cniht* – youth, servant, soldier, feudal tenant bound to serve as a mounted soldier, knight, servant in a knight's household; in Ireland also (Mac) Knight, *Mac an Ridire*, Ir. *ridire* – knight. (Reaney, MacLysaght, Turk).

Found widespread by Guppy in the south and Midlands.

In Newfoundland:

Early instances: Elizabeth, of Carbonear, 1755, property "in possession of the Family for upwards of 80 years," that is, before 1675 (CO 199.18); John, of Salvage, 1676 (CO 1); ——, of Quidi Vidi, 1703 (CO 194.3); William, of Bonavista, 1708–09 (CO 194.4); John, of St. John's, 1708 (CO 194.4); John, ? of Placentia, 1751 (Kirwin); Robert, of Brigus, 1800 (CO 199.18); Miss, schoolmistress of Harbour Grace, 1810 (CO 194.49); Anne, from Glasgow, Scotland, married at St. John's, 1814 (Nfld. Archives BRC); Henry, of Moreton's Harbour, 1819 (D'Alberti 29); Richard, fisherman of Blackhead (Bay de Verde district), 1827 (DPHW 52A); Honor Kight, from Co. Galway, married at St. John's, 1831 (Nfld. Archives BRC); Thomas Knight, merchant of Ferryland, 1832 (DPHW 31); John, planter of Broad Cove (Bay de Verde district), 1834, of Adams Cove, 1834 (DPHW 52A); John, of Nipper's Harbour, 1845 (DPHW 86); Thomas, granted land at Hall's Bay, 1850 (Nfld. Archives, Registry Crown Lands); Captain William Skinner, from Devon, married at St. John's, 1856 (*Newfoundlander* 1 May 1856); Jonathon, of Black Island (Exploits district), 1859 (DPHW 92); Jonathon, of Jackson's Harbour (Exploits district), 1861 (DPHW 92); John, of the French Shore, 1867 (Nfld. Archives HGRC); Robert, of Burtons Pond (Green B.), 1871 (Lovell); Richard, of Pouch Cove, 1871 (Lovell); Josiah, of Rogues Harbour (Green B.), 1871 (Lovell).

Modern status: Scattered, especially at Jackson's Cove and St. John's.

Place names: Knights Arm 47-31 52-58; —— Brook 48-53 58-14; —— Cove 48-32 53-19; —— Island 49-25 54-56; —— Point 48-33 53-18.

KNOLL, a surname of England, from Old English *cnoll* – (dweller at the) top of the hill, or from the English place names Knoll (Kent, Sussex), Knowle

(Devon, Dorset, Somerset, Warwickshire). (Reaney, Cottle). *See also* KNOWLING, KNOWLTON.

In Newfoundland:

Early instance: Joseph Knill, of St. John's, 1708, of Bay Bulls, 1708 (CO 194.4)

Modern status: Unique, at St. John's (*Electors* 1955).

Place name: Knoll Lake (Labrador) 52-54 66-54.

KNOTT, a surname of England and Ireland, from the Old Norse personal name *Knútr* (Canute), Old Norse *knútr* – knot, or from Old English *cnotta* – knot, thick-set, or from Middle English *knot* – (dweller on the) hill. (Reaney, Cottle). *See* NOTT.

Traced by Guppy in Derbyshire and by MacLysaght mainly in Dublin since the 17th century.

In Newfoundland:

Early instance: John, fisherman of Harbour Le Cou, 1860 (DPHW 99).

Modern status: Scattered in the south and west coast districts.

KNOWLAND, a variant of the surname of Ireland, (O)NOLAN or Knowlan, *Ó Nualláin*, Ir. *nuall* – shout. (MacLysaght).

Traced by MacLysaght as a principal name in Cos. Westmeath and Longford in 1659 and still extant.

In Newfoundland:

Early instances: Patrick Knowlan, from Ireland, labourer ? of St. John's, 1776 (CO 194.33); Morlough, of Bay Bulls, 1786 (CO 194.36); Daniel, from Killegny Parish (unidentified) (Co. Wexford), married at St. John's, 1808 (Nfld. Archives BRC); Alice Knowlin, of Harbour Main, 1809 (Nfld. Archives BRC).

Modern status: Unique, at St. John's (*Electors* 1955).

KNOWLING, a surname of England, from Old English **cnolling* – (dweller at the) hilltop. (Reaney). *See also* KNOLL, KNOWLTON.

Traced by Spiegelhalter in Devon.

In Newfoundland:

Early instances: Michael Knowline, of St. John's, 1775 (DPHW 26D); Simeon and Thomas Knowling, of Rencontre (Fortune B.), 1871 (Lovell); William, planter of Sagona (Island), 1871 (Lovell).

Modern status: Rare, at St. John's.

KNOWLTON, a surname of England, from the English place name Knowlton (Dorset, Kent), or (dweller at the) farm, village by the knoll. (Ekwall, E.C. Smith). *See also* KNOLL, KNOWLING.

In Newfoundland:

Early instance: David, from Parrsborough, Nova Scotia, married at St. John's, 1855 (DPHW 26D).

Modern status: Unique, at St. John's (*Electors* 1955).

KNOX, a surname of Scotland and Ireland, from the Scots place name Knock (Renfrewshire), "from the remarkable prominence there called 'The Knock.' The *s* is English plural." (Black).

Traced by MacLysaght in Ulster.

In Newfoundland:

Early instances: William, from Soho Square, London, in possession of fishing room at Fermeuse, 1788, 1792 (D'Alberti 4); Robin, of Harbour Grace Parish, 1809 (Nfld. Archives HGRC); Bartholomew, from Inistioge (Co. Kilkenny), married at St. John's, 1811 (Nfld. Archives BRC); Jeremiah, from Co. Cavan, of the Royal Newfoundland Co., died at St. John's, 1845, aged 44 (*Times* 4 Jan 1845); Thomas, from Southampton, England, married Joanna Maddicks of King's Cove, 1849 (*Royal Gazette* 5 Jun 1849); J. Knok, on the *True Blue* in the seal fishery out of Carbonear, 1853 (*Newfoundlander* 28 Mar 1853); —— Knox, Captain of the *Express*, in the seal fishery out of Harbour Grace, 1857 (*Newfoundlander* 19 Mar 1857); James Nocks, of Bay of Islands, 1871 (Lovell).

Modern status: At St. Shotts and Clarenville (*Electors* 1955), Shalloway Cove (Bonavista B.) and St. John's.

Place names: Knox Bay (Labrador) 54-53 66-23; —— Lake (Labrador) 54-46 65-19.

KORBAI, a surname of Hungary.

In Newfoundland:

Early instance: ——, from Hungary to St. John's during the Second World War. (Family).

Modern status: Unique, at St. John's.

KREIGER, ? a misspelling of the surnames of Germany Krieger – warrior, soldier, or Krüger – publican, landlord.

In Newfoundland:

Early instance: Otto Kruger, cooper of Harbour Grace, 1871 (Lovell).

Modern status: Unique, at St. John's.

KUNG, a surname of China – hob; great, respectful, decorous; give, present. (So).

In Newfoundland:

Family tradition: ——, from Canton, China, settled at Corner Brook (MUN Folklore).

Modern status: Rare, at St. John's (*Electors* 1955), and Corner Brook.

L

LABOUBON, LEBOUBAN, ? Newfoundland variants of the surname of France (Le) Boubon, the Auvergne form of Boubée, from Old French *bobée* – malady of the eyes. (Dauzat).

In Newfoundland:

Modern status: LaBoubon, unique, at George's Lake (*Electors* 1955); LeBouban, rare, at Mainland and Corner Brook (*Electors* 1955).

LABOUR, a surname of France – possessor of ploughland, or from a not uncommon place name of estates and hamlets. (Dauzat).

In Newfoundland:

Modern status: At English Harbour East and Grand Le Pierre.

LACE, a surname of England, from Old French *las, laz,* Middle English *lace* – (maker of) cord, string. (Reaney).

In Newfoundland:

Early instances: William, fisherman of Belleoram Reach, married at Rencontre

East, 1858 (DPHW 104); George, planter of Rencontre East, 1859 (DPHW 104).

Modern status: In the Fortune Bay and Hermitage district including Rencontre East (*Electors* 1955).

(DE)LACEY, surnames of England, Ireland and Guernsey (Channel Islands), from the French place name Lassy (Calvados); in Ireland also Lacy, *Ó Laitheasa,* originally *Ó Flaithgheasa,* Ir. *flaith* – prince. (Reaney, MacLysaght, Turk).

Lacey traced by Guppy in Leicestershire and Rutlandshire, by Spiegelhalter in Devon, and (de)-Lacy by MacLysaght in Cos. Meath, Limerick and Wexford.

In Newfoundland:

Family tradition: Diocletian Lacey, a Spanish soldier, deserted to England and was later smuggled to Newfoundland and settled at The Dock near Port de Grave, in the early 18th century (MUN Folklore).

Early instances: George, of Great St. Lawrence (now St. Lawrence), 1765 (CO 194.16); Francis, from Deimoth Castle (Co. Kildare), Irish convict landed at Petty Harbour or Bay Bulls, 1789 (CO 194.38); Bridget Leacy, of St. John's, 1805 (Nfld. Archives BRC); Richard Lacy, from Kilmacthomas

(Co. Waterford), married at St. John's, 1814 (Nfld. Archives BRC); Robert Lacey, shoemaker of Mulley's Cove (Conception B.), 1819 (DPHW 52A); William, planter of Exploits Burnt Island, 1820 (USPG); John Lacy, from Newton Barry (Co. Wexford), deserted service at St. John's, 1828 (*Newfoundlander* 22 May 1828); Daniel Lacey, of Harbour Grace Parish, 1830 (Nfld. Archives HGRC); Daniel Lacy or Lecy, planter of Carbonear, 1838 (DPHW 48); James Lacey, of the Portugal Cove and Torbay area, 1850 (Nfld. Archives, Registry Crown Lands); Diocletian, fisherman of The Dock, Port de Grave, 1859 (DPHW 38); Daniel, of Herring Neck, 1871 (Lovell); John Leacy, of Little Placentia (now Argentia), 1871 (Lovell); James Lacey, farmer of Torbay, 1871 (Lovell); Thomas, planter of Twillingate, 1871 (Lovell).

Modern status: Delacey, rare, at St. John's; Lacey, scattered, especially at St. John's.

Place names: Lac(e)y Head 49-32 55-05; Lacy Point 49-31 55-04; Lacey Island 49-20 55-04.

LA COSTA, LE CASTA, ? Newfoundland variants of the surname of France, Lacoste – (dweller on) the coast. (Dauzat). Traced by Dauzat in Southern France. *See* COSTARD.

In Newfoundland:

Family tradition: Raphaël Lacosta, from Brittany, settled on the Port-au-Port Peninsula (Thomas, "French Fam. Names").

Early instance: W. Le Caste on the *Eliza* (*Newfoundlander* 18 May 1854).

Modern status: LaCosta, at Campbell's Creek and Piccadilly; LeCasta, at Cape St. George (*Electors* 1955).

LA COUR(E), LE COURE, variants of the surname of France, Lacour of Jersey (Channel Islands), Le Cour – (dweller at the) court. (Dauzat, Turk).

In Newfoundland:

Family tradition: Joseph LeCour (b. 1879), settled in L'Anse-à-Canards between 1895 and 1900 (Butler, 19); —— LeCour, a French Huguenot, came to Harbour Main via Jersey (Channel Islands) (MUN Hist.).

Early instances: Edward Lacour, of Harbour Main, 1777 (CO 199.18); Grace LeCour, married at

St. John's, 1799 (Nfld. Archives BRC); Mary La-
Cour, of Harbour Grace Parish, 1809 (Nfld. Archives
HGRC).

Modern status: LaCour, rare, especially at Harbour Main; LeCoure, rare, in the Port-au-Port and St.
George's districts.

LAFFIN, a ? Newfoundland variant of the surname
of Ireland, Laffan, ? from the French surname La
Font – (dweller by) the spring. (MacLysaght).

Traced by MacLysaght in Cos. Tipperary and
Wexford.

In Newfoundland:

Early instance: —— Laffin, on the *Richard
Brown*, 1848 (*Newfoundlander* 1 Jun 1848).

Modern status: Unique, at Stephenville.

LA FITTE, a surname and place name of France –
(dweller by) the boundary mark of a property.

Traced by Dauzat in southern France.

In Newfoundland:

Family tradition: —— La Fitte, formerly resident
of St. Pierre, moved via a French fishing vessel to
Port-au-Port about 1790 (MUN Hist.).

Modern status: In the Port-au-Port district.

LA FOSSE, a surname and place name of France –
(dweller by) the ditch, moat, or ? gravedigger.
(Dauzat).

In Newfoundland:

Early instances: —— Lefosse, of Oderin, 1709
(CO 194.4); William Lafosse, fisherman of New
(now Parsons) Harbour, 1857 (DPHW 102).

Modern status: Scattered, in the Burgeo-La Poile
district and at St. John's.

LAGATDU, ? a Newfoundland variant of the surnames of France, Breton Lagade(u)c – (one with) big
eyes. (Dauzat). The final element *du* forms a compound meaning black eye (Thomas, "French Fam.
Names").

In Newfoundland:

Family tradition: The first Lagatdu, a Breton
speaker, settled at Cape St. George (Thomas,
"French Fam. Names"); the Lacadue family settled at
Cape St. George in 1900 (MUN Geog.).

Modern status: At Cape St. George (*Electors*
1955).

LAHEY, a variant (not recorded by MacLysaght but
found in Matheson and Census 1794–5) of the
surname of Ireland, Lahy, basically distinct from,
but often used synonymously with (O)Leahy, *Ó*

Laochdha, Ir. *laochdha* – heroic. (MacLysaght). *See
also* LEAHEY.

MacLysaght traced (O)Leahy in Cos. Cork, Kerry
and Tipperary.

In Newfoundland:

Family tradition: William, from Ireland, settled at
Cape Broyle in 1790 (MUN Folklore).

Early instances: Patrick, married at St. John's,
1754 (DPHW 26D); Mary Lahey, from Trinity Parish
(Co. Waterford), married at St. John's, 1813 (Nfld.
Archives BRC); Edward Lahee, of Harbour Grace
Parish, 1816 (Nfld. Archives HGRC); William Lahy,
from Ireland, of King's Cove, 1817 (*Royal Gazette*
27 May 1817); Edward Lahy or Leahy, of Heart's
Content, 1819 (Nfld. Archives KCRC); Richard
Lahey, of Harbour Grace, 1828 (*Newfoundlander* 27
Nov 1828); Thomas, of Bay du Nord, 1871 (Lovell);
Michael, of Heart's Desire, 1871 (Lovell).

Modern status: Scattered, especially at Bell
Island.

LAIDLEY, a variant of the surname of Scotland,
Laidlaw, ? of English origin, ? from the English
place name Ludlow (Shropshire). (Black).

Traced by Matthews as a merchant in Lisbon.

In Newfoundland:

Family tradition: ——, from Portugal, settled at
St. John's (MUN Folklore).

Early instance: A.C.G. Laidley arrived in
Harbour Grace, 1829 (*Newfoundlander* 9 Jul 1829).

Modern status: Rare, at St. John's.

LAINEY, a ? Newfoundland variant of the surname
of the Channel Islands Lainé, or of France, Lainay,
from the French place name Ainay (Allier, Cher) –
one from Ainay, or for Lainiez (*see* LAINEZ).
(Dauzat, Turk).

In Newfoundland:

Family tradition: The Lainé family, from France,
or St. Pierre, settled throughout the St. George's
region about 1830–50 (MUN Geog.); Adolphe
Lainey, La Grand'Terre, settled in 1872 in Maisons-
d'Hiver (Butler 15–16).

Modern status: In the Port-au-Port district and at
Stephenville Crossing.

LAINEZ, ? a Newfoundland variant of the surname
of the Channel Islands Lainé, or of France, Lainiez,
itself a variant in the north and northeast of La(i)nier
– wool merchant or manufacturer of woollen goods,
or a variant of Lainay (*see* LAINEY). (Dauzat, Turk).

In Newfoundland:

Modern status: At Cape St. George (*Electors* 1955).

LAING, a surname of Scotland, the Scots variant of LANG, LONG.

Guppy found Laing widespread in Scotland.

In Newfoundland:

Family tradition: ——, from the Isle of Man, to Carbonear; some of the family later settled at Champneys West (MUN Folklore).

Early instance: John, of Swail Bight (Labrador), 1849 (DPHW 113).

Modern status: Scattered, especially at Carbonear.

LAITE, LAYTE, LEYTE, surnames of England, ? from the English place name Leat (Devon), or from Old English *gelǣt* – (dweller by the) conduit or watercourse. (Reaney, Spiegelhalter).

Spiegelhalter traced Leat in Devon.

In Newfoundland:

Family tradition: —— Leyte, from England, settled at Fogo in the late 1700s (MUN Folklore).

Early instances: George Late, of Trinity (Trinity B.), 1802 (DPHW 64); John Laite, of Harbour Grace Parish, 1806 (Nfld. Archives HGRC); James Late, of King's Cove Parish, 1839 (Nfld. Archives KCRC); Thomas Leit or Lete, of Fogo, 1852, of Eastern Tickle (Fogo district), 1858 (DPHW 83); John Late, granted land at Upper Lance Cove, Smith Sound (Trinity B.), 1855 (Nfld. Archives, Registry Crown Lands).

Modern status: Laite, scattered, especially at Petley (*Electors* 1955); Layte, scattered, in the Twillingate district and at Lewisporte; Leyte, scattered, especially at Fogo and Rogers Cove (Fogo district).

LAKE, a surname of England from the English place name Lake (Devon, Wiltshire, etc.), or from Old English *lacu* – (dweller by the) stream. (Reaney, Spiegelhalter).

Traced by Guppy in Devon, Kent, Lincolnshire, Norfolk and Northamptonshire.

In Newfoundland:

Family traditions: Several Lake brothers, from Wales came to work at Harbour Buffett about 1800. John, resident of Placentia, 1740 (MUN Geog.).

Early instances: Jn. in St. John's, 1725, 1726 (CO 194/8, ff. 98–108 per P.E.L. Smith); Abraham in Placentia, 1731–40 (CO 194/9 f. 101 per P.E.L. Smith); George, of Placentia ? district, 1744 (CO 194.24); Archibald, of St. John's, 1752 (DPHW 26C); Ann, of Paradise Sound, wife of George, planter, suit in the court at Placentia, 1758 (Col. Secy. Office, Outgoing Corres. 1749–70, vol. 2, p. 455, PANL GN/2/1A, microfilm Box 1, per P.E.L. Smith); John, of Fortune, 1801 (Duckworth Papers 1810–12 Provincial Archives); George (about 1798–1868), mar-

ried at Fortune, 1817, of Grand Bank, 1817 (DPHW 106, 109); Patrick, fisherman of Batchelor's Cove (Placentia B.), 1871 (Lovell); Patrick, of Toslow, 1871 (Lovell); John, of Great St. Lawrence (now St. Lawrence), 1871 (Lovell); William, of Little St. Joseph (Placentia B.), 1871 (Lovell); John (and others), of Oderin, 1871 (Lovell); John, of St. Kyran's, 1871 (Lovell).

Modern status: Scattered, especially at Oderin (*Electors* 1955) and Fortune.

Place names: Lakes Cove, —— Hill 47-40 55-03.

LAKIN, a surname of England, ? a diminutive of the baptismal name Lawrence (*see* LAWRENCE), or ? from the Old Irish personal name *Lochán* or Old Norse byname **Hlakkandi*, as in the English place name Lackenby (Yorkshire NR). (Long, A. H. Smith, Ekwall, Reaney Notes).

Traced by Guppy in Staffordshire.

In Newfoundland:

Modern status: Rare, at St. John's.

LAMB(E), surnames of England, Scotland and Ireland, from the animal, or a shortened form of the baptismal name Lambert (*see* LAMBERT), or from an inn sign, or ? in Scotland from an Old Norse personal name *Lamb*, or also in Ireland from a more than usually absurd pseudo-translation (*uan* – lamb) or (O)Loan(e), *Ó Luain, luan*, – hound and hence warrior. (Reaney, Cottle, Black, MacLysaght).

Found widespread by Guppy, in Devon by Spiegelhalter, and in Co. Monaghan by MacLysaght.

In Newfoundland:

Early instances: Richard Lamb, of Port de Grave, 1776, property "in possession of the Family for 62 years," that is, since 1714 (CO 199.18); John, planter of Green Point, Placentia, 1789 (Kirwin); William (and others) Lamb(e), of Placentia, 1794 (D'Alberti 5); John Lamb, of St. John's, 1799 (DPHW 26D); John, of Carbonear, 1810 (DPHW 48); Michael, of Harbour Grace Parish, 1825 (Nfld. Archives HGRC); Margaret, of Harbour Main, 1828 (Nfld. Archives BRC); Adam, planter of Bay du Nord, 1871 (Lovell); Thomas, of Burin, 1871 (Lovell); Patrick, of Point Verde, 1871 (Lovell); John (and others), of Red Island (Placentia B.), 1871 (Lovell).

Modern status: Lamb, especially at St. John's; Lambe, scattered in the Placentia East and West and Burin districts.

Place name: Lamb Tickle (Labrador)

LAMBERT, a baptismal name and surname of England, Scotland, Ireland and the Channel Islands, from Old German personal names such as *Landoberct, Landebert, Lambert* containing the elements *land* and *bright,* popular as a baptismal name from the 12th to the 15th century after St. Lambert, a 7th century bishop of Maestricht, Flanders; or from Old English *lamb* and *hierde* – lamb-herd. (Withycombe, Reaney, Black, MacLysaght, Turk).

Traced by Guppy in Essex, Kent, Norfolk, Nottinghamshire and Yorkshire, by Spiegelhalter in Devon, and by MacLysaght in southeast Leinster.

In Newfoundland:

Family tradition: ——, rope maker from Salisbury (Wiltshire), settled at Twillingate; the family later moved to Lewisporte (MUN Folklore).

Early instances: Thomas Lampert, fisherman of St. John's, 1794–5, "30 years in Newfoundland," that is, 1764–5 (Census 1794–5); James Lambert, of Trinity Bay, 1768 (DPHW 64); Thomas, of Trinity (Trinity B.), 1790 (DPHW 64); William, proprietor and occupier of fishing room at Old Perlican, Winter 1800–01 (Census Trinity B.); Ellen, of Toad's (now Tors) Cove, 1810 (Nfld. Archives BRC); Moses, of Harbour Grace Parish, 1813 (Nfld. Archives HGRC); Mary Lambeth, of Ragged Harbour, 1813 (Nfld. Archives BRC); Nicholas Lambert, of Bay Bulls district, 1813 (D'Alberti 23); Stephen, of Torbay, 1817 (DPHW 26B); Ellen Lamberd, from Permoy (Co. Cork), married at St. John's, 1819 (Nfld. Archives BRC); Mary Lambert, of King's Cove, 1822 (Nfld. Archives KCRC); George, planter of Grates Cove, 1825 (DPHW 58); Ellen Lambard, of Harbour Grace, 1828 (Nfld. Archives HGRC); John Lambert, from Whitechurch (Dorset), deserted service at Harbour Grace, 1829 (*Weekly Journal and General Advertiser* 30 Apr 1829); Catherine, of Seal Cove (now New Chelsea), 1838 (DPHW 59); Mary, of Greenspond, 1846 (DPHW 26B); William, granted land at Bay Bulls Road, 1849 (Nfld. Archives, Registry Crown Lands); James, of Fox Harbour (Trinity B.), 1854 (DPHW 59A); Solomon, fisherman of Great St. Lawrence (now St. Lawrence), 1860 (DPHW 100); John, of Fox Harbour (Placentia B.), 1871 (Lovell); William, of Logy Bay, 1871 (Lovell); Richard, of Miller's Passage, 1871 (Lovell).

Modern status: Widespread, especially at Southport (Trinity B.), and Grates Cove.

Place name: Lambert Island (Labrador) 59-47 64-09.

LAM(P)KIN, surnames of England, variants of Lambkin, a diminutive of LAMB or LAMBERT. In Newfoundland, however, for the Chinese name Kim Lee, borne by a laundryman who came to St. John's

in the early 1900s and married a local girl, and changed by his descendants. (F.G. Adams).

In Newfoundland:

Modern status: Lamkin, rare, at St. John's; Lampkin, unique, at St. John's.

LAMSWOOD, a surname of England, ? from an unidentified English place name, or ? (dweller in the) wood (? near which) lambs were kept.

Traced by Matthews as a manufacturer in Brixham (Devon).

In Newfoundland:

Modern status: Rare, at Bell Island, St. Phillips and St. John's.

LANDER, a surname of England, from Old French *lavandier(e)* – washerman, washerwoman, or from the English place name Landare (Cornwall). (Reaney, Spiegelhalter). *See also* LA(U)NDRY, LAVENDER.

Traced by Guppy in Cornwall and by Spiegelhalter in Devon.

In Newfoundland:

Early instances: John, planter of Bonavista, 1790 (D'Alberti 4); Captain William, of Trinity (Trinity B.), 1799 (DPHW 64); Mary Landers, of St. John's, 1804 (Nfld. Archives BRC); Stephen Lander, of Bonavista, owner of fishing room at Bayleys Cove, "built by the family before 1805" (Bonavista Register 1806); William, of Catalina, 1808 (DPHW 64); James Landers, of Harbour Grace Parish, 1822 (Nfld. Archives HGRC); Charles Lander, fisherman of Ship Cove (now part of Port Rexton), 1871 (Lovell).

Modern status: At Windsor (*Electors* 1955), Port Rexton, Bonavista and Gander.

LANDRIGAN, LUNDRIGAN, variants of the surnames of Ireland, (O)Lonergan, Londrigan, *Ó Longargáin.* (MacLysaght).

Traced by MacLysaght in Co. Tipperary.

In Newfoundland:

Early instances: Michael ? Landricon, of Harbour Main, 1755 (MUN Hist.); John Lonnergan, labourer of Bonavista, 1774 (CO 194.32); Thomas Lonergan, fisherman of St. John's, 1794–5, "20 years in Newfoundland," that is, 1774–5 (Census 1794–5); Edward Lunergan, of Cupids, 1789 (CO 199.18); John, of (Upper) Island Cove, 1802 (CO 199.18); Phillip Longergan, from Clonmel (Co. Tipperary), married at St. John's, 1805 (Nfld. Archives BRC); Lawrence Londregan, of Harbour Grace Parish, 1812 (Nfld. Archives HGRC); Mary Londrigan alias Kelson, of Fogo, 1814 (Nfld. Archives BRC); James

Lundrigan, of Hearts Content, 1819 (Nfld. Archives KCRC); James Lundrigan or Lundergan, of Catalina, 1820 (Nfld. Archives KCRC); James Lundrigan, of Trinity, 1833 (Nfld. Archives KCRC); John Lonergan, ? of Harbour Grace, 1845 (*Newfoundlander* 16 Jan 1845); Anne Lonergan, of Plate Cove (Bonavista B.), 1862 (Nfld. Archives KCRC); Patrick Lunergan, farmer of Bay Bulls Road (St. John's), 1871 (Lovell); Patrick, of Witless Bay, 1871 (Lovell); Matthew Londergan, of Distress (now St. Bride's), 1871 (Lovell); John and Thomas Lundrigan, of Burin, 1871 (Lovell); Joseph (and others) Lundergan, of Little St. Lawrence, 1871 (Lovell); Robert Lonergan, of Bay Bulls, 1871 (Lovell); David (and others) Lundrigan, of Peters River and Holyrood, 1871 (Lovell).

Modern status: Landrigan, rare, at St. John's; Lundrigan, widespread, especially at Upper Island Cove, Burin, Little St. Lawrence and St. Bride's.

LA(U)NDRY, surnames of England and Ireland, from the Old German personal name *Landric(us)*, Old French *Landri* – land-ruler, or from Middle English *lavendrie* – (worker in a) wash-house; in Ireland, as Landry, a variant of Landers, *de Londras* – (the man) from London. (Reaney, MacLysaght). *See also* LANDER, LAVENDER.

Spiegelhalter traced Landray in Devon; MacLysaght traced Landers and presumably Landry in Munster.

In Newfoundland:

Early instance: John Landry, of St. John's, 1788 (DPHW 26C).

Modern status: Landry, rare, at New Harbour (Trinity B.), Corner Brook (*Electors* 1955), and St. John's; Laundry, rare, at St. John's and New Chelsea.

LANE, a surname of England and Ireland, from Old English *lanu* – (dweller in the) lane, or from the English place name Lane (Devon), or in Ireland also as the anglicized form of several Gaelic surnames – Lehane, Lyne, LYONS. (Reaney, Spiegelhalter, MacLysaght).

Found widespread by Guppy and in Cos. Cork and Limerick by MacLysaght.

In Newfoundland:

Early instances: John, of Renews, 1675 (CO 1); Hugh, of Salvage, 1681 (CO 1); Edward, of St. John's, 1706 (CO 194.22); William, of Brigus, 1760, property "in possession 37 years," that is, since 1723 (CO 199.18); Richard, of Bay de Verde, 1730 (CO 194.23); John, of Trinity Bay, 1766 (DPHW 64);

William, of Fogo, Twillingate or Tilton (now Tilting), 1771 (CO 194.30); Roger, of Bonavista, 1789 (DPHW 70); Thomas, of Lower Island Cove, 1791 (CO 199.18); Elizabeth, of Fermeuse, 1798 (Nfld. Archives BRC); Joseph, of Barrow Harbour (Bonavista B.), owner of fishing room at Stockley's Cove, Barrow Harbour, 1805 (Bonavista Register 1806); Roger (and Co.), of Vere (now Fair) Island, Greenspond, owner of fishing room there, 1806 (Bonavista Register 1806); Mary, of Harbour Grace Parish, 1806 (Nfld. Archives HGRC); Cornelius, of Tilton Harbour (now Tilting), 1817 (Nfld. Archives BRC); John, of Greenspond, 1823 (DPHW 76); Samuel, of Open Hole (now Open Hall), 1830 (DPHW 70); Patrick Leyne or Lane, of Ragged Harbour (now Melrose), 1833 (Nfld. Archives KCRC); James, of Tickle Cove (Bonavista B.), 1834 (Nfld. Archives KCRC); John, of Gambo Brook (Bonavista North district), 1838 (DPHW 76); Charles, of Indian Arm (Bonavista B.), 1843 (DPHW 73A); John, granted land at Catalina, 1851 (Nfld. Archives, Registry Crown Lands); Joseph, of King's Cove, 1853 (DPHW 73A); Joseph Leyne, of Plate Cove (Bonavista B.), 1856 (Nfld. Archives KCRC); James Lane, of Fox Harbour (Trinity B.), 1856 (DPHW 59A); Edmond Leyne or Lane, of Broad Cove (now Duntara), 1857 (Nfld. Archives KCRC); Joseph Lane, of Sailor's Island (Bonavista B.), 1865 (DPHW 81); Johanna, of Bloody Bay (Bonavista B.), 1869 (Nfld. Archives KCRC); widespread in Lovell 1871.

Modern status: Widespread, especially at Dark Cove East and West, Grand Falls and St. John's.

Place names: Lane Pond 48-26 55-34; Lane's Lookout 49-43 54-15.

LANEY, ? a variant of the surname of Ireland (O)Leany, *Ó Laighnigh* – descendant of the Leinsterman. (MacLysaght).

Found rare in Munster by MacLysaght.

In Newfoundland:

Family tradition: Adolphus, from Acadia, settled at Degras (St. George's B.) before 1850 (MUN Folklore).

Modern status: Rare, at Stephenville.

LANG, a surname of England, Scotland and Ireland, from Old English *lang*, *long* – long, tall, in a Scots and northern English form. (Reaney). *See also* LAING, LONG.

Traced by Guppy in Devon and in the Glasgow and Paisley districts.

In Newfoundland:

Family tradition: —— Laing, from Glasgow,

Scotland, settled at St. John's; later the family changed the spelling to Lang on conversion from Presbyterianism to Roman Catholicism (MUN Folklore).

Early instances: Jeffrey, of St. John's Harbour, 1703 (CO 194.3); Oliver, of Ferryland, 1708 (CO 194.4); John, of Bay Bulls, 1802 (USPG); John, of Placentia, 1803 (D'Alberti 13); Andrew, of Carbonear, 1813 (DPHW 48); Lang, Baine & Co., merchants trading from the River Clyde, Scotland, to Newfoundland, 1817 (D'Alberti 27); Peter, of Harbour Grace Parish, 1822 (Nfld. Archives HGRC); William, from Greenock, Scotland, married at Open Hall, 1851, of Greenspond, 1856 (DPHW 73A, 76); William, of Ship Island (Bonavista B.), 1871 (Lovell).

Modern status: Rare, at St. John's and Corner Brook.

LANGDON, a surname of England, from the English place name Langdon (Devon, Dorset, Essex, Kent). (Reaney, Cottle, Spiegelhalter).

Traced by Guppy in Cornwall, Devon and Somerset.

In Newfoundland:

Family tradition: James, from England, settled at Seal Cove (Fortune B.), about 1840 (MUN Hist.).

Early instances: James, collector of Greenwich Hospital dues in the district of Little St. Lawrence, 1810–14 (D'Alberti 20, 24); Charles, planter of Twillingate, 1820 (USPG); John, of St. John's, 1821 (DPHW 26D); William, from Penton (unidentified), England, married at St. John's, 1822 (Nfld. Archives BRC); John Langdonna or Langdown, of Nipper's Harbour, 1842 (DPHW 86); George Langdon, of Harbour Grace Parish, 1845 (Nfld. Archives HGRC); Charles, of Torbay, 1848 (DPHW 32); John Langdon or Langdown, of Fogo, 1855 (DPHW 83); Charles Langdown, of Jackson's Arm, 1858 (DPHW 92); Thomas, of Exploits Burnt Island, 1858 (DPHW 92); David Langdon, of Merritt's Harbour, 1858 (DPHW 85); Ann, of Herring Neck, 1860 (DPHW 85); George, of Harbour Grace, 1867 (Nfld. Archives HGRC); Job Langdown, planter of Channel, 1871 (Lovell); William Langdon, planter of Grole, 1871 (Lovell); James, planter of Seal Cove (Fortune B.), 1871 (Lovell).

Modern status: Scattered, especially at Seal Cove (Fortune B.), Botwood, Northern Arm (Gander district) and Norris Arm.

Place names: Langdon's or Langdown's Cove, Langdon's or Langdown's Point 49-42 55-49; Langdon's Cove 49-32 55-45; Langdown Cove 49-39 55-56; Langsdown's Brook 48-57 55-53.

LANGER, LANGOR, surnames of England, from the English place name Langer (Nottinghamshire), or (dweller on or near the) long gore, a long triangular-shaped piece of land. (Ekwall).

Langer traced by Matthews as a captain at Southampton (Hampshire).

In Newfoundland:

Early instances: David Langer, constable of Trinity district, ? 1730, 1732 (CO 194.9); William, of Trinity Bay, 1765 (DPHW 64); Thomas Langher, of Heart's Ease, 1807 (DPHW 64); Thomas, planter of Heart's Content, 1823 (DPHW 64B); James Langor, of Come-by-Chance, 1835 (DPHW 30); Thomas Langher or Langer, of Trinity (Trinity B.), 1837, of Rider's Harbour, 1844, of Thoroughfare, 1853 (DPHW 64B); Joseph Languir, of Harbour Grace Parish, 1841 (Nfld. Archives HGRC); Ellen Langor, of Fox Harbour (Trinity B.), 1856 (DPHW 59); William Langer, of St. John's, 1871 (Lovell); James, of Gooseberry Cove (Trinity B.), 1880 (DPHW 68).

Modern status: Langer, scattered, especially at Heart's Desire; Langor, rare, in the Trinity North district.

LANGFORD, a surname of England and Ireland, from the common English place names Lang(a)ford, Longford in at least seven counties. (Reaney, Cottle, Spiegelhalter).

Traced by Spiegelhalter in Devon, and by MacLysaght mainly in southwest Munster.

In Newfoundland:

Early instances: Patience, of Herring Neck, 1850 (DPHW 85); Maria, of Harbour Grace, 1867 (Nfld. Archives HGRC).

Modern status: Scattered, in the White Bay South district.

LANGILLE, a surname of England and Scotland; in England from the English place name Langhole (Norfolk) – (dweller by the) long flat land; in Scotland from the Scots place name Langwell (Caithness, Ross and Cromarty) – (dweller by the) long field; or ? a Newfoundland variant of the surname of France, Languille – the fisher of eels. (E.C. Smith, Dauzat).

In Newfoundland:

Modern status: Langille, rare, at St. Jacques (*Electors* 1955) and St. John's; Languille, rare, at St. John's (*Electors* 1955).

Place names (not necessarily from the surname): Cape Anguille 47-55 59-24; Anguille Mountains 48-00 59-11.

LANGINS, ? a Newfoundland variant of the surname of Germany, Langhans – long Hans. (Weekley *Surnames*).

In Newfoundland:

Early instance: Mary Ann ? Langin, of Trinity (unspecified), 1863 (Nfld. Archives KCRC).

Modern status: Rare, at Corner Brook.

LANGLEY, a surname of England, from the English place name in sixteen counties from Northumberland to Wiltshire, or from Old English *lang lēah* – (dweller by the) long wood or clearing. (Reaney, Cottle).

Traced by Guppy in Cheshire and Sussex and by Spiegelhalter in Devon.

In Newfoundland:

Early instances: ——, of St. John's Harbour, 1703 (CO 194.3); Nicholas Lan(g)ley, of Petty Harbour, 1708 (CO 194.4); Richard, merchant, juror, of St. John's, 1809, with others purchased the lease of Little Bell Island in 1814, deceased 1844 (D'Alberti 19, 24, *Newfoundlander* 14 Mar 1844); James, of Pouch Cove, 1819 (DPHW 26B); Catherine, of King's Cove Parish, 1852 (Nfld. Archives KCRC).

Modern status: Unique, at Corner Brook.

Place name: Langley Cove 46-56 53-32.

LANGMEAD, a surname of England, from the English place name Langmead (Devon). (Spiegelhalter).

Traced by Spiegelhalter in Devon.

In Newfoundland:

Family tradition: Robert, from Plymouth (Devon), settled at Pouch Cove about 1825 (MUN Hist.).

Early instances: William Langmayd, of Petty Harbour, 1708 (CO 194.4); James Langmeade, of Pouch Cove, 1816 (DPHW 26B); Richard Langmeed, planter of St. John's, 1841 (DPHW 29); Richard Langmead, granted land at Back Arm, Harbour Breton, 1851 (Nfld. Archives, Registry Crown Lands); Mrs. Elizabeth, from Ditsan (? for Dittisham) (Devon), of St. John's, 1852 (*Newfoundlander* 15 Jul 1852); Uriah, of Fortune, 1871 (Lovell).

Modern status: At Pouch Cove and St. John's.

LANGOR. *See* LANGER

LANNIGAN, a variant of the surname of Ireland (O)Lanigan, *Ó Lonagáin*. (MacLysaght).

Traced by MacLysaght mainly in Co. Kilkenny and adjacent areas.

In Newfoundland:

Early instances: Joseph, ? labourer of St. John's, 1779 (CO 194.34); William Lanigan, of Harbour

Grace Parish, 1811 (Nfld. Archives HGRC); William, from Old Court (Co. Kilkenny), of Carbonear, died 1815 (*Royal Gazette* 15 Jun 1815); William Lannagin, fisherman of Harbour Grace, deceased, 1829 (*Newfoundlander* 28 Feb 1829); Margaret La(n)nigan, from Garth Nahough (unidentified), Ireland, married at St. John's, 1829 (Nfld. Archives BRC).

Modern status: Rare, at St. John's.

LANNING, a surname of England, ? a variant of LANNON.

In Newfoundland:

Modern status: Rare, especially at Botwood.

Place names: Lanning Ground 49-33 55-08; Lannings Cove 49-30 55-22.

LANNON, a surname of Ireland, the Co. Kilkenny form of (O)Lennon, Lennan, *Ó Leannáin*, ? Ir. *leann* – cloak, mantle, or ? Ir. *leanán* – paramour. (MacLysaght).

In Newfoundland:

Family tradition: ——, from Kilkenny, Ireland, settled at Harbour Main (MUN Folklore).

Early instances: Lawrence Lannan, from Gowran (Co. Kilkenny), married at St. John's, 1809 (Nfld. Archives BRC); Martin Lannon, fisherman of St. John's, 1814 (DPHW. 26D); Kyran Lannan, of Harbour Grace Parish, 1823 (Nfld. Archives HGRC); Patrick Lannen, of Fogo, 1825 (Nfld. Archives KCRC); Joanna Lannan, of Bonavista, 1828 (Nfld. Archives KCRC); Joanna Lannen, from Arristown (unidentified) (Co. Wexford), married at King's Cove, 1829 (Nfld. Archives KCRC); Michael Lannan, granted land near the "Narrows," Great Placentia, 1851 (Nfld. Archives, Registry Crown Lands); James Lannen, from Co. Carlow, of Harbour Grace, 1844 (*Indicator* 27 Jul 1844); George Lannan or Landon, of Exploits Burnt Island, 1854 (DPHW 86); Patrick (and others) Lannan, farmers of Chapel's Cove (Conception B.), 1871 (Lovell); David Lannen, planter of Fortune Harbour, 1871 (Lovell).

Modern status: Scattered, especially at South East Placentia.

Place names: Lannon Cove, —— Point 46-54 55-57.

LA PAGE, a surname of France and the Channel Islands, LEPAGE of England, from Middle English, Old French *page* – page, young boy, servant. (Reaney, Dauzat, Turk).

In Newfoundland:

Early instance: Frederick Lepage, shipping agent of St. John's, 1829 (*Newfoundlander* 1 Jan 1829).

Modern status: LaPage, at Abraham's Cove; LePage, at Ship Cove (Port-au-Port district) (*Electors* 1955).

LARACY, a variant of the surname of Ireland, (O)Larrissey, *Ó Learghusa,* Ir. *lear* – sea, *gus* – vigour. (MacLysaght).

Traced by MacLysaght mainly in Co. Kilkenny and adjacent areas.

In Newfoundland:

Family tradition: Patrick, from Dublin, Ireland, settled at Conception Harbour about 1715 (MUN Folklore).

Early instances: Patrick Laricy, of Harbour Grace Parish, 1820 (Nfld. Archives HGRC); James Larracy, of St. John's, ? 1821 (CO 194.64); Mary Larricy or Larisey, from Thomastown (Co. Kilkenny), of King's Cove, 1830 (Nfld. Archives KCRC); Mary Laresy, married at St. John's, 1831 (Nfld. Archives BRC); Thomas Laracy, granted land at Cat's Cove (now Conception Harbour), 1856 (Nfld. Archives, Registry Crown Lands); Thomas Larrissey, planter of Salmon Cove (now Avondale), 1871 (Lovell).

Modern status: At Kitchuses, St. John's and with large concentrations at Conception Harbour and Cupids.

LARKIN, a surname of England and Ireland, in England, a diminutive of *Lar,* a pet-form of Lawrence; in Ireland (O)Larkin, *Lorcáin,* "probably from *Lorc,* an old name denoting rough or fierce." (Reaney, Cottle, MacLysaght).

Traced by Guppy in Kent and by MacLysaght in Cos. Galway, Monaghan, Tipperary and Wexford.

In Newfoundland:

Early instances: Jerome, from Mullinahone (Co. Tipperary), married at St. John's, 1810 (Nfld. Archives BRC); Moses, of St. John's, ? 1821 (CO 194.64); Edmond Larken, of Harbour Grace Parish, 1828 (Nfld. Archives HGRC); Patrick Larken or Larkins, of King's Cove, 1833 (Nfld. Archives KCRC); Peter Larkin, married on the French Shore, 1839 (Nfld. Archives BRC); William Larkins, of Torbay, 1844 (DPHW 32); Ellen Larkin, of Broad Cove (now Duntara), 1847 (Nfld. Archives KCRC); Edward, granted land at Great Placentia, 1857 (Nfld. Archives, Registry Crown Lands); Thomas, of Flowers Cove to Point Ferrolle area, 1871 (Lovell).

Modern status: In the St. John's and White Bay North districts.

Place names: Larkin Point 47-46 59-20; —— Shoal 47-19 54-38.

LARNER, a surname of England and Ireland, ? from the common French place name and surname Launay – (dweller by the) plantation of elders; in Ireland for the English surname Lardner – the official in charge of the larder or in charge of pig food (acorns, mast) in the forest. (Reaney, Cottle, MacLysaght, Dauzat).

Traced by MacLysaght in Co. Galway.

In Newfoundland:

Modern status: Rare, at St. John's (*Electors* 1955), and Whitbourne.

Place name: Larner Cove 47-52 56-10.

LARSEN, LARSON, surnames of Scandinavia son of Lar (Lawrence) (*see* LAWRENCE).

In Newfoundland:

Modern status: Larsen, unique, at Gander; Larson, rare, at Curling (*Electors* 1955).

LASAGA, LASAGE, Newfoundland variants of the French Basque surnames Lissagaray, a variant of Elissagaray – (dweller by the) church on the hill, or Lissaragay – (dweller by the) ash plantation. (Dauzat).

In Newfoundland:

Modern status: Scattered, in the St. George's and Humber West districts.

LASH, ? a variant of the surnames of England, Latch, Leach etc., from the English place names Lach Dennis or Lache (Cheshire) or Eastleach or Northleach (Gloucestershire), or from Old English *læcc, lecc* – (dweller by the) stream, or from Old English *lǣce* – leech, physician. (Reaney, Cottle).

Traced by Matthews as a merchant in Paignton (Devon).

In Newfoundland:

Early instances: ——, of St. John's, 1828 (*Newfoundlander* 28 Aug 1828); W., of Witless Bay, 1830 (*Newfoundlander* 22 Apr 1830); William, from Paignton (Devon), accountant of St. John's, 1838 (DPHW 26B); Frederick, member of the Board of Road Commissioners for Salvage, 1844 (*Nfld. Almanac*); William Lash or Lush, member of the Board of Road Commissioners for St. Mary's Harbour, Placentia and St. Mary's district; 1844–8 (*Nfld. Almanac*); John Sr., of Shambler's Cove (Bonavista B.), 1871 (Lovell).

Modern status: Rare, at Witless Bay, Bay Roberts (*Electors* 1955) and St. John's.

LASKEY, a surname of England, from the English place name Lesquite (Cornwall). (Spiegelhalter).

Traced by Spiegelhalter in Devon.

In Newfoundland:
Early instance: James, of Lamaline, 1832 (DPHW 109).

Modern status: Rare, at Grand Bank (*Electors* 1955), Fortune and St. John's.

LATREILLE, a surname of France, ? from *treille* – vine (arbour). (Dauzat).
In Newfoundland:
Modern status: Rare, at St. John's.

LAUNDRY. *See* LANDRY

LAURIE, a surname of England and Scotland, a diminutive of the baptismal name Lawrence. *See* LAWRENCE.
Traced by Guppy in Northumberland and south of the Forth and Clyde, and by Spiegelhalter in Devon.
In Newfoundland:
Family tradition: ——, from Queen's County (now Co. Leix), Ireland, settled at St. Thomas about 1870 (MUN Folklore).
Early instance: Robert Lawrie, clerk of St. John's, 1871 (Lovell).
Modern status: Rare, at Bell Island, St. Thomas and St. John's.

LAVALLEE, a surname of France, Lavallée, from a common French place name or (dweller in) the valley. (Dauzat).
In Newfoundland:
Early instances: Bryan Lavalle, from Castle Barr (Connacht), married at St. John's, 1804 (Nfld. Archives BRC); Sara Levelle, of Toad's (now Tor's) Cove, 1805 (Nfld. Archives BRC); Theophile Lavelle, of Labrador, 1883 (Nfld. Archives HGRC); Peter Lavallee, of Blanc Sablon, 1896 (Nfld. Archives HGRC).
Modern status: Lavalle, rare, at Flower's Cove; LaVallee, rare, at Port Saunders (*Electors* 1955) and Stephenville.

LAVENDER, a surname of England, from the Old French *lavandier(e)* – washerman, washerwoman. (Reaney). *See also* LANDER, LA(U)NDRY.
In Newfoundland:
Early instance: James, planter of Trouty, 1830 (DPHW 64B).
Modern status: Rare, at Corner Brook and Trouty.

LAVERS, a surname of England, Laver of England and France, in England from the English place name

Laver (Essex), or from Old English *lǣfer* – (dweller near the) bulrush, wild iris; in France from *l'avoir* – property, probably a nickname for the owner of a flock of sheep. (Spiegelhalter, Ekwall, Dauzat).
Laver traced by Guppy in Dorset and Somerset, by Spiegelhalter in Devon, and by Reaney *Origin* in Essex.
In Newfoundland:
Family tradition: ——, from France, settled at Flowers Cove; the family later moved to Port Saunders (MUN Folklore).
Early instance: Edmond, of Harbour Grace Parish, 1822 (Nfld. Archives HGRC).
Modern status: In the Humber East and St. Barbe districts especially at Port Saunders.

LAVHEY for LAVEY, a surname of Ireland, ? the Co. Westmeath form of (Mac)Leavy, Levy, *Mac Con Shléibhe*, Ir. *cú* – hound, *sliabh* – mountain, of Co. Longford. (MacLysaght).
In Newfoundland:
Modern status: At Terrenceville and Channel.

LAVIS, a surname of England of unknown origin, ? a variant of the surname of France Lavisse – (dweller at the house with the outside) staircase, or the French ducal name Lévis. Henry James Johnston-Lavis, M.D., M.R.C.S., B. ès Sc., F.G.S. (b. 1856) was descended from a Huguenot family and settled in Devon. (*Devonshire Association* Vol. XLVII, 1915).
In Newfoundland:
Early instances: Robert, of St. John's Harbour, 1703 (CO 194.3); William, of Port au Choix, 1873 (MUN Hist.).
Modern status: Rare, at St. John's and Corner Brook (*Electors* 1955).

LAW(E)S, surnames of England, Law(e) of Ireland, Law of Scotland, from Old English *hlāw* – (dweller by the) hill, burial mound (*see* LOWE), or ? from a not uncommon Scots place name, Law, or a diminutive of the baptismal name Lawrence. *See* LAWRENCE. (Reaney, Cottle, Black, MacLysaght).
Guppy traced Law in Essex, Lancashire, Northamptonshire, Nottinghamshire and Yorkshire WR, and found it scattered in Scotland, Laws in Durham, Northumberland and with Lawes in Suffolk. Spiegelhalter traced Law(s) in Devon; and MacLysaght Law(e) mainly in northeast Ulster.
In Newfoundland:
Early instances: James Law, married at St. John's, 1786 (DPHW 26D); Henry, fisherman of

(Indian) Burying Place (Twillingate district), 1871 (Lovell).

Modern status: Lawes, rare, at Renews; Laws, rare, at St. John's.

Place name: Cape Law (Labrador) 53-44 60-50.

LAWLESS, a surname of England and Ireland, from Middle English *laweles*, *laghles* – law-breaking, licentious; for *lawless man* – outlaw. (Reaney, Cottle, MacLysaght).

Traced by MacLysaght in Cos. Dublin and Galway.

In Newfoundland:

Family tradition: ——, from Ireland, settled at North River (Conception B.); the family later moved to Flower's Cove (MUN Folklore).

Early instances: Lawrence, of St. John's, 1757 (DPHW 26C); James, of Harbour Grace Parish, 1806 (Nfld. Archives HGRC); Sarah, from Tintern (Co. Wexford), married at St. John's, 1827 (Nfld. Archives BRC); Michael, of Labrador, 1877 (Nfld. Archives HGRC); Maurice Lawles(s), of Flower's Cove, 1885 (Nfld. Archives HGRC).

Modern status: In the St. Barbe district, including Flower's Cove.

LAWLOR, a variant of the surnames of Ireland, (O)Lalor, Lawler, *Ó Leathlobhair*, Ir. *leath* – half, *lobhar* – sick person, leper. (MacLysaght, Cottle).

Traced by MacLysaght in Co. Leix.

In Newfoundland:

Family tradition: Edward, from Co. Waterford, Ireland, emigrated to St. John's about 1800; the family moved to Trinity East (Trinity B.), about 1834 (MUN Folklore).

Early instances: Maurice Lawler, fisherman of St. John's, 1794–5, "21 years in Newfoundland," that is, 1773–4 (Census 1794–5); John, from Dublin, Irish convict landed at Petty Harbour or Bay Bulls, 1789 (CO 194.38); Bridget Lawlor, from Newbown (unidentified) (Co. Wexford), married at St. John's, 1812 (Nfld. Archives BRC); Dennis, from Laughlan Bridge (Co. Carlow), Ireland, shoreman of St. John's, deceased 1814 (*Royal Gazette* 31 Mar 1814); John Lawler, of Trepassey, 1815 (D'Alberti 25); Stephen, magistrate of Oderin district, 1816 (D'Alberti 26); Bridget, of Harbour Grace Parish, 1819 (Nfld. Archives HGRC); ——, of Burin, 1822 (CO 194.65); Timothy Lawlor, of Renews, 1829 (Nfld. Archives BRC); Lawrence Lawler, of Greenspond, 1830 (Nfld. Archives KCRC); Dennis, from Waterford, of Tilting Harbour (now Tilting), 1831 (Nfld. Archives KCRC); Catherine, of King's Cove,

1832 (Nfld. Archives KCRC); Garret, of Torbay, 1839 (Nfld. Archives BRC); Gus Lawlor, from Co. Kilkenny, Ireland, married Ann Hart of Fermeuse, 1841 (Dillon); Stephen Lawler, of Fogo, 1843 (*Newfoundlander* 31 Aug 1843); Michael Lawlor or Laughlor, of Trinity (unspecified), 1856 (Nfld. Archives KCRC); Edward Lalor, of Ship Cove (unspecified), 1868 (Nfld. Archives KCRC); Martin and Robert Lawler, of Horse Cove (now St. Thomas), 1871 (Lovell); Michael Lawlor, farmer of Renews to Cape Race area, 1871 (Lovell); Robert, planter of Trinity (Trinity B.), 1871 (Lovell).

Modern status: Scattered, especially at St. Thomas and in the St. John's districts.

Place name: Lawler Bay 47-00 52-54.

LAWRENCE, (or Laurence), a baptismal name and surname of England, Ireland and the Channel Islands, from the Latin *Laurentius* – of Laurentum (a city), ? ultimately from Latin *laurus* – bay tree. St. Laurence the Deacon, martyred at Rome in 258, was a favourite saint in the Middle Ages. (Withycombe, Reaney, Cottle, MacLysaght, Turk). *See also* REEVE(S).

Traced by Guppy especially in the south and west of England, and by MacLysaght in Ireland though "not closely identified with any particular locality."

In Newfoundland:

Early instances: William Laurence, of Porta Grace (? for Port de Grave), 1676 (CO 1); Edward Lawrence, of Blackhead (Conception B.), 1790 (CO 199.18); Daniel Luverance or Lawrance, of St. John's, 1816 (DPHW 23); John Lawrence, of Bonavista, 1816 (D'Alberti 26); Patrick, of Joe Batt's Arm, 1818 (Nfld. Archives KCRC); Mary Lawrence or Laurence, of Harbour Grace Parish, 1829 (Nfld. Archives HGRC); Benjamin Lawrence, of Bay L'Argent, 1835 (DPHW 30); Stephen Laurance, of Bay de l'Eau Island, 1835 (DPHW 30); Thomas, of St. Jacques, 1835 (DPHW 30); William Laurance or Lawrence, planter of Carbonear, 1843 (DPHW 48); Elizabeth Lawrence, of Adam's Cove, married at St. John's, 1845 (DPHW 26D); Robert, fisherman of Morgan's Island (Burgeo-La Poile district), 1856 (DPHW 101); Robert Isaac, from Bath, England, married at St. John's, 1859 (DPHW 26D); Robert, schoolteacher of Brigus, 1871 (Lovell); William, of Burnt Island (Burgeo-La Poile district), 1871 (Lovell); John, planter of Cinque Cerf, 1871 (Lovell); George, of Exploits Burnt Island, 1871 (Lovell); Thomas, of Little Bay (Burgeo-La Poile district), 1871 (Lovell); Robert, of Lower Burgeo, 1871 (Lovell); John, of Manuels, 1871 (Lovell)

Modern status: Scattered, especially at Bay L'Argent, Channel, Isle aux Morts and St. John's.

Place names (not necessarily from the surname): Lawrence Harbour, —— Head 49-25 55-11; —— Ledge 49-41 54-45; —— Point 47-41 58-05; —— Pond 47-28 53-03; Laurences (or Laurance Rock) 47-06 55-04; Lawrenceton (or Laurenceton) 49-12 55-17; St. Lawrence 46-55 55-24; —— —— Point (or Middle Head) 46-54 55-22; St. Lawrence River 46-56 55-22.

LAWS. *See* LAW(E)S

LAWSON, a surname of England, Scotland and Ireland, – son of Law, diminutive of Lawrence. *See* LAWRENCE.

Traced by Guppy in the north of England, especially in Durham, and found "irregularly dispersed, but more frequent in the south of Scotland." MacLysaght found Lawson in most Ulster counties since the early 17th century.

In Newfoundland:

Early instances: Michael, married at St. John's, 1782 (DPHW 26D); Henry, fisherman of St. John's, 1841 (DPHW 29).

Modern status: At Corner Brook (*Electors* 1955) and St. John's.

LAWTON, a surname of England and Ireland from the English place name Lawton (Cheshire, Herefordshire), or from Old English *hlāw-tūn* – (dweller at the) farm or village on the hill; also in Ireland for *Ó Lachtnáin*, Ir. *lachtna* – grey. (Ekwall, Cottle, MacLysaght).

Traced by Guppy in Cheshire and Staffordshire and by MacLysaght in Co. Cork.

In Newfoundland:

Family traditions: Thomas, born at Youghal (Co. Cork), about 1804, came to Newfoundland at an early age as a cooper at Carbonear, and settled at King's Cove about 1834 (P.K. Devine). Louis (1888–1972), born in Pettigo (Co. Donegal), came with his parents to Harbour Grace at an early age and later settled on Bell Island (*Evening Telegram* 4 Apr 1972).

Early instances: Edward ? Laughten, one of 72 impressed men who sailed from Ireland to Newfoundland ? 1811 (CO 194.51); Thomas Lau(gh)ton or Lawton, of King's Cove Parish, 1840, of King's Cove, 1855 (Nfld. Archives KCRC); Thomas, of Broad Cove (now Duntara), 1856 (Nfld. Archives KCRC).

Modern status: At Bell Island (*Electors* 1955), King's Cove and St. John's.

LAYDEN, a surname of England and Ireland, ? a variant of the surnames of England, Ledden, Leddon, from the English place name Leddon (Devon), or of Leaden, Leadon from Highleadon or Upleadon (Gloucestershire) or Leadon or Upleadon (Herefordshire), or of the surnames of Ireland (O)Lydon (Leyden in Cos. Connacht and Clare), *Ó Loideáin*. (Spiegelhalter, Reaney Notes, MacLysaght).

Spiegelhalter traced Leddon, Ledden in Devon, MacLysaght traced Leyden in Connacht and Co. Clare.

In Newfoundland:

Early instances: William Leaden or Ledden, planter of Catalina, 1823, of Trinity, 1827, of Trouty, 1836 (DPHW 72, 64B); John Ledden, of Keels, 1849 (DPHW 73); Maria Ledden, Ladden, or Lidden, of King's Cove Parish, 1873 (Nfld. Archives KCRC).

Modern status: At Lewisporte, Corner Brook, St. John's and Victoria.

LAYMAN, a surname of England, from Old English *lēah* and *mann* – dweller by the wood or clearing. (Reaney). *See also* LEAMAN.

In Newfoundland:

Early instances: Ellis, of Bay Bulls, ? 1753 (CO 194.13); Gregory, of Burnt Point (Bay de Verde district), 1799 (CO 199.18); Alexander, of St. John's, 1814 (DPHW 26B); Alexander, planter of Old Perlican, 1823 (DPHW 58); William, carpenter of Ferryland, 1828 (DPHW 31); John, planter of Lower Island Cove, 1851 (DPHW 55); Thomas, fisherman of Fogo, 1851 (DPHW 83); John, of Gull Island (Conception B.), 1857 (DPHW 55); Peter, fisherman of Harbour Round, 1871 (Lovell); John Leyman, of Spaniard's Bay, 1871 (Lovell).

Modern status: Scattered, especially at Gull Island.

LAYTE. *See* LAITE

LAYTON, a surname of England, from the English place name Layton (Lancashire, Yorkshire NR). (Cottle).

In Newfoundland:

Early instance: Captain Charles, of Harbour Grace, 1870, 1871 (Lovell, Nfld. Archives HGRC).

Modern status: Unique, at St. John's (*Electors* 1955).

LEAHEY. *See* LAHEY

MacLysaght traced (O)Leahy in Cos. Cork, Kerry and Tipperary.

In Newfoundland:

Early instances: John Leahy, from Cloyne (Co. Cork), married at St. John's, 1804 (Nfld. Archives BRC); Patrick, from Youghal (Co. Cork), of Harbour Grace, deceased 1810 (*Royal Gazette* 28 Jun 1810); William, of St. John's, 1847 (*Newfoundlander* 16 Sep 1847); Thomas, of Bell Island, 1871 (Lovell); Michael, of Cape Broyle, 1871 (Lovell).

Modern status: Unique, at Witless Bay (*Electors* 1955).

Place names: Leahy Cove 48-59 58-01; —— Pond 47-17 53-26.

LEAMAN, LEAMON, LOVEMAN, LUFFMAN, surnames of England, from the Old English personal name *Lēofmann* – beloved man, or Middle English *leofman, lem(m)an* – lover, sweetheart. Leaman, Leamon may also be variants of LAYMAN, or, in Newfoundland, ? anglicizations of the French surname LE MOINE. In Ireland, Lemon may also be an abbreviated form of MacLamond, later Mac-Clement. *See* CLEMENS. (Reaney, Spiegelhalter, MacLysaght). *See also* LOMOND.

Spiegelhalter traced Leaman, Lemman, Lem-(m)on in Devon. Guppy traced Lem(m)on in Norfolk and Sussex. MacLysaght traced Lemon in Ulster.

In Newfoundland:

Early instances: Thomas Lemon, juror of St. John's, 1752 (CO 194.13); John Leamon, merchant of Brigus, 1828 (DPHW 34); Gregory Lemon or Layman, planter of Burnt Point (Bay de Verde district), 1834 (DPHW 52A); Henry Lemmon, fisherman of Bird Island Cove (now Elliston), 1835 (DPHW 72); William Lemons, of Brigus, married at La Poile, 1861, of East Point (La Poile district), 1871 (Lovell, DPHW 99) .

Modern status: Leaman, at St. John's; Leamon, in the Burgeo-La Poile district, at Brigus and St. John's; Luffman, at Bell Island (*Electors* 1955), Harbour Grace, Markland and St. John's.

LEAMEY, a variant of the surname of Ireland, (O)Leamy, *Ó Laomdha*, ? Ir. *laomdha* – bent, later *Ó Léime.* (MacLysaght).

Traced by MacLysaght in Co. Tipperary.

In Newfoundland:

Early instances: Denis Leamy, of Harbour Grace Parish, 1826 (Nfld. Archives HGRC); Philip, from Co. Tipperary, of Portugal Cove, 1860, 1871 (Lovell, MUN Hist.); Michael Leamey, farmer of Blackhead (St. John's), 1871 (Lovell); Michael Lamey, of St. John's, 1871 (Lovell); Louis, planter of Green Cove (Bonne B.), 1871 (Lovell).

Modern status: Rare, at St. John's.

Place names: Leamys Brook, —— Ponds 47-32 52-41.

LEAMON. *See* LEAMAN

LEAR, a surname of England, ? from the Old English personal name *Lēofrīc* as in the English place name Learchild (Northumberland) – *Lēofrīc*'s slope, ? from the English place name Leire (Leicestershire), or from Old Norse *leirr* – (dweller at the) clayey place, or from Old English *hlear* – face, cheek. (Spiegelhalter, Reaney Notes, Ekwall). *See also* LOVERIDGE.

Traced by Guppy in Devon.

In Newfoundland:

Family traditions: ——, from Jersey (Channel Islands), settled at Hibbs Hole, about 1760 (MUN Folklore). John (1823–1915), son of the first Lear from Wales, who settled at Hibbs Hole (MUN Geog.).

Early instance: Henry (and others), fishermen of Hibbs Hole, 1871 (Lovell); Henry, son of John and Mary of Dartmouth (Devon), gamekeeper and blacksmith, married at Harbour Breton, 1872 (Harbour Breton Anglican Church Records per D.A. Macdonald).

Modern status: Scattered, especially at Hibbs Hole and Seal Cove (Harbour Main district).

Place names: Lear's Cove 46-52 54-12, 47-36 53-11.

LEARIE. *See* O'LEARY

LEARNING, a surname of Newfoundland, of unknown origin, ? of Guernsey (Channel Islands).

In Newfoundland:

Family tradition: ——, from Guernsey (Channel Islands), settled at Cartwright (Labrador), before 1852; some of the family later settled at Happy Valley (Labrador), St. John's and Gander. Another tradition maintains direct English descent and suggests the possibility of a change of name. (MUN Folklore).

Early instances: James, of Salvation Cove (Labrador), 1850 (DPHW 113); George Bennett, of Alexis Bay (Labrador), married at Battle Harbour (Labrador), 1854 (DPHW 114).

Modern status: At Gander (*Electors* 1955) and St. John's.

LEAWOOD, a surname of England, not apparently recorded elsewhere, ? from the English place name Leawood Ho (Devon). (Gover).

In Newfoundland:
Early instance: John, planter of Hants Harbour, 1841 (DPHW 59A).
Modern status: At Britannia (*Electors* 1955), New Chelsea and St. John's.

LEBANS, a variant of the surname of Ireland Levens, *Mac Dhuinnshléibhín,* itself a variant of Dunlevy which has been changed to Levinge, Leviston, Levingstone and LIVINGSTONE. (MacLysaght).
Levens traced by MacLysaght in Co. Louth since before 1659.
In Newfoundland: From New Brunswick in 1952 (Family).
Modern status: Rare, at St. John's.

LEBLANC, a surname of France, Le Blancq of the Channel Islands, Fr. *le blanc* – the man with white hair (Dauzat, Turk). Le Blanc has sometimes been changed to WHITE in Newfoundland and the Channel Islands.
Traced by Dauzat especially in the north of France.
In Newfoundland:
Family tradition: Stephen, from the Magdalen Islands, was one of the original settlers of Stephenville, and the settlement was named after him (MUN Geog.) Etienne [Stephen] and Célestine LeBlanc of Margaree, N.S., settled in Stephenville about 1840; family name now WHITE. Cécine, Guillaume and Antoine LeBlanc, sons of a Marin LeBlanc, of Margaree, settled at St. George's, 1847. (G.R. Thomas).
Modern status: At Corner Brook (*Electors* 1955), Gander and St. John's.

LEBOUBAN. *See* LABOUBON

LE CASTA. *See* LA COSTA

LECOINTRE The predominant spelling and pronunciation of the current name in the Cape St. George area (Thomas, "French Fam. Names"). *See* LEQUANT.

LECOQ, a surname of France, Le Cocq of the Channel Islands, French *le coq,* a nickname applied to one who carries himself well, speaks well and runs after the girls. (Dauzat, Turk).
In Newfoundland:
Modern status: Rare, at St. Teresa's (St. George's district) (*Electors* 1955).

LECOUNTRE, ? a surname of France, not in Dauzat or Chapuy, of unknown origin. Turk. *See also* LECOINTRE.

In Newfoundland:
Modern status: At Mainland and Cape St. George (*Electors* 1955).

LECOURE. *See* LACOUR

LEDINGHAM, a surname of England, from the English place name Leadenham (Lincolnshire). (E.C. Smith).
In Newfoundland:
Modern status: Rare, at St. John's.

LEDREW, an anglicization of the surname of France and Jersey (Channel Islands), Ledru – vigorous, lively, lady's man. (Dauzat, Turk). Drew is also found in Jersey.
In Newfoundland:
Family traditions: ——, from Jersey (Channel Islands), settled at Cupids; later the family moved to Change Islands and Ship Cove (Botwood) (MUN Folklore).
Early instances: Mary La Dros, of Cupids, 1762 (CO 199.18); Ive, of Brigus, 1780 (CO 199.18); George Le Drew, of Cupids, 1807 (DPHW 34); George Le(a)drow or Ledgrow, planter of Careless (now Kerley's) Harbour, 1822 (DPHW 64); Maria LeDrowe, of Harbour Grace Parish, 1823 (Nfld. Archives HGRC); —— Ledroe, on the *Venus,* in the seal fishery out of Port de Grave, 1838 (*Newfoundlander* 29 Mar 1838); Tobias LeDrow, of Change Islands, 1841 (DPHW 83); Moses Ledrew, of British Harbour (Trinity B.), 1854 (DPHW 64B); Isaac and William Ledroe, of Kelligrews, 1871 (Lovell); Isaac LeDrew, of St. John's, 1871 (Lovell); Robert, of Ward's Harbour (now Beaumont North), 1871 (Lovell); George, of Trinity (Trinity B.), 1871 (Lovell).
Modern status: Widespread, especially at Cupids, Change Islands, Botwood and St. John's.
Place name: Ledrew Rock 49-30 55-43.

LEDWELL, a surname of England, from the English place name Ledwell (Oxfordshire). (E.C. Smith).
In Newfoundland:
Family tradition: Sebastian, of English descent, came from Ireland and settled at Little Placentia (now Argentia) (MUN Folklore).
Early instances: Thomas, enlisted in the Nova Scotia Regiment of Fencible Infantry at St. John's, 1806–07 (CO 194.46); Robert, of Placentia, 1838 (Nfld. Archives BRC); James, granted land at Birds Cove, Little Placentia (now Argentia), 1859 (Nfld. Archives, Registry Crown Lands).

Modern status: At Trepassey (*Electors* 1955), Calvert, Ship Harbour (Placentia East district) and St. John's.

LEE, a surname of England, Ireland and the Channel Islands, one of several variant forms derived from common English place names, Lea, Lee, Leigh, Lye, or from Old English *lēah* – (dweller by the) wood, clearing; in Ireland also for *Mac Laoidhigh*, Ir. *laoidheach* – poetic, or *Mac an Leagha* – son of the physician. (Reaney, MacLysaght, Turk).

Found widespread by Guppy in England and by MacLysaght in Ireland.

In Newfoundland:

Early instances: Richard, of Fermeuse, 1675 (CO 1); Richard, of Ferryland, 1676 (CO 1); J., of Petty Harbour, 1703 (CO 194.3); John, of St. John's, 1705 (CO 194.4); John, of Colliers, 1781 (CO 199.18); Patrick, from Drogheda (Co. Drogheda), Irish convict landed at Petty Harbour or Bay Bulls, 1789 (CO 194.38); Edward, of Bay Bulls, 1793 (USPG); Daniel, of Placentia, 1794 (D'Alberti 5); Mary, from Waterford City, married at St. John's, 1813 (Nfld. Archives BRC); Betsy, of King's Cove, 1815 (Nfld. Archives KCRC); Rev. John Leigh, magistrate of Twillingate, 1816 (D'Alberti 26); Elinor Lee, of Greenspond, 1817 (Nfld. Archives KCRC); William, of Round Harbour (Burin district), 1818 (DPHW 109); Thomas, of Harbour Grace Parish, 1821 (Nfld. Archives HGRC); Edward Leigh, from St. Mary's (unspecified), married at Tilting Harbour (now Tilting), 1829 (Nfld. Archives KCRC); Darby Lee, of Harbour Grace, 1831 (Nfld, Archives HGRC); Robert, of St. Jacques, 1835 (DPHW 30); William, of Pushthrough, 1835 (DPHW 30); Michael, of Ferryland district, 1838 (*Newfoundlander* 25 Oct 1838); Robert, of Harbour Breton, 1839 (DPHW 106); Matthew, fisherman of Bonne Bay (Fortune B.), 1841 (DPHW 102); John, member of the Board of Road Commissioners for Gaultois area, 1857 (*Nfld. Almanac*); William, of Grand Bank, 1859 (DPHW 106); Edward, ? of Northern Bay, 1862 (DPHW 57); John, of Belleoram, 1871 (Lovell); Sylvester, of Burn Cove (Ferryland district), 1871 (Lowell); Edward (and others), of St. Mary's, 1871 (Lovell); John, farmer of Torbay, 1871 (Lovell); Thomas, of Witless Bay, 1871 (Lovell).

Modern status: Widespread, especially at Riverhead (St. Mary's district), Petty Harbour, Round Harbour (Fortune B.) and St. John's.

Place names: Lee Bight (now Adeytown) 48-05 53-56; —— Cove 47-40 56-04, 47-54 55-49; (Lee) Beach Cove, (——) —— Point 47-01 55-57; Lees

Gully, —— Pond 47-23 53-12; —— Pond (or Miller's Pond) 47-37 52-50.

LEE-WHITING. *See* LEE and WHITING

In Newfoundland:

Early instances: Robert Lee Whiting, carpenter of St. John's, 1806 (CO 194.45); Robert Lee, granted land at Point of Beach, Harbour Grace, 1834 (Nfld. Archives, Registry Crown Lands).

Modern status: Rare, at Harbour Grace (*Electors* 1955).

LEFE(U)VRE, LEFEVER. *See* FE(A)VER

LEFRESNE, with a misspelling LEFRENSE, for the surname of Jersey (Channel Islands) Du Fresne, from Fr. *frêne* – (dweller by the) ash tree. (Turk).

In Newfoundland:

Modern status: LeFrense, at Isle aux Morts and Burnt Island (Burgeo-La Poile district); LeFresne, at St. John's (*Electors* 1955) and Windsor.

LEGER, a surname of England, Leger an old baptismal name and surname of France, St. Leger of Ireland, from an Old German personal name *Leodegar*, Old French *Legier* containing the elements *people* and *spear*, popular through the martyrdom of St. Léger, bishop of Autun, who died in 678. (Reaney, Cottle, Dauzat).

In Newfoundland:

Early instance: John Legger, of Newfoundland, ? 1706 (CO 194.24).

Modern status: Rare, at Grand Falls (*Electors* 1955), and St. John's.

LEGGE, a surname of England, Scotland and Ireland, from Old Norse *leggr*, Middle English *legg*, a nickname; or in Scotland and Devon according to Black and Spiegelhalter from Old English *lēah* (dative *lēage*) – (dweller) at the lea, wood, clearing; or in Ireland ? as the anglicized form of *Mac Coise*, Ir. *cos* – foot, leg. (Reaney, Cottle, Black, Spiegelhalter, MacLysaght).

Legg traced by Guppy in Dorset, by Spiegelhalter in Devon and by MacLysaght in Ulster.

In Newfoundland:

Family tradition: Seven Legge brothers, from England, came to Newfoundland and settled on the south and east coasts (MUN Folklore).

Early instances: William Legg, of Old Perlican, 1708–09 (CO 194.4); William, of Trinity Bay, 1768 (DPHW 64); William, of Heart's Content, 1793 (DPHW 64); Catherine, of Bonavista, 1803 (Nfld.

Archives BRC); John, of Scilly Cove (now Winterton), 1807 (DPHW 64); James, of Carbonear, 1816 (DPHW 48); John Legge, planter of New Perlican, 1823, of Heart's Delight, 1823 (DPHW 64B); Frances, of Harbour Grace Parish, 1824 (Nfld. Archives HGRC); J. Legg, of St. John's, 1832 (*Newfoundlander* 8 Mar 1832); Thomas Legge, of Barrisway (St. George's B.), 1835 (DPHW 30); Richard Legg, fisherman of Bay d'Espoir, 1850, skipper of Gaultois, 1857 (DPHW 102); John Leg, of Open Hole (now Open Hall), 1857 (Nfld. Archives KCRC); Anne, of Tickle Cove (Bonavista B.), 1859 (Nfld. Archives KCRC); John, of Indian Arm (Bonavista B.), 1862 (Nfld. Archives KCRC); Isaac, of Broad Cove (now Duntara), 1864 (Nfld. Archives KCRC); Philip Legge, of Robinson's Head, 1870 (DPHW 96); scattered in Lovell 1871.

Modern status: Widespread, especially at Heart's Delight, Garnish, Robinson's and St. John's.

LEGGO, ? a variant of the surname of France Ligot, French *lien* – tie, bond, nickname for a binder of sheaves etc. (Dauzat).

In Newfoundland:

Early instance: Robert Ligo, planter of Bay of Islands, 1871 (Lovell).

Modern status: At Corner Brook.

LEGROW, a surname of Scotland and Jersey (Channel Islands), in Scotland from the Scots place name Legrow (Orkney), in Jersey a variant of the surname of France Legros – the fat one. (Black, Dauzat, Turk).

In Newfoundland:

Early instances: The five children of John Le Grow, of Broad Cove (Bay de Verde district), 1776 (CO 199.18); Thomas, of Small Point (Bay de Verde district), 1804 (CO 199.18); Jonathan Legrow, planter of Mulley's Cove (Bay de Verde district), 1835 (DPHW 52A); —— Legros, of St. John's, 1832 (*Newfoundlander* 13 Dec 1832); John Legro, fisherman of East Cul de Sac, 1851 (DPHW 102); Henry Legrow, of Madox Cove, 1871 (Lovell); James P. LeGros, merchant of Petites, 1871 (Lovell).

Modern status: Scattered, especially at Bauline (St. John's North district), Broad Cove (Bay de Verde district) and St. John's.

LEITCH, a surname of Scotland, the Scots form of Leach, Leech, from Old English *lǣce* – leech, physician. (Black).

In Newfoundland:

Early instances: ——, of St. John's, 1832 (*New-foundlander* 20 Dec 1832); John, from Greenock, Scotland, married at St. John's, 1838 (*Times* 27 Jun 1838).

Modern status: At St. John's and Corner Brook.

Place name: Leitch (or Leech) Brook 48-57 55-50.

LELIEVRA, a Newfoundland variant of the surname of France and Guernsey (Channel Islands), Lelièvre – the rabbit, a nickname for a coward, the rabbit being the symbol of cowardice. (Dauzat, Turk).

In Newfoundland:

Early instances: Francis Lelievre, ? Of St. John's, 1795 (CO 194.41); Tito, lessee of land in the vicinity of St. John's, 1803–5 (CO 194.45).

Modern status: Rare, at Bell Island (*Electors* 1955).

LEM, a surname of China – forest. (So).

In Newfoundland:

Modern status: Unique, at St. John's.

LEMAIRE, for Lemerre, a surname of France, usually Maire, – mayor, an occupational name or nickname, or from the French place name Maire (Isère). (Dauzat).

Dauzat traced Lemerre on the Contentin peninsula.

In Newfoundland:

Early instance: John Lemer, of St. John's, 1706 (CO 194.22).

Modern status: At Locks Cove (White B.) (*Electors* 1955) and St. Anthony.

LEMEE, for the surnames of France and the Channel Islands, Lemée, Le Mée, from the French place name in several localities. (Dauzat).

In Newfoundland:

Family tradition: John La Mee, from Benock, France, settled at Coachman's Cove about 1850–70 (MUN Folklore).

Modern status: Rare, at Coachman's Cove (White B.) and St. John's (*Electors* 1955).

LEMESSURIER, a surname of the Channel Islands, a variant of the French surname Mesureur – (land) surveyor. (Dauzat, Turk).

In Newfoundland:

Family tradition: G., from the Channel Islands, settled at St. John's in 1838; later that year he moved to Isle Valen (MUN Folklore).

Early instances: Peter, of St. John's, 1811–12 (CO 194.52); Peter, merchant of Ferryland, 1844, of

Aquaforte, 1845 (DPHW 31); George Lemesurier, merchant of Twillingate, 1871 (Lovell).

Modern status: At Marquise (*Electors* 1955), Corner Brook and St. John's.

LEMOINE, a surname of France and the Channel Islands – the monk, a nickname perhaps to be associated with the expression "fat as a monk." (Dauzat, Turk). *See* LEAMAN.

In Newfoundland:

Family tradition: Yves, a deserter, settled in the Cape St. George area about 1895 (MUN Hist.).

Early instances: John Lemoine, fisherman of Lower Burgeo, 1842 (DPHW 101); George, of Petites, 1860 (DPHW 99); John, granted land at Channel, 1861 (Nfld. Archives, Registry Crown Lands).

Modern status: Scattered, especially at Cape St. George.

Place names: Bay Le Moine 47-39 58-38; —— —— —— Gulch 47-41 58-35; —— —— —— Rock 47-38 58-38.

LENCH, a surname of England, from the English place name Lench (Worcestershire), or from Old English *hlenc* – (dweller on the) ? hill. (Cottle).

In Newfoundland:

Early instance: Rev. Charles (1859–1931), born near Dudley, Staffordshire; came to Newfoundland as a probationer in the Methodist Church in 1883; died at Brigus (Swain).

Modern status: Unique, at St. John's.

LEONARD, a baptismal name and surname of England, the Channel Islands and Ireland, Léonard of France, from the Old German personal name *Leonhard* containing the elements *lion* and *bold*; in Ireland as an anglicized form of Irish surnames including Lennon (*see* LANNON), Linnane, Linneen. (Withycombe, Reaney, MacLysaght, Turk).

Traced by Guppy in Cambridgeshire, Gloucestershire and Yorkshire NR, ER.

In Newfoundland:

Family traditions: Four brothers named Leonard, Lynard or Lenard, from ? Co. Cork, Ireland, came to Newfoundland about 1720, settled at British Harbour (Trinity B.) and other parts of the island (MUN Folklore). Thomas Leonard, from England, settled at Olivers Cove (Placentia B.), later renamed St. Leonard's after the family (MUN Folklore).

Early instances: Patrick, from Kinnegad (Co. Westmeath), Irish convict landed at Petty Harbour or Bay Bulls, 1789 (CO 194.38); Francis Linnard, of Placentia, 1794 (D'Alberti 5); Thomas Leonard, of

Trinity Bay, 1800, of Trinity (Trinity B.), 1809 (DPHW 64); Thomas Lenard, from Dublin, married at St. John's, 1821 (Nfld. Archives BRC); Thomas Linnard, of Careless (now Kerley's) Harbour, 1825 (Nfld. Archives KCRC); Jeremiah Leonard or Lenard, of Harbour Grace Parish, 1826 (Nfld. Archives HGRC); Martha Lenard, of Catalina, 1832 (Nfld. Archives KCRC); Martin Lenart, of Harbour Grace, 1839 (Nfld. Archives HGRC); Thomas Lennard, member of the Board of Road Commissioners for the area Presque to Oliver's Cove (now St. Leonard's) (Placentia B.), 1844 (Nfld. Almanac); Patrick, member of the Board of Road Commissioners for the area Isle Valen, 1844 (*Nfld. Almanac*); John Leonard, fisherman of British Harbour (Trinity B.), 1851 (DPHW 64B).

Modern status: Widespread, especially in the Placentia West district and at St. John's.

Place names: Leonard's Cove 48-00 53-50; —— —— Pond 47-20 53-15; St. Leonard's 47-28 54-27.

LEPAGE. *See* LA PAGE.

LEPRIEUR, a surname of France – the prior (of an abbey), an ironic nickname. (Dauzat). *See also* PRIOR, PRESS.

Traced by Dauzat especially in northwestern France.

In Newfoundland:

Family tradition: The Leprieur family emigrated from France or St. Pierre to Winterhouse, La Barre or L'Anse au Canard, Newfoundland, between 1890 and 1900 (MUN Geog.); Jean Leprieure (b. 1877), settled at L'Anse au Canard in 1900 (Butler 19).

Modern status: At Winterhouse (*Electors* 1955), West Bay (Port-au-Port district), Piccadilly and Corner Brook.

LEQUANT, ? a Newfoundland variant of the surnames of Jersey (Channel Islands) Le Quesne and CAIN, of France Le Quesne, ? from the French place name Caen (Calvados). Other possible derivatives are from Fr. Le Quesne – (dweller at the house with) the oak tree, or ? (strong as) the oak; Le Qui(e)n – dog, monkey; Le Quint – the fifth (child of a family); Le Quen – rogue, thief, villain. (Dauzat, Turk).

In Newfoundland:

Modern status: Lequant, rare, at Deer Lake; LaQuant, unique, at Harmon Field (*Electors* 1955).

LERICHE, a surname of France and of Jersey (Channel Islands) – the rich one (a nickname). *See also* RICH(E). (Dauzat, Turk).

Traced by Dauzat in north and northwestern France.

In Newfoundland:

Early instance: John, ? of Port de Grave, 1778 (Nfld. Archives T22).

Modern status: At Badger (*Electors* 1955).

LEROUX, a surname of France and of Jersey (Channel Islands) – the red (-haired one). (Dauzat, Turk).

Traced by Dauzat in northwestern France.

In Newfoundland:

Early instances: Charles LeRue, fisherman of Lower Burgeo, 1861 (DPHW 101); Edward Leroux, from France, trader of Sandy Point (St. George's B.), 1870 (DPHW 96, D. W. Prowse).

Modern status: Scattered, in the west coast districts and at St. Joseph's (Fortune B.).

LEROY, a surname of France and the Channel Islands – the king. *See* KING. (Dauzat, Turk).

Traced by Dauzat especially in northwestern France.

In Newfoundland:

Family tradition: The Leroi family from France or St. Pierre, settled at Winterhouse, La Barre or L'Anse au Canard between 1890 and 1910 (MUN Geog.).

Early instances: Andrew, of St. John's, 1812 (CO 194.52); Charles, of Burgeo, married at Harbour Breton, 1855 (DPHW 72).

Modern status: Rare, in the Port-au-Port district (*Electors* 1955).

LESELLEUR, a surname of Jersey (Channel Islands) and a variant of the surname of France, Le S(c)ellier – saddler, harness-maker. (Dauzat).

In Newfoundland:

Family tradition: ——, from Jersey (Channel Islands) to Quebec; the family settled at Grand Falls in the 1960s (MUN Folklore).

Modern status: Rare, at La Poile (*Electors* 1955) and Grand Falls.

LESEMAN, ? a variant of the surname of England Leachman, of Scotland L(e)ishman, from Old English *lǣce* – physician and *mann* – servant of the physician. (Reaney). *See also* LUSHMAN.

In Newfoundland:

Early instance: Henry G. (1855–1901), ? of St. John's (General Protestant Cemetery, St. John's).

Modern status: Rare, at St. John's.

LESHANA, LESHANE, SHANO, variants of the surnames of Jersey (Channel Islands), Le Chanu, or of the surnames of France, Chanu, Chenu, – white-haired.

LeChana traced in Jersey (Channel Islands).

In Newfoundland:

Family tradition: Philip LeShane (1749–1806), from Normandy, settled at Burnt Woods, near Lower Island Cove (Conception B.) (MUN Geog.).

Early instances: Philip Shano, of Pissing Mare (North Shore, Conception B.), 1796, of Kettle Cove, 1804, of Lower Island Cove, 1805 (CO 199.18); Simeon Shane, of Burnt Woods (Lower Island Cove), 1857 (DPHW 55); Henry, planter of Twillingate, 1871 (Lovell).

Modern status: Leshana, rare, at St. John's; LeShane, at Lower Island Cove; Shano, at Harbour Grace (*Electors* 1955) and St. John's.

LESLIE, a surname of Scotland and Ireland, from the Scots place name Leslie (Aberdeenshire, Fife). (Reaney, Cottle, MacLysaght, Withycombe).

"Its use as a christian name in England seems to have begun in about the last decade of the 19th C, and no explanation of it can be offered. *Leslie* is now a common man's name but is sometimes also given to girls, when it is usually spelt *Lesley*." (Withycombe).

Found scattered in Scotland by Guppy, and in Co. Monaghan by MacLysaght.

In Newfoundland:

Early instances: Peter, soldier of St. John's, 1811 (DPHW 26B); Makem Leseley, fisherman of Coley's Point, 1843 (DPHW 39); —— Leslie, son of an English army ? doctor, at Conne River since 1880, telegraph operator in 1905. (Millais).

Modern status: At Coley's Point (*Electors* 1955), Corner Brook, Topsail and St. John's.

LESTER, a surname of England, (Mac) Lester of Ireland; in England from the French place name Lestre (La Manche), or the English place name Leicester (Leicestershire), or a variant of Lister, from Middle English *lit(t)e* – to dye, hence a dyer; in Ireland a variant of MACAL(L)ISTER. *See also* LIDSTER. (Reaney, MacLysaght).

Traced by Spiegelhalter in Devon.

In Newfoundland:

Early instances: Benjamin, J.P. of Trinity district, 1750 (CO 194.12); Michael, of St. John's, 1762 (CO 194.15); Benjamin, from Poole, lessee of land at Bay de Verde, 1802, —— and Co., operated salmon fishery at Dog Bay, Indian Arm, Fogo, Indian Bay, Freshwater Bay, Trouty and New Harbour, 1804 (CO 199.18, CO 194.45); John, granted land on Old

Placentia Road, 1854 (Nfld. Archives, Registry Crown Lands).

Modern status: At St. John's and Gander.

Place name: Lester Point (Labrador) 54-12 58-21.

LETACNOUX, ? a variant of the surname of France, Estagnol – (dweller in the) house near the pond, or ? from the place name L'Etacq (Jersey, Channel Islands). (Dauzat).

In Newfoundland:

Family tradition: ——, from France or St. Pierre, settled at Winterhouse, La Barre or L'Anse au Canard between 1890 and 1910 (MUN Geog.).

Modern status: Unique, at Winterhouse (*Electors* 1955).

LETHBRIDGE, a surname of England, ? from an unidentified English or Scots place name.

Traced by Guppy in Devon.

In Newfoundland:

Family tradition: ——, from Bristol to Lethbridge in the 18th century (MUN Folklore).

Early instances: Andrew, fisherman of Brigus, 1834 (DPHW 34); Andrew, of Catalina, 1857 (DPHW 72); George and William, merchants of Twillingate, 1871 (Lovell).

Modern status: At St. John's, Clarenville and Lethbridge.

Place name: Lethbridge 48-22 53-52.

LETIEC, a surname of Jersey (Channel Islands), ? a variant of the surname of France Tièche, from Old French *tieis* – German (Dauzat); Breton *tieg* – farmer, family head, with French *le* (Thomas, "French Fam. Names").

In Newfoundland:

Modern status: Rare, at Mooring Cove (*Electors* 1955) and Stephenville Crossing.

LEVALLIANT, for the surname of France and Jersey (Channel Islands), Vaillant – valiant, courageous, or in Old French robust, sturdy. (Dauzat).

In Newfoundland:

Family tradition: Fred (–1942), from Jersey (Channel Islands), settled at Port-aux-Basques; some of the family later moved to St. John's (MUN Folklore).

Modern status: At St. John's, Gander and Grand Falls.

LEVER, a surname of England, from Old French *levre* – hare, or a short form of *leverer* – hunter of the hare, harrier, or from the English place names Great or Little Lever (Lancashire), or from Old English *lǣfer* – (dweller near the) rush(es), reed(s), iris(es). (Reaney, Cottle).

Traced by Guppy in Lancashire.

In Newfoundland:

Early instance: Eve, of Heart's Content, 1871 (Lovell).

Modern status: Rare, at St. John's.

LEVITZ, a shortened form of the surname of Russia, Levítskij, from Hebrew *lēwī* – Levite, or a clergy surname of non-Hebrew origin. (Unbegaun).

In Newfoundland:

Modern status: At St. John's and Corner Brook.

LEWIS, also spelt LOUIS, a baptismal name and surname of England, Wales, Ireland, France and the Micmac Indians of Newfoundland; in England from the Old Frankish personal name *Hlúdwig* (Latin *Ludovicus*, Old French *Clovis*, French Louis) containing the elements *loud* and *battle*, or from the English place name Lewes (Sussex); in Wales as an anglicization of the Welsh personal name Llewel-(l)yn, ? containing the element *llyw* – leader. (Withycombe, Reaney, Cottle, Spiegelhalter).

Found widespread by Guppy especially in Monmouthshire, South and North Wales, and also widespread in Ireland by MacLysaght.

In Newfoundland:

Family traditions: Jean Louis Du Malin, ex-member of the French navy, settled at Fleur de Lys, dropped Du Malin and was known as Jean Louis, now spelt Lewis (R. Sparkes). John Lewis (1757–1827), of Grand Bank (MUN Hist.). Philip Louis (–1825), from Jersey (Channel Islands), settled at Lower Island Cove about 1785 (MUN Geog.).

Early instances: Robert Lewis, of Newfoundland, 1724 (CO 194.3); Thomas, of St. John's, killed by the French, ? 1705 (CO 194.22); William, from Sherborne (Dorset), apprenticed to Captain James Brooks of Bay Bulls, 1759 (Dorset County Record Office per Kirwin); William, of Port de Grave, 1771 (Nfld. Archives T22); Thomas, of Chapels Cove, 1792 (CO 199.18); John, of Bay de Verde, 1800 (DPHW 64); George, occupier of fishing room at Grates Cove, Winter 1800–01 (Census Trinity B.); John, of Lower Island Cove, 1801 (CO 199.18); Philip Louis, of Harbour Grace Parish, 1809 (Nfld. Archives HGRC); Thomas Lewis, one of the party of men led by William Cull of Fogo who went up the Exploits River in quest of the residence of the native Indians, 1810 (D'Alberti 20); John Lewis, Luis, or Luse, of King's Cove, 1816 (Nfld. Archives KCRC);

David Lewis, from Glamorganshire, Wales, married at St. John's, 1817 (Nfld. Archives BRC); James, planter of Barr'd Islands, 1821 (USPG); Newell, of Fogo, 1823 (Nfld. Archives KCRC); Moses, of Holyrood, 1828 (Nfld. Archives BRC); John, an Indian in pursuit of the Aborigines, 1828 (*Newfoundlander* 13 Feb 1828); William, planter of Greenspond, 1829 (DPHW 64B); John Louis, from Canada, married at King's Cove, 1829 (Nfld. Archives KCRC); Patrick Lewis, of Broad Cove (now Duntara), 1831 (Nfld. Archives KCRC); Maurice Louis, Micmac Indian of Bay d'Espoir, 1835 (Wix); John Lewis, of Herring Neck, 1856, of Stone Harbour (Twillingate district), 1859 (DPHW 85); George Louis, of Grates Cove, 1858 (DPHW 58); Robert Lewis, of Bonne Bay, 1862 (MUN Hist.); Anne, of Tickle Cove (Bonavista B.), 1864 (Nfld. Archives KCRC); Anne, of Stock Cove (Bonavista B.), 1865 (Nfld. Archives KCRC); Anne, of Knight's Cove (Bonavista B.), 1870 (Nfld. Archives KCRC); scattered in Lovell 1871; Noel and Reuben Louis, Micmac Indians of Conne River about 1872 (MacGregor); Reuben Lewis, Micmac Indian trapper with hunting grounds at Kaegudeck, 1900–06 (Millais).

Modern status: Lewis, widespread, especially at Holyrood, Fleur de Lys and St. John's; Louis, unique, at St. John's.

Place names: Lewis Brook 48-49 58-35; —— Gulch 48-06 59-06; —— Head 48-58 53-45; —— Hill 47-06 55-44; —— Hills 48-48 58-30; —— Island 48-58 53-48, 49-36 55-44, (Labrador) 52-48 55-55; —— Lake 49-17 55-32, (Labrador) 53-45 66-21; —— Point 48-06 59-05, 50-08 56-11; —— Pond 48-35 53-23; —— Rock (Labrador) 54-27 57-03; —— Tickle (Labrador) 52-47 55-55; Lewisporte, —— Harbour 49-15 55-03; Louis (or Douglas) Lake 48-28 56-41; —— Point 49-10 57-59; —— Pond 47-20 53-11; —— Ridge (Labrador) 53-37 64-06.

LEYTE. *See* LAITE

LIDDY, a surname of Ireland, (O)Liddy, *Ó Lideadha*, Leddy in Co. Cavan. (MacLysaght).
Traced by MacLysaght in Co. Clare.
In Newfoundland:
Early instance: Patrick, of St. John's, 1843 (DPHW 29).
Modern status: Unique, at Torbay.

LIDSTER, a variant of the surname of England Lister, a derivative of Middle English *lit(t)e* – to dye, hence a dyer. *See also* LESTER. (Reaney).

In Newfoundland:
Modern status: Rare, at Cupids.

LIDSTONE, a surname of England, from the English place name, Lidstone (Devon, Oxfordshire). (Spiegelhalter, Bardsley).
Traced by Guppy in Devon.
In Newfoundland:
Family tradition: —— Lidsten, from Germany, settled at South River (Conception B.); the family later changed their name to Lidstone (MUN Folklore).
Early instances: John Lidston(e), of Port de Grave, 1779 (CO 199.18); Thomas Lidstone, of St. John's, 1780 (D'Alberti 6).
Modern status: Scattered, especially at Corner Brook and Botwood.

LIGHT(S), surnames of England, from Old English *leoht* – ? (dweller in a) light (place), ? a glade, a clearing; or *leoht* – light, active, bright, gay, or Old English *lȳt* – little. (Reaney).
Traced by Guppy in Hampshire and by Spiegelhalter in Devon.
In Newfoundland:
Early instance: Charles Light, of Isle of Glue (Fortune B.), 1871 (Lovell).
Modern status: Light, rare, at St. John's (*Electors* 1955); Lights, at Rose Blanche (*Electors* 1955), and Belleoram.

LILLINGTON, a surname of England from the English place name Lillington (Dorset, Warwickshire). (Spiegelhalter, Ekwall).
Traced by Spiegelhalter in Devon.
In Newfoundland:
Modern status: At Channel and Isle aux Morts.

LILLY, a surname of England, Scotland, Ireland and the Channel Islands, ? from a pet-form of the baptismal name Elizabeth, or from the English place names Lilley (Hertfordshire) or Lilly (Berkshire, Devon), or from Old English *lin-lēah* – (dweller by or worker in the) flax field, or in Scotland from the Scots place name Lillock (Fife), or in Ireland for (Mac) Lilly, *Mac Ailghile*. (Reaney, Spiegelhalter, Cottle, Black, MacLysaght, Turk).
Lilly traced by Guppy in Lincolnshire and by Spiegelhalter in Devon. Black found Lilley "not a common name anywhere in Scotland." MacLysaght describes (Mac) Lilly as the name of a branch of the MacGuires of Co. Fermanagh.
In Newfoundland:

Family tradition: Three Lilly brothers, from Wales came to Newfoundland; one settled at Harbour Grace, William (–1870) and the other at St. John's about ? 1830 (MUN Folklore).

Early instances: John Lillie, heir to Lillies Plantation at St. John's, 1765 (CO 194.21); William Lilly, of Bay Roberts, 1765, of Harbour Grace, 1765, of Port de Grave, 1774 (CO 199.18, Nfld. Archives T22); Samuel, of Carbonear, 1780 (CO 199.18); John, of Lower Island Cove, 1784 (CO 199.18); James, fisherman of Bay of Exploits, ? 1797 (CO 194.39); William, of (Upper) Island Cove, 1798 (CO 199.18); William, magistrate of Conception Bay, 1814 (CO 194.55); John, of Fortune, 1823 (DPHW 109); Duncan James, of Ragged Harbour (now Melrose), 1829 (Nfld. Archives KCRC); James Lill(e)y, planter of Trinity (Trinity B.), 1843 (DPHW 64B); John Lilley, fisherman of Pushthrough, 1853 (DPHW 102); James, of Fox Island (Burgeo-La Poile district), 1856 (DPHW 101); James Lilly, of Bay de Este (Fortune B.), 1871 (Lovell); William, of Exploits Burnt Island, 1871 (Lovell).

Modern status: Scattered, especially in the Fortune Bay and Hermitage district.

Place names: Lilly Bank 49-31 55-23; —— Rocks (Labrador) 56-58 61-27.

LIND, a surname of England, from Old English *lind* – (dweller by the) linden, lime tree. (Reaney, Cottle).

Traced by Spiegelhalter in Devon.

In Newfoundland:

Early instances: H., of Port de Grave Parish, 1829 (*Newfoundlander* 5 Nov 1829); Rev. H., of Harbour Grace, 1847, of south shore of Trinity Bay, 1855, of Sandy Point (St. George's B.), 1871 (*Newfoundlander* 7 Oct 1847, 26 Jul 1855, Lovell); Henry, schoolteacher of Greenspond, 1871 (Lovell).

Modern status: Rare, at Corner Brook and Little Bay (Green B.) (*Electors* 1955), and Grand Falls.

Place name: Linds Pond 48-40 53-40.

LINDAHL, a surname of Sweden – (dweller in the) linden, limetree valley. Lindall and Lindell are surnames of England from the English place name Lindel (Lancashire) with the same meaning.

In Newfoundland:

Modern status: At Grand Falls.

LIN(D)FIELD, surnames of England, from the English place name Lindfield (Sussex), or (dweller by the) field of lime trees.

In Newfoundland:

Early instance: Robert Linfield, planter of Twillingate, 1819 (USPG).

Modern status: Lindfield, unique, at Corner Brook; Linfield, at Twillingate and Loon Bay.

LINDSAY, a surname of England, Scotland and Ireland, from the French place name Limésy (Seine-Maritime) or the English place name Lindsey (Lincolnshire, Suffolk); also in Ulster for *Ó Loingsigh*, elsewhere anglicized as LYNCH, and sometimes adopted by some families of MacClintock. (Reaney, Cottle, Black, MacLysaght).

Traced by Spiegelhalter in Devon, by Guppy in Ayrshire, and by MacLysaght in Ulster and elsewhere in Ireland.

In Newfoundland:

Early instances: Alexander, planter of Brigus, 1825 (DPHW 34); James, fisherman of Harbour Grace, 1851 (DPHW 43).

Modern status: At Bell Island, Corner Brook (*Electors* 1955) and St. John's.

Place name: Lindsay Rock (Labrador) 53-46 56-37.

LINDSTROM, a surname of Sweden, Lindström, – (dweller by the) stream by which lime trees grow.

In Newfoundland:

Modern status: Rare, at St. John's.

LINEGAR, a surname of England, (O)Linnegar of Ireland, in England from the English place names Linacre (Lancashire, Cambridgeshire), Linacre Court (Kent), or (dweller by or worker in the) flax field; in Ireland, a variant of (O)Linneen, LANNON. (Reaney, MacLysaght).

Traced by MacLysaght in Co. Fermanagh.

In Newfoundland:

Early instances: Bridget Linogar, from Glanmore (Co. Kilkenny), married at St. John's, 1809 (Nfld. Archives BRC); Michael (and others) Linegar, of St. John's, 1871 (Lovell); Ellen, of Trinity Bay, 1874 (Nfld. Archives HGRC).

Modern status: At Bell Island (*Electors* 1955), Placentia and St. John's.

LINEHAN, a surname of Ireland (O)Linehan, Lenihan, Lenaghan, *Ó Leannacháin* or *Ó Luingeachán*. (MacLysaght).

Traced by MacLysaght in Cos. Roscommon, Cork and Limerick.

In Newfoundland:

Early instances: Cornelius Lanahan, fisherman of Quidi Vidi, 1794–5, "40 years in Newfoundland," that is, 1754–5 (Census 1794–5); John Linam, carpenter of St. John's, 1794–5, "25 years in Newfoundland," that is, 1769–70 (Census 1794–5); John Linahen, of Harbour Grace Parish, 1817 (Nfld. Archives HGRC); Patrick Linehan, from Waterford, married at St. John's, 1822 (Nfld. Archives BRC); P., of St. John's, 1822 (CO 194.65); Patrick, planter of Mall Bay, Mosquito, Mother Ixxes area, 1871 (Lovell); Edward (and others) Linnahan, of North Harbour, John's Point, Tickles and Colinet area, 1871 (Lovell).

Modern status: Scattered, in the St. Mary's district, especially at Colinet and Mosquito (*Electors* 1955) and St. John's.

LINFIELD. *See* LINDFIELD

LING, a surname of England and China, in England from the English place names Ling, Lyng in several counties, or from Old English *hlinc* – (dweller on the) hill, or from Old Norse *lyng* – (? dweller among the) ling, heather; in China – forest. (Cottle, E.C. Smith).

Traced by Guppy in Norfolk, Suffolk and Somerset.

In Newfoundland:

Modern status: Rare, at St. John's.

LINGARD, a surname of England, from the English place names Lingards (Yorkshire WR) or Lingart (Lancashire), or from Old English *līn*, Old Norse *garthr* – (dweller near or worker in the) flax enclosure. (A.H. Smith).

Traced by Guppy in Derbyshire and Lincolnshire.

In Newfoundland:

Modern status: At Bishop's Falls.

LINTHORNE, LINTON, surnames of England, LINTON of Scotland and Ireland, from the common English and Scots place name Linton, or Lynton (Devon); in Ireland also for MacClinton, *Mac Giolla Fhionntáin* – devotee of St. Fintan. (Cottle, MacLysaght).

Spiegelhalter traced Lintern, Linton in Devon.

In Newfoundland:

Early instances: Shad. Linthorn, of Placentia ? district, 1744 (CO 194.24); Benjamin Linthorne, merchant or agent of Conception Bay, 1784 (D'Alberti 2); George, of Bonavista, 1801 (DPHW 70); Elinor ? Linnton, of King's Cove Parish, 1842 (Nfld. Archives KCRC); Robert Lintern, fisherman of Brigus, 1858 (DPHW 35).

Modern status: Linthorne, scattered, especially at

Bonavista; Lintern, unique, at St. John's (*Electors* 1955).

Place name: Linton Lake 47-12 55-08.

LITTLE, a surname of England, Scotland and Ireland, from Old English *lȳtel* – little, small; in Ireland a synonym by translation of Begg(ane), Biggane, Ir. *beag* – little, and Petty, Pettit; in Scotland sometimes a variant of Liddell, ? from the English or Scots place name Liddel (Cumberland, Roxburghshire). (Reaney, MacLysaght, Black).

Traced by Spiegelhalter in Devon, and by Guppy in Cambridgeshire, Cornwall, Cumberland, Westmorland and Northumberland, and in the Scots Border counties, especially Dumfriesshire.

In Newfoundland:

Family tradition: John G., from England, settled at Otterbury (Carbonear) in the 1870s (MUN Hist.); ——, from England, settled in the Bonavista area about 1830; he later moved to Musgravetown (MUN Folklore).

Early instances: Michael, high constable of St. John's, 1794–5, "34 years in Newfoundland," that is, 1760–1 (Census 1794–5); Giles Little(s), of Bonavista, 1791–2 (DPHW 70, USPG); Thomas Little, of (Upper or Lower) Amherst Cove, 1871 (Lovell); John George and John Richard, of Goulds Road (Brigus district), 1871 (Lovell); John, planter of Musgravetown, 1871 (Lovell); John, fisherman of Victoria Village, 1871 (Lovell).

Modern status: Scattered, especially at Bonavista and Upper Amherst Cove.

LITTLEJOHN, a surname of England, a nickname doubtless used ironically. (Reaney, Cottle).

Traced by Guppy in Cornwall and by Spiegelhalter in Devon.

In Newfoundland:

Family tradition: William, from Ipplepen (Devon), settled at Coley's Point (MUN Hist.).

Early instances: ? Bisset, of St. John's, 1787 (DPHW 26C); John and William Littlejohns, of Coley's Point, 1871 (Lovell).

Modern status: Scattered, including Coley's Point.

LIVINGSTONE, a surname of Scotland and Ireland, from the Scots place name Livingston (West Lothian); also in Ireland for Levens, *Mac Dhuinnshléibhín.* (Reaney, Cottle, Black, MacLysaght).

Traced by MacLysaght in Ulster.

In Newfoundland:

Early instances: John, merchant of St. John's,

1794–5, "30 years in Newfoundland," that is, 1764–5 (Census 1794–5); John Livingston, of Quidi Vidi Cove, 1771 (CO 194.18, 30).

Modern status: Rare, at Deer Lake.

Place name: Livingston Bay (Labrador) 53-54 66-28.

LLOYD, a baptismal name and surname of England and Wales, a surname of Ireland, from Welsh *llwyd* – grey, hoary. (Withycombe, Reaney, Cottle).

Traced by Guppy in the Welsh Border counties and in North and South Wales, by Spiegelhalter in Devon, and by MacLysaght in Co. Waterford.

In Newfoundland:

Early instances: Thomas, of Harbour Grace Parish, 1826 (Nfld. Archives HGRC); Edward Thomas, of St. John's, 1839 (DPHW 26B).

Modern status: At St. John's (*Electors* 1955) and Norris Point.

Place names: Lloyds Lake 48-23 57-31; ―――― River 48-33 57-13.

LOCKE, a surname of England and Ireland from Old English *loc(c)* – lock (of ? curly hair), or Old English *loc(a)* – (keeper of the) fold, enclosure, or Middle English *loke* – (keeper of the) bridge or lock on a river. (Reaney, Cottle, MacLysaght 73).

Guppy traced Lock in Devon, Dorset, Norfolk, Somerset, Suffolk and Locke in Hampshire. MacLysaght found Locke fairly numerous but not identified with any particular area.

In Newfoundland:

Early instances: J. Lock, of St. John's Harbour, 1703 (CO 194.3); Elizabeth, of Lower Island Cove, 1754 (CO 199.18); Thomas, of Fogo, Twillingate or Tilton (now Tilting), 1771 (CO 194.30); John, planter of Tizzard's Harbour, 1820 (USPG); David, planter of New Harbour (Trinity B.), 1823 (DPHW 59A); David Locke, of Heart's Desire, 1832 (Nfld. Archives KCRC); Aaron Lock(e), fisherman of Trinity (Trinity B.), 1845 (DPHW 64B); Isaac Lock, of Moreton's Harbour, 1851 (DPHW 86); Benjamin, of Lower Burgeo, 1856 (DPHW 101); John Locke (formerly of Tizzard's Harbour), of Little Bay Islands, 1860 (DPHW 92, MUN Hist.); Henry Lock, of Cape Norman (Cook's Harbour), 1871 (Lovell); Frederick and John, of Little Bay Island, 1871 (Lovell); Thomas and William, miners of Tilt Cove, 1871 (Lovell).

Modern status: Scattered, especially at St. John's, Little Bay Islands and Corner Brook.

Place names: Lockport (or Locks Harbour), Lockport Harbour 49-27 55-30; Locks Cove 47-38 56-31, 51-20 55-57, 49-28 55-31, 49-44 54-16,

51-20 55-57; ―――― Harbour 49-28 55-36; ―――― Island, ―――― Mountain 51-20 55-47; ―――― Rock (Labrador) 53-07 55-46; Lockston 48-24 53-23.

LOCKYER, a surname of England, from Old English *loc* – lock (-maker), lock (-smith). (Reaney, Cottle).

Traced by Guppy in Dorset, Hampshire and Somerset.

In Newfoundland:

Early instances: Richard, of Trinity (Trinity B.), 1760 (DPHW 64); William, of Bay de Verde, 1774 (CO 199.18); George, of Trinity Bay, 1793 (DPHW 64); George, occupier of fishing room at Heart's Content, Winter 1800–01 (Census Trinity B.); George Lockyear, from Chard (Somerset), fisherman of Grates Cove, deceased 1812 (*Royal Gazette* 2 Jul 1812); Margaret Lockier, of Heart's Desire, 1825 (Nfld. Archives KCRC); Susanna Lokier or Lokyer, of Harbour Grace Parish, 1828 (Nfld. Archives HGRC); William Lockyer, of Isle Valen, 1835 (DPHW 30); James Samuel, of Greenspond, 1856 (DPHW 76); James, planter of Burin, 1871 (Lovell).

Modern status: Scattered, especially at Woody Island and Isle Valen (Placentia B.) (*Electors* 1955).

Place names: Mount Lockyer 49-31 56-53; Lockyers or Lockers Bay 48-54 53-57; Lockyers Waters 47-21 53-17.

LODER, a surname of England, ? from the English place names Loders, Uploders (Dorset), or from Old English *(ge)lād* – (dweller by the) path, road or watercourse, or from Middle English *lode* – to load, hence a carrier. (Reaney, Cottle).

Guppy traced Lod(d)er in Dorset.

In Newfoundland:

Early instances: Celas Loader, of Bay de Verde, 1800 (CO 199.18); James, of St. John's, 1801 (DPHW 26B); Silas, planter of Old Perlican, 1819 (DPHW 58); James, of Harbour Grace Parish, 1826 (Nfld. Archives HGRC); James, planter of Hants Harbour, 1830 (DPHW 59A); Solomon Loder, fisherman of Fogo, 1846 (DPHW 83); Silas, planter of Ireland's Eye, 1848 (DPHW 64B); ――――, from Dorset, of Gillams Cove (now Gillams), 1849 (Feild); George, of Clarke's Cove (Twillingate district), 1852 (DPHW 85); Sarah, of Herring Neck, 1852 (DPHW 85); Solomon, fisherman of Green Cove (Twillingate district), 1857 (DPHW 85); David Loader, of Harbour Grace, 1867 (Nfld. Archives HGRC); John, planter of Bay of Islands, 1871 (Lovell); Solomon Loder, of Fogo, 1871 (Lovell); Richard, of Great St. Lawrence (now St. Lawrence), 1871 (Lovell); William Loader, schoolteacher of Perry's Cove, 1871 (Lovell).

Modern status: Scattered, especially at Summerside (Humber West district) and St. Anthony.

Place names: Loaders Pond 47-47 53-18; Loders Cove, —— Pond 48-26 53-44.

LODGE, a surname of England, from Middle English *logge* – cottage, hut, mason's lodge. (Reaney, Cottle).

Traced by Guppy in Yorkshire WR.

In Newfoundland:

Family tradition: ——, from Devon, settled at Catalina in 1864 (MUN Folklore).

Early instances: John, of Trinity Harbour, 1772 (CO 194.30); Philip, servant of Battle Harbour (Labrador), 1795 (MUN Hist.); James, planter of Catalina, 1836 (DPHW 72).

Modern status: Scattered, especially at Port Union.

Place names: Lodge Pond (Labrador) 52-13 55-59.

LOGAN, a surname of Scotland and Ireland, from the Scots place name Logan (Ayrshire and elsewhere); also in Ireland a variant of Lohan, *Ó Leocháin*. (Black, MacLysaght).

In Newfoundland:

Early instances: Humphrey, merchant of St. John's, 1815 (DPHW 26B, 26D); William, fisherman of the Flowers Cove to Point Ferolle area, 1871 (Lovell); John G., from Upper Stewiacke, Nova Scotia, married at Corner Brook, 1878 (DPHW 96).

Modern status: Rare, at Gander (*Electors* 1955).

Place name: Logan Lake (Labrador) 53-35 64-09.

LOMASSNEY, a variant of the surname of Ireland (O)Lomasney, *Ó Lomasna*, Ir. *lom* – bare, *asna* – rib. (MacLysaght).

MacLysaght traced (O)Lomasney in Co. Tipperary.

In Newfoundland:

Modern status: Rare, at Ferryland (*Electors* 1955).

LOMOND, ? a variant of the surname of England, Lowman, from the English place names Uplowman, Craze Loman or River Loman (Devon), or of Loveman, LEAMAN, LEAMON.

Spiegelhalter traced Lowman in Devon.

In Newfoundland:

Early instances: —— Lowman, of St. John's, 1782 (DPHW 23); George, fisherman of Cape Ray, 1841 (DPHW 101); George and Isaac Lomond, of Point Rosy (Burgeo-La Poile district), 1871 (Lovell).

Modern status: Scattered, especially at Grand Bay and Channel.

Place names: Lomond, —— Cove 49-27 57-46; —— River 49-26 57-44.

LONG, a surname of England, Scotland and Ireland, from Old English *long, lang* – long, tall, the southern and Midlands form in contrast to LANG, LAING in the north and in Scotland, though Long is also recorded in Scotland; also in Ireland for a Norman name *de Long*, or *Ó Longáin* or *Ó Longaigh*.

Traced by Guppy in the south and Midlands, especially in Wiltshire, by Spiegelhalter in Devon, and by MacLysaght especially in Cos. Cork and Donegal.

In Newfoundland:

Early instances: Francis, fisherman of Trinity (Trinity B.), 1758 (DPHW 64); Alexander, gardener of St. John's, 1794–5, "35 years in Newfoundland," that is, since 1759–60 (Census 1794–5); Mary, of Bonavista, 1803 (Nfld. Archives BRC); Thomas, from Youghal (Co. Cork), married at King's Cove, 1803 (Nfld. Archives BRC); Francis, of English Harbour (Trinity B.), 1804, of Salmon Cove (now Champneys), 1817 (DPHW 64); Moses, from Rosegarland (Co. Wexford), planter of Brigus, deceased 1814 (*Royal Gazette* 3 Nov 1814); Mary, from Holy Cross Parish (Co. Tipperary), married at St. John's, 1814 (Nfld. Archives BRC); Michael, of King's Cove, 1815 (Nfld. Archives KCRC); John, of Carbonear, 1816 (DPHW 48); ——, of Bell Isle (now Bell Island), 1817 (Nfld. Archives BRC); John, of Harbour Grace Parish, 1823 (Nfld. Archives HGRC); Dennis, of Tilton Harbour (now Tilton), 1824 (Nfld. Archives KCRC); James, from Co. Wexford, of Tickle Cove (Bonavista B.), 1826 (Nfld. Archives KCRC); Maria, of Open Hole (now Open Hall), 1826 (Nfld. Archives KCRC); Joseph, of Ragged Harbour (now Melrose), 1831 (Nfld. Archives KCRC); William, of Keels, 1843 (DPHW 73A); William, of Plate Cove (Bonavista B.), 1857 (Nfld. Archives KCRC); Lucas, of North River (Conception B.), 1867 (Nfld. Archives HGRC); Archibald and Daniel, fishermen of Bonne Bay, 1871 (Lovell); Joseph, of Brigus (South), 1871 (Lovell); Edward, lumberman of Castle Cove (Bonavista B.), 1871 (Lovell); George, of Ferryland, 1871 (Lovell); Dennis, of Fox Cove (Burin district), 1871 (Lovell); John and Timothy, of Great Jervis, 1871 (Lovell); William, of Mortier, 1871 (Lovell).

Modern status: Scattered, especially at St. John's.

Place names: Some 150 or more place names contain the specific Long, but it is unlikely that any derive from the surname.

LORENZEN, ? a variant of the surnames of France, Lorenceau, Lorenz(i), from the baptismal name Laurent. *See* LAWRENCE. (Dauzat).

In Newfoundland:

Early instances: Emilius William, son of Peter and Ann-Margaret of Copenhagen, married at Harbour Breton 1858, aged 26, cooper at Jersey Harbour, moved to Harbour Breton in the 1870s (Harbour Breton Anglican Church Records per D.A. Macdonald; DPHW 104); William Lorenson, of Jersey Harbour, 1871 (Lovell).

Modern status: Rare, at Garnish and St. John's.

LOUGHLIN, a surname of Ireland, Mac Loughlin, *Mac Lochlainn*, from a Norse personal name, or (O)Loughlin, *Ó Lochlainn*, or (O)Loughnane, *Ó Lachtnáin*, Ir. *lachtna* – grey, in Co. Meath. (MacLysaght).

MacLysaght found MacLoughlin widespread and as MacLaughlin in Cos. Donegal and Derry, (O)Loughlin in Cos. Clare and Meath.

In Newfoundland:

Early instances: William Laughlen, innholder of St. John's, ? 1730 (CO 194.24); Mary Loughlin alias McDuggle, from Isle of Mull, Scotland, married at St. John's, 1818 (Nfld. Archives BRC); Michael Laughlin, of Trinity (unspecified), 1818 (Nfld. Archives KCRC); John Laughlan, of Tilton Harbour (now Tilting), 1822 (Nfld. Archives KCRC); Catherine Loughlan, from Thomastown (Co. Kilkenny), married at St. John's, 1828 (Nfld. Archives BRC); Thomas, of Harbour Grace Parish, 1828 (Nfld. Archives HGRC); Francis, of King's Cove Parish, 1834 (Nfld. Archives KCRC); Patrick Locklen, granted land at Harbour Grace, 1849 (Nfld. Archives, Registry Crown Lands); James Loughlan, of English Harbour West (Fortune B.), 1871 (Lovell); William Lachlan, of Flat Island (now Port Elizabeth), 1871 (Lovell); James, farmer of Red Cove (Placentia B.), 1871 (Lovell).

Modern status: Scattered.

Place name: Loughlins Hill 47-00 55-28.

LOUIS. *See* LEWIS

LOUVELLE, a surname of France, from the French place name Louville (Eure-et-Loir, Ruy-de-Dôme). (Dauzat). *See also* LOVELL with which confusion is possible.

In Newfoundland:

Modern status: At Cape St. George (*Electors* 1955), Shallop Cove and Stephenville Crossing.

LOVELACE, LOVELESS, surnames of England, from Old English *lufu-lēas* – loveless, heartwhole, or from Middle English compounds containing the elements *love* and *lass*, or *love* and *cord* or *girdle*, a love-token or keepsake. (Reaney, Cottle).

In Newfoundland:

Family tradition: Joseph Loveless, from England, was the first settler of Seal Cove (Fortune B.) in the early 1800s (MUN Hist.).

Early instances: Thomas Lovelace, sailor dwelling in Newfoundland, 1661–2 (Dorset County Record Office per Kirwin); Anthony Love[l]ace, merchant of Brigus, 1828 (DPHW 34); William Lovelace, of Greenspond, 1832 (DPHW 76); Joseph Loveless, of Grand Bank, 1836 (DPHW 106); Josiah, of Lamaline, 1840 (DPHW 109); Josiah Lovelace, fisherman of Seal Cove (Fortune B.), 1854 (DPHW 102); —— Loveless, of Bull Cove (Conception B.), 1870 (MUN Hist.).

Modern status: Lovelace, at St. John's and Greenspond; Loveless, scattered, especially at Seal Cove (Fortune B.).

LOVELL, a surname of England and Ireland from Anglo-French *lovel* – wolf-cub. (Reaney, Cottle, MacLysaght 73). *See also* LOVETT, LOWE, LOUVELLE.

Traced by Guppy in Bedfordshire, Hampshire, Huntingdonshire, Northamptonshire, Somerset and Sussex, and by Spiegelhalter in Devon.

In Newfoundland:

Family traditions: Benjamin (1776–1828), from England, settled at Grand Bank (MUN Hist.). Thomas (1845–1906), from England, was the first settler of McIvers, about 1867 (MUN Geog.).

Early instances: Benjamin, fisherman of Grand Bank, 1817 (DPHW 109); Jonathon, of St. Jacques, 1835 (DPHW 30); Thomas, of Bay of Islands, 1871 (Lovell); James, of Lamaline, 1871 (Lovell); John, printer and publisher of St. John's, 1871 (Lovell).

Modern status: Scattered, especially at McIvers.

LOVEMAN. *See* LEAMAN

In Newfoundland:

Family tradition: Simon, from Leading Tickles, of Pacquet about 1890 (MUN Hist.).

Modern status: Scattered, especially in the Green Bay district.

Place name: Loveman Bank 49-31 55-23.

LOVERIDGE, a surname of England and the Channel Islands, from the Old English personal name *Lēofrīc* – beloved ruler. (Reaney, Miller). *See also* LEAR.

Traced by Guppy in Devon, Dorset and Gloucestershire.

In Newfoundland:

Early instances: Thomas, of Pouch Cove, 1845 (DPHW 32); Henry, of Twillingate, 1871 (Lovell).

Modern status: Scattered.

LOVETT, a surname of England and Ireland, from Old French *lovet* – wolf-cub (*see* LOVELL); also in Ireland from the Scots surname Lovat. (Reaney, MacLysaght).

Guppy traced Lovett in Hertfordshire, Lovett and Lovitt in Leicestershire and Rutlandshire, and Lovatt in Staffordshire. MacLysaght traced Lovett in Co. Kerry.

In Newfoundland:

Early instances: John, of King's Cove, 1821 (Nfld. Archives KCRC); Thomas, of Aquaforte, 1871 (Lovell); William, of Ferryland, 1871 (Lovell); Richard, of Renews, 1871 (Lovell); William, of St. John's, 1871 (Lovell).

Modern status: Rare, at Aquaforte (*Electors* 1955) and St. John's.

LOVEYS, a surname of England, ? from the Old English personal names *Lēofa* (masculine) *Lēofe* (feminine) – beloved, or *Lēofwīg* – beloved warrior. (Reaney). *See* LAVIS.

Traced by Matthews in Devon.

In Newfoundland:

Early instances: William Loveys, of Western Bay, 1777 (CO 199.18); William, of Harbour Grace, 1791 (USPG); William Loveys or Lovays, of St. John's, 1813 (DPHW 26B); William Lovey, planter of Mulleys Cove, 1851 (DPHW 52A); Mrs. E. Loveys, of Brigus, 1871 (Lovell).

Modern status: Scattered.

LOWE, a surname of England, Ireland and the Channel Islands, Low of England and Scotland, from Old French *lou* – wolf, or from Old Norse *lágr* – low, short, or from Old English *hláw* – (dweller near the) hill, (burial) mound (*see* LAW(E)S), or a pet-form of Lawrence (*see* LAWRENCE), or in Ireland an anglicized form of Irish *Mac Lughadha*. (Reaney, Cottle, MacLysaght, Turk).

Guppy traced Lowe in ten counties in England and Low in the Aberdeen district; Spiegelhalter traced Lowe in Devon; and MacLysaght traced Lowe in Dublin and Ulster.

In Newfoundland:

Early instances: John Low, of Torbay, married at St. John's, 1775 (DPHW 26D); Edward Lowe, of Lower Island Cove, 1790, of Northern Bay, 1796 (CO 199.18); Mary, of Harbour Grace Parish, 1806 (Nfld. Archives HGRC); George Low, married at St. John's, 1832 (Nfld. Archives BRC); Jane Lowe, of Hants Harbour, 1838 (DPHW 59); John, planter of Catalina, 1840 (DPHW 72); Elizabeth, of Russells Cove (now New Melbourne), 1860 (DPHW 59); Allen Lowes, of Daniel's Harbour, 1871 (Lovell); William, of Port au Choix, 1871 (Lovell); Anthony (and others) Lowiss, of Western Bay, 1871 (Lovell).

Modern status: Scattered, especially at St. John's.

Place name: Lowe Rock 48-30 53-04.

LUBY, a surname of Ireland, (O)Luby (or Looby), *Ó Lúbaigh*, Ir. *lúbach* – cunning. (MacLysaght).

Traced by MacLysaght in Co. Tipperary.

In Newfoundland:

Early instances: David and Thomas, of Toads (now Tors) Cove, 1871 (Lovell).

Modern status: At St. John's and Tors Cove.

LUCAS, a surname of England, Ireland, France and the Channel Islands, (Mac) Lucas of Scotland, the learned form of the baptismal name Luke – the man from Lucania (a district in Lower Italy). (Withycombe, Reaney, MacLysaght, Turk).

Traced by Guppy in the Midlands and southwest and by Spiegelhalter in Devon; by MacLysaght in all provinces except Connacht; west coast families may be descended from Acadian settlers (Thomas, "French Fam. Names").

In Newfoundland:

Early instances: Peter, boat-keeper of St. John's Harbour, 1682 (CO 1); T., occupier of fishing room at Trinity (Trinity B.), Winter 1800–01 (Census Trinity B.); Thomas Lucus, of Harbour Grace Parish, 1823 (Nfld. Archives HGRC); Francis Lucas, planter of Catalina, 1833 (DPHW 72); Josiah, of Grand Bank, 1846 (DPHW 106); John G., teacher of Flat Island (unspecified), 1857 (*Nfld. Almanac*).

Modern status: Scattered, especially at Stephenville Crossing.

LUDLOW, a surname of England and Ireland, from the English place name Ludlow (Shropshire) – the hill by the rapid, loud or babbling river. (Cottle, MacLysaght 73).

Traced by Matthews as a captain and merchant of Dartmouth (Devon); by MacLysaght formerly in Dublin, Cos. Louth and Meath but now scattered and also in Ulster and Co. Cork.

In Newfoundland:

Early instances: John Lidlow, planter of Fogo, 1821 (USPG); James Lidrow, planter of Cupids, 1821; his son William was baptized at Change Islands, 1823 (USPG); —— Ledlow, fisherman of South Shore (? of Conception B.), 1838 (DPHW 30); John and William Ludlow, of Back Cove (Twillingate district), 1871 (Lovell); John, miner of Tilt Cove (White B.), 1871 (Lovell).

Modern status: Scattered.

LUDWIG, a baptismal name and surname of Germany, the German form of Lewis, Louis (*see* LEWIS). However, Bardsley records Lutwyche, Lutwidge, from the English place name Lutwich or Lutwyche (Shropshire). (Bardsley, Ekwall).

In Newfoundland:

Early instance: John, justice of Ferryland district ? 1730, 1732 (CO 194.9).

Modern status: Unique, at St. John's (*Electors* 1955).

LUEDEE, ? a Newfoundland variant of the surname of France Leudet – collector of customs. Leudier is a Norman form. (Dauzat). Luhédé has been recorded as the name of a pioneer settler at Chéticamp, N.S., born in France of French parents, perhaps the same as Louis Luidé, ? a deserter from the French navy. (G.R. Thomas). Neither form is recorded in Dauzat.

In Newfoundland:

Modern status: Scattered, in St. George's district.

LUFF, a surname of England, from an Old English personal name *Leof* or *Luffa*, or from Old English *lēof* – beloved. (Reaney).

Traced by Guppy in Monmouthshire, Somerset and Sussex, and by Spiegelhalter in Devon.

In Newfoundland:

Early instance: George, fisherman of Exploits Burnt Island, 1815 (D'Alberti 29).

Modern status: Scattered, especially at Bishop's Falls.

Place name: Luff Point (Labrador) 53-50 56-59.

LUFFMAN. *See* LEAMAN

LUKEMAN, a surname of England – servant of Luke (*see* LUCAS) (Reaney).

In Newfoundland:

Early instances: Alexander ? Luck(i)man, of St. John's, 1822 (CO 194.65); Alice Lukeman or Luckman, of Fogo, 1830 (Nfld. Archives KCRC); John

Lukeman, fisherman of Lions Den (Fogo district), 1811 (Lovell).

Modern status: At Fogo (*Electors* 1955), Corner Brook and St. John's.

Place name: Lukeman Head 48-56 54-54.

LUKINS, a surname of England, from the Old English personal names *Lufu* (feminine) or *Lufa* (masculine) and the diminutive suffix -*kin* – little love; or from Old French *lou* – wolf and -*kin* – little wolf.

In Newfoundland:

Family tradition: ——, from Yorkshire, settled at St. John's in 1884 (MUN Folklore).

Early instance: Frederick T., born in Yeovil (Somerset) 1870, came to Newfoundland as a fisherman in 1885 and settled at St. John's (*Nfld. Who's Who* 1927).

Modern status: Rare, at Buchans (*Electors* 1955), and St. John's.

LUNDRIGAN. *See* LANDRIGAN

LUNNEN, a surname of England, – (the man from) London.

In Newfoundland:

Early instance: William, fisherman of Twillingate, 1871 (Lovell).

Modern status: Rare, at Twillingate and Little Harbour East (*Electors* 1955) and St. John's.

Place names: Lunnon (or Lannon) Cove, —— Point 46-54 55-57.

LUSCOMBE, a surname of England, the English place name Luscombe (Devon) – ? pig-sty valley. (Spiegelhalter, Gover).

Traced by Guppy in Devon.

In Newfoundland:

Early instances: Arthur Liscom or Liscum, of Petty Harbour about 1720–5 (CO 194.7); Samuel Liscom, of Fogo, 1803 (D'Alberti 13); Honour Liscombe, of Herring Neck, 1821 (USPG); Edward Luscombe, of St. John's, 1823 (DPHW 26D); Joseph Liscomb, of Moreton's Harbour, 1853 (DPHW 86); Levi, fisherman of Clarke's Cove (Twillingate district), 1854 (DPHW 85); John Luscomb, miner of Trump Island (Twillingate district), 1871 (Lovell).

Modern status: Scattered, especially at Loon Bay (Twillingate district).

LUSH, a surname of England and Ireland, from Old French *l'uis* – the portal, hence doorkeeper, usher. (Spiegelhalter, MacLysaght).

Traced by Guppy in Dorset and Wiltshire.

In Newfoundland:

Early instances: Josiah, of St. John's, 1775 (DPHW 26D); William and Edward, of Bonavista, 1792 (USPG); Robert, proprietor and occupier of fishing room at Old Perlican, Winter 1800–01 (Census Trinity B.); William, of Brigus, 1817 (DPHW 34); John, of Greenspond, 1824 (DPHW 76); Benjamin, of Pools Island (Bonavista B.), 1830 (DPHW 76); W., J.P. of Placentia and St. Mary's district, 1847 (*Nfld. Almanac*); Sarah Mary, of Shoal Bay (unspecified), married at St. John's, 1854 (DPHW 26D); John (and others), of English Cove (Harbour Main district), 1871 (Lovell); John Sr., planter of Pinchard's Island, 1871 (Lovell).

Modern status: Scattered, especially at Marysvale and Middle Brook (Bonavista North district).

Place name: Lush's or Lushes Bight 49-36 55-43.

LUSHMAN, a surname of England – servant of LUSH, or ? for Leachman, Leishman, from Old English *lǽce* – servant of the physician. *See also* LESEMAN.

In Newfoundland:

Early instances: Thomas, of New (now Parsons) Harbour, 1825 (DPHW 30); Francis and Thomas, fishermen of Little (now Grey) River, 1871 (Lovell).

Modern status: In the Burgeo-La Poile district especially at Grey River.

LUTER, a surname of England, from Old French *leuteor* or from Middle English *lute* – lute-player, (*see* LUTHER), or from Old French *loutre* – otter (hunter). (Reaney).

In Newfoundland:

Early instance: Jehu, of Carbonear, 1810 (DPHW 48).

Modern status: Rare, at Buchans.

LUTHER, a surname of England and Ireland, in England from French *luthier* – lute-player (*see also* LUTER); in Ireland a variant of Lowther from the English place name Lowther (Westmorland). (Reaney, MacLysaght).

MacLysaght traced Lowther in Co. Fermanagh.

In Newfoundland:

Early instances: Bernard, of Carbonear, 1681 (CO 1); Stephen, of Adams Cove, 1790 (CO 199.18); John, of Harbour Grace Parish, 1811 (Nfld. Archives HGRC); George, fisherman of New Perlican, 1871 (Lovell); Job, constable of Twillingate, 1871 (Lovell); James and Silas Lother, fisherman of Hants Harbour, 1871 (Lovell).

Modern status: Scattered.

Place name: Luthers Gullies 47-43 53-22.

LYDALL, a surname of England, ? from an unidentified place name, ? a variant of Liddel (Cumberland), Old English *Hlȳdan-dæl* – valley of the river *Hlȳde*, the roaring stream, torrent. (Ekwall).

In Newfoundland:

Modern status: Unique, at St. John's.

LYE, a surname of England, from the English place name Lye (Herefordshire, Worcestershire), or from Old English *lēah* – (dweller by the) field, pasture, clearing, wood. *See* LEE. (Cottle).

In Newfoundland:

Modern status: Rare, at Placentia.

LYNCH, a surname of England and Ireland, in England from Old English *hlinc* – (dweller by the) hill, or from the English place names East Lynch (Somerset) or Lynch (Devon); in Ireland from the Norman *de Lench*, or for *Ó Loingsigh*, Ir. *loingseach* – mariner, or (O)Lynchehan, *Ó Loingseacháin*. (Reaney, Cottle, Spiegelhalter, MacLysaght). *See also* LENCH.

Traced by Spiegelhalter in Devon and by MacLysaght in Cos. Antrim, Down, Cavan, Clare, Cork, Tipperary, Donegal and Tyrone.

In Newfoundland:

Early instances: Thomas, of Petty Harbour, 1753 (DPHW 26C); Michael, shoreman of St. John's, 1794–5, "37 years in Newfoundland," that is, 1757–8 (Census 1794–5); Elizabeth, of (Upper) Island Cove, 1789 (CO 199.18); Thomas, of Salmon Cove (now Champneys), 1790 (DPHW 64); Thomas, of Bay de Verde, 1791 (CO 199.18); Honor, of Harbour Grace, 1795 (CO 199.18); James, of Trinity (Trinity B.), 1797 (DPHW 64); Thomas, from Castletown Parish (unidentified) (Co. Limerick), married at St. John's, 1806 (Nfld. Archives KCRC); William and Patrick, two of 72 impressed men who sailed from Ireland to Newfoundland, ? 1811 (CO 194.51); Thomas, of Tickle Harbour (now Bellevue), 1817 (Nfld. Archives KCRC); Nancy, of Burin, 1824 (Nfld. Archives BRC); Edward, of New Harbour (Trinity B.), 1826 (Nfld. Archives KCRC); Peter, of King's Cove, 1831 (Nfld. Archives KCRC); Sister Mary Xaverius Lynch, Presentation Sister, from Waterford, of St. John's, 1833 (*Carbonear Star* 2 Oct 1833); Michael, ? of Northern Bay, 1846 (DPHW 54); Thomas, of Bonavista, 1857 (Nfld. Archives KCRC); Joseph, of Cat Harbour (now Lumsden), 1862 (Nfld. Archives KCRC); Edward, of South Dildo, 1866 (Nfld. Archives KCRC); William and Lewis, of Ferryland, 1871 (Lovell); Michael (and others), of Little Placentia (now Argentia), 1871

(Lovell); John, of Spaniard's Bay, 1871 (Lovell); David and Michael, of Western Bay, 1871 (Lovell).

Modern status: Scattered, especially at Upper Island Cove and St. John's.

Place names: Lynch Cove 47-52 55-46; —— Island (Labrador) 53-33 55-56; Lynch's Pond 47-48 53-17.

LYONS, a surname of England and Ireland, Lyon of England and Scotland, "Either from *Lyon*, the popular pronunciation of *Leo* and *Leon*, or a nickname from the lion," or from the French place name Lyons-la-Forêt (Eure), or from an inn sign; in Ireland for *Ó Laighin* in Co. Galway, elsewhere usually Lyne, or for *Ó Liatháin* in Co. Cork, elsewhere Lehane. (Reaney, Cottle, MacLysaght, Black).

Guppy traced Lyon in Lancashire; Spiegelhalter traced Lyon(s) in Devon; and MacLysaght traced Lyons in Cos. Cork and Galway.

In Newfoundland:

Family tradition: Denis (O)Sullivan, from Ireland, settled at Avondale and changed his name to Lyons to escape English persecution, about mid-1800s (MUN Folklore).

Early instances: Martin Lyon, of St. John's, 1779 (DPHW 26D); Timothy Lines, of Lower Bacon Cove (Conception B.), 1788 (CO 199.18); James Lyons, of Harbour Grace Parish, 1807 (Nfld. Archives HGRC); Cornelius, from Ballinclare (unidentified) (Co. Kerry), married at St. John's, 1808 (Nfld. Archives BRC); Mary, of Trepassey, 1815 (Nfld. Archives BRC); Mary, of Carbonear, 1829 (Nfld. Archives BRC); Alice, daughter of James of Waterford, married at St. John's, 1822 (*Nfld. Mercantile Journal* 27 Jun 1822); John, of Petty Harbour, 1835 (Nfld. Archives BRC); William Lyne, from Dorchester, England, married at St. John's, 1839 (Nfld. Archives

BRC); Thomas Lines, fisherman of Long Pond, 1841 (DPHW 39); Richard Lyons, fisherman of The Ponds (Port de Grave district), 1860 (DPHW 38); John Lyon, from Liverpool, of St. John's, deceased 1869 aged 70 (*Morning Chronicle* 16 Oct 1869); Thomas Lyons, of Bareneed, 1871 (Lovell); Edward W. Lyon, agent of Harbour Grace, 1871 (Lovell); Jeremiah Lyons, farmer of Mosquito (now Bristol's Hope), 1871 (Lovell); Dennis, farmer of Salmon Cove and Gasters (now Avondale), 1871 (Lovell).

Modern status: At Argentia, Bell Island (*Electors* 1955), and Avondale.

LYTHCOTT, a surname of England, ? from the English place name Lyd(a)cott (Devon).

In Newfoundland:

Modern status: Rare, at St. John's.

LYTHGOE or Lithgow, a surname of England and Scotland, from the Scots place name Linlithgow (West Lothian), Scots Gaelic from British – wet hollow. (Reaney, Cottle, Black).

Traced by Guppy in Lancashire.

In Newfoundland:

Early instance: Samuel Lythgoe, from Liverpool, England, married at St. John's, 1821 (Nfld. Archives BRC).

Modern status: Rare, at St. John's.

LYVER, a surname, ? of England, of unknown origin.

In Newfoundland:

Early instances: James (and others) Liver, of Waldron's Cove, 1871 (Lovell); Garland (and others) Levier, of Salmon Cove and Gasters (now Avondale), 1871 (Lovell).

Modern status: Scattered.

M

In the following pages, Mac and its abbreviation Mc, meaning son, are treated as if spelt uniformly Mac, the form preferred by MacLysaght and Black.

No attempt has been made to differentiate such variations in the use of lower and upper case as, for example, Macdonald and MacDonald.

McABEE, a surname of Ireland, one of several forms of *Mac an Beatha*, Ir. *bioth*, genitive *beatha* – life. *See* McEVOY, VEY.

In Newfoundland:

Modern status: Unique, at St. John's.

McALLISTER, a surname of Scotland – son of Alexander. *See* ALEXANDER. (Black).

In Newfoundland:

Early instances: Walter Macallister, from Greenock, Scotland, married at St. John's, 1808 (Nfld. Archives BRC); Walter Macallaster, Macallister or McAlaster, of St. John's, 1809 (CO 194. 48, 50, D'Alberti 19); John McAllister, from Isle of Aaron (? Arran, Scotland), married at St. John's, 1823 (DPHW 26D); James McAlister or McCalister, of Harbour Grace Parish, 1835 (Nfld. Archives HGRC).

Modern status: At Deer Lake and St. John's.

MacARTHUR, a surname of Scotland – son of Arthur, a baptismal name of uncertain origin. (Withycombe, Black).

Traced by Guppy in Argyllshire and Stirlingshire.

In Newfoundland:

Early instances: Alexander McArthur, soldier of St. John's, 1844 (DPHW 29); Allen, of Cod Roy and Rivers, 1871 (Lovell).

Modern status: In the St. George's district especially at Doyles (*Electors* 1955) and Corner Brook.

MacASKILL, a surname of Scotland, Gaelic *Mac-Asgaill*, son of Askell, an Old Norse personal name – "the kettle or sacrificial vessel of the gods." *See also* HASKELL. (Reaney, Black).

In Newfoundland:

Modern status: Rare, at St. Anthony (*Electors* 1955); Macaskill, unique, at St. John's.

M(a)cAULEY, surnames of Ireland and Scotland, *Mc Amhalghaidh* or *Mac Amhlaoibh*, both derived from personal names. (MacLysaght, Black).

McAuly traced by MacLysaght in Cos. Westmeath and Fermanagh; Macaulay traced by Guppy in Leicestershire and Rutland.

In Newfoundland:

Early instances: Lochlan McCauley, of St. John's, 1772 (DPHW 26C); Catherine McAuley, ? of St. John's, 1774 (CO 194. 32); Edward Macawley, master in R.C. School, Bonavista, 1810 (CO 194.49); Dr. McCauley, ? of Oderin, 1843 (Frecker).

Modern status: At Winterhouse Brook, Summerside (Electors 1955), and St. John's; McCauley, at Dunville.

McBAY, a surname of Scotland, Gaelic *MacBeatha (Bheatha)*. (Black).

In Newfoundland:

Family tradition: ——, from Linlithgow, Scotland, settled in Newfoundland (MUN Folklore).

Early instances: Michael MacBay, from St. Kerry Parish (Co. Kilkenny), married at St. John's, 1814 (Nfld. Archives BRC); Peter McBey or McBay, of St. John's, 1856 (DPHW 23); Peter McBey, high constable of Carbonear, 1871 (Lovell).

Modern status: At St. John's.

MACBETH, a surname of Scotland and Ireland. Black comments: "A personal name like Macrae, not a patronymic. It was common in Scotland in early times from the eleventh to the fourteenth century. In Old Gaelic it was spelled *Maccbethad*, and means 'son of life,' 'a religious person,' 'man of religion,' or 'one of the elect.'" In Ulster it is confused with MacVeagh and McEVOY. (Black, MacLysaght).

Traced by MacLysaght in Ulster.

In Newfoundland:

Early instances: Adam, of Greenspond, 1821 (DPHW 76); Elizabeth McBath, baptized at Swain's Island, 1830, aged 40 (DPHW 76); Jane McBeth (about 1843–1893), from Paisley, Scotland, deceased 1893, aged 50 (General Protestant Cemetery, St. John's.

Modern status: Unique, at Buchans (*Electors* 1955).

McBURNEY, a surname of Scotland and Ireland, from the Old Norse personal name *Bjarni* – bear. (Black, MacLysaght).

Traced by MacLysaght as a "comparatively recent introduction in Ireland, now numerous in north-east Ulster."

In Newfoundland:

Early instance: John McBarnie or MacBurney, of St. John's, 1787 (DPHW 26C).

Modern status: Rare, at Botwood (*Electors* 1955) and Gander.

McCABE, a surname of Scotland and Ireland, Gaelic *M'Caibe*, Ir. *MacCába*, ? of Norse origin. (Black, MacLysaght).

Traced by Black as widespread in the midland counties of Ireland, especially in Cos. Leitrim, Cavan, Monaghan and Meath.

In Newfoundland:

Family tradition: ——, from Northern Ireland, settled at Clarke's Beach (MUN Folklore).

Early instances: Michael, soldier of St. John's, 1813 (DPHW 26D); James, of Harbour Grace Parish, 1823 (Nfld. Archives HGRC); James, married at St. John's, 1834 (Nfld. Archives HGRC); James, of Port de Grave, 1834 (*Newfoundlander* 23 Jan 1834).

Modern status: At Blackhead (Bay de Verde district), in the Harbour Grace district, at Corner Brook (*Electors* 1955), in the Port de Grave district and at St. John's.

M(a)cCALLUM, surnames of Scotland and Ireland, Gaelic *MacC(h)aluim*, earlier *Mac Gille Chaluim* – son of the devotee of (St.) Columba; in Ireland a variant of Mac Colum, *Mac Coluim*, Ir. *colm* – dove. (Cottle, Black, MacLysaght).

Traced by Guppy in Argyllshire and Perthshire; by MacLysaght, as Mac Colum in Ulster.

In Newfoundland:

Early instances: C. McCallum, of St. John's, 1829 (*Newfoundlander* 5 Mar 1829); Charles, from Manchester, England, married at St. John's, 1831 (DPHW 26D).

Modern status: MacCallum, rare, at St. John's; McCallum, rare, at Corner Brook.

Place names: MacCallum (or Bonne) Bay 47-39 56-13; McCallum 47-38 56-14.

McCANN, a surname of Ireland, *Mac Cana*, Ir. *cano* – wolf cub. (MacLysaght).

Traced by MacLysaght in Co. Armagh.

In Newfoundland:

Family tradition: Neil, from Donegal, Ireland,

settled at Gull Island (North Shore, Conception Bay), about 1787; some of the family later moved to Port-au-Port (MUN Folklore).

Early instances: Catherine McCan, of Harbour Grace Parish, 1818 (Nfld. Archives HGRC); R. McCann, of St. John's, 1831 (*Newfoundlander* 29 Dec 1831); Philip, ? of Northern Bay, 1842 (DPHW 54); John (and others), of Gull Island (Conception B.), 1871 (Lovell); Rosa McKan, of Harbour Grace, 1891 (Nfld. Archives HGRC).

Modern status: At Carbonear, Gull Island (Conception B.), Port-au-Port district and St. John's.

McCARTHY, a surname of Ireland, *Mac Cárthaigh*, Ir. *cárthach* – loving. "The most numerous Mac name in Ireland." (MacLysaght).

Traced by MacLysaght in Cos. Cork and Kerry.

In Newfoundland:

Family traditions: Thomas (–1845), from Co. Cork, Ireland, was one of the first settlers of Red Island (Placentia B.), about 1813 (MUN Hist.). Robert, from Ireland, settled at St. Jacques in the early 1800s (MUN Folklore). Tim, from Co. Kerry, came to Newfoundland about 1820–25; he eventually settled at Terrenceville (MUN Folklore). Patrick (1812–1900), from Ireland, settled at Upper Island Cove in the early 1800s (MUN Geog.).

Early instances: Florence, servant at Salmon Cove (Conception B.), ? 1752 (CO 194.13); Julia McCartre, of St. John's, 1753 (DPHW 26C); Charles McCarthy, in possession of property in fishery at Petty Harbour, 1794-5, "25 years in Newfoundland," that is, 1769–70 (Census 1794-5); John, of Crockers Cove (Carbonear), 1771 (Nfld. Archives L118); William, fisherman of Quidi Vidi, 1794-5, "20 years in Newfoundland," that is, 1774–5 (Census 1794-5); John, ? fisherman of Ship Cove (Port de Grave district), 1779 (Nfld. Archives T22); John McCarty, of Harbour of Quirpon (Island of Jack), 1787 (CO 194.21); Charles McCarthy, from Bally Murphy (Co. Cork), Irish convict landed at Petty Harbour or Bay Bulls, 1789 (CO 194.38); Daniel, of Bay de Verde, 1791 (CO 199.18); Callaghan, of Carbonear, 1792 (CO 199.18); John ? McCarty, of Greenspond, in possession of fishing room at Pond Island, Greenspond Harbour, 1801 (Bonavista Register 1806); Mary McCarthy, from ? Gragew (unidentified) (Co. Carlow), married at St. John's, 1803 (Nfld. Archives BRC); Patrick McCarty, of Bay Bulls, 1803 (Nfld. Archives BRC); Anne McCarthy, from Waterford City, married at Bay Bulls, 1804 (Nfld. Archives BRC); Richard, of Small Point (North Shore, Conception B.), 1804, of Western

Bay, 1806 (CO 199.18); Felix, of Harbour Grace Parish, 1806 (Nfld. Archives HGRC); Mary, of Harbour Grace, 1808 (Nfld. Archives BRC); Thomas, one of 72 impressed men who sailed from Ireland to Newfoundland, ? 1811 (CO 194.51); Charles, of Renews, 1813 (Nfld. Archives BRC); Mary McCarty, of Trepassey, 1815 (Nfld. Archives BRC); Charles McCarthy, of Trinity (unspecified), 1816 (Nfld. Archives KCRC); Michael McCarty, of Joe Batts Arm, 1817 (Nfld. Archives KCRC); Daniel, of Tickle Harbour (now Bellevue), 1817, of Careless (now Kerley's) Harbour, 1821 (Nfld. Archives KCRC); William M'Carthy, from Youghal (Co. Cork), dealer and chapman of St. John's, died 1817 (*Nfld. Mercantile Journal* 18 Apr 1817); Charles McCarthy, from Tallan (unidentified), of Bonavista, 1820 (Nfld. Archives KCRC); John Carty, of Broad Cove (now Duntara), 1821 (Nfld. Archives KCRC); John, of King's Cove, 1825 (Nfld. Archives KCRC); Michael McCarty, of Hearts Desire, 1825 (Nfld. Archives KCRC); Dennis McCarthy, of New Harbour (Trinity B.), 1825 (Nfld. Archives KCRC); Owen, of Hearts Content, 1825 (Nfld. Archives KCRC); John, married on the French Shore, 1839 (Nfld. Archives BRC); Charles, ? of Northern Bay, 1843 (DPHW 54); Charles, of New Perlican, 1847 (*Newfoundlander* 1 Apr 1847); Martin, from Lismore (Co. Waterford), (? of St. John's), died 1847, aged 38 (*Royal Gazette* 29 Jun 1847); Daniel, granted land at Outer Cove (St. John's district), 1848 (Nfld. Archives, Registry Crown Lands); Patrick McCarty, granted land at Chance Cove (near Renews), 1853 (Nfld. Archives, Registry Crown Lands); John McCarthy, of Beau Bois, died 1855, aged 59 (MUN Hist.); Thomas, granted land at Spaniards Bay, 1856 (Nfld. Archives, Registry Crown Lands); William, of Green Bay, died 1857 (*Newfoundlander* 15 Jan 1857); Mary, of Ship Cove (now part of Port Rexton), 1857 (Nfld. Archives KCRC); Allen, of Knight's Cove (Bonavista B.), 1866 (Nfld. Archives KCRC); widespread in Lovell 1871.

Modern status: Widespread, especially at St. John's, Carbonear, Upper Island Cove, Renews, Bellevue, Terrenceville and Woods Island Harbour.

Place name: McCarthys Pond 47-42 53-18.

McCONNELL, a surname of Ireland and Scotland, a variant of MacDONNELL, *Mac Domhnaill* – son of Daniel. *See* DANIELS. (Black, MacLysaght).

Traced by MacLysaght in Cos. Antrim, Down and Tyrone, and by Black in Argyllshire, Ayrshire and Wigtownshire.

In Newfoundland:

Modern status: Rare, at the Goulds (St. John's).

MacCORMAC, M(a)cCORMACK, McCORMICK, surnames of Scotland and Ireland – son of Cormac. *See* CORMACK. (Black, MacLysaght).

MacLysaght found MacCormack "numerous throughout all the provinces, the spelling MacCormick being more usual in Ulster." Black found Maccormick "more common in the Highlands."

In Newfoundland:

Family tradition: Martin McCormack, from Co. Cork, Ireland, settled at St. John's (MUN Folklore).

Early instances: Peter McCormick, soldier of St. John's, 1767 (DPHW 26C); Alex McCormack, of St. John's, 1797 (D'Alberti 6); Patrick McCormick, of Ragged Harbour (now Melrose), 1816 (Nfld. Archives KCRC); Patrick McCormack or McCormick, of Bonavista, 1820 (Nfld. Archives KCRC); Mary McCormic, from Ross (unspecified), married at St. John's, 1830 (Nfld. Archives BRC); Ellen McCormick, of Trinity (unspecified), 1832 (Nfld. Archives KCRC); Thomas, granted land at Snug Cove (near Bonavista), 1850 (Nfld. Archives, Registry Crown Lands); Patrick McCormack, of Tickle Cove (Bonavista B.), 1868 (Nfld. Archives KCRC); John, of Indian Arm (Bonavista B.), 1870 (Nfld. Archives KCRC); Thomas McCormick, of Catalina, 1871 (Lovell); James McCormack, fisherman of Southern Bay (Bonavista B.), 1871 (Lovell).

Modern status: MacCormac, unique, at St. John's; M(a)cCormack, scattered, especially at St. John's; McCormick, rare, at St. John's and Placentia.

Place name: McCormick (or McCornick) River 59-00 63-45.

McCOUBREY, a surname of Scotland, *Mac Cuithbreith* – son of Cuthbert, a common Old English personal name containing the elements *cuth* – famous, *beorht* – bright. (Withycombe, Black).

In Newfoundland:

Family tradition: Andrew, from Ballynahinch near Belfast, Ireland, came to St. John's as King's Printer in the early 1800s (MUN Folklore).

Early instance: Andrew, of St. John's, 1816 (CO 194.66).

Modern status: Rare, at St. John's.

McCOURT, a surname of Ireland and Scotland, *Mac Cuarta* or *Mac Cuairt*. (MacLysaght, Black).

Traced by MacLysaght in Cos. Louth and Armagh, and by Black at Ballantrae (Ayrshire).

In Newfoundland:

Early instance: Philip and Philip, traders of St. John's, 1871 (Lovell).

Modern status: Rare, at St. John's (*Electors* 1955)

McCRAE, McRAE, variants of the surname of Scotland and Ireland Macrae, a personal name like Macbeth, not a patronymic, Gaelic *Macrath* – son of grace or prosperity. (Black, MacLysaght). *See also* McCRATE, McCROWE, McGRATH.

Traced by Guppy in Inverness-shire and the Hebrides, by Black in Ayrshire, and by MacLysaght in Ulster.

In Newfoundland:

Early instances: William McRay, soldier of St. John's, 1778 (DPHW 26C); Patrick McRae, fisherman of Black River (Placentia B.), 1871 (Lovell); Roderick, clerk of Harbour Grace, 1871 (Lovell); Ellen McCray or McCrae, of Harbour Grace Parish, 1884 (Nfld. Archives HGRC).

Modern status: McCrae, rare, at St. John's (*Electors* 1955); McRae, rare, at Harbour Grace (*Electors* 1955) and St. John's.

McCRATE, ? a variant of MacCraith, a form of McCRAE.

In Newfoundland:

Early instances: Thomas McGrate, of Harbour Grace Parish, 1832 (Nfld. Archives HGRC); James (and others) McCrate, fishermen of Salmonier (St. Mary's), 1871 (Lovell).

Modern status: McCrate, rare, at St. John's; McCrate, McRate, rare, at Mount Carmel.

McCRINDLE, a surname of Scotland, a variant of MacRanald, Gaelic *Macraonuill* – son of *Ranull*. (Black).

Traced by Black in Ayrshire and Galloway.

In Newfoundland:

Modern status: At St. John's.

McCROWE, a surname of Scotland and ? of Ireland, a variant of Macrae. *See* McCRAE. (Black). *See also* CROWE.

In Newfoundland:

Modern status: At Oderin (*Electors* 1955), Placentia and St. John's.

McCRUDDEN, a surname of Ireland and Scotland, *MacRodáin*, Ir. *rod* – strong, spirited. (MacLysaght, Black).

Traced by MacLysaght in Co. Donegal and by Black in Glasgow.

In Newfoundland:

Early instance: John McCruden, policeman of St. John's, 1871 (Lovell).

Modern status: Rare, at St. John's (*Electors* 1955).

McCUE, a surname of Ireland, formerly MacCoo, a form of MacHUGH, *Mac Aodha* – son of Hugh. (MacLysaght). *See* McHUGH, MACKAY.

Traced by MacLysaght especially in Co. Fermanagh.

In Newfoundland:

Family tradition: Michael, from Ireland, settled at Fox Harbour (Placentia B.), before 1857 (MUN Folklore, MUN Hist.).

Early instances: Charles McKue, of Turks Gut (now Marysvale), 1805 (CO 199.18); John McCue, of Harbour Grace Parish, 1821 (Nfld. Archives HGRC); Thomas McCue, ? of Oderin, 1834 (Frecker); Philip and Thomas, fishermen of Little Placentia (now Argentia), 1871 (Lovell); Maurice, fisherman of Oliver's Cove (Placentia B.), 1871 (Lovell).

Modern status: Scattered, especially at Fox Harbour (Placentia B.).

McCURDY, a surname of Scotland and Ireland, *Mac Muircheartaigh*, Gaelic *muircheartach* – sea-ruler, sea-director. (Black, MacLysaght).

Traced by Black on the islands of Arran and Bute, and by MacLysaght in Co. Antrim.

In Newfoundland:

Early instances: John Macurdy, surgeon of St. John's, 1787, 89 (DPHW 26D, CO 194.38); Simon Micurty, of Harbour Grace Parish, 1842 (Nfld. Archives HGRC).

Modern status: Rare, at St. John's.

McDERMOTT, a surname of Ireland, with several variants in Scotland, Mac Dermot, *Mac Diarmada* – son of the unenvious one. (MacLysaght, Black).

Traced by MacLysaght in Cos. Galway and Roscommon.

In Newfoundland:

Early instances: Thomas McDermot, from Edgerstown (Co. Longford), Irish convict landed at Petty Harbour or Bay Bulls, 1789 (CO 194.38); Patrick McDermott, of Harbour Grace Parish, 1827 (Nfld. Archives HGRC); Michael McDermot, from Roscommon, married at St. John's, 1839 (Nfld. Archives BRC).

Modern status: At West Point (Burgeo-La Poile district) (*Electors* 1955).

M(a)cDONALD, surnames of Scotland and Ireland and of the Micmacs of Newfoundland, *Mac Dhomhnuill* – son of Donald, from primitive Celtic *Dubno-walos* containing the elements *world* and *mighty*, in Old Irish *Domnall*, in Gaelic *Domhnall*.

Black comments: "Properly speaking there is no such surname as Macdonald. *MacDhomhnuill* means 'son of (a particular) Donald': all others of the name are simply *Domhnullach*, 'one of the Donalds.'" But, as Cottle remarks, "be that as it may, it was the second commonest surname (after SMITH) in Scotland in 1858, dropping to third (after SMITH and BROWN) by 1958 ..." In Ireland, sometimes a synonym of the Irish MacDONNELL. (Withycombe, Black, Cottle, MacLysaght). *See* O'DONALD.

Traced by Guppy in Inverness-shire.

In Newfoundland:

Family traditions: Philip McDonald, from Ireland, was the first settler of Penny's Point, Salmonier, about 1850 (MUN Geog.). Michael and Francis, from Waterford, settled at Salmonier, St. Mary's Bay, between 1850–60 (MUN Folklore). James, from England, settled at Gaultois in the late 1600s (MUN Folklore). Patrick, from Waterford, settled at Kilbride about 1825 (MUN Folklore). Mary MacDonald (–1880), from Catalina, married and settled at Topsail (MUN Geog.).

Early instances: Paul McDonald, accused of robbery and murder of William Keen, St. John's, 1753 (CO 194.13); Ronald or George MacDonald, of Harbour Main, 1755 (MUN Hist.); James McDonald, of Western Bay, 1771 (CO 199.18); Laurence, fisherman of Quidi Vidi, 1794-5, "14 years in Newfoundland," that is, 1780–1 (Census 1794–5); ——, of Bay de Verde, 1789 (CO 199.18); Bartholomew, of Trinity Bay, 1795 (DPHW 64); John, planter of Tilton Harbour (now Tilting), ? 1797 (CO 194.39); William, from Fahy Parish (unidentified) (Co. Waterford), married at St. John's, 1808 (Nfld. Archives BRC); John, of Cats Cove (now Conception Harbour), 1816 (D'Alberti 26); William MacDonald, from Belfast, married at St. John's, 1821 (DPHW 26D); Thomas McDonald, of Ragged Harbour (now Melrose), 1824 (Nfld. Archives KCRC); Ann, of Harbour Grace, died 1830, aged 27 (*Newfoundlander* 3 Jun 1830); James MacDonald, of Furby's Cove, 1835 (DPHW 30); William McDonald, ? of Northern Bay, 1843 (DPHW 54); Robert, navigator of Trinity (Trinity B.), 1844 (DPHW 64B); James, fisherman of Dragon (Fortune B.), 1854 (DPHW 102); Henry MacDonald, of Ramea, 1855 (DPHW 101); George McDonald, of Burnt Island (Bonavista B.), 1857 (Nfld. Archives KCRC); Michael, of Outer Cove, 1858 (*Newfoundlander* 1 Apr 1858); Ann, of Bloody Bay (Bonavista B.), 1869 (Nfld. Archives KCRC); widespread in Lovell 1871; John Sr. and Jr., and James, Micmac Indians of Conne River, about 1872 (MacGregor).

Modern status: Widespread, especially at St. John's, St. Albans, Norris Arm and Colliers.

Place names: Macdonald Cove 47-15 53-56; MacDonald Falls (Labrador) 54-58 60-22; McDonald (or Mugford) Bay (Labrador) 57-48 62-02; —— Shoal 50-50 57-08.

MacDONNELL, a surname of Scotland and Ireland, a variant of either MacDONALD or McCONNELL. (Black, MacLysaght).

Traced by MacLysaght in Cos. Antrim, Clare and Fermanagh.

In Newfoundland:

Early instances: Elizabeth MacDonnel, of St. John's, 1778 (DPHW 26C); John McDonnell, from Clonmel (Co. Tipperary), married at St. John's, 1800 (Nfld. Archives BRC); Bridget McDonnel, of Trinity (unspecified), 1803 (Nfld. Archives BRC); Patrick MacDonell, of Harbour Grace Parish, 1807 (Nfld. Archives HGRC); Ellen McDonnell, of Torbay, 1817 (Nfld. Archives BRC); Catherine, of Ragged Harbour (now Melrose), 1829 (Nfld. Archives KCRC); Betsy McDonnal or McDonald, of Broad Cove (now Duntara), 1831 (Nfld. Archives KCRC); George McDonnell, of Greenspond, 1829 (Nfld. Archives KCRC); Matthew, of Ferryland, married at Fortune Harbour, 1831 (Nfld. Archives KCRC); Margaret, of Herring Neck, 1833 (Nfld. Archives KCRC); Thomas, of Upper Burgeo, 1843 (DPHW 101); John, of Burnt Island (Bonavista B.), 1857 (Nfld. Archives KCRC); Elizabeth, of Tickle Cove (Bonavista B.), 1863 (Nfld. Archives KCRC); Margaret, of Open Hall, 1865 (Nfld. Archives KCRC); Jacob, of Harbour Grace, 1866 (Nfld. Archives HGRC); Thomas, farmer of Flat Rock (St. John's district), 1871 (Lovell); Patrick and William, farmers of Outer Cove (St. John's district), 1871 (Lovell); Richard MacDonnell, dealer of Harbour Main, 1871 (Lovell).

Modern status: Rare, at St. George's (*Electors* 1955).

M(a)cDOUGAL(L), surnames of Scotland with several variants, *Mac Dhúghaill* – son of Dougal, from "Old Irish *dubhgall* 'black stranger,' a name originally given by the Irish to the Norwegians, which later became a common christian name. It is now chiefly used in the Highlands of Scotland. The word *dubhgall* is still used in Irish and Gaelic to indicate an Englishman and in Modern Breton for a Frenchman." (Withycombe).

Traced by Guppy in Argyllshire.

In Newfoundland:

Early instances: Archibald McDougal, of St. John's, 1813 (DPHW 26B); Thomas McDuggle, of Tickle Cove (Bonavista B.), 1862 (Nfld. Archives KCRC); Laughlin McDougall, fisherman of Cape Ray, 1871 (Lovell); ——, farmer of Topsail, 1871 (Lovell); Angus and John McDougal, of Cod Roy and Rivers, 1871 (Lovell); Michael MacDougall, farmer of Colliers, 1871 (Lovell).

Modern status: MacDougall, at Gander and St. John's; McDougal, at McDougall's Gulch (St. George's district) (*Electors* 1955) and Stephenville Crossing; McDougall, at St. John's and Burin.

M(a)cEACHERN, surnames of Scotland, *MacEachthigh-earna* – son of the horse-lord.

In Newfoundland:

Early instance: Angus McEachin, fisherman of Bonavista, 1871 (Lovell).

Modern status: MacEachern, at Campbells Creek, Highlands (*Electors* 1955), and Port au Port; McEachern, at St. John's (*Electors* 1955), Stephenville and Jeffrey's.

McEVOY, a surname of Ireland, *Mac Fhíodhbhuidhe*, probably from Ir. *fíodhbhadhach* – woodman, or for MacElwee, *Mac Giolla Bhuidhe*, Ir. *buidhe* – yellow, *giolla* – fellow, youth. (MacLysaght). *See also* McABEE, VEY.

Traced by MacLysaght in Co. Leix.

In Newfoundland:

Family tradition: ——, from Co. Kerry, Ireland, settled at St. Jacques (Fortune B.) (MUN Folklore).

Early instances: Michael, ? labourer of St. John's, 1779 (CO 194.34); Paul Macaboy, from Ross Parish (unspecified), married at St. John's, 1800 (Nfld. Archives BRC); Bridget McEvoy, of Broad Cove (now Duntara), 1889 (Nfld. Archives KCRC).

Modern status: At Deer Lake, Regina, St. Jacques (*Electors* 1955), and St. John's.

MacEWAN, MacEWEN, surnames of Scotland and Ireland, *MacEoghain(n)* – son of Ewen, Gaelic *Eòghann*, Old Irish *Eogán* – well-born. (Black, MacLysaght).

Guppy traced MacEwan, MacEwen in Perthshire.

In Newfoundland:

Modern status: MacEwan, McEwen, unique, at St. John's.

MACEY, a surname of England, and as Mace, Mass(e)y etc. of Guernsey (Channel Islands), a pet-form of the baptismal name Matthew, or from various place names in France, Macey (La Manche),

Massy (Seine-Inférieure), Macé-sur-Orne, La Forté Macé (Orne). (Reaney, Turk).

Spiegelhalter traced Macey, Mace, Massey in Devon; Guppy traced Mace in Gloucestershire and Oxfordshire, Massey in Cheshire, Derbyshire, Lancashire, Shropshire and Staffordshire.

In Newfoundland:

Early instances: James, of Battle Harbour (Labrador), 1795 (MUN Hist.); Ann, occupier of fishing room at Scilly Cove (now Winterton), Winter 1800–01 (Census Trinity B.); Edward Macey, of Shoe Cove (Twillingate district), 1846 (DPHW 86); J., of St. Mein Bay (now St. Anthony Bight), 1849 (Feild); Thomas, clerk of Harbour Grace, 1871 (Lovell).

Modern status: At St. John's (*Electors* 1955), Woods Island Harbour and Green Island Brook.

Place names: Macy Island (Labrador) 52-56 55-50; —— Tickle (Labrador) 52-55 5S-51.

M(a)cFARLANE, a surname of Scotland, MacFarland of Scotland and Ireland, variants, with others, of MacParlan, Gaelic *MacPharlain*, from Old Irish *Partholon*, containing the elements *sea* and *waves*, *billows*, but erroneously confused with the baptismal name Bartholomew. (Black).

Guppy traced McFarlane in Stirlingshire and Ayrshire; MacLysaght traced MacFarland in Cos. Tyrone and Armagh.

In Newfoundland:

Early instances: James Thomas McFarlane, of St. John's, 1834 (DPHW 23); Peter MacFarlene, passenger on the *Atlantic* wrecked at Pouch Cove, 1840 (*Newfoundlander* 14 May 1840); William McFarlane, fisherman of Ram's Islands, 1871 (Lovell); Charles, fisherman of Trinity (Trinity B.), 1871 (Lovell).

Modern status: MacFarlane, rare, at St. John's; McFarlane, at Port Royal (*Electors* 1955), Freshwater (Placentia B.), St. John's and Grand Falls.

Place name: Macfarlane (Bank) (Labrador) 53-47 56-35.

McFATRIDGE, a Nova Scotian and Irish variant of the surname of Scotland MacFetridge, Gaelic *MacPhetruis, MacPheadruis* – son of Peter. (Black, MacLysaght).

MacLysaght traced MacFettridge in Co. Antrim.

In Newfoundland:

Early instance: James, of Sandy Point (St. George's B.), 1870 (DPHW 96).

Modern status: At Sandy Point (St. George's B.), St. Davids (*Electors* 1955), Stephenville, Stephenville Crossing and Freshwater (Placentia B.).

McGEE, a surname of Ireland and Scotland, *Mao Aoidh* – son of *Aodh* (Hugh), and so the same as MACKAY, McKIE, Mackie. The name is usually spelt Magee in east Ulster. (Black, MacLysaght).

Traced by MacLysaght in Cos. Antrim and West-meath.

In Newfoundland:

Early instances: John, of Placentia, 1713–20 (CO 194.7); John Magee, of St. John's, 1768 (DPHW 26C); Nicholas, of Harbour Grace Parish, 1807 (Nfld. Archives HGRC); Mary McGee, of Ferryland, 1823 (Nfld. Archives BRC); Michael Magee, ? of Harbour Grace, 1845 (*Newfoundlander* 9 Jan 1845); John McGhee, granted land at Cats Cove (now Conception Harbour), 1857 (Nfld. Archives, Registry Crown Lands); John, granted land at Salmon Cove (unspecified), 1857 (Nfld. Archives, Registry Crown Lands); George Magee, of Bonne Bay, 1871 (Lovell); John (and others), farmers of Salmon Cove and Gasters, 1871 (Lovell); Thomas McGee, farmer of Gastus (Conception B.), 1871 (Lovell); Francis, fisherman of Cod Roy and Rivers, 1871 (Lovell).

Modern status: At Avondale and Placentia.

McGETTIGAN, a surname of Ireland, also Mac Ettigan, *Mag Eiteagáin*. (MacLysaght).

Traced by MacLysaght mainly in Co. Donegal.

In Newfoundland:

Modern status: At St. Mary's, Gander (*Electors* 1955), and St. John's.

MacGIBBON, a surname of Scotland and Ireland; in Scotland, – son of Gibbon, a double diminutive of Gilbert (*see* GILBERT); in Ireland a variant of Mac-Kibben or MacKibbin, *Mag Fhibín* – son of (little) Philip. (Black, MacLysaght).

In Newfoundland:

Early instance: John McGibbon, of St. John's, 1821 (CO 194.64).

Modern status: Rare, at Corner Brook.

McGILL. *See* MAGILL

MacGILLIVARY, MacGILLIVRAY, variants of a surname of Scotland which occurs in several forms, Gaelic *Mac Gille-bhrath* – son of the servant of judgement. (Black).

Traced by Black as "an old Argyllshire clan or sept."

In Newfoundland:

Early instances: William McGillivary, from Glasgow, married at St. John's, 1842 (DPHW 26D); Thomas McGilvray, cooper of St. John's, 1871 (Lovell).

Modern status: MacGillivary, at Topsail (*Electors* 1955) and St. John's; MacGillivray, at St. George's (*Electors* 1955), Corner Brook and St. John's.

McGINN, a surname of Ireland, *Mag Fhinn*, Ir. *fionn* – fair. (MacLysaght).

MacLysaght traced MacGing in Cos. Mayo and Antrim, MacGinn in Co. Tyrone and Maginn in Cos. Antrim and Down.

In Newfoundland:

Early instance: John, police constable of St. John's, 1825 (D'Alberti 35).

Modern status: At Sunnyside (Twillingate district) (*Electors* 1955), Pilley's Island, Corner Brook and St. John's.

McGORY, McGRORY, surnames of Scotland and Ireland, *Mac Ruaidhrí*. (MacLysaght, Black).

Traced by MacLysaght in Cos. Tyrone and Derry.

In Newfoundland:

Modern status: McGory, at St. John's; McGrory, at Old Petty Harbour Road (St. John's).

McGOWAN, a surname of Ireland and Scotland, Ir. *Mac an Ghabhann, Mac Gabhann*, Gaelic *Mac a'ghobhainn, MacGhobhainn* – son of the smith. (MacLysaght, Black).

Traced by MacLysaght in Co. Cavan and by Black in Stirling.

In Newfoundland:

Family tradition: ——, of the Elliston area, in the early 1880s (MUN Hist.).

Modern status: Unique, at Buchans (*Electors* 1955).

McGRATH, a surname of Ireland *Mac Graith*, the Irish equivalent of the surname of Scotland McCRAE. (MacLysaght).

Traced by MacLysaght in Cos. Clare, Donegal, Fermanagh and Waterford.

In Newfoundland:

Family traditions: Bartley, from Ireland, settled at Devil's (now Patrick's) Cove, before 1810 (Mannion). ——, from Carrick-on-Suir (Co. Waterford), settled at Little Placentia (now Argentia) in 1799 (MUN Folklore). Tobias (1765–1841), of Tilton Harbour (now Tilting) (Green).

Early instances: Thomas, servant at Salmon Cove (Conception B.), ? 1752 (CO 194.13); Phillip Mckgra, fisherman of Trinity (Trinity B.), 1757 (DPHW 64); James McGrath, fisherman of St. John's, 1794–5, "30 years in Newfoundland," that is, 1764–5 (Census 1794–5); John, cooper of Torbay,

1794–5, "12 years in Newfoundland," that is, 1782–3 (Census 1794–5); Jer. Magrath, of Placentia, 1794 (D'Alberti 5); Roger McGrath, shoreman of Battle Harbour (Labrador), 1795 (MUN Hist.); Dennis, of Harbour Grace, 1796 (CO 199.18); John, of Mosquito (now Bristols Hope), 1796 (CO 199.18); William, deserter of Burin, 1802 (D'Alberti 12); Toby, of Fogo Island, 1805 (D'Alberti 15); Catherine Magrath, from Shanren (unidentified) (Co. Kilkenny), married at St. John's, 1808 (Nfld. Archives BRC); Roger, one of 72 impressed men who sailed from Ireland to Newfoundland, ? 1811 (CO 194.51); Tobias McGrath, of Tilton Harbour (now Tilting), 1815 (Nfld. Archives KCRC); Michael, from Limerick, shipwright of St. John's, died 1816 (*Royal Gazette* 31 Dec 1816); William, of Ragged Harbour (now Melrose), 1819 (Nfld. Archives KCRC); Thomas, from Co. Waterford, of Kings Cove, 1819 (Nfld. Archives KCRC); George, of "Gransway on the French Shore," 1822 (Nfld. Archives BRC); John, planter of Old Bonaventure, 1827 (DPHW 64B); John, of Catalina, 1829 (Nfld. Archives KCRC); John Magrath, of Perry's Cove, 1829 (Nfld. Archives BRC); Thomas McGrath, granted land at White Hills (St. John's), 1848 (Nfld. Archives, Registry Crown Lands); James, granted land at Little Placentia (now Argentia), 1856 (Nfld. Archives, Registry Crown Lands); Philip, fisherman of Delby's Cove (Trinity North district), 1857, of Riders Harbour, 1859 (DPHW 63, 64B); T., of Placentia Bay, 1858 (*Newfoundlander* 1 Apr 1858); Thomas, of Round Cove (Bonavista B.), 1866 (Nfld. Archives KCRC); James, of Keels, 1867 (Nfld. Archives KCRC); Mary Anne, of (Little) Hearts Ease, 1870 (Nfld. Archives KCRC); widespread in Lovell 1871.

Modern status: Widespread, especially at St. John's, Tilting, Torbay, Patrick's Cove and Colliers.

Place names: Magrath Cove 47-40 55-22; McGrath Lake (Labrador) 54-56 60-14; —— Pond 47-19 53-20; McGraths Cove 48-10 53-50.

McGUIRE, a surname of Ireland and Scotland, *Mag Uidhir*, Ir. *odhar*, genitive *uidhir* – dun-coloured, hence son of the pale (-faced) man. (MacLysaght, Black).

Traced by MacLysaght in Co. Fermanagh and by Black in Ayrshire.

In Newfoundland:

Early instances: John, of St. John's, 1787 (DPHW 26C); James, from Truhousewater (Co. Fermanagh), Irish convict landed at Petty Harbour or Bay Bulls, 1789 (CO 194.38); James Maguire, labourer from Iniskilling (for Enniskillen) (Co. Fermanagh), put

ashore as a convict at Bay Bulls, 1789 (CO 194.41); Patrick McGuire, of Musketta (now Bristol's Hope), 1805 (CO 199.18); Patrick Maguire, of Harbour Grace Parish, 1815 (Nfld. Archives HGRC); Luke McGuire, from Co. Kilkenny, married at St. John's, 1817 (Nfld. Archives BRC); John Meguire, of Torbay, 1835 (Nfld. Archives BRC); Michael McGuire, ? of Northern Bay, 1841 (DPHW 54); Thomas MacGuire, granted land at Cupids, 1847 (Nfld. Archives, Registry Crown Lands); John McGuire, fisherman of Bay Roberts, 1852 (DPHW 39); Jacob Maguire, of Harbour Grace, 1869 (Nfld. Archives HGRC); Thomas McGuire, of Salmonier (St. Mary's B.), 1871 (Lovell); James and Martin Maguire, fishermen of Torbay, 1871 (Lovell); Michael, fisherman of Western Bay, 1871 (Lovell).

Modern status: At Carbonear, Gander, Lower Goulds, Port Saunders (*Electors* 1955), and St. John's.

McGURK, a surname of Ireland and Scotland, *Mag Oirc*. (MacLysaght, Black).

Traced by MacLysaght in Cos. Tyrone and Antrim.

In Newfoundland:

Modern status: At Carbonear.

McHUGH, a surname of Ireland and Scotland, *Mac Aodha*. *See* McCUE. (MacLysaght, Black).

Traced by MacLysaght in north Connacht and west Ulster, and by Black in Edinburgh "probably of Irish origin."

In Newfoundland:

Early instances: Charles, fisherman of St. John's, 1794–5, "12 years in Newfoundland," that is, 1782–3 (Census 1794–5); Charles, of Harbour Grace Parish, 1810 (Nfld. Archives HGRC); John McHugo, farmer of Chapel's Cove, 1871 (Lovell); Charles (and others) McKew and James McQue, of Turks Gut (now Marysvale), 1871 (Lovell).

Modern status: Scattered, including Marysvale.

M(a)cINNIS, surnames of Scotland and Ireland, *Mac Aonghuis* – son of Angus. "The Scottish form of MacGuinness." (MacLysaght).

In Newfoundland:

Early instance: Daniel McInnis, soldier of St. John's, 1812 (DPHW 26B).

Modern status: MacInnis, at Highlands (*Electors* 1955), O'Regans and St. John's; McInnis, rare, at Grand Falls.

McINTOSH, a surname of Scotland, Gaelic *Mac an toisich* – son of the leader. (Black).

Traced by Guppy in Inverness-shire and Perth-shire.

In Newfoundland:

Early instance: Lucy MacIntosh, married at St. John's, 1834 (DPHW 26D).

Modern status: At Stephenville Crossing and Corner Brook.

McINTYRE, a surname of Scotland, Gaelic *Mac an t-saoir* – son of the carpenter, wright or craftsman; in Ireland often substituted for MacAteer of similar derivation. (Black, MacLysaght).

Traced by Guppy in Argyllshire and by MacLysaght in Ulster.

In Newfoundland:

Early instances: Richard Mackintire, married at St. John's, 1793 (DPHW 26D); William Machintire, of Harbour Grace Parish, 1816 (Nfld. Archives HGRC); James McIntyre, from Pictou (Nova Scotia), married at St. John's, 1847 (*Newfoundlander* 28 Oct 1847); James (1844–), from Saltcoats, Ayrshire came to St. John's initially in 1869, settled there in 1883 (Mott).

Modern status: Rare, at Curling and St. John's.

Place name: McIntyre Bay (Labrador) 54-41 66-21.

M(a)cISAAC, surnames of Scotland, Gaelic *Mac Isaac* or *Mac Iosaig* – son of Isaac. *See* ISAACS.

In Newfoundland:

Early instances: Dougal McIsaac, of Sandy Point (St. George's B.), 1870, of Kippens, 1871 (DPHW 95, 96); Alexander (and others), of Cod Roy and Rivers, 1871 (Lovell).

Modern status: Scattered in the west coast districts; McIsaac, especially at Port au Port; MacIsaac, especially at St. Andrews.

Place name: McIsaacs Brook 49-20 57-00.

MACKAY, M(a)cKAY, MACKEY, McKIE, surnames of Scotland, MacKay, (Mac)Kee, (O)MacKey of Ireland; Gaelic *Mac Aoidh* – son of *Aed(h)*, later *Aodh*, a Gaelic name meaning 'fire,' but (O)MacKey in Ireland, *Ó Macdha*. According to Black, "In the later Middle Ages, it was mistakenly equated with Teutonic Hugh or Hugo." *See* McCUE, McKIE. (Black, MacLysaght).

Guppy traced McKay and Mackay in the northern counties of Scotland, especially Caithness, and McKie and Mackie in Ayrshire and Aberdeenshire. MacLysaght traced MacKay, MacKee in Ulster, Kee in Co. Donegal, and (O)MacKey in Co. Tipperary.

In Newfoundland:

Family traditions: —— McKay (1860–), born on Cape Breton Island, of Scots descent, but recently of Boston, USA, moved to western Newfoundland and founded the settlement of McKays (MUN Folklore). —— MacKay or Mackey, from Kilkenny, Ireland, settled at Bar Haven (Placentia B.), in the 17th century; some of the family later moved to Grand Falls (MUN Folklore).

Early instances: John McKay, soldier of St. John's, 1780 (DPHW 26C); Edward Mackey, of Chapels Cove, 1785 (CO 199. 18); Mary, of Bricas (for Brigus) (unspecified), 1801 (Nfld. Archives BRC); Thomas, from Faha, Waterford City, married at Bonavista, 1803 (Nfld. Archives BRC); Mary, from Inistioge (Co. Kilkenny), married at St. John's, 1806 (Nfld. Archives BRC); Michael, of Harbour Grace Parish, 1806 (Nfld. Archives HGRC); Patrick MacKey, from Featherd (Co. Tipperary), of Mobile, died 1817 (*Royal Gazette* 3 Jun 1817); Mary Mackay or Macky, married at Ragged Harbour (now Melrose), 1818 (Nfld. Archives KCRC); Nicholas McKee, of Carbonear, 1820 (D'Alberti 30); Elenor Mackey, of Catalina, 1823 (Nfld. Archives KCRC); William, of Ferryland, 1823 (Nfld. Archives BRC); Michael, of Hearts Content, 1825 (Nfld. Archives KCRC); Bridget, of Brigus-by-South, 1828 (Nfld. Archives BRC); Mary, of Hants Harbour, 1828 (Nfld. Archives BRC); ——, of Mackey and McCarthy, Carbonear, 1830 (*Newfoundlander* 2 Dec 1830); Richard, janitor of Harbour Grace Chapel, 1831 (Nfld. Archives HGRC); George, of Hearts Desire, 1832 (Nfld. Archives KCRC); James, of Trinity, 1832 (Nfld. Archives KCRC); William Mackey or Mackay, ? of Northern Bay, 1840 (DPHW 54); Richard Mackay, member of Board of Road Commissioners for Barren Island (now Bar Haven), 1844 (*Nfld. Almanac*); Daniel, member of Board of Road Commissioners for Burin, 1844 (*Nfld. Almanac*); Richard Mackey, member of R.C. Board of Education, Brigus, 1844 (*Nfld. Almanac*); John McKay, of Grand Bank, 1849 (MUN Hist.); Edward Mack(e)y, of Shoe Cove (Twillingate district), 1849, of Tilt Cove (Twillingate district), 1854 (DPHW 86); John Mackey, of Sholes [sic] Cove (Bonavista B.), 1855 (Nfld. Archives KCRC); Edward, of Cotterels Island (Bonavista B.), 1856 (Nfld. Archives KCRC); Anastasia, of Hayward's Cove (Bonavista B.), 1859 (Nfld. Archives KCRC); Mary Mackey or Muckey, of Beaver Cove (Twillingate district), 1860 (DPHW 87); John Mackey, of Dog Cove (Bonavista B.), 1861 (Nfld. Archives KCRC); Bridget, of Gooseberry Island (Bonavista B.), 1863 (Nfld. Archives KCRC); Richard Maky, of Harbour Grace, 1869 (Nfld.

Archives HGRC); Peter McKay, of Middle Barachoix (St. George's district), 1870 (DPHW 96); John, of Pacquet, 1871 (Lovell); John, of Renews to Cape Race area, 1871 (Lovell); Samuel, trader of Sandy Point (St. George's district), 1871 (Lovell); Edward and Thomas Mackay, of Shoal Cove (Bonavista B.), 1871 (Lovell); William Mackay, of Bay de Verde, 1871 (Lovell).

Modern status: MacKay, Mackay, rare, at Heart's Content (*Electors* 1955), and St. John's; McKay, scattered; Mackey, scattered, especially at Melrose and St. Brendans.

Place names: McKay Island 47-51 53-56, 49-11 53-33; —— Lake (Labrador) 53-44 65-37; Mount —— (Labrador) 53-42 57-03; —— River (Labrador) 53-41 65-21; McKays 48-14 58-49.

McKENNA, a surname of Ireland and Scotland, Ir. *Mac Cionaoith*, Gaelic *Mac Cionaodha*. (MacLysaght, Black).

Traced by MacLysaght in Co. Monaghan and also in Leinster and Munster, with the last syllable stressed in Cos. Clare and Kerry, and by Black in Glasgow.

In Newfoundland:

Early instances: Johanna McKinna, of Harbour Grace Parish, 1831 (Nfld. Archives HGRC); Rev. James, from Waterford, of St. John's, 1833 (*Carbonear Star* 2 Oct 1833); John McKinna or McKenna, of Harbour Grace, 1868 (Nfld. Archives HGRC); S.T. and William McKenney, of St. John's, 1871 (Lovell).

Modern status: At Island Harbour (Fogo district) (*Electors* 1955), Tilting and Badger.

M(a)cKENZIE, surnames of Scotland and Ireland, Gaelic *MacCoinnich* or *MacC(h)oinnich*, containing the element *cann* – fair, bright. (Black).

Traced by Guppy in Ross-shire and Invernessshire.

In Newfoundland:

Family tradition: Hugh MacKenzie, from Scotland, settled in Bonne Bay, at a place he named Glenburn (now Glenburnie), about 1870 (MUN Hist.).

Early instances: Dugale Karr McKenzie, soldier of St. John's, 1779 (DPHW 26C); Duncan MacKenzie, of Humber Sound, ? 1839 (DPHW 96); Alexander McKenzie, passenger on the *Atlantic*, wrecked at Pouch Cove, 1840 (*Newfoundlander* 14 May 1840); John, from Nova Scotia, married at St. John's, 1848 (*Royal Gazette* 11 Apr 1848); T., painter, married at Carbonear, 1852 (*Newfoundlander* 12 Aug 1852); Francis, of Harbour Grace, 1866 (Nfld. Archives

HGRC); Alexander, doctor of Rose Blanche, 1871 (Lovell); Henry Mackenzie, telegraph operator of Heart's Content, 1871 (Lovell); Daniel, of Plate Cove, 1872 (Nfld. Archives KCRC); William McKenzie, of Bay of Islands area, 1877 (DPHW 96).

Modern status: MacKenzie, at Grand Falls and St. John's; McKenzie, at Glenburnie, Neddy's Harbour (*Electors* 1955), Norris Point and St. John's.

Place names: Mackenzie Lake (Labrador) 54-05 63-30; McKenzie River (Labrador) 53-15 60-45, 54-10 65-09; McKenzies Brook 49-26 57-53.

MACKEY. *See* MACKAY

McKIE. *See* MACKAY

In Newfoundland:

Early instances: Peter, from Wigtown, North Britain, of St. John's, 1787, died at St. John's, 1836, aged 88 (*Times* 13 Apr 1836, DPHW 26C); John, from Scotland, married at St. John's, 1812 (Nfld. Archives BRC); ——, magistrate of Bay Bulls district, 1812 (D'Alberti 22); John L., doctor, J.P. of Bay Bulls, 1817 (CO 194.60).

Modern status: Rare, at Gander (*Electors* 1955) and St. John's.

McKIM, a surname of Scotland, *MacShim* – son of Sim(on). *See* SIMON. (Black, Cottle).

In Newfoundland:

Early instance: Robert A. MacKim, marble cutter of St. John's, 1871 (Lovell).

Modern status: Rare, at St. John's.

McKINLAY, McKINLEY, surnames of Scotland and Ireland, the Gaelic form of the surname Finlayson (*see* FINLAY); also in Ireland for Mac Alee, *Mac an Leagha*. (Black, MacLysaght).

Traced by MacLysaght in Ulster.

In Newfoundland:

Early instances: Laurence McKinnally, from Johnstown (unspecified), married at St. John's, 1829 (Nfld. Archives BRC); John McKinlay, of St. John's, 1849 (General Protestant Cemetery, St. John's); Alexander Anderson McKinley (1862–1923), from Glasgow, Scotland, of St. John's, 1891 (*Nfld. Who's Who* 1937, General Protestant Cemetery, St. John's).

Modern status: McKinlay, McKinley, at St. John's.

McKINNON, a surname of Scotland, Gaelic *MacFhionghuin* or *MacFhionnghain* – son of ? Fairborn. (Black, Cottle).

In Newfoundland:

Early instances: John, of St. John's, 1826 (Dispatches 1825–6); Archibald, fisherman of Cod Roy and Rivers, 1871 (Lovell); Murdock, tailor of Harbour Grace, 1871 (Lovell).

Modern status: In the St. George's district, at Gander (*Electors* 1955), Corner Brook and St. John's.

McKNIGHT, a surname of Scotland and Ireland; in Scotland a variant of MacNaught, in Ireland also from *Mac an Ridire*, Ir. *ridire* – knight. (Black, MacLysaght).

Traced by Black in Ayrshire and Galloway.

In Newfoundland:

Modern status: At Placentia (*Electors* 1955) and St. John's.

McLAUGHLIN, McLOUGHLAN, M(a)cLOUGHLIN, surnames of Ireland, McLaughlin of Scotland, Ir. *Mac Lochlainn*, Gaelic *Mac Lachlainn* – son of Lachlann, a Norse personal name meaning Norway. (Black, MacLysaght).

MacLysaght found MacLoughlin widespread and MacLaughlin especially in Cos. Donegal and Derry.

In Newfoundland:

Early instances: James McLaughlin, of Trepassey, 1792 (D'Alberti 4); James Maghloughlin, from Bagg Bay (unidentified), married at St. John's, 1807 (Nfld. Archives BRC); Michael McLoughlan, from Tintern (Co. Wexford), married at St. John's, 1818 (Nfld. Archives BRC); Patrick McLaughlin, of St. John's, ? 1821 (CO 194.64); Michael McLoughlan, of Catalina, 1824 (Nfld. Archives KCRC); John McLaughlan, of Tilting Harbour (now Tilting), 1827 (Nfld. Archives KCRC); Michael, from Co. Tipperary, of King's Cove, 1828 (Nfld. Archives KCRC); Michael, of Ragged Harbour (now Melrose), 1828 (Nfld. Archives KCRC); Michael, of Trinity (unspecified), 1829 (Nfld. Archives KCRC); John McLoughlan, of Ship Cove (now part of Port Rexton), 1830 (Nfld. Archives KCRC); —— M'Laughlan, from Ireland, of Broad Cove (unspecified), 1836 (*Nfld. Patriot* 24 Sep 1836); Anty [sic] McLoughnan, of Broad Cove (now Duntara), 1856 (Nfld. Archives KCRC); William M'Laughlan, bookkeeper of St. Peter's (St. Pierre),1860 (DPHW 99); Stephen McLochlan, fisherman of Fortune Harbour, 1871 (Lovell); Mrs. Margaret McLochlan and James McLachlan, of St. John's, 1871 (Lovell); Catherine McLoughlan, of Bloody Bay (Bonavista B.), 1872 (Nfld. Archives KCRC).

Modern status: McLaughlin, at Fortune Harbour (*Electors* 1955), Grand Falls, Bishop's Falls and St. John's; McLoughlan, rare, at St. John's; MacLoughlin, rare, at St. John's; McLoughlin, rare, at Duntara.

M(a)cLEAN, surnames of Scotland and Ireland, Gaelic *Mac Gille Eoin* – son of the servant of (St.) John (*see* JOHN). (Black, MacLysaght).

Traced by Guppy especially in Argyllshire and by MacLysaght in Cos. Antrim and Derry.

In Newfoundland:

Family tradition: Daniel McLean, from Cape Ann, Cape Breton, settled at Sandy Point (St. George's B.), before 1866 (MUN Folklore).

Early instances: John MacLane, of Harbour Grace Parish, 1810 (Nfld. Archives HGRC); Donald M'Lean, from Argyllshire, Scotland, cooper of St. John's, died 1813 (*Royal Gazette* 10 Jun 1813); Mary McLean, from Waterford, married at St. John's, 1817 (Nfld. Archives BRC); William McLean or McCleane, of King's Cove Parish, 1840 (Nfld. Archives KCRC); Donald McLean, planter of Carbonear, 1842 (DPHW 48); Elizabeth, granted land at Monday's Brook (unspecified), 1846 (Nfld. Archives, Registry Crown Lands); Allan M'Lean, from Greenock, tinsmith ? of St. John's, died 1847 (*Nfld. Patriot* 9 Jun 1847); John McClean or McLean, of Harbour Grace, 1866 (Nfld. Archives HGRC); Daniel McLean, of Sandy Point (St. George's district), 1870 (DPHW 96); Angus, of Channel, 1871 (Lovell); Hugh (and others), of Cod Roy and Rivers, 1871 (Lovell); Hugh (and others), of (Upper) Island Cove, 1871 (Lovell); John, fisherman of Rose Blanche, 1871 (Lovell); James, fisherman of Green Island Cove (St. Barbe district), 1874 (DPHW 95); John, of Bay of Islands area, 1878 (DPHW 96); Lauchlin, from Richmond County, Cape Breton, married at Bay of Islands, 1882 (DPHW 96).

Modern status: MacLean, at Woody Point, Corner Brook, Springdale and St. John's; McLean, scattered, especially at Green Island Cove (St. Barbe district).

Place names: MacLean Lake (Labrador) 53-55 65-30; McLean Lake (Labrador) 53-28 60-28; —— Point (Labrador) 53-30 59-52.

M(a)cLELLAN, surnames of Scotland and Ireland, Gaelic *Mac Gill'Fhaolain* – son of the servant of (St.) Fillan. Fillan (d. 734), the son of St. Kentigerna, was an abbot near St. Andrews, and on his retirement built a church in Perthshire. (Black, Coulson).

In Newfoundland:

Early instances: John and William McLellan, of Cod Roy and Rivers, 1871 (Lovell); Timothy, of Bay of Islands area, 1888 (DPHW 96).

Modern status: MacLellan, at Doyles (*Electors* 1955), Corner Brook and St. John's; McLellan, in the St. George's district and at Stephenville, Corner Brook and St. John's.

McLENNAN, McLENNON, surnames of Scotland and Ireland, Gaelic *Mac Gill'inein* for *Mac Gill-Fhinnein* – son of the servant of (St.) Finnan. Finnan (or Finnian) (d. about 579) founded schools at Moville (Co. Down) and Dromin (Co. Louth). In Ireland, MacLennan is also a variant of MacLenaghan, *Mac Leanacháin*, Ir. *leanach* – possessing mantles. (Black, MacLysaght, Coulson).

In Newfoundland:

Early instances: John ? Miclenan, of St. John's, ? 1821 (CO 194.64); Rev. J. McLennan, of St. Andrew's Kirk, St. John's, 1846 (*Newfoundlander* 16 Feb 1846).

Modern status: McLennan, rare, at St. John's; McLennon, at South East Placentia and Corner Brook.

M(a)cLEOD, surnames of Scotland, Gaelic *Mac Leòid* – son of *Leod*, from a Norse personal name *Ljót(r)* – ugly, which was probably the first element of a compound name such as *Ljót-ulf* – ugly wolf. (Black).

Traced by Guppy in Inverness-shire and Ross-shire.

In Newfoundland:

Early instances: William McLeod, of St. John's, 1810 (CO 194.49); Peter, from Stornoway, Ross-shire, Scotland, ? of Harbour Grace, 1858 (*Newfoundlander* 8 Mar 1858); George, clerk of Harbour Grace, 1871 (Lovell); Alexander, of Bay of Islands area, 1878 (DPHW 96).

Modern status: MacLeod, rare, at Corner Brook; McLeod, scattered, especially at St. John's.

Place name: McLeod Point 47-34 53-38.

McLOUGHLAN, M(a)cLOUGHLIN. *See* McLAUGHLIN

McMAHON, a surname of Ireland *Mac Mathghamhna*, Ir. *mathgamhan* – bear. (MacLysaght). *See also* MAHONEY.

Traced by MacLysaght in Cos. Clare and Monaghan.

In Newfoundland:

Early instances: James, ? of St. John's, 1752 (CO 194.13); Elizabeth, of Petty Harbour, 1810 (Nfld. Archives BRC).

Modern status: Rare, at Bishop's Falls and Grand Falls.

McMANUS, a surname of Scotland and Ireland, *Mac Maghnuis* – son of Magnus, from an Old Norse personal name *Magnúss*, ultimately from Latin *Magnus* – great. (Withycombe, Black, MacLysaght).

Traced by MacLysaght in Cos. Fermanagh and Roscommon.

In Newfoundland:

Early instances: James, in fishery at Petty Harbour, 1794–5, "50 years in Newfoundland," that is, 1744–5 (Census 1794–5); James, of St. John's, 1806 (Nfld. Archives BRC); Brien, of Placentia, 1836 (Nfld. Archives BRC); John, miner of Tilt Cove, 1871 (Lovell).

Modern status: At St. John's.

M(a)cMILLAN, surnames of Scotland and Ireland, Gaelic *Mac Mhaolain* or *Mac Gille Mhaoil* – son of the bald or tonsured one; also in Ireland for Mac Mullan, MacMULLEN, *Mac Maoláin*, Ir. *maol* – bald. (Black, MacLysaght).

Traced by Guppy in Argyllshire and by MacLysaght in Ulster.

In Newfoundland:

Early instances: John McMillin, soldier of St. John's, 1779 (DPHW 26C); John McMillan, general importer of St. John's, 1871 (Lovell).

Modern status: MacMillan, rare, at Botwood (*Electors* 1955) and St. John's; McMillan, rare, at St. John's.

MacMORRAN, a surname of Scotland and Ireland, Old Gaelic *mugh-ròn* – slave of the seal, a suggested explanation by Cottle being that seals were humans under a curse. (Black, Cottle, MacLysaght). *See also* MORAN.

Traced by MacLysaght in Co. Fermanagh where, however, it has inevitably been changed to Moran.

In Newfoundland:

Modern status: Rare, at St. John's.

McMULLEN. *See* M(a)cMILLAN

In Newfoundland:

Early instance: ——, of St. John's, 1832 (*Newfoundlander* 8 Mar 1832).

Modern status: Unique, at Bell Island.

McMURRAY, a surname of Ireland and Scotland, Irish *Mac Muireadhaigh* – son of *Muireadach*, a common early Irish personal name. (MacLysaght, Black).

Traced by MacLysaght in Co. Donegal and by Black in Galloway.

In Newfoundland:

Early instance: John, Wesleyan missionary of Brigus, 1840 (DPHW 34).

Modern status: Unique, at Buchans (*Electors* 1955).

MacNAB, a surname of Scotland and Ireland, Gaelic *Mac an Aba* – son of the abbot. (Black, MacLysaght).

Traced by Guppy in central Scotland and by MacLysaght in Ulster.

In Newfoundland:

Family tradition: James, from Edinburgh, Scotland, settled in Nova Scotia; some of the family later moved to St. John's (MUN Folklore).

Early instances: —— McNab, of St. John's, 1832 (*Newfoundlander* 8 Mar 1832); Thorburne Ashley (1876–), from Mahone Bay, Nova Scotia, of St. John's, 1907 (*Nfld. Who's Who* 1927).

Modern status: Rare, at St. John's.

McNAMARA, a surname of Scotland and Ireland, *Mac Conmara* – son of the hound of the sea. (Black, MacLysaght).

Traced by MacLysaght in Co. Clare.

In Newfoundland:

Early instances: Augustine, publican of St. John's, 1794–5, "24 years in Newfoundland," that is, 1770–1 (Census 1794–5); John M(a)cNamera, from Dungarvon (Co. Waterford), fisherman of Quidi Vidi, 1794–5, "16 years in Newfoundland," that is, 1778–9, died 1810 (Census 1794–5, *Royal Gazette* 14 Jun 1810); William McNamara, of Harbour Grace, 1782 (CO 199.18); Michael, from Waterford City, married at St. John's, 1797 (Nfld. Archives BRC); William MacNamara, planter of Isle of Spears, 1818 (D'Alberti 12); John McNamara, from Co. Kilkenny, married at Trinity (unspecified), 1819 (Nfld. Archives KCRC); John, from Co. Cork, married at King's Cove, 1825 (Nfld. Archives KCRC); John, of Fogo, 1821 (Nfld. Archives KCRC); Michael, of Catalina, 1822, of Ragged Harbour (now Melrose), 1825 (Nfld. Archives KCRC); Naston, of Tilting Harbour (now Tilting), 1824 (Nfld. Archives KCRC); John, of Herring Neck, 1828 (Nfld. Archives KCRC); Thomas, of Old Perlican, 1828 (DPHW 58); Michael, of Turks Cove, 1829 (Nfld. Archives KCRC); Michael Machnamara, of Trinity (unspecified), 1829 (Nfld. Archives BRC); Margaret MacNamara, of Northern Bay, 1831 (Nfld. Archives BRC); John McNamara, of Fortune Harbour, 1832 (Nfld. Archives KCRC); Maurice, of Low Point (Conception B.), 1871 (Lovell).

Modern status: At Grand Falls (*Electors* 1955), Port Union, Harbour Grace and St. John's.

MacNAUGHTON, a surname of Scotland and Ireland, Gaelic *Mac Neachdainn* – son of *Neachdain*, from earlier *Nectan* or *Necton*, the Old Gaelic form of Pictish *Naiton* – the pure one. (Black, MacLysaght).

Traced by Guppy in Perthshire.

In Newfoundland:

Early instance: John Naughton, shoreman of St. John's, 1794–5, "8 years in Newfoundland," that is, 1786–7 (Census 1794–5).

Modern status: Rare, at St. John's.

M(a)cNEIL(L), variants of the surname of Scotland and Ireland, Gaelic *Mac Nèill* – son of *Neil*, from a diminutive of Irish *Nía* – champion. (Withycombe, Black, MacLysaght).

Traced by Guppy in Argyllshire and Renfrewshire and by MacLysaght in Cos. Antrim and Derry since the 14th century; and in Co. Mayo.

In Newfoundland:

Early instances: John McNeil, soldier of St. John's, 1812 (DPHW 26B); Hector, from Greenock, Scotland, married at St. John's, 1816 (Nfld. Archives BRC); John M'Neil, Scotsman, age 30, deserted from ship *Perseverance*, St. John's, 1818 (*Nfld. Mercantile Journal* 28 Aug 1818); Charles McNeil, planter of Brigus, 1833 (DPHW 34); Israel, merchant of Carbonear, 1853 (DPHW 49); John McNiel (1842–), druggist, from Perthshire, Scotland, settled in St. John's in 1861 (Mott); James and John McNeil, farmers of Cod Roy and Rivers, 1871 (Lovell); Patrick, planter of Trepassey, 1871 (Lovell).

Modern status: MacNeil(l), at Doyles, Millertown (*Electors* 1955), St. Andrews, Stephenville and St. John's; McNeil(l), scattered.

McNEILLY, a surname of Ireland and Scotland, *Mac an Fhilidh*, Ir. *fileadh* – poet. (MacLysaght, Black).

Traced by MacLysaght in Co. Antrim and by Black in Galloway.

In Newfoundland:

Early instances: Alexander J. W. (1845–1911), born at Armagh, Ireland, and his brother Isaac Robert (1848–1891) born at Ballycastle, Antrim, Ireland, settled at St. John's in 1849 (Mott).

Modern status: At St. John's.

McNIVEN, a surname of Scotland, Gaelic *Mac Naiomhin* – son of the holy one. (Black).

In Newfoundland:

Modern status: At St. John's and Gander.

M(a)cPHEE, McPHIE, variants of the surname of Scotland MacFee, Gaelic *Mac Dhubhshith* – son of the black (one) of peace. (Black).

In Newfoundland:

Early instance: Neile Mcphee, from Prince Edward Island, married at St. John's, 1855 (*Newfoundlander* 8 Nov 1855).

Modern status: M(a)cPhee, rare, at Corner Brook (*Electors* 1955) and St. John's; McPhie, unique, at St. John's.

M(a)cPHERSON, surnames of Scotland, Gaelic *Mac a' Phearsain* or *Mac a' Phearsoin* – son of the parson. (Black).

Traced by Guppy in Inverness-shire and adjacent counties.

In Newfoundland:

Family tradition: Peter Macpherson (–1826), from Greenock, Scotland commenced business at Port de Grave in the early 1800s, and died there in 1826, aged 39 (MUN Hist.).

Early instances: Peter McPherson, of St. John's, 1813 (DPHW 23); Peter Mcpherson, of Port de Grave, deceased 1834 (*Newfoundlander* 31 Jul 1834); John, from Scotland, of St. John's, 1856 (*Newfoundlander* 22 Sep 1856); Rory McPherson, of Flat Bay (St. George's B.), 1871 (Lovell); Samuel, of Fogo, 1871 (Lovell).

Modern status: MacPherson, at Highlands, Heatherton, Grand Falls (*Electors* 1955), and St. John's; McPherson, at Baie Verte, Sandy Point, Fogo (*Electors* 1955), and Stephenville.

M(a)cQUARRIE, surnames of Scotland – son of *Guaire*, "an old Gaelic personal name meaning 'proud' or 'noble.'" (Black).

In Newfoundland:

Modern status: MacQuarrie, rare, at Stephenville and St. John's; McQuarrie, rare, at St. George's and Tompkins (*Electors* 1955).

McRAE. *See* McCRAE

McWHIRTER, a surname of Scotland and Ireland, Gaelic *Mac Cruitéir* – son of the harper. (Black, MacLysaght).

Traced by Black in Ayrshire and by MacLysaght in Cos. Armagh and Antrim.

In Newfoundland:

Early instance: Alexander McWhirter, of Bay of Islands area, 1876 (DPHW 96).

Modern status: At Corner Brook.

MADDEN, a surname of Ireland, *Ó Madáin*, earlier *Ó Madadháin*, Ir. *mada* – dog. (MacLysaght).

Traced by MacLysaght in Cos. Galway and Kildare. In Co. Kildare, "an English family of the same name also settled."

In Newfoundland:

Early instances: Michael Madan, of St. John's, 1775 (DPHW 26C); Thomas Madden, from Ballyneil Parish (unidentified), Diocese of Lismore, married at St. John's, 1793 (Nfld. Archives BRC); William, of Chapels Cove, 1796 (CO 199.18); Mary, of Harbour Grace Parish, 1819 (Nfld. Archives HGRC); Catherine, of Petty Harbour, 1821 (Nfld. Archives BRC); Timothy, fisherman of Bryant's Cove, 1871 (Lovell); John (and others), of Maddox Cove, 1871 (Lovell); William Maiden, of Brigus, 1871 (Lovell).

Modern status: Scattered, especially in the St. John's South district.

MADDICK(S), MADDOCK, MADDOX, surnames of England, Wales and Ireland, Maduc in Scotland, from the Old Welsh personal name *Matōc*, Welsh *Madowc, Madog* – goodly, or ? fox. (Reaney, MacLysaght, Black).

Guppy traced Maddock(s) in Cheshire, Devon, Shropshire and South Wales, Maddox in Herefordshire. MacLysaght traced Maddock and Maddox in Co. Wexford, Mayduck in Co. Down.

In Newfoundland:

Early instances: John Madox, of Fermeuse, 1675 (CO 1); John Maddock, of St. John's, 1708–09 (CO 194.4); John, J.P., Placentia district, 1750 (CO 194.2); Stephen, from Carrick (Diocese of Lismore), married at St. John's, 1799 (Nfld. Archives BRC); Thomas, of Petty Harbour, 1803 (Nfld. Archives BRC); Elizabeth, of Harbour Grace Parish, 1806 (Nfld. Archives HGRC); Michael Madick, of Carbonear, 1810 (Nfld. Archives BRC); Luke Maddock, from Waterford, dealer and chapman of St. John's, died 1813 (*Royal Gazette* 9 Sep 1813); John, from Abbotskerswell (Devon), of St. John's, 1823 (DPHW 26B); Thomas Maddock(s), Maddicks, Maddix or Maddox, of King's Cove, 1824 (Nfld. Archives KCRC); John Maddock, of Greenspond, 1827 (Nfld. Archives KCRC); Pat Madox, of Bay Bulls, 1829 (Nfld. Archives BRC); John Madick, of Twillingate, 1832 (Nfld. Archives KCRC); John Maddick, of Fogo, 1833 (Nfld. Archives KCRC); Joanna Maddocks, daughter of Thomas Mad[d]ocks, of Southampton (Hampshire), of King's Cove, 1849 (*Newfoundlander* 7 Jun 1849); John Maddock, granted land near Torbay, 1850 (Nfld. Archives, Registry Crown Lands); Henry Maddick, of Harbour Grace,

1857 (DPHW 43); John Maddox, of Keels, 1858 (Nfld. Archives KCRC); Thomas, of Dog Cove (Bonavista B.), 1863 (Nfld. Archives KCRC); John, of Knight's Cove (Bonavista B.), 1868 (Nfld. Archives KCRC); Thomas Maddox, Madix, or Maddicks, of Stock Cove (Bonavista B.), 1870 (Nfld. Archives KCRC); Michael Maddix, of Oderin, 1871 (Lovell); John M. Maddock, of Ship Cove (Brigus district), 1871 (Lovell).

Modern status: Maddick(s), at St. John's; Maddock, at Carbonear (*Electors* 1955), Corner Brook and St. John's; Maddox, scattered, especially at King's Cove (*Electors* 1955).

Place names: Maddox Cove 47-28 52-42; —— Pond 47-30 52-42.

MADDIGAN, a surname of Ireland, *Ó Madagáin*, "a branch of the O'Maddens." *See* MADDEN. (MacLysaght).

Traced by MacLysaght in Cos. Clare and Limerick.

In Newfoundland:

Early instances: Edmond Madigan, of Bay Bulls, 1793 (USPG); —— Maddigan, from Shenren Parish (unidentified) (Co. Kilkenny), married at St. John's, 1813 (Nfld. Archives BRC); John Madigan, of Witless Bay, 1820 (Nfld. Archives BRC); Eleanor Mad(d)igan, of Harbour Grace Parish, 1831 (Nfld. Archives HGRC); Edward Maddigan, of Lamaline, 1860 (DPHW 106); Richard, tailor and clothier, of Harbour Grace, 1867, 1871 (Nfld. Archives HGRC, Lovell); James Madigan, farmer of Point aux Gauls, 1871 (Lovell).

Modern status: Scattered, especially at Witless Bay (*Electors* 1955) and St. John's.

MADDOCK, MADDOX. *See* MADDICK(S)

MADORE, ? a Newfoundland variant of the surname of France Madamour, from Fr. *mal d'amour* – (one suffering from) love sickness. (Dauzat).

In Newfoundland:

Family tradition: ——, from Acadia, settled at Stephenville (MUN Geog.).

Early instance: George and William, fishermen of Flat Bay (St. George's B.), 1871 (Lovell).

Modern status: Scattered, in the west coast districts, especially at Stephenville Crossing (*Electors* 1955).

MAGILL, McGILL, surnames of Ireland, MacGill of Scotland; in Ireland *Mac an Ghaill*, Ir. *gall* – foreigner, or an abbreviation of one of the many names

beginning with *Mac Giolla* – son of the devotee or servant of; in Scotland, Gaelic *Mac an ghoill* – son of the stranger or Lowlander. (MacLysaght, Black).

MacLysaght traced Magill in Ulster; Black traced MacGill in Galloway.

In Newfoundland:

Early instances: William McGill, of St. John's, 1812 (D'Alberti 22); William Magell or Magill, deputy naval officer, Placentia district, 1821 (D'Alberti 31); Frederick McGill, granted land near Brady's Path, St. John's, 1849 (Nfld. Archives, Registry Crown Lands).

Modern status: Magill, McGill, rare, at St. John's.

MAHANEY, MEHANEY, ? Newfoundland variants of the surname of Ireland MAHONEY.

In Newfoundland:

Early instances: Daniel Mahanney, ? of Little Placentia (now Argentia) about 1730–5 (CO 194.5); James Mahaney, of St. John's, 1768 (DPHW 26D); James Mahany, of Salmon Cove, Northern Arm (Conception B.), 1775 (CO 199.18); Maurice, of Cat's Cove (now Conception Harbour), 1781 (CO 199.18); John, of Musketta (now Bristol's Hope), 1783 (CO 199.18); Thomas, of Gull Island (Conception B.), 1798 (CO 199.18); David, of Colliers, 1798 (CO 199.18); Nicholas Mehany, Meheny or Mahoney, of Carbonear, 1806 (DPHW 48); Valentine Mahany, planter of Exploits Burnt Island, 1818 (USPG); Paul Mahiny, of Trinity (unspecified), 1820 (Nfld. Archives KCRC); David, of Tilton Harbour (now Tilting), 1831 (Nfld. Archives KCRC); Francis Mahany, planter of Carbonear, 1835 (DPHW 48); Patrick, of Stock Cove (Bonavista B.), 1876 (Nfld. Archives KCRC); Alice, of Knight's Cove (Bonavista B.), 1877 (Nfld. Archives KCRC); Joanna, of King's Cove, 1887 (Nfld. Archives KCRC).

Modern status: Mahaney, at Gander (*Electors* 1955), Victoria, Carbonear and St. John's; Mehaney, scattered in the Twillingate district and at Springdale.

MAHAR, MAHER, MEAGHER, surnames of Ireland, Meagher also of England, in Ireland, *Ó Meachair*, Ir. *michair* – kindly, in England from Old French *megre*, Latin *macer* – thin, lean. MacLysaght notes that Maher is now the more usual spelling of the name in Ireland. (MacLysaght, Reaney).

Traced by MacLysaght in Cos. Offaly and Tipperary.

In Newfoundland:

Family traditions: Thomas Mahr, from Ireland,

settled at St. Brendan's about 1818; he later moved to Valleyfield (MUN Folklore). Denis Maher (about 1780–), from Tipperary, Ireland, settled in Nova Scotia, then at St. John's in 1818; he later moved to Flatrock (St. John's) (MUN Geog.).

Early instances: Michael Maher, shoreman of St. John's, 1794–5, "23 years in Newfoundland," that is, 1771–2 (Census 1794–5); Jeremiah, planter of Harbour Grace, 1783 (D'Alberti 2); John Meagher, of Trinity Bay, 1785 (DPHW 64); William Magher, of Carbonear, 1795 (CO 199.18); John Meagher, proprietor and occupier of fishing room, Trinity (Trinity B.), Winter 1800–01 (Census Trinity B.); B., occupier of fishing room at Bonaventure (unspecified), Winter 1800–01 (Census Trinity B.); Mary, of Belle Isle (now Bell Island), 1803 (Nfld. Archives BRC); Edward, from Gambourfield (unidentified) (Co. Tipperary), married at St. John's, 1805 (Nfld. Archives BRC); Mary Maghan or Maghar, of Trepassey, 1814 (Nfld. Archives BRC); Patrick Magher, from Labrador, married at St. John's, 1814 (Nfld. Archives BRC); John Meagher, of Careless (now Kerleys) Harbour, 1821 (Nfld. Archives KCRC); Edward, of Riders Harbour (Trinity B.), 1821 (Nfld. Archives KCRC); Patrick, of Twillingate, 1822 (Nfld. Archives KCRC); Mary, of Ferryland, 1828 (Nfld. Archives BRC); Mary, of King's Cove, 1830 (Nfld. Archives KCRC); Bridget Maher, from Co. Wexford, married at Trinity (unspecified), 1830 (Nfld. Archives KCRC); Patrick, of Tickle Cove (Bonavista B.), 1834 (Nfld. Archives KCRC); James, of Madix (for Maddox) Cove (Petty Harbour), 1837 (Nfld. Archives BRC); John, of Renews, 1837 (Nfld. Archives BRC); Michael Meagher, from Piltown (Co. Kilkenny), and William, from Co. Tipperary, of Harbour Grace, 1844 (Indicator 27 Jul 1844); Edward, of Flowers Island (Bonavista B.), 1851 (DPHW 76); Patrick Maher, of Greenspond, 1857 (Nfld. Archives KCRC); John, granted land at Little Placentia (now Argentia), 1859 (Nfld. Archives, Registry Crown Lands); James, planter of Aquaforte, 1871 (Lovell); Joseph, farmer of Flat Rock (St. John's), 1871 (Lovell); Daniel (and others) Mahar, of Marquise (Placentia B.), 1871 (Lovell); James and Thomas Maher, of Mobile, 1871 (Lovell).

Modern status: Mahar, at Hawke's Bay (Electors 1955), Seal Cove (near Stephenville Crossing) and Grand Bank; Maher, scattered, especially at St. John's, Flatrock (St. John's), and Bird Cove (St. Barbe district); Meagher, at Aquaforte and St. John's (Electors 1955).

Place names: Mahers 47-24 53-22; —— Brook 53-37 64-19; —— Point 49-08 53-37.

MAHON, a surname of Ireland much used for Mohan, Ó Mócháin, and for Mahan, and occasionally for MacMAHON. (MacLysaght).

MacLysaght traced Ma(g)han in Co. Galway and Mohan in Connacht, where both have been widely changed to Mahon.

In Newfoundland:

Early instances: Archibald Mahone, of Witless Bay, 1675 (CO 1); William Mahen or Mahon, constable of St. John's, 1809 (D'Alberti 19); William Mahon, from Laghmon Parish (Co. Wexford), married at St. John's, 1809 (Nfld. Archives BRC); Sibilla Mahen, of Harbour Grace Parish, 1812 (Nfld. Archives HGRC); John, from Co. Carlow, married at Fortune Harbour, 1830 (Nfld. Archives KCRC); William Mahin, of Trinity (unspecified), 1834 (Nfld. Archives KCRC); Patrick Mahon, from Co. Kilkenny, of Port de Grave, 1844 (Indicator 24 Aug 1844); Michael, granted land near Edghills Farm (unidentified), 1854 (Nfld. Archives, Registry Crown Lands); William, of Ferryland, 1871 (Lovell); Edward Mahan, of Flower's Island (Bonavista B.), 1871 (Lovell); Michael Mahen, of Torbay, 1871 (Lovell).

Modern status: At St. John's and Torbay.

MAHONEY, a surname of Ireland, (O)Mahony, Ó Mathghamhana, of the same derivation as MacMAHON. (MacLysaght). See also MAHANEY.

Traced by MacLysaght especially in west Munster.

In Newfoundland:

Family tradition: Richard, from Co. Cork, Ireland, settled at St. John's, about 1855 (MUN Folklore).

Early instances: Pat, fisherman of St. John's, 1794–5, "20 years in Newfoundland," that is, 1774–5 (Census 1794–5); Darby Mahony, shoreman of Torbay, 1794–5, "20 years in Newfoundland," that is, 1774–5 (Census 1794–5); John, from Mitchelstown (Co. Cork), Irish convict landed at Petty Harbour or Bay Bulls, 1789 (CO 194.38); Michael, of Harbour Grace Parish, 1806 (Nfld. Archives HGRC); Michael, from Carrick-on-Suir (Co. Tipperary), married at St. John's, 1812 (Nfld. Archives BRC); Maurice Mahoney, of Bonavista district, 1814 (D'Alberti 6); Maurice Mahony, of Trinity (unspecified), 1816 (Nfld. Archives KCRC); Maurice, from Co. Cork, married at Rider's Harbour (Trinity B.), 1819 (Nfld. Archives KCRC); Michael, of King's Cove, 1824 (Nfld. Archives KCRC); James Mahoney, from Co. Waterford, of Harbour Grace, 1844 (Indicator 27 Jul 1844); Bridget, of Knights

Cove (Bonavista B.), 1852 (Nfld. Archives KCRC); Mary, of Plate Cove (Bonavista B.), 1853 (Nfld. Archives KCRC); Bridget, of Stock Cove (Bonavista B.), 1855 (Nfld. Archives KCRC); Johana Mahony, of Broad Cove (now Duntara), 1859 (Nfld. Archives KCRC); Anne Mahoney, of Barrow Harbour (Bonavista B.), 1863 (Nfld. Archives KCRC); James (and others), of Cat's Cove (now Conception Harbour), 1871 (Lovell); William, of Crocker's Cove (Carbonear), 1871 (Lovell); Patrick, of Muscle Point (St. Mary's B.), 1871 (Lovell); Michael Mahony, farmer of Renews to Cape Race area, 1871 (Lovell); Daniel and Michael, of St. Mary's, 1871 (Lovell); Michael Jr. and Sr., of Tilton Harbour (now Tilting), 1871 (Lovell).

Modern status: Scattered, especially at Conception Harbour and Stock Cove.

MAIDMENT, a surname of England – servant of the maidens or ? nuns. (Reaney, Cottle).

Traced by Guppy in Dorset and Wiltshire.

In Newfoundland:

Early instances: Elijah, planter of Twillingate, 1818 (USPG); Samuel Maidmont, Mademont or Maidment, of Hant's Harbour, 1823 (DPHW 58); Richard Maidment, of Trinity (Trinity B.), 1836 (DPHW 64B); George, servant of Brigus, 1859 (DPHW 35); George, of Smart's Island (Bonavista B.), 1871 (Lovell); Eli Mardment, of St. Anthony, 1871 (Lovell); Samuel Maidment, of French Beach (Twillingate district), 1880 (DPHW 86).

Modern status: Scattered, especially in the Trinity North district.

Place names: Maidmonts Harbour (Labrador), —— Island (Labrador) 58-23 62-34.

MAINWARING, a surname of England, Ireland and Jersey (Channel Islands), pronounced as also spelt Mannering, "from a place name Mesnilwarin, the manor of Warin"; in Ireland also as the anglicized form of Ó Manaráin, otherwise Marrinan and Manron. (Reaney, Cottle, MacLysaght, Turk).

Traced by Guppy in Herefordshire.

In Newfoundland:

Family tradition: Gilbert Clapp, whose family originated from Devon, England and settled in St. John's, changed the family name to Mainwaring by Deed Poll (MUN Folklore).

Early instances: Patrick Manwaring, of St. John's, 1810 (CO 194.50); Patrick Mainwarring, fisherman of Petty Harbour, 1871 (Lovell).

Modern status: Rare, at St. John's.

MAIR, a surname of England and Scotland; in England from the English place name Maire (Devon); in Scotland from Gaelic *maor* – "officer who executed summonses and other legal writs." (Spiegelhalter, Reaney, Black).

Traced by Guppy in Ayrshire and by Spiegelhalter in Devon.

In Newfoundland:

Early instances: John ? Mair, of St. John's, 1762 (CO 194.15); Thomas Mairs, of Chapels Cove, 1801, fenced property from Chapels Cove to Harbour Main, 1815 (CO 199.18, D'Alberti 25).

Modern status: Unique, at Holyrood (*Electors* 1955).

MAJOR, MAUGER, (pronounced major), surnames of England, Major of Ireland, from a personal name Old German *Madalgar*, *Malger*, Old French *Maugier*, containing the elements *council* and *spear*. (Reaney, MacLysaght). *See* MAUGER.

Major traced by Guppy in Cheshire, by Spiegelhalter in Devon, and by MacLysaght in Ulster.

In Newfoundland:

Family tradition: George Major, of French origin, came to Newfoundland from England in 1853; some of his descendants settled at Stephenville (MUN Folklore).

Early instances: Thomas Major, of Mortier, 1780 (D'Alberti 6); Nancy, of Fortune, 1817 (DPHW 106); Degory, ship master of Carbonear, 1841 (DPHW 48); ——, fisherman of Petites, 1842 (DPHW 101); Elias Mager, granted land at Fortune, 1855 (Nfld. Archives, Registry Crown Lands); George Major, of Bonne Bay, 1869 (DPHW 93); Thomas, of Channel, 1871 (Lovell); John and John, farmers of St. John's, 1871 (Lovell).

Modern status: Scattered, in the west coast districts, at Fortune and St. John's.

Place names (not necessarily from the surname): Major Point 47-16 55-53, 49-56 55-44; —— Rock 47-37 58-39; —— Shoal 46-51 55-43; Majors Path (St. John's).

MAKING, a surname of England, one of several variants from *Maykin*, a diminutive of *May*, a pet-form of *Mayhew* (Matthew). *See* MATTHEWS. (Reaney).

Guppy traced Makens in Suffolk, Makins in Norfolk.

In Newfoundland:

Family tradition: Benjamin, a deserter from the

Royal Navy or Artillery at St. John's, was one of the first settlers at St. Stephen's (St. Mary's district) (Nemec, MUN Hist.).

Early instance: Denis Makin, ? of St. John's, 1843 (*Newfoundlander* 16 Mar 1843).

Modern status: At St. Stephen's (*Electors* 1955), and St. John's.

MAKINSON – son of Makin. *See* MAKING.

In Newfoundland:

Family tradition: George, from Liverpool, settled at Harbour Grace; acquired the property formerly known as the Goulds or Cochrane Dale, now Makinsons, ? in 1863 (Family).

Early instance: George, engineer proprietor of Harbour Grace, 1871 (Lovell).

Modern status: Rare, at Makinsons (Port de Grave district), and Buchans.

Place name: Makinsons 47-31 53-17.

MALCOLM, a baptismal name and surname of Scotland and Ireland, Gaelic *Mael Coluimb* – devotee of (St.) Columba of Iona (521–597); in Ireland also *Ó Maolcholuim* – St. Columcille (Columba). Black notes that as a surname it is "comparatively modern." (Withycombe, Black, MacLysaght). Guppy found Malcolm "general."

In Newfoundland:

Early instances: James (and others), of St. John's, 1871 (Lovell).

Modern status: Unique, at Corner Brook (*Electors* 1955).

Place name (not necessarily from the surname): Malcolm Island 49-34 54-19.

MALEY, ? a variant of the surname of Ireland, O'Malley, Mailey. *See* MALLAY.

In Newfoundland:

Early instances: Patrick, of St. John's, 1796 (CO 194.39); James, granted land at Old Coots Marsh Road (unidentified), 1850 (Nfld. Archives, Registry Crown Lands).

Modern status: Unique, at Twillingate.

MALLAM, a surname of England, from the English place name Malham (Yorkshire WR), or (dweller at the) stony or gravelly place. (Ekwall, Cottle).

Traced by Guppy in Durham.

In Newfoundland:

Early instances: Robert Malom, of Greenspond, 1822 (DPHW 76); Mrs. Emma Mallom, of St. John's, 1871 (Lovell).

Modern status: Rare, at Heart's Content and St. John's.

MALLARD, a surname of England and France, a variant of the English surname Maylard, from Old German *Madalhard*, Old French *Maillart*, containing the elements *council* and *strong*, or a variant of the French surname Malard (Normandy), a Latin-German hybrid containing the elements *malus* – bad and *hard* – strong, or a variant of the French surname Mallet, a pet-form of an old baptismal name *Malo*, the popular name of the 6th century saint Maclovius who gave his name to St. Malo (Ille-et-Vilaine), or from Old French *mal(l)art*, English mallard – wild duck or drake. (Reaney, Dauzat).

In Newfoundland:

Family tradition: ——, of Placentia, 1820; the family later moved to St. John's (MUN Folklore).

Early instances: William, of St. John's, 1796 (CO 194.39); Bridget Mallart, of Quidi Vidi, 1812 (Nfld. Archives BRC); Thomas Mallard, of Old Perlican, 1814 (Nfld. Archives BRC); Richard, of Quidi Vidi, 1835 (Nfld. Archives BRC).

Modern status: At Quidi Vidi and St. John's.

MALLAY, a variant of the surname of Ireland O'Malley, Mailey, *Ó Máille*. "One of the few O names from which the prefix was seldom dropped." (MacLysaght). *See* MALEY, and MELAY with which confusion may have occurred in Newfoundland. *See also* MEALEY.

Traced by MacLysaght in Co. Mayo.

In Newfoundland:

Family tradition: Thomas and family, from Ireland, were the first settlers of Mooring Cove (Mortier B.), before 1836 (MUN Hist.).

Early instances: Charles Malley, of St. John's, 1771 (CO 194.18); Thomas, of Greenspond, 1824–5 (Dispatches 1825–6); Edward Mallay, of Exploits Burnt Island, 1844 (DPHW 86); Patrick Malay, fisherman of Burin, 1871 (Lovell); Patrick Molay, farmer of Torbay, 1871 (Lovell).

Modern status: At Mooring Cove, Marystown, St. John's, Stephenville and Corner Brook.

MALONE, a surname of Ireland (O)Malone, *Ó Maoileoin* – devotee of St. John. (MacLysaght).

MacLysaght found Malone scattered, but numerous in Co. Clare "where it is pronounced Maloon and is probably really Muldoon."

In Newfoundland:

Family tradition: James, from Waterford, came to

St. John's in the early 1800s; he later moved to Carbonear (MUN Folklore).

Early instances: Jacob, of Newfoundland, ? 1706 (CO 194.24); P., fisherman of Torbay, 1794–5, "16 years in Newfoundland," that is, 1778–9 (Census 1794–5); James, fisherman of St. John's, 1794–5, "10 years in Newfoundland," that is, 1784–5 (Census 1794–5); William, of Trinity (Trinity B.), 1786 (DPHW 64); Patrick, from Dublin, Irish convict landed at Petty Harbour or Bay Bulls, 1789 (CO 194.38); William, watchmaker of Bonavista, 1789 (CO 194.38); Michael, proprietor and occupier of fishing room, Rider's Harbour, Winter 1800–01 (Census Trinity B.); John, of Harbour Grace Parish, 1806 (Nfld. Archives HGRC); Anne, from Glenmore Parish (Co. Kilkenny), married at St. John's, 1808 (Nfld. Archives BRC); Stephen, of Ragged Harbour (now Melrose), 1824 (Nfld. Archives KCRC); Andrew, of Tilting Harbour (now Tilting), 1826 (Nfld. Archives KCRC); Edmund, from Ballyadams (unidentified), (Queens Co. now Leix), married at Harbour Grace, 1829 (Nfld. Archives BRC); Andrew Melone, of Fogo, 1830 (Nfld. Archives KCRC); Philip Malone, of Freshwater (unspecified), married at St. John's, 1836 (Nfld. Archives BRC); Thomas, from Co. Carlow, of Harbour Grace, 1844 (*Indicator* 27 Jul 1844); Thomas, from Waterford City, Ireland, cooper of Carbonear, 1871, died 1896, aged 90 (Lovell, Carbonear R.C. Cemetery); Thomas, farmer of Logy Bay, 1871 (Lovell); Michael and Philip, farmers of Middle Cove (St. John's), 1871 (Lovell); John, farmer of Mosquito (now Bristol's Hope), 1871 (Lovell).

Modern status: At Logy Bay and St. John's.
Place name: Malone Rock 47-04 55-06.

MALONEY, a variant of the surname of Ireland (O)Moloney, *Ó Maoldhomhnaigh* – servant of the Church. "In Co. Tipperary Maloughgney has become Molony in some cases; there too the Mulumby family ... has been changed to Moloney." (O)MULLOW-NEY is the Connacht form of (O)Moloney. (MacLysaght).

MacLysaght traced (O)Moloney in Cos. Clare and Tipperary.

In Newfoundland:
Early instances: Walter ? Mallonowy, from Waterford, Ireland, of Little Placentia (now Argentia) about 1730–5 (CO 194.9); Andrew Mal(l)oney, of Trinity (Trinity B.), 1772 (CO 194.30, DPHW 64); Andrew Maloney, of St. John's, about 1780–4 (CO 194.35); James Malouny, from Tipperary (Co. Tipperary), married at St. John's, 1808 (Nfld. Archives BRC); Elizabeth Malowny, of Harbour Grace Parish,

1812 (Nfld. Archives HGRC); Thomas Maloney, granted land in the Witless Bay to Ferryland area, 1847 (Nfld. Archives, Registry Crown Lands); Peter, tinsmith of Harbour Grace, 1871 (Lovell).

Modern status: Widespread, especially at Holyrood, Bay Bulls, Sweet Bay (Bonavista B.), and St. John's.

Place names: Maloneys Beach 47-23 53-08; —— Hill 47-05 55-45; —— River 47-26 53-10.

MANDERSON, ? a Newfoundland variant of the surname of Scotland Manderston, from the Scots place name in Berwickshire, or a variant of the surname Magnusson – son of Magnus. *See* McMANUS.

Traced by Bardsley in the Shetlands.
In Newfoundland:
Early instance: Harvey Adams, engineer of St. John's, 1846 (DPHW 26B).
Modern status: Rare, at St. John's.

MAND(E)(R)VILLE, variants of a surname of England and Ireland, from the French surname and not uncommon place name Manneville; in Ireland, de Mandeville, *de Móinbhíol*, or for de Maydewell, both names of Norman families. *See* MANSFIELD. (MacLysaght).

Traced by MacLysaght in Co. Tipperary.
In Newfoundland:
Early instances: Patrick Mandavile, from Clonmel (Co. Tipperary), married at St. John's, 1805 (Nfld. Archives BRC); Mary Mandasel or Mandaval, of Harbour Grace Parish, 1815 (Nfld. Archives HGRC); Catherine Mandeville, of Bareneed, 1828 (Nfld. Archives BRC); Mary Mandevill, of Grates Cove, 1831 (Nfld. Archives KCRC); Geoffery Mandeville, from Carrick-on-Suir (Co. Tipperary), of St. John's, died 1832 (*Royal Gazette* 22 May 1832); ——, of Port de Grave, 1833 (*Newfoundlander* 12 Sep 1833); Richard Mandeville or Mandaville, from Carrick-on-Suir (Co. Tipperary), of Brigus, 1844–55 (*Nfld. Almanac* 1844, *Newfoundlander* 25 Jan 1855, 25 Jun 1855); William Mandeville, fisherman of Gaskin, Point La Hays, 1871 (Lovell); Stephen, planter of Peters River and Holyrood, 1871 (Lovell).

Modern status: Manderville, at St. John's and Point La Haye; Mandeville, unique, at Marquise (*Electors* 1955); Mandville, at Point La Haye, Dunville and St. John's.

MANN, a surname of England, Scotland and Ireland; in England and Ireland from Old English *mann* – man, servant, bondman, vassal; in Scotland, a form of Main, shortened from Magnus (*see* McMANUS). (Reaney, Cottle, Black, MacLysaght).

Traced by Guppy in East Anglia and the west Midlands, especially in Cambridgeshire, Norfolk and Warwickshire and by MacLysaght in Ulster.

In Newfoundland:

Early instances: Thomas Man(n), from Totnes (Devon), of St. John's, 1751–77 (CO 194.13, 33); Thomas Mann, of Carbonear, 1804 (CO 199.18).

Modern status: Rare, at St. John's and Corner Brook (*Electors* 1955).

Place names: Mann Point 49-22 54-26; —— —— (Labrador) 54-28 57-15; —— Rocks 49-30 54-53.

MANNING, a surname of England, Ireland and the Channel Islands, from an Old English personal name *Manning* based on *mann* (*see* MANN); also in Ireland sometimes a synonym of (O)Manni(o)n. In Newfoundland, in popular usage, not recognized by MacLysaght, (O)Mangan, *Ó Mongáin*, Ir. *mongach* – hairy, is sometimes a variant of Manning. (Reaney, Cottle, MacLysaght, Turk).

Traced by Guppy in Cheshire, Devon, Essex, Gloucestershire and Northamptonshire, and by MacLysaght in Cos. Cork and Dublin.

In Newfoundland:

Early instances: Michael, ? fisherman of Port de Grave, 1782 (Nfld. Archives T22); Joseph Mangan, of Catalina, in possession of property at Bay de Verde, 1793, of Bay de Verde, 1794 (CO 199.18, DPHW 48); John, of St. John's, 1796 (CO 194.39); John Mangen, of Torbay, 1804 (Nfld. Archives BRC); William Manning, from England, married at St. John's, 1808 (Nfld. Archives BRC); Edward Mannein, of Brigus, 1809 (DPHW 34); Lena Manning, of Harbour Grace Parish, 1810 (Nfld. Archives HGRC); Thomas, from Dingle (Co. Kerry), married at St. John's, 1821 (Nfld. Archives BRC); Elizabeth Mangan, of Trepassey, 1827 (Nfld. Archives BRC); Cornelius, from Lismore (Co. Waterford), of St. John's, died 1829 (*Royal Gazette* 19 May 1829); Abigale Maning or Mangin, of Twillingate, 1832, of Fortune Harbour, 1833 (Nfld. Archives KCRC); Walter Mangan, granted land at Cuslett, 1850 (Nfld. Archives, Registry Crown Lands); Maria Manning, of Harbour Grace, 1868 (Nfld. Archives HGRC); Matthew, farmer of Cuslett (Placentia B.), 1871 (Lovell); William, of Oderin, 1871 (Lovell); John (and others), of Torbay, 1871 (Lovell).

Modern status: Scattered, especially at Torbay and St. John's.

MANSFIELD, a surname of England and Ireland; in England from the English place name Mansfield (Nottinghamshire) – the field by the hill called *Mam* – ? breast; in Ireland for de Mandeville. *See* MAND(E)(R)VILLE. (Cottle, Ekwall, MacLysaght).

Traced by Guppy in Essex and Oxfordshire, and by MacLysaght in Cos. Tipperary and Waterford.

In Newfoundland:

Family tradition: ——, from England, settled at Conception Harbour (MUN Folklore).

Early instances: John Mansfeild, ? labourer of St. John's, 1779 (CO 194.34); Walter Mansfield, from Lismore (Co. Waterford), married at St. John's, 1812 (Nfld. Archives BRC); Robert, of Harbour Grace Parish, 1815 (Nfld. Archives HGRC); George, planter of Seal Cove (now New Chelsea), 1826 (DPHW 58); Robert Mansfie(l)d, planter of Lance Cove (now Brownsdale), 1844, of Little Islands (Trinity South district), 1846 (DPHW 59A); Peter, planter of Russell's Cove (now New Melbourne), 1848, of Indian Point (Trinity South district), 1850 (DPHW 59A); William Maishfield, of English Harbour (Bonavista district), 1871 (Lovell); John (and others) Mansfield, of Cats Cove (now Conception Harbour), 1871 (Lovell); Edward, miner of La Manche (Placentia B.), 1871 (Lovell).

Modern status: Scattered, especially at New Melbourne.

Place names: Mansfield Cove 49-30 55-59; —— (or Manful Bight) 49-57 55-29; —— Head 49-30 56-00.

MANSTON, a surname of England from the English place names Manston (Dorset, Kent, Yorkshire WR), Manston Farm (Devon) – *Mann*'s homestead, village. (Ekwall, Spiegelhalter). *See* MANN.

Traced by Matthews in Devon and Dorset.

In Newfoundland:

Early instance: Henry, of Greenspond, 1831 (DPHW 76).

Modern status: Rare, at St. John's.

MANUEL, a baptismal name and surname of England, a surname of Scotland; in England a shortened form of Em(m)anuel, Hebrew 'God with us,' "First used as a Christian name by the Greeks ... it spread westward and became particularly common in Spain and Portugal ... *Manuel* and *Emanuel* are found as Christian names in Cornwall in the 15th and 16th centuries" (Withycombe), or a variant of the surname Manwell, itself a variant of MAND(E)(R)VILLE; in Scotland from the Scots place name Manuel (Stirlingshire). (Withycombe, Ewen, Bardsley, Black).

Traced by Matthews in Devon.

In Newfoundland:

Family tradition: In the early 1700s, John Manuel of England owned a fleet of sailing vessels engaged in the Newfoundland fishery. His three sons, Joseph, Samuel, and William came to Newfoundland in 1758 and settled at Exploits. (Rev. G.C. Lacey).

Early instances: William, of Twillingate, in possession of fishing room, Pond Island, Greenspond Harbour, 1755 (Bonavista Register 1806); Robert, from Stoborough (Dorset), planter of Newfoundland, 1766 (Dorset County Record Office per Kirwin); John, of St. John's, 1806–7 (CO 194.46); William, planter of Salvage, 1817 (DPHW 72); Joseph, of Catalina, 1827 (DPHW 70); Thomas, of Bonavista, 1840 (DPHW 70); Joseph, of Exploits Burnt Island, 1841 (DPHW 88); Benjamin, of Channel, 1871 (Lovell); Luke, of Griquet, 1871 (Lovell); Thomas and Titus W., of Loon Bay (Twillingate district), 1871 (Lovell); Alfred and John, of (Lower) Island Cove, 1871 (Lovell).

Modern status: Widespread, especially at Corner Brook, Deer Lake, Norris Arm and Lewisporte.

Place names (not necessarily from the surname): Manuel Arm 47-41 56-10; Manuel(s) Cove 49-37 54-44; Manuel Gulch 49-32 55-05; —— Island(s), —— Point, —— Stores 49-31 55-04; Manuels, —— River 47-31 52-57; —— River 51-08 56-47; —— Long Pond (or Long Pond) 47-31 52-58.

MARCH, a surname of England, from Old French, Middle English *marche* – (dweller by the) boundary, frontier, or from the English place name March (Cambridgeshire). *See also* MARCHE, with which confusion may occur, and MARSH. (Reaney, Cottle).

Traced by Spiegelhalter in Devon.

In Newfoundland:

Family tradition: Abraham Eli (1853–1922), of English descent, was the first settler of Philip's Head, Bay of Exploits (MUN Folklore).

Early instances: Stephen, of Trinity Bay, 1767 (DPHW 64); Jacob, of St. John's, 1783 (DPHW 26C); George, of Bonavista, 1791 (USPG); Stephen and others), occupiers of fishing rooms, Old Perlican, Winter 1800–01 (Census Trinity B.); George, of Harbour Grace Parish, 1822 (Nfld. Archives HGRC); William, shoemaker of Harbour Grace, 1845 (DPHW 43); ——, on the *Iron Duke*, in the seal fishery out of New Perlican, 1853 (*Newfoundlander* 17 Mar 1853); ——, on the *Frederick*, in the seal fishery out of Trinity (unspecified), 1853 (*Newfoundlander* 17 Mar 1853); Simion, ? of Northern Bay, 1856 (DPHW 54); Edgar, of Green's Harbour (Trinity B.), 1858 (DPHW 59A).

Modern status: Widespread, especially at Green's Harbour, St. John's and Lady Cove (Trinity B.).

MARCHE, ? a shortened form of the surname of France Lamarche, from the French place name Lamarche (Côte d'Or, Meuse, Vosges) – the frontier. (Dauzat). *See* MARCH, MARSH.

In Newfoundland:

Family tradition: ——, from Acadia, settled at "du Cric," St. George's Bay (MUN Geog.).

Early instances: Frank and John March, of Indian Head (St. George's B.), 1871 (Lovell).

Modern status: Scattered, in the Port-au-Port district.

Place name: March(e)s Point 48-30 59-08.

MARGINSON, a variant of the surname of England Marg(e)r(i)son – son of Margery, a female baptismal name said to be derived from the name of the herb marjoram. (Cottle, Withycombe).

Traced by Guppy in Lancashire.

In Newfoundland:

Modern status: Rare, at Gander. (Margeson, at St. John's, *Electors* 1955).

Place name: Margesson Island 49-29 55-44.

MARKNETTE, ? a variant of a surname of Portugal such as Marques – (descendant of) Marcos, the Portuguese and Spanish form of Marcus – belonging to the god Mars. (E.C. Smith).

In Newfoundland:

Tradition: John, from Portugal, 1918, married at Fortune 1929 (Methodist marriages, P.E.L. Smith).

Modern status: Rare, at Fortune (*Electors* 1955).

MARKS, a surname of England and Ireland, from the baptismal name Mark, Latin *Marcus*, ultimately from *Mars* the god of war, the name of the second Evangelist, or from Old English *mearc* – (dweller by the) boundary, or from the English place name Mark (Somerset), (*see* MARCH, MARCHE), or from the French place name Marck (Pas-de-Calais). Cottle notes that the original surname Marks was common only in Devon and Cornwall but is now chiefly Jewish. (Withycombe, Cottle, MacLysaght). *See also* MARSH.

Traced by Guppy in Cornwall and Devon, and by MacLysaght in Co. Leix and elsewhere in the 17th century.

In Newfoundland:

Early instances: James, of Bonavista, 1795 (DPHW 70); William, of Carbonear, 1812 (DPHW 48); Thomas, of Harbour Grace Parish, 1822, of Harbour

Grace, 1830 (Nfld. Archives HGRC); William, carpenter of Mosquito (now Bristol's Hope), 1829 (DPHW 43); Mrs., of St. John's, 1844 (*Newfoundlander* 29 Feb 1844); John, fisherman of Lower Burgeo, 1847 (DPHW 101); John, of King's Cove, 1860 (DPHW 26D); John Mark, of East Cul de Sac, 1871 (Lovell); Charles and Thomas Marks, of Grole, 1871 (Lovell).

Modern status: Scattered, in the south and west coast districts including Grole.

Place names (not necessarily from the surname): Cape Mark 47-44 55-52; ——— Island (or Big Rookery Island) 57-29 61-24; ——— Islands (Labrador) 53-24 55-44; ——— Point 48-40 53-57; ——— Rocks 47-34 57-40; ——— ———, ——— ——— Shoal 47-37 56-10; Markland 47-23 53-33; Marks Bight (Labrador) 55-04 59-24; ——— Island 54-30 57-14; ——— Lake 49-18 55-50; ——— Shute Cove, ——— ——— Pond 48-34 53-47.

MARNELL, a surname of Ireland, "originally Warnell, a derivative of Warner." (MacLysaght).

Traced by MacLysaght in Kilkenny since 1550.

In Newfoundland:

Early instance: James, of St. John's, 1846 (*Newfoundlander* 2 Jul 1846).

Modern status: Rare, at St. John's.

MARQUIS, a surname of England, France, the Channel Islands and Scotland; in the first three from Old French *marchis* – marquis, a nickname and, as Bardsley notes, also a baptismal name like Duke and Earl formerly common in Yorkshire WR which, it may be added, are still common in North America. In Scotland, Marquis is a shortened form of the West Highland name (Mac) Marquis – son of Mark (*see* MARKS), now rare. (Bardsley, Dauzat, Black, Turk).

Traced by Dauzat in Normandy-Picardy and by Black as MacMarquis in Argyllshire.

In Newfoundland:

Modern status: Rare, at St. John's.

Place name: Marquise.

MARRIE, a variant of the surname of Ireland MARRY, of uncertain origin, probably cognate with Merry, *Ó Mearadhaigh, Ó Meardha* – from adjectives meaning lively. (MacLysaght).

Traced by MacLysaght in Co. Louth and north Connacht.

In Newfoundland:

Family tradition: John Marrie, from Wales, went to St. Pierre at the age of 6; ten years later he left St. Pierre and settled at Mount Carmel (MUN Folklore).

Modern status: Marrie, at St. Catherines (*Electors* 1955), Mount Carmel and St. John's; Marry, rare, at St. John's.

MARSDEN, a surname of England, from the English place name Marsden (Lancashire, Yorkshire WR, Gloucestershire), or from Old English *mercels* – mark, boundary and *denu* – valley, hence (dweller by the) boundary-valley. (Cottle, Ekwall).

Traced by Guppy in Derbyshire, Lancashire and Yorkshire WR.

In Newfoundland:

Family tradition: James, from England, settled at François, about 1850 (MUN Hist.).

Early instances: James, fisherman of Transway [Fransway] (Fortune B.), 1858 (DPHW 102); James, of François, 1873 (MUN Hist.).

Modern status: In the Burgeo-La Poile district especially at François (*Electors* 1955).

MARSH, a surname of England and Ireland, from Old English *mersc* – (dweller near the) marsh, or from the English place name Marsh (11 places in Devon), or a variant of MARCH or MARKS. (Reaney, Cottle, MacLysaght, Spiegelhalter). *See also* MESH.

Traced by Guppy in 14 counties and by MacLysaght in Ireland since the 17th century.

In Newfoundland:

Early instances: Richard, of Salvage, 1681 (CO 1); James, of Perlican (unspecified), 1815 (Nfld. Archives KCRC); Benjamin, of Bonavista, 1823 (DPHW 70); Joseph, planter of Bonaventure (unspecified), 1825 (DPHW 64B); William, servant of Trinity (Trinity B.), 1832 (DPHW 64B); Joseph, of King's Cove, 1834 (Nfld. Archives KCRC); William, from Canterbury, England, married at St. John's, 1835 (DPHW 26D); George, of Herring Neck, 1857 (DPHW 85); David, of Burin, 1871 (Lovell); Mark, of Channel, 1871 (Lovell); John, of Gooseberry Islands (Bonavista B.), 1871 (Lovell); William, of Green Harbour (Trinity B.), 1871 (Lovell).

Modern status: Scattered, especially at Deer Harbour (Trinity B.) and Bonavista.

Place name: Marsh's Rock 49-10 53-32.

MARSHALL, a surname of England, Scotland and Ireland, from Old French *maresc(h)al* etc., "one who tends horses, especially one who treats their diseases; a shoeing smith, a farrier" (*OED*), or a high officer of state as in Earl Marshal. (Reaney, Cottle, Black, MacLysaght).

Found widespread in England and in central and

southern Scotland by Guppy, and widespread but particularly numerous in Ulster by Maclysaght

In Newfoundland:

Early instances: Nicholas, of Carbonear, 1790, property "in possession of the Family for upwards of 120 years," that is, before 1670 (CO 199.18); Frances, of Harbour Grace, 1775, property "in possession of the Family for upwards of 90 years," that is, before 1680 (CO 199. 18); John, of Keels, 1681 (CO 1); Henry, boatkeeper of St. John's, 1681 (CO 1); Henry, of Brigus, 1681 (CO 1); Robert, of Conception B., 1706 (CO 194.4); John, of Petty Harbour, 1708 (CO 194.4); Richard, of Harbour Main, 1762 (CO 199. 18); Simon, fisherman of Bay de Verde, 1782 (D'Alberti 2); Richard, of Freshwater (Carbonear), 1792 (CO 199.18); William, of Gooseberry Cove (near Carbonear), 1802 (CO 199.18); Jonathan Marshel(l) or Marshal, of Crocker's Cove (Carbonear), 1810 (DPHW 48); Robert Marshall, fisherman of Broad Cove (Bay de Verde district), 1828 (DPHW 52A); William, planter of Bear's Cove (Harbour Grace), 1831 (DPHW 43); John, granted land at Bell's Cove (Little Burin), 1835 (Nfld. Archives, Registry Crown Lands); John, of Burin, 1840 (*Newfoundlander* 11 Jun 1840); Rev. William, of Hermitage Bay, 1841 (*Newfoundlander* 3 Jun 1841); Robert, planter of Blow-me-down (Carbonear), 1841 (DPHW 48); William, of Sound Island (Placentia B.), 1857 (DPHW 105); Joseph and William, of Bay of Islands, 1871 (Lovell); Robert and Thomas, of Flat Rock (Carbonear), 1871 (Lovell); John, of Little Bay Island, 1871 (Lovell); Isaac and Robert, of Salmon Cove (Brigus district), 1871 (Lovell).

Modern status: Widespread, especially at St. John's and Carbonear.

Place names: Marshall Beach 49-38 55-48; —— Ground 49-40 55-45; —— Falls (Labrador) 54-47 60-24; —— Island 47-38 54-12, (Labrador) 56-43 61-01; —— Rapids (Labrador) 53-09 66-18.

MARSHFIELD, a surname of England, from the English place name Marshfield (Gloucestershire, Cheshire, Monmouthshire), or (dweller in the) field by a marsh. (Cottle).

In Newfoundland:

Family tradition: William, settled at Greenspond about 1846 (MUN Folklore).

Early instances: Cornelius Mashfield, of Bonavista, 1792 (USPG); William Marshfield, of Greenspond, 1846 (DPHW 76); Robert, of Keels, 1859 (DPHW 73B).

Modern status: Rare, at King's Cove, Keels (*Electors* 1955), Greenspond and St. John's.

MARTIN, a baptismal name and surname of England, Scotland, Ireland, France, the Channel Islands and Germany and of the Micmacs of Newfoundland, in all of these from Latin *Martinus*, a diminutive of *Martius* – of Mars. St. Martin of Tours (4th century), who shared his cloak with a beggar, was a favourite saint in England and France. "A very popular Christian name and an early surname" (Reaney). In England, Martin is also from the English place name Martin found in six counties, or from Old English *meretūn*, *mærtūn* – (dweller at the) homestead, village near the lake, or ? as a nickname, from marten – polecat, or the bird; in Ireland also for Gilmartin, *Mac Giolla Mhártain* – devotee of St. Martin; in Scotland, also ? a shortened form of St. Martin, "a once great family in East Lothian," or ? a shortened form of MacMartin, Gaelic *Mac Mhàrtainn* or *Mac Mhàrtuinn* – son of the servant of (St.) Martin. (Withycombe, Reaney, Cottle, Dauzat, MacLysaght, Black, Turk).

Found widespread in England and the southern half of Scotland by Guppy, and "one of the most numerous surnames in Ireland" by MacLysaght.

In Newfoundland:

Family traditions: —— from England, settled at Salvage and changed his name from Crisby to Martin (MUN Folklore). George, of French descent, from Middlefield, Nova Scotia, settled in the Exploits River area between 1900–05 (MUN Folklore). —— Martineau, from the Channel Islands, settled at Harbour Grace; the name was subsequently changed to Martin (MUN Folklore). Joseph, of Bird Island Cove (now Elliston), 1825 (MUN Hist.).

Early instances: Gilbert, of Witless Bay, 1675 (CO 1); Christopher, of Salvage, 1681 (CO 1); William (also Elias and Robert in 1682), boatkeeper of St. John's, 1681 (CO 1); William, of Trinity (unspecified), 1708–9 (CO 194.4); John Martyn, of Petty Harbour about 1720–5 (CO 194.7); William Martin, of Harbour Grace, 1735 (CO 199.18); Emmanuel, fisherman of Trinity (Trinity B.), 1761 (DPHW 64); John, fisherman of Torbay, 1794–5, "30 years in Newfoundland," that is, 1764–5 (Census 1794–5); Joseph, of Grates Cove, 1784 (CO 199.18); William, from Ireland, boatkeeper of Bay Bulls, 1786 (CO 194.36); Nicholas, of Adams Cove, 1790 (CO 199.18); James, of Placentia, 1794 (D'Alberti 5); James, proprietor and occupier of fishing room at Heart's Delight, Winter 1800–01 (Census Trinity B.); Henry, of Hants Harbour, 1804 (DPHW 64);

Abraham, of Lower Island Cove, 1805 (CO 199.18); Sarah, from Devon, married at St. John's, 1814 (Nfld. Archives BRC); Mary, of King's Cove, 1815 (Nfld. Archives KCRC); James, of Port de Grave, 1816 (DPHW 58); Michael, of Fogo, 1819 (Nfld. Archives KCRC); ? May, of Ferryland, 1824 (DPHW 31); Henry, of Fortune, 1825·(DPHW 106); John, mason of Brigus, 1827 (DPHW 34); Henry M., from Poole, married at Great Placentia, 1828 (*Newfoundlander* 22 Jun 1828); Mary, of Renews, 1829 (DPHW 31); Stephen, of Catalina, 1832 (DPHW 70); J. W., of St. Mary's, 1832 (*Newfoundlander* 26 Jan 1832); Michael, of Bonavista, 1833 (Nfld. Archives KCRC); William, of Flat Rock (unspecified), married àt St. John's, 1834 (Nfld. Archives BRC); John, of Grates Cove, 1837 (Nfld. Archives BRC); John, of ? Northern Bay, 1839 (DPHW 54); Richard, of Black Island (Twillingate district), 1841 (DPHW 86); Edward, of Lamaline, 1842 (DPHW 109); ——, of White Hills (St. John's), 1843 (DPHW 26B); Richard, of Moreton's Harbour, 1849 (DPHW 86); Joseph Marten, of Bareneed, 1854 (*Newfoundlander* 18 Dec 1854); William Martin, fisherman of Herring Neck, 1850 (DPHW 50); Elizabeth, of Plate Cove (Bonavista B.), 1856 (Nfld. Archives KCRC); Henry, of New Perlican, 1857 (DPHW 59A); Capt. William, from Coombeinteignhead (Devon), of St. John's, 1857 (*Newfoundlander* 16 Nov 1857); James, of Stock Cove (Bonavista B.), 1858 (Nfld. Archives KCRC); Mary, of Tickle Cove (Bonavista B.), 1858 (Nfld. Archives KCRC); Ellen, of Keels, 1860 (Nfld. Archives KCRC); Sarah, of Fox Harbour (Trinity South district), 1860 (DPHW 59); widespread in Lovell, 1871; Norah, from Middleton (Co. Cork), of Trepassey, died 1895, aged 62 (Dillon); John, Micmac Indian, of Conne River, 1908 (MacGregor).

Modern status: Widespread, especially at St. John's, Harbour Grace, Grates Cove, Flatrock (St. John's), Little Heart's Ease, Elliston, Hickman's Harbour, Bunyan's Cove and Lewisporte.

Place names (not necessarily from the surname): Martin Bank (or Rock) 47-12 56-03; —— Bank (Labrador) 52-18 55-34; —— Bay (Labrador) 52-56 55-50, 60-05 64-24; —— Island 48-48 53-48, (Labrador) 57-29 62-16; —— Lake 48-43 55-34, (Labrador) 54-56 66-06; —— Point 49-46 57-55; —— River (Labrador) 53-57 66-27; Martin's Cove 49-56 55-47; —— Ledge 48-12 52-55.

MARTRET, a surname of France from the French place name Martret (Saône-et-Loire, etc.) – field of the martyrs and by extension cemetery. (Dauzat).

In Newfoundland:

Modern status: Rare, at St. John's.

MASON, a surname of England, Scotland and Ireland, from Old Norman French *machun*, Old Central French *maçon*, *masson* – mason, or from the English place name Mason (Northumberland). (Reaney, Cottle, MacLysaght, Black, Ekwall).

Found widespread by Guppy, especially in Cambridgeshire but rarer in the north, and numerous in all provinces of Ireland except Connacht by MacLysaght.

In Newfoundland:

Early instances: Samuel, fisherman of St. John's, 1794–5, "25 years in Newfoundland," that is, 1769–70 (Census 1794-5); John, of Gasters, 1780 (CO 199. 18); George, of Harbour Main, 1806 (CO 199.18); John, of Harbour Grace Parish, 1807 (Nfld. Archives HGRC); John, of Bonavista, 1815 (DPHW 70); John Mason or Meason, of Ragged Harbour (now Melrose), 1820 (Nfld. Archives KCRC); Matthew Mason, of Catalina, 1821 (Nfld. Archives KCRC); John, of Tilting Harbour (now Tilting), 1826 (Nfld. Archives KCRC); James, of Rencontre, 1835 (DPHW 30); Thomas Ma(i)son, ? of Northern Bay, 1839 (DPHW 54); Thomas, fisherman of Fogo, 1851 (DPHW 83); Richard, of Greenspond, 1857 (DPHW 76B); ——, Capt. of the *Haldee* in the seal fishery out of Harbour Grace, 1857 (*Newfoundlander* 19 Mar 1857); Joseph, farmer of Broad Cove (now St. Phillips), 1871 (Lovell).

Modern status: Scattered, especially at Avondale and St. John's.

Place names: Masons Cove 49–19 52-02; —— Pond 48-43 54-22.

MASTERS, a surname of England and the Channel Islands, Master of England and Scotland, from Middle English *maister*, Old French *maistre* – master of a school, farm, house, apprentice, a servant at the master's house. "In Scotland, the eldest sons of barons are designed 'Masters,' and the uncles of lords were also called Masters." It was also given to a person whose name was not known, and was also the title of one who had charge of a hospital. (Reaney, Cottle, Black, Turk).

Traced by Guppy in Dorset, Leicestershire, Rutland and Somerset.

In Newfoundland:

Early instances: John, born in Newfoundland, 1687 (Dorset County Record Office per Kirwin); William, watchmaker of St. John's, 1794–5, "18 years in Newfoundland," that is, 1776–7 (Census 1794–5); William, of Placentia, 1794 (D'Alberti 6); William, mason of Brigus, 1831 (DPHW 34); Samuel, fisherman of Harbour Buffett, 1871 (Lovell).

Modern status: Scattered, especially in the Placentia West district.

Place name: Masters Head 47-43 53-50.

MASTERTON, a surname of Scotland, from the Scots place name Masterton (Fife). (Black).

In Newfoundland:

Modern status: Rare, at St. John's.

MATCHEM, MATCHIM, surnames of England, ? from the English place name Matchams (Hampshire). *See* CUFF.

Guppy traced Matcham in Kent.

In Newfoundland:

Family tradition: Joseph Cuff came to Bonavista between 1794–1805, and changed his name to Matcham, spelt at various times Matchim, Matchem, Machin. He was the forefather of the Matchims at Gaultois, Catalina, Musgravetown, Savage Cove, Sandy Cove and Barrow Harbour (MUN Hist.).

Early instances: Joseph Matcham, of Bonavista, 1811 (DPHW 70); William, of Barrow Harbour, 1846 (DPHW 73); Robert, of Hardy Cove (Fortune B.), 1854 (DPHW 104); William, fisherman of Barrosway Cove (Fortune B.), 1854 (DPHW 102); Joseph Matchen, fisherman of Happy Adventure, 1871 (Lovell); James Matcher, of Green Harbour (Trinity B.), 1871 (Lovell); Robert Matchern, of Gaultois, 1871 (Lovell); Ed Matchim, of Savage Cove, 1911 (Nfld. Archives HGRC).

Modern status: Matchem, scattered, especially in the Fortune Bay and Hermitage district; Matchim, especially at Sandy Cove (Bonavista B.).

Place name: Matchim Cove 48-36 53-50.

MATE, a surname of England, ? from Middle English *mate* – fellow or, as an adjective, dejected, or ? from Old English *mæd* – meadow, or ? from the French surname Mette ? from Old French *mete* – (dweller by the) boundary. Barber identified Mate as a Huguenot name in London in 1618. (Reaney Notes, Weekley *Surnames*, Dauzat, Barber).

In Newfoundland:

Early instances: Henry, fisherman of Robin Hood (now part of Port Rexton), 1854 (DPHW 64B); Henry, of Ship Cove (now part of Port Rexton), 1871 (Lovell).

Modern status: Rare, at Pushthrough (*Electors* 1955), and St. John's.

MATHESON, a surname of England and Scotland – son of *Mathi*, a pet-form of Matthew. *See* MATTHEWS. (Reaney, Cottle).

Guppy traced Mattison, Matson, Mathison, Matterson, and Matteson in Yorkshire WR, and found Math(i)eson scattered in Scotland.

In Newfoundland:

Early instance: John Garland, fisherman at Port de Grave, 1871 (Lovell).

Modern status: Rare, at St. John's.

Place name: Mathison Island 49-41 54-24.

MATTERFACE, a surname of England, from the French place name Martinvast (La Manche). (Reaney *Origin*).

In Newfoundland:

Early instances: Stephen, of Newfoundland ? 1706 (CO 194.24); Thomas, of Little St. Lawrence, 1821 (D'Alberti 31); William, master-mariner of St. John's, 1844 (DPHW 26B); Charles, of Boat Harbour (Placentia B.), 1871 (Lovell).

Modern status: At Boat Harbour, Baine Harbour (Placentia B.) (*Electors* 1955), and St. John's.

MATTHEWS, a surname of England and Ireland and of the Micmacs of Newfoundland, Matthew, a baptismal name and surname traced by Guppy in Cornwall, Gloucestershire and Suffolk and also as Mathew by MacLysaght in Ireland, Mathews in the Channel Islands. Hebrew *Mattathiah* – gift of Jehovah, Latin *Matthaeus* or *Matthias*. The name was introduced into England by the Normans and from it and its diminutives in both English and French have derived several surnames: MAY(E), MAYO, MACEY, Machin, MAKING, Matthewson, Maycock, MATHESON and many others. In Ireland, Matthews is also a synonym of MacMAHON. (Withycombe, Reaney, MacLysaght, Cottle, Turk).

Found widespread by Guppy in the Midlands and south and west England especially in Wiltshire, Gloucestershire and Herefordshire, and by MacLysaght in Ulster and Co. Louth.

In Newfoundland:

Family traditions: John, from Torquay (Devon), settled at Lance Cove (now Brownsdale) (MUN Folklore). John Goodwin (1861–), from London, came to Newfoundland via New Brunswick in 1880, and settled at King's Point (Green B.), in 1886 (MUN Hist.). John, from England, settled at Grand Bank before 1821 (MUN Hist.). Mary Ann (1852–1937), born at Rose Blanche (MUN Geog.).

Early instances: Elizabeth Mathews, of St. John's or ? Bay Bulls, 1680, "39 years an inhabitant," that is, since 1641 (CO 1); John Matthews, of Ferryland about 1650 (Prowse); William Mathews, of St.

John's, 1675 (CO 1); Joshua and Jonathan Matthews, of Newfoundland, ? 1706 (CO 194.24); Henry, in fishery at Petty Harbour, 1794–5, "40 years in Newfoundland," that is, 1754–5 (Census 1794–5); Robert, of Trinity Bay, 1772 (DPHW 64); Thomas, of Harbour Main, 1783 (CO 199.18); James, of Trinity (Trinity B.), 1804 (DPHW 64); Joseph, of Greenspond, 1816 (DPHW 76); William, of King's Cove, 1816 (Nfld. Archives KCRC); George, planter of New Perlican, 1823 (DPHW 64B); John, of Grand Bank, 1826 (DPHW 109); William, of Broad Cove (now Duntara), 1828 (Nfld. Archives KCRC); John, baptized at Cape Island (Bonavista B.), 1830, aged 17 (DPHW 76); John, of Burgeo Islands, 1830 (DPHW 30); John, of Bay L'Argent, 1835 (DPHW 30); John, planter of Broad Cove (Bay de Verde district), 1837 (DPHW 52A); William, of Tickle Cove (Bonavista B.), 1838 (DPHW 73A); Thomas, fisherman of Channel, 1840 (DPHW 101); Edward, fisherman of Eastern Point (Burgeo-La Poile district), 1840 (DPHW 101); William, of Indian Arm (Bonavista B.), 1841 (DPHW 73A); James, of Fogo, 1842 (DPHW 83); William, of Cairns Island (Bonavista B.), 1843 (DPHW 76); George, of Catalina, 1845 (DPHW 67); ——, of Burnt Islands (Burgeo-La Poile district), 1849 (Feild); Jane Mathews, of Keels, 1855 (Nfld. Archives KCRC); Ellen, of Ragged Harbour (now Melrose), 1857 (Nfld. Archives KCRC); John Matthews, of Petites, 1857 (DPHW 98); John, of Lower Island Cove, 1858, of Canvas Town (Lower Island Cove), 1860 (DPHW 55); widespread in Lovell 1871; Noel, Micmac Indian of Conne River, about 1872, with hunting grounds at Great Burnt Lake and Crooked Lake about 1900–07 (MacGregor, Millais).

Modern status: Widespread, especially at St. John's, Musgravetown, Brownsdale and Grand Bank.

Place names (not necessarily from the surname): Matthew Cove 48-28 53-36; —— Rock 47-32 54-04; —— Rocks (Labrador) 59-48 63-57; Matthews Bank (Labrador) 52-51 55-47; —— Brook 49-00 57-43; —— Cove (Labrador) 52-17 55-36; —— Ground 48-44 53-07; —— Island 49-37 54-47; —— Pond 48-11 55-42, 48-19 53-52.

MAUGER, a variant of, and having the same pronunciation as, MAJOR. (Turk).
In Newfoundland:
Early instances: P., ? fisherman of Port de Grave, 1773 (Nfld. Archives T22); William, of Upper Burgeo, 1846 (DPHW 101); James Maujor, of Petites, 1857 (DPHW 98); Thomas, of Channel, 1863 (DPHW 97).

Modern status: At Burin, La Poile, Petites (Electors 1955) and Channel.

MAUNDER, a surname of England, from Old English mand, mond, Old French ma(u)nde – (maker of) woven basket(s) with a handle or handles. (Hardy, The Woodlanders, has mawn-basket, a word used in Newfoundland for a trout-bag.) The verb maund(er) has several meanings: to bed (Lower), grumble, mutter, growl, move or act in a dreamy, idle or inconsequent manner, talk in the dreamy and foolish manner characteristic of dotage or imbecility, ramble or wander in one's talk. (EDD, Spiegelhalter, Lower, MUN student, Weekley Romance).
Traced by Guppy in Devon.
In Newfoundland:
Family tradition: Richard, from England, settled at St. John's (MUN Folklore).
Early instances: Richard, of St. John's, 1848 (DPHW 26D); Richard (1871–1889), born at Deancombe (Devon), died at St. John's (General Protestant Cemetery, St. John's).
Modern status: At St. John's.

MAVIN, a surname of England of unknown origin.
In Newfoundland:
Early instances: Richard Maven, fisherman of Lower Burgeo, 1844 (DPHW 101); George (and others), fisherman of Fortune, 1871 (Lovell).
Modern status: At Ramea (Electors 1955), and Fortune.

MAXWELL, a surname of England, Scotland and Ireland – (dweller by the) big spring, or from the Scots place name Maxwell, a parish of Kelso (Roxburghshire), which probably received its name "from a salmon pool on the Tweed near Kelso Bridge, still locally known as Maxwheel." In Ireland it is also a synonym of Mescall, Ó Mescal. (E. C. Smith, Black, MacLysaght).
Traced by Guppy in Cambridgeshire and Dumfriesshire and by MacLysaght in Ulster.
In Newfoundland:
Early instances: William, soldier of St. John's, 1821 (DPHW 26B); William, married at St. John's, 1830 (Nfld. Archives BRC).
Modern status: At Corner Brook and Pasadena.

MAY(E), surnames of England and Ireland, petforms of Matthew (see MATTHEWS), from Mayhew, or from Middle English may – young lad or girl; in Ireland also from Ó Miadhaigh, Ir. miadhach – honourable. (Reaney, Cottle, MacLysaght).

Guppy traced May in ten counties and noted that Maye is a rare Devon form.

In Newfoundland:

Early instances: Peter Maye, of Bay Bulls, 1675 (CO 1); Samuel May, fisherman of St. John's, 1696–7 (CO 194.1); William, planter of Twillingate, 1818 (USPG); Thomas, of Harbour Grace Parish, 1828 (Nfld. Archives HGRC); Thomey, from Grage (unidentified), ? Ireland, married at St. John's, 1830 (Nfld. Archives HGRC); John, of Indian Burial Place (Twillingate district), 1843 (DPHW 86); James, of Garnish, 1850, planter of Point Enragée (Fortune B.), 1858 (DPHW 104); Owen, planter of Lally Cove, 1859 (DPHW 104); Charles and John, of Belleoram, 1871 (Lovell); Robert, of Hermitage Cove, 1871 (Lovell); Abraham, of Little Bay (East and West) (Fortune B.), 1871 (Lovell).

Modern status: May, scattered, especially at Point Enragée; Maye, in the Green Bay district.

Place names (not necessarily from the surname): May Cove 47-33 54-53; —— ——, —— Head 47-44 55-53; —— Point 46-53 55-56; —— Pond (or Point —— Pond) 46-54 55-55.

MAYBEE, a surname of England, ? from a pet-form of the female baptismal names Amabel, Mabel, ? from Latin *amabilis* – lovable, or ? a variant of the surname of Guernsey (Channel Islands) Mabey. (Turk).

In Newfoundland:

Early instances: John Maybe(y), of Trinity (Trinity B.), 1811, of Trouty, 1822 (DPHW 64); George Mabin, farmer of Springfield (Conception B.), 1871 (Lovell).

Modern status: At Corner Brook, Trinity (*Electors* 1955) and St. John's.

MAYE. *See* MAY

MAYNARD, a surname of England and Ireland, from a personal name, Old German *Maganhard, Meginard*, Old French *Mainard, Meinhard*, containing the elements *strength* and *strong*. (Reaney).

Traced by Guppy in Cornwall and Devon, and by MacLysaght in Co. Cork.

In Newfoundland:

Early instances: William Manyard, boatkeeper of St. John's, 1682 (CO 1); James Mainard, of Bay de Verde, 1730 (CO 194.23); Thomas Mannard, planter of Bull Cove (Brigus district), 1832 (DPHW 34); Henry Maynard, from Ringwood (Hampshire), married at St. John's, 1833 (DPHW 26D); Henry Manyard, farmer of Flatrock (St. John's), 1871 (Lovell).

Modern status: Scattered, especially at Norris Point (St. Barbe district).

MAYNE, a surname of England, Ireland and Scotland, from the Old German personal names *Maino, Meino* – strength, or from Old French *magne, maine* – great, or from Old French *mayns*, a nickname for a man "with the hands," or from the French place name Maine or Mayenne; in Ireland also for Mac-MANUS in Co. Fermanagh; in Scotland, usually spelt Main, from the baptismal name Magnus (*see* Mc-MANUS). (Reaney, Cottle, MacLysaght, Black).

Traced by Guppy in Cornwall, by MacLysaght in Cos. Fermanagh and Antrim, and, as Main, by Black at Nairn and in Aberdeenshire and the southern counties of Scotland.

In Newfoundland:

Early instances: Nicholas Maine, "2 years an inhabitant of St. John's or Bay Bulls," in 1680, of St. John's, 1682 (CO 1); John Mayne, of St. John's, 1777 (DPHW 26D); John, of Bonavista, 1789 (DPHW 70); John Jr., of Harbour Grace, 1813 (D'Alberti 5); Thomas, of Bonne Bay, deceased 1846 (*Newfoundlander* 29 Oct 1846); Roger Maine, fisherman of Hopeall, 1871 (Lovell); Simeon, of Port au Port, 1871 (Lovell); Joseph, of Scilly Cove (now Winterton), 1871 (Lovell).

Modern status: At Corner Brook (*Electors* 1955), Hopeall and Millertown.

MAYO, a surname of England and Ireland, in England from Old French *Mahieu*, a Norman form of Matthew (*see* MATTHEWS); in Ireland (Mac) Mayo, *Mac Máighiú*, from the same source. (Reaney, MacLysaght).

Traced by Guppy in Dorset and by MacLysaght in Co. Mayo, though the surname is not taken from the name of the county.

In Newfoundland:

Early instances: William, of St. John's, 1798 (DPHW 26B); John, of Burin, 1805 (D'Alberti 15); Fanny, of Ferryland, 1848 (DPHW 31); George Mayho, fisherman of Pardy's Island (Burin district), 1860 (DPHW 108); James John, Fortune, married Margaret Lake, 1869 (Grand Bank Methodist marriages, P.E.L. Smith); Robert, of Rock Harbour (Placentia B.), 1871 (Lovell).

Modern status: Scattered, especially in the Burin district and at Creston South.

MEADE(S), surnames of England, Meade a surname of Ireland, from Old English *mǣd* – (dweller in or by the) meadow, or from the English place name

Mead (Devon), or ? from Old English *meodu* – (maker or seller of) mead; also in Ireland, – the man from Meath. (Reaney, MacLysaght).

Guppy traced Mead in Buckinghamshire, Essex, Hertfordshire, Somerset, Wiltshire and Yorkshire NR, ER, noting that Meade is a Somerset form. Spiegelhalter traced Mead(e) in Devon, and MacLysaght Meade in Co. Cork.

In Newfoundland:

Early instances: Richard Mead, of St. John's, 1804 (Nfld. Archives BRC); Garret Meade, from Waterford, of St. John's, died 1817 (*Royal Gazette* 20 May 1817); John, of Harbour Grace Parish, 1820 (Nfld. Archives HGRC); Samuel Mead, of Jersey Harbour, 1829 (DPHW 109); George Mead(e), of Brigus, 1830 (DPHW 34); George Mede, of Hermitage Cove, 1835 (DPHW 30); William Mead, of Upper Burgeo, 1846 (DPHW 101); George, of Aquaforte, 1848 (DPHW 31); George, from Gillingham (Dorset), married at St. John's, 1850 (DPHW 26D); Meshack, fisherman of Cape La Hune, ? 1851 (DPHW 101); Meshack, of Eastern Cul de Sac, 1854 (DPHW 102); William, of Little La Poile, 1860 (DPHW 99); Michael Meade, of Harbour Grace, 1866 (Nfld. Archives HGRC); James Mead, of Burnt Island (Burgeo-La Poile district), 1871 (Lovell); George, of Ferryland, 1871 (Lovell); Henry, of Furby's Cove, 1871 (Lovell); John (and others), of Little Placentia (now Argentia), 1871 (Lovell); Charles (and others) Meade, of Ramea Islands, 1871 (Lovell); Jeremiah, of Ship Harbour (Placentia B.), 1871 (Lovell); William Mead, planter of West Point (Burgeo-La Poile district), 1871 (Lovell).

Modern status: Meade, scattered, especially in the Burgeo-La Poile district; Meades, rare, at St. John's.

Place name: Meade Shoal (Labrador) 53-53 56-26.

MEADEN, a surname of England – (dweller by the) meadow-end. (Reaney).

Traced by Guppy in Dorset.

In Newfoundland:

Early instances: John Meadon, of St. John's, 1779 (DPHW 26D); George, of Brigus, at Exploits B[urnt] Island, 1822 (USPG).

Modern status: Rare, at St. John's (*Electors* 1955).

MEADUS, a surname of England, from Old English *meodu* – mead, *hūs* – house (dweller or worker at the) mead-house, or a variant of Meadows – (dweller by the) meadows. (Weekley *Surnames*).

Traced in Dorset.

In Newfoundland:

Family traditions: William Meadows, from Great Canford near Poole (Dorset), settled at Grates Cove, the family name becoming Meadus (MUN Folklore). Edmund Meadus (1819–1905), from Poole (Dorset), came to Newfoundland with his brother in the 1830s; Edmund settled at Greenspond and his brother at Grates Cove (MUN Folklore).

Early instances: J. Medies or Madies, planter of St. John's, 1702 (CO 194.2); John Medis or Meadows, planter of Western Bay, 1824–29 (DPHW 52A); John Brooks Medus, from Poole (Dorset), married at St. John's, 1829 (DPHW 26D); Thomas Meadows, of Salmon Cove (now Champneys), 1834 (DPHW 64B); Thomas Meadus, of Salmon Cove (now Champneys), 1843 (DPHW 64B); John, merchant's clerk of Fogo, 1845 (DPHW 83); John, of Twillingate, 1858 (DPHW 26D); Fanny Meadows, of Grates Cove, 1858 (DPHW 58); Edmond and Malachie Meadows, of Greenspond, 1871 (Lovell); William Meadus, of Trinity (Trinity B.), 1871 (Lovell); William Meadas, Medis or Medirs, of King's Cove, 1871 (Nfld. Archives KCRC).

Modern status: Scattered, especially at St. John's and Grates Cove.

MEAGHER. *See* MAHER

MEALEY, a surname of Ireland (O)Meally, properly a synonym of (O)Melly, *Ó Meallaigh*, Ir. *meall* – pleasant, but often used for a quite distinct name O'Malley (MALLAY). (MacLysaght).

MacLysaght traced (O)Melly in north Connacht and Co. Donegal.

In Newfoundland:

Early instances: Thomas Mealy, fisherman of St. John's, 1794–5, "14 years in Newfoundland," that is, 1780–1 (Census 1794–5); Patrick, from Dublin, Irish convict landed at Petty Harbour or Bay Bulls, 1789 (CO 194.38); Edward, of Western Bay, 1798 (DPHW 48); William Mealey, proprietor and co-occupier of fishing room, Riders Harbour (Trinity B.), Winter 1800–01 (Census Trinity B.); Joanna Meal(l)y, of Trepassey, 1810 (Nfld. Archives BRC); John Mealy, from Limerick, shoreman of St. John's, died 1816 (*Nfld. Mercantile Journal* 27 Nov 1816); Laurence, of Harbour Grace Parish, 1822 (Nfld. Archives HGRC); Thomas, from Co. Carlow, married at Bonavista, 1822 (Nfld. Archives KCRC); Michael Mealy, from Ireland, of Carbonear, 1837 (*Nfld. Patriot* new series II., 4); Edward and James Mealy, of Foxtrap, 1871 (Lovell).

Modern status: At St. John's.

Place name (not necessarily from the surname): Mealey Mountains (Labrador) 53-10 60-00.

MEANEY, a surname of Ireland (O)Meany, a Munster form of (O)MOONEY, *Ó Maonaigh,* Ir. *moenach –* dumb or Ir. *maonach –* wealthy. (MacLysaght).

Traced by MacLysaght in Cos. Clare and Kilkenny.

In Newfoundland:

Early instances: William Meany, of Harbour Main, 1784 (CO 199.18); Edward, of St. John's, 1789 (CO 194.38); Nicholas, of Carbonear, 1795 (CO 199.18); Bridget, of Harbour Grace Parish, 1806 (Nfld. Archives HGRC); Matthew, from Old Laughlin Parish (unidentified) (Co. Carlow), married at St. John's, 1813 (Nfld. Archives BRC); William, fisherman of Bonavista Bay, 1821 (D'Alberti 31); Michael, from Ballyberrigan (Co. Cork), fisherman of Carbonear, died 1839 (*Star and Conception B.J.* 8 Jan 1840); Robert Meaney, of Fermeuse, 1835 (Nfld. Archives BRC); ——, ? of Harbour Grace, 1837 (*Newfoundlander* 5 Jan 1837); Mary, of King's Cove Parish, 1846 (Nfld. Archives KCRC); John Mean(e)y, of Harbour Grace, 1866 (Nfld. Archives HGRC); scattered in Lovell 1871; Michael Meany, of Bird Cove (St. Barbe district), 1873 (MUN Hist.).

Modern status: Scattered, especially at Avondale.

Place name: Meany Island (Labrador) 53-46 56-39.

MEEHAN, a surname of Ireland (O)Meehan, *Ó Miadhacháin,* Ir. *miadhach –* honourable, or a variant of (O)Meegan of the same derivation, or of (O)Mehegan, *Ó Maothagáin,* Ir. *maoth –* soft. (MacLysaght).

Traced by MacLysaght in all four provinces.

In Newfoundland:

Early instances: Catherine Mehan, from Furless (unidentified), Ireland, married at St. John's, 1804 (Nfld. Archives BRC); James Meehan, of Fogo Island, 1805 (D'Alberti 15); Patrick, from Carrick-on-Suir (Co. Tipperary), married at St. John's, 1806 (Nfld. Archives BRC); Michael, tailor of St. John's, 1809–10 (CO 194.50); David, of Harbour Grace Parish, 1816 (Nfld. Archives HGRC); James, of Tilton Harbour (now Tilting), 1817 (Nfld. Archives KCRC); John Meaghen, of Fortune Harbour, 1830 (Nfld. Archives KCRC); D. Mehan, of Harbour Grace, 1832 (*Newfoundlander* 23 Aug 1832); John Meehan, of Bay de Verde, 1871 (Lovell); Daniel, of Gaskin (Point La Hays), 1871 (Lovell); William, of Mall Bay, Mother Ixxes (now Regina) and Mosquito area, 1871 (Lovell); John, of St. Mary's, 1871 (Lovell).

Modern status: At St. John's and in St. Mary's district especially at Point La Haye.

MEHANEY. *See* MAHANEY

MELAMED, a Jewish surname, Hebrew *melammed –* teacher, schoolmaster.

In Newfoundland:

Modern status: Rare, at St. John's.

MELANSON, ? a Newfoundland variant of the surname of France Melesson, containing the element *melle –* ring or *mêle –* medlar (the fruit). (Dauzat).

In Newfoundland:

Modern status: Rare, at Mouse Island (Burgeo-La Poile district) (*Electors* 1955) and St. John's.

MELAY, MELEE, variants of the surname Ireland (O)Millea, *O Maol Aoidh –* devotee of St. Aodh or Hugh. (MacLysaght). *See also* MALLAY.

MacLysaght traced (O)Millea in Kilkenny and adjacent counties from the 16th century.

In Newfoundland:

Early instances: John Millay and William Mellee, of St. John's, 1871 (Lovell); William Melley, of Three Arms (Twillingate district), 1871 (Lovell).

Modern status: In the Placentia West district and at St. John's.

MELBOURNE, a surname of England from the English place name Melbourne (Derbyshire, Yorkshire ER, Cambridgeshire). (Cottle, Ekwall).

In Newfoundland:

Early instances: James, of Bay de Loup, 1852 (DPHW 101); Edward, fisherman of Frenchman's Cove (Burgeo-La Poile district), 1860 (DPHW 99); Edward Melborne, fisherman of Cinque Cerf, 1871 (Lovell).

Modern status: At Grand Bruit, Burgeo (*Electors* 1955) and Channel.

Place names: New Melbourne, —— —— Cove 48-03 53-09.

MELEE. *See* MELAY

MELENDY, MELINDY, ? surnames of England of unknown origin.

In Newfoundland:

Early instances: Thomas Mallandy, Mellondy, Milandy or Melundy, of Cape Island (Bonavista B.), 1835, of Cape Freels, 1849 (DPHW 76).

Modern status: Melendy, at St. John's, Lumsden, Corner Brook and Templeman; Melindy, at Lumsden.

MELVIN, a surname of England, Ireland and Scotland, in England and Scotland a variant of Melville, from the Scots place name Melville (Midlothian) named after Geoffrey de Mallaville of Emalleville (Seine-Inférieure); in Ireland for (O)Mulvin, *Ó Maoilmhín*, Ir. *mín* – gentle, or for (O)Bleahan, Bleheen, *Ó Blichín*. (Reaney, Black, MacLysaght).

Traced by MacLysaght in east Galway.

In Newfoundland:

Family tradition: Michael, ? from Ireland, was the first settler of La Manche (Southern Shore) in the mid-1800s (MUN Folklore).

Early instances: Elizabeth, of St. John's, 1751 (CO 194.13); Matthew, of Bay Bulls district, 1803 (Nfld. Archives BRC); Lucinda, of Harbour Grace, 1828 (Nfld. Archives BRC); Stephen, planter of Bauline (Conception B.), 1871 (Lovell); David, of Burn Cove (Ferryland district), 1871 (Lovell); William, of Caplin Cove (Twillingate district), 1871 (Lovell); George and Thomas, planters of La Manche (Southern Shore), 1871 (Lovell); Garret and Matthew, fishermen of La Manche to Cape Race area, 1871 (Lovell).

Modern status: Scattered, especially in the Ferryland district with a large concentration at La Manche (*Electors* 1955).

Place name (not necessarily from the surname): Melvins Point 49-07 55-13.

MENCHENTON, MENCHINTON, surnames of England, from the English place names Minchinhampton (Gloucestershire), Minchington (Dorset), Michendown (Devon). (Cottle). *See* MENCHIONS.

Spiegelhalter traced Minchington in Devon.

In Newfoundland:

Family tradition: —— Menchenton, from England, went to Exploits at the age of 5 (in the early 19th century); the family later moved to Norris Arm (MUN Folklore).

Early instances: Jonathan Minchington, carpenter of St. John's, 1847 (DPHW 26B); Alfred, fisherman of Great Harbour (Fortune B.), 1851 (DPHW 104); —— Menchinton, on the *Mary Jane* in the seal fishery out of Catalina, 1853 (*Newfoundlander* 17 Mar 1853); William Minchington, member of the Board of Road Commissioners for the area of Exploits Burnt Island, 1857 (*Nfld. Almanac*).

Modern status: Menchenton, at Norris Arm and St. John's; Menchinton, rare, at St. John's.

MENCHIONS, a variant of the surname of England Minchin, from Old English *mynecen* – nun (a nickname), or from the English place name Minchin-

hampton (Gloucestershire) – the nun's high farm or homestead. (Reaney, Cottle, Ekwall). *See also* MENCHENTON.

Guppy traced Minchin in Gloucestershire.

In Newfoundland:

Family tradition: Thomas, from England, settled at ? Bishop's Cove (MUN Folklore).

Early instances: Thomas Minchum, of Ragged Harbour (unspecified), 1681 (CO 1); Thomas Menshen, of St. John's or place adjacent, 1706, of Petty Harbour, 1708 (CO 194.4); Matthew Minshon, of Coopers Head (Bishop's Cove, Conception B.), 1801 (CO 199.18); Thomas Minchens, of Bird Island Cove (now Elliston), 1825 (MUN Hist.); Matthew (and others), of Bishop's Cove, 1871 (Lovell); John, planter of Spaniards Bay, 1871 (Lovell).

Modern status: Scattered, especially at Bay Roberts and Bishop's Cove.

MERCER, a surname of England and Ireland, Old French *merc(h)ier* – merchant, especially a dealer in silks, velvets and other costly fabrics. (Reaney).

Traced by Guppy in Kent and Lancashire, by Spiegelhalter in Devon and by MacLysaght in Cos. Antrim and Down and as Mercier in Co. Offaly and other midland counties.

In Newfoundland:

Family traditions: Jacob, from Poole (Dorset), settled at Bay Roberts about 1810 (MUN Folklore). ——, from Jersey (Channel Islands), settled at Bay Roberts about 1727 (MUN Folklore). Joseph (1818–1899), of Blaketown (Trinity B.) (MUN Geog.).

Early instances: Charles, Thomas and Edward Merser, of Bay Roberts, 1790, property "in possession of the Family for upwards of 108 years," that is, before 1682 (CO 199.18); Robert, of Morrison, on the western shore (? of Placentia B.), about 1730–5 (CO 194.9); John Mercer, of Placentia ? district, 1744 (CO 194.24); Owen, of Point Verd(e) (Placentia district), before 1751 (Kirwin); Charles, one of four Newfoundland inhabitants in possession of Little Belle Isle (Conception B.), 1757 (Nfld. Archives L118); Thomas Merser, of (Upper) Island Cove, 1773 (CO 199.18); Charles, of Port de Grave, 1775 (CO 199.18); John, of the Harbour of Quirpon (Island of Jack), 1787 (CO 194.21, 37); Francis, of Great Bell Isle (now Bell Island), before 1797 (D'Alberti 7); John Mercer, planter of Chamberlains, 1826 (DPHW 34); George, fisherman of Topsail, 1840 (DPHW 39); Thomas, of Ship Cove (Conception B.), 1842 (DPHW 39); James, planter of Cupids, 1848 (DPHW 34); William Merser, of Joe Batts Arm, 1857 (DPHW 83); Jonathan, granted land at Spaniards Bay Pond, 1859 (Nfld. Archives, Registry Crown Lands); Thomas, of Bareneed, 1871 (Lovell); John and Thomas, of Coley's Point, 1871 (Lovell); William, of Kelligrews, 1871 (Lovell); George and William Jr., of St. John's, 1871 (Lovell).

Modern status: Widespread, especially at Upper Island Cove, Shearstown, Bay Roberts, St. John's, Blaketown, Whitbourne, Coley's Point and Chamberlains.

Place names: Mercer('s) Cove 47-16 55-53; Mercer Cove 47-37 57-38; —— Head 47-15 55-51, —— —— (or Little Cape) 47-16 55-50; —— Island (Labrador) 52-38 55-51; —— Point 47-36 57-38; —— Rocks 47-15 55-52; Mercer's Cove 47-36 53-14.

MERCHANT, a surname of England, a variant of Marchant, from Old French *marchand, marchëant* – merchant, trader. (Reaney, Cottle).

Traced by Spiegelhalter in Devon.

In Newfoundland:

Early instances: ——, of St. John's, 1800 (D'Alberti 7); James, of Harbour Grace Parish, 1821 (Nfld. Archives HGRC); John Mercant, fisherman of Bears Cove (Harbour Grace), 1824 (DPHW 43); Valentine Merchant, from Co. Waterford, married at St. John's, 1831 (Nfld. Archives BRC); John, of Harbour Grace, 1847 (*Newfoundlander* 11 Nov 1847); Thomas, granted land at New Perlican, 1857 (Nfld. Archives, Registry Crown Lands); Valentine, trader of Heart's Content, 1871 (Lovell).

Modern status: Rare, at St. John's (*Electors* 1955).

Place names (not necessarily from the surname): Merchant Cove 47-32 55-36, 47-34 54-09; —— Island 47-24 53-58, 51-36 55-27.

MERILS, a surname of England, one of several variants from the feminine baptismal name Muriel, of Celtic origin, in Welsh *Meriel, Meryl*, in Irish *Muirgel*, later *Muirgheal*, containing the elements *sea* and *bright*. It is found in Brittany and Normandy in the 11th century and was brought to England by the Normans, though, as Reaney remarks, in Staffordshire and the Welsh border counties it may have come direct from Wales, and in Yorkshire it may have been introduced by Scandinavians from Ireland. Another source may be (dweller on or near the) pleasant hill. (Withycombe, Reaney, Cottle).

Guppy traced Merrils in Nottinghamshire. Spiegelhalter traced Merrell in Devon.

In Newfoundland:

Modern status: Rare, at St. John's.

MERNER, ? a Newfoundland variant of the surname of Ireland Mernagh, *Meirtneach* – dispirited. (MacLysaght).

MacLysaght traced Mernagh in Co. Wexford.

In Newfoundland:

Early instances: Peter Mernaugh, of Harbour Grace Parish, 1818 (Nfld. Archives HGRC); Patrick Merner, from Sutton's Parish (Co. Wexford), married at St. John's, 1820 (Nfld. Archives BRC); James, married at St. John's, 1831 (Nfld. Archives BRC); James, farmer of Harbour Main, 1871 (Lovell); Denis, farmer of St. John's, 1871 (Lovell).

Modern status: At Placentia (*Electors* 1955), Harbour Main and St. John's.

MERRICK, a surname of England and Ireland, Merricks of Scotland, from the Old German personal name *Amalricus* containing the elements *work* and *ruler*, or from the Welsh form *Meuric* of the baptismal name Maurice, or from the Scots place name Merrick (Kirkcudbrightshire); also in Ireland a variant of Merry, *Ó Mearadhaigh, Ó Meardha*, from adjectives meaning lively. (Withycombe, Cottle, E. C. Smith, Black, MacLysaght). *See* MYRICK.

Traced by Guppy in Herefordshire, Middlesex and Shropshire, with Meyrick also a Shropshire form, by Spiegelhalter in Devon, and by MacLysaght from Wales in Connacht since the 13th century, and in west Waterford and adjoining areas.

In Newfoundland:

Early instance: Patrick Merrick, of St. John's, 1856 (*Newfoundlander* 11 Dec 1856).

Modern status: Rare, at St. John's (*Electors* 1955).

MERRIGAN, a surname of Ireland, (O)Merrigan, *Ó Muireagáin*, ? a diminutive of a name beginning with *Muir*. (MacLysaght). *See also* MORGAN.

Traced by MacLysaght originally in Cos. Longford and Westmeath, now scattered.

In Newfoundland:

Early instances: Bridget, of Trinity (unspecified), 1772 (CO 194.30); Mary, of Harbour Grace Parish, 1807 (Nfld. Archives HGRC); Stephen Merragen, from Waterford City, married at St. John's, 1807 (Nfld. Archives BRC); Thomas Merigan, of St. John's, 1830 (Nfld. Archives BRC); Jeremiah Merrigan, granted land near Monday's Pond, 1840 (Nfld. Archives, Registry Crown Lands); Mary, of King's Cove Parish, 1841 (Nfld. Archives KCRC); Edmond (and others) Merigan, of Colliers, 1871 (Lovell); James and William Merrigan, planters of Renews, 1871 (Lovell).

Modern status: Scattered.

MESH, ? a variant of the surname of England Mash, itself ? a variant of MARSH.

Guppy traced Mash in Huntingdonshire.

In Newfoundland:

Early instances: Richard, of Bonavista, 1789 (DPHW 70); Rachael, of Bonavista, in possession of fishing room, Bayley's Cove, Bonavista before 1805 (Bonavista Register 1806); Patience, of Broad Cove (now Duntara), 1825 (Nfld. Archives KCRC); Joseph, of Keels, 1826 (DPHW 70); Joseph Mish, planter of Bonaventure (unspecified), 1826 (DPHW 64B); John Mesh, Mish or Mash, of Gooseberry Island (Bonavista B.), 1850 (Nfld. Archives KCRC); Benjamin Mesh, fisherman of Riders Harbour (Trinity B.), 1853 (DPHW 64B); Benjamin and John, of Deer Harbour (Trinity B.), 1871 (Lovell); Samuel Mash, of Salvage, 1871 (Lovell).

Modern status: Scattered, especially at Keels.

MESHER, a surname of England, a variant of Measure from French *masure* – (dweller in the) hovel, shanty, or ? from the English place name Meshaw (Devon), or ? a variant of Masheder, ? a nickname for one who steeped malt, or ? a variant of Messer, from Old French *mess(i)er* – harvester, hayward. (Weekley *Surnames*, Ekwall, Reaney).

In Newfoundland:

Early instances: Charles Messer, of Harbour Grace Parish, 1828 (Nfld. Archives HGRC); John Mesher, of Spotted Islands (Labrador), 1835 (DPHW 26B).

Modern status: At St. Anthony and Gander.

Place name: Meshers Harbour (Labrador) 54-55 58-58.

MESSERVEY, a surname of Jersey (Channel Islands). (Turk).

In Newfoundland:

Family tradition: ———, from Jersey (Channel Islands), settled at Sandy Point (St. George's B.) in the latter part of the 18th century (MUN Folklore).

Early instances: Capt. Masservey, of Harbour Grace, 1760 (CO 199.18); Philip Misservey, of St. George's Bay, 1820 (DPHW 26B); Benjamin Messervey, of Sandy Point (St. George's B.), 1870 (DPHW 96); John Messewey, of La Poile, 1871 (Lovell).

Modern status: In the St. George's district, especially at Sandy Point (*Electors* 1955).

Place name: Messerv(e)y Point 48-27 58-30.

METCALF(E), surnames of England and Ireland, of uncertain origin, ? from Old English **mete-cealf* – a calf fattened for food, hence a nickname for a fat man. (Reaney).

Traced by Guppy in Cumberland, Westmorland, Durham, Lancashire and Yorkshire, by Spiegelhalter in Devon, and by MacLysaght in Ireland since the 17th century.

In Newfoundland:

Early instances: James Midcaff, of St. John's, 1798 (DPHW 26B); Nicholas and James, of Chamberlains, 1801 (CO 199.18); ——— Metcalf, of Portugal Cove, 1830 (*Newfoundlander* 12 Aug 1830); John Metcalfe, of Topsail, 1835 (DPHW 26D).

Modern status: Metcalf, at Millertown Junction (*Electors* 1955); Metcalfe, at Bell Island and in the Harbour Main district.

MEWS, a surname of England from the English place name Meaux (Yorkshire ER) "pronounced *mews* to rhyme with sluice." (Reaney).

In Newfoundland:

Early instances: John ? Mew, merchant of St. John's, 1805 (CO 194.44); Joseph Mew, one of the party of men led by William Cull of Fogo, who went up the Exploits (River) in quest of the native Indians, 1810 (D'Alberti 20); Honour, of Change Islands, 1821 (USPG); James, J.P. for Northern district of the Colony, 1834 (*Newfoundlander* 10 Jul 1834); James, fisherman of Joe Batts Arm, 1849, of Barr'd Island, 1861 (DPHW 80, 83); James Collis, of Hants Harbour, 1860 (DPHW 59); James L., of Old Perlican, 1871 (Lovell).

Modern status: Scattered, especially at St. John's and Birchy Bay (Twillingate district).

MEYERS, with Meyer, surnames of England and Ireland, from Old French *maire* – mayor, or from Old French *mire*, Middle English *mire, meir, meyre* – physician, or from German Meier – steward, bailiff, farmer, a Jewish and German surname; also in Ireland *Ó Meidhir*, Ir. *meidhir* – mirth.

Traced by MacLysaght in the west of Ireland.

In Newfoundland:

Modern status: At St. John's.

MICHAEL(S), surnames of England, Ireland, Syria-Lebanon and the Micmacs of Newfoundland, Mac Michael of Scotland, Michel of France and Mi(t)chel(e) of the Channel Islands, from Hebrew – Who is like God? Mac Michael is from Gaelic *Mac Mìcheil*, earlier *Mac Gille Mhìcheil* – son of the servant of (St.) Michael. In Ireland, Michael has to some extent been changed to MITCHELL and is also a synonym of Mulvihil, *Ó Maoilmhichil* – devotee of (St.)

Michael. (Withycombe, Reaney, Cottle, Black, MacLysaght, Turk).

Michael was traced by Spiegelhalter in Devon and by MacLysaght in Connacht and elsewhere.

In Newfoundland:

Early instances: John Michael, of King's Cove, 1815 (Nfld. Archives KCRC); Mary Micha(e)l, of Harbour Grace Parish, 1823 (Nfld. Archives HGRC); Margery Michael, married at St. John's, 1830 (Nfld. Archives BRC); John Michel, of South Shore (Conception B.), 1830 (DPHW 26B); James Michall, fisherman of Bay of Islands, 1871 (Lovell); L'aime Michel, fisherman of Petites, 1871 (Lovell); Antonio Michael (1875 –), born at Mount Lebanon, Syria, son of Michael Michael, came to Newfoundland in 1898, settled at St. John's and later Corner Brook; his brothers arrived soon afterwards (*Nfld. Who's Who* 1930, Family); Matty Michel and son, Micmac Indian trappers whose hunting ground was Bonne Bay, 1900–06 (Millais).

Modern status: Michael, at St. John's and Corner Brook; Michaels, at St. John's.

Place names (not necessarily from the surname): Lake Michael (Labrador) 54-36 58-27; Michael's Harbour 49-18 54-59; Michaels River (Labrador) 52-06 59-27.

MIDDLETON, a surname of England, Scotland and Guernsey (Channel Islands), Midleton of Ireland, from the place name Middleton which occurs in some seventy localities in England and in Kincardineshire, generally with the meaning of the middle place or farm. (Cottle, Spiegelhalter, Black, MacLysaght, Turk).

Traced by Guppy in 10 counties in England, including Devon, and in the Aberdeen district.

In Newfoundland:

Early instances: John Middlecom or Mildcum, of Old Perlican, 1681, 1682 (CO 1); William Middleton, shoreman at St. John's, "30 years in Newfoundland," that is, 1764–5 (Census 1794–5); Mary Midleton, of Bay Bulls, 1800 (Nfld. Archives BRC); Abraham Middleton, one of 72 impressed men who sailed from Ireland to Newfoundland ? 1811 (CO 194.51).

Modern status: Rare, at Gander (*Electors* 1955), Nippers Harbour and John's.

Place name: Middleton Lake 49-02 55-58.

MIESSEAU. *See* MUSSEAU

MIFFLEN, MIFFLIN, surnames of England of unknown origin.

Traced by Kirwin in Poole (Dorset).

In Newfoundland:

Early instances: Samson Mifflen, of Bonavista, 1791 (USPG); Sampson, of Catalina, 1843 (*Newfoundlander* 31 Aug 1843); George, granted land at Lance Cove (unspecified), 1855 (Nfld. Archives, Registry Crown Lands).

Modern status: Mifflen, at St. John's; Mifflin, at Catalina, Bonavista and St. John's.

MILES, MYLES, surnames of England and Ireland, from the Old German personal name *Milo*, Old French *Miles*, *Milon*, possibly connected with Old Slavonic *milu* – merciful, or from Latin *miles* – soldier, or from French *Mi(h)el*, a popular form of Michael (*see* MICHAEL); also in Ireland sometimes a variant of (O)Mullery, Mulry, *Ó Maolmhuire* – devotee of the Blessed Virgin Mary. (Reaney, MacLysaght).

Guppy traced Miles in 12 counties, Spiegelhalter in Devon, and MacLysaght found Miles and Myles scattered, with the variant MOYLES mainly in Co. Mayo.

In Newfoundland:

Family traditions: James Miles, from Shaftesbury(Dorset), was the first settler of the community in Fortune Bay now known as Terrenceville, about 1820–30 (MUN Geog.). Sarah (1795–1855), of Bird Island Cove (now Elliston) (MUN Geog.). James Myles (1840–1904), of Boxey (MUN Geog.).

Early instances: Charles Miles, of Bonavista, 1787 (DPHW 70); John Miles or Myles, planter of Bayley's Cove, 1817, of Bird Island Cove (now Elliston), 1823 (DPHW 72); Martha Miles, of Cat Island (Bonavista B.), 1824 (Nfld. Archives KCRC); James, of King's Cove, 1826 (Nfld. Archives KCRC); Thomas Myles, of St. Jacques, 1827, of Jersey Harbour, 1827 (DPHW 109); Catherine Miles, of Keels, 1830 (Nfld. Archives KCRC); Edward, of Ragged Harbour (now Melrose), 1831 (Nfld. Archives KCRC); Michael Myles, of Harbour Grace Parish, 1832 (Nfld. Archives HGRC); Honor, of Catalina, 1833 (Nfld. Archives KCRC); James Miles, of Fortune Bay Bottom, 1835 (DPHW 30); Thomas, of Coombs Cove (Fortune B.), 1835 (DPHW 30); Stephen, of Herring Neck, 1842, of Salt Harbour (Twillingate district), 1851 (DPHW 85, 86); Thomas, blacksmith of Fogo, 1846 (DPHW 83); John, granted land at Colliers Pond near Bonavista, 1850 (Nfld. Archives, Registry Crown Lands); Rachael Myles, of Fortune, 1855 (DPHW 106); Andrew Miles, school-master of Stone Harbour (Twillingate district), 1857 (DPHW 85); Ellen, of Haywards Cove, 1857 (Nfld. Archives KCRC); Robert, planter of

Head of Fortune Bay, 1858 (DPHW 104); John, of Dog Cove (? Bonavista B.), 1869 (Nfld. Archives KCRC); scattered in Lovell 1871.

Modern status: Miles, scattered, especially at Boxey and Salt Harbour Island (Twillingate district); Myles, scattered, especially at Frenchman's Cove (Burin district).

Place names (not necessarily from the surname): Miles Brook 47-45 52-47; —— Cove 49-32 55-47; —— Pond 47-44 52-47.

MILLER, a surname of England, Ireland and Scotland, from Middle English *mylne* – mill or Old Norse *mylnari* – miller. Miller is an assimilated form of Milner. Millar is a Scots form. (Reaney, Cottle, MacLysaght, Black).

Guppy traced Miller in 14 counties in England, and Millar and Miller over the greater part of Scotland though rare in the north. MacLysaght found Millar and Miller very numerous in Co. Antrim and adjacent counties.

In Newfoundland:

Family tradition: ——, from Poole (Dorset), settled at New Bonaventure; the family later moved to Trinity (Trinity B.), and St. John's (MUN Folklore).

Early instances: Richard, of Fermeuse, 1675 (CO 1); John, of St. John's, 1705 (CO 194.22); Samuel Miller or Millar, of Trinity Bay, 1766 (DPHW 64); Samuel Jr. and Thomas Miller, of Fogo, Twillingate or Tilton Harbour (now Tilting), 1771 (CO 194.30); Grace, of Heart's Content, 1773 (DPHW 64); William, of Bonaventure (unspecified), 1785 (DPHW 64); ——, salmon fisherman of Exploits, 1786 (MUN Hist.); George, of English Harbour (Trinity B.), 1792 (DPHW 64); William and Patrick, of Placentia, 1794 (D'Alberti 5); Robert, in fishery at Portugal Cove, 1794–5 (Census 1794–5); John, of St. Mary's, 1797 (D'Alberti 7); William, of Bay Bulls, 1802 (USPG); Thomas, of Fogo, 1803 (D'Alberti 13); Hanna, of Greenspond, 1803 (Nfld. Archives BRC); John, of Kerley's Harbour, 1807 (DPHW 64); Samuel Jr., of New Bonaventure, 1808 (DPHW 64); William, of Fortune Bay, 1815 (D'Alberti 25); Ewing, Miller & Co., merchants trading from the River Clyde to Newfoundland, 1817 (D'Alberti 27); John, from Ireland, married at Joe Batts Arm, 1819 (Nfld. Archives KCRC); Thomas, of Trinity (unspecified), 1819 (Nfld. Archives KCRC); James, clerk of Ferryland, 1821 (D'Alberti 31); Thomas, of Brunette (Island), 1825 (DPHW 109); Samuel Millar, planter of Trouty, 1827 (DPHW 64B); Robert Miller, of Topsail Bite, 1830 (DPHW 30); John, of Pick Hart (Burin

district), 1831 (DPHW 109); Samuel Millar, planter of Salmon Cove (now Champneys), 1832 (DPHW 64B); James Miller, of Harbour Grace Parish, 1832 (Nfld. Archives HGRC); John, of Riders Harbour (Trinity B.), 1833 (Nfld. Archives KCRC); Elizabeth, of Chamberlains, 1837 (DPHW 26D); Thomas, of Manuels, 1838 (DPHW 30); William, fisherman of Gillis Harbour (Trinity North district), 1841 (DPHW 64B); John, ? of Northern Bay, 1844 (DPHW 54); John, planter of Lower Island Cove, 1851 (DPHW 55); ——, of Harbour Grace, 1851 (*Newfoundlander* 2 Oct 1851); Johanna, of Hants Harbour, 1853 (DPHW 59); William Millar, fisherman of Robin Hood (now part of Port Rexton), 1853 (DPHW 64B); William Miller, of New Harbour (unspecified), 1857 (*Newfoundlander* 24 Sep 1857); Joseph, fisherman of Ireland's Eye, 1859 (DPHW 64B); James, of Broad Cove (now Duntara), 1867 (Nfld. Archives KCRC); widespread in Lovell 1871.

Modern status: Widespread, especially at St. John's, New Bonaventure, Kerley's Harbour and Topsail.

Place names: Miller Head, —— Rock 46-57 55-14; —— Head 47-29 55-06; —— Peninsula (Labrador) 59-42 64-07; —— Point 47-36 55-57; —— Rock 49-33 55-10; —— Shoal 47-41 56-00; Millers Brook 49-05 54-40; —— Island 49-34 56-51; —— Passage 47-31 55-39; —— Pond 46-46 53-21; —— ——, —— —— River 47-37 52-50; —— Rock 49-41 54-45; Millertown 48-49 56-33; —— Junction 49-01 56-21.

MILLEY, a ? Newfoundland variant of the surname of Ireland (O)Millea, ? *Ó Maol Aoidh* – devotee of (St.) Aodh or Hugh. (MacLysaght). *See* MELAY, McCUE, McHUGH, HUGHES, MULLEY, MOLLOY.

Traced by MacLysaght in Kilkenny adjacent counties and by Woulfe in Connacht.

In Newfoundland:

Family tradition: John (1797–), born in Western Bay, of Spanish descent, (the name was formerly Millea), was the first Milley to settle at Burnt Point (Conception B.) (MUN Folklore). ——, from Ireland, settled at St. John's (MUN Folklore).

Early instances: Edward, of Western Bay, 1783 (spelt Mellea, 1803) (CO 199. 18); Edward, of St. John's, 1797 (D'Alberti 6); Thomas, of Northern Bay, 1801 (CO 199.18); James ? Milly, one of 72 impressed men who sailed from Ireland to Newfoundland ? 1811 (CO 194.51); William Minney, planter of Adams Cove, 1821 (DPHW 52A); William Milley or Mulley, planter of Mulley's Cove, 1832 (DPHW 52A); John Milley, planter of Burnt Point

(Conception B.), 1832 (DPHW 52A); Francis, of Exploits Burnt Island, 1843 (DPHW 86); Sarah Mily, of Torbay, 1853 (DPHW 32); John Milley, of Trinity (Trinity B.), 1871 (Lovell).

Modern status: Scattered, especially at Burnt Point.

MILLS, a surname of England and Ireland – (dweller by the) mill(s), or son of Miles or Mill; also in Ireland, except Ulster, from the Irish *an Mhuilinn* – of the mill. (Reaney, MacLysaght).

Found widespread by Guppy in England, and in Ulster and elsewhere in Ireland by MacLysaght.

In Newfoundland:

Family tradition: John Joseph Leite, from Portugal, settled in Newfoundland about 1920, adopted the surname Mills; the family settled at Marystown (MUN Folklore).

Early instance: Edward, of Little Placentia (now Argentia), about 1730–5 (CO 194.9); John, of Trinity Bay, 1769 (DPHW 64); Simon, labourer of St. John's, 1795 (D'Alberti 5); Nathaniel, proprietor and occupier of fishing room at Old Perlican, Winter 1800–01 (Census Trinity B.); Elizabeth, of Harbour Grace Parish, 1823 (Nfld. Archives HGRC); James, planter of Fogo, 1823 (USPG); Samuel, joiner of Carbonear, 1823 (DPHW 48); John, of Petty Harbour, 1830 (DPHW 31); John, sailmaker of Trinity (Trinity B.), 1831 (DPHW 64B); Antestatia [sic], of Seal Cove (now New Chelsea), 1831 (DPHW 59); John, of Kings Cove Parish, 1836 (Nfld. Archives KCRC); John, of Western Head (Twillingate district), 1846 (DPHW 86); Eliza, of Crockers Cove (Carbonear), 1847 (DPHW 48); William J., granted land at Brigus, 1850 (Nfld. Archives, Registry Crown Lands); Ralph and William, drowned in Bay Bulls, 1853 (*Newfoundlander* 14 Feb 1853); Ambrose, of Moreton's Harbour, 1860 (DPHW 87); scattered in Lovell 1871.

Modern status: Widespread, especially at St. John's and Burlington (Green B.).

Place names: Mills Harbour (Labrador) 56-54 61-31; —— Siding 48-12 53-58.

MINNETT, a surname of England, from Old French *mignot* – dainty, pleasing, or a diminutive of the personal name *Minn*. (Reaney).

Guppy traced Minett in Gloucestershire.

In Newfoundland:

Early instance: J. Minnet, of St. John's, 1832 (*Newfoundlander* 20 Sep 1832).

Modern status: At St. John's.

MINTY, a surname of England and Scotland, in England from the English place name Minety (Wiltshire) from Old English *minte* – mint, in Scotland of unknown origin. (Guppy, A. H. Smith, Black).

Guppy traced Mint(e)y in Wiltshire.

In Newfoundland:

Early instances: Joseph, fisherman of Twillingate, 1821 (USPG); William, of Bird Island Cove (now Elliston), 1825 (MUN Hist.).

Modern status: At Durrell's Arm, Windsor, Lewisporte (*Electors* 1955), Twillingate and St. John's.

MISCHAUDE, ? a Newfoundland variant of the surname of France Michaut, from the baptismal name Michel – (St.) Michael. (Dauzat). *See* MICHAEL(S).

In Newfoundland:

Modern status: Rare, at Corner Brook.

MISKELL, a surname of Ireland, a variant of (O)Mescal, *Ó Meiscill* (MacLysaght).

Traced by MacLysaght mainly in Co. Clare and adjacent parts of Cos. Galway and Limerick and to a lesser extent in the Waterford area.

In Newfoundland:

Modern status: At St. John's.

MITCHAM, a surname of England from the English place name Mitcham (Surrey), or (dweller or worker at the) big homestead. (Reaney, Cottle).

Traced by Spiegelhalter in Devon.

In Newfoundland:

Family tradition: ——, shipwright, from England, settled at Green's Harbour (Trinity B.) (MUN Folklore).

Early instances: James Mitcham or Mitchem, of New Perlican, 1790, occupier of fishing room at Turks Cove, Winter 1800–01 (Census Trinity B., DPHW 64).

Modern status: Rare, at St. John's (*Electors* 1955).

MITCHELL, a surname of England, Scotland, Ireland, the Channel Islands and of the Micmacs of Newfoundland, from the baptismal name Michael (*see* MICHAEL(S)), or from Old English *mycel*, Middle English *michel* etc. – big; also in Connacht often a synonym of (O)Mulvihill, *Ó Maoilmhichil* – devotee of (St.) Michael. (Reaney, MacLysaght, Turk).

Found widespread by Guppy in England and Scotland as far north as Aberdeen and by MacLysaght in all provinces except Munster.

In Newfoundland:

Family traditions: George, an Englishman, moved from Herring Neck to Little Bay Islands in 1850 (MUN Hist.). ——, from St. Pierre settled at Shoal Point (Mortier B.), in the 18th century (MUN Hist.). William, from Scotland, settled at St. John's (MUN Folklore).

Early instances: Henery, of St. John's Harbour, 1680 (CO 1); John, of Bay Bulls, 1708 (CO 194.4); John Michell or Mitchell, planter of Hermitage, 1710–15 (CO 194.5); Richard Mitchell, fisherman of Quidi Vidi, 1731 (CO 194.9); John, of Petty Harbour, 1789 (D'Alberti 4); William Mitchel, in possession of property in fishery at Portugal Cove, 1794–5 (Census 1794–5); William Mitchell, of Harbour Grace Parish, 1820 (Nfld. Archives HGRC); William, of Harbour Grace, 1830 (Nfld. Archives HGRC); Emmanuel Mitchel, planter of Brigus, 1831 (DPHW 34); James, of New Perlican, 1836 (DPHW 59); Mrs. Mitchell, from Youghal (Co. Cork), of Harbour Grace, 1844 (*Indicator* 27 Jul 1844); Eliza, from Plymouth, married at St. John's, 1847 (*Royal Gazette* 30 Nov 1847); William Mitchel, of Deer Island (Burgeo-La Poile district), 1849 (DPHW 101); Alexander Mitchell, granted land at Chamberlains, 1850 (Nfld. Archives, Registry Crown Lands); George Mitchel, fisherman of Green Cove (Twillingate district), 1851, of Little Bay Islands, 1858 (DPHW 85, 92); George, of Shoe Cove (Twillingate district), 1851 (DPHW 86); William Mitchell, of Garia, 1855 (DPHW 98); James, of Hants Harbour, 1856 (DPHW 59); Arthur Bambrick, from Dublin, of St. John's, 1858 (*Newfoundlander* 8 Feb 1858); Laurie, fisherman of Bay d'Est (Burgeo-La Poile district), 1860 (DPHW 99); John Mitchel, of Greenspond, 1870 (Nfld. Archives KCRC); scattered in Lovell 1871; John Mitchell, Indian engaged in salmon fishery at Grandy's Brook, 1874 (MUN Hist.).

Modern status: Widespread, especially at Portugal Cove, St. John's, Marystown and Terrenceville.

Place names: Mitchell Brook 49-20 58-07; —— Cove 47-33 56-52; Mitchells Brook 47-08 53-31, 47-53 58-07; —— Pond 49-21 57-46; —— —— North 47-36 52-51; —— —— South 47-33 52-52.

MITCHELMORE, a surname of England, ? from the English place name Mutter's Moor (Devon), or some unidentified place name.

Spiegelhalter traced Mi(t)chelmore in Devon.

In Newfoundland:

Family tradition: Thomas was the first settler of Green Island Cove (St. Barbe district), in the late 1800s (MUN Hist.).

Early instances: William, of St. John's, 1828 (DPHW 26D); Henry, fisherman of Green Island (St. Barbe district), 1871 (Lovell).

Modern status: Scattered, especially at Green Island Cove (St. Barbe district).

MOAKLER, a surname of England, Mockler of Ireland, from Old French *mal, mau* – bad and *clerc* – cleric. (Reaney, Dauzat, MacLysaght).

MacLysaght traced Mockler in Co. Tipperary since 1210.

In Newfoundland:

Family tradition: ——, from Tipperary, settled at St. John's about 1830 (MUN Folklore).

Early instances: William Mockler, from Cashel (Co. Tipperary), married at St. John's, 1797 (Nfld. Archives BRC); Catherine Mokeler, of Bay Bulls, 1820 (Nfld. Archives BRC); Margaret Mockler, of Harbour Grace Parish, 1826 (Nfld. Archives HGRC); T., of St. John's, 1831 (*Newfoundlander* 29 Dec 1831); J., of Harbour Grace, 1832 (*Newfoundlander* 23 Aug 1832).

Modern status: At Bay Bulls, St. John's and Topsail.

MOFFAT(T), surnames of England, Scotland and Ireland, from the Scots place name Moffat (Dumfriesshire).

Traced by Guppy in Cumberland, Westmorland and Northumberland and south of the Forth and Clyde especially on the Scots border in Dumfriesshire, and by MacLysaght in Ulster since the early 17th century.

In Newfoundland:

Early instance: William Moffett, soldier of St. John's, 1819 (DPHW 26B).

Modern status: Rare, at Corner Brook (*Electors* 1955).

MOGRIDGE, MUG(G)RIDGE, surnames of England from the English place name Mogridge (Devon). (Reaney).

Mogridge traced by Spiegelhalter in Devon, Muggeridge by Guppy in Surrey and Sussex.

In Newfoundland:

Family tradition: Aaron Mogridge (1795–1875), born in Exeter, came with wife and children to St. John's as a carpenter working on the Anglican Cathedral in 1843, settled in the Goulds-Kilbride area in 1847 (MUN Geog.).

Early instances: Gilbert Maugridge, of St. John's, 1762 (CO 194.15); Bartholomew Mokridge, of Tickle Cove (Bonavista B.), 1832 (DPHW 70); Robert Moggridge, granted land at Bay Bulls Road,

1849 (Nfld. Archives, Registry Crown Lands); John Mogeridge, farmer of St. John's, 1871 (Lovell).

Modern status: Mogridge, rare, at Kilbride; Muggridge, at Winter Brook, Open Hall and Tickle Cove (Bonavista B.), and Bay Bulls Road; Mugridge, rare, at Musgravetown.

MOLLON, ? a Newfoundland variant of the surname of France Molon, from French *meule* – millstone, or an obscure nickname – stack, pile. (Dauzat).

In Newfoundland:

Early instance: John Molum, of Placentia, 1681 (CO 1).

Modern status: At Lark Harbour and Cox's Cove (Humber West district) (*Electors* 1955).

MOLLOY, a surname of Ireland, (O)Molloy, Mulloy, *Ó Maolmhuaidh*, Ir. *muadh* – big, soft, noble, or an anglicized form of *Ó Maolaoidh* (*see* MILLEY), or for a number of other Irish names (MacLysaght).

Traced by MacLysaght in Cos. Offaly and Roscommon and elsewhere.

In Newfoundland:

Family tradition: Patrick, from Ireland, settled at Trepassey about 1750–5 (MUN Folklore).

Early instances: William, fisherman of St. John's, 1794–5, "30 years in Newfoundland," that is, 1764–5 (Census 1794–5); Michael Mulloy, from Lismoline (unidentified) (Co. Tipperary), married at St. John's, 1803 (Nfld. Archives BRC); Edward, of Burin, 1804 (D'Alberti 14); Richard Molloy, one of 72 impressed men who sailed from Ireland to Newfoundland ? 1811 (CO 194.51); Joanna Mulloy alias Meany, of St. Mary's Bay, 1814 (Nfld. Archives BRC); Pat, of Harbour Grace Parish, 1821 (Nfld. Archives HGRC); Mary Molloy, of Trepassey, 1823 (Nfld. Archives BRC); Edward Moloy, doctor of Carbonear, 1824 (DPHW 48); Honora ? Maloy, from Co. Kilkenny, married at. Trinity (unspecified), 1826 (Nfld. Archives KCRC); John Molloy, of Tilting Harbour (now Tilting), 1829 (Nfld. Archives KCRC); George Moloy, of Torbay, 1830 (Nfld. Archives BRC); M. Molloy, of Brigus, 1831 (*Newfoundlander* 24 Nov 1831); William Mulloy, surgeon, from New Ross (Co. Wexford), spent 24 years in Newfoundland [1813], 11 at Harbour Grace, died at Harbour Grace, 1837 aged 47 (*Times* 25 Oct 1837); Mrs. Molloy, from Co. Tipperary, of Brigus, 1844 (*Indicator* 24 Aug 1844); John, planter of Harbour Breton, 1859 (DPHW 104); Michael, of Biscay Bay, Portugal Cove area, 1871 (Lovell); John (and others), of Great St. Lawrence, 1871 (Lovell); Michael Mulloy, of Little St. Lawrence, 1871

(Lovell); John Molloy, of Pursell's Cove (Twillingate district), 1871 (Lovell); Thomas, planter of Salmon Cove and Gasters, 1871 (Lovell); Andrew Mulloy, of Aquaforte, 1871 (Lovell); James, of St. Mary's, 1871 (Lovell); John, planter of St. Shotts, 1871 (Lovell).

Modern status: Scattered, especially at St. John's, St. Shotts, Trepassey, Portugal Cove South and St. Lawrence.

Place name: Molloy Ledge 48-11 53-30.

MONA(G)HAN, surnames of Ireland (O)Monaghan, *Ó Manacháin*, Ir. *manach* – monk. (MacLysaght).

Traced by MacLysaght in Roscommon and adjacent counties.

In Newfoundland:

Early instances: ? Rosey Monahan, of Bay Bulls, 1808 (Nfld. Archives BRC); Mary, of Harbour Grace Parish, 1823 (Nfld. Archives HGRC); Margaret, of Harbour Grace, 1829 (Nfld. Archives BRC); Mary Minagin, married at St. John's, 1831 (Nfld. Archives BRC); Michael Minigan, labourer of St. John's, 1871 (Lovell).

Modern status: Monaghan, rare, at Corner Brook (*Electors* 1955); Monahan, rare, at Dunville and Otterbury (Port de Grave district) (*Electors* 1955), and St. John's.

MONK, a surname of England and Scotland, from Old English *manuc, munec* – monk, from service in a monastery or, as Cottle puts it, "in scandalous jest." (Reaney, Cottle, Black). *See also* MONKS with which confusion has occurred.

Traced by Guppy in Buckinghamshire, Kent, Lancashire, Northamptonshire, by Spiegelhalter in Devon and by Black in the Outer Isles.

In Newfoundland:

Family tradition: Timothy, from the west of England, settled at Davis Island (now Port Elizabeth) in the early 1800s; his youngest son William was the first settler of Monkstown about 1850 (MUN Hist.).

Early instance: James, of Oderin, 1871 (Lovell).

Modern status: At Monkstown (Placentia West district) and St. John's.

Place names: Monks Bank 47-13 54-57; —— Ground 47-40 54-11, 48-42 52-58; Monkstown 47-35 54-26.

MONKS, a surname of England and Ireland – servant of the monks, one employed at a monastery; in Ireland also a synonym of MONAGHAN and MacEvanny from *manach* – monk. (Reaney, MacLysaght). *See also* MONK.

In Newfoundland:

Early instances: James, of Bonavista, 1797 (DPHW 70); Hanna, of Kings Cove, 1817 (Nfld. Archives KCRC); William, fisherman of Red Harbour (Burin district), 1860 (DPHW 108); John and William, of Tacks Beach (Placentia B.), 1871 (Lovell).

Modern status: At Woody Island (Placentia B.) (*Electors* 1955), and Kings Cove.

MONNIER, a surname of France, from Old French *monier* – money-changer, or a dialect form of *meunier* – miller, or from the personal name Aymonier.

In Newfoundland:

Modern status: Rare, at St. John's.

MONROE, MUNRO, surnames of Scotland and Ireland, Gaelic *Rothach* – (the man from the) mouth of the (River) Roe (Co. Londonderry). "According to a tradition which may be substantially correct the ancestors of the Munros came [to Scotland] from Ireland, from the foot of the river Roe in Derry, whence the name *Bunrotha*, giving *Munrotha* by eclipsis of *b* after the preposition *in*" (W. J. Watson, *The History of the Celtic Place-names of Scotland*, Edinburgh, 1926, p. 116, cited by Black and Reaney). The name has been adopted in Ireland by some O'Mellans and some Milroys. (Black, MacLysaght).

Traced by Guppy in the north of Scotland, especially Ross-shire.

In Newfoundland:

Family traditions: —— Munro, from Scotland, came to Newfoundland via Prince Edward Island and Nova Scotia; his son lived at Campbellton (Notre Dame B.). ——, from Scotland, settled at Glenwood in the late 1800s (MUN Folklore).

Early instances: Thomas Munro, fisherman of St. John's, ? 1730 (CO 194.24); Moses Monroe (1842–), born in Co. Down, Ireland, settled in St. John's about 1860 (Mott); William Munroe, clerk of Harbour Grace, 1871 (Lovell).

Modern status: Monroe, at St. John's; Munro, at Port Blandford (*Electors* 1955), Glenwood and St. John's.

Place names: Monroe 48-12 53-48; Munroes Pond 49-08 55-04.

MONSTER, a ? Newfoundland variant of the surname of Ireland, Munster, changed from (O)Moynihan, *Ó Muimhneacháin*, Ir. *Muimhneach* – Munsterman. (MacLysaght).

Traced by MacLysaght in Co. Mayo.

In Newfoundland:

Family tradition: —— Monster, also spelt Monstur or Morster, from Ireland, settled at Fortune (MUN Folklore).

Early instance: James and Thomas signed petition, 1811 (Duckworth Papers P1/5, pp. 1081–4 per P.E.L. Smith); James 1816 (Lench 1916, pp. 41,43); Thomas, of Fortune, 1825, 1829 (DPHW 109; Grand Bank Methodist baptisms per P.E.L. Smith).

Modern status: At Fortune.

MOODY, a surname of England, Scotland, Ireland and the Channel Islands, from Old English *mōdig* – bold, brave, impetuous, passionate. (Reaney, Cottle, Black, MacLysaght, Turk).

Traced by Guppy in Hampshire, Lincolnshire and Somerset, by Spiegelhalter in Devon and by MacLysaght mainly in Ulster and in Co. Offaly since 1600.

In Newfoundland:

Early instances: John, ? of St. John's, ? 1753 (CO 194.13); John, from Greenock, Scotland, married at St. John's, 1809 (Nfld. Archives BRC); James Moodey, planter of Salmon Cove (now Champneys), 1827 (DPHW 64B).

Modern status: At White Rock (Trinity B.) (*Electors* 1955), Champneys West and St. John's.

MOONEY, a surname of Ireland, (O)Mooney, *Ó Maonaigh*, Ir. *moenach* – dumb or *maonach* – wealthy. (MacLysaght). *See also* MEANEY.

Found widespread by MacLysaght.

In Newfoundland:

Early instances: Will Money, ? labourer of St. John's, 1779 (CO 194.34); James Mooney, fisherman of St. John's, 1794–5, "12 years in Newfoundland," that is, 1782–3 (Census 1794–5); Bartholomew, from Dublin, Irish convict landed at Petty Harbour or Bay Bulls, 1789 (CO 194.38); Pat and Robert, of Placentia, 1794 (D'Alberti 5); Pat Moony, of Harbour Grace Parish, 1810 (Nfld. Archives HGRC); Thomas Mooney, one of 72 impressed men who sailed from Ireland to Newfoundland ? 1811 (CO 194.51); Patrick, of Trinity (Trinity B.), 1812 (DPHW 64); Patrick, of Hearts Content, 1819 (Nfld. Archives KCRC); Eleanor, from Stradbally (Co. Waterford), married at St. John's, 1828 (Nfld. Archives BRC); Sarah, of Brigus, 1853 (*Newfoundlander* 12 Sep 1853); Patrick, of Harbour Grace, 1869 (Nfld. Archives HGRC); John, planter of Branch, 1871 (Lovell); John and Andrew, planters of Gaskin (Point La Hays), 1871 (Lovell); Patrick, of St. Mary's, 1871 (Lovell).

Modern status: Scattered, especially in the Placentia East and St. Mary's districts.

Place name: Mooneys Cove (or Big Seal Cove) 47-22 53-55.

MOOR(E)(S), surnames of England, MUIR, Mure, Mo(o)r(e), of Scotland, Moore of Ireland, from a personal name *More*, Old French *Maur*, Latin *Maurus* – a Moor or dark as a Moor, swarthy, the name of a 6th century saint, or from the English place names Moor(e) (Devon), Moore (Cheshire), More (Shropshire), or from Old English *mōr* – (dweller on or near the) moor, marsh, fen, waste land; in Ireland also for (O)More, *Ó Mórdha*, Ir. *mordha* – majestic. (Reaney, Black, MacLysaght, Spiegelhalter). *See also* MUIR.

Guppy found Moore widespread in England and Muir in Ayrshire and Dumfriesshire. MacLysaght found Moore widespread in Ireland but numerous only in Co. Antrim and Dublin.

In Newfoundland:

Family traditions: John Moore, from Northern Ireland settled at Bareneed about 1800 (MUN Folklore). ——, an Englishman, one of the first four settlers at Twillingate, settled at Back Harbour in the early 1700s (*Nfld. Quarterly* Dec 1905). James Moore (?1803–94), planter of Codroy (Rev. W.J. Moore). Thomas Moore Fitzgibbon, from Ireland or France, settled in Newfoundland and changed his name to Thomas Fitzgibbon Moore; he was the mail carrier for Trinity Bay and member of House of Assembly for Trinity in 1837; the family settled in Dildo, but later moved to Eastport (MUN Folklore, MUN Hist.). Edmund Moores, from Co. Kilkenny, settled at Bay de Verde about 1820 (MUN Hist.).

Early instances: John Moores, of Freshwater (Carbonear), 1773, property "in possession of the Family for upwards of 105 years," that is, before 1668 (CO 199.18); Mary and Ann Moore, of Harbour Grace, 1800, property "in possession [of the Family] for 102 years," that is, 1698 (CO 199.18); Hannah Moore(s), of Brigus, 1708 (CO 194.4); Thomas Moores, of Blackhead (Bay de Verde district), 1708–9 (CO 194.4); John Mo(o)re, fisherman of St. John's or Petty Harbour about 1739–43 (CO 194.11, 24); William Moores, of Harbour Main, 1746 (CO 199.18); Ann Moore, of St. John's, 1751 (CO 194.13); John Moorse, fisherman of Trinity (Trinity B.), 1763 (DPHW 64); William Moors, of Trinity Bay, 1776 (DPHW 64); Christopher Moore, agent of Fogo, 1780 (D'Alberti 6); Richard Moores, of Mulley's Cove, 1783 (CO 199.18); Charles, of Northern Bay, 1790 (CO 199.18); Stephen Moore, of Ferry-

land, 1791 (USPG); James Moores, of Cuckold's Cove (now Dunfield), 1791 (DPHW 64); Richard, of Small Point (Bay de Verde district), 1794 (CO 199.18); Charles, of Ochre Pit Cove, 1794 (CO 199.18); John, of Port de Grave, 1800 (CO 199.18); John Moors, proprietor of fishing room, Old Perlican, Winter 1800–01 (Census Trinity B.); James, occupier of fishing room, Hearts Content, Winter 1800–01 (Census Trinity B.); George Moores, of Lower Island Cove, 1802 (CO 199.18); Robert, of Adams Cove, 1804 (CO 199.18); Philip Moore, from Gowran (Co. Kilkenny), married at St. John's, 1808 (Nfld. Archives BRC); Joanna, of Trepassey, 1808 (Nfld. Archives BRC); Isaac Moors, salmon fisherman of Twillingate, 1808 (CO 194.48); James Moore, one of 72 impressed men who sailed from Ireland to Newfoundland ? 1811 (CO 194.51); John Moor, of Clowns Cove (Carbonear), 1811 (DPHW 48); William Kellond Moore, of Portugal Cove, 1813 (DPHW 26B); George, from Birmingham, England, married at St. John's, 1814 (Nfld. Archives BRC); James Moors, from the Island of Guernsey, married at Ragged Harbour (now Melrose), 1818 (Nfld. Archives KCRC); James Moore, of Kings Cove, 1819 (Nfld. Archives KCRC); Bridget, from Carrick (unspecified), Ireland, married at Ragged Harbour (now Melrose), 1820 (Nfld. Archives KCRC); John Moors, constable of Bareneed, 1821 (CO 194.64); Thomas Fitzgibbon Moore, planter of Durell's Harbour (Trinity North district), 1823, of New Harbour (Trinity B.), 1826 (DPHW 64); Catherine Moors, of Riders Harbour (Trinity B.), 1826 (Nfld. Archives KCRC); Mary Moore, of Torbay, 1827 (Nfld. Archives BRC); Lorenzo, of Carbonear, 1828 (*Newfoundlander* 30 Jan 1828); Thomas More, planter of Cupids, 1828 (DPHW 34); Henry Moore, baptized at Greenspond, 1830, aged 31 (DPHW 76); William Moor(e)s, fisherman of Perrys Cove, 1830 (DPHW 52A); Nicholas Moores, fisherman of Biscayen Cove (Bay de verde district), 1830 (DPHW 52A); John Moore, clerk of Crockers Cove (Carbonear), 1830 (DPHW 48); James Moor, of Fortune, 1830 (DPHW 106); Catherine Moores, of Turks Cove, 1830 (Nfld. Archives KCRC); Isaac Moore, merchant of Isle Valen, 1835 (Wix); Edmund, fisherman of New Bay (Green Bay), 1836 (DPHW 88); John, from Dartmouth, England, sailmaker of St. John's, died 1838, aged 48 (*Times* 7 Nov 1838); Elizabeth, of Torbay, 1838 (DPHW 26D); Joseph, planter of Jigging Hole (Trinity North district), 1842 (DPHW 64B); Michael, from Dingle (Co. Kerry), of Harbour Grace, 1844 (*Indicator* 27 Jul 1844); John, of Pouch Cove, 1844 (DPHW 32);

James, fisherman of Codroy, 1845 (DPHW 101); Charles Moors, granted land near Petty Harbour, 1850 (Nfld. Archives, Registry Crown Lands); William Moores, of Merritts Harbour, 1851 (DPHW 85); Edward Lee Moore, granted land at Placentia Road, 1852 (Nfld. Archives, Registry Crown Lands); Adam Moores, of Broad Cove (Bay de Verde district), 1853 (DPHW 52A); Joel Moore, of Pushthrough, 1853 (DPHW 102); James Mores, of Ramea, 1856 (DPHW 101); Catherine Moore, of Scilly Cove (now Winterton), 1856 (Nfld. Archives KCRC); Rob., of Port Patrick (Burin district), 1858, of Jersey Harbour, 1860 (DPHW 104, 106); Joseph Moores, of Bay Roberts, 1859 (DPHW 39); William Moore, of Indian Arm, 1860 (Nfld. Archives KCRC); William, of Change Islands, 1861 (DPHW 88); Edward, of Dildo, 1862 (DPHW 62); widespread in Lovell 1871.

Modern status: Moore, widespread, especially at St. John's, Carbonear, Avondale and Dildo; Moores, widespread, especially at St. John's, Harbour Grace, Carbonear Adams Cove and Pouch Cove; Moors, in the Twillingate district (*Electors* 1955).

Place names: Moore Point (Labrador) 51-44 56-25; Moores Cove 49-30 55-18; —— Point, —— Gulch 46-40 53-04; —— Harbour (Labrador), —— Island (Labrador) 57-32 61-45; —— Point 51-22 55-34; —— Island Tickle (Labrador) 57-30 61-46; Moors Point 48-40 53-38.

MOOTREY, MUTREY, variants of the surname of Scotland Moutray, from the Scots place name Moutray, an estate in Edinburgh.

In Newfoundland:

Modern status: Mootrey, at St. John's; Mutrey, at Adam's Cove (*Electors* 1955), Carbonear and St. John's.

MORAN, a surname of Ireland, (O)Moran, the anglicized form of *Ó Moráin* and *Ó Moghráin* and (Mac) Morran. (MacLysaght). *See* MURREN.

Traced by MacLysaght especially in Connacht.

In Newfoundland:

Early instances: Daniel, fisherman of Quidi Vidi, 1794–5, "24 years in Newfoundland," that is, 1770–1 (Census 1794–5); Daniel, fisherman of St. John's, 1794–5 (Census 1794–5); Edmond, from Rossparicome Parish (unidentified), Ireland, married at St. John's, 1803 (Nfld. Archives BRC); Margaret, of Harbour Grace Parish, 1806 (Nfld. Archives HGRC); John, of Blackhead (Bay de Verde district), 1806 (CO 199.18); Mary Morin alias ? Chekny, of Port de Grave, 1810 (Nfld. Archives BRC); Barbara Moran, of Blackhead (unspecified), 1813 (Nfld.

Archives BRC); Gabriel, of King's Cove, 1832 (Nfld. Archives KCRC); Edward, granted land at Upper Long Pond, 1838 (Nfld. Archives, Registry Crown Lands); Quen, ? of Northern Bay, 1841 (DPHW 48); James, of Burin district, 1845 (*Nfld. Almanac*); John, ? of Harbour Grace, 1845 (*Newfoundlander* 9 Jan 1845); ——, on the *St. Ann*, in the seal fishery out of Carbonear, 1847 (*Newfoundlander* 25 Mar 1847); James, of Brigus, 1856 (*Newfoundlander* 5 Jun 1856); Francis, of Burin, 1858 (*Newfoundlander* 14 Jan 1858); Jacob, of Harbour Grace, 1866 (Nfld. Archives HGRC); Edward Moran and Joseph Moren, of Bay of Islands, 1871 (Lovell); John Moran, of Fermeuse, 1871 (Lovell); James, farmer of Pouch Cove, 1871 (Lovell).

Modern status: At Blackhead (Bay de Verde district), South River, Pouch Cove and St. John's.

MORASH, ? a variant of the surnames of England Morrish (*see* MORRIS) and ? MARSH. Cottle observes that the pronunciation Morrish is as vulgar as saying *liquorish*. (Cottle, Spiegelhalter).

Guppy traced Morrish especially in Somerset and in Devon.

In Newfoundland:

Modern status: At South Dildo, Harbour Buffett (*Electors* 1955), and St. John's.

MORASSIE, MORAZIE, MORAZÉ ? Newfoundland variants of the surname of France Morancé, from the French place names Marancé (Rhône), Marancez (Eure-et-Loir). (Dauzat); MORAZÉ is a Saint-Pierre name (Thomas, "French Fam. Names").

In Newfoundland:

Family tradition: Pierre Morazé settled at Mainland about 1904 (Thomas, "French Fam. Names").

Modern status: Morassie, rare, at St. John's (*Electors* 1955); Morazie, at Mainland (Port-au-Port).

MORDEN, a surname of England, from the English place name Morden (Cambridgeshire, Dorset, Surrey), Old English *mōr-dūn* – (dweller on the) hill on the moor or in the fens.

In Newfoundland:

Early instance: William Henry, of St. John's, 1830 (DPHW 26D).

Modern status: Unique, at St. John's (*Electors* 1955).

MORECOMBE, a surname of England, from the English place names Morecombe and Morecombe Wood (Devon), Old English *mōr* – moor and *cumb* – hollow, valley, coomb. (Spiegelhalter).

Guppy traced Morcom and Morkam in Cornwall; Spiegelhalter traced Morcom in Devon.

In Newfoundland:

Modern status: At St. John's and South River.

MORET, a surname of France, a diminutive of the personal name *More* (*see* MOORES) or from several places so-called. (Dauzat).

In Newfoundland:

Modern status: Rare, at St. John's.

MOREY, a surname of Ireland sometimes a synonym of MOORE and MORIARTY and confused with MORRY. (MacLysaght).

In Newfoundland:

Early instances: James, of Twillingate, 1768 (MUN Hist.); Edward, fisherman of St. John's, 1794–5, "17 years in Newfoundland," that is, 1777–8 (Census 1794–5); William, from Passage Parish (Co. Waterford), married at St. John's, 1797 (Nfld. Archives BRC); James, from Castle Hyde (Co. Cork), married at Bonavista, 1803 (Nfld. Archives BRC); Daniel Mor(e)y or Morea, of Harbour Grace Parish, 1809, 1820 (Nfld. Archives HGRC); Johanna Morey, of Torbay, 1814 (Nfld. Archives BRC); Patrick Morea, of Carbonear, died 1820, aged 65 (Carbonear R.C. Cemetery); Honora, of Tickle Cove (Bonavista B.), 1834 (Nfld. Archives KCRC); Thomas Graham Morey, of Ferryland, 1840 (DPHW 26D); Mary, of Caplin Bay (now Calvert), 1843 (DPHW 31); George Mor(e)y, of Ward's Harbour (now Beaumont North), 1846 (DPHW 86); John Morey, of Newman's Cove, 1870 (Nfld. Archives KCRC).

Modern status: Scattered, especially at La Scie.

MORGAN, a surname of England, Wales, Scotland and Ireland, and a baptismal name in Wales, from an Old Celtic name *Morcant*, *Morgan* containing the elements *sea* and ? *bright*; in Ireland also the anglicized form of several Irish surnames. *See* MERRIGAN. (Reaney, Cottle, MacLysaght, Black, Withycombe).

Traced by Guppy especially in Monmouthshire and South and North Wales, by Black in Aberdeenshire, and by MacLysaght in Cos. Armagh, Monaghan, Belfast and Dublin and elsewhere.

In Newfoundland:

Early instances: John, of St. Mary's, 1720 (D'Alberti 7); William, of Port de Grave, 1783, property "in possession of the Family for 53 years," that is, since 1730 (CO 199.18); Marshall, married at St. John's, 1769 (DPHW 26D); William, of Cupids, 1768 (CO 199.18); John, of Brigus, 1805 (CO

199.18); Thomas, of Harbour Grace Parish, 1808 (Nfld. Archives HGRC); George, of Bull Cove (Conception B.), 1824 (DPHW 34); William, of Wild Cove (Fogo district), 1835 (DPHW 83); Maurice, of St. John's, 1838 (Nfld. Archives BRC); John, of Grand Bank, 1842 (DPHW 106); James, granted land between Ferryland and Aquaforte, 1851 (Nfld. Archives, Registry Crown Lands); Edmin, of Brazils (Burgeo-La Poile district), 1857 (DPHW 98); Martin, of Petites, 1858 (DPHW 98); Samuel, of North River, 1859 (DPHW 38); Robert, of Great St. Lawrence, 1860 (DPHW 100); Abraham and Isaac, granted land at Bay Roberts, 1863 (Nfld. Archives, Registry Crown Lands); William, granted land at Lance Cove (near Holyrood), 1863 (Nfld. Archives, Registry Crown Lands); scattered in Lovell 1871.

Modern status: Widespread, especially at St. John's, Indian Pond (Harbour Main district), Seal Cove, Upper Gullies, Blow-me-Down and Coward's Island (Bonavista North district).

Place names: Morgan Arm, —— Brook 47-43 56-31; —— Arm 47-46 55-49; —— Cove 49-35 56-51; —— Island 47-36 57-37; —— Shoal (Labrador) 52-10 55-42; Morgans Cove (Labrador) 55-09 59-09; —— Island 46-51 55-50.

MORIAR(I)TY, surnames of Ireland (O)Moriarty, *Ó Muircheartaigh*, Ir. *muircheartach* – navigator. (MacLysaght). *See also* MOREY.

Traced by MacLysaght especially in Co. Kerry.

In Newfoundland:

Early instances: Richard Morarthy, of Harbour Grace Parish, 1827 (Nfld. Archives HGRC); Edmond Moriarty, married at St. John's, 1832 (Nfld. Archives BRC); James, from Co. Kerry, of Harbour Grace, 1844 (*Indicator* 27 Jul 1844); Patrick, tailor of St. John's, 1846 (DPHW 23) John Morrity, fisherman of Cuckolds Cove (now Dunfield), 1857 (DPHW 64B); Patrick, granted land at Carbonear, 1860 (Nfld. Archives, Registry Crown Lands); Thomas Moriarty, farmer of Turks Gut (now Marysvale), 1871 (Lovell); Jeremiah and John, of Witless Bay, 1871 (Lovell).

Modern status: Moriarity, scattered; Moriarty, at Harbour Grace, Marysvale and St. John's.

Place name: Moriartys Pond 47-34 52-51.

MORRELL, a surname of England, Ireland and Jersey (Channel Islands), Morrel of France, a diminutive of the personal name *More* or from Old French *more* – dark, swarthy (*see* MOORES). (Reaney, Dauzat, Turk).

Traced by Guppy in Yorkshire.

In Newfoundland:

Modern status: Rare, at Millertown Junction (*Electors* 1955) and St. John's.

MORRIS, a surname of England, Wales, Scotland and Ireland, with Maurice the usual form of the baptismal name, Latin *Mauritius* – Moorish, dark, swarthy, from *Maurus* – a Moor. *"Maurice* is the learned form, *Morris* the common popular one." Morris may also be a nickname – the swarthy, dark one. In Ireland it is sometimes used for MORRISSEY and Fitzmaurice. (Reaney, Cottle, MacLysaght, Black). *See also* MOORES, MORASH, MORRISON, MORSE.

Found widespread by Guppy in Wales, the Welsh border counties and the south of England.

In Newfoundland:

Family traditions: James, from Carnarvon, Wales, settled in Trinity (Trinity B.), in the early 1800s (MUN Folklore). Thomas (1820–80) and Roland, from Belfast, Ireland, arrived in Newfoundland between 1840–50; Roland settled in St. John's and Thomas settled at St. George's (MUN Geog.).

Early instances: Thomas, of Bonavista, 1676 (CO 1); Edward, of St. John's Harbour, 1703 (CO 194.3); John (and others), of Lower Island Cove, 1766 (CO 199.18); Samuel Mor(r)ice, of Trinity (Trinity B.), 1786 (DPHW 64); Geoffrey Morris, of Bay Bulls, 1793 (USPG); Geoffry, from Carrick (unspecified), Ireland, married at St. John's, 1802 (Nfld. Archives BRC); John, of Placentia, 1803 (D'Alberti 13); Elizabeth, of Harbour Grace Parish, 1806 (Nfld. Archives HGRC); Joseph Morice or Morris, of Cuckolds Cove (now Dunfield), 1808 (DPHW 64); John ? Moris, apprentice, one of 72 impressed men who sailed from Ireland to Newfoundland ? 1811 (CO 194.51); John Morrice, from Mullinshore (unidentified), Ireland, butcher of St. John's, deceased, 1811 (*Royal Gazette* 17 Oct 1811); Geoffrey Morris, of the western side of Placentia Bay, 1817 (D'Alberti 27); Thomas, of Cupids, 1828 (Nfld. Archives BRC); Thomas, of New Harbour (Trinity B.), 1825 (Nfld. Archives KCRC); Benjamin Morris or Morrisy, planter of Trouty, 1828 (DPHW 64B); Robert Morris, of Pool's Harbour (Burin district), 1829 (DPHW 109); Bridget, from Waterford, married at Wilting Harbour (now Tilting), 1830 (Nfld. Archives KCRC); Geoffrey, of Burin, deceased, 1831 (*Newfoundlander* 27 Jan 1831); Robert, of Round Harbour (Burin district), 1832 (DPHW 109); Clemence, of the First Barrisway (St. George's B.), 1835 (Wix); David Morise, of Pick Heart (Burin district), 1835 (DPHW 106); Robert Morris, of Long Island (Fortune B.),

1835 (DPHW 30); Matthew, of Freshwater (unspecified), 1841 (Nfld. Archives, Registry Crown Lands); Thomas, of Channel, 1843 (DPHW 101); Ambrose, of Gaultois, 1844 (DPHW 102); Honorable Patrick, granted land "Windermere Lake," Bay Bulls, 1844, granted land at Sugar Loaf Pond, Logy Bay, 1845 (Nfld. Archives, Registry Crown Lands); Robert, sailmaker of Harbour Grace, 1846 (DPHW 43); Abigal, of Cat Harbour (now Lumsden), 1850 (Nfld. Archives KCRC); Samuel, seaman of Goose Cove, Trinity (Trinity North district), 1854, of Bar Point (Trinity North district), 1856 (DPHW 64B); David, fisherman of Dragon (Fortune B.), 1854 (DPHW 102); John, of South Side (St. George's district), 1871 (DPHW 96); scattered in Lovell 1871.

Modern status: Widespread, especially at St. John's, Lower Island Cove and Robinsons.

Place names: Morris Bank (Labrador) 53-33 55-50; —— Channel 48-44 53-47; —— Cove 49-41 55-51; —— Island 48-45 53-45, —— Lake (Labrador) 54-48 63-35, —— Rocks 48-29 53-02; Morrisville 47-52 55-46.

MORRISON, a surname of England, Scotland and Ireland – son of Maurice (*see* MORRIS); in Ireland confused with MORRISSEY.

Found by Guppy in Northumberland and well distributed in Scotland, and numerous by MacLysaght in Ulster.

In Newfoundland:

Early instances: John, of St. John's, 1764 (DPHW 26D); Andrew, magistrate of Ferryland, 1816 (D'Alberti 26); James Morison, from Edinburgh, of Ferryland, died 1832 (*Royal Gazette* 22 May 1832); William Downie (1820–92), born at Stornoway, Island of Lewis, Scotland, settled in St. John's, via Pictou, Nova Scotia, in 1845 (Mott); John Mareson, of Bay of Islands, 1871 (Lovell); John Morrisen, of Harbour Grace Parish, 1878 (Nfld. Archives HGRC).

Modern status: At Petries (*Electors* 1955), Corner Brook and St. John's.

Place name: Mor(r)ison Island (Labrador) 54-55 58-01.

MORRISSEY, a surname of Ireland and Jersey (Channel Islands); in Ireland *Ó Muirgheasa*, Ir. *muir* – sea, *geas* – action, or from the Norman surname *de Marisco*, in Jersey ? from the latter. (MacLysaght, Turk). *See* MORRIS, MORRISON.

Traced by MacLysaght especially in Cos. Waterford, Limerick and Cork.

In Newfoundland:

Early instances: John Morrisey, from Ireland,

labourer of St. John's, 1774 (CO 194.32); Samuel Morrisey or Morricey, of Trinity Bay, 1782, of Trinity (Trinity B.), 1790 (DPHW 64); Mary Morisey, of St. John's, 1793 (Nfld. Archives BRC); R. Morrissey, in fishery at Portugal Cove, 1794–5 (Census 1794–5); Margaret Morissy, from Mooncoin (Co. Kilkenny), married at St. John's, 1808 (Nfld. Archives BRC); Mary Morricey, of Harbour Grace Parish, 1812 (Nfld. Archives HGRC); Morris Moracey, of Cape Broyle, 1817 (Nfld. Archives BRC); Thomas Morrisy, of Bonavista, 1821 (Nfld. Archives KCRC); Thomas, of Fogo, 1823 (Nfld. Archives KCRC); Daniel, of Tilting Harbour (now Tilting), 1825 (Nfld. Archives KCRC); John Morrassy, of Brigus, 1828 (Nfld. Archives BRC); Catherine Morrisy, of King's Cove, 1829 (Nfld. Archives KCRC); John, planter of Cuckolds Cove (now Dunfield), 1829 (DPHW 64B); Michael Morissey, of Greenspond, 1830 (Nfld. Archives KCRC); Thomas Morrisey, of New Harbour (Trinity B.), 1832 (Nfld. Archives KCRC); Thomas, of Heart's Content, 1832 (Nfld. Archives KCRC); R., of Harbour Grace, 1832 (Newfoundlander 23 Aug 1832); Denis Morrissey, teacher of Outer and Middle Cove, 1839 (Newfoundlander 1 Aug 1839); Thomas Mourissy, ? of Northern Bay, 1842 (DPHW 54); Patrick Morrissey, from Waterford, of Port de Grave, 1844 (Indicator 24 Aug 1844); Thomas, from Co. Waterford, of Brigus, 1844 (Indicator 24 Aug 1844); Terence Morissy, schoolteacher of Bay Bulls, 1871 (Lovell); Lawrence Morrissey, of Burin, 1871 (Lovell); Michael, of Placentia, 1871 (Lovell); Thomas, of Salmon Cove (Brigus district), 1871 (Lovell).

Modern status: Scattered, especially at St. John's and North River.

MORROW, a surname of England and Ireland, from the English place name Morrowe (Cumberland), or from Old English *mōr* – moor, *raw* – row (of houses), hence (dweller in the) hamlet on the moor. (Bardsley).

Traced by MacLysaght in Ulster where, he remarks, it is more common than in England where it originated.

In Newfoundland:

Modern status: At Shoal Harbour (Trinity B.) (*Electors* 1955), Grand Falls and St. John's.

MORRY, ? a variant of MURRAY or MOREY.

In Newfoundland:

Early instances: John, of Newfoundland, ? 1706 (CO 194.24); John Mory, fisherman of St. John's or Petty Harbour about 1739–43 (CO 194.11); James Morry, of Fogo, Twillingate or Tilton (now Tilting), 1771 (CO 194.30); William Morrey or Maney, from Ireland, labourer of Bonavista, 1774 (CO 194.32); Matthew Morry, merchant of Caplin Bay (now Calvert), ? 1815, 1823 (CO 194.56, DPHW 31); Benjamin, ? of Ferryland, 1838 (*Newfoundlander* 25 Oct 1838); John Morr(e)y, of Ferryland, 1848 (DPHW 31); Elizabeth Morry, of St. John's, married at Torbay, 1859 (DPHW 32); William, of Aquaforte, 1871 (Lovell).

Modern status: At Ferryland and St. John's.

MORSE, a variant of MORRIS. (Reaney *Origin*).
Traced by Guppy in Wiltshire.
In Newfoundland:
Early instances: Philip, of Trinity Bay, 1767 (DPHW 64); Ben, a Welshman, aged 30, deserted from ship *Perseverance*, (? at St. John's), 1818 (*Nfld. Mercantile Journal* 28 Aug 1818).

Modern status: Unique, at St. John's (*Electors* 1955).

Place name: Morse Islands (Labrador) 57-20 61-23.

MORTON, a surname of England, Ireland and Scotland from a widespread English or Scots place name – the farm, homestead on the moor. (Reaney, Cottle, MacLysaght, Black).

Guppy traced Morton in Cambridgeshire, Cheshire, Derbyshire, Staffordshire and Yorkshire NR, ER, and Kilmarnock, Moreton in Cheshire and Staffordshire. MacLysaght traced Morton in Ireland since the 13th century, now mainly in Ulster and Dublin.

In Newfoundland:

Early instances: Thomas Moreton, fisherman of St. John's, 1794–5, "45 years in Newfoundland," that is, 1749–50 (Census 1794–5); Thomas Morton, of Port de Grave before 1850 (MUN Hist.); John Moreton, of Greenspond, 1853, of King's Cove, 1855 (DPHW 76, 73B).

Modern status: Rare, at Gander (*Electors* 1955), and St. John's.

Place names: Moreton's Harbour, —— —— Head 49-34 54-52; Morton Cove 49-33 54-54.

MOSDELL, a surname of England from the English place name Mosedale (Cumberland) – valley with a moss or peat bog. (Ekwall).

In Newfoundland:

Early instances: William Mosdel, of Brigus, at Exploits Burnt Island, 1822 (USPG); William Mosdill, planter of Green Bay (Brigus and Cupids districts), 1826 (DPHW 34); William Mosdell, granted land at Bay Roberts, 1834 (Nfld. Archives, Registry Crown Lands); James Mosedale, of St. John's, 1851 (*Newfoundlander* 26 Jun 1851).

Modern status: At Bell Island, Whitbourne (*Electors* 1955), Bay Roberts and St. John's.

MOSHER, ? a Newfoundland variant of the surname of France Mosser, or of the Channel Islands Moser, *mou sire* – sir, master, an ironic nickname, or the surname of Germany Mosher – dweller by the marsh. (Dauzat, Turk). P.E.L. Smith reports that the Fortune name is derived from the Channel Islands name Malzard. (Malzard in Turk).

In Newfoundland:

Family tradition: ——, from Nova Scotia, settled on the West Coast of Newfoundland in ? early or mid-nineteenth century.

Early instances: Capt. Philip Malzard, Harbour Breton, 1811 (Surrogate Court Fortune Bay, 1803–19, 1821, pp. 149–52, PANL GN/5/1/C/5); Francis Maluzard, of Lamaline, 1835; Henry Malzard, son of Francis, married Mary Ann Major, Fortune, 1855 (Methodist marriages, Grand Bank per P.E.L. Smith); Saul, 1900, George, 1901, sons of Malzards, baptized with the name Mosher (P.E.L. Smith); John William, of Bay of Islands area, 1874 (DPHW 96).

Modern status: At Fortune, Gander and Corner Brook.

MOSS, a surname of England, Ireland and Scotland, from the English place name Moss (Yorkshire WR) or the Scots place name Moss (Orkney), or from Old English *mos* – (dweller by the) moss, morass, marsh, or from *Mosse* "a common form of Jewish *Moses*"; also in Ireland "a partial translation" of *Ó Maol-móna*, Ir. *móin*, genitive *móna* – moorland, turf-bog. (Reaney, Black, MacLysaght).

Traced by Guppy in Cheshire, Essex, Lancashire, Staffordshire and Worcestershire, by Spiegelhalter in Devon and by Black in Orkney.

In Newfoundland:

Family tradition: ——, from Devon, England, settled at Jamestown and Happy Adventure (Bonavista B.) (MUN Folklore).

Early instances: John, of Trinity (Trinity B.), 1794 (DPHW 64); Barnaby, of Bonavista, 1825 (DPHW 70); Thomas, of Keels, 1825 (DPHW 70); Sera, of Open Hole (now Open Hall), 1826 (Nfld. Archives KCRC); Joseph, of Tickle Cove (Bonavista B.), 1827 (Nfld. Archives KCRC); Mary, of Kings Cove, 1829 (Nfld. Archives KCRC); Henry, of Barrow Harbour (Bonavista B.), 1843 (DPHW 73A);

Henry, of Red Cliff Island (Bonavista B.), 1852 (DPHW 73A); William, of Salvage, 1854 (DPHW 73A); William, of Burn Island (? Bonavista B.), 1861 (Nfld. Archives KCRC); Enos, of Plate Cove, 1869 (Nfld. Archives KCRC); scattered in Lovell 1871.

Modern status: Scattered, especially at Jamestown and Happy Adventure.

Place names (not necessarily from the surname): Moss Harbour (Labrador) 57-45 61-59; —— Lake (Labrador) 54-52 65-55; Mosses Cove 48-36 53-45.

MOTT, a surname of England and as Motte of Jersey (Channel Islands), from Old French *motte* – (dweller by or on the) mound, or a pet-form of the baptismal name Matilda. (Spiegelhalter, Weekley *Romance*, Turk).

Traced by Spiegelhalter in Devon and by Guppy in Essex.

In Newfoundland:

Early instances: Andrew, of St. John's, 1784 (DPHW 26D); William Mote, fisherman of Flat Bay (St. George's B.), 1871 (Lovell); Henry Youmans (1856–1946), from Dartmouth, Nova Scotia, settled in St. John's in 1877 (Mott).

Modern status: Rare, at Placentia (*Electors* 1955).

MOTTY, a surname of England, ? a variant of Mottee or Mottie of Jersey (Channel Islands), ? for the French surname Mottet – (dweller by or on the) little mound, or a diminutive of Mott (Matilda). *See* MOTT. (Dauzat, Turk).

Traced in Devon.

In Newfoundland:

Early instances: Nicholas, of St. John's, 1824 (DPHW 26B); Capt. Nicholas and Sarah, from Dartmouth (Devon), of St. John's, deceased, 1851 (*Newfoundlander* 20 Feb 1851).

Modern status: At St. John's.

MOULAND, a variant of the surname of England Molland, from the English place name Molland (Devon). (Spiegelhalter).

Spiegelhalter traced Molland in Devon.

In Newfoundland:

Family tradition: Thomas, from England, settled at Bonavista (MUN Folklore).

Early instances: William Moulen, fisherman of Trinity (Trinity B.), 1762 (DPHW 64); James Moulam, of Bonavista, 1790 (DPHW 70); Maurice Molland, cooper of St. John's, 1820 (D'Alberti 30); Andrew Mowling, of Dolan (for Doting Cove)

(Green B.), 1851 (DPHW 76); Hannah Belle Moulan, of Scilly Cove (now Winterton), 1854 (DPHW 59).

Modern status: Scattered, especially at Mockbeggar, Doting Cove, Musgrave Harbour and Bonavista.

Place name: Moulands Pond 49-18 57-32.

MOULTON, a surname of England from the English place names North or South Molton (Devon) or Moulton (Cheshire, Lincolnshire, Norfolk, Northamptonshire, Suffolk, Yorkshire NR). (Bardsley, Spiegelhalter).

Traced by Spiegelhalter in Devon.

In Newfoundland:

Early instances: George and Thomas, of Burin, 1805 (D'Alberti 15); George Monthen, Motton, Molten or Moulton, of Adam's Cove, 1822, of Biscayan Cove, 1830, of Pouch Cove, 1842 (DPHW 52A, 32); George Moulton, of Garnish, 1838 (DPHW 109); Richard Maulton, fisherman of Inkpen's Point (Burin district), 1860 (DPHW 108); John and Henry Moulton, of Flat Island (now Port Elizabeth), 1871 (Lovell).

Modern status: Scattered, especially at Epworth and Burin Bay (Burin district).

MOURNE, ? a variant of the surname of Scotland Mouren, Old Irish *Muirgen* – sea-begotten, a mermaid, Old Welsh *Morgen* – sea-born. (Black).

In Newfoundland:

Modern status: At Cox's Cove (Humber West district) (*Electors* 1955).

MOWAT, a surname of Scotland, from Norman French *Mont Hault* – high mount.

In Newfoundland:

Early instance: John, from Edinburgh, married at St. John's, 1833 (DPHW 26D).

Modern status: Rare, at St. John's (*Electors* 1955).

MOWDAY, a surname ? of England, of unknown origin.

In Newfoundland:

Modern status: Rare, at Gilesport (Twillingate district) (*Electors* 1955).

MOXLEY, a surname of England from the English place name Moxley (Somerset) or Mowsley (Leicestershire). (A.H. Smith, E.C. Smith).

In Newfoundland:

Early instances: John, of Harbour Grace Parish, 1813 (Nfld. Archives HGRC); John, of Carbonear, deceased, 1838 (*Newfoundlander* 15 Mar 1838);

Jonas Moxly, of Harbour Grace, 1866 (Nfld. Archives HGRC).

Modern status: Unique, at Winterhouse Brook (St. Barbe district) (*Electors* 1955).

MOYLES, a surname of England and Ireland, Cornish *moel*, Irish Gaelic *maol* – bald; in Ireland for MILES. (Reaney, MacLysaght).

Traced by Spiegelhalter in Devon and by MacLysaght mainly in Co. Mayo. Guppy traced Moyle in Cornwall.

In Newfoundland:

Early instances: John, of Fogo, 1843 (DPHW 83); John, of Port au Choix, 1871 (Lovell); John, of Tilt Cove, 1871 (Lovell); Catherine, of Gooseberry Island (Bonavista B.), 1872 (Nfld. Archives KCRC); Catherine, of Haywards Cove (Bonavista B.), 1873 (Nfld. Archives KCRC); Martha, of Cottells Island (Bonavista B.), 1876 (Nfld. Archives KCRC).

Modern status: Scattered, especially at Lewisporte.

MOYSE, a surname of England and Jersey (Channel Islands), Hebrew *Moses*, French *Moise* – of obscure origin. (Withycombe, Reaney, Turk). *See also* MOYST.

Traced by Spiegelhalter in Devon.

In Newfoundland:

Early instance: ——, Captain of Brig *Constantia* (at St. John's), 1828 (*Newfoundlander* 14 Aug 1828).

Modern status: Rare, at St. John's.

MOYST, a surname of England, a variant of MOYSE. (Weekley *Surnames*).

In Newfoundland:

Early instance: William Moist, of St. John's, 1842 (DPHW 26B).

Modern status: At Corner Brook and St. John's.

MUDGE, a surname of England, from the Old English personal name *Mucga* or Old English *mucga* – midge, a nickname, or a dialect word in Devon and Cornwall, mudge – (dweller near the) mud, swamp. (Spiegelhalter, Weekley *Surnames*).

Traced by Weekley in Devon and Cornwall.

In Newfoundland:

Early instances: John, fisherman of St. John's or Petty Harbour, about 1739–43, juror of St. John's, 1751 (CO 194.11, 13, 24); ——, of Petty Harbour, 1794–5 (Census 1794–5); Anora, of Port de Grave, 1797 (Nfld. Archives BRC).

Modern status: Scattered, in the St. Barbe district.

MUGFORD, a surname of England from the English place names Muckford or Mogworthy (formerly *Moggeford*) (Devon) – *Mocca*'s ford. (Spiegelhalter, Gover).

Guppy traced Mugford, Mogford in Devon.

In Newfoundland:

Family tradition: George (1802–77), from England, came to Port de Grave about 1833, and settled in Clarke's Beach about 1835 (MUN Geog.).

Early instances: John, of Port de Grave, 1784, property "possessed by the Family for 110 years," that is, 1674 (CO 199.18); G. and William, of Conception Bay [1706] (CO 194.4); George, of Brigus, 1708–9 (CO 194.4); Robert, of Salmon Cove (Brigus and Cupids district), 1854 (DPHW 34); John, granted land at Clarkes Beach, 1855 (Nfld. Archives, Registry Crown Lands); John (and others) Mudford, of Twillingate, 1871 (Lovell); Benjamin Magford, Isaac and Reuben Mugford, of Drogheda, 1871 (Lovell); Henry and James Mugford, of Bishop's Cove, 1871 (Lovell); George, of Flower's Cove (St. Barbe district), 1874 (DPHW 95).

Modern status: Scattered, especially at Clarke's Beach and St. John's.

Place names: Mugford Bay (Labrador) 57-48 62-02; Cape —— (Labrador) 57-50 61-43; —— Harbour (Labrador) 57-48 61-42; —— Rock 47-34 53-11; —— Tickle (Labrador) 57-48 61-52; The Mugfords (or Cod Island) (Labrador) 57-47 61-47.

MUG(G)RIDGE. *See* MOGRIDGE

MUIR, a surname of Scotland – (dweller by the) moor. (Black). *See* MOORES.

Traced by Guppy in Ayrshire and Dumfriesshire.

In Newfoundland:

Early instances: Rev. A. S., of St. John's, 1851 (*Newfoundlander* 6 Mar 1851); James Landers, from Newcastle on Muir, married at St. John's, 1858 (DPHW 23).

Modern status: Rare, at the Goulds (St. John's).

MUISE, traced as Mius at Chéticamp, N.S., as Muce at Margaree (1809 Census), and as Miousse in the Magdalen Islands (G.R. Thomas); ? a Newfoundland variant of the surname of France Muse – one who likes to amuse himself. (Dauzat).

In Newfoundland:

Modern status: At St. George's and South Branch (St. George's district).

Place name: ? Mouse Island 47-34 59-10.

MULCAHY, a surname of Ireland (O)Mulcahy, *Ó Maolchathaigh*, derived from St. Cathach, not [as in Cottle] from *cathach* – warlike. (MacLysaght).

Traced by MacLysaght throughout Munster.

In Newfoundland:

Early instances: Tabitha, of Broad Cove (Bay de Verde district), 1750 (CO 199.18); William, of Western Bay, 1784 (CO 199.18); John, of Harbour Grace, 1805 (CO 199.18); Mary, of Bay Bulls, 1808 (Nfld. Archives BRC); Eleanor, from Carrich (unspecified) (Co. Tipperary), married at St. John's, 1809 (Nfld. Archives BRC); Michael, ? of St. John's, 1810 (CO 194.50); Andrew, of Careless (now Kerley's) Harbour, 1821 (Nfld. Archives KCRC); Andrew, of Catalina, 1823 (Nfld. Archives KCRC); Catherine Mulcahey, of Tilting Harbour (now Tilting), 1830 (Nfld. Archives KCRC); Thomas Mulcahy, of King's Cove, 1833 (Nfld. Archives KCRC); Anne, of Tickle Cove (Bonavista B.), 1856 (Nfld. Archives KCRC); Elizabeth Muchahy or Mulchahy, of Open Hall, 1861 (Nfld. Archives KCRC).

Modern status: At Tickle Cove (*Electors* 1955), Cape Broyle, Bay Bulls and St. John's.

MULLAL(L)(E)Y, variants of the surname of Ireland (O)Mullally, *Ó Maolalaidh*, ? Ir. *aladh* – speckled. (MacLysaght).

Traced by MacLysaght in Co. Galway.

In Newfoundland:

Early instances: James Mullally, fisherman of St. John's, 1794–5, "23 years in Newfoundland," that is, 1771–2 (Census 1794–5); Michael, from Mullinahone (Co. Tipperary), married at St. John's, 1809 (Nfld. Archives BRC); Edward Mullaly, of Bonavista, 1810 (USPG); Laurence, of Harbour Grace Parish, 1813 (Nfld. Archives HGRC); Michael Mulaney alias Mollally, from Thurles (Co. Tipperary), cooper of St. John's, sought in a charge of murder, 1818 (*Nfld. Mercantile Journal* 10 Dec 1818, D'Alberti 28); Michael Mullaly, from Co. Kilkenny, of Trinity (unspecified), 1818 (Nfld. Archives KCRC); Michael, of Riders Harbour (Trinity B.), 1819 (Nfld. Archives KCRC); Lawrence, of Joe Batts Arm, 1819 (Nfld. Archives KCRC); Lawrence Mullally, of Tilting Harbour (now Tilting), 1830 (Nfld. Archives KCRC); Ellen Mullaly, of Bonavista Bay, 1839 (Nfld. Archives BRC); John Mullally, ? of Northern Bay, 1847 (DPHW 54); John, of Harbour Grace, 1858 (*Newfoundlander* 18 Jan 1858).

Modern status: Mullaley, rare, at Little Harbour (Placentia West district) (*Electors* 1955), St. John's and Freshwater (Placentia); Mullalley, rare, at Oderin (*Electors* 1955); Mullally, unique, at St.

John's; Mullaly, scattered, especially at Northern Bay.

Place name: Mullally Lake (Labrador) 53-48 57-42.

MULLETT, a surname of England and Ireland, in England ? from Old French *mule* – mule, or ? from Old French *mulet* – a seller of mussels, or ? from Old French *molet* – five-pointed star (a shop sign); in Ireland ? a variant of Millett, a diminutive of Miles (*see* MILES). (Reaney, Spiegelhalter, MacLysaght).

Traced by Spiegelhalter in Devon and by MacLysaght in Co. Wexford.

In Newfoundland:

Family tradition: Thomas, from England, settled at Wesleyville (MUN Folklore).

Early instances: Thomas, born at Swain's Island (now Wesleyville), 1814 (DPHW 76); Thomas, of Greenspond, 1816 (DPHW 76); Catherine Mullet, from Taghmon (Co. Wexford), 1823 (Nfld. Archives BRC); Edward Mullett, of Bonavista, 1823 (Nfld. Archives KCRC); Laurent Mullet, planter of Trinity (Trinity B.), 1836 (DPHW 64B); Patrick Mullett, of St. John's, deceased, 1851 (*Newfoundlander* 6 Mar 1851).

Modern status: Scattered, especially at Wesleyville and St. John's.

MULLEY, a surname of England, not apparently recorded elsewhere, and of Ireland; in England ? from the Old English personal name *Mūl(a)*, as in the place name Mulwith (Yorkshire WR); in Ireland a variant of (O)Mullea, (O)Millea. *See* MILLEY with which confusion has occurred in Newfoundland. (Ekwall, MacLysaght).

In Newfoundland:

Early instances: John, of Blackhead (Bay de Verde district), 1776 (CO 199.18); Adam Mull(e)y, of Mulleys Cove (Bay de Verde district), 1802, property "bequeathed by their father's will" (CO 199.18); Thomas Mulley, of Harbour Grace Parish, 1827 (Nfld. Archives HGRC); Michael, planter of Broad Cove (Bay de Verde district), 1840 (DPHW 52A); Peter, planter of Western Bay, 1855 (DPHW 52B); Colin Mully, of Pouch Cove, 1871 (Lovell).

Modern status: At Blackhead, Broad Cove (Bay de Verde district) and Pouch Cove.

MULLINGS, a surname of England, from Old English **mulling* – darling, or ? a variant of MULLINS. (Reaney).

In Newfoundland:

Early instance: Joseph R., of St. John's, 1853 (*Newfoundlander* 27 Jan 1853, 6 Mar 1856).

Modern status: Unique, at St. John's.

MULLINS, a surname of England and Ireland, in England from the common French place name Moulins, or ? from the Old English personal name *Mūl(a)*; in Ireland a form of (O)Mullan(e), *Ó Maoláin,* Ir. *maol* – bald, tonsured. (Spiegelhalter, A. H. Smith, MacLysaght).

Traced by Guppy in Dorset and Somerset, by Spiegelhalter in Devon, and by MacLysaght in Cos. Clare and Cork.

In Newfoundland:

Family traditions: Augustus (1820–93), from Wiltshire, England, settled at Rencontre East (Fortune B.), in 1840 (MUN Folklore). George, from Ireland, settled at Rencontre East; his son John was born there in 1857 (MUN Folklore).

Early instances: William Mullens, of St. John's, 1803 (Nfld. Archives BRC); William Mullins, of Harbour Grace Parish, 1810 (Nfld. Archives HGRC); Richard, of Tilton Harbour (now Tilting), 1819, of Fogo, 1824, of Herring Neck, 1829 (Nfld. Archives KCRC); James, from Co. Kilkenny, married at St. John's, 1831 (Nfld. Archives BRC); James, granted land at Little Placentia (now Argentia), 1839 (Nfld. Archives, Registry Crown Lands); Daniel Mullen, fisherman of Pouch Cove, 1839 (DPHW 30); Philip Mullins, granted land at Mondays Pond, 1845 (Nfld. Archives, Registry Crown Lands); John, of Jersey Harbour, 1853 (DPHW 104); James, of Harbour Grace, 1853 (DPHW 43); Augustus, planter of Rencontre East, 1856 (DPHW 104); Susan and Thomas, of Greenspond, 1871 (Lovell); William, of Hare (now Deep) Bay (Fogo district), 1871 (Lovell); Charles and John, of Jean de Baie (Placentia B.), 1871 (Lovell); Jonathan, of Sagona, 1871 (Lovell); James, of Spaniards Bay, 1871 (Lovell).

Modern status: Scattered, especially at Rencontre East and St. John's.

Place names: Mullins Cove (Labrador) 53-44 56-25; —— ——, —— Head (Labrador) 54-14 58-12; —— Hill 47-38 55-58.

MULLOWNEY, the Connacht variant of the surname of Ireland (O)Moloney, *Ó Maoldhomhnaigh* – servant of the church, or (O)Maloughney, *Ó Maolfhachtna* – devotee of St. Fachtna, or Malumby. (MacLysaght). *See* MALONEY.

MacLysaght traced (O)Moloney in Cos. Tipperary and Clare.

In Newfoundland:

Early instances: William and Co., of Harbour Main, 1764 (CO 199.18); Henry Molloney, of St. John's, 1758 (DPHW 26C); Andrew Melowny, blacksmith of Trinity Bay, 1767 (DPHW 64); James

Mulloney, from Waterford, tailor of ? St. John's, 1777 (CO 194.33); John Molloney, of Harbour Grace, 1780 (D'Alberti 6); Cornelius Moloney, of Trinity (Trinity B.), 1790 (DPHW 64); Thomas Mullowney, of Placentia, 1794 (D'Alberti 5); Thomas Moloney, of Bonavista, 1799 (DPHW 70); William Mullowney, of Western Bay, 1799 (CO 199.18); William, ? of Port de Grave, 1801 (Nfld. Archives T22); Samuel, of Burin, 1805 (D'Alberti 15); Joseph ? Mullowney, one of 72 impressed men who sailed from Ireland to Newfoundland ? 1811 (CO 194.51); Mary Mullownay, from Powerstown (Co. Tipperary), married at St. John's, 1815 (Nfld. Archives BRC); William Mullawny or Mullowny, of King's Cove, 1815 (Nfld. Archives KCRC); Cornelius Molony, of Western side of Placentia Bay, 1817 (D'Alberti 27); Mary Mullowny or Moloney, of Tickle Cove (Bonavista B.), 1820 (Nfld. Archives KCRC); William Mullowney, of Harbour Grace, died in Bristol, 1828 (Newfoundlander 2 Apr 1828); Michael, of Carbonear, 1829 (Nfld. Archives BRC); ——, of Witless Bay, 1830 (Newfoundlander 22 Apr 1830); David, granted land at Holyrood, 1835 (Nfld. Archives, Registry Crown Lands); Elizabeth, from Co. Tipperary, of St. John's, died 1849, aged 78 (Nfld. Patriot 3 Nov 1849); Thomas Mullowny, of Burned (? for Burnt) Islands (Bonavista B.), 1855 (Nfld. Archives KCRC); John, of Indian Arm (Bonavista B.), 1858 (Nfld. Archives KCRC); Ellen, of Open Hall, 1864 (Nfld. Archives KCRC); Andrew Moloney, of Red Cliff Island (Bonavista B.), 1867 (Nfld. Archives KCRC); scattered in Lovell 1871.

Modern status: At Trepassey (Electors 1955), Clarke's Beach, Grand Falls, St. John's and Witless Bay.

MUL(L)ROONEY, surnames of Ireland, (O)Mulrooney, Ó Maolruanaidh. (MacLysaght).

Traced by MacLysaght in Cos. Fermanagh and Galway. In Galway, however, it has been changed to Moroney.

In Newfoundland:

Family tradition: Ellen Mullrooney (1843–1900), of Fox Harbour (Placentia B.) (MUN Geog.).

Early instances: Patrick Mulrooney, of Harbour Grace Parish, 1816 (Nfld. Archives HGRC); Catherine Mulroney, married at King's Cove Parish, 1842 (Nfld. Archives KCRC); Elizabeth Marooney, of Bellevue, 1885 (Nfld. Archives HGRC).

Modern status: Mullrooney, at Bar Haven (Electors 1955); Mulrooney, scattered, especially at Red Island (Placentia B.) and Windsor.

MUNDEN, MUNDON, surnames of England, from the English place names Great and Little Munden (Hertfordshire) or Mundon (Essex). (Bardsley, Reaney Origin).

Traced by Matthews in Poole (Dorset).

In Newfoundland:

Family tradition: Azariah, sent out to Newfoundland as agent by a firm from Bridport, Dorset; he settled at Brigus in 1760 (MUN Hist.).

Early instances: Azariah Mondon, of Brigus, 1770 (CO 199.18); Joseph Munden (? 1792–1881), from Broadwinsor (Dorset), of Twillingate, resident in Newfoundland 70 years, that is, since about 1811 (Kirwin); Thomas, ? of St. John's, 1822 (CO 194.65); Robert, fisherman of Pouch Cove, 1837 (DPHW 30); ——, on the Jane Elizabeth in the seal fishery out of Port de Grave, 1838 (Newfoundlander 29 Mar 1838); John, of Burin, 1871 (Lovell); Joseph, planter of East Point (Burgeo-La Poile district), 1871 (Lovell).

Modern status: Munden, in the Burgeo-La Poile district especially at Burnt Island; Mundon, rare, at Baine Harbour (Electors 1955) and Whitbourne.

Place name: Munden Island (Labrador) 53-52 57-05.

MUNDY, a surname of England, Monday, Munday of Ireland, in England from the Old Norse personal name Mundi; in Ireland "a far-fetched synonym of MacAloon," a variant of MacGloin, Mac Giolla Eoin – devotee of St. John, "due to the similarity in sound of the word Luain – Monday." (Reaney, MacLysaght).

Guppy traced Mund(a)y in Berkshire, Buckinghamshire, Hampshire, Oxfordshire and Wiltshire. MacLysaght traced Monday in Co. Fermanagh.

In Newfoundland:

Family tradition: Robert Mundy, from Leicester, England, was an early settler of Pouch Cove; he settled there about 1825 (MUN Hist.).

Early instances: William Monday, proprietor and occupier of fishing room at Old Perlican, Winter 1800–01 (Census Trinity B.); John, of Fogo, 1803 (D'Alberti 13); Robert Monday or Munday, of Pouch Cove, 1831 (DPHW 30); William H. Mundy, schoolteacher of Carbonear, 1871 (Lovell); Robert, of St. John's, 1871 (Lovell).

Modern status: Unique, at Carbonear (Electors 1955).

Place names: Monday Bank (Labrador) 52-18 55-39; Monday (or Munday) Bank (Labrador) 53-50 56-40; Monday Pond 48-03 52-58; Mondays (or Mundy) Pond 47-29 53-15; Mondays Rock 49-43 54-16; Mundy Pond 47-21 52-52, 47-33 52-44.

MUNN, a surname of England, (Mac) Munn of Scotland and Ireland, in England a variant of Moon(e), from the French place name Moyon (La Manche), or from Anglo French *moun, mun* – monk; in Scotland and Ireland from Gaelic *Mac Gille Mhunna* – son of the servant of (St.) Munn, Fintán Mocumoie (d. 635). (Reaney, Black, MacLysaght).

Traced by Guppy in Worcestershire. MacLysaght traced MacMunn in Co. Donegal.

In Newfoundland:

Early instances: Thomas Muns, fisherman of St. John's, 1732 (CO 194.9); J., of Twillingate, 1768 (MUN Hist.); John Munn, merchant of Ferryland, ? 1815, 1825 (CO 194.56, DPHW 31); John, of Harbour Grace, brother of —— from Port Bannatyne, Scotland, 1838 (*Newfoundlander* 26 Jul 1838, 8 Mar 1858); John, from Scotland, of St. John's, 1845 (*Newfoundlander* 1 Sep 1845); Robert S. (1829–), born at Isle of Bute, Scotland, came to Newfoundland to join the firm of Punten and Munn in 1851 (Mott).

Modern status: At St. John's and Buchans.

MUNRO. *See* MONROE

MURCELL, ? a surname of England of unknown origin.

In Newfoundland:

Family traditions: William Mursell, from Herring Neck, settled at what is now known as Mursell's Cove, Little Bay Islands in 1851 (MUN Hist.). —— Murcell, from Herring Neck, settled at Harbour Deep (White B.) in 1894 (MUN Folklore).

Early instances: William, of Conception Bay, [1706] (CO 194.4); Charles Mursell, fisherman of Stone Harbour (Twillingate district), 1854 (DPHW 85); Charles and William, of Herring Neck, 1871 (Lovell); William, planter of Little Bay Islands, 1871 (Lovell).

Modern status: Rare, at Great Harbour Deep (White B.) (*Electors* 1955).

Place name: Murcell Cove 49-39 55-49.

MURDOCH, MURDOCK, variant spellings of a baptismal name of Scotland and a surname of England, Scotland and Ireland, originally from two Gaelic names *Muireach* – belonging to the sea, mariner or *Murchadh* – sea-warrior, "of different origin ... [but] hopelessly confused in this name." "Introduced into Yorkshire before the Conquest by Norwegians from Ireland." In Ireland Murdoch is used occasionally as a synonym of Murtagh, *Ó Muircheartaigh*, Ir. *muircheatach* – navigator. (Black, Reaney, Withycombe, MacLysaght).

Traced by Guppy in Ayrshire and by MacLysaght in Ulster.

In Newfoundland:

Modern status: Murdoch, at St. John's; Murdock, at Aguathuna, Roddickton (*Electors* 1955), and Corner Brook.

MURLEY, a surname of Ireland, (O)Murley, *Ó Murthuile*, a variant of HURLEY. (MacLysaght).

Traced by MacLysaght in west Cork.

In Newfoundland:

Family tradition: Sam, from England, settled at what is now known as Tides Brook (Mortier B.), about 1840 (MUN Hist.).

Early instances: Samuel, granted land at Mortier Bay, 1862 (Nfld. Archives, Registry Crown Lands); Samuel Sr. and Jr. Murlay, of Butters Cove (? now Creston), 1871 (Lovell); William, farmer of Muddy Hole (Burin district), 1871 (Lovell).

Modern status: At Corner Brook, Petries, Gander and Creston North.

MURPHY, a surname of Ireland and Scotland, (O)Murphy, *Ó Murchadha*, Ir. *murchadh* – sea-warrior, or Mac Murphy, *Mac Murchada*. MacLysaght notes that the "resumption of the prefixes O and Mac, which is a modern tendency with most Gaelic names, has not taken place in the case of Murphy," that the majority of the Murphys in Ulster were probably originally Mac Murphy, and that Murphy is the most common name in Ireland. It occurs in Scotland from Irish immigration. (MacLysaght, Cottle).

In Newfoundland:

Family traditions: ——, from Co. Limerick, settled at Sunny Hill (Ferryland) (MUN Geog.). William (1800–60), from Co. Cork, settled at Bird Island Cove (now Elliston), about 1820 (MUN Geog.). ——, from Northern Ireland, came to St. John's from Nova Scotia about 1900 (MUN Folklore). ——, from Co. Kilkenny, settled at Dunville (MUN Folklore). ——, from Dublin, settled at Kilbride about 1840 (MUN Folklore).

Early instances: William, from Ireland, of Fermeuse, 1752 (CO 194.13); Andrew, assistant constable ? Bay Bulls ? 1753 (CO 194.13); M., smith of St. John's, 1794-5, "40 years in Newfoundland," that is, 1754-5 (Census 1794-5); William, of Harbour Main, 1755 (MUN Hist.); David, fisherman of Quidi Vidi, 1794-5, "16 years in Newfoundland," that is, 1778-9 (Census 1794-5); Pat., of Bay de Verde, 1783 (CO 199.18); Thomas, of Petty Harbour, 1783 (DPHW 26C); Joseph, of Devils (now

Jobs) Cove, 1786 (CO 199.18); Richard, fisherman of Harbour Grace, 1786 (CO 194.36); Peter, of Adams Cove, 1788 (CO 199.18); John, from Dublin, Irish convict landed at Petty Harbour or Bay Bulls, 1789 (CO 194.38); Stephen, ? of Port de Grave, 1790 (Nfld. Archives T22); Arthur, of Ferryland, 1791 (USPG); Maurice, of North Side, Trinity (Trinity B.), 1792 (DPHW 64); Patrick, of Placentia, 1794 (D'Alberti 5); Michael, of Chapels Cove, 1796 (CO 199.18); James, from Co. Wicklow, married at St. John's, 1797 (Nfld. Archives BRC); Maurice, of Colliers, 1799 (CO 199.18); P. and James, proprietors and occupiers of fishing room, Grates Cove, Winter 1800–01 (Census Trinity B.); James, of Trepassey, 1802 (D'Alberti 12); James, of Kit Hughes (now Kitchuses), 1803 (CO 199.18); James, of Conception Harbour, 1803 (MUN Hist.); Walter, from Waterford, merchant of St. John's, deceased, 1810 (*Royal Gazette* 22 Nov 1810); John, one of 72 impressed men who sailed from Ireland to Newfoundland ? 1811 (CO 194.51); Thomas, from Sutton's Parish (Co. Wexford), shopkeeper of St. John's, died 1814 (*Royal Gazette* 8 Dec 1814); Michael, of Open Hole (now Open Hall), 1815 (Nfld. Archives KCRC); Capt. Peter, of King's Cove, 1815 (Nfld. Archives KCRC); James, of Bonavista, 1815 (Nfld. Archives KCRC); John, of Ragged Harbour (now Melrose), 1815 (Nfld. Archives KCRC); William, from Dunkate (Co. Kilkenny), of St. John's, died 1816 (*Royal Gazette* 4 Jan 1816); Edward, of New Harbour (Trinity B.), 1818 (Nfld. Archives KCRC); Dennis, from Co. Cork, married at Plate Cove, 1820 (Nfld. Archives KCRC); Thomas, of Broad Cove (now Duntara), 1820 (Nfld. Archives KCRC); John, of Catalina, 1820 (Nfld. Archives KCRC); Thomas, of Tickle Cove (Bonavista B.), 1821 (Nfld. Archives KCRC); Honour, of Old Perlican, 1821 (DPHW 58); Michael, of Riders Harbour (Trinity B.), 1825 (Nfld. Archives KCRC); William, from Co. Kilkenny, married at Bird Island Cove (now Elliston), 1826 (Nfld. Archives KCRC); Dennis, of Gussets Cove (unidentified), married at Harbour Grace, 1828 (Nfld. Archives BRC); ———, from Co. Kilkenny, married at Kings Cove, 1829 (Nfld. Archives KCRC); Margaret, from Graigue (unidentified) (Co. Kilkenny), married at Chapels Cove, 1829 (Nfld. Archives BRC); Judith, of Twillingate, 1829 (Nfld. Archives KCRC); Thomas, of Greenspond, 1829 (Nfld. Archives KCRC); Anne, of Turks Cove, 1829 (Nfld. Archives KCRC); James Murphey, of Heart's Content, 1832 (Nfld. Archives KCRC); James Murphy, granted land near Middle Long Pond, 1836 (Nfld. Archives, Registry Crown Lands); Edward, ? of Northern Bay, 1838 (DPHW

54); John, from Co. Wexford, married at Renews, 1841 (Dillon); Patrick, granted land at Gotts Cove, Trinity Harbour, 1842 (Nfld. Archives, Registry Crown Lands); John, from Midleton (Co. Cork), of Harbour Grace, 1844 (*Indicator* 27 Jul 1844); Thomas, from Co. Cork, of Brigus, 1844 (*Indicator* 24 Aug 1844); John, granted land at Catalina, 1847 (Nfld. Archives, Registry Crown Lands); John, granted land at San Croie, near Keels, 1848 (Nfld. Archives, Registry Crown Lands); John, granted land at Holyrood, 1849 (Nfld. Archives, Registry Crown Lands); Thomas, of Red Clift Island (Bonavista B.), 1850 (Nfld. Archives KCRC); Edmond, of Stock Cove (Bonavista B.), 1855 (Nfld. Archives KCRC); John, of Keels, 1857 (*Newfoundlander* 22 Oct 1857); Mary, of Indian Arm (Bonavista B.), 1857 (Nfld. Archives KCRC); Lawrence, granted land at Barren Island (now Bar Haven), 1857 (Nfld. Archives, Registry Crown Lands); James, granted land at Distress (now St. Bride's), 1857 (Nfld. Archives, Registry Crown Lands); Sylvester, of Torbay, 1858 (*Newfoundlander* 1 Apr 1858); John, of Burin, 1858 (*Newfoundlander* 14 Jan 1858); Johana, of Fortune Harbour, 1862 (Nfld. Archives KCRC); Patrick, of Shoels Cove (Bonavista B.), 1863 (Nfld. Archives KCRC); James, of Knights Cove (Bonavista B.), 1864 (Nfld. Archives KCRC); Jacob, of the French Shore, 1868 (Nfld. Archives HGRC); John, of Bonne Bay, 1869 (DPHW 93); widespread in Lovell 1871; Richard, from Co. Kilkenny, of Carbonear, died 1883, aged 55 (Carbonear R.C. Cemetery); James, from Co. Kilkenny, died at Cape Race, 1895, aged 76 (Dillon).

Modern status: Widespread, especially at St. John's, Old Petty Harbour Road, Open Hall, Bell Island, Crawley's Island (Placentia B.), Parker's Cove and Little Bay (Placentia B.).

Place names: Murphy(s) Cove 47-27 54-28; Murphy Cove 47-36 53-55; ——— Head (Labrador) 59-31 63-43; ——— Point 46-58 53-35; ——— River (Labrador) 53-51 57-54; ——— Rock 46-56 55-32, 47-21 54-14, 48-32 52-59; Murphys Cove 46-56 55-29; Murphys (or Lomonds) Cove 49-28 57-46; ——— Pond (Labrador) 52-56 55-55; ——— River 47-08 53-24; ——— First Pond 47-54 53-18.

MURRAY, a surname of England, Scotland and Ireland generally from the province of Moray, Scotland, but in England also from the English place names Moorhay or Moor(e)-Hayes (Devon), and in Ireland for O'Murry, *Ó Muireadhaigh*, MacElmurray or Gilmore, *Mac Giolle Mhuire*, MacMurray, *Mac Muireadhaigh*, and (O)Murrihy, *Ó Muirghthe*.

(Black, Reaney, Spiegelhalter, MacLysaght). *See also* MOREY, MORRY.

Traced by Guppy fairly generally in Scotland but rather more numerous south of the Forth and Clyde and in Durham and Northumberland, by Spiegelhalter in Devon, and by MacLysaght in Cos. Tyrone, Fermanagh, Clare, MacMurray in Co. Down, O'Murray in Co. Roscommon.

In Newfoundland:

Early instances: James, in possession of property and fisherman of St. John's, 1794–5, "10 years in Newfoundland," that is, 1784–5 (Census 1794–5); Patrick, boatkeeper of Tilton Harbour (now Tilting), ? 1786 (CO 194.36); John, of Adams Cove, 1786 (CO 199.18); James, from Drumclan (Co. Monaghan), Irish convict landed at Petty Harbour or Bay Bulls, 1789 (CO 194.38); William, of Western Bay, 1796 (CO 199.18); John, from Ross (unspecified) (Co. Wexford), married at St. John's, 1798 (Nfld. Archives BRC); Marg Murry, proprietor and occupier of fishing room, New Harbour, Winter 1800–01 (Census Trinity B.); Patrick, of Fogo Island, 1805 (D'Alberti 13); Margaret Murray alias Gibbons, of Ferryland, 1805 (Nfld. Archives BRC); John Murr(a)y, of Harbour Grace Parish, 1808 (Nfld. Archives HGRC); Biddy Murrey, born at Placentia, 1810, baptized in Trinity North district, 1811 (DPHW 64); Thomas Murray, of Heart's Content, 1819 (Nfld. Archives KCRC); Hannah, of St. Mary's, 1827 (Nfld. Archives BRC); Lawrence, of Holyrood, 1829 (Nfld. Archives BRC); Michael Murry, of King's Cove Parish, 1835 (Nfld. Archives KCRC); John Murray, of Freshwater (unspecified), 1836 (Nfld. Archives BRC); ——, of Maggoty Cove, deceased, 1851 (*Newfoundlander* 13 Nov 1851); James, from Waterford, of St. John's, 1856 (*Newfoundlander* 25 Aug 1856); John, granted land at Cape Broyle, 1861 (Nfld. Archives, Registry Crown Lands); Michael Murr(a)y, of Trinity, (unspecified), 1861 (Nfld. Archives KCRC); John, of Harbour Grace, 1866 (Nfld. Archives HGRC); scattered in Lovell 1871.

Modern status: Scattered, especially at St. John's, Carbonear and Fox Harbour (Placentia B.).

Place names: Murray Barasway 47-19 53-55; —— Harbour (Labrador) 52-27 55-43; —— Head (Labrador) 59-54 64-08; —— Lake (Labrador) 54-28 65-38; —— Mountains 49-07 58-23; —— Point 47-40 57-59, —— —— (Labrador) 52-54 55-50; Murrays Pond 47-37 52-49, 47-48 54-46; —— —— River 47-37 52-50.

MURRIN, a surname of Ireland, (O)Murrin, *Ó Muireáin*, and according to Le Messurier of the Channel Islands, a variant of Mourant.

Traced by MacLysaght in Cos. Mayo and Sligo where, however, the name has been changed to MORAN.

In Newfoundland:

Early instances: Daniel Murran, of St. John's, 1796 (DPHW 26B); Sara Murren, from Kitchrily [sic] (unidentified) ? Ireland, married at St. John's, 1797 (Nfld. Archives BRC); William, of Bay Roberts, 1804 (CO 199.18); Bryan, from Ross (unspecified) Ireland, fisherman of St. John's, died 1815 (*Royal Gazette* 27 Apr 1815); John Murrin, of Quidi Vidi, 1814 (DPHW 26B); John Murren, of Pouch Cove, 1821 (DPHW 26B); Thomas, of White Hills (St. John's), 1821 (DPHW 26B); John (and others) Murrne, of Spaniards Bay, 1871 (Lovell).

Modern status: Scattered, especially at St. John's and Spaniards Bay.

MUSHROW. *See* MUSSEAU

MUSSEAU, MIESSEAU, MUSHROW, ? Newfoundland variants of the surname of France Mousseau, French *moussu* – (dweller in the) mossy place. (Dauzat).

In Newfoundland:

Early instances: Prosper Moisson, of Channel, 1871 (Lovell); Joseph (and others), of Mouse Island (now Channel West), 1871 (Lovell).

Modern status: Musseau, at Petries (*Electors* 1955), Channel, Curling and Mouse Island; Miesseau, rare, at Stephenville Crossing; Mushrow, rare, at Channel and St. John's.

MUTFORD, a surname of England, from the English place name Mutford (Suffolk), ? from Old English *(ge)mōtford* – ford at which moots were held. (Ekwall).

In Newfoundland:

Modern status: Rare, at Twillingate.

MUTREY. *See* MOOTREY

MUTTON, a surname of England, from Old French *mouton* – sheep, a nickname or for shepherd, or from English place names Mutton Farm, Mutton Mill (Cornwall), Mytton (Shropshire), Myton (Warwickshire, Yorkshire NR), Mitton (Lancashire, Yorkshire WR, Worcestershire). (Reaney, Spiegelhalter).

Traced by Guppy in Cornwall and by Spiegelhalter in Devon.

In Newfoundland:

Early instance: Thomas, fisherman of Petty Harbour, 1871 (Lovell).

Modern status: Unique, at St. John's (*Electors* 1955).

Place names: Mutton Bay, Cape 46-42 53-22.

MYERS, MYRES, surnames of England, Myre(s) of Scotland, Myers of Ireland, in England and Scotland from Norse *mýrr* – (dweller near the) marsh, bog; in England also from Old French *mire* – physician; in Scotland also from the Scots place name Myres (Fifeshire); in Ireland a variant of (O)Meere, *Ó Midhir*, Ir. *meidhir* – mirth. (Reaney, Black, MacLysaght).

Myers traced by Guppy in Yorkshire WR, by Spiegelhalter in Devon, and by MacLysaght in Co. Clare.

In Newfoundland:

Early instances: Alice Myers, from Clonmel (Co. Tipperary), married at St. John's, 1811 (Nfld. Archives BRC); John, of St. John's, 1814 (D'Alberti 24); Mary, of Harbour Grace Parish, 1825 (Nfld. Archives HGRC); Robert, planter of Trinity (Trinity B.), 1828 (DPHW 64B).

Modern status: Myers, scattered; Myres, unique, at St. John's.

MYLER, ? a variant of the surname of Ireland Meyler, *Maoilir*, "the name of a Welsh family in Ireland since 1200." (MacLysaght).

Traced by MacLysaght in Co. Wexford.

In Newfoundland:

Early instances: John Miler, of St. John's, 1774 (DPHW 26C); James Myler, from Donashadee (Co. Down), Irish convict landed at Petty Harbour or Bay Bulls, 1789 (CO 194.38); Patrick, of St. John's, 1803 (Nfld. Archives BRC); Bridget, of Harbour Grace Parish, 1815 (Nfld. Archives HGRC).

Modern status: At Bell Island (*Electors* 1955), and St. John's.

MYLES. *See* MILES

MYRDEN, ? a variant of the surname of England Murden, ? from the English place names Morden (Cambridgeshire, Dorset, Surrey) or Mordon (Durham). (Bardsley).

In Newfoundland: Gerald H., born in North Sydney, NS, settled at Corner Brook.

Modern status: At Corner Brook.

MYRES. *See* MYERS

MYRICK, a variant of the surname of England and Wales Meyrick, and of the surname of Ireland Merrick. Cottle comments: "Welsh form (*Meuric*) of Maurice. Preceded by Welsh *Ap* – son of, it is the probable origin of the name *America*, since when John Cabot returned to Bristol after his second transatlantic voyage in 1498, the king's pension of £20 was handed to him by the two collectors of customs for Bristol, the senior being Richard Ameryk ... who was 'probably the heaviest investor' in the expedition ... His title to be the eponym of the continent is surely stronger than the frivolous claim of the Italian Amerigo Vespucci." In Ireland, MacLysaght comments: "Merrick of triple origin: a Welsh name in Connacht from the thirteenth century and gaelicized *Mac Mibhric*; in west Waterford and adjoining areas probably *Ó Mearadhaigh* (alias Merry); or occasionally an English name."

In Newfoundland:

Family tradition: —— ? Merrick (later Myrick), from Tipperary settled in St. John's about 1820; a son moved to Cape Race about 1870 (MUN Folklore).

Early instances: Honora Myrick, from Cashel Vame (unidentified) (Co. Tipperary), married at St. John's, 1809 (Nfld. Archives BRC); Michael Meyrick, ? of St. John's, 1822 (CO 194.65); John (and others) Myrick, of St. John's, 1871 (Lovell).

Modern status: Scattered, especially at St. John's and in the Ferryland district.

MYRON, ? a shortened form of various surnames of Russia, from the baptismal name Miron.

In Newfoundland:

Modern status: At St. John's.

N

NAGLE, a surname of Ireland, the Co. Cork form of the Norman name *de Angulo* which in Connacht and Leinster was anglicized NANGLE except where some branches of the family became COSTELLO(E) after one of the sons of Gilbert de Nangle. (MacLysaght).

In Newfoundland:

Family tradition: Patrick, from ? Cork, Ireland, settled at Tors Cove in the early 1800s; the family later moved to Bay Bulls (MUN Folklore).

Early instances: John Neagle, in fishery at Petty Harbour, 1794–5, "28 years in Newfoundland," that is, 1766–7 (Census 1794–5); John, of St. John's, 1780 (DPHW 26C); Thomas, of South Side Musketta (now Bristol's Hope), 1782 (CO 199.18); Garret, from Camih Parish (unidentified), Diocese of Waterford, married at St. John's, 1793 (Nfld. Archives BRC); John Nagle, of Harbour Grace Parish, 1823 (Nfld. Archives HGRC); Thomas Neagle, of Brigus, 1828 (Nfld. Archives BRC); Patrick, of Harbour Grace, 1830 (Nfld. Archives BRC); Patrick, granted land at Rocky Hill, near Bay Bulls, 1847 (Nfld. Archives, Registry Crown Lands); Patrick, fisherman of Toad's (now Tors) Cove, 1871 (Lovell); Peter Nagle, fisherman of St. Mary's, 1871 (Lovell).

Modern status: Rare, at Riverhead (St. Mary's), Chamberlains (Electors 1955), Bay Bulls and St. John's.

Place name: Nagle's Hill (St. John's).

NANGLE. *See* NAGLE

In Newfoundland:

Early instance: Matthew, of St. John's, 1796 (CO 194.39).

Modern status: Rare, at St. John's (Electors 1955).

NAPIER, with a variant Napper, surnames of England and Scotland, Napper of Ireland, from Old French *nap(p)ier* – keeper of the table-linen (in a great household). (Reaney, Cottle, Black, MacLysaght).

Napper traced by Guppy in Berkshire and by MacLysaght in Co. Meath.

In Newfoundland:

Early instances: Mary Napper, of Salvage, 1842 (MUN Hist.); Mary Ann, of Tickle Cove (Bonavista South district), 1843 (DPHW 73A).

Modern status: At George's Brook (Electors 1955) and Sandy Cove (Bonavista South district).

NARDINI, a surname of France, a diminutive of *Nardi*, the Corsican form of *Bernardi*. (Dauzat). *See* BERNARD.

In Newfoundland:

Family tradition: ——, from Italy, operated a sawmill and store at Nardines and settled at Stephenville Crossing, about 1909 (MUN Hist.).

Early instance: Antonio, of Sandy Point, operated sawmill at Main Gut, 1889 (J.P. Howley, "Reminiscences").

Modern status: Rare, at Stephenville Crossing.

NASH, a surname of England and Ireland – (dweller) at the ash tree. *See* ASH.

Traced by Guppy in Buckinghamshire, Gloucestershire, Hertfordshire and Surrey, by Spiegelhalter in Devon, and by MacLysaght in Cos. Limerick and Kerry.

In Newfoundland:

Early instances: Samuel, of Newfoundland, 1752 (St. Patrick's Parish Records, Waterford per Kirwin); Edward, of St. John's, 1763 (DPHW 26C); John, of Pick Hart (Burin district), 1831 (DPHW 109); Charles, fisherman of Bonne Bay (Fortune B.), 1833 (DPHW 102); William Narsh, ? of Northern Bay, 1842 (DPHW 54); T. Nash, one of the road commissioners for opening a road from Branch to Distress Cove (now St. Bride's), 1848 (Nfld. Almanac); John, fisherman of Furby's Cove, 1851 (DPHW 104); Charles, of Sam Hitches (Harbour), 1853 (DPHW 104); Charles, of Bay de Este, 1871 (Lovell); Patrick (and others), of Branch, 1871 (Lovell); Thomas, planter of Garnish, 1871 (Lovell); Thomas, of Piccaire, 1871 (Lovell); John and Thomas, of Seal Islands (Burgeo district), 1871 (Lovell); John, planter of West Point (Burgeo district), 1871 (Lovell).

Modern status: Scattered, especially at Branch.

Place name: Nash Lake (Labrador) 55-01 67-18.

NEAL(E), (O)NEIL(L), variants of a baptismal name and surname of England, Scotland, Ireland and as Neal(e) of the Channel Islands, Neil and formerly Neel of Jersey, probably from an Old Irish and

Gaelic personal name *Niáll* – champion. Reaney comments: "The name was carried to Iceland by the Scandinavians as *Njáll*, taken to Norway, then to France and brought to England by the Normans. It was also introduced direct into north-west England by Norwegians from Ireland. It was usually latinized as *Nigellus* through an incorrect association with *niger* – black." (Withycombe, Reaney, Black, Mac-Lysaght, Turk).

Guppy found Neal(e) widespread in England, Neil in Ayrshire. MacLysaght found Mac Neill, from the western isles of Scotland in Cos. Antrim and Derry since the fourteenth century, and (O)Neill numerous throughout Ireland, especially in Cos. Tyrone and Antrim.

In Newfoundland:

Family traditions: Harry O'Neill (–1853), shipwrecked Irishman, married a Miss Casey and settled at Conche in the early 1800s (Casey). John, from Belfast, married Mary Brothers and settled at Admirals Cove, Fermeuse (MUN Folklore). Isaac Neil (1820–86), from Wales, settled at Spaniards Bay in the 1840s (MUN Geog.). Seven Neil brothers, from Ireland settled in Newfoundland: 3 in Spaniards Bay, 3 in Harbour Grace and 1 on the southeast coast (MUN Folklore). Thomas O'Neil, from Shangarry Mongara (Co. Cork), settled at Boney; he later moved to Bay de Verde (MUN Hist.). —— O'Neill, from Waterford, settled at St. John's about 1855 (MUN Folklore).

Early instances: Paul Neal, of Little Placentia (now Argentia) about 1730–5 (CO 194.9); Patrick O'Neil, of St. John's, 1753 (DPHW 26C); Patrick Neil, in fishery at Petty Harbour, 1794–5, "30 years in Newfoundland," that is, 1764–5 (Census 1794–5); Edward Neal, of Western Bay, 1783 (CO 199.18); John Neale, Irish convict sent to Newfoundland ? 1789 (CO 194.38); John O'Neal, from Dublin, Irish convict landed at Petty Harbour or Bay Bulls, 1789 (CO 194.38); George Neil, of Bryants Cove, 1793 (CO 199.18); Mary Neill, from Camih (unidentified), Diocese of Waterford, married at St. John's, 1793 (Nfld. Archives BRC); Julianna O'Neal or O'Neill, from Waterford, Ireland, of Harbour Main, 1793, died 1810 (CO 199.18, *Royal Gazette* 8 Nov 1810); John Neal, of Kettle Cove (North Shore, Conception B.), 1796 (CO 199.18); Constantine (O)Neal, from Co. Kilkenny, of Fermeuse, 1797, died 1810 (D'Alberti 7, *Royal Gazette* 8 Nov 1810); Martin Neil, from Faha (unidentified), Diocese of Waterford, married in the Bay Bulls district, 1805 (Nfld. Archives BRC); John Neill, of Fermeuse, 1806 (Nfld. Archives BRC); Margaret O'Neal or O'Neill, of

Harbour Grace Parish, 1806 (Nfld. Archives HGRC); Martin Neill, from Co. Tipperary, labourer of St. John's, deceased 1810 (*Royal Gazette* 6 Dec 1810); Patrick Neil, of Kings Cove, 1816 (Nfld. Archives KCRC); Margaret Neal, of Renews, 1820 (Nfld. Archives BRC); Clemence, planter of Carbonear, 1820 (DPHW 48); Edward Neil or Neal, of Bonavista, 1821 (Nfld. Archives KCRC); Thomas Neil, of Tickle Cove (Bonavista B.), 1822 (Nfld. Archives KCRC); Patrick, of Catalina, 1823 (Nfld. Archives KCRC); Edward Neal, of Keels, 1824 (Nfld. Archives KCRC); Arthur Neil, of Bay Bulls, 1831 (Nfld. Archives BRC); Moses O'Neill, of Freshwater (unspecified), 1832 (Nfld. Archives BRC); Margaret O'Neil, of Ragged Harbour (now Melrose), 1832 (Nfld. Archives KCRC); J. O'Neill, of Burin, 1832 (*Newfoundlander* 26 Jan 1832); Elinor Neil, of Trinity (unspecified), 1833 (Nfld. Archives KCRC); Mary O'Neel, of Fortune Harbour, 1833 (Nfld. Archives KCRC); James Neill, "one of the first Irish settlers in the valley" (Freshwater, St. John's), died 1834 (Mannion); Henry Neals, of Furby's Cove, 1835 (DPHW 30); Thomas (O)Neil, ? of Northern Bay, 1838 (DPHW 54); Michael Neil, from Co. Cork, of Port de Grave, 1844 (*Indicator* 24 Aug 1844); John Neill, ? of Harbour Grace, 1845 (*Newfoundlander* 16 Jan 1845); Michael O'Neil, granted land at Gasters, 1850 (Nfld. Archives, Registry Crown Lands); Patrick, granted land at Cats Cove (now Conception Harbour), 1852 (Nfld. Archives, Registry Crown Lands); Richard Neyle, from Newton Abbot (Devon), married at St. John's, 1853 (*Weekly Herald* 31 Aug 1853); Thomas Neill, of Red Cliff Island (Bonavista B.), 1857, of Plate Cove, 1858 (Nfld. Archives KCRC); Rev. Jeremiah, granted land at Trepassey, 1859 (Nfld. Archives, Registry Crown Lands); Peter Neil, fisherman of La Plante, 1860 (DPHW 99); Philip O'Neil, of Bay Roberts, 1871 (Lovell); George and Humphrey Neile, of Spaniards Bay, 1871 (Lovell); James and John Neill, of Madox Cove, 1871 (Lovell); Charles and John Neil, of East Point (Burgeo-La Poile district), 1871 (Lovell); Patrick Neill, of Duricle (Placentia B.), 1871 (Lovell); John Neille, planter of Cape Race, 1871 (Lovell); Thomas Neil and Son, traders of Bay de Verde, 1871 (Lovell); Peter Neale, of West Cul de Sac, 1871 (Lovell); James and Martin Neal, farmers of Torbay, 1871 (Lovell); Samuel (and others), of Manuels, 1871 (Lovell); Patrick O'Neill, farmer of Outer Cove, 1871 (Lovell); John O'Neil, farmer of Holyrood, 1871 (Lovell).

Modern status: Neal, scattered, especially at St. John's; Neale, unique, at St. John's; Neil, scattered, especially at Spaniard's Bay; O'Neil, scattered, especially at St. John's; O'Neill, scattered, especially at Admirals Cove, Fermeuse (*Electors* 1955) and St. John's.

Place names: Neils Pond 47-21 53-27, 47-32 52-52; O'Neale Rock (Labrador) 53-24 55-38.

NEARY, a surname of Ireland, (O)Neary, *Ó Nárdhaigh*, possibly from *nardach* – skilful. (MacLysaght).

Traced by MacLysaght in north Connacht.

In Newfoundland:

Family tradition: Peter, from Ireland, settled at Portugal Cove in the late 1600s (MUN Folklore).

Early instances: Mark, married at St. John's, 1778 (DPHW 26D); Francis, in possession of property in fishery at Portugal Cove, 1794–5 (Census 1794–5); Francis, from Ratho (unidentified) (Co. Carlow), married at St. John's, 1804 (Nfld. Archives BRC); Nicholas, of Harbour Grace Parish, 1807 (Nfld. Archives HGRC); Thomas, of Bonavista, 1828 (Nfld. Archives KCRC).

Modern status: Scattered, especially at Bell Island and St. John's.

Place name: Nearys (or Piccos) Pond 47-40 52-49.

NECHO, NICHO, ? Newfoundland variants of the surnames of France Nicaud, Nicod, Nicot, pet-forms of an old baptismal name and surname *Nicodème* – (St.) Nicodemus. (Dauzat).

In Newfoundland:

Early instance: Mary Nicco, of Harbour Grace Parish, 1828 (Nfld. Archives HGRC).

Modern status: Rare, Necho at Catalina (*Electors* 1955); Necho, Nicho, at Horwood.

(O)NEIL(L). *See* NEAL(E)

NEILSON, a surname of Scotland and Ireland – son of Neil. *See* NEALE. (Black, MacLysaght). *See* NELSON.

Traced by Guppy in the Glasgow district and by MacLysaght, from Scotland, especially in Dublin and Ulster since the early seventeenth century.

In Newfoundland:

Early instance: James N., teacher of St. Andrew's School, St. John's, 1857 (*Nfld. Almanac*).

Modern status: At St. John's, Burin (*Electors* 1955) and Corner Brook.

NELDER, a variant of the surname of England Needler, from Old English **nædlere* – maker of needles. (Reaney).

In Newfoundland:

Early instance: William, mason of St. John's, 1845 (DPHW 26B).

Modern status: At St. John's.

NELSON, a surname of England and Ireland, a variant of NEILSON. *See* NEAL(E).

Traced by Guppy in Bedfordshire, Cumberland, Westmorland, Lancashire, Lincolnshire, Norfolk and Yorkshire, and by MacLysaght (with Neilson) in Dublin and Ulster since the seventeenth century.

In Newfoundland:

Early instance: John, planter of Freshwater (Carbonear), 1845 (DPHW 48).

Modern status: At St. John's.

NETTEN, a surname of England from the English place name Netton (Devon, Wiltshire). (Spiegelhalter).

Traced by Spiegelhalter in Devon.

In Newfoundland:

Early instances: William, schoolmaster and missionary of St. John's, 1833 (DPHW 26B); William, of Petty Harbour, 1835 (DPHW 31); William, of Bonavista, 1845 (DPHW 70); Rev. William, of Catalina, 1871 (Lovell); Rev. T. S., of Rose Blanche, 1871 (Lovell).

Modern status: Rare, at St. John's.

NEVILLE, a surname of England, Ireland and Jersey (Channel Islands), from the French place names Neville (Seine-Inférieure) or Neuville (Calvados and elsewhere); also in Ireland for Nee, *Ó Niadh*, Ir. *niadh* – champion, and (Mac) Nevin, *Mac Cnáimhín*, ? Ir. *cnámh* – bone. (MacLysaght, Turk).

Traced by Spiegelhalter in Devon and by MacLysaght in Cos. Limerick, Clare, Kilkenny and Waterford.

In Newfoundland:

Early instances: Walter Nevill, of St. John's, deceased 1730 (CO 194.9); John Nevil, from Dunbrady Parish (unidentified), (Co. Wexford), married at St. John's, 180' (Nfld. Archives BRC); Lawrence Nevill, of Harbour Grace Parish, 1806 (Nfld. Archives HGRC); Richard ? Nevile, one of 72 impressed men who sailed from Ireland to Newfoundland ? 1811 (CO 194.51); Michael Nevill, arrived (at St. John's) from Ross, Ireland, in the spring of 1814 (*Royal Gazette* 22 Sep 1814); Mrs. Nevel, of Trinity (unspecified), 1816 (Nfld. Archives KCRC); James Neville, of Tilting Harbour (now Tilting), 1829 (Nfld. Archives KCRC); Frances, of Salmon Cove (unspecified) (Conception B.), married at St. John's,

1839 (DPHW 26D); Nicholas, granted land at Northern Gut (now North River), 1859 (Nfld. Archives, Registry Crown Lands); Peter, fisherman of Logy Bay, 1871 (Lovell); Gregory and James, farmers of Topsail, 1871 (Lovell).

Modern status: Scattered, especially at St. John's.

Place names: Nevile Island (Labrador) 52-32 56-06; Nevilles (or Octagon) Pond 47-31 52-53.

NEWBURY, a surname of England, from the English place name Newbury (Berkshire, Essex, Somerset, Wiltshire). (Cottle).

Traced by Guppy (as Newber(r)y) in Bedfordshire, Devon and Warwickshire. Spiegelhalter traced Newber(r)y, Newbury in Devon.

In Newfoundland:

Early instances: Nicholas Newberry, of St. John's, 1751 (CO 194.13); Nicholas, of Quidi Vidi Cove, 1771 (CO 194.18); Elias Newbury, of Caribou Tickle (Labrador), 1787, of Fogo, 1789 (MUN Hist.); Richard Newbery, of Shoe Cove (Twillingate district), 1846 (DPHW 86); Frederick, fisherman of Brigus, 1851 (DPHW 34).

Modern status: Scattered, especially in the Green Bay district.

NEWCOMBE, a surname of England and Ireland, from Old English *nīw* and *cumen, cuma* – newly-arrived stranger; in Ireland also for (O)Nee, *Ó Niadh*, Ir. *niadh* – champion. (Reaney, Cottle, MacLysaght).

Traced by Guppy in Devon and by MacLysaght as Newcomon formerly in Dublin since the end of the sixteenth century, as Newcombe mainly in Co. Mayo in the nineteenth century.

In Newfoundland:

Early instances: George, of Flower's Cove, 1873 (MUN Hist.).

Modern status: At Castors River and Bartlett's Harbour (St. Barbe district) (*Electors* 1955).

NEWELL, a surname of England and Ireland, a variant of NEVILLE or NOEL, or from the English place names Newell (Kent) or Newhall (Devon); in Ireland also (O)Newell, *Ó Tnúthghail*, Ir. *tnúth-gal* – envy, valour. (Reaney, Spiegelhalter, MacLysaght).

Traced by Spiegelhalter in Devon and by MacLysaght in Co. Kildare and especially in Co. Down.

In Newfoundland:

Early instances: Thomas, of English Harbour (Trinity B.), 1675 (CO 1); Thomas, of Bonavista, 1675 (CO 1); Thomas, of Harbour Main, 1676 (CO 1); Thomas Sr. and Jr., of Green Island (Bonavista

B.), 1708–9 (CO 194.4); ——, constable of Trinity district ? 1730 (CO 194.9); Jonah Newel or Newals, fisherman of Goose Cove (Trinity North district), 1758, of Trinity (Trinity B.), 1760 (DPHW 64); Joseph Newell, of St. John's, 1763 (DPHW 26C); Thomas, of Old Perlican, 1770 (DPHW 64); John, of Western Bay, 1776 (CO 199.18); Nicholas Newall, fisherman of Quidi Vidi, 1794–5, "born in Newfoundland," (Census 1794–5); Thomas Newell, occupier of fishing room at Heart's Content, Winter 1800–01 (Census Trinity B.); Thomas, of Greenspond, 1809 (DPHW 64); John, of Pouch Cove, 1814 (DPHW 26B); Eliza Newel, of Grates Cove, 1830 (DPHW 58); T. Newell, of Harbour Grace, 1830 (*Newfoundlander* 14 Oct 1830); Jonathan, planter of Clown's Cove (Carbonear), 1832 (DPHW 48); T., ? of Carbonear, 1832 (*Newfoundlander* 8 Nov 1832); John (or Joseph) Newell (or Nowell), from Brixham (Devon), of St. John's, deceased 1835, aged 38 (*Times* 25 Mar 1835, *Star and Conception B.J.* 15 Apr 1835); John Newel, planter of Bear's Cove (Harbour Grace), 1839 (DPHW 43); John Newell, planter of Freshwater (Carbonear), 1852 (DPHW 49); Stephen Nuel or Newell, fisherman of Brigus, 1856 (DPHW 35); William Newell, fisherman of Northern (now North) River, 1860 (DPHW 34); Isaac (and others), of Burnt Head (Brigus district), 1871 (Lovell); Josiah, of Flat Bay (Green B.), 1871 (Lovell); Abraham, of Kelligrews, 1871 (Lovell).

Modern status: Scattered, especially at Pouch Cove, St. John's, and in the Port de Grave district.

Place name: Newell Island 49-04 53-34.

NEWHOOK, a surname of England (1 in *London Telephone Directory*) and Newfoundland; in Newfoundland ? from Flemish Nieuhoek – New Harbour. (Wix).

In Newfoundland:

Family tradition: Charles Newick (later Newhook) (1752–1799), of French Huguenot descent, settled at Trinity (Trinity B.) in 1775 (MUN Folklore).

Early instances: Charles Newick, of Trinity Bay, 1778 (DPHW 64); ? Elijah Newhook, proprietor and occupier of fishing room at Trinity (Trinity B.), Winter 1800–01 (Census Trinity B.); James, planter of Durrells Arm (Trinity North district), 1823 (DPHW 64B); Martha, of New Harbour (Trinity B.), 1825 (Nfld. Archives KCRC); Charles, J.P., Northern District of the Colony, 1834 (*Newfoundlander* 10 Jul 1834); Sarah, of St. John's, 1845 (DPHW 26D); William, of Dog Cove (Trinity North district), 1859 (DPHW 63); John and Mrs. Sarah Newhock, of Old

Shop, 1871 (Lovell); Charles and William New hook, shipwrights of Catalina, 1871 (Lovell); Jonas, of Jackson's Arm, 1871 (Lovell); William, of Ship Cove (now part of Port Rexton), 1871 (Lovell); Charles (and others) Newick, of Chapel Arm (Trinity B.), 1871 (Lovell).

Modern status: Widespread, especially at Norsman's Cove and Long Cove (Trinity South district).

NEWMAN, a surname of England and Ireland, from Old English *nēowe* etc. and *mann* – new man, newcomer. (Reaney).

Found widespread by Guppy especially in the west Midlands, and by MacLysaght numerous, except in Ulster, and especially in Cos. Cork and Meath.

In Newfoundland:

Early instances: Robert and William, of Bonavista, 1675, 1681 (of Harbour Main, 1676) (CO 1); Henry, merchant of St. John's, 1701 (CO 194.2); Robert, of Torbay, 17-8-9 (CO 194.4); William, from Dartmouth (Devon), in possession of property at Cupids, 1755 (CO 199.18); John, of Greenspond, 1776 (MUN Hist.); William, of Trinity Bay, 1779 (DPHW 64); William, of Brigus, 1801 (CO 199.18); William, of Northern Bay, 1804 (CO 199. 18); William, planter of Joe Batts Arm, 1821 (USPG); Richard, of Twillingate, 1823 (D'Alberti 33); Samuel, planter of Carbonear, 1833 (DPHW 48); John, of Catalina, 1834 (DPHW 70); William, of Barr'd Islands, 1842 (DPHW 83); George, fisherman of Dark Tickle (Notre Dame B.), 1865 (DPHW 91); scattered in Lovell 1871.

Modern status: Scattered, especially at Joe Batts Arm and Boyd's Cove (Twillingate district).

Place names: Newman Sound 48-36 53-47; Newmans Cove 48-35 53-12.

NEWPORT, a surname of England, from the English place name Newport (Devon, Essex, Monmouthshire). (Cottle).

Traced by Guppy in Cheshire and Somerset.

In Newfoundland:

Early instances: James, fisherman of Whale Cove (Burin district), 1860 (DPHW 108); James (and others), of Burin, 1871 (Lovell); Richard, of Moreton's Harbour, 1871 (Lovell); Anthony, of Witless Bay, 1871 (Lovell); Thomas, of Garnish, 1874 (DPHW 103).

Modern status: At Garnish, Grand Bank and St. John's.

Place name: ? Newport, Newport Harbour 49-02 53-38.

NEWTON, a surname of England, from the commonest English place name – the new place, homestead, farm, village. (Cottle).

Traced by Guppy from Northumberland to Cornwall.

In Newfoundland:

Early instances: Thomas, of Salmon Cove (now Champneys), 1794 (DPHW 64); John, of St. John's, 1806 (CO 194.45); Thomas, planter of Trinity (Trinity B. 1830, of Ship Cove (now part of Port Rexton), 1832 (DPHW 64B); Elizabeth, baptized at Greenspond, 1830, aged 56 (DPHW 76); Elinor, of King's Cove Parish, 1836 (Nfld. Archives KCRC); Mary Ellen, of Deer Harbour, 1866 (Nfld. Archives KCRC).

Modern status: Rare, at Southport (*Electors* 1955), Bell Island and St. John's.

NICHO. *See* NECHO

NICHOLAS, a baptismal name and surname of England and the Channel Islands, Mac Nicholas of Ireland; in England from Latin *Nicolaus* in turn from a Greek name containing the elements *victory* and *people*. St. Nicholas, bishop of Myra about 300, is the patron saint of children, sailors, pawnbrokers and wolves. The English form of the name *Nicol* is the origin of several surnames. In Ireland, Mac Nicholas, *Mac Nicoláis*, is "the name of a gaelicized branch of the Norman de Burgos, sometimes corrupted to Clausson" (*see* CLAYSON). (Withycombe, Reaney, MacLysaght, Turk).

Traced by Guppy in Cornwall and Monmouthshire and by Spiegelhalter in Devon.

In Newfoundland:

Early instances: William, of St. John's, 1705 (CO 194.22); Jean, of Trinity Bay, 1781 (DPHW 64); ——, of Bryant's Cove, 1794 (MUN Hist.); Thomas, planter of Harbour Grace, 1822 (DPHW 43); ——, from Co. Cork, married in Trinity (unspecified), 1829 (Nfld. Archives KCRC); John Nichollas, granted land at Cupids, 1845 (Nfld. Archives, Registry Crown Lands).

Modern status: Scattered.

NICHOL(L)(E)(S), NICOL(L)(E), variants of a surname of England, Ireland, Scotland, France and the Channel Islands, diminutives of Nic(h)olas. *See* NICHOLAS.

Guppy traced Nichol in Cumberland, Westmorland and Northumberland, and found Nichol(l)s widespread, Nicols and Nickels in Devon, Nickolls in Worcestershire and elsewhere, and Nicol(l) over a

large part of Scotland. In Ireland Nicholls and Nicholson are occasional synonyms of Mac Nicholl, *Mac
Niocaill*, a Co. Tyrone name.

In Newfoundland:

Family traditions: —— Nicholle, from Jersey
(Channel Islands), settled at Grand Bank in the early
1800s (MUN Hist.). George Nichols (1840–1901),
born at Goldmills, Cape Breton Island, settled at
what is now known as Nicholsville, Deer Lake,
about 1870 (MUN Hist.). —— Nichols (1875–),
from England, came as an Anglican missionary to
Newfoundland in 1907 (MUN Folklore).

Early instances: William Nichols, of Quidi Vidi,
1708–9 (CO 194.4); Mary, of St. John's, 1722
(Exeter Public Library Archives per Kirwin); John
Nicholls, of Harbour Grace, 1770 (CO 199.18); Jane,
of Trinity (Trinity B.), 1780 (DPHW 64); Clem.
Nicolle Jr., of Placentia, 1794 (D'Alberti 5); John
Nicholl, of Carbonear, 1799 (CO 199.18); Winter,
Nicholl and Co., operated salmon fishery at Harbour
Breton, 1808 (CO 194.48); Edward Nichel, planter of
Blackhead (Bay de Verde district), 1816 (DPHW
52A); Philip Nicole, fisherman of Grand Bank, 1818
(DPHW 109); Edward Nichol(l) or Nichole, planter of
Crocker's Cove (Carbonear), 1823 (DPHW 48); Mary
Niccole, of Harbour Grace Parish, 1827 (Nfld. Ar-
chives HGRC); Jonathon Nicholls, from Coleraine
(Co. Derry), Ireland, of Carbonear, deceased 1832
(*Royal Gazette* 10 Jun 1832); Philip Nicolle, granted
land at Jerseyman's [sic] Harbour (Fortune B.), 1833
(Nfld. Archives, Registry Crown Lands); Joseph
Nicolle, J.P. for Southern District of the Colony,
1834, of La Poile, 1843 (*Newfoundlander* 10 Jul
1834, 31 Aug 1843); Joshua M., granted land at La
Poile Bay, 1851, at Petites, 1860 (Nfld. Archives,
Registry Crown Lands); Richard Nichol, of Fresh-
water (Carbonear), 1858 (DPHW 49); Philip W.
Nicolle, granted land at Channel Harbour, 1860
(Nfld. Archives, Registry Crown Lands).

Modern status: Nichol, at Seldom, Stag Harbour,
Lewisporte and Carbonear; Nicholl, at Bell Island,
Carbonear, Harbour Grace and St. John's; Nicholle,
at Grand Bank and St. John's; Nicholls, rare, at St.
John's; Nichols, scattered, especially at Nicholsville
(Deer Lake); Nicol, at St. John's; Nicolle, unique, at
St. John's; Nicolle, in the St. Barbe district, espe-
cially at Rocky Harbour.

Place names: Nichols Brook 49-11 53-23;
Nicholsville 49-11 57-28.

NICHOLSON, a surname of England, Scotland and
Ireland – son of Nichol(as). *See* NICHOLAS.

Traced by Guppy in the northern counties of

England and in Essex, Lincolnshire and Norfolk,
and in the Scots Border counties, especially Dumfriesshire, and by MacLysaght in Co. Tyrone.

In Newfoundland:

Early instance: James, of St. John's, 1791 (DPHW
26C).

Modern status: Rare, at St. John's and Gander.

NICK(ER)SON, variants of NICHOLSON. *See*
NICHOLAS.

In Newfoundland:

Early instances: Charles and Thomas Nickson,
carpenters of St. John's, 1871 (Lovell).

Modern status: Rare, at St. John's.

NICOL(L)(E). *See* NICHOL(L)(E)(S)

NIGHTINGALE, a surname of England and the
Channel Islands, from Old English *nihtegale* –
night-singer, nightingale, "a common nickname for a
sweet singer." (Reaney, Turk).

Traced by Guppy in Lancashire, Surrey and
Sussex and by Spiegelhalter in Devon.

In Newfoundland:

Early instances: Peter, of St. John's, 1753 (DPHW
26C); Rev. Adam, Methodist missionary of Old
Perlican, 1832, of Port de Grave, 1841 (DPHW 58,
(*Newfoundlander* 3 Jun 1841).

Modern status: Rare, at St. John's.

Place name: Nightingale Rock (Labrador) 55-26
60-12.

NIPPARD, a variant of a surname of England,
Neppard, Nipprod, Neppred, ? from Old English
næp and *weard* – turnip-guard, or dialect neep-head
– turnip head, a nickname for a stupid person.
(Brocklebank, *EDD*).

Traced by Brocklebank as Nipprod and Neppred
in Dorset in 1718. She comments: "The name
Neppred or Nipprod (and various other spellings) is
not uncommon locally. Another form is Neppard,
occurring frequently in Newfoundland among families of Dorset and West Country origin." (Brocklebank, Joan, *Affpuddle in the County of Dorset*,
Bournemouth, 1968, p. 70).

In Newfoundland:

Early instances: Thomas Neppard, of Fogo,
1842 (DPHW 83); James Nipper or Nippard, of
Hare (now Deep) Bay (Fogo district), 1857, 1871
(DPHW 83, Lovell) Martin and Thomas Nippard,
fishermen of Little Seldom-Come-By, 1871
(Lovell).

Modern status: In the Fogo and Gander districts,

especially at Deep Bay (Fogo district) and Salt Pond (Gander district).

Place names: Nipper Cove (Labrador) 55-09 59-01; —— Head 47-21 54-55; —— Shoal 47-39 58-07; —— Cove Point (Labrador) 55-09 59-02; Nippers Harbour 49-48 55-52, 49-32 55-51; —— Islands 49-47 55-50.

NIXON, a surname of England, Ireland and Scotland – son of Nick. *See* NICHOLAS.

Traced by Guppy in Cheshire, Cumberland, Westmorland, Durham, Lincolnshire, Northumberland, Staffordshire, by Black on both sides of the Scottish border, and by MacLysaght as "numerous in Ulster" and also in Co. Wicklow.

In Newfoundland:

Early instances: Charles, carpenter of St. John's, 1836 (DPHW 26B); Susanna S., from Edinburgh, married at St. John's, 1842 (*Star and Nfld. Advocate* 3 Nov 1842).

Modern status: At St. John's and Topsail.

Place name: Nixon Hill (Labrador) 56-39 61-32.

NOAH, a baptismal name of England and a surname of Lebanon-Syria, from a Hebrew and Arabic personal name – long(lived), "a shortened representation of the name of the Sumerian Noah, *Zi-ud-sudda* – life of days long." (Withycombe).

In Newfoundland:

Early instances: Kalleem Bacile, born 1868, at Hadeth, North Lebanon, son of Bacele Noah, emigrated to New York, U.S.A. in 1887; in 1891 moved to Yarmouth, Nova Scotia, conducted a business on the southwest coast of Newfoundland and settled at St. John's in 1896 (*Nfld. Who's Who* 1937).

Modern status: Rare, at St. John's and Corner Brook.

NOBLE, a surname of England, Scotland and Ireland, French *noble* – noble, well-known. (Reaney).

Traced by Guppy in Yorkshire WR, by Spiegelhalter in Devon, and by MacLysaght continuously in Ireland since the thirteenth century and especially in Ulster.

In Newfoundland:

Family tradition: John, from England, came to Newfoundland at an early age and settled at Nipper's Harbour (Green B.) (MUN Folklore).

Early instances: John, from Bristol, purchaser of Eales plantation, St. John's, 1780 (D'Alberti 6); John, merchant of St. John's, 1794-5, operated salmon fishery at Nippers Harbour, 1804 (Census 1794–5, CO 194.45); Richard, of Brigus, 1815 (DPHW 26D); Richard, of Harbour Grace Parish, 1816 (Nfld. Archives HGRC); Sarah, baptized at Greenspond, 1830, aged 63 (DPHW 76); John, of Vere (now Fair) Island, 1830 (DPHW 76); Edward, of King's Cove, 1842 (DPHW 73); Edward, of Amherst Cove (Bonavista B.), 1846 (DPHW 70); John, of Rogue's Harbour, 1851 (DPHW 86); Thomas, of Stocking Harbour (Twillingate district), 1853, of Kiry's Island (Twillingate district), 1854 (DPHW 86); Ann, of Herring Neck, 1860 (DPHW 85); William, clerk of Harbour Grace, 1871 (Lovell).

Modern status: Scattered, especially at Nipper's Harbour.

Place names: Noble Cove, —— Head 49-47 55-52; —— Cove, —— Point 51-35 55-26; —— Pond 49-49 55-56; Nobles Brook 49-44 56-53.

NOEL, a baptismal name and surname of England and the Channel Islands, Noël of France, from Old French *noël* – Christmas, a name given to one born at that festival (*see* CHRISTMAS). In France, also, according to Dauzat, from the name of a saint "too little known," *Saint-Nadeau*. (Withycombe, Reaney, Dauzat, Turk). *See also* NEWELL.

Traced by Spiegelhalter in Devon and by Matthews in Jersey (Channel Islands).

In Newfoundland:

Family tradition: Clemence or John, from Jersey (Channel Islands), settled in Harbour Grace (MUN Folklore).

Early instances: John, of Freshwater (Carbonear), 1777 (CO 199.18); John, of Brigus, 1786 (CO 199.18); Philip, of Port de Grave, 1786 (CO 199.18); John, of Carbonear, 1790 (CO 199.18); John, of Southside, Harbour Grace, 1816 (DPHW 48); Richard Nouell, planter of Western Bay, 1826 (DPHW 52A); Peter Nowell, fisherman of Grates Cove, 1850 (DPHW 58); Jonathan, from North Sydney (Nova Scotia), of Woody Point (Bonne B.), 1870 (MUN Hist.); Rev. John Noell, of Upper Island Cove, 1871 (Lovell).

Modern status: Widespread, especially at Freshwater (Carbonear), Harbour Grace and St. John's.

Place names: Noels Pond 48-33 58-32; Nowell Lake (Labrador) 52-40 66-00.

NOFTALL, NOFTLE, variants of the surname of Guernsey (Channel Islands) Naftel, of unknown origin. (Turk).

In Newfoundland:

Family tradition: Of Channel Islands origin.

Early instances: Peter Nofty, of Broad Cove (Bay de Verde district), 1783 (CO 199.18); Peter Noftle, planter of Broad Cove (Bay de Verde district), 1816 (DPHW 52A); William Noftle or Noftel, of Mulley's Cove (Bay de Verde district), 1820 (DPHW 52A); Thomas Noftle, fisherman of Blackhead (Bay de Verde district), 1826 (DPHW 52A); Jacob Noffter, of Harbour Grace Parish, 1828 (Nfld. Archives HGRC); William Noftal, of St. John's, 1855 (DPHW 26D); Hugh and Joseph Nofty, of Pouch Cove, 1871 (Lovell).

Modern status: Noftall, scattered, especially at St. John's and Fleur de Lys; Noftle, in the Carbonear-Bay de Verde district, at Buchans and St. John's.

NOLAN. *See* KNOWLAND
In Newfoundland:
Early instances: Thomas Noland, of Petty Harbour, 1681 (CO 1); William Nowlan, fisherman of St. John's, 1794–5, "17 years in Newfoundland," that is, 1777–8 (Census 1794–5); Patrick, shoreman of Quidi Vidi, 1794–5, "16 years in Newfoundland," that is, 1778–9 (Census 1794–5); John, of Harbour Main, 1799 (CO 199.18); Ellice [sic] Nowlen, of Harbour Grace Parish, 1807 (Nfld. Archives HGRC); Patrick Nowlan, from Old Ross (Co. Wexford), married at St. John's, 1811 (Nfld. Archives BRC); James ? Nowlan, one of 72 impressed men who sailed from Ireland to Newfoundland ? 1811 (CO 194.51); Simon Nowland, occupier of fishing room, Momables Bay (now Mobile), 1812 (D'Alberti 22); Michael Nowlan, from Co. Carlow, deserted from service at Bay Bulls, 1818 (*Nfld. Mercantile Journal* 19 Jun 1818); Michael, of Bonavista, 1825 (Nfld. Archives KCRC); James, of King's Cove, 1829 (Nfld. Archives KCRC); Martin, of Ragged Harbour (now Melrose), 1830 (Nfld. Archives KCRC); John, of St. Mary's, 1837 (Nfld. Archives BRC); Thomas, of Carbonear, 1839 (*Newfoundlander* 31 Oct 1839); Jeremiah, from Fethard (Co. Wexford), of Brigus, 1844 (*Indicator* 24 Aug 1844); John, of Black Island (? Bonavista B.), 1845 (Nfld. Archives KCRC); Johannah, of Broad Cove (now Duntara), 1855 (Nfld. Archives KCRC); Michael No(w)lan, of Catalina, 1857 (Nfld. Archives KCRC); Margaret Nowlan, of Tickle Cove (Bonavista B.), 1857 (Nfld. Archives KCRC); John, granted land at Salmon Cove (unspecified), 1857 (Nfld. Archives, Registry Crown Lands); Henry, fisherman of Trouty, 1859 (DPHW 64B); scattered in Lovell 1871.

Modern status: Widespread, especially at Mount Carmel and St. John's.

Place names: Nolan Pond 48-32 53-04, Nolans Point 48-27 53-39; Nowlan Harbour (Labrador) 52-46 55-49.

NOLANDER, a surname of Norway of unknown origin.
In Newfoundland:
Family tradition: ——, from Norway, settled at Fermeuse (Family).
Modern status: Rare, at Admirals (Fermeuse) (*Electors* 1955), and St. John's.

NOONAN, a surname of Ireland, (O)Noonan, Nunan, *Ó Nuanáin*, formerly *Ó hIonmhaineáin*, Ir. *ionmhain* – beloved. (MacLysaght).
Traced by MacLysaght mainly in Co. Cork.
In Newfoundland:
Early instances: James, shoreman of Quidi Vidi, 1794–5, "15 years in Newfoundland," that is, 1779–80 (Census 1794–5); Edward, of Bay Bulls, 1780 (D'Alberti 6); John, ? of St. John's, ? died 1795 (CO 194.40); Dennis, proprietor and occupier of fishing room, Old Perlican, Winter 1800–01 (Census Trinity B.); Thomas, of Harbour Grace Parish, 1806 (Nfld. Archives HGRC); Hanna, from Co. Wexford, of St. John's, 1811 (Nfld. Archives BRC); Joanna, of Catalina, 1826 (Nfld. Archives KCRC); John Nonnon, planter of Cupids, 1835 (DPHW 34); John Noonan, from Waterford, of Harbour Grace, 1844 (*Indicator* 27 Jul 1844); Michael, ? of Northern Bay, 1849 (DPHW 54); Philip, son of the late Denis Morris Noonan, of Freemont (Co. Cork), of St. John's, deceased 1853 (*Newfoundlander* 14 Mar 1853); James Lyons, of Greenspond, 1859 (DPHW 75); Denis (and others), of Bay de Verde, 1871 (Lovell).

Modern status: Scattered, especially at Bay de Verde.

NORBERG, ? a variant of the surname of Sweden Nordberg – (dweller on or by the) north mountain. (E.C. Smith).
In Newfoundland:
Family tradition: ——, from Sweden, settled at St. John's in the late 1800s (MUN Folklore).
Modern status: At St. John's.

NORMAN, a surname of England, Ireland and the Channel Islands, Old English *Northmann* – dweller in the north, a Scandinavian especially a Norwegian, "recorded as a personal name from the second half of the 10th century and fairly common in 1066," or from Old French *Normund, Normant* – a Norman. (Reaney, MacLysaght 73, Turk). *See also* NORMORE.
Traced by Guppy in twelve counties including Devon, Dorset and Somerset, and by MacLysaght now mainly in Dublin, previously especially in Co. Derry.

In Newfoundland:

Family tradition: ——, from Jersey (Channel Islands), settled at the Battery, Brigus, in the early 18th century (MUN Hist.).

Early instances: James and William, of Brigus, 1774, property "in possession of the Family for upwards of 60 years," that is, before 1714 (CO 199.18); Henry, merchant of St. John's, ? 1765 (CO 194.16); Thomas and Sons, of Port de Grave, 1783 (CO 199.18); Daniel, of Bay Roberts, 1802 (CO 199.18); Gregory, of Bell Isle (now Bell Island), 1813 (DPHW 26B); William, of Salmon Cove (Brigus district), 1815 (DPHW 34); James Narmin, of Harbour Grace Parish, 1819 (Nfld. Archives HGRC); William Norman, planter of Bareneed, 1826 (DPHW 34); Ann Norms or Normo, of Grates Cove, 1828 (DPHW 58, Nfld. Archives BRC); William Norman, planter of Catalina, 1829 (DPHW 64B); John, married at St. John's, 1832 (Nfld. Archives BRC); William, planter of Cupids, 1837 (DPHW 34); Joseph, of Greenspond, 1838 (DPHW 76); Georgiana, daughter of John Norman, St. Thomas', Exeter (Devon), married at St. John's, 1852 (Newfoundlander 21 Jun 1852); Nathan, J.P., Labrador, 1857 (Nfld. Almanac); Garret and John, of Long Harbour (Placentia B.), 1871 (Lovell); Thomas, of Red Island (Placentia B.), 1871 (Lovell); Richard, of Flower's Cove, 1873 (MUN Hist.); Richard, fisherman of French Island Harbour (St. Barbe district), 1871 (Lovell).

Modern status: Widespread, especially at St. John's, Long Harbour, and Red Island (Placentia B.) (Electors 1955), Bay Roberts, Pacquet and Port Union.

Place names: Cape Norman 51-38 55-54; —— Head 47-38 57-42; —— Island (Labrador) 53-52 57-06; —— Lake (Labrador) 52-00 63-43; —— Reef (Labrador) 54-15 57-13; —— Rock 47-41 58-11, (Labrador) 51-38 55-49; —— Bay Pond (Labrador) 52-52 55-56; Norman's Cove 47-33 53-40, 51-37 55-53; —— Pond 47-35 53-22, 48-53 57-55.

NORMORE, a surname of England, ? a variant of Narramore, Narrowmore or Northmore, from the English place names Narramore (Devon), Northmore (Lancashire, Oxfordshire, Somerset), or (dweller) north of the moor or (dweller on the) northern moor; but probably confused with NORMAN in some early instances in Newfoundland.

Spiegelhalter traced Narramore and Northmore, Guppy Northmore in Devon.

In Newfoundland:

Family tradition: Gregory, from Jersey (Channel Islands), settled at Bell Island about 1740, died about 1785 (MUN Hist.).

Early instances: Charles, of Lower Island Cove, 1754 (CO 199.18); Thomas Narrowmore, of Bay Bulls, 1793 (USPG); Catherine Normore, in possession of property, Bell Island, 1794-5, "born in Newfoundland" (Census 1794-5); Peregrine, of St. John's, 1800 (DPHW 26B); Henry, proprietor and occupier of fishing room, Grates Cove, Winter 1800-01 (Census Trinity B.); Giles Narmore, of Cutwell Arm (Twillingate district), 1851 (DPHW 86); —— Normore, of Cann Islands (near Seldom, Fogo district), 1859 (DPHW 84); John, fisherman of Sunday Cove Island, 1866 (DPHW 91).

Modern status: Scattered, especially at Bell Island (Electors 1955).

NORRIS, a surname of England, Scotland and Ireland, from Anglo-French nor(r)eis – northerner – "A very common name, particularly in the midlands and the south" – also a personal name, or from Old French norrice – nurse, or (dweller at the) north house. (Reaney, MacLysaght). See also NURSE.

Traced by Guppy in Berkshire, Dorset, Lancashire and Somerset, as Norrish in Devon, and by MacLysaght as of Elizabethan origin in Co. Cork and now fairly numerous in all provinces except Connacht.

In Newfoundland:

Family tradition: Neddie, first settler of Bonne Bay before 1800, after whom Norris Point and Neddie's Harbour are named (MUN Hist.).

Early instances: Richard, fisherman of St. John's, 1794-5, "28 years in Newfound land," that is, 1766-7 (Census 1794-5); Thomas, of Ferryland, 1789 (DPHW 26C); John, proprietor and occupier of fishing room, Old Perlican, Winter 1800-01 (Census Trinity B.); John, of Pinchard's Island, 1802 (Bonavista Register 1806); Susana [sic], of Bonavista, 1803 (Nfld. Archives BRC); Philip, of Witless Bay, 1807 (Nfld. Archives BRC); David, from Carrick-on-Suir (Co. Tipperary), married at St. John's, 1810 (Nfld. Archives BRC); John, of Bay Bulls, 1812 (Nfld. Archives BRC); John, of Harbour Grace Parish, 1814 (Nfld. Archives HGRC); Thomas, planter of Ferryland ? 1815 (CO 194.56); Patrick, of King's Cove, 1815 (Nfld. Archives KCRC); James, of Keels, 1824 (Nfld. Archives KCRC); Mary, of Petty Harbour, 1828 (Nfld. Archives BRC); Anne, baptized at Swain's Island (now Wesleyville), 1830, aged 12 (DPHW 76); J., of Witless Bay, 1830 (Newfoundlander 22 Apr 1830); James Norriss, from Glasgow, Scotland, married at St. John's, 1835 (DPHW 26D); Levi Norris, of Inner Islands (now Newtown), 1850 (DPHW 76); William, of Bay de Verde, 1855 (DPHW

59); Francis and John, of Grates Cove, 1871 (Lovell); William Norriss, of Random Sound, 1871 (Lovell); John Norris, planter of Salmonier (St. Mary's), 1871 (Lovell); James, trader of Three Arms (Twillingate district), 1871 (Lovell).

Modern status: Scattered, especially at Bay de Verde, Witless Bay, Newtown and St. John's.

Place names: Norris Arm 49-06 55-15; —— Cove 49-30 57-50, 49-31 57-53; —— Point 49-31 57-53; —— Rock 49-15 53-24.

NORTH, a surname of England and Ireland – the man from the north or the dweller in the north. In Ireland, North is a synonym in Co. Westmeath of Ultagh, *Ultach* – Ulsterman. (Reaney, MacLysaght).

Traced by Guppy in Hampshire, Leicestershire, Rutlandshire, Lincolnshire and Oxfordshire, by Spiegelhalter in Devon, and by MacLysaght in Co. Westmeath.

In Newfoundland:

Early instances: Thomas, of Harbour Grace Parish, 1810 (Nfld. Archives HGRC); Thomas, of Ireland's Eye, 1810 (DPHW 64); Mary, from Old Ross (Co. Wexford), married at St. John's, 1812 (Nfld. Archives BRC); Bridget, of Bay de Verde, 1830 (Nfld. Archives BRC); John, fisherman of Bay Roberts, 1837 (DPHW 39); William, ? of Northern Bay, 1840 (DPHW 54); Thomas, planter of New (now Parsons) Harbour, 1871 (Lovell); Patrick, cooper of St. John's, 1871 (Lovell).

Modern status: At Bay de Verde, Bay Roberts, Corner Brook and St. John's.

Place names: Many place names contain North as specific but few, if any, are likely to be from the surname.

NORTHCOTT, a surname of England from the English place names Northcott or Northcote (Devon) or Norcott (Hertfordshire), or (dweller in the) cottage to the north. (Reaney).

Traced by Guppy in Cornwall and Devon.

In Newfoundland:

Early instances: John Norcott, fisherman of St. John's or Petty Harbour, about 1739–43, of St. John's, 1750 (CO 194.11, 12, 24); John Northcott, petitioner re improvements at White's Arm (? Hare B.), ? 1761 (CO 194.15); Mary Narrowcot, of Colliers, 1781 (CO 199.18); Abram Norcott, of Harbour Grace Parish, 1807 (Nfld. Archives HGRC); Thomas Northcot, of Carbonear, 1816 (DPHW 48); William Norcott, of Harbour Grace, 1831 (Nfld. Archives HGRC); John Norkett or Northcutt, fisherman of Lower Burgeo, 1845 (DPHW 101); Henry Northcote,

fisherman of Furby's Cove, 1841 (DPHW 102); Anthony Norcotte, fisherman of Barrasway Cove (Fortune B.), 1854 (DPHW 102); Michael and Patrick Norcott, fishermen of Bryant's Cove, 1871 (Lovell); Anthony, of Gaultois, 1871 (Lovell).

Modern status: Scattered.

NORTHOVER, a surname of England, from the English place name Northover (Somerset) or (dweller on the) north river bank or north shore. (Cottle, Spiegelhalter).

Traced by Spiegelhalter in Devon.

In Newfoundland:

Early instances: Martha, of Lamaline, 1838 (DPHW 106); Thomas, granted land at Robin Hood (now part of Port Rexton), 1855 (Nfld. Archives, Registry Crown Lands); James and Matthew, fishermen of New Perlican, 1871 (Lovell); Samuel, of Red Island (Placentia B.), 1871 (Lovell); Thomas, of Ship Cove (now part of Port Rexton), 1871 (Lovell).

Modern status: At Red Island (Placentia B.) (*Electors* 1955), Long Harbour (Placentia B.), New Perlican and St. John's.

NOSEWORTHY, a surname of England from the English place name Norsworthy (Devon) – North's homestead. (Spiegelhalter, Gover).

Guppy traced Nosworthy, Spiegelhalter also Norsworthy in Devon.

In Newfoundland:

Family traditions: ——, from Dorset, was one of the early settlers at Pouch Cove in the early 1900s (MUN Hist.). ——, from Devon, settled at Bryant's Cove, about the early 19th century (MUN Hist.).

Early instances: William, of Bread and Cheese (now Bishop's) Cove, 1765 (CO 199.18); John, fisherman of St. John's, 1794–5, "28 years in Newfoundland," that is, 1766–7 (Census 1794–5); Jacob, of Cupids, 1782 (CO 199.18); Thomas, of Green Head (Spaniards B.), 1796, of Bryant's Cove, 1797 (CO 199.18); Charity, of Port de Grave, 1798 (CO 199.18); John, of Kelligrews, 1799 (CO 199.18); William, ? of Pouch Cove, 1805 (DPHW 23); John, of Brigus, 1809 (DPHW 34); James Nosworthy, of Northern Cove (Harbour Grace district), 1820 (DPHW 43); Elizabeth, of Harbour Grace Parish, 1826 (Nfld. Archives HGRC); Jacob Noseworthy, of Long Pond (? Manuels), 1832 (DPHW 30); Elizabeth, of Kelligrews, 1836 (DPHW 26D); Sarah, of Biscayan Cove (unspecified), 1839 (DPHW 26D); James, of Leading Tickles, 1844 (DPHW 86); Alfred, of Cat Harbour (now Lumsden), 1855 (DPHW 76); Simon, Fortune, married Fanny Higgins, 1869 (Grand Bank

Methodist marriages, P.E.L. Smith); Isaac Nose-warthy, of Bay Roberts, 1871 (Lovell).

Modern status: Widespread, especially at Bell Island, St. John's, Pouch Cove, Spaniards Bay, Long Pond and Harbour Grace,

Place name: Nosworthy Point 49-31 55-24.

NOTT, a surname of England from Old English *hnott* – bald-headed, close-cropped, or ? a short form of such an Old English personal name as *Wulfnoth*. (Reaney, Spiegelhalter). *See also* KNOTT.

Traced by Guppy in Devon, Essex, Herefordshire, Hertfordshire, Worcestershire.

In Newfoundland:

Early instances: James Nott, of Bonne Bay (Fortune B.), 1835 (DPHW 30); Thomas, fisherman of New (now Parsons) Harbour, 1853 (DPHW 102); Benjamin, planter of Brazils (Burgeo-La Poile district), 1871 (Lovell); Thomas, of Lower Burgeo, 1871 (Lovell).

Modern status: Rare, at Belleoram (*Electors* 1955) and St. John's.

NUGENT, a surname of Ireland, *Nuinseann*, from the Norman surname *de Nogent*. (MacLysaght).

Traced by MacLysaght in Cos. Cork and Westmeath.

In Newfoundland:

Family tradition: John (approximately 1835–87), of Kelligrews (MUN Folklore).

Early instances: Patrick, from Omagh (Co. Tyrone), Irish convict landed at Petty Harbour or Bay Bulls, 1789 (CO 194.38); Edmund, of Harbour Grace Parish, 1808 (Nfld. Archives HGRC); Maurice, of St. John's, 1817 (CO 194.59); Margaret, of Kelligrews, 1818 (Nfld. Archives BRC); Mary, of Port de Grave, 1833 (*Newfoundlander* 6 Jun 1833); John Valentine, from Ireland, emigrated to St. John's in 1833 (*Star and Conception B.J.* 9 Jan 1839);

Thomas, granted land at Barren Island (now Bar Haven), 1849 (Nfld. Archives, Registry Crown Lands); John, granted land on Petty Harbour Road, 1848 (Nfld. Archives, Registry Crown Lands); Edward (and others), of Lower Gully (now Riverdale), 1871 (Lovell); Michael, of King's Cove, 1884 (Nfld. Archives KCRC).

Modern status: Scattered, especially at St. John's, Riverdale and Kelligrews.

Place name: Nugent Bank (Labrador) 53-38 56-04.

NURSE, a surname of England and Ireland, from Old French *nurice* – nurse. *See* NORRIS. (Reaney, MacLysaght).

Traced by Guppy in Norfolk and by Spiegelhalter in Devon.

In Newfoundland:

Early instances: Bernard, resident of St. John's for 60 years in 1783, that is, since 1723 (D'Alberti 2); Edward, fisherman of St. John's or Petty Harbour, about 1739–43 (CO 194.11); Richard, planter of Salmon Cove (now Champneys), 1823 (DPHW 64B); Moses, of Pushthrough, 1830 (DPHW 30); Mrs. Elizabeth, from Hampshire, of St. John's since 1785, died 1835, aged 70 (*Times* 4 Mar 1835); Jabez ? Nurse, granted land at Quidi Vidi, 1853 (Nfld. Archives, Registry Crown Lands); Richard, of Brunette (Island), 1871 (Lovell); John, trader of Twillingate, 1871 (Lovell).

Modern status: Scattered.

NUTBEEM, a surname of England, from the English place name Nutbane (Hampshire), or from Old English *hnutbēam* – (dweller near a) nut-tree. (Reaney, Cottle).

In Newfoundland:

Modern status: Rare, at Harbour Grace.

O

OAK(E), OKE, surnames of England from Old English *āc* – (dweller by the) oak tree(s), or from the English place names Oak (Devon), Oake (Somerset). (Reaney, Cottle, Spiegelhalter).

Oke traced at Shapwick (Dorset) in 1350 (Nfld. Archives z42), Oakes traced by Guppy in Cheshire and by Spiegelhalter in Devon.

In Newfoundland:

Family tradition: Robert Oke whose family originated in Dorset, came to Newfoundland from England to work with the Slade firm at Burin about 1820; his family later went into business at Harbour Grace and St. John's (Nfld. Archives z42).

Early instances: Joseph Oak Sr. and Jr., of Fogo, 1803 (D'Alberti 13); John and William Oake, planters of Change Islands, 1821 (USPG); —— Oke, express packet agent of Harbour Grace, 1830 (*Newfoundlander* 11 Feb 1830); James Oake, of Lions Den (Fogo district), 1845 (DPHW 83); Robert Oke, of Portugal Cove, 1853 (*Newfoundlander* 12 Dec 1853); William Robert, of Halls Bay, 1854 (DPHW 86); Charles Oake, of Eastern Tickle (Fogo district), 1854 (DPHW 83); Henry Oke, of Ward's Harbour (now Beaumont North), 1855 (DPHW 86); Robert, of Round Harbour (Twillingate district), 1856 (DPHW 86); R., of St. John's, 1856 (*Newfoundlander* 1 May 1856); Robert Oak, miner of Tilt Cove, 1871 (Lovell).

Modern status: Oak, unique, at Salt Pond (Gander district) (*Electors* 1955); Oake, scattered, especially at Fogo, Corner Brook and in the Green Bay district; Oke, scattered.

Place name: Oke Ground 49-38 55-39.

OAKLEY, a surname of England, from the English place names Oakley, Oakleigh, traced by Cottle in twelve Midland and southern counties, or from Old English *āc* – oak and *lēah* – wood, clearing. (Cottle, A. H. Smith, Spiegelhalter).

Traced by Guppy in Staffordshire and Warwickshire, and by Spiegelhalter in Devon.

In Newfoundland:

Family tradition: Walter, from England, settled at Greenspond in the early 19th century (MUN Folklore).

Early instances: James, surgeon, appointed J.P., of Placentia district, 1792, of Trinity district, 1800 (D'Alberti 4, 11); R.G., proprietor and co-occupier

of fishing room, Shole [sic] Harbour (Trinity B.), Winter 1800–01 (Census Trinity B.); James, of Bonavista, 1813 (DPHW 70); Robert, shipowner of Scilly Cove (now Winterton), 1823 (DPHW 64B); John, of Greenspond, 1826 (DPHW 76); John Oakly, J.P. in the Northern District of the Colony, 1834 (*Newfoundlander* 10 Jul 1834); George Oakley, servant of Trinity (Trinity B.), 1844 (DPHW 64B); Samuel, fisherman of Old Bonaventure, 1847 (DPHW 64B); Charles, of Fair Island (Bonavista B.), 1871 (Lovell); Jacob and Robert, of Freshwater Bay (Bonavista B.), 1871 (Lovell); A. T., Jr., of Ship Island (Bonavista B.), 1871 (Lovell); Rev. Alfred M., of Fogo, 1871 (Lovell); Mrs. Sarah, of St. John's, 1871 (Lovell).

Modern status: Scattered, especially at St. John's.

OATES, a surname of England and Ireland, from an Old German personal name *Odo*, *Otto*, Old French *Odes*, *Otes* – riches; in Ireland "a synonym by pseudo-translation of Quirke" (*see* QUIRK), Ir. *coirce* – oats. (Reaney *Origin*, MacLysaght).

Guppy traced Oat(e)s in Cornwall; Spiegelhalter traced Oates in Devon.

In Newfoundland:

Early instances: George Oats, of Carbonear, 1780 (CO 199.18); Patrick, of St. John's, 1804 (Nfld. Archives BRC); Ann Oates, of Harbour Grace Parish, 1812 (Nfld. Archives HGRC); Annie Oats, of Bell Isle (now Bell Island), 1817 (Nfld. Archives BRC); Thomas Oat(e)s, planter of English Harbour (Trinity B.), 1839 (DPHW 64B); Thomas Oates, ? of St. John's, deceased, 1839 (*Newfoundlander* 5 Dec 1839); Andrew and Robert, fishermen of Fermeuse, 1871 (Lovell).

Modern status: Scattered, especially at Carbonear.

O'BRIEN. *See* BRIAN(D)

O'CONNELL, a surname of Ireland, *Ó Conaill.* MacLysaght notes that though "the prefixes Mac and O were very widely dropped during the period of the submergence of Catholic and Gaelic Ireland which began in the early seventeenth century," they were generally resumed in the 1880s with the revival of national consciousness. In particular, he notes that the use of O with Connell rose from 9 per cent in 1866 to 33 per cent in 1890, "due perhaps to the use of O by 'Liberator' Daniel O'Connell." But, he adds, "It is of interest to recall that his father was plain Morgan Connell, at least for legal purposes, though he was doubtless known as O'Connell by his neighbours in Kerry, most of whom, of course, normally spoke the Irish not the English language."

Traced by MacLysaght in Co. Kerry.

In Newfoundland: Connell occurs twice in *Electors* 1955, but had been completely superseded by O'Connell by 1972.

Early instances: N. Connell, of Newfoundland ? 1706 (CO 194.24); Henry, carpenter of St. John's, 1794–5, "31 years in Newfoundland," that is, 1763–4 (Census 1794–5); Michael, of Western Bay, 1786 (CO 199.18); Thomas, of Carbonear, 1789 (CO 199.18); Robert, of Salmon Cove, Northern Arm (Conception B.), 1798 (CO 199.18); Morris or Maurice, of Musketta (now Bristol's Hope), 1799 (CO 199.18); Richard, an agent of Bay de Verde, 1804 (CO 199.18); Robert, of Harbour Grace Parish, 1806 (Nfld. Archives HGRC); Dennis Connel, from Tullon Parish (unidentified) (Co. Kilkenny), married at St. John's, 1808 (Nfld. Archives BRC); Jeremiah, from Co. Cork, married in the Northern district, 1813 (Nfld. Archives BRC); Jeremiah Connell, of Bonavista, 1815 (Nfld. Archives KCRC); James, of Trinity (unspecified), 1817 (Nfld. Archives KCRC); James, of Rider's Harbour (Trinity B.), 1817 (DPHW 64); Dennis, of Greenspond, 1824 (Nfld. Archives KCRC); John, of Harbour Grace, 1829 (Nfld. Archives BRC); Thomas, ? of Labrador, 1829 (*Newfoundlander* 28 Feb 1829); William O'Connel, of Harbour Grace Parish, 1832 (Nfld. Archives HGRC); Margaret Connell, of Riverhead (unspecified), 1835 (Nfld. Archives BRC); David Connel, ? of Northern Bay, 1844 (DPHW 54); Michael Connell, from Co. Kerry, of Harbour Grace, 1844 (*Indicator* 27 Jul 1844); Maurice, of Broad Cove (now Duntara), 1850 (Nfld. Archives KCRC); Daniel O'Connell, granted land at Cats Cove (now Conception Harbour), 1853 (Nfld. Archives, Registry Crown Lands); Julia Connall, of Bay of Islands, 1868 (Nfld. Archives HGRC); John O'Connell and David Connell, of Broad Cove (Bay de Verde district), 1871 (Lovell); Thomas, of Torbay, 1871 (Lovell); Daniel (and others), of Fermeuse, 1871 (Lovell).

Modern status: Connell, rare, at St. John's and Bonavista (*Electors* 1955); O'Connell, scattered.

Place name: Connells Pond 47-24 53-10.

O'CONNOR. *See* CONNORS

O'DEA, a surname of Ireland, *Ó Deághaidh*, modern form *Ó Deá*. MacLysaght comments: "Away from its homeland it is usually mispronounced as O'Dee which, though cognate, is a distinct name viz. *Ó Diaghaidh*. This, no doubt accounts for the use of GODWIN in Mayo as its synonym. The prefix O is now almost always used, but a century ago Dea was quite usual and the English DAY was regarded as synonymous."

Traced by MacLysaght in Co. Clare.

In Newfoundland:

Family tradition: Michael O'Dea (1774–1849) from Templemore, Co. Tipperary, settled at St. John's in 1808; he was a stone mason by trade, but devoted himself to farming in Freshwater Valley (S. O'Dea).

Early instances: Dennis Dea, of Newfoundland, 1783 (D'Alberti 2); William, proprietor and occupier of fishing room, Old Perlican, Winter 1800–01 (Census Trinity B.); Thomas, of Salmon Cove (now Champneys), 1807 (DPHW 64); George, ? of Scilly Cove (now Winterton), 1808 (DPHW 64); William Dea, of Harbour Grace Parish, 1810 (Nfld. Archives HGRC); Patrick, planter of Bay Bulls, 1871 (Lovell).

Modern status: At Bay Bulls, St. John's and Renews.

Place name: Odea's Pond 48-27 54-03.

O'DEADY. *See* DEADY

ODELL, a surname of England and Ireland, from the English place name Odell (Bedfordshire), or from Old English *wād* – woad "used as a dye and apparently cultivated in England in O[ld] English times and later" and *hyll* – hill (dweller by the) hill where woad grows. Of its use in Ireland, MacLysaght comments: "An English name, formerly Odle and quite incorrectly written O'Dell." (A.H. Smith, Cottle, MacLysaght).

Traced by Guppy in Bedfordshire, Buckinghamshire and Hertfordshire, and by MacLysaght in Co. Limerick since the mid-seventeenth century.

In Newfoundland:

Early instances: William Odle, of Carbonear, 1790 (CO 199.18); John Odel, ? of St. John's, 1810 (CO 194.50); Richard Odle, of Harbour Grace Parish, 1811 (Nfld. Archives HGRC); Mary Odell, of Fortune Harbour, 1830 (Nfld. Archives KCRC); Richard, of The Labrador, married at St. John's, 1837 (Nfld. Archives BRC).

Modern status: Unique, at St. John's.

Place name: Odell Lake (Labrador) 59-53 64-14.

O'DONALD, a surname apparently of Ireland but not recorded by MacLysaght, ? for O'DONNELL.

In Newfoundland:

Early instances: Richard, of Bay de Verde, 1802 (CO 199.18); Edward O'Donald or O'Donnell, of Isle Valen, deceased 1828 (*Newfoundlander* 11 Sep 1828, 16 Jul 1829); John Donald, labourer of Harbour Grace, 1871 (Lovell); John and Richard O'Donald, of Bloody Bay (Bonavista B.), 1871 (Lovell); Edward, fisherman of Ragged Harbour (now Melrose), 1871 (Lovell).

Modern status: Rare, at South Brook (Humber East district) (*Electors* 1955).

O'DONNELL, a surname of Ireland, *Ó Domhnaill*. (MacLysaght). *See* O'DONALD.

Traced by MacLysaght in Cos. Clare, Donegal and Galway.

In Newfoundland:

Early instances: James R. O'Donnel, clergyman of St. John's, 1794–5, "12 years in Newfoundland," that is, 1782–3 (Census 1794–5); Thomas O'Donel, from Feathard (Co. Tipperary), married at St. John's, 1793 (Nfld. Archives BRC); William O'Donnal, of Ragged Harbour (now Melrose), 1815, of Riders Harbour, ? 1816 (Nfld. Archives KCRC); Michael O'Donnell alias Michael Clarke, from Modiling (Co. Waterford), of Paradise (unspecified), died 1816 (*Royal Gazette* 16 Jul 1816); Joanna O'Donnal, of Catalina, 1821 (Nfld. Archives KCRC); John O'Donnel, of Greenspond, 1823 (Nfld. Archives KCRC); John O'Donnell, of Harbour Grace Parish, 1824 (Nfld. Archives HGRC); Edward O'Donnell or O'Donald, of Isle Valen, deceased 1828 (*Newfoundlander* 11 Sep 1828, 16 Jul 1829); Catherine O'Donnoll, of Bonavista, 1831 (Nfld. Archives KCRC); John O'Donnell, of Placentia, 1838 (*Newfoundlander* 6 Dec 1838); John F., from Capir (Co. Tipperary), of St. John's, deceased, 1855 (*Newfoundlander* 16 Aug 1855); Catherine, of Harbour Grace, 1866 (Nfld. Archives HGRC); Rev. R., of Burin, 1871 (Lovell).

Modern status: Scattered, especially at St. John's.

Place name: O'Donnells 47-04 53-34.

O'DRISCOLL. *See* DRISCOLL

O'DWYER. *See* DWYER

OFFREY, a ? Newfoundland variant of the surnames of France Offray, Auffray, etc., old baptismal names from a German personal name *Adalfrid*, containing the elements *noble* and *peace*. (Dauzat).

In Newfoundland:

Modern status: At Eddies Cove West (Electors 1955), Port aux Choix and Hawkes Bay.

O'FLAHERTY. *See* FLAHERTY

O'FLYNN. *See* FLYNN

OGDEN, a surname of England from the English place name Ogden (Lancashire). (Cottle).

In Newfoundland:

Early instances: Jonathan, J.P. for St. John's district, 1789 (D'Alberti 4); Michael Ogsen, fisherman of Bonne Bay, 1871 (Lovell).

Modern status: Rare, at Felix Cove, Piccadilly (*Electors* 1955) and Stephenville.

OGILVIE, a surname of Scotland and Ireland from the Scots place name Ogilvie (Angus). (Black).

Guppy found Ogilvie and Ogilvy "fairly dispersed, but especially characteristic of Forfarshire."

In Newfoundland:

Modern status: Unique, at Gander.

O'GORMAN. *See* GORMAN

O'GRADY, a surname of Ireland (O)Grady, *Ó Grádaigh*, Ir. *gráda* – illustrious, or for a rarer name Gready of Co. Mayo. "An important branch [of the O'Grady family] changed their name to BRADY in the late sixteenth century." The prefix O is retained more in Co. Clare than elsewhere. (MacLysaght).

Traced by MacLysaght in Cos. Clare and Limerick.

In Newfoundland:

Early instances: John ? Grady, one of 72 impressed men who sailed from Ireland to Newfoundland ? 1811 (CO 194.5); James Grady, of Harbour Grace Parish, 1816 (Nfld. Archives HGRC); Thomas, from Kilish Parish (unidentified) (Co. Tipperary), married at St. John's, 1820 (Nfld. Archives BRC); James, of Portugal Cove, 1832 (DPHW 30); J., of St. John's, 1832 (*Newfoundlander* 20 Sep 1832); William, of Outer Cove, 1836 (Nfld. Archives BRC); James, of Ferryland area, 1838 (*Newfoundlander* 25 Oct 1838); John, of Petty Harbour, 1871 (Lovell).

Modern status: At Marquise (*Electors* 1955), Carbonear, Gander and St. John's.

O'HALLIGAN, a surname of Ireland (O)Halligan, *Ó hAileagáin*. (MacLysaght).

Traced by MacLysaght in Cos. Louth and Armagh.

In Newfoundland:

Early instance: J. Halligan, of St. John's, 1832 (*Newfoundlander* 20 Sep 1832).

Modern status: Rare, at Long Pond (Harbour Main district), Windsor (*Electors* 1955) and St. John's.

O'HANLEY. *See* HANLEY

O'HANLON. *See* HANLON

OKE. *See* OAK(E)

O'KEEFE. *See* KEEFE

O'KELLY. *See* KELLY

OL(D)FORD, surnames of England from the English place name Yellowford (Devon). (Gover, Spiegelhalter).

Spiegelhalter traced Olford in Devon.

In Newfoundland:

Early instances: George Ol(d)ford, of Bonavista, 1791 (DPHW 70); William Oldford, proprietor of fishing room, Salmon Cove (now Champneys), Winter 1800–01 (Census Trinity B.); Andrew, of Greenspond, 1815 (DPHW 77); James, planter of Salvage, 1819 (DPHW 72); George, of Bird Island Cove (now Elliston), 1824 (DPHW 70); Susan Ol(d)ford, of Kings Cove, 1830 (Nfld. Archives KCRC); Sarah Oldford, baptized at Swain's Island, 1830, aged 26 (DPHW 76); Thomas, of Cobbler's Island (Bonavista B.), 1830 (DPHW 76); John, of Eastern Cul de Sac, 1835 (DPHW 30); John, of New (now Parsons) Harbour, 1835 (DPHW 30); Morgan, of Fortune, 1846 (DPHW 106); Benjamin, fisherman of Sailor's Island (Bonavista B.), 1865 (DPHW 81); George (and others), of Musgravetown, 1871 (Lovell).

Modern status: Olford, rare, at St. John's; Oldford, scattered, especially at Elliston, Musgravetown, Bunyans Cove, Burnside and Salvage.

Place name: Olfords Point 48-22 53-53.

OLDRIDGE, a surname of England, a variant of ALDRICH or from the English place name Oldridge (Devon). (Spiegelhalter).

In Newfoundland:

Early instance: Henry, from Dartmouth, married at St. John's, 1854, of St. John's, 1871 (*Newfoundlander* 26 Jan 1854, Lovell).

Modern status: Unique, at Cape Broyle (*Electors* 1955).

O'LEARY, a surname of Ireland (with a ? Newfoundland variant LEARIE not recorded by MacLysaght), (O)Leary, *Ó Laoghaire*. "*Laoghaire* was one of the best known personal names in ancient Ireland," interpreted by Woulfe as calf-keeper. (MacLysaght, Woulfe).

Traced by MacLysaght in Co. Cork.

In Newfoundland:

Family tradition: Patrick, Michael and Matthew O'Leary, from Ireland, settled at Fox Harbour (Placentia B.) between 1836–57 (MUN Hist.).

Early instances: Dennis Leary, of Harbour Main, 1760 (CO 199.18); Thomas, of Cupids, 1790 (CO 199.18); Timothy, of Small Point (North Shore Conception B.), 1794 (CO 199.8); John, from Midleton (Co. Cork), married at St. John's, 1799 (Nfld. Archives BRC); Catherine O'Leary, from the city of Cork, married at St. John's, 1803 (Nfld. Archives BRC); John Leary, of Harbour Grace Parish, 1806 (Nfld. Archives HGRC); S., of Upper Bacon Cove (Conception B.), 1806 (CO 199.18); James and Dennis ? Leary, two of 72 impressed men who sailed from Ireland to Newfoundland ? 1811 (CO 194.51); Bridget Leary, of Renews, 1829 (DPHW 31); John, from Midleton (Co. Cork), of Harbour Grace, 1844 (*Indicator* 27 Jul 1844); ——, from Co. Wexford, of Brigus, 1844 (*Indicator* 24 Aug 1844); Edward, granted land at Upper Long Pond, 1852 (Nfld. Archives, Registry Crown Lands); Maria J. O'Leary, of Harbour Grace, 1870 (Nfld. Archives KCRC); Patrick Leary, planter of Biscay Bay and Portugal Cove, 1871 (Lovell); Daniel, of Carbonear, 1871 (Lovell); John, of Cat Harbour (now Lumsden), 1871 (Lovell); Michael and Nicholas, of Cats Cove (now Conception Harbour), 1871 (Lovell); James, of Channel, 1871 (Lovell); Nicholas and Thomas, farmers of English Cove (Conception B.), 1871 (Lovell); Michael, of Flowers Cove, 1871 (Lovell); Michael, of South Side Turks Gut (now Marysvale), 1871 (Lovell); John, of Upper Small Point (now Kingston), 1871 (Lovell); John Nelson Learie, engineer ? on Newman and Co's steamship *Greyhound*, son of James and Elizabeth of Ayrshire, married at Harbour Breton, 1880 (Harbour Breton Anglican Church Records per D.A. Macdonald).

Modern status: Learie, rare, at St. John's; O'Leary, scattered, especially at St. John's and Portugal Cove South.

Place name: Learys Brook 47-35 52-42.

OLFORD. *See* OLDFORD

OLIVER, a baptismal name and surname of England, Scotland, Ireland and with Olivier, of the Channel Islands, of uncertain origin. Cottle summarizes the difficulties: "Charlemagne's peer, Roland's friend, Oliver, must have borne a Germanic name, but Germanic *Alfihar* 'elf army' ... would need to be much changed, and Old Norse *Olaf* ... is even less likely; anyway, in the popular mind the shaping influence was Old French *Oliv(i)er* – olive branch. Naturally, the F [font, baptismal name] lost face at the Restoration, but it now has some currency again." (Withycombe, Reaney, Cottle, Turk).

Found widespread by Guppy especially in Northumberland and Durham and the Scottish border counties, and by MacLysaght in Cos. Louth and Limerick.

In Newfoundland:

Early instances: William, of Bay of Bulls, 1681 (CO 1); John, boatkeeper of St. John's, 1681 (CO 1); Thomas, fisherman of Devil's (now Job's) Cove (Conception B.), 1796 (Nfld. Archives T51); Thomas, of Gull Island (Conception B.), 1798 (CO 199.18); Joseph, of Harbour Grace Parish, 1812 (Nfld. Archives HGRC); John, from Wales, Methodist missionary, Grand Bank, 1820 (Grand Bank Methodist baptisms, P.E.L. Smith); John, of Western Bay, 1835 (Nfld. Archives BRC); Joseph, ? of Northern Bay, 1839 (DPHW 54); James, shoemaker of Trinity (Trinity B.), 1849 (DPHW 64B); Louis, fisherman of Burnt Point (Conception B.), 1851 (DPHW 55).

Modern status: Scattered, especially at St. John's, Burnt Point and Gull Island (Conception B.).

Place names (not necessarily from the surname): Oliver (or Shark Gut) Island (Labrador) 57-56 62-13; Oliver's Cove 49-42 54-03; —— Pond 47-36 52-50.

OLIVIOUS, a surname of Portugal.

In Newfoundland:

Modern status: Rare, at St. John's, since ? early 1900s.

OLLERHEAD, a surname of England, ? from an unidentified English place name, or from Old English *alor* – alder and *hēafod* – head, (dweller on the) headland with alders or at the head of the alder trees. (Bardsley).

Traced by Bardsley in Cheshire and Lancashire.

In Newfoundland:

Family tradition: —— Ollerhead, a Welsh sailor, settled at Heart's Content in 1866, later moved to St. Anthony; some of the family moved to Corner Brook (MUN Folklore).

Early instance: Robert, merchant of St. John's, 1825, of Heart's Content, 1826 (DPHW 26D, 64B).

Modern status: At St. Anthony, Main Brook (White B.) and Corner Brook.

OLSEN, a surname of Scandinavia – son of Olaf.

In Newfoundland:

Early instances: Henry, seaman of St. John's, 1871 (Lovell); Captain Olaf (1881–), born at Tjotto, Norway, settled at St. John's in 1921 (*Nfld. Who's Who* 1927).

Modern status: Rare, at St. John's.

O'MARA, a surname of Ireland, O'Meara, Mara, *Ó Meadhra*, Ir. *meadhar* – merry. "This is one of the O names from which the prefix was never very widely dropped." (MacLysaght).

Traced by MacLysaght in Co. Tipperary.

In Newfoundland:

Early instances: David Mara, fisherman of St. John's, 1794–5, "30 years in Newfoundland," that is, 1764–5 (Census 1794–5); William, from Kilmaden (unidentified), Ireland, married at St. John's, 1804 (Nfld. Archives BRC); Patrick, from Carrick-on-Suir (Co. Tipperary), house carpenter of St. John's, died 1814 (*Royal Gazette* 2 Jun 1814); Thomas, of Harbour Grace Parish, 1815 (Nfld. Archives HGRC); William, of Greenspond, 1818 (Nfld. Archives KCRC); Michael, from Thurles (Co. Tipperary), dealer and chapman of St. John's, 1828 (*Newfoundlander* 9 Apr 1828); John O'Mara, ? of Ferryland, 1830 (*Newfoundlander* 7 Jan 1830); John, from Waterford, married at St. John's, 1831 (*Newfoundlander* 3 Nov 1831); Michael Mara, from Ireland, employed at Carbonear, deserted 1833 (*Carbonear Star* 30 Oct 1833); John O'Mara, granted land at Duggins Gully (unidentified), 1835 (Nfld. Archives, Registry Crown Lands); John, granted land on Placentia Road, 1846 (Nfld. Archives, Registry Crown Lands); John, granted land at Quidi Vidi Harbour, 1859 (Nfld. Archives, Registry Crown Lands); Catherine Mara, of Cat Harbour (now Lumsden), 1861 (Nfld. Archives KCRC); John, of Bay Bulls, 1871 (Lovell).

Modern status: At Bay Bulls (*Electors* 1955) and St. John's.

O'NEIL(L). *See* NEAL(E)

O'QUINN. *See* QUINN

ORAM, a surname of England, where a variant of Orme is from the Old Norse personal name *Ormr*,

Old Danish, Old Swedish *Orm* – serpent, or from the English place name Oreham (Sussex). Cottle comments: "... but it is a Somerset name, and the Norse did not penetrate Somerset, so it may be a concealed place-name in -ham." (Reaney, Spiegelhalter, Cottle).

Traced by Guppy in Somerset and by Spiegelhalter in Devon.

In Newfoundland:

Family tradition: William and Anne, from ? Devon, settled at Goose Cove (near St. Anthony) in the early 19th century; some of the family later moved to Bragg's Island (Bonavista B.) (MUN Folklore).

Early instances: William Oram or Orme, of Greenspond, 1838 (DPHW 76); William Oram, of Goose Cove (near St. Anthony), 1873 (DPHW 94).

Modern status: At Corner Brook, St. John's and in the Bonavista North district especially Bragg's Island and Saunders Cove (*Electors* 1955).

O'REGAN, a surname of Ireland (O)Regan, *Ó Riagain, Ó Réagain* (Co. Waterford) – little king. (Reaney, Cottle, MacLysaght).

Traced by MacLysaght in Cos. Clare, Cork and Leix.

Tradition: The O'Regans of O'Regans were formerly ORGANs, the change of name being made by James O'Regan (1879–1966), previously of Gaultois.

In Newfoundland:

Early instances: Timothy Regan, shoreman of St. John's, 1794–5, "10 years in Newfoundland," that is, 1784–5 (Census 1794–5); Richard Re(a)gan, of Harbour Grace Parish, 1807 (Nfld. Archives HGRC); Anne, of Perlican (unspecified), 1815 (Nfld. Archives KCRC); William O'Reegan, arrived (? St. John's), from Cork, 1815 (*Royal Gazette* 26 Oct 1815); John Regan, of Labrador, married at St. John's, 1817 (Nfld. Archives BRC); Ellen O'Regan, of St. John's, 1829 (*Newfoundlander* 10 Sep 1829); —— Reagan, of Donovan and Reagan, of Harbour Grace, 1832 (*Newfoundlander* 23 Aug 1832); John Regan, J.P. for the Northern district of the Colony, 1834, granted land at Old Perlican, 1834 (*Newfoundlander* 10 Jul 1834, Nfld. Archives, Registry Crown Lands).

Modern status: At Great Codroy and St. John's.

Place name: O'Regan's 47-52 59-14. The place name, formerly Bucklands (*see* BUCKLAND), was changed to O'Regan [sic] by Proclamation 8 Aug 1911 after the Rev. Dr. O'Regan.

O'REILLY, O'RIELLY, surnames of Ireland, *Ó Raghailligh* – valiant. (Cottle, MacLysaght).

Found widespread by MacLysaght, especially in Co. Cavan. *See also* RILEY with which confusion has occurred in Newfoundland.

In Newfoundland:

Family traditions: Thomas O'Riely, from Ireland, settled at St. Brendan's in the 1800s (MUN Folklore).

—— O'Reilley, from Boston (Mass.), settled at Corbin (MUN Folklore).

Early instances: John Reiley, from Cavan (Co. Cavan) and James Rieley, from Coat Hill (Co. Cavan), Irish convicts landed at Petty Harbour or Bay Bulls, 1789 (CO 194.38); James Reily, from Coole Hill (Co. Cavan), linen bleacher ? of St. John's, 1789 (CO 194.38); Pat, of Harbour Grace Parish, 1813 (Nfld. Archives HGRC); Patrick Riley or Reily, of Ragged Harbour (now Melrose), 1818 (Nfld. Archives KCRC); Margaret O'Reily, from Gorey (Co. Wexford), married at St. John's, 1820 (Nfld. Archives BRC); Rosalie Rielley, of Placentia, 1830 (*Newfoundlander* 23 Dec 1830); John Riley or Reilly, fisherman of Biscayan Cove, 1833, of Pouch Cove, 1843 (DPHW 30, 32); John Rielley, of Herring Bay (Placentia B.), 1847 (*Nfld. Almanac*); Andrew Riely, planter of Catalina, 1851 (DPHW 72); John Rielley, from Waterford, of Little Placentia (now Argentia), 1854 (*Newfoundlander* 2 Feb 1854); Thomas Ryly or Riel(l)y, of Gooseberry Island (Bonavista B.), 1856, of Cottells Island, 1870 (Nfld. Archives KCRC); John Reilly, planter of Musgravetown, 1871 (Lovell); Patrick, of Shoal Bay (Ferryland district), 1871 (Lovell); John Rielley, farmer of Cape St. Mary's, 1871 (Lovell); Edward and John, of Gaskin (Point La Hays), 1871 (Lovell); Nathaniel Rielly, of Port de Grave, 1871 (Lovell); Phillip, of Ship Harbour (Placentia B.), 1871 (Lovell).

Modern status: O'Reilly, scattered, especially at St. John's and Freshwater (Placentia B.); O'Rielly, at Gander and St. John's.

ORGAN, a surname of England and Ireland, in England from Middle English *organ* – (player or maker of the) organ which, however, in early times denoted a variety of musical instruments, especially wind instruments, or ? from a personal name, probably from Latin *origanum* – marjoram; in Ireland, a south Tipperary variant of (O)Horgan, *Ó hArgáin*. (Reaney, Spiegelhalter, MacLysaght).

Traced by Guppy in Gloucestershire and by MacLysaght in Co. Tipperary.

In Newfoundland:

Early instances: Michael, of Isle aux Morts, 1835 (DPHW 30); ——, of St. John's, 1839 (*Newfoundlander* 17 Jan 1839); Michael, fisherman of B(r)azils (Burgeo-La Poile district), 1840 (DPHW 101); David, of Brunette (Island), 1840 (DPHW 109); George, fisherman of Red Island (Burgeo-La Poile district), 1845 (DPHW 101); George, fisherman of Little Bay (Burgeo-La Poile district), 1860 (DPHW 99); Mel, of St. John's Island (Northwest coast), 1862 (MUN Hist.); James, of Bonne Bay, 1866 (DPHW 93); James, of Gaultois, 1871 (Lovell); David and John, of Harbour Gulley (Fortune B.), 1871 (Lovell).

Modern status: Scattered, especially at St. Veronica (Fortune B.) and St. Albans.

Place names: Organ Bight 47–49 56-08; —— Island 47-41 58-07.

O'RIELLY. *See* O'REILLY

O'ROURKE, RORKE, surnames of Ireland (O)Rourke, *Ó Ruairc*, "The family is not of Norse origin though *Ruairc* is from a Norse personal name." (MacLysaght).

Traced by MacLysaght in Co. Leitrim.

In Newfoundland:

Family traditions: —— O'Rourke, from southern Ireland, settled at Holyrood (MUN Folklore). John Rorke (1807–1896), born at Athlone (Co. Westmeath), raised in ? Kilman Parish (Co. Cavan), settled at Harbour Grace in 1825 and later moved to Carbonear (MUN Hist.).

Early instances: John ? Rourk, from Pallas (for Pallas Green New) (Co. Limerick), married at St. John's, 1803 (Nfld. Archives BRC); James O'Rourke, schoolmaster of St. John's, 1806 (CO 194.45); John Rurk, of Harbour Grace Parish, 1819 (Nfld. Archives HGRC); Honorable John Rourke (1807 –), born at Athlone (Co. Westmeath), raised in Kelmon Parish (Co. Cavan), came to St. John's as clerk in the firm of Bennett and Ridley, 1824, started a fish supply business at Carbonear in 1830 (Mott); Kitty Roorke, of Outward (? for Outer) Cove (St. John's), 1824 (Nfld. Archives BRC); Thomas Rourke, fisherman of Caplin Bay (now Calvert), died 1825 (*Newfoundlander* 28 Feb 1829); Timothy, of Harbour Grace, deceased 1834 (*Newfoundlander* 2 Jan 1834); Michael, of St. Mary's Bay, 1837 (Nfld. Archives BRC); Edward Rorke, from Co. Cork, of Brigus, 1844 (*Indicator* 24 Aug 1844); Bartholomew Rourke, granted land at Bay Roberts, 1854 (Nfld. Archives, Registry Crown Lands); James and John, of Mall Bay, Mosquito and Mother Ixxes (now Regina) area, 1871 (Lovell); Martin (and others), of

New Bay (Notre Dame B.), 1871 (Lovell); Michael, of North Harbour, John's Point, Tickles and Colinet area, 1871 (Lovell).

Modern status: Rorke, ot Carbonear; O'Rourke, scattered.

Place name: O'Rourke Shoal 50-47 57-17.

OSBO(U)RNE, surnames of England, Osborn of the Channel Islands, OSBORNE of Ireland, and Osborn a baptismal name, from the Old English personal name *Osbeorn* containing the elements *god* and *man*, or from the corresponding Norse name *Asbjorn* containing the elements *god* and *bear*. Both the Old English and Norse forms were in use in England before 1066, but it was also a common name in Normandy and was taken to England by the Normans after the Conquest. (Withycombe, Reaney, MacLysaght, Turk). *See* OSMOND with which confusion has occurred in Newfoundland.

Guppy found Osborn(e) widespread especially in the Midlands and south of England; Spiegelhalter traced Osborn(e), Osbourne in Devon; and MacLysaght traced the first Irish settling in Cos. Waterford and Tipperary about 1550 though the name is now found in all the provinces.

In Newfoundland:

Family tradition: —— Osbourne, from England, settled in Seal Cove (White B.) in the early 1800s (MUN Hist.).

Early instances: Wadham Osbourne, fisherman of Barr'd Islands, 1821 (USPG); Dinah, of Joe Batts Arm, 1821 (USPG); William Osbourne or Osmond and John Osbourne, planters of Change Islands, 1821 (USPG); Mary Osburn, of Bay Bulls, 1821 (Nfld. Archives BRC); Mary, of Harbour Grace Parish, 1826 (Nfld. Archives HGRC); Thomas Osborne, of Petty Harbour, 1829 (DPHW 31); Sibonah, baptized at Greenspond, 1830, aged 32 (DPHW 76); Thomas Osbourne, of St. John's, 1830 (*Newfoundlander* 2 Sep 1830, 9 Jun 1831); John Osborn, planter of Carbonear, 1843 (DPHW 48); John, planter of Brunette (Island), 1855 (DPHW 104); James, planter of Grand Bank, 1859 (DPHW 104); James and Thomas Hosborn, of (Upper) Island Cove, 1871 (Lovell); John Osborne, miner of Tilt Cove, 1871 (Lovell).

Modern status: Osborne, scattered, especially at Blaketown and Seal Cove (White B.); Osbourne, scattered.

Place names: Osberns Pond (Labrador) 52-56 55-55; Osborne Point (Labrador) 59-40 63-56.

O'SHAUGHNESSY, a surname of Ireland *Ó Seachnasaigh*. (MacLysaght).

Traced by MacLysaght in Cos. Galway and Limerick.

In Newfoundland:

Early instances: Terence, murdered ? in St. John's before 1821 (Dispatches 1818–21); Eliza, from the Parish of Saints Peter and Paul (unspecified), Ireland, married at St. John's, 1835 (Nfld. Archives BRC); John O'Shaughnasy, O'Chounisy or O'Shaughnicy, of Kings Cove Parish, 1843 (Nfld. Archives KCRC); John S. O'Shaughnessy, M.D., from Limerick, Ireland, of Carbonear, died 1863, aged 72 (Carbonear R.C. Cemetery); John Shaughnessy, fisherman of Fermeuse, 1871 (Lovell).

Modern status: Rare, at Kingmans (Ferryland district) and St. John's.

O'SHEA. *See* SHEA

OSMOND, a baptismal name and surname of England, Osmond and Osmont of the Channel Islands, from Old English *Osmund* or Norse *Asmundr*, both containing the elements *god* and *protection*; after 1066 it was reinforced by the Norman version *Osmond*. (Withycombe, Reaney, Turk). *See* OSBO(U)RNE with which confusion has occurred in Newfoundland.

Traced by Guppy in Berkshire and Somerset and by Spiegelhalter in Devon.

In Newfoundland:

Family tradition: John, from Cornwall, England, settled at Indian Bay (Bonavista B.) about 1800 (MUN Folklore).

Early instances: David, of Trinity Bay, 1768 (DPHW 64); Joseph, of Crockers Cove (Carbonear), 1785 (CO 199.18); Richard, of Carbonear, 1797 (CO 199.18); Benjamin, fisherman of Grand Bank, 1817 (DPHW 109); Julia, of Greenspond, 1820 (DPHW 76); William Osmond or Osborne, planter of Change Islands, 1821 (USPG); William Osmond, of Catalina, 1822 (Nfld. Archives KCRC); John, married at St. John's, 1834 (Nfld. Archives BRC); Richard, of Cape Island (Bonavista North district), 1836 (DPHW 70); Benjamin, granted land at Frenchman's Cove (Fortune B.), 1838 (Nfld. Archives, Registry Crown Lands); James, of Barr'd Islands, 1842 (DPHW 83); Joseph, fisherman of Moreton's Harbour, 1842 (DPHW 88); John, of Fox Island (Burgeo-La Poile district), 1844 (DPHW 101); Reuben, fisherman of Brunette (Island), 1852 (DPHW 104); James, planter of Little Bay (Burin district), 1857 (DPHW 104); Basil, of River Head (White B.), 1864 (DPHW 94); scattered in Lovell 1871.

Modern status: Widespread, especially at St.

John's, Cape Ray, Mouse Island (Burgeo-La Poile district), Channel and Beaches (White B.).

Place names: Osmond 47-37 59-16; —— Cove 47-33 54-52; —— Hill 47-16 54-55; Osmondville (or The Beaches) 49-35 56-50; Osmonton Arm 49-27 55-24.

O'TOOLE. *See* TOOLE

OTTENHEIMER, a surname of Switzerland, from ? a German place name Ottenheim, or (dweller at or near the) home of otters, vipers or adders.

In Newfoundland:

Early instance: ——, from Switzerland, settled in St. John's in 1934 (Family).

Modern status: Rare, at St. John's.

OUTERBRIDGE, a surname of England, from the English place name Oughtibridge (Yorkshire WR), or (dweller at the) outer bridge. (Bardsley).

In Newfoundland:

Early instance: Joseph (1843–), born at Bermuda, settled at St. John's in 1862 (*Nfld. Who's Who* 1930).

Modern status: Rare, at St. John's.

OVER, a surname of England, from the English place names Over (Cheshire, Gloucestershire), Littleover and Mickleover (Derbyshire), from Old English *ofer* – (dweller on or near the) bank or steep slope. (Reaney, Cottle).

Traced by Spiegelhalter in Devon.

In Newfoundland:

Early instances: James, of Lower Island Cove, 1791 (CO 199.18); Henry, of Tickle Cove (Bonavista B.), in possession of fishing room there, 1806 (Bonavista Register 1806).

Modern status: Rare, at Chamberlains and Southern Bay (Bonavista B.).

Place names: Overs Islands 48-32 53-45; —— Rocks 48-38 53-30.

OWEN, a baptismal name and surname, and OWENS a surname, of Wales, England and Ireland, Owen(s) of Guernsey (Channel Islands), from the Old Welsh personal name *Ou(e)in*, ? from Latin *Eugenius* – well-born, and connected with Ewan, EWING etc.; also in Ireland Owens is a synonym of MacKeown and "equated with HINES and HYNES in Ulster, but not in Connacht." (Withycombe, Reaney, Cottle, MacLysaght, Turk).

Guppy traced Owen(s) in North and South Wales and in the Welsh border counties with Owens "mostly confined to Wales"; Spiegelhalter traced Owen in Devon; and MacLysaght traced Owens in Ulster and Connacht.

In Newfoundland:

Early instances: Thomas Owen, of St. John's, 1766 (DPHW 26C); William, of Port de Grave, 1769 (CO 199.18); Peter Owens, of Harbour Grace Parish, 1814 (Nfld. Archives KCRC); James, of New Harbour (Trinity B.), 1817 (Nfld. Archives KCRC); Richard Owen, of Bonavista, 1826 (Nfld. Archives KCRC); Bridget Owens, from Thurles (Co. Tipperary), married at St. John's, 1830 (Nfld. Archives BRC); Charles Owen, of Fogo, 1832 (Nfld. Archives KCRC); George, of Eastern Tickle (Twillingate district), 1871 (Lovell); Thomas J. Owens, of Bay of Islands district, 1876 (DPHW 96).

Modern status: Owen, unique, at St. John's; Owens, at Norris Arm North and St. John's.

Place name: Owen Rock 47-21 54-17.

OXFORD, a surname of England from the English place name Oxford (Oxfordshire) – ford for oxen. (Reaney).

Traced by Spiegelhalter in Devon.

In Newfoundland:

Early instances: Thomas, merchant of St. John's, 1675 (CO 1, Prowse); Maria, of Herring Neck, 1852 (DPHW 85); Henry, fisherman of Stone Harbour (Twillingate district), 1857 (DPHW 85); Joseph, of Little Bay Islands (Exploits district), 1857 (DPHW 92); Elijah, of East Cul de Sac (Burgeo-La Poile district), 1871 (Lovell); John (and others), of Twillingate, 1871 (Lovell).

Modern status: Scattered, especially at Little Bay Islands and Springdale.

Place names: Oxford Point 47-28 55-51; Oxfords (Stage or Cove) in St. John's Harbour (Visscher about 1680).

OZON, a surname of France from the French place name Ozon (Ardèche, Hautes-Pyrénées, Nièvre), but probably also confused with Ozannes, also a surname of England and of Guernsey (Channel Islands), from Ozanne and Osanne, Old French names for Palm Sunday, baptismal names ? for one born on that day. (Dauzat, Reaney, Turk).

Spiegelhalter traced Ozanne in Devon.

In Newfoundland:

Early instances: John, of St. George's Bay, 1835 (DPHW 30); John Ozong, fisherman of Sandy Point (St. George's B.), 1871 (Lovell).

Modern status: At Cape St. George, Corner Brook (*Electors* 1955) and St. John's.

P

PACHNOWSKI, a surname ? of White Russia (or Byelorussia) of Polish origin containing ? the element *pach* – young, with the suffix *-owski* denoting high social status. (Unbegaun).

In Newfoundland:

Early instance: Stephen, from Winnipeg, Manitoba, settled in 1954.

Modern status: Rare, at Manuels.

PACK, a surname of England and ? of Guernsey (Channel Islands), from Old French *Pasques, Paque* – (one born at Easter. *See also* CHRISTMAS, NOEL. (Reaney, Turk).

Traced by Spiegelhalter in Devon

In Newfoundland:

Early instances: Richard, of St. John's, 1814, of Quidi Vidi, 1815 (DPHW 26B, 26D); Robert, merchant of Carbonear, 1820 (DPHW 48); Robert, granted land at Bay Roberts, 1834 (Nfld. Archives, Registry Crown Lands); Stephen Olive, granted land at Spaniards Bay, 1842 (Nfld. Archives, Registry Crown Lands); Stephen ? O'Pack, granted land at Lamaline Harbour, 1851 (Nfld. Archives, Registry Crown Lands); William Pack, fisherman of Richard's Harbour (Fortune Bay district), 1851 (DPHW 102); Thomas, granted land at Bay Bulls, 1855 (Nfld. Archives, Registry Crown Lands).

Modern status: Scattered.

Place names: Packs Harbour (Labrador) 53-51 56-59; —— Pond 47-48 53-17.

PACKWOOD, a surname of England from the English place name Packwood (Warwickshire), apparently *Pac(c)a*'s wood though the personal name is not known in Old English. (Bardsley, Ekwall).

In Newfoundland:

Early instance: George, of Round Harbour (Twillingate district), 1852 (DPHW 86).

Modern status: At Howley (*Electors* 1955), and Woodstock (White B.).

PADDLE, a surname of Newfoundland apparently arbitrarily changed from the English surname Padley, from the English place name Padley (Derbyshire) – the clearing, glade notable for toads or frogs, or belonging to *Padda*. (Bardsley, Ekwall).

Bardsley traced Padley in Nottinghamshire.

In Newfoundland:

Family tradition: —— Padley, from England, came to the Burin Peninsula in 1840, the next year he settled at Flat Island (now Port Elizabeth) (Placentia B.); the surname was later changed to Paddle (MUN Folklore).

Early instance: John Padley, fisherman of Flat Island (now Port Elizabeth), 1871 (Lovell).

Modern status: At Port Elizabeth (*Electors* 1955).

PADDOCK, a surname of England from Old English *padduc* – frog, or a variant of the surname of England Parrock – (dweller by the) paddock or enclosure, or from the English place name Paddock Wood (Kent). (Reaney, Cottle, Ekwall).

Traced by Guppy in Shropshire.

In Newfoundland:

Early instances: James, fisherman of Trinity (Trinity B.), 1837 (DPHW 64B); Thomas, of Ward's Harbour (now Beaumont North), 1843 (DPHW 86); George Paddick, of Hall's Bay, 1854 (DPHW 86); Eli Paddock, of Sunday Cove Island, 1868 (DPHW 91).

Modern status: Scattered, especially in the Green Bay district.

Place names: Paddock Shoal 46-58 53-32; Paddock's (or Paddox) Bight 49-34 55-47.

PADDON, a surname of England from the English place name Paddon (Devon) – ? *Peatta's tun* – *Peatta*'s farm, enclosure. (Spiegelhalter, Gover). *See also* PATTEN.

Traced by Guppy in Devon.

In Newfoundland:

Early instance: William, boatkeeper of St. John's, 1794–5, "30 years in Newfoundland," that is, 1764–5 (Census 1794–5).

Modern status: Rare, at St. John's.

Place name: Paddon Point (Labrador) 53-43 60-01.

PAFFORD, a surname of England from the English place name Pafford (Devon), or (dweller on the) path to the ford. (Spiegelhalter, Gover).

Traced by Spiegelhalter in Devon.

In Newfoundland:

Family tradition: Samuel (about 1825–51), from England, came to Newfoundland between 1835–40 and settled at Harbour Buffett (MUN Geog.).

Early instance: William, fisherman of Burgeo, 1871 (Lovell).

Modern status: At Harbour Buffett (*Electors* 1955) and Corner Brook.

PAGE, a surname of England and Ireland, (Le) Page of the Channel Islands, from Old French *page* – page, originally a subordinate personal attendant on a knight. (Reaney, Black, Turk). *See* PEACH.

Page found widespread by Guppy in the Midlands and south of England, including Devon and especially in Essex, and by MacLysaght in east Galway and Ulster.

In Newfoundland:

Early instances: James, trader who sustained losses when St. Pierre was surrendered to the French in 1763 (CO 194.16); Peter, servant of Battle Harbour, 1795 (MUN Hist.); Steven, from Puddington Parish (Bedfordshire), married at St. John's, 1809 (Nfld. Archives BRC); Frederick R., son of Thomas, from Stornington, near Bedford, Beds., England, of Burin, 1832, of St. John's, 1847 (*Newfoundlander* 26 Jan 1832, 5 May 1842, 12 Aug 1847); Solomon, planter of Marshalls Folly (Carbonear district), 1836 (DPHW 48); Abraham, planter of Small Point (Bay de Verde district), 1840 (DPHW 52A); Thomas, fisherman of Otterbury (Carbonear district), 1847 (DPHW 48); Thomas, of Cupids, 1871 (Lovell).

Modern status: Rare, at Lower Island Cove (*Electors* 1955) and St. John's.

Place name: Page Rock 46-50 55-49.

PALFREY, a surname of England and ? of Ireland, from Old French *palefrei* – (man in charge of the) palfrey(s), saddle-horse(s). (Reaney, Cottle).

Traced by Guppy in Devon.

In Newfoundland:

Early instances: Richard, from Teignmouth (Devon), married at St. John's, 1845, died 1881, aged 60 (*Newfoundlander* 27 Feb 1845, General Protestant Cemetery, St. John's); Patrick and Michael, of Clattice Harbour

(Placentia B.), 1871 (Lovell); John, of Isle Valen, 1871 (Lovell).

Modern status: At Davis Cove (Placentia B.) (Electors 1955), Placentia and St. John's.

PALMER, a surname of England, Ireland and the Channel Islands, from Old French *palmer*, *paumer* – palmer, pilgrim so-called from the palm-branch he brought back from the Holy Land. Spiegelhalter, however, maintains that it was more usually a nickname than for a real palmer. In Ireland, it is also an

occasional synonym of (O)Mullover, *Ó Maolfhoghmhair*, Ir. *foghmhar* – harvest. (Reaney, Cottle, Spiegelhalter, MacLysaght, Turk).

Found widespread by Guppy in the Midlands and south of England including Devon, and by MacLysaght in Ireland since the thirteenth century.

In Newfoundland:

Early instances: James, of Harbour Grace, 1677 (CO 1); Andrew, of Ferryland, 1708–9 (CO 194.4); Mary, of St. John's, 1794–5 (Census 1794–5); Palmer and Adams, operated salmon fishery at Indian Burying Place, 1804 (CO 194.45); William, of Bonavista, 1820, of Plate Cove (Bonavista B.), 1839 (DPHW 70, 73A); David, of Hant's Harbour, 1826 (DPHW 58); George, planter of Salmon Cove (Brigus and Cupids district), 1848, of Springfields, 1850 (DPHW 34); David, fisherman of Shoal Harbour (Trinity B.), 1854 (DPHW 59A); John, of Indian Arm (Bonavista B.), 1856 (DPHW 73A); David, of Random Sound, 1871 (Lovell).

Modern status: Scattered.

Place names: Palmer Point (Labrador) 54-28 57-16; —— River (Labrador) 58-55 63-53.

PAPAIL, ? a Newfoundland variant of the surnames of France Papillon, Parpaillon, from French *papillon* – butterfly, a symbol of lightness in all its forms. (Dauzat).

In Newfoundland:

Early instance: ? Peter Pallah, fisherman of Lamaline, 1871 (Lovell).

Modern status: Rare, at St. Lawrence and Lord's Cove (*Electors* 1955).

PAQUETTE, a surname of France, Pacquet of Jersey (Channel Islands), Paquette being the feminine form of *Paquet* – (dealer in) faggot(s), (carrier of) packet(s), or a variant of *Pâquerette*, an old feminine baptismal name. (Dauzat, Turk).

In Newfoundland:

Modern status: Rare, at St. John's.

Place names: Pacquet, —— Brook, —— Harbour 49-59 55-53.

PARADIS, a surname of England and France, in England a worker in a paradise, a pleasure-garden of a convent, monastery or cathedral, or ? a dweller at Paradise, a name given sometimes ironically to a place, "a perfect Paradise"; in France ? a nickname for an actor in a mediaeval religious play. (Bardsley, Weekley *Surnames*, Dauzat). *See* PARDY.

In Newfoundland:

Modern status: Rare, at St. John's.

PARDY, a surname of England, Pardieu of France, an oath-name *(de) par Dieu* – in God's name; in Newfoundland probably confused with PARADIS. (Reaney, Cottle, Dauzat).

Guppy traced Pardre in Shropshire and Worcestershire, Spiegelhalter traced Pardew in Devon, and Matthews Pardy as captains and planters in Poole (Dorset).

In Newfoundland:

Family tradition: John (1818–90), of Grand Bank (MUN Hist.).

Early instances: Thomas Pardey, of Placentia ? district, 1744 (CO 194.24); William Pardy, of Bonavista, 1786 (DPHW 70); Samuel, born at St. John's, 1794, baptized in Trinity North district, 1816 (DPHW 64); Christopher and Joseph, of Burin, 1805 (D'Alberti 15); John, of Trouty, 1815 (DPHW 64); William Parady, granted land at Grand St. Pierre, Barrisway, 1833 (Nfld. Archives, Registry Crown Lands); Thomas Pardy, of Bay d'Este at Shelter Point, 1835 (DPHW 30); Henry, of Catalina, 1846 (DPHW 67); George, of Moreton's Harbour, 1848 (DPHW 86); James, of Twillingate, 1855 (DPHW 85); Samuel, planter of Jacfontain (Jacques Fontaine), 1856 (DPHW 104); William, planter of Harbour Mille, 1858 (DPHW 104); James, of Little Harbour (Twillingate district), 1861 (DPHW 88); William, of Doting Cove (Bonavista B.), 1862 (DPHW 77); Sarah, of Broad Cove (now Duntara), 1866 (Nfld. Archives KCRC); John and Thomas, of Upper and Lower Amherst Cove, 1871 (Lovell); James and Joseph, of Burn Island (Placentia B.), 1871 (Lovell); Samuel, miner of Tilt Cove, 1871 (Lovell).

Modern status: Widespread, especially at Harbour Mille, Bonavista and Wild Cove (White B.).

Place names: Pardy Head, —— —— Cove, Little —— Head 47-57 55-46; —— Island, —— Point 47-02 55-09; Pardys Folly 47-09 55-06; Barth (Pardy) Island (Labrador) 56-36 61-46.

PARK, a surname of England and Scotland, Parke(s), of England and Ireland, from Old French *parc*, Middle English *parc*, *parke* – (worker at or dweller near the) lists, park, enclosure, or a contraction of the surname Parrack, Parrock which have the same meaning. (Reaney, Cottle). *See also* PARKER.

Guppy traced Park in Cumberland, Westmorland, Lancashire, Nottinghamshire and in the Glasgow and Paisley districts, Parke in Suffolk, and Parkes in Warwickshire and Worcestershire; Spiegelhalter traced Park(es) in Devon; and MacLysaght traced Park from Scotland and Parkes from England in Northern Ireland.

In Newfoundland:

Early instances: J., soldier of St. John's, 1779 (DPHW 26C); Thomas Parke and Robert Park, of Bay of Islands, 1835 (DPHW 30); —— Park, from Burin, of McIvers (Bay of Islands district), 1849 (Feild); John, fisherman of Cape Ray, 1871 (Lovell).

Modern status: Scattered, especially in the Humber West district at McIvers, Cox's Cove, Lark Harbour and Corner Brook.

Place names: Park Cove 51-03 55-48; —— Harbour 48-32 53-48; Parkes Beach 49-08 58-06; —— Cove 49-07 58-03; Park(e)s Rock 49-13 58-08; —— Shoal 49-10 58-08; Park Harbour Hill 48-32 53-51; —— —— Point 48-33 53-46; —— —— Pond 48-31 53-49.

PARKER, a surname of England, Scotland and Ireland from Old French *parquier* etc., Anglo French *parker* – park-keeper. *See* PARK. (Reaney, Cottle, Black).

Found widespread by Guppy, by Spiegelhalter in Devon, and by MacLysaght in Ulster.

In Newfoundland:

Early instances: Henry, of Petty Harbour, 1703, of St. John's, 1708 (CO 194.3, 4); John, of Gooseberry Harbour (Trinity North district), 1786–89 (DPHW 64); Peter, from Carlow (Co. Carlow), Irish convict landed at Petty Harbour or Bay Bulls, 1789 (CO 194.38); John, of Greenspond, in possession of fishing room, Newells Island, 1806 (Bonavista Register 1806); John, of Harbour Grace Parish, 1808 (Nfld. Archives HGRC); Michael, from Co. Cork, married at St. John's, 1814 (Nfld. Archives BRC); Joseph, from Bridgport (Dorset), of Burin, died 1816 (*Royal Gazette* 22 Oct 1816); Michael, planter of Hants Harbour, 1817 (DPHW 58); John ? Parker, planter of Cupids, 1828 (DPHW 34); Frederick Parker, agent of Brigus, 1830 (DPHW 34); John, from London, married at St. John's, 1835 (DPHW 26D); Nicholas, of Torbay, 1841 (DPHW 32); Charles, fisherman of Salmon Cove (now Champneys), 1853 (DPHW 64B); Thomas T., of Middle Bull (? for Middle Bill) Cove (Bonavista B.), 1871 (Lovell); William, of Bay of Islands, 1871 (Lovell).

Modern status: At Champneys and St. John's.

Place names: Parker Beach 49-08 58-24; —— River 51-30 55-44; Parkers Cove 47-24 54-51; —— Pond 47-36 52-47; Parker Tooth 49-40 55-46.

PARKINS, a surname of England, from the personal name *Per(es)* and *kin* – son of Perkin, Little Peter. (Reaney). *See* PETER *and also* PERKS.

Guppy traced Parkin in six counties, Parkyn in Cornwall, but Parkins only in Hertfordshire. Spiegelhalter traced Parkin(s), Parkyns in Devon.

In Newfoundland:

Early instances: William, merchant of Harbour Grace, 1821 (DPHW 43); Patrick Parkin, from Co. Tipperary, married at St. John's, 1831 (Nfld. Archives BRC); Walter Parkins, labourer of St. John's, 1850 (DPHW 29); Fanny Constantine, born ? at Grand Bank, 1874 (MUN Hist.).

Modern status: Rare, at St. John's.

PARKINSON, a surname of England – son of *Perkin*. *See* PARKINS. (Reaney).

Traced by Guppy in Cheshire, Durham, Lancashire, Lincolnshire, Nottinghamshire and Yorkshire WR.

In Newfoundland:

Modern status: At St. John's.

PARMENTER, PARMITER, surnames of England from Old French *parme(n)tier* – tailor, or ? Old French *parcheminier* – maker or seller of parchment. (Reaney, Cottle, Spiegelhalter).

Guppy traced Parminter in Devon, especially in the Barnstaple district.

In Newfoundland:

Early instances: Richard Parmiter, of Manuels, 1825, of Middle Bight (now Codner), 1838 (DPHW 26B, 30); John Parmter, granted land at Topsail, 1857 (Nfld. Archives, Registry Crown Lands); William Parmiter, of Ha-Ha (now Raleigh) (St. Anthony district), 1871 (DPHW 94); Joseph, of Kelligrews, 1871 (Lovell).

Modern status: Parmenter, rare, at St. John's; Parmiter, at St. John's, Goulds, Harbour Grace and Point Leamington (Green B.).

Place name: Parmenter Island (Labrador) 60-18 64-23.

PARNELL, a surname of England and Ireland from the baptismal names Petronella, Petronilla, feminine diminutives of the Roman name *Petronius*, possibly from Latin *petra* – stone. *Petronilla* was thought to be the name of a daughter of St. Peter, and, as St. *Petronilla*, she was invoked against fevers. The name was very common in the Middle Ages, when it was used as a convenient feminine form of Peter. The contracted forms *Pernel* or *Parnel* came to be used for a priest's concubine or later for any loose woman. (Withycombe, Reaney, Cottle, MacLysaght). *See also* PENNELL.

Traced by Guppy in Cambridgeshire, Cornwall

(where he also found a rare form Parnall), and Devon; and by MacLysaght in Cos. Wicklow, Longford and Dublin.

In Newfoundland:

Early instances: ——, of Quidi Vidi, 1703 (CO 194.3); Thomas, of St. John's, 1704 (CO 194.3); Mary Ann, from Clifton (? England), married at St. John's, 1834 (DPHW 26D); William, planter of Petty Harbour, 1871 (Lovell); John, of Tilt Cove, 1871 (Lovell).

Modern status: Rare, at St. John's.

PARRELL, PARRILL, surnames of Ireland, variants of Parle, Parill from a diminutive of the baptismal name Peter. *See* PETERS. (MacLysaght).

Traced by MacLysaght in Cos. Wexford and Clare.

In Newfoundland:

Early instances: William Parell, of Bonavista, 1792 (USPG); Ambrose Parrel, of Placentia, 1794 (D'Alberti 5); James Parril, of Harbour Grace Parish, 1808 (Nfld. Archives HGRC).

Modern status: Parrell, in the St. Barbe district especially at Payne's Cove, and St. John's; Parrill, at St. Anthony.

PARROTT, a surname of England and the Channel Islands, one of many diminutives of the personal name *Perre* (Peter) (*see* PETERS), or a nickname from the parrot named after *Perot*. (Reaney, Cottle, Turk).

Traced by Guppy in Buckinghamshire and Oxfordshire and in the forms Parrett, Parrott, Perrott by Spiegelhalter in Devon.

In Newfoundland:

Family tradition: Three brothers John (1790–), Peter (1795–) and William (1791–), from Poole (Dorset), wintered in Scilly Cove (now Winterton) about 1810–12 and then settled there; William later moved to Port Rexton (MUN Geog.).

Early instances: Roger Parrit, of St. John's, 1705 (CO 194.22); Matthew Parrot, of Trinity Bay, 1766 (DPHW 64); Ruth Parrott, of Bonavista, 1774 (CO 194.32); Samuel Parrot, of Trinity (Trinity B.), 1790 (DPHW 64); Pieter [sic] Parrott, planter of Scilly Cove (now Winterton), 1825 (DPHW 64B); Samuel, planter of Old Bonaventure, 1849 (DPHW 72); Nathaniel and William Parritts, planters of Bay of Islands, 1871 (Lovell).

Modern status: Scattered, especially at Winterton and St. John's.

PARRY, a surname of England and Wales – son (from Welsh *Ap-*) of Harry, or ? from Pierre (Peter). *See* PETERS. (Withycombe, Cottle, Spiegelhalter).

Traced by Guppy in the Welsh border counties and in North and South Wales, and by Spiegelhalter in Devon.

In Newfoundland:

Early instances: Pasco, ? of St. John's, 1730 (CO 194.9); Joseph, baptized at Flowers Island (Bonavista B.), 1830, aged 18 (DPHW 76); John and Thomas, of Bay of Islands, 1871 (Lovell); William, of Daniel's Harbour, 1871 (Lovell).

Modern status: Rare, at Gander (*Electors* 1955).

PARSLEY, a surname of England from Old French *Passelewe* – cross the water (a nickname). (Reaney, Cottle).

Spiegelhalter traced Parsley, Parslow in Devon; Guppy traced Parslow in Gloucestershire.

In Newfoundland:

Early instances: Arthur Par(s)ley, planter of St. John's, 1706 (CO 194.4); William Parcly, Pastley or Parsley, of Harbour Grace Parish, 1821 (Nfld. Archives HGRC); William Parsley, from Annandale, Scotland, married at St. John's, 1833 (DPHW 26D); William, granted land at Harbour Main, 1850 (Nfld. Archives, Registry Crown Lands); William, farmer of Salmon Cove and Gasters, 1871 (Lovell).

Modern status: Scattered, especially in the Harbour Main district.

PARSONS, a surname of England and Ireland – the parson's servant, or one who lived or worked at the parson's (house); in Ireland also for *Mac an Phearsain* (MACPHERSON in Scotland). (Reaney, Cottle, MacLysaght). *See also* WILLIAMS.

Guppy found Parsons widespread in the south of England, especially in Wiltshire.

In Newfoundland:

Family traditions: —— Williams, from England, deserted from the Royal Navy, settled at Diamond Cove where he changed his surname of Parsons (MUN Folklore). Meshach Parsons (1828–), born at Rose Blanche, son of —— from Guernsey, settled at Rocky Harbour (Bonne B.), in 1878 (MUN Geog.). Samuel, from Devon, settled at Running Brook, Bay Roberts about 1825 (MUN Folklore). Edward (about 1725–), from Devon, settled at Parsons Cove (Bryants Cove), between 1750 and 1775 (MUN Geog.). Thomas (1799–), from Bristol, settled at Freshwater (Carbonear), about 1821 (MUN Geog.).

Early instances: John, of Clowns Cove (Carbonear), 1755, property "in possession of the family for upwards of 90 years," that is, before 1665 (CO 199.18); Joseph, of Clowns Cove (Carbonear), 1675 (CO 1); James and William, of Bay Roberts, 1769,

property "in possession of the Family for 102 years," that is, 1667 (CO 199.18); Patience, of Harbour Grace, 1765, property "possessed by the Family for 92 years," that is, 1673 (CO 199.18); Anthony, of St. John's, 1705, of Ferryland, 1708 (CO 194.4); Joseph, of Blackhead (North Shore Conception B.), 1708–9 (CO 194.4); Edward, of Bryants Cove, 1801, property "possessed by the Family for 56 years," that is, 1745 (CO 199.18); John, of Ochre Pit Cove, 1780 (CO 199. 18); John, of Carbonear, 1790 (CO 199. 18); John, mariner of St. John's, 1794–5 (Census 1794–5); Robert and William, of Crockers Cove (Carbonear), 1795 (CO 199. 18); Phil., of Trinity (Trinity B.), 1798 (DPHW 64); Thomas, given possession of fishing room at Pacquet Harbour, 1804 (D'Alberti 14); John, of Otterbury Cove (Carbonear), 1805 (CO 199.18); Henery [sic], of Freshwater (Carbonear), 1808 (DPHW 48); Charles, of Bears Cove (Harbour Grace), 1810 (DPHW 48); W., of Fortune Bay, 1811 (D'Alberti 21); George, of Greenspond, 1816 (DPHW 76); William, fisherman of Codroy, 1821 (DPHW 109); George, planter of Twillingate, 1823 (USPG); Ambrose, born at Codroy Island, baptized at Little Burgeo, 1830, aged 4 (DPHW 30); James, of St. George's Harbour (St. George's B.), 1830 (DPHW 30); John, fisherman of Perry's Cove, 1830 (DPHW 52A); Thomas, baptized at Pinchards Island (Bonavista B.), 1830, aged 35 (DPHW 76); Thomas, of Cat Harbour (now Lumsden), 1831 (DPHW 76); John, planter of Hangman's Cove (Carbonear district), 1831 (DPHW 48); John, planter of Sculpin Bay (Bay de Verde district), 1831 (DPHW 52A); George, of Middle Bill Cove (Bonavista B.), 1832 (DPHW 76); Catherine, born at Jersey Harbour, baptized at Rencontre, 1835, aged 17 (DPHW 30); James, of Sandy Point (St. George's B.), 1835 (DPHW 30); William, of Pushthrough, 1835 (DPHW 30); James, from Kilkenny, married at St. John's, 1835 (Nfld. Archives BRC); William Thomas, granted land at Bay Bulls, 1844 (Nfld. Archives, Registry Crown Lands); George, fisherman of Change Islands, 1846 (DPHW 83); Thomas, of Grand Bank, deceased, 1846 (*Newfoundlander* 20 Aug 1846); James, of Leading Tickles (Twillingate district), 1847, of Donier Harbour, 1848 (DPHW 86); ——, of Codroy Road (West Coast), 1849 (Feild); William, of New (now Parsons) Harbour, 1853 (DPHW 102); Benjamin, of Cottels Island (Bonavista B.), 1853 (Nfld. Archives, Registry Crown Lands); Robert, granted land at Gooseberry Island (Bonavista B.), 1855 (Nfld. Archives, Registry Crown Lands); Sampson, of Lower Island Cove, 1856 (DPHW 55); Thomas, fisherman of Morgans Island (Burgeo-La Poile district), 1856 (DPHW 101); Martha, of Garnish, 1856 (DPHW 106); Meshach, of Rose Blanche, 1860 (DPHW 99); James, of Lush's Bight (Exploits district), 1860 (DPHW 92); William, of Burin, 1861 (DPHW 100); James, of Englee, 1864 (DPHW 94); John Henry, of The Gut (St. George's district), 1870 (DPHW 96); widespread in Lovell 1871.

Modern status: Widespread throughout Newfoundland with especially concentrated numbers at Parsonsville (Bell Island), Bay Roberts, Corner Brook, Lumsden North, St. John's, Indian Bay and Greenspond (Bonavista B.), Rose Blanche, Harbour Grace, Coleys Point, Salmon Cove and Freshwater (Carbonear) and Carbonear.

Place names: Parsons Brook 48-58 57-47; —— Cove 47-41 53-11, 47-44 55-22, 49-09 57-55, 49-32 55-00, 47-41 53-15; —— Ground 49-32 55-32, (Labrador) 52-17 55-41; —— Harbour 47-36 56-39; —— Point 49-02 55-53, (Labrador) 52-36 55-46; —— Pond 50-02 57-43, 48-55 57-53, 49-59 57-37; —— Tickle (Labrador) 52-36 55-47; —— Pond Hill (or Mill) 49-59 57-43; —— —— River 50-02 57-43; Parsonsville 47-36 53-01.

PASHA, PASHER, ? Newfoundland variants of the surname of the Channel Islands PERCHARD (Le Messurier).
  In Newfoundland:
  Early instance: Charles Parshar, servant of Clowns Cove (Carbonear), 1820 (DPHW 48).
  Modern status: Rare, at Corner Brook and Harbour Grace.

PATERSON. *See* PATTERSON

PATEY, a surname of England, diminutive of *Pate* (Patrick). *See* PATRICK. (Reaney).
  Traced by Spiegelhalter in Devon.
  In Newfoundland:
  Family tradition: The Pateys, from Conception Bay, were the first settlers of St. Lunaire in 1849 (MUN Hist.).
  Early instances: Anne Paty, married at St. John's, 1839 (Nfld. Archives BRC); Keziah Patey, of St. Anthony, married at Battle Harbour (Labrador), 1854 (DPHW 114); John, of Braha (now Brehat), 1871 (Lovell); John, of Cape Norman, 1871 (Lovell); John, planter of St. Lunaire, 1871 (Lovell); Patrick Patty, of the Flowers Cove to Point Ferolle area, 1871 (Lovell).
  Modern status: Scattered, especially at St. Anthony and River of Ponds (St. Barbe district).

Place names: Pateyville (St. Anthony) 51-21 55-34; Jack Patey's Point 51-13 56-02.

PATON, a surname of England and Scotland, *Patun,* a diminutive with an Old French suffix of Pat(e) (Patrick). *See* PATRICK, and FATTEN, PAYTON, PEYTON with which confusion may have occurred. (Reaney, Cottle).
  Traced by Spiegelhalter in Devon and by Guppy mostly in the southern half of Scotland.
  In Newfoundland:
  Early instance: Thomas Patton, of St. John's, 1822 (D'Alberti 32).
  Modern status: Rare, at Gander.

PATRICK, a baptismal name and surname of England, Scotland and Ireland from Latin *patricius* – patrician, aristocrat, the name adopted by the apostle of Ireland on his consecration as a missionary. The baptismal name was common in Ireland, Scotland and the north of England, in Scotland being sometimes interchangeable with Peter. In Ireland, most people bearing the surname are of Scots origin. (Withycombe, Reaney, Cottle, MacLysaght, Black). *See also* FITZPATRICK, KILPATRICK and KIRKPATRICK.
  Traced by Spiegelhalter in Devon, by Reaney in the north of England, and by Black in Ayrshire.
  In Newfoundland:
  Early instances: Onoris [sic], married at St. John's, 1836 (Nfld. Archives BRC); David and John, of St. John's, 1871 (Lovell).
  Modern status: At Cox's Cove (*Electors* 1955), Corner Brook and St. John's.
  Place names (not necessarily from the surname): Patrick(s) Harbour, Patrick Harbour Rock 47-41 56-01; Patrick Island 47-17 54-50; —— Point 47-08 53-40; Patricks Cove 47-03 54-07; —— Point 49-42 55-59; —— Pond 49-01 56-26; —— Rock 47-03 54-09.

PATRY, a surname of Scotland, PETRIE (pronounced Paitrie in Aberdeen); or Patry of France, from the baptismal name *Patrie* (Patrick). *See* PATRICK. (Black, Dauzat, Reaney).
  In Newfoundland:
  Early instance: Alfred (1883–), from Quebec City, became lighthouse keeper at Cape Anguille, in 1908 (*Nfld. Who's Who* 1930).
  Modern status: Rare, at Cape Anguille (*Electors* 1955).

PATTEN, a surname of England and Ireland, from Middle English *paten* – (maker or seller of) patten(s), clogs, or from the English place name Paddon (Devon), or a variant of PATON or Patton; also in Ireland, especially in Co. Donegal, with PEYTON and Patton, an anglicized form of *Ó Peatáin*, "probably another diminutive of Patrick" (*see* PATRICK). (Reaney, Spiegelhalter, MacLysaght).

Traced by Guppy in Hertfordshire, by Spiegelhalter (with Patton) in Devon, and by MacLysaght in Co. Donegal.

In Newfoundland:

Family tradition: Samuel (1789–1829), of Grand Bank (MUN Hist.).

Early instances: Edward Patten or Pettin, of New Perlican, 1681, 1682 (CO 1); Edward Patten, of St. John's, 1780 (DPHW 26C); John, from Bristol, married at St. John's, 1809 (Nfld. Archives BRC); Charles, planter of Grand Bank, 1819 (DPHW 109); Thomas Paten, of Cupids, 1826 (DPHW 34); Michael Patten, of Harbour Grace Parish, 1829 (Nfld. Archives HGRC); Robert, of Cape Ray, 1871 (Lovell); William, of Port de Grave, 1871 (Lovell).

Modern status: At Port de Grave, St. John's, Grand Bank and Codroy.

PAT(T)ERSON, surnames of England, Scotland and Ireland – son of Patrick (*see* PATRICK); in Co. Galway for Cussane, Ir. *casáin* – path. (Reaney, MacLysaght).

Guppy traced Patterson, Patti(n)son in Northumberland, Cumberland, Westmorland and Yorkshire, and Paterson commonly, Patterson less frequently, over a large part of Scotland though rare in the north. MacLysaght found Patterson, Pattison very numerous in Ulster and also in Co. Galway.

In Newfoundland:

Early instances: Robert ? Patason (for ? Paterson), ? of St. John's, 1730 (CO 194.9); Thomas Patterson, of St. John's, 1768 (DPHW 26C); Paterson and Foster, merchants of Harbour Grace, 1871 (Lovell).

Modern status: Paterson, rare, at St. John's; Patterson, at Placentia, Dunville, Bishop's Falls and St. John's.

PAUL, a baptismal name and **PAUL(S)** surnames of England, PAUL of Scotland and of the Micmacs of Newfoundland, from Latin *paulus* – small, the name of Saul of Tarsus after his conversion, or from the English place name Paul (Cornwall), after the church of St. Paulinus. (Withycombe, Reaney, Cottle, Spiegelhalter, Black, MacLysaght). *See also* POLLARD, POLLETT, POOLE, POWLEY, BOULOS.

Paul(l) traced by Guppy in Cornwall, Dorset and Somerset, and by Spiegelhalter in Devon, with Paull

more characteristic of Cornwall; and by Black in Daviot (? Aberdeenshire), Fintry (? Forfarshire), and the Lothians and Fife where it is considered "by family tradition a Flemish name," but, as Black comments, "not necessarily so."

In Newfoundland:

Family tradition: —— Pauls, from Scotland, settled at St. Bernards (Fortune B.); some of the family later moved to Rencontre East (MUN Folklore).

Early instances: Robert Paul, carpenter of St. John's, 1794–5, "14 years in Newfoundland," that is, since 1780–1 (Census 1794–5); William Paull, of Bonavista, 1786 (DPHW 70); Henry Paul, of Placentia, 1794 (D'Alberti 5); John, of Bay de Verde, 1796 (CO 199.18); John, of Greenspond, 1815 (DPHW 76); John, planter of Old Perlican, 1820 (DPHW 58); Patrick, of Harbour Grace Parish, 1824 (Nfld. Archives HGRC); Sarah, baptized at Deer Island (Bonavista B.), 1830, aged 9 (DPHW 76); Robert, planter of Cuckold's Cove (now Dunfield), 1834, of Trouty, 1839, of Ireland's Eye, 1852 (DPHW 64B); George, born ? 1836, servant, son of Richard and Hannah of Dorset, married at Harbour Breton, 1861 (Harbour Breton Anglican Church Records per D.A. Macdonald); William, of Catalina area, 1847 (Nfld. Archives, Registry Crown Lands); John, of Fortune, 1855, of Grand Bank, 1860 (DPHW 106); Henry, of Mud Cove (Burin district), 1860 (DPHW 108); Noel, of Exploits River, 1871 (Lovell); Thomas, of Newman's Cove, 1871 (Lovell); Noel, of Grandy's Brook (Burgeo-La Poile district), 1871 (Lovell); Charles Pauls, of New (now Parsons) Harbour, 1871 (Lovell); Ben, Abraham and Noel, Micmac Indian trappers whose hunting ground was the Exploits River about 1900–06 (Millais).

Modern status: Paul, scattered, especially at Dark Cove East and West, and Bonavista; Pauls, rare, at Rencontre East, Mose Ambrose and St. John's.

Place names (not necessarily from the surname): Paul Island 51-11 56-00, (Labrador) 56-30 61-25; L'Anse a Paul 47-05 55-49; Pauls Gulch 48-07 59-03; —— Lake 49-06 56-04; —— Pond 48-40 55-08; John Paul Rock 53-48 56-17; Noel Paul's Brook 48-49 56-19.

PAWLETT, a surname of England from a diminutive of the baptismal name Paul (*see* PAUL), or ? a variant of POLLETT, or ? from the English place name Pawlett (Somerset). (Bardsley, Spiegelhalter).

Traced by Spiegelhalter in Devon.

In Newfoundland:

Early instance: Charles Paulett, planter of Wreck Cove (Burin district), 1855 (DPHW 104).

Modern status: Rare, at Robinson's (*Electors* 1955).

PAWLEY, a surname of England, from the French place name Pavilly (Seine-Inférieure), or ? a pet-form of the baptismal name Paul (*see* PAUL). (Reaney, Spiegelhalter).

Traced by Spiegelhalter in Devon.

In Newfoundland:

Early instances: John, of Hants Harbour, 1834 (DPHW 58); John, planter of Caplin Cove (Trinity South district), 1843 (DPHW 59A); Charles Pauley, of Harbour Breton, 1851 (DPHW 104).

Modern status: Rare, at Hants Harbour (*Electors* 1955), and Curling.

PAYNE, a surname of England with many variants, Paine of the Channel Islands, from Latin *paganus*, Old French *Paien* – villager, rustic, later heathen. Reaney notes: "Lebel explains this as a name given to children whose baptism had been postponed. Dauzat prefers to regard it as a derogatory term applied to adults whose religious zeal was not what it should be." (Reaney, Turk).

Guppy traced Pain(e) and Payne in nineteen counties in the south and Midlands noting that there is no geographical difference between the two principal forms of this name but that Payne is twice as frequent, that Pain and Paine have much the same frequency, and that wherever Payne is common it is associated with Pain and Paine.

In Newfoundland:

Family traditions: Thomas, from England, came to St. John's and worked as a boat builder; he and his three brothers later built a whale factory at Aquaforte (MUN Folklore). Samuel and Matthew, from Yorkshire, settled at Parsons Pond and Chimney Cove (St. Barbe district) respectively (MUN Folklore).

Early instances: William Paine, of Harbour Grace, 1765, property "in possession of the Family for 60 years," that is, 1705 (CO 199.18); Nicholas Pain, of Fogo, Twillingate or Tilton (now Tilting), 1771 (CO 194.30); —— Payne, of St. John's, 1787 (DPHW 23); Thomas, of Placentia, 1794 (D'Alberti 5); Norris and Pain, occupiers of fishing room, Old Perlican, Winter 1800–01 (Census Trinity B.); Thomas Payne, from Teignmouth (Devon), married at St. John's, 1803 (Nfld. Archives BRC); William Pain, of Fogo, 1803, 1805 (D'Alberti 13); James Paine, of Greenspond, 1816 (DPHW 76); Thomas Payne, planter of Salmon Cove (now Champneys), 1823 (DPHW 64B); Charles ? Pain, of Brigus, 1825 (DPHW 34); Elizabeth Payne, of Aquaforte, 1834

(DPHW 26D); James, of Newell's Island (Bonavista B.), 1839 (DPHW 76); James Paine, of Ramea, 1843 (DPHW 101); Charles, of Bonne Bay, 1848 (DPHW 93); ——, from England, of Little or Rocky Harbour (Bonne B.), 1849, resident there since about 1809 (Feild); Francis Payn, granted land at Port aux Basques, 1851 (Nfld. Archives, Registry Crown Lands); James Blagdon Payne, of Burgeo, 1852 (DPHW 101); Peter, of Ferryland, 1854 (*Newfoundlander* 28 Dec 1854); Captain William, from Sheldon (Devon), of St. John's, 1856 (*Newfoundlander* 11 Feb 1856); Philip Payn, of Rose Blanche, 1860 (DPHW 99); W. B. Payne, from Jersey (Channel Islands), came to Burin in 1866 (*Nfld. Quarterly* March 1907); scattered in Lovell 1871.

Modern status: Widespread, especially at Rocky Harbour, Cow Head, Parsons Pond (St. Barbe district), Cox's Cove, Fogo, St. John's and Aquaforte.

Place names: Paine Island (Labrador) 53-24 55-44; Paine's Cove 49-40 54-26; Payne Brook 49-08 57-58; —— Rock 49-43 57-17; Payne's Cove 51-22 56-37, 49-28 57-47; —— Head 49-35 57-56; —— Point 49-29 57-55; —— Cove Rock 51-23 56-37.

PAYNTER, a surname of England, the Cornish form of Painter, from Old French *peinto(u)r*, Anglo-French *peintour* – painter. (Reaney).

Traced by Guppy in Cornwall and Spiegelhalter in Devon.

In Newfoundland:

Early instances: John Painter, servant of Battle Harbour (Labrador), 1795 (MUN Hist.); Hannah Paynter, of Fortune, 1859 (DPHW 106); George Painter, fisherman of Coomb's Cove (Fortune B.), 1871 (Lovell); Thomas, Hare (now Deep) Bay (Fogo district), 1871 (Lovell).

Modern status: Rare, at Horwood and Gander.

Place name: The Painter 49-39 57-59.

PAYTON, a surname of England and Ireland from the English place names Paddon (Devon) or Payton (Herefordshire), or a variant of PATON, PATTEN, PATTON or PEYTON.

Traced by Spiegelhalter in Devon.

In Newfoundland:

Early instance: Richard Pa(y)ton, of Brigus, 1797 (DPHW 48).

Modern status: Rare, at Riverdale (Harbour Main district) (*Electors* 1955) and St. John's.

PEACH, a surname of England from ? the Old English personal name *Pæcci* as in Patchill (Devon), or ? from the French surname *Pêche* – (seller of) peach(es), or ? from Old French *peche* – sin (a nick-name). (Spiegelhalter, Reaney, Dauzat). *See* PAGE.

Traced by Guppy in Dorset and by Spiegelhalter in Devon.

In Newfoundland:

Family tradition: Henry, James and George Page, from England, came to Newfoundland, changed their name to Peach, and settled at Arnold's Cove, Red Harbour and Spencer(s) Cove (Placentia B.), respectively (MUN Folklore).

Early instances: John, of Trinity (Trinity B.), 1805 (DPHW 64); Thomas, planter of Small Point (North Shore Conception B.), 1817 (DPHW 52A); John, from Chippenhow (Dorset), married at St. John's, 1838 (DPHW 26D); Rev. J. S., of Perlican and Hant's Harbour, 1841 (*Newfoundlander* 3 Jun 1841); Thomas, planter of Otterbury (Carbonear), 1845 (DPHW 48); John, of Lower Island Cove, 1859 (DPHW 55); John, fisherman of Spencer's Cove, 1871 (Lovell).

Modern status: Scattered, especially at Flat Island (Placentia West district) (*Electors* 1955) and in the Carbonear Bay de Verde district.

Place name: Peaches Cove 47-40 54-04.

PEAR, a surname of England from Middle English *pere*, Old French *pe(e)r* – peer, paragon, match, companion. (Reaney).

In Newfoundland:

Modern status: At Corner Brook and St. John's.

PEARCE, PIERCE, with several other variants including Pearse, surnames of England and Ireland, from Old French *Piers* – Peter (*see* PETERS). (Reaney, Cottle, MacLysaght).

Guppy found Pearce and Pearse widespread especially in southwest England, with Pearse mostly in Devon and Somerset, and Pierce in North Walues and Sussex; MacLysaght traced Pierce and Pearce mainly in east Leinster.

In Newfoundland:

Family traditions: Charles, of Bird Island Cove (now Elliston), drowned there in 1812, aged 62 (MUN Hist.). Susan (1830–98), of Carbonear (MUN Geog.).

Early instances: Robert and John Peirce or Peirse, of Bay Bulls, 1675, (Robert "12 years an inhabitant in 1680," that is, since 1668, John, "10 years an inhabitant in 1680," that is, since 1670) (CO 1); John Peirce, of St. John's Harbour, 1677 (CO 1); John Pearce, of Twillingate, 1768 (MUN Hist.); Charles, of Bonavista, 1788 (DPHW 70); Andrew, of Fogo, 1800 (D'Alberti 11); Mary Pierce, of Joe Batts Arm, 1817

(Nfld. Archives KCRC); Richard Pierce or Pearce, of Petty Harbour, 1830 (DPHW 31); Joseph Pierce, planter of Western Bay, 1831 (DPHW 52A); Samuel, of Tilton Harbour (now Tilting), 1831 (Nfld. Archives KCRC); Robert Pierce or Pearce, of Catalina, 1838 (DPHW 67); Thomas Pierce, of Fortune, 1839 (DPHW 106; P.E.L. Smith); Andrew Pearce, from Puddletown (Dorset), of Twillingate, died 1841, aged 70 (*Times* ?1 Sep 1841); George Pearce or Pierce, of Old Perlican, 1841 (DPHW 48); William Pierce, of Black Island (Twillingate district), 1843 (DPHW 86); Jasper, from Co. Wexford, of Harbour Grace, 1844 (*Indicator* 27 Jul 1844); James Pearce, Methodist preacher of Hant's Harbour, 1846 (DPHW 59A); John, of Port de Grave, 1852 (DPHW 26D); John Pierce, of Normans Cove, 1858 (DPHW 59A); Edward, fisherman of The Dock (Port de Grave district), 1860 (DPHW 38); scattered in Lovell 1871.

Modern status: Pearce, scattered, especially at Maberly and Neck (Trinity North district) and St. John's; Pierce, scattered, especially at Harbour Breton.

Place names: Pearce Ground 49-42 54-45; —— Harbour 49-35 54-54; —— Head 47-48 54-13; —— Peak 47-17 53-58; —— Rock 49-39 54-46; Pierces Pond 47-48 53-22.

PEARCEY, PIERC(E)Y, surnames of England from Old French *perce-haie* – pierce hedge, in which "hedge" may be the protection around a forest or enclosure or a military work, hence "poacher" or "warrior renowned for forcing his way through fortifications," or a variant of PERCY. (Reaney, Spiegelhalter).

Guppy traced Pearcey and Spiegelhalter, Piercy in Devon.

In Newfoundland:

Family tradition: Henry Piercey, from Northam (Devon), settled at Scilly Cove (now Winterton) in 1792 (MUN Folklore).

Early instances: George Peircy, of St. John's Harbour, 1675 (CO 1); James Pierc(e)y, of Trinity Bay, 1789, occupier of fishing room at Trinity (Trinity B.) and Heart's Content, Winter 1800–01 (DPHW 64, Census Trinity B.); William Pearcey, planter of Brigus, 1797 (D'Alberti 7); Francis Piercey, occupier of fishing room at New Perlican, Winter 1800–01 (Census Trinity B.); Robert, occupier of fishing room at Scilly Cove (now Winterton), Winter 1800–01 (Census Trinity B.); Nathan Pearcey, of Bonavista, 1808 (DPHW 70); Joseph Piercey, Pearsey, or Percey, fisherman of Western Bay, 1827 (DPHW 52A); James Piercey, of Fortune,

1830 (DPHW 109); James Pearcey, planter of Trouty, 1833 (DPHW 64B); William Piercy, planter of Little Catalina, 1844 (DPHW 64B); John, planter of Robin Hood (now part of Port Rexton), 1846 (DPHW 64B); John Piercey, of Jersey Harbour, 1847 (DPHW 106); Joseph Pearcey, of Walters Point (Trinity North district), 1849 (DPHW 64B); Henry, of Bull Cove (Conception B.), 1857 (DPHW 35); scattered in Lovell 1871.

Modern status: Pearcey, at Riverdale (Harbour Main district), Hants Harbour (*Electors* 1955), Point Leamington, Gander and St. John's; Piercey, widespread, especially at Normans Cove, Winterton, Heart's Content, New Perlican, Fortune, Pass Island (Fortune B.), Port Rexton and St. John's; Piercy, scattered.

Place names: Piercey Brook, —— Hill 46-52 55-52; —— Point 46-52 55-53.

PEARL, a surname of England from Old French *perle* – (dealer in) pearl(s). (Reaney).

In Newfoundland:

Early instances: Mary, of Harbour Grace Parish, 1814 (Nfld. Archives HGRC); Sir James (1790–1840), a retired naval officer, given 600 acres of land now known as Mount Pearl, St. John's, between 1825–34 (*Place Names of the Avalon Peninsula* p. 247); Thomas Pearil, fisherman of Bell Isle (now Bell Island) and Lance Cove, 1871 (Lovell).

Modern status: Rare, at Bell Island.

Place names (not necessarily from the surname): Pearl Island 47-39 56-11; —— Island (Labrador), —— River (Labrador) 53-51 59-48; —— Lake (Labrador) 54-16 66-02; Pearl (Big) Island 49-13 58-16; Mount Pearl (St. John's).

PEARSON, PIERSON, surnames of England and Scotland, Pearson of Ireland, – son of *Piers* (Peter). *See* PETERS. (Reaney, Cottle, Black, MacLysaght 73).

Guppy found Pearson widespread in the north and Midlands, with Pierson and Peirson rare in Yorkshire NR and ER; MacLysaght found Pearson in many parts of Ireland.

In Newfoundland:

Early instances: Robert Pearson, of Harbour Grace Parish, 1824 (Nfld. Archives HGRC); John A., from Manchester, married at St. John's, 1845 (*Newfoundlander* 11 Sep 1845); Michael Pierson, ? of Northern Bay, 1857 (DPHW 54)1 John and Thomas Pearson, of Great Paradise (Placentia B.), 1871 (Lovell); George, of Griquet, 1871 (Lovell).

Modern status: Pearson, rare, at Merasheen

(*Electors* 1955), and St. John's; Pierson, at Great Paradise, Petit Forte (Placentia B.) and St. John's.

PEATTIE, PEATY, surnames of England, PEATTIE, Peaddie of Scotland; in England ? variants of Beattie – son of Beatrice; in Scotland ? diminutives of Peat, itself a diminutive of Peter (*see* PETERS), or of Pate, a diminutive of Patrick (*see* PATRICK), or of Batey, a pet-form of *Bate* (Bartholomew) or from the place name Peattie (Kincardineshire, Angus). (Bardsley, Reaney, Black).

Black traced Peattie, Peaddie in Fife.

In Newfoundland:

Early instances: William Peaty, ? of St. John's, 1751 (CO 194.13); —— and family, of St. Lunaire, 1849 (Feild); John, fisherman of Cape Ray, 1871 (Lovell).

Modern status: Peattie, at Glovertown, ? late 1950s; Peaty, rare, at Grand Falls.

PEAVIE, PEAVY, PE(E)VIE, ? Newfoundland variants of the surname of England Pavey, from *Pavia*, a woman's name, ? from Old French *pavie* – peach or *Pavie* – (the woman from) Pavia (Italy). (Reaney).

Guppy traced Pavey in Devon.

In Newfoundland:

Modern status: Peavie, Peavy, Pe(e)vie, at St. Joseph's and Port Anne (Placentia West district) (*Electors* 1955).

PECK, a surname of England, from Old English *pēac* – (dweller by the) peak, hill, or from the English place names Peak Hill, Peek or Peck Hill (Devon), or from Middle English *pekke* – (maker of) peck(s) or vessels used as a peck measure. (Reaney, Spiegelhalter, Gover).

Traced by Guppy in Bedfordshire, Cambridgeshire, Norfolk, Nottinghamshire and Suffolk, and with Peake by Spiegelhalter in Devon.

In Newfoundland:

Early instances: Ann, of Harbour Grace Parish, 1825 (Nfld. Archives HGRC); Susan M., ? of St. John's, 1856 (*Newfoundlander* 10 Apr 1856); Charles and John, fisherman of Cod Roy and Rivers, 1871 (Lovell).

Modern status: Rare, at St. John's (*Electors* 1955).

PECKFORD, ? a variant of the surnames of England PICKFORD, Beckford or BICKFORD.

In Newfoundland:

Early instances: William, occupier of fishing room, Ireland's Eye, Winter 1800–01 (Census Trinity B.); Thomas and John, of Fogo, 1803 (D'Alberti 13); Thomas, of Change Islands, 1832 (M HW 30); Thomas, of Greenspond, 1839 (DPHW 76); Thomas and William Veckford, of Loon Bay, 1871 (Lovell).

Modern status: Scattered, especially at Change Islands.

Place names: Peckford Island 49-33 53-51; ——— Lake (Labrador) 54-50 66-18.

PECKHAM, a surname of England from the English place name Peckham (Kent, Surrey) – (dweller at the) homestead by the hill or peak. (Cottle, Ekwall).

In Newfoundland:

Early instances: William Peckham or Pecham, fisherman of Trinity (Trinity B.), 1763 (DPHW 64); John, of Bonavista, 1792 (USPG); Henry, planter of Salmon Cove (Carbonear district), 1837 (DPHW 48); James, of Greenspond, 1842 (DPHW 76); James, of St. John's, 1857 (DPHW 29); Elias, of Twillingate, 1861 (DPHW 88).

Modern status: Scattered, especially in the Carbonear-Bay de Verde district.

Place name: Peckham Cove (Labrador) 52-36 55-55.

PEDDIGREW, a variant of Pettigrew a surname of England, Scotland and Ireland, from *petit cru* (Old French *petit* – little and *cru* – growth, increase) – a man of little growth, a dwarf. (Reaney, Cottle, Black, MacLysaght).

Pettigrew traced by Spiegelhalter in Devon, by Black especially in Lanarkshire, and by MacLysaght with a variant Petticrew in Belfast and adjacent areas.

In Newfoundland:

Family tradition: ———, from Wales, settled at St. John's (MUN Folklore).

Early instance: Christopher and Martin Pedigrew, of St. John's, 1871 (Lovell).

Modern status: At St. John's.

PEDDLE, a surname of England and of Jersey (Channel Islands), a variant of Peddell, from the English place names Peadhill, Pethill, Pithil (Devon), or ? Pedwell (Somerset), or ? Piddle (Dorset), a river which gave its name as Piddle or Puddle to several places, or ? Bedwell (Essex, Hertfordshire), or ? Bidwell (Northamptonshire, Bedfordshire, Devon, Somerset), or a variant of Beadle, Bedle, etc., from Old English *bydel* – beadle. (Bardsley, Reaney, Spiegelhalter, Ekwall, Turk).

Spiegelhalter traced Peddell in Devon.

In Newfoundland:

Family traditions: Peter, from Wales, settled at Bishop's Cove (Conception B.), about 1820 (MUN Folklore). John, from Portsmouth, England, settled at Bloomfield about 1870 (MUN Folklore).

Early instances: Francis Piddle, of Bread and Cheese (now Bishop's) Cove, 1775 (CO 199.18); William Piddle or Peddle, of (Upper) Island Cove, 1780, of Harbour Grace, 1805 (D'Alberti 15, CO 199.18); Samuel Piddle, of Musketta (now Bristol's Hope), 1785 (CO 199.18); Piddle and Weatheral, occupiers of fishing room at Trinity (Trinity B.), Winter 1800–01 (Census Trinity B.); Samuel, of Bryants Cove, 1802 (CO 199.18); William, of Green Head (Spaniards B.), 1803 (CO 199.18); John Peddle, in possession of property on Holyrood Island between St. Mary's and Trepassey, 1808 (D'Alberti 18); William Piddle or Peddle, of Brigus, 1810 (DPHW 34); Edward Piddle, of Carbonear, 1814 (DPHW 48); John Peddle, of St. Mary's, 1816 (Nfld. Archives BRC); John, of Keels, 1822 (DPHW 70); John Poddle, of Bulls Cove (Conception B.), 1831 (DPHW 34); John Piddel, of Cattle (for Castle) Cove (Bonavista B.), 1831 (DPHW 76); Thomas Piddle or Riddle, planter of Mulleys Cove, 1832 (DPHW 52A); Tabitha Peddle, of Hants Harbour, 1834 (DPHW 59); Edward, planter of Seal Cove (now New Chelsea), 1839 (DPHW 59A); Francis, of King's Cove Parish, 1842 (Nfld. Archives KCRC); William Piddle or Peddle, of Leading Tickles, 1849 (DPHW 86); Job Peddle, fisherman of New (now Parsons) Harbour, 1849 (DPHW 102); John, of Chance Cove, 1862 (DPHW 62); James Piddle, of Gulleys (Conception B.), 1871 (Lovell); Henry, of New Perlican, 1871 (Lovell); George, of Pearce's Harbour (Twillingate district), 1871 (Lovell); Michael Peddle, fisherman of Salmonier (St. Mary's B.), 1871 (Lovell); Robert Peadle, of Gaskin (Point La Hays), 1871 (Lovell).

Modern status: Widespread, especially at Harbour Grace, Corner Brook, Hodges Cove, Port Blandford, Bishop's Cove and St. John's.

Place names: Peddles Pond 47-35 53-23; ——— Waters 47-21 53-25.

PEET, a variant of the surname of England and Scotland Peat, a diminutive of Peter. *See* PETERS. (Spiegelhalter, Black).

Guppy traced Peet in Lancashire and Nottinghamshire, Peat in Derbyshire; Spiegelhalter traced Peate, Peatt in Devon.

In Newfoundland:

Family tradition: ——, from Cape Breton Island, settled at St. John's in the twentieth century (MUN Folklore).

Early instance: William, of St. John's, 1846 (DPHW 23).

Modern status: At St. John's.

PE(E)VIE. *See* PEAVIE

PELL(E)Y, surnames of England, PELLY of Ireland, (Le) Pelley of Guernsey (Channel Islands), from Old French *pele*, Modern French *pelé* – bald, or a diminutive of *Pell*, a pet-form of Peter (*see* PETERS), or from Old French *pel* – (dealer in) skin(s), or ? a variant of the surname Pilley from the English place name Pilley (Hampshire, Yorkshire WR). (Reaney, Turk).

Pelly traced by Spiegelhalter in Devon and by MacLysaght mainly in Cos. Galway and Roscommon.

In Newfoundland:

Family traditions: —— Pelley, from the west country of England, father of John (1816–1903), settled in Hants Harbour in the early 1800s (MUN Folklore). —— Pilly, from Dorset, settled in Twillingate in the early 1800s (*Nfld. Quarterly* Dec 1905).

Early instances: William Jr. ? Pelly, of Harbour Grace, 1792 (USPG); James Pelley, of Carbonear, 1793 (CO 199.18); Mark Pelly, of St. John's, 1798 (DPHW 26B); James, proprietor and occupier of fishing room, Hant's Harbour, Winter 1800–01 (Census Trinity B.); Arch, fisherman of Jersey Harbour, 1818 (DPHW 109); John, of Old Perlican, 1822 (DPHW 58); George, of Fogo, 1842 (DPHW 83); John Pilley, of Brook Cove (Trinity B.), 1846 (DPHW 59A); Thomas, fisherman of Fox Harbour (? Trinity B.), 1850 (DPHW 59A); Job, granted land at Deep Bight, Random Sound, 1856, on Random Island, 1858 (Nfld. Archives, Registry Crown Lands); Joseph Pelly, of Shoal Bay (Fogo district), 1858 (DPHW 83); Josiah, of Black Island (Exploits district), 1859 (DPHW 92); Joseph (and others), of Broad Cove (Trinity B.) (now Somerset), 1871 (Lovell); John, of Change Islands, 1871 (Lovell); George and Joseph, of Eastern Tickle, 1871 (Lovell); Charles Pelly, of Twillingate, 1871 (Lovell); George and John Pilly, of Exploits Burnt Island, 1871 (Lovell).

Modern status: Pelley, scattered, especially at Somerset, Bishop's Falls and St. John's; Pelly, rare, at Dover and Cormack (*Electors* 1955).

Place names: Pelleys Brook 48-31 58-26; Pelly Ground 49-33 55-01.

PENDER, a surname of England, Scotland and Ireland, in England from Old English *(ge)pyndan* – to impound, hence an impounder (of stray animals); in Ireland a shortened form of PENDERGAST. (Reaney, Cottle, MacLysaght).

Guppy traced Pender in Cornwall and Pinder in Lincolnshire and Nottinghamshire with Pindar a rare Lincolnshire form. Spiegelhalter traced Pender and Pinder in Devon.

In Newfoundland:

Early instances: Richard Pinder, of Bonavista, 1791 (USPG); Elenor Pender, of St. John's, 1807 (Nfld. Archives BRC); John, of Harbour Grace Parish, 1831 (Nfld. Archives HGRC); Patrick Pindar, of Harbour Grace, 1866 (Nfld. Archives HGRC).

Modern status: At Marquise (*Electors* 1955), Corner Brook and St. John's.

PENDERGAST, a surname of England and Ireland and recorded in Scotland by Black, from the Welsh place name Prendergast (Pembrokeshire), ? – castle village. (Cottle, Black, MacLysaght).

Traced by Spiegelhalter in Devon and by MacLysaght especially in Cos. Mayo and Tipperary.

In Newfoundland:

Early instances: William Pendergrast, publican of St. John's, 1794–5, "30 years in Newfoundland," that is, 1764–5 (Census 1794–5); William Pendergrass, of Petty Harbour, 1776 (DPHW 26C); William Pendergrast, in possession of property and shoreman of Quidi Vidi, 1794–5, "14 years in Newfoundland," that is, 1780–1 (Census 1794–5); Michael Pendergast, from Dublin, Irish convict landed at Petty Harbour or Bay Bulls, 1789 (CO 194.38); Thomas, from Suttons Parish (Co. Wexford), married at St. John's, 1793 (Nfld. Archives BRC); Ann Pendergrast, of Lower Island Cove, 1796 (CO 199.18); Mary Pendergast, of Harbour Grace Parish, 1806 (Nfld. Archives HGRC); William Prendergast, from Co. Wexford, cooper of St. John's, died 1812 (*Royal Gazette* 14 May 1812); James Pendergast, of King's Cove, 1816 (Nfld. Archives KCRC); William, of Ragged Harbour (now Melrose), 1817 (Nfld. Archives KCRC); James Prendergast, of Harbour Grace, 1830 (Nfld. Archives HGRC); James L., of Carbonear, 1837 (*Newfoundlander* 18 May 1837); Catherine, from Co. Kilkenny, of Brigus, 1844 (*Indicator* 24 Aug 1844); Sarah Ann Perdergoss, of Hants Harbour, 1848 (DPHW 59); Edward Prendergast, granted land at Admirals Cove (north side of Cape Broyle), 1857 (Nfld. Archives, Registry Crown Lands); William Prendergrast, of Cupids, 1871 (Lovell); Peter, of Holyrood, 1871 (Lovell);

Matthew, farmer of Logy Bay, 1871 (Lovell); Michael, farmer of Salmon Cove and Gasters (Conception B.), 1871 (Lovell); Philip Prendergrass, of Barren Island (now Bar Haven), 1871 (Lovell).

Modern status: Scattered in the east coast districts.

PENNELL, a surname of England and Jersey (Channel Islands), from the English place names Penn Hall (Worcestershire) or Penhill (Devon, Yorkshire NR), or a variant of PARNELL, PENWELL or PINEL. (Reaney, Baring-Gould, Turk).

Traced by Spiegelhalter in Devon.

In Newfoundland:

Family tradition: Lovell, from Topsham (Devon), established a business at Trepassey in the 1750s or 1760s (Nemec).

Early instances: David and Danile [sic], merchants of Trepassey, 1797 (CO 194.39); Thomas, of Renews before 1798 (D'Alberti 8); Thomas Pennel, of Harbour Grace Parish, 1812 (Nfld. Archives HGRC); John, of Western Bay, 1828 (DPHW 52A); John Pennel(l), of Ochre Pit Cove, 1829 (DPHW 52A); Clement Pennell, of St. George's Harbour (St. George's B.), 1830 (DPHW 30); John Pennel, of St. George's Bay, 1835 (DPHW 30); Thomas Pennell, farmer of Chapel's Cove, 1871 (Lovell); John (and others), of Harbour Main, 1871 (Lovell); Henry, clerk of St. John's, 1871 (Lovell).

Modern status: Scattered, especially at Daniel's Point (Ferryland district), Curling, Carmanville and St. John's.

Place name: Pennell Shoal 47-31 55-00.

PENN(E)Y, surnames of England, Scotland, Ireland and Guernsey (Channel Islands), from Old English *peni(n)g* – penny, a nickname from the coin, or a personal name *Pening*, or from the English place name Penny Hill Farm (Devon). (Reaney, Spiegelhalter, Turk).

Penn(e)y traced by Spiegelhalter in Devon, Penny by Guppy in Hampshire and Somerset, and by MacLysaght in Dublin as early as 1296 and comparatively recently in Co. Cork.

In Newfoundland:

Family traditions: —— Penn(e)y, from Devon, settled at Carbonear in 1690 (MUN Folklore). Oliver Penney or Pinney (1769–1818), from Jersey (Channel Islands), settled at Carbonear in the 1790s and shortly afterwards moved to Western Bay (MUN Folklore). Elizabeth (1792–1871), of Carbonear (MUN Geog.). Three brothers, from Devon or Cornwall, came to Newfoundland, two settled at English Harbour (Trinity B.) and the third at Indian Islands (MUN Folklore). John Penny, from England, came to Ramea as apprentice to Newman & Co. in 1865; about 1872, he established his own business there (MUN Hist.).

Early instances: Benedict Penny, of Carbonear, 1770, property "in possession of the Family for upwards of 71 years," that is, before 1699 (CO 199.18); Richard Pen(n)y, of St. John's, 1705 (CO 194.22); Margaret Penny, of Bay Bulls, 1751 (Mannion); Hugh, of Freshwater (Carbonear), 1761 (CO 199.18); Thomas, of Harbour Main, 1766 (CO 199.18); William Peney, of Trinity Bay, 1780 (DPHW 64); William Penny, of Burin, 1780 (D'Alberti 1); Pinney and Frampton, of St. Mary's, 1782 (D'Alberti 2); William Pinney or Penney, of English Harbour (Trinity B.), 1785 (DPHW 64); Hugh Penny, of Brigus, 1790 (CO 199.18); John Penney, servant of Battle Harbour, 1795 (MUN Hist.); John Penney, of Clowns Cove (Carbonear), 1796 (CO 199.18); Oliver, of Western Bay, 1797 (CO 199.18); Thomas, of Chapels Cove, 1800 (CO 199.18); Mary, of Harbour Grace Parish, 1806 (Nfld. Archives HGRC); Clements Penn(e)y, planter of Blow-me-down (Carbonear), 1816, of Otterbury (Carbonear), 1846 (DPHW 48); Solomon, of Bull Cove (Conception B.), 1823 (DPHW 34); William Penny, of Gooseberry Cove (Carbonear), 1829 (DPHW 48); William, of Cattle (for Castle) Cove (Bonavista B.), 1831 (DPHW 76); Edward, from Ashburton (Devon), of St. John's, 1834 (DPHW 26D); George Penn(e)y, of Keels, 1836 (DPHW 73A); Richard Penney, merchant of Poole (Dorset), and Little Placentia (now Argentia), 1836 (Nfld. Archives *Prelim. Inventory* p. 46); William Penny, planter of Flat Rock (Carbonear), 1836 (DPHW 48); Charles, of Ward's Harbour (now Beaumont North), 1845 (DPHW 86); John, of Tickle Cove (Bonavista B.), 1845 (DPHW 73A); Edward, of Fortune, 1845 (Grand Bank Methodist baptisms 1845, P.E.L. Smith); Isaac, of Long Island (Bonavista B.), 1846 (DPHW 73A); ——, on the *John* in the seal fishery out of Harbour Grace, 1847 (*Newfoundlander* 25 Mar 1847); Charles, granted land at Salmon Cove (now Champneys), 1851 (Nfld. Archives, Registry Crown Lands); Henry, of Seldom Come By, 1855 (DPHW 92); Richard, of Scilly Cove (now Winterton), 1857 (DPHW 59A); Samuel, of Burgeo, 1858 (DPHW 101); Charles, of Indian Islands (Fogo district), 1858 (DPHW 83); Ambrose, fisherman of Salmon Cove (Carbonear), 1859 (DPHW 49); Richard Pinney, of Pease Cove (Trinity B.), 1870 (DPHW 65); widespread in Lovell, 1871.

Modern status: Penney, widespread, especially at

St. John's, Carbonear, Salmon Cove (Carbonear), Holyrood, Corner Brook, English Harbour (Trinity B.), and Canning's Cove; Penny, scattered.

Place names: Penny Brook 47-51 56-10; —— Cove 49-59 56-08; —— Harbour (Labrador) 53-09 55-46; —— Hill 46-52 55-50; —— Hills, —— Point 49-51 56-34; —— Island (Labrador) 51-44 56-25; —— Rock 49-45 54-19; —— Hook Cove (Labrador) 53-29 55-48; Pennys Brook 49-23 55-42; —— Pond 47-16 53-16.

PENSTON, a surname of Scotland from the Scots place name Penston (East Lothian, otherwise Haddington). (Black).
In Newfoundland:
Modern status: Rare, at St. John's.

PENTON, a surname of Scotland from the Scots place name Penton (Dumfriesshire) (pronounced Pentón), or of England, though apparently not recorded elsewhere, from the English place name Penton (Hampshire), or ? a shortened form of the English surname Pennington from Pennington (Hampshire, Lancashire), probably a farm paying a penny rent. (Cottle, Ekwall). *See also* PEYTON.
In Newfoundland:
Family tradition: —— Peyton, settled in Joe Batts Arm between 1869–84; the name was later changed to Penton (MUN Hist.).
Early instance: Ann Penton or Pinton, of Joe Batts Arm, 1823 (Nfld. Archives KCRC).
Modern status: Scattered, especially at Joe Batts Arm.

PENWELL, PENWILL, surnames of England, ? from an unidentified place name in Devon, or ? a variant of PENNELL.
Traced in Devon (Devonshire Assoc. Vol. LVIII).
In Newfoundland:
Family tradition: William Penwill or Pennell (1800–1850), from England, came to Harbour Breton to work with Newman & Co.; some of the family later settled at Grand Bank (MUN Hist.).
Early instance: William Penwell or Penwill, of Grand Bank, 1841, 1871 (DPHW 109, Lovell).
Modern status: Penwell, Penwill, rare, at Grand Bank.

PEPPER, a surname of England and Ireland, in England from Old English *pipor* – (dealer in) pepper, spices; in Ireland a synonym of Peppard, "A Norman family identified with Co. Louth from 1185." (Reaney, Cottle, MacLysaght).

Traced by Guppy in Leicestershire, Rutlandshire, Lincolnshire and Suffolk, and by Spiegelhalter in Devon. MacLysaght traced Peppard (and presumably Pepper) in Cos. Louth and Wexford.
In Newfoundland:
Family Tradition: Robert, from Wexford, died at Bay Roberts, 1861, aged 75 years. (R.D. Pepper).
Early instances: Peter, of Harbour Grace, 1792 (USPG); Robert, of St. John's, 1827 (DPHW 26B).
Modern status: Rare, at Bay Roberts and Portugal Cove.

PERC(E)Y, surnames of England, PERCY of Scotland from the French place name Percy (La Manche, Calvados), or ? a variant of PEARC(E)Y. (Reaney, Cottle).
Spiegelhalter traced Percy in Devon.
Early instances: William Percey, of Brigus, 1770, property "in possession of the Family for 120 years or upwards," that is, before 1650 (CO 199.18); Joseph, of Western Bay, 1786 (CO 199.18); Jasper Percy, planter of Trouty, 1822 (DPHW 64); John, of Keels, 1830 (DPHW 70); ——, on the *St. John's* in the seal fishery out of Port de Grave, 1838 (*Newfoundlander* 29 Mar 1838); George, fisherman of Pass Island (Fortune B.), 1848 (DPHW 102); Stephen, of St. John's, 1857 (*Nfld. Almanac*); Joseph, of Trinity (Trinity B.), 1871 (Lovell); Caroline Percy, schoolteacher of Horse Cove (now St. Thomas), 1871 (Lovell).
Modern status: Percey, at Spruce Brook (St. George's district) (*Electors* 1955), Brigus and St. John's; Percy, scattered, especially at Brigus.

PERCHARD, a surname of Jersey and Guernsey (Channel Islands), ? a variant of the surname of France Perchaud, ? for one who cut or used poles, or was as thin as a pole, or for a surveyor. (Dauzat, Turk). *See also* PASHA, PASHER.
In Newfoundland:
Early instances: Richard, of St. John's, 1792 (DPHW 26D); John, from Island of Jersey, of Bay Roberts, 1792, deceased 1810 (CO 199.18, *Royal Gazette* 29 Nov 1810); Charles, planter of Trinity (Trinity B.), 1825 (DPHW 64B); Mary, from Dartmouth, England, of Newfoundland, died 1839, aged 70 "resided in Newfoundland for 50 years," that is, since 1789 (*Royal Gazette* 28 May 1839).
Modern status: At St. John's.

PERCIVAL, a surname of England from Old French *percer* – to pierce and *val* – valley (Reaney notes that such names were not uncommon in France), or from the French place name Perceval (Calvados), or from a French baptismal name *Perceval*, after a hero of Breton romances. (Reaney, Cottle, Dauzat).

Traced by Guppy in Cheshire, Derbyshire and Northamptonshire.

In Newfoundland:

Modern status: Rare, at St. John's.

PERCY. *See* PERC(E)Y

PERFECT, a surname of England, a late form ("a pedantic Latinized respelling") of Parfait, from Latin *perfectus*, Old French *parf(e)it*, Middle English *perfit*, *parfit* – perfect. (Reaney, Cottle).

Spiegelhalter traced Perfect and Parfitt in Devon.

In Newfoundland:

Family tradition: William, from Bathurst (Sussex), settled at Ochre Pit Cove about 1830–1840; his brother settled in Western Bay (MUN Folklore).

Early instances: Richard, of St. John's, 1756 (DPHW 26C); Samuel, mason of Western Bay, 1821 (DPHW 52A); William, planter of Ochre Pit Cove, 1849 (DPHW 52A).

Modern status: Rare, at St. John's.

PERHAM, a surname of England from the English place names Perham (Wiltshire) or Parham (Suffolk). (Spiegelhalter). *See also* PERRAN.

Traced by Guppy in Somerset and by Spiegelhalter in Devon.

In Newfoundland:

Family tradition: ——, from Placentia B., early settler of Pool's Cove (Fortune B.) (MUN Hist.).

Early instances: Robert Perram or Perrim, of St. John's, 1802, 1809 (DPHW 26D, CO 194.50); —— Perham, from Dorset, of Red Bay, Straits of Belle Isle, 1849 (Feild); James, of Burin, 1871 (Lovell); James, of Bay du Nord (Fortune B.), 1871 (DPHW 103); Robert, fisherman of Savage Cove (St. Barbe district), 1873 (DPHW 95).

Modern status: At Bar Haven (*Electors* 1955) and in the Fortune Bay-Hermitage district, especially at Pool's Cove.

PERIERA, a misspelling of the surname of Spain and Portugal Pereira – (owner of or dweller by the) pear tree.

In Newfoundland:

Modern status: Rare, at Burin Bay (Burin district).

PERKS, a surname of England, a contraction of Perkins, a diminutive of Piers (Peter). *See* PETERS. (Cottle). *See also* PARKINS.

Traced by Guppy in Warwickshire and Worcestershire and by Spiegelhalter in Devon.

In Newfoundland:

Early instance: Henry, of Trinity (unspecified), 1889 (Nfld. Archives KCRC).

Modern status: At Flat Bay (St. George's district) (*Electors* 1955), Corner Brook and St. John's.

PERLIN, a surname of Russia, from Perle – pearl, the Yiddish equivalent of Margólin from the Greek *margarites*, Latin *margarita* – pearl, used as a woman's name. (Unbegaun).

In Newfoundland:

Early instance: Israel (1871–), born in Russia, came to Newfoundland from the United States in 1891 and established business in St. John's (*Nfld. Who's Who* 1930).

Modern status: At St. John's.

PERRAN, a surname of England from the English place names Perranarworthal, Perran Uthnoe or Perranzabuloe (Cornwall), named after St. Peran. (Ekwall). *See also* PERHAM.

In Newfoundland:

Modern status: Rare, at St. John's.

PERRETT, a surname of England, Perret and Perrot of France, Perrot of Ireland and Guernsey (Channel Islands), like PARROTT, diminutives of P(i)erre – Peter (*see* PETERS), or also in England from the English place name Perrott (Dorset, Somerset). (Reaney, MacLysaght, Spiegelhalter, Turk).

Guppy traced Perrett and Perrott in Dorset, Monmouthshire, Somerset and Wiltshire, with Perrett the more usual form though the two are usually associated. Spiegelhalter traced both forms in Devon. MacLysaght traced Perrot mainly in Co. Cork.

In Newfoundland:

Early instances: James Perritt, of Greenspond, 1776 (CO 194.33); John Perret, fisherman of Bay of Islands, 1875 (DPHW 95).

Modern status: Rare, at Mount Moriah (Corner Brook).

Place names: Perret Bight, Perret's Point (Labrador) 55-06 59-10; Perrett Tickle (Labrador) 56-09 61-15.

PERRIER, a surname of England, France and Jersey (Channel Islands), from Old French *perrie(u)r* – quarrier, or in England from Old English *pirige* – (owner of or dweller by the) pear tree, or ? a variant of POIRIER. (Reaney, Dauzat, Turk).

In Newfoundland:

Early instance: Dominick and Simon, fishermen of Sandy Point (St. George's B.), 1871 (Lovell).

Modern status: At Buchans and in the St. George's district especially at St. George's.

PERRIN, a surname of England, France and the Channel Islands, a diminutive of P(i)erre (Peter). *See* PETERS. (Reaney, Cottle, Dauzat, Turk).

Traced by Guppy in Devon.

In Newfoundland:

Early instances: Barrington, of St. John's, 1806 (CO 194.45); John, of Long Pond (? Manuels), 1832 (DPHW 30); James, fisherman of Turnip Cove (Fortune B.), 1871 (Lovell).

Modern status: At Long Pond, Manuels.

PERRY, a surname of England, Ireland, France and the Channel Islands, in England from Old English *pirige* – (owner of or dweller by the) pear tree, or a variant of PARRY; in France from the place name Perry (Aude, Charente, etc.). (Reaney, Cottle, Dauzat, Turk).

Traced by Guppy in the Midlands and southwest of England, and by MacLysaght mainly in Ulster but also elsewhere in Ireland.

In Newfoundland:

Family traditions: William, from England, settled at Indian Islands (? Fogo district) before 1848 (MUN Folklore). ——, from Channel Islands, settled at Fogo in the late 1700s (MUN Folklore). Three brothers, from Devon or Cornwall were early settlers at Harbour Grace, Cape Freels and Fogo respectively (MUN Folklore).

Early instances: John, ? of Little Placentia (now Argentia) "wronged by Samuel Adams" about 1730–5 (CO 194.9); Noah, of Western Bay, 1760 (CO 199.18); John, publican of St. John's, 1794–5, "22 years in Newfoundland," that is, 1772–5 (Census 1794–5); John, of Northern Bay, 1802 (CO 199.18); Jane, of Harbour Grace Parish, 1809 (Nfld. Archives HGRC); Henry, born ? 1843, servant, of Sherborne (Dorset), in Harbour Breton 1863, married there 1874 (Harbour Breton Anglican Church Records per D.A. Macdonald); Charles, of Exploits Burnt Island, 1843 (DPHW 86); Philip, planter of Perry's Cove, 1843 (DPHW 52A); ——, on the *Success* in the seal fishery out of Harbour Grace and Carbonear, 1849 (*Newfoundlander* 22 Mar 1849); Charles, of Ward's Harbour (now Beaumont North), 1851, of Cutman (? Cutwell) Arm, 1856 (DPHW 86); Nicholas, fisherman of Seldom Come By, 1851, of Indian Island (Fogo district), 1856 (DPHW 83); William, of Broad Cove (Bay de Verde district), 1851 (DPHW 52B);

Benjamin, of Pinchards Island, 1852 (DPHW 76); Jane, of Harbour Grace, 1857 (*Newfoundlander* 10 Dec 1857); Isaac John, of Catalina, 1866 (DPHW 66); Joseph, planter of Cape Race, 1871 (Lovell); Joseph, of Gooseberry Islands (Bonavista B.), 1871 (Lovell); Francis, telegraph operator of Heart's Content, 1871 (Lovell); Thomas, of Inner Islands (Bonavista B.), 1871 (Lovell); John, of Musgravetown, 1871 (Lovell); Nicholas and Philip Perrey, of Stocking Harbour (Green B.), 1871 (Lovell).

Modern status: Widespread, especially at St. John's and Daniel's Harbour.

Place names: Perry Cove 48-26 53-43; —— Point 49-31 55-04; Perry's Bight 49-32 54-16; —— Cove 47-48 53-09; —— Gulch (Labrador) 57-09 61-27; —— Point 49-12 53-31.

PETERMAN, a surname of England – servant of Peter. *See* PETERS. (Bardsley).

In Newfoundland:

Modern status: Unique, at St. John's.

PETERS, a surname of England, Wales, Scotland and Ireland, Peter of England and Scotland, from the baptismal name Peter, Latin *Petrus*, from the Greek – rock, a translation of the Aramaic *Cephas*, the name given by Jesus to Simon, son of Jonas. "St. *Peter* appealed to the imagination of the medieval Church more than any other of the apostles ... and his name was one of the commonest christian names in every country. It was introduced into England by the Normans and soon became a favourite. The usual form was the French *Piers,* which gave rise to numerous surnames." They include PARKINS(ON), PARRELL, PARROTT, PARRY, PEARCE, PIERCE, PEARSON, PIERSON, PEET, PELL(E)Y, PERKS, PERRETT, ? PERRAN, PERRIN, PETERMAN, PETER(S), PETERSON. In Ireland, Mac Feeters, *Mac Pheadair* – son of Peter, is often translated PETERS(ON). (Withycombe, Reaney, Cottle, Black, MacLysaght).

Traced by Guppy in Cornwall, Somerset and North Wales with Peter also in Cornwall, and by MacLysaght in Cos. Tyrone and Derry. Black traced Peter in Angus, Aberdeenshire and Kincardineshire.

In Newfoundland:

Family tradition: J., from England, was magistrate at Harbour Grace about 1812; the family later moved to St. John's (MUN Folklore).

Early instances: Richard, of St. John's, killed by the French, ? 1705 (CO 194.22): Mary, from Tipperary Parish, married at St. John's, 1808 (Nfld. Archives BRC); Philip, of Ragged Harbour (now Melrose), 1815 (Nfld. Archives KCRC); Joseph, of

Harbour Grace, 1821 (D'Alberti 31); Joseph, merchant of Broad Cove (Bay de Verde district), 1824 (DPHW 52A); Joseph, schoolmaster of Carbonear, 1839 (DPHW 48); George Henry, of Lower Burgeo, 1860 (DPHW 101); John, cooper of Gaultois, 1871 (Lovell); Philip, fisherman of Rogues Harbour (Green B.), 1871 (Lovell).

Modern status: Scattered, especially at St. John's.

Place names (not necessarily from the surname): Peters Arm (or Peterview), —— —— South, 49-07 55-20; —— Brook 46-53 55-52; —— (or Peterel) Islands 52-04 55-42; —— Point (Labrador) 54-07 58-26; —— Pond 49-05 55-26; Peters (or Fosters) Pond 49-43 54-17; —— River 46-46 53-37; ——, —— Arm Brook 49-07 55-22.

PETERSON, a surname of England, Wales and Ireland – son of Peter; in Ireland, with PETERS, a translation of MacFeeter. *See* PETERS. (Withycombe, Cottle, MacLysaght).

Traced by Withycombe in Wales and by MacLysaght in Cos. Tyrone and Derry.

In Newfoundland:

Early instances: Mary, of Ferryland, 1804 (Nfld. Archives BRC); William, of Harbour Grace Parish, 1819 (Nfld. Archives HGRC); Hans Petersen, of St. John's, 1861 (DPHW 26D).

Modern status: Rare, at Main Brook (White B.) (*Electors* 1955), St. John's and Botwood.

PETIPAS, a surname of England, Petitpas of France and Jersey (Channel Islands), from the French place name Petitpas (Loire-Inférieure, etc.) – little passage, or for one who took little steps when walking. A lost place name of Devon Pettypace, said, however, to survive as a field name, "is to be associated with the family of William Petitpas, who flourished about 1249." (Bardsley, Dauzat, Gover).

In Newfoundland:

Family tradition: ——, ship carpenter from Quebec, worked on the construction of the Reid Newfoundland Railroad; he was the first settler of Whitbourne (MUN Folklore).

Early instances: Montford Petitpas, of Humber Arm, Bay of Islands, 1871 (MUN. Hist.); Mansfield Petipas, of Harbour Grace Junction, 1890 (Nfld. Archives HGRC); Catherine, of Whitbourne, 1891 (Nfld. Archives HGRC).

Modern status: At Whitbourne.

Place names: Petitpas (or Pettitpas) Cove, Petitpas Point 48-59 57-59.

PETITE, a surname of France, Petit(t) etc. of England and Ireland, – short (Bardsley, Dauzat, MacLysaght).

Guppy traced Petit(t) in Bedfordshire, Essex, Kent, Suffolk and Sussex; Spiegelhalter traced Pettitt in Devon. MacLysaght traced Pet(t)it(t) in Co. Meath.

In Newfoundland:

Early instances: Noel Petit or Pessit, of Connaigre, 1710–15, of Cap Nigro (Connaigre), 1714 (CO 194.5, 6); John and Levent Petit, of Pass Island, 1765 (CO 194.16); Jeremiah Petite, of St. Jacques, 1856 (DPHW 104); Jeremiah, of Grole, 1857 (DPHW 104); Jeremiah and William, of Mose Ambrose, 1871 (Lovell).

Modern status: At Mose Ambrose, Belleoram (*Electors* 1955), English Harbour West and Channel.

Place name: Petites 47-37 58-38.

PETLEY, a surname of England, from the English place name Pitley (Devon). (Spiegelhalter).

Traced by Spiegelhalter in Devon.

In Newfoundland:

Early instance: Rev. Henry, of Hearts Content, 1857 (*Newfoundlander* 8 Oct 1857).

Modern status: Rare, at Curling (*Electors* 1955), and St. John's.

Place names: Petley, —— Rock 48-09 53-45; Petleys Pond 48-52 58-23.

PETRIE, a surname of Scotland, a diminutive of Peter (*see* PETERS) or of Patrick (*see* PATRICK). (Black). *See also* PATRY.

In Newfoundland:

Early instance: Alexander, of Bay of Islands district, 1877 (DPHW 96).

Modern status: At St. John's, Bell Island, Grand Falls and Gander.

Place names: Petries, Petrie(s) Brook, Petries Point 48-58 58-01.

PETTEN, ? a variant of the surname of England Petton, from the English place name Petton (Devon, Shropshire).

Spiegelhalter traced Petton in Devon.

In Newfoundland:

Early instances: Edward Pettin or Petten, of New Perlican, 1681, 2 (CO 1); John Petten, of Brigus, 1708–9 (CO 194.4); Edward, of Harbour Grace, 1708–9 (CO 194.4); William Petton, of Bay Roberts, 1765 (CO 199.18); Edward, of Hibbs Hole, 1781 (CO 199.18); William, of Port de Grave, 1793 (CO

199.18); George Petten, of St. John's, 1796 (CO 194.39); John Petten or Petton, of Middle Bight (now Codner), 1832 (DPHW 30); Edward Petton, of Southern Shore (Conception B.), 1840 (DPHW 30); William Petten, of Flat Islands (Bonavista B.), 1851 (DPHW 83A); John and Nathaniel, of Foxtrap, 1871 (Lovell).

Modern status: Scattered, especially at Pick Eyes (Port de Grave district), Foxtrap and Codner.

PEVIE. *See* PEAVIE

PEYTON, a surname of England and Ireland, in England ? from the English place names Peyton (Essex, Suffolk) or Petton (Devon, Shropshire), or a variant of PATON, PATTEN, PATTON or PAYTON; in Ireland, with PAYTON and PATTON, an anglicized form of *Ó Peotáin*, ? a diminutive of Patrick (*see* PATRICK). (Bardsley, Ekwall, MacLysaght). *See also* PENTON.

Traced by Matthews in Hampshire and by MacLysaght especially in Donegal.

In Newfoundland:

Family tradition: John Sr., from ? Wimbourne, Christchurch, Hampshire, settled in Fogo, then Exploits; John Jr. joined him at Exploits about 1812 but later moved to Twillingate; some of his descendants settled at Grand Falls and Gander (MUN Folklore).

Early instances: John Jr., of Bay of Exploits, 1818 (D'Alberti 28); John, of Fogo, 1837 (*Newfoundlander* 20 Apr 1837); Edward, of Port de Grave, 1838 (DPHW 26D); John, granted land between Back Harbour and Front Harbour, Twillingate, 1841 (Nfld. Archives, Registry Crown Lands); Thomas, of Barr'd Islands, 1871 (Lovell); Henry, of Seal Cove and Indian Pond (Conception B.), 1871 (Lovell); Thomas, of Seldom-Come-By, 1871 (Lovell).

Modern status: Scattered, especially at Botwood.

Place names: Mount Peyton 48-57 55-06; —— Point 47-47 55-49; Peytons Brook 47-20 52-56; —— Gullies 47-22 53-19; —— Pond 47-21 52-56, 47-44 52-45.

PHAIR, a surname of England and Ireland; in England from Old English *fæger* – fair, beautiful, used occasionally as a personal name; in Ireland a translation of *fionn* – fair. (Reaney, MacLysaght).

Found scattered but not numerous in Ireland by MacLysaght.

In Newfoundland:

Modern status: Rare, at Windsor.

PHELAN, a surname of Ireland (O)Phelan, *Ó Faoláin*, Ir. *faol* – wolf. (MacLysaght).

Traced by MacLysaght in Cos. Kilkenny and Waterford.

In Newfoundland:

Early instances: James, ? of St. John's, 1779 (CO 194.34); David, of Northern Cove (Conception B.), 1785 (CO 199.18); Father, of Harbour Grace, 1786 (CO 194.36); Patrick, of Bay de Verde, 1797 (CO 199.18); William, of Brigus, 1802 (CO 199.18); Walter, of Brigus, 1802, in possession of property at Cupids (CO 199.18); Luke, of Trinity (Trinity B.), 1803 (DPHW 64); Richard, from Mothel (unidentified) (Co. Waterford), married at St. John's, 1806 (Nfld. Archives BRC); Tabita, of Broad Cove (Bay de Verde district), 1806 (Nfld. Archives BRC); John, of Ferryland, 1808 (Nfld. Archives BRC); Ann, of Torbay, 1813 (Nfld. Archives BRC); John, of Carbonear, 1819 (D'Alberti 29); Rebecca, of Keels, 1820, of Kings Cove, 1826 (Nfld. Archives KCRC); Robert, from Clonmel (Co. Tipperary), of Greenspond, 1831 (Nfld. Archives KCRC); Frances, of Pouch Cove, 1835 (DPHW 26D); William, from Halifax, married at St. John's, 1837 (Nfld. Archives BRC); Owen, from Callan (Co. Kilkenny), of St. John's, 1844 (*Newfoundlander* 25 Jan 1844); Thomas, of St. Mary's (St. Mary's B.), 1844 (*Nfld. Almanac*; Honora, of Indian Arm (Bonavista B.), 1858 (Nfld. Archives KCRC); Ann, of Cottles Island (Bonavista B.), 1860 (Nfld. Archives KCRC); John, of Gooseberry Island (Bonavista B.), 1860 (Nfld. Archives KCRC); Mary, of Broad Cove (now Duntara), 1862 (Nfld. Archives KCRC); scattered in Lovell 1871.

Modern status: At St. John's.

PHILLIPS, a surname of England, Wales, Scotland, Ireland and Guernsey (Channel Islands) from the baptismal name Philip, Latin *Philippus* from the Greek – horse-lover, after the apostle, common in England in the Middle Ages and the origin of many surnames such as Philip(s), Phelps, PHILPOTT, PHIPPARD. In Ireland in modern times Phillips has to some extent superseded (Mac) Philbin, *Mac Philbín* – little Philip. (Withycombe, Reaney, Cottle, MacLysaght, Turk).

Traced by Guppy in the Midlands and south and west of England, especially in Monmouthshire, in South Wales and Scotland, and by MacLysaght in Cos. Galway and Mayo.

In Newfoundland:

Family tradition: Residents with this name at Cape St. George recall an earlier French form Philippe (Thomas, "French Fam. Names").

Early instances: Thomas Philips, of St. John's Harbour, 1703 (CO 194.3); G. Phillips, of Placentia, 1724 (CO 194.8); John, of Lower Island Cove, 1756 (CO 199.18); Absalom, of Bonaventure, 1777, of Kerleys Harbour, 1779 (DPHW 64); Tim, of Bonavista, 1791 (USPG); Isaac, of New Bonaventure, 1813 (DPHW 64); Thomas Philips, of Harbour Grace Parish, 1822 (Nfld. Archives HGRC); George Phillips, planter of Twillingate, 1823 (USPG); John, planter of Seal Cove (now New Chelsea), 1824 (DPHW 59A); James Philips, from Devizes (Wiltshire), married at St. John's, 1828 (Nfld. Archives BRC); John, fisherman of Carbonear, 1840 (DPHW 48); Matthew Phillips, planter of British Harbour, 1842 (DPHW 64B); John, of Round Harbour (Twillingate district), 1849, of Indian Burying Place, 1851 (DPHW 86); George, fisherman of Colliers, 1852 (DPHW 34); Levi, fisherman of Burgeons [sic] Cove (Trinity B.), 1855 (DPHW 64B); scattered in Lovell 1871.

Modern status: Scattered, especially at Bonavista and St. John's.

Place names (not necessarily from the surname): Phillips Brook 47-44 58-07, 48-44 58-31; —— Cove, —— Head 49-13 55-19; —— Island (Labrador) 56-59 61-21; —— Pond 47-22 53-23.

PHILPOTT, a surname of England, a diminutive of Philip. *See* PHILLIPS and *also* POTTLE. (Reaney, Cottle).

Traced by Guppy especially in the west Midlands and south. He notes that Philpott is characteristic of Kent, Wiltshire and Shropshire.

In Newfoundland:

Family tradition: Jim, from Yorkshire, settled at Plate Cove in 1850 (MUN Folklore).

Early instances: John Philpot(t), of Bonavista, 1786 (DPHW 70); Sera Philpot or Filpot, of King's Cove, 1823, of Catalina, 1823 (Nfld. Archives KCRC); Susan Phil(l)pott, of Keels, 1824 (Nfld. Archives KCRC); Jean Philpot, of Open Hole (now Open Hall), 1830 (Nfld. Archives KCRC); James, of Tickle Cove (Bonavista B.), 1846 (Nfld. Archives KCRC); Thomas Philpott, of Plate Cove, 1848 (DPHW 73); Richard, of Herring Neck, 1851 (DPHW 85); John, of Stone Harbour (Twillingate district), 1854 (DPHW 85); John Philpot, of Indian Arm (? Bonavista B.), 1855 (Nfld. Archives KCRC); Jane, of Burnt Island (Bonavista B.), 1857 (Nfld. Archives KCRC); James, of Flat Island (Bonavista B.), 1862 (DPHW 77).

Modern status: Scattered, especially at Plate Cove East and Coachman's Cove.

PHIPPARD, a surname of England a derivative of Philip, or a contracted form of the surname of France Philippard, a pejorative form of Philippe. (Reaney, Dauzat). *See* PHILLIPS.

Reaney notes that Phippard survives in England but is not well-evidenced. Dauzat traced Philippard in the Côtes-du-Nord.

In Newfoundland:

Early instances: Henry, ? of Harbour Grace, 1778 (D'Alberti 7); William, and Co., carried on fishery in Great Salmonier, 1803, claimed fishing rights to certain salmon brooks in St. Mary's Bay, 1804–5 (CO 194.45, D'Alberti 15); William Phipard, watchmaker of St. John's, 1806 (CO 194.45); William Phippard, of Placentia, 1871 (Lovell).

Modern status: Rare, at Placentia.

PICCO(TT), variants of Picot, a surname of England and the Channel Islands, ? from an Old French personal name *Pic* with the suffix *-ot*, or ? from a nickname from Old French *picot* – point, pointed object, or ? a variant of the surname of France Picaud, a pejorative form of *piqueur* – user of a pickaxe. (Reaney, Dauzat, Turk). *See also* PICKETT.

In Newfoundland:

Early instances: Elias Picoc or Picoe, of Portugal Cove, 1781 (DPHW 26C); William and Elias Pico, from the Island of Jersey, of Port de Grave, 1783 (D'Alberti 2); James, of St. John's, 1790 (DPHW 26D); John Piccott of Vire (? now Fair) Islands, 1832 (DPHW 30); Nathan Picot, cooper of Lower Burgeo, 1845 (DPHW 101); ——, agent at Burgeo, 1849 (Feild); Moses, planter of Pass Island (Hermitage B.), 1871 (Lovell).

Modern status: Picco, scattered, especially at St. John's; Piccott, at St. John's, Cartyville, Robinsons and Heatherton.

Place names: Piccos Brook 47-43 52-42; Piccos (or Nearys) Pond 47-40 52-49; —— —— South 47-37 52-51; Picot Hole 47-37 58-40.

PICKERING, a surname of England from the English place name Pickering (Yorkshire NR). (E.C. Smith).

Traced by Guppy in Cheshire, Cumberland, Westmorland, Durham, Leicestershire, Rutlandshire, Northumberland, Yorkshire ER, NR, and by Spiegelhalter in Devon.

In Newfoundland:

Early instances: William, of St. John's, 1704 (CO 194.3); Joseph, of Catalina, 1836 (DPHW 67).

Modern status: Rare, at Corner Brook.

PICKETT, a surname of England, a variant of PIC-CO(TT); in Newfoundland also ? a variant of the surnames of Ireland Pigot or Piggott, from the Old French personal name *Pic*. (Spiegelhalter, MacLysaght).

Traced by Guppy in Wiltshire and by Spiegelhalter in Devon.

In Newfoundland:

Family tradition: Mary (1798–1839), born at Fair Island (Bonavista B.) (MUN Geog.).

Early instances: Patrick Picket, from Lismore (Co. Waterford), married at St. John's 1803 (Nfld. Archives BRC); Michael Pickett, of St. John's, 1803 (Nfld. Archives BRC); Thomas, of Fogo, 1803 (Nfld. Archives BRC); Pat Picket, of Harbour Grace Parish, 1811 (Nfld. Archives HGRC); Samuel, baptized at Vere (now Fair) Island, 1830, aged 50 (DPHW 76); Bridget, of Lions Den, 1833, of Herring Neck, 1833 (Nfld. Archives KCRC); J. Pickett, Road Commissioner for the area of Deer Island (Bonavista B.), 1847 (*Nfld. Almanac*).

Modern status: Scattered, especially at Fair Island (Bonavista B.) and Fogo.

PICKFORD, a surname of England, from the English place names Pickford (Sussex), or ? Pitchford (Shropshire), or ? a variant of BICKFORD or PECKFORD. (Bardsley, A. H. Smith).

Traced by Guppy in Cheshire, Derbyshire, Somerset and Wiltshire.

In Newfoundland:

Early instance: James, of St. John's, 1871 (Lovell).

Modern status: Rare, at Grand Falls and St. John's.

PIDGEON, a surname of England, Ireland and the Channel Islands, in England and the Channel Islands from Old French *pipjon* – (? keeper of) pigeon(s) or one easy to pluck, to swindle, or ? for French *Petit Johan* – Little John; in Ireland for Mac Wiggin, Mac Guigan, *Mag Uiginn*. (Reaney, Cottle, MacLysaght, Turk).

Traced by Spiegelhalter in Devon and by MacLysaght in Co. Monaghan.

In Newfoundland:

Early instance: William, constable of Ferryland district, ? 1730, 1732 (CO 194.9).

Modern status: Rare, at Marystown and St. John's.

Place name (not necessarily from the surname): Pidgeon ? (or Pigeon) Point 48-10 53-45.

PIERCE. *See* PEARCE

PIERC(E)Y. *See* PEARCEY

PIEROWAY, ? a Newfoundland variant of the surname of the Channel Islands Pirouet, ? from the French surname and place name Pirou (La Manche).

In Newfoundland:

Early instance: Phillip, of Sandy Point (St. George's B.), 1870 (DPHW 96).

Modern status: At Stephenville, Corner Brook and scattered in the St. George's district.

Place name: Pierways Hill 48-32 58-52.

PIERPOINT, a surname of England from the French *pierre* and *pont* – stone bridge, place names in Seine-Inférieure, Calvados, La Manche, etc. (Reaney, Cottle).

In Newfoundland:

Modern status: Unique, at St. John's.

PIERSON. *See* PEARSON

PIKE, a surname of England, Ireland and Guernsey (Channel Islands), in England from Old English *pīc* – pike (man), pick-axe, (dweller near the) point (hill), or from Middle English *pike* – (seller of) pike (the fish) hence fishmonger, or from a Scandinavian personal name *Pik* – tall, lanky, or from Old French *pic* – woodpecker; in Ireland also for Mac Peake, *Mac Péice*, ? from Old English **peac* – a stout, thickset man or (dweller by the) peak, hill. (Reaney, Cottle, MacLysaght, Turk).

Traced by Guppy in Berkshire, Buckinghamshire, Devon, Dorset, Hampshire, Northamptonshire, Somerset, Wiltshire and Worcestershire and by MacLysaght in Ulster.

In Newfoundland:

Family traditions: Thomas (1755–1855), from Falmouth (Cornwall), settled at Carbonear in 1788 (MUN Geog.). Gilbert Pike, a lieutenant in the crew of Peter Easton, the pirate, married an Irish princess Sheila Nagira, who had been captured by Easton; Gilbert and his wife settled in Bristols Hope before 1610 and later moved to Carbonear (MUN Hist.).

Early instances: Thomas, of Carbonear, 1681 (CO 1); Francis, Samuel and Edward, of Clowns Cove (Carbonear), 1800, property "in possession of the Family for upwards of 56 years," that is, before 1744 (CO 199.18); Samuel, of Mosquitto (now Bristol's Hope), 1751 (CO 194.13); Charlotte, of Harbour Grace, 1760 (CO 199.18); Jeane, of Trinity Bay, 1764 (DPHW 64); William, from Poole, in possession of property at Carbonear, 1770 (CO 199.18); Francis, of Crockers Cove (Carbonear), 1785 (CO

199.18); Edward, of Broad Cove (Bay de Verde district), 1788 (CO 199.18); Elizabeth, ? of St. John's, 1795 (CO 194.40); ——, of Bay Roberts, 1798 (DPHW 48); Anastasia, from Ross (unspecified), Ireland, married at St. John's, 1806 (Nfld. Archives BRC); John, planter of British Harbour (Trinity B.), 1823 (DPHW 64); George, planter of New Harbour (Trinity B.), 1824 (DPHW 64B); George, of Old Perlican, 1836 (DPHW 58); Edward, planter of Freshwater (Carbonear), 1839 (DPHW 48); Timothy, fisherman of Channel, 1841 (DPHW 101); Elisha, fisherman of Cape Ray, 1841 (DPHW 101); William, of Lower Burgeo, 1843 (DPHW 101); Joseph Pyke, of Kings Cove Parish, 1849 (Nfld. Archives KCRC); Jabez Pike, planter of Blackhead (Bay de Verde district), 1855 (DPHW 52B); Anne, of Tickle Harbour (now Bellevue), 1855 (Nfld. Archives KCRC); John, of Heart's East, 1855 (Nfld. Archives KCRC); W., of Spaniard's Bay, 1858 (*Newfoundlander* 21 Jan 1858); John, granted land at Channel, 1859 (Nfld. Archives, Registry Crown Lands); John, of Lance Cove (now Brownsdale), 1859 (DPHW 58); Manuel, of Great St. Lawrence, 1861 (DPHW 100); Charles, of Flat Island (Bonavista B.), 1862 (DPHW 77); widespread in Lovell 1871.

Modern status: Widespread, especially at Carbonear, Harbour Grace, St. John's, St. Lawrence, Corner Brook and St. Davids.

Place names: Pike Lake (Labrador) 53-54 62-58; Pike (Back) Run (Labrador) 54-07 58-21; Pikes Arm 49-39 54-35 —— Cove (Labrador) 52-46 55-54; —— Island 47-35 59-08; —— Pond 47-45 53-16; (Pikes) Ponds 47-44 53-14.

PILGRIM, a surname of England from Middle English *pelegrim* etc. – one from foreign parts, a pilgrim to the Holy Land or Rome. (Reaney, Cottle).

Traced by Guppy in Essex.

In Newfoundland:

Family tradition: Thomas Butler Pilgrim (1860–1939), son of —— Pilgrim from England who settled in Carbonear (MUN Folklore).

Early instances: Thomas Lambert, of Trinity (Trinity B.), 1818 (DPHW 64); Henry, fisherman of Carbonear, 1836 (DPHW 48); John, of the French Shore, 1859 (DPHW 49); John, of St. Anthony Bight, 1864 (DPHW 94); William, of Cape Norman (now Cook's Harbour), 1871 (Lovell); George (and others), of St. Anthony, 1871 (Lovell); William, of Brandy Harbour (St. Barbe district), 1875 (DPHW 95).

Modern status: Scattered, especially at Griquet and St. Anthony Bight.

PINE, PYNE, surnames of England, PYNE of Ireland, from Old English *pīn*, Old French *pin* – (dweller by the) pine-tree or a nickname for a tall, upright man, or from the French place name Le Pin (Calvados) or a place marked by a conspicuous pine. (Reaney). *See also* PENNELL, PINEL.

Traced by Spiegelhalter in Devon. MacLysaght traced Pyne in Co. Cork since 1599.

In Newfoundland:

Family tradition: —— Pine, an early settler of Conche (White B.) in the early 1800s, guarded the French rooms there (Casey).

Early instances: R. Pine, of Conception Bay, [1706] (CO 194.4); Michael, shoreman of St. John's, 1794–5, "30 years in Newfoundland," that is, 1764–5 (Census 1794–5); William, from Thomastown (Co. Kilkenny), married at St. John's, 1811 (Nfld. Archives BRC); Thomas, of Harbour Grace Parish, 1817 (Nfld. Archives HGRC); Thomas, fisherman of English Harbour (Trinity B.), 1821 (DPHW 64); Patrick Pyne, from Ross Perkin (Co. Wexford), deserted from service of Wise, Baker and Howard, ? at St. John's, 1828 (*Newfoundlander* 22 May 1828); Owen, of Belleoram, 1838 (DPHW 106); Thomas, from Co. Cork, of Harbour Grace, 1844 (*Indicator* 27 Jul 1844); Owen and Philip, of Burin, 1871 (Lovell); John, planter of Conche, 1871 (Lovell); William Pyne, farmer of Outer Cove (St. John's district), 1871 (Lovell).

Modern status: Pine, at Prowsetown (Placentia West district) (*Electors* 1955), Outer Cove and St. John's; Pyne, rare, at St. John's.

PINEL, a surname of England and Jersey (Channel Islands) from Old French *pinel* – little pine-tree. Reaney notes: "A nickname (not uncommon) applied either affectionately to a tall, thin man, or derisively to a small weedy man." (Reaney, Turk). *See also* PINE, PENNELL.

In Newfoundland:

Early instances: Thomas, master of the brig *James and Ellen*, ? Newfoundland, 1828 (*Newfoundlander* 2 Oct 1828); Amice, of Petites, 1871 (Lovell).

Modern status: Rare, at Burgeo (*Electors* 1955).

PING, a surname of China – even; equal, average; weigh.

In Newfoundland:

Early instance: Sarah Pinng, prisoner in gaol at St. John's, 1802 (D'Alberti 12).

Modern status: Rare, at St. John's.

PINHORN, a surname of England, ? from an unidentified place name ? containing the Old English elements *pīn* – pine and *horn* – a projecting headland, a horn-shaped hill.

Matthews traced Pinhorne as a captain in Poole (Dorset).

In Newfoundland:

Family tradition: Four Pinhorn brothers, from Devon, settled at Scilly Cove (now Winterton) in the late 1600s (MUN Folklore).

Early instances: Benjamin, fisherman of Trinity (Trinity B.), 1757 (DPHW 64); John, of Scilly Cove (now Winterton), 1780 (DPHW 64).

Modern status: At St. John's, Winterton and Trinity (Trinity B.).

Place name: Pinhorns Pond 47-56 53-15.

PINK, a surname of England from Old English *pinc(a)* – chaffinch. (Reaney, Cottle). *See also* PINSENT.

Traced by Spiegelhalter in Devon.

In Newfoundland:

Family tradition: James, a farmer from southern England, settled at Cape La Hune about 1877 (MUN Geog.).

Early instances: Anne, baptized at Oar (or Aviron) Bay, 1835, aged 22 (DPHW 30); Charlotte, baptized at La Hune Bay, 1835, aged 11 (DPHW 30); Mary, baptized at Western Cul de Sac, 1835, aged 24 (DPHW 30); Dr., of the Garrison, St. John's, 1844 (*Newfoundlander* 21 Nov 1844); William, trader of Jersey Harbour (Fortune B.), 1871 (Lovell); John Jr. and Sr., of Cape La Hune, 1871 (Lovell).

Modern status: In the Burgeo-La Poile district especially at Cape La Hune.

Place name (not necessarily from the surname): Pink Bottom 47-37 55-56.

PINKS(T)EN, PINKSTOM, PINKSTON, variants of the surname of England otherwise Pin(c)kstone, Pingstone from the English place name Pinxton (Derbyshire). (Bardsley, Reaney).

Traced by Bardsley in various forms in Lancashire.

In Newfoundland:

Family tradition: John Pinkson, was an early settler of Seal Cove (White B.) in the early 1800s (MUN Hist.).

Early instances: Lavinia Pinksen (1878–1943), of St. John's (General Protestant Cemetery, St. John's).

Modern status: Pinksen, at Corner Brook, Deer Lake and in the White Bay South district, especially at Seal Cove; Pinksten, unique, at Broad Cove (Bay de Verde district); Pinkstom, Pinkston, unique, at Brigus.

PINSENT, a surname of England, from Old French *pinçon, pinson* – finch, used as a personal name and nickname – gay as a finch, or ? from Old French *pinçon, pinchon* – pincers, forceps, also used as a nickname, or ? an anglicization of the French surname Poinson or Poinçon (Reaney, Ekwall, Dauzat, Spiegelhalter). *See also* PINK.

Traced by Spiegelhalter in Devon.

In Newfoundland:

Early instances: Andrew Pinson, seaman from Abbotskerswell, with Henry Study, in possession of property called St. George's Increase in St. John's, 1736, 1741 (Exeter Public Library Archives per Kirwin); James Penson, fisherman of Trinity (Trinity B.), 1761 (DPHW 64); William Pinsent (about 1759–1837), from Teignmouth (Devon), agent at Port de Grave between 1773–5; later with his brother John (– 1823) established business there and at Hussey's Cove and Cupids (Nfld. Archives T22, MUN Hist., CO 199.18); William, of Ochre Pit Cove, 1800 (CO 199.18); Jame(s) Pinson, of Scilly Cove (now Winterton), 1800 (DPHW 64); Elenor Penson, of Harbour Grace Parish, 1807 (Nfld. Archives HGRC); Benjamin Pinson, of Freshwater (Carbonear), 1808 (DPHW 48); Andrew, of Lance a Loup, 1816–20 (D'Alberti 26, 30); John Penson, aged 45, from Devon, deserted from the brig *Devon*, St. John's, 1820 (*Nfld. Mercantile Jour.* 18 May 1820); William Pincent, of Old Perlican, 1835 (DPHW 58); John, of Cat Harbour (now Lumsden), 1839 (DPHW 76); —— Pinsent, junior magistrate of Harbour Grace, 1853 (*Newfoundlander* 21 Mar 1853); Helen, of New Harbour (Trinity B.), 1866 (Nfld. Archives HGRC); Jacob, of Chapel Arm, 1866, of South Dildo, 1866, of Tickle Harbour (now Bellevue), 1866 (Nfld. Archives KCRC); John, of Dildo Cove, 1871 (Lovell).

Modern status: Scattered, especially at Bellevue.

Place names: Pinsent 49-26 54-03; Pinsent (or Pensons) Arm 52-41 55-53; Pensent Arm (Labrador) 52-41 55-54; Pinsent Island (Labrador) 52-42 55-50.

PINTO, a surname of Spain and Portugal, a nickname for one with a scar or blemish. (E.C. Smith).

In Newfoundland:

Early instance: John (1900–1967), born in Vigo, Spain, of St. John's (Mount Carmel Cemetery, St. John's).

Modern status: At St. John's.

PIPPY, a surname of England, ? a variant of Pippet – ? a diminutive of Philip (*see* PHILLIPS) or Pep(p)in, Pepys, or of Pepin, Pepis, Peppy or Pipet of Jersey (Channel Islands), from the Old French personal name *Pepin*, or from Old French *pepin*, *pipin* – seed of a fleshy fruit, used for a gardener. (Reaney, Cottle, Turk).

Spiegelhalter traced Pippet in Devon.

In Newfoundland:

Family tradition: Two Pippy brothers, from England, came to Newfoundland; one settled at Twillingate and the other settled on the Avalon Peninsula (MUN Folklore).

Early instances: Joseph, of St. John's, 1791 (DPHW 26C); Joseph Peppy, carpenter of Bell Island, 1794–5, "born in Newfoundland" (Census 1794–5); Elizabeth Pippy, of St. John's, in possession of property at Musketta (now Bristols Hope), 1796 (CO 199.18); George, of Harbour Grace, 1804 (CO 199.18); Dinah, of Blackhead (Bay de Verde district), 1806 (CO 199.18); Charles Pippey, planter of Broad Cove (Bay de Verde district), 1816 (DPHW 52A); George Pippy, fisherman of Cape St. Francis, 1826 (DPHW 52A); Jane, of Kings Cove Parish, 1835 (Nfld. Archives KCRC); William, of Bay de Verde, 1844 (*Newfoundlander* 18 Jun 1844); William, of Pouch Cove, 1871 (Lovell); John Pippey, of Fogo, 1871 (Lovell).

Modern status: Scattered, especially at St. John's.

Place name: The Pippies (Labrador) 53-12 55-41.

PITCHER, a surname of England from Old English *(ge)pician* – to pitch, for one who covers or caulks with pitch. (Reaney).

Traced by Guppy in Buckinghamshire and Sussex and by Spiegelhalter in Devon.

In Newfoundland:

Early instances: Richard, of Trinity Bay, 1769 (DPHW 64); John, of New Perlican, 1789 (DPHW 64); Richard and John, proprietors and occupiers of fishing room, Hearts Content, Winter 1800–01 (Census Trinity B.); William, of Scilly Cove (now Winterton), 1805 (DPHW 64); Ann, of Harbour Grace Parish, 1816 (Nfld. Archives HGRC); James, planter of Old Bonaventure, 1824–34 (DPHW 64B); Israel, of Burgum's Cove (Trinity B.), 1871 (Lovell); Charles and James, of Burin, 1871 (Lovell); Cabet, of Hope All, 1871 (Lovell); Jacob, of Salmon Cove (now Champneys), 1871 (Lovell).

Modern status: Scattered, especially at Green's Harbour and St. John's.

Place names: Pitchers Pond, —— Brook 47-41 53-28.

PITT(S), surnames of England from Old English *pytt* – (dweller by the) pit(s), excavation(s) or hollow(s), or from the English place names Pit(t) of which Spiegelhalter recorded 22 in Devon, Pitt (Hampshire) or Pett (Kent). (Reaney, Cottle, Spiegelhalter). *See also* PUTT.

Guppy traced Pitt in Gloucestershire, Herefordshire and Worcestershire, Pitts in Devon and Norfolk; Spiegelhalter traced Pitt(s) in Devon.

In Newfoundland:

Family tradition: James Pitts, born at Kennford (Devon), of Lance Cove, Bell Island, died 1805, aged 70 (MUN Hist.).

Early instances: Andrew Pitt, of New Perlican, 1708–9 (CO 194.4); James Pitts, planter of Bell Island, 1794–5, "43 years in Newfoundland," that is, since 1751–2 (Census 1794–5); Elizabeth, of St. John's, 1774 (DPHW 26C); J., a soldier, 1798, in possession of house in Maggotty Cove bought by his father 20 years previously, that is, 1778 (D'Alberti 8); Capt., in possession of property at Quidi Vidi, 1794–5 (Census 1794–5); Betsy Pitt, of Keels, 1829 (Nfld. Archives KCRC); Jane, of Ferryland, 1832 (DPHW 31); James, of Greenspond, 1840 (DPHW 76); Richard, ? of Castle Cove (Bonavista B.), 1849 (DPHW 73); Thomas, ship master of Harbour Grace, 1849 (DPHW 43).

Modern status: Pitt, rare, at St. John's and Musgravetown; Pitts, at Bell Island, New Perlican and Cannings Cove.

Place names: Pitts Harbour (Labrador), —— Point (Labrador), —— Hill (Labrador) 52-01 55-54; —— Pond, —— Park 48-28 54-12; Pitt Sound Reach, —— —— Island 48-52 53-44.

PITTMAN, a surname of England from Old English *pytt* and *mann* – dweller by the pit or excavation or in the hollow. (Reaney).

Guppy traced Pitman in Dorset and Somerset; Spiegelhalter traced Pit(t)man in Devon.

Family tradition: William (1746–1808), from Abbotsbury (Dorset), to Trinity, 1788. William (1778–1836), son of the preceding, was the first Pittman to settle at New Perlican, 1800.

In Newfoundland:

Early instances: Samuel, of St. John's, 1785 (DPHW 26D); —— Pitman, from England, of Lamaline, 1849, aged 88, had not been home for 60 years, that is, since 1789 (Feild); William Pittman, of Trinity (Trinity B.), 1789, occupier of fishing room, New Perlican, Winter 1800–01 (Census Trinity B.); William Pitman, planter of Moretons Harbour, 1820 (USPG); William Pitman, planter of White Bay, 1830

(DPHW 29); George Pittman, carpenter of Carbonear, 1835 (DPHW 48); John, fisherman of Spout Cove (Bay de Verde district), 1837, of Small Point, 1839 (DPHW 52A); James Pitman, of Greenspond, 1853 (DPHW 76); Deborah, of Burin, 1857 (DPHW 106); Julia Pittman, of Hants Harbour, 1858 (DPHW 59); Joseph Pitman, of Harbour Le Cou, 1859 (DPHW 98); William, of Meadow[s] (Burin district), 1860 (DPHW 107); Elias Pittman, of Grandvache, 1864 (DPHW 94); Thomas Pitman, of Sop's Island, 1864 (DPHW 94); scattered in Lovell 1871.

Modern status: Widespread, especially at St. John's, Sop's Island, Rocky Harbour (St. Barbe district) and Marystown.

Place names: Pittman Bight 49-48 55-51; —— Point 48-07 53-55; Pittmans Pond 49-30 56-32.

PITTS. *See* PITT

PLANKE, a surname of England from Middle English *planke* – (dweller by the) plank or narrow footbridge. (Reaney).

In Newfoundland:

Early instances: J. ? Planke, planter of St. John's, 1701 (CO 194.2); James Plank, fisherman of Brule (Placentia B.), 1871 (Lovell); John, fisherman of St. Kyrans (Placentia B.), 1871 (Lovell).

Modern status: At Mortier and Port au Bras.

PLOUGHMAN, PLOWMAN, surnames of England, from Old English *plōh* – plough and *mann* – man.

Spiegelhalter traced Plowman, which seems to be the usual English form, in Devon.

In Newfoundland:

Early instances: John Plowman, of Brigus, 1782 (CO 199.18); —— Ploughman or Plowman, of Harbour Grace Parish, 1813 (Nfld. Archives HGRC); John Ploughman, of Ship Cove (now part of Port Rexton), 1816 (DPHW 64); Henry Plowman, of Trinity (unspecified), 1833 (Nfld. Archives KCRC); Henry, of Port au Choix, 1873 (MUN Hist.).

Modern status: Ploughman, scattered, especially in the Trinity North district; Plowman, at Corner Brook and in the St. Barbe district especially at Port Saunders.

POIRIER, a surname of France and Jersey (Channel Islands) – (owner of or dweller by the) pear tree. (Dauzat, Turk). *See also* PERRIER.

In Newfoundland:

Family tradition: ——, an Acadian from the Magdalen Islands, settled at St. George's about 1850 (MUN Geog.).

Modern status: Rare, at Doyles, St. John's and Stephenville.

POLEM, ? a surname of England, apparently not recorded elsewhere, ? from the English place name Poolham (Lincolnshire). (Ekwall).

In Newfoundland:

Early instances: Thomas Polham, of Hearts Content, 1772 (DPHW 64); Eliza Polum, of Hearts Desire, 1832 (Nfld. Archives KCRC); William Polin, of Harbour Grace Parish, 1839 (Nfld. Archives HGRC); William Polam, of New Perlican, 1871 (Lovell).

Modern status: Rare, at Hearts Content, Windsor (*Electors* 1955) and New Perlican.

POLLARD, a surname of England, Ireland and the Channel Islands, a derivative of the baptismal name Paul (*see* PAUL), or from Middle English *poll* – to clip or *poll* – head, giving nickname *pollard* – one with a big or close-cropped head. (Reaney).

Traced by Guppy in Cambridgeshire, Cornwall, Derbyshire, Lancashire, Leicestershire and Rutlandshire, by Spiegelhalter in Devon, by MacLysaght in Co. Westmeath in the fourteenth century.

In Newfoundland:

Early instances: Christopher, of Capling Bay (now Calvert), 1675 (CO 1); Richard, of St. John's, 1770 (DPHW 26D); Thomas, of Goose Cove (Labrador), 1787, of Matthews Cove (Labrador), 1789 (MUN Hist.); Ellen Penelope, from Charlottetown, Prince Edward Island, married at Twillingate, 1850 (*Royal Gazette* 24 Sep 1850); Fawlon, of Black Island (Exploits district), 1859 (DPHW 92); Thomas, of Coney Arm (White B.), 1864 (DPHW 94); John, of Great Harbour Deep (White B.), 1871 (Lovell); Ambrose and John, miners of Tilt Cove, 1871 (Lovell).

Modern status: Scattered, especially in the White Bay North and South districts.

Place name: Pollards Point 49-45 56-54.

POLLETT, a surname of England, Pollet, Paulet of France, diminutives of Paul (*see* PAUL), or ? in England a variant of Pollitt a diminutive of the Greek personal name *Hippolytus* – letting horses loose. In Greek legend Hippolytus was the son of the Amazon Queen *Hippolyta*, but the use of the baptismal name stems from a Roman saint martyred in 252. Also in England ? from the English place name Pawlett (Somerset). (Reaney, Cottle, Bardsley).

Traced by Spiegelhalter in Devon.

In Newfoundland:

Family tradition: Two Paulet brothers settled in New Harbour (Trinity B.), about 1770; the surname was later changed to Pollett (MUN Folklore).

Early instances: Priscilla Pollet, of New Perlican, 1776, of New Harbour, 1794 (DPHW 64); Thomas Pollett, of Bonavista, 1792 (USPG); Joseph Pollet, of Western Bay, 1798 (DPHW 48); Mary, of Trinity (unspecified), 1833 (*Newfoundlander* 3 Oct 1833); Thomas and William, miners of La Manche, 1871 (Lovell).

Modern status: Scattered, especially at New Harbour (Trinity B.).

POLLIS, ? a variant of the surname of France Police, ? from a nickname of unknown origin. (Chapuy).

In Newfoundland:

Family tradition: Jean Marie (? born about 1800–20), from France to ? Cape Breton (Nova Scotia) and later to Halfway Point (Humber Arm), where his son John Mary was born in 1857. (J.P. Pollis).

Modern status: Rare, at Corner Brook.

POLLOCK, a surname of Scotland and Ireland from the Scots place name Pollock (Renfrewshire, Glasgow). (Black, Guppy).

Traced by Guppy in the Glasgow district and by MacLysaght in northeast Ulster.

In Newfoundland:

Modern status: Rare, at St. John's and Lewisporte.

Place name: Pollock Rocks 47-24 53-59.

POM(E)ROY, surnames of England from the French place names La Pommeraie (Vendée), La Pommeraye (Calvados etc.), or from Old French *pommeraie* – (dweller near or owner of the) apple-orchard. (Reaney, Dauzat *Noms de Lieux*). Traced by Guppy in Dorset and by Spiegelhalter in Devon.

In Newfoundland:

Family traditions: —— Pomeroy, from Ireland, settled at Merasheen about 1820 (MUN Folklore).

——, from Breadport [? Bridport], England, settled at Lamaline in 1854; he later moved to Paradise (Placentia B.) (MUN Folklore).

Early instances: John Pom(m)ery, of Brigus, 1806 (DPHW 34); —— Pomeroy, of Bull Cove (Conception B.), 1843 (MUN Hist.); William, of Fogo, 1843 (DPHW 83); ——, on the *Argo* in the seal fishery out of St. John's, 1851 (*Newfoundlander* 13 Mar 1851); George Pomer(o)y, boatkeeper of Catalina, 1852 (DPHW 72, Nfld. Archives, Registry Crown Lands); William Pomroy, of Great Paradise (Placentia B.),

1871 (Lovell); John and Joseph, of Merasheen, 1871 (Lovell).

Modern status: Pomeroy, scattered, especially at Merasheen (*Electors* 1955); Pomroy, rare, at St. John's and Placentia.

POND, a surname of England from Middle English *pond* – (dweller by the) pond, or ? from Old English *pund* – (dweller by or keeper of the) pound (for stray animals) or (maker of) weight(s). (Reaney, Cottle).

Traced by Spiegelhalter in Devon.

In Newfoundland:

Early instances: John, born in Newfoundland, 1795 (CO 194.65); Edward, of Greenspond, 1804 (Bonavista Register 1806); James, planter of Fogo, 1821 (USPG); James, baptized at Vere (now Fair) Islands (Bonavista B.), 1830, aged 21 (DPHW 76); Diana, baptized at Cape Cove (Bonavista B.), 1830, aged 35 (DPHW 76); William, baptized at Swain's Island, 1830, aged 26 (DPHW 76); Thomas, planter of Salmon Cove (now Champneys), 1840 (DPHW 64B); James, of Fox Harbour (Placentia B.), 1871 (Lovell); Adam and George, of Twillingate, 1871 (Lovell).

Modern status: Scattered, especially in the Bonavista North district.

Place names: Greenspond, —— Harbour, —— Island 49-04 53-34. Many other place names contain the specific Pond but these are not necessarily from the surname.

POOLE, a surname of England and Ireland, ? a variant of the baptismal name Paul (*see* PAUL), or from English place names Pool(e) of which Spiegelhalter recorded 17 in Devon, Pool (Dorset, Gloucestershire, Yorkshire WR), or from Old English *pōl* – (dweller by the) pool, tidal stream. (Reaney, Cottle, Ekwall).

Guppy traced Poole in Cambridgeshire, Dorset, Essex, Gloucestershire, Shropshire, Staffordshire, Wiltshire and (with Pool occasionally) in Somerset. Spiegelhalter traced Po(o)le in Devon.

In Newfoundland:

Early instances: Richard Pooley (Pool in 1677), of Renews, 1675 (CO 1); William Poole (Pole in 1681), of Trepassey, 1677 (CO 1); John Pool, of St. John's, 1764 (DPHW 26D); John Poole, of Quidi Vidi Cove, 1771 (CO 194.18, 30); Nicholas, a Newfoundland planter, 1784 (Dorset County Record Office per Kirwin); John, of Harbour Breton, 1811 (D'Alberti 21); William Absalom, of Bay of Islands, 1816 (Dispatches V.2, 1816); Henry, planter of Lance Cove (now Brownsdale), 1833 (DPHW 58);

Catherine, baptized at Rencontre, 1835, aged 62 (DPHW 58); Elizabeth, baptized at New (now Parsons) Harbour, 1835, aged 16 (DPHW 30); William, of Grand Bank, 1836 (DPHW 106); Elizabeth, of Fortune, 1840 (DPHW 106); Henry, planter of Little Islands (Trinity South district), 1843 (DPHW 59A); Jane, of Hants Harbour, 1845 (DPHW 59); Simon, of Little Harbour (Twillingate district), 1846 (*Newfoundlander* 4 Jun 1846, DPHW 88); John, of Channel, 1853 (DPHW 98); Thomas, of Fortune, married Jane Piercey 1853 (Grand Bank Methodist marriages, P.E.L. Smith); Stephen, planter of Belleoram, 1871 (Lovell); George and Thomas, of Burnt Island (Burgeo-La Poile district), 1871 (Lovell); William, of Cape Ray, 1871 (Lovell); John and Philip, of Corbin, 1871 (Lovell).

Modern status: Pool, unique, at Grand Bay (Burgeo-La Poile district) (*Electors* 1955); Poole, scattered, especially at Belleoram and Corbin.

Place names (not necessarily from the surname): Pool Cove, —— Island 47-38 58-34; Poole Cove, —— Rock 47-30 55-47; —— Island 47-38 56-13; —— Point 47-43 56-03; Pool's Cove 47-41 55-26; —— Harbour 49-07 53-37; —— Island, —— —— Tickle 49-07 53-36; —— Island 47-42 58-05.

POPE, a surname of England, Ireland and Scotland from Old English *pāpa*, Middle English *pope* – pope, used "? for an austere man, a killjoy, one who had played the part in a pageant, one who had even been abroad in the pope's service." (Cottle, Reaney, MacLysaght 73).

Traced by Guppy in Devon, Dorset, Gloucestershire, Hampshire, Kent and Worcestershire, by Black in Caithness, Sutherland and Orkney where the name is pronounced Paip, and by MacLysaght in Co. Waterford.

In Newfoundland:

Early instances: John and Samuel, of St. John's, 1794–5 (Census 1794–5); Robert, of Fogo, 1841 (DPHW 83); John, of Fools (now Pools) Island, 1852 (DPHW 76); William, planter of Long Harbour (Burin district), 1856 (DPHW 104); William, planter of Stone's Cove (Burin district), 1858 (DPHW 104); Abel, of Shoal Bay (Fogo district), 1858 (DPHW 83); Mary Ann, of Craints Cove, 1863 (MUN Hist.); John, of Ram's Islands (Placentia B.), 1871 (Lovell).

Modern status: Scattered, especially at Stone's Cove and St. John's.

Place names: Pope Point 47-53 54-13; Popes Harbour 48-14 53-33; —— Rock 46-59 55-11; —— Harbour Pond 48-15 53-36.

PORTER, a surname of England, Scotland and Ireland, from Old French *portier*, Anglo-French *porter* – door-keeper, gatekeeper (of a castle or monastery), or from Old French *porteour* – carrier, porter. Of the first function, Black comments: "The porter was one of the most important officials connected with the castle or monastic institution. Lands and privileges were attached to the office, and in the case of a royal castle the position was often hereditary. The porter of a religious house was also the distributor of the alms of the convent, for the poor were always supplied *ad portam monasterii*, at the gate of the monastery. He also kept the keys and had power to refuse admission to those whom he deemed unworthy." (Reaney, Cottle, Black).

Traced by Guppy in thirteen counties and by Spiegelhalter also in Devon. MacLysaght comments: "Though essentially English in origin there are few names which occur more widely in every kind of Irish record relating to all the provinces, except Connacht, from the thirteenth century to modern times. It is numerous now especially in Ulster."

In Newfoundland:

Family tradition: ——, from Bristol, settled at Change Islands (MUN Folklore).

Early instances: William, of Hibbs Hole, 1777, property "in possession of the Family for 106 years," that is, since 1671 (CO 199.18); Richard, constable of Carbonear district, ? 1730, 1732 (CO 194.9); ——, of Fortune, 1765 (CO 194.16); J., of St. John's, 1782 (DPHW 26C); Mary, of Cupids, 1783 (CO 199.18); William, of Harbour Grace, 1790 (CO 199.18); William, of Bonavista, 1792 (USPG); William, of Green Head (Spaniards B.), 1796 (CO 199.18); Richard, of Port de Grave, 1802 (CO 199.18); James, planter of Bird Island Cove (now Elliston), 1811 (DPHW 72); George, planter of Fogo, 1816 (MUN Hist.); George, planter of Change Islands, 1821 (USPG); Patience, of Foxtrap, 1838 (DPHW 26D); Theophilus, fisherman of Long Pond, 1840 (DPHW 30); Julia, of Harbour Grace Parish, 1844 (Nfld. Archives HGRC); scattered in Lovell 1871.

Modern status: Widespread, especially at Foxtrap, Long Pond, Blow me Down (Port de Grave district), Elliston and St. John's.

Place name: Porters Brook 48-55 57-33; —— Cove, Porterville 49-15 55-11.

POTTER, a surname of England and Ireland from Late Old English *pottere* or Old French *potier* – potter, a maker of earthenware vessels or of metal pots, or a bell-founder. (Reaney).

Traced by Guppy in eleven counties and by Mac-Lysaght in small numbers in all the provinces.

In Newfoundland:

Early instances: ——, of Quidi Vidi, 1703 (CO 194.3); Barnardt of St. John's Harbour, 1703 (CO 194.3); William, of Harbour Grace Parish, 1809 (Nfld. Archives HGRC); Ellen Potter alias Daniel, of Trinity (unspecified), 1828 (Nfld. Archives BRC); William Potter, of Black Island (Twillingate district), 1842 (DPHW 86); William, planter of Bird Island Cove (now Elliston), 1844 (DPHW 72).

Modern status: In the Twillingate and Gander districts.

POTTLE, a surname of England a diminutive of *Pot* from *Philipot* – little Philip, or a variant of POTTER, or ? from Old French *potol* – post, stake, perhaps applied to a lean, tall man. (Reaney, Cottle, Spiegelhalter). *See* PHILLIPS, PHILPOT(T), POTTER, POTTS.

Traced by Spiegelhalter in Devon.

In Newfoundland:

Early instances: James, of English Harbour (? Trinity B.), 1708, of South West Catalina, 1709 (CO 194.4); Lawrence, of Placentia ? district, 1744 (CO 194.24); Joseph, of St. John's, ? 1752 (CO 194.13); Thomas, of Clowns Cove (Carbonear), 1766 (CO 199.18); Martin, of Trinity Bay, 1767 (DPHW 64); Thomas, of Bunkers Hill (Carbonear), 1786 (CO 199.18); Martin, of Bonavista, 1792 (USPG); Manuel, occupier of fishing room, Heart's Content, Winter 1800–01 (Census Trinity B.); Robert, of Torbay, 1801 (Nfld. Archives BRC); Robert, of St. John's, 1802 (Nfld. Archives BRC); John, fisherman of Colliers, 1834 (DPHW 34); William, planter of Blow me Down (Carbonear district), 1837 (DPHW 48); Thomas, of Harbour Grace Parish, 1838 (Nfld. Archives HGRC); George J., of Harbour Grace, 1846 (DPHW 43); Mary, of Cat Harbour (now Lumsden), 1859 (Nfld. Archives KCRC); William, of Flat Rock (Carbonear), 1860 (DPHW 49); William Pottles, of Jobs Cove, 1871 (Lovell).

Modern status: Scattered, especially at Jobs Cove and St. John's.

Place names: Pottles Bay (Labrador), —— Cove (Labrador) 54-29 57-30; —— Cove (Labrador), —— —— Head (Labrador) 54-10 57-22.

POTTS, a surname of England, a shortened form of *Philipot* – little Philip (*see* PHILLIPS), or for POTTER, or from Old English *pott* – (dweller by the) hole, pit. (Reaney, Cottle). *See also* PHILPOT(T), POTTLE.

Traced by Guppy in Cheshire, Durham and Northumberland, and by Spiegelhalter in Devon.

In Newfoundland:

Early instances: William, publican of St. John's, 1794–5 (Census 1794–5); Mary, from Ballymire (unidentified) (Co. Wexford), married at St. John's, 1819 (Nfld. Archives BRC).

Modern status: Rare, at Grand Falls (*Electors* 1955), and St. John's.

POULAIN, a surname of France and the Channel Islands – a nickname for one who is lively, animated. (Dauzat, Turk).

In Newfoundland:

Early instance: Gestina Poulin, of Tickle Cove (Bonavista B.), 1890 (Nfld. Archives KCRC).

Modern status: Rare, at Little Bay (Burin district) (*Electors* 1955).

POULLETT, a surname of the Micmac Indians of Newfoundland, a variant of the surname of France and Jersey (Channel Islands) Poul(l)et, from French *poule* – hen, hence a nickname for one who is chicken-hearted, fearful. (Dauzat, Turk).

In Newfoundland:

Modern status: Rare, at St. Albans.

POWELL, a surname of England, Wales, Ireland and the Channel Islands, a shortened form of the Welsh *ap Howell* – son of Howel, Welsh *hywel* – eminent (*see* HOWELL), or a variant of PAUL, or of POOLE; in Ireland also an occasional synonym of GUILFOYLE. (Withycombe, Reaney, Cottle, MacLysaght, Turk).

Found widespread by Guppy in the south and west of England, especially in Herefordshire and Monmouthshire and in South Wales, and by MacLysaght in small numbers in all the provinces.

In Newfoundland:

Family tradition: The Powell family were Welsh rock miners who came to Nova Scotia; later one branch of the family moved to Newfoundland and settled at Carbonear and Happy Adventure (MUN Folklore).

Early instances: Nicholas, of Carbonear, 1765, property "in possession of the Family for upwards of 124 years," that is, before 1641 (CO 199.18); Richard Powel(l), fisherman of Trinity (Trinity B.), 1759 (DPHW 64); Richard Powell, of Bonavista, 1787 (DPHW 70); Benjamin, of Fogo, 1805 (D'Alberti 15); Jane Powel, of Harbour Grace Parish, 1810 (Nfld. Archives HGRC); Robin Powell, of Tickle Cove (Bonavista B.), 1825 (DPHW 70); Robert, from Devon, married at Bonavista, 1829 (Nfld. Archives KCRC); John, of King's Cove, 1829 (Nfld. Archives KCRC); John, from Callan (Co.

Kilkenny), married at St. John's, 1830 (Nfld. Archives BRC); Mary Anne, of St. John's, 1837 (DPHW 26D); Robert, of Merritts Harbour, 1846, of Herring Neck, 1851 (DPHW 85, 86); Thomas, fisherman of Burnt Head (Carbonear district), 1847 (DPHW 47); ——, on the *Isabella* in the seal fishery out of Catalina, 1853 (*Newfoundlander* 17 Mar 1853); William, of Sandy Cove (Bonavista B.), 1857 (DPHW 73B); Nicholas, granted land on Hearts Content Road, 1859 (Nfld. Archives, Registry Crown Lands); Thomas, of Red Bay (St. Barbe district), 1863 (DPHW 95); Charles, of Barrow Harbour (Bonavista B.), 1865 (DPHW 81); Joseph and Thomas, of Crockers Cove (Carbonear), 1871 (Lovell); Len, of Hearts Content, 1871 (Lovell); Sarah, schoolteacher of Victoria Village, 1871 (Lovell); Robert Powels, of Ferryland, 1871 (Lovell); Charles and Robert Powell, of Happy Adventure, 1871 (Lovell).

Modern status: Scattered, especially at Happy Adventure, Carbonear and Corner Brook.

Place names: Powell Cove 48-59 53-52; —— Point 47-18 53-55; —— Rapids (Labrador) 53-37 64-22; Powells Brook 47-44 53-14, 49-22 58-07; —— Peak 49-21 58-05; —— Pond 48-21 53-52.

POWER, a surname of England and Ireland, from Old French *Pohier* – the man from Poix (Picardy), or from Old French *povre, poure* – poor, or ? from Old French *poer* – one (em)power(ed) to do something, a herald. MacLysaght notes that the *de* in the Irish form *de Paor* should be *le*, – the poor man, consequent on a vow. POWERS – son of Power appears to be rare. (Reaney, Cottle, MacLysaght).

Guppy traced the variant Poore in Hampshire; Spiegelhalter traced Poore and Power in Devon; MacLysaght traced Power mainly in Waterford and adjacent counties, among the fifty most numerous Irish names.

In Newfoundland:

Family traditions: ——, one of the first settlers of Conche in the early 1800s, was a guardian of the French rooms there (Casey). ——, from Co. Cork, settled at Robin Hood (now part of Port Rexton) about 1800 (MUN Folklore). Richard Della de Poeur, from the north of France, settled at Portugal Cove South; the name was later changed to Power (MUN Folklore).

Early instances: Maurice, John and Thomas, of Little Placentia (now Argentia), about 1730–5 (CO 194.9); Thomas, from Waterford, thief of St. John's, 1751 (CO 194.13); Robert, of Freshwater Bay (unspecified), ? 1753 (CO 194.13); John, butcher of Bell Island, 1794–5, "40 years in Newfoundland," that is, 1754–5 (Census 1794–5); Edward, of Port de Grave, 1760 (CO 199. 18); Maurice, of Trinity Bay, 1766 (DPHW 64); John, of Crockers Cove (Carbonear), 1771 (Nfld. Archives L118); Michael, fisherman of Torbay, 1794–5, "25 years in Newfoundland," that is, 1769–70 (Census 1794–5); John, fisherman of Quidi Vidi, 1794–5, "20 years in Newfoundland," that is, 1774–5 (Census 1794–5); Michael, of Petty Harbour, 1779 (DPHW 26C); Thomas and Pious, of Harbour Main, 1779 (MUN Hist.); John Poor, of Placentia, 1780 (D'Alberti 1); Michael Power, of Cupids, 1781 (CO 199.18); Stephen Power or Poor, servant of Renews, 1784 (D'Alberti 2); Michael Power, of Spoon Cove (Conception B.), 1784 (CO 199.18); Patrick (–1811), from Kilbronan (Co. Waterford), planter of Low Point (Conception B.), 1789 (CO 199.18, *Royal Gazette* 31 Oct 1811); Nickles [sic], of Bonavista, 1790 (DPHW 70); Thomas, of Broad Cove (North Shore, Conception B.), 1790 (CO 199.18); Michael, from Tintern Parish (Co. Wexford), married at St. John's, 1793 (Nfld. Archives BRC); John, of Turks Gut (now Marysvale), 1802 (CO 199.18); John, given permission to build fish flake and stage at Nippers Harbour, 1803 (D'Alberti 13); Bridget, of Witless Bay, married at St. John's, 1803 (Nfld. Archives BRC); Mary, of Harbour Grace Parish, 1806 (Nfld. Archives HGRC); Mary Power alias Furlong, from Waterford City, married at St. John's, 1807 (Nfld. Archives BRC); Patrick Power, of Great St. Julians, 1810 (D'Alberti 20); Thomas, appointed to protect the birds on the Penguin Islands, 1810 (D'Alberti 20); John Poor, of Carbonear, 1810 (DPHW 48); Thomas, from Ireland, fisherman of Ferryland, deceased, 1810 (*Royal Gazette* 6 Dec 1810); Thomas Power, one of 72 impressed men who sailed from Ireland to Newfoundland, ? 1811 (CO 194.51); Pierce Poor, from the parish of New Gate (Co. Waterford), married at St. John's, 1811 (Nfld. Archives BRC); Mary, from Northern Bay, married at St. John's, 1812 (Nfld. Archives BRC); James Power, from Powerstown (Co. Tipperary), married at St. John's, 1813 (Nfld. Archives BRC); Charles, from Mothele (Co. Waterford), publican of St. John's, deceased 1815 (*Royal Gazette* 2 Mar 1815); John, of Trinity (unspecified), 1817 (Nfld. Archives KCRC); James, from Co. Waterford, of Tilton Harbour (now Tilting), 1817 (Nfld. Archives KCRC); Mary, from Co. Waterford, married at New Harbour (Trinity B.), 1817 (Nfld. Archives KCRC); Edmund, of Ragged Harbour (now Melrose), 1818 (Nfld. Archives KCRC); Patrick, from Ballymitten (unidentified), Ireland, fisherman of St. John's, deceased 1818 (*Nfld. Mercantile Journal* 17 Jul 1818); Michael, of King's Cove, 1822 (Nfld. Archives KCRC); Mary, of Moretons Harbour, 1822 (Nfld. Archives KCRC); Doctor, of Fogo, 1825 (Nfld. Archives KCRC); Samuel, of Toads (now Tors) Cove, 1825 (Nfld. Archives BRC); Robert, of Joe Batts Arm, 1826 (Nfld. Archives KCRC); Bridget, from Co. Kilkenny, married at Riders Harbour (Trinity B.), 1826 (Nfld. Archives KCRC); Margaret, of Brigus South, 1828 (*Newfoundlander* 27 Nov 1828); Patrick, of Broad Cove (now Duntara), 1828 (Nfld. Archives KCRC); Michael, of Caplin Bay (now Calvert), 1828 (*Newfoundlander* 27 Nov 1828); Richard, from Western Bay, married at Harbour Grace, 1828 (Nfld. Archives HGRC); Michael, of Twillingate, 1829 (Nfld. Archives KCRC); Mary, from Tintern (Co. Wexford), married at Harbour Grace, 1829 (Nfld. Archives BRC); Bridget, from Waterford, married at Brigus, 1829 (Nfld. Archives BRC); Richard, of Cape Cove (Bonavista B.), 1829 (Nfld. Archives KCRC); ——, of St. Mary's, 1830 (Nfld. Archives BRC); ——, from Co. Wexford, of King's Cove, 1830 (Nfld. Archives KCRC); James, of Fortune Harbour, 1830 (Nfld. Archives KCRC); Michael, from Co. Kilkenny, married at Ship Cove (now part of Port Rexton), 1830 (Nfld. Archives KCRC); Richard, of Middle Bill Cove (Bonavista B.), 1833 (Nfld. Archives KCRC); Thomas, planter of Blackhead (Bay de Verde district), 1834 (DPHW 52A); William Power or Poor, planter of Adam's Cove, 1840 (DPHW 52A); Walter Power, granted land at Outer Cove (St. John's district), 1843 (Nfld. Archives, Registry Crown Lands); Ambrose, of Shoe Cove (Twillingate district), 1844 (DPHW 86); Philip, granted land at Cod Seine Cove (Bay Bulls), 1847 (Nfld. Archives, Registry Crown Lands); Edward, of Flat Island (Bonavista B.), 1849 (DPHW 73); John de la Power, of St. John's, 1851 (*Newfoundlander* 13 Feb 1851); Patrick Power, of Hallow Wood (? for Holyrood) (Conception B.), 1856 (Nfld. Archives KCRC); Anne, of Indian Arm (Bonavista B.), 1857 (Nfld. Archives KCRC); Ann, of Greenspond, 1860 (Nfld. Archives KCRC); Thomas, of Dog Cove (Bonavista B.), 1861 (Nfld. Archives KCRC); Thomas, of Chapel Arm, 1866 (Nfld. Archives HGRC); Mary, of Barrow Harbour (Bonavista B.), 1868 (Nfld. Archives KCRC); Power, widespread, Poor, rare, in Lovell 1671.

Modern status: Power, widespread in all districts, especially at St. John's, Bell Island, Tors Cove, Branch, Grand Falls, Chapel Arm and Marystown; Powers, rare, at St. John's.

Place names: Powers Cove, —— —— Head 47-11 55-08; Powers Cove, —— Pond 47-34 52-50; —— Rock 47-05 55-04.

POWLEY, a surname of England, a variant of Pawley, ? a diminutive of Paul (*see* PAUL), or ? from some unidentified place name (Bardsley).
In Newfoundland:
Modern status: Rare, at Corner Brook (*Electors* 1955).

POYNTER, a surname of England from Middle English *poynte* – a tagged lace or cord of twisted yarn, silk or leather, hence a maker of points used for fastening hose and doublet together, or one who points tiles, stones or bricks with mortar. (Reaney).
Traced by Spiegelhalter in Devon.
In Newfoundland:
Early instances: Edward Pointer, of Grand Bank, 1852 (DPHW 106); Fanny, of Grand Beach, 1855 (MUN Hist.).
Modern status: Rare, at Seal Cove (Harbour Main district), St. Lawrence (*Electors* 1955) and St. John's.
Place names (not necessarily from the surname): Pointer Lake (Labrador) 53-02 66-57, 54-24 66-54.

PRADO, ? a Newfoundland variant of the surname of France Pradeau from various French place names with the general sense of meadow – (dweller by the) meadow. (Dauzat).
In Newfoundland:
Modern status: At Felix Cove and Aguathuna (*Electors* 1955).

PRATT, a surname of England and Ireland from Old English *prætt* – a trick or an Old English adjective **prætt* – cunning, astute. Cottle also suggests a derivative from a slang term for buttocks. (Reaney, Cottle). *See also* PRETTY.
Traced by Guppy mainly in the eastern and Midland counties but also in Devon, and by MacLysaght in southeast Ireland.
In Newfoundland:
Early instance: Rev. John (1841–1904), born at Barnard Castle (Co. Durham), spent his early life at Gunnerside, Yorkshire NR, came to Newfoundland in 1874 where he served as minister in many communities until his death at Grand Bank in 1904 (Pitt).
Modern status: At St. John's.

PREBLE, a surname of England ? from the French place name Préval (Sarthe). (E.C. Smith).

Guppy traced Prebble in Kent.

In Newfoundland:

Modern status: Rare, at Woody Point (St. Barbe district) (*Electors* 1955).

Place name: Prebble Rocks (Labrador) 59-13 63-24.

PREDHAM. *See* PRIDHAM

PRESH(Y)ON, PRESUYON, ? Newfoundland variants of the surnames of France Perrichon or Perruchon, the former a pet-form of Pierre (*see* PETERS), both - (dweller on) stony ground. (Dauzat).

In Newfoundland:

Modern status: Preshon, at Flat Bay (St. George's district) (*Electors* 1955);

Preshyon, rare, at Corner Brook; Presuyon, rare, at St. Teresa's (St. George's district) (*Electors* 1955).

PRESS, a surname of England from Old English *prēost* – priest, "in early examples denoting office but later usually a nickname for a man of 'priestly' appearance or behaviour or, no doubt, often for one of a most unpriestly character." (Reaney, Cottle). *See also* PRIOR.

In Newfoundland:

Family tradition: —— from London, England, settled at St. John's (MUN Folklore).

Modern status: At St. John's.

PRESTON, a surname of England and Ireland from a common English place name in 24 counties – the priest's place or farm, or ? sometimes – the priest's son. (Reaney, Cottle).

Traced by Guppy in Lancashire, Norfolk, Nottinghamshire, Shropshire and Yorkshire, by Spiegelhalter in Devon, and by MacLysaght in Co. Meath.

In Newfoundland:

Early instances: James, ? of St. John's, 1776 (CO 194.33); John, of Renews appointed J.P. for Ferryland district, 1823 (D'Alberti 33); Jacob, of Fools (now Pool's) Island (Bonavista B.), 1823 (DPHW 76); John, from Drewsteignton (Devon), married at St. John's, 1834 (DPHW 26D); James, of Twillingate, deceased, 1845 (*Newfoundlander* 9 Oct 1845).

Modern status: At Corner Brook, St. John's and in the Bonavista North and Twillingate districts.

PRESUYON. *See* PRESH(Y)ON

PRETTY, a surname of England from Old English *prættig* – crafty, cunning, skilled. (Reaney, Cottle). *See also* PRATT.

Traced by Guppy in Leicestershire, Rutlandshire and Suffolk.

In Newfoundland:

Early instances: Samuel, of Dildo Cove (Trinity B.), 1835, came to Newfoundland from Chard (Somerset) 60 years previously, that is, 1775 (Wix); Joseph ? Pretten (for ? Prettey), of Bonavista, 1791 (USPG); Samuel Pretty, of Trinity Bay, 1792, of Shoal Harbour (now Cavendish), Winter 1800–01 (Census Trinity B., DPHW 64); Joseph Pretty or Pritty, of Dureles [sic] Cove (Trinity North district), 1823 (DPHW 64B); Joseph Pretty, of New Harbour, 1857 (*Newfoundlander* 24 Sep 1857); John, fisherman of New Bonaventure, 1857 (DPHW 64B); Elias Pritty, of Chapel Arm, 1866 (Nfld. Archives HGRC); Jesse Pretty, of Harbour Grace, 1869 (Nfld. Archives HGRC); Samuel, of Freshwater Bay (Bonavista B.), 1871 (Lovell).

Modern status: Scattered, especially at Dildo and St. John's.

Place names (not necessarily from the surname): Pretty Island, —— —— Harbour, —— Tickle 49-29 55-42; —— Islands 48-44 53-50.

PRICE, a surname of England, Wales, Ireland and Guernsey (Channel Islands), a shortened form of the Welsh *ap Rhys* – son of Rhys, or from Old French *pris* – (a fixer or setter of) price(s). (Reaney, Cottle, MacLysaght, Turk). *See also* REES(E) and RICE.

Traced by Guppy especially in the Welsh Border counties and in North and South Wales, and found by MacLysaght in Ireland since the fourteenth century but not especially associated with any particular locality.

In Newfoundland:

Early instances: Walter, clergyman of St. John's, 1786 (DPHW 26C); William, of Bonavista, 1804 (DPHW 70); Benjamin, planter of Hants Harbour, 1823 (DPHW 58); Sarah, of Ragged Harbour (now Melrose), 1824 (Nfld. Archives KCRC); Mary, of Tilton Harbour (now Tilting), 1824 (Nfld. Archives KCRC); Sarah, of Brunette, 1829 (DPHW 106); William, from Bristol, England, married at St. John's, 1830 (Nfld. Archives BRC); James, of Grand Bank, 1842 (DPHW 109); James, of Back Cove (Twillingate district), 1871 (Lovell); John, farmer of Logy Bay, 1871 (Lovell); Philip, planter of Petty Harbour, 1871 (Lovell).

Modern status: Scattered, especially at Brunette.

PRIDDLE, a surname of Wales, a shortened form of the Welsh *ap Riddle*. (Long).

In Newfoundland:

Early instances: Job, fisherman of New (now Parsons) Harbour, 1854 (DPHW 102); Issa[h] and Jacob, of Carbonear, 1871 (Lovell); George, planter of Fortune, 1871 (Lovell).

Modern status: Scattered, especially at Victoria.

PRIDE, PRYDE, surnames of England from Middle English *pride* – pride, a nickname or pageant name, or ? from Welsh *prid* – precious, dear. (Reaney).

Traced by Reaney especially in the Welsh Border counties.

In Newfoundland:

Early instance: Philip and Thomas Pride, fishermen of Twillingate, 1871 (Lovell).

Modern status: Pride, at Twillingate and Grand Falls; Pryde, rare, at Corner Brook.

PRIDEAUX, a surname of England and the Channel Islands from the English place name Prideaux (Cornwall). (Reaney, Turk).

Traced by Spiegelhalter in Devon.

In Newfoundland:

Early instance: Thomas, from Shaldon (Devon), master of ? *Carteretta*, married at St. John's, 1846 (*Newfoundlander* 21 May 1846, DPHW 26D).

Modern status: Unique, at St. John's.

PRIDHAM, PREDHAM, surnames of England from Old French *prudhomme* – upright, honest man or an expert. (Reaney).

Spiegelhalter traced Pridham in Devon.

In Newfoundland:

Early instance: James Pridam, of Petty Harbour, 1813 (DPHW 26B).

Modern status: Predham, at St. John's and Petty Harbour; Pridham, at St. John's and Blackhead (St. John's district).

PRIM, a surname of England, ? a variant of Prime from Old French *prim(e)* – fine, delicate, or of Prin(n) from Latin *primus*, Old French *prin* – first, superior; small, slender. (Reaney). *See also* PRIMMER.

Spiegelhalter traced Prin in Devon.

In Newfoundland:

Early instances: John, of St. John's Harbour, 1703 (CO 194.3); Peter, from Tintern Parish (Co. Wexford), married at St. John's, 1805 (Nfld. Archives BRC); Peter, from Dunmain Parish (unidentified) (Co. Wexford), carpenter of St. John's, deceased, 1816 (*Nfld. Mercantile Journal* 23 Oct 1816); Henry, of Grand Bank, 1871 (Lovell).

Modern status: Rare, at St. John's.

PRIMMER, a surname of England ? from French *premier* – first, or ? a priest whose function was to conduct the office of prime, or ? from Mediaeval Latin *primarius* – chief forester, foreman. (Weekley *Surnames*, Bardsley, Spiegelhalter). *See also* PRIM.

Spiegelhalter traced Primer in Devon.

In Newfoundland:

Early instances: John Primer, planter of Fogo, 1792 (MUN Hist.); William Primmer, planter of Barr'd Islands, 1821 (USPG); James, of Joe Batts Arm, 1842 (DPHW 83).

Modern status: Scattered, especially at Barr'd Islands.

Place name: Primer Rock 49-40 54-44.

PRINCE, a surname of England and Jersey (Channel Islands) from French *prince* – prince, a nickname or pageant name or from service in a prince's household. (Reaney, Cottle, Turk).

Traced by Guppy in Cheshire, Derbyshire, Staffordshire and by Spiegelhalter in Devon.

In Newfoundland:

Early instances: Samuel, son of John and Mary, baptised 14 Jul 1814 at Bonavista (DPHW 71, S. Prince); Anne, of King's Cove, 1825 (Nfld. Archives KCRC); John, of Tickle Cove (Bonavista B.), 1840 (DPHW 73); John (and others), planters of Southern Bay (Bonavista B.), 1871 (Lovell).

Modern status: Scattered, especially at Princeton.

Place names (not necessarily from the surname): Princes Pond 47-20 52-48; —— Horny Rock 49-44 54-19; —— Lookout 47-37 52-51; Princeton 48-25 53-36.

PRIOR, PRYOR, surnames of England, PRIOR of Scotland and Ireland, from Old English *prior* or Old French *pri(o)ur* – prior, a monastic official next in rank below an abbot, the surname being based on a nickname deriving often from employment in a prior's service. (Reaney, Cottle, MacLysaght, Black). *See also* PRESS, LEPRIEUR.

Guppy traced Prior, Pryor in Bedfordshire, Cambridgeshire, Cornwall, Hampshire, Hertfordshire, Norfolk and Suffolk, with Prior the usual form, Pryor chiefly characteristic of Cornwall and Pryer a rare form found in Norfolk. MacLysaght traced Prior in Cos. Cavan and Leitrim and also elsewhere in Ireland.

In Newfoundland:

Early instances: Edward Prior, of St. John's, 1835 (DPHW 26B); William Pryor, from Halifax, granted land at Port aux Basques, 1846 (Nfld. Archives, Registry Crown Lands); John, of Bay de Verde,

1860 (DPHW 56); Joseph, servant, son of John and Ann of Crewkerne (Somerset), married at Harbour Breton, 1868 (Harbour Breton Anglican Church Records per D.A. Macdonald); William, of Channel, 1871 (Lovell).

Modern status: Prior, Pryor, scattered.

PRITCHARD, a surname of England, Wales and Ireland, a shortened form of the Welsh *ap Richard* – son of Richard (*see* RICHARDS), or a variant of PRITCHETT. (Reaney, Cottle).

Traced by Guppy in North Wales and the Welsh Border counties, and by MacLysaght in Co. Armagh and other parts of Ulster.

In Newfoundland:

Early instances: John Prichard, of Salvage, 1676 (CO 1); Charles Pritchard, shoe-maker of Trinity (Trinity B.), 1827 (DPHW 64B); James, of Open Hole (now Open Hall), 1830 (DPHW 70); —— Pricherd, of St. John's, 1839 (*Newfoundlander* 18 Apr 1839); William Pridget or Prichard, fisherman of Brigus, 1839, 1848 (DPHW 34); John Pritchard, fisherman of Bay Roberts, 1843 (DPHW 39).

Modern status: At Brigus, Corner Brook and Buchans.

PRITCHETT, a surname of England and Wales, ? a variant of Prickett from Middle English *priket* – a buck in his second year, a nickname; or a variant of PRITCHARD. (Reaney).

In Newfoundland:

Family tradition: James, ? from Devon, settled at Goose Bay (Bonavista B.); the family later moved to Domino Point, Freshwater Bay (Bonavista B.), then to Middle Brook, Gambo (MUN Folklore).

Early instances: James Pritchell, of Greenspond, 1815 (DPHW 76); James Pritchet, of Goose Bay (Bonavista B.), 1832 (DPHW 76); Job (and others), of Freshwater Bay (Bonavista B.), 1871 (Lovell).

Modern status: Scattered, especially at Middle Brook (Bonavista B.).

Place name: Pritchetts 48-50 54-17.

PROBERT, a surname of England and Wales, a shortened form of the Welsh *ap Robert* – son of Robert (*see* ROBERTS). (Reaney).

Traced by Guppy in Herefordshire, Monmouthshire and South Wales.

In Newfoundland:

Family tradition: —— (1879–) from Gateshead, England, went to Quebec in 1906; his son moved to Newfoundland in 1954 (MUN Folklore).

Modern status: Unique, at St. John's.

PROCTOR, a surname of England and Ireland from Latin *procurator*, Middle English *prok(e)tour* – steward, agent, tithe-collector, attorney in a spiritual court, one licensed to collect alms for lepers or enclosed anchorites. (Reaney, Cottle).

Traced by Guppy in the north and Midlands, and by MacLysaght in Cos. Armagh and Donegal since the seventeenth century.

In Newfoundland:

Early instances: Thomas, of Placentia, 1725 (CO 194.8); Mark, of St. John's, 1816 (CO 194.60); James, of Grand Bank, 1850 (DPHW 106).

Modern status: Unique, at St. John's.

PROLE, a surname of England from the English place names East and West Prawle (Devon), from Old English **prǣ(w)hyll* or **prā(w)hyll* – (dweller on the) look-out hill. (Spiegelhalter, Ekwall).

Guppy traced Prole in Bedfordshire; Spiegelhalter traced Proll in Devon.

In Newfoundland:

Early instances: John Proule, of St. John's, 1819 (DPHW 26B); James Prole or Proal, of Indian Burying Place (Twillingate district), 1843 (DPHW 86).

Modern status: At Winterton and Indian Burying Place.

PROSPER, a baptismal name and surname of France, after a Christian historian of the fifth century. (Dauzat).

In Newfoundland:

Early instance: James, fisherman of Bay of Islands, 1871 (Lovell).

Modern status: At Corner Brook.

Place name: Prosper Island 51-36 55-51.

PROSSER, a surname of England and Wales, a shortened form of the Welsh *ap Rosser* – son of Rosser. (Cottle).

Traced by Guppy in Gloucestershire, Herefordshire, Monmouthshire and South Wales.

In Newfoundland:

Early instance: William, of St. John's, 1751 (CO 194.13).

Modern status: At Harbour Breton, Parsons Harbour (*Electors* 1955) and Channel.

Place name: Prosser Rock 47-34 52-42.

PROUDFOOT, a surname of England and Ireland from Old English *prūd*, *prūt* – proud and *fōt* – foot, a nickname for one who walks with a haughty gait. (Reaney, Cottle).

Traced by Spiegelhalter in Devon and by MacLysaght in Co. Meath.

In Newfoundland:

Early instance: Robert, from Scotland, married at St. John's, 1828 (Nfld. Archives BRC).

Modern status: At Bell Island (*Electors* 1955) and St. John's.

PROWSE, a surname of England from Old French and Middle English *prous, prouz* – valiant, brave, doughty. (Reaney, Cottle).

Guppy traced Prouse and Prowse in Devon and Cornwall, with Prouse confined to Devon.

In Newfoundland:

Early instances: George, of Bay Bulls, 1682 (CO 1); Benjamin Prouse, fisherman of St. John's or Petty Harbour, ? 1745 (CO 194.24); Henry Prowse or Prowce, soldier of St. John's, 1753 (DPHW 26C); Robert Prowse (1798–), born at Torquay (Devon), came to St. John's in 1808, later went into business at Port de Grave and St. John's (MUN Hist.); Samuel, appointed magistrate for the coast of Labrador, 1814 (D'Alberti 19); John, from South Bovey (Devon), carpenter of St. John's, died 1835, aged 54 (*Times* 18 Feb 1835); Samuel, from Torquay (Devon), sub-collector of H.M. Customs at Twillingate, 1843, died in Okehampton (Devon), 1856 (*Royal Gazette* 30 May 1843, *Newfoundlander* 10 Jul 1856).

Modern status: Scattered, especially at St. John's.

Place name: Prowseton 47-40 54-21.

PRYDE. *See* PRIDE

PRYOR. *See* PRIOR

PUDDESTER, PUDDISTER, English variants of the surname of Jersey (Channel Islands) Poingdestre from Old French *Poingdestre* – right fist, a nickname. (Weekley *Romance*, Cottle, Turk).

In Newfoundland:

Early instances: Henry Poingdestre, of Western Bay, 1770 (CO 199.18); George Puddester or Poddister, planter of Broad Cove (Bay de Verde district), 1816 (DPHW 52A); John Puddester or Pudister, planter of Northern Bay, 1818 (DPHW 52A); Stephen Puddester, fisherman of Blackhead (Bay de Verde district), 1827 (DPHW 52A); George Podester, of Harbour Grace Parish, 1834 (Nfld. Archives HGRC); Thomas Puddester, of St. John's, 1843 (DPHW 26D); Thomas Pudista, of King's Cove, 1871 (Lovell); George Pudister, of Bay Bulls, 1871 (Lovell).

Modern status: Puddester, scattered, especially at St. John's and Bay Bulls; Puddister, at St. John's and Bay Bulls.

PUDDICOMBE, a surname of England from Puddicombe House (Devon). (Spiegelhalter).

Traced by Spiegelhalter in Devon.

In Newfoundland:

Early instance: William Puddicumb, of Harbour Grace Parish, 1888 (Nfld. Archives HGRC).

Modern status: At Lock's Cove (White B.), and St. John's.

PUDDISTER. *See* PUDDESTER

PUGH, a surname of England and Wales, a shortened form of the Welsh *ap Hugh* – son of Hugh (*see* HUE, HUGHES). (Reaney, Cottle).

Traced by Guppy in Herefordshire, Monmouthshire, Shropshire, Worcestershire, South Wales and especially North Wales.

In Newfoundland:

Early instance: Edward, of Heart's Content, 1871 (Lovell).

Modern status: At Harbour Grace, Corner Brook (*Electors* 1955) and St. John's.

PULLIN, a surname of England from Old French *poulain* – colt, a nickname. (Nfld. Archives KCRC). (Reaney). *See* POULAIN.

Guppy traced Pullon, Pullen, Pullin in Berkshire, Buckinghamshire, Gloucestershire, Monmouthshire, Oxfordshire, Wiltshire and Yorkshire WR, with Pullen the most frequent form, followed by Pullin which is usually associated with Pullen and is characteristic of Gloucestershire; Pullan is mostly found in Yorkshire WR. Spiegelhalter traced Pulling in Devon.

In Newfoundland:

Early instances: Mary Pullen, from Brixham (Devon), ? of St. John's, died 1813 (*Royal Gazette* 17 Jun 1813); William Arthur, planter of Twillingte, 1823 (USPG).

Modern status: Rare, at Corner Brook.

PUMPHREY, a surname of England and Wales, a shortened form of the Welsh *ap Humphrey* – son of Humphrey (*see* HUMPHRIES), or a variant of Pomfret, Pontefract (Yorkshire WR), from Latin *Pontefracto* – broken bridge, locally pronounced pumfrit. (Reaney, Ekwall).

Spiegelhalter traced Pumfrey in Devon.

In Newfoundland:

Early instances: Jerry Pumphry, of Harbour Grace Parish, 1817 (Nfld. Archives HGRC); Michael, Jeremiah and John Pumphrey, granted land at Southside Carbonear, 1847 (Nfld. Archives, Registry

Crown Lands); ——, captain of the *Glide* in the seal fishery out of Harbour Grace, 1857 (*Newfoundlander* 19 Mar 1857).

Modern status: Scattered.

PURCELL, a surname of England and Ireland from Old French *pourcel* – piglet, a nickname. (Reaney, MacLysaght).

Guppy traced Purssell in Buckinghamshire, Spiegelhalter Purcell in Devon and MacLysaght Purcell in Co. Tipperary.

In Newfoundland:

Early instances: Patrick, cooper of St. John's, 1794–5, "30 years in Newfoundland," that is, 1764–5 (Census 1794–5); Matthew Purcill, of St. Mary's, married at St. John's, 1803 (Nfld. Archives BRC); Mary Purcel, from Gartorahoe [sic], Cashel (Co. Tipperary), married at St. John's, 1804 (Nfld. Archives BRC); Elizabeth Purcell, of Portugal Cove, 1811 (Nfld. Archives BRC); Michael Purcel(l) or Purcil, of Harbour Grace Parish, 1818 (Nfld. Archives HGRC); William Purcel, of Bonavista, 1826 (Nfld. Archives KCRC); John Purcell, teacher of Brookfield (unspecified), 1839 (*Newfoundlander* 1 Aug 1839); James, granted land near Upper Long Pond, 1844 (Nfld. Archives, Registry Crown Lands); Maria, of Harbour Grace, 1866 (Nfld. Archives HGRC; Margaret, of British Harbour, 1868 (Nfld. Archives KCRC).

Modern status: Scattered, especially at St. John's.

Place name: Purcell's Harbour 49-37 54-43.

PURCHASE, a surname of England from Old French *purchas* – pursuit, pillage, later used for a messenger, courier. (Reaney, Cottle).

Guppy traced Purkis in Cambridgeshire, Spiegelhalter Purchase in Devon.

In Newfoundland:

Early instances: Thomas, from Bristol, fisherman of Bream-Head, Newfoundland, deceased 1810 (*Royal Gazette* 8 Nov 1810); John, from Hampshire, married in the Northern District, 1812 (Nfld. Archives BRC); Joshua, of Joe Batts Arm, 1817, of Fogo, 1819 (Nfld. Archives KCRC); ——, 1827, Thomas, of Lamaline, 1835 (DPHW 109; Grand Bank Methodist baptisms, 1827 per P.E.L. Smith); Thomas, of Round Harbour (Burin district), 1827 (DPHW 109); Joseph, planter of Ship Cove (Trinity North district), 1831 (DPHW 64B); James, of Cat Harbour (now Lumsden), 1845 (DPHW 76); John, of Exploits Burnt Island, 1845 (DPHW 86); Charles Purchas, planter of Trinity (Trinity B.), 1845 (DPHW 64B); Cabel Purchase, of Tilton Harbour (now Tilt-

ing), 1859 (DPHW 92); Joseph, fisherman of Pease Cove (Trinity North district), 1859 (DPHW 64B); Thomas, fisherman of Fortune, 1860 (DPHW 106); George, of Great St. Lawrence, 1860 (DPHW 100); William, of Meadows (Burin district), 1860 (DPHW 107); Joseph, of Deer Harbour (Trinity B.), 1871 (Lovell); George, of Garia, 1871 (Lovell); Jonas, of St. John's 1871 (Lovell).

Modern status: Scattered, especially at Corner Brook, St. John's and in the Gander district.

PURDY, a surname of England and Ireland, a nickname for one who used the oath *pour Dieu* – by (literally for) God, an interpretation accepted by, for example, Reaney and Cottle but dismissed contemptuously by Black.

Traced by Guppy in Norfolk, by Spiegelhalter in Devon, and by MacLysaght in northeast Ulster since the seventeenth century.

In Newfoundland:

Early instances: Joseph, of Bay of Islands, 1848 (DPHW 96); George, of Long Harbour (Fortune B.), 1871 (Lovell).

Modern status: At Corner Brook.

Place name: Purdy Cove 50-27 56-20.

PUSHIE, ? a surname of England, a variant of Pusey etc. from the English place name Pusey (Berkshire), or a variant of BUSH(E)Y.

In Newfoundland:

Modern status: At St. John's.

PUTT, a surname of England, a variant of PITT. (Reaney).

Traced by Spiegelhalter in Devon and by Cottle in the West Midland and southwestern counties.

In Newfoundland:

Early instance: James, of Petty Harbour, 1848 (DPHW 31).

Modern status: At St. John's and Lower Goulds.

PYE, a surname of England from Old French, Middle English *pye*, *pie* – magpie, or from Middle English *pie* – (maker or seller) of pie(s), or (dweller at the sign of the) *Pie*. (Reaney, Cottle).

Traced by Guppy in Kent, Lancashire and Northumberland, and by Spiegelhalter in Devon.

In Newfoundland:

Early instances: Elisha, of Carbonear, 1799 (CO 199.18); Roger Pies, of Portugal Cove, 1802 (DPHW 26B); Thomas Pie, fisherman of Brigus, 1834 (DPHW 34); Thomas Pye, of Catalina, 1842 (DPHW 67); Elijah and Samuel, of Crockers Cove (Carbonear),

1871 (Lovell); Samuel, fisherman of Hopeville (Bonavista South district), 1872 (DPHW 80).

Modern status: Scattered, especially at St. John's.

PYGAS, a ? Newfoundland variant of the surname of France *Pigasse* – (user or seller of) pick(s), axe(s). (Dauzat).

In Newfoundland:

Modern status: Rare, at Corner Brook.

PYNE. *See* PINE

PYNN, a surname of England, ? from the English place name Pinn (Devon). (Gover).

Traced by Matthews in Dorset.

In Newfoundland:

Early instances: Henry Pin (Pinn in 1676, Pynne in 1677), of Carbonear, 1675 (CO 1); Henry Pynn, of Harbour Grace, 1775, property "possessed by the Family for upwards of 70 years," that is, before 1705 (CO 199.18); Robert Pinne, of St. John's, 1706 (CO 194.3); Patience Pynn, of St. John's, in possession of property at Musketta (now Bristol's Hope), 1765 (CO 199.18); George, of (Upper) Island Cove, 1770 (CO 199.18); Henry Pinn, of Seal Cove (now New Chelsea), 1822 (DPHW 58); Elizabeth Pynn, of Hants Harbour, 1823 (DPHW 58); William Pinn, shipmaster of Trinity (Trinity B.), 1833 (DPHW 64B); —— Pynne, of Quirpon, 1849, from Harbour Grace, 1835 (Feild); Mary Pynn, of Quidi Vidi, 1835 (DPHW 26D); John Pinn or Pynn, of Bonavista, 1841 (DPHW 70); Henry Pynn, of Russell's Cove (now New Melbourne), 1852 (DPHW 59A); William, of Fortune, married Leah Collier 1870 (Grand Bank Methodist marriages, P.E.L. Smith); scattered in Lovell 1871.

Modern status: Widespread, especially at Harbour Grace, New Chelsea and St. John's.

Place names (not all necessarily from the surname): ? Pin Hill 47-21 55-12; Pynns, —— Brook 49-06 57-33; —— Brook 48-57 55-53, 48-59 57-59, 49-05 57-32; —— Pond 49-00 57-58.

Q

QUAN(N), variants of the surnames of Ireland (O)Quane, Quan, *Ó Cuain* from the personal name *Cuan*. (MacLysaght).

MacLysaght traced (O)Quan(e) originally in Co. Sligo but for the last three centuries mainly in Co. Waterford.

In Newfoundland:

Early instances: Honora Quan, from RathGormick (unidentified) (Co. Waterford), married at St. John's, 1816 (Nfld. Archives BRC); James, from Berry (Devon) married at St. John's, 1827 (Nfld. Archives BRC).

Modern status: Quan, rare, at St. John's; Quann, at Miller's Passage (*Electors* 1955), Harbour Breton, Stephenville, Lourdes and St. John's.

QUEHE,·? a variant of the surname of Ireland Quee, possibly for the Scots MacQuey, Ir. *Mac Aodhe* – son of *Aodh* or Hugh. (MacLysaght, Black).

MacLysaght traced Quee in Co. Antrim.

In Newfoundland:

Modern status: Rare, at Corner Brook.

QUICK, a surname of England and Ireland from Old English *cwic* – nimble, lively, or from various English place names including the element *quick* – poplar, aspen, or (dweller near the) poplar, aspen; or in Ireland sometimes a variant of QUIRK. (Reaney, MacLysaght).

Traced by Guppy in Cornwall and Devon and by MacLysaght in Co. Cork.

In Newfoundland:

Early instances: Richard, of Quidi Vidi Cove, 1771 (CO 194.18, 30); John Quick or Quirk, of St. John's, 1796 (CO 194.39); John Quick, of St. John's, 1809 (D'Alberti 19).

Modern status: At St. John's.

QUIGLEY, a surname of Ireland (O)Quigley, *Ó Coigligh*, ? Ir. *coigeal* – one with unkempt hair. (MacLysaght).

MacLysaght found (O)Quigley dispersed throughout Ireland but most numerous in Cos. Donegal and Derry.

In Newfoundland:

Early instances: Garret(t), of St. John's, 1759 (DPHW 26C, CO 194.18); Patrick Quigly, from Co.

Wexford, married at St. John's, 1803 (Nfld. Archives BRC); Pat, of Harbour Grace Parish, 1813 (Nfld. Archives HGRC); Mary, from Co. Wexford, married at Trinity (unspecified), 1816 (Nfld. Archives KCRC); P. Quigley, of Carbonear, 1832 (*Newfoundlander* 4 Oct 1832); John, of Torbay, 1839 (Nfld. Archives BRC); James, from Co. Tipperary, of Port de Grave, 1844 (*Indicator* 24 Aug 1844); Edward, Road Commissioner for the area, Harry Cove Point and Path from Limber Grass to Harry Cove (Placentia B.), 1848 (*Nfld. Almanac*); Peter, from Bree Parish (unidentified) (Co. Wexford), of St. John's, 1857 (*Newfoundlander* 30 Mar 1857); John, of King's Cove, 1862 (Nfld. Archives KCRC); John, of Barrow Harbour (Bonavista B.), 1863 (Nfld. Archives KCRC); Michael Quigly, of Keels, 1871 (Nfld. Archives KCRC); Peter Quigley, farmer of Belle Isle (now Bell Island) and Lance Cove, 1871 (Lovell); Dominic (and others), of the North Harbour, John's Point, Tickles and Colinet area, 1871 (Lovell).

Modern status: Scattered, especially at St. John's, Torbay and in the Humber West district.

QUILTY, a surname of Ireland (O)Quilty, *Ó Caoilte*. (MacLysaght).

Traced by MacLysaght mainly in Munster and especially in Co. Limerick.

In Newfoundland:

Family tradition: ——, from Ireland, settled at Bishop's Cove (Conception B.), in the 1700s; the family later moved to St. Thomas (Harbour Main district) (MUN Hist.).

Early instances: Nicholas, of Coopers Head (Bishop's Cove), 1780 (CO 199.18); J., of Harbour Grace Parish, 1806 (Nfld. Archives HGRC); William, of Harbour Grace, 1868 (Nfld. Archives HGRC); John (and others), of Bishop's Cove, 1871 (Lovell); William, fisherman of St. Mary's, 1871 (Lovell).

Modern status: Scattered, including St. Thomas.

QUINLAN, a surname of Ireland (O)Quinlan, *Ó Caoinleáin*, the Munster form of *Ó Caoindealbháin*. (MacLysaght).

Traced by MacLysaght mainly in Co. Tipperary.

In Newfoundland:

Family tradition: ——, from Co. Tipperary, Ireland, settled in Newfoundland; the family lived at Holyrood and later at Red Head Cove (Conception B.) (MUN Folklore).

Early instances: Peter, of Gasters (Conception B.), 1775 (CO 199.18); Thomas, of Brigus, 1792 (CO 199.18); Terry, of Harbour Grace Parish, 1806 (Nfld. Archives HGRC); Bridget, of St. John's, 1806 (Nfld. Archives BRC); John Quinland, of Trinity (Trinity B.), 1807 (DPHW 64); Thomas Quinlan, from Portlaw Parish (Co. Waterford), married at St. John's, 1812 (Nfld. Archives BRC); Maurice, from Dingle (Co. Kerry), married at Bonavista, 1822 (Nfld. Archives KCRC); Mrs., of Harbour Grace, 1832 (*Newfoundlander* 23 Aug 1832); Peter, ? of Northern Bay, 1838 (DPHW 54); Jeremiah (and others), of North Arm, Holyrood, 1871 (Lovell); Jeremiah, planter of Red Head Cove, 1871 (Lovell); Edward and Richard, of Renews, 1871 (Lovell); Joseph Quinlin, of Fortune (Harbour), 1871 (Lovell).

Modern status: Scattered, especially at Birchy Bay (Twillingate district) and St. John's.

(O)QUINN, surnames of Ireland, Quinn of the Channel Islands, (O)Quin(n), *Ó Cuinn*, from the personal name *Conn*, but in Ulster often *Ó Coinne* "more correctly anglicized Quinney." (MacLysaght, Turk).

Found by MacLysaght very numerous in all provinces and especially in Co. Tyrone.

In Newfoundland:

Some West Coast families named AUCOIN have hibernicized their family name to O'QUINN.

Early instances: William Quinn, of Fermeuse, murdered in 1752 (CO 194.13); Patrick Quin, fisherman of St. John's, 1794–5, "16 years in Newfoundland," that is, 1778–9 (Census 1794–5); Samuel Quinn, of Trinity Bay, 1798 (DPHW 64); Darby, proprietor and occupier of fishing room, Riders Harbour, Winter 1800–01 (Census Trinity B.); John Quin, from Grulnahir [sic] (unidentified) (Co. Tipperary), married at St. John's, 1813 (Nfld. Archives BRC); Mary, of Harbour Grace Parish, 1813 (Nfld. Archives HGRC); William, from Co. Kilkenny, fisherman of Conception Bay, died 1814 (*Royal Gazette* 8 Sep 1814); Jeremiah Quinn, from Cahier (Co. Tipperary), fisherman of Harbour Grace, died 1815 (*Royal Gazette* 6 Jul 1815); Lawrence Quin, of King's Cove, 1817 (Nfld. Archives KCRC); Jeremiah, of Trinity (unspecified), 1819 (Nfld. Archives KCRC); Stephen Quinn, of Joe Batts Arm, 1824 (Nfld. Archives KCRC); —— Quin, merchant of Rose Blanche, 1849 (Feild); John Quinn, of Burin, 1871 (Lovell); James and M., of Cod Roy and

Rivers, 1871 (Lovell); Tassian, of Indian Head (St. George's B.), 1871 (Lovell); Richard, of Placentia, 1871 (Lovell); Michael, of Salmonier (St. Mary's B.), 1871 (Lovell).

Modern status: Quinn, at Carbonear, Harbour Grace, Stephenville and St. John's; O'Quinn, scattered, especially at Stephenville and in the St. George's district.

Place name: Quinn Lake 48-29 56-51.

QUINTON, a surname of England from the English place name Quinton (Gloucestershire, Northamptonshire, Worcestershire), or from the French place name Saint-Quentin (La Manche) or ? Saint-Quentin-en-Tourmout (Somme); or from the personal name Latin *Quintinus*, popularized by Saint Quentin of Amiens martyred in the third century; or ? a nickname for one who tilted at the quintain, a post or a target mounted on a post tilted at by horsemen or footmen. (Reaney, Cottle).

In Newfoundland:

Family tradition: 2 or 3 brothers named Quinton or Quenton whose ancestors originated in France, came to Newfoundland from the Channel Islands and settled at Red Cliff (Island), (Bonavista B.) (MUN Folklore).

Early instances: William, servant of Battle Harbour (Labrador), 1795 (MUN Hist.); William, of St. John's, 1798 (DPHW 26D); John Quintum and Brothers, of Red Cliff Island, in possession of fishing room there before 1806 (Bonavista Register 1806); James Quinten, of Tickle Cove (Bonavista B.), 1830 (DPHW 70); Charles Quinton, of Open Hall, 1834 (DPHW 70); William, of Keels, 1843–45 (DPHW 73A); Edward, agent of Harbour Grace, 1854 (DPHW 43); Sarah, of Plate Cove (Bonavista B.), 1864 (Nfld. Archives KCRC); John, of King's Cove, 1871 (Lovell); Charles (and others), of Southern Bay (Bonavista B.), 1871 (Lovell).

Modern status: Scattered, especially in Bonavista South district, in particular at Red Cliff and Southern Bay.

Place names: Quinton Cove, —— —— Rocks 49-37 55-40; Quintons Cove 48-26 53-43.

QUIRK, a surname of Ireland (O)Quirke, *Ó Cuirc*, or sometimes a variant of QUICK. (MacLysaght).

Traced by MacLysaght in Co. Tipperary.

In Newfoundland:

Early instances: John, an accountant, and Thomas, a fisherman of St. John's, 1794–5, "20 years in Newfoundland," that is, 1774–5 (Census 1794–5); Thomas, of Musketta (now Bristol's

Hope), 1787 (CO 199.18); Richard, in possession of property at Quidi Vidi, 1794–5 (Census 1794–5); Cornelius, from Killcash (Co. Tipperary), married at St. John's, 1798 (Nfld. Archives BRC); Mary, of Harbour Grace Parish, 1809 (Nfld. Archives HGRC); ——, on the vessel *Sea Rover* out from Co. Wexford to St. John's, settled in Mobile in the 1820s (Dillon); William Guirk or Quirk, of King's Cove, 1822 (Nfld. Archives KCRC); John Quirk, of Burin, 1837 (Nfld. Archives BRC); Hugh, of Harbour Grace, 1866 (Nfld. Archives HGRC); William, of Bay Bulls, 1871 (Lovell); Edward, of Ferryland, 1871 (Lovell); Thomas and William, of Fortune Harbour, 1871 (Lovell); Henry (and others), of Great St. Lawrence, 1871 (Lovell).

Modern status: Scattered, especially at St. Lawrence.

Place name: Quirk Island 49-31 55-16.

R

RABBIT(T)S, surnames of England, Rabbitt(e) of England and Ireland, from the Old German personal names *Radbodo, Rabbodo*, containing the elements *counsel* and *messenger*, or from pet-forms of Robert (*see* ROBERTS); but "hardly ever of English origin in Ireland: *coinín* being the Irish for rabbit it does duty for Cunneen, Cunneeny, Conheeny, Cunnane and Kinneen in Cos. Clare, Galway and Mayo." (Reaney, Cottle, MacLysaght).

Guppy traced Rabbetts in Dorset.

In Newfoundland:

Early instances: John Rabbits Sr. and Jr., of Brigus, 1805, property "in possession of the Family for 55 years," that is, since 1755 (CO 199.18); Matthew Rabbit, of Pass Island (Burin district), 1835 (DPHW 106); —— Rabbitts, on the *Hebe* in the seal fishery out of Port de Grave, 1838 (*Newfoundlander* 29 Mar 1838); William Rabbits, granted land at Mad Rock Cove (Brigus), 1846 (Nfld. Archives, Registry Crown Lands); James and Joseph, of New (now Parsons) Harbour, 1871 (Lovell).

Modern status: Rabbits, rare, at Brigus and Corner Brook; Rabbitts, at St. John's.

RADFORD, a surname of England, Ireland and Guernsey (Channel Islands) from the English place names Radford (Devon, Nottinghamshire, Oxfordshire, Warwickshire, Worcestershire), Ratford Farm, Redford (Sussex) or Retford (Nottinghamshire), or (dweller by the) red (from the colour of the nearby soil) or reedy ford. (Reaney, Cottle, MacLysaght 73, Turk).

Traced by Guppy in Derbyshire, Essex, Nottinghamshire and Oxfordshire, by Spiegelhalter in Devon, and by MacLysaght in Co. Wexford since the sixteenth century.

In Newfoundland:

Early instances: Samuel, soldier of St. John's, 1753 (DPHW 26C); Nathaniel, from Milmannan Parish (unidentified) (Co. Wexford), married at St. John's, 1808 (Nfld. Archives BRC); Simon, from Exeter (Devon), married at St. John's, 1820 (Nfld. Archives BRC); James, of Hare Bay (Fogo district), 1841 (DPHW 83).

Modern status: At St. John's, Stephenville and St. George's.

RAHAL, a variant of the surnames of Ireland (O)Rahill, R(h)all, *Ó Raghaill.* (MacLysaght).

Traced by MacLysaght in Co. Cavan and West Leitrim.

In Newfoundland:

Family tradition: Michael, from Ireland, settled in Newfoundland; his son J. J. resided at St. John's (MUN Folklore).

Early instances: Michael Rahil, of Harbour Grace Parish, 1837 (Nfld. Archives HGRC); Michael Rall, fisherman of St. John's, 1871 (Lovell).

Modern status: At St. John's.

RAIKE, a surname of England from Old English *hraca* – (dweller near a) pass or narrow valley, or from the English place names The Rake (Sussex), Raikes Farm (Surrey) or Raikes (Yorkshire WR). (Reaney, Cottle).

Guppy found Raike uncommon in Yorkshire.

In Newfoundland:

Family tradition: ——, from England, settled in Bonne Bay (MUN Folklore).

Early instance: William Rake, fisherman of Bonne Bay, 1871 (Lovell).

Modern status: At Silver Point (St. Barbe district) (*Electors* 1955), Glenburnie, Birchy Head (St. Barbe district) and Deer Lake.

RAINES, RAYNES, surnames of England, Rain of Scotland, from Latin *Regina*, French *Reine* – queen, a personal name or nickname, or from an Old English personal name beginning with *Regen* – as in *Reynold* (*see* REYNOLDS), or from the French place names Rennes or Rheims, or from the Scots place name Rayne (Aberdeenshire), or from French *raine* – frog, or from the English dialect word *rain* – (dweller by the) strip of land or boundary. (Reaney, Weekley *Surnames*, Black).

Guppy traced Raine in Cumberland, Westmorland, Durham and Yorkshire NR and ER, Rain in Durham and Rains in Derbyshire. Spiegelhalter traced Rains and Raynes in Devon.

In Newfoundland:

Early instances: Walter Raine, of St. John's, 1809 (D'Alberti 19); Francis Rean(e)s or Raines, planter of Adams Cove, 1816 (DPHW 52A); William Reans, fisherman of Pouch Cove, 1830 (DPHW 52A);

William Reenes, planter of Harbour Grace, 1838 (DPHW 43); William Reins, of Ward's Harbour (now Beaumont North), 1851 (DPHW 86).

Modern status: Raines, at Corner Brook and Grand Falls; Raynes, at St. John's and Chamberlains.

RALPH, a baptismal name and surname of England, Scotland and Ireland from the Old Norse personal name *Rathulfr* or Old German *Radulf*, containing the elements *counsel* and *wolf*. In Ireland it is used as a synonym of ROLFE. (Withycombe, Reaney, Black, MacLysaght). *See also* RAWLINS, ROFFE.

Traced by Spiegelhalter in Devon and by MacLysaght in east Leinster.

In Newfoundland:

Family tradition: ——, from Scotland, settled at Port de Grave; in the 18th century some of the family moved to Flat Island and Cowards Island (Bonavista B.) (MUN Folklore).

Early instances: John, of St. John's, ? 1753 (CO 194.13); John, of Port de Grave, 1816 (DPHW 58); James, of Flat Island (Bonavista B.), 1849 (DPHW 73); James, of Clarke's Beach, 1860 (DPHW 38); Robert, from England, married at Grand Bank, 1872 (MUN Hist.).

Modern status: Scattered, especially at St. John's, Port de Grave, Flat Island and Traytown.

RAMSAY, RAMSEY, surnames of England, Scotland and Ireland, from the English place names Ramsey (Essex, Huntingdonshire) or Ramsey Farm (Devon). (Reaney, Black, MacLysaght, Spiegelhalter).

Traced by Spiegelhalter in Devon, and found scattered in Scotland by Guppy, and in Ulster by MacLysaght.

In Newfoundland:

Early instances: Robert Ramsey, soldier of St. John's, 1780 (DPHW 26C); Thomas Ramsay, of Grand Bank, 1868 (MUN Hist.).

Modern status: Ramsay, at Channel, Ramsay and Ramsey at St. John's.

RANDELL, a surname, Randal a baptismal name, of England, with a variant Randall also in England, Scotland and Guernsey (Channel Islands) and Randles in Ireland, from the Old English personal name *Randwulf*, Old Norse *Ranthulfr*, containing the elements *shield* and *wolf*. "The vernacular forms in the Middle Ages were *Ranulf* and *Randol*, which were latinized as *Rannulfus* and *Randulfus* respectively. The abbreviated form *Rand* and the diminutive *Rankin* were also common ... 18th century antiquarianism coined the form Randolph from Latin *Randulfus.*" (Withycombe, Reaney, Black, MacLysaght, Turk). *See also* RENDELL, RANKIN, RANSOME.

Guppy found Randell less frequent than Randall with both forms occurring in Dorset, but Randell alone in Worcestershire. Spiegelhalter traced Randall, Randle in Devon.

In Newfoundland:

Family traditions: John Randell (1780–), born Symondsbury (Dorset), (his ancestors who had emigrated from Norway to Northern Scotland, thence to Symondsbury, had changed their name from Randolph), settled in Trinity (? Trinity B.) and married there in 1795 (MUN Folklore). ——, from England, settled at Twillingate about 1839; some of the family later settled in White Bay (MUN Folklore).

Early instances: Richard Randall, fisherman of St. John's or Petty Harbour, ? 1745 (CO 194.24); Joseph Randale and Co., of Bonavista, 1796 (D'Alberti 5); John Randal(l) or Randell, of Ship Cove (now part of Port Rexton), 1798 (DPHW 64); William Randall, of Fogo, 1803 (D'Alberti 13); John, of Greenspond, 1815 (DPHW 76); William, planter of Trinity (Trinity B.), 1823 (DPHW 64); Richard Randel, of Bird Island Cove (now Elliston), 1828 (DPHW 70); William Randle, of Vere (now Fair) Island, 1830 (DPHW 76); Richard Randles, of Harbour Grace Parish, 1838 (Nfld. Archives HGRC); Reuben Randal(l), of Barr'd Islands, 1842 (DPHW 83); Samuel Randall, of Nippers Harbour, 1842 (DPHW 86); John, of Salmon Cove (now Champneys), 1842 (DPHW 64B); Joseph Randell, of Catalina, 1849 (DPHW 64); Eli Randle or Randell, of Halls Bay (Twillingate district), 1854, of Grandvache (White B.), 1864 (DPHW 86, 94); Thomas Randall, fisherman of Robin Hood (now part of Port Rexton), 1855 (DPHW 64B); scattered in Lovell 1871.

Modern status: Widespread, especially at Champney's Arm, St. John's, Hooping Harbour, Williamsport (White B.) and Port Rexton.

Place names: Randall Cove, —— Point 49-34 55-42.

RANKIN, a surname of England, Scotland and Ireland. *See* RANDELL.

Traced by Guppy in Lanarkshire and by MacLysaght in Derry and adjacent counties.

In Newfoundland:

Family tradition: Richard, from England, moved to Lower Island Cove from Harbour Grace and established a mercantile business there in the 19th century (MUN Hist.).

Early instances: Richard, merchant of Lower Island Cove, 1828 (DPHW 26D); Richard, J.P. for the

Northern District of the Colony, 1834 (*Newfound-lander* 10 Jul 1834); Charles, of St. John's, 1835 (DPHW 23); William, clerk of Harbour Grace, 1871 (Lovell).

Modern status: Rare, at Hearts Content, Harmon Field (*Electors* 1955) and St. John's.

RANSOME, a surname of England – son of *Rand*. *See* RANDELL.

Guppy traced Ransom, Ranson in Suffolk.

In Newfoundland:

Early instance: Charles Ranson, fisherman of West Point (Burgeo-La Poile district), 1871 (Lovell).

Modern status: At Burnt Island (Burgeo-La Poile district).

RAWLINS, a surname of England, Rawlin(e) and Rawling of Scotland, from a French diminutive *Raoulin* – little Ralph (*see* RALPH). (Withycombe, Reaney, Black).

Guppy traced Rawlin(g)s in Shropshire, Somerset and Wiltshire; Spiegelhalter traced Rawlin(g)(s) in Devon; and Black traced Rawlin(e), Rawling in Dumfriesshire.

In Newfoundland:

Early instances: Thomas Rawlings, of Bay de Verde, 1682 (CO 1); John Rawlins, of Harbour Grace Parish, 1823 (Nfld. Archives HGRC); Mary, married at St. John's, 1836 (Nfld. Archives BRC); Thomas Rawlings, of St. John's, 1842 (DPHW 23).

Modern status: Unique, at St. John's (*Electors* 1955).

Place name: Rawlins Cross (St. John's).

RAYMOND, a baptismal name and surname of England and Ireland, from an Old German personal name *Raginmund*, Old French *Raimund* or *Reimund*, containing the elements *counsel* or *might* and *protection*; in Ireland a variant of REDMOND. (Withycombe, Reaney, MacLysaght). *See also* REMO.

Guppy traced Raymo(u)nt, Spiegelhalter Rayment, Raymond, Raymont in Devon; MacLysaght traced Raymond mainly in Cos. Cork and Kerry.

In Newfoundland:

Early instances: Thomas Raymon, of Colliers, 1791 (CO 199.18); James Raymond, planter of Catalina, 1826 (DPHW 64B); Robert, married at St. John's, 1834 (Nfld. Archives BRC); Robert, farmer of Goulds, 1871 (Lovell); Daniel (and others), of Shoal Bay (Ferryland district), 1871 (Lovell)

Modern status: At South Brook (Humber East district), Gander, Catalina, Lower Goulds and St. John's.

Place names (not necessarily from the surname): Raymond Brook 47-27 52-49, 48-23 53-51; —— Head 47-23 52-43 —— Island, —— Passage 47-44 56-08; —— Point 47-42 52-Sh: —— Shoal

RAYNES. *See* RAINES

READ, REID, surnames of England, Scotland and Ireland and Reed in the Channel Islands, with Reid the commoner form in Scotland and Ireland, from Old English *rēad* – red (of complexion or hair), or from the English place names Read (Lancashire), Rede (Suffolk), or Reed (Hertfordshire), or from Old English **rīed, rȳd* – (dweller in the) clearing; in Ireland also for (O)Mulderrig, *Ó Maoildeirg* – red chief, or an abbreviation of (O)Mulready, *Ó Maoilbhrighde* – devotee of St. Brigid. (Reaney, Cottle, MacLysaght, Turk).

Guppy found Read widespread in the south and Midlands, Reade in Berkshire and Cheshire, Reed mainly in Cornwall, Devon, Durham and Northumberland, Reid in Durham and Northumberland and over the greater part of Scotland but mainly south of Aberdeen. MacLysaght traced Reid and Read(e) in Ulster.

In Newfoundland:

Family traditions: Moses Reid (1814–), from Devon, England, settled at Dildo in 1834 (MUN Geog.). Bliss (1825–1895), born in Carbonear, settled at Heart's Delight in 1845 (MUN Geog.).

Early instances: Michael Reid, constable of Bonavista district, ? 1730–32 (CO 194.9); David, of Trinity Bay, 1766 (DPHW 64); John Reed, of St. John's, 1767 (DPHW 26C); William Read, of Old Perlican, 1782 (DPHW 64); Roger, of Bay de Verde, 1796 (DPHW 64); David, of Lower Island Cove, 1799 (CO 199.18); Thomas, occupier of fishing room, Trinity (Trinity B.), Winter 1800–01 (Census Trinity B.); John, occupier of fishing room, Green's Harbour, Winter 1800–01 (Census Trinity B.); James Reed, occupier of fishing room, Hant's Harbour, Winter 1800–01 (Census Trinity B.); William, proprietor and occupier of fishing room, New Perlican, Winter 1800–01 (Census Trinity B.); —— Read, joint purchaser of fishing room on Pond Island, Greenspond Harbour, 1802 (Bonavista Register 1806); John, of Fogo, 1803 (D'Alberti 13); Thomas, merchant of Greenspond, 1804 (D'Alberti 14); Elizabeth Reid, of Harbour Grace Parish, 1806 (Nfld. Archives HGRC); Thomas Read and Co., operated salmon fishery at Ragged Harbour and Deadman's Bay, 1808 (CO 194.48); John Reed, of Brigus, 1813 (DPHW 34); Michael, from Mullinahone (Co.

Tipperary), married at St. John's, 1820 (Nfld. Archives BRC); David Read, from Greenock, Scotland, married at St. John's, 1820 (Nfld. Archives BRC); Moses, planter of New Harbour (Trinity B.), 1823 (DPHW 64); Stephen, of Hearts Delight, 1823 (DPHW 64B); William Reid, planter of Ship Cove (now part of Port Rexton), 1823 (DPHW 64B); John Reid, Reed or Read, of Adam's Cove, 1827 (DPHW 52A); Francis Reid, of Bonavista, 1830 (Nfld. Archives KCRC); Edward Read, of Keels, 1831 (DPHW 70); George Reed or Ried, ? from Exeter (Devon), of Petty Harbour, 1831 (DPHW 31); David Reed, granted land at Morley's Marsh Road (unidentified), ? 1839 (Nfld. Archives, Registry Crown Lands); Francis Augustus Read, of Lower Burgeo, 1843 (DPHW 101); Thomas, of La Poile, 1843 (*Newfoundlander* 31 Aug 1843); William Reed, of Ward's Harbour (now Beaumont North), 1846 (DPHW 86); William, of Little Bay Islands, 1847 (DPHW 86); James, fisherman of Salmon Cove River (Brigus district), 1849 (DPHW 34); James Reid or Read, fisherman of Carbonear, 1850 (DPHW 49); James Reed, fisherman of Change Islands, 1852 (DPHW 83); Stephen Reid, of Old Placentia, 1857 (*Newfoundlander* 22 Jan 1857); Joseph Reed, of Russels Cove (now New Melbourne), 1858 (DPHW 59A); William Read, of Norman's Cove (Trinity B.), 1858 (DPHW 62); Mary Ann Reed, of Little Catalina, 1860 (DPHW 67); Moses, of Dildo Cove, 1862 (DPHW 62); widespread in Lovell 1871.

Modern status: Read, rare, at Corner Brook and Channel; Reid, widespread, especially at St. John's, Neddy's Harbour (St. Barbe district), Chapel Arm, Dildo, Green's Harbour, Hearts Delight, Corner Brook, Little Catalina and Bishops Falls.

Place names: Reed Point (Labrador). 53-57 58-51; Reeds Pond (Labrador) 53-26 56-06, Reid Brook (Labrador) 56-18 62-05; Reidville 49-13 57-23.

READER, a surname of England, from Middle English *redyn* – to thatch with reed, hence a thatcher. (Reaney, Cottle).

Traced by Reaney especially in Norfolk.

In Newfoundland:

Early instances: Thomas, of Bonavista, 1797 (DPHW 70); John, of Knight's Cove (Bonavista B.), 1848 (DPHW 73); Robert, agent of Cupids, 1856 (DPHW 35); James (and others), of Musgravetown, 1871 (Lovell); Robert, of St. John's, 1871 (Lovell).

Modern status: Scattered, especially at Bloomfield (Bonavista B.).

REARDIGAN, ? a variant, apparently not recorded elsewhere, of the surnames of Ireland (O)Redahan, (O)Redican, *Ó Roideacháin.* (MacLysaght). *See also* REDDIGAN.

MacLysaght traced (O)Redahan in Co. Mayo, (O)Redican in Co. Clare.

In Newfoundland:

Early instances: Denis, smith of St. John's, 1794–5 (Census 1794–5); Mary Redigan or Redigar, from Waterford City, married at St. John's, 1814 (Nfld. Archives BRC); Martin Reardigan, of Caplin Bay (now Calvert), "died while buying molasses in St. John's," 1827 (*Newfoundlander* 21 Nov 1827).

Modern status: At St. John's.

REARDON, a variant of the surnames of Ireland (O)Rearden, (O)Riordan, *Ó Riordáin,* Ir. *riogh* and *bhard* – royal bard. (MacLysaght).

Traced by MacLysaght exclusively in Munster.

In Newfoundland:

Family tradition: Albert, from Ireland, settled in Newfoundland; his son was born at Tilting (MUN Folklore).

Early instances: Gilbert Peardon or Beardon (? for Reardon), of St. John's, 1704–06 (CO 194.3); Denis Reardon, barber of St. John's, 1794–5, "16 years in Newfoundland," that is, 1778–9 (Census 1794–5); John, fisherman of Quidi Vidi, 1794–5, "16 years in Newfoundland," that is, 1778–9 (Census 1794–5); Timothy Riordan, of Port de Grave, 1788 (CO 199.18); Jim Reardon or Riardon, of Harbour Grace Parish, 1807 (Nfld. Archives HGRC); Peter Reardan, from Abbey Parish (unidentified) (Co. Limerick), married at St. John's, 1811 (Nfld. Archives BRC); Peter Reardon, from Limerick, cooper of St. John's, died 1813 (*Royal Gazette* 18 Nov 1813); Michael Riordan or Reardin, of Tilton Harbour (now Tilting), 1815 (Nfld. Archives KCRC); Mary Rearden, of Brigus, 1828 (Nfld. Archives BRC); William Reardon, granted land near Perry's Cove, 1847 (Nfld. Archives, Registry Crown Lands); William, of Cape Fogo, 1871 (Lovell); Stephen, of Perry's Cove, 1871 (Lovell); Thomas, of Portugal Cove, 1871 (Lovell); Patrick, of Sandy Cove (Fogo district), 1871 (Lovell).

Modern status: Scattered, especially at St. John's and Goose Cove (White B.).

REBIC, ? a variant of the surname of England Rebbeck – ? son of Rebecca, or of the surname of France Rebec(q) – (player on the) rebeck, a mediaeval three-stringed fiddle, or ? the French place name Rebesques (Pas-de-Calais). (Bardsley, Dauzat).

In Newfoundland:
Modern status: Unique, at St. John's.

RECCORD, a variant of the surname of England and France Record, in England from an Old German personal name *Ricward*, Old French *Ricoart* – powerful guardian; in France ? a nickname – witness. (Reaney, Dauzat).

Spiegelhalter traced Record in Devon.

In Newfoundland:
Family tradition: George, from Fogo, settled at Victoria Cove (Gander B.) in the 1890s (MUN Hist.).

Modern status: Rare, at Victoria Cove and St. John's.

REDDICK, a surname of England, from the English place name Redwick (Gloucestershire), or ? a variant of Ruddick or Ruddock, from Old English *ruddoc* – robin-redbreast.

In Newfoundland:
Early instances: J. Roddick, schoolteacher of Harbour Grace, 1845–47 (*Nfld. Almanac* 1847, *Nfld. Quarterly* Dec 1911); John, planter of Herring Neck, 1850, of Salt Harbour (Twillingate district), 1852, of Stone Harbour (Twillingate district), 1860 (DPHW 85); Mrs. J. Radix and John (and others) Reddix, of St. John's, 1871 (Lovell).

Modern status: At Seldom, Salt Harbour Island, Herring Neck and Sunnyside (Twillingate district) and Bauline (West).

Place name: Reddick Bight (Labrador) 58-57 63-10.

REDDIGAN, ? a variant, apparently not recorded elsewhere, of the surnames of Ireland (O)Redahan, (O)Redican, *Ó Roideacháin*. (MacLysaght). *See also* REARDIGAN.

MacLysaght traced (O)Redahan in Co. Mayo, (O)Redican in Co. Clare.

In Newfoundland:
Early instances: James Redigan, of Harbour Grace Parish, 1830 (Nfld. Archives HGRC); James and John Reddigan, of St. John's, 1871 (Lovell); Richard Redigan Sr., of Caplin Bay (now Calvert), 1871 (Lovell).

Modern status: At Calvert, Dunville and St. John's.

REDDY, a surname of England and Ireland, in England from Middle English *readi* etc. – prompt, quick, prepared; in Ireland, (O)Reddy, *Ó Roidigh*. (Reaney, MacLysaght).

Traced by Spiegelhalter in Devon and by MacLysaght mainly in Co. Kilkenny.

In Newfoundland:
Early instances: Michael, of St. John's, 1782 (DPHW 26D); Daniel, of Bay Bulls, 1781 (D'Alberti 2); Michael Ready, from Castletown (Co. Kilkenny), fish splitter, late of Bay Bulls, 1788–91 (CO 194.38); Michael, boatkeeper of Fermeuse, 1797 (D'Alberti 7); John Reddy, from Owning (unidentified) Diocese of Ossery, Ireland, married at St. John's, 1801 (Nfld. Archives BRC); Richard, of Ferryland, 1806 (Nfld. Archives BRC); Darby Ready, from Co. Waterford, shoreman of Harbour Grace, died 1812 (*Royal Gazette* 4 Jun 1812); John, of Torbay, 1817 (Nfld. Archives BRC); Thomas Reddy, of King's Cove, 1827 (Nfld. Archives KCRC); James Ready, of Flat Rock (? St. John's district), 1838 (Nfld. Archives BRC); Edward Reddy, farmer of Duricle (Placentia B.), 1871 (Lovell); James, farmer of Flat Rock (St. John's), 1871 (Lovell); Richard, of Little Paradise (Placentia B.), 1871 (Lovell); Michael, of Red Island (Placentia B.), 1871 (Lovell); Thomas, of South East Bight (Placentia B.), 1871 (Lovell); John and William, miners of Tilt Cove, 1871 (Lovell); Richard Riddy, of Burin, 1871 (Lovell).

Modern status: Scattered, especially at St. John's.

Place name: ? Ready Rocks (Labrador) 53-31 55-44.

REDMAN, a surname of England and Guernsey (Channel Islands) – red-man, a cutter of weeds or a thatcher (*see* READER), or from Old English *rēad* – red (of complexion or hair) (*see* READ), or from the English place name Redmain (Cumberland) – red cairn, or a variant of REDMOND. (Reaney, Cottle, Turk).

Traced by Guppy in Wiltshire and Yorkshire WR and by Spiegelhalter in Devon.

In Newfoundland:
Family traditions: ——, of Sussex and Irish ancestry, from Portadown (Co. Armagh) to Newfoundland about 1902 (MUN Folklore).

Early instances: Michael, labourer of Bay Bulls, 1786 (CO 194.36); William, of St. John's, 1851 (DPHW 23).

Modern status: Rare, at St. John's (*Electors* 1955).

Place names (not necessarily from the surname): Redman Cove (Labrador), —— Point (Labrador) 52-39 55-46; Redmans Head 47-39 52-55.

REDMOND, a surname of Ireland, a variant of RAYMOND. (MacLysaght). *See also* REDMAN.

Traced by MacLysaght especially in South Wexford.

In Newfoundland:

Early instances: Patrick, publican of St. John's, 1794–5, "20 years in Newfoundland," that is, 1774–5 (Census 17945); Patrick, from Tintern (Co. Wexford), married at St. John's, 1805 (Nfld. Archives BRC); Daniel, of Placentia, 1806 (D'Alberti 16); Joseph Redmond(s), of Harbour Grace Parish, 1808 (Nfld. Archives HGRC); James Redmond, from Newtown (Co. Waterford), fisherman of St. John's, died 1814 (*Royal Gazette* 24 Mar 1814); James, of Catalina, 1825 (DPHW 70); J., of Carbonear, 1831 (*Newfoundlander* 25 Aug 1831); John, of King's Cove Parish, 1838 (Nfld. Archives KCRC); Jacob, of Harbour Grace, 1868 (Nfld. Archives HGRC); Patrick, of Belle Isle (now Bell Island) and Lance Cove, 1871 (Lovell); Lawrence, farmer of Salmon Cove and Gasters, 1871 (Lovell).

Modern status: At Avondale South (*Electors* 1955), Corner Brook and St. John's.

Place name: Redmond Lake (Labrador) 54-40 66-42.

REELIS, ? a variant of the family name of Ireland Rellis, ? *Mag Riallghuis*. (MacLysaght).

MacLysaght traced Rellis in Leinster, especially in Co. Wexford.

In Newfoundland:

Modern status: At Grand Falls, Shoe Cove (St. John's) (*Electors* 1955) and St. John's.

REES(E), surnames of Wales and England, from the Old Welsh personal name *Ris*, Welsh *Rhys* – ardour. (Reaney, Cottle). *See also* PRICE, RICE.

Guppy traced Rees in Herefordshire, Monmouthshire, North Wales and especially South Wales. Spiegelhalter traced Reese in Devon.

In Newfoundland:

Family tradition: George Rees (of Welsh ancestry) (1772–), born at Bristol, England, came as shipwright to work at shipyards at Lance Cove (Bell Island) in 1797 (MUN Hist.).

Early instances: James Rese, of St. John's, 1797 (D'Alberti 6); George Rees or Reece, of Belle Isle (now Bell Island] 1818, of Lance Cove (Bell Island), 1821 (DPHW 26B); Mary Rease, of Greenspond, 1831 (Nfld. Archives KCRC).

Modern status: Rees, scattered, especially at Bell Island and St. John's; Reese, rare, at St. John's.

REEVE(S), surnames of England, Reeves of Ireland, Reeve from Old English *(ge)rēfa* – reeve, sheriff, chief magistrate, bailiff, overseer, Reeves – servant, ? son, (dweller at the house) of the reeve, or from Old English *efes* – (dweller at the) edge (of a wood

or hill); in Ireland also formerly for *Ó Rímheadha*. (Reaney, Cottle, MacLysaght). *See also* LAWRENCE.

Guppy traced Reeve in Essex, Norfolk, Northamptonshire, Suffolk, Sussex and Wiltshire, Reeves in Berkshire, Buckinghamshire, Derbyshire, Devon, Hampshire, Kent, Northamptonshire, Somerset, Staffordshire and Wiltshire.

In Newfoundland:

Family tradition: John Henry Reeves, from England, deserted the British Navy by jumping overboard at Channel Head and swimming to Port aux Basques and then changed his name to Lawrence to avoid detection, in the early 1800s (MUN Folklore).

Early instances: William Reave(s), of Bell Island, 1708–09 (CO 194.4); Henry ? Reve, constable of Ferryland district ? 1730, 1732 (CO 194.9); John Reeves, appointed Chief Justice of Newfoundland, 1791 (Prowse); John, one of 72 impressed men who sailed from Ireland to Newfoundland ? 1811 (CO 194.51); Herbert Reevis, of St. John's, 1833 (DPHW 26B); James Reeves, of English Harbour (unspecified), 1835 (DPHW 30); William, planter of Channel, 1871 (Lovell); James (and others), of Great St. Lawrence, 1871 (Lovell).

Modern status: Reeve, rare, at Bell Island (*Electors* 1955) and St. John's; Reeves, scattered.

REGULAR, a variant of the surname of England Reglar – a member of a religious or monastic order, one subject to or bound by a religious rule, as opposed to "secular." (Weekley *Surnames*).

In Newfoundland:

Family tradition: William, from England, settled at Harbour Grace (MUN Folklore).

Modern status: Scattered, especially at Hampden and Ming's Bight (White Bay district).

REID. *See* READ

REINHARD(T), surnames of Germany, from the Old German personal name *Raginhard* containing the elements *counsel* and *hard*. (Dauzat).

In Newfoundland:

Modern status: Reinhard, Reinhardt, rare, at Carbonear.

REMO, a Newfoundland variant of the surnames of France Rémon(d), Rémont, of Jersey (Channel Islands), Remon, from the Old German personal name *Raginnmund*, Old French *Raimund*, *Reimund* (*see* RAYMOND). (Withycombe, Dauzat, Turk). *See also* REYNOLDS.

In Newfoundland:

Early instances: Peter Remon, fisherman of Little La Poile, 1860 (DPHW 99); Peter Remmo, of West Point (Burgeo-La Poile district), 1871 (Lovell).

Modern status: Rare, at The Reach (Burgeo-La Poile district) (*Electors* 1955) and Burgeo.

RENAUD, a surname of France, from the Old German personal name *Raginwald* containing the elements *counsel* and *govern, rule.* (Dauzat).

In Newfoundland:

Family tradition: Julien Renaud, from St. Pierre or France was the first inhabitant of Grand Jardin, Cape St. George, in the early 1800s (MUN Geog.).

Modern status: Unique, at Bishop's Falls (*Electors* 1955).

RENDELL, a surname of England, a variant of RAN-DELL or RENNIE, or from a diminutive of Reynold (Reginald) (*see* REYNOLDS). (Spiegelhalter, Black).

Guppy traced Rendall, Rendell in Devon, Dorset and Somerset, noting that Rendell is the usual form and that Rendle also occurs in Devon.

In Newfoundland:

Family traditions: Charles Rendle, from Devon, settled at Heart's Content in 1798; the spelling of the name later changed to Rendell (MUN Folklore). Stephen Rendell, son of Elias of Coffinswell (Devon), settled at Old Perlican (MUN Folklore).

Early instances: John, fish merchant of St. John's, 1793 (D'Alberti 5); Elias, of Ferryland, 1818 (D'Alberti 28); Richard Rendall, of Bonavista, 1824 (DPHW 70); John Rendle, agent of Brigus, 1832 (DPHW 34); Stephen Rendell, from Coffinswell (Devon), apprentice at Bulley, Job and Co., St. John's, 1834 (Nfld. Archives Tll); John, fisherman of Furby's Cove (Fortune B.), 1839 (DPHW 102); John Rendell, Renales or Reynolds, of Caplin Cove (Bay de Verde district), 1845 (DPHW 58); John Rendle, from Paignton (Devon), joiner of St. John's, died 1849 (*Nfld. Patriot* 17 Mar 1849); William Rendall, granted land at Ship Cove (now part of Port Rexton), 1851 (Nfld. Archives, Registry Crown Lands); Elias Rendell, planter of Green Cove (Twillingate district), 1851 (DPHW 85); Stephen, of Mulleys Cove, 1853 (DPHW 52B); William Sr., from Shaldon (Devon), of St. John's, 1854 (*Newfoundlander* 2 Feb 1854); Joseph, of Herring Neck, 1860 (DPHW 85); Stephen Rendal, John and Richard Rendel, of Bird Island Cove (now Elliston), 1871 (Lovell); John and Joseph Rendall, of Grandfathers Cove (White B.), 1871 (Lovell); Charles (and others) Rendle, of Hearts Content, 1871 (Lovell).

Modern status: Scattered, especially at St. John's.
Place name: Rendells Cove 49-21 55-11.

RENNIE, a surname of Scotland, a double diminutive or pet-form of Reynold (Reginald) (*see* REYNOLDS). (Black). *See also* RENDELL.

Traced by Guppy in the Aberdeen district.

In Newfoundland:

Early instances: Stuart and Rennie, merchants of St. John's, trading from the River Clyde to Newfoundland, 1794–5, "14 years in Newfoundland," that is, 1780–1 (Census 1794–5, D'Alberti 12, 27); William Frederick, from Glasgow, married at St. John's, 1835 (DPHW 26D); David, trader of Catalina, 1871 (Lovell).

Modern status: At St. John's, Little St. Lawrence, St. Lawrence and Allan's Island (Burin district).

Place name: Rennie's River 47-35 52-41; Rennies Mill Road (St. John's).

RENOUF, a surname of England, France and the Channel Islands from the Old German personal name *Raginwulf,* Old English *Regenwulf,* containing the elements *counsel* and *wolf.* (Dauzat, Spiegelhalter, Turk).

Traced by Spiegelhalter in Devon, by Dauzat in Calvados and Contentin, and in Jersey and Guernsey.

In Newfoundland:

Early instances: Thomas Renout or Renoul (? for Renouf), of St. John's, 1778 (CO 194.34); Thomas Renouf, of La Poile, 1843, of Green Harbour (Burgeo-La Poile district), 1844, J.P. for Fortune Bay district, 1845 (*Nfld. Almanac, Newfoundlander* 31 Aug 1843, DPHW 101); John, from the Island of Jersey, of St. John's, died at his residence Jersey Cottage, 1849 (*Nfld. Patriot* 24 Feb 1849); James, of Crabbes (St. George's district), 1870 (DPHW 96); Clement, of Robinson's Head (St. George's B.), 1871 (Lovell); Isaac (and others), of Sandy Point (St. George's B.), 1871 (Lovell).

Modern status: Scattered, especially in the St. George's district.

RETEIFF, RETIEFF, variants of the surnames of France Restif or Rétief – restive, stubborn, disobedient, mulish. (Dauzat).

In Newfoundland:

Family tradition: Frédéric Retieffe in the mid-nineteenth century deserted from the French fishery, settling in Three Rock Cove (Thomas, "French Fam. Names").

Modern status: Reteiff, at Piccadilly and

Stephenville Crossing (*Electors* 1955); Retieff, in the Port-au-Port district (*Electors* 1955), and at Stephenville and Torbay.

REVELLIS, ? a variant of the surname of France Revel(l)y etc., from various French place names, or a nickname for a rebel or mutineer. (Dauzat).

In Newfoundland:

Modern status: Rare, at Benoits Cove (*Electors* 1955).

REX, a surname of England – the son of Rich (Richard) (*see* RICHARDS, RIX), or for one who played the part of the *Rex* – king in a pageant. (Bardsley).

In Newfoundland:

Family tradition: Two Rex brothers, from Devon, settled at Ship Cove (now part of Port Rexton) in the 18th century; Ship Cove and Robin Hood were later named Port Rexton, so-named to commemorate the surname of the first male child born there (MUN Folklore).

Early instances: Henery, of Ferryland, 1706–08 (CO 194.4, 24); John, of Petty Harbour, 1708 (CO 194.4); John, of Bay Bulls, 1708 (CO 194.4); John Rex, Rix or Ricks, of Ship Cove (now part of Port Rexton), 1796 (DPHW 64); R. Rex, of Fogo, 1803 (D'Alberti 13); George, planter of Trinity (Trinity B.), 1850 (DPHW 64B); George, of Round Harbour (Fogo district), 1871 (Lovell); Joseph, master mariner of St. John's, 1871 (Lovell).

Modern status: At Corner Brook, St. John's and Port Rexton.

Place name: Port Rexton 48-23 53-20.

REYNOLDS, a surname of England and Ireland from the Old German personal name *Raginald*, latinized as *Reginaldus*, Old French *Reinald*, *Reynaud*, containing the elements *counsel* and *might*, *power*; in Ireland for Mac Rannald, *Mac Raghnaill*, *Raghnal* – Reginald. (Reaney, Cottle, MacLysaght). *See also* RAINES, RENDELL, RENNIE, REMO.

Traced by Guppy in the Midlands and south of England, by Spiegelhalter in Devon, and by MacLysaght in Co. Leitrim and, often with the prefix Mac, in Ulster.

In Newfoundland:

Family traditions: James, from England, settled at Salmon Cove (Carbonear) between 1880–1890 (MUN Folklore). William (1840–1929), of English descent, born at Caplin Cove (Bay de Verde district), was one of the earliest settlers of Small Point (Bay de Verde district) (MUN Geog.).

Early instances: Thomas, of Carbonear, 1770 (CO 199.18); James, of Mullys Cove, 1783 (CO 199.18); ——, ? of St. John's, 1797 (D'Alberti 6); William, of Harbour Grace Parish, 1809 (Nfld. Archives HGRC); John, planter of Northern Bay, 1833 (DPHW 52A); John Reynolds, Rendell or Renales, of Caplin Cove (Bay de Verde district), 1856 (DPHW 55); William Reynolds or Rayolds, of Perry's Cove, 1857 (DPHW 49); Bridget, of Harbour Grace, 1869 (Nfld. Archives HGRC); John, cooper of Gaultois, 1871 (Lovell).

Modern status: Scattered, especially in the Carbonear-Bay de Verde district, at Caplin Cove, Riverhead (Harbour Grace) and St. John's.

Place name: Reynolds Shoal 49-29 55-43.

R(H)UELOKKE, ? variants of the surnames of Germany Ruhlicke or Ruhlke from the Old German personal name *Hrodo* containing the element *fame*. (Heintz-Cascorbi). *See also* ROFFE.

In Newfoundland:

Modern status: Rhuelokke, rare, at Grand Bank; Ruelokke, rare, at Fortune (*Electors* 1955) and St. John's.

RHYMES, a Newfoundland variant of the surname of France Reims – one from Rheims (Marne). (Dauzat).

In Newfoundland:

Early instances: James Rheims, ? of St. John's, 1822 (CO 194.65); Esau Rimes or Rymes, of Lower Burgeo, 1847, 1871 (DPHW 101, Lovell).

Modern status: Rare, at Muddy Hole (Burgeo-La Poile district) (*Electors* 1955) and Burgeo.

RICE, a surname of Wales, England and Ireland, from the Old Welsh personal name *Ris*, Welsh *Rhys* – ardour; in Ireland also a puzzling anglicization of *Ó Maolchraoibhe*, Ir. *craobh* – branch. (Reaney, MacLysaght). *See also* PRICE, REES(E).

Traced by Guppy in Devon and Norfolk, and by MacLysaght in Munster and Armagh, Monaghan and neighbouring counties.

In Newfoundland:

Family tradition: ——, from England, was the first settler of Bear Cove (White B.) in the early 1800s (MUN Folklore).

Early instances: Elizabeth, from Co. Kilkenny, married at St. John's, 1810 (Nfld. Archives BRC); John, of St. John's, 1817 (DPHW 26D); John, planter of Little Harbour (Twillingate district), 1820 (USPG); James, of Twillingate, 1823 (D'Alberti 33); Patrick, of Harbour Grace Parish, 1827 (Nfld. Archives HGRC); Patrick, of Grates Cove, 1828 (Nfld. Ar-

chives BRC); George, farmer of Carbonear, 1835
(DPHW 48); Patrick, ? of Northern Bay, 1838 (DPHW
54); John, of Friday's Bay (Twillingate district),
1845 (DPHW 86); Arundel, of Herring Neck, 1856
(DPHW 85); Hannah, of Riverhead (White B.), 1864
(DPHW 94); George and Thomas, of Bell Island, 1871
(Lovell); James, planter of Red Head Cove (Concep-
tion B.), 1871 (Lovell).

Modern status: Widespread, especially at Red
Head Cove (Conception B.), at Bear Cove, Western
Arm, Seal Cove (White Bay South district) and St.
John's.

Place names: Rice Head 49-20 55-12; —— Island
49-16 55-01; —— Mountain 49-49 56-33.

RICH(E), surnames of England, Rich of the Channel
Islands, Riche of France, from Old French *riche* –
rich; in England also from Old English **ric* –
(dweller by the) stream, or a diminutive of Richard
(*see* RICHARDS). (Reaney, Turk). *See also* LERICHE.

Guppy traced Rich in Cornwall, Devon, Somerset
and Wiltshire.

In Newfoundland:

Family tradition: I.J. Riche, from England, settled
at North West River (Labrador); the family later
moved to St. John's (MUN Folklore).

Early instances: Allen Rich, of St. John's, 1776
(CO 194.33); Arthur, of Port de Grave, in possession
of property at Salmon Cove (Port de Grave), 1805
(CO 199.18).

Modern status: Rich, rare, at South River (*Electors* 1955), and St. John's; Riche, at St. John's and
Springdale.

Place names: Pointe Riche (or Point Rich), ——
—— Rock (or Rich Point Rock) 50-42 57-25; Riche
Lake 47-47 55-48; Riches Island 47-47 55-50; Point
Riche Peninsula (or Rich Point Peninsula) 50-40 57-
23.

RICHARDS, a surname of England, Wales and
Guernsey (Channel Islands), Richard of Jersey, from
the Old German personal name *Ric(h)ard*, Central
French *Richard*, Anglo-Norman *Reiard*, containing
the elements *powerful* and *brave*. With its nicknames
and diminutives, such as *Rich(ie)*, *Hitch*, *Rick(et)*,
Hick(et), *Dick(on)*, it has given rise, as Withycombe
comments, to an immense number of surnames
including DICK(S), DICK(IN)SON, DIXON, HICKMAN,
HICKS, HIGDEN, HISCOCK, HITCHENS, HUDDY, HUDSON,
PRITCHARD. (Withycombe, Reaney, Cottle, Turk).

Found widespread by Guppy in the Midlands,
north and south Wales, and especially in Cornwall
and Monmouthshire.

In Newfoundland:

Early instances: William, of Port de Grave, 1782,
property "in possession of the Family for upwards of
90 years," that is, before 1692 (CO 199.18); Thomas,
from Lympstone (Devon), of Newfoundland, 1734
(Kirwin); William, of St. John's, 1762 (CO 194.15);
Abraham, of Port de Grave, in possession of property at Back Cove (Port de Grave), 1775 (CO
199.18); John, in possession of plantation at St.
Mary's, 1780 (D'Alberti 6); William, from Ross
(unspecified) (Co. Wexford), married at St. John's,
1803 (Nfld. Archives BRC); Charlotte, of Harbour
Grace Parish, 1806 (Nfld. Archives HGRC); Richard,
schoolmaster of Trinity (Trinity B.), 1827 (DPHW
64B); Isabella, of Harbour Grace, 1828 (Nfld. Archives BRC); Thomas, of Jersey Harbour, 1828, of
Harbour Breton, 1832 (DPHW 109); James Riccards,
of King's Cove, 1829 (Nfld. Archives KCRC); Abraham Richards, planter of Bareneed, 1838 (DPHW 34);
Thomas, of Seldom Come By, 1842 (DPHW 83);
John, from the city of Cork, of Harbour Grace, 1844
(*Indicator* 27 Jul 1844); William, granted land at
Southern Gut (now South River), Salmon Cove,
1847 (Nfld. Archives, Registry Crown Lands);
William James, of Herring Neck, 1850, schoolmaster of Clark's Cove (Twillingate district), 1851
(DPHW 85); Elizabeth, of St. Anthony, 1854 (DPHW
114); Peter, of Round Harbour (Twillingate district),
1856 (DPHW 86); scattered in Lovell 1871.

Modern status: Scattered, especially at St. Carols
(White B.) and St. John's.

Place names (not necessarily from the surname):
Richards Brook 48-55 54-48; —— Harbour 47-37
56-24; —— Head 47-37 57-36; —— Island 48-40
53-37.

RICHARDSON, a surname of England, Ireland,
Scotland and the Channel Islands – son of Richard
(*see* RICHARDS). (Turk).

Traced by Guppy in the Midlands and north, especially Cumberland and Westmorland, and in
Dumfriesshire, and by MacLysaght in Ulster.

In Newfoundland:

Early instances: John Richeson, ? of St. John's,
? 1706 (CO 194.24); Edward Richardson, soldier of
St. John's, 1756 (DPHW 26C); Thomas, from Balla-
loobyto Parish (? for Ballylooby) (Co. Tipperary),
married at St. John's, 1802 (Nfld. Archives BRC);
Joseph, of Brigus, 1803 (CO 199.18); William, of
Harbour Grace Parish, 1818 (Nfld. Archives HGRC);
Mary Jane, from Halifax, married at St. John's, 1833
(*Times* 19 Jun 1833); Mark, fisherman of Bonne
Bay (Burin district), 1853 (DPHW 102).

Modern status: At Botwood (*Electors* 1955) and
St. John's.

RICHE. *See* RICH

RICHMOND, a surname of England, Ireland and
Scotland, from the English place name Richmond
(Yorkshire NR, Surrey), or from the common French
place name Richemont – splendid hill. (Cottle, Mac-
Lysaght 73).

Traced by Guppy in Lancashire, Yorkshire,
Norfolk, Nottinghamshire and Warwickshire and in
Ayrshire, and by MacLysaght in Ulster.

In Newfoundland:

Early instances: John, of Trinity Bay, 1767
(DPHW 64); William, fisherman of Bay of Exploits,
? 1797 (CO 194.39); William, of Fogo, 1805 (D'Alberti 15); Michael Richmon, of Harbour Grace
Parish, 1843 (Nfld. Archives HGRC); William Richmond, planter of Green Cove (Twillingate district),
1854 (DPHW 85); William, of Herring Neck, 1871
(Lovell); William, of Little Bay Islands, 1871 (Lovell); Mrs. Ellen, of St. John's, 1871 (Lovell).

Modern status: At Green Cove (Twillingate district) (*Electors* 1955), Pikes Arm and Herring Neck.

Place name: Richmond Rock 49-40 55-47.

RICKERT, a surname of England, Holland and
Germany. *See* RICHARDS. (Reaney, E.C. Smith).

In Newfoundland:

Family tradition: James Frederick, of St. John's,
from Danzig, 1883. (Mrs. J. Rickert).

Modern status: At St. John's.

RICKETTS, a surname of England, a variant of
RICHARDS, from a pet-form Rick of Richard, or from
other variants Rickard in Cornwall and Rickards in
Devon. (Reaney, Cottle, Spiegelhalter).

Guppy traced Rickett in Essex and Ricketts in
Gloucestershire.

In Newfoundland:

Early instances: William Rickett, of Newfoundland, ? 1706 (CO 194.24); Catherine, of St. John's,
1805 (Nfld. Archives BRC); Catherine, of Bonavista
Bay, 1805 (Nfld. Archives BRC); James Ricketts, of
King's Cove, 1820 (Nfld. Archives KCRC); Robert
Rickets, from Dorset, married at Trinity (unspecified), 1825 (Nfld. Archives KCRC); James Ricketts,
of Smart's Island (Bonavista B.), 1836 (DPHW 76);
James Rickets, of Knight's Cove (Bonavista B.),
1852 (Nfld. Archives KCRC); John, of Broad Cove
(now Duntara), 1862 (Nfld. Archives KCRC); Johanna, of Stock Cove (Bonavista B.), 1864 (Nfld.
Archives KCRC); James Ricketts, of Big Island

(White B.), 1864 (DPHW 94); Ellen, of Plate Cove,
1868 (Nfld. Archives KCRC).

Modern status: Scattered, especially in the
Burgeo-La Poile, Bonavista South and White Bay
South districts with a large concentration at Knight's
Cove (Bonavista B.).

Place name: Ricketts Bridge 47-36 52-44.

RICKS, RIX, surnames of England, pet-forms of
Richard (*see* RICHARDS) or from Old English (West
Saxon) *rixe* – (dweller by the) rush(es), of which the
dative plural has given RIXON. (Reaney, Cottle). *See
also* REX, RIGGS.

Spiegelhalter traced Ricks in Devon; Guppy
traced Rix in Norfolk.

In Newfoundland:

Early instances: John Ricks, of Trinity (Trinity
B.), 1793 (DPHW 64); James Rix, married at St.
John's, 1798 (DPHW 26D); John, proprietor and
occupier of fishing room, Ship Cove (now part of
Port Rexton), Winter 1800–01 (Census Trinity B.);
Mary Ricks, of King's Cove Parish, 1851 (Nfld.
Archives KCRC); John, of Charles Brook (White B.),
1871 (Lovell); James and Joseph, of Wiseman's
Cove (White B.), 1871 (Lovell).

Modern status: Ricks, at Corner Brook and in the
White Bay North and South districts; Rix, rare, at
Millertown (*Electors* 1955).

Place names: Rix Cove, —— Island, —— Point
49-44 56-00; —— Harbour 47-45 53-48.

RIDDLE, a surname of England, Scotland and as
Riddell of Ireland, from the English place names
Ruddle (Cornwall) or Ryedale (Yorkshire NR), or
the Scots place name Riddell (Roxburghshire), or
? as a nickname from mediaeval Latin *ridellus* –
sieve or curtain. (Spiegelhalter, Black, MacLysaght).

Guppy traced Riddle in Cornwall and Northumberland, Riddell in Northumberland; Spiegelhalter
traced Riddell in Devon, and Black traced Riddal,
Riddel(l) in Ayrshire.

In Newfoundland:

Early instances: Thomas, fisherman of Mulley's
Cove, 1830 (DPHW 52A); Thomas, planter of Small
Point (Bay de Verde district), 1837 (DPHW 52A);
James, planter of Trinity (Trinity B.), 1843 (DPHW
64B).

Modern status: Rare, at St. John's and Small
Point (Bay de Verde district).

RIDEOUT, a surname of England, ? a nickname for a
rider, probably as Cottle suggests from some lost
joke. (Reaney, Cottle).

Guppy traced Ridout in Dorset; Spiegelhalter traced Rideout in Devon.

In Newfoundland:

Family traditions: ——, from Yorkshire, settled at Long Pond (Conception B.) (MUN Folklore). Henry (1810 –), from England, settled at Whales Gulch (Twillingate district) (MUN Geog.). Richard Ridout (1815–1907), from England, settled in Conception Bay South area; the spelling of the surname was later changed to Rideout (MUN Geog.). Richard (1840–1928), from England, came to Newfoundland in 1870 and was the first settler of Pilleys Island (Notre Dame B.) (MUN Geog.).

Early instances: William, planter of Fogo, 1792 (MUN Hist.); John, of Trinity (Trinity B.), 1794 (DPHW 64); Richard, operated salmon fishery at New Bay, John, operated salmon fishery at Nippers Harbour, 1804 (CO 194.45); Richard Ridout, of St. John's, 1814 (DPHW 26D); William Rideout, planter of Twillingate, 1820 (USPG); Richard, planter of Western Head (Twillingate district), 1821 (USPG); John Ridout, of Greenspond, 1823 (DPHW 76); Mary, baptized at Cape Cove (Bonavista B.), 1830, aged 27 (DPHW 76); J. Rideout, of Carbonear, deceased, 1831 (*Newfoundlander* 14 Jul 1831); Richard Ridout, of Long Pond, 1832 (DPHW 30); Robert Rideout, fisherman of Pass Island (Fortune B.), 1831 (DPHW 102); John Ridout, of Bay de l'Eau Island, 1835 (DPHW 30); Rennie, of Middle Bill Cove (Bonavista B.), 1835 (DPHW 76); Susanna Rideout, of Foxtrap, 1836 (DPHW 26D); Henry Ridoute, of Moreton's Harbour, 1838 (DPHW 86); William Ridout, of Round Harbour (Twillingate district), 1847 (DPHW 86); John, Road Commissioner for the area Cape Freels to Cobblers Island (Bonavista B.), 1847 (*Nfld. Almanac*); Joseph, of Rogue's Harbour (Twillingate district), 1849 (DPHW 86); Philip Rideout, of King's Cove Parish, 1850 (Nfld. Archives KCRC); George Ridout, of Harbour Breton, 1853 (DPHW 104), same as George, of Great Harbour (Burin district), 1856, returned to Harbour Breton about 1859 (Harbour Breton Anglican Church Records per D.A. Macdonald); Samuel Rideout, of Frenchman's Cove (Burin district), 1853 (DPHW 106); Thomas Ridout, of Ward's Harbour (now Beaumont North), 1854 (DPHW 86); Alfred, of Tilt Cove, 1855 (DPHW 86); Ann Rideout, of Herring Neck, 1855 (DPHW 85); George, planter of Great Harbour (Burin district), 1856 (DPHW 104); Jonathon, of Exploits Burnt Island, 1859 (DPHW 92); William Ridout, of Beaver Cove (Twillingate district), 1860 (DPHW 87); Samuel, fisherman of Fortune, 1860 (DPHW 106); Thomas, of Harbour Le Cou, 1860 (DPHW 99); widespread in Lovell 1871.

Modern status: Widespread, especially at Long Pond, Corner Brook, St. John's, Beaumont South, Kings Point (Green B.) and Whales Gulch (Twillingate district).

RIDG(E)LEY, surnames of England, ? variants of Ridley from the English place name Ridley (Essex, Cheshire, Northumberland), or (dweller in or near the) wood cleared by burning or cutting, or the seedy clearing, or from an unidentified place name. (Cottle).

In Newfoundland:

Early instances: Robert Rigly, of Harbour Grace Parish, 1821 (Nfld. Archives HGRC); Thomas Ridgley, of Miller's Passage (Bay de l'Eau), 1835 (DPHW 30); Jonathon, of Red Cove (Fortune B.), 1858 (DPHW 104); Sarah, of Lower Burgeo, 1859 (DPHW 101).

Modern status: Ridgeley, at Lourdes and St. John's; Ridgley, at Little Bay West, Miller's Passage (*Electors* 1955) and St. John's.

RIGGS, a surname of England, ? a variant of RICKS, or from Old English *hrycg* – (dweller on the) ridge. (Cottle, Spiegelhalter). *See also* DUFF.

Traced by Spiegelhalter in Devon.

In Newfoundland:

Family traditions: —— Duff, from England, deserted ship, settled at Bulls Cove (Burin district), and changed his surname to Riggs (MUN Folklore). George (1790–1863), from Lawn, settled at Grand Bank (MUN Hist.).

Early instances: Thomas, of Twillingate, 1768 (MUN Hist.); Thomas, planter of Fogo, 1780 (D'Alberti 6); Thomas, of Counch (? for Conche), 1787 (MUN Hist.); Thomas and William, of Bay de Verde, 1804 (CO 199.18); James, of Harbour Grace Parish, 1806 (Nfld. Archives HGRC); John, apprentice, one of 72 impressed men who sailed from Ireland to Newfoundland ? 1811 (CO 194.51); Elizabeth, of St. John's, deceased, 1831 (*Newfoundlander* 27 Oct 1831); Joseph, planter of Adam's Cove, 1832 (DPHW 52A); Stephen, ? of Northern Bay, 1840 (DPHW 54); George, of Grand Bank, 1850 (DPHW 106); Susannah, of Lawn, 1858 (DPHW 106); Andrew and William, of Burin, 1871 (Lovell); Jonathon, of Butter's Cove (Placentia B.), 1871 (Lovell); William, of Western Bay, 1871 (Lovell).

Modern status: Scattered, especially at Bay de Verde and Grand Bank.

RILES, RYLES, variants of the surname of England RYALL. *See* ROIL.

Guppy traced Ryle(s) formerly in Cheshire; Spiegelhalter traced Ryle and Ryall in Devon.

In Newfoundland:

Early instances: Charles Ryle or Ryal(e), skipper, of Harbour Breton, 1847 (D.A. Macdonald); Sarah Ryle, of Russell's Cove (now New Melbourne), 1858 (DPHW 59).

Modern status: Riles, in the Burgeo-La Poile district; Ryles, at Corner Brook.

Place name: Ryle Barrisway 47-39 54-46.

RILEY, a surname of England from the English place name Riley (Devon, Lancashire and ? elsewhere), or (dweller in or near the) rye clearing, or for the surname of Ireland O'REILLY. (Bardsley, Spiegelhalter).

Traced by Guppy in Derbyshire, Essex, Lancashire, Nottinghamshire, Staffordshire, Warwickshire and Yorkshire WR, and by Spiegelhalter in Devon.

In Newfoundland:

Early instances: Patrick Riely, of St. John's, 1805 (Nfld. Archives BRC); Patrick Riley, of Tilton Harbour (now Tilting), 1823 (Nfld. Archives KCRC); Margaret Reily, from Thurles (Co. Tipperary), married at St. John's, 1824 (Nfld. Archives BRC); Daniel Rily, of Bonavista, 1824 (Nfld. Archives KCRC); Rosilla Reily, of Placentia, 1830 (Nfid. Archives BRC); Daniel Riley, of Tickle Cove (Bonavista B.), 1830 (Nfld. Archives KCRC); Dan, of King's Cove, 1830 (Nfld. Archives KCRC); J.F., from Woolwich (Kent), ? of St. John's, deceased, 1831 (*Newfoundlander* 18 Aug 1831); John, granted land at Little Placentia (now Argentia), 1838 (Nfld. Archives, Registry Crown Lands); Thomas, granted land at Cuslett (Placentia B.), 1850 (Nfld. Archives, Registry Crown Lands); David and Edward, of Burin, 1871 (Lovell); Peter, cooper of Carbonear, 1871 (Lovell); William, miner of Tilt Cove, 1871 (Lovell).

Modern status: Unique, at St. John's.

Place name: Riley's Brook 49-01 58-27.

RIMMER, a surname of England, from Middle English *rimen* – to rime, or Anglo-French *rimour*, *rymour* – rimer, poet. (Reaney).

Traced by Guppy in Lancashire.

In Newfoundland:

Early instance: Frederick, hatter of St. John's, 1871 (Lovell).

Modern status: Rare, at Phillips Head (*Electors* 1955) and Little Burnt Bay (Gander district).

RING, a surname of England and Ireland, in England for *Ringer* – bell-ringer or ? one who made or wore

rings; in Ireland (O)Ring, *Ó Rinn*, ? Ir. *reann* – spear. (Reaney, Cottle, MacLysaght).

Traced by MacLysaght in east Cork.

In Newfoundland:

Early instances: Gabriel Ring, King or Bing, of Chapels Cove, 1766 (CO 199.18); William Ring, of Harbour Grace Parish, 1827 (Nfld. Archives HGRC); T., of Harbour Grace, deceased 1831 (*Newfoundlander* 14 Jul 1831); David, ? of Northern Bay, 1842 (DPHW 54); John, fisherman of Heart's Content, 1871 (Lovell); William, cooper of St. John's, 1871 (Lovell).

Modern status: At St. John's.

Place names (not necessarily from the surname): Ring Island (Labrador) 56-52 61-22; —— Rocks 49-09 53-34.

RINGER, a surname of England, ? from the Old English personal name *Hringhere*, containing the elements *ring* and *army*, or from Old English *hringan* – to ring, hence a bell-ringer, or from Old English *wringan* – to wring, squeeze, hence ? a wringer or presser of cheese. (Reaney, Cottle).

Traced by Guppy in Norfolk.

In Newfoundland:

Modern status: Rare, at Deer Lake.

RINGMAN, a surname of England of the same value as RINGER. (E.C. Smith).

In Newfoundland:

Modern status: Unique, at St. John's.

RIOUX, a surname of France from the Old German personal name *Rîdwulf* containing the elements *ride* and *wolf*. (Dauzat).

In Newfoundland:

Family tradition: Yves Boloche (b. 1874), deserted from the French fishery and settled in Winterhouses in 1892, adopting the name RIOUX (Butler 19).

Early instance: François Roix, fisherman of Great Jervis, 1871 (Lovell).

Modern status: In the Port au Port district and at Corner Brook.

Place name: Rioux 48-12 54-02.

RITCEY, a surname of Nova Scotia, from German family name Henericie.

In Newfoundland:

Family tradition: Robert Willoughby Ritcey (1883–1955) came to St. John's from Bridgewater, N.S., in 1906. (J. Ritcey)

In Newfoundland:

Modern status: At St. John's.

RITEMAN, ? an anglicization of the surnames of Germany Rüttemann, Ritt(e)mann, or Riedemann – dweller near the marsh or bog.

In Newfoundland:

Modern status: Rare, at St. John's.

RIX. *See* RICKS

RIXON, a surname of England – son of *Rick*, or dweller by the rushes, different from WRIXON. *See* RICKS, RICHARDS.

In Newfoundland:

Family tradition: The surname Rixon at Lower Island Cove, was once Rexford (MUN Hist.).

Early instances: John, in possession of fishing room at Trinity (? Trinity B.), 1762 (D'Alberti 6); John Rixom, of Devils (now Job's) Cove, 1798 (DPHW 48); Lydia Rixon, proprietor of fishing room, Grates Cove, Winter 1800–01 (Census Trinity B.); John Rixim, of Harbour Grace Parish, 1811 (Nfld. Archives HGRC); Sarah Rixin, of Conception Bay, 1812 (Nfld. Archives BRC).

Modern status: At Lower Island Cove, Paradise (Harbour Main district) and Job's Cove.

ROACH(E), **ROCHE**, surnames of England, Roche of France, the Channel Islands, and Ireland, from Old French, Middle English *roche* – (dweller by the) rock, or from various French and English place names. (Reaney, Cottle, MacLysaght, Dauzat).

Guppy traced Roach in Cornwall and Gloucestershire; Spiegelhalter traced Roach and Roch in Devon; MacLysaght found Roche widespread in Ireland.

In Newfoundland:

Family traditions: —— LeRoche, French settler at Harbour Main about 1720 (MUN Hist.). Edward Roche, from Co. Cork, came to Newfoundland in 1812; he settled at Placentia and later moved to Branch (MUN Folklore). ——, from Waterford, settled at Branch about 1790 (MUN Folklore). John Roach, from Ireland, settled at Coley's Point about 1832 (MUN Folklore).

Early instances: John Roach, of St. John's, 1708–9 (CO 194.4); John, of Placentia ? district, 1744 (CO 194.24); Jacob Roche, of Newfoundland, 1762 (St. Patrick's Parish Records, Waterford, per Kirwin); Michael Roach, of Back Cove (Port de Grave), 1783 (CO 199.18); Edmund, of Bay de Verde, 1800 (CO 199. 18); Phillip, boatkeeper of Placentia, 1800 (D'Alberti 8); Michael Rouche [sic], of St. Mary's Harbour (unspecified), 1802 (D'Alberti 12); Patrick Roach, from Macoumb (uniden-

tified) (Co. Carlow), married in the Bay Bulls district, 1805 (Nfld. Archives BRC); Edmund Roach or Roche, of Harbour Grace Parish, 1806 (Nfld. Archives HGRC); Anne Roach, from Adamstown (Co. Wexford), married at St. John's, 1807 (Nfld. Archives BRC); Thomas, of Ragged Harbour (now Melrose), 1815, of Heart's Content, 1819 (Nfld. Archives KCRC); Richard Roche, of Ferryland, 1816 (Nfld. Archives BRC); Ellen, of Outer Cove (St. John's district), 1821 (Nfld. Archives BRC); Thomas Roach, of Bonavista, 1822 (Nfld. Archives KCRC); Garrett, of King's Cove, 1824, of Keels, 1825 (Nfld. Archives KCRC); John, of Carbonear, died 1827, aged 27 (*Newfoundlander* 21 Jan 1828); Pat, of Catalina, 1829 (Nfld. Archivet KCRC); M., from Ross (unspecified) (Co. Wexford), of St. John's, 1832 (*Newfoundlander* 22 Mar 1832); Robert, from Waterford, of St. John's, died 1834, aged 39 (*Times*); Patrick, of Trinity (unspecified), 1834 (Nfld. Archives KCRC); ——, granted part of Ship's Room Beach (Bay Roberts), 1839 (Nfld. Archives, Registry Crown Lands); Nicholas, granted land at Middle Cove (St. John's district), 1841 (Nfld. Archives, Registry Crown Lands); P., lighthouse keeper, Fort Amherst, 1844 (*Nfld. Almanac*); William Roche, of Lower Burgeo, 1845 (DPHW 101); Edward Roach, granted land between Topsail and Kelligrews, 1847 (Nfld. Archives, Registry Crown Lands); Patrick, granted land at Branch River, 1851 (Nfld. Archives, Registry Crown Lands); Patrick, granted land at Renews Harbour, 1852 (Nfld. Archives, Registry Crown Lands); Michael, of Plate Cove, 1857 (Nfld. Archives KCRC); Patrick, of Indian Arm (Bonavista B.), 1857 (Nfld. Archives KCRC); scattered in Lovell 1871.

Modern status: Roach, scattered, especially at Coleys Point; Roache, at Topsail, Jerseyside (Placentia), Brigus and St. John's; Roche, scattered, especially in the St. John's districts at Torbay and Middle Cove, and at Branch.

Place names: Roaches Line 47-30 53-19; —— Marsh 47-18 52-49; Roche (or Rocky) Harbour 49-35 57-56; —— Peak 47-16 54-55; —— Point 47-19 53-58; —— (or Shoal) Point (Labrador) 53-24 60-00.

ROBBINS, a surname of England and the Channel Islands, a diminutive of Rob(ert) (*see* ROBERTS, ROBIN). (Turk).

Guppy traced Robbins in Nottinghamshire, Oxfordshire and Warwickshire, Robins in Cornwall, Devon, Hertfordshire and Warwickshire. Spiegelhalter traced Rob(b)ins in Devon.

In Newfoundland:

Family traditions: Henry Robbins or Robins, from Bridport (Dorset) came to Harbour Grace about 1861, aged 18; he later moved to Cat Harbour (now Lumsden) and was one of the earliest settlers there (MUN Hist.). —— Robbins, from Wales, settled at Lower Island Cove; some of the family later moved to Hatchet Cove (Trinity B.) (MUN Folklore).

Early instances: William Rob(b)ins, of St. John's, 1677, "12 years an inhabitant in 1680," that is, since 1668 (CO 1); John Robins, of Renews, 1703–4 (CO 194.3, 22); Thomas Robbins, of Lower Island Cove, 1789 (CO 199.18); George Robins, of Bonavista, 1808 (DPHW 70); Charles, of Lower Burgeo, 1845 (DPHW 101); Eli, of Petites, 1858 (DPHW 98).

Modern status: Scattered, especially at St. John's, Lumsden and Hatchet Cove.

Place names (not necessarily from the surname): Robin Cove 47-08 55-05, —— Lake (Labrador) 54-55 63-24; Robins Cove 49-39 54-46; —— Pond 47-39 52-46.

ROBERE, ? a phonetic spelling of the surname of France Robert. *See* ROBERTS.

In Newfoundland:

Modern status: Rare, at St. Lawrence and Point au Gaul.

ROBERGE, a surname of France from Old French *roberge* – man-of-war, hence a nickname for a sailor. (Dauzat).

In Newfoundland:

Modern status: Unique, at Stephenville Crossing (*Electors* 1955).

ROBERTS, a surname of England, Wales and Ireland from the baptismal name Robert, from the Old German personal name *Hrodebert*, Old English *Hreodbeorht*, Old French *Ro(d)bert*, containing the elements *fame* and *bright*. Robert, introduced into England at the time of the Norman Conquest, and its pet-forms and diminutives Rob(in), Hob, Dob, Nob and (later) Bob, have been the source of many surnames including ROBERTS(ON), ROBBINS, ROB(IN)SON, HOBBS, BOBBETT, PROBERT, HOPKINS, DOBBIN, DOBSON, RABBIT(T)S and ? DIBBON. (Withycombe, Reaney, Cottle). *See also* ROPSON.

Found widespread by Guppy in the south and Midlands and especially in North Wales; and by MacLysaght in all provinces though rare in Connacht.

In Newfoundland:

Family traditions: Mark R. (1815–1898), born at

Sturminster Newton (Dorset), settled at Portugal Cove about 1835; he moved to Woody Point (Bonne Bay) about 1870 (MUN Folklore). ——, from Devon, settled at Rocky Harbour (Bonne Bay) in 1835 (MUN Hist.). Mary Ann (1813–), born at Twillingate (MUN Folklore). John (1860–1920), fisherman of Woody Point (Bonne Bay) (MUN Geog.).

Early instances: Philip, of St. John's, 1675, 23 years an inhabitant in 1680, that is, since 1657 (CO 1); William, of Ferryland, 1675 (CO 1); Dinah, of Brigus, 1771, property "in possession of the Family for 80 years," that is, since 1691 (CO 199.18); ——, of Quidi Vidi, 1703 (CO 194.3); William, of Renews, 1703–4 (CO 194.3, 22); William, of Bonavista, 1708–9 (CO 194.4); Thomas, of Bay de Verde, 1730 (CO 194.23); Bartholomew, from Ireland, of Little Placentia (now Argentia) about 1730–5 (CO 194.9); Hugh, merchant of Harbour Grace, 1771 (Nfld. Archives L118); John, of Portugal Cove, 1790 (DPHW 26C); Stephen, juror of Greenspond, 1804 (D'Alberti 14); Abraham, of Cupids, 1805 (DPHW 34); Joseph, of Hermitage Cove (Burin district), 1821 (DPHW 109); Elizabeth, of Carbonear, 1821 (Nfld. Archives BRC); Joseph, of Fogo, 1827 (Nfld. Archives KCRC); Morgan, of Grand Jervis, 1830 (DPHW 30); John, of Cobblers Island (Bonavista B.), 1833 (DPHW 76); Matthew, married on the French Shore, 1839 (Nfld. Archives BRC); Nathan, fisherman of Aquaforte, 1840 (DPHW 31); John, of Herring Neck, 1852, of Stone Harbour (Twillingate district), 1856 (DPHW 85); Hugh, of Donier (Twillingate district), 1854, of Triton Harbour, 1856 (DPHW 86); Joshua, of Fortune, 1855 (DPHW 106); Frederick, of Seal Bay Head (Twillingate district), 1856 (DPHW 86); Jeremiah, of Little Bay Islands, 1859 (DPHW 92); Joseph, of Burin, 1860 (DPHW 100); George, of Mud Cove (Burin district), 1861 (DPHW 108); John, of Lush's Bight (Exploits district), 1861 (DPHW 92); Stephen, of Bluff Head Cove, 1861 (DPHW 88); Andrew, of Twillingate, 1861 (DPHW 88); John, of Bonne Bay, 1865 (DPHW 93); widespread in Lovell 1871.

Modern status: Widespread, especially at Brigus, Hermitage, Corner Brook, Jim's Cove (Green B.), Twillingate and St. John's.

Place names (not necessarily from the surname): Robert 50-47 56-02; Robert's Arm 49-29 55-49; Bay Roberts 47-37 53-13; —— Brook 48-35 58-22; —— Lookout 47-36 53-15.

ROBERTSON, a surname of England, Scotland and Ireland – son of Robert. *See* ROBERTS.

Traced by Guppy in Norfolk and Northumberland and generally in Scotland, and by MacLysaght in Ulster.

In Newfoundland:

Early instances: R., merchant of St. John's, 1794–5, "12 years in Newfoundland," that is, 1782–3 (Census 1794–5); John, of Trinity Bay, 1785 (DPHW 64); John, from Bristol, married at St. John's, 1839 (DPHW 26D); James, passenger on the *Atlantic*, wrecked at Pouch Cove, 1840 (*Newfoundlander* 14 May 1840); John, from Halifax, married at St. John's, 1848 (*Newfoundlander* 30 Nov 1848); Stephen, of Isle aux Morts, 1857 (DPHW 98).

Modern status: At Corner Brook, Bishop's Falls, Gander and St. John's.

ROBIN, a surname of France and the Channel Islands, a diminutive of Robert (*see* ROBBINS, ROBERTS, and RUBIA). (Dauzat, Turk).

In Newfoundland:

Family tradition: Guillaume, from Roche-Devrien [*sic*] (Brittany), a deserter, was the first settler of Cape St. George (MUN Hist.).

Early instance: Juan Robie, fisherman of Bay of Islands, 1871 (Lovell).

Modern status: At St. John's and Cape St. George (*Electors* 1955).

Place names (not necessarily from the surname): Robin Cove 47-08 55-05; —— Lake (Labrador) 54-55 63-24; Robins Cove 49-39 54-46; —— Pond 47-39 52-46.

ROBINSON, a surname of England, Ireland and Guernsey (Channel Islands), usually – son of Robin (*see* ROBERTS), but also for ROBERTSON. (Reaney, Cottle, Turk).

Found widespread by Guppy in England, especially in the north, and by MacLysaght in Ireland, especially in Ulster.

In Newfoundland:

Family traditions: John, from Cornwall, was an early settler at Seal Cove (White B.) about 1815–20 (MUN Hist.). Stephen, English fisherman of La Poile, 1862 (MUN Hist.).

Early instances: William, of Ferryland, 1677 (CO 1); John, boatkeeper of St. John's, 1681 (CO 1); John, of Trinity (Trinity B.), 1787 (DPHW 64); Thomas, from Wareham (Dorset), of St. John's, deceased 1817 (*Royal Gazette* 26 Aug 1817); William, from Co. Tipperary, married at St. John's, 1831 (Nfld. Archives BRC); Rev. Christopher, of Glebe House, Granard, Ireland, deceased, father of Bryan Robinson, barrister of St. John's, 1838 (*Newfoundlander*

12 Apr 1838); Mary, of Harbour Grace, 1850 (DPHW 26D); George, of Petites, 1860 (DPHW 99); John, of Aspey Cove (Twillingate district), 1871 (Lovell); John, of Bareneed, 1871 (Lovell); John, of Coleys Point, 1871 (Lovell); Stephen, of Isle aux Morts, 1871 (Lovell); Andrew, of Renews, 1871 (Lovell).

Modern status: Scattered, especially in the Humber West, Green Bay and White Bay South districts.

Place names: Robinson Bight 48-06 53-48; Robinsons, Robinson Brook (or Robinsons River) 48-15 58-48; Robinson Island 50-36 57-16, (Labrador) 60-20 64-27; —— Point 47-54 53-44; Robinsons Cove 49-30 57-47; —— Head 48-16 58-49; —— Ponds 48-48 58-21; —— River 47-46 52-46.

ROBSON, a surname of England, Ireland and Scotland – son of Rob(ert). *See* ROBERTS, ROPSON. (Reaney, Cottle, Black, MacLysaght 73).

Traced by Guppy in Cumberland, Westmorland, Durham, Lincolnshire, Northumberland and Yorkshire NR, ER, and in the Scots Border counties, and by MacLysaght in Ulster.

In Newfoundland:

Early instance: Thomas, from New Brunswick, granted patent on fog bell by House of Assembly, St. John's, 1850 (*Royal Gazette* 16 Apr 1850).

Modern status: At Corner Brook, Deer Lake and St. John's.

ROCHE. *See* ROACH

ROCKETT, a surname of Ireland, a variant of Rockell, from the surname of France Rochelle, from the place name La Rochelle (Charente), or dweller by the rock. (MacLysaght).

Traced by MacLysaght in Co. Waterford since before 1393.

In Newfoundland:

Early instances: Robert Rocket, of Harbour Grace, 1817, 1830 (Nfld. Archives HGRC); Robert Rocket, from Carrick (unspecified) (Co. Tipperary), married at St. John's, 1821 (Nfld. Archives BRC); Mary ? Rocket, of Ragged Harbour (now Melrose), 1833 (Nfld. Archives KCRC); Robert Rocket, of Port de Grave, deceased, 1853 (*Newfoundlander* 9 May 1853).

Modern status: Rare, at Corner Brook.

Place name: Rocketts Cove (Labrador) 51-55 55-59.

ROCKWELL, a surname of England from the English place name Rockwell (Somerset). (Spiegelhalter).

Traced by Spiegelhalter in Devon.

In Newfoundland:

Modern status: Rare, at St. John's.

ROCKWOOD, a surname of England from an unidentified place name, or dweller in or near a rocky wood or a wood frequented by rooks. (E.C. Smith).

In Newfoundland:

Family tradition: Two Rockwood brothers, from England, settled in Heart's Content in the early 1800s (MUN Folklore).

Early instances: William, of Trinity Bay, 1772 (DPHW 64); Elizabeth, of Change Islands, 1821 (USPG); William, planter of Heart's Content, 1823 (DPHW 64B); Elizabeth, of Harbour Grace Parish, 1830 (Nfld. Archives HGRC); A., on the *Britannia* in the seal fishery out of Carbonear, 1847 (*Newfoundlander* 25 Mar 1847); ——, on the *Pacquet* in the seal fishery out of St. John's, 1849 (*Newfoundlander* 29 Mar 1849).

Modern status: Scattered, especially at Heart's Content and St. John's.

RODDEN, a surname of England and Ireland, in England from the English place names Rodden (Somerset) or Rowden (Devon, Herefordshire), the first from Old English *rā-denu* – (dweller in the) roe valley, the second from Old English *ruh dūn* – (dweller on or near the) rough hill; in Ireland (O)Rodden, *Ó Rodáin*, Ir. *rod* – strong, or *Mac Rodáin* usually anglicized MacCrudden. (Spiegelhalter, Cottle, Ekwall, MacLysaght).

Traced by Spiegelhalter in Devon and by MacLysaght in Co. Donegal.

In Newfoundland:

Early instance: John Rodon, of Petty Harbour, 1682 (CO 1).

Modern status: Rare, at St. John's.

RO(D)GERS, surnames of England, Wales, Scotland, Ireland, Roger of Guernsey (Channel Islands), from the baptismal name Roger, from the Old German personal name *Hrodgar*, Old English *Hrothgar*, Old French *Roger*, containing the elements *fame* and *spear*. Roger, introduced into England at the time of the Norman Conquest, and its pet-forms and diminutives, Hodge and Dodge, have given rise to such surnames as RO(D)GER(S), DODGE, HODGE and HODGSON. In Ulster Ro(d)gers usually stood for MacRory, *Mac Ruaidhrí*. (Reaney, Cottle, MacLysaght, Black, Turk).

Guppy found Rogers widespread in the south and

Midlands, especially in Cornwall, Herefordshire and Shropshire, with Rodgers characteristic of Derbyshire, and Rodger of Scotland where the name is scattered. MacLysaght found Ro(d)gers numerous throughout Ireland, except in Munster.

In Newfoundland:

Family traditions: Richard Rogers, from Sheffield, England, settled at Fair Island (Bonavista B.) about 1800; some of the family later moved to Silver Fox Island, Deer Island, Sydney Cove and Round Harbour (MUN Folklore). John (1815–98), from England, settled at Channel about 1830 (MUN Geog.). Bethana (1822–86), from Fortune Bay, settled at Grand Bank (MUN Hist.). The spelling Rogers was changed to Rodgers at Old Perlican (MUN Hist.).

Early instances: George Rogers, soldier of St. John's, 1759 (DPHW 26D); George, of Trinity Bay, 1765 (DPHW 64); N., of Twillingate, 1768 (MUN Hist.); Joseph, merchant of Conception Bay, 1784 (D'Alberti 2); David, of Northern Bay, 1790 (CO 199.18); John, of Ferryland, 1792 (D'Alberti 4); Davis, of Ochre Pit Cove, 1792 (CO 199.18); William, of Placentia, 1794 (D'Alberti 5); James, of Burnt Point (North Shore, Conception B.), 1797 (CO 199.18); James, proprietor and occupier of fishing room, Trinity (Trinity B.), Winter 1800–01 (Census Trinity B.); James, of Kettle Cove (North Shore, Conception B.), 1804 (CO 199.18); Mary, from Rosteercan (unidentified) (? Co. Kilkenny), married at St. John's, 1807 (Nfld. Archives BRC); Samuel, of Harbour Grace Parish, 1810 (Nfld. Archives HGRC); James, of Pouch Cove, 1812 (DPHW 26B); James, of Torbay, 1817 (DPHW 26B); William, of Greenspond, 1821 (DPHW 76); David, planter of Old Perlican, 1822 (DPHW 58); John, of Grand Bank, 1822 (DPHW 109); Thomas, of Fortune, 1825 (DPHW 109); Harriet, of Burin, 1828 (*Newfoundlander* 22 Jun 1828); James Rodgers, planter of Seal Cove (now New Chelsea), 1828 (DPHW 59A); Rebecca Rogers, of Vere (now Fair) Island, 1830 (DPHW 76); Mary, of Flowers Island (Bonavista B.), 1830 (DPHW 76); Frances, of Gooseberry Island (Bonavista B.), 1830 (DPHW 76); Luke, fisherman of Grole, 1848 (DPHW 102); James Rudger, of Change Islands, 1849 (DPHW 83); Thomas Rogers, of Salvage, 1849 (DPHW 72); David, of Harbour Grace, 1855 (DPHW 43); Ellen, of Russells Cove (now New Melbourne), 1856 (DPHW 59); Joseph, of Catalina, 1859 (DPHW 67); Samuel, of Cottle Island (Bonavista B.), 1861 (Nfld. Archives KCRC); widespread in Lovell 1871.

Modern status: Rodgers, scattered, especially at Old Perlican and St. John's; Rogers, scattered, especially at Paul's Island and Sydney Cove (Bona-vista B.), Durrell's Arm and St. John's.

Place names (not necessarily from the surname): Rodger(s) Cove 49-22 54-31; Rodgers Brook 47-32 53-14; —— Cove 49-22 54-31; —— (or Pigeon) Point (Labrador) 54-27 57-15; Cape Roger, —— Island 47-21 54-44; —— Lake (Labrador) 54-27 66-20; Rogers Cove 49-35 54-19; —— Gullies 47-48 52-49; —— Harbour (Labrador) 54-58 58-40; —— Head 47-38 56-12; —— Island (Labrador) 53-15 55-44, 54-54 58-05; —— Point 49-35 54-19; —— Rocks 46-51 55-46; —— Tilt Pond 47-42 52-50.

RODWAY, a surname of England from the English place names Rodway (Somerset) – road way, or Rodway (Warwickshire, Devon), or Reddaway, Roadway (Devon) – red way. (Reaney, Cottle, A.H. Smith).

Guppy traced a variant Radway in Gloucestershire.
In Newfoundland:
Family tradition: Sir Richard, from England, jumped ship and settled at Kingwell (Placentia B.) (MUN Folklore).

Early instances: John, of Spencer's Cove (Placentia B.), 1854 (DPHW 105); Richard, of Baine Harbour (Placentia B.), 1868–1907 (Nfld. Archives Prelim. Inventory); James, fisherman of Mussel Harbour (Placentia B.), 1871 (Lovell).

Modern status: Scattered, especially in the Placentia West district.

ROE, a surname of England and Ireland, in England from Old English *rā*, Middle English *rō* – roe, ? a nickname for one noted for his speed, shyness or prowess in hunting, or confused with ROWE; in Ireland, a synonym of Ormond, *Ó Ruaidh*, Ir. *ruadh* – red, or an abbreviated form of Mac Enroe, *Mac Conruabha*, where *Ruabha* is probably a place name, or of English origin confused with ROWE. (Reaney, Cottle, MacLysaght).

Traced by Guppy in Lincolnshire, Nottinghamshire and Somerset, and by MacLysaght in Co. Waterford.

In Newfoundland:
Early instances: John, ? labourer of St. John's, 1779 (CO 194.34); Thomas, of Trinity Bay, 1779 (DPHW 64); Richard, from Mooncoin (Co. Kilkenny), married at St. John's, 1806 (Nfld. Archives BRC); William, of Harbour Grace Parish, 1822 (Nfld. Archives HGRC); Christian Roe or Rowe, of Trinity (unspecified), 1831 (Nfld. Archives KCRC); Michael Roe or Row(e), of Tickle Cove (Bonavista B.), 1846

(Nfld. Archives KCRC); Benjamin Roe, of Chance Cove (Trinity B.), 1862 (DPHW 62).

Modern status: Rare, at Corner Brook (*Electors* 1955) and St. John's.

ROEBOTHAM, RO(E)BOTHAN, ROWBOTTOM, surnames of England – (dweller in the) rough valley, according to Reaney, probably a place in Lancashire. (Reaney, Cottle).

Guppy traced Rowbotham and Rowbottom in Derbyshire and Staffordshire.

In Newfoundland:
Family tradition: —— Rowbottom, from England, settled at Goose Cove (White B.) (MUN Hist.).

Modern status: Roebotham, at Pound Cove and Seldom; Roebothan, unique, at St. John's; Robothan, unique, at Goose Cove (White B.); Rowbottom, at Lush's Bight (Green B.).

ROFF, ROLFE, ROLLS, surnames of England, Rolfe of Ireland, a few of twenty-six variants, of German origin especially in the Old Norse form *Hrólfr*, in Old French *Roul*, often latinized as *Rollo*, containing the elements *fame* and *wolf*. These have been confused both in England and Ireland with RALPH. (Withycombe, Reaney, Cottle, MacLysaght). *See* ROLFE, ROLLS and *also* R(H)UELOKKE.

Guppy traced Rofe in Kent, Roffe in Hertfordshire, Roofe in Norfolk and Rolfe in Buckinghamshire, Hertfordshire, Kent, Norfolk and Suffolk.

In Newfoundland:
Early instances: John Roff, fisherman of Port de Grave, 1839 (DPHW 39); James ? Rueff, of King's Cove Parish, 1853 (Nfld. Archives KCRC); George Roff, of Conche, 1871 (Lovell); Joseph Rouf, miner of La Manche, 1871 (Lovell).

Modern status: At Mortier.
Place name: Joseph Roff Cove 47-41 53-57.

ROGERS. *See* RO(D)GERS

ROGERSON, a surname of England – son of Roger. (*See* RO(D)GERS).

Traced by Guppy in Lancashire.
In Newfoundland:
Early instances: James, merchant of St. John's, 1803 (D'Alberti 13); Richard, merchant of Harbour Grace, 1820 (DPHW 48).

Modern status: Rare, at St. John's.
Place name: Rogerson Lake 48-31 56-46.

ROHAN, a surname of England and Ireland, in England from the French place name Rohan

(Morbihan); in Ireland (O)Rohan, *Ó Robhacháin* (Munster), *Ó Ruadhacháin* (Ulster). (Reaney, Mac-Lysaght).

Traced by MacLysaght mainly in Co. Kerry.

In Newfoundland:

Early instances: Patrick, of Harbour Grace Parish, 1816 (Nfld. Archives HGRC); Catherine, of Harbour Main, 1828 (Nfld. Archives BRC); Patrick, shoemaker of Harbour Grace, 1867, 1871 (Nfld. Archives HGRC, Lovell).

Modern status: At Mount Carmel (*Electors* 1955) and Harricot (St. Mary's district).

ROIL, ROYAL, ROYLE, RYALL, surnames of England; (O)RYLE, Riall of Ireland, with ROYAL, RYLES and RILES Newfoundland variants. On the names in England, Weekley *Surnames* comments: "Loyal and Royal are doubtful. Though quite possible nicknames, they are perhaps rather for *Lyle, Ryle* or *Lyall, Ryall*. The first two are local and the second two baptismal, though they have of course been confused. *Lyall* is for Lyulph, representing an Old Danish Lithwulf ... and *Ryall* is for Riulf ... A[nglo] S[axon] Riewulf [containing the elements *power* and *wolf*]." The place names are Ryle (Northumberland), Ryhill (Yorkshire ER, WR), Ryall (Devon) – (dweller by the) rye hill. In Ireland (O)Ryle, Riale, *Ó Raghaill*, ? an abbreviated form of O'REILLY. (Weekley *Surnames*, Cottle, Spiegelhalter, MacLysaght). *See* RILES, RYALL.

Guppy traced Royle in Cheshire and Lancashire, Spiegelhalter traced Ryall, Ryle and Royle in Devon; MacLysaght traced Ryle mainly in Co. Kerry.

In Newfoundland:

Early instances: John Royall, ? of St. John's, ? 1706 (CO 194.24); John Royal, of Trinity Bay, 1770 (DPHW 64); Charlotte Reule, of Little Bay (Burin district), 1839 (DPHW 106); Henry Roil, planter of Carbonear, 1842 (DPHW 48); Patrick Royale, of Harbour Grace Parish, 1845 (Nfld. Archives HGRC); Joseph Royal, ? of Northern Bay, 1853 (DPHW 54); Bernard, of Harbour Grace, 1870 (Nfld. Archives HGRC); Henry Royle, of Fortune, married Mary Maria Penny, 1871 (Grand Bank Methodist marriages per P.E.L. Smith); James (and others), of Job's Cove, 1871 (Lovell); Silas, of Victoria Village, 1871 (Lovell).

Modern status: Roil, at St. John's; Royal, rare, at Grand Bank and St. John's; Royle, at Paradise (Harbour Main district), Grand Bank and St. John's.

Place name (not necessarily from the surname): Port Royal 47-32 54-06.

ROLANDS, ROWLANDS, surnames of England and Wales, Rowland of Ireland and the Channel Islands, also Rol(l)and(s) of Jersey (Channel Islands), from the baptismal name Ro(w)land, from the Old German personal name *Hrodland*, Old French *Rol(l)ant* etc., containing the elements *famous* and *land*, or from the English place names Rowland (Derbyshire) or Rowland Wood (Sussex) – roe wood, or for the French surname Rol(l)and; in Ireland, with ROWLEY, also for (O)Rolan, *Ó Rothláin*. (Reaney, Cottle, MacLysaght, Turk).

Guppy traced Rowland in Cheshire, Derbyshire and Devon, Rowlands in Monmouthshire and North and South Wales; Spiegelhalter traced Ro(w)land in Devon; MacLysaght Rowland and Rowley in Co. Mayo and Ulster.

In Newfoundland:

Early instances: Andrew Rowland (Rowlin in 1677, Roling in 1682), of Petty Harbour, 1675 (CO 1); Elisha Rowlands, planter of Little Placentia (now Argentia), 1726 (CO 194.8); David Rowland, Episcopal minister of St. John's, 1810, missionary at Moreton's Harbour, 1821 (CO 194.49, 52); Catherine Rowlan, from Newtown (unidentified) (Co. Wexford), married at St. John's, 1817 (Nfld. Archives BRC); James Rowland, servant of Rock Harbour (Placentia B.), 1871 (Lovell).

Modern status: Rolands, at Stephenville (*Electors* 1955); Rowlands, at Jean de Baie (Placentia B.) and Marystown.

Place names (not necessarily from the surname): Mount Roland, —— Point 51-20 55-54; Rowland Head 48-32 53-03; —— Point 49-44 55-58, (Labrador) 60-10 64-22; —— Rock 47-24 54-01.

ROLFE. *See* ROFF, RALPH

In Newfoundland:

Early instances: John Rolf, granted land at Clarke's Beach, 1844 (Nfld. Archives, Registry Crown Lands); Andrew Rolfe, sub-collector of customs, of St. John's, 1871 (Lovell).

Modern status: At Paradise (Green B.) (*Electors* 1955), Badger, Corner Brook, St. John's and Deer Lake.

Place name: Rolf Rock 47-10 55-08.

ROLLINGS, a surname of England, a diminutive of *Roll* (*see* ROFF) or of *Roland* (*see* ROLANDS), or a late spelling of *Rawl(g)* (*see* RALPH), or from the English place names Rowling Court or Rowling Street (Kent). (Reaney).

Spiegelhalter traced Rollin, Rawlin(s) in Devon.

In Newfoundland:

Early instances: Lewis Rollins, tailor of St. John's, 1768 (DPHW 26C); John, of Harbour Grace Parish, 1828 (Nfld. Archives HGRC).

Modern status: At St. John's.

ROLLS. *See* ROFF

Spiegelhalter traced Rolle in Devon; Matthews traced Rolles in Dorset, Hampshire and Gloucestershire (Bristol).

In Newfoundland:

Early instances: John Role, of Bay de Verde, 1708 (CO 194.4); John Rolles, of Bonavista, 1784 (DPHW 64); Samuel Rolls, from Poole, in possession of property at Bay de Verde, 1788 (CO 199.18); Charles, servant of Battle Harbour (Labrador), 1795 (MUN Hist.); Samuel Rolles, proprietor and occupier of fishing room, Trinity (Trinity B.), Winter 1800–01 (Census Trinity B.); Samuel Rolls, from Poole, in possession of fishing room, Ship Island, Greenspond Harbour, 1805, in possession of fishing room, Mockbeggar room, Bonavista, before 1806 (Bonavista Register 1806); Mark Rol(l)s, of Tickle Cove (Bonavista B.), 1841 (DPHW 73A); Thomas Rolls, of Grates Cove, 1856 (DPHW 29); James, merchant of Barr'd Islands, 1871 (Lovell); Richard Rholes, master mariner of St. John's, 1871 (Lovell).

Modern status: Especially at Bonavista.

Place name: Rolls Cove 47-34 52-41.

ROMAINE, a surname of England, Old French *Romeyn* – the man from Rome, or *romeyn* – a Roman. Reaney comments: "*Romanus* was the name of two martyrs and a 7th-century bishop of Rouen. Only one English example of this personal name has been noted, but it may sometimes be the source of the surname." (Reaney).

Spiegelhalter traced Roman, which he derives from the name of a Celtic saint Rumon, in Devon.

In Newfoundland:

Early instances: John, planter of Bonavista, 1822 (DPHW 72); —— Romaine, a Frenchman, in Bay St. George area, 1856 (Butler 4, n. 14). Benjamin Romain, fisherman of Musgravetown, 1871 (Lovell).

Modern status: At Port-au-Port and Newman's Cove.

Place names: Romaine River 50-21 63-28; Romaines 48-33 58-42; —— Brook 48-33 58-40.

ROMPKEY, an anglicization of the surname of Germany Ramgen.

In Newfoundland:

Family tradition: Johan Wendel Ramgen (1677–1757) migrated from the Palatinate to Nova Scotia in 1750. Two descendants settled at Belleoram, Newfoundland, of whom Jacob became the forerunner of the Rompkey family (R. G. Rompkey).

Early instance: Jacob and John Romkey, planters of Belleoram, 1871 (Lovell).

Modern status: Rare, at St. John's.

RONAN, RONAYNE, surnames of Ireland (O)Ronan, Ronayne, *Ó Ronain*, and of Scotland. "The well-known personal name *Ronan* may from *rón* – seal," or for (O)Roughneen, *Ó Reachtnín*. (MacLysaght, Black).

Traced by MacLysaght chiefly in Co. Cork and also in Dublin and Mayo.

In Newfoundland:

Early instances: John Ronan, of St. John's, 1804 (Nfld. Archives BRC); Mary, of Harbour Main, 1806 (Nfld. Archives BRC); John, from Ross (unspecified) (Co. Wexford), married at St. John's, 1806 (Nfld. Archives BRC); William, of Harbour Grace Parish, 1807 (Nfld. Archives HGRC); James Ronay, of St. Mary's Harbour, married at St. John's, 1820 (DPHW 26D); Anastasia Ronan, from Sutherland, Scotland, married at Tilton Harbour (now Tilting), 1823 (Nfld. Archives KCRC); Joanna, of Joe Batts Arm, 1823 (Nfld. Archives KCRC); Mary ? Ronan, of Trinity (unspecified), 1828 (Nfld. Archives KCRC); Francis, from Carrick-on-Suir (Co. Tipperary), of Harbour Grace, 1830, 1844 (*Indicator* 27 Jul 1844, Nfld. Archives HGRC); Bridget, servant of Job's Cove, 1835 (DPHW 52A); John Ronayne, ? of Northern Bay, 1853 (DPHW 54); John and William, of Tizzard's Harbour, 1871 (Lovell).

Modern status: Ronan, rare, at St. John's; Ronayne, at Marystown, Tors Cove (*Electors* 1955), Witless Bay and St. John's.

ROONEY, a surname of Ireland (O)Rooney, *Ó Ruanaidh*, or an abbreviation of MUL(L)ROONEY, or for (O)Rooneen, *Ó Rúnaidhin*. (MacLysaght).

Traced by MacLysaght originally in Co. Down and now numerous in all provinces except Munster.

In Newfoundland:

Early instances: Gordon ? Rooney, of Conception Bay, 1706 (CO 194.4); Michael Rooney, operated salmon fishery at Trepassey, 1808 (CO 194.48); William, St. John's, 1816 (CO 194.60); Ann, of Fortune Harbour, 1832 (Nfld. Archives KCRC).

Modern status: Rare, at St. John's and Lower Island Cove.

ROOST, a variant of the surname of England and Scotland Rust, in Scotland also Roust, from ? Old

English *rust* – red-haired or of red complexion, though Cottle finds this derivation unconvincing. (Reaney, Cottle, Black).

Black traced R(o)ust in Aberdeenshire.

In Newfoundland:

Early instances: Thomas (and others) Rewst, and William Roust, of St. John's, 1871 (Lovell).

Modern status: Unique, at St. John's (*Electors* 1955).

ROPER, a surname of England from Old English *rāp* – rope, hence rope-maker. (Reaney).

Traced by Guppy in Dorset, Suffolk and Worcestershire, and by Spiegelhalter in Devon.

In Newfoundland:

Early instances: Andrew, of ? Little Placentia (now Argentia), about 1730–5 (CO 194.9); Henry, of St. John's, 1845 (DPHW 26D).

Modern status: At St. John's.

Place name: Roper River (Labrador) 53-49 57-45.

ROPSON, ? a variant of ROBSON (*see* ROBERTS), or of Rapson – son of *Rap* (*see* RALPH).

In Newfoundland:

Modern status: At Gold Cove, Great Harbour Deep (White B.) (*Electors* 1955), and Beaches (White B.).

RORKE. *See* O'ROURKE

ROSE, a feminine baptismal name and a surname of England, Scotland, Ireland, France, also in Jewish usage. The baptismal name derives from the Old German *Hrodohaidis* containing the elements *fame* and *kind*, introduced into England by the Normans in the forms *Ro(h)ese*, later *Royse*, in Middle English *Rose*, as if derived from Latin *rosa* – rose, whence the surnames Rose, Royce. Other origins of the surname are from an inn-sign – at the sign of the rose; from Scots Gaelic and Irish *ros* – promontory, headland, cape; from Welsh *rhôs* – moor, heath, plain; from the English place names Roos (Yorkshire ER), Roose (Lancashire), Ross (Herefordshire, Northumberland), derived from the preceding. The Jewish surname is usually an abbreviated form of German compound names based on the flower, such as *Rosenbaum* – rose-tree, *Rosenthal* – rose-valley, ROSENBERG – rose-hill. (Withycombe, Reaney, Cottle, Ekwall). *See* ROSS *and also* ROUZES.

Traced by Guppy in contiguous counties from Lincolnshire to Dorset, by Spiegelhalter in Devon; and found scattered by MacLysaght, but settled in Co. Limerick since the mid-seventeenth century.

In Newfoundland:

Family traditions: Manuel Rozes, a Spaniard, settled at Degras (MUN Geog.). Robert Rose (1785–1863), of Grand Bank (MUN Hist.).

Early instances: John, of St. Mary's, 1720 (D'Alberti 7); John, constable of Ferryland district, ? 1730–1732 (CO 194.9); Richard, J.P. of Trepassey, 1753 (CO 194.13); Ezekiel, of Western Bay, 1783 (CO 199.18); William, of Placentia, 1794 (D'Alberti 5); John, of Battle Harbour (Labrador), 1795 (MUN Hist.); Robert, proprietor and occupier of fishing room, Grates Cove, Winter 1800–01 (Census Trinity B.); John, of Marshalls Folly (Carbonear district), 1801 (CO 199.18); James and Thomas, of Turks Gut (now Marysvale), 1801 (CO 199.18); Thomas, of Brigus, 1802 (CO 199.18); Joseph, of St. John's, 1814 (D'Alberti 24); Grace, of Harbour Grace Parish, 1817 (Nfld. Archives HGRC); William, fisherman of Grand Bank, 1818 (DPHW 109); James, planter of Twillingate, 1820 (USPG); John, planter of Bull Cove (Conception B.), 1824 (DPHW 34); John, planter of Ochre Pit Cove, 1826 (DPHW 52A); Thomas, of Fortune, 1827 (DPHW 106); Henry, of Hermitage Cove (Burin district), 1828 (DPHW 109); Mary, of Old Perlican, 1828 (DPHW 58); John, planter of Perry's Cove, 1830 (DPHW 48); Thomas, of Belleoram, ? about 1830–5 (DPHW 30); Robert, of Big Harbour (Burin district), 1831 (DPHW 109); Morgan, of King's Cove, 1831 (Nfld. Archives KCRC); James, planter of Spout Cove (Carbonear district), 1831 (DPHW 48); Henry, planter of Bird Island Cove (now Elliston), 1832 (DPHW 72); William, planter of Otterbury (Carbonear district), 1833 (DPHW 48); William, of Little Bay (Bay de l'Eau), 1835 (DPHW 30); John, of Pushthrough, 1836 (DPHW 106); Thomas, of Renews, 1837 (Nfld. Archives BRC); Joseph, ? of Northern Bay, 1839 (DPHW 54); Margaret, of Catalina, 1841 (DPHW 67); Ann, of Gaultois, 1846 (DPHW 102); John, of Lower Burgeo, 1846 (DPHW 101); James, servant of Fogo, 1847 (DPHW 83); ——, of Rose Blanche, 1849 (Feild); William, fisherman of Green Cove (Twillingate district), 1851 (DPHW 85); Charlotte Ross [for Rose], married at Harbour Breton, 1851 (Harbour Breton Anglican Church Records per D.A. Macdonald); Thomas, fisherman of Bay d'Espoir, 1852 (DPHW 104); Richard, of Great Harbour (Burin district), 1854 (DPHW 104); Robert, of Channel, 1857 (DPHW 98); William, of Plate Cove, 1859 (Nfld. Archives KCRC); James, granted land at Salmon Cove (Port de Grave), 1860 (Nfld. Archives, Registry Crown Lands); Thomas, of Burin, 1860 (DPHW 100); Martin, of Harbour Grace, 1867 (Nfld. Archives

HGRC); Margaret, of Trinity (unspecified), 1868 (Nfld. Archives KCRC); William, of Red Cliff Island (Bonavista B.), 1869 (Nfld. Archives KCRC); widespread in Lovell 1871.

Modern status: Widespread, especially at Bell Island, Salmon Cove (Carbonear district), Grand Bank, Hermitage and St. John's.

Place names (not necessarily from the surname): Rose Cove 47-35 55-26, 47-40 56-13; —— Head 49-41 54-45; —— Island (Labrador) 58-32 62-58; —— Lake (Labrador) 53-45 57-42; Rose Point (or Point Enragée) 47-23 55-18; Rose au Rue 47-31 54-11; —— —— —— Island 47-30 54-10; —— —— —— Point 47-32 54-09; —— —— —— Sunker (Rock) 47-29 54-10; —— Blanche, —— —— Bay, —— —— —— Brook, —— —— Harbour, —— —— Point 47-36 58-42; Rosedale 48-41 53-58; Rosée Harbour 47-24 55-18; Roses Bank 47-33 55-24; Jas Rose Point 47-38 56-14; Tom Roses Pond 51-06 55-58.

ROSENBERG. *See* ROSE

In Newfoundland:

Early instance: Lazarus (1886–), born in Russia, came to St. John's from England in 1924 (*Nfld. Who's Who* 1937).

Modern status: Rare, at St. John's.

ROSS, a surname of England, Scotland and Ireland, from Old German *Rozzo*, a pet-form of compound names containing the element *Hrod* – fame, or from the English place names Roos (Yorkshire ER), Roose (Lancashire), Ross (Herefordshire, Northumberland), the Scots place name Ross(shire), or the French place name Rots (Calvados). (Reaney, Cottle). *See* ROSE.

Traced by Guppy in Dorset and generally in Scotland but with its chief home in Ross-shire; by Spiegelhalter in Devon; and by MacLysaght in Ulster where it is of Scots origin and in Dublin and Cork where it may be of English origin.

In Newfoundland:

Early instances: John, of St. John's, 1778 (DPHW 26C), Stephen, of Flat Island (Bonavista B.), 1839 (DPHW 76); Rev. Alexander, of Harbour Grace, 1856, deceased 1857 (*Newfoundlander* 2 Jun 1856, 25 May 1857); Walter, telegraph operator of Heart's Content, 1871 (Lovell).

Modern status: At Harbour Grace, Burin, Stephenville and St. John's.

Place names: Ross Bay (Labrador) 52-55 66-12, 53-00 66-14; —— —— Junction (Labrador) 53-03 66-12; —— Lake (Labrador) 54-58 63-16; —— Rock 49-55 55-32.

ROSSITER, a surname of England and Ireland from the English place names Rochester (Kent) – the town at the bridges, or ? Wroxeter (Shropshire), *Rochecestre* in *Domesday Book*. (Cottle, Ekwall, Spiegelhalter).

Traced by Guppy in Dorset, by Spiegelhalter in Devon, and by MacLysaght especially in Co. Wexford.

In Newfoundland:

Family tradition: Tom, from Ireland, settled at St. John's in the late 1800s (MUN Folklore).

Early instances: Phillip, soldier of St. John's, 1766 (DPHW 26C); Catherine Rositer, from Co. Wexford, married at St. John's, 1817 (Nfld. Archives BRC); Joseph Rossiter, fisherman of Carbonear, 1837 (DPHW 48); Richard Rositer, of Ferryland, 1841 (*Newfoundlander* 25 Feb 1841); Anne Roseter, of Caplin Bay (now Calvert), 1849 (DPHW 31); George Rossiter, fisherman of Ramea, 1858 (DPHW 101); Benjamin, planter of Twillingate, 1871 (Lovell).

Modern status: Scattered, especially at Ramea and St. John's.

Place name: Rossiters Pond 47-44 5314.

ROTCHFORD, a surname of England and Ireland from the English place name Rochford (Essex, Worcestershire), or ? the French surname and place name Rochefort (in several localities); in Ireland, Co. Cork, for de Ridlesford. (Reaney, Cottle, MacLysaght).

Traced by Spiegelhalter in Devon and MacLysaght especially in Cos. Meath and Kilkenny.

In Newfoundland:

Early instances: —— Rochford, French planter of Placentia, 1714 (CO 194.6); William, of St. John's, 1777 (DPHW 26C); Bridget, from Laughman (unidentified) (Co. Wexford), married at St. John's, 1815 (Nfld. Archives BRC); John, of Harbour Grace, 1823, 1828 (Nfld. Archives HGRC, *Newfoundlander* 31 Jul 1828); John, farmer of Cat's Cove (now Conception Harbour), 1871 (Lovell).

Modern status: In the Harbour Main district.

ROTHMAN, a surname of England from Old English *roth* – (dweller in the) clearing. (Reaney).

In Newfoundland:

Modern status: At Bell Island (*Electors* 1955) and Portugal Cove.

ROUD, ? a Newfoundland variant of the surname of France Roudet – wheelwright, or a nickname for one who groans like a wheel. (Dauzat).

In Newfoundland:

Early instances: John Roudy, planter of St. John's, 1706 (CO 194.4); ? William Rude, fisherman of Bay of Islands, 1871 (Lovell).

Modern status: Unique, at St. John's.

ROUL, a surname of France from an Old German personal name *Hrogwulf* containing the elements *rest* and *wolf* or *Hrodwulf* containing the elements *glory* and *wolf*. (Dauzat).

In Newfoundland:

Modern status: At Webbers (*Electors* 1955), St. Lawrence and Lawn.

ROUSSEAU, a surname of France and the Channel Islands – red-haired. (Dauzat).

In Newfoundland:

Modern status: Rare, at Corner Brook.

ROUZES, a Newfoundland variant of the surname of France Rouzé – rosy-cheeked, or (dweller near or worker in the) rose-garden. (Dauzat). *See also* ROSE with which confusion may have occurred.

In Newfoundland:

Family tradition; Manuel Rouzes, a Breton speaker, from La Roche, Brittany, or La Rochelle (Thomas, "French Fam. Names").

Modern status: At Cape St. George (*Electors* 1955).

ROWBOTTOM. *See* ROEBOTHAM

ROWE, a surname of England, Ireland and Guernsey (Channel Islands) from Old English *rūh* – rough, or Old English *rāw* – (dweller in the) row (of houses) or (by the) hedgerow, or a variant of ROE, ROLF (*see* ROFF), or RALPH. (Reaney, Cottle, MacLysaght, Turk).

Traced by Guppy especially in Cornwall and also in Devon, Lincolnshire, Somerset and Suffolk, with Row a rare form in Cornwall and Suffolk.

In Newfoundland:

Family traditions: George, from Devon, settled at Fogo (MUN Folklore). James, born at Yeovil (Somerset) about 1740–50, settled first at Trinity (? Trinity B.) and moved to Heart's Content in 1784 (MUN Geog.).

Early instances: D. Row, of St. John's, 1705 (CO 194.22); George Rowe, of Newfoundland ? 1706 (CO 194.22); Thomas, fisherman of Trinity (Trinity B.), 1757 (DPHW 64); Edward Row, of Trinity Bay, 1778 (DPHW 64); Anne Rowe, of Carbonear, 1783 (CO 199.18); James, of Heart's Content, 1786 (DPHW 64);

John Row, ? of Port de Grave, 1800 (Nfld. Archives T22); John, from Torquay (Devon), merchant of St. John's, deceased 1811 (*Royal Gazette* 11 Oct 1811); ——, of Ferryland, 1818 (D'Alberti 28); Richard, of Harbour Grace Parish, 1823 (Nfld. Archives HGRC); John Rowe, from Ballyhone (? for Ballynahone) (Co. Westmeath), married at St. John's, 1824 (Nfld. Archives BRC); Henry and James, of Bird Island Cove (now Elliston), 1825 (MUN Hist.); William, planter of Old Perlican, 1826 (DPHW 58); D'Ewes Coke Pattington, of Harbour Grace, died 1830, aged 34 (*Newfoundlander* 3 Jun 1830); Dr., of Burin, 1832 (*Newfoundlander* 26 Jan 1832); John Row, granted part of Vice Admirals Room (Renews), 1833 (Nfld. Archives, Registry Crown Lands); John Rowe, from Torbryan (Devon), married at St. John's, 1835 (DPHW 26D); James, planter of Salmon Cove (Carbonear), 1839 (DPHW 48); Edward, of Deer Island (Trinity B.), 1844 (DPHW 59A); Alford (? for Alfred), planter of Cupids, 1848 (DPHW 34); Mary Ann Row, of Seldom-Come-By, 1855 (DPHW 26D); Thomas Rowe, of Catalina, 1857 (DPHW 67); Susanna, of Lower Island Cove, 1860 (DPHW 58); Catherine, of Indian Arm (Bonavista B.), 1868 (Nfld. Archives KCRC); scattered in Lovell 1871.

Modern status: Widespread, especially at Carbonear, Heart's Content, Chance Cove, Corner Brook and St. John's.

Place name: Jimmy Rowes Pond 47-41 53-29.

ROWLANDS. *See* ROLANDS

ROWLEY, a surname of England and Ireland, in England from the English place name Rowley (Devon, Durham, Somerset, Yorkshire ER, WR); in Ireland, with ROWLAND (*see* ROLANDS), for (O)Rolan, Ó *Rothláin*. (Cottle, MacLysaght).

Traced by Guppy in Hertfordshire and Staffordshire, and by Spiegelhalter in Devon.

In Newfoundland:

Early instances: Anthony Rowly, of Petty Harbour, 1681 (CO 1); John Rowley, of St. John's, 1708 (CO 194.4); Richard Rowly, of Harbour Grace Parish, 1823 (Nfld. Archives HGRC).

Modern status: Unique, at Lewisporte (*Electors* 1955).

ROWSELL, a surname of England, a variant of RUSSELL, or ? an anglicization of the surname of France and Guernsey (Channel Islands) Roussel (*see* ROUSSEAU). (Bardsley, Turk).

Traced in Dorset, and by Bardsley in Somerset.

In Newfoundland:

Family tradition: Three Rowsell brothers of Huguenot ancestry (the surname was originally Rouselle), came to Newfoundland from Poole or Bristol in the early 1700s; they settled in Bonavista Bay, Notre Dame Bay and Pushthrough (Fortune Bay and Hermitage district) (MUN Folklore).

Early instances: George Sr. and Jr., planters of Fogo, 1792, 1808, George Sr., operated salmon fishery at Halls Bay and New Bay, 1804 (CO 194.45, MUN Hist.); Thomas, fisherman of Bay of Exploits, ? 1797 (CO 194.39); Henry Rosewell (? for Rowsell), of Bay Roberts, 1805 (CO 199. 18); Thomas Rowsall, fisherman of Change Islands, 1821 (USPG); Elizabeth, of Twillingate, 1822 (USPG); Henry Rousel, of Leading Tickles, 1843 (DPHW 86); John Rowsaill, of Exploits Burnt Island, 1846 (*Newfoundlander* 4 Jun 1846); Edward Rousal, fisherman of Pushthrough, 1844 (DPHW 102); Joseph Rousell, of Ward's Harbour (now Beaumont North), 1844 (DPHW 86); John, of Exploits, 1846 (DPHW 86); John Rowsell, of Round Harbour (Twillingate district), 1847 (DPHW 86); Samuel Rowsal, granted land at Bonavista, 1855 (Nfld. Archives, Registry Crown Lands); William Rowsell, of Little Bay Islands (Notre Dame B.), 1867 (DPHW 91); Henry Rousel, of Bareneed, 1871 (Lovell); Henry Rousell, of Coley's Point, 1871 (Lovell); Abram (and others) Rowsell, of Sunday Cove Island, 1871 (Lovell).

Modern status: Widespread, especially at Corner Brook, Leading Tickles (Green B.) and Grand Falls.

Place names: Rowsell Cove 49-30 55-19, 49-35 55-48; —— Harbour (Labrador) 58-58 63-14; —— Head (Labrador) 58-59 63-10; —— Hill 49-25 56-05; Rowsells Brook 49-18 56-18; —— River (or South Brook) 49-26 56-06; Jim Rowsell Ground 49-38 55-39; Thomas Rowsell Island 49-30 55-29.

ROYAL, ROYLE. *See* ROIL

RUBIA, ROBIA ? a Newfoundland variant of the surname of France Roubieu, or ? from the French place name Roubia (Aude). (Dauzat).

In Newfoundland: An anglicization of Robin in western Newfoundland (Thomas, "French Fam. Names").

Modern status: At Loretto (Port-au-Port district), Waterchute (Humber East district) (*Electors* 1955) and St. John's.

RUBY, a surname of England and Ireland, according to Spiegelhalter from an Old French personal name, but according to Weekley and MacLysaght from the French place name Roubaix (Nord). (Spiegelhalter, Weekley *Surnames*, MacLysaght).

Traced by Spiegelhalter in Devon and by MacLysaght in Co. Cork since the seventeenth century.

In Newfoundland:

Early instances: William, ? of Northern Bay, 1841 (DPHW 54); William, granted land at Bay Bulls Road, 1849 (Nfld. Archives, Registry Crown Lands); William, worked a 10 acre farm near St. John's in 1862 (Mannion); George and Samuel Rhuby, farmers of St. John's, 1871 (Lovell).

Modern status: In the St. John's district especially at Heavy Tree Road (St. John's South district).

Place names (not necessarily from the surname): Ruby Rock 47-34 52-41; Ruby Line (St. John's).

RUDDERHAM, a surname of England a variant of Rotherham from the English place name Rotherham (Yorkshire WR). (Reaney).

In Newfoundland:

Modern status: Rare, at St. George's (*Electors* 1955).

RUELOKKE. *See* R(H)UELOKKE

RUMBOL(D)T, surnames of England from the Old German personal name *Rumbald* containing the elements *glory* and *bold*, "popular through the precocious Saint Rumbald, or Rumwald [? 7th century], who at birth confessed himself a Christian, demanded baptism, preached a sermon, and died aged three days," or from the English place names Rumbold Farm or Rumbolds-Wyke (Sussex). (Reaney, Cottle, Guppy).

Traced by Guppy in Hampshire.

In Newfoundland:

Early instances: John Rumbolt, of Hawkes Bay (Labrador), 1787, of Hawkes Post (Labrador), 1789–1795, had planter account with Slades' firm at Fogo, 1808 (MUN Hist.); Alfred Rinnbolt, of Port au Choix, 1871 (Lovell); John Rimbald, of Flowers Cove, 1871 (Lovell); Patrick and John Rumbolt, of New Ferolle Cove (St. Barbe district), 1873 (MUN Hist.).

Modern status: Rumboldt, at St. John's, Coley's Point and Corner Brook; Rumbolt, scattered in the St. Barbe, Humber East and West districts.

Place name: Rumbolts Cove (Labrador) 52-18 55-49.

RUMSEY, a surname of England from the English place name Romsey (pronounced Rumsey) (Hampshire). (Spiegelhalter, Ekwall).

Traced by Spiegelhalter in Devon.

In Newfoundland:

Early instance: Frances, of Broad Cove (Bay de Verde district), 1752 (CO 199.18).

Modern status: At St. John's.

RUMSON, ? a variant of the surname of England Rumsam, from the English place name Rumsam (Devon). (Spiegelhalter).

Spiegelhalter traced Rumsam in Devon.

In Newfoundland:

Early instance: Samuel Rumson, schoolmaster of Carbonear, 1820 (DPHW 48).

Modern status: Rare, at Carbonear and St. John's (*Electors* 1955).

RUSSELL, a surname of England, Scotland and Ireland, from Old French *rousel*, a diminutive of *rous* – red, used also as a personal name. *See also* ROWSELL. (Reaney, Cottle, Black, MacLysaght).

Traced by Guppy in twelve counties, by Spiegelhalter in Devon, by Guppy also over a large part of Scotland but rare in the north, and by MacLysaght in Ulster and Leinster.

In Newfoundland:

Family traditions: ——, from Devon, settled in Bonavista Bay in the late 1700s (MUN Folklore). Three brothers, Edward, Stephen and William, from Bristol, England, settled at Bay Roberts about 1800 (MUN Geog.). Jane (1796–1858), born at Mercer's Cove, Bay Roberts (MUN Geog.). George (1830–), from Liverpool, England, came to Bonavista in 1846; he later settled at Catalina (MUN Folklore).

Early instances: Matthew Russle or Russell, of Toads (now Tors) Cove, 1681, of Witless Bay, 1682 (CO 1); Samuel Russell, of Old Perlican, 1681 (CO 1); Griffen, of St. John's, 1704 (CO 194.3); Denis, of Placentia ? district, 1744 (CO 194.24); John, from Sherborne (Dorset), apprenticed to Captain Nathaniel Brooks, of St. John's, 1755 (Dorset County Record Office per Kirwin); Henry Russet, of Bay Roberts, 1797 (DPHW 48); Thomas Russell, of Bonavista, 1799 (DPHW 70); Anastasia Russel, from Carrick (unspecified), Ireland, married at St. John's, 1802 (Nfld. Archives BRC); Matthew Russell, of Burin, 1814 (D'Alberti 21); Joseph, of Quidi Vidi, 1819 (DPHW 26B); Patrick Rus(s)ell, of Harbour Grace Parish, 1821 (Nfld. Archives HGRC); Thomas Russell, of Moreton's Harbour, 1822 (Nfld. Archives KCRC); Thomas, of Tickle Cove (Bonavista B.), 1831, of King's Cove, 1834 (DPHW 70, 73C); James, of Catalina, 1835 (DPHW 67); Johns ? of Harbour Grace, 1845 (*Newfoundlander* 16 Jan 1845); ——, captain of the *Hebe* in the seal fishery out of Brigus, 1857 (*Newfoundlander* 16 Mar 1857); John, of

Muddy Hole (now Maberly), 1862 (DPHW 77); Joana, of Carbonear, 1868 (Nfld. Archives HGRC); Jane, of Hopeville (Bonavista South district), 1870 (DPHW 80); scattered in Lovell 1871.

Modern status: Widespread, especially at St. John's, Coley's Point, Bay Roberts, Port Union, Bonavista and Winter Brook (Bonavista B.).

Place names: Russel Rock 47-01 55-08, 49-41 54-45; Russell (Station) 48-58 57-48; —— Cove (Labrador) 52-38 55-47; —— Head 47-41 55-40; —— Pond 48-56 54-09; Russells Cove 48-08 53-57; Russels Cove 48-04 53-06.

RUSTED, a surname of England ? from Old English *rust* – red and *hēafod* – head. Reaney has Greated as a variant of Greathead.

Traced at Royston (Hertfordshire).

In Newfoundland:

Family tradition: Ernest (1879–) born at Royston, England, settled at Salvage in 1903 (MUN Folklore).

Modern status: At St. John's.

RUTH, a surname of England, Ireland and France, in England from Middle English *reuthe* – pity; in Ireland a variant of an older name Rothe, *Rút*, "from a Norse word meaning red"; in France from a surname of Alsace-Lorraine, a pet-form of the Old German personal name *Hrodo* containing the element *glory*. (Reaney, MacLysaght, Dauzat).

Traced by MacLysaght in Co. Kilkenny.

In Newfoundland:

Early instances: William, soldier of St. John's, 1774 (DPHW 26C); Patrick, from Inistioge (Co. Kilkenny), married at St. John's, 1820 (Nfld. Archives BRC).

Modern status: Scattered, especially at Summerside (Humber West district).

Place names (not necessarily from the surname): Ruth Island 49-41 54-23; —— Lake (Labrador) 54-46 66-52.

RUTHERFORD, a surname of England, Scotland and Ireland, from the English and Scots place name Rutherford (Yorkshire NR, Roxburghshire). (Reaney, Black, MacLysaght).

Traced by Guppy in Northumberland and Warwickshire and the Scots Border counties, and by MacLysaght in Ulster.

In Newfoundland:

Early instances: Thomas, passenger on the *Atlantic* wrecked at Pouch Cove, 1840 (*Newfoundlander* 14 May 1840); R. and J. S., of St. John's,

1841 (*Newfoundlander* 17 Jun 1841); Robert, ? of Portugal Cove, 1846 (*Newfoundlander* 19 Feb 1846); George C., of Harbour Grace, 1857 (*Newfoundlander* 2 Jul 1857); ? James Rutford, of Fogo, 1871 (Lovell).

Modern status: Rare, at St. John's and Brookfield (Bonavista North district) (*Electors* 1955).

RYALL. *See* ROIL

In Newfoundland:

Early instances: Thomas, of Placentia ? district, 1744 (CO 194.24); John Ryal(e), of Trinity (Trinity B.), 1787 (DPHW 64); William Ryal, proprietor of fishing room, Salmon Cove (now Champneys), Winter 1800–01 (Census Trinity B.); Thomas Ryall, wheelwright of St. John's, 1806 (CO 194.45); Richard Ryal(e), of Cuckold's Cove (now Dunfield), 1812 (DPHW 64); John, from ? Harrington (Northamptonshire), fisherman of St. John's, deceased 1814 (*Royal Gazette* 12 May 1814); John Ryal, carpenter of Brigus, 1833 (DPHW 34); Henry Ryal, Royal, Ryles or Roil, gardener of Carbonear, 1835 (DPHW 48); Thomas Ryal, of King's Cove Parish, 1838 (Nfld. Archives KCRC); Thomas Ryall, from Somerset, ? of St. John's, in Newfoundland 36 years, that is, since 1803, died 1839, aged 68 (*Times* 20 Mar 1839); John Ryal, planter of Spaniards Bay, 1841 (DPHW 64); John Ryall, granted land at Salmon Cove (Port de Grave), 1850 (Nfld. Archives, Registry Crown Lands).

Modern status: At Botwood, Job's Cove and St. John's.

Place name: Ryalls Pond 47-33 52-52.

RYAN, a surname of Ireland (O)Ryan, *Ó Maoilriain* now abbreviated to *Ó Riain*, "from an old personal name of obscure meaning." (MacLysaght).

Traced by MacLysaght especially in Co. Tipperary.

In Newfoundland:

Early instances: George, surgeon of Fermeuse, 1752 (CO 194.13); James, of Bay Bulls, ? 1753 (CO 194.13); Edmund, of St. John's, 1755 (DPHW 26C); Thomas, of Harbour Main, 1755 (MUN Hist.); James, of Harbour Grace, 1763 (CO 199.18); Thomas Rhine, of Trinity (Trinity B.), 1764 (DPHW 64); Jeremiah, of Trinity Bay, 1767 (DPHW 64); Margaret Ryan, of Bonavista, 1774 (CO 194.32); John, of Torbay, 1777 (DPHW 26C); John, farmer of Quidi Vidi, 1794–5, "8 years in Newfoundland," that is, 1786–7 (Census 1794–5); Martin, from Humewood (Co. Wicklow), Irish convict landed at Petty Harbour or Bay Bulls, 1789 (CO 194.38); James, of Carbonear, 1790 (CO

199.18); Edmond, of St. Mary's, 1792 (D'Alberti 6); Joseph, from Kill (unidentified) (Co. Waterford), married at St. John's, 1793 (Nfld. Archives BRC); Roger, of Bay de Verde, 1794 (CO 199.18); Darby, of Brigus, in possession of property at Holyrood, 1802 (CO 199.18); James, of King's Cove, 1803 (Nfld. Archives BRC); Michael, from Carrick (unspecified) (Co. Tipperary), married at Bay Bulls, 1804 (Nfld. Archives BRC); John, from Newport (Rhode Island), editor of *Royal Gazette*, St. John's, 1806 (D'Alberti 23); John, schoolmaster of Grand Bank, 1810 (CO 194.49); Richard, of Ship Cove (now part of Port Rexton), 1810 (DPHW 64); William, from Cashel (Co. Tipperary), dealer of St. John's, deceased 1810 (*Royal Gazette* 11 Oct 1810); Dennis, one of 72 impressed men who sailed from Ireland to Newfoundland ? 1811 (CO 194.51); Mary, of Trepassey, 1812 (Nfld. Archives BRC); ——, ? merchant of Burin, 1816 (CO 194.57); Michael, from Co. Tipperary, of St. John's, died 1817, aged 47 (*Nfld. Mercantile Journal* 14 Feb 1817); Honora, of Ragged Harbour (now Melrose), 1817 (Nfld. Archives KCRC); Patrick, of New Harbour (Trinity B.), 1817 (Nfld. Archives KCRC); Luke, of Logy Bay, 1818 (Mannion); Thomas, of Heart's Content, 1819 (Nfld. Archives KCRC); Jeremiah, of Riders Harbour (Trinity B.), 1819 (Nfld. Archives KCRC); David, of Keels, 1820 (Nfld. Archives KCRC); Michael, of Tilting Harbour (now Tilting), 1821 (Nfld. Archives KCRC); John, of Broad Cove (now Duntara), 1822 (Nfld. Archives KCRC); John, of Gooseberry Island (Bonavista B.), 1825 (Nfld. Archives KCRC); Allice [sic], from Co. Kilkenny, married at Herring Neck, 1829 (Nfld. Archives KCRC); Thomas, of Turks Cove (Trinity B.), 1829 (Nfld. Archives KCRC); William, of Fortune Harbour, 1830 (Nfld. Archives KCRC); Edward Ryan or Rian, planter of Salmon Cove (now Champneys), 1830 (DPHW 64B); Phillip Ryan, of Pouch Cove, 1833 (DPHW 30); John, of Shoe Cove (South Shore, Conception B.), 1836 (DPHW 30); Matthew, of Ferryland, 1839 (Nfld. Archives BRC); William Rhine, of New Bay Head (Twillingate district), 1844 (DPHW 86); Elizabeth Ryan, of Bobby's Cove (Twillingate district), 1844 (DPHW 86); James, from Co. Tipperary, Lawrence from Waterford, Thomas from Co. Kilkenny, of Brigus, 1844 (*Indicator* 24 Aug 1844); William, from Co. Tipperary, Michael, from Co. Carlow, David, from Co. Waterford, of Harbour Grace, 1844 (*Indicator* 27 Jul 1844); John, of Plate Cove, 1845 (Nfld. Archives KCRC); Thomas Ryna [sic], of Harbour Green (Bonavista North district), 1847 (DPHW 76); —— Ryan, of Greenspond, 1849 (Nfld. Archives KCRC); John Ryan(s), planter of Adams Cove, 1850 (DPHW 52A); Patrick Ryan, of Red Cleft (? for Cliff) Island (Bonavista B.), 1850 (Nfld. Archives KCRC); Edward and John, granted land at Colliers, 1852 (Nfld. Archives, Registry Crown Lands); Catherine, of Knights Cove, 1853 (Nfld. Archives KCRC); John, ? of Northern Bay, 1853 (DPHW 54); William, of Ward's Harbour (now Beaumont North), 1854 (DPHW 86); Johanna, of Stock Cove (Bonavista B.), 1854 (Nfld. Archives KCRC); Augustine, of Scilly Cove (now Winterton), 1856 (Nfld. Archives KCRC); Rev. John, granted land at Salmonier Arm, 1856 (Nfld. Archives, Registry Crown Lands); Patrick, granted land at Great Placentia, 1857 (Nfld. Archives, Registry Crown Lands); Michael, granted land at North Harbour (St. Mary's B.), 1857 (Nfld. Archives, Registry Crown Lands); Matthew, granted land at Cats Cove (now Conception Harbour), 1857 (Nfld. Archives, Registry Crown Lands); John, of Tickle Cove (Bonavista B.), 1859 (Nfld. Archives KCRC); Bridget, of Pinchers (? for Pinchards) Island, 1861 (Nfld. Archives KCRC); John, of Open Hall, 1861 (Nfld. Archives KCRC); William, of Indian Arm (Bonavista B.), 1865 (Nfld. Archives KCRC); James D. (1844–), from Kedra Cahir (Co. Tipperary), settled at St. John's, 1866 (Mott); Patrick, from Thomastown (Co. Kilkenny), cooper of St. John's, deceased 1869 (*Morning Chronicle* 13 Jul 1869); widespread in Lovell 1871.

Modern status: Widespread, throughout all districts with large concentrations at Bell Island, St. John's, Corner Brook, Birchy Cove (Bonavista B.), Roberts Arm (Green B.), O'Regans (St. George's district), St. Joseph's (St. Mary's district) and Riverhead, Fermeuse.

Place names: Ryan Rock 49-39 55-38; Ryans Bay (Labrador) 59-35 64-03; —— Brook 47-36 53-18, 47-51 59-14; —— Head 47-28 53-13; —— Hill 46-57 55-25; —— Pond 57-22 53-21.

RYDER, a surname of England, Wales and Ireland, in England and Wales from Late Old English *rīdere* – rider, probably knight, mounted warrior, or from Old English *rīed*, *rӯd* – (dweller in the) clearing; in Ireland for (O)Markahan, *Ó Marcacháin* or (O)Markey, *Ó Marcaigh*, Ir. *marcach* – rider. (Reaney, MacLysaght, Cottle).

Traced by Spiegelhalter in Devon, by Guppy in North Wales and by MacLysaght in Cos. Louth, Monaghan and especially north Connacht.

In Newfoundland:

Early instances: Henry, of Bay Bulls, 1681, 1682 (CO 1); Martha Rider, of Scylly (? for Scilly) Cove (now Winterton), 1754 (DPHW 64); Richard Ryder, of Bonavista, 1787 (DPHW 70); ——, ? in possession of fishing room, Newman's Point, Bonavista, before 1805 (Bonavista Register 1806); Allen, of St. John's, 1848 (DPHW 26D); John Rider, of Knights Cove, 1851 (DPHW 73); John Weeks ? Rider, of King's Cove, 1855 (DPHW 73B).

Modern status: Scattered, especially at Bonavista.

Place names: Rider Harbour 48-11 53-32; —— Hill 48-22 53-22; Riders (or Ryders) Brook 48-14 53-56.

RYLAND, a surname of England and Ireland from the English place name Ryland (Cambridgeshire, Lincolnshire). Cottle interprets the name as "land where rye grows," but A. H. Smith sees the place in Cambridgeshire as "island." (Cottle, A.H. Smith).

Traced by MacLysaght in Co. Waterford.

In Newfoundland:

Early instance: John D., of St. John's, 1822 (D'Alberti 32, CO 194.65).

Modern status: Rare, at Shoal Cove West (St. Barbe district) (*Electors* 1955).

RYLES. *See* RILES

S

SABB, a surname of Syria-Lebanon, from the Arabic – hard, difficult. *See also* SAPP.

In Newfoundland:

Modern status: Rare, at St. John's.

SACREY, an anglicization of the surname of France and Jersey (Channel Islands) Sacré, that is *consacré* – consecrated, a nickname for a priest. (Dauzat).

In Newfoundland:

Family tradition: Two Sacré brothers from Jersey (Channel Islands) came to Harbour Grace; one brother settled there and the other moved to Twillingate. The surname was later spelt Sacrey (MUN Folklore).

Early instances: Thomas Sac(a)ry, of Leading Tickles, 1850, of Black Island (Twillingate district), 1851 (DPHW 86); John Sacry, of Harbour Grace, 1867 (Nfld. Archives HGRC); Thomas, miner of Tilt Cove, 1871 (Lovell).

Modern status: Scattered, especially at Pacquet (White B.).

SAGE, a surname of England, France and Ireland, in England and France from Old French *sage* – wise, in Ireland an occasional synonym of SAVAGE. (Reaney, Dauzat, MacLysaght).

Traced by Guppy in Devon and Somerset.

In Newfoundland:

Early instances: Charles, of St. John's, 1830 (DPHW 26D); James, telegraph employee of Head of Bay D'Espoir, 1871 (Lovell).

Modern status: Rare, at Doyles (*Electors* 1955) and St. John's.

SAINSBURY, a surname of England from the English place name Saintbury (Gloucestershire). (Reaney).

In Newfoundland:

Early instances: Thomas Saintsbury, of Trinity Bay, 1785 (DPHW 64); Phoebe Sansberry, of Cape Cove (Bonavista B.), 1827 (Nfld. Archives KCRC); Japheth Sainsbury, baptized at Pouch Island (Bonavista B.), 1830 (DPHW 76); John, of Keels, 1834 (DPHW 70); John, of Cold Harbour (Bonavista B.), 1850 (DPHN 76); John, granted land at Pinchers (for Pinchards) Island (Bonavista B.), 1852 (Nfld. Archives, Registry Crown Lands); John Sansbury, of Ragged Harbour (now Melrose), 1857 (Nfld. Archives KCRC); ——, captain of *New Packet* in the seal fishery out of Greenspond, 1858 (*Newfoundlander* 1 Apr 1858); Japhet Sansbury, granted land at Sleepy Cove (Swains Island) (Bonavista B.), 1863 (Nfld. Archives, Registry Crown Lands); Francis (and others) Samsbury, of Inner Islands (now Newtown) (Bonavista B.), 1871 (Lovell).

Modern status: Scattered, especially at Newtown.

SAINT, a surname of England and France, in England from Middle English *saint, seint*, Old French *sant*, Anglo-French *seint* – saint, a nickname, as Cottle has it, "for excessive or exiguous piety"; in France from an old baptismal name or the numerous place name Sains. (Reaney, Cottle, Dauzat).

Traced by Guppy in Derbyshire.

In Newfoundland:

Early instances: Charles, of St. John's, 1804 (DPHW 23); Charles, of Bonavista, 1805 (Bonavista Register 1806); George, fisherman of Langue de Cerf (Fortune B.), 1871 (Lovell); Thomas and John, of Musgravetown, 1871 (Lovell).

Modern status: Scattered, especially in Musgravetown.

Place names (not necessarily from the surname): Saint Island 48-58 53-45; —— Rock 46-50 55-45.

ST. CLAIR, SINCLAIR, surnames of England, St. Clair of France, usually Sinclair of Scotland and Ireland, from the French place name St. Clair (Calvados, La Manche) after a seventh century Norman saint and a third century bishop of Nantes, from Latin *clarus* – bright, shining. (Reaney, Cottle, Dauzat, Black, MacLysaght).

Sinclair traced by Guppy in Hertfordshire and Surrey, and found scattered in Scotland especially in Caithness and the Orkneys, and by MacLysaght in Ulster.

In Newfoundland:

Early instances: Charles Sinclair, of St. John's, 1812 (DPHW 26B); Duncan, from Isle of Scotland, married at St. John's, 1828 (Nfld. Archives BRC); Daniel Pilkington S., from Newcastle-on-Tyne, England, married at King's Cove, 1843 (DPHW 73A); Charles, planter of Little Catalina, 1846 (DPHW 72); Edward, planter of Western Bay, 1850 (DPHW 52A);

Joseph Sanclair or Sinclair, servant of Trinity (Trinity B.), 1858 (DPHW 64B); Charles Sinclair, of White Rock (Trinity B.), 1871 (Lovell); George L., of Bay of Islands area, 1878 (DPHW 96); Mary St. Clair, of King's Cove, 1893 (Nfld. Archives KCRC).

Modern status: St. Clair, Sinclair, scattered.

ST. CROIX, a surname of France and the Channel Islands after a saint. (Dauzat, Turk).

In Newfoundland:

Early instances: Richard and John, of Placentia, 1794 (D'Alberti 5); Christopher, of Bay Bulls, 1802 (USPG); William, planter of Cape Race, 1871 (Lovell); Benjamin and John, of Gaskin (Point La Hays), 1871 (Lovell); William, of Peter's River and Holyrood, 1871 (Lovell); Thomas St. Croix and Christopher Ste. Croix, of Port au Bras (Placentia B.), 1871 (Lovell); Philip de St. Croix, fisherman of Flowers Cove, 1874 (DPHW 95).

Modern status: Scattered, especially in the St. Mary's district at St. Vincent's and Gulch.

Place names: St. Croix Bay 47-26 53-51; —— —— Point 47-26 53-55.

ST. GEORGE, a surname of England and Guernsey (Channel Islands), for one who played the saint's part in a pageant or drama or from a common inn-sign (especially with the Dragon). (Weekley *Surnames*, Turk). *See* GEORGE.

In Newfoundland:

Early instance: Edward, schoolteacher of St. John's, 1871 (Lovell).

Modern status: Scattered, especially at Heart's Desire.

Place names (not necessarily from the surname): Cape St. George 48-28 59-16; Lake —— —— (or George's Lake) 48-45 58-10; —— —— Peninsula (or Port-au-Port Peninsula) 48-35 59-03; St. George's 48-26 58-29; —— —— Bay 48-24 58-53; —— —— Harbour 48-26 53-29; —— —— Leads 47-34 52-39; —— —— River 48-29 58-26.

ST. JOHN, a surname of England and Ireland from the common French place name S. Jean, or from the English place name St. John's Chapel (Devon), once the site of "an ancient chapelry ... of the Knights Templars, later of St. John of Jerusalem." (Spiegelhalter, MacLysaght, Gover). *See also* JOHN.

Traced by Spiegelhalter in Devon and by MacLysaght in Co. Tipperary since the thirteenth century.

In Newfoundland:

Early instances: Jane St. John or Singeon, of Harbour Grace, 1783 (CO 199.18); Andrew St.

Johns, carpenter of Quidi Vidi, 1794–5, "9 years in Newfoundland," that is, 1785–6 (Census 1794–5); Oliver St. John, of Bay Bulls, 1793 (USPG); Charlotte Garland, inherited property at Carbonear Island, Salmon Cove (Carbonear) and Perry's Cove, 1810 (Nfld. Archives T3); Alice, of St. John's, 1811 (Nfld. Archives BRC); Oliver, magistrate of Conception Bay, 1813 (D'Alberti 26); John, from Fethard (Co. Tipperary), married at St. John's, 1819 (Nfld. Archives BRC); John, of Greenspond, 1829 (Nfld. Archives KCRC); John, of Trinity (unspecified), 1830 (Nfld. Archives KCRC); Edward, from Fethard (Co. Tipperary), of Harbour Grace, 1844 (*Indicator* 27 Jul 1844); Edward, granted land at Riverhead, Cats Cove (now Conception Harbour), 1853 (Nfld. Archives, Registry Crown Lands).

Modern status: Scattered.

Place names: Many surnames contain the specific St. John, but rarely from the surname.

SALT, a surname of England from Old English **selte* – (worker at the) salt (-pit), or from the English place name Salt (Staffordshire). (Cottle, Ekwall).

Traced by Guppy in Derbyshire and Staffordshire, and by Cottle also in Yorkshire WR.

In Newfoundland:

Modern status: Rare, at St. John's (*Electors* 1955).

Place names: Many place names contain the specific Salt, but rarely from the surname.

SALTER, a surname of England, Scotland and the Channel Islands from Old English *sealtere* – maker or seller of salt, or from Old French *sautere, saltere* – (player on the) psaltery, a stringed instrument like a harp. (Reaney, Cottle, Black, Turk).

Traced by Guppy in Devon and Suffolk and by Black in Stirlingshire.

In Newfoundland:

Early instances: William ? Saltor, of St. John's Harbour, 1703 (CO 194.3); James Salter, from Dartmouth (Devon), of St. John's, 1821 (DPHW 26D).

Modern status: At St. John's.

Place names: Salter Island (Labrador) 53-19 55-47; Salters Rock 47-07 55-03.

SALTMAN, a surname of England – dealer in salt. (Reaney *Origin*).

In Newfoundland:

Modern status: Rare, at Harbour Grace.

SAMMS, a surname of England, a pet-form of Samson. *See* SAM(P)SON. (Reaney).

In Newfoundland:

Early instances: Thomas Sams, of Fortune, 1826 (DPHW 109); Catherine Samms, baptized at Eastern Cul de Sac (Burgeo-La Poile district), 1835, aged 32 (DPHW 30); Reuben Sam(m)s, of Bay Chaleur (Burgeo-La Poile district), 1835, of Rose Blanche, 1844 (DPHW 30, 101); Benjamin Samms, baptized at Rencontre (Burgeo-La Poile district), 1835, aged 21 (DPHW 30); Reuben Sams, of Bonne Bay, 1867 (DPHW 93); Benjamin (and others), of Cod Roy and Rivers, 1871 (Lovell).

Modern status: Scattered, on the southwest and northwest coasts, especially at Cape Anguille.

SAM(P)SON, SANSOM(E), SANSON, surnames of England, Sam(p)son of Guernsey (Channel Islands), Sampson of Ireland, and Samson, Sanson of France, from the Hebrew "child of Shamash (the sun-god)," the name of the champion of the Israelites against the Philistines. "*Samson* was the name of a Welsh bishop (fl. 550) who crossed over to Brittany and founded the abbey of Dôl, where he was buried and later venerated as a saint. It is impossible to say whether he was named after the Biblical *Samson*, or whether his name was of Celtic origin, but there is no doubt that the prevalence of the name in Brittany and Normandy, whence it was carried to England, was due to his fame." Occasionally the name may be of local origin from the French place names Saint-Samson (Seine-Inférieure, Calvados), Saint-Samson-de-Bonfosse (La Manche) or Saint-Samson-de-la-Roque (Eure). (Withycombe, Reaney, Dauzat, Turk).

Guppy traced Sampson in Cornwall, Derbyshire, Devon and Kent and found Sansome rare in Nottinghamshire. MacLysaght found Sampson scattered. Spiegelhalter traced Sam(p)son, Sansom and Sanson in Devon.

In Newfoundland: *See also* SAMSON, SANSOM(E), SANSON.

Family traditions: William Sampson (–1858), from southwest England, settled at Fox Harbour (Placentia B.) about 1830 (MUN Geog.). John, from Little Placentia (now Argentia), settled at Fox Harbour (Placentia B.) between 1836–57 (MUN Hist.).

Early instances: William Sampson, of St. John's, ? 1706, 1708 (CO 194.4), Thomas, fishing admiral of Twillingate, 1768 (MUN Hist.); John, fisherman of Brigus, 1833 (DPHW 34); Margaret Sampsan, of Harbour Grace Parish, 1843 (Nfld. Archives HGRC); Elizabeth Sampson, of Plate Cove (Bonavista B.), 1858 (Nfld. Archives KCRC); Joseph, of Bull's Cove (Burin district), 1861 (DPHW 100); William, of

Bonne Bay, 1871 (Lovell); Mary Jane, of Tickle Cove (Bonavista B.), 1872 (Nfld. Archives KCRC).

Modern status: Scattered.

SAMSON. *See* SAM(P)SON

In Newfoundland:

Family traditions: ——, from Devon, settled at Flat Island (Bonavista B.) (MUN Folklore). Francis Peter (1863–), born at Dinan (Côtes du Nord), settled at Daniel's Harbour (St. Barbe district) (MUN Folklore). George (1814–), from Dorchester (Dorset), settled at Twillingate in 1826; he later moved to Black Island (Notre Dame B.) in 1830 (MUN Folklore).

Early instances: Elizabeth, of King's Cove, 1827 (Nfld. Archives KCRC); Mary, of Turks Cove, 1830 (Nfld. Archives KCRC); Thomas, of Flat Island (Bonavista B.), 1838 (DPHW 73); George, of Exploits Burnt Island, 1848 (DPHW 86); Jane, of Knights Cove, 1864 (Nfld. Archives KCRC); Andrew, of Salvage, 1865 (DPHW 81); Joseph, of Burin, 1871 (Lovell); James, of English Harbour (Greenspond Island, Bonavista B.), 1871 (Lovell); Nicholas, of Little Placentia (now Argentia), 1871 (Lovell); James, of Sandy Cove (Placentia B.), 1871 (Lovell); Thomas and Andrew, of St. John's, 1871 (Lovell).

Modern status: Scattered, especially at Flat Island (Bonavista B.).

Place names: Samson (or Samson Island or Flat Island) 48-48 53-38; —— Point 47-19 53-56; —— Tickle, Samsons Island 49-30 54-57; Samson Point Shoal 47-23 54-00.

SAMUELSON, a surname of England – son of Samuel, from the Hebrew meaning "'name of God' or 'Shum (is) God,' for there is much evidence for a god called *Shum* or *Shem*." Samuel, one of the greatest Hebrew prophets, anointed Saul as first king of Israel. The surnames Samuel(s), Samwell are not necessarily of Jewish origin. (Withycombe, Reaney).

In Newfoundland:

Modern status: At St. John's.

SAMWAYS, a surname of England from Old English *sāmwās* – dull, foolish. (Reaney, Cottle).

Traced by Guppy in Dorset.

In Newfoundland:

Family tradition: Peter, from Poole (Dorset), settled in Newfoundland in the 19th century (MUN Folklore).

Early instances: James Samway, planter of Carbonear, 1829 (DPHW 43); Charles Samsways, of Lower Burgeo, 1871 (Lovell).

Modern status: Scattered.

SANDEMAN, a surname of Scotland – servant of Sa(u)nder, a pet-form of Alexander (*see* ALEXANDER), or according to Black, "The first of the name may have been an incomer from Denmark. In Jutland the *sandemaend* (*sandemand* sing.) 'men of truths,' were a constant institution, and had in the local parliament to swear about murders, assaults, rapes, and the like (Prof. Alexander Bugge)." (Reaney, Black).

In Newfoundland:

Modern status: Rare, at Torbay.

SANDERS, SAUNDERS, surnames of England, Scotland and Ireland, Saunders of Guernsey (Channel Islands) – son of Sa(u)nder, a pet-form of Alexander (*see* ALEXANDER). (Turk).

Found widespread by Guppy in the Midlands and south, especially in Devon, with both forms often associated, Sanders being most frequent in Devon and Worcestershire, Saunders in Dorset, Cambridgeshire and Oxfordshire. Traced by MacLysaght in Ulster.

In Newfoundland:

Family traditions: Philip Sanders (1828–1905), born at Totnes (Devon) settled at Carbonear before 1855; the name later became Saunders when a blacksmith making an iron cooper stamp inserted a "u" in the surname in error (MUN Folklore, Family). —— Saunders, a ship-builder from Blackpool (Lancashire), settled at Change Islands in the 1890s; he later moved to Clarke's Head (Gander B.) (MUN Hist.).

Early instances: William Saunders or Landers, of Green Island (Bonavista area), 1708–9 (CO 194.4); Henry Saunders, soldier of St. John's, 1766 (DPHW 26C); Adam Sanders, merchant from Plymouth (Devon), of St. John's, 1780 (Exeter Public Library Archives per Kirwin); William Saunders, of Placentia, 1780 (D'Alberti 1); Robert, in possession of fishing room, Pond Island, Greenspond Harbour, 1788 (Bonavista Register 1806); Joshua, of Bonavista, 1800 (DPHW 70); Charles Sanders or Senders, of Brigus, 1812 (DPHW 34); Joseph Sauders (? for Saunders), of King's Cove, 1816 (D'Alberti 26); Robert, of Greenspond, 1818 (DPHW 76); John William, of Ferryland, 1822 (CO 194.65); Nathaniel Sanders, of Harbour Grace, baptized 1825 (DPHW 58); William Saunders, of Renews, 1829 (DPHW 31); Daniel Sanders, of Aquaforte, 1835 (Nfld. Archives BRC); —— Saunders, on the *Tyro* in the seal fishery out of Colliers, 1838 (*Newfoundlander* 29 Mar 1838); Edward, of Change Islands, 1841 (DPHW 83); Edward, of Aquaforte, 1841 (*Newfoundlander* 4 Feb 1841); John, of Beaver Cove (Twillingate district),

1844 (DPHW 86); William, granted land at Carbonear, 1850 (Nfld. Archives, Registry Crown Lands); Edward, of Cupids, 1851 (DPHW 34); Joseph, planter of Head of Fortune Bay, 1858 (DPHW 104); George, planter of Harbour Mille (Fortune B.), 1858 (DPHW 104); Henry, of Herring Neck, 1858 (DPHW 85); Anthony Sanders, fisherman of Burin, 1860 (DPHW 100); Henry Saunders, fisherman of Clarke's Cove (Twillingate district), 1860 (DPHW 85); Joseph, of Caplin Cove (Exploits district), 1860 (DPHW 92); scattered in Lovell 1871.

Modern status: Sanders, rare, at Grand Falls and St. John's; Saunders, widespread, especially at Carbonear, Shearstown, Glovertown, Dark Cove, Hare Bay, Springdale and St. John's.

Place names: Sanders Brook 48-35 58-22; Saunders Brook 49-40 56-00; —— Cove 48-42 54-01, 49-21 55-18; —— Knob (Labrador) 52-12 55-36; —— Point 50-38 57-18; —— Ponds 47-07 53-09; Port —— 50-39 57-16.

SANGER, a surname of England from Old English *sangere*, *songere* – (church) singer, chorister. (Reaney, Cottle).

In Newfoundland:

Early instances: Joel, of Greenspond, 1804 (D'Alberti 14); Charles, planter of Bird Island Cove (now Elliston), 1820 (DPHW 72).

Modern status: At Elliston, Grand Falls and St. John's.

SANN, a surname of Germany of uncertain origin. (Gottschald).

In Newfoundland: From Germany to St. John's in 1953 (Family).

Modern status: Rare, at St. John's.

SANSFORD, ? a variant of the surnames of England San(d)ford – (dweller by the) sandy ford, or from the English place names Sandford (in eleven counties) or Sampford (Devon), or ? an anglicization of the surname of France Sansfaute – without fault (a nickname). (Cottle, Spiegelhalter, Dauzat).

Dauzat traced Sansfaute in Isle-Adam (Seine-et-Oise) as the name of an immigrant.

In Newfoundland:

Early instances: William, planter of Old Perlican, 1828 (DPHW 58); Mary Sandford, baptized at Pinchard's Island (Bonavista B.), 1830, aged 14 (DPHW 76); Joseph Saneford, of Grate's Cove, 1831 (DPHW 64B); James Sand(s)ford, of Harbour Grace Parish, 1831, ? of Northern Bay, 1840 (Nfld. Archives HGRC, DPHW 54); Mary Sandford, of St. John's,

1854 (DPHW 26D); Joseph Sansford, of Turks Cove, 1871 (Lovell); Henry and John Santsford, of Silly Cove (now Winterton), 1871 (Lovell); John Sandford, of Charles Brook (White B.), 1871 (Lovell); Stephen, of Wiseman's Cove (White B.), 1871 (Lovell).

Modern status: Rare, at St. Anthony.

Place name: Sanfords Pool 48-36 58-19.

SANSOM. *See* SAM(P)SON

In Newfoundland:

Early instances: Isaac, of Turks Cove, 1797 (DPHW 64); James (and others), of Flat Island (Bonavista B.), 1871 (Lovell).

Modern status: Rare, at Winterton and George's Brook (Trinity B.) (*Electors* 1955) and St. John's.

Place name: Sansom Islands (or North Samson Island) 49-30 54-57.

SANSOME. *See* SAM(P)SON

In Newfoundland:

Family tradition: —— Samson, from Dorchester (Dorset), settled at Twillingate in 1826; he moved to Black Island (Notre Dame B.) in 1830, then to Seal Cove (now Hillgrade) in 1844. The spelling of the surname over the years changed to Sansome (MUN Folklore).

Modern status: Scattered, especially at Hillgrade and Black Island (Twillingate district).

SANSON. *See* SAM(P)SON

In Newfoundland:

Early instances: Thomas, of Flat Island (Bonavista B.), 1835 (DPHW 76); John Sapson or Sanson, of Salvage, 1871 (Lovell).

Modern status: Rare, at Monroe (Trinity B.).

SAPP, a surname of Syria-Lebanon, a variant of SABB.

In Newfoundland:

Modern status: Rare, at Bell Island (*Electors* 1955).

SARGENT, SERJEANT, two of seventeen variants recorded by Reaney of the surname of England and Ireland from Old French *sergent, serjant* – servant, officer of the courts, tenant by military service below the rank of knight. (Reaney, Cottle).

Guppy traced Sarg(e)ant in Cornwall, Northamptonshire, Staffordshire, Suffolk and Wiltshire, noting that Sargent is most frequent and that both forms are usually associated, except in Cornwall and Wiltshire, where Sargent alone occurs, and Sergeant in Lincolnshire. Spiegelhalter traced Sargent, Sergeant and Serjeant in Devon. MacLysaght traced Sergeant in Co. Armagh and adjacent areas.

In Newfoundland:

Early instances: William Sergeant (Sarpeant in 1682), of St. John's, 1677, "10 years an inhabitant in 1680," that is, since 1670 (CO 1); John Sergeant, of Twillingate, 1768 (MUN Hist.); John Sergeant or Sargent, of Fogo, 1815 (Nfld. Archives KCRC); Abigail Sarge(a)nt or Serjent, of Fortune Harbour, 1831 (Nfld. Archives KCRC); Francis Sargent, of Back Cove (Twillingate district), 1871 (Lovell); Dennis Sargeant, of Greenspond, 1871 (Lovell).

Modern status: Sargent, at Fogo, Lewisporte and St. John's; Serjeant, rare, at St. John's (*Electors* 1955).

SATURLEY, a surname of England, otherwise Satterlee or Satterl(e)y, from the English place name Satterleigh (Devon), or from Old English *sǣtere* and *lēah* – robber's wood or clearing, with the spelling ? influenced by Saturday. (Cottle, Ekwall).

Spiegelhalter traced Satterl(e)y in Devon.

In Newfoundland:

Early instances: Thomas Satterly, fisherman of St. John's, 1846 (DPHW 26B); John Satorly, of Petty Harbour, 1871 (Lovell).

Modern status: At St. John's.

Place name: Saturday Ledge 47-06 52-55, (Saturdays Ledge in Lane's *Chart of Part of the Coast of Newfoundland, from Point Lance to Cape Spear,* 1773) is probably for Satterl(e)y.

SAUNDERS. *See* SANDERS

SAVAGE, a surname of England, Ireland and Guernsey (Channel Islands) from Old French *salvage, sauvage,* Latin *silvāticus,* popular Latin *salvāticus* – savage, wild, (originally) of the woods; in Ireland *Mac an t-Sábhaisigh,* or for (O)Savin, *O Sabháin* in south Munster. (Reaney, Cottle, MacLysaght, Turk). *See also* SAGE.

Traced by Guppy in Cambridgeshire, Gloucestershire, Norfolk, Northamptonshire, Shropshire, Warwickshire and Worcestershire, by Spiegelhalter in Devon, and by MacLysaght in Cos. Kilkenny and Down.

In Newfoundland:

Early instances: Michael, of Harbour Grace Parish, 1830 (Nfld. Archives HGRC); John, granted land near Outer Cove (St. John's), 1842 (Nfld. Archives, Registry Crown Lands); John, ? of Harbour Grace, 1845 (*Newfoundlander* 9 Jan 1845); John (and others), of Logy Bay, 1871 (Lovell).

Modern status: At St. John's.

Place names: Many place names contain the specific Savage but rarely from the surname.

SAVERY, SAVO(U)RY, surnames of England, ? Sauvary of Guernsey (Channel Islands) from the Old German personal names *Sabarieus, Savarieus,* Old French *Saveri.* (Reaney, Turk).

Guppy traced Savory in Norfolk, Spiegelhalter Savary, Savery and Savory in Devon.

In Newfoundland:

Early instances: Joseph ? Savory, of St. John's, 1752 (CO 194.13); John Savery, of St. John's, 1760 (DPHW 26C); Samuel Savory, proprietor and occupier of fishing room, Old Perlican, Winter 1800–01 (Census Trinity B.); Charity, of Harbour Grace Parish, 1807 (Nfld. Archives HGRC); Robert Savary, fisherman of Channel, 1871 (Lovell); John and Abram Savery, fishermen of Corban (Fortune B.), 1879 (DPHW 103).

Modern status: Savery, rare, at Channel; Savory, at Grand Bank, Fortune and Port aux Basques; Savoury, scattered, especially at Belleoram.

SAVIDON, ? an anglicization of the surnames of France Savordin or Savournin, from an old baptismal name *Saturnin,* derived from Latin *Saturnus,* a mythological god, after the third century bishop and martyr of Toulouse, or from the French place name St. Savournin (Bas du Rhin). The form Savordin is recorded by Chapuy. (Chapuy, Dauzat *Noms de lieux*).

In Newfoundland:

Family tradition: first settler of this name from Saint-Pierre, where the name is currently attested (Thomas, "French Fam. Names").

Modern status: Rare, at West Bay (Port-au-Port district).

SAVO(U)RY. *See* SAVERY

SAWYER, a surname of England from Middle English *saghe, sawe* – to saw, hence a sawer of timber, especially in a saw-pit. (Reaney). *See also* SAYERS.

Sawyer traced by Guppy in Suffolk and by Spiegelhalter in Devon.

In Newfoundland:

Early instances: John Sawer, king's carpenter of St. John's, 1794–5, "24 years in Newfoundland," that is, 1770–1 (Census 1794–5); Samuel Sawyer, of St. George's Harbour (St. George's B.), 1830 (DPHW 30).

Modern status: Rare, at St. John's and Musgravetown.

Place names: Sawyer Lake (Labrador) 54-26 65-58; Mount —— (Labrador) 53-56 61-07; Sawyers Hill 47-11 53-52.

SAYERS, a surname of England and Ireland, from a Norman personal name of Old German origin ? *Sigiheri* containing the elements *victory* and *army*, or a variant of SAWYER, or from Old English *secgan* – to say, hence a reciter, professional story-teller, or ? from Anglo-French *assaio(u)r,* Middle English *assayer* – assayer (of metals), food-taster, or from Old French *saier* – (maker or seller of) say (silk), or from Cornish *saer* – carpenter; in Ireland also for SEARS. (Reaney, Cottle, Spiegelhalter, MacLysaght).

Guppy traced Sayer in Norfolk and Yorkshire NR, ER, Sayers in Sussex. Spiegelhalter traced Sayers in Devon, MacLysaght traced Sayers in Co. Kerry and northeast Ulster.

In Newfoundland:

Early instance: Robert, soldier of St. John's, 1839 (DPHW 26B).

Modern status: Unique, at St. John's.

Place name: Sayers Gut 47-38 54-11.

SCAMMELL, a surname of England, from Old English *scamol* – bench (on which meat was exposed for sale), hence a worker in a shambles or slaughterhouse or a fish or meat market; or related to *scramble* – to struggle in an indecorous and rapacious manner to obtain something, hence one notorious for unseemly behaviour; or lean, scraggy. (Weekley *Romance*, Spiegelhalter, Cottle). *See also* SHAMBLER.

Traced by Spiegelhalter in Devon.

In Newfoundland:

Early instances: F. Scammel, of Fogo, 1803 (D'Alberti 13); Susannah Samnell, of Change Islands, 1821 (USPG).

Modern status: At Change Islands and St. John's.

SCANLON, a variant of the surnames of Ireland (Mac) and (O)Scanlan, *Mac Scannláin, Ó Scannláin,* or a variant in Co. Sligo of (O)Scannell, *Ó Scannail,* all from Ir. *scannal* – contention. (MacLysaght).

Traced by MacLysaght in Cos. Clare, Sligo, Cork, Fermanagh and Galway.

In Newfoundland: ——, from Ireland, settled at Bartletts Harbour (St. Barbe district) in 1820 (MUN Folklore).

Early instances: Daniel, shoreman of St. John's, 1794–5, "20 years in Newfoundland," that is, 1774–5 (Census 1794–5); Darby Scanlan, of Carbonear, 1797 (CO 199.18); B. Scan(d)lon, of Harbour

Grace Parish, 1807 (Nfld. Archives HGRC); Daniel Scanlan, from Castletown Reach (Co. Cork), planter of St. John's, died between 1807–10 (D'Alberti 34); Alice Scanlon, from Mellow (Co. Cork), of St. John's, deceased 1811 (*Royal Gazette* 17 Oct 1811); Michael Scanlan, from New Ross (Co. Wexford), married at St. John's, 1820 (Nfld. Archives BRC); James, of Harbour Grace, 1832 (Nfld. Archives HGRC); John, of Ragged Harbour (now Melrose), 1834 (Nfld. Archives KCRC); Patrick, from Dingle (Co. Kerry), of Harbour Grace, 1844 (*Indicator* 27 Jul 1844); Jeremiah, of Trinity (unspecified), 1856 (Nfld. Archives KCRC); George Scanlon, of Lower Island Cove, 1857 (*Newfoundlander* 21 May 1857); Rev. Matthew Scanlan, of Bonavista, 1871 (Lovell); John, planter of Colliers, 1871 (Lovell).

Modern status: Scattered, especially in the St. Barbe district.

SCAPLEN, a surname of unascertained origin.

Traced by Matthews in Poole (Dorset).

In Newfoundland:

Early instances: James, granted land at Bay Roberts, 1841 (Nfld. Archives, Registry Crown Lands); James Scaplin, granted land at Spaniards Bay, 1842 (Nfld. Archives, Registry Crown Lands); James L., granted land at Burnt Head (Port de Grave district), 1855 (Nfld. Archives, Registry Crown Lands); John and Mrs. Sarah, of Carbonear, 1871 (Lovell); Elizabeth C., of St. John's, 1871 (Lovell).

Modern status: At St. John's.

SCIEVO(U)R, SEVIOUR, variants of a surname of England derived from Old English *sife* – (maker or seller of) sieve(s). (Reaney, Cottle).

Matthews traced Scevior in Hampshire.

In Newfoundland:

Early instances: William Sievier or S(e)iv(i)er, of Trinity Bay, 1772, of Rider's Harbour, 1782 (DPHW 64); Ann Sevier, widow of St. John's, 1794–5 (Census 1794–5); William, proprietor and occupier of fishing room, Riders Harbour (Trinity B.), Winter 1800–01 (Census Trinity B.); John Scivior, of Gasters (Conception B.), 1802 (CO 199.18); John Sevier, of Harbour Grace Parish, 1809 (Nfld. Archives HGRC); Garland Seiver or Sivier, of St. John's, 1813, of White Hills (St. John's), 1821, of Quidi Vidi, 1823 (DPHW 26B); William Sevior, of Trinity (Trinity B.), 1816 (DPHW 64); Elinor Sciver, Scivier, Civier or Sevior, of King's Cove Parish, 1834 (Nfld. Archives KCRC); William Sivier, Sevier or Scevior, planter of British Harbour (Trinity B.), 1843 (DPHW 64B); John Sevier, planter of Bonavista, 1840 (DPHW

72); Joseph Sceviour, of Exploits Burnt Island, 1858 (DPHW 92); Alexander Sivier, fisherman of Bay of Islands, 1871 (Lovell).

Modern status: Scevior, rare, at Colliers; Sceviour, scattered; Seviour, rare, at St. John's.

SCHUMPH, a surname of ? German-French origin of unknown meaning. Jean Schumph, son of Christian and Monique of Quebec City, first of the name in Chéticamp, N.S., whence many Acadian settlers came to Stephenville. (G.R. Thomas).

In Newfoundland:

Modern status: At Stephenville and Kippens.

SCHWARTZ, SWARTZ, variants of a surname of Germany and France from German *schwarz* – black-haired or of dark complexion. (Dauzat).

Traced by Dauzat in Alsace-Lorraine.

In Newfoundland:

Modern status: Schwartz, at St. John's and Deer Lake; Swartz, at Stephenville.

SCOTT, a surname of England, Scotland and Ireland; in Scotland from Old English *Scott* – an Irishman, later a Gael from Scotland, a name of mysterious origin ? associated with Welsh *ysgwthr* – cutting, carving, hence the tattooed people; in England – a man from Scotland not necessarily a Gael, and also a personal name; also ? confused with Scutt, ? from Old French *escoute*, Middle English *scut* – scout, spy. (Reaney, Cottle, Black).

Traced by Guppy especially in the Border counties of England and Scotland, in eastern England, Devon, and (as Scutt) in Dorset, and by MacLysaght in Ulster and Dublin.

In Newfoundland:

Family traditions: Philip, from Co. Wexford, settled at ? Bay Bulls after 1798 (MUN Folklore). Arthur, from Aberdeen, Scotland, settled in Fortune Bay in the 1880s (MUN Folklore).

Early instances: Thomas, of St. John's, 1757 (DPHW 26C); Philip, from Tintern (Co. Wexford), married at St. John's, 1810 (Nfld. Archives BRC); Thomas, of Pouch Cove, 1817 (DPHW 26B); Daniel Scot(t), of Harbour Grace Parish, 1818 (Nfld. Archives HGRC); John Scott, of Heart's Content, 1826 (Nfld. Archives KCRC); Benjamin, of Harbour Grace, 1829 (DPHW 43); William, planter of South Shore (Conception B.), 1828 (DPHW 34); Ellen, of Turks Cove, 1829 (Nfld. Archives KCRC); John, of Fools (now Pools) Island, 1830 (DPHW 76); Sarah, of Brunette (Island), 1830 (DPHW 106); William, from Enniskillen (Co. Fermanagh), of St. John's, died 1832 (*Royal Gazette* 10 Jul 1832); Charles, planter of Upper Gullies, 1832 (DPHW 34); Nicholas, of Scilly Cove (now Winterton), 1832 (Nfld. Archives KCRC); Benjamin, of Trinity (Trinity B.), 1834 (DPHW 64B); Michael, of Bay Bulls, 1838 (Nfld. Archives BRC); Joseph, fisherman of Cape Ray, 1841 (DPHW 101); Daniel, from Castle Durrah, Ireland, of Harbour Grace, 1844 (*Indicator* 27 Jul 1844); Peter, of Ramea, 1851 (DPHW 101); James, of Belleoram, 1852 (DPHW 104); Ann, of Grand Bank, 1858 (DPHW 106); scattered in Lovell 1871.

Modern status: Widespread, especially at St. John's and Upper Gullies.

Place names: Scott Brook 47-29 55-05; —— Falls (Labrador) 53-31 64-32; —— Point 47-22 55-18, 50-52 56-08; —— Rock 47-09 55-23; Scotts Point 47-34 59-08; —— Tickle 48-39 53-40.

SCURR(E)Y, variants of the surnames of Ireland (O)Scarry, Scurry, *Ó Scurra* and *Ó Scoireadh*. (MacLysaght).

Traced by MacLysaght from *Ó Scurra* in Co. Galway and from *Ó Scoireadh* in Cos. Waterford and Kilkenny.

In Newfoundland:

Early instances: Michael Scurry, of King's Cove, 1831 (Nfld. Archives KCRC); Thomas, of Harbour Grace Parish, 1833 (Nfld. Archives HGRC).

Modern status: Scurr(e)y, Scurry at St. John's.

SEABRIGHT, a surname of England from the Old English personal names *Sǣbeorht* – sea-bright or *Sigebeorht* – victory-bright, both names of early kings of Essex. (Reaney).

In Newfoundland:

Early instance: James, fisherman of Waldron's Cove (Fogo district), 1871 (Lovell).

Modern status: At Corner Brook (*Electors* 1955), in the Gander district and at St. John's.

SEARLE, a surname of England from the Old German personal names *Sarilo*, *Serila*, in Norman-French *Serlo*, ? related to Old English *searu* – armour. "The name was frequent in Normandy and common in England after the Conquest." (Reaney). *See also* EARLE.

Guppy traced Searle in Cambridgeshire, Cornwall and Devon. Searles traced in Cornwall.

In Newfoundland:

Family tradition: ——, from Cornwall, settled at Bell Island in 1750 (MUN Folklore). John Searle, from the west country of England, of Little Bell Island 1696; one of his sons moved to Bell Island,

the other settled at Portugal Cove where the name was changed to Earle (MUN Hist.).

Early instances: James, of Petty Harbour, 1811 (DPHW 26B); Robert Searl, of St. John's, 1812 (DPHW 23); John ? Sarrell, missionary of Twillingate, 1816, of Moretons Harbour, 1819 (CO 194.57, D'Alberti 29); Richard Searle, joiner of Carbonear, 1823 (DPHW 48); John Sarell, of Port de Grave Parish, 1829 (*Newfoundlander* 5 Nov 1829); Charles Serle, planter of Middle Bight (now Codner), 1838 (DPHW 30); Thomas Sarell, teacher of Lance Cove (Bell Island), 1839 (*Newfoundlander* 1 Aug 1839); Samuel Serle, of Long Pond (Manuels), 1871 (Lovell).

Modern status: At Bell Island, St. John's, Jerseyside (Placentia), and in the Harbour Main district.

SEARS, a surname of England and Ireland, a variant of SAYERS, but also in Ireland (Co. Kerry) the anglicized form of *Mac Saoghair*. (Reaney, MacLysaght).

Traced by Guppy in Hertfordshire, and by MacLysaght in Co. Kerry and elsewhere.

In Newfoundland:

Family tradition: ——, of Scots, Irish and English ancestry, settled on the northeast coast of Newfoundland; some of the family moved to St. John's before 1890 (MUN Folklore).

Early instances: Edward Sears, ? merchant of Newfoundland, 1770 (CO 194.29); Robert Seares, gaoler of St. John's, 1815–1816 (D'Alberti 26); Robert, from ? Dorchester (Dorset), married at St. John's, 1822 (Nfld. Archives BRC); Rev. Sears, Roman Catholic priest of Bay of Islands, 1871 (Lovell), [same as] Rev. Thomas, Roman Catholic priest of Sandy Point (St. George's B.), 1871 (Lovell).

Modern status: At Paradise (Harbour Main district) and in the St. John's district.

Place names: Searston 47-50 59-19; —— Bay 47-49 59-21.

SEARY, a surname of Ireland and England, a variant of (O)Seery, *Ó Saoraidhe*. "A small sept of Westmeath also called Freeman and Earner. But according to Woulfe the derivation is from a Norse personal name not from Ir. *saor* – free." (MacLysaght).

Traced by MacLysaght in Co. Westmeath, by Woulfe in Cos. Donegal, Mayo and Galway; and in Oxfordshire, Berkshire and Yorkshire WR.

In Newfoundland:

Modern status: Rare, at St. John's since 1953.

Place name: Searys Park 47-57 53-49 (1984).

SE(A)WARD, surnames of England, Seward (former-ly Seaward) of Ireland, from the Old English personal names *Sǣweard* – sea-lord or *Sigeweard* – victory-lord, or from the Old English *sū-hierde* – sow-herd. (Reaney, MacLysaght).

Guppy traced Seaward in Hampshire and Seward in Devon; Spiegelhalter traced Se(a)ward in Devon, and MacLysaght traced Seward in Co. Cork since the mid-seventeenth century.

In Newfoundland:

Early instances: Thomas Seward, of St. John's, 1752 (CO 194.13); William Soward, of Trinity Bay, 1772 (DPHW 64); John Seaward, of Bonavista, 1792 (USPG); Edward Seward, of New Perlican, 1792 (DPHW 64); Robert, of Harbour Grace Parish, 1815 (Nfld. Archives HGRC); James, of Trinity (unspecified), 1818 (Nfld. Archives KCRC); Mary, of Heart's Content, 1819 (Nfld. Archives KCRC); Solomon Soward, of Fox Harbour (Trinity B.), 1854 (DPHW 59A); Robert, of Heart's Ease, 1855 (Nfld. Archives KCRC); Mary Ann, of Scilly Cove (now Winterton), 1858 (DPHW 59); Thomas Seaward, fisherman of Gooseberry Cove (Trinity B.), 1880 (DPHW 68).

Modern status: Seaward, scattered, especially at Clarenville; Seward, especially at New Perlican and Gooseberry Cove.

Place name: Seward Lake (Labrador) 54-27 65-52.

SEELEY, a surname of England with some seventeen variants, Sealy and Seely of Ireland, from Old English *sælig* – happy, blessed, later innocent, simple, later silly, used as a woman's name; in Ireland also for (O)Shally, *Ó Sealbhaigh*, Ir. *sealbach* – having possessions. (Reaney, Cottle, MacLysaght 73).

Guppy traced Seal(e)y in Somerset; Spiegelhalter traced Sealy and Seel(e)y in Devon; MacLysaght traced Sealy mainly in Cos. Kerry and Cork.

In Newfoundland:

Family tradition: Robert, from England, settled at Bareneed (Conception B.), about 1800 (MUN Geog.).

Early instances: John Selley, of Bonavista, 1792 (USPG); Thomas Silly, of Port de Grave in possession of property at Cupids, 1805 (CO 199.18); Robert Sealy, of St. John's, 1810 (CO 194.50); William Maddick Silly, merchant of Brigus, 1827, of Cupids, 1841 (DPHW 34); John, of Old Perlican or Hants Harbour, 1838 (*Newfoundlander* 20 Sep 1838); John Sealey, fisherman of Herring Neck, 1850, of Salt Harbour (Twillingate district), 1852 (DPHW 85); William, carpenter of Bareneed, 1850 (DPHW 39); Thomas, of Northern (now North) River (Conception B.), 1860 (DPHW 38).

Modern status: Rare, at Isle aux Morts and Gilesport (Twillingate district) (*Electors* 1955).

SELBY, a surname of England from the English place names Selby (Yorkshire WR), or ? Sileby (Leicestershire), or ? Selaby (Durham). (Cottle, Spiegelhalter, Ekwall).

Traced by Guppy in Nottinghamshire and by Spiegelhalter in Devon.

In Newfoundland:

Early instances: Samuel ? Selby, of Newfoundland, 1730 (CO 194.23); Thomas Scammel Selby, from Plymouth (Devon), of St. John's, 1834 (DPHW 26D); Joseph, fisherman of Grole (Fortune B.), 1850 (DPHW 102); John Sebley, of Cape La Hune (Burgeo-La Poile district), 1871 (Lovell); Frank Selby, miner of Tilt Cove, 1871 (Lovell).

Modern status: At Grole (*Electors* 1955) and St. John's.

SELLARS, SELLERS, surnames of England, from Old French *selier*, *seller* – sadler, of Middle English *seller* – seller, dealer, or Middle English, Anglo-French *celerer* – cellarer, storeman, purveyor. (Reaney, Cottle).

Traced by Guppy in Yorkshire NR and ER, and by Spiegelhalter in Devon.

In Newfoundland:

Family tradition: William Sellars, from England, settled at Harbour Grace in the early sixteenth century (MUN Folklore).

Early instances: William Sellor, of St. John's Harbour, 1703 (CO 194.3); William Sellars, of Bonavista, 1817 (DPHW 70); Bond Sellers, planter of Western Bay, 1826 (DPHW 52A); Elisa Scellar, of Harbour Grace Parish, 1833 (Nfld. Archives HGRC).

Modern status: Sellars, scattered, especially at St. John's and Western Bay; Sellers, rare, at St. John's and Western Bay.

Place name: Sellars Brook 49-26 57-54.

SENIOR, a surname of England from Old French *seignour* – lord (of the manor etc.) from Latin *senior* – older, or ? a nickname ? for a swaggerer. (Reaney, Cottle). *See also* SINYARD.

Traced by Guppy in Dorset and Yorkshire WR, and by Spiegelhalter in Devon.

In Newfoundland:

Early instances: Samuel, occupier of fishing room, Heart's Content, Winter 1800–01 (Census Trinity B.); Charles (and others), of Flat Islands (Placentia B.), 1871 (Lovell); Jacob, fisherman of Hope All (Trinity B.), 1871 (Lovell).

Modern status: Especially in the Placentia West district (*Electors* 1955).

SERJEANT. *See* SARGENT

SERRICK, a surname of England from the Old English personal names *Sǣrīc* – sea-ruler or *Sigerīc*, containing the elements *victory* and *powerful*, or Old Norse *Sigrikr* or Old Danish *Sigrik*. (Reaney).

Traced by Reaney in Sussex. Spiegelhalter traced the variants Serrage, Serridge and Surridge in Devon.

In Newfoundland:

Family tradition: ——, from England emigrated to the southern United States, then to Cupids (Newfoundland) about 1800 (MUN Folklore).

Early instances: Daniel Sirrick or Ser(r)ick, ship's carpenter of Cupids, 1835 (DPHW 34); Alexander Serrick, schoolmaster of Clarke's Beach, 1859 (DPHW 35).

Modern status: At Pynn's Brook (Humber East district), Corner Brook (*Electors* 1955), Carbonear and Deer Lake.

SESK, a variant of the surname of Ireland Sisk, of uncertain origin, but ? a modern variant of the mediaeval surname Seix, (*saghas*) of Cos. Kilkenny and Kildare, now almost extinct. (MacLysaght).

MacLysaght traced Sisk in east Cork.

In Newfoundland:

Early instance: William and James Sisk, of Ferryland, 1815 (D'Alberti 31).

Modern status: At Corner Brook (*Electors* 1955), Ferryland and St. John's.

SEVIOUR. *See* SCEVIO(U)R

SEVERN, a surname of England, ? (dweller by the river) Severn.

Traced by Guppy in Derbyshire and Nottinghamshire, and in Worcestershire.

In Newfoundland:

Family tradition: ——, from Worcestershire, settled at St. John's in the 19th century (MUN Folklore).

Modern status: Unique, at St. John's (*Electors* 1955).

SEWARD. *See* SE(A)WARD

SEXTON, a surname of England and Ireland from Mediaeval Latin *sacristanus* – "the officer in a church in charge of the sacred vessels and vest-

ments," not the modern grave-digger, or from the English place name Sexton (Devon); in Ireland for *Ó Seasnáin* and rarely of English origin. (Reaney, Spiegelhalter, MacLysaght).

Traced by Spiegelhalter in Devon and by MacLysaght in Co. Limerick.

In Newfoundland:

Early instances: Robert Sex(t)on, of Trinity Bay, 1779 (DPHW 64); Phillip Sexton, fisherman of St. John's, 1794–5, "born in Newfoundland" (Census 1794–5); Robert, occupier of fishing room, Trinity (Trinity B.), Winter 1800–01 (Census Trinity B.); Patrick, from Kilcash (Co. Tipperary), shoreman of St. John's, deceased 1810 (*Royal Gazette* 15 Nov 1810); Stephen, planter of Canale (Bonavista B.), 1815 (DPHW 72); James, of Harbour Grace Parish, 1816 (Nfld. Archives HGRC); Margaret, of Greenspond, 1817 (Nfld. Archives KCRC); Mary Sexten, from Carrick-on-Suir (Co. Tipperary), married at St. John's, 1818 (Nfld. Archives BRC); Stephen Sexton, planter of Bonavista, 1819 (DPHW 72); Thomas Sexton, cooper, son of William and Mary Ann of Dartmouth (Devon), married at Harbour Breton, 1858, aged 26 (DPHW 104; Harbour Breton Anglican Church Records per D.A. Macdonald); Timothy Sexton, fisherman of Goose Cove (White Bay North district), 1871 (Lovell); Patrick, fisherman of Tilton Harbour (now Tilting), 1871 (Lovell).

Modern status: Scattered, especially at Bonavista.

SEYMORE, SEYMOUR(E), surnames of England and Ireland from the French place name Saint-Maur-des-Fossés (Seine), or the English place name Seamer (Yorkshire NR), or ? from such Old English personal names as *Sǣmar*, *Sigemar*, *Sǣmær*. (Reaney, Cottle, Spiegelhalter, MacLysaght 73).

Seymour traced by Guppy in Berkshire and Buckinghamshire, by Spiegelhalter in Devon, and by MacLysaght in Cos. Cork and Tipperary, Dublin and Belfast.

In Newfoundland:

Early instances: John Seamour, of New Perlican, 1708 (CO 194.4); John Seymour, of Newfoundland, 1730 (CO 194.23); Richard, ? labourer of St. John's, 1779 (CO 194.34); Richard, shoreman of Torbay, 1794–5, "12 years in Newfoundland," that is, 1782–3 (Census 1794–5); Henry, of Northern Cove (Spaniard's B.), 1805 (CO 199.18); George, from Poole (Dorset), married at St. John's, 1834 (DPHW 26D); Henry W., from Exeter (Devon), married at St. John's, 1854 (*Newfoundlander* 11 Sep 1854); Isaac, of Exploits, 1859 (DPHW 92); Charles and John, of

Hiscock's Point (Burgeo-La Poile district), 1871
(Lovell); Thomas, of Shoal Bay (Fogo district), 1871
(Lovell); Henry and Nathaniel, of Spaniard's Bay,
1871 (Lovell).

Modern status: Seymore, rare, at Exploits
(*Electors* 1955) and Mouse Island (Burgeo-La Poile
district); Seymour, scattered, especially at Spaniard's
Bay and Isle aux Morts; Seymoure, unique, at Mouse
Island (Burgeo-La Poile district).

Place name: Seymours Gullies 47-33 53-28.

SHAGARHUE. *See* SHUGARUE

SHALLOW, a surname of Ireland, a variant of
(O)Shally etc., *Ó Sealbhaigh,* Ir. *sealbach* – having
possessions. (MacLysaght). *See also* SEELEY,
SHELLEY.

Traced by MacLysaght in Co. Cork.

In Newfoundland:

Early instances: Patrick, from Lismore (Co.
Waterford), married at St. John's, 1805 (Nfld. Ar-
chives BRC); Patrick, of Gooseberry Island (Bona-
vista B.), 1822 (Nfld. Archives KCRC); J., of St.
John's, 1826 (Dispatches 1825–6); John, of King's
Cove, 1826 (Nfld. Archives KCRC); Patrick, from
Co. Kilkenny, of Keels, 1829, of Broad Cove (now
Duntara), 1830 (Nfld. Archives KCRC); Michael,
from Co. Wexford, of Harbour Grace, 1844 (*Indi-
cator* 27 Jul 1844); Philip, of Tickle Cove (Bonavista
B.), 1855 (Nfld. Archives KCRC); Phillip, of Plate
Cove (Bonavista B.), 1860 (Nfld. Archives KCRC);
Andrew (and others), of Fermeuse, 1871 (Lovell);
Andrew and Richard, of Renews, 1871 (Lovell).

Modern status: At Grand Falls.

Place names; A few place names contain the
specific Shallow, but rarely from the surname.

SHAMBLER, a surname of England, ? worker in a
shambles or slaughterhouse. *See* SCAMMELL.

Traced by Matthews in Christchurch (Hampshire).

In Newfoundland:

Early instances: James, of Port Bonavist
(Bonavista), 1675, of Harbour Main, 1676 (CO 1);
Joseph, of Keels, 1681 (CO 1); Samuel, of Green
Island (Bonavista area), 1708–9 (CO 194.4); John,
proprietor of fishing room, Bonaventure (unspeci-
fied) (Trinity B.), Winter 1800–01 (Census Trinity
B.); George, of St. John's, 1816 (DPHW 26); Samuel,
from St. Mary Church (Devon), of St. John's, 1854
(*Newfoundlander* 30 Jan 1854).

Modern status: Unique, at St. John's (*Electors*
1955).

Place name: Shamblers Cove 49-04 53-36.

SHANNAHAN, a variant of the surname of Ireland
(O)Shanahan, *Ó Seanacháin,* Ir. *sean* – old. (Mac-
Lysaght).

Found widespread throughout Munster by Mac-
Lysaght.

In Newfoundland:

Early instances: James Shanahan, ? labourer of
St. John's, 1779 (CO 194.34); Mary, of St. John's,
1797 (Nfld. Archives BRC); John, from Thurles (Co.
Tipperary), married at St. John's, 1817 (Nfld. Ar-
chives BRC); James, of Harbour Grace Parish, 1817
(Nfld. Archives HGRC); Anastasia, from Kilmacow
(Co. Kilkenny), married at Harbour Grace, 1829
(Nfld. Archives BRC); John Shanahan or Shannon,
of Herring Neck, 1833 (Nfld. Archives KCRC); Jo-
hanna Shanrahan, granted land at Ferryland, 1838
(Nfld. Archives, Registry Crown Lands); Pierce
Shanahan, from Co. Waterford, of Brigus, 1844
(*Indicator* 24 Aug 1844); Nicholas, of Harbour
Grace, 1866 (Nfld. Archives HGRC); James (and
others), of Renews, 1871 (Lovell).

Modern status: Scattered, especially in the Ferryland district.

Place name: Shanahans Gully 47-38 53-21.

SHANO. *See* LESHANA

SHAPLEIGH, a surname of England from the English place name Shapley (Devon).

Spiegelhalter traced Shapley in Devon.

In Newfoundland:

Early instances: Mary Shapley, heir to Bennetts
Cove (St. John's) between 1717–1784 (D'Alberti 2);
Samuel, of Bay Bulls, 1793 (USPG).

Modern status: Rare, at Grand Falls.

SHAPTER, a surname of England from the English
place name Shapter (Devon). (Spiegelhalter). *See
also* CHAPTER.

Traced by Spiegelhalter in Devon.

In Newfoundland:

Modern status: At St. John's.

SHARP(E), surnames of England and Scotland,
Sharp of the Channel Islands,

Sharpe of Ireland, from Old English *scearp* –
sharp, quick, smart, in Ireland an anglicization of *Ó
Géaráin,* Ir. *géar* – sharp. (Reaney, Cottle, MacLysaght, Turk).

Found widespread but rare in southwest England
and in Perthshire by Guppy, in Devon by
Spiegelhalter, and in Co. Donegal by MacLysaght.

In Newfoundland:

Family tradition: Joseph Sharp (1830–1900), of English descent, was born at Bay Roberts (MUN Geog.).

Early instances: William Sharp, of St. John's Harbour, 1703 (CO 194.3); William, of Spoon Cove (Conception B.), 1790 (CO 199.18); James, of Bonavista, 1826 (DPHW 70); James, of Port de Grave Parish, 1829 (*Newfoundlander* 5 Nov 1829); Isaac Sharpe, baptized at Greenspond, 1830, aged 35 (DPHW 76); William Sharp, of Harbour Grace Parish, 1830 (Nfld. Archives HGRC); James Sharpe, granted land at Ship's Head Beach (Harbour Grace), 1839 (Nfld. Archives, Registry Crown Lands); William Sharp, of Western Bay, 1856 (DPHW 52B); Joshua, fisherman of Ward's Harbour (now Beaumont North), 1864 (DPHW 91); James (and others), of (Upper) Island Cove, 1871 (Lovell); James (and others) Sharpe, of Twillingate, 1871 (Lovell).

Modern status: Sharp, rare, at Stephenville and St. John's; Sharpe, scattered, especially at St. John's, Corner Brook, Twillingate and Upper Island Cove.

Place names (not necessarily from the surname): Sharp Hill 50-07 57-28; —— Peak 47-03 55-27, 47-23 53-52; —— Point 47-29 55-08, 47-35 54-51; Tommy Sharpe Rock 47-45 53-59.

SHARRON, SHERRAN, SHERREN, SHERRING, SHIRRAN, ? variants of the surname of England Sherwin – cut wind, from Old English *sceran* – to cut and *wind*, used of a swift runner, or of the surname of Ireland (O)Sheeran, Sheerin, *Ó Sirín*. (Reaney, MacLysaght).

Guppy traced Sherrin(s) in Dorset and Somerset; MacLysaght traced (O)Sheeran, Sheerin in Cos. Donegal, Fermanagh and Leix.

In Newfoundland:

Family tradition: —— Sharron, from England, settled at Wild Bight (Green B.); branches of the family later spelt the name Shirren and Sherran (MUN Folklore).

Early instances: Samuel, Richard and Stephen Shearing, of Bonavista, 1792 (USPG); Sara Shieran, of St. John's, 1803 (Nfld. Archives BRC); Richard Shearing, from Bonavista B., died at St. John's, 1820, aged 62 (*Nfld. Mercantile Journal* 30 Mar 1820); William Sharon, of Bonavista, 1825 (DPHW 70); Stephen Sharen or Shearing, of Fleury Bight (Twillingate district), 1842–1848 (DPHW 86); Stephen Sherron, of New Bay Head (Twillingate district), 1846 (DPHW 86); Samuel Sherren or Sharon, planter of Bonavista, 1848–1850 (DPHW 72); Stephen and William Sharon, of New Bay (Notre Dame B.), 1871 (Lovell); James Sharen, of Three

Arms (Twillingate district), 1871 (Lovell); Alexander Fraser Shirran, born at Macduff, Scotland, died at St. John's, 1911, aged 79 (General Protestant Cemetery, St. John's).

Modern status: Sharron, scattered, especially at Botwood; Sherran, rare, at Corner Brook; Sherren, rare, at St. John's; Sherring, rare, at Glenwood; Shirran, at Bonavista.

SHAVE, a surname of England from Old English *sceaga* – (dweller in or near the) shaw, wood. (Reaney). *See also* SHAW, SHEA and SHEAVES.

Traced by Guppy in Essex.

In Newfoundland:

Family tradition: ——, from England, settled at Baine Harbour (Placentia B.) in the late 18th century; some of the family later moved to Burin (MUN Folklore).

Early instances: John, of Oderin about 1730–5 (CO 194.9); William ? Shave, of St. John's, 1816 (CO 194.57); Thomas Shave, of Famish Gut (now Fairhaven) (Placentia B.), 1835 (DPHW 30); Charles, of Port aux Basques, 1835 (DPHW 30); George Shaves, planter of Catalina, 1839 (DPHW 72); Benjamin Shave, trader of Harbour Buffett, 1871 (Lovell).

Modern status: Scattered, especially in the Burin district.

Place name: Shave Island 49-41 54-23.

SHAW, a surname of England, Scotland and Ireland of the same derivation as SHAVE, or in northern Scotland from a Gaelic personal name. (Reaney, Cottle, Black, MacLysaght). *See also* SHEA, SHEAVES.

Found widespread by Guppy in England, by Black in Kirkcudbrightshire, Ayrshire, Stirlingshire, Aberdeenshire and Argyllshire, and by MacLysaght in all the provinces and especially in Ulster.

In Newfoundland:

Early instances: Charles, of St. John's, 1767 (DPHW 26D); William, of Harbour Grace Parish, 1827 (Nfld. Archives HGRC); James, planter of Grate's Cove, 1829 (DPHW 64B); Samuel, of St. George's Harbour (St. George's B.), 1830 (DPHW 30); Robert, granted land at Bay Bulls, 1859 (Nfld. Archives, Registry Crown Lands); John, of Heart's Ease, 1868 (Nfld. Archives KCRC); James, of Sandy Point (St. George's B.), 1871 (Lovell); George and John, planters of Random Sound (Trinity B.), 1871 (Lovell).

Modern status: Scattered, especially at Little Heart's Ease.

Place name: Shaw Lake (Labrador) 54-07 65-46.

SHEA, a surname of England, (O)SHEA of Ireland; in England a variant of SHAVE, SHAW; in Ireland (O)Shea, *Ó Séaghdha,* Ir. *séaghdha* – hawklike, stately. (MacLysaght).

Traced by MacLysaght primarily in Co. Kerry, later in Cos. Kilkenny and Tipperary.

In Newfoundland:

Family traditions: ——, from Ireland, settled at Pouch Cove in the early 1800s (MUN Hist.). Henry, from Ireland, settled at St. John's in the late 18th century (*Nfld. Quarterly* Dec 1902).

Early instances: Timothy, of Bay Bulls, 1731 (CO 194.9); Dennis, fisherman of St. John's, 1794–5, "40 years in Newfoundland," that is, 1754–5 (Census 1794–5); Richard, of Port de Grave, 1768 (CO 199.18); Richard Shai, of Petty Harbour, 1776 (DPHW 26D); John Shea, of Quidi Vidi, 1793 (Nfld. Archives BRC); Mary, from Grange Parish (unidentified) (Co. Tipperary), married at St. John's, 1804 (Nfld. Archives BRC); Mary, of Adams Cove, 1804 (Nfld. Archives BRC); Pat, of Harbour Grace Parish, 1806 (Nfld. Archives HGRC); C., one of 72 impressed men who sailed from Ireland to Newfoundland, ? 1811 (CO 194.51); John, from Waterford, soldier of St. John's, died 1814 (*Royal Gazette* 20 Oct 1814); Joseph, of Pouch Cove, 1817 (Nfld. Archives BRC); Nicholas, of Joe Batts Arm, 1821 (Nfld. Archives KCRC); Patrick, of Twillingate, 1822 (Nfld. Archives KCRC); Patrick, of Moreton's Harbour, 1822 (Nfld. Archives KCRC); William, of King's Cove, 1823 (Nfld. Archives KCRC); John, of Ragged Harbour (now Melrose), 1824 (Nfld. Archives KCRC); John, of Tilton Harbour (now Tilting), 1824 (Nfld. Archives KCRC); James, of Greenspond, 1826 (Nfld. Archives KCRC); Mary, from Co. Tipperary, of Catalina, 1829 (Nfld. Archives KCRC); Moses, of Fortune Harbour, 1830 (Nfld. Archives KCRC); Richard, of Harbour Grace, 1830 (Nfld. Archives HGRC); Joseph, from Carrick-on-Suir (Co. Tipperary), of Harbour Grace, 1833 (*Newfoundlander* 21 Mar 1833); David, of Bay of Islands, 1868 (Nfld. Archives HGRC); scattered in Lovell 1871.

Modern status: Shea, widespread, especially at St. John's; O'Shea, rare, at Freshwater (Placentia B.).

Place names: Shea Brook 48-52 54-55; Sheas Gully 47-44 53-24.

SHEARS, a surname of England, Sheares of Ireland, from Old English *scīr,* *scære – fair, bright, or ? from Old English *scēarra* – shear (-smith), a maker of shears or scissors, or from the English place name Shere (Surrey, ? Devon). (Reaney, Spiegelhalter, MacLysaght).

Guppy traced Shears in Devon and Surrey; MacLysaght traced Sheares in Co. Cork since the late seventeenth century.

In Newfoundland:

Family traditions: Jonas (1830–), born at Rose Blanche, moved to Woody Point (Bonne B.) and in 1878 settled at Rocky Harbour (St. Barbe district) (MUN Geog.). Henry, of King's Cove, 1824; the family later moved to Open Hall (Devine *Old King's Cove*).

Early instances: Walter Shares, of St. John's, 1783 (DPHW 26C); Mary Shears, of Harbour Grace Parish, 1811 (Nfld. Archives HGRC); Richard, from Broadhempston(Devon), storekeeper of St. John's, died 1822, aged 34 (*Nfld. Mercantile Journal* 25 Jul 1822); John, of Frenchman's Cove (Burin district), 1828 (DPHW 26B); Stephen, of Barrisways (St. George's B.), 1835 (DPHW 30); John, of Garnish, 1836 (DPHW 109); John, of Tickle Cove (Bonavista B.), 1848, of Open Hall, 1841 (DPHW 73); ——, old resident of Harbour Le Cou, 1849 (Feild); Rev. William, of Bay Roberts, 1871 (Lovell); Richard, of Crabb's Brook (now Crabbe's River), 1871 (Lovell); James (and others), of Robinson's Head, 1871 (Lovell); John, planter of Sandy Point (St. George's B.), 1871 (Lovell); John C., of Trinity (Trinity B.), 1871 (Lovell).

Modern status: Scattered in the west coast districts especially at Rocky Harbour (St. Barbe district).

Place names: Shearstown, —— Brook 47-36 53-18.

SHEAVES, a variant of SHAVE(S) or ? SHAW.

In Newfoundland:

Family tradition: Edward, settled at Sheaves Cove (Channel Harbour) in 1789 (MUN Geog.).

Early instances: George Sheave or Shaves, planter of Catalina, 1842 (DPHW 72); Samuel Sheave, of Beau (now Boat) Harbour (Placentia B.), 1871 (Lovell); Charles and John Sheaves, of Channel, 1871 (Lovell).

Modern status: At St. John's and in the Burgeo-La Poile district especially at Port aux Basques.

Place names: Sheaves Cove, —— Head 48-31 59-03; Tom Sheaves Rock 47-33 53-57.

SHEEHAN, a surname of Ireland, (O)Sheehan, Sheahan, *Ó Síodhacháin,* ? Ir. *síodhach* – peaceful and ? an anglicization of a surname of Lebanon. (MacLysaght).

Traced by MacLysaght especially in Cos. Cork, Kerry and Limerick.

In Newfoundland:

Family tradition: ——, from Co. Kilkenny, settled at Broad Cove (now Cappahayden) in the early 19th century (MUN Folklore).

Early instances: Thomas Shehan, ? labourer of St. John's, 1779 (CO 194.34); John Shean, from Droning Parish (unidentified), Ireland, married at St. John's, 1807 (Nfld. Archives BRC); John Sheen or Shean, of Harbour Grace Parish, 1812 (Nfld. Archives HGRC); John Shean, fisherman of Grand Bank, 1819 (DPHW 109); Doctor Sheehan, of Tilton Harbour (now Tilting), 1820 (Nfld. Archives KCRC); John, of Joe Batts Arm, 1824 (Nfld. Archives KCRC); George Sheen, planter of Brigus, 1827 (DPHW 34); Bridget Shehan, of King's Cove, 1833 (Nfld. Archives KCRC); Dr. Richard Sheehan, died at Harbour Breton, 1834 (*Newfoundlander* 13 Nov 1834); William Shean, granted land at Caplin Bay (unspecified), 1838 (Nfld. Archives, Registry Crown Lands); William Sheen, ? of Ferryland, 1838 (*Newfoundlander* 25 Oct 1838); —— Shehan, on the *Margaret* in the seal fishery out of Port de Grave, 1838 (*Newfoundlander* 29 Mar 1838); Stephen Sheehan, from Co. Wexford and ? Darby, from Co. Waterford, of Brigus, 1844 (*Indicator* 24 Aug 1844); Charles Sheane, granted land at Channel Harbour, 1847 (Nfld. Archives, Registry Crown Lands); John Sheehan, member of Board of Road Commissioners for the area of Grates Cove to Hants Harbour (Trinity B.), 1857 (*Nfld. Almanac*); John (about 1780–1861), from Thomastown (Co. Kilkenny), of Renews, died 1861, aged 81 (Dillon); John, of Greenspond, 1863 (Nfld. Archives KCRC); scattered in Lovell 1871; Suliman (1879–), from Beirut, Syria (now Lebanon), settled at Deer Lake about 1912 (*Nfld. Who's Who* 1930).

Modern status: Scattered, especially at St. John's.

SHEFFIELD, a surname of England from the English place name Sheffield (Sussex, Berkshire, Yorkshire WR).

Traced by Guppy in Leicestershire and Rutlandshire.

In Newfoundland:

Modern status: Unique, at Corner Brook,

Place names: Sheffield Hill 49-14 56-33; —— Lake 49-20 56-34.

SHELLEY, a surname of England and Ireland, in England from the English place name Shelley (Essex, Suffolk, Yorkshire WR, Northumberland); in Ireland a variant of SHALLOW. (Cottle, MacLysaght).

Traced by Guppy in Staffordshire and by Spiegelhalter in Devon.

In Newfoundland:

Family tradition: Robert Shelly, from Hampshire, England, settled first at Barr'd Islands then at Aspen Cove (Notre Dame B.), in the early 1800s; the spelling of the name changed to Shelley (MUN Hist.).

Early instances: Patrick Shilley, of Trinity Bay, 1778 (DPHW 64); John Shelly, of St. John's, 1796 (CO 194.39); Josiah Shilly, of Bonavista, 1801 (DPHW 70); Phillip Shelly, from Port Law (Co. Waterford), married at St. John's, 1811 (Nfld. Archives BRC); John, of Harbour Grace Parish, 1816 (Nfld. Archives HGRC); Patrick, of Catalina, 1826 (Nfld. Archives KCRC); Edward, of Harbour Grace, 1830 (Nfld. Archives HGRC); James, of Bareneed, 1834 (*Newfoundlander* 23 Jan 1834); Edward, from Co. Tipperary, of Harbour Grace, 1844 (*Indicator* 27 Jul 1844); George, of Stocking Harbour (Twillingate district), 1853 (DPHW 86); Mary, of Keels, 1855 (Nfld. Archives KCRC); Walter, of Halfway House, Salmonier (unspecified), 1856 (*Newfoundlander* 15 Sep 1856); Sarah, of Tickle Cove (Bonavista B.), 1868 (Nfld. Archives KCRC); Walter Shelley, of Burnt Island (Burgeo-La Poile district), 1871 (Lovell); George, of Jackson's Arm (Fogo district), 1871 (Lovell); Robert Shelly, of Apsey (now Aspen) Cove, 1871 (Lovell); Patrick, of Coachman's Cove, 1871 (Lovell); Charles, of Shoal Bay (Ferryland district), 1871 (Lovell).

Modern status: Scattered, in the North East coast districts.

SHEPHERD, SHEPPARD, surnames of England, Scotland, Ireland and the Channel Islands from Old English *scēaphyrde* – shepherd, or **scēap-weard* – sheepward, or *scipweard* – shipmaster. (Reaney, MacLysaght, Turk).

Found widespread by Guppy with Shepherd nearly three times as numerous as Sheppard, the latter being most numerous in Somerset and Gloucestershire, Shephard in Cornwall, Shepheard in Norfolk and Shropshire, Shepperd in Buckinghamshire, and Shepard in Gloucestershire. He found Shepherd scattered in Scotland. MacLysaght found Shepherd and Sheppard numerous in all provinces except Connacht.

In Newfoundland:

Family tradition: —— Sheppard, from Channel Islands, settled at Harbour Grace (MUN Folklore).

Early instances: Thomas Shepard and Richard Sheppard, of Salvage, 1681 (CO 1); Francis Sheppard, of Harbour Grace, 1775, property "in possession of the Family for upwards of 90 years," that is, before 1685 (CO 199.18); David Shepherd, of St.

John's Harbour, 1703 (CO 194.3); Stephen, of Bona-vista, 1708 (CO 194.4); William Sheppard, constable of Carbonear district, ? 1730–32 (CO 194.9); James, of Port de Grave, 1775 (CO 199.18); Jonathan of Mint Cove (Spaniards B.), 1783 (CO 199.18); William, of Bay de Verde, 1788 (CO 199.18); William Shepherd or Sheppard, of Cuckold's Cove (now Dunfield), 1796 (DPHW 64); James Sheppard, pro-prietor and occupier of fishing room, Trinity (Trinity B.), Winter 1800–01 (Census Trinity B.); John, of Cupids, 1802 (CO 199.18); William Shepherd, ope-rated salmon fishery at Shoe Cove, 1804 (CO 194.45); William Sheperd, from Widmerpool (Nottinghamshire), married at St. John's, 1817 (Nfld. Archives BRC); John Sheppard, baptized at Fool's (now Pool's) Island, 1830, aged 43 (DPHW 76); John, of Catalina, 1833 (DPHW 70); William Shepherd, of Rock Cove (Bay de l'Eau), 1835 (DPHW 30); Joseph, of Miller's Passage (Bay de l'Eau), 1835 (DPHW 30); John, of Bay de l'Eau Island, 1835 (DPHW 30); William Sheppard, from Nottinghamshire, of St. John's, died 1848 (Nfld. Patriot 12 Apr 1848); Jona-than Shepherd, granted land at Bryant's Cove, 1851 (Nfld. Archives, Registry Crown Lands); Ann, of Wreck Cove (Burin district), 1855 (DPHW 104); George Sheppard, of Leading Tickles (Twillingate district), 1856 (DPHW 86); Absalom, of Muddy Hole (Fogo district), 1858, of Indian Island, 1862 (DPHW 83, 84); John Shepherd, of Blanchet (Burin district), 1858 (DPHW 104); scattered in Lovell 1871.

Modern status: Shepherd, scattered; Sheppard, widespread, especially at St. John's, Harbour Grace, Spaniards Bay, Lark Harbour (Humber West dis-trict), Stag Harbour and Indian Islands (Fogo district), Botwood, Corner Brook and Catalina.

Place names: Shepherd Cove 47-29 55-40, 48-31 53-03; —— Point 48-31 53-03, 47-50 54-09; —— Island, —— —— Rock 50-44 55-40; —— Rock 47-24 55-37.

SHERRAN, SHERREN, SHERRING. *See* SHARRON

SHIELDS, a surname of England, Scotland and Ireland, in England from Old English *scild, sceld* – (maker of) shield(s), or (dweller by the) shelter, or from Old English **scieldu* – (dweller by the) shallow place; in Scotland from Middle English *schele* – a shepherd's summer hut, a small house; in Ireland for *Ó Siadhail*, of obscure origin. (Reaney, Black, Mac-Lysaght).

Guppy traced Shields in Gloucestershire, Shield in Northumberland; MacLysaght traced Shields in Donegal and Offaly.

In Newfoundland:
Early instances: Thomas Shiels, fisherman of St. John's, 1794–5, "20 years in Newfoundland," that is, 1774–5 (Census 1794–5); William Shields, from Edinburgh, keeper of Cape Spear lighthouse, died 1836 (*Star and Conception B.J.* 14 Sep 1836).
Modern status: At St. John's.

SHINAR, SHINER, ? variants of the surname of Eng-land Shinner from Middle English *scinnere* – magi-cian, or a variant of SKINNER, or of the surname of Ireland Shinnagh, *Sionnach, Ó Sionnaigh,* Ir. *sion-nach* – fox. (Spiegelhalter, MacLysaght).

Shiner traced in London (Tel. Dir. 1961). Spie-gelhalter traced Shinner in Devon; MacLysaght traced Shin(n)agh in Cos. Mayo and Galway.
In Newfoundland:
Early instances: Levi Shiner or Shinar, of Nip-per's Harbour, 1843, of Kiry's Island (Twillingate district), 1854 (DPHW 86); George Shinners, of Harbour Grace, 1866 (Nfld. Archives HGRC); Levi Shiner, of St. John's, 1871 (Lovell).
Modern status: Shinar, at South Brook (Green B.); Shiner, at Smith's Harbour (Green B.).
Place name: Shiner Point 49-44 55-57.

S(H)INNICKS, ? Newfoundland variants of the sur-names of England Senneck and Sinnocks which reflect the old pronunciation of the English place name Sevenoaks (Kent), or of the surname of Ire-land (O)Shinnick, *Ó Sionnaigh,* ? Ir. *sionnach* – fox. (Reaney, MacLysaght). *See* SNOOK.

Matthews traced Sinnox in Dorset and MacLy-saght (O)Shinnick almost exclusively in Co. Cork.
In Newfoundland:
Early instances: James Sinnex, of Trinity (Trinity B.), 1788 (DPHW 64); James, planter of Trouty, 1824 (DPHW 64B); John Chennix, of Spear Harbour (Lab-rador), 1850 (DPHW 113); James Senex, fisherman of St. John's, 1871 (Lovell); James Chennix, of Ponds River (Northwest coast), 1873 (MUN Hist.).
Modern status: Shinnicks, at River of Ponds (Sinnicks in *Electors* 1955); Sinnicks, at Anchor Point (Sinnix in *Electors* 1955).

SHIRLEY, a surname of England, Scotland and Ire-land, from the English place name Shirley (Derby-shire, Hampshire, Surrey, Warwickshire), or dweller in the clearing or wood belonging to the shire, or the clearing where the shire moot (assembly) was held, or the bright clearing. The common female, and rare male, baptismal name derives from the surname. (Withycombe, Cottle, Ekwall, Black, MacLysaght).

Traced by Guppy in Staffordshire and by Spiegelhalter in Devon.

In Newfoundland:

Family tradition: Clifford (–1860), of Welsh ancestry, was baptized at English Harbour West (Fortune B.) in 1820 (MUN Geog.).

Early instances: Benjamin, of Burin, 1805 (D'Alberti 15); John, fisherman of Coomb's Cove (Fortune B.), 1851 (DPHW 104).

Modern status: Rare, at English Harbour West.

Place name (not necessarily from the surname): Shirley Lake 49-02 55-02.

SHIRRAN. *See* SHARRON

SHORT, a surname of England, Ireland and the Channel Islands from Old English *sceort* – short. (Reaney, Turk).

Traced by Guppy in Devon, Northumberland, Surrey and Sussex, and by MacLysaght in Ulster and Dublin.

In Newfoundland:

Early instances: William, of St. John's Harbour, 1703 (CO 194.3); William Shortt, of Ferryland, 1708 (CO 194.4); Walter Short, of Island of Spear, 1708–9 (CO 194.4); Sarah, of Bay Bulls, 1708 (CO 194.4); John, of Conche, 1787, of Battle Harbour (Labrador), 1789–1795, of Fogo, 1808 (MUN Hist.); Isaac, of Bonavista, 1790 (DPHW 70); S., occupier of fishing room, Old Perlican, Winter 1800–01 (Census Trinity B.); Samuel, of Trinity (Trinity B.), 1800, of (Old) Bonaventure, 1805 (DPHW 64); Samuel, planter of Hants Harbour, 1821 (DPHW 58); Joseph, of Grand Bank, 1823 (DPHW 109); William, of Harbour Grace Parish, 1827 (Nfld. Archives HGRC); Ann, of Fortune, 1829 (DPHW 109); John, of Little Codroy River, 1835 (DPHW 30); John, of Triton Harbour, 1852 (DPHW 86); William, fisherman of Western Bay, 1853 (DPHW 52B); Rebecca, of Twillingate, 1860 (DPHW 87); George, servant, son of Charles and Elizabeth of ? Hinton le May (untraced) (Dorset), married at Harbour Breton, 1865, aged 22 (Harbour Breton Anglican Church Records per D.A. Macdonald); scattered in Lovell 1871.

Modern status: Widespread, especially at Kingston, Hants Harbour and St. John's

Place names (not necessarily from the surname): Short Ground 49-33 55-36; —— Point 47-37 56-13, 49-32 55-46; —— Reach 47-37 57-37; Shorts Brook 46-54 55-57; —— Harbour 50-50-51-14.

SHORTALL, a surname of England and Ireland, *Soirtéil* or *Seartal*, ? from Old English *sceort –*

short and *h(e)als* – neck. (MacLysaght). *See also* SHORTIS.

Traced by MacLysaght in Co. Kilkenny since the thirteenth century.

In Newfoundland:

Family tradition: Thomas, from Co. Wexford, settled in the St. John's or Bonavista area (MUN Folklore).

Early instances: Nicholas Shortill, from Ireland, soldier ? of St. John's, 1774 (CO 194.32); James Shortall, in possession of land on Scroggins Headland near Caplin Bay (now Calvert) and Ferryland, 1798 (*Nfld. Quarterly* Mar 1909); Mary Shortel, from Waterford, married at St. John's, 1805 (Nfld. Archives BRC); Margaret Shortill, of Harbour Grace Parish, 1819 (Nfld. Archives HGRC); John, of King's Cove Parish, 1839 (Nfld. Archives KCRC); Thomas Shortle, of Blackhead (St. John's), 1871 (Lovell).

Modern status: At St. John's.

SHORTIS, a surname of England and ? also of Ireland, a translation of *Curthose* – short boot, or from Old English *sceort* – short and *h(e)als* – neck. (Reaney). *See also* SHORTALL.

In Newfoundland:

Early instance: Michael, from Carrick-on-Suir (Co. Tipperary), of Harbour Grace, 1845 (*Newfoundlander* 9 Jan 1845, *Nfld. Who's Who* 1830).

Modern status: Unique, at St. John's (*Electors* 1955).

SHUGARUE, SHAGARHUE, Newfoundland variants of the surnames of Ireland (O)S(h)ugrue, *Ó Siochfhradha* from a Norse personal name. (MacLysaght).

Traced by MacLysaght in Co. Kerry.

In Newfoundland:

Early instances: Dennis Shoughro or Shoughrow, of Harbour Grace Parish, 1820 (Nfld. Archives HGRC); Barth Shugrue or Shagaraw, of Harbour Grace, 1867–8 (Nfld. Archives HGRC); Timothy Shoghrew, farmer of St. John's, 1871 (Lovell).

Modern status: Shugarue, at Riverhead (Harbour Grace) and Gander; Shagarhue, unique, at Inglewood (Trinity B.) (*Electors* 1955).

SHUTE, a surname of England from the English place names Shute and Shewte (Devon) or from Old English **sciete, scyte* – (dweller in the) land in the angle or corner of a parish boundary. (Cottle, A.H. Smith, Spiegelhalter).

Traced by Guppy in Dorset and by Spiegelhalter in Devon.

In Newfoundland:

Early instance: Robert, agent of St. John's, 1780 (D'Alberti 1).

Modern status: Scattered.

SIBLEY, a surname of England from the feminine baptismal name Sibyl, Mediaeval Latin *Sibilla*, *Sibylla* (from the Greek), the name of women who acted as mouthpieces of the ancient oracles and later were accepted as blessed with divine revelations and admitted to the Christian heaven along with the Prophets. Hence *Sibylla* came into use as a baptismal name, was introduced into England after the Norman Conquest and became the source of a number of surnames. (Withycombe, Reaney, Cottle).

Spiegelhalter traced Sibla, Sibly in Devon.

In Newfoundland:

Family traditions: ——, from England, settled at Harbour Breton in the 19th century (MUN Folklore). Peter (1829–), from ? Bolden, England, settled on Fogo Island in the 1860s (MUN Folklore).

Early instances: Thomas, of Bay Bulls, 1679, of New Perlican, 1681 (CO 1); James Cybley for Sibley, of Heart's Content, 1708–9 (CO 194.4); James, stoker on Newman and Co's steamship *Greyhound*, son of James and Anne of Crewkerne (Somerset), married at Harbour Breton, 1879, aged 23 (Harbour Breton Anglican Church Records per D.A. Macdonald).

Modern status: Scattered.

Place name: Sibleys Cove 48-02 53-06.

SIDEL, ? a variant of the surname of Germany Seidel from a German place name or from a personal name containing the element *Sieg* – victory. (E.C. Smith, Gottschald).

In Newfoundland:

Modern status: Rare, at St. John's.

SILK, a surname of England from Old English *seolc* – (worker or dealer in) silk, Silke in Ireland for Sheedy, *Ó Síoda*, Ir. *síoda* – silk. (Reaney, Cottle, MacLysaght).

Traced by Spiegelhalter in Devon. MacLysaght traced Silke in east Galway.

In Newfoundland:

Family tradition: ——, from London, England, settled at Pelley's Island (Notre Dame B.) in the 20th century (MUN Folklore).

Early instance: Catherine, of Harbour Grace Parish, 1817 (Nfld. Archives HGRC).

Modern status: Rare, at Grand Falls.

SILVA, a surname of Portugal and Spain – (dweller in or near the) wood, thicket, bush.

In Newfoundland:

Family tradition: Origins in Tomar, Portugal, thence to Lisbon (MUN Folklore).

Modern status: Rare, at St. John's.

SILVER, a surname of England and Scotland from Old English *silfre* – silver(smith), or **seolfre*, **sylfre* – (dweller by the) silvery stream, as in the place names Monksilver (Somerset) or Silver Beck (Cumberland), or an anglicization of the German-Jewish surname Silber. (Reaney, Cottle).

Traced by Black in Kincardineshire.

In Newfoundland:

Early instance: James, merchant of Bay of Islands, 1871 (Lovell).

Modern status: At St. John's.

Place names: Many place names contain the element Silver, but only Silverton 49-27 57-54 appears to be from the surname.

SILVEY, ? an anglicization of the surname of France Silvy from an obscure French saint *Silvius*, patron saint of Saint-Selve (Gironde); a nickname from Latin *silva* – wood, forest. (Dauzat).

Traced in London (Tel. Dir. 1961).

In Newfoundland:

Early instances: Thomas, of St. John's, 1787 (DPHW 26C); Sara Silvy, of St. John's, 1806 (Nfld. Archives BRC); Elizabeth Sylvy, of Maggotty Cove (St. John's district), 1835 (Nfld. Archives BRC).

Modern status: Rare, at Fleur de Lys.

SIMMON(D)S, SYMONDS, surnames of England, SYMONS of the Channel Islands, from the Old Norse personal name *Sigmundr*, Old Danish *Sigmund*, containing the elements *victory* and *protector*, confused with the baptismal name Simmond (Simon) (*see* SIMON). (Reaney, Cottle, Turk).

Of the many variants, Guppy found Simmon(d)s in the south and west, with Simmons much the more frequent form, Simmonds being associated with it in Berkshire, Hampshire, Oxfordshire and Sussex, and Semmens characteristic of Cornwall. He traced Symon(d)s and Simons in the Midlands and west, with Symonds the most generally diffused, Symons being characteristic of Cornwall and Devon, Simons of Lincolnshire, Leicestershire, Rutlandshire and Northamptonshire, Simon(d)s of Northamptonshire, and all three variants of Cornwall. Spiegelhalter traced Simmon(d)s, Sym(m)ons, Symonds in Devon.

In Newfoundland:

Family tradition: George Symonds (1835–),

from Exeter (Devon), settled at St. John's in 1856 (MUN Folklore).

Early instances: John Simons, boatkeeper of St. John's Harbour, 1682 (CO 1); William Simmon, of Newfoundland, ? 1706 (CO 194.24); William Simmonds, of Musketta (now Bristol's Hope), 1779 (CO 199.18); —— Symmonds, of Bay Bulls, 1780 (D'Alberti 1); Samuel Simmonds, of Trinity Bay, 1783, of Trinity (Trinity B.), 1787 (DPHW 64); Samuel, of Lower Island Cove, 1785 (DPHW 48); Thomas Simmons, of Joe Batts Arm, 1815 (Nfld. Archives KCRC); Michael Simmens or Simons, of Harbour Grace Parish, 1815 (Nfld. Archives HGRC); Betsy Simmons, of Catalina, 1821 (Nfld. Archives KCRC); W. Simmonds, of Carbonear, 1821 (D'Alberti 31); Catherine Simmons, of King's Cove, 1822 (Nfld. Archives KCRC); John, fisherman of Grand Bank, 1826 (DPHW 109); Catherine, of Ragged Harbour (now Melrose), 1827 (Nfld. Archives KCRC); James Simmonds, of Keels, 1831 (DPHW 70); William Symons, from Whitchurch (Devon), 1835 (DPHW 26D); William Simmons, from Laverstoft, ? for Laverstock (Wiltshire), married at Petty Harbour, 1838 (DPHW 31); James, planter of Little Catalina, 1842 (DPHW 72); Samuel, of Salt Harbour (Twillingate district), 1858 (DPHW 85); Edward, of Green's Harbour (Trinity B.), 1867 (DPHW 61); Elizabeth ? Simmons, of Cottells Island, 1870 (Nfld. Archives KCRC); scattered in Lovell 1871.

Modern status: Simmonds, scattered, especially at St. John's and Cannings Cove; Simmons, scattered, especially at Green's Harbour and St. John's; Symonds, at Goose Cove (White B.), Barachoix Brook (St. George's district) (*Electors* 1955) and St. John's.

Place names: Simmonds Barasway 47-45 55-51; —— Cove 48-36 53-46; —— Pond 48-27 54-07; Simmons Brook 47-39 55-29; —— Island 47-03 55-10.

SIMMS, SYMES, surnames of England, SIMMS of Ireland, from *Sim(m)* a pet-form of *Simmond* (*see* SIMMONDS) or *Sime* a pet-form of *Simon* (*see* SIMON). (Reaney, Cottle).

Guppy traced Sim(m) in Cumberland and Westmorland, Sims in Cheshire, Derbyshire, Gloucestershire, Somerset and Wiltshire and Symes in Dorset. Spiegelhalter traced Simes, Simms and Syms in Devon. MacLysaght traced Simms in Cos. Antrim and Donegal.

In Newfoundland:

Family tradition: John Symes, from England, settled at Grand Bank in the early 1800s; the surname later changed to Simms (MUN Hist.).

Early instances: Samuel Syms, of St. John's, 1762 (CO 194.15); John ? Symes, of Fogo, Twillingate or Tilton (now Tilting), 1771 (CO 194.30); John Sims, of Turks Gut (now Marysvale), 1803 (CO 199.18); Benjamin, son of Robert (1787–1874) from Blandford (Dorset), planter, baptised at Harbour Breton, 1838 (Harbour Breton Anglican Church Records per D.A. Macdonald); Henry Sym(e)s, of Fogo, 1803–05 (D'Alberti 13); John Sims, of Brigus, 1815 (DPHW 34); James Simms, of Twillingate, 1812 (D'Alberti 22); William, of Carbonear, 1815 (DPHW 48); George Symms, of Harbour Grace Parish, 1822 (Nfld. Archives HGRC); John, of Burin, 1823 (DPHW 106); George Simms, merchant of Trepassey, 1824 (DPHW 26B); John, of Hermitage Cove, 1824 (DPHW 109); George Syms, of Fortune Harbour, 1830 (Nfld. Archives KCRC); Thomas Sims, of Brunett(e) (Island), 1838 (DPHW 106); Ann Simms, of Grand Bank, 1842 (DPHW 106); Emanuel Symes, fisherman of Grole, 1846 (DPHW 102); George Syms or Sims, of Donier Harbour (Twillingate district), 1848 (DPHW 86); Robert Simms, fisherman of Pass Island (Fortune B.), 1848 (DPHW 102); Joseph Sim(m)s, fisherman of Crocker's Cove (Carbonear), 1848 (DPHW 49); Robert Sims, of St. Anthony, 1854 (DPHW 114); Emanuel Symes, of New (now Parsons) Harbour, 1859 (DPHW 101); Benjamin Simms, of Hunt's Island (Burgeo-La Poile district), 1859 (DPHW 101); Benjamin, of Harbour Breton, 1860 (DPHW 99); scattered in Lovell 1871.

Modern status: Simms, widespread, especially at Pass Island (Fortune B.), Corner Brook, St. Anthony Bight, St. Anthony and St. John's; Symes, in the Burgeo-La Poile district (*Electors* 1955).

Place names: Simms Bay (Labrador) 52-11 55-44; —— Brook 48-54 58-20; —— Island, —— Rock 49-44 54-16; —— Ridge 49-44 56-54; Sims Lake (Labrador) 54-00 65-55; —— Point 46-45 53-22, 49-31 55-15; —— River (Labrador) 53-47 65-27.

SIMON, a baptismal name and surname of England and France, the Channel Islands and Syria-Lebanon, the usual New Testament form of the Hebrew personal name *Shimeon* (Simeon) – hearkening or ? little hyena or ? influenced by a Greek personal name from an adjective meaning "snub-nosed." Simon was popular as a baptismal name in the Middle Ages after the apostle *Simon Bar-Jonah* surnamed Peter (*see* PETERS) and gave rise to several surnames including SIMMON(D)S, SIMMS, SYMES, SIMPSON. (Withycombe, Reaney, Cottle, Dauzat, Turk).

Traced by Spiegelhalter in Devon and found widespread by Dauzat in France.

In Newfoundland:

Family tradition: ——— Simon from France or St. Pierre in 1880s, was the first settler of that name at Cape St. George (Thomas, "French Fam. Names").

Early instance: John, of Newfoundland, ? 1706 (CO 194.24).

Modern status: Scattered, especially at Cape St. George.

SIMPSON, a surname of England, Scotland and Ireland – son of Simon (see SIMON) or from the English place name Simpson (Devon). (Reaney, Spiegelhalter, Black, MacLysaght).

Found widespread by Guppy in England and Scotland except north of Aberdeen, and by MacLysaght in Ulster.

In Newfoundland:

Early instances: Richard, of Newfoundland, 1704 (CO 194.3); Andrew, of Great Bellisle (now Bell Island), 1771 (DPHW 26C); Andrew, of St. John's, 1811 (CO 194.52); William Simbson or Sim(p)son, of Trinity (Trinity B.), 1816-18 (Nfld. Archives KCRC, DPHW 64); William Simpson (about 1795–1844), from Aberdeen, Scotland, druggist of St. John's, died 1844, aged 49 (*Times* 18 Dec 1844); James, from Scotland, married at Lower Burgeo, 1853 (DPHW 101); Robert, merchant of Bay Roberts, 1871 (Lovell).

Modern status: At St. John's and Long Pond (Harbour Main district).

SINCLAIR. See ST. CLAIR

SINGLE, a surname of England from Old English *sengel – (dweller by the) burnt clearing, or tufts of grass, or gleanings. (Reaney, A. H. Smith). *See* SINGLETON.

In Newfoundland:

Early instance: William, fisherman of Russell's Cove (now New Melbourne), 1859, of Seal Cove (now New Chelsea), 1859 (DPHW 59, 59A).

Modern status: At New Chelsea.

SINGLETON, a surname of England, Scotland and Ireland from Old English *sengel and *tūn – farm in a burnt clearing etc. (*see* SINGLE) whence the place name Singleton (Sussex), or from Old English *scingol and *tūn – farm built on shingle or with a shingled roof, whence the place name Singleton (Lancashire). (Cottle, A. H. Smith, Black, MacLysaght).

Traced by Guppy in Lancashire, found uncommon by Black in Scotland, and by MacLysaght in Ireland as early as 1387.

In Newfoundland:

Family tradition: ———, left a British ship at Carbonear in the early 1800s and later moved to St. Joseph's (St. Mary's B.) (MUN Folklore).

Early instances: Thomas, of Bonavista, 1792 (USPG); Thomas, planter of Trinity (Trinity B.), 1842 (DPHW 64B); Richard, of Harbour Grace Parish, 1843 (Nfld. Archives HGRC); John, fisherman of Salmonier (St. Mary's B.), 1871 (Lovell); John and Richard, of Spaniard's Bay, 1871 (Lovell).

Modern status: Scattered, especially in the Harbour Grace and St. Mary's districts.

SINNOTT, a surname of England and Ireland from the Old English personal name *Sigenōth* containing the elements *victory* and *bold*. (Reaney).

Traced by Spiegelhalter in Devon and by MacLysaght in Co. Wexford since the thirteenth century.

In Newfoundland:

Early instances: Edward Sennott, shoreman of Torbay, 1794–5, "20 years in Newfoundland," that is, 1774–5 (Census 1794–5); Edward Sinnot, of St. John's, 1806 (Nfld. Archives BRC); Father, of Joe Batts Arm, 1818 (CO 194.61); Peter Sinnott, from Chanrache (unidentified) (Co. Wexford), married at St. John's, 1819 (Nfld. Archives BRC); V., of Harbour Grace, 1821 (USPG); Betsy, of Catalina, 1823 (Nfld. Archives KCRC); Mary, of Placentia, 1823 (Nfld. Archives BRC); Rev. James, R.C. priest, of St. John's, 1827 (*Newfoundlander* 24 Oct 1827); Patrick, of Moreton's Harbour, 1830 (Nfld. Archives KCRC); Patrick, of Fortune Harbour, 1830 (Nfld. Archives KCRC); J. Sinnot, inspector of pickled fish at Placentia, 1844 (*Nfld. Almanac*); William Sinnott, granted land at Sweeney's Marsh Road (unidentified), 1846 (Nfld. Archives, Registry Crown Lands); Martin, of Flat Rock (unspecified), 1847 (*Newfoundlander* 18 Jan 1847); Francis Senett, of Greenspond, 1871 (Lovell); David Synnot, miner of La Manche (Placentia B.), 1871 (Lovell).

Modern status: Scattered.

SINYARD, SYN(Y)ARD, surnames of England, variants of SENIOR.

In Newfoundland:

Early instances: Samuel Singard, of Trinity Bay, 1791 (DPHW 64); Samuel Sinyard, planter of Heart's Content, 1823 (DPHW 64B).

Modern status: Sinyard, at St. John's, Heart's Content and Harbour Grace; Synard, at Riverhead

(St. Mary's B.), and Parkers Cove (*Electors* 1955); Synyard, at Mall Bay (St. Mary's B.).

SKANES, a surname of England, ? of Scandinavian origin, but probably confused with the surname of Ireland (Mac) Skehan (*see* SKEHANS).

Matthews traced Skains, Scaines in Devon.

In Newfoundland:

Family tradition: ——, from Cornwall, England, settled at Bell Island about 1750 (MUN Folklore).

Early instances: James Skenes, shoreman of St. John's, 1794–5, "7 years in Newfoundland," that is, 1787–8 (Census 1794–5); John Skean, from Grange (unidentified) (Co. Tipperary), married at St. John's, 1813 (Nfld. Archives BRC); William Skane, of Harbour Grace Parish, 1814 (Nfld. Archives HGRC); Charles Skaines, from Ide (Devon), planter of St. John's, died 1815 (*Royal Gazette* 9 Mar 1815); Michael Skean, of Ragged Harbour (now Melrose), 1820 (Nfld. Archives HGRC); John Scanes or Skains, of Belle Isle (now Bell Island), 1822 (DPHW 26B); John Skanes or Skeanes, of Broad Cove (Bay de Verde district), 1829 (DPHW 52A); Mary Skean, of Carbonear, 1829 (Nfld. Archives BRC); John Skannes, of Round Harbour (Twillingate district), 1846 (DPHW 86); James Skein, granted land at Northern Gut (now North River), 1857 (Nfld. Archives, Registry Crown Lands); Richard Skean, of Springfield (Conception B.), 1871 (Lovell).

Modern status: Scattered, especially at Bell Island and St. John's.

SKEARD, ? a variant of the surname of England Skarth from a Scandinavian personal name – harelip. An Old English word *sceard* – notch(ed), gap survives in a number of place names such as Shardlow, Sharstone etc. (Reaney *Origin*, Ekwall).

In Newfoundland:

Early instances: ? John Skard, of Grand Bank, 1827 (MUN Hist.); Thomas (and others) Skeard, of Channel, 1871 (Lovell).

Modern status: Scattered, especially at Channel.

SKEFFINGTON, SKIFFINGTON, surnames of England, SKEFFINGTON of Ireland, from a Scandinavianized form of Old English *Sc(e)aftinga-tūn* – the farm of *Sceaft*'s people or from the English place name Skeffington (Leicestershire). (Cottle, Ekwall, MacLysaght).

Traced by Reaney *Origin* in Leicestershire, and by MacLysaght in Ireland since 1534.

In Newfoundland:

Early instances: George Skimington, of St. John's Harbour, 1703 (CO 194.3); George Sciffinton, chief Quaker, of Bonavista, 1705 (CO 194.3); —— Skaffington, from Bonavista, granted sole fishery for salmon in Freshwater Bay, Ragged Harbour, Gander Bay and Dog Creek (now Horwood), 1723 (Prowse); Samuel Skiffington, of Greenspond, joint possessor of fishing room, Pond Island, Greenspond, 1802 (Bonavista Register 1806); Margaret Skimiton, of King's Cove, 1803 (Nfld. Archives BRC); John Skiffington, of Broad Cove (now Duntara), 1825 (Nfld. Archives KCRC); John, of Tickle Cove (Bonavista B.), 1841 (DPHW 73A); George, of Knight's Cove (Bonavista B.), 1844 (DPHW 73A); J. S. Keffington [sic], member of Board of Road Commissioners for Keels to Plate Cove (Bonavista B.) area, 1844 (*Nfld. Almanac*); John Skiffington, granted land at Cannaile (near Bonavista), 1850 (Nfld. Archives, Registry Crown Lands); George (and others) Skeffington, of Upper and Lower Amherst Cove (Bonavista B.), 1871 (Lovell); James (and others) Skiffington, of Newman's Cove (Bonavista B.), 1871 (Lovell).

Modern status: Skeffington, at Newmans Cove, and Upper and Middle Amherst Cove; Skiffington, scattered, especially at Musgravetown.

SKEHANS, SKEHEN, variants of the surname of Ireland (Mac) Skehan, *Mac Sceacháin*, ? Ir. *sceach* – briar, or confused with SKANES. (MacLysaght).

MacLysaght traced (Mac) Skehan in Cos. Monaghan, Louth and Tipperary.

In Newfoundland:

Family tradition: —— Skean, from Carrick (unspecified), Ireland, settled at St. John's in the 19th century (MUN Folklore).

Early instances: Edmund Skehan, of Port de Grave, 1784 (CO 199.18); Richard, of Carbonear, 1792 (CO 199.18); William, of Colliers, 1793 (CO 199.18); John Skehen, of Harbour Grace Parish, 1811 (Nfld. Archives HGRC); Ellen Skeahan, married at St. John's, 1833 (Nfld. Archives BRC).

Modern status: Skehans, rare, at Hallstown (Port de Grave district) and St. John's; Skehen, unique, at St. John's.

SKIFFINGTON. *See* SKEFFINGTON

SKINNER, a surname of England and the Channel Islands from Old Norse *skinn* – skin, hence a skinner. (Reaney, Cottle, Turk). *See also* SHINAR.

Traced by Guppy in Cornwall, Devon, Kent, Lincolnshire, Norfolk, Surrey, Sussex and Worcestershire.

In Newfoundland:

Family tradition: ———, from England, settled at Ochre Pit Cove (MUN Folklore).

Early instances: R., of Newfoundland, ? 1706 (CO 194.24); Richard, of St. John's, 1762 (CO 194.15); William, of Ochre Pit Cove, 1776 (CO 199.18); James, of Fogo, 1805 (D'Alberti 15); John, of Renews, 1815 (Nfld. Archives BRC); Samuel, planter of Northern Bay, 1826 (DPHW 52A); Mary, of Harbour Grace Parish, 1828 (Nfld. Archives HGRC); James, fisherman of Cuckold's Cove (now Dunfield), 1832, of Trouty, 1837 (DPHW 64B); Anne, baptized at Leconte (? Burgeo-La Poile district), 1835 (DPHW 30); James, planter of Trinity (Trinity B.), 1835 (DPHW 64B); Thomas, of Richard's Harbour, 1835 (DPHW 30); Matthew, fisherman of Sagona, 1850 (DPHW 107); George Schinner, of Greenspond, 1854 (DPHW 76); Abraham Skinner, of Rose Blanche, 1860 (DPHW 99); John, of Twillingate, 1861 (DPHW 88); John Skinnar, of Harbour Grace, 1868 (Nfld. Archives HGRC); scattered in Lovell 1871.

Modern status: Scattered, especially at Harbour Breton, Richard's Harbour and St. John's.

Place names: Skinner (or Brake) Cove 49-32 58-03; Skinner Cove, ——— Rock, ——— Ledge 49-40 54-24; ——— Ledge 49-32 55-09; ——— Rocks 46-42 53-24; Skinners Cove 47-38 55-04.

SKIRVING, a surname of Scotland, of unknown origin. "As Skirvane it was one of the commonest surnames in the parish of Haddington in the eighteenth century." (Black).

In Newfoundland:

Modern status: At St. John's.

SLADE, a surname of England from Old English *slæd* – (dweller in the) valley, or from the English place name Slade (Lancashire, Devon). (Reaney, Cottle, Spiegelhalter).

Traced by Guppy in Devon and especially in Somerset.

In Newfoundland:

Early instances: John, of Fogo, Twillingate or Tilton (now Tilting), 1771 (CO 194.30); John, of Marshalls Folly (Carbonear), 1801 (CO 199.18); John and Co., operated salmon fishery at Fogo, 1804 (CO 194.45); John, of Perry's Cove, 1813 (DPHW 48); Henry, soldier of St. John's, 1818 (DPHW 26D); William G., of Harbour Grace, 1828 (Nlfd. Archives HGRC); James, of Woody Island (Placentia B.), 1835 (DPHW 30); James, granted land at Trinity (Trinity B.), 1836 (Nfld. Archives, Registry Crown Lands); Thomas and Co., of Twillingate, 1837 (*Newfound-*

lander 6 Apr 1837); ———, of Slade, Elson and Co., Carbonear, 1845 (*Newfoundlander* 10 Apr 1845); John, of Ward's Harbour (now Beaumont North), 1846 (DPHW 86); Robert, Thomas and James, granted land at Catalina, 1850 (Nfld. Archives, Registry Crown Lands); James, of Harbour Buffett, 1854 (MUN Hist.); George, fisherman of Little Bay (Burgeo-La Poile district), 1860 (DPHW 99); scattered in Lovell 1871.

Modern status: Scattered, especially at Carbonear, Salmon Cove (Carbonear) and Victoria.

Place name: Slades Rock 48-40 53-01.

SLANEY, a surname of Ireland, *de Sláine*, "one of the few Irish toponymics" presumably from Slane (Co. Meath). (MacLysaght).

In Newfoundland:

Family tradition: Michael, of Irish descent, of St. Lawrence in the early 19th century (MUN Geog.).

Early instances: Patrick Sliney, of Harbour Grace Parish, 1823 (Nfld. Archives HGRC); David Slaney, granted land at Great St. Lawrence (now St. Lawrence), 1844 (Nfld. Archives, Registry Crown Lands); Henry, member of Board of Road Commissioners of Burin district, 1844 (*Nfld. Almanac*); Mrs., schoolteacher of Ferryland, 1845 (*Nfld. Quarterly* Dec 1911); David and Thomas Sliney, farmers of Chapel's Cove, 1871 (Lovell).

Modern status: Scattered, especially at St. Lawrence.

SLATTERY, a surname of Ireland, (O)Slattery, *Ó Slatara*, *Ó Slatraigh*, Ir. *slatra* – strong. (MacLysaght).

Traced by MacLysaght in Co. Clare and adjacent counties of Munster.

In Newfoundland:

Early instances: John, servant at ? Little Placentia (now Argentia), about 1730–5 (CO 194.9); Edmond, from Clonmel (Co. Tipperary), married at St. John's, 1793 (Nfld. Archives BRC); William, of St. John's, 1794–5 (Census 1794–5); William, of Trinity (unspecified), 1820 (Nfld. Archives KCRC); Thomas Slatery, of Harbour Grace Parish, 1824 (Nfld. Archives HGRC); Thomas Slattery, of Portugal Cove, 1832 (DPHW 30); Margaret, from Co. Tipperary, of Brigus, 1844 (*Indicator* 24 Aug 1844); James, miner of Tilt Cove, 1871 (Lovell).

Modern status: At Mount Carmel (*Electors* 1955) and St. John's.

SLOAN, a surname of Ireland and Scotland, (O)Sloan(e), *Ó Sluagháin*, Ir. *sluagh* – hosting, army. (MacLysaght, Black).

Traced by MacLysaght in Cos. Armagh, Down and Antrim, and as Sloyan in Co. Mayo, and by Guppy in Aryshire.

In Newfoundland:

Early instances: Thomas Sloan, from Co. Waterford, married at St. John's, 1827 (Nfld. Archives BRC); Elenor Slone, of Harbour Grace Parish, 1828 (Nfld. Archives HGRC); George Sloan, soldier of St. John's, 1841 (DPHW 29).

Modern status: Rare, at Riverhead (Harbour Grace district) (*Electors* 1955), and St. John's.

Place name: Sloans Gully 47-44 53-23.

SMALL, a surname of England and Ireland from Old English *smæl* – small, slender, thin; in Ireland also for BEGG and Kielty (*see* QUILTY). (Reaney, Cottle, MacLysaght).

Traced by Guppy in Nottinghamshire, Somerset and Worcestershire, by Spiegelhalter in Devon, and by MacLysaght in Co. Galway and Ulster.

In Newfoundland:

Family traditions: Reuben, of English descent, from Conception Bay, settled in Moreton's Harbour about 1810 (MUN Hist.). ——, from Scotland, settled at Moreton's Harbour (MUN Folklore).

Early instances: William, of St. John's, 1756 (DPHW 26C); John, of Moreton's Harbour, 1845 (DPHW 86); Israel, of Fogo, 1855 (DPHW 86); Richard, of Tizzard's Harbour, 1860 (DPHW 88); Joseph, merchant of Lower Burgeo, 1871 (Lovell); Joseph, miner of Tilt Cove, 1871 (Lovell).

Modern status: Scattered, especially at Moreton's Harbour and Wild Cove (White B.).

Place names: Many place names contain the element Small, but only Small's Island 47-37 57-36 appears to be from the surname.

SMALLCOMBE, a surname of England from Old English *smæl* – small and *cumb* – hollow, valley, coomb, or from the English place names Smallcombe, Smallicombe, Smallacomb(e) (Devon). (A.H. Smith).

Spiegelhalter traced Smallacombe in Devon.

In Newfoundland:

Family tradition: —— Smallcomb, from England, settled first in Boston, then at Riverhead (Harbour Grace) in 1871 (MUN Folklore).

Early instances: Michael Smalkom or Smallcombe, of Harbour Grace Parish, 1844 (Nfld. Archives HGRC); —— Smallcombe, on the *Experiment* in the seal fishery out of Harbour Grace, 1847 (*Newfoundlander* 25 Mar 1847); Patrick Smallcomb, fisherman of St. John's, 1871 (Lovell).

Modern status: Rare, at Bell Island (*Electors* 1955) and Harbour Grace.

SMALLWOOD, a surname of England – (dweller in or near the) narrow wood, or from the English place name Smallwood (Cheshire, Lancashire, Suffolk). (Cottle).

In Newfoundland:

Family tradition: Randle or Randall, from England, settled in Virginia, U.S.A. in 1620. Joseph, a Loyalist descendant settled at Prince Edward Island about 1783. His grandson David, from Charlottetown (Prince Edward Island) settled at St. John's in 1861 (Smallwood, *I Chose Canada*).

Early instance: David, trader of Ship Island (Bonavista B.), 1871 (Lovell).

Modern status: At St. John's, Brigus and Roaches Line.

SMART, a surname of England and Scotland from Old English *smeart* – quick, smart, brisk, prompt. (Reaney, Cottle).

Traced by Guppy in Northamptonshire and Wiltshire and by Spiegelhalter in Devon.

In Newfoundland:

Family tradition: ——, from the British Isles, settled on a small island near Change Islands; the Family later moved to Change Islands (MUN Folklore).

Early instances: A. ? Smart, of Placentia, 1724 (CO 194.8); William Smart, ? of St. John's, ? died 1795 (CO 194.40); John, from Mahelin (unidentified) (Co. Down), married at St. John's, 1808 (Nfld. Archives BRC); Emmos (? for Amos), of Harbour Grace Parish, 1810 (Nfld. Archives KCRC); Mary, of Trinity (unspecified), 1815 (Nfld. Archives BRC); Robert, of Woody Point, 1816 (DPHW 95); Mary, of Harbour Grace, 1829 (Nfld. Archives BRC); George, planter of Catalina, 1847 (DPHW 72); ——, on the *Elizabeth* in the seal fishery out of Brigus, 1847 (*Newfoundlander* 25 Mar 1847); Thomas, planter of Stone Harbour (Twillingate district), 1851 (DPHW 85); Robert, from Somerset, England, married at Fortune, 1856 (DPHW 106); Robert, of Herring Neck, 1857 (DPHW 85); Edward, of Little Bay Island (Twillingate district), 1871 (Lovell).

Modern status: Scattered, especially at Lethbridge (Bonavista B.).

SMEATON, a surname of England and Scotland – the place of the smiths or workers in metal, or from the English place names Smeaton (Cornwall, Yorkshire NR, WR) or Smeeton (Leicestershire); in Scot land from Smytheton or Smythetun (now Smeaton) (Midlothian). (Cottle, Black).

In Newfoundland:

Modern status: Rare, at St. John's.

SMITH, SMYTH, surnames of England, Scotland, Ireland and Guernsey (Channel Islands) from Old English *smith* – smith, blacksmith, farrier, metalworker, or *smiththe* – (worker at the) smithy; in Ireland also a synonym of Gow and McGOWAN. "The primate and patriarch of our surnames, its form unchanged for over 1,000 years; forms with medial -y and final -e are usually both ignorant and affected, though the first may sometimes have been used for clarity next to the minim letter m, and -e may rarely represent 'smithy' ... Easily the commonest surname in England and Wales (though JONES is far ahead in Wales alone), Scotland, and USA, and the fifth in Ireland in 1890 ... It is thus a frequent victim of hyphenation, either in a sincere effort to avoid ambiguity or in an insincere one to sound distingué; and it has recently gathered to itself many changed foreign surnames. Yet it remains primitive: a smith *smites*, and his honoured name rings down the ages like an anvil." (Cottle, Turk).

Smith found widespread by Guppy in England and Scotland, especially south of the Forth and Clyde and by MacLysaght in Co. Cavan; Smyth traced by Guppy in Devon and Suffolk and by Cottle in Northern Ireland. *See also* SMYTH.

In Newfoundland:

Family traditions: John George Smith, from England, settled at Dildo (Trinity B.) before 1844 (MUN Folklore). ——, from England, settled at Bishop's Cove about 1710 (MUN Geog.). ——, from England, one of the earliest residents of Twillingate, settled at The Point, Twillingate in the late 17th century, (*Nfld. Quarterly* Dec 1905); John, from Chance Cove (Trinity B.) was the first Smith to settle at Norman's Cove in the early 1800s (MUN Hist.). —— Brown, from England, deserted ship, changed his name to Smith, and became the first settler of Rock Harbour (Placentia B.) about 1800 (MUN Hist.). Margaret Smith, of Irish descent, of Calvert, 1818 (MUN Geog.). Charles, from England, was one of the earliest settlers of Flat Island (now Port Elizabeth). Elizabeth (about 1801–74), born at Argentia (MUN Geog.). Robert C., from Nairn, Scotland, emigrated to Newfoundland in the mid-19th century; some of the family later settled at Gander (MUN Geog.); George Frederick (died 1892), sea captain from Southampton, settled at St. John's about 1885. (P.E.L. Smith).

Early instances: Humphrey Smith, of Witless Bay, 1675, of Toads (now Tors) Cove, 1681 (CO 1); Pierce, of Bay de Verde, 1675 (CO 1); William, of Harbour Main, 1676 (CO 1); Peter, of Torbay, 1676 (CO 1); J., of St. John's, 1705 (CO 194.22); William, of Bread and Cheese Cove (now Bishop's Cove), 1785, property "in possession of the Family for more than 80 years," that is, before 1705 (CO 199.18); William, fisherman of Trinity (Trinity B.), 1757 (DPHW 64); Elizabeth, of (Upper) Island Cove, 1776 (CO 199.18); John, planter of Fogo, 1792 (MUN Hist.); Thomas, proprietor and occupier of fishing room, Heart's Delight, Winter 1800–01 (Census Trinity B.); Thomas, proprietor and occupier of fishing room, New Perlican, Winter 1800–01 (Census Trinity B.); Isaac, of Cooper's Head (Bishop's Cove), 1801 (CO 199.18); James, of Placentia, 1803 (D'Alberti 13); Nath., of Greenspond, 1804 (D'Alberti 14); Thomas, of Burin, 1805 (D'Alberti 15); James, from Londonderry (Co. Derry), married at St. John's, 1807 (Nfld. Archives BRC); Abraham, ? of Carbonear, 1810 (DPHW 48); Caleb, of Twillingate, 1811 (D'Alberti 22); Francis, one of 72 impressed men who sailed from Ireland to Newfoundland, ? 1811 (CO 194.51); Elizabeth Smyth or Smith, of Harbour Grace Parish, 1814 (Nfld. Archives HGRC); George Smith, of Gasters, 1816 (D'Alberti 26); Jane, of Ferryland, 1817 (Nfld. Archives BRC); Caleb, planter of Merritt's Harbour, 1820, of Moreton's Harbour, 1822 (USPG); James, planter of Scilly Cove (now Winterton), 1823 (DPHW 64B); Samuel, of Keels, 1825 (DPHW 70); Robert, planter of Cupids, 1826 (DPHW 34); John, from Co. Tipperary, married at King's Cove, 1828 (Nfld. Archives KCRC); Thomas, planter of Hants Harbour, 1831 (DPHW 59A); Robert, of Manuels, 1832 (DPHW 30); Captain Alfred, of Brigus, 1833 (Nfld. Archives L165); Jane, of Herring Neck, 1833 (Nfld. Archives KCRC); Hartwick Mansell Schmidt, from Deptford, England, married at St. John's, 1835 (DPHW 26D); John Smith, fisherman of Blow-me-down (Carbonear), 1836 (DPHW 48); Robert, planter of New Harbour (Trinity B.), 1836 (DPHW 64B); George, of Deadman's Bay (Bonavista B.), 1837 (DPHW 76); Juliana, of Topsail, 1838 (DPHW 26D); ——, on the *Nelson* in the seal fishery out of Port de Grave, 1838 (*Newfoundlander* 29 Mar 1838); George, planter of Chamberlains, 1841 (DPHW 26B); Thomas, of Open Hole (now Open Hall), 1847 (Nfld. Archives KCRC); Job, of South Harbour (Fortune B.), 1849 (DPHW 102), of Greeps Head (Fortune B.), 1851 (DPHW 102); William, of Dog Cove (Bonavista B.), 1850 (Nfld. Archives KCRC); John, of Triton Harbour (now Triton), 1851 (DPHW 86); Benjamin, fisherman of Fox Harbour (Trinity B.), 1855 (DPHW 59A); Catherine, of Pichers (? for Pinchards) Island, 1856 (Nfld. Archives KCRC); Isabella, of Heart's Ease, 1856 (DPHW 59); Edward, of Spaniard's Bay, died 1856 (*Newfoundlander* 18 Sep 1856); Susana, of Haywards Cove (Bonavista B.), 1857 (Nfld. Archives KCRC); Charles, from Stockholm, Sweden, married at St. John's, 1858 (*Newfoundlander* 19 Jul 1858); Charles, of Petty Harbour, 1859 (DPHW 31); John, of Garia, 1860 (DPHW 99); William, of Gooseberry Island (Bonavista B.), 1861 (Nfld. Archives KCRC); George, of Little Harbour (Twillingate district), 1861 (DPHW 88); Emmanuel Reed, of Chance Cove, 1862 (DPHW 62); Maria Smith or Smyth, of Chapel Arm, 1866 (Nfld. Archives KCRC); Samuel Smith, of Cottell's Island (Bonavista B.), 1867 (Nfld. Archives KCRC); Maria, of Harbour Grace, 1868 (Nfld. Archives HGRC); Richard, fisherman of Robin Hood (now part of Port Rexton), 1869 (DPHW 65); widespread in Lovell 1871.

Modern status: Widespread throughout all districts with large concentrations at St. John's, Spaniard's Bay, Bishop's Cove, Dildo, Chance Cove, Norman's Cove, Boat Harbour (Placentia B.) and Corner Brook.

Place names: Smith Island (Labrador) 54-13 58-18; —— Point 48-11 53-51; —— Shoal 47-11 54-50, 47-38 58-32; —— Sound 48-10 53-40; —— Lookout 49-39 54-47; Smiths Cove 47-34 54-14; —— Harbour 49-44 55-58; —— Point 47-22 54-53; —— Rock (Labrador) 52-15 55-36; Smitt Pond (Labrador) 52-57 55-57; John Smith Harbour, —— —— Island 49-44 55-58.

SMURRIDGE, a variant of the surnames of England Smal(l)bridge, Smaridge,

Small(d)ridge, from the English place name Smallridge (Devon), or ? a mistake name for Snurridge (Devon). (Reaney).

Guppy traced Smal(l)bridge, Smaridge and Spiegelhalter Small(d)ridge, Smaridge in Devon.

In Newfoundland:

Early instance: Henry and Robert Smerridge, of Burnt Island (Burgeo-La Poile district), 1871 (Lovell).

Modern status: Rare, at Burnt Island (Burgeo-La Poile district) (*Electors* 1955).

SMYTH. *See* SMITH

In Newfoundland:

Early instances: William Smyth, of St. John's Harbour, 1703 (CO 194.3); Jacob, from Tintern (Co.

Wexford), married at St. John's, 1814 (Nfld. Archives BRC); Elizabeth Smyth or Smith, of Harbour Grace Parish, 1814 (Nfld. Archives HGRC); John Smyth, of Greenspond, 1820 (Nfld. Archives KCRC); John, of Bonavista, 1822 (Nfld. Archives KCRC); John, from Co. Cork, married at King's Cove, 1822 (Nfld. Archives KCRC); Susanna, of Keels, 1827 (Nfld. Archives KCRC); Catherine, of Ferryland, 1830 (Nfld. Archives BRC); Mary, of Cape Cove (Bonavista B.), 1831 (Nfld. Archives KCRC); Charles, from New York, married at St. John's, 1834 (DPHW 26D); Thomas, fisherman of Southern Harbour (Placentia B.), 1871 (Lovell); Isaac fisherman of Sound Island (Placentia B.), 1871 (Lovell).

Modern status: At Baine Harbour, Parker's Cove (Placentia B.) (*Electors* 1955) and St. John's.

SNELGROVE, a surname of England – (dweller in the) grove or wood infested by snails. (E.C. Smith).

In Newfoundland:

Early instances: Ann, of Lower Island Cove, 1756 (CO 199.18); John Snellgrove, sailmaker of St. John's, 1794–5, "born in Newfoundland" (Census 1794–5); John Snelgrove, of Western Bay, 1799 (CO 199.18); John, proprietor and occupier of fishing room, Grates Cove, Winter 1800–01 (Census Trinity B.); Roger, of Harbour Grace, 1804 (CO 199.18); Isaac, planter of Catalina, 1816 (DPHW 72); Abraham, planter of Hants Harbour, 1817 (DPHW 58); Thomas, of Torbay, 1836 (DPHW 26D); George Robert Snellgrove, planter of Brunet (Island), 1859 (DPHW 104); Jacob (and others) Snelgrove, of Caplin Cove (Bay de Verde district), 1871 (Lovell); Moses, of Exploits Burnt Island, 1871 (Lovell); George T. R., of Garnish, 1871 (Lovell).

Modern status: Scattered, especially at St. John's and Lower Island Cove.

Place names: Snelgrove Lake (Labrador) 54-37 65-50; Snelgroves Hill 48-31 53-05.

SNOOK(S), surnames of England, previously thought to be derived from Sevenoaks (Kent) (*see* SHINNICKS), but more probably from Old English *snōc* – point, projection (of land), used as a nickname for one with a long nose, or from Old English *snōc* – snake, also ? a personal name. (Reaney, Cottle).

Guppy traced Snook in Berkshire, Dorset, Somerset and Wiltshire; Spiegelhalter traced Snook(e) in Devon.

In Newfoundland:

Family tradition: Morgan Sr. and Jr. Snook, English settlers forced to leave St. Pierre under terms of the Treaty of Paris, became the first recorded English settlers of Fortune (MUN Hist., P.E.L. Smith).

Early instances: John Snooke, of Old Perlican, 1677 (CO 1); James Snook, fisherman of Trinity (Trinity B.), 1759 (DPHW 64); Morgan Sr. and Jr., traders who sustained losses when St. Pierre was surrendered to the French in 1763 (CO 194.6); Morgan, local pilot with James Cook for the survey of Fortune Bay, 1765 (Whiteley); William and Elijah, proprietors and occupiers of fishing room, New Perlican, Winter 1800–01 (Census Trinity B.); Robert, of St. John's, 1813 (DPHW 26B); John, planter of Catalina, 1818 (DPHW 72); John, planter of Carbonear, 1820 (DPHW 48); Susanna Snuke, of Heart's Content, 1825 (Nfld. Archives KCRC); Benjamin Snook, of Fortune, 1827 (DPHW 106); Samuel, of Western Cul-de-sac (Burgeo-La Poile district), 1835 (DPHW 30); Robert, fisherman of Sagona, 1853 (DPHW 104); George Snoke, of Petit Fort, 1871 (Lovell); John Snook, of Bay of Islands, 1871 (Lovell); Samuel, cooper of Gaultois, 1871 (Lovell).

Modern status: Snook, scattered, especially at Sunnyside (Trinity B.), Grand Bank, Sagona Island and St. Albans; Snooks, scattered, especially in the Humber West districts.

Place names: Snook Bank 47-36 59-19; —— Cove (Labrador), —— Point (Labrador) 54-13 57-46; Snook(s) Cove (Labrador) 54-04 58-34; Snooks Arm 49-51 55-42; —— —— (or East) Pond 49-52 55-44; Snooks Brook 46-56 55-59, 48-13 53-54; —— Harbour 48-10 53-53, 47-44 55-57, 47-35 59-07, —— Island 47-35 59-07; —— Head 49-50 55-42; —— Island (Labrador) 52-22 55-43; —— Point 47-53 55-49; —— Rocks (Labrador) 54-16 58-11; —— Colt 47-44 54-58.

SNOW, a surname of England and Ireland from Old English *snāw – (one with) snow (-white hair), or born or baptized at a time of great snow. (Reaney, Cottle, MacLysaght 73).

Traced by Guppy in Devon, Essex and Staffordshire.

In Newfoundland:

Family tradition: William John and his brother from England, deserted their ship at Salmon Cove Point (Port de Grave district) and settled at Salmon Cove (Port de Grave district) about 1830 (MUN Geog.).

Early instances: John and Sons, of Harbour Grace, 1765, property "in possession of the Family for upwards of 90 years," that is, before 1675 (CO 199.18); John, of Port de Grave, 1760, property "in possession of the Family for 82 years," that is, 1678

(CO 199.18); John, of Kelly's Island, 1708–9 (CO 194.4); William, of Bay Roberts, 1795, property "in possession of the Family for 81 years," that is, 1714 (CO 199.18); William, married at St. John's, 1782 (DPHW 26D); Edward, John and William, of Cole Lees (now Coley's) Point, (CO 199.18); James, of Fogo, 1803 (D'Alberti 13); Jacob, of Bareneed (Port de Grave district), 1816 (Nfld. Archives L165); George, planter of Clowns Cove (Carbonear), 1836 (DPHW 48); George, fisherman of Freshwater (Carbonear), 1840 (DPHW 48); William, of Herring Neck, 1842, of Stone Harbour, 1852 (DPHW 85, 86); James, of Black Island (Twillingate district), 1844 (DPHW 86); George, granted land at Carbonear, 1847 (Nfld. Archives, Registry Crown Lands); Charles, granted land at Clarke's Beach, 1855 (Nfld. Archives, Registry Crown Lands); Isaac, fisherman of Brigus Goulds, 1857 (DPHW 35); John, of Quidi Vidi, 1857 (DPHW 29); Thomas, of Salmon Cove (Port de Grave), 1858 (DPHW 35); Thomas, of Little Bay Islands, 1859 (DPHW 92); William, of Exploits, 1860 (DPHW 92); John (and others), granted land at Spaniards Bay Pond, 1861 (Nfld. Archives, Registry Crown Lands); widespread in Lovell 1871.

Modern status: Widespread, especially at Bay Roberts, Hallstown (Port de Grave district), Clarke's Beach, Botwood, Lewisporte and in the Carbonear-Bay de Verde district.

Place names (not necessarily from the surname): Snow (or Snow's) Island (Labrador) 55-21 59-40; —— Lake (Labrador) 53-26 65-39; Snows Pond 47-28 53-23.

SODERO, a surname of Italy traced by Dr. G.W. Sodero; the Frenchified form Sodereau, untraced in France, indicates the pronunciation of Sodero.

Family traditions: Joseph Sodereau (?1830–1910), of Italian-French descent, having fought with Garibaldi and in the Crimean War, settled in Harbour Breton in the 1860s; J.W. Sodero, son of the preceding, telegraphist of Harbour Breton.

In Newfoundland:

Early instances: Joseph Sodero (? 1832–1910), son of Giuseppi and Rosa, shopkeepers of Pisa (Italy), married at English Harbour West, 1864 (D.A. Macdonald); J.W. Soders [for Sodero], merchant of Harbour Breton, 1871 (Lovell).

Modern status: Rare, at Harbour Breton and St. Andrews (St. George's district) (Electors 1955).

SOLO, a surname of unascertained origin.
In Newfoundland:
Modern status: Rare, at Corner Brook.

SOM(M)ERS, SUMMERS, surnames of England and Ireland, ? from Old French *somier* – sumpter, packhorse man, muleteer; also in Ireland in Connacht for (O)Somahan, *Ó Somacháin*, Ir. *somachán* – soft, innocent person, in Ulster occasionally a synonym of MacGovern, *Mag Shamhráin*, Ir. *samhradh* – summer. (Reaney, Cottle, MacLysaght).

Guppy traced Somers in Somerset, Summers in Devon, Gloucestershire, Northumberland and Somerset; MacLysaght traced Somers, Summers in Leinster, Connacht and Ulster.

In Newfoundland:

Early instances: James Summers, merchant of St. John's, ? 1765, 1768 (CO 194.16, DPHW 26C); Joseph, of Gooseberry Cove (Carbonear), 1800 (CO 199.18); Elizabeth ? Summers, of Portugal Cove, 1807 (Nfld. Archives BRC); Agnes ? Somers, of Belle Isle (now Bell Island), 1813 (Nfld. Archives BRC); Thomas Summers, from Paulpesty Parish (unidentified) (Co. Wexford), married at St. John's, 1815 (Nfld. Archives BRC); John, of King's Cove, 1816 (Nfld. Archives KCRC); Catherine, from Co. Wexford, married at Catalina, 1827 (Nfld. Archives KCRC); Judith, of Harbour Grace Parish, 1827 (Nfld. Archives HGRC); Edward, of Harbour Main, 1828 (Nfld. Archives BRC); William, of Hants Harbour, 1828 (DPHW 59); George Summers or Somers, "sometimes known as Somerton," of Portugal Cove, 1830, 1838 (DPHW 26B, 30); Joseph Summers, planter of Flat Rock (Carbonear), 1836 (DPHW 48); Thomas, from England, planter of Portugal Cove, died 1837 (*Times* 9 Aug 1837); Peter Summers or Somers, of Blow-me-down (Carbonear), 1849, of Otterbury (Carbonear), 1856 (DPHW 49); Milo Summers, from New Ross (Co. Wexford), of Harbour Main, 1851 (*Newfoundlander* 27 Mar 1851); Philip Somers, of Topsail, 1871 (Lovell); John Summers, butcher and cattle dealer of Brigus, 1871 (Lovell); James, of Random Sound, 1871 (Lovell); John, of Victoria Village, 1871 (Lovell).

Modern status: Somers, scattered, especially at Carbonear; Sommers, at Victoria (Carbonear district) and Buchans; Summers, scattered, especially at St. John's.

Place names (not necessarily from the surname): Somers Rock 48-36 53-30; Summer Cove (Labrador) 54-08 58-25, 55-13 59-12; Summerford 49-29 54-47; —— Arm 49-29 54-40; Summerside 48-59 57-59; Summerville 48-27 53-33.

SOMERTON, a surname of England from Old English *sumortūn* – summer dwelling, a place to which cattle were taken and people removed during the summer, or from the English place name Somerton (Lincolnshire, Norfolk, Oxfordshire, Somerset, Suffolk). (Cottle, Ekwall). *See also* SOMERS.

In Newfoundland:

Early instance: T., in possession of property in fishery at Portugal Cove, 1794–5 (Census 1794–5).

Modern status: Scattered, especially at Bell Island and Portugal Cove.

SOOLEY, SUL(L)EY, surnames of England, ? from the French place name Sully (Calvados). (Spiegelhalter).

Guppy traced Sully in Somerset; Spiegelhalter traced Sull(e)y in Devon.

In Newfoundland:

Family traditions: Alfred Sooley, of Hearts Content, was the son of William ——, a Norwegian whaler who settled in Newfoundland and changed his name to Sooley (MUN Folklore). Ned (1814–), from England, settled at Hearts Delight in 1860 (MUN Geog.).

Early instances: Daniel Sulys, fisherman of Trinity (Trinity B.), 1757 (DPHW 64); Richard Suly(s), of Trinity Bay, 1766 (DPHW 64); Thomas Sooley, of Trinity Bay, 1780 (DPHW 64); Edward, occupier of fishing room, Hearts Content, Winter 1800–01 (Census Trinity B.); Thomas, proprietor and occupier of fishing room, Turks Cove (Trinity B.), Winter 1800–01 (Census Trinity B.); William Sul(e)y, planter of New Harbour (Trinity B.), 1823 (DPHW 64); John Sooley, planter of Hearts Delight, 1823 (DPHW 64B); Margaret Sully, of Harbour Grace Parish, 1827 (Nfld. Archives HGRC); M., of St. John's, 1832 (*Newfoundlander* 20 Sep 1832); Mark Sully and William Sulley, of Dildo Cove, 1871 (Lovell); John Sully, of Old Shop (Trinity B.), 1871 (Lovell).

Modern status: Sooley, especially at Hearts Delight; Suley, scattered; Sulley, at St. John's and St. Anthony.

Place names: Sooleys Gullies 47-50 53-16.

SOPER, a surname of England and Jersey (Channel Islands) from Old English *sāpe* – (maker or seller of) soap. (Reaney, Turk).

Traced by Guppy in Devon.

In Newfoundland:

Family tradition: Thomas (–1760), a boatbuilder from Halifax (Yorkshire WR), settled near Cupids (MUN Folklore).

Early instances: John Soaper, ? of St. John's, 1751 (CO 194.13); John Soper, planter of Freshwater (Carbonear), 1812 (DPHW 48); Jonas, captain of

Cupids, 1824 (DPHW 34); Esther, of Grand Bank, 1824 (DPHW 106); George Soaper, planter of Carbonear, 1825 (DPHW 48); Thomas Soper, of Bonavista, 1826 (DPHW 70); John So(a)per, planter of Hants Harbour, 1827 (DPHW 58); —— Soper, of Harbour Grace, 1832 (*Newfoundlander* 19 Jul 1832); John, from Devon, of St. John's, died 1835, aged 41 (*Times* 28 Oct 1835); Thomas, of Caplin Cove (Trinity South district), 1842 (DPHW 59A); Henry Sopen, of Old Shop (Trinity B.), 1871 (Lovell).

Modern status: Scattered, especially at Hants Harbour and St. John's.

Place names: Sopers 48-57 58-02; —— Rock 47-34 53-11.

SORENSEN, SORENSON, surnames of Sweden and Norway – son of *Soren*.

In Newfoundland:

Early instance: George Sorenson, of Harbour Breton ? 1857 (DPHW 104).

Modern status: Sorensen, unique, at St. John's; Sorenson, rare, at St. John's.

SOULIER(S), surnames of France, variants of Solier – dweller in a bungalow or flat-roofed house, or a maker or seller of shoes. (Dauzat).

Traced by Dauzat in the region of Lyons.

In Newfoundland:

Modern status: Soulier, Souliers, rare, at St. John's.

SOUTHCOTT, a surname of England – (dweller in the) southern cottage, or from the English place names Southcott (Devon, Berkshire, Buckinghamshire, Wiltshire), Southcote, Southacott (Devon). (Cottle, Spiegelhalter).

Traced by Spiegelhalter in Devon.

In Newfoundland:

Family tradition: James (1824–), from Essex, England, settled at St. John's about 1875 (MUN Folklore).

Early instances: James, soldier of St. John's, 1813 (DPHW 26B); J. and J.T., builders of St. John's, 1852 (*Newfoundlander* 21 Jun 1852).

Modern status: At Ship Cove (Burin district) (*Electors* 1955) and Grand Falls.

SOUTHWELL, a surname of England and Ireland – (dweller by the) southern spring or well, or from the English place names Southwell (Dorset, Nottinghamshire) or Southill (Devon). (Cottle, Spiegelhalter).

Traced by Guppy in Hampshire, by Spiegelhalter in Devon, and by MacLysaght ? in Co. Cork.

In Newfoundland:

Early instances: ——, of St. John's, 1830 (*Newfoundlander* 30 Dec 1830); William, of Harbour Grace Parish, 1844 (Nfld. Archives HGRC); William, of Upper Small Point (now Kingston), 1871 (Lovell).

Modern status: Scattered, especially at Carbonear.

SPARK(E)S, surnames of England from Old Norse *sparkr*, *spræk* – lively, sprightly, or ? Old English *spearca* – spark, small portion, or ? the Old English personal name *Spearh(e)afoc* – sparrowhawk. (Reaney, Cottle, Spiegelhalter).

Guppy traced Sparkes in Sussex, Sparks in Devon and Somerset; Spiegelhalter traced Spark(e)s in Devon.

In Newfoundland:

Family traditions: George Sparkes, from England, settled at Lance Cove (Bell Island) in the early 1800s (MUN Hist.). John, from Northern Ireland, settled at Greenspond; his son later moved to Glovertown (MUN Folklore). William, from England, settled at Greenspond; some of his descendants moved to Glovertown (MUN Folklore). Joseph and his parents, from England, settled at Bull Cove (Conception B.); later, in the mid-19th century, he moved to French's Cove (Bay Roberts) (MUN Folklore). Eliab Sporks, from Ireland, settled in Newfoundland about 1847 and changed his name to Sparkes to avoid being pressed into the army; his son Ephraim John was born at Lower Island Cove (MUN Folklore).

Early instances: George Spark(e), of Witless Bay, 1676, of Balene (now Bauline), 1677 (CO 1), William, of St. John's Harbour, 1703 (CO 194.3); Ambrose Sparks, of Brigus, 1804, property "in possession of the Family for 40 years," that is, 1764 (CO 199.18); John, of Bay Roberts, 1787 (CO 199.18); Ambrose Spark(e)s, of Harbour Grace, 1791–2 (USPG); Jenny Sparke and Thomas Sprake, of Fogo, 1821 (USPG); Ambrose Spark(e)s, planter of Bull Cove (Conception B.), 1825 (DPHW 34); Basil Sparks, of Greenspond, 1826 (Nfld. Archives KCRC); Anastasia, of Joe Batts Arm, 1826 (Nfld. Archives KCRC); Ambrose, of Lower Island Cove, 1856 (DPHW 55); William, granted land at Spaniards Bay Pond, 1858 (Nfld. Archives, Registry Crown Lands); William, of Bell Island, 1871 (Lovell); John, planter of Bloody Bay (Bonavista B.), 1871 (Lovell).

Modern status: Sparkes, scattered, especially at Lower Island Cove, Georgetown (Port de Grave district), Glovertown and St. John's; Sparks, rare, at St. John's.

Place names: Sparks Cove 49-31 55-25; —— Gully 47-28 53-20.

SPARROW, a surname of England and Ireland from Old English *spearwa* – sparrow, flutterer. (Reaney, Cottle, MacLysaght 73).

Traced by Guppy in Essex, Gloucestershire and Suffolk, by Spiegelhalter in Devon, and by MacLysaght mainly in Co. Wexford since the seventeenth century.

In Newfoundland:

Early instances: Martin, of Brunet (Island) (Fortune B.), 1871 (Lovell); James (and others), of Little Placentia (now Argentia), 1871 (Lovell); Robert and Thomas, fishermen of Ship Harbour (Placentia B.), 1871 (Lovell).

Modern status: At St. John's, Holyrood and in the Placentia East, Humber West districts.

Place names (not necessarily from the surname): Sparrow Point 47-21 53-55; —— Cove Point 49-24 55-34.

SPEARNS, ? a Newfoundland variant of the surnames of England Spearon, Sperring, Spurren from Old French *esperon* – (maker or seller of) spur(s), or ? a variant of the surname of Ireland Mac Sparran, *Mac an Sparáin*, Ir. *sparán* – purse. (Weekley *Surnames*, MacLysaght).

Mac Sparran traced by MacLysaght in Cos. Derry and Antrim.

In Newfoundland:

Early instances: Thomas Speering, of Great St. Lawrence, 1765 (CO 194.16); John (and others) Spearns, of Great St. Lawrence, 1871 (Lovell).

Modern status: At St. John's, Kingmans (Ferryland district), St. Lawrence and Little St. Lawrence.

Place names: Speerin Cove, —— Point 46-55 55-21.

SPECKER, a surname of Germany containing the element *Speck* – bacon, lard, fat, blubber, or one who lives on the corduroy road, a road of tree-trunks laid across a swamp or marsh. (Heinzte-Cascorbi).

In Newfoundland:

Modern status: Rare, at Corner Brook.

SPENCE, a surname of England, Scotland and Ireland from Old French *despense*, Middle English *spense*, *spence* – (one who worked at or was in charge of the) larder, buttery. (Reaney, Cottle, Black, MacLysaght). *See also* SPENCER.

Traced by Guppy in Yorkshire, by Spiegelhalter in Devon, and by MacLysaght in Cos. Antrim and Down where it is the name of a branch of the Scottish clan MacDuff.

In Newfoundland:

Early instances: Richard, of Trinity (unspecified), 1821 (Nfld. Archives KCRC); Daniel, of Harbour Grace Parish, 1822 (Nfld. Archives HGRC); Richard Spense, from Waterford, married at St. John's, 1823 (Nfld. Archives BRC); Ann Spence, of Greenspond, 1823 (Nfld. Archives KCRC); Richard, of St. John's, 1841 (*Newfoundlander* 2 Dec 1841); Levinia, of Old Perlican, 1849 (DPHW 58); James, fisherman of French Island Harbour (St. Barbe district), 1865 (DPHW 95); George and Samuel, of Flower's Cove (St. Barbe district), 1871 (Lovell); John, sailor, and John, master mariner, of Harbour Grace, 1871 (Lovell); Alexander, fisherman of Port de Grave, 1871 (Lovell).

Modern status: At Corner Brook, Whitbourne (*Electors* 1955), Deer Lake and in the St. Barbe district.

SPENCER, a surname of England, Spenser of England and Ireland, from Old French *despensier*, Anglo-French *espenser* – dispenser (of provisions), butler, house steward; in Ireland also for (Mac) Spillan(e), *Mac Spelláin*, Ir. *speal* – scythe.

Traced by Guppy in the Midlands (especially Warwickshire and Yorkshire), by Spiegelhalter in Devon, and by MacLysaght ? in Co. Offaly.

In Newfoundland:

Early instances: Matthew, of Bay de Verde, 1709 (CO 194.4); William, of Newfoundland, 1730 (CO 194.23); Christopher, of Trinity Harbour (unspecified), 1772 (CO 194.30); Maurice, ? of Greenspond, 1776 (CO 194.33); Christopher Spenser, of Carbonear, 1795 (CO 199.18); William Spencer, of Trinity (Trinity B.), 1795 (DPHW 64); Rev. Aubry, appointed J.P. for Ferryland district, 1819 (D'Alberti 29); Thomas and John, planters of Twillingate, 1820 (USPG); William, of Grand Bank, 1822 (DPHW 106); John, of Fortune, 1824 (DPHW 109); William, planter of Jigging Hole (Trinity North district), 1829 (DPHW 64B); Margaret Spenser, married at St. John's, 1833 (Nfld. Archives BRC); Matthew Spencer, of Hermitage Cove (Hermitage B.), 1835 (DPHW 30); Stephen, fisherman of West Cul de Sac, 1837 (DPHW 102); George Spencer or Spenser, fisherman of Port de Grave, 1839 (DPHW 39); Josiah, of New Bay (Green B.), 1841 (DPHW 88); Abram, of Pass Island (Fortune B.), 1845 (DPHW 102); Robert, born 1846, labourer, son of John and Priscilla of Sturminster

Newton (Dorset), servant to Newman and Co., Harbour Breton 1862, married there 1876 (D.A. Macdonald); Eliakim, of Seal Bay Head (Twillingate district), 1856 (DPHW 86); scattered in Lovell 1871.

Modern status: Scattered, especially at Channel.

Place names: Spencer Bank (Labrador) 51-42 56-26; Spencer(s) Cove 47-40 54-05; Spencer Point 47-53 54-13; Spencers (or Collett) Cove 47-35 54-05; —— Dock 49-30 55-45; Josiah Spencer Cove 49-30 55-19.

SPICER, a surname of England from Old French *espicier, especier* – spice-seller, grocer, druggist, apothecary. (Reaney, Cottle).

Traced by Guppy in Dorset and by Spiegelhalter in Devon.

In Newfoundland:

Early instances: John, of Greenspond, 1820 (DPHW 76), John, planter of Silly Cove (now Winterton), 1825 (DPHW 64B); Ellén, from Waterford, married at St. John's, 1829 (Nfld. Archives BRC); James, of New Perlican, 1830 (DPHW 30); Stephen, fisherman of La Plante (Burgeo-La Poile district), 1864 (DPHW 97).

Modern status: At Winterton (*Electors* 1955) and in the Burgeo-La Poile district.

Place name: Spicer Rock 47-14 54-41.

SPINGLE, ? a Newfoundland variant of the surnames of England Spigurnel, Spick(er)nell, Middle English *spigurnel* from Anglo-Latin – sealer of the King's writs in Chancery. (Spiegelhalter, Cottle).

Spiegelhalter traced Spigurnel in Devon.

In Newfoundland:

Early instances: John Spikernell (Pikernell in 1677, Spikenell in 1681), of Old Perlican, 1675 (CO 1); James Spic(k)nell, of Cold Harbour (Bonavista North district), 1850, 1856 (DPHW 76).

Modern status: Rare, at Brig Bay (St. Barbe district).

SPOONER, a surname of England from Old English *spōn* – (maker of) roofing-shingle(s) or ? spoon(s). (Reaney, Cottle).

Traced by Reaney as mainly a northern name.

In Newfoundland:

Early instances: Charles, foreman for Grand Jury, Fortune Bay, 1811 (D'Alberti 21); George, of Brigus, 1816 (Nfld. Archives L165).

Modern status: Rare, at Brigus.

SPRACKLIN, a surname of England from Old Norse *Sprakaleggr,* Old English *Spracaling* – man with creaking legs. (Reaney).

In Newfoundland:

Family traditions: ——, of German descent, came to Newfoundland from the British Isles and settled at Brigus about 1800 (MUN Folklore). The community of Charlottetown (Bonavista B.) was named after Mrs. Charlotte (Hussey) Spracklin who was the first woman settler there, in the 19th century (Anon).

Early instances: Samuel Sprackling, of Brigus, 1772, property "in possession of the Family for 70 years," that is, 1702 (CO 199.18); Samuel, planter of Cupids, 1826 (DPHW 34); —— Spracklin, on the *Dandy* in the seal fishery out of Port de Grave, 1838 (*Newfoundlander* 29 Mar 1838); Elizabeth, of Bonavista, deceased, 1854 (*Newfoundlander* 28 Sep 1854); Elizabeth, of St. John's, 1860 (DPHW 26D).

Modern status: Scattered, especially at Brigus and St. John's.

Place name: Spracklings (or Spracklins) Island (Labrador) 56-09 60-47.

SPRATT, a surname of England and Ireland, Sprot(t) of England and Scotland, from an Old English personal name **Sprot(t)* – sprout, shoot, or ? from Old English *sprot* – sprat (fish), a nickname for a short person. (Reaney, Spiegelhalter).

Spiegelhalter traced Spratt, Sprott in Devon, Guppy traced Spratt in Devon, and MacLysaght Spratt in Ulster.

In Newfoundland:

Early instances: Samuel, from Wareham (Dorset), planter in Newfoundland, 1747 (Dorset County Record Office per Kirwin); Samuel, J.P., Placentia, 1753 (CO 194.13); E. Sprett, of St. John's, 1831 (*Newfoundlander* 29 Dec 1831); Margaret Sprat, married at St. John's, 1833 (Nfld. Archives BRC); Edward, of King's Cove Parish, 1836 (Nfld. Archives KCRC).

Modern status: At St. John's.

SPRY, a surname of England – (dweller on the) land overgrown with brushwood, as in the place name Sprytown (Devon), or a nickname from Middle English *sprei* – quick, active. (Spiegelhalter, Gover).

Traced by Guppy in Cornwall and Devon.

In Newfoundland:

Early instances: John, surgeon of ? St. John's, ? 1753 (CO 194.13); John, of St. John's, 1802 (DPHW 26D); John, of Harbour Grace Parish, 1834, ? of Northern Bay, 1838 (Nfld. Archives HGRC, DPHW 54); Thomas, printer of Carbonear, 1838, of St. John's, 1854 (DPHW 48, *Newfoundlander* 21 Dec 1854, 14 Jan 1858).

Modern status: At St. John's.

SPURRELL, a surname of England, a variant of Spurwell, as in the English place name Spurrells Cross (Devon) or from the place name Spirewell (Devon) – the spring by the reeds or sedges. (Spiegelhalter, Gover).

Traced by Guppy in Devon.

In Newfoundland:

Early instances: John Spurdel, fisherman of Trinity (Trinity B.), 1758 (DPHW 64); John Spurdle or Spurrle, of Trinity Bay, 1782 (DPHW 64); John Spurrell, of Greenspond, 1815 (DPHW 76); Thomas, of Old Bonaventure, 1815 (DPHW 64); William Spurrel(l), planter of Cuckold's Cove (now Dunfield), 1833, of Island Cove (now Dunfield), 1842 (DPHW 64B); Moses Spurrel, planter of Sulley's Cove (Trinity North district), 1841 (DPHW 64B); J. Spurrell, Road Commissioner for Flower Cove to Fools (now Pools) Island area (Bonavista B.), 1847 (*Nfld. Almanac*); Amelia, baptized at Heart's Ease, 1849 (DPHW 64B); John, granted land at Pools Island, 1854 (Nfld. Archives, Registry Crown Lands); Mary, of St. John's, 1858 (DPHW 26D); Susanna Spiral (for Spurrell), of Fox Harbour (Trinity South district), 1858 (DPHW 59).

Modern status: Scattered, especially at Badger's Quay, Valleyfield, St. John's and in the Trinity North district with large concentrations at Butter Cove, Dunfield and Gooseberry Cove.

SPURVEY, a surname of England from the English place names Spurway Barton, Spurways (Devon) or a variant of the surname Spurrier – spur-maker. (Gover, Spiegelhalter).

Spiegelhalter traced Spurrier and Spurway in Devon.

In Newfoundland:

Family tradition: George, Martin and Matthew Spurrier, Sporier or Spurrvey, from England, were the first settlers of Fox Harbour (Placentia B.) in the late 1790s or early 1800s; the name later became Spurvey (MUN Hist.).

Early instances: Richard Spurway, boatkeeper of Bay Bulls, 1681 (CO 1); William Spurrier, of Oderin (Placentia B.), 1774, merchant of St. Mary's, 1774 (CO 194.32); Christopher and Co., of Poole (Dorset), at Burin, 1812 (D'Alberti 22).

Modern status: At Fox Harbour (Placentia B.).

SQUAREY, SQUARRY, surnames of England, ? anglicizations of the French surname Esquerré – recalcitrant, stubborn, a name of Spanish or Basque origin. (Dauzat, Barber).

Matthews found Squarry widespread in Devon.

In Newfoundland:

Early instances: —— Squarry, of Quidi Vidi, 1703 (CO 194.3); Thomas Squary, of St. John's, 1705 (CO 194.3); William, of Bay Bulls, 1708 (CO 194.4); John Squarey, from Shaldon (Devon), married at St. John's, 1845 (*Royal Gazette* 9 Aug 1845); Robert Thomas, editor, proprietor and printer of *Harbour Grace Standard and Conception Bay Advertiser*, of Harbour Grace, 1871 (Lovell).

Modern status: Squarey, at Channel; Squarry, unique, at Channel.

Place name: Squarey Islet (or Squarry Island) 48-39 53-08.

SQUIBB, a surname of England – an insignificant, paltry fellow. (Bardsley, *OED*).

Traced by Matthews in Dorset.

In Newfoundland:

Early instance: Francis, Justice of Trinity district, ? 1730 (CO 194.9).

Modern status: At St. John's and Carbonear.

Place name: Squib Point 47-48 53-46.

SQUIRE(S), surnames of England from Old French *escuyer*, Middle English *squyer* – shield-bearer, esquire, a young gentleman attending a knight. (Reaney, Cottle). *See also* SWYERS.

Traced by Guppy in Bedfordshire, Devon, Leicestershire, Rutlandshire and Nottinghamshire, with Squires "far the least frequent, occurring in Leicestershire and Nottinghamshire."

In Newfoundland:

Family traditions: George Squire, from Winterborne Zelstone (Dorset), settled at Catalina; he later moved to Salvage (Bonavista B.). His son Joseph, from Salvage, was the first settler of Eastport in 1868 (MUN Folklore, Family). Apollus Squires, from England, settled at Greenspond (MUN Folklore).

—— Squires, from Ireland, settled in the St. John's area (MUN Folklore).

Early instances: Benjamin Squires, of Bay Roberts, 1765, property "in possession of the Family for more than 90 years," that is, before 1675 (CO 199.18); Benjamin Squire, of Great Belle Isle (now Bell Island), 1770 (DPHW 26C); John Squires, fisherman of Torbay, 1794–5, "24 years in Newfoundland," that is, 1770–1 (Census 1794–5); William, shoreman of St. John's, 1794–5, "20 years in Newfoundland," that is, 1774–5 (Census 1794–5); John, of Southside Broad Cove (now St. Phillips), 1790 (CO 199.18); Sarah, of Freshwater (Carbonear), 1791 (CO 199.18); James and George Squire, of Placentia, 1794 (D'Alberti 5); John, servant of

Battle Harbour (Labrador), 1795 (MUN Hist.); Simon Squires, of Bonavista, 1798 (DPHW 70); John Squire, of Fogo, 1803 (D'Alberti 13); William Squires, of Harbour Grace Parish, 1828 (Nfld. Archives HGRC); Maria, of Brine's (? for Bryants) Cove, 1839 (DPHW 26D); George, of Salvage, 1840 (DPHW 76); Simon, planter of Herring Neck, 1850, of Canister Cove (Twillingate district), 1855, of Pike's Arm (Twillingate district), 1859 (DPHW 85); Thomas, of Seldom-Come-By, 1852 (DPHW 84); Henry Squire, from Dartmouth (Devon), married at St. John's, 1852 (*Newfoundlander* 26 Aug 1852); John Squires, of Salt Harbour (Twillingate district), 1856 (DPHW 85); Thomas, of Leading Tickles, 1856 (DPHW 86); James, of Stone Harbour (Twillingate district), 1857 (DPHW 85); scattered in Lovell 1871.

Modern status: Squire, in the Bonavista North and South districts especially at Eastport (Bonavista South district); Squires, widespread, especially at St. John's, St. Phillips, Sibley's Cove and Old Perlican.

Place names (not necessarily from the surname): Squier Cove 47-36 57-20; Squire Island 49-26 54-56; The Squire (Labrador) 53-07 55-44; Squier Back Cove 47-35 57-18; Sir Richard Squires Park

STABB, a surname of England, ? a variant of Stubb, from Old English *stubb* – (dweller by the) tree-stump, or *stybb* – stub, stumpy. (Spiegelhalter, Reaney, Cottle).

Traced by Spiegelhalter in Devon.

In Newfoundland:

Early instances: Thomas, of St. John's, 1809 (CO 194.48); Esau, merchant of Ferryland, 1823 (DPHW 31); Nicholas, deputy sheriff of Harbour Grace, 1829 (*Newfoundlander* 19 Feb 1829); John, captain of Carbonear, 1836 (DPHW 48); William, from Torquay (Devon), married at St. John's, 1842 (DPHW 26D).

Modern status: Unique, at St. John's, in the name of the firm Henry J. Stabb & Co.

STACEY, a surname of England and Ireland, a diminutive of *Stace* the vernacular form of the baptismal name Eustace, ? from the Greek – fruitful, the name of two saints, one of them, with St. Hubert, a patron saint of huntsmen. (Withycombe, Reaney, Cottle, MacLysaght 73).

Traced by Guppy in Cornwall, Devon, Hampshire, Hertfordshire, Somerset, Surrey and Sussex, and by MacLysaght in Cos. Wicklow and Wexford.

In Newfoundland:

Family tradition: Charles, from England, settled at Rushoon (Placentia B.) in the mid 1800s (MUN Folklore).

Early instances: Moses Stacy, married at St. John's, 1767 (DPHW 26D); Thomas Stacey, of Battle Harbour (Labrador), 1787, of Fogo, 1789 (MUN Hist.); John, of Garia, 1856 (DPHW 98); James (and others) Stacy, of Lamaline, 1871 (Lovell); Charles Stacey, of Rushoon, 1871 (Lovell); Thomas, fisherman of Sound Island (Placentia B.), 1871 (Lovell).

Modern status: Scattered, especially at St. John's, Swift Current and Point May (Burin district).

Place name: Stacey's Point 47-50 54-08.

STACK, a surname of England and Ireland from Old Norse *stakkr* – (builder of or one as big as a) haystack. (Reaney).

Traced by MacLysaght in Co. Kerry since the thirteenth century.

In Newfoundland:

Early instances: Thomas, of St. John's, 1797 (DPHW 26D); Garret, of Northern Bay, 1806 (CO 199.18); James, from Moore (unidentified) (Co. Kerry), married at St. John's, 1813 (Nfld. Archives BRC); William, of Harbour Grace Parish, 1819 (Nfld. Archives HGRC); Mary, of Petty Harbour, 1821 (Nfld. Archives BRC); Thomas and John, granted land at Outer Cove (St. John's), 1851 (Nfld. Archives, Registry Crown Lands); John, of Cat's Cove (now Conception Harbour), 1871 (Lovell).

Modern status: At Gander, Outer Cove, St. John's and Petty Harbour.

STAFFORD, a surname of England, Ireland and Guernsey (Channel Islands) from the English place names Stafford (Devon, Somerset, Dorset), Stowford (Devon, Wiltshire) or Stoford (Somerset, Wiltshire); in Ireland sometimes for Mac Stocker, *Mac an Stocaire* – trumpeter. (Cottle, MacLysaght, Turk).

Traced by Guppy in Derbyshire, Leicestershire, Rutlandshire, by Spiegelhalter in Devon, and by MacLysaght in Co. Wexford and Ulster.

In Newfoundland:

Early instances: John Staford, of St. John's, about 1795 (Exeter Public Library Archives per Kirwin); Robert Stafford, from Rose Garland Parish (Co. Wexford), married at St. John's, 1805 (Nfld. Archives BRC); John, of Harbour Grace Parish, 1816 (Nfld. Archives HGRC); Maurice, of King's Cove, 1826 (Nfld. Archives KCRC); Michael, aged 28, from Ireland, deserted the brig *Ardent* at St. John's, 1837 (*Times* 14 Jun 1837); Martin, of ? Ferryland, 1838 (*Newfoundlander* 25 Oct 1838); John, ? of Northern Bay, 1840 (DPHW 54); John, of Harbour Grace, 1868 (Nfld. Archives HGRC); Michael, miner of La Manche (Placentia B.), 1871 (Lovell).

Modern status: At St. John's and Topsail.

STAGG, a surname of England from Old English *stagga* – stag, a nickname for which "various reasons suggest themselves." (Cottle).

Traced by Spiegelhalter in Devon.

In Newfoundland:

Early instances: Edward Stag, of Bonavista, 1792 (USPG); Thomas, of Kings Cove Parish, 1837 (Nfld. Archives KCRC); Thomas Stag(g), of Catalina, 1838 (DPHW 67); Joseph, of Little Catalina, 1842 (DPHW 67); Robert Stagg, of Birchy Cove (Bonavista B.), 1871 (Lovell); John, fisherman of English Harbour (Bonavista B.), 1871 (Lovell).

Modern status: Scattered, especially at Bonavista, Little Catalina and Cape Freels.

Place names: Many place names contain the specific Stag not from the surname.

STAINER, a surname of England from Middle English *steyne* – to stain, hence stainer, painter, or ? from Old French *estanier* – tin-worker. (Reaney, Spiegelhalter).

Traced by Spiegelhalter in Devon.

In Newfoundland:

Early instances: John Stayner, of St. John's, 1824 (DPHW 26B); George Stainer, fisherman of Flat Islands (Placentia B.), 1871 (Lovell).

Modern status: Rare, at Woody Island (Placentia B.) (*Electors* 1955).

STAMP, a surname of England and Ireland (though not given in MacLysaght etc.), ? from the French place name Étampes (Aisne, Seine-et-Oise). (Weekley *Romance*, Reaney *Origin*).

Traced by Guppy in Lincolnshire, and in Ireland (Tel. Dir.).

In Newfoundland:

Family tradition: ———, from Wexford, settled at St. John's (MUN Folklore).

Early instances: Anty [sic], of Trepassey, 1830 (Nfld. Archives BRC); Sara, married at St. John's, 1837 (Nfld. Archives BRC); Richard and Richard, of Flat Rock (St. John's), 1871 (Lovell); John (and others), of Peter's River and Holyrood, 1871 (Lovell); John (and others), of St. John's, 1871 (Lovell).

Modern status: Scattered, especially at St. Vincent's and St. John's.

STANBURY, a surname of England from the English place names Stanborough (Devon), Stanbury (Devon, Yorkshire WR) – stone-fortress, or ? from an Old English personal feminine name *Stanburh – "of

the same tough meaning." (Reaney, Cottle). *See also* STANSBURY.

Traced by Guppy in Devon and by Reaney in Lancashire.

In Newfoundland:

Early instance: Edward, of St. John's, 1790 (DPHW 26C).

Modern status: Unique, at St. John's.

STANDING, a variant of the surname of England Standen from the English place name Standen (Berkshire, Kent, Lancashire, Wiltshire). (Reaney, Cottle).

Guppy traced Standen in Kent and Sussex, Standing also in Sussex; Reaney traced Standen and Standing in Lancashire.

In Newfoundland:

Modern status: Rare, at Messieurs (Burgeo-La Poile district) (*Electors* 1955).

STANFIELD, a surname of England and Scotland from the English place name Stanfield (Norfolk, Staffordshire) or – (dweller by the) stony field. (Cottle, Black). *See also* STANSFIELD.

In Newfoundland:

Early instance: Samuel, fisherman of English Harbour (Bonavista B.), 1871 (Lovell).

Modern status: Unique, at Port Blandford (*Electors* 1955).

STANFORD, a surname of England, Scotland and Ireland, from the English place name Stanford (in nine counties) – stony ford. (Cottle, MacLysaght). *See also* STANSFORD.

Traced by Guppy in Dorset, Suffolk and Sussex (though Cottle would expect it in other counties), by Spiegelhalter in Devon, and by MacLysaght mainly in Co. Cavan.

In Newfoundland:

Family tradition: Henry (1845–) born at Carbonear, of English descent, [the family having] settled at Adams Cove about 1800 (MUN Geog.).

Early instance: Owen, joiner of St. John's, 1850 (DPHW 29).

Modern status: Scattered, especially at St. John's.

Place names: Stanford River 49-57 57-45; Stanfords River (Labrador) 54-29 59-29.

STANLEY, a surname of England and Ireland from the English place name Stanley (in twelve counties) – stony field or clearing. (Cottle, MacLysaght).

Traced by Guppy in Gloucestershire and Warwickshire, by Spiegelhalter in Devon and by MacLysaght in Leinster and Munster.

In Newfoundland:

Family traditions: John (1810–70), from England, settled at Long Pond (Conception Bay South) in 1840 (MUN Geog.). Levi and Sons were the first settlers of Red Beach (now part of Clarenville) (MUN Hist.).

Early instances: William, planter of Hants Harbour, 1827 (DPHW 59A); Charles, of Long Pond, 1832 (DPHW 30); John, shoreman of Bird Island Cove (now Elliston), 1841 (DPHW 72); Charles, of Barr'd Islands, 1856 (DPHW 83).

Modern status: Scattered, especially at Clarenville, George's Brook (Trinity North district) and Bay Bulls Road (St. John's).

Place names (not necessarily from the surname): Stanley Cove 47-42 56-10; —— Rocks 47-15 54-59.

STANSBURY, a variant of STANBURY.

In Newfoundland:

Early instance: Edward Stainsbury or Stansbury, fisherman of St. John's, 1794–5, "20 years in Newfoundland," that is, 1774–5 (Census 1794–5).

Modern status: Unique, at St. John's.

STANSFIELD, a surname of England from the English place name Stansfield (Norfolk, Suffolk, Yorkshire WR) – stony field or ? *Stan*'s field, or ? a variant of STANFIELD.

Traced by Guppy in Yorkshire WR.

In Newfoundland:

Modern status: Rare, at Corner Brook (*Electors* 1955).

STANSFORD, ? a variant, apparently not recorded elsewhere, of STANFORD.

In Newfoundland:

Modern status: Unique, at St. John's.

STAPLES, a surname of England from the English place name Staple (Devon, Kent, Somerset), or Old English *stapol* – (dweller by the) post, pillar, or ? from the French place names Étaples (Pas-de-Calais) or Staple (Nord). (Reaney, Cottle, Spiegelhalter).

Traced by Guppy in Nottinghamshire. Spiegelhalter traced Staple(s) in Devon.

In Newfoundland:

Family tradition: John C. Staple, from Bristol, settled at English Harbour West (Fortune B.) about 1840 (MUN Folklore).

Modern status: At Corner Brook and Gander.

STAPLETON, a surname of England and Ireland, from the English place name Stapleton (in seven counties) – farm by a pillar or post or ? Stapledon (Devon). *See also* GAUL(E), *Mac an Ghaill* – son of the foreigner, adopted by some Stapletons. (Cottle, MacLysaght).

Traced by MacLysaght mainly in Cos. Kilkenny and Tipperary.

In Newfoundland:

Family tradition: William (1797–), from England or Ireland, came to St. John's in 1813 and settled at Horse Cove (now St. Thomas, Conception B.) in 1817 (MUN Geog.).

Early instances: Bruce Stappeton, married at St. John's, 1765 (DPHW 26D); William Stapleton; fisherman of St. John's, 1794–5, "20 years in Newfoundland," that is, 1774–5 (Census 1794–5); John Stapleton or Stepelton, of Harbour Grace Parish, 1808 (Nfld. Archives HGRC); James Stapleton, of Harbour Grace, 1813 (D'Alberti 23); John, of Tilting Harbour (now Tilting), 1829 (Nfld. Archives KCRC); Michael, from Ballingarry (Co. Tipperary), married at St. John's, 1830 (Nfld. Archives BRC); James, schoolmaster of Carbonear, 1845 (DPHW 48); John, fisherman of Flower's Cove, 1871 (Lovell).

Modern status: Scattered, especially at St. Thomas and Marystown.

STARES, ? a variant of the surnames of England STEAR, Steer(e)(s), from Old English *stēor* – (one like, or a keeper of the) steer(s), young ox(en). (Reaney, Cottle).

Guppy traced Stares in Hampshire; Spiegelhalter traced Stear, Steer(e) in Devon.

In Newfoundland:

Early instances: Moses Stares or Stears, of St. John's, 1772 (DPHW 26C); John Steer, of Greenspond, 1818 (DPHW 72); John, of Ferryland, 1818 (D'Alberti 28); John (1824–), from Torquay (Devon), settled at St. John's in 1827 (Mott); Richard Stears, from Totnes (Devon), of St. John's, 1835 (DPHW 26D); Captain John Steer, from Abbotskerswell (Devon), died at Anchor Point (Straits of Bell Isle), 1848 (*Nfld. Patriot* 30 Aug 1848); William Stares or Stores, of Petty Harbour, 1856 (DPHW 31); William Stears, granted land at Bay Bulls Road, 1859 (Nfld. Archives, Registry Crown Lands); John Steer, granted land at Upper Long Pond, 1863 (Nfld. Archives, Registry Crown Lands); Frank Stares, fisherman of Brooklyn (Bonavista South district), 1879 (DPHW 74).

Modern status: Stares, at Bell Island, Bonavista, Brooklyn (*Electors* 1955), Corner Brook and St. John's; Stears, unique, at Corner Brook.

Place name: Stares Point 48-24 53-51.

STARK(E), STARKS, surnames of England from Old English *stearc* – firm, stiff, tough, harsh, unyielding. (Reaney, Cottle).

Matthews traced Stark(s) in Dorset.

In Newfoundland:

Family traditions: Thomas Starkes (1799–1869), from Fordingbridge (Hampshire), settled at Nippers Harbour (Green B.), between 1820 and 1830 (MUN Geog.). William, from Yorkshire, settled at Nippers Harbour (MUN Folklore).

Early instances: Nicholas ? Starkes, ? of St. John's, ? 1706 (CO 194.24); John Starks, from Hampshire, married in the northern district, 1812 (Nfld. Archives BRC); Joshua, from Christchurch (Hampshire), planter of Joe Batts Arm, 1815, 1818 (CO 194.61, Nfld. Archives KCRC); James Stark, of Greenspond, 1815 (DPHW 76); Joshua, of Fogo, 1816 (MUN Hist.); Mary, baptized at Pinchard's Island (Bonavista B.), 1830, aged 15 (DPHW 76); George Starks, baptized at Fools (now Pools) Island (Bonavista B.), 1830, aged 16 (DPHW 76); John Stark, of Harbour Grace, 1831 (*Newfoundlander* 5 May 1831); George Starks, of Nippers Harbour, 1860 (DPHW 87); John (and others) Stark, of Groats Island (Bonavista B.), 1871 (Lovell); Henry and William Starks, of Little Fogo Islands, 1871 (Lovell).

Modern status: Stark, unique, at Corner Brook; Starkes, scattered, especially at Nippers Harbour; Starks, at Pools Island (*Electors* 1955) and Corner Brook.

Place name: Starks Bight 51-19 55-40.

STARR, a surname of England, Starrs of Ireland, from Middle English *sterre* – star, a nickname, personal name or sign-name, or ? from Old English *stær* – starling. (Reaney, Cottle, Spiegelhalter, MacLysaght).

Guppy traced Starre (? now Starr) in Lincolnshire, Spiegelhalter traced Starr in Devon, and MacLysaght traced Starr in north Tipperary and Starr(s) in Ulster.

In Newfoundland:

Modern status: Rare, at Bay Roberts.

STEAD, STEED, surnames of England from Old English *stede* – farm, estate (-worker) or the English place name Stead (Yorkshire WR), or from Old English *stēda* – stallion, stud-horse (-keeper), or as a nickname for a man of spirit, of mettle. (Reaney, Cottle).

Guppy traced Stead in Monmouthshire and Yorkshire, Steeds in Somerset. Spiegelhalter traced Stead and Steed in Devon.

In Newfoundland:

Family tradition: ―― Stead, from Devon, settled at Salvage (Bonavista B.) (MUN Folklore).

Early instances: William ? Steeds, of Bonavista, 1792 (USPG); John Steeds, planter of Bird Island Cove (now Elliston), 1821 (DPHW 72); Mary Steed, baptized at Salvage, 1831, aged 13 (DPHW 76); W.J., from Belfast, ? of St. John's, 1857 (*Newfoundlander* 18 May 1857); Frederick, of Little Catalina, 1864 (DPHW 66).

Modern status: Stead, scattered, especially at Little Catalina; Steed, in the Trinity North district (*Electors* 1955).

STEARS. *See* STARES

STEELE, a surname of England, Scotland, Ireland and Jersey (Channel Islands) from Old English *styæle*, *stēle* – steel (-worker), one hard as steel, firm, reliable; in Scotland from the Scots place name Steel (Ayrshire, Berwickshire, Dumfriesshire). (Reaney, Cottle, Black, Turk).

Guppy traced Steel(e) in Cheshire, Cumberland, Westmorland, Staffordshire, Suffolk and Yorkshire WR, with Steel the more frequent but both forms usually associated, and Steel south of the Forth and Clyde. MacLysaght traced Steele in Ulster.

In Newfoundland:

Family tradition: John (1827–), from southern England, settled in the Smith Sound area in 1850 (MUN Geog.).

Early instances: Anthony Steel, of Newfoundland, ? 1706 (CO 194.24); John, of St. John's, 1762 (CO 194.15); Charles, occupier of fishing room, Trinity (Trinity B.), Winter 1800–01 (Census Trinity B.); Robert Steels, from Greenock, married at St. John's, 1846 (*Newfoundlander* 8 Oct 1846); Charles Steel, fisherman of Change Islands, 1849 (DPHW 83); Charles Steel(e), fisherman of Northern Bay, 1854 (DPHW 52B); John Steel, of Herring Neck, 1855, of Salt Harbour (Twillingate district), 1856, of Pike's Arm (Twillingate district), 1858 (DPHW 85); George Steele, of Muddy Hole (Bonavista North district), 1862 (DPHW 77); George Steel, of Brooklyn (Bonavista B.), 1871 (Lovell); John, of Burgum's Cove (Trinity B.), 1871 (Lovell).

Modern status: Scattered, especially at St. John's.

Place names (not necessarily from the surname): Steel (or Cairn) Mountain 48-24 58-24; ―― Point 46-58 52-56; Steele Creek (Labrador) 53-55 57-42; Steeles Brook 48-29 55-18.

STEEVES, a surname of England – son of Ste(e)ve, a diminutive of Stephen (*see* STEPHENS). (E.C. Smith).

In Newfoundland:

Modern status: Rare, at St. John's and Pouch Cove.

STEIN, a surname of England and Germany, in England from the personal names in Old Norse *Steinn*, Old Danish *Sten*; also in England and in Germany of late German origin, Old High German *stein* – stone, hence stone-worker, mason. (Reaney, Gottschald, E.C. Smith).

In Newfoundland:

Modern status: At Grand Falls, Botwood and St. John's.

STEINBRINK, a surname of Germany – (dweller in or owner of the) high-lying stony meadow or clearing. (Heintze-Cascorbi).

In Newfoundland:

Modern status: Unique, at St. John's.

STENTAFORD, a surname of England from the English place name Stentaford Land (Devon), or (dweller by the) stony ford. (Spiegelhalter).

Spiegelhalter traced Stentiford in Devon.

In Newfoundland:

Family tradition: ——, from southern England, settled at ? Hearts Content about 1830 (MUN Folklore).

Early instances: John, of St. John's, 1804 (DPHW 23); William Thomas Stentaford or Stantaford, agent of Brigus, 1831 (DPHW 34); John Stentaford, from Cornwall, inhabitant of St. John's for many years, died at Brigus, 1849, aged 74 (*Nfld. Patriot* 10 Nov 1849); Charles, of Gullys (Conception B.), 1871 (Lovell); Samuel, of Hearts Content, 1877 (DPHW 60).

Modern status: At Hearts Content (*Electors* 1955), Carbonear and St. John's.

STEPHENS, STEVENS, surnames of England and Wales, STEPHENS of Ireland and Guernsey (Channel Islands), Stephen and Steven of Scotland, and Stephen of the Micmac Indians of Newfoundland, from the baptismal name Stephen from a Greek personal name – crown, wreath, garland, borne by the first Christian martyr, occurring in England only as a monk's name before the Norman Conquest but soon afterwards a common baptismal name. In Ireland it may also be an anglicization of *Mac Giolla Stiofáin* – devotee of St. Stephen. Surnames derived from it include STEEVES, STEPHENS(ON), STEVENS(ON). (Withycombe, Reaney, Cottle, Black, MacLysaght, Turk).

Guppy found Stephens and Stevens widespread in the Midlands and south and west England, with Stephens very numerous in Cornwall, the Welsh Border counties and South Wales, and Stevens well-distributed throughout the area but best represented in the south and east. He also traced Stephen in Aberdeenshire, though Black found Stevens less common than Steven or Stephen.

In Newfoundland:

(a) Stephens: Early instances: William, of Keels, 1681 (CO 1); ——, of Quidi Vidi, 1703 (CO 194.3); Nicholas, of St. John's, 1705–06 (CO 194.22); Edward, of Conception Bay [1706] (CO 194.4); William, of Petty Harbour, 1708 (CO 194.4); Richard Stephens or Stevens, of Port de Grave, 1708–9 (CO 194.4); Edward Stephens, of Harbour Grace, 1708–9 (CO 194.4); William, in fishery at Bell Island, 1794–5, "26 years in Newfoundland," that is, 1768–9 (Census 1794–5); Thomas, of Bonavista, 1793 (USPG); Henry, of Bay de Verde, 1807 (DPHW 64); William Stephen(s), from London, married at St. John's, 1813 (Nfld. Archives BRC); Thomas Stephens, of Brigus, 1818 (Nfld. Archives L165); Richard Stephans, from Waterford, married at St. John's, 1823 (Nfld. Archives BRC); Robert Stephens, Stevens or Stephenson, of Blow-me-down (Carbonear), 1835 (DPHW 48); William Stephens, of Bareneed, 1848 (DPHW 39); Thomas, servant of Butters Cove (Placentia B.), 1871 (Lovell); Thomas, of Tacks Beach (Placentia B.), 1871 (Lovell); —— Stephen, Indian trapper, 1902 (Millais).

(b) Stevens: Early instances: William Stevens or Stephens, of St. John's Harbour, "10 years an inhabitant in 1680," that is, since 1670 (CO 1); —— Stevens, constable for Ferryland district, ? 1730, 1732 (CO 194.9); Charles Steven(s), of Bay de Verde, 1766, of Old Perlican, 1770 (DPHW 64); James Stevens, of Port de Grave, 1770 (CO 199.18); Anne, of Bell Isle (now Bell Island), 1809 (Nfld. Archives BRC); William, of Quidi Vidi, 1819 (DPHW 26B); Joseph, of White Hills (St. John's), 1822 (DPHW 26B); John, an Indian in pursuit of the Aborigines, 1828 (*Newfoundlander* 13 Feb 1828); Thomas Stevens or Stephens, of Brigus, 1825 (DPHW 34); Magdalen Stevens, of King's Cove, 1827 (Nfld. Archives KCRC); Richard, of Venison Island (Labrador), 1831 (DPHW 30); Mary, of Harbour Grace Parish, 1831 (Nfld. Archives HGRC); John, of Irelands Eye (Trinity B.), 1843 (DPHW 64B); James, ship carpenter of Little Catalina, 1845 (DPHW 72); Thomas, fisherman of Rock Harbour (Burin district), 1860 (DPHW 100) .

Modern status: Stephens, at St. John's; Stevens, scattered.

Place names (not necessarily from the surname): Stephens Pond 47-21 52-51; Stephenville 48-33 58-35; —— Pond 48-32 58-32; —— Crossing 48-30 58-26; Stevens Lake (Labrador) 53-04 66-58.

STEPHENSON, STEVENSON, surnames of England, Scotland and Ireland, and Stephenson of the Micmac Indians of Newfoundland – son of Stephen (*see* STEPHENS), or in England also from the English place name Stevenstone (Devon). (Cottle, Spiegelhalter, MacLysaght).

Guppy found Stephenson and Stevenson widespread in the Midlands, the north of England and Sussex, with Stephenson characteristic of the northern counties and Stevenson characteristic of the Midlands, Sussex and Scotland south of the Forth and Clyde. Spiegelhalter traced Stephenson and Stevenson in Devon, and Black also traced both forms in Scotland. MacLysaght traced Stephenson in Co. Limerick and Ulster, and Stevenson, Ste(e)nson and Stinson in Ulster. He found Stevenson also a synonym of the Anglo-Norman Fitzstephen.

In Newfoundland:

Family traditions: Robert Stephenson (–1880), from England, settled at Victoria (Conception B.) (MUN Geog.). ——, from Malangarie [sic], Ayrshire, settled at Corner Brook in 1917 (MUN Folklore).

Early instances: Joseph Stephenson, servant at ? Little Placentia (now Argentia) about 1730–5 (CO 194.9); William and Matthew Stevenson, of Harbour Grace, 1760 (CO 199.18); —— Stephenson, soldier of St. John's, 1767 (DPHW 26C); Henry Stevenson, of St. John's, 1797 (DPHW 26B); Matthew, of Trinity (Trinity B.), 1798 (DPHW 64); George Stephenson, of Burin, 1804 (D'Alberti 14); William Stevenson, planter of Fogo, 1808 (MUN Hist.); William, missionary of Moreton's Harbour, 1811, of Twillingate, ? 1815 (D'Alberti 21, CO 194.56); ——, of St. Mary's, 1812 (D'Alberti 22); Alexander Stephenson or Stevenson, from Oban, Argyllshire, merchant of Bay Bulls, "lived 25 years in Newfoundland," that is, since about 1814, married at St. John's, 1819, died about 1839, aged 47 (*Royal Gazette* 15 Jan 1839, *Times* 9 Jan 1839, Nfld. Archives BRC); John Stevenson, from Newcastle (Durham), of St. John's, 1834 (DPHW 26D); Thomas Stephenson, planter of Otterbury (Carbonear), 1846 (DPHW 48); Robert Stephenson or Stevens, planter of Blow-me-down (Carbonear), 1851 (DPHW 49); Collis Stephenson, planter of Western Bay, 1852 (DPHW 52A); James Stevenson, carpenter of Catalina, 1856 (DPHW 72); John Stephenson, of Harbour Grace, 1858 (*Newfoundlander* 22 Apr 1858); John Stevenson, of Victoria Village,

1871 (Lovell); Thomas Stephenson, of Bryants Cove, 1871 (Lovell); John, fisherman of Ferryland, 1871 (Lovell); John, of Halls Bay (Notre Dame B.), 1871 (Lovell); Stephen (–1952), Micmac Indian of Deer Lake (MUN Hist.).

Modern status: Stephenson, scattered; Stevenson, scattered, especially at St. John's and Harbour Grace.

Place names: Stephensons Pond 47-54 57-30; Stevenson Rocks (Labrador) 53-04 66-58; —— Islets 49-10 53-25; Stevensons Village 47-41 53-15.

STERLING, a surname of England and Ireland from Old English *stærling* – starling, used also as a personal name, or for *Easterling* – the man from the Baltic, or for Middle English *easterlin* – (maker of) coin with a star design, or a variant of STIRLING. (Weekley *Romance*, Spiegelhalter).

Traced by Spiegelhalter in Devon and by MacLysaght in Ulster.

In Newfoundland:

Early instances: John, of Harbour Grace, 1800 (CO 199.18); Edgar, merchant of Brigus, 1857 (DPHW 35); Albert Stirling or Sterling, son of William and Emma of Harbour Grace, customs officer at English Harbour West, married at Harbour Breton, 1867 (Harbour Breton Anglican Church Records per D.A. Macdonald); James, fisherman of Bay of Islands, 1871 (Lovell); Albert, of English Harbour West (Fortune B.), 1871 (Lovell).

Modern status: Rare, at Corner Brook.

STEVENS (ON). *See* STEPHENS (ON)

STEWART, a surname of England, Scotland and Ireland, with a number of variants including Steward and Stuart – steward (of a manor), keeper of a household, officer of the royal household. (Reaney, Cottle, Black, MacLysaght).

Guppy traced Stewart in Northumberland, Steward in Essex, Norfolk and Suffolk, Stuart in Lancashire, and Stewart general and Stuart scattered in Scotland. Spiegelhalter traced Stewart and Stuart in Devon. MacLysaght traced both forms in Ulster.

In Newfoundland:

Early instances: Nicholas Steward, of Petty Harbour, 1703 (CO 194.3); Thomas Stuard, servant of Trinity (? Trinity B.), 1731 (CO 194.9); Anthony Steward, carpenter of St. John's, 1794–5, "16 years in Newfoundland," that is, 1778–9 (Census 1794–5); David Stewart, from Baltinglass (Co. Wicklow), Irish convict landed at Petty Harbour or Bay Bulls, 1789 (CO 194.38); —— Stuart, carpenter of Ferry land, 1790 (D'Alberti 4); —— and Rennie, merchants trading from the River Clyde to Newfoundland, 1802, 1817 (D'Alberti 12, 27); Anthony Steward, presented petition to erect flakes etc. on Cully's Plantation on the north side of Bay Bulls, 1807 (D'Alberti 17); Eleanor Stuart, of Harbour Grace, 1830 (Nfld. Archives HGRC); Miss ——, from Greenock, married Judge Des Barres, ? at St. John's, 1833 (*Carbonear Star* 24 Jul 1833); William Stewart, of Rack [for Wreck] Cove, Bay de l'Eau, 1835 (DPHW 30); James, of King's Cove Parish, 1838, of King's Cove, 1843 (Nfld. Archives KCRC, DPHW 73A); James, of Bonavista, 1843 (*Newfoundlander* 31 Aug 1843); William Stuart, fisherman of Miller's Passage (Burin district), 1850 (DPHW 104); John Stewart, fisherman of Salmonier (Burin district), 1853, planter of Mose Ambrose, 1858 (DPHW 104); William, of Burgeo, 1855 (DPHW 101); Edward, of Fox Cove (Fortune B.), 1871 (Lovell); John, planter of Langue de Cerf (Fortune B.), 1871 (Lovell); George and Neil Stuart, clerks of Harbour Grace, 1871 (Lovell).

Modern status: Scattered, especially in the Fortune Bay and Hermitage district.

Place name: Stewart Lake (Labrador) 54-29 65-55.

STICK, a surname of England from Old English *sticca* – rod, staff of wood, slender branch, probably a nickname for a tall, slender man. (Reaney).

Traced by Spiegelhalter in Devon.

In Newfoundland:

Early instance: Robert Sticks, fisherman of St. John's, 1833 (DPHW 26B).

Modern status: Rare, at Bay Roberts and St. John's.

Place names (not necessarily from the surname): Stick Pond, —— —— Brook 47-38 52-42.

STICKLAND, a surname of England said by Barber to be from an English place name Stickland (Dorset) not, however, recorded in Fägersten, from ? Old English *sticol* – steep and *land*. *See also* STRICKLAND with which confusion may have occurred.

In Newfoundland:

Early instances: Mary, of Harbour Grace Parish, 1819 (Nfld. Archives HGRC); Susanna, of Hants Harbour, 1832 (DPHW 59); Elizabeth, of Seal Cove (now New Chelsea), 1832 (DPHW 59); Henry, of Fortune, 1835 (DPHW 106); Rachel, of Long Island Harbour (Burin district), 1836 (DPHW 106); William, of Dead Island (Burgeo-La Poile district), 1842 (DPHW 101); William, of West Point (Burgeo-La Poile district), 1843 (DPHW 101); Robert, of Grole,

1845 (DPHW 102); Aaron, of Sibleys Cove or Scilly Cove (now Winterton), 1850 (DPHW 58); Robert, agent of Harbour Breton, 1851 (DPHW 104); William, of Bay de Loup (? for Bay de l'Eau), 1858 (DPHW 101); John, of Meadow(s) (Burin district), 1860 (DPHW 107); Thomas, of Little Bay (Burgeo-La Poile district), 1861 (DPHW 99); scattered in Lovell 1871.

Modern status: Scattered, especially in the Humber West district.

Place names: Stickland Cove 47-39 55-56, 47-47 55-52; —— Point 47-36 58-53, 47-41 54-08; —— Rock 47-09 55-00; —— Shoal 47-37 58-32.

STICKLEY, a surname of England ? from the English place name Stickley Coppice (Dorset) – steep meadow (by the) wood. (Fägersten, Bardsley).

Traced by Bardsley in Somerset in 1327–8.

In Newfoundland:

Family tradition: Lorenzo (1863–), of Birchy Head (Bonne B.) (MUN Geog.).

Early instances: William, of Lewis Bay (Labrador), 1787, of Fogo, 1789, servant of Battle Harbour, 1795 (MUN Hist.); John, of Bay de Verde, 1796 (CO 199.18); James, of St. John's, 1803 (D'Alberti 13); Thomas, of Chamberlains, 1804 (CO 199.18); William, of Catalina, 1807 (DPHW 64); —— Stickly, of Portugal Cove, 1831 (Nfld. Archives BRC); William Stickley, of Carbonear, 1858 (DPHW 49); John and Joseph, fishermen of Hants Harbour, 1871 (Lovell).

Modern status: Rare, at Catalina.

STIRLING, a surname of England and Scotland from the Scots place name Stirling (Stirlingshire) or a variant of STERLING. (Black).

Traced by Guppy in Stirlingshire and adjacent counties.

In Newfoundland:

Family tradition: William, M.D., from Scotland, settled in Harbour Grace, 1794 (MUN Folklore).

Early instances: Joseph Thomas, of St. John's, 1785 (DPHW 26D); W., of Harbour Grace, 1818 (CO 194.61); W., magistrate, Conception Bay, 1830 (*Newfoundlander* 14 Oct 1830); Edgar, member of Board of Road Commissioners for the Brigus to Port de Grave area, 1857 (*Nfld. Almanac*); William, M.D., of Twillingate, 1871 (Lovell).

Modern status: At St. John's, Harbour Grace and Gander.

STOCKLEY, a surname of England from the English place names Stockley, Stockleigh (in six counties including Devon), Old English *Stocc-lēah* – wood from which stocks (logs) were got, or *Stoc-lēah* – wood or clearing belonging to a religious house. (Reaney, Cottle, Ekwall).

In Newfoundland:

Family tradition: ——, from Wales, settled at Greenspond ? in the early 18th century (MUN Folklore).

Early instances: George, of Barrow Harbour (Bonavista B.), 1783 (DPHW 64); ——, in possession of fishing room, Stockley's Cove, Barrow Harbour before 1805 (Bonavista Register 1806); Samuel and Co., in possession of fishing room, Pinchard's Island (Bonivista B.), 1802 (Bonavista Register 1806); James, of Greenspond, 1815 (DPHW 76); James, born at Swain's Island (Bonavista B.), 1818 (DPHW 76); John, from Hampshire, married at Trinity (unspecified), 1826 (Nfld. Archives KCRC); William, fisherman of Robin Hood (now part of Port Rexton), 1857 (DPHW 64B); George, planter of Rose Blanche, 1871 (Lovell); William, of Ship Cove (now part of Port Rexton), 1871 (Lovell).

Modern status: Scattered, especially at St. John's, Wesleyville, and in the Twillingate district.

Place name: Johnny Stockley Island 49-09 53-34.

STOCKMAN, a surname of England, from Old English *stocc* – (dweller by the) tree-stump or footbridge, or a cutter of logs, or ? a cattle raiser or dealer. (Reaney, Spiegelhalter).

Traced by Spiegelhalter in Devon.

In Newfoundland:

Early instance: William, of Petty Harbour, 1802 (DPHW 26B).

Modern status: Rare, at Petty Harbour and Petty Harbour Road (*Electors* 1955).

STOCKWOOD, a surname of England from the English place names Stoke Woods (Devon), Stockwood (Dorset, Somerset, Devon) – wood belonging to a religious house or tree-stump wood, meanings similar to STOCKLEY. (Cottle, Ekwall).

In Newfoundland:

Family tradition: John, from England, settled at Gull Island (Conception B.) (MUN Folklore).

Early instance: John, of Gull Island (Conception B.), 1853 (DPHW 55).

Modern status: At Gull Island, Burnt Point (Conception B.) and St. John's.

STOKES, a surname of England and Ireland from the English place names Stoke(s) (Devon, Somerset,

Warwickshire, Derbyshire, Northamptonshire, Staffordshire), Old English *stoc* – place, religious site, outlying settlement. (Reaney, Cottle, MacLysaght).

Traced by Guppy in Essex, Leicestershire, Rutlandshire, Northamptonshire, Nottinghamshire, Shropshire, Staffordshire and Worcestershire, by Spiegelhalter in Devon, and by MacLysaght in Ireland since the fourteenth century.

In Newfoundland:

Family tradition: ——, from England, settled at Cape Freels; some of his descendants moved to Newtown (Bonavista B.) (MUN Folklore).

Early instances: Nicholas Stoke(s), of Newfoundland, 1704, of St. John's, 1705 (CO 194.3, 22); Nicholas Stokes, planter and fisherman of Point Vert about 1730–5 (CO 194.9); Edward, of St. John's, 1751 (CO 194.13); John, from Kingstag (Dorset), married at Greenspond, 1803 (Nfld. Archives BRC); Mary, of St. Mary's Bay, 1805 (Nfld. Archives BRC); Catherine, of Greenspond, 1826 (Nfld. Archives KCRC); Elizabeth, of Harbour Grace Parish, 1828 (Nfld. Archives HGRC); Malachi, of Flowers Island (Bonavista B.), 1830, of Middle Bill Cove (Bonavista B.), 1834 (DPHW 76; Francis, of Cape Freels, 1849 (DPHW 76); Francis Stoke, of Pool's Island, 1871 (Lovell); Joseph Stokes, farmer of Logy Bay, 1871 (Lovell).

Modern status: Scattered, especially at Cape Freels, Deadman's Bay (Fogo district) and St. John's.

STONE, a surname of England, Ireland and Guernsey (Channel Islands) from the English place name Stone (Staffordshire, Devon (22), Worcestershire etc.), or (dweller by or among the) stone(s) or rock(s); in Ireland also a synonym of Clogherty and Mulclohy, Ir. *cloch* – stone. (Reaney, Cottle, MacLysaght, Turk).

Traced by Guppy in the southwest and southeast of England and in Derbyshire, and by MacLysaght, but nowhere numerous, in Ireland.

In Newfoundland:

Family traditions: John, of Big Bell Isle (now Bell Island), 1824 (MUN Hist.). Henry William (–1888), from Glastonbury (Somerset) came to St. John's, moved to Old Bonaventure (Trinity B.) and was the first settler of Upper Rocky Brook (now Monroe) in 1870 (MUN Geog.).

Early instances: John, of Bay Bulls, 1675 (CO 1); ——, of Quidi Vidi, 1703 (CO 194.3); John, of Bay de Verde, 1708–9 (CO 194.4); Thomas, constable, Trinity district ? 1730, 1732 (CO 194.9); Robert, of

Trinity Bay, 1765 (DPHW 64); George, married at St. John's, 1772 (DPHW 26D); Thomas, from Poole (Dorset), in possession of property at Cornaille (now Canaille), 1789 (CO 199.18); Henry, of Old Bonaventure, 1795, 1814 (DPHW 64); S., of Trinity (? Trinity B.), 1796 (D'Alberti 5); Richard Cornish, of Harbour Grace, 1801 (USPG); Maria, of St. John's, 1807 (Nfld. Archives BRC); William, from Shenren (unidentified) (Co. Kilkenny), married at St. John's, 1812 (Nfld. Archives BRC); Jonas, of Trepassey, 1821 (Nfld. Archives BRC); Richard, of Greenspond, 1824 (DPHW 76); John, cooper of Brigus, 1827 (DPHW 34); Sarah, of Fortune Harbour, 1830 (Nfld. Archives KCRC); John, carpenter of New Harbour (Trinity B.), 1836 (DPHW 64B); Thomas, shoemaker of Carbonear, 1837 (DPHW 48); Thomas, planter of Salmon Cove (Carbonear), 1838 (DPHW 48); Ambrose, of Catalina, 1840, of Little Catalina, 1846 (DPHW 67); Thomas, planter of Perry's Cove, 1841 (DPHW 48); James Stone(s), master of boat, at Harbour Breton, 1841. (D.A. Macdonald); Robert, of Grand Bank, 1843 (DPHW 106); Henry, of King's Cove Parish, 1848 (Nfld. Archives KCRC); Martin, merchant's clerk, of Fogo, 1850 (DPHW 83); George, fisherman of Merritts Harbour, 1851 (DPHW 85); Henry, fisherman of Pike's Arm, Herring Neck, 1851 (DPHW 85); Thomas, of Coomb's Cove, 1853 (DPHW 104); Thomas, of Bay de l'Eau Island, 1853 (DPHW 104); James, of Harbour Breton, 1853 (DPHW 104); Robert, of Petites, 1854 (DPHW 98); Thomas Stones, of English Harbour (Burin district), 1855 (DPHW 104); scattered in Lovell 1871.

Modern status: Widespread, especially at Corner Brook, Lower Lance Cove (Trinity B.), Bryant's Cove and St. John's.

Place names (not necessarily from the surname): Stone (or Stowbergs) Brook 49-13 58-05; Stone Cove 47-35 55-07; Stone (or Graves) Island 47-25 53-58; Stone Island 47-43 56-09, 48-21 53-21, 48-42 53-09, 49-43 54-19; —— (or Offer Stone) Island 49-46 54-18; Stone Islands 47-03 52-52; —— Point 47-45 56-06; —— Shoal 47-38 58-31, 48-20 53-22; —— Valley 47-37 56-02; Stone's Cove 47-35 55-07; —— Rock 47-34 55-07; Stoneville 49-28 54-32.

STONEMAN, a surname of England – dweller by the (conspicuous) stone or worker in stone, mason. (Reaney).

Traced by Guppy in Devon.

In Newfoundland:

Early instances: John, married at St. John's, 1788 (DPHW 26D); George, planter of Twillingate, 1822

(USPG); W., member of Board of Road Commissioners, Trinity Bay North, 1844, of Trinity (? Trinity B.), 1847, deceased 1856 (Nfld. Almanac, New-foundlander 1 Apr 1847, 21 Aug 1856); George, from Albany, New York, married at St. John's, 1851 (DPHW 23).

Modern status: Rare, at St. John's.

STOODLEY, a surname of England and Jersey (Channel Islands) from the English place names Stoodleigh, Stoodley (Devon) – the clearing or pasture for a stud, a herd of horses. (Cottle, Turk).

Traced by Spiegelhalter in Devon.

In Newfoundland:

Family tradition: George (1809–1893), of English descent, of Grand Bank; his brother John's descendants settled at Jersey Harbour (MUN Hist.).

Early instances: Jonathan, planter ? Of Fogo, 1792, of Battle Harbour (Labrador), 1795 (MUN Hist.); George, of Grand Bank, 1837 (DPHW 109); Thomas, of Indian Burying Place (Twillingate district), 1842 (DPHW 86).

Modern status: Scattered, especially at Grand Bank and in the Fortune Bay and Hermitage district.

STOR(E)Y, surnames of England and Scotland, Storey of Ireland, from an Old Norse personal name Stori – ? big. (Reaney, Cottle, Black, MacLysaght).

Traced by Guppy in Cumberland, Westmorland, Durham, Lincolnshire, Norfolk, Northumberland and Yorkshire NR, ER, with Storey the usual form, and by MacLysaght in Ulster and Dublin since the seventeenth century.

In Newfoundland:

Family tradition: Rev. George Philliskirk Story, 1853–94, from Filey (Yorkshire), came to Newfoundland as a schoolteacher at Carbonear between 1870–4; he later became a Methodist minister and was stationed at various places including Carbonear, Channel, until his death at St. John's in 1892; his descendants settled at St. John's (Family, General Protestant Cemetery, St. John's).

Early instance: William Storey, of St. John's, 1843 (DPHW 29).

Modern status: Storey, unique, at St. John's; Story, rare, at St. John's.

STOTT, a surname of England and Scotland, from Middle English stott – bullock (-keeper), or a nickname. (Reaney, Cottle, Black).

Traced by Guppy in Lancashire, Northumberland, Somerset and Yorkshire WR.

In Newfoundland:

Early instance: James (1845–), from Fyvie (Aberdeenshire), settled at St. John's in 1860 or 1867 (Mott).

Modern status: Rare, at Botwood (*Electors* 1955) and St. John's.

STOWE, a surname of England from Old English *stow* – (dweller by the) (holy) place, church, monastery, or from the English place name Stow(e) in eleven counties. (Reaney, Cottle).

Traced by Guppy in Lincolnshire and by Spiegelhalter in Devon.

In Newfoundland:

Early instances: Stephen, soldier of St. John's, 1756 (DPHW 26C); William, of Harbour Grace, 1765 (CO 199.18); Benjamin Stow, of Greenspond, 1849 (DPHW 76); —— Stowe, on the *Two Brothers* in the seal fishery out of Trinity (unspecified), 1853 (*Newfoundlander* 17 Mar 1853); Mrs. E., schoolteacher of Carbonear, 1871 (Lovell); Hannibal, of Twillingate, 1871 (Lovell).

Modern status: At Harbour Grace (*Electors* 1955), Corner Brook and St. John's.

Place name: Stow (or Gambles) Tickle (Labrador) 52-49 55-51.

STOYLES, a surname of England from Old French *estoile*, Middle English *stoyle* – star, or ? from an unidentified place name, or ? a variant of STYLES. (Reaney, Spiegelhalter).

Traced by Spiegelhalter in Devon.

In Newfoundland:

Family tradition: William Stoyles or Stiles (about 1800–1882), from Devon, settled at Lance Cove (Bell Island), in 1832 (MUN Hist.).

Early instances: Thomas W., ? of St. John's, 1821 (CO 194.64); John, planter of Grates Cove, 1837 (DPHW 58); Alfred (and others) Stoyls, of Random Sound (Trinity B.), 1871 (Lovell); William Stiles, fisherman of Bell Isle (now Bell Island), and Lance Cove, 1871 (Lovell).

Modern status: Scattered, especially at Lance Cove (Bell Island), Hillview (Trinity B.) and St. John's.

STRAND, a surname of England from the English place name Strand (Cornwall) or from Old English *strand* – (dweller by the) shore. (Spiegelhalter).

Traced by Spiegelhalter in Devon.

In Newfoundland:

Modern status: Rare, at Flat Bay and St. Teresa's (St. George's district) (*Electors* 1955).

Place name (not necessarily from the surname): Strand Rock 46-52 55-46.

STRANG, a surname of England and Scotland, ? originally from Old French *estrange*, Middle English *strange* – foreign(er), later from Scots and Northern English *strang* – strong. *See also* STRANGE, STRONG. (Reaney, Cottle, Black).

Traced by Cottle in the north of England and by Black in Orkney.

In Newfoundland:

Early instances: John, of St. John's, 1816 (D'Alberti 26); Andrew and Martin, fishermen of Lawn, 1871 (Lovell); John, fisherman of Port de Grave, 1871 (Lovell).

Modern status: At Lawn and St. John's.

STRANGE, a surname of England and ? of Ireland from Old French *estrange*, Middle English *strange* – foreigner, stranger, newcomer. (Reaney). *See also* STRANG.

Traced by Guppy in Berkshire and Dorset and by Spiegelhalter in Devon.

In Newfoundland:

Early instances: Edmond (Edward in 1681), of Renews, 1677 (CO 1); Pat, of Harbour Grace Parish, 1806 (Nfld. Archives HGRC); Bridget, of Harbour Main, 1809 (Nfld. Archives BRC); Mary, from New Ross (Co. Wexford), married at St. John's, 1811 (Nfld. Archives BRC); John, fisherman of Port de Grave, 1838 (DPHW 39); ——, on the *Ann* in the seal fishery out of Brigus, 1847 (*Newfoundlander* 25 Mar 1847); Joseph, of Lower Burgeo, 1854 (DPHW 101).

Modern status: At Port de Grave (*Electors* 1955) and St. John's.

STRANGEMORE, ? a surname of England ? from an unidentified English place name.

In Newfoundland:

Modern status: At Cooks Harbour (*Electors* 1955), Mouse Island (Burgeo-La Poile district) and St. Anthony.

STRAPP, a surname of Ireland, not recorded by MacLysaght. "The forebears of the Strapp family, whose original name was O'Meara [*see* O'MARA], are traced to Fetherd, Co. Tipperary. In the rebellion of 1798 a member of the family incurred the wrath of English law, and had to flee Ireland with a price on his head. This fugitive went to Germany where he married and lived under the assumed name Strasse, which, on his return to Ireland he changed to Strappe, now written without the final "e." During the exodus from Ireland in the early nineteenth century two young brothers of the Strapp family embarked for America on a ship which was wrecked. The passengers were rescued by vessels bound for different ports. One of the Strapp boys was brought to Newfoundland, the other, to the United States." (Bro. J.P. Keane, "Brother Patrick Vincent Strapp 1866–1952," *The Christian Brothers' Educational Record, 1953*. Dublin: Bray Printing Co. Ltd., p. 318).

In Newfoundland:

Family tradition: At Harbour Main since the early nineteenth century (Ibid).

Early instances: Patrick Strap(pe), of Harbour Grace Parish, 1812 (Nfld. Archives HGRC); Citty (? for Kitty) Strap, married at St. John's, 1837 (Nfld. Archives BRC); Patrick Strapp, member of Board of Road Commissioners of Harbour Main, 1844 (*Nfld. Almanac*); ——, on the *Eliza* in the seal fishery out of Carbonear, 1847 (*Newfoundlander* 25 Mar 1847); ——, on the *Eliza* in the seal fishery out of Harbour Grace, 1853 (*Newfoundlander* 28 Mar 1853); ——, captain of the *Ellen* in the seal fishery out of Brigus, 1857 (*Newfoundlander* 16 Mar 1857).

Modern status: At Harbour Main, Conception Harbour and St. John's.

STRATHIE, a surname of Scotland from the Scots place name Strathie (Aberdeenshire, Ross, Cromarty and Caithness-shire). (Black).

In Newfoundland:

Early instances: Alexander, joiner of Bonavista, 1821 (DPHW 72); Robert Strathie or Strethie, carpenter of English Harbour (Trinity B.), 1837, of Catalina, 1845 (DPHW 64B, 67); John Strathie, of Harbour Grace, 1871 (Lovell); Robert, farmer of Musgravetown, 1871 (Lovell).

Modern status: Rare, at Bonavista.

STRATTON, a surname of England and Scotland from the English place name Stratton in nine southern and eastern counties of England and in Midlothian and Fifeshire, usually – place on a Roman road. (Cottle, Black). *See also* STREET, STRETTON.

Traced by Guppy in Bedfordshire, Hampshire, Surrey and Wiltshire and by Spiegelhalter in Devon.

In Newfoundland:

Family traditions: Mary Ann, from Yorkshire, settled at Greenspond before 1856 (MUN Folklore). ——, from Devon or Cornwall, settled at Greenspond in the 1700s (MUN Folklore).

Early instance: Thomas Jr., of Greenspond, 1819 (DPHW 76).

Modern status: Scattered, especially at Corner Brook and in the Bonavista North district.

Place names: Stratten's Point 49-08 53-37; Strattons Pond 48-56 57-53.

STRAWBRIDGE, STROWBRIDGE, surnames of England from the English place name Strawbridge (Devon).

Spiegelhalter traced Strawbridge in Devon.

In Newfoundland:

Early instances: John Strawbridge, boatkeeper of St. John's, 1794–5, "20 years in Newfoundland," that is, 1774–5 (Census 1794–5); Thomas, of Bay de l'Eau Island, 1835 (DPHW 30); Miles Stradridge or Suadridge, mariner of Trinity (Trinity B.), 1837 (DPHW 64B); George Stubbridge, fisherman of Red Cove (Fortune B.), 1853 (DPHW 104); George Stabridge, fisherman of Burin, 1871 (Lovell); Samuel Strowbridge, of Belleoram, 1871 (Lovell); John, planter of English Harbour West (Fortune B.), 1871 (Lovell); Clarence and George, planters of Point Enragée (Fortune B.), 1871 (Lovell); John Stowbridge, of Isle Valen (Placentia B.), 1871 (Lovell).

Modern status: Strawbridge, rare, at St. John's; Strowbridge, scattered, especially at Red Cove and other parts of the Fortune Bay and Hermitage district.

STREET, a surname of England from Old English *stræt* – (dweller by the) street, Roman road, (or later hamlet), or from the English place name Street (Herefordshire, Kent, Somerset, Devon). (Reaney, Cottle). *See also* STRATTON, STRETTON.

Traced by Guppy in Bedfordshire, Hampshire, Surrey and Wiltshire and by Spiegelhalter in Devon.

In Newfoundland:

Family traditions: Mary Ann (1790–) born at Ochre Pit Cove (Conception B.) (MUN Folklore). Abraham, from Street or Epworth (Somerset), settled first at Burin Bay about 1840, later at Spoon Cove (now Epworth) (Files – Dr. Kirwin).

Early instances: Thomas, of Hearts Content, 1772 (DPHW 64); ——, in charge of ordnance, Trinity (unspecified), 1779 (CO 194.34); Thomas, salmon fisherman at Gander Bay, 1785 (MUN Hist.); John, of Bonavista, 1792 (USPG); John, merchant of St. John's, 1793 (DPHW 26D); John, of Trinity (Trinity B.), 1798 (DPHW 64); Thomas, occupier of fishing room, Old Perlican, proprietor of fishing room at Silly Cove (now Winterton), Winter 1800–01 (Census Trinity B.); Thomas, of Bay de Verde, 1802 (CO 199.18); George, of Lower Island Cove, 1803 (CO 199.18); Thomas, from Poole (Dorset), lessee of fishing room, Ship Island, Greenspond Harbour, 1805 (Bonavista Register 1806); Jasper, of King's

Cove, 1837, of Knights Cove, 1840 (DPHW 73); James, of Catalina, 1841 (DPHW 67); Charles, planter of Northern Bay, 1851 (DPHW 55); William James, fisherman of New (now Parsons) Harbour, 1851 (DPHW 102); James, fisherman of Bull Cove (Conception B.), 1853 (DPHW 34); Abraham and Isaac, of Burin, 1871 (Lovell); James, farmer of English Cove (Conception B.), 1871 (Lovell); Matthew, fisherman of Lower Burgeo, 1871 (Lovell); James, planter of Spillars Cove (Bonavista B.), 1871 (Lovell).

Modern status: Scattered, especially at Spillars Cove.

STREETER, a surname of England, identical with STREET.

In Newfoundland:

Modern status: Rare, at St. John's.

STRETTON, a surname of England, same as STRATTON, from the English place name Stretton in eight Midland counties. (Cottle). *See also* STREET.

Traced by Guppy in Derbyshire, Leicestershire and Rutlandshire and by Spiegelhalter in Devon.

In Newfoundland:

Early instances: John, of Harbour Grace, 1775 (CO 199.18); John, of Carbonear, 1790 (CO 199.18); Thomas ? Strotten (for Stretton), of Greenspond, in possession of fishing room, Pond Island, Greenspond Harbour, 1802 (Bonavista Register 1806).

Modern status: Unique, at Exploits (Twillingate district) (*Electors* 1955).

STRICKLAND, a surname of England from the English place name Strickland (Westmorland), from Old English *styrc*, *steorc* – stirk, that is land or pasture for young bullocks or heifers. (Cottle, Ekwall). *See also* STICKLAND with which confusion may have occurred.

Traced by Guppy in Cumberland, Westmorland, Lancashire and Yorkshire NR, ER.

In Newfoundland:

Early instances: Joseph, of Riders Harbour (Trinity B.), 1811 (DPHW 64); William, of Joe Batts Arm, 1815, of Fogo, 1819, of Tilton Harbour (now Tilting), 1822 (Nfld. Archives KCRC); William, of Dead Man's Island (unspecified), 1830 (DPHW 30); Thomas, of Cornelius Island, Burgeo, 1830 (DPHW 30); John, of Hermitage Cove, 1831 (DPHW 109); George, of Rencontre, 1835 (DPHW 30); Robert, from Poole (Dorset), married at St. John's, 1840 (DPHW 26D); Henry, from Lymington (Hants), married at Kings Cove, 1842, of Tickle Cove (Bonavista B.), 1844 (DPHW 73A); William, of Brigus, 1844 (DPHW

26D); John, from Bridport (Dorset), married at King's Cove, 1845, of Knights Cove, 1845, of Newman's Cove (Bonavista B.), 1851 (DPHW 72, 73A); ——, of La Poile, 1849 (Feild); John, of Harbour Breton, 1853 (DPHW 104); Susanna, of Deadman's Bay (Bonavista North district), 1862 (DPHW 79); Thomas, of Isle aux Morts, 1871 (Lovell); John, of Twillingate, 1871 (Lovell); George, of Waldron's Cove (Fogo district), 1871 (Lovell); James and William Stricklin, of Bay of Islands, 1871 (Lovell).

Modern status: Widespread, especially at Little Bay (Fortune B.), Channel, Hunts Island and other parts of the Burgeo-La Poile district, Newmans Cove (Bonavista B.) and St. John's.

Place names: Strickland Pond 47-38 58-12, —— —— Brook 48-22 53-40.

STRIDE, STRYDE, surnames of England, STRIDE, of the Micmac Indians of Newfoundland, of uncertain meaning.

Guppy traced Stride in Hampshire.

In Newfoundland:

Early instances: Henry Stride, of Exploits Burnt Island, 1843 (DPHW 86); George, fisherman of Northern Harbour (Exploits B.), 1871 (Lovell); Peter and Ellen, Micmacs of Bay D'Espoir, 1872 (MacGregor); John, Micmac Indian trapper whose hunting grounds were the north side of Mt. Sylvester about 1900–06 (Millais).

Modern status: Stride, scattered, especially in the Gander district; Stryde, especially in the Twillingate district.

STRINGER, a surname of England from Old English *streng* – string, cord, hence a maker of strings for bows. (Reaney).

Traced by Reaney in Yorkshire.

In Newfoundland:

Early instances: Joseph, of Grate's Cove, 1835 (DPHW 58); John, of St. John's, 1838 (DPHW 26B); Henry and James, of Random Sound, 1871 (Lovell).

Modern status: At St. John's and in the Trinity North district especially at Hodges Cove and Little Hearts Ease.

STRONG, a surname of England, Ireland and Jersey (Channel Islands), Old English *strang*, Middle English *strong* – strong. (Reaney, Cottle, Turk). *See also* STRANG.

A Midlands and southern surname traced by Guppy in Devon, Nottinghamshire and Wiltshire, and by MacLysaght in Ulster.

In Newfoundland:

Family traditions: William, from England, settled at Greenspond (MUN Folklore). Joseph was the first settler of Broad Cove (now part of Clarenville) (MUN Hist.).

Early instances: William, of St. John's, 1682 (CO 1); George, of Newfoundland, 1730 (CO 194.23); James Stronge, of Bay de Verde, 1730 (CO 194.23); John Strong, of Trinity Bay, 1767 (DPHW 64); George and John, of Old Perlican, 1787 (Nfld. Archives T18); Solomon, of Three Arm Island (Twillingate district), 1846 (DPHW 86); William, planter of Lance Cove (now Brownsdale), 1852 (DPHW 33); William, of Little Bay Islands, 1859 (DPHW 42); William, fisherman of Burin, 1860 (DPHW 100); George, of Twillingate, 1871 (Lovell).

Modern status: Scattered, especially at Clarenville.

Place names (not necessarily from the surname): Strong Island, —— Tickle 48-06 53-42; —— Island 49-25 55-19; —— Tickle 47-54 53-43; —— Island Sound 49-24 55-20; Strongs Island 49-29 54-47; —— Point 48-10 53-57.

STROUD, a surname of England from the English place names Stroud (Gloucestershire, Hampshire), Strode (Devon), Strood (Kent), or Old English *strōd* – (dweller by the) marshy land overgrown with brushwood. (Reaney, Cottle, Ekwall).

Guppy traced Strode in Somerset; Spiegelhalter traced Strode and Stroud in Devon.

In Newfoundland:

Family tradition: Richard Elliott, from the west country of England, settled at Greenspond; he later moved to the Glovertown area (MUN Hist.).

Early instances: Richard, of Greenspond, 1829 (DPHW 76); Richard, of Bloody Bay (Bonavista B.), 1834, of Middle Arm (Bonavista South district), 1844 (DPHW 73A, 76); William, of Burin, 1871 (Lovell).

Modern status: Scattered.

Place name: Strouds Pond 47-02 55-20.

STROWBRIDGE. *See* STRAWBRIDGE

STRUGNELL, a surname ? of England, of unascertained origin.

Traced by Matthews as a captain in Plymouth (Devon).

In Newfoundland:

Early instances: ——, on the brig *Triton*, 1831, captain of the brig *Triton*, 1833 (*Newfoundlander* 4 Aug 1831, 8 Aug 1833); John, fisherman of Pouch Cove, 1849 (DPHW 32).

Modern status: At Pouch Cove.

STRYDE. *See* STRIDE

STUCKEY, a surname of England from the English place names Stiffkey (Norfolk) pronounced Stiffkey as spelt or Stooky – island with stumps of trees, or Stockey (Devon) – enclosure made with stumps of trees. (Weekley *Surnames*, Spiegelhalter, Ekwall).

Traced by Guppy in Somerset and by Spiegelhalter in Devon.

In Newfoundland:

Early instances: Joseph, planter of Herring Neck, 1821 (USPG); Thomas, planter of Clark's Cove (Twillingate district), 1854 (DPHW 85).

Modern status: Scattered, especially at Pike's Arm and other parts of the Twillingate district.

Place names: Stuckey Cove, Point 49-32 55-41.

STUCKLESS, a surname of England, ? from the English place names Stockleigh, Stokeley, Stockley (Devon). The Devon place name Stuckleys is probably associated with the family of George Stucley (1667). (Gover). *See also* STUCKLEY.

Probably a Devon surname but not recorded by Spiegelhalter or elsewhere.

In Newfoundland:

Family traditions: ——, from the west country of England settled at Twillingate in the nineteenth century; a descendant, Isaac (1837–1902) born in Twillingate, settled at Point Leamington in 1860 (MUN Geog.). ——, from Wales, settled in the Twillingate area; descendants settled at Smooth Cove and Purcells Harbour (Twillingate district) (MUN Folklore).

Early instances: Lydia, of Twillingate, 1821 (USPG); John, of Catalina, 1822 (Nfld. Archives KCRC); John, of Ragged Harbour (now Melrose), 1823 (Nfld. Archives KCRC); John, of Trinity (unspecified), 1828 (Nfld. Archives KCRC); Joseph, of Tizzard's Harbour, 1843 (DPHW 86); Richard, of Moreton's Harbour, 1846 (DPHW 86); Richard, of Joe Batts Arm, 1853 (DPHW 83); Isaac Stucklas, of New Bay (Exploits district), 1859 (DPHW 42); Joseph, of Exploits Burnt Island, 1861 (DPHW 42); William Stuckless, of River Head (White B.), 1864 (DPHW 94).

Modern status: Widespread, especially at Corner Brook, Point Leamington and Twillingate North Side.

Place name: Stuckless Cove 49-51 56-33.

STUCKLEY, a surname of England, from the English place names Stockleigh, Stockley, Stokeley (Devon), all containing the Old English elements *stoc* – place, religious site, outlying settlement and *lēah* – wood, clearing. (Spiegelhalter, A. H. Smith). *See also* STOKES, STUCKLESS.

Spiegelhalter traced Stucley in Devon.

In Newfoundland:

Early instances: Edward, planter of Fogo, 1808 (MUN Hist.); John Stukley, of St. John's, 1845 (DPHW 29); Richard Stuckley, of Joe Batts Arm, 1856 (DPHW 83); Eli and John, of Tilt Cove, 1871 (Lovell).

Modern status: Rare, at Burt's Cove (Twillingate district) (*Electors* 1955).

STURGE, a surname of England from the personal names Old Norse *Thorgils*, Old Danish, Old Swedish *Thorgisl* – Thor's hostage. (Reaney, Cottle). Traced in Gloucestershire (Mrs. M. Artiss, *née* Sturge).

In Newfoundland:

Early instances: Thomas Sturgys, of St. John's, 1821 (CO 194.64); John Sturge, baptized at Greenspond, 1817, aged 23 (DPHW 76); John, of Flowers Island (Bonavista B.), 1830 (DPHW 76); Mark Sturges, fisherman of Harbour Le Cou, 1871 (Lovell).

Modern status: Scattered, especially at St. John's, Wesleyville, Brookfield and other parts of the Bonavista North district.

Place name: Sturges Islands 49-08 53-35.

STURGEON, a surname of England and Scotland from Old French *esturgeon*, the fish, originally meaning "agitator" (Reaney, Spiegelhalter, Black).

Traced by Guppy in Suffolk, by Spiegelhalter in Devon, and by Black mainly in Dumfriesshire and Kirkcudbrightshire.

In Newfoundland:

Early instance: Thomas, fisherman of Quidi Vidi, 1794–5, "9 years in Newfoundland," that is, 1785–6 (Census 1794–5).

Modern status: Unique, at Grand Bank (*Electors* 1955).

STYLES, a surname of England and Ireland from Old English *stigol* – (dweller by the) stile, steep ascent, or ? a variant of STOYLES. (Reaney, Cottle).

Guppy traced Stiles and Styles in Kent, Northamptonshire and Sussex, Spiegelhalter traced Stiles and Style in Devon.

In Newfoundland:

Early instances: John, of Hawkes Bay (Labrador), 1787, of Hawkes Post (Labrador), 1789 (MUN Hist.); George Stiles, planter of Twillingate, 1817 (USPG); James Styles, fisherman of Little River (Burgeo-La Poile district), 1835 (DPHW 101); James, fisherman

of Grates Cove, 1849 (DPHW 58); James, of Swires Cove (Burgeo-La Poile district), 1849 (DPHW 101); Phoebe, of Wild Cove (Twillingate district), 1860 (DPHW 87); William, schoolteacher of Kelligrews, 1871 (Lovell); George, planter of Petites, 1871 (Lovell).

Modern status: Scattered.

Place names: Styles Harbour (Labrador) 53-02 55-46; —— Hill 49-41 54-48; —— Point 47-33 56-49.

SUL(L)EY. *See* SOOLEY

SULLIVAN, a surname of Ireland (O)Sullivan, *Ó Súileabháin*, Ir. *súil* – eye, with last part of the name uncertain. (MacLysaght).

The third most numerous name in Ireland, traced by MacLysaght especially in Cos. Cork and Kerry.

In Newfoundland:

Early instances: John Sullyvan, ? of Little Placentia (now Argentia), about 1730–5 (CO 194.9); William Sullivan, married at St. John's, 1768 (DPHW 26D); Richard, of Bay Bulls, 1781 (D'Alberti 2); Denis, fisherman of Quidi Vidi, 1794–5, "10 years in Newfoundland," that is, 1784–5 (Census 1794–5); James, of King's Cove, 1785 (Bonavista Register 1806); Michael, from Bruff (Co. Limerick), Irish convict landed at Petty Harbour or Bay Bulls, 1789 (CO 194.38); Daniel, of Carbonear, 1793 (CO 199.18); Dennis, of Salmon Cove, Northern Arm (Conception B.), 1798 (CO 199.18); John, of Harbour Main, 1801 (CO 199.18); Thomas, of Port de Grave, 1802 (CO 199.18); James, from Clonmel (Co. Tipperary), married at King's Cove, 1803 (Nfld. Archives BRC); Daniel of Harbour Grace, 1804 (CO 199.18); Catherine, of Bonavista, 1805 (Nfld. Archives BRC); John, of Northern Bay, 1806 (CO 199.18); James Sulivan, of Trinity (Trinity B.), 1807 (DPHW 64); Luke, Patrick, Michael, John, William, Daniel Sullivan, 6 of 72 impressed men who sailed from Ireland to Newfoundland, ? 1811 (CO 194.51); John, from Carrick-on-Suir (Co. Tipperary), married at St. John's, 1813 (Nfld. Archives BRC); Thomas, from Scull (Co. Cork), fisherman of St. Lawrence, deceased 1814 (*Royal Gazette* 18 Aug 1814); Elinor Sulivan, of New Harbour (Trinity B.), 1815 (Nfld. Archives KCRC); James Sullivan or Solivan, of Riders Harbour, 1817 (Nfld. Archives KCRC); John Sulivan, of Tilton Harbour (now Tilting), 1818 (Nfld. Archives KCRC); John Solovan, of Pouch Cove, 1818 (DPHW 26B); John Sullivan, of Chapels Cove, 1824 (Nfld. Archives BRC); Jeremiah, of Careless (now Kerleys) Harbour, 1826 (Nfld.

Archives KCRC); Anne, of Cats Cove (now Conception Harbour), 1828 (Nfld. Archives BRC); Daniel, of Heart's Content, 1829 (Nfld. Archives KCRC); Bridget, of Broad Cove (now Duntara), 1831 (Nfld. Archives KCRC); John, of Fortune Harbour, 1832 (Nfld. Archives KCRC); Richard, of Ferryland district, 1838 (*Newfoundlander* 25 Oct 1838); Joseph, from Co. Wexford, married at Renews, 1841 (Dillon); Elizabeth, from Dingle (Co. Kerry), of Harbour Grace, 1844 (*Indicator* 27 Jul 1844); Michael, from Co. Kilkenny, of Brigus, 1844 (*Indicator* 24 Aug 1844); ——, on the *Margaret* in the seal fishery out of Flat Island (? Bonavista B.), 1853 (*Newfoundlander* 17 Mar 1853); John, granted land at Branch, 1854 (Nfld. Archives, Registry Crown Lands); Margaret Sulivan, of Tickle Cove (Bonavista B.), 1857 (Nfld. Archives KCRC); Patrick, of Indian Arm (Bonavista B.), 1857 (Nfld. Archives KCRC); James, of Barrow Harbour, 1865 (Nfld. Archives KCRC); Mary Sullivan, of Stock Cove, 1866 (Nfld. Archives KCRC); Patrick, of Deer Harbour, 1866 (Nfld. Archives KCRC); widespread in Lovell 1871.

Modern status: Widespread, especially at St. John's, Calvert, Pouch Cove and Brent's Cove (White B.).

Place names: Sullivan Island 48-11 53-32; —— Lake (Labrador) 53-46 57-42.

SUMMERS. *See* SOMERS

SUMMERVILLE, Sommerville in *Electors* 1955, usually Somerville, a surname of England, Scotland and Ireland, ? from ? the English place name Summerwell (Devon) or the French place name Graveron-Sémerville (Nord), or in Ireland a synonym of *Ó Somacháin*, Ir. *somachán* – soft, innocent. (Reaney, Black, MacLysaght). *See also* SOMERS.

Somerville traced by Spiegelhalter in Devon and by MacLysaght in Ulster and Co. Galway.

In Newfoundland:

Early instance: John Somerville, trader of Bay Bulls, 1871 (Lovell).

Modern status: Rare, at St. John's.

Place name: Summerville 48-27 53-33.

SUMNER, a surname of England from Old French *somoner* etc., Anglo-French *somenour* etc. – summoner, a petty officer who cites and warns people to appear in court. (Reaney, Cottle).

Traced by Guppy in Cheshire and Lancashire and by Spiegelhalter in Devon.

In Newfoundland:

Modern status: Rare, at St. John's.

SUTHERBY, a surname of England from Old Norse *suthr í bý* – (dweller in the) south of the village. (Reaney).

Traced by Guppy in Yorkshire, formerly in Lincolnshire.

In Newfoundland:

Modern status: Rare, at St. John's.

SUTHERLAND, a surname of Scotland from the Scots county. (Cottle).

Traced by Guppy in the north of Scotland.

In Newfoundland:

Early instances: William, ? of St. John's, 1810 (CO 194.50); Angus, native of Pictou, Nova Scotia, died at St. John's, 1849, aged 55 (General Protestant Cemetery, St. John's).

Modern status: At Grand Falls, Bishops Falls and St. John's.

Place name: Sutherland Inlet (or Anchorstock Bight) (Labrador) 57-47 61-50.

SUTTON, a surname of England and Ireland from the common English place name – the southern or south-facing farm, or south of the farm or village, or a minor settlement lying south of the main one; in Ireland possibly from the Irish place name. (Reaney, Cottle, MacLysaght).

Traced by Guppy in eleven counties and by MacLysaght in Cos. Kildare and Wexford since the thirteenth century.

In Newfoundland:

Family tradition: George (about 1750–1830), ? from England, settled at Trepassey about 1775 (MUN Geog.).

Early instances: Richard, of Torbay, 1708–9 (CO 194.4); Thomas, from Sutton's Parish (Co. Wexford), boatkeeper of Trepassey, 1788 (D'Alberti 4, Nemec); John, of Bay de Verde, 1798 (DPHW 64); Miss, schoolmistress, of St. John's, 1810 (CO 194.49); Catherine, of Harbour Grace Parish, 1817 (Nfld. Archives HGRC); George, of Brigus, 1817 (Nfld. Archives L165); John, of Catalina, 1822, of Ragged Harbour (now Melrose), 1825 (Nfld. Archives KCRC); Martin, from Co. Wexford, married at St. John's, 1830 (Nfld. Archives BRC); C., of Harbour Grace, deceased, 1831 (*Newfoundlander* 14 Jul 1831); Jeremiah, fisherman of Pushthrough, 1842 (DPHW 102); Jeremiah, lumberman of Head of Bay d'Espoir, 1871 (Lovell).

Modern status: Scattered, especially at Trepassey.

Place names: Sutton Island (Labrador) 57-11 61-25, 57-12 61-51; Suttons Island (Labrador) 53-47 57-08; —— Pond 47-35 53-28.

SWAIN, a surname of England, Swayne of Ireland, from a personal name Old Norse *Sveinn*, Old Danish, Old Swedish *Sven*, "often anglicized as *Swan*" (*see* SWAN), or Old Norse *sveinn* – boy, servant, peasant, swineherd; in Ireland Swayne may also be a synonym of SWEENEY, Swiney, but not of SWAN. (Reaney, Cottle, MacLysaght).

Guppy traced Swain in Derbyshire, Devon, Hertfordshire, Leicestershire, Rutlandshire, Lincolnshire and Swayne in Surrey.

In Newfoundland:

Early instances: Richard Swaine (Swan in 1677), of Old Perlican, 1675 (CO 1); John Swain, of St. John's, 1808 (D'Alberti 18); John Swain(e), fisherman of Blow-me-down (Carbonear), 1838 (DPHW 48); Eliza Swayne, of Stone Island, Caplin Bay (now Calvert), 1841 (Dillon); John Swane, schoolteacher of Perry's Cove (Conception B.), 1846 (DPHW 48).

Modern status: Scattered, especially at Perry's Cove.

Place names: Swaine Point (Labrador) 60-15 64-23; Swain's Island, —— Tickle, —— Green Tickle, —— Island Tickle 49-09 53-33; —— Shag Rock 49-09 53-31.

SWAN, a surname of England, Scotland and Ireland, from the Old English personal name *Swan* from Old Norse *sveinn* (*see* SWAIN), or from Old English *swān* – herdsman, peasant, swineherd, or from Old English *swan* (the bird), a nickname or inn-sign. (Reaney, Cottle).

Guppy found Swan(n) in Derbyshire and Northumberland, Swan in Durham, Swann in Essex, and Swan in the south of Scotland, especially towards the Scots Border. MacLysaght traced Swan in Co. Antrim and other parts of Ulster.

In Newfoundland:

Early instances: James, from Stevenstone (Ayrshire), married at St. John's, 1830 (DPHW 26D); ——, daughter of Thomas, from Dunse (Berwickshire), Scotland, married at St. John's, 1857 (*Newfoundlander* 10 Sep 1857).

Modern status: Rare, at Clarenville.

Place names (not necessarily from the surname): Swan Island(s), —— Island Harbour 49-28 55-03.

SWANSON, a surname of England – son of *Swan* (*see* SWAN), or ? from the English place name Swainstone (Devon). (Spiegelhalter).

Traced by Spiegelhalter in Devon.

In Newfoundland:

Modern status: Rare, at Buchans.

SWARTZ. *See* SCHWARTZ

SWEENEY, a surname of Ireland, (Mac) Sweeney, *Mac Suibhne*, Ir. *suibhne* – pleasant. (MacLysaght). *See* SWAIN.

Traced by MacLysaght in Cos. Donegal, Cork and Kerry.

In Newfoundland:

Early instances: Cornelius, of St. John's, 1796 (CO 194.39); Sara, from Feedown (unidentified) (Diocese of Ossery), married at St. John's, 1804 (Nfld. Archives BRC); James Sweeny, farmer of Bell Isle (now Bell Island), 1814, came to Bell Isle from Ireland 10 or 11 years previously, that is, 1804–5 (D'Alberti 24); John, of Harbour Grace Parish, 1808 (Nfld. Archives HGRC); ? Owen, of Tilton Harbour (now Tilting), 1820 (Nfld. Archives KCRC); Thomas, of Ross (unspecified), married at Bonavista, 1831 (Nfld. Archives KCRC); Mary, of Joe Batts Arm, 1823 (Nfld. Archives KCRC); Miles Sweeney, ? of Harbour Grace, 1845 (*Newfoundlander* 9 Jan 1845); Solomon Sweeny, granted land at Ferryland, 1846 (Nfld. Archives, Registry Crown Lands); Margaret, of Petty Harbour, 1867 (Nfld. Archives HGRC); Edward (and others) Sweeney, fishermen of Carbonear, 1871 (Lovell); Michael, of Fleury Bight (Gander B.), 1871 (Lovell); John, of Fortune Harbour, 1871 (Lovell); Edward, of Ram's Islands (Placentia B.), 1871 (Lovell).

Modern status: Scattered, especially at Bell Island.

Place names: Sweeney Island 49-32 5S-15; Sweeneys Pond 47-46 53-17.

SWEET, a surname of England from the Old English personal name *Swēt(a)* – sweet, or from Old English *swēte* – sweet (a nickname, perhaps ironic). (Reaney, Cottle).

Traced by Guppy in Somerset and by Spiegelhalter in Devon.

In Newfoundland:

Early instances: Phillip, of Trinity (? Trinity B.), 1708–9 (CO 194.4); William, of Trinity Bay, 1774 (DPHW 64); John, of Freshwater (Carbonear), 1791 (CO 199.18); William, proprietor of fishing room, Salmon Cove (now Champneys), Winter 1800–01 (Census Trinity B); Daniel, of Twillingate, 1811 (D'Alberti 22); Francis, granted land at Catalina, 1847 (Nfld. Archives, Registry Crown Lands); George, of Bay of Islands, 1871 (Lovell); Richard, of Rose Blanche, 1871 (Lovell); Thomas, sailor of St. John's, 1871 (Lovell).

Modern status: At Channel (*Electors* 1955), Corner Brook and Catalina.

Place names (not necessarily from the surname): Sweet Bay 48-26 53-39, 48-30 53-39.

SWEETAPPLE, a surname of England, presumably a nickname, a term of endearment, or from residence near a particular sweet apple-tree. (Reaney, Bardsley).

In Newfoundland:

Early instances: William, of Greenspond, 1815 (DPHW 76); Charles, of Harbour Grace, 1819 (D'Alberti 29); John, of Deer Island (Bonavista B.), 1830 (DPHW 76); John, fisherman of Gooseberry Island (Bonavista B.), 1864 (DPHW 81).

Modern status: Scattered, especially at Glovertown and St. John's.

SWEETLAND, a surname of England from the English place name Sweetlands Farm (Devon). (Spiegelhalter).

Traced by Spiegelhalter in Devon.

In Newfoundland:

Early instances: Henry, of St. John's, 1787 (DPHW 26C); William, of English Harbour (Trinity B.), 1790 (DPHW 64); Henry, J.P., Ferryland district, 1790 (D'Alberti 4); Ann, of Ferryland, 1791 (USPG); Edward, of Carbonear, 1802 (CO 199.18); Joseph, of Bonavista, 1807 (DPHW 70); Mary, of Harbour Grace, 1813 (Nfld. Archives BRC); William, merchant of Caplin Bay (now Calvert), ? 1815 (CO 194.56); ——, of Placentia Bay, 1830 (*Newfoundlander* 21 Oct 1830); Benjamin, of Trinity Bay, 1837 (*Newfoundlander* 20 Apr 1837); Henry, fisherman of Brigus, 1856 (DPHW 35); Benjamin, lawyer of Trinity (Trinity B.), 1871 (Lovell).

Modern status: Scattered, especially at Bonavista.

SWERSKY, SWIRSKY, anglicizations of ? the surname of Russia Zveruchivskij, from the Polish Zwierzchowski, containing the element *zwierzch* – above. (Unbegaun).

In Newfoundland:

Modern status: Swersky, unique, at St. John's; Swirsky, unique, at Corner Brook.

SWIFT, a surname of England and Ireland from Old English *swift* – swift, quick, also used as a personal name; in Ireland also sometimes by pseudo-

translation of (O)Fodaghan, *Ó Fuadacháin* or (O)Foody, *Ó Fuada* or *Ó Fuadaigh*. (Reaney, MacLysaght).

Traced by Guppy in Derbyshire, Lancashire, Nottinghamshire and Yorkshire WR, by Spiegelhalter in Devon and by MacLysaght in Co. Mayo.

In Newfoundland:

Early instances: John, of Harbour Grace Parish, 1834 (Nfld. Archives HGRC); William, fisherman of Bay de Loup (Burgeo-La Poile district), 1859 (DPHW 101); William, of Red Island (Burgeo-La Poile district), 1871 (Lovell); William, of St. John's, 1871 (Lovell).

Modern status: At Seal Cove (Harbour Main district), Muddy Hole and The Reach (Burgeo-La Poile district) (*Electors* 1955).

SWYER(S), surnames of England, northern forms of SQUIRE(S), or from Old English *swīra, swēora* – (dweller by the) neck, cob, hollow on a ridge, or from the English place name Swyre (Dorset). (Reaney, Cottle).

In Newfoundland:

Family traditions: —— Swyers, from Pomerania, Germany, settled at Bonavista in 1859 (MUN Folklore). —— Swyer, from Somerset, settled at Port aux Basques in the 18th century (MUN Folklore). ——, from Jersey, Channel Islands, settled at Sandy Point (St. George's B.) in the 1700s (MUN Folklore).

Early instances: Phillip Swyer, planter of Bayley's Cove (Bonavista B.), 1817 (DPHW 72); Robert Swire(s), planter of Hants Harbour, 1821 (DPHW 58); Richard Swyor, of Kings Cove Parish, 1839 (Nfld. Archives KCRC); John Swires, planter of Bonavista, 1842 (DPHW 72); James, of Old Perlican, 1850 (DPHW 58); Thomas Swyers, fisherman of Little Seldom-Come-By, 1871 (Lovell); William Swiers and Bennett Swyer, of Sandy Point (St. George's B.), 1871 (DPHW 96, Lovell).

Modern status: Swyer, at Barachois Brook, Cartyville (St. George's district) and Stephenville; Swyers, scattered.

Place name: Swyers Pool 48-36 58-19.

SYMES. *See* SIMMS

SYMONDS. *See* SIMMON(D)S

SYN(Y)ARD. *See* SENIOR, SINYARD

T

TAAFFE, a surname of Ireland – son of David (*see* DAVEY), the name of a family of Welsh origin which went to Ireland in the thirteenth century. (MacLysaght).

Traced by MacLysaght in Cos. Louth and Sligo.

In Newfoundland:

Early instances: John Tafe or Tufe, of St. John's, 1809–10 (CO 194.50); Mary Taffe, of St. John's, 1814 (Nfld. Archives BRC).

Modern status: Rare, at Corner Brook.

TAIT(E), surnames of England, Scotland and Ireland from Old Norse *teitr* – gay, cheerful, or a variant of Tate from an Old English personal name *Tāt(a)* – dear, glad, hilltop, dice, lock of hair, daddy, teat. (Reaney, Cottle, Black, MacLysaght).

Guppy traced Tait and Tate in Durham and Northumberland and Tait in the Scots Border counties; Spiegelhalter traced Tait and Tate in Devon; and MacLysaght traced Tait and Tate in northern Ulster.

In Newfoundland:

Early instances: George Tait, planter of Trinity (Trinity B.), 1822 (DPHW 64); Richard Teate, Tate or Tait, from Fealhurd [sic], (unidentified) (Co. Waterford), of Tilton Harbour (now Tilting), 1823 (Nfld. Archives KCRC).

Modern status: Taite, at Corner Brook, Glovertown, St. John's and Grand Falls; Tait, at St. John's and Grand Falls.

Place name: Tait Point (Labrador) 60-03 64-16.

TALBOT, a surname of England and Ireland from an Old German personal name **Talabod* or **Dalabod*, Old French *Talebot*, of obscure meaning. (Reaney, Cottle, Dauzat).

Traced by Guppy in Dorset, Lancashire, Nottinghamshire and Somerset, by Spiegelhalter in Devon, and by MacLysaght in Dublin.

In Newfoundland:

Early instances: George Talbott, of English Harbour (Trinity B.), 1675, of Bonavista, 1677 (CO 1); John, of St. Pierre area, about 1714 (CO 194.6); James Talbot, of Trinity Bay, 1774 (DPHW 64); Thomas Talbott, of Harbour Grace, 1820 (Nfld. Archives HGRC); James Talbot, of St. John's, 1829 (DPHW 26D); William, from Ooning (unidentified)

(Co. Kilkenny), married at Harbour Grace, 1829 (Nfld. Archives BRC); Thomas, of Bird Island Cove (now Elliston), 1830 (Nfld. Archives KCRC); Thomas, schoolmaster of Mosquito (now Bristols Hope), 1839 (MUN Hist.); Thomas, of Carbonear, 1856 (*Newfoundlander* 19 Jun 1856); William, fisherman of Rose Blanche, 1871 (Lovell).

Modern status: Rare, at Canada Harbour (White B.) (Electors 1955).

TALECK, TALLACK, TALLECT, variants of the surnames of France Tal(l)ec, a Breton name – one who has a big forehead or brow. (Dauzat).

In Newfoundland:

Family tradition: A Breton name (Thomas, "French Fam. Names").

Early instances: Phillip Tallick or Tallack, of St. John's Harbour, 1703, 1706, of Quidi Vidi, 1708–9 (CO 194.3,4).

Modern status: Taleck (*Electors* 1955), Talick (1970 Telephone Directory), rare, at Corner Brook; Tallack, unique, at West Bay (Port au Port district); Talleck, rare, at Cape St. George (*Electors* 1955).

Place names: Tallek Arm, Tallek (South Arm) (Labrador) 59-02 63-54.

TANCOCK, a surname of England for Dancock, a pet-form of Daniel (*see* DANIELS). (Bardsley, Spiegelhalter).

Traced by Guppy in Devon.

In Newfoundland:

Modern status: Unique, at St. John's.

TANSLEY, a surname of England from the English place name Tansley (Derbyshire), ? containing the Old English personal name *Tān* and *lēah* – wood, clearing.

In Newfoundland:

Modern status: Rare, at St. John's.

TAPLIN, a variant of the surnames of England Tam(p)lin, Tambling etc., double diminutives of *Tam* (Tom) (*see* THOMAS). (Bardsley, Reaney, Cottle). *See also* TOMLINSON, TOMPKINS.

Guppy traced Tamblyn in Cornwall.

In Newfoundland:

Early instances: James, farmer of Holyrood (Conception B.), 1871 (Lovell); James Tapling, of King's Cove, 1877 (Nfld. Archives KCRC).

Modern status: At Grand Falls (*Electors* 1955), Holyrood and Bell Island.

TAPP, a surname of England from the Old English personal name **Tæppa*, unrecorded but found in such place names as Taplow (Buckinghamshire), Tapton (Derbyshire), etc. (Reaney).

Traced by Guppy in Devon and Somerset.

In Newfoundland:

Early instances: Benjamin, of Broad Cove (now St. Phillips) or Portugal Cove, married at St. John's, 1791 (DPHW 26D); William Tappe, of Cape Ray, 1835 (DPHW 30); —— Tapp, of Harbour Grace, 1844 (*Newfoundlander* 13 Jun 1844); John and Benjamin, farmers of Broad Cove (now St. Phillips), 1871 (Lovell); John, fisherman of Caplin Bay (now Calvert), 1871 (Lovell).

Modern status: Scattered.

TAPPER, a surname of England from Old English *tæppere* – tapper (of casks), ale-seller, inn-keeper. (Reaney, Cottle).

Traced by Spiegelhalter in Devon.

In Newfoundland:

Family tradition: ——, from Lancaster (Lancashire), settled at Tapper's Cove (Torbay) (MUN Folklore).

Early instances: John Taper, boatkeeper of St. John's, 1682 (CO 1); Charles Tapper, planter in possession of property, Torbay, 1794–5, "30 years in Newfoundland," that is, 1764–5 (Census 1794–5); Charlotte, of Port de Grave, 1814 (Newfoundland Archives BRC); John, fisherman, from Sturminster Newton (Dorset), of Harbour Breton, 1857 (DPHW 104; D.A. Macdonald); John, of Frenchman's Cove (Burin district), 1871 (Lovell).

Modern status: Scattered, especially at Torbay.

Place name: Tappers Cove (Torbay).

TARBETT, a surname of England, Tarbe(r)t of Scotland; in England variants of Turbard from Scandinavian *thor-*, *thur-* and Old German *-bert*, in Norman French *Turbert*, ? as in Thouberville (Eure), or confused with the Old Norse personal name *Thorbiorn*, Old English *Thurbeorn* – Thor-warrior which also gives THORBURN; in Scotland ? from the Scots place name Tarbat (Ross and Cromarty). (Reaney, Black).

Spiegelhalter traced Tarbutt, Turbett in Devon.

In Newfoundland:

Modern status: At Corner Brook and Mount Carmel.

TARGETT, a surname of England, Target of France; in France a diminutive of Targe – (wearer or maker of) targe(s), shield(s), buckler(s), or from the French place name Target (Allier), or ? confused with the surname Targit from Old French *targif* – slow; in England, according to Bardsley – dweller by the target, where archers practised, but according to Weekley from the Old English personal name *Thurgod*. Reaney, however, does not cite Target(t) as variants of either Thorogood or Thurgood. (Dauzat, Weekley *Romance*, Bardsley, Reaney).

In Newfoundland:

Family tradition: —— Target, tinsmith, from England, settled at Hants Harbour before 1850 (MUN Folklore).

Early instances: John Targate, of Harbour Grace Parish, 1813 (Nfld. Archives HGRC); John Targett, of Hants Harbour, 1841 (DPHW 59); Richard and William Targate, farmers of Holyrood, 1871 (Lovell).

Modern status: At Corner Brook, Port au Port and Kippens.

TARRANT, a surname of England and Ireland from a British river name, a variant of Trent, of unknown meaning, ? trespasser, flooder, whence eight places in Dorset and one in Hampshire; in Ireland used in Co. Cork with Thornton as the anglicized form of *Ó Toráin*. (Cottle, Ekwall, MacLysaght).

Traced by Spiegelhalter in Devon and by MacLysaght in Co. Cork.

In Newfoundland:

Early instances: John Tarrant or Tarrent, of St. John's, 1708–9 (CO 194.4); Robert Tarrant, of Black Island (Twillingate district), 1840 (DPHW 86); William, of Fogo, 1840 (DPHW 83); William, of Shoal Bay (Fogo district), 1871 (Lovell).

Modern status: Scattered, especially at Lawn.

TAVENOR, TAVERNER, TAVERNOR, surnames of England from Old French *tavernier*, Anglo-French *taverner* – tavern-keeper, inn-keeper. (Reaney, Cottle).

Guppy traced Taverner in Devon, where Spiegelhalter also traced Taven(d)er and Taviner.

In Newfoundland:

Family tradition: Benjamin and his brother Jacob Tavenor were among the first settlers of Trinity (Trinity B.), in 1725 (Family).

Early instances: Margaret (and others) Taverner, of Bay de Verde, 1675 (CO 1); Jacob Tavernor, of Trinity, 1708–9 (CO 194.4); William Taverner, of Newfoundland, ? 1713 (CO 194.5); Abraham

Tavener, of St. John's, 1801 (DPHW 26D); Bridget Tavernor, from Dublin, married at St. John's, 1818 (Nfld. Archives BRC); William, planter of Salmon Cove (now Champneys), 1837 (DPHW 64B).

Modern status: Tavenor, at St. John's, Port aux Basques, Corner Brook and Shoal Harbour; Taverner, unique, at Stephenville; Tavernor, at Shoal Harbour, St. John's and Corner Brook.

TAYLOR, a surname of England, Scotland, Ireland and the Channel Islands, with Tayler of Guernsey from Old French *tailleor*, Anglo-French *tailleur* – tailor. (Reaney, Black, MacLysaght, Turk).

Found widespread by Guppy in England and Scotland, and by MacLysaght in Ulster and Dublin.

In Newfoundland:

Family tradition: ——, from Hampshire, settled at Bishops Cove (Conception B.) in the 18th century (MUN Folklore).

Early instances: Thomas, of Old Perlican, 1675 (CO 1); Laurence Tayler, of Harbour Grace, 1677 (CO 1); —— Taylor, merchant of St. John's, 1700 (CO 194.2); William, of Port de Grave, 1782, property "possessed by the Family for upwards of 80 years," that is, before 1702 (CO 199.18); Robert, of Cupids, 1788, in possession of property at Port de Grave, property "possessed by the Family for upwards of 80 years," that is, before 1708 (CO 199.18); Richard, of Carbonear, 1765 (CO 199.18); Susanna, of Southside Musketta (now Bristols Hope), 1779 (CO 199.18); William, of Bonavista, 1786 (DPHW 70); Samuel, constable of Aquaforte, 1797 (D'Alberti 6); Thomas, fisherman of Bay of Exploits, ? 1797 (CO 194.39); Richard, of Crockers Cove (Carbonear), 1804 (CO 199.18); Robert, of Brigus, 1809 (DPHW 34); Bazil, of Moretons Harbour, 1812 (DPHW 48); James, planter of Joe Batts Arm, 1823 (USPG); William, planter of Cupids, at Change Islands, 1823 (USPG); Bridget Talor, of Gooseberry Island (Bonavista B.), 1829 (Nfld. Archives KCRC); Jacob Taylor, of Middle Bight (now Codner), 1832 (DPHW 30); Richard, of Salmon Cove (Port de Grave district), 1834 (*Newfoundlander* 23 Jan 1834); Joseph, of Long Pond, 1837 (DPHW 26D); James, of Red Island (Burgeo-La Poile district), 1840 (DPHW 101); John, of Tickle Cove (Bonavista B.), 1843 (DPHW 73A); Morgan, of Grole, 1847 (DPHW 102); Thomas, of Western Head (Twillingate district), 1847 (DPHW 86); William Henry, deacon of Spaniard's Bay, 1847 (DPHW 26D); James, of Harbour Breton, 1851 (DPHW 104); Robert, of Burnt Head (Cupids district), 1851 (DPHW 34); Wm. C., from Teignmouth (Devon), married at St. John's,

1855 (*Newfoundlander* 9 Aug 1855); Richard Wm., of Lower Burgeo, 1857 (DPHW 101); William Tailor, of Harbour Le Cou, 1860 (DPHW 99); John Taylor, of Burin Bay, 1860 (DPHW 100); widespread in Lovell 1871.

Modern status: Widespread, especially at Forrester's Point (St. Barbe district), Corner Brook, Moretons Harbour, Raleigh (White B.), St. John's, Cupids, Carbonear, Bishop's Cove, Long Pond and Grole.

Place names: Taylor Bay 47-33 55-39; —— Brook 49-33 57-06; —— Inlet (Labrador) 57-50 61-43; —— Island 47-38 56-12, 47-44 55-51; —— Point 48-05 53-01, 48-06 53-45; —— Pond 46-40 57-00; —— Rock 47-37 56-12; —— —— (Labrador) 54-35 57-12; —— Shoal 47-36 58-39; —— Island Rocks 47-44 55-51; Taylor's Bay 46-53 55-44; —— Point 49-43 54-18; —— Bay Point, —— —— Rock 46-52 55-42; —— —— Shoal 46-49 55-43; —— Table Cove (Labrador) 55-07 59-05.

TEE, a surname of England from Old English *ēa* – (dweller by the) stream, or ? a variant not recorded by MacLysaght of the surnames of Ireland (O)Tighe, Tigue, Teague, *Ó Taidhg*. (Reaney, MacLysaght).

In Newfoundland:

Early instances: John Teage Jr., of Bay Bulls about 1773–5 (USPG); Sylvester Tee, from Ross (unspecified) (Co. Wexford), married at St. John's, 1793 (Nfld. Archives BRC); John Teage, of St. John's, 1817 (CO 194.59); Silvester Tea, of Toads (now Tors) Cove, 1820 (Nfld. Archives BRC).

Modern status: At Burn Cove (Ferryland district) (*Electors* 1955) and St. John's.

TEMPLE, a surname of England and France from Old French *temple*, Old English *templ* – (dweller in or near the) temple, especially one of the houses associated with the Knights Templars, a "military and religious order founded to protect pilgrims to the Holy Land and taking its name from Solomon's Temple, but suppressed in 1312 for alleged vice and heresy," though "many eighteenth century foundlings were given the surname at their baptism in Temple Church, London," also in England from Combe Temple, now Templeton (Devon) (*see* TEMPLETON). (Cottle, Spiegelhalter, Reaney).

In France, Temple is a not uncommon place name associated with a house of the Knights Templars. (Reaney, Cottle, Spiegelhalter, Dauzat).

Traced by Guppy in Lincolnshire and by Spiegelhalter in Devon.

In Newfoundland:

Family tradition: George, from England, was one of the earliest settlers of Norman's Cove (Trinity B.) in the early 1800s (MUN Hist.).

Early instances: Thomas, of Bonavista, 1816 (Nfld. Archives KCRC); George, planter of Selby Cove (Bay de Verde district), 1824 (DPHW 58); George, planter of Norman's Cove, 1829 (DPHW 59A); William, planter of Upper Island Cove, 1846 (DPHW 59A); Matthew and William, of Chapel Arm (Trinity B.), 1871 (Lovell); James, planter of Cobblers Island (Bonavista B.), 1871 (Lovell).

Modern status: Scattered, especially at Long Cove (Trinity B.).

Place names: Temple Bay (Labrador), —— Pass (Labrador) 51-59 55-55; —— Brook (Labrador) 52-02 55-59.

TEMPLEMAN, a surname of England – servant or tenant of the Templars. *See* TEMPLE. (Reaney, Cottle).

Traced by Guppy in Nottinghamshire.

In Newfoundland:

Early instances: James, of Bonavista, 1803 (DPHW 70); Joseph, of St. John's, 1817 (CO 194.59); Joseph, granted land at "Longlands" Old Topsail Road, 1840 (Nfld. Archives, Registry Crown Lands).

Modern status: Scattered, especially at St. John's and Bonavista.

Place names: Templeman 49-12 53-32; —— Lake 49-01 55-08.

TEMPLETON, a surname of England, Scotland and Ireland, in England from the English place name Templeton (Devon, Berkshire), – the Templars' place; in Scotland ? from the Scots place name in Ayrshire. (Cottle, Ekwall, Black, MacLysaght). *See* TEMPLE.

Traced by Guppy in Ayrshire and Lanarkshire and by MacLysaght in Ulster.

In Newfoundland:

Early instance: Robert, native of Glenluce, Scotland, died at St. John's, 1904, aged 65 (General Protestant Cemetery, St. John's).

Modern status: At St. John's.

TERRY, a surname of England and Ireland, in England from the Old German personal name *Theudoric*, Old French *T(h)ierri*, *Terri*, containing the elements *people* and *rule*; also in Ireland an anglicization of *Mac Toirdealbhaigh*. (Reaney, Cottle, MacLysaght).

Traced by Guppy in Buckinghamshire, Kent and Yorkshire WR, by Spiegelhalter in Devon, and by MacLysaght especially in the city and county of Cork since the thirteenth century.

In Newfoundland:

Early instances: James, of Newfoundland, ? 1706 (CO 194.24); Thomas, of North Side Harbour Grace, 1760 (CO 199.18); Thomas (and others), of Harbour Main, 1774 (CO 199.18); Thomas, of St. John's, 1803 (Nfld. Archives BRC); Patrick, of Bonavista, 1820 (Nfld. Archives KCRC); Mary, of Numins (? for Newman's) Cove, 1850 (Nfld. Archives KCRC); Edward, of King's Cove, 1860 (Nfld. Archives KCRC); Michael and William, fishermen of Newman's Cove, 1871 (Lovell).

Modern status: Scattered, especially in the Harbour Main district.

TESSIER, a surname of France and the Channel Islands, from the French *tisserand* – weaver. (Dauzat, LeMessurier).

In Newfoundland:

Early instances: ——, of St. John's, 1841 (*Newfoundlander* 18 Feb 1841); James C. (1842–) from London, England, joined the firm of P. & L. Tessier at St. John's, 1853 (Mott).

Modern status: At St. John's and Grand Bank.

TETFORD, TITFORD, surnames of England from the English place names Tetford (Lincolnshire) or Thetford (Cambridgeshire, Norfolk), or (dweller by the) people's ford, or a variant of the surname Thetford. (Cottle, Ekwall).

Titford traced by the family in Fordingbridge (Hampshire).

In Newfoundland:

Early instance: George Titford, mariner of Harbour Grace, 1849 (DPHW 43).

Modern status: Tetford, at St. John's, Harbour Grace and Lawrenceton (Gander district); Titford, at St. John's and Shearstown.

THATCHELL, ? a variant of the surname of England Tatchell – ? son of *Tachel* (untraced). (Bardsley).

Bardsley traced Tatchell in Somerset.

In Newfoundland:

Early instances: Henry, of St. John Island (St. Barbe district), 1873 (MUN Hist.); George, of Bartlett's Harbour, 1911 (Nfld. Archives HGRC).

Modern status: At Castor River, Bartletts Harbour, Ferolle (St. Barbe district) (*Electors* 1955) and Port Saunders.

THISTLE, a surname of England – dweller near the thistles, or a Newfoundland variant of the surname of France and Jersey (Channel Islands) TOUZEL, from a nickname – young man with hair cut short (Dauzat, Turk).

In Newfoundland:

Family tradition: ——, one of four Thistle brothers, from Guernsey (Channel Islands) who came to Newfoundland, settled at Harbour Grace. A descendant moved to Boot Harbour (near Springdale) about 1825 (MUN Folklore).

Early instances: Amy, of Harbour Grace, 1765, property "possessed by the Family for 102 years," that is, since 1663 (CO 199.18); Henery [sic] Thistle, of Bell Island, 1708–9 (CO 194.4); Thomas Thistle, constable of Carbonear district ? 1730, 1732 (CO 194.9); Frances, of Carbonear, 1772 (CO 199.18); William, of Mulleys Cove, 1777 (CO 199.18); William, of Pouch Cove, 1818 (DPHW 26B); Samuel, of Broad Cove (Bay de Verde district), 1821 (DPHW 52A); Alice, of Cat Harbour (now Lumsden), 1868 (Nfld. Archives KCRC); Thomas, of Bay of Islands, 1871 (Lovell); John, clerk of St. John's, 1871 (Lovell); Samuel Tistle, of Random Sound, 1871 (Lovell).

Modern status: Scattered, especially at St. John's and Corner Brook.

Place names (not necessarily from the surname): Thistle Island (Labrador) 53-41 60-03; —— Rock 51-43 56-23; —— Shoal 51-12 55-46.

THOMAS, a baptismal name and surname of England, Wales, Scotland, Ireland, France and the Channel Islands from an Aramaic word meaning 'twin,' the name of one of the Apostles, also known as *Didymus*, Greek for a twin. In England, according to Withycombe, *Thomas* is found before the Norman Conquest only as a priest's name but thereafter came into general use and was popularized by the fame of St. Thomas of Canterbury (Thomas Becket 1118–70) whose martyrdom made Canterbury the greatest object of pilgrimage in the country. From the thirteenth century onwards Thomas became one of the commonest male baptismal names (Every Tom, Dick and Harry) and even a generic term for males as in tomcat, tomboy. In France, Dauzat ascribes its popularity also to St. Thomas Aquinas (1225–74). Several surnames were formed from it including THOMAS(on), T(h)omlin(e), TAPLIN, T(H)OMS, THOM(P)SON, TOMLINSON, TOMPKINS, TUMA. (Withycombe, Reaney, Cottle, Black, MacLysaght, Dauzat, Turk).

Found widespread by Guppy especially in Monmouthshire and South Wales, and by MacLysaght throughout Ireland but especially in Dublin and Belfast.

In Newfoundland:

Family tradition: Edward, from Wales, settled at Cupids about 1850; his son moved to Salvage (Bonavista B.) about 1880 (MUN Folklore).

Early instances: Henry, of Harbour Grace, 1765, property "in possession of the Family for upwards of 80 years," that is, before 1685 (CO 199.18); Jacob, carpenter of St. John's, 1794–5, "52 years in Newfoundland," that is, 1742–3 (Census 1794–5); William Bevil (1757–), born at St. John's was one of the Thomases who carried on business at Dartmouth (Devon) and St. John's in partnership as Thomas and Stokes (Prowse); Jacob, of Trinity Bay, 1767 (DPHW 64); James, of Western Bay, 1784 (CO 199.18); Nile and Co., of Ferryland, 1791 (USPG); Henry (1794–1879), from Daccombe (Devon) to St. John's, 1837 (G.S. Thomas); John, proprietor and occupier of fishing room at Silly Cove (now Winterton), Winter 1800–01 (Census Trinity B.); Isabella, from Co. Wexford, married at St. John's, 1811 (Nfld. Archives BRC); Maria, of Torbay, 1822 (Nfld. Archives BRC); Grace, of Heart's Content, 1825 (Nfld. Archives KCRC); M., from Mevagissey (Cornwall), late of St. John's, 1832 (*Newfoundlander* 19 Apr 1832); Benjamin, of Grand Bank, 1834 (DPHW 109); Joseph, planter of Hants Harbour, 1839 (DPHW 59A); William, cooper, married at Harbour Breton, 1841, ? same as William, of Lower Burgeo, 1845 (DPHW 101; D.A. Macdonald); George, of Harbour Le Cou, 1849 (Feild); Nicholas, of Carbonear, married at Square Island (Labrador), 1851 (DPHW 114); John, of Catalina, deceased, 1858 (*Newfoundlander* 7 Jan 1858); scattered in Lovell 1871.

Modern status: Scattered, especially at St. John's, Grand Falls and Carbonear.

Place names (not necessarily from the surname): Thomas Falls (Labrador) 53-31 64-30; —— Island (or Graveyard) Island (Labrador) 57-12 61-28; —— Point (Labrador) 60-19 64-26; —— Pond 47-27 52-55; —— River (Labrador) 54-14 61-31; —— Rock 47-08 55-03; John Thomas Rock 46-51 55-46.

THOMASEN, a surname of Denmark – son of Thomas (*see* THOMAS). (A. Horwood).

In Newfoundland:

Modern status: Rare, at Grand Bank.

THOMEY, ? a Newfoundland variant of the surnames of Ireland, (O)TWOMEY, Toomey, *Ó Tuama*, or ? of the surname of France Thoumieu, a shortened form of Bartoumieu (Bartholomew).

MacLysaght traced Twomey in Cos. Cork and Kerry, Toomey in Co. Limerick, and LeMessurier Thoume in the Channel Islands.

In Newfoundland:

Family tradition: —— Thomey, Toomey, Twomey or Tumey, from Co. Cork, settled at Bristol's Hope about 1835 (MUN Folklore).

Early instances: Arthur, of Harbour Grace, 1771 (Nfld. Archives L118); John T(h)omey, ? of Port de Grave, 1775, 1783 (Nfld. Archives T22); John Thomey, ? of St. John's, 1795 (CO 194.40); —— and Co., of Carbonear, 1798 (CO 199.18); Roger, of Musketta (now Bristol's Hope), 1802 (CO 199.18); Honora, of King's Cove Parish, 1838 (Nfld. Archives KCRC).

Modern status: Thomey, scattered, especially at Harbour Grace; Twomey, rare, at Botwood.

Place names: Thomey Cove 47-52 56-10; —— Island (Labrador) 54-32 57-12; Toomie Point (Labrador) 53-45 56-37.

THOM(P)SON, surnames of England, Scotland and Ireland, with Thomson more commonly in Scotland, – son of T(h)om (Thomas). *See* THOMAS. (Reaney, Cottle, Black, MacLysaght).

Guppy traced Thompson especially in Northumberland, but found it widespread except in the southwest of England, and Thomson distributed over a large part of Scotland especially south of the Forth and Clyde. MacLysaght found Thom(p)son mainly in Ulster.

In Newfoundland:

Family tradition: Alexander Thomson (about 1810–1885) from Moffat (Dumfriesshire), Scotland, settled at St. John's about 1833 (MUN Folklore). William Thompson, from Scotland, settled at Coley's Point in 1863 (MUN Hist.).

Early instances: Thomas Thompson, of St. John's, 1756 (DPHW 26C); Andrew Thomson, of Harbour Grace, 1801 (USPG); James Thompson, of Bay Bulls, 1803 (Nfld. Archives BRC); John, planter of Hants Harbour, 1827 (DPHW 58); John, from Co. Kilkenny, married at St. John's, 1828 (Nfld. Archives BRC); John Thom(p)son, of Grates Cove, 1828 (DPHW 58); John Thompson, of Catalina, 1832 (DPHW 70); John, planter of Old Perlican, 1833 (DPHW 58); Edward Thomson, of Trinity (unspecified), 1834 (Nfld. Archives KCRC); John, from Dumbarton, Scotland, of Catalina, died 1842 (*Times* 13 Apr 1842); Henry Thompson, M.D., of Broad Cove (Bay de Verde district), 1845 (*Newfoundlander* 19 Jun 1845); John, M.D. of Carbonear, 1848 (DPHW 48); R., at Harbour Breton, 1848 (D.A. Macdonald); Silas Thomson, of Herring Neck, 1850, of Salt Harbour (Twillingate district), 1854 (DPHW 85); Leonard, of The Ponds (Port de Grave district), 1860 (DPHW 38); Charles R. (1851–), from Perth, Scotland, moved with his family to Nova Scotia; he settled at St. John's in 1871 (Mott); scattered in Lovell 1871.

Modern status: Thompson, scattered, especially at Point Leamington (Green B.), Botwood and St. John's; Thomson, at St. John's.

Place names: Thompson Beach 47-29 55-48; —— Point (Labrador) 59-55 64-09; Lake Thomson (or Eastern Blue Pond) 50-27 57-07.

T(H)OMS, surnames of England, Thoms of Scotland, Toms of the Channel Islands, pet-forms of Thomas (*see* THOMAS); also in Scotland for Mac Thomas – son of Thomas. (Reaney, Black, Turk).

In Newfoundland:

Early instances: William Thoms, of Ferryland, 1675 (CO 1); John, of Bonavista, 1787 (DPHW 70); James Thom, of St. John's, 1822 (CO 194.65); Mary, of New Harbour (Trinity B.), 1828 (DPHW 59A); Jacob Thomas or Thombs, of Shoe Cove (Twillingate district), 1842, 1850 (DPHW 86); James Toms, of Shoe Cove, 1851 (DPHW 86); Elias Thombs, of Joe Batts Arm, 1856 (DPHW 83); John Thom, of Burnt Island (Burgeo-La Poile district), 1871 (Lovell); William, of New (now Parsons) Harbour, 1871 (Lovell); Henry (and others) Thom, of Torbay, 1871 (Lovell).

Modern status: Thoms, scattered; Toms, scattered, especially at La Scie.

Place names (not necessarily from the surname): Tom Hole 47-39 55-03, —— Rock 47-22 55-47, 47-37 57-29; —— Holt 47-00 55-09; —— Rock Head 47-37 57-30; Toms Cove 49-47 56-48, —— —— (Labrador) 55-07 59-11; —— Point (Labrador) 55-06 59-14; —— Pond (Labrador) 54-58 67-13.

THOMSON. *See* THOMPSON

THORBURN, a surname of England and Scotland from an Old Norse personal name *Thorbiorn* in Old English *Thurbeorn*. (Reaney, Cottle, Black). *See also* TARBETT.

Traced by Spiegelhalter in Devon.

In Newfoundland:

Early instances: Sir Robert, K.C.M.G. (1836–1906) from Juniper Bank (Peebleshire) Scotland, came to St. John's in 1852 (Mott); Michael (and others), of St. John's, 1871 (Lovell); Thomas J., of Gambo, 1889 (Nfld. Archives KCRC).

Modern status: At St. John's.

Place names: Thorburn Hills 47-27 52-44; —— Lake 48-16 54-10; —— Road 47-35 52-51.

THORNE, a surname of England and Ireland from the English place names Thorn(e) (Devon, Somerset, Yorkshire WR), or – (dweller by the) (haw)thorn;

in Ireland occasionally a variant of Thoran or a shortened form of Thornton. (Reaney, Cottle, Spiegelhalter, MacLysaght).

Traced by Guppy in Berkshire, Buckinghamshire, Devon, Dorset, Kent, Somerset and Wiltshire, with Thorne the usual form but associated with Thorn in Devon, Somerset and Kent.

In Newfoundland:

Early instances: William Thorn, of St. John's, 1762 (CO 194.15); Richard Thorne, in possession of property and fisherman of Torbay, 1794–5, "20 years in Newfoundland," that is, 1774–5 (Census 1794–5); John Thorn, of Trinity (Trinity B.), 1775, of New Harbour (Trinity B.), 1795 (DPHW 64); John, of Fortune Bay, 1811 (D'Alberti 21); William, of Harbour Grace, 1816 (Nfld. Archives HGRC); William, planter of Durrell's Harbour (Trinity B.), 1826 (DPHW 64B); Catherine, of Kings Cove Parish, 1836 (Nfld. Archives KCRC); ——, of St. Lawrence, 1843 (*Newfoundlander* 31 Aug 1843); William, of New (now Parsons) Harbour, 1856 (DPHW 102); William, of Lower Island Cove, 1857 (DPHW 55); William, of Burin, 1871 (Lovell); John, of Chapel Arm (Trinity B.), 1871 (Lovell); William, of Whales Brook (Trinity B.), 1871 (Lovell).

Modern status: Widespread, especially at Torbay, New Harbour (Trinity B.), Thornlea, Norman's Cove, Burnt Islands (Burgeo-La Poile district), Grand Falls and St. John's.

Place name: Thornlea 47-36 53-43.

THORNHILL, a surname of England, Scotland and Ireland from the English place name Thornhill (Derbyshire, Dorset, Wiltshire, etc.), or ? from the Scots place name Thornhill (Dumfriesshire), or – (dweller by the) (haw)thorn(-covered) hill. (Cottle, MacLysaght, Black).

Traced by Guppy in Cheshire and by MacLysaght in Cos. Cork and Limerick since the seventeenth century.

In Newfoundland:

Family tradition: Ann (Thornhill) Penwill (1805–1903), of Grand Bank (MUN Hist.).

Early instances: Nancy, of Fortune, 1817 (DPHW 106); William, planter of Grand Bank, 1819 (DPHW 109); William Thornall, of Brunett (Island), 1829 (DPHW 106); Ann Thornhill, of Fox Island (Burgeo-La Poile district), 1844 (DPHW 101); John, of Blue Pinion (Fortune B.), 1856 (DPHW 104); Robert, of Bay L'Argent, 1871 (Lovell); James (and others), of East and West Little Bay, 1871 (Lovell); George (and others), of Mose Ambrose, 1871 (Lovell).

Modern status: Scattered, especially at Grand Bank and Fortune.

Place names: Thornhill Cove, —— Point 46-36 55-56; —— Shoal 46-51 55-55.

THORPE, a surname of England from the English place name common in many counties settled by the Danes in the Midlands and northeast, from Old English *Thorp* – (dweller or worker in a) hamlet, village or outlying dairy-farm. (Reaney, Cottle).

Thorp(e) traced by Spiegelhalter in Devon and by Guppy in Cheshire, Derbyshire, Hampshire, Kent, Leicestershire, Rutlandshire, Lincolnshire, Norfolk and Yorkshire WR, with Thorpe twice as frequent as Thorp but nearly always associated except in Leicestershire, Rutlandshire and Norfolk, where Thorpe alone occurs.

In Newfoundland:

Early instance: John, shopkeeper of St. John's, 1814 (CO 194.55).

Modern status: Rare, at St. Phillips.

THOURET, THURIOT, ? Newfoundland variants of the surnames of France, Thoret, Thoreau. (Dauzat).

In Newfoundland:

Modern status: Thouret, unique, at Robinsons (*Electors* 1955); Thuriot, at North East Brook (White B.) (*Electors* 1955) and Roddickton.

TIBBO, a Newfoundland variant of the surnames of France T(h)ibaud, etc., from the Old German personal name *Theudbold* (Theobald in England) containing the elements *people* and *bold*. (Dauzat). A variant Tipple has been noted.

In Newfoundland:

Family tradition: Three Tibbo brothers (the name was originally Thibeau or Thibeault) from Jersey (Channel Islands), came to Newfoundland via England in the mid-18th century. Jonathan settled at Grand Bank before 1817; another settled in Fortune Bay and the other in Placentia Bay (MUN Hist.).

Early instances: Thomas, soldier of Placentia, 1780 (D'Alberti 6); Christian Tybo, from Copenhagen, Denmark, married at St. John's, 1816 (Nfld. Archives BRC); John Tibbo, fisherman of Grand Bank, 1816 (DPHW 109); John, of Long Island (Burin district), 1816 (DPHW 109); Peter (1778–1856), son of Matthew and Sarah of Sagona, of Rack (for Wreck) Cove, Bay de l'Eau, 1835 (DPHW 30; D.A. Macdonald); John Tibbot or Tippet, of Coleys Point, 1842 (DPHW 39); James Tibbut, planter of Catalina, 1849 (DPHW 72); William Tibboe, of Harbour Breton, 1858 (DPHW 104); scattered in south coast communities in Lovell 1871.

Modern status: Scattered, especially at Grand Bank.

Place names: Tibbos Hill 47-30 55-36; Thibaud Shoal 47-37 58-36; —— Cove 47-37 54-11; —— (or Tiheay) Cove 49-06 58-12; Thibauds Head 47-41 55-08.

TIBBS, a surname of England. "In the 13th century *Tibbe* was used as a pet-name for both men and women, from *Isabel* or *Tibold* (Theobald)." (Reaney). *See also* TIPPETT, TIPPLE.

Traced by Spiegelhalter in Devon.

In Newfoundland:

Early instances: Robert, fisherman of Trinity (Trinity B.), 1756 (DPHW 64); John Tibs, of Trinity Bay, 1769 (DPHW 64); Robert Tibbs, proprietor and occupier of fishing room, New Perlican, Winter 1800–01 (Census Trinity B.); John, married at St. John's, 1808 (Nfld. Archives BRC); Margaret, of Petty Harbour, 1831 (Nfld. Archives BRC); William Tibs, of Harbour Grace Parish, 1840 (Nfld. Archives HGRC); William, ? of Northern Bay, 1841 (DPHW 54).

Modern status: At St. John's and Trinity (Trinity B.).

TILLER, a surname of England, from Middle English *tiliere*, *tilyer*, from Old English *tilian* – to till, rather than from Old English *tilia* (*see* TILLEY) – tiller of the soil, farmer, farm labourer. (Reaney, Cottle).

In Newfoundland:

Family tradition: ——, from England, settled at Wesleyville (Bonavista B.); his son, Darius later moved to St. John's (MUN Folklore).

Early instances: Thomas, proprietor of fishing room, Bonaventure (unspecified), Winter 1800–01 (Census Trinity B.); Thomas, of Trinity (Trinity B.), 1857 (DPHW 64); William Tillers, of Greenspond, 1815 (DPHW 76); Anne Tiller, baptized at Swain's Islands 1830, aged 28 (DPHW 72); John, of St. John's, 1855 (DPHW 26D).

Modern status: Scattered, especially at St. John's.

Place names: Tiller Cove, —— (or Drunkards) Point 46-55 55-31.

TILLEY, a surname of England, Tilly of Ireland and France; in England from Old English *tilia*, Middle English *tilie* – tiller, farmer, or diminutive of *Till* (Matilda), or from the English place names Tilley (Shropshire) or Tiley (Dorset), or from the French place name Tilly (Aube, Calvados, etc.); in Ireland a

variant of (Mac) Tully, *Mac an Tuile* or of (O)Tally, *Ó Taithligh*, Ir. *taithleach* – peaceable. (Reaney, Spiegelhalter, Dauzat, MacLysaght).

Guppy traced Tilley in Somerset and Spiegelhalter Till(e)y in Devon.

In Newfoundland:

Family traditions: Robert Till(e)y (about 1824–72), from Bonavista, settled at Bird Island Cove (now Elliston) about 1853 and opened a small business there. The surname was spelt Tilly until about 1923 when Clarence, a descendant of Robert, misspelt the name as Tilley on a blind for his shop window. The name has been spelt Tilley ever since (MUN Hist., Nfld. Archives Z66). John Tilley, from Hants Harbour, was the first permanent settler of Shoal Harbour (Trinity B.), in 1845 (MUN Hist.). Joseph and sons were the first settlers of Lower Shoal Harbour (now part of Clarenville) (MUN Hist.).

Early instances: William, of Port Bonavist (Bonavista), 1675 (CO 1); William Tilly, of Harbour Main, 1675 (CO 1); Elizabeth Tilley, of New Perlican, 1708–9 (CO 194.4); William Tilledge or Tillage, of Bay de Verde, 1708–9 (CO 194.4); Richard Tilleys, of Green Island (near Bonavista), 1708–9 (CO 194.4); —— Tilley, constable of Bonavista district, ? 1730 (CO 194.9); George Tilly, of Newfoundland, 1730 (CO 194.23); Thomas, married at St. John's, 1784 (DPHW 26D); Jane, in possession of property at St. John's and Petty Harbour, 1794–5 (Census 1794–5); James, proprietor and occupier of fishing room, Old Perlican, Winter 1800–01 (Census Trinity B.); J. Tilsey (or Tilley), operated salmon fishery at Shoe Cove (unspecified), 1804 (CO 194.45); Anne Tilly, married at Harbour Grace, 1808 (Nfld. Archives HGRC); John, planter of Hants Harbour, about 1821 (DPHW 58); John, of Fortune, 1830 (DPHW 109); John, J.P. for the Northern district of the Colony, 1834 (*Newfoundlander* 10 Jul 1834); Thomas Tiling, planter of Bird Island Cove (now Elliston), 1835 (DPHW 72); —— Tilley, of Kelligrews, 1839 (DPHW 30); Thomas Tilly, of Indian Burying Place, 1847 (DPHW 86); Robert Till(e)y, of Open Hall, 1847 (DPHW 73A); Joseph Tilly, fisherman of Shoal Harbour (? Trinity B.), 1848 (DPHW 58); James Tilley, ? of Northern Bay, 1852 (DPHW 54); William, of Indian Arm (Bonavista B.), 1853 (DPHW 73B); John Tilly, of Round Harbour (Twillingate district), 1857 (DPHW 86); Felix, of Grates Cove, 1858 (DPHW 58); Luke Tiley, from England, married at Grand Bank, 1859 (DPHW 106); scattered in Lovell 1871.

Modern status: Widespread, especially at St. John's and Kelligrews.

Place names: Tilley Cove, —— Head 49-29 55-46; Tilleys Cove, —— Hill, —— Point 48-40 53-38; —— Cove Ponds 48-37 53-50.

TIMBURY, a surname of England, from the English place name Timsbury (Somerset, Hampshire), or ? a variant of TIMPERLEY. (Bardsley).

In Newfoundland:

Early instance: Job Timbuary, fisherman of Bay de l'Eau, 1846 (DPHW 101).

Modern status: Unique, at Ramea (*Electors* 1955).

TIMMINS, TIMMONS, surnames of England, Timmons of Ireland; in England – son of Tim(othy), according to Bardsley, but since Timothy did not come into use in England until after the Reformation, the name may derive from a diminutive of an Old English personal name *Tuma* or *Tyma*; in Ireland for *Mac Toimin*, a diminutive of Thomas (*see* THOMAS) or for Timon, *Ó Tiomáin*. (Withycombe, Bardsley, Spiegelhalter, MacLysaght).

Timmons traced by MacLysaght in Cos. Wicklow and Carlow, and in Co. Mayo where, however, it has been almost replaced by Timon or Tymon.

In Newfoundland:

Early instances: Margaret ? Timmins, from St. Mullins (Co. Carlow), married at St. John's, 1819 (Nfld. Archives BRC); Laurence Timmons, of Harbour Grace, 1822 (Nfld. Archives HGRC); Edward Timmins, planter of Holyrood, 1871 (Lovell).

Modern status: Timmins, rare, at St. John's; Timmons, at Holyrood (*Electors* 1955), St. John's and Glenwood.

Place names: Timmins Bay (Labrador) 54-52 66-27; —— Lake (Labrador) 54-03 65-39.

TIMPERLEY, a surname of England from the English place name Timperleigh (Cheshire). (Bardsley). *See also* TIMBURY.

Traced by Guppy in Cheshire.

In Newfoundland:

Modern status: Unique, at St. John's (*Electors* 1955).

TIPPETT, a surname of England, a diminutive of *Tipp* which is a variant of *Tibb*, a pet-form of Theobald. (Reaney, Cottle). *See also* TIBBS, TIPPLE.

Traced by Guppy in Cornwall and by Spiegelhalter in Devon.

In Newfoundland:

Early instances: William, of Bay Roberts, 1801 (CO 199.18); Mary Tippet, of Harbour Grace, 1809 (Nfld. Archives HGRC); James Tippet(t), planter of Little Catalina, 1846, 1851 (DPHW 72); William Tippett, of Ragged Harbour (now Melrose), 1871 (Lovell).

Modern status: Scattered, especially at Little Catalina.

TIPPING, a surname of England from the Old English personal name **Tipping* – son of *Tippa*, found only in place names. (Reaney).

Traced by Guppy in Worcestershire.

In Newfoundland:

Modern status: At Corner Brook (*Electors* 1955) and St. John's.

Place name: Tippings Pond 48-56 57-53.

TIPPLE, a surname of England, another diminutive of *Tipp*. (Reaney, Cottle). *See* TIBBS, TIPPET.

In Newfoundland:

Family tradition: Thomas, from England married at Grand Bank, 1848; his family later settled at Burin Bay (MUN Hist.).

Early instance: Thomas, of Petites, 1856 (DPHW 98).

Modern status: At Topsail, Bay Roberts and Corner Brook.

TITFORD. *See* TETFORD

TIZZARD, a surname of England, also Tizard. Reaney *Origin* on the interchange of T and D comments somewhat cryptically: "The name of Robert *Disard* (1220 Cur) may well be an early form of *Tizard*, surviving as *Dysart*," ? from the Scots place name Dysart (Fifeshire). Another account of the name, current in the family, states that Tizzard originated at Mevagissey (Cornwall) about the time of the Spanish Armada 1588 in the form Tizzaro and is Spanish and not French as some suppose. (Rev. H.M. Tizzard).

Matthews traced Tizard in Dorset.

In Newfoundland:

Family traditions: ——, from Poole (Dorset), settled at Old Perlican in the 1700s (MUN Hist.). Rebecca (1832–1923), born at Tizzards Harbour (MUN Geog.). —— Tizard, of Twillingate, 1768 (MUN Hist.).

Early instances: Peter, proprietor and occupier of fishing room, Old Perlican, Winter 1800–01 (Census Trinity B.); Thomas, planter of Twillingate, 1822 (USPG); Thomas, soldier of St. John's, 1824 (DPHW 26B); William, fisherman of Carbonear, 1857 (DPHW 49); George, of Fogo, 1857 (DPHW 83).

Modern status: Scattered, especially at St. John's.

Place names: Tizzard Cove 47-10 55-04; Tizzard's Harbour, —— —— Head 49-36 54-48.

TOBIN, a surname of England and Ireland, a variant of the surname of England St. Aubyn, or of France St.-Aubin, both from various localities in France St. Aubin (Aisne, Aube, etc.). (Spiegelhalter, MacLysaght).

Traced by Spiegelhalter in Devon and by MacLysaght in Cos. Kilkenny and Tipperary.

In Newfoundland:

Family tradition: Thomas, from Co. Cork, was one of the earliest settlers of Red Island (Placentia B.), about 1815 (MUN Hist.).

Early instances: Nicholas, of St. John's, ? 1753–57 (CO 194.13, DPHW 26D); John, of Harbour Main, 1755 (MUN Hist.); Maurice, from Cappaginn (? for Cappoquin, Co. Waterford), married at St. John's, 1793 (Nfld. Archives BRC); Mark, of Trinity (Trinity B.), 1804 (DPHW 64); David, from Co. Kilkenny, married at St. John's, 1807 (Nfld. Archives BRC); John, of Harbour Grace, 1808 (Nfld. Archives HGRC); Maurice, from Rogamuck (Co. Waterford), fisherman of St. John's, deceased 1810 (*Royal Gazette* 27 Sep 1810); John, of King's Cove, 1815 (Nfld. Archives KCRC); Thomas, of Tickle Harbour (now Bellevue), 1817 (Nfld. Archives KCRC); Thomas, of Riders Harbour, 1820 (Nfld. Archives KCRC); John, of Broad Cove (now Duntara), 1821 (Nfld. Archives KCRC); John, of Bonavista, 1824 (Nfld. Archives KCRC); Mary, of Witless Bay, 1827 (Nfld. Archives BRC); John, planter of Trouty, 1828 (DPHW 64B); John, of Open Hole (now Open Hall), 1830 (Nfld. Archives KCRC); Patrick, dentist of Carbonear, 1830 (*Newfoundlander* 2 Dec 1830); John, planter of Salmon Cove (now Champneys), 1833 (DPHW 64B); Richard, ? of Northern Bay, 1838 (DPHW 54); Patrick, of Flatrock (unspecified), 1840 (*Newfoundlander* 16 Jan 1840); William, granted land at Wigmore's Gully Road, 1849 (Nfld. Archives, Registry Crown Lands); Thomas, magistrate of St. George's Bay, 1852 (*Newfoundlander* 26 Aug 1852); Patrick, cooper of Riverhead (St. John's), 1854 (*Newfoundlander* 10 Jul 1854); Margaret, granted land between Topsail and Kelligrews, 1857 (Nfld. Archives, Registry Crown Lands); James, granted land near Holyrood, 1860 (Nfld. Archives, Registry Crown Lands); John, of Trepassey, 1862 (*Nfld. Almanac* 1863); widespread in Lovell 1871.

Modern status: Widespread, especially at St. John's, Gaskiers, Ship Cove (Placentia B.), and Witless Bay.

Place names: Tobins Point 47-43 54-12; —— Pond 47-18 53-15.

TOMLINSON, a surname of England – son of Tomlin, a double diminutive of Thomas (*see* THOMAS and *also* TAPLIN, TOMPKINS). (Reaney, Cottle).

Traced by Guppy in Cheshire, Derbyshire, Lancashire, Lincolnshire, Nottinghamshire, Staffordshire and Yorkshire WR, with Thomlinson in Cumberland and Westmorland.

In Newfoundland:

Modern status: At St. John's.

TOMPKINS, a surname of England, Tomkins of Jersey (Channel Islands) – son of little Tom. *See* THOMAS and *also* TOMLINSON, TAPLIN. (Reaney, Cottle, Turk).

Traced by Guppy in Buckinghamshire and as Tom(p)kins by Spiegelhalter in Devon.

In Newfoundland:

Early instances: T. Tomkins, ? of St. John's, 1832 (*Newfoundlander* 27 Dec 1832); Christopher, fisherman of Fortune, 1871 (Lovell).

Modern status: At Corner Brook, Stephenville, Tompkins and Gander.

Place name: Tompkins 47-48 59-13.

TOMS. *See* THOMS

(O)TOOLE, surnames of Ireland, *Ó Tuathail*, Ir. *tuathal*, containing the elements *people* and *mighty*. (MacLysaght).

Traced by MacLysaght originally in Co. Kildare and later in Co. Wicklow.

In Newfoundland:

Family tradition: The O'Tooles of Renews were Toole in the nineteenth century.

Early instances: Maurice Tool(e), of St. John's, 1757 (DPHW 26C); Timothy Tool, of Harbour Main and Gasters, 1803 (CO 199.18); Margaret Toole, of Trepassey, 1811 (D'Alberti 21); Johanna, of Harbour Grace, 1813 (Nfld. Archives HGRC); Bridget, from Tintern (Co. Wexford), married at St. John's, 1813 (Nfld. Archives BRC); Terence Tool, of Ferryland area, 1838 (*Newfoundlander* 25 Oct 1838); Michael O'Toole, from Co. Wexford, married at Renews, 1841 (Dillon); Terence Toole, planter of Caplin Bay (now Calvert), 1871 (Lovell); Timothy and John, farmers of Cats Cove (now Conception Harbour), 1871 (Lovell); Michael Tool, farmer of Torbay, 1871 (Lovell).

Modern status: O'Toole, scattered, especially at St. John's; Toole, rare, at Little Paradise (Placentia B.) (*Electors* 1955).

Place names: Billy Toole Cove 49-36 55-40; Toole Rock (Labrador) 53-45 56-37.

TOOPE, a surname of England from the Old Danish personal name *Topi.* (Reaney).

Spiegelhalter traced Toop in Devon.

In Newfoundland:

Family tradition: James, from Somerset, England, came to Newfoundland in 1812, settling first in Rise's [sic] Harbour and later at Ireland's Eye (Trinity B.) (MUN Folklore).

Early instances: Silvester Tope, of St. John's, 1752 (CO 194.13); James Toop or Toup, of Ireland's Eye, 1810 (DPHW 64); George Toop, planter of Twillingate, 1819 (USPG); Francis Toup, planter of Salmon Cove (now Champneys), 1823 (DPHW 64B); Benjamin Toppe, of Broad Cove (unspecified), married at St. John's, 1827 (Nfld. Archives BRC); John Toop, planter of Careless (now Kerleys) Harbour, 1837 (DPHW 64B).

Modern status: Scattered, especially at Ireland's Eye.

TOOTON, a surname of Syria-Lebanon of unknown, ? Armenian origin.

In Newfoundland:

Family tradition: Anthony, from Damascus, Syria, settled at St. John's in the early 20th century.

Modern status: At St. John's.

TORRAVILLE, earlier Terrifield, a surname of England, ? from the English place names Therfield (Hertfordshire) or Turville (Berkshire), both from Old English *thyrre* and *feld* – (dweller by the) dry field, plain, open country. (Ekwall).

In Newfoundland:

Family tradition: —— Torraville or Terrifield, from France, settled at Change Islands (MUN Folklore).

Early instances: Joseph Terrifield, planter of Herring Neck, 1821 (USPG); Benjamin Torreville, of Fogo, 1843 (DPHW 83); Jeremiah Terrafield, fisherman of Stone Harbour (Twillingate district), 1856 (DPHW 85); Thomas, fisherman of Clark's Cove (Twillingate district), 1858 (DPHW 85); George and Thomas Torravelle, of Change Islands, 1871 (Lovell).

Modern status: Scattered, especially at Victoria Cove (Fogo district) and Fogo.

TOUCHER, ? a Newfoundland variant of the surnames of Ireland (O)Tougher, Tooher, *Ó Tuachair,* earlier *Ó Tuathchair,* containing the elements *people* and *dear* (MacLysaght). *See also* TUCKER.

MacLysaght traced (O)Tougher, Tooher in the Ely-O'Carroll territory and in north Connacht.

In Newfoundland:

Early instance: Matthew Tutcher, labourer of St. John's, 1871 (Lovell).

Modern status: Rare, at St. John's.

TOUCHING(S), ? Newfoundland variants of the surname of France Touchon, or of France and the Channel Islands Tostevin, Tostivin. (Dauzat).

In Newfoundland:

Family tradition: John, from Rencontre West, of Pass Island (Hermitage B.), 1860 (MUN Hist.).

Early instance: John Touchings, fisherman of Grole, 1846 (DPHW 102).

Modern status: Touching, unique, at Round Harbour (Fortune B.) (*Electors* 1955); Touchings, at Pass Island, François and Corner Brook.

TOULMAN, ? a variant of the surname of England Tollman from Old English *toll* and *mann* – tollman, collector of tolls or taxes, or a variant of Toulmin, a metathesized form of Tomlin (*see* TOMLINSON). (Reaney, Weekley *Romance*). Spiegelhalter traced Toulmin in Devon.

In Newfoundland:

Modern status: Rare, at Gander.

TOURANT, ? a variant of the surnames of France Tourencq or Torrent. (Dauzat).

In Newfoundland:

Modern status: Tourant, at Three Rock Cove (Port au Port district) (*Electors* 1955).

TOUROUT, ? a variant of the surname of France Turot, a pet-form of Arthur.

In Newfoundland:

Family tradition: the first settler deserted from the French fishery (Thomas, "French Fam. Names"). Anglicized to TURRETT.

Modern status: At West Bay and St. Teresa's (*Electors* 1955), Lourdes and Stephenville.

TOUZEL, a surname of France and Jersey (Channel Islands), usually anglicized in Newfoundland as THISTLE.

In Newfoundland:

Modern status: Unique, at Harbour Breton (*Electors* 1955).

TOWER, a surname of England and Scotland, in England from Old English *tūr,* Old French *tour* – (dweller by the) tower, or from Old English *tāwian* –

to taw, hence tawer, leather-dresser; in Scotland
? originally De Tour. (Reaney, Cottle, Black).

Traced by Spiegelhalter in Devon and by Black in
Aberdeen.

In Newfoundland:

Modern status: Unique, at St. John's

Place name (not necessarily from the surname):
Tower Mountain (Labrador) 59-20 64-08.

TRACEY, a surname of England and Ireland, in England from the French place names Tracy-Bocage or
Tracy-sur-Mer (Calvados); in Ireland (O)Tracey,
Treacy, *Ó Treasaigh,* Ir. *treasach* – warlike. (Reaney, MacLysaght).

Traced by Spiegelhalter in Devon and by Mac-
Lysaght as fairly numerous in every province.

In Newfoundland:

Family tradition: Michael, from Waterford,
settled at Kilbride about 1825 (MUN Folklore).

Early instances: Thomas Tracy, married at St.
John's, 1767 (DPHW 26D); Daniel Treacy, from
Cashel (Co. Tipperary), married at St. John's, 1805,
died 1818 (Nfld. Archives BRC, *Royal Gazette* 6 Jan
1818); Mary Tracey, of Harbour Grace, 1807 (Nfld.
Archives HGRC); Thomas Treacy or Tracy, of Kings
Cove Parish, 1834 (Nfld. Archives KCRC); John
Tracey, granted land at Coots Marsh, 1847 (Nfld.
Archives, Registry Crown Lands); James, of Plate
Cove (Bonavista B.), 1856 (Nfld. Archives KCRC);
Matthew Treacey, of Chapel's Cove, 1871 (Lovell);
John Tracey, of Cape Norman, 1871 (Lovell);
William, merchant of Herring Neck, 1871
(Lovell).

Modern status: Scattered, especially at Plate Cove
East.

Place name: Tracey Hill (Labrador) 51-43 56-26.

TRAHEY, a surname of Ireland, a variant of
(O)Tro(h)y, *Ó Troighthigh,* Ir. *troightheach* – foot-
soldier. (MacLysaght). *See also* TROY.

Traced by MacLysaght in Co. Tipperary.

In Newfoundland:

Early instances: Michael Trehey, in possession of
property at Petty Harbour, 1794–5 (Census 1794–5);
Thomas Trahee, married at Harbour Grace, 1813
(Nfld. Archives HGRC); John Trehy, farmer of Cats
Cove (now Conception Harbour), 1871 (Lovell).

Modern status: At St. John's and in the Harbour
Main district.

TRAINOR, a surname of England and Ireland, in
England from Middle English *trayne* – to lay a train
or snare, to set a trap, hence trapper; in Ireland (Mac)

Traynor, Treanor, *Mac Thréinfhir,* Ir. *tréan* – strong
and *fear* – man. (Reaney, MacLysaght).

Traced by MacLysaght in Cos. Armagh,
Monaghan etc.

In Newfoundland:

Family tradition: William came to Newfoundland
via Portsmouth (Hampshire) and settled at Admirals
Cove (Southern Shore) in the 17th century (*Evening
Telegram* 19 Dec 1964).

Early instances: William, granted land at Clears
Cove, Fermeuse, 1848 (Nfld. Archives, Registry
Crown Lands); Dennis and William Treanor, fisher-
men of Fermeuse, 1871 (Lovell).

Modern status: At Admirals (Fermeuse) and St.
John's.

TRAPNELL, a surname of England from Old French
trop isnel – too swift. (Reaney).

Traced by Spiegelhalter in Devon.

In Newfoundland:

Early instances: John, of Harbour Grace, 1792
(USPG); George, from Poole (Dorset) of St. John's,
died 1852, aged 65 (*Weekly Herald and C.B. General Advertiser* 8 Dec 1852).

Modern status: At Corner Brook (*Electors* 1955)
and St. John's.

TRASK, a surname of England from the English
place name Thirsk (Yorkshire NR). (Weekley *Surnames*).

In Newfoundland:

Family traditions: Samuel (1800–), from
Merriott (Somerset), settled at Bird Island Cove
(now Elliston) (MUN Hist.). Caleb (1850–1910),
from southwest England, settled at Northern Cove
(Bird Island Cove) (MUN Folklore).

Early instances: Samuel Trap or Trass, fisherman
of Bird Island Cove (now Elliston), 1828, 1832
(DPHW 72).

Modern status: Scattered, especially at Elliston.

TRAVERS(E), surnames of England and Ireland;
from Middle English *travers,* used of a toll paid on
passing the boundary of a town or lordship, or a
tollgate or tollbridge, and hence perhaps the surname
of the keeper and collector of such tolls; in Ireland
also for (O)Trower, *Ó Treabhair,* Ir. *treabhair* –
skilful. (Reaney, Cottle, MacLysaght).

Guppy traced Travis in Derbyshire, Lancashire
and, with Traves, in Lincolnshire; Spiegelhalter
traced Travers in Devon; and MacLysaght Travers
in Co. Leitrim. Traverse may be a Newfoundland
variant.

In Newfoundland:

Family tradition: —— Travers, from France, settled at Lark Harbour (MUN Folklore).

Early instances: Ralph Trevers, of Barrow Harbour (Bonavista B.), 1681 (CO 1); Robert Travers, of Placentia ? district, 1744 (CO 194.24); Nicholas, of St. John's, 1796 (CO 194.39); John, of St. Mary's, 1797 (D'Alberti 7); ——, ? of Port de Grave, 1801 (Nfld. Archives G22); William, from Waterford, shopkeeper of St. John's, 1811 (*Royal Gazette* 28 Nov 1811); Patrick, of Portugal Cove, 1829 (Nfld. Archives BRC); John, of Harbour Grace, 1831 (DPHW 26B); Jabez Travis, planter of Hants Harbour, 1831 (DPHW 59A); Thomas Traves, of Kings Cove Parish, 1842 (Nfld. Archives KCRC); Mary Travers, from Kildare, of St. John's, 1854 (*Newfoundlander* 27 Apr 1854); James, of Twillingate, 1861 (DPHW 88); scattered in Lovell 1871.

Modern status: Travers, scattered; Traverse, scattered, especially at Jerseyside (Placentia B.).

Place names: Travers Cove, —— —— Point 47-18 53-59; Traverse Brook 48-51 54-06; —— Island 48-49 54-05.

TRELEGAN, a surname of England ? from an unidentified Cornish place name.

In Newfoundland:

Early instances: Richard Trilegan, of St. John's, 1826 (Dispatches 1825–6); William Trelegan, blacksmith of St. John's, deceased, 1852 (*Newfoundlander* 29 Apr 1852).

Modern status: Rare, at St. John's.

TREMBLET, a surname of France – (dweller near the) trembling poplar or aspen with a diminutive; TREMBLETT, a variant of the foregoing and also of the surname of England Tremlett from the English place name Trembleath (Cornwall). (Dauzat, Spiegelhalter).

Guppy traced Tremlett in Devon.

In Newfoundland:

Family traditions: Five Tremblett brothers, from France, settled in Newfoundland: two at St. John's, one at Burin, one at Bonavista and the fifth at some unknown locality (MUN Folklore). ——, from Ireland, settled at Bonavista in the mid-nineteenth century (MUN Folklore).

Early instances: John Tremlett, of Port de Grave, 1751 (CO 194.13); Robert, from West Teignmouth (Devon), merchant of St. John's since 1775–6, died 1812 (Census 1794–5, *Royal Gazette* 20 Aug 1812); John Tremblet, of St. Mary's, 1802 (Nfld. Archives BRC); Joshua Tremblett, of Bonavista, 1819 (DPHW

70); Robert Tremlett, of Twillingate, 1823 (D'Alberti 33); Henry (and others) Tremblett, of Bird Island Cove (now Elliston), 1825 (MUN Hist.); John and Thomas, of North Harbour, John's Point, Tickles and Colinet area, 1871 (Lovell); William Tremlett, miner of Tilt Cove, 1871 (Lovell); Richard Tremlet, of Gull Cove (St. Mary's B.), 1871 (Lovell); William Trimlett, of Rushoon (Placentia B.), 1871 (Lovell).

Modern status: Tremblett, scattered, especially at Bonavista.

TREMILLS, a surname of England, from the English place name Tremail (Cornwall).

In Newfoundland:

Early instance: Thomas, of Petty Harbour, 1839 (DPHW 31).

Modern status: At Petty Harbour (*Electors* 1955) and St. John's.

TRENCHARD, a surname of England from Old French *trenchier* – to cut, cleave, with a ? pejorative suffix – ? swordsman or ? butcher. (Reaney, Bardsley).

Traced by Spiegelhalter in Devon.

In Newfoundland:

Early instances: Benjamin Trencher, blacksmith of Lower Island Cove, 1838 (? DPHW 55); Benjamin C. Trenchard, fisherman of Bay Roberts, 1860 (DPHW 39); Benjamin and John, of Lower Island Cove, 1871 (Lovell); Charles Trenchar, blacksmith of Harbour Grace, 1871 (Lovell).

Modern status: At Bay Roberts and St. John's.

TRICCO, a Newfoundland variant of the surname of France Tricot, etc. – ? (one who wields a) stick, cudgel. (Dauzat).

In Newfoundland:

Early instance: Joseph Trecco, farmer of Torbay, 1871 (Lovell).

Modern status: At St. John's.

TRICKETT, a surname of England from the Norman-Picard form of French Trichet, Trichot, ? pet-forms of Trichard, Tricard – cheat, deceiver. (Reaney, Dauzat).

Traced by Guppy in Cheshire.

In Newfoundland:

Family traditions: John Tricket, from the Bristol area of England, settled at Salmon Cove (Carbonear) about 1870 (MUN Folklore). —— Crickett, from England, was the first settler of Spout Cove (Conception B.) in the 17th century. The surname was later changed to Trickett (*Compass* 29 Apr 1971).

Early instances: John, of Salmon Cove (unspecified), 1840 (*Newfoundlander* 13 Feb 1840); John Tricket, granted land at Spout Cove (North Shore, Conception B.), 1849 (Nfld. Archives, Registry Crown Lands); Mark Cricket, fisherman of Perry's Cove (Conception B.), 1856 (DPHW 49).

Modern status: Scattered, especially at Spout Cove.

TRIMM, ? a surname of England, ? from the English river name Trym (Gloucestershire), or a variant of the surname of Ireland, Trim, *de Truim*, "one of the few Irish toponymics," from the Irish place name Trim (Co. Meath) – the town of the ford of the elder trees. (MacLysaght, *Illustrated Road Book of Ireland*).

In Newfoundland:

Early instances: William Trim(m), planter of Seal Cove (now New Chelsea), 1829 (DPHW 59A); Job Trim, of Northern Bay, 1841 (DPHW 52A); Henry Trimm (1813–94), from England, married at Grand Bank, 1848 (DPHW 106, MUN Hist.); John Trim, of Seal Island (Burgeo-La Poile district), 1858 (DPHW 98).

Modern status: At St. John's, Grand Bank and New Chelsea.

Place names: Trimms Beach 47-06 55-45; —— Brook 49-58 56-03.

TRO(A)KE, surnames of England from Cornish *troc* – (dweller by the) tree trunk, stump. (Spiegelhalter).

Spiegelhalter traced Troake in Devon.

In Newfoundland:

Early instances: John Troke, of Harbour Grace, 1812 (Nfld. Archives HGRC); John, planter of Twillingate, 1821 (USPG); James Troak, fisherman of Garia, 1844 (DPHW 101); George Troake, of Harbour Breton, 1854 (DPHW 104), recorded as George Noakes in 1853 (D.A. Macdonald); George Troke, boatmaster of La Poile, 1860 (DPHW 99); William Troak, fisherman of Salvage, 1865 (DPHW 81).

Modern status: Troake, at Daniels Cove (*Electors* 1955), St. John's, Little Burnt Bay and Durrells Arm; Troke, scattered.

Place name: Troak Point 47-02 55-10.

TROWBRIDGE, a surname of England from the English place names Trowbridge (Wiltshire) or Trobridge House, Crediton (Devon). (Reaney, Spiegelhalter).

Guppy traced Trowbridge in Dorset; Spiegelhalter traced Trobridge in Devon.

In Newfoundland:

Early instances: Samuel Tro(w)bridge, of Belleo-

ram, 1835 (DPHW 30); Sarah Trowbridge, of Sagona, 1857 (DPHW 104); Benjamin Trobridge, of Burgeo (now Chambers Island) (Placentia B.), 1871 (Lovell).

Modern status: At St. John's and in the Placentia East and West districts.

TROY, a surname of England and Ireland from the French place name Troyes (Aube); in Ireland also a variant of (O)Trohy (*see* TRAHEY). (Cottle, MacLysaght).

Traced by MacLysaght in Co. Tipperary.

In Newfoundland:

Early instances: James, from Inch Parish (unidentified) (Co. Tipperary), married at St. John's, 1811 (Nfld. Archives BRC); Mary, of Bonavista, 1813 (Nfld. Archives BRC); Catherine, of Harbour Grace, 1814 (Nfld. Archives HGRC); Richard, of King's Cove, 1826 (Nfld. Archives KCRC); ——, of St. John's, 1832 (*Newfoundlander* 20 Dec 1832); Rev. Edward, of Torbay, 1855, 1871 (*Newfoundlander* 1 Nov 1855, Lovell); Michael Try, fisherman of Goose Cove (White B.), 1871 (Lovell).

Modern status: At Main Brook (White B.) (*Electors* 1955) and Goose Cove (White B.).

Place names: Troytown (or Great Triton) Harbour, Troytown (or Triton) Island 49-32 55-37.

TRUSCOTT, a surname of England from the English place names Truscott, Launceston (Cornwall) or Trescott (Staffordshire). (Spiegelhalter, Reaney).

Traced by Guppy in Cornwall and by Spiegelhalter in Devon.

In Newfoundland:

Modern status: At St. John's.

TUBRETT, a variant of the surnames of Ireland (O)Tubridy, Tubrit, *Ó Tiobraide*, Ir. *tiobraid* – a well. (MacLysaght).

Traced by MacLysaght in Co. Clare.

In Newfoundland:

Early instances: Walter Tubrid, of St. John's, 1804 (Nfld. Archives BRC); Anne Tubbert, from Tintern (Co. Wexford), married at St. John's, 1810 (Nfld. Archives BRC); James Tubrid, granted land at Freshwater Road, 1841 (Nfld. Archives, Registry Crown Lands).

Modern status: At Holyrood and Windsor.

TUCK, a surname of England, ? from the Old Danish personal name *Tuk*.

Traced by Guppy in Norfolk and Wiltshire and by Spiegelhalter in Devon.

In Newfoundland:

Family tradition: ——, from Hampshire, England, settled at Hants Harbour (Trinity B.) (MUN Folklore).

Early instances: Farwell, proprietor and occupier of fishing room, Old Perlican, Winter 1800–01 (Census Trinity B.); Benjamin (about 1798–1860), planter of Fortune, 1821 (DPHW 109); Peter, planter of Hants Harbour, 1839, of Brook Cove (Trinity South district), 1851 (DPHW 59A); Susan, of Ragged Harbour (now Melrose), 1857 (Nfld. Archives KCRC).

Modern status: Scattered, especially at Hants Harbour.

Place name: Tucks High Point 49-24 54-17.

TUCKER, a surname of England and Ireland from Old English *tucian* – to torment, later to tuck or full (cloth), associated with FULLER and WALKER, or rarely from French *tout coeur* – brave, courageous; in Ireland also sometimes a synonym of O'Tougher (*see* TOUCHER). (Reaney, Cottle, MacLysaght).

Traced by Guppy especially in Devon and also in Cornwall, Dorset, Hampshire, Monmouthshire, Somerset and South Wales.

In Newfoundland:

Family traditions: John (and family), from Teignmouth (Devon), settled at Port de Grave in the mid 1700s (MUN Hist.). Robert (about 1815–), from Poole (Dorset), settled at Scilly Cove (now Winterton) about 1827 (MUN Folklore). George, from England, moved from Little Bay Islands to Indian Burying Place in 1850 (MUN Hist.).

Early instances: John and Richard, of St. John's, 1676, Richard "8 and one half years an inhabitant" in 1680, that is, since about 1671 (CO 1); John and James, of Port de Grave, 1757, property "in possession of the Family for upwards of 74 years," that is, before 1683 (CO 199.18); John, of Ferryland, 1708–09 (CO 194.4); John, of Brigus South, 1708–09 (CO 194.4); Frances, of Harbour Grace, in possession of property at Carbonear, 1800, property "possessed by the Family for 72 years," that is, 1728 (CO 199.18); Thomas, of Petty Harbour, 1765 (DPHW 26C); R., of Broad Cove (now St. Phillips), 1765 (CO 199. 18); Robert, of Trinity (Trinity B.), 1808 (DPHW 64); Nebuchadnezza, of Bonavista, 1823 (DPHW 70); Ann, of Trepassey, 1822 (Nfld. Archives BRC); Joseph, from Poole (Dorset), of Little Placentia (now Argentia), J.P. for Burin and Placentia districts, 1823 (D'Alberti 33, *Newfoundlander* 2 Mar 1837); George, ? of Fogo, 1824 (Nfld. Archives KCRC); Nebuchard, planter of Bird Island Cove (now Ellis-

ton), 1827 (DPHW 72); William, clerk of Carbonear, 1828 (DPHW 48); William Tucker or Tucher, of Tilting Harbour (now Tilting), 1829 (Nfld. Archives KCRC); Elizabeth Tucker, of Harbour Grace Parish, 1830 (Nfld. Archives HGRC); Henry, of Portugal Cove, 1837 (Nfld. Archives BRC); Thomas, planter of Burnt Point (Bay de Verde district), 1834 (DPHW 52A); Robert, captain of Scilly Cove (now Winterton), 1838 (DPHW 59A); William, planter of Western Bay, 1840 (DPHW 52A); William, blacksmith of Old Perlican, 1841 (DPHW 58); John, of Flower's Cove, 1843 (DPHW 76); George, of Indian Burying Place, 1848 (DPHW 86); Henry M., ship-master of Harbour Grace, 1853 (DPHW 49); Eliza, from Shaldon (Devon), of St. John's, 1854 (*Newfoundlander* 28 Sep 1854); James, from Teignmouth or Shaldon (Devon), married at St. John's, 1855 (*Newfoundlander* 18 Jan 1855, DPHW 23); George, of Little Bay Islands, 1860 (DPHW 92); widespread in Lovell 1871.

Modern status: Widespread, especially at St. John's, Little Bay Islands (Green B.), Burnt Point (Conception B.), Port de Grave, St. Phillips, Reefs Harbour (St. Barbe district), Elliston, Bunyans Cove (Bonavista B.) and Corner Brook.

Place names: Tucker Head 48-59 57-56; —— Shoal 49-08 53-34; Tuckers Gully 47-44 53-20; —— Head 49-28 57-46.

TUFF, a surname of England from Old English *tōh*, Middle English *togh* – tough, vigorous, steadfast, stubborn. (Weekley *Surnames*).

Traced by Guppy in Kent.

In Newfoundland:

Early instances: William, of Western Bay, 1794 (CO 199.18); John, planter of Ochre Pit Cove, 1824 (DPHW 52A); Captain George Tough, from Dorchester (Dorset), died at St. John's, 1835 (*Star and Conception B.J.* 2 Sep 1835); John, schoolmaster of Catalina, 1839 (DPHW 72); George Tuff, of Exploits Burnt Island, 1841 (DPHW 86); Joseph, of Cat Harbour (now Lumsden), 1850 (DPHW 76); Joseph, of Lower Island Cove, 1856 (DPHW 55); William Tough, member of Board of Road Commissioners for the area of Greenspond, 1857 (*Nfld. Almanac*); George Tuff, of Bennett Island (Bonavista North district), 1862 (DPHW 77); William Tough, fisherman of Clarkes Beach, 1871 (Lovell).

Modern status: Scattered, especially at St. John's and in the Bonavista North district.

TUFFIN, ? a variant of the surname of England Tiffen, from the Greek and Low Latin *Theophania* –

manifestation of God, Epiphany. In France Tiphaine was a baptismal name given to girls born on the Feast (January 6). (Reaney).

Traced by Guppy in Dorset.

In Newfoundland:

Early instances: George, of Carbonear, 1795 (CO 199.18); William, of Battle Harbour (Labrador), 1795 (MUN Hist.); James, planter of Herring Neck, 1821 (USPG); Charles, labourer of St. John's, 1857 (DPHW 29); Thomas, of Little Bay Islands, 1859 (DPHW 92).

Modern status: At Little Bay Islands, Sullivan's Cove (Green B.) (*Electors* 1955) and Too Good Arm (Twillingate district).

TULK, a surname of England, ? from Old Norse *tulkr* – interpreter, spokesman.

Traced by Spiegelhalter in Devon.

In Newfoundland:

Early instances: William, fisherman of Old Perlican, 1822 (DPHW 58); James, of Pinchard's Island (Bonavista B.), 1830 (DPHW 76); Charles, of Harbour Beaufit (for Buffett) (Placentia B.), 1836 (DPHW 30); Mary, of Belleoram, 1838 (DPHW 106); George, planter of Hants Harbour, 1844 (DPHW 59A); John Togue or Tulk, of Deadman's Bay (Bonavista North district), 1850 (DPHW 76); John, planter of Inner Islands (now Newtown) (Bonavista B.), 1871 (Lovell); William, of St. Jacques (Fortune B.), 1871 (Lovell).

Modern status: Scattered, especially at Ladle Cove, Aspen Cove (Fogo district) and St. John's.

TUMA, a surname of Syria-Lebanon, the Christian Arabic form of Thomas (*see* THOMAS).

In Newfoundland:

Modern status: At Corner Brook.

TURNBULL, a surname of England and Scotland, a nickname indicative of bravery or strength. (Reaney, Cottle).

Traced by Guppy especially in Northumberland and also in Durham and Roxburghshire.

In Newfoundland:

Early instance: George W., moulder of St. John's, 1871 (Lovell).

Modern status: Unique, at St. John's.

TURNER, a surname of England, Scotland, Ireland and the Channel Islands, from Old French *to(u)rn(e)or* – "turner, one who turns or fashions objects of wood, metal, bone, etc., on a lathe" (*OED*), but also, as Reaney suggests, possibly – turnspit, translator, one who takes part in a tournament, or as a nickname, "turn hare" – one who could outstrip

and turn a hare. (Reaney, Cottle, Black, MacLysaght, Turk).

Found widespread by Guppy in England and in the Greenock and Glasgow districts and in Dumfriesshire, and by MacLysaght widely distributed in Ireland.

In Newfoundland:

Early instances: William, in possession of fishing room, Keels (Bonavista B.), 1765 (Bonavista Register 1806); William, fisherman of St. John's, 1794–5 (Census 1794–5); Robert, occupier of fishing room, Catalina, Winter 1800–01 (Census Trinity B.); Mary, of Bay Bulls district, 1804 (Nfld. Archives BRC); Joanna, of King's Cove, 1815 (Nfld. Archives KCRC); John, of Bonavista, 1824 (Nfld. Archives KCRC); Thomas, fisherman of Old Perlican, 1830 (DPHW 58); Patrick, of Tickle Cove (Bonavista B.), 1845 (Nfld. Archives KCRC); Edwin, planter of Lower Island Cove, 1851 (DPHW 55); Naomi, of Seldom-Come-By, 1855 (DPHW 67); Patrick, of Cottels Island (Bonavista B.), 1858 (Nfld. Archives KCRC); James, of Rose Blanche, 1860 (DPHW 99); Patrick, of Shoels Cove (? Bonavista B.), 1863 (Nfld. Archives KCRC); David, of Gooseberry Island (Bonavista B.), 1866 (Nfld. Archives KCRC); John, of Plate Cove, 1869 (Nfld. Archives KCRC); Charles, of Black Island, Exploits Bay, 1871 (Lovell); Robert, of Clarke's Beach, 1871 (Lovell).

Modern status: Scattered, especially at Happy Adventure and St. Brendan's.

Place names: (though turner is also a type of seal, *DNE*) Turner Bay (or Turner's Bight) 54-13 58-07; Turner Head (Labrador) 53-16 55-45; Turner(s) Head (Labrador) 54-14 58-10; Turner (or Fish) Island (Labrador) 57-28 61-25; Turner Bight (Labrador) 57-46 61-39.

TURPIN, a surname of England and France, in England from the Old Norse personal name *Thorfinnr* containing the elements *Thor*, the god, and *Finnr*, the ethnic name; in France also from a personal name *Turpinus* from Latin *turpis* – disgraceful, base, a name taken by early Christians as a token of humility, revived in the eleventh century, with its original meaning forgotten, after an eighth-century bishop of Rheims. (Reaney, Dauzat).

Traced by Guppy in Devon and Essex.

In Newfoundland:

Family tradition: Michael, Irish immigrant killed and scalped by Red Indians at Sandy Cove (Tilting), 1809 (Nfld. Dictionary Centre).

Early instances: Sarah, of Bay Bulls, 1780 (D'Alberti 1); John (and others), of Great St. Lawrence (now St. Lawrence), 1871 (Lovell).

Modern status: Scattered, especially at St. Lawrence.

TURRETT. *See* TOUROUT

TURTLE, TUTTLE, surnames of England and Ireland, two of seventeen variants recorded by Reaney, commonly from the Old Norse personal name *Thorketill*, but also from Old English *turtle, turtla* – turtledove, or from French *tourtel* – crooked, TUTTLE from Old English **tōt-hyll* – (dweller by the) lookout-hill, or from such English place names as Toot Hill (Essex), Tothill (Lincolnshire, Middlesex), Tootle Height (Lancashire), Tuttle Hill (Warwickshire) or Tidwell Barton (Devon); but the two names appear to be inextricably confused, at least in Newfoundland. (Reaney, Spiegelhalter, MacLysaght). *See also* DURDLE.

Spiegelhalter traced Tuttle, Tottle, Tootell in Devon; MacLysaght traced Tuthill, Tuttle, Tothill in Co. Limerick and Turtle in Ulster.

In Newfoundland:

Family tradition: Charles Tuttle, rock mason, from Bradford, England, was the first settler of Shearstown, about 1855 (MUN Folklore).

Early instance: Charles Turtle, fisherman of Freshwater (Carbonear), 1839 (DPHW 48).

Modern status: Turtle, at Shearstown; Tuttle, at Shearstown, Bay Roberts and St. John's.

Place names: Names containing the specific Turtle are not thought to be from the surname. Tuttle Island (Labrador) 57-14 61-33.

TWOMEY. *See* THOMEY

TWYNE, a surname of England from Old English *twīn* – (maker or seller of) thread, string. (Reaney).

In Newfoundland:

Family tradition: —— Twyne (earlier spelt Twyner), from Devon, settled at Twillingate in the early 1800s (MUN Folklore).

Early instances: Charles Tyane or Tzane, soldier of Harbour Grace, 1853 (DPHW 43); George Twine, fisherman of Black Island, Exploits Bay, 1871 (Lovell).

Modern status: Scattered, especially in the White Bay South district.

U, V

UDELL, UDLE, surnames of England, Udle of the Channel Islands, in England from the English place name Yewdale (Lancashire). (Bardsley, Miller).

Guppy traced Udall in Derbyshire; Miller traced Udle in the Channel Islands.

In Newfoundland:

Early instances: William Udle, of Carbonear, 1798 (DPHW 48); John, planter of St. John's, 1871 (Lovell).

Modern status: Udell, at Carbonear and St. John's; Udle, at St. John's.

UNDERHAY, a surname of England from the English place name Underhays (Devon) or from Old English *under* and *hæg* – (dweller) below (the) meadow, enclosure. (Gover, Spiegelhalter).

Traced by Guppy in Devon.

In Newfoundland:

Early instances: William, merchant of St. John's, 1794–5 (Census 1794–5); C. Richard, member of Board of Road Commissioners for Hearts Content, 1844 (*Nfld. Almanac*).

Modern status: At St. John's and Hearts Content.

UPSHALL, a surname of England from the English place name Upsall (Yorkshire NR) – upper hall, dwelling. (Cottle).

In Newfoundland:

Family tradition: —— Baker, from Wales, settled at Harbour Buffett and changed his name to Upshall; he later moved to Little Harbour (Placentia B.) (MUN Folklore).

Early instances: Peter Upshore or Upshall of Famish Gut, (now Fairhaven) (Placentia B.), 1835–6 (DPHW 30); George Upshall, of Harbour Beaulette (for Buffett) (Placentia B.), 1856 (*Newfoundlander* 22 Sep 1856); Elizabeth, of Harbour Breton, 1856 (D.A. Macdonald); Joseph, fisherman of Hay Stack (Placentia B.), 1871 (Lovell); Christopher, miner of La Manche, 1871 (Lovell).

Modern status: Scattered, especially at Little Harbour East (Placentia B.).

Place name: Upshall (Station) 47-40 53-54.

UPWARD(S), surnames of England from the English place name Upwood (Huntingdonshire). (Bardsley).

In Newfoundland:

Family tradition: Jeremiah Upward, from England, settled at Harry's Harbour (Green B.) about 1820 (MUN Folklore).

Early instances: Edward Upward, of New (now Parsons) Harbour, 1835 (DPHW 30); Nehemiah Upwood, of ? Harris Cove (Exploits district), 1856 (DPHW 92); William Upward, of Harry's Harbour, 1874 (DPHW 90).

Modern status: Upward, especially at Harry's Harbour; Upwards, at West Point (Burgeo-La Poile district), Silver Point (St. Barbe district) (*Electors* 1955) and Shoal Brook (St. Barbe district).

USHER, a surname of England, Ussher of Ireland, from Old French *huisser*, Middle English *usher* – usher, door-keeper, chamberlain. (Reaney, Cottle, MacLysaght).

Traced by Guppy in Northumberland and by MacLysaght in Ireland since the fourteenth century.

In Newfoundland:

Early instances: John, of Harbour Grace, 1823 (Nfld. Archives HGRC); John, soldier of St. John's, 1825 (DPHW 26B); Patrick, tailor of St. John's, 1871 (Lovell).

Modern status: Rare, at Corner Brook (*Electors* 1955) and Seal Cove (Harbour Main district).

VAIL, VALE, surnames of England and Ireland from Old French *val*, Middle English *val(e)* – dweller in the) valley, or from the French place name Val (Calvados, etc.), or a variant of Veil from Old French *de la veille* – of the watch, watchman, or a variant of Veal(e) from Old French *vieil*, Anglo-French *viel* – old, or from Old French *veel, viel* – calf. (Reaney, Spiegelhalter, Cottle, MacLysaght).

Guppy traced Veal(e) in Cornwall and Devon, Vale in Herefordshire. MacLysaght traced Vail, Vale, Veale in Co. Waterford.

In Newfoundland:

Family tradition: The Vale family came from Co. Wexford on the vessel *Sea Rover* and settled at Mobile in the 1820s (Dillon).

Early instances: Nicholas Veal, cooper of St. John's, 1794–5, "18 years in Newfoundland," that is, 1776–7 (Census 1794–5); David Veil, of Bay Bulls district, 1804 (Nfld. Archives BRC); David Vale, from Co. Waterford, married at St. John's,

1808 (Nfld. Archives BRC); Pennis (? for Dennis) Veale, of Harbour Grace, 1824 (Nfld. Archives HGRC); Sybilla Vaile, of St. John's, deceased, 1851 (*Newfoundlander* 25 Sep 1851); Thomas Vail, of Lower Island Cove, 1858 (DPHW 55); Michael, fisherman of St. Mary's, 1871 (Lovell); Thomas and William Vale, of Mobile, 1871 (Lovell).

Modern status: Vail, at Lower Island Cove (*Electors* 1955), St. Mary's and St. John's; Vale, unique, at St. John's (*Electors* 1955).

Place name: Vails Point 49-58 55-40.

VALLIS, a surname of England from the name of the old province of Valois (Ille-de-France) or a variant of the surname of France Vallois, a variant of Vallon, the name of numerous hamlets. (Reaney, Dauzat).

Dauzat traced Vallois in Normandy and elsewhere.

In Newfoundland:

Early instances: James, proprietor and occupier of fishing room, Bonaventure (unspecified) (Trinity B.), Winter 1800–01 (Census Trinity B.); William Vallers, from Redhill (Hampshire), of Burin, deceased 1815 (*Royal Gazette* 15 Jun 1815); J. Vallis, of Bonavista, deceased 1831 (*Newfoundlander* 14 Jul 1831); James Vallice, of Coombs Cove, Bay de l'Eau, 1835 (DPHW 30).

Modern status: Scattered, especially at Coombs Cove.

VAN ALSTYNE, VANALSTYNE, surnames of Holland from an unidentified Dutch place name.

In Newfoundland: From the U.S.A. during World War II.

Modern status: Rare, Van Alstyne at St. John's, Vanalstyne, at Coley's Point.

VANNAN, a surname of Scotland, "not likely to be from Gaelic *(Mac) Mhannain*" (Black).

In Newfoundland:

Early instance: A., from Edinburgh, Scotland, settled at St. John's in 1946 (Family).

Modern status: Unique, at St. John's.

VARDY, a surname of England, a variant of Varty, Verity from French *vérité* – truth. (Reaney, Weekley *Surnames*).

Traced by Weekley in Yorkshire WR.

In Newfoundland:

Family traditions: George (1819–82) and two brothers, from Devon, settled ? at Clay Pits (Trinity B.) in the early 19th century (MUN Folklore). ——,

of French ancestry, from England, settled at Clay Pits (Trinity B.) and later at Hickman's Harbour. The name in France was originally Fertitate, became Vertie in England and on settling in Newfoundland, was further changed to Vardy (MUN Hist.).

Early instances: George Vardey, of Grates Cove, 1841 (DPHW 59); William Vardy, of Lower Burgeo, 1845 (DPHW 101); George, fisherman of Random Sound (Trinity B.), 1871 (Lovell); Moses, fisherman of Clay Pits (Trinity B.), 1879 (DPHW 60).

Modern status: Scattered, especially at Clarenville.

Place names: Vardy Brook 48-59 58-06; Vardys Island 47-35 59-08; Vardyville 48-08 53-44.

VASLETT, a ? Newfoundland variant of the surname of France Vaslet, an archaic form of Valet, French *valet* – man-servant. (Dauzat). *See also* VASS, VAVASOUR.

In Newfoundland:

Modern status: Rare, at Terrenceville.

VASS, a surname of England from Latin *vassus*, Old French *vasse* – servant, also used occasionally as a personal name. (Reaney). *See also* VASLETT, VAVASOUR.

In Newfoundland:

Early instance: Edmund, shoemaker of Harbour Grace, 1866, 1871 (Nfld. Archives HGRC, Lovell).

Modern status: Rare, at Clarenville (*Electors* 1955).

VATCHER, a surname of England from Old French *vachier* – cowherd. (Reaney, Cottle).

Traced by Matthews in Devon.

In Newfoundland:

Early instances: Philip, fisherman of Freshwater (Carbonear), 1818 (DPHW 48); John, of Grand Bank, 1842 (DPHW 106); James, on the *Corfe Mullen* in the seal fishery out of Carbonear, 1847 (*Newfoundlander* 25 Mar 1847); Charles, fisherman of Merritt's Harbour, 1851 (DPHW 85); Emanuel, of Lower Burgeo, 1851 (DPHW 101); Ann, of Filthy (now British) Harbour, 1853 (DPHW 59); Joseph, planter of Crocker's Cove (Carbonear), 1854 (DPHW 49); Eli (and others), of Twillingate, 1871 (Lovell).

Modern status: Scattered, especially at St. John's.

VATER(S), ? West Country variants, not apparently recorded elsewhere, of the surnames of England Fayter, Fetters, from Anglo-French, Middle English *faitour* – imposter, cheater. (Reaney).

Reaney traced Vatters in Devon in 1524.

In Newfoundland:

Family traditions: ——, from England, settled at Victoria (Carbonear district), about 1840 (MUN Geog.). N., from Bristol, England, settled at St. Brendans, about 1855 (MUN Folklore).

Early instances: James Vater, planter of Otterbury (Carbonear), 1830 (DPHW 48); Edmond, from Belchalwell (Dorset), married at Gooseberry Island (Bonavista B.), 1849, of Cottel's Island (Bonavista B.), 1851 (DPHW 73A, 76); Joseph, of Perry's Cove, 1871 (Lovell).

Modern status: Vater, rare, at St. John's; Vaters, scattered, especially Victoria (Carbonear district).

VAUGHAN, a surname of Wales, England and Ireland from Welsh *fychan*, *bychan* – small, little; also in Ireland for Mohan, Maughan or Mahon, *Ó Macháin*. (Reaney, Cottle, MacLysaght 73).

Traced by Guppy in Herefordshire, Monmouthshire, Shropshire, North and South Wales, and by MacLysaght in Ireland since the early sixteenth century.

In Newfoundland:

Early instances: George Vens or Vaughan, fisherman of Small Point (Bay de Verde district), 1820, 1831 (DPHW 52A); John Vaughen, from Milford Haven (Pembrokeshire), married at St. John's, 1825 (Nfld. Archives BRC); —— Vaughan, master of the *Belinda*, died at Seal Island (unspecified), 1829 (*Newfoundlander* 8 Oct 1829); William, planter of Mulleys Cove (Conception B.), 1844 (DPHW 52A).

Modern status: At Small Point (Bay de Verde district) and St. John's.

VAVASOUR, a surname of England from Latin *vassus vassorum* – servant of servants, Old French *vavas(s)our*. Reaney comments: "A feudal tenant ranking immediately below a baron ..." (Reaney, Cottle). *See also* VASLETT, VASS.

Traced by Spiegelhalter in Devon.

In Newfoundland:

Family tradition: James (1846–), from Dorset, came with his parents to Tilt Cove, Newfoundland between 1850–60; he moved to St. John's in 1892 (MUN Folklore).

Early instances: James Vavasor, of St. John's, 1813 (DPHW 26B); Hugh Vavasseur, of Great St. Lawrence (now St. Lawrence), 1871 (Lovell).

Modern status: At St. John's.

VEITCH, a surname of England, Scotland and Ireland, ? from a common French place name Vic, or ? from an Old English personal name *Ucca* or *Uacca*. (E.C. Smith, Black (Amendments and Additions), MacLysaght 73).

Traced by MacLysaght from Scotland in Cos. Fermanagh and Cavan since the end of the seventeenth century.

In Newfoundland:

Family tradition: ——, of Irish descent, from St. Mary's Bay, settled at Holyrood in the 1870s (MUN Folklore).

Early instances: John Vitch, granted land at George's Cove Marsh (near Holyrood), 1859 (Nfld. Archives, Registry Crown Lands); George (and others) Veitch, of Holyrood, 1871 (Lovell).

Modern status: At Corner Brook, Buchans, Marystown (*Electors* 1955), Holyrood and St. John's.

VERGE, a surname of England – (dweller by the) verge, boundary (? of a village) or ? from Old French *verge* – (owner of a) rood, quarter of an acre, hence ? orchard, garden. (Weekley *Surnames*, Bardsley).

In Newfoundland:

Family tradition: Joe, from Liverpool, settled at Carbonear in the early 1800s; he later moved to Harbour Grace (MUN Folklore).

Early instances: John Vinge, fisherman of Bonaventure (unspecified), 1758 (DPHW 64); Mary Verge, of Trinity Bay, 1773 (DPHW 64); John, of Trinity (Trinity B.), 1785 (DPHW 64); John Verges, servant of St. John's, 1799 (D'Alberti 10); Thomas Verge, proprietor of fishing room, Irelands Eye (Trinity B.), Winter 1800–01 (Census Trinity B.); George, planter of Twillingate, 1818 (USPG); John, planter of Old Bonaventure, 1834 (DPHW 64B); Thomas, of Bonavista, 1841 (DPHW 70); William, planter of Trouty (Trinity B.), 1843 (DPHW 64B); John, planter of Cat Cove (Trinity North district), 1849 (DPHW 64B); Charity, of Scilly Cove (now Winterton), 1854 (DPHW 59A); Susanna Virge, of New Perlican, 1859 (DPHW 58); William Verge, fisherman of Smith Sound (Trinity B.), 1859 (DPHW 63); George, of Bay of Islandst 1871 (Lovell); Heli [sic] and John, labourers of Harbour Grace, 1871 (Lovell).

Modern status: Scattered, especially at Harbour Grace and Old Bonaventure.

Place names: Verge Island, —— Rock 48-07 53-32.

VERRAN, a surname of England from the English place name Veryan (Cornwall) or from Old French *vairon* – wall-eyed. (Spiegelhalter).

Guppy traced Verran, Verrin in Cornwall, Spiegelhalter traced Verren in Devon.

In Newfoundland:

Modern status: Rare, at Placentia.

VEY, a surname of England, France and Ireland, in England and France from the French place names Le Vey (Calvados, Orne) or Les Veys (Manche) or from Old French *veie, voie* – way, road; in England also ? a variant of the surname of England Vye, a pet-form of the baptismal name Vivian (*see* VIVIAN); in France also from French *fois* (an obscure nickname); in Ireland Mac Vey, Veugh, Veigh, *Mac an Beatha,* Ir. *boith,* genitive *beatha* – life, sometimes changed to Mac Evoy (*see* McEVOY, McABEE). (Spiegelhalter, E. C. Smith, Dauzat, MacLysaght 73).

MacLysaght traced Mac Vey in Co. Armagh.

In Newfoundland:

Family tradition: —— Vyse, from Ireland, settled at Grates Cove where the surname changed to Voy then Vey; the family moved to Long Beach (Trinity B.) about 1836 (MUN Folklore).

Early instances: Charles, of Trinity (Trinity B.), 1787 (DPHW 64); George, of Port de Grave, 1797 (DPHW 48); George Vey or Vye, of St. John's, 1803, died 1835, aged 75, having spent nearly 50 years in Newfoundland, that is, since about 1785 (DPHW 23, *Times* 7 Jan 1835); Joseph Vye, from Sherborne (Dorset), of St. John's, 1833 (DPHW 26D); James Vise or Vey, fisherman of Grates Cove, 1850 (DPHW 58); William Vie, sailmaker of Bay Roberts, 1871 (Lovell); Philip Vey, of Bird Island Cove (now Elliston), 1871 (Lovell); James, of Random Sound (Trinity B.), 1871 (Lovell).

Modern status: Scattered, especially at Long Beach (Trinity B.).

Place names: Vey Point 48-23 53-53; Vyse Cove 47-52 55-47.

VICARS, VICKERS, surnames of England, Vicars, Mac Vicar, Mac Vicker of Ireland – servant (or, according to MacLysaght, son) of the vicar. (Reaney, Cottle, MacLysaght 73). *See also* VIGUERS with which confusion may have occurred.

Guppy traced Viccars in Buckinghamshire, Vickers in Derbyshire, Durham and Lincolnshire; Spiegelhalter traced Viccars in Devon; and MacLysaght Vicars, Mac Vicar, Mac Vicker in Ulster.

In Newfoundland:

Early instances: Joseph Vicax, of Salvage, 1681 (CO 1); Thomas Vickers, soldier of St. John's, 1802 (DPHW 26B); Eleanor Vicars, from Co. Kilkenny, married at St. John's, 1813 (Nfld. Archives BRC); Rev. J., of Port de Grave, 1843 (*Newfoundlander* 2 Nov 1843); John Vickers, miner of Tilt Cove, 1871

(Lovell); Michael Vicors, of Logy Bay, 1871 (Lovell).

Modern status: Vicars, at St. John's; Vickers, scattered, especially at Witless Bay (*Electors* 1955).

VIGUERS, a variant of the surnames of England Vigar(s), Vigers etc., Vigors of Ireland, Vigour of France, from Old French *vigoro(u)s,* Anglo-French *vigrus* – hardy, lusty, strong. (Reaney, Cottle, MacLysaght, Dauzat). *See also* VICARS with which confusion may have occurred.

Guppy traced Vigar(s), Vigors in Somerset; Mac-Lysaght traced Vigors in Co. Carlow since the seventeenth century; and Dauzat Vigou(r) in Ille-et-Vilaine and Ouest.

In Newfoundland:

Early instances: John, Lewis, George and Robert Vigours, traders who sustained losses when St. Pierre was surrendered to the French in 1763 (CO 194.16); John and Thomas Viquers, of Placentia, 1794, 1803 (D'Alberti 5, 13); John (and sons) Viguers, of Bay Bulls, 1802 (USPG); Francis Vigears, baker of St. John's, 1871 (Lovell).

Modern status: At St. John's.

Place name: Vigors Island 47-37 54-20.

VINCENT, a baptismal name and surname of England, Ireland, France and Jersey (Channel Islands) from Latin *vincens* – conquering, the name of a third-century Spanish martyr; in Ireland also sometimes for MacAvinchy. (Withycombe, Reaney, Cottle, Dauzat, MacLysaght, Turk).

Traced by Guppy in Cornwall, Devon, Norfolk, Somerset, Suffolk and Wiltshire, and by MacLysaght in Cos. Limerick and Dublin since the mid-seventeenth century, and in Co. Derry (for Mac-Avinchy),

In Newfoundland:

Family tradition: ——, from Scotland, settled at Cape Freels (MUN Folklore).

Early instances: Giles Vinsant or Vincent, planter of Connaigre, 1710–15, of Isle Grole, 1714 (CO 194.5, 6); John, fisherman of St. John's or Petty Harbour, about 1739–43 (CO 194.11); Joanna Vinsen, of Bay de Verde, 1774 (CO 199.18); Joseph Vincent, soldier of St. John's, 1802 (DPHW 26B); John, planter of Fogo, 1808 (MUN Hist.); John, of Greenspond, 1819 (DPHW 76); Alice, of Harbour Grace, 1825 (Nfld. Archives HGRC), William, of Bonavista, 1826 (Nfld. Archives KCRC); John, baptized at Cape Island (Bonavista B.), 1830, aged 18 (DPHW 76); William, of King's Cove Parish, 1834 (Nfld. Archives KCRC); William, of Three Arms

(Twillingate district), 1841 (DPHW 86); R., Road Commissioner for the Cape Freels to Cobblers Island area, 1847 (*Nfld. Almanac*); ——, of Cow Cove (near Cow Head, St. Barbe district), 1849 (Feild); Joseph, of Cape Freels, 1849 (DPHW 76); William, of Herring Neck, 1857 (DPHW 85); ——, of Black Island (Exploits district), 1859 (DPHW 92); William, of Merritts Harbour, 1859 (DPHW 85); James, of Stock Cove (Bonavista B.), 1860 (Nfld. Archives KCRC); William, of Knights Cove, 1866 (Nfld. Archives KCRC); John, of Main River (St. George's district), 1870 (DPHW 96); Philip, of Burin, 1871 (Lovell); Thomas, farmer of Logy Bay, 1871 (Lovell); John (and others), of Sandy Point (St. George's B.), 1871 (Lovell).

Modern status: Widespread, especially at Corner Brook, Newtown, Triton and St. John's.

Place names (not necessarily from the surname): Vincent Island 51-35 55-27; Mount —— 47-09 55-08.

VINCER, a surname of England of unknown origin, ? like Vince(y) a derivative of VINCENT.

In Newfoundland:

Modern status: Rare, at St. John's.

VINEHAM, apparently a variant (one in London Telephone Directory) of the surname of England Vining, from the English place name Vining (Sussex) from Old English *fīning* – place where wood is heaped, possibly clearing. (A.H. Smith).

In Newfoundland:

Early instances: Thomas Vining, in possession of property at Torbay, 1794–5 (Census 1794–5); Charles, planter of Twillingate, 1820 (USPG).

Modern status: At Pilley's Island, Durrell's Arm and Botwood.

VIN(N)ICOMBE, surnames of England from the English place name Vin(n)icombe (Devon). (Spiegelhalter).

Traced by Spiegelhalter in Devon.

In Newfoundland:

Early instances: William Vinicomb, of St. John's, 1753 (DPHW 26C); —— Vinnicombe, in possession of land at Quidi Vidi, 1780 (D'Alberti 1); Mrs. Jean, renting a meadow near Maggotty Cove (St. John's), 1796 (D'Alberti 12); Richard Vinecum, of Maggotty Cove, 1813 (Nfld. Archives BRC); Jean Vinican, of Catalina, 1821 (Nfld. Archives KCRC); Mary Jane Vilicombe, of Plate Cove (Bonavista B.), 1866 (Nfld. Archives KCRC); Charles Vinecomb, of Cow Harbour (Bonne B.), 1871 (Lovell).

Modern status: Vin(n)icombe, at St. John's.

VISCOUNT, a surname of England, (Le) Vesconte of Jersey (Channel Islands) from the office – a vice-count, one who takes the place of a count. Bardsley comments: "This surname, unlike many others of the same official class, does not seem to have lasted long. I find no modern instances." (Bardsley, Turk).

In Newfoundland:

Modern status: At Fox Island River (Port au Port district), Placentia and St. John's.

VIVIAN, a baptismal name and surname of England, with also Vivyan of Guernsey (Channel Islands) and Vyvyan of Jersey from Latin *vivus* – alive, whence the personal name *Vivianas*, the name of a fifth-century saint and martyr. (Reaney, Cottle, Turk).

Traced by Guppy in Cornwall and by Spiegelhalter in Devon.

In Newfoundland:

Early instances: Richard, planter of Careless (now Kerley's) Harbour, 1830, of Old Bonaventure, 1840–45, of Cat Cove (Trinity B.), 1843 (DPHW 64B); William, of Twillingate, 1841 (DPHW 88); James, of Greenspond, 1841 (DPHW 76); George, of Shambler's Cove (Bonavista B.), 1871 (Lovell); James, of Smart's Island (Bonavista B.), 1871 (Lovell).

Modern status: Scattered, especially at Hare Bay.

VOISEY, a surname of England. *See* FACEY.

Matthews traced Voysey in Devon.

In Newfoundland:

Early instances: Richard Voysey, of St. John's, 1813 (DPHW 26B); Richard, from Buckfastleigh (Devon), of St. John's, 1822 (DPHW 26D); Sarah Vesey, from Ipplepen (Devon), married at St. John's, 1850 (DPHW 26D); Richard Voisey, granted land at Quidi Vidi Road, 1854 (Nfld. Archives, Registry Crown Lands); George Voisy, rigger of Harbour Grace, 1871 (Lovell).

Modern status: At St. John's.

Place names: Voicey(s) or Voisies Bay (Labrador) 56-15 61-50; Voiseys Brook 47-38 52-49.

VOKEY, a surname of England and ? of Jersey (Channel Islands), ? from the English place name Voghay (Devon), from Old English *focga* – aftermath, coarse reeds, or from *Focga* a personal name. (Gover, E.C. Smith).

In Newfoundland:

Family tradition: William, from Jersey (Channel Islands), settled at Spaniards Bay about 1775 (MUN Folklore).

Early instances: Thomas, of Western Bay, 1783

(CO 199.18); Philip, of Port de Grave, 1787, of (Upper) Island Cove, 1790, of Northern Cove (Spaniard's Bay), 1799 (CO 199.18); Philip, of Spaniard's Bay, 1832 (DPHW 30); Nathaniel Valky or Vokey, fisherman of Delby's Cove (Trinity B.), 1856 (DPHW 64B).

Modern status: Scattered, especially at Bell Island (*Electors* 1955) and Spaniard's Bay.

VOORHOEVE, a surname of Holland – ? (worker in the) forecourts, outer courts.

In Newfoundland:

Modern status: Unique, at St. John's.

VOUTIER, ? a Newfoundland variant of the surname of France and Jersey (Channel Islands) Vautier, a regional form (Franche-Comté, Lorraine, Normandy, etc.) of Gautier (*see* GAUDET). (Dauzat, Turk).

In Newfoundland:

Early instances: Richard Voucher, of Burgeo Island, 1830 (DPHW 30); Francis Vautier, fisherman of Lower Burgeo, 1842 (DPHW 101); Samuel Viltore, of Red Island (Burgeo-La Poile district), 1845 (DPHW 101); Peter Vautier, from Jersey (Channel Islands), married at St. John's, 1856 (DPHW 26D); James and William Voter, of English Harbour East, 1871 (Lovell); John Vautier, of Indian Harbour (Burgeo-La Poile district), 1871 (Lovell); Francis Jr. and Sr., of La Poile, 1871 (Lovell).

Modern status: At Petites, La Poile (*Electors* 1955) and Bishop's Falls.

W

WADDEN, a variant of the surname of Ireland Wadding, *Uaidín*. (MacLysaght).

MacLysaght traced Wadding in Co. Wexford.

In Newfoundland:

Family tradition: ——, from Co. Wexford, settled at St. John's about 1840 (MUN Folklore).

Early instances: Ephrim Waden, of St. John's, 1804 (Nfld. Archives BRC); Nicholas (1815–1911), from New Ross (Co. Wexford), arrived in St. John's 1830 and opened business as shoemaker 1843–44. (B. Wadden); Margaret Wadden, from Co. Wexford, married at St. John's, 1838 (Nfld. Archives BRC); John, of Change Islands, 1877 (DPHW 89).

Modern status: At Buchans and St. John's.

WADDLETON, a surname of England from the English place names Waddington (Yorkshire WR, Surrey); in Newfoundland a variant of the surname Warrington from Warrington (Lancashire). (Cottle).

Guppy traced Warrington in Derbyshire and Staffordshire.

In Newfoundland:

Family tradition: —— Warrington, from England, settled at Trepassey; the family on conversion to Roman Catholicism changed its name to Waddleton (MUN Geog.).

Early instances: John Waddleton, of St. John's, 1789 (DPHW 26C); Samuel, of Trepassey, 1839 (Nfld. Archives BRC); J. Warrington, of St. John's, 1857 (*Newfoundlander* 23 Apr 1857); John Warington, of Torbay, 1871 (Lovell).

Modern status: At Trepassey and St. John's.

WADE, a surname of England and Ireland from the Old English personal name *Wada* from *wadan* – to go, or Old German *Wado*, or from the English place name Wade (Suffolk), or from Old English *(ge)wæd* – (dweller by the) ford. Reaney comments: "The persistence of the personal name may be due, in part, to the tale of Wade [a legendary hero], originally a sea-giant, dreaded and honoured by the coast tribes of the North Sea and Baltic." (Reaney, Cottle, MacLysaght).

Traced by Guppy in Cheshire, Derbyshire, Durham, Norfolk, Northamptonshire, Suffolk and Yorkshire, by Spiegelhalter in Devon, and by MacLysaght in all provinces since the thirteenth century.

In Newfoundland:

Early instances: Maurice, of Northern Arm, Salmon Cove (now Avondale), 1778 (CO 199.18); Edward, of Cats Cove (now Conception Harbour), 1791 (CO 199.18); Patrick, of Trinity (Trinity B.), 1792 (DPHW 64); Ed, of Harbour Grace, 1809 (Nfld. Archives HGRC); James, ? of St. John's, 1822 (CO 194.65); T., of Brigus, 1831 (*Newfoundlander* 24 Nov 1831); Michael, of Flat Rock (St. John's), 1838, 1871 (Nfld. Archives BRC, Lovell); Robert, fisherman of Bird Island Cove (now Elliston), 1840 (DPHW 72); John, farmer of Caplin Bay (now Calvert), 1871 (Lovell); John, of Salmonier (St. Marys), 1871 (Lovell).

Modern status: Scattered, especially at Conception Harbour and Flatrock (St. John's).

Place name: Wade Lake (Labrador) 54-20 65-38.

WADLAND, a surname of England from the English place name Wadland Barton (Devon). (Spiegelhalter).

Traced by Guppy in Devon.

In Newfoundland:

Early instance: George, of St. John's, 1802 (D'Alberti 12).

Modern status: At St. John's.

WADMAN, a surname of England and ? of Ireland (though not included by MacLysaght), from Old English *wād* – woad and *mann* – dyer with or dealer in woad, or from Middle English *wodeman* – woodman, forester. (*See* WOODMAN). (Reaney).

In Newfoundland:

Family tradition: ——, from Ireland, settled at Barren Island (now Bar Haven) (Placentia B.), about 1880 (MUN Folklore).

Early instances: Richard Wadmen, of Trinity Bay, 1774 (DPHW 64); Matthew Wadman, of Pushthrough, 1835 (DPHW 30); Charles, fisherman of Grole, 1846 (DPHW 102); William, of Firby's Harbour (Burgeo-La Poile district), 1850 (DPHW 101); William, of Harbour Le Cou, 1860 (DPHW 99); Martin Wadhan, fisherman of Barren Island (now Bar Haven), 1871 (Lovell); William Wadman, of Rose Blanche, 1871 (Lovell).

Modern status: At Bar Haven (*Electors* 1955) and Arnold's Cove.

Place name: Wadman Point 47-28 54-23.

WAGG, a surname of England, ? a nickname, shake-(head), as in Waggett. (Bardsley, Weekley *Surnames*).

In Newfoundland:

Early instances: James Sr., of Burin, 1814 (D'Alberti 24); Ann, of Harbour Grace, 1825 (Nfld. Archives HGRC); John, of Fogo, 1855 (DPHW 83); Thomas, fisherman of Step-Aside (Burin district), 1861 (DPHW 100).

Modern status: Scattered.

WAGNER, a surname of England and Germany, in English – waggoner, carter, in German – wheelwright. (Bardsley).

In Newfoundland:

Modern status: Rare, at Corner Brook (*Electors* 1955) and Riverhead (Harbour Grace).

WAKEHAM, a surname of England from the English place name Wakeham (Devon, Sussex). (Cottle, Spiegelhalter).

Traced by Guppy in Devon.

In Newfoundland:

Family tradition: Three brothers Jim, John and Ben, from ? Sheffield, England, migrated to Newfoundland. Jim and John went to Placentia Bay and Ben settled in St. John's (Family).

Early instances: John, of Salvage, 1681 (CO 1); Samuel Wakham, of Petty Harbour, 1703, of St. John's, 1706 (CO 194.3, 22); John Wakam, of Bonavista, 1708 (CO 194.4); Thomas Wakeham, in possession of property and planter of St. John's, 1794–5, "48 years in Newfoundland," that is, 1746–7 (Census 1794–5); William, of Cupids, 1871 (Lovell).

Modern status: At St. John's and in the Placentia East and West districts.

WAKELIN, a surname of England from the Norman-French baptismal name *Walchelin*, double diminutive of the Old German personal names *Walho* or *Walico*. (Reaney). *See also* WALKINS.

Traced by Guppy in Cambridgeshire, Essex and Suffolk.

In Newfoundland:

Modern status: Rare, at Harbour Grace.

WAKLEY, a surname of England ? from the English place name Wakeley (Hertfordshire). (Reaney, Cottle).

Guppy traced Wakely in Dorset.

In Newfoundland:

Early instances: Isaac Wakeley, of Greenspond, 1824 (DPHW 76); John Wakely, granted land at Corbin Harbour (Fortune B.), 1833 (Nfld. Archives, Registry Crown Lands); Isaac, fisherman of Haystack (Placentia B.), 1871 (Lovell).

Modern status: At Safe Harbour (Bonavista B.) and Greenspond (*Electors* 1955).

WALBOURNE, a surname of England, from the Old French personal name *Walebron*, or from the English place name Walburn (Yorkshire NR). (Reaney).

Guppy traced Walburn in Durham.

In Newfoundland:

Early instances: Samuel Walburne, planter of Fogo, 1816 (MUN Hist.); Elizabeth Walbourne, of Change Islands, 1821 (USPG).

Modern status: Scattered, especially at Fogo.

WALDRON, a surname of England and Ireland from the Old German personal names *Walahram*, *Waleran*, Old French *Galeran(t)*, or ? from the English place name Waldron (Sussex), or from Old English *weald-ærn* or *weald-renn* – house in a wood; in Ireland also an anglicization of *Mac Bhaildrin* and *Mac Bhalronta*. (Reaney, Cottle, MacLysaght).

Traced by Guppy in Berkshire, Wiltshire and Worcestershire, by Spiegelhalter in Devon, by Cottle in Hampshire, and found widespread in Ireland.

In Newfoundland:

Early instances: J., merchant from Poole (Dorset), J.P. of Fortune Bay, 1784, at Harbour Breton, 1797 (CO 194.24, D'Alberti 4, 6, 12); William, of Trinity (Trinity B.), 1813 (DPHW 64); —— Walderen, ? of St. John's, 1833 (*Newfoundlander* 7 Nov 1833); Joseph Waldron or Walden, planter of Spaniards Bay (now Spaniards Cove) (Trinity B.), 1845, 1871 (DPHW 64B, Lovell); Rev. Thomas Waldron or Walderen, from the Archdiocese of Tuam, Ireland, Parish Priest of King's Cove, 1854 (*Carbonear Star* 2 Oct 1833, *Newfoundlander* 7 Dec 1854.

Modern status: At Cormack, Trouty and Kearley's Harbour (*Electors* 1955).

Place names: Waldron Cove, —— —— Point 49-31 55-10; —— Islands (Labrador) 59-14 63-34; Tom Waldrons Pond 47-22 52-47.

WALKER, a surname of England, Scotland, Ireland and the Channel Islands from Old English *wealcere* – fuller. (Reaney, Cottle, Black, MacLysaght, Turk). *See also* FULLER and TUCKER.

Found widespread by Guppy especially in Durham, and generally in Scotland except in the extreme north; and by MacLysaght in northeast Ulster and Dublin.

In Newfoundland:

Family tradition: Arthur B. (1877–), from Windsor (Berkshire), emigrated to New Brunswick and later settled at St. John's (MUN Folklore).

Early instances: Thomas, in possession of property and mason of St. John's, 1794–5, "21 years in Newfoundland," that is, 1773–4 (Census 1794–5); William, merchant of St. John's or Harbour Grace, 1780 (D'Alberti 1); James, of Placentia, 1794 (D'Alberti 5); Grace, of Brigus, 1797 (CO 199.18); Honora, from Shenren (unidentified) (Co. Kilkenny), married at St. John's, 1808 (Nfld. Archives BRC); James, of Harbour Grace, 1810 (Nfld. Archives HGRC); James, planter of Heart's Content, 1823 (DPHW 64B); William, of King's Cove, 1824 (Nfld. Archives KCRC); Mark, of Tickle Cove (Bonavista B.), 1825 (Nfld. Archives KCRC); ——, on the *George* in the seal fishery out of Port de Grave, 1838 (*Newfoundlander* 29 Mar 1838); John, of New Harbour (Trinity B.), 1841 (DPHW 59); Mary Ann, servant of Carbonear, 1843 (DPHW 48); James, planter of Bird Island Cove (now Elliston), 1847 (DPHW 72); Mary, of Open Hole (now Open Hall), 1856 (Nfld. Archives KCRC); Catherine, of Stock Cove (Bonavista B.), 1863 (Nfld. Archives KCRC); John, of Gullys (Conception B.), 1871 (Lovell); Robert, of Salvage, 1871 (Lovell); Joseph, of Waldron's Cove, 1871 (Lovell).

Modern status: Scattered, especially at St. John's.

Place names: Walker Island (Labrador) 53-19 55-45; —— Lakes (Labrador) 59-49 64-12; —— Ledge 49-32 55-09; Walker's Cove 49-50 56-32; —— Point 49-07 53-36.

WALKINS, ? a variant, untraced elsewhere, of the surname of England WAKELIN, from Norman-French *Walchelin*, a double diminutive of the Old German personal names *Walho* or *Walico*. (Reaney).

In Newfoundland:

Early instances: Henry Walkins, of Tilton Harbour (now Tilting), 1818 (Nfld. Archives KCRC); Henry, of Little Harbour (unspecified), 1846 (*Newfoundlander* 4 Jun 1846); Solomon Walkens, planter of Bonne Bay, 1871 (Lovell).

Modern status: Rare, at St. John's.

WALL, a surname of England and Ireland, in England from Old English *weall* – (dweller by the town, sea, or ruined Roman) wall, or in the West Midlands dialect area where *walle* is for *welle* – (dweller by

the) spring or stream; in Ireland for the Norman surname *de Valle* gaelicized as *de Bhál*. (Reaney, Cottle, MacLysaght).

Traced by Guppy in Derbyshire, Durham, Herefordshire, Shropshire, Somerset and Worcestershire, by Spiegelhalter in Devon, and by MacLysaght in Limerick and Connacht.

In Newfoundland:

Early instances: John ? Walls, servant of Little Placentia (now Argentia), about 1730–5 (CO 194.9); Philip Walls, fisherman of St. John's or Petty Harbour, ? 1745 (CO 194.24); Lawrence Wall, of St. John's, 1757 (DPHW 26C); James, of Harbour Main, 1780 (CO 199.18); Patt, of Musketta (now Bristols Hope), 1789 (CO 199.18); John, of Colliers, 1801 (CO 199.18); Philip, from Owen (unidentified) (Co. Kilkenny), married at St. John's, 1806 (Nfld. Archives BRC); James, of Harbour Grace, 1807 (Nfld. Archives HGRC); Edward, one of 72 impressed men who sailed from Ireland to Newfoundland, ? 1811 (CO 194.51); Garret, of Tilton Harbour (now Tilting), 1821 (Nfld. Archives KCRC); Mary Wall alias Keating, of Petty Harbour, 1821 (Nfld. Archives BRC); Elizabeth Wall, from Carbonear, married at Fortune Harbour, 1831 (Nfld. Archives KCRC); Samuel, of Moreton's Harbour, 1843 (DPHW 86); Garrett, from Dungarvan (Co. Waterford), of Harbour Grace, 1844 (*Indicator* 27 July & 1844); Garret, granted land at Chapels Cove Pond (Conception B.), 1859 (Nfld. Archives, Registry Crown Lands); Jeremiah, of Petites, 1859 (DPHW 98); scattered in Lovell 1871.

Modern status: Widespread, especially at Grand Falls, Harbour Main and St. John's.

Place names (not necessarily from the surname): Wall Bight (or Seal Bay) (Labrador) 51-19 56-06; —— Island (Labrador) 52-13 55-37; —— Rock 48-07 52-50, 48-41 52-58; —— Shoal (Labrador) 52-13 55-36; The Wall (Labrador) 52-28 55-43; Walls Pond 47-25 53-09; Tom Wall Harbour 49-32 55-03.

WALLACE, a surname of England, Scotland and Ireland, the Scots form of WALLIS, normally referring to Strathclyde Welshmen; in Ireland also occasionally a synonym of WALSH. (Reaney, Black, MacLysaght).

Traced by Guppy in Durham, Northumberland and Yorkshire and over the south of Scotland.

In Newfoundland:

Early instances: Robert Wallice, of St. John's, 1771 (DPHW 26D); Michael Wallace or Wallis, from Waterford, married at Tilton Harbour (now Tilting), 1817 (Nfld. Archives KCRC); Edmund Wallace, of

Harbour Grace, 1828 (Nfld. Archives HGRC); Edward, ? of Northern Bay, 1840 (DPHW 54); R.W., from Greenock, married at St. John's, 1852 (*Newfoundlander* 27 Sep 1852); John, fisherman of Placentia, 1871 (Lovell).

Modern status: At St. John's.

Place names: Wallace Brook 49-32 58-08; —— Cove, —— Head 47-43 56-19; —— Cove 48-31 58-23.

WALLIS, a surname of England, Ireland and the Channel Islands from Anglo-French *Waleis*, *Walais* – Welshman, Celt, referring in the Welsh Border counties to the Welsh, in the east probably to Bretons. *See* WALLACE. (Reaney, Cottle, MacLysaght, Turk).

Traced by Guppy in Berkshire, Cambridgeshire, Cornwall, Derbyshire, Kent, Somerset, Staffordshire, Wiltshire and Yorkshire NR, ER, and by Spiegelhalter in Devon.

In Newfoundland:

Early instances: Richard, of Bonavista, 1675 (CO 1); John, of St. John's, 1708–9 (CO 194.4); John, in possession of property and fisherman of Torbay, 1794–5, "30 years in Newfoundland," that is, 1764–5 (Census 1794–5); Thomas, from Waterford City, married at St. John's, 1812 (Nfld. Archives BRC); John, from Abbotskerswell (Devon), of St. John's, deceased 1818 (*Royal Gazette* 6 Jan 1818); Edward, of Harbour Grace, 1827 (Nfld. Archives HGRC); Patrick, drowned near Cape Race, 1834 (*Newfoundlander* 1 Aug 1834).

Modern status: Rare, at St. John's.

WALSH, a surname of England, Scotland and Ireland from Old English *wælisc*, Middle English *walsche* – foreigner. (Reaney, Cottle, Black, MacLysaght). *See also* WALLACE, WALLIS, WELSH.

Traced by Guppy in Lancashire, by Spiegelhalter in Devon, and by MacLysaght as the fourth numerous of Irish surnames.

In Newfoundland:

Family traditions: John (–1827) and Ellen (Lyons) Walsh, were married in Co. Wexford, 1785. That year they emigrated to Newfoundland, settled first at Petty Harbour, then, in 1786, moved to Cape Broyle (MUN Folklore, Dillon). Avalon, of Southern Welsh ancestry, was born at Great Burin Islands, 1883 (MUN Folklore). ——, from Co. Cork, settled at Burin or St. Lawrence, ? in the 19th century (MUN Folklore).

Early instances: John Walsh or Welch, soldier of St. John's, 1756 (DPHW 26C); Philip Walsh, of

Chapels Cove, 1766 (CO 199.18); William, of Kit Hughes (now Kitchuses), 1776 (CO 199.18); John, of Western Bay, 1784 (CO 199.18); John, of Bay de Verde, 1785 (CO 199.18); Walter, of Cupids, 1787 (CO 199.18); John, from Carrick-on-Suir (Co. Tipperary), and Thomas, from Mayvoir (Co. Westmeath), Irish convicts landed at Petty Harbour or Bay Bulls, 1789 (CO 194.38); James and ? Edmond, of Placentia, 1794 (D'Alberti 5); Thomas, of Harbour Grace, 1796 (CO 199.18); Thomas, of Adams Cove, 1796 (CO 199.18); Patrick, from Mooncoin (Co. Kilkenny), married at St. John's, 1797 (Nfld. Archives BRC); James, of Holyrood, 1797 (CO 199.18); Catherine, of Lower Island Cove, 1798 (CO 199.18); Michael, of Carbonear, 1800 (CO 199.18); Thomas, from Youghal (Co. Cork), married at King's Cove, 1803 (Nfld. Archives BRC); Mary, of Keels, 1803 (Nfld. Archives BRC); Michael, encroacher on property at Holyrood Island between St. Mary's and Trepassey, 1808 (D'Alberti 18); Thomas, of Burin, 1809 (DPHW 26B); William, one of 72 impressed men who sailed from Ireland to Newfoundland, ? 1811 (CO 194.51); William, from Monaghan (Co. Kilkenny), fisherman of St. John's, died 1811 (*Royal Gazette* 5 Dec 1811); Garret, from Carrigtohill (Co. Cork), of Carbonear, died 1811 (*Royal Gazette* 26 Dec 1811); Robert, aged 20, from Co. Wexford, deserted from the employ of Wm. B. Pendergast & Sons, St. John's, 1812 (*Royal Gazette* 4 Jun 1812); James, of Devils (now Jobs) Cove, 1812 (*Royal Gazette* 11 Jun 1812); Walter, of Harbour Main, 1813 (Nfld. Archives BRC); Lawrence, given permission to erect fishing conveniences at Mobile, 1813 (D'Alberti 23); Peter, petitioned to occupy a fishing room at Low Point (Conception B.), 1814 (D'Alberti 24); Walter, from Carrick-on-Suir (Co. Tipperary), cooper of St. John's, died 1814 (*Royal Gazette* 6 Jan 1814); Patrick Walch, of Joe Batts Arm, 1815 (Nfld. Archives KCRC); Bridget Walsh, of Bonavista, 1815 (Nfld. Archives KCRC); Thomas, from Co. Cork, married at Trinity (unspecified), 1816 (Nfld. Archives KCRC); Peter, from Waterford, dealer and chapman of Fermeuse, deceased 1817 (*Nfld. Mercantile Journal* 18 Apr 1817); John, planter of Blackhead (Bay de Verde district), 1818 (DPHW 52A); ——, from Ireland, fisherman of Fortune Bay, 1818 (D'Alberti 28); Eliner [sic], of Ragged Harbour (now Melrose), 1818 (Nfld. Archives KCRC); Pierce, of Fogo, 1819 (Nfld. Archives KCRC); Thomas, of Heart's Content, 1819 (Nfld. Archives KCRC); John, of Tickle Cove (Bonavista B.), 1820 (Nfld. Archives KCRC); Mary, of Bay Bulls, 1820 (Nfld. Archives BRC); Mary, of

Petty Harbour, 1820 (Nfld. Archives BRC); Thomas, of Catalina, 1821 (Nfld. Archives KCRC); Martin, of Manuels, 1822 (CO 194.65); Richard, of Broad Cove (now Duntara), 1823 (Nfld. Archives KCRC); Ellen, of Greenspond, 1824 (Nfld. Archives KCRC); Honor, of Brigus, 1828 (Nfld. Archives BRC); Robert, of Cats Cove (now Conception Harbour), 1828 (Nfld. Archives BRC); Mary, of Plate Cove (Bonavista B.), 1828 (Nfld. Archives KCRC); Thomas, from Carrickbeg (Co. Waterford), of Carbonear, 1828 (*Newfoundlander* 6 Feb 1828); Patrick, of Open Hole (now Open Hall), 1829 (Nfld. Archives KCRC); Patrick, of Fortune Harbour (Exploits district), 1830 (Nfld. Archives KCRC); John, of Heart's Desire, 1832 (Nfld. Archives KCRC); Mary, of Turks Cove, 1832 (Nfld. Archives KCRC); Catherine, of Bonaventure (unspecified), 1832 (Nfld. Archives KCRC); Patrick, of Port de Grave, 1834 (*Newfoundlander* 23 Jan 1834); James, of Outer Cove (St. John's), 1837 (Nfld. Archives BRC); Richard, of Ferryland, 1837 (Nfld. Archives BRC); Edward, of Little Placentia (now Argentia), 1838 (Nfld. Archives, Registry Crown Lands); William, ? of Northern Bay, ? 1839 (DPHW 54); James, of Fortune, 1841 (DPHW 109); Patrick, of Knights Cove (Bonavista B.), 1853 (Nfld. Archives KCRC); John, of Sholes [sic] Cove, 1856 (Nfld. Archives KCRC); Patrick, of Mosquito (now Bristol's Hope), 1857 (MUN Hist.); Richard, granted land at Hatchers Arm (Corbin B.), 1857 (Nfld. Archives, Registry Crown Lands); John, of Hayward's Cove, 1857 (Nfld. Archives KCRC); Charles, missionary of Upper Island Cove, 1857 (*Newfoundlander* 23 Apr 1857); John, of Dog Cove, 1858 (Nfld. Archives KCRC); John, of Cottles Island, 1860 (Nfld. Archives KCRC); John, of Gooseberry Island (Bonavista B.), 1861 (Nfld. Archives KCRC); Hannah, of Burnt Island (Bonavista B.), 1867 (Nfld. Archives KCRC); James, of Indian Arm, 1870 (Nfld. Archives KCRC); widespread in Lovell 1871.

Modern status: Widespread in all districts, with large concentrations at St. John's, Corner Brook, Plate Cove West, Marystown, Bay de Verde, Ferryland and Holyrood.

Place names: Walsh (Station) 48-35 54-12; John —— Shoal 46-50 55-46; Tom —— Cove, —— —— Lookout 47-24 53-54.

WALTER(S), surnames of England, Wales and the Channel Islands, (Mac) Walter of Ireland, from the Old German personal names *Walter* or *Waldhar* containing the elements *mighty* and *army*, introduced into England in the reign of Edward the Confessor and very popular after the Norman Conquest, giving

the surnames WALTER(S), WATERS, WATKINS, WATSON, WATT(S). (Withycombe, Reaney, Cottle, MacLysaght, Turk).

Guppy traced Walter in Devon, Kent, Lincolnshire, Oxfordshire, Somerset and Sussex, Walters in Devon, Monmouthshire, Staffordshire and South Wales.

In Newfoundland:

Early instances: William Walters, fisherman of Trinity (Trinity B.), 1757 (DPHW 64); Henry, gunmaker of St. John's, 1806 (CO 194.45); William, of Salmon Cove (now Champneys), 1814 (DPHW 64); John, planter of Robin Hood (now part of Port Rexton), 1823 (DPHW 64B); Ann, of Lamaline, 1835 (DPHW 106); John, from Ogwell (Devon), of St. John's, died 1840, aged 62 (*Times* 14 Oct 1840); James, fisherman of Maggeridge [sic] (Burgeo-La Poile district), 1846 (DPHW 101); William, from East Ogwell (Devon), of St. John's, 1855 (*Newfoundlander* 29 Nov 1855); John, planter of English Harbour (Trinity B.), 1869 (DPHW 65); George, of Fox Roost (Burgeo-La Poile district), 1871 (Lovell); Charles, of Hiscock's Point, 1871 (Lovell); William, of Upper Lance Cove (Trinity district), 1871 (Lovell).

Modern status: Walter, unique, at St. John's; Walters, scattered, especially at St. John's and Champneys.

Place name (not necessarily from the surname): Walter Point 48-23 53-22.

WARD, a surname of England and Ireland from Old English *weard* – watchman, guard, or Middle English *werd*, *ward* – (dweller in or near the) marsh, or from the English place name Ward (Devon); in Ireland usually for *Mac an Bháird* – son of the bard. (Reaney, Cottle, MacLysaght).

Found widespread by Guppy and by MacLysaght in Cos. Donegal and Galway.

In Newfoundland:

Family traditions: William Michael, from Gibraltar or England, came to Newfoundland in 1838 and taught school at Harbour Grace, Isle Valen (Placentia B.), Harbour Buffet and Portugal Cove (MUN Folklore). Daniel, from Dorchester (Dorset), of Moreton's Harbour, 1888 (Nfld. Dictionary Centre).

Early instances: Thomas, of St. John's, 1757 (DPHW 26C); Patrick, of Fogo, 1764 (MUN Hist.); Richard, in fishery at Petty Harbour, 1794–5, "20 years in Newfoundland," that is, 1774–5 (Census 1794–5); Patrick, from Co. Kilkenny, married at St. John's, 1802 (Nfld. Archives BRC); William, Methodist missionary of Bonavista, 1810 (CO 194.49);

Joseph, planter of Twillingate, 1800–18 (D'Alberti 22, USPG); Anastasia, of Heart's Content, 1819 (Nfld. Archives KCRC); Margaret, of Trinity (unspecified), 1827 (Nfld. Archives KCRC); William, of Rock Harbour (Placentia B.), 1837 (Nfld. Archives BRC); Patrick, of Harbour Main, 1838 (*Newfoundlander* 27 Sep 1838); John, teacher of Logy Bay, 1839 (*Newfoundlander* 1 Aug 1839); Johanna, of Harbour Grace Parish, 1841 (Nfld. Archives HGRC); Simon, of Leading Tickles, 1842 (DPHW 86); William James, from Halifax, editor of St. John's *Morning Post* 1843 (*Nfld. Patriot* 17 May 1843); John, ? of Northern Bay, 1844 (DPHW 54); Benjamin, of Cape Island (Bonavista B.), 1857 (DPHW 76); William, of Harbour Grace, 1868 (Nfld. Archives HGRC); scattered in Lovell 1871.

Modern status: Scattered, especially at St. John's and Portugal Cove South.

Place names: Ward Cove, —— Head 49-27 55-20; —— Harbour 49-37 55-41; —— Island 49-29 55-28; Wards Harbour 49-36 55-53; —— Rock 47-05 55-04.

WARE, a surname of England and Ireland from Old English ˈwær, Middle English *war(e)* – wary, astute, prudent, or Old English *wær* – (dweller near or worker at the fishing) weir, dam, or from the English place name Ware (Hertfordshire, Devon, Dorset, Kent). (Reaney, Cottle, MacLysaght). *See also* WAREHAM, WEIR, WARR.

Traced by Guppy in Devon and by MacLysaght in Cos. Cork and Dublin in the sixteenth century.

In Newfoundland:

Early instances: William, of St. John's Harbour, 1703–4 (CO 194.3); James, planter of Twillingate, 1821 (USPG); Isaac, of Tizzards Harbour, 1842 (DPHW 86); Emanuel Warre, lighthouse keeper, Cape Spear, 1844–46 (*Nfld. Almanac, Newfoundlander* 6 Apr 1846); John Weare, planter of Burin, 1871 (Lovell).

Modern status: Rare, at Corner Brook (*Electors* 1955).

WAREHAM, a surname of England from the English place name Wareham (Dorset) or (dweller at the) homestead (near the) weir (*see* WARE). (Cottle).

Traced by Guppy in Dorset and by Spiegelhalter in Devon.

In Newfoundland:

Family tradition: Thomas, from Wareham (Dorset), settled at Otterbury (Carbonear) in the 1830s (MUN Geog.).

Early instances: Warehams or Wakehams flake,

St. John's, 1780 (D'Alberti 1); Stephen Wareham, of Keels, 1834, of Tickle Cove (Bonavista B.), 1838 (DPHW 73A); Thomas, planter of Otterbury (Carbonear), 1840 (DPHW 48); John, of Spencer's Cove (Placentia B.), 1871 (Lovell); Willis Whareham, of Perry's Cove, 1871 (Lovell).

Modern status: Scattered, especially at St. John's and Carbonear.

Place names: Wareham (Village) 49-01 53-52; —— Rock 47-42 54-09.

WARFIELD, a surname of England from the English place name Warfield (Berkshire) – the field by the wrens' stream. (Cottle, Ekwall).

Traced by Spiegelhalter in Devon.

In Newfoundland:

Modern status: At New Melbourne (*Electors* 1955), Charlottetown and St. John's.

WARFORD, a surname of England from the English place name Warford (Cheshire) or (dweller by the) ford (by the) weir. *See* WARE, WEIR.

In Newfoundland:

Early instances: Richard Wafford, of Newfoundland, ? 1706 (CO 194.24); Henry (and others) Warford, of Port de Grave, 1771, property "in possession of the Family for 60 years," that is, 1711 (CO 199.18); Hugh, of Harbour Grace, 1771 (Nfld. Archives L118); John, of Mint Cove (Spaniards Bay), 1795 (CO 199.18); John, ? of St. John's, 1810 (CO 194.50); Anastasia, of Holyrood, 1828 (Nfld. Archives BRC); John, planter of Bear's Cove (Harbour Grace), 1830 (DPHW 43); William, of Fogo, 1856 (DPHW 83); Henry, of Scilly Cove (now Winterton), 1871 (Lovell); Isaac and John, of Upper Gully (Conception B.), 1871 (Lovell); Jacob Wharford, of Ship Cove (Brigus), 1871 (Lovell).

Modern status: Scattered, especially at Upper Gullies and South River (Conception B.).

WARR, a surname of England from Old French *(de la) warre, guerre* – (of the) war, hence warrior, or ? a variant of WARE. (Reaney, Cottle, Spiegelhalter).

Traced by Guppy in Buckinghamshire and by Spiegelhalter in Devon.

In Newfoundland:

Early instances: John, of St. John's, 1780 (DPHW 26C); William War(r), of Trinity (Trinity B.), 1803 (DPHW 64); Charles Warr, of Little Harbour (Twillingate district), 1845 (DPHW 86); Francis (and others), of Twillingate, 1871 (Lovell).

Modern status: Scattered, especially at Springdale.

WARREN, a surname of England and Ireland from the French place name La Varenne (Seine-Inférieure), or a variant of the surname of England War(e)ing, or from the Old French personal name Warin, Guarin; in Ireland also a synonym of (0) Murnane, *Ó Murnáin*. (Reaney, Cottle, Spiegelhalter, MacLysaght).

Found by Guppy in fourteen counties, especially Dorset, and by MacLysaght in the Dublin area and Co. Kerry.

In Newfoundland:

Early instances: Robert Warren, Warrin or Warring, of St. John's, 1675, "11 years an inhabitant in 1680," that is, since 1669 (CO 1); John Warren, of Salvage, 1676 (CO 1); William, fisherman of Trinity (Trinity B.), 1761 (DPHW 64); Henry, fisherman of Petty Harbour, 1794–5, "29 years in Newfoundland," that is, 1765–6 (Census 1794–5); William and Son, proprietors and occupiers of fishing room, Old Perlican, Winter 1800–01 (Census Trinity B.); J. and Son, proprietors and occupiers of fishing room, New Perlican, Winter 1800–01 (Census Trinity B.); William, of Brigus, 1808 (DPHW 34); Samuel, planter of Herring Neck, 1821 (USPG); James, planter of New Harbour (Trinity B.), 1823 (DPHW 64); John, planter of Heart's Content, 1824 (DPHW 64B); John, of Grand Bank, 1824 (DPHW 109); Sarah, of Fortune, 1825 (DPHW 106); Matthew, of Maggotty Cove (St. John's), 1828 (*Newfoundlander* 9 Apr 1828); Stephen, planter of Heart's Ease, 1830 (DPHW 64B); Mary, of Hants Harbour, 1830 (DPHW 59); William, fisherman of Fox Island (Burgeo-La Poile district), 1831 (DPHW 101); Edward, from Broadhempston (Devon), married at St. John's, 1835 (DPHW 26D); Capt. John, from Dover (Kent), married at St. John's, 1835 (Nfld. Archives BRC); James, from ? Broadhempston (Devon), married at Petty Harbour, 1837 (DPHW 31); John, of Open Hall, 1838 (DPHW 73A); Charles, of King's Cove Parish, 1838 (Nfld. Archives KCRC); William, of Tickle Cove (Bonavista B.), 1840 (DPHW 73); Besy, of Harbour Grace Parish, 1844 (Nfld. Archives HGRC); John, planter of Salt Harbour (Twillingate district), 1851, of Stone Harbour (Twillingate district), 1856 (DPHW 85); Joseph, fisherman of Grates Cove, 1851 (DPHW 58); George, from Devon, of St. John's, died 1853, aged 35 (*Weekly Herald and C. B. Advertiser* 16 Mar 1853); Matthew H., J.P. for the Labrador Coast, 1853 (*Newfoundlander* 23 Jun 1853); William, from Exeter (Devon), of St. John's, 1856 (*Newfoundlander* 15 May 1856); William, granted land at Channel, 1860 (Nfld. Archives, Registry Crown Lands); Ambrose, of Chapel Arm (Trinity B.), 1861 (DPHW 62);

Joseph, of Gooseberry Island (Bonavista B.), 1865 (DPHW 87); widespread in Lovell 1871.

Modern status: Widespread, especially at Chapel Arm (Trinity B.), Tack's Beach (Placentia B.) (*Electors* 1955), Corner Brook and St. John's.

Place names: Warren Cove 47-39 56-20, —————— (Labrador) 53-35 55-59; Warrens Island 51-36 55-32.

WARRICK, a surname of England and Scotland from Middle English *warroke* – (maker or builder of) scaffold(s), or a variant of WARWICK, of which Warrick is the pronunciation. (Reaney).

In Newfoundland:

Early instances: John, of Fogo, 1803–05 (D'Alberti 13, 15); George, soldier of St. John's, 1853 (DPHW 23).

Modern status: At Fogo and St. John's.

WARWICK, a surname of England and Scotland from the English place name Warwick (Warwickshire, Cumberland). (Reaney). *See also* WARRICK.

Traced by Guppy in Northamptonshire, by Spiegelhalter in Devon, and by Reaney in Dumfriesshire and Kirkcudbrightshire.

In Newfoundland:

Early instances: James, of Placentia, 1784 (Kirwin); James, planter of Fogo, 1821 (USPG); Sarah, of Herring Neck, 1858 (DPHW 85).

Modern status: Unique, at St. John's (Electors 1955).

Place name: Warwick Harbour 48-12 53-35.

WASS, a surname of England from the English place name Wass (Yorkshire NR) or from Old English *wæsse* – (dweller by the) swamp or from Old Scandinavian *vath* – (dweller by the) ford, or a variant of GASH. (Reaney, Cottle, Ekwall). *See also* WAYSON.

Traced by Guppy in Lincolnshire.

In Newfoundland:

Early instance: Richard, of Harbour Grace Parish, 1871 (Nfld. Archives HGRC).

Modern status: Unique, at Corner Brook.

WATERFIELD, a surname of England from the French place names Vatierville (Seine-Maritime) or ? Vatteville (Eure). (Reaney, Cottle, Spiegelhalter).

Traced by Spiegelhalter in Devon.

In Newfoundland:

Modern status: At St. John's.

WATERMAN, a surname of England – servant of Walter (*see* WALTER), or water-bearer, water-carrier, boatman. (Reaney, Cottle).

Traced by Guppy in Kent, and in Hampshire.

In Newfoundland:

Early instances: Joseph Watterman, of Bell Isle (now Bell Island), 1681 (CO 1); Richard Waterman, J.P. for Trinity district, ? 1730, 1732 (CO 194.9); John, fisherman of Trinity (Trinity B.), 1757 (DPHW 64); William, from Burton (Christchurch), Southampton, purchased land at Old Perlican, 1751 (Nfld. Archives T18); James, ship's carpenter of St. John's, 1783, 1794–5, "born in Newfoundland" (DPHW 26C, Census 1794–5); James, of Torbay, 1813 (DPHW 26B); Richard, of Flatrock (St. John's), 1820 (DPHW 26B); Robert, planter of Fogo, 1821 (USPG); David, of Hare Bay (now Deep Bay) (Fogo district), 1871 (Lovell); John and William, of Waterman and Co., Twillingate, 1871 (Lovell).

Modern status: Scattered, especially at Deep Bay (Fogo district).

WATERS, a surname of England and Ireland – son of Walter, (Water being the normal mediaeval pronunciation of Walter), or (dweller by the) waters or streams; in Ireland also a synonym of several Gaelic-Irish surnames such as Hiskey, Whoriskey, Toorish, etc., or a later form of the Norman name *de Auters.* (Reaney, Cottle, MacLysaght). *See* WALTER with which confusion seems to have occurred.

Traced by Guppy in Cornwall, Kent, Monmouthshire, Norfolk, Wiltshire, by Spiegelhalter in Devon and by MacLysaght in Co. Cork and ? elsewhere.

In Newfoundland:

Early instances: Edward, of Conception Bay [1706], of Harbour Grace, 1708–9 (CO 194.4); Samuel, married at John's, 1800 (DPHW 26D); Henry, from Kilkenny, married at St. John's, 1805 (Nfld. Archives BRC); John, of Bay L'Argent, 1871 (Lovell); William, of Garnish, 1871 (Lovell); David and Thomas, of Jersey Harbour, 1871 (Lovell); John, of Lamaline, 1871 (Lovell); Lambert, of Point Enragee, 1871 (Lovell); George, of Pouch Cove, 1871 (Lovell).

Modern status: Unique, at St. John's (Electors 1955).

WATKINS, a surname of England, Wales and Ireland – son of *Watkin,* a diminutive of Walter (*see* WALTER, WATERS). (Reaney, Cottle, MacLysaght 73).

Traced by Guppy especially in Herefordshire, Monmouthshire and South Wales, and also in Devon, Gloucestershire, Shropshire, Worcestershire and North Wales, and by MacLysaght in Ireland mainly from the seventeenth century.

In Newfoundland:

Early instances: Henry, fisherman of Little Harbour, Twillingate, 1814 (DPHW 88); Ally, from Killinick (Co. Wexford), married at St. John's, 1819 (Nfld. Archives BRC); Robert, planter of Twillingate, 1820 (USPG); Elizabeth, of Barr'd Islands, 1821 (USPG); Henry, from Enniscorthy (Co. Wexford), married at St. John's, 1835 (DPHW 26D); William, planter of Stone Harbour (Twillingate district), 1852 (DPHW 85); Abel, of Hall's Bay, 1855 (DPHW 86); James, son of James and Susannah of Teignmouth (Devon), married at Harbour Breton, 1867 (Harbour Breton Anglican Church Records per D.A. Macdonald); James, merchant of Rencontre, 1871 (Lovell); William, of Herring Neck, 1871 (Lovell); Isaac, of Ward's Harbour (now Beaumont North), 1871 (Lovell).

Modern status: Scattered, especially in the Twillingate district.

WATSON, a surname of England, Scotland and Ireland – son of *Wat* (Walter) (*see* WALTER, WATERS); in Ireland also an anglicized form of Scots *Mac Bhaididh,* Mac Whatty, MacWatt, MacQuatt. (Reaney, Cottle, Black, MacLysaght).

Found widespread by Guppy in England, especially in Durham, and over a large part of Scotland but most numerous south of the Forth and Clyde; by Spiegelhalter in Devon; by Black in the northeastern counties of Scotland; and by MacLysaght especially in northeast Ulster.

In Newfoundland:

Early instances: David, of St. John's, 1783 (DPHW 26C); Arthur, of Bay of Islands district, 1868 (DPHW 96); James H., (1845–), from Torquay (Devon), joined the fishery business of his brother at Hants Harbour in 1869 (Mott).

Modern status: Scattered, especially at Corner Brook.

Place names: Watsons Brook 48-57 57-56; —— Pond 48-55 57-55.

WATT(S), surnames of England and Scotland, Watt of Ireland – a pet-form of Wa(l)ter. *See* WALTER, WATERS. (Reaney, Cottle, Black, MacLysaght).

Spiegelhalter traced Watt(s) in Devon; Guppy traced Watts in the southern counties, especially Gloucestershire, Somerset and Wiltshire, and mostly in Scotland in Aberdeenshire and the neighbouring region; MacLysaght found Watt numerous in northeast Ulster.

In Newfoundland:

Early instances: William Watts, of Newfoundland, 1704 (CO 194.3); Robert, of Bonavista, 1708–9

(CO 194.4); Philip, fisherman of St. John's or Petty Harbour about 1739–43 (CO 194.11); ——, of St. John's, 1755 (DPHW 26C); Henry, of Carbonear, 1800 (CO 199.18); Richard, of Heart's Content, 1825 (Nfld. Archives KCRC); Sera, of Harbour Grace Parish, 1831 (Nfld. Archives HGRC); Richard, of King's Cove Parish, 1836 (Nfld. Archives KCRC); Henry Corban, of Harbour Grace, 1838 (*Newfoundlander* 27 Sep 1838); Arthur, cooper of New Harbour (Trinity B.), 1841, of Trinity (Trinity B.), 1843 (DPHW 64B); Henry, fisherman of Brigus, 1849 (DPHW 34); John Watt, of Petty Harbour, 1850 (DPHW 31); Helen, from Aberdeen, married at St. John's, 1854 (*Newfoundlander* 3 Jul 1854); William Watts, fisherman of Clark's Cove (Twillingate district), 1858 (DPHW 85); William, of Whale Cove (Burin district), 1860 (DPHW 108); William Watt, of Burin, 1871 (Lovell).

Modern status: Watt, rare, at St. John's and Corner Brook; Watts, scattered, especially at Rocky Harbour (St. Barbe district).

Place names: Watts Bight 51-35 56-01; —— Point 51-27 56-21; —— Pond 47-40 52-44.

WATTON, a surname of England from the English place name Watton (Devon, Hertfordshire, Norfolk, Yorkshire ER). (Cottle).

Traced by Spiegelhalter in Devon. In Newfoundland:

Early instances: T. ? Watten, of St. John's, 1822 (CO 194.65); John Watten or Watton, fisherman of Change Islands, 1846, 1856 (DPHW 83); Elizabeth Andrews Watton, of St. John's, 1851 (DPHW 26D); William, of Ireland's Eye, 1871 (Lovell).

Modern status: Scattered, especially in the Trinity North and Fogo districts.

WATTS. *See* WATT

WAUGH, a surname of England, Scotland and Ireland from Old English *w(e)alh* – foreigner. (Reaney, Cottle, Black, MacLysaght). *See also* WALSH, WALLIS, WELSH.

Traced by Guppy in Northumberland and Durham and in the Scots Border counties, especially Dumfriesshire, by Spiegelhalter in Devon, and by MacLysaght in small numbers in all provinces since the mid-seventeenth century.

In Newfoundland:

Early instance: Matthew, soldier of St. John's, 1837, deceased 1856 (DPHW 26B, *Newfoundlander* 27 Oct 1856).

Modern status: Rare, at Grand Falls.

WAY(E), WHEY, surnames of England, Way of Guernsey (Channel Islands) from the English place name Waye (Devon, where it occurs seventeen times, Dorset, etc.), or from Old English *weg* – (dweller near the) road, path. (Reaney, Cottle, Turk).

Guppy traced Way in Devon, Hampshire, Kent and Oxfordshire.

In Newfoundland:

Early instances: Richard Way, ? merchant of St. John's, 1778–80 (CO 194.34, D'Alberti 1); John Whey, married at St. John's, 1778 (DPHW 26D); Phillip and William, of Bonavista, 1792 (USPG); Henry Way, of Trinity (? Trinity.B.), 1796 (D'Alberti 5); John (and others) Wey, of Northern Bay, 1802 (CO 199.18); John Way, from Dartmouth (Devon), merchant of St. John's, deceased 1814 (*Royal Gazette* 7 Jul 1814); Michael W(h)ey, builder of Brigus, 1825 (DPHW 34); John Way, planter of Cuckold's Cove (now Dunfield), 1828 (DPHW 64B); Sarah, baptized at Vere (now Fair) Island, 1830, aged 25 (DPHW 76); William, planter of Bear's Cove (Harbour Grace), 1835 (DPHW 43); John, fisherman of Herring Neck, 1850, of Stone Harbour, 1853 (DPHW 85); John, of Flowers Cove to Point Ferolle area, 1871 (Lovell); Nathaniel, of Greenspond, 1871 (Lovell); James, of Inner Islands (now Newtown), 1871 (Lovell); John, of Little Catalina, 1871 (Lovell); Philip Way, of Bird Island Cove (now Elliston), 1871 (Lovell).

Modern status: Way, widespread, especially at Bonavista, Savage Cove (St. Barbe district) and St. John's; Waye, at Bishop Falls, Windsor, Lethbridge and St. John's; Whey, rare, at Trinity (Bonavista B.).

Place names: Way Bay (Labrador), —— Lake 53-35 65-25.

WAYSON, a surname of England. (Reaney). *See* GASH, WASS.

In Newfoundland:

Early instance: William, from North Sydney, of Woods Island (Bay of Islands district), 1878 (DPHW 96).

Modern status: Rare, at Benoits Cove (Humber West district) (*Electors* 1955).

WEATHERDON, a surname of England from the English place name Witherdon (Devon). (Spiegelhalter).

Traced by Spiegelhalter in Devon.

In Newfoundland:

Early instance: William, of St. John's, 1825–26 (DPHW 26B, 26D).

Modern status: Rare, at St. John's.

WEBB, a surname of England and Ireland from Old English *webba* (masculine), *webbe* (feminine) – weaver. (Reaney, Cottle, MacLysaght). *See also* WEBBER, WEBSTER.

Traced by Guppy in the Midlands and south, especially in Somerset and Wiltshire, and by MacLysaght especially in Dublin and Belfast.

In Newfoundland:

Early instances: Richard, of Brigus, 1675, 77 (CO 1); Robert, boatkeeper of St. John's Harbour, 1675 (CO 1); William, fisherman of St. John's or Petty Harbour about 1739–43 (CO 194.11, 24); ——, purchased fishing room at Northern Bay, 1789 (CO 194.45); John, of Western Bay, 1789 (CO 199.18); John, from Youghal (Co. Cork), of Harbour Grace, died 1813 (*Royal Gazette* 19 Aug 1813); Anne Whebe, of Catalina, 1834 (DPHW 67); John Webb, of Flat Bay (St. George's B.), 1871 (Lovell); John, of Robinsons Head, 1871 (Lovell).

Modern status: Scattered, especially in the west coast districts.

Place names: Web Island (Labrador) 56-37 61-16; Webb(s) Bay (Labrador) 56-46 61-45; —— Brook (Labrador) 56-48 61-56; —— Hill (Labrador) 56-48 61-47; —— Knoll (Labrador) 56-44 61-44; —— Point (Labrador) 56-43 61-42.

WEBBER, a surname of England and the Channel Islands – weaver, a later formation than WEBB. (Reaney, Cottle, Turk).

Traced by Guppy especially in Devon, and also in Cornwall, Somerset, Suffolk, Surrey and Sussex.

In Newfoundland:

Early instances: Henry, of Harbour Grace, 1782, property "in possession of the Family for upwards of 105 years," that is, before 1677 (CO 199.18); Alexander, of Fermeuse, 1681 (CO 1); Jonathan, of Carbonear, 1702 (CO 194.2); Edmond, of Ferryland, 1704–09 (CO 194.2, 4); Bartholomew, of St. John's, 1708-9 (CO 194.4); Thomas, of Port de Grave, 1708–09 (CO 194.4); Samuel, of Greenspond, 1776 (MUN Hist.); William, from ? Staverton (Devon), of Port de Grave, deceased 1810 (*Royal Gazette* 6 Dec 1810); George, of Trinity (Trinity B.), 1827 (Nfld. Archives KCRC); George Wibber or Webber, of Old Perlican, 1832–33 (DPHW 58, 64B); William Webber, of Petty Harbour, 1838 (DPHW 30); George, fisherman of Pouch Cove, 1843 (DPHW 32); John, from Yeovil (Somerset), married at King's Cove, 1843 (DPHW 73A); Andrew, of Shoal Bay (unspecified), married at St. John's, 1854 (DPHW 26D); Thomas, house carpenter of Cupids, 1860 (DPHW 35); Andrew, miner of Tilt Cove, 1871 (Lovell).

Modern status: Scattered, especially at St. John's.

Place names: Webber Bight 49-32 55-13, 49-36 54-49; —— Brook 48-40 55-15; —— Harbour (Labrador) 53-17 55-45, —— Island (Labrador) 57-14 61-31, —— Pond 48-42 55-21; Webbers (settlement), —— Cove 46-56 55-33; —— Pond 47-34 53-16.

WEBSTER, a surname of England, Scotland and Ireland from Old English *webbestre* – female weaver (compare *spinster*), but in Middle English used more often of men. (Reaney, Cottle, Black, MacLysaght 73). *See also* WEBB(ER).

Found widespread by Guppy especially in Derbyshire, Lancashire and Yorkshire and in the Midlands, and scattered in Scotland; and by MacLysaght as numerous in Leinster and Ulster since the mid-seventeenth century.

In Newfoundland:

Early instances: Charles Webister, of Ochre Pit Cove, 1801 (CO 199.18); James Webster, of St. John's, 1818 (DPHW 26B); John, ? of Northern Bay, 1853 (DPHW 54); Henry, miner of Tilt Cove, 1871 (Lovell).

Modern status: At Pope's Harbour (Trinity North district), Corner Brook and St. John's.

WEEKS, a surname of England from Old English *wīc* – abode, hamlet, and later and commonly (worker at the) dairy-farm, or from the English place names Week(s), Wick, Wyke (Devon), Wix (Essex). (Reaney, Cottle, Spiegelhalter). *See also* WICKS, WICKENS, WITCHER.

Traced by Guppy in Devon, Gloucestershire, Hampshire, Kent, Somerset and Wiltshire.

In Newfoundland:

Early instances: Edward, of St. John's, 1708–9, of Bay Bulls, 1708 (CO 194.4); John, fisherman of St. John's or Petty Harbour, about 1739–43 (CO 194.11, 24); Robert Weekes, of Bay Bulls, about 1772–5 (USPG); William Weeks, of St. John's, 1789 (CO 194.38); Richard, of Bonavista, 1808 (DPHW 70); James Weekes, of Harbour Grace, 1822 (Nfld. Archives HGRC); William Weeks or Wix, stone mason of Brigus, 1827 (DPHW 34); Margaret Weeks, baptized at Vere (now Fair) Island, aged 44 (DPHW 76); James Weeks, fisherman of Burnt Point (Bay de Verde district), 1830 (DPHW 52A); John Weeks, of King's Cove, 1835 (DPHW 73A); Richard, of Catalina, 1836, of Little Catalina, 1850 (DPHW 67); John, planter of Bull Cove (Brigus district), 1846 (DPHW 34); James, trader of Muddy Hole (Fogo district), 1871 (Lovell).

Modern status: At Baie Verte, St. John's (*Electors* 1955) and Duntara.

Place name: Weeks Point 48-26 53-42.

WEIR, a surname of England, Scotland and Ireland, in England a variant of WARE, in Scotland, according to Black, from the French place name Vere (Calvados etc.) or an anglicization of the Gaelic personal name *Mac Amhaoir* – son of the officer, or for MacNair; in Ireland also for *Mac an Mhaoir*, Ir. *maor* – steward, officer, or *Mac Giolla Uidhir*, Ir. *odhar*, genitive *uidhir* – dun-coloured, weather-beaten, or *Ó Corra*, Ir. *corra* – edge by mistranslation. (Reaney, Cottle, Black, MacLysaght).

Found widespread by Guppy in Scotland except in the north and especially in Lanarkshire, and by MacLysaght in Co. Armagh and elsewhere in Ulster and in Co. Westmeath.

In Newfoundland:

Early instances: Richard and Thomas, of St. John's, 1814 (D'Alberti 24); Robert, a joiner, from Glasgow, married at St. John's, 1847 (*Newfoundlander* 25 Nov 1847); Thomas, of Petty Harbour, 1850 (DPHW 31); Isaac (and others), of Little Bay Islands (Notre Dame B.), 1871 (Lovell).

Modern status: Scattered, especially at Little Bay Islands.

Place names: Weir's Brook 49-10 54-32; ——— Pond 49-13 54-23.

WELCHER, ? a variant, apparently not recorded elsewhere, of the surname of England WILTSHIRE, or ? a derivative of Welch (*see* WELSH).

In Newfoundland:

Early instance: John Wilcher, of Catalina, 1834 (DPHW 67).

Modern status: At Badger's Quay and Valleyfield (Bonavista North district).

WELLMAN, a surname of England from Old English *wella* and *mann* – dweller by the well, spring or stream, or from Old French *Guillemin*, Northern *Willemin*, diminutives of Guillaume, Willelm (*see* WILLIAMS). (Reaney, Cottle). *See also* ATWILL, WELLON, WELLS.

Spiegelhalter traced Welman in Devon.

In Newfoundland:

Family tradition: John, from Twillingate, settled at Wellman's Bight, Little Bay Islands, 1847; his sons settled at Port Anson, Wellman's Cove and Springdale (MUN Hist.).

Early instances: Joannah, of Harbour Grace, 1825 (Nfld. Archives HGRC); John Wil(l)man, of Little Bay Islands, 1847, of Sunday Cove Island (Twillingate district), 1859 (DPHW 86, 92); Edward Wellman, fisherman of Carbonear, 1850 (DPHW 49); Robert Willman, soldier of St. John's, 1858 (DPHW 29).

Modern status: Scattered, especially in the Green Bay district.

Place names: Wellman Bight 49-39 55-47; Wellmans Cove 49-34 55-48.

WELLON, a surname of England, ? from Middle English *wellen* – (dweller by the) springs, streams, wells. (Spiegelhalter). *See also* ATWILL, WELLS, WELLMAN.

Traced by Spiegelhalter in Devon.

In Newfoundland:

Family tradition: Robert Gaff, from Poole (Dorset), resided at Greenspond, Fogo Island, Wadham Island, Doting Cove, and settled at Ladle Cove (Fogo district) in 1868 (MUN Hist.).

Early instances: William Welen, of Brigus, 1806 (DPHW 34); William Welland, of Cat Harbour (now Lumsden), 1835 (DPHW 76); Robert Wellon, of Herring Neck, 1843, of Seldom Come By, 1855 (DPHW 83, 86); John and Richard Whellon, fishermen of Greenspond, 1871 (Lovell).

Modern status: Scattered, especially at Ladle Cove (Fogo district).

WELLS, a surname of England, Scotland and Ireland from the English place name Wells (Norfolk, Somerset), or from Old English *wella* – (dweller by the) well(s), spring(s), stream(s). (Reaney, Cottle, Black, MacLysaght 73). *See also* ATWILL, WELLON, WILLS, WELLMAN.

Found widespread by Guppy, in Devon by Spiegelhalter, in Dumfriesshire by Black (where it is pronounced Walls), and mainly in northeast Ulster by MacLysaght, though in Munster and Leinster in the thirteenth century.

In Newfoundland:

Family traditions: ———, from Durham, England, settled at the Horse Islands (MUN Folklore). ——— (1852–1927), from Norton (Yorkshire), died at Grand Falls (MUN Folklore). John, from Ringwood (Hampshire), settled at Joe Batts Arm in 1797, died in 1851, aged 72 (MUN Hist.).

Early instances: Thomas, of Trinity Bay, 1769, of English Harbour (Trinity B.), 1783 (DPHW 64); James and William, of Port de Grave, 1776 (CO 199.18); Ann, of Carbonear, 1786 (CO 199.18); Henry, of Bonavista, 1794 (DPHW 70); Theophilus, of Cupids, 1796, of Colliers, 1798 (CO 199.18); H., proprietor and occupier of fishing room, Old Perlican, Winter 1800–01 (Census Trinity B.); R., of Ochre Pit Cove, 1801 (CO 199.18); John, of Lower Island Cove, 1802 (CO 199.18); Richard, of Northern Bay, 1802 (CO 199.18); Edward, of Bay de Verde, 1805 (CO 199.18); John, a soldier from Lisburn (Co. Antrim), married at St. John's, 1805 (Nfld. Archives BRC); John, of Harbour Grace, 1807 (Nfld. Archives HGRC); Isaac, fisherman of Salmon Bay (Petty Harbour district), 1840 (DPHW 31); Joseph, of Greenspond, 1815 (DPHW 76); John, fisherman of Joe Batts Arm, 1816 (USPG); William, planter of Twillingate, 1820 (USPG); William, fisherman of Mosquitto (now Bristols Hope), 1828 (DPHW 43); William, of Pouch Cove, 1831 (DPHW 30); George, fisherman of Brigus, 1835 (DPHW 34); John, of Three Arms (Twillingate district), 1841 (DPHW 86); William B., of St. John's, 1843 (*Newfoundlander* 4 May 1843); Henry, of Exploits Burnt Island, 1844 (DPHW 86); ——, on the *Isabella* in the seal fishery out of Bay Roberts, 1849 (*Newfoundlander* 5 Apr 1849); Sarah, of Catalina, 1843 (DPHW 67); George, of Barrow Harbour (Bonavista South district), 1853 (DPHW 73A); Elizabeth, of Gooseberry Island, 1856 (Nfld. Archives KCRC); William, of Shoal Bay (Fogo district), 1858 (DPHW 83); Matthew, of Harbour Grace, 1866 (Nfld. Archives HGRC); Francis, of Cottells Island, 1870 (Nfld. Archives KCRC); widespread in Lovell 1871.

Modern status: Widespread, especially at St. John's, Hare Bay, Corner Brook, Springdale and Sandyville (Fortune Bay and Hermitage district).

Place names (not necessarily from the surname): Well Bay, —— Point 50-48 57-13; Wells Cove 49-41 55-51, (Labrador) 52-38 55-46; —— Rock (Labrador) 52-12 55-39.

WELSH, a surname of England, Scotland and Ireland, Welch of Guernsey (Channel Islands) from Old English *wēalisc* – foreigner, Welsh, British, Celtic, though, as Cottle comments, "the Welsh called and call themselves no such thing," or a variant of WALSH, reflecting in Ireland, "the pronunciation of Walsh in Munster and Connacht." (Reaney, Cottle, Black, MacLysaght, Turk).

Guppy traced Welch in Buckinghamshire, Essex, Nottinghamshire, Somerset and Wiltshire, Welsh in Scotland south of the Forth and Clyde; Spiegelhalter traced Welch, Welsh in Devon; MacLysaght traced Welsh in Munster and Connacht.

In Newfoundland:

Early instances: Philip Welch, fisherman of St. John's, ? 1730–32 (CO 194.9, 24); Daniel Welsh, fisherman of Petty Harbour, 1794–5, "40 years in Newfoundland," that is, 1754–5 (Census 1794–5); John Welch, of Harbour Main, 1755 (MUN Hist.); Joseph Welsh, of Trinity Bay, 1765 (DPHW 64); Thomas, of King's Cove, 1800 (Bonavista Register 1806); Thomas, planter of Flatrock (St. John's), 1803 (D'Alberti 13); Thomas, of Burin, 1805 (D'Alberti 15); John, of Bay de Verde, 1806 (D'Alberti 16); William W(h)elch or Whealch, of Brigus, 1807 (DPHW 34); George Welch, of Harbour Grace, 1813 (Nfld. Archives HGRC); James, planter of Herring Neck, 1822 (USPG); Jerry Welsh, of Witless Bay, 1828 (Nfld. Archives BRC); David, of Round Harbour (Burin district), 1836 (DPHW 106); Daniel Welch, merchant of Carbonear, 1849 (DPHW 49); David Welsh, fisherman of Little Bay (Burin district), 1853 (DPHW 104); Thomas, farmer of Bacon Cove (Conception B.), 1871 (Lovell); Misal, of Ochre Pit Cove, 1871 (Lovell); Thomas, of Tizzards Harbour, 1871 (Lovell); Patrick Welch, of Lamaline, 1871 (Lovell); Robert, of Lord's Cove, 1871 (Lovell); Michael, of Point aux Gauls (Placentia B.), 1871 (Lovell).

Modern status: Scattered, especially at Islington (Trinity B.).

Place names: Welch Hill 47-42 53-13; Welchs Hill 46-57 55-29; Welsh Cove 49-40 55-56; —— Island 49-42 54-44.

WELSHMAN, a surname of England, "probably in a more modern and restricted sense (a man from present-day Wales) than that of WELSH." (Cottle).

Spiegelhalter traced Welchman in Devon.

In Newfoundland:

Early instances: James Welchman, of Old Perlican, 1675 (CO 1); George Welshman, of Trinity (Trinity B.), 1794 (DPHW 64); John Wilshman or Welshman, of Shoe Cove (Twillingate district), 1843 (DPHW 86); Isaac Welshman, from England, married at Grand Bank, 1849 (DPHW 106).

Modern status: At Corner Brook and in the Green Bay district.

WENTZELL, an anglicization of the surname of Germany Wen(t)zel from the Slavic personal name *Wenzeslaus* (as in Good King Wenceslas). (Gottschald).

In Newfoundland:

Modern status: At Portland Creek, Daniel's Harbour and Corner Brook.

WEST(E), surnames of England, Scotland and Ireland – (the man from the) west or (the dweller to the) west (of the village, place). (Reaney, Cottle,

Black, MacLysaght). The form Weste does not appear to be recorded elsewhere.

West found widespread by Guppy, in Devon by Spiegelhalter, in Banffshire, Perthshire and West Lothian by Black, and in Cos. Down, Wicklow and Wexford by MacLysaght.

In Newfoundland:

Family tradition: Four brothers Charles, Jacob, Joseph and William, from Harbour Grace, settled at Ladle Cove (Fogo district) in 1868 (MUN Hist.).

Early instances: Briente Weste, of Newfoundland, 1730 (CO 194.23); Robert West, merchant of St. John's, Southside, 1794–5 (Census 1794–5); Sarah, baptized at Greenspond, 1830, aged 20 (DPHW 76); Thomas, of Bay L'Argent, 1835 (DPHW 30); Joseph, of Cat Harbour (now Lumsden), 1845 (DPHW 76); John, of Harbour Grace Parish, 1845 (Nfld. Archives HGRC); Joseph, of Garnish, 1853 (DPHW 104); John, fisherman of Rock Harbour (Burin district), 1860 (DPHW 100); John, of Muddy Hole (Burin district), 1871 (Lovell).

Modern status: West, scattered, especially at Ladle Cove (Fogo district); Weste, rare, at Lumsden.

Place names: Many place names contain the specific West not from the surname.

WESTCOTT, a surname of England from the English place names Westcot, Westcote, Westcott, Westacott in nine counties including Devon. (Reaney, Cottle).

Guppy traced Wescott in Somerset and West(a)cott in Devon.

In Newfoundland:

Early instances: John Wescott, shoreman of St. John's, 1794–5, "20 years in Newfoundland," that is, 1774–5 (Census 1794–5); Robert Westcott, of Torbay, 1778 (DPHW 26C).

Modern status: At Petty Harbour and St. John's.

WESTE. *See* WEST

WESTGUARD, ? a variant of the surname of Denmark Westergaard – dweller at the western farm. (E.C. Smith).

Modern status: Unique, at Curling.

WEYMOUTH, a surname of England from the English place name Weymouth (Dorset). (Cottle).

Spiegelhalter traced Waymouth, Weymouth in Devon.

In Newfoundland:

Family tradition: William (1819–88), from England, of Grand Bank (MUN Hist.).

Early instances: William Waymuth, of Toads (now Tors) Cove, 1676 (CO 1); Michael Weymoth, of St. John's or Bay Bulls, 1680 (CO 1); Robert Weymouth, boatkeeper of St. John's, 1682 (CO 1); Gregory Wheymouth, of St. John's, 1781 (DPHW 26C); W. Weymouth, of Grand Bank or Fortune, 1841 (*Newfoundlander* 4 Feb 1841); William, fisherman of Grand Bank, 1859 (DPHW 106).

Modern status: At Grand Beach (Burin district) (*Electors* 1955) and Grand Bank.

Place names: Weymouth Cove, —— Point 50-51 56-10.

WHALEN. *See* WHELAN

WHATLEY, a surname of England from the English place name Whatley (Dorset, Somerset). (Cottle).

Traced by Guppy in Wiltshire and by Spiegelhalter in Devon.

In Newfoundland:

Modern status: At Belleoram (*Electors* 1955).

WHEADON, a surname of England and Guernsey (Channel Islands) from the English place names Whiddon, Wheadown (Devon). (Spiegelhalter, Turk).

Spiegelhalter traced Wheadon, Whidden and Whiddon in Devon.

In Newfoundland:

Early instances: William Whiddon, of St. John's, 1758 (DPHW 26C); John Wheaden, of Fogo, 1803 (D'Alberti 13); James Wheadon or Wheaden, planter of Bradley's Cove (Conception B.), 1817 (DPHW 52A); Henry Wadon or Weedon, planter of Ochre Pit Cove, 1843 (DPHW 52A); John Weydon, of Old Perlican, 1846 (*Newfoundlander* 30 Jul 1846); Robert Wheadon, of Noggin Cove (Twillingate district), 1871 (Lovell); Ezia Weedon, telegraph operator of Heart's Content, 1871 (Lovell).

Modern status: In the Bay de Verde district.

WHEATON, a surname of England from the English place name Wheaton Aston (Staffordshire). (Spiegelhalter).

Traced by Spiegelhalter in Devon.

In Newfoundland:

Early instances: Thomas Wheatten, of Trinity Bay, 1777 (DPHW 64); Thomas Wheton, of Harbour Grace Parish, 1831 (Nfld. Archives HGRC); William Wheaton, of St. John's, 1836 (DPHW 26B); Robert, of Gander Bay, 1854 (DPHW 83); Thomas, of Little Catalina, 1871 (Lovell); George and William Whetham, of Fogo, 1871 (Lovell).

Modern status: Scattered, especially at Frederickton (Fogo district).

WHEELER, a surname of England and Ireland, from Old English *hweogol, hwēol* – wheel, hence wheelwright, wheel-maker; in Co. Limerick perhaps of a different origin. (Reaney, Cottle, MacLysaght).

Traced by Guppy in Berkshire, Buckinghamshire, Gloucestershire, Oxfordshire, Wiltshire and Worcestershire, by Spiegelhalter in Devon; and by MacLysaght in Ireland since 1603, now fairly numerous in Co. Limerick.

In Newfoundland:

Early instances: John and William Wheller, of Bonavista, 1792 (USPG); John Wheeler, of Bonavista, 1793 (DPHW 70); John, of Salmon Cove (now Champneys), 1796 (DPHW 64); William, fisherman of Twillingate, 1796 (DPHW 88); James, occupier of fishing room, Heart's Content, Winter 1800–01 (Census Trinity B.); John, of St. John's, 1801 (DPHW 26B); Jane, of Harbour Grace, 1809 (Nfld. Archives KCRC); Anne, of King's Cove, 1825 (Nfld. Archives KCRC); William, of Bay of Islands, 1835 (DPHW 30); John, of Keels, 1835 (DPHW 73A); William, of Cat Harbour (now Lumsden), 1837 (DPHW 76); James Richard, fisherman of Torbay Road, 1840 (DPHW 26B); James, schoolmaster of Trinity (Trinity B.), 1841 (DPHW 64B); James, of Torbay, 1851 (DPHW 32); John, of Lower Island Cove, 1853 (DPHW 55); George, of Greenspond, 1856 (DPHW 26D); William, of Tizzard's Harbour, 1861 (DPHW 88); John B., schoolmaster of Musgrave Harbour, 1865 (MUN Hist.); John, miner of Tilt Cove, 1871 (Lovell); Eleazar Wheller, of Loon Bay (Twillingate district), 1871 (Lovell); Elijah, miner of Trump Island (Twillingate district), 1871 (Lovell).

Modern status: Widespread, especially at St. John's, Windsor, Daniel's Cove (Twillingate district), Corner Brook and Lower Island Cove.

Place names: Wheeler Brook 48-31 58-18; —— Mountain (Labrador) 57-34 62-18; William Wheeler Point 49-10 57-52; Wheelers Brook 48-53 58-20.

WHELAN, a surname of Ireland, with a variant WHALEN, (O)Whelan, *Ó Faoláin*, Ir. *faol* – wolf, a variant of PHELAN, or sometimes an abbreviation of Whelehan, or occasionally a synonym of Hyland. Whalen is recorded by E.C. Smith but not by MacLysaght.

MacLysaght found Whelan numerous in the country between Cos. Tipperary and Wexford, and rare in Ulster.

In Newfoundland:

Family traditions: —— Whelan, from Ireland, settled at Little Placentia (now Argentia), about 1805 (MUN Folklore). Edward Thomas Whalen (1832–91),

born at Bradley's Cove (Conception B.), moved to Caplin Cove in 1855 (MUN Geog.).

Early instances: Richard Whelan, servant of Little Placentia (now Argentia), about 1730–5 (CO 194.9); Edward Wheyland, of St. John's, 1751 (CO 194.13); William Whealon and Co., of Bradley's Cove, 1756 (CO 199.18); Thomas Whaling, of Trinity Bay, 1774 (DPHW 64); Mary Whealon, of Colliers, 1778 (CO 199.18); John Whelan, of Ferryland, 1783 (D'Alberti 2); Davis Whealon, of Broad Cove (North Shore, Conception B.), 1778, of Small Point (North Shore, Conception B.), 1804 (CO 199.18); Michael Whelan, from Tipperary (Co. Tipperary), married at St. John's, 1808 (Nfld. Archives BRC); William Whealin, of Brigus, 1809 (DPHW 34); William Whelan, from Clanragh (Co. Kilkenny), farmer of St. John's, died 1810 (*Royal Gazette* 19 Jul 1810); William ? Whelen, one of 72 impressed men who sailed from Ireland to Newfoundland ? 1811 (CO 194.51); Jane Whelan, of Harbour Grace Parish, 1812 (Nfld. Archives HGRC); William, from Waterford, trader of Bay Roberts, died 1812 (*Royal Gazette* 5 Nov 1812); Martin, from Waterford, fisherman of Bonavista, died 1814 (*Royal Gazette* 22 Sep 1814); Elinor, of King's Cove, 1815 (Nfld. Archives KCRC); Edward Whalen, fisherman of Adams Cove, 1820 (DPHW 52A); Bridget Whelan, of Gooseberry Island (Bonavista B.), 1824 (Nfld. Archives KCRC); Rebecca, of Keels, 1824 (Nfld. Archives KCRC); Thomas, of Bay de Verde, 1828 (Nfld. Archives BRC); Catherine, of Brigus, 1829 (Nfld. Archives BRC); Thomas, of Broad Cove (now Duntara), 1829 (Nfld. Archives KCRC); James, of Cape Royal (for Cape Broyle), 1831 (Nfld. Archives BRC); Robert, of Greenspond, 1832 (Nfld. Archives KCRC); Henry Whelan or Whealon, planter of Ochre Pit Cove, 1835 (DPHW 52A); Thomas Whelan, ? of Northern Bay, 1838 (DPHW 54); ——, on the *True Blue* in the seal fishery out of Port de Grave, 1838 (*Newfoundlander* 29 Mar 1838); ——, teacher of Petty Harbour, 1839 (*Newfoundlander* 1 Aug 1839); Edmond, from Co. Waterford, and James from Co. Kilkenny, of Harbour Grace, 1844 (*Indicator* 27 Jul 1844); John Whalen, of Leading Tickles, 1847 (DPHW 86); John Whelan, granted land at Cupids, 1847 (Nfld. Archives, Registry Crown Lands); James Whealen, Road Commissioner for the area Harry Cove Point and Path from Limber Grass to Harry Cove, 1848 (*Nfld. Almanac* 1848); Patrick Whelan, granted land at Indian Arm (Bonavista B.), 1849 (Nfld. Archives, Registry Crown Lands); James, of Black Island, 1850 (Nfld. Archives KCRC); Robert Walton, of Cape Fogo, 1851 (DPHW 83);

James Whelan, planter of Crocker's Cove (Carbonear) 1851 (DPHW 52A); Michael, of Dog Cove (Bonavista B.), 1854 (Nfld. Archives KCRC); Mary, of Knight's Cove (Bonavista B.), 1855 (Nfld. Archives KCRC); Margaret, of Trinity (unspecified), 1855 (Nfld. Archives KCRC); Bridget, of Sholes [sic] Cove, 1855 (Nfld. Archives KCRC); Bridget, of Haywards Cove (Bonavista B.), 1857 (Nfld. Archives KCRC); Catherine, of Burnt Island (Bonavista B.), 1858 (Nfld. Archives KCRC); Abby, of Plate Cove (Bonavista B.), 1858 (Nfld. Archives KCRC); Mary, of Stock Cove (Bonavista B.), 1859 (Nfld. Archives KCRC); John, granted land at St. Mary's Harbour, 1860 (Nfld. Archives, Registry Crown Lands); Catherine, of Cape Freels, 1861 (Nfld. Archives KCRC); Michael, granted land at Bryants Cove, 1861 (Nfld. Archives, Registry Crown Lands); Edward, farmer of Flatrock (St. John's), 1863 (Mannion); Maria, of Spaniard's Bay, 1866 (Nfld. Archives HGRC); Martha, of Cottles Island (Bonavista B.), 1867 (Nfld. Archives KCRC); William, of Cat Harbour (now Lumsden), 1868 (Nfld. Archives KCRC); Whalen and Whelan, scattered in Lovell 1871; Mary, from Thomastown (Co. Kilkenny), of Carbonear, died 1891, aged 77 (Carbonear R.C. Cemetery).

Modern status: Whalen, widespread, especially at St. John's, Western Bay, Flowers Cove (St. Barbe district), Caplin Cove (Trinity B.), and Pilley's Island (Green B.); Whelan, widespread, especially at St. John's, Colliers and Bauline.

Place names: Whalen (or Valen) Harbour 47-28 54-23; Whalens Brook 47-28 53-14; —— Pond 47-15 53-24, 47-23 53-21.

WHEY. *See* WAY(E)

WHIFFEN, WHIFFIN, surnames of unknown origin, ? variants of GIFFIN.

In Newfoundland:

Family traditions: Herbert Whiffen, from Cardiff, Wales, married Mary Brennan of Ship Cove (Placentia B.) (MUN Folklore). Sarah (about 1839–1900), born at Bonavista (MUN Geog.).

Early instances: William Wiffen, of Bonavista, 1828 (DPHW 70); Herbert Whiffen, granted land at Little Southern Harbour and Grassy Island (Placentia B.), 1838 (Nfld. Archives, Registry Crown Lands); Herbert, trader of Harbour Buffett, 1871 (Lovell); Patrick and William Whiffin, miners of La Manche, 1871 (Lovell); Henry and Thomas, of Long Harbour, 1871 (Lovell); William Weffin, of Trinity (unspecified), 1881 (Nfld. Archives KCRC).

Modern status: Whiffen, scattered, especially at

Bonavista and Fox Harbour (Placentia B.); Whiffin, rare, at Corner Brook.

Place name: Whiffen Head 47-46 54-01.

WHITE, WHYTE, surnames of England, Scotland and Ireland, White of the Channel Islands from the Old English personal name *Hwita*, a shortened form of names beginning with *Hwīt-*, or a nickname from Old English *hwīt* – white, fair (of complexion or hair), or from Old English **wiht* – (dweller by the) bend, curve (in a river or road), or from Norman French *waite* – lookout, place to watch from, or by confusion with WIGHT; also in Scotland an anglicization of the Gaelic *M'Illebhàin* (*MacGhillebhàin*); in Ireland also for such names as Bane, Bawn, Galligan, Kilbane, by translation of Ir. *bán* – white, *geal* – white. (Reaney, Cottle, Black, MacLysaght, Turk). *See also* WHITT, LEBLANC.

Guppy found White widespread in England, White and Whyte south of the Forth and Clyde; MacLysaght found White numerous in every province since the fourteenth century and especially in Cos. Down and Sligo.

In Newfoundland:

Family traditions: Thomas (1846–1928), from Portsmouth area, settled at Jersey Harbour about 1864 (MUN Geog.). Ancestors of the White family at Stephenville were French speaking Acadians (MUN Folklore). ——, from Co. Tipperary, settled in Placentia Bay (MUN Folklore). ——, English youngster, was one of the first settlers of Sandy Cove (St. Barbe district) in the late 1800s (MUN Hist.). Some families named Leblanc on the west coast anglicized their surname to White.

Early instances: Peter White, of Witless Bay, 1676, of Balene (now Bauline, Southern Shore Avalon Peninsula), 1677 (CO 1); Ann, of St. John's Harbour, 1703 (CO 194.3); Arthur, of Ferryland, 1706, 1708 (CO 194.4, 24); George, of Trinity (Trinity B.), 1760 (DPHW 64); ——, of Twillingate, 1768 (MUN Hist.); James, in possesion of property in fishery at Bell Island, 1794–5, "25 years in Newfoundland," that is, 1769–70 (Census 1794–5); Aaron, of Placentia, 1780 (D'Alberti 1); heirs of George, of Harbour Grace, 1785 (CO 199.18); George, of Bacon Cove (Harbour Grace), 1785 (CO 199.18); William, of Conche, 1787, of Fogo, 1789 (MUN Hist.); Edward and George, of Bonavista, 1792 (USPG); Henry, in possession of property at Petty Harbour, 1794–5 (Census 1794–5); Samuel, of Bay de Verde, 1797 (CO 199.18); Joseph, of Gooseberry Cove (Carbonear), 1800 (CO 199.18); William, of Lower Island Cove, 1803 (CO 199.18); Catherine

White alias Walsh, from Killenaule (Co. Tipperary), married at St. John's, 1803 (Nfld. Archives BRC); John White, of Greenspond, 1804 (Bonavista Register 1806); Samuel, in possession of fishing room, Ship Island (Greenspond Harbour), before 1805 (Bonavista Register 1806); Samuel, of Mockbeggar room, Bonavista before 1805 (Bonavista Register 1806); John, from Waterford, shoreman of St. John's, died 1814 (*Royal Gazette* 15 Sep 1814); Robert, from ?Hulstaff (Somerset), married at St. John's, 1815 (Nfld, Archives BRC); George, of King's Cove, 1815 (Nfld. Archives KCRC); John, from Slade (Co. Wexford), fisherman of Mobile, died 1816, (*Nfld. Mercantile Journal* 12 Oct 1816); John, of Clowns Cove (Carbonear), 1816 (DPHW 48); Mary, of St. Mary's, 1817 (Nfld. Archives BRC); Thomas, of Ragged Harbour (now Melrose), 1818 (Nfld. Archives KCRC); James, of Salmon Cove (now Champneys), 1819 (DPHW 64); Thomas, of Torbay, 1820 (DPHW 26B); James, fisherman of Trouty, 1821 (DPHW 64); James, of Emanuels (Manuels), 1822 (DPHW 26B); Caleb, servant of New Harbour (Trinity B.), 1823 (DPHW 64); George, planter of New Perlican, 1823 (DPHW 64B); Edward, planter of Heart's Content, 1823 (DPHW 64B); William, planter of Catalina, 1825 (DPHW 72); William, fisherman of Salmon Cove (Carbonear district), 1825 (DPHW 48); William, from Totnes (Devon), of St. John's, died 1829 (*Royal Gazette* 8 Sep 1829); Ann, of Job's Cove, 1829 (Nfld. Archives BRC); Sam, of Keels, 1830 (Nfld. Archives KCRC); Michael, planter of Seal Cove (now New Chelsea), 1833 (DPHW 59A); Edward, planter of Ochre Pit Cove, 1833 (DPHW 52A); Catherine, of Port de Grave, 1834 (*Newfoundlander* 23 Jan 1834); William, planter of P. (? for Perry's) Cove (Carbonear district), 1835 (DPHW 48); Belinda, of Long Pond (Harbour Main district), 1837 (DPHW 26D); Michael, ? of Northern Bay, 1839 (DPHW 54); William, of Indian Arm (Bonavista B.), 1841 (DPHW 73A); James, of Indian Burying Place, 1844 (DPHW 86); John, of Fortune, 1846 (DPHW 106); James, granted land at Cupids, 1847 (Nfld. Archives, Registry Crown Lands); John Richard, of Kingston (Dorset), married at King's Cove, 1847 (DPHW 73A); Susannah, of Bird Island Cove (now Elliston), 1849 (DPHW 67); John, of Tickle Cove (Bonavista B.), 1849 (DPHW 73); Richard, granted land at Aquaforte, 1850 (Nfld. Archives, Registry Crown Lands); Charles, fisherman of Jersey Harbour, 1850 (DPHW 104); Martin, granted land near Beaver Pond (Bonavista B.), 1850 (Nfld. Archives, Registry Crown Lands); Mary, of Gooseberry Island (Bonavista B.), 1850 (Nfld. Archives KCRC); John,

granted land at Great Paradise (Placentia B.), 1851 (Nfld. Archives, Registry Crown Lands); John, granted land at the Goulds, 1852 (Nfld. Archives, Registry Crown Lands); Charles, of Moreton's Harbour, 1854 (DPHW 86); Samuel, of Dog Cove (Bonavista B.), 1854 (Nfld. Archives KCRC); Nicholas, granted land at Cape Bonavista Shore, 1854 (Nfld. Archives, Registry Crown Lands); Roger, fisherman of Otterbury (Carbonear district), 1847 (DPHW 49); Charles, of Herring Neck, 1854 (DPHW 85); William Kepple White (1821–86), Anglican priest, born Camberwell (Surrey), son of George Keppel [sic] White and Sarah, missionary at Harbour Buffett 1854 and Harbour Breton. (J. House of Assembly 1850, 24; Harbour Breton Anglican Church Records per D.A. Macdonald); Charles, fisherman of Merritt's Harbour, 1855 (DPHW 85); Robert Whight, fisherman of Hants Harbour, 1856 (DPHW 59A); Joseph White, of Cotterels Island (Bonavista B.), 1856 (Nfld. Archives KCRC); Mary Anne, of Sholes [sic] Cove (Bonavista B.), 1856 (Nfld. Archives KCRC); William, fisherman of Green Cove (Twillingate district), 1856 (DPHW 85); Samuel, of Garia, 1857 (DPHW 98); Joseph, of Haywards Cove, 1857 (Nfld. Archives KCRC); William, missionary and rural dean, of Harbour Breton, 1857 (DPHW 104); John, fisherman of Salt Harbour (Twillingate district), 1857 (DPHW 85); John, of Petites, 1858 (DPHW 98); James, of Three Arms (Exploits district), 1860 (DPHW 42); Philip Whyte, granted land at New Perlican, 1860 (Nfld. Archives, Registry Crown Lands); Charles White, fisherman of Mortier Bay, 1860 (DPHW 100); Samuel, of Muddy Hole (Bonavista North district), 1862 (DPHW 77); Joseph, of Burnt Island (Bonavista B.), 1866 (Nfld. Archives KCRC); Anne Whyte, of Open Hall, 1868 (Nfld. Archives KCRC); White, widespread in Lovell 1871.

Modern status: White, widespread in all districts with large concentrations at St. John's, Stephenville, Corner Brook, Kippens (Port au Port district), Sandy Cove (St. Barbe district), and Trout River (St. Barbe district); Whyte, rare, at Corner Brook.

Place names: There are over 180 place names containing the specific White, some of which are derived from the family name.

WHITEHORN(E), surnames of England from Old English *hwīt* – white, fair, splendid and *horn* – (owner of a) bright (drinking) horn, trumpet, or from the English place name Whitethorn (Devon). (Reaney, Cottle, Spiegelhalter).

Traced by Spiegelhalter in Devon.

In Newfoundland:

Early instances: James Whitehorn, fisherman of Twillingate, 1871 (Lovell); W. G. Whitehorne, of Springdale, 1917 (MUN Hist.).

Modern status: Whitehorn, at Cottrells Cove (*Electors* 1955), Stephenville and Corner Brook; Whitehorne, at Springdale and Twillingate.

WHITELEY, a surname of England and Jersey (Channel Islands) from the English place names Whitleigh (Berkshire), Whitley (Cheshire, Northumberland, Warwickshire, Wiltshire, Yorkshire WR), Higher Whiteleigh, Whitel(e)y, Whitleigh Hall, Whitley (Devon), etc. (Reaney, Cottle, Spiegelhalter, Turk).

Traced by Guppy in Yorkshire WR and by Spiegelhalter in Devon.

In Newfoundland:

Family tradition: William Henry, from Tadley (Hampshire), settled at Boston in 1800. His grandson William Henry (1834–1903), settled at Bonne Espérance (Labrador) about 1849 (Mott, Nfld. Archives T58).

Early instance: Andrew, planter of Catalina, 1846 (DPHW 72).

Modern status: Rare, at St. John's.

WHITEMARSH, a surname of England from the English place names Whit(e)marsh (Wiltshire), or dweller by the white (? chalky, shining) marsh. (Cottle).

Spiegelhalter traced Whitmarsh in Devon.

In Newfoundland:

Early instances: Robert, of Greenspond, 1863 (DPHW 77); Robert Whitemark, fisherman of English Harbour (Bonavista B.), 1871 (Lovell).

Modern status: At St. John's.

WHITEWAY, a surname of England from the English place names Whiteway House, Whiteway Barton (Devon), Whiteway (Farm) (Dorset), etc., or (dweller by the) white way, road. (Reaney, Cottle, Spiegelhalter). The Newfoundland pronunciation is reflected in the alternative spelling Whiteaway.

Traced by Guppy in Devon.

In Newfoundland:

Family traditions: John Whiteway, from Western Bay, three generations out from Devonshire, was the first settler of Muddy Hole (now Musgrave Harbour) in the early 1830s (MUN Hist., MUN Folklore). The town of Clarenville was named Clarenceville, later shortened to Clarenville, after the son of Sir William Whiteway about 1900 (MUN Hist.).

Early instances: Silvester Whitway, boat-keeper of St. John's, 1682 (CO 1); Hugh Whiteway, fisherman of St. John's or Petty Harbour about 1739–43 (CO 194.11); William (about 1736–1834), from the west of England came to Newfoundland aged 20, of Western Bay, 1771, died at Western Bay (*Star and Conception B.J.* 15 Oct 1834, CO 199.18); Thomas Whitaway, of Harbour Grace, 1812 (Nfld. Archives HGRC); William Whiteway, from Staverton (Devon), married at St. John's, 1820 (Nfld. Archives BRC); John, merchant from Stokeinteignhead (Devon), given possession of part of Virginia or Battons Plantation, St. John's, 1826 (Exeter Public Library Archives per Kirwin); Edward, planter of Brigus, 1833 (DPHW 34); John, fisherman of Muddy Hole (? Carbonear district), 1840 (DPHW 52A); Sir William Vallance (1828–), from Buckyett House (Devon), settled at St. John's, 1843 (Mott); William, fisherman of Ochre Pit Cove, 1843 (DPHW 52A); Ford, ? of Northern Bay, 1844 (DPHW 54); James Whiteaway, fisherman of Change Islands, 1849 (DPHW 83); John Whiteway, of Seal Cove (now New Chelsea), 1856 (DPHW 59); William Whitaway, of Job's Cove, 1856 (DPHW 55); Nicholas Whiteway, of Muddy Hole (Fogo district), 1858 (DPHW 83); Samuel Whitway, of Herring Neck, 1871 (Lovell); James (and others) Whiteway, of Brooklyn, 1871 (Lovell); John Whiteday, of St. Juliens, 1871 (Lovell).

Modern status: Scattered, especially at Musgrave Harbour and St. John's.

Place names: Whiteway, —— Bay 47-41 53-29; —— Pond 47-39 52-46.

WHITING, a surname of England from the Old English personal name *Hwīting* – son of *Hwīta*, or a nickname from Old English *hwīta* – the white or fair one. (Reaney, Cottle). *See also* LEE-WHITING.

Traced by Guppy in Buckinghamshire and Yorkshire NR, ER, and by Spiegelhalter in Devon.

In Newfoundland:

Early instances: William, of Newfoundland, ? 1706 (CO 194.24); Daniel, fisherman of Petites, 1871 (Lovell); George, of St. John's, 1871 (Lovell).

Modern status: At Round Harbour and Gaultois (Fortune Bay and Hermitage district) (*Electors* 1955).

WHITMAN, a surname of England from the Old English personal name *Hwītmann* – the white, fair man, or servant of WHITE. (Reaney, Cottle).

Guppy traced Whiteman in Huntingdonshire and Shropshire.

In Newfoundland:

Early instances: Robert, of Old Perlican, 1677 (CO 1); ——, captain of the schooner *Tropic*, 1829 (*Newfoundlander* 18 Jun 1829); ——, manager of Glenwood Mills, 1903 (Millais).

Modern status: Rare, at Gander (*Electors* 1955) and Harbour Grace.

Place name: Whitmans Pond 48-59 54-35.

WHITMEE, a surname of England from Middle English *whyt* – white, fair and *may* – young man or maid. (Reaney).

In Newfoundland:

Modern status: Rare, at St. John's.

WHITT, a variant of the surname of England WHITE.

In Newfoundland:

Early instance: Thomas Witt, fisherman of Twillingate, 1871 (Lovell).

Modern status: Scattered.

WHITTAKER, a surname of England, Whitaker (also an English variant) of Ireland, from the English place names Wheatacre (Norfolk), Whiteacre (Kent), Whitacre (Warwickshire) or High Whitaker (Lancashire), or (dweller by the) wheat field or white (chalky or limed) field. (Reaney, Cottle, MacLysaght).

Guppy traced Whit(t)aker in Cheshire, Derbyshire, Lancashire, Staffordshire and Yorkshire WR; MacLysaght traced Whitaker (formerly Whiteacre) in Cos. Meath and Louth since the fourteenth century.

In Newfoundland:

Modern status: At St. Anthony (*Electors* 1955) and St. John's.

WHITTEN, ? a variant of the surname of England Whitton, and formerly as Whitton of Ireland, from the English place names Whitton in six counties or Whiddon (Devon), or (dweller or worker at the) white farm, or the place or farm of (an Anglo-Saxon called) White or of a family called WHITE. (Cottle, Spiegelhalter, MacLysaght 73).

Whitton traced by Guppy in Northamptonshire and by Spiegelhalter in Devon, Whitten by MacLysaght in Co. Armagh and in other parts of Ulster.

In Newfoundland:

Early instances: Gregory Whitten or Whitton, of St. John's, 1708–09 (CO 194.4); William Whiten, of Trinity Bay, 1764 (DPHW 64); George Whitten or Whittan, of White Hills or Southside (St. John's),

1817 (DPHW 26B); Robert Whitten, of Petty Harbour, 1817 (DPHW 26B); Martha, of Torbay, 1854 (DPHW 32); Josiah Whiten, miner of Kelligrews, 1871 (Lovell).

Modern status: Scattered, especially at St. John's and Petty Harbour.

WHITTLE, a surname of England and Ireland from the English place name Whittle (Lancashire, Northumberland), or (dweller near the) white hill or clear stream (as in Whitwell (pronounced Wittle)) (Cambridgeshire). (Reaney, Cottle, MacLysaght).

Traced by Guppy in Dorset, Lancashire, Leicestershire, Rutlandshire and Somerset, and by MacLysaght formerly in Co. Waterford but now more numerous in adjacent Leinster counties.

In Newfoundland:

Early instances: George Whittle, of Trinity Bay, 1780 (DPHW 64); Thomas Whittle, shoemaker of St. John's, 1794–5, "12 years in Newfoundland," that is, 1782–3 (Census 1794–5); Joseph, of Trinity (Trinity B.), 1789 (DPHW 64); John, of Harbour Grace Parish, 1834 (Nfld. Archives HGRC); John, of Petites, 1859 (DPHW 98); Charles (and others), of Flat Islands (Burin district), 1871 (Lovell); Patrick, fisherman of Frenchman's Cove (Burin district), 1871 (Lovell); Benjamin, servant of Little Bay (Burin district), 1871 (Lovell).

Modern status: Scattered, especially at St. Bernards and St. John's.

Place names: Whittle Hill 47-41 58-10; —— Rock 47-37 58-39; Whittles Point (Labrador) 54-09 58-27.

WHITTY, a surname of England, and Ireland where it was formerly Whitey, from Old English *hwīt* and *ēage* – white eye, or Old English *witega* – wise man, prophet, or Old English *hwīt-(ge)hæg* – (dweller by the) white enclosure, or ? confused with the surname Witty from Old English *wit(t)ig* – wise, in Middle English – witty. (Reaney).

Traced by Matthews in Devon and by MacLysaght in Co. Wexford since the thirteenth century.

Early instances: James, a shoreman in possession of property at Torbay, 1794–5, "30 years in Newfoundland," that is, 1764–5 (Census 1794–5); Stephen Whity, of Trinity (Trinity B.), 1793 (DPHW 64); James Whitty, from Old Ross (Co. Wexford), married at St. John's, 1810 (Nfld. Archives BRC); William, of Harbour Grace, 1823 (Nfld. Archives HGRC).

Modern status: Especially at Torbay and St. John's.

WHYATT. *See* WYATT

WICKENS, a surname of England from the English place names Wicken (Cambridgeshire, Northamptonshire) or Wicken Bonurst (Essex), etc., or Old English *atte wicken* – (dweller or worker) at the airy farms, or ? confused with Wicking(s) from Old Norse *Vikingr*, etc. – pirate, or from Wickens (Kent). (Reaney, Cottle). *See also* WEEKS, WICKS, WITCHER.

Wickens traced by Guppy in Sussex, Wickin(g)s by Spiegelhalter in Devon.

In Newfoundland:

Early instances: Charles Wickins, from Mullinahone (Co. Tipperary), married at St. John's, 1824 (Nfld. Archives BRC); Mrs. Wickan, of St. John's, 1871 (Lovell); Martin Wickens, planter of Renews to Cape Race area, 1871 (Lovell).

Modern status: At Renews, Cappahayden (*Electors* 1955), Rushy Pond, Grand Falls and St. John's.

WICKHAM, a surname of England and Ireland, formerly Wycomb in Ireland, from the English place names Wickham (Gloucestershire, Berkshire, Cambridgeshire, etc.) or Wycombe (Buckinghamshire) – generally homestead with a dairy farm, or manor, dwelling-place. (Cottle, Spiegelhalter, MacLysaght). *See* WEEKS, WICKS.

Traced by Guppy in Somerset and Sussex, by Spiegelhalter in Devon, and by MacLysaght in Dublin and Co. Wexford.

In Newfoundland:

Early instances: Patrick, granted land near Freshwater (St. John's), 1839 (Nfld. Archives, Registry Crown Lands); James J., of Harbour Grace Parish, 1884 (Nfld. Archives HGRC).

Modern status: At St. John's.

WICKS. *See* WEEKS and *also* WICKENS, WITCHER.

Traced by Spiegelhalter in Devon.

In Newfoundland:

Family tradition: Thomas, from the London area of England, settled around Wesleyville about 1835 (MUN Folklore).

Early instances: William Wick, of St. John's, 1798 (DPHW 26B); William Wicks, of Greenspond, 1815 (DPHW 76); Sera Wicks or Wix, of Bird Island Cove (now Elliston), 1826 (Nfld. Archives KCRC); Sera Wicks alias Murphy, of Bonavista, 1827 (Nfld. Archives KCRC); Samuel Wicks, of Fair Island (Bonavista B.), 1837 (DPHW 76); John, fisherman of Barr'd Islands, 1847 (DPHW 83); Charles, of Burnt Point (Bay de Verde district), 1855 (DPHW 55); John,

of Broad Cove (now Duntara), 1855 (Nfld. Archives KCRC); John, fisherman of Jackson's Arm, 1871 (Lovell); Samuel, of Swain's Island (Bonavista B.), 1871 (Lovell).

Modern status: Scattered, especially at St. John's, and in the Bonavista district.

Place name: Wicks Cove 49–52 56-46.

WIDGER, a surname of England and ? the Channel Islands from the Old English personal name *Wihtgār*, containing the elements *elf* and *spear*, or from an Old German personal name containing the elements *battle* and *army*. (Reaney, Cottle, Turk).

Traced by Spiegelhalter in Devon.

In Newfoundland:

Early instances: Stephen, of St. John's, 1774 (DPHW 26C); Richard Widgen or Widger, house-carpenter of Carbonear, 1838, 1843 (DPHW 48).

Modern status: Unique, at Carbonear.

WIGH, ? a variant of the surname of England Wigg, from ? Old English *wicga* – beetle, or ? from Middle English *wygge* – (maker or seller of) wedge (-shaped cakes or buns). (Reaney).

In Newfoundland:

Modern status: Rare, at St. John's.

WIGHT, a surname of England from Middle English *wi(g)ht* – agile, valiant, strong, or rarely from the Isle of Wight (? from a Celtic name meaning raised land, island), or confused with WHITE. (Reaney, Cottle).

Traced by Spiegelhalter in Devon.

In Newfoundland:

Early instances: George, of St. John's, 1842 (*Newfoundlander* 17 Nov 1842); Susanna, of Grand Bank, 1850 (DPHW 106); Arthur (and others), of South East Bight (Placentia B.), 1871 (Lovell).

Modern status: Scattered, especially at Deer Lake.

WILANSKY, a Jewish surname, ? of Polish origin, ? from Vilna (Vilnius) capital of Soviet Lithuania.

In Newfoundland:

Modern status: At St. John's.

WILCOX, a surname of England, a diminutive of *Will* (William) (*see* WILLIAMS) and *cock* (*see* COX). (Reaney, Cottle). *See also* WILLCOTT.

Guppy traced Wilcock, Wilcox etc. in Cornwall, Devon, Gloucestershire, Lancashire, Monmouthshire, Nottinghamshire, Somerset and Yorkshire WR. He comments, "Less common forms are Willcocks,

Willcox, Wilcocks, and Willcock. All six varieties of the name occur in Cornwall. In fact, in 1883 there were eleven Cornish farmers of this name, and it may be truly said that scarcely two of them spelt it in the same way. Wilcox is characteristic of Somersetshire, Gloucestershire, and Nottinghamshire, Willcox of Somersetshire, Willcocks and Willcock of Devonshire, and Wilcock of Lancashire and the West Riding."

In Newfoundland:

Early instances: John Willcocks, shoreman of St. John's, 1794–5, "40 years in Newfoundland," that is, 1754–5 (Census 1794–5); John Wilcock or Woolcock, of Brigus, 1801 (CO 199.18); Samuel Wilco, planter of Western Bay, 1827 (DPHW 52A); James Wilcock, of Harbour Grace Parish, 1832 (Nfld. Archives HGRC); William Wilcox, of Rack (for Wreck) Cove, Bay de l'Eau, 1835 (DPHW 30); —— Wilcocks, on the *Water Witch* in the seal fishery out of Port de Grave, 1838 (*Newfoundlander* 29 Mar 1838); Thomas Wilcox, ? of Northern Bay, 1856 (DPHW 54); Benjamin, granted land at Bay Roberts, 1857, at Spaniard's Bay Head, 1857 (Nfld. Archives, Registry Crown Lands); James, of Aquaforte, 1871 (Lovell); James, of Englee Harbour, 1871 (Lovell); Benjamin, of Renews, 1871 (Lovell).

Modern status: Scattered, especially in the White Bay North district.

WILDISH, a surname of England from Old English **wealdisc* – Wealdish(man), man of the Weald, a district including parts of Kent, Surrey, Hampshire and Sussex. (Reaney).

In Newfoundland:

Family traditions: From the Isle of Sheppey (Kent).

Modern status: At Gander (*Electors* 1955) and St. John's.

WILKINS, a surname of England from the English personal name *Wilkin*, a diminutive of Will(iam) with a Flemish suffix (*see* WILLIAMS). (Reaney, Cottle). *See also* WILCOX, WILKINSON, WILLETT.

Traced by Guppy in Berkshire, Norfolk, Somerset and Wiltshire, and by Spiegelhalter in Devon.

In Newfoundland:

Early instances: Nicholas Wilking, juror of St. John's, ? 1753 (CO 194.13); N. H. Wilkins or Wilking, of St. John's, 1822, 1827 (D'Alberti 32, (*Newfoundlander* 7 Nov 1827); Jacob Wilkine, of Harbour Grace Parish, 1834 (Nfld. Archives HGRC); George Hughes Wilkins, from Southampton (Hampshire), captain of Rifle Brigade, married at St.

John's, 1851 (DPHW 26D); Robert, of Cobbler's Island (Bonavista B.), 1856 (DPHW 76).

Modern status: Scattered, especially at Wesleyville and Hare Bay (Bonavista North district).

WILKINSON, a surname of England and Ireland – son of *Wilkin. See* WILKINS.

Found widespread by Guppy, especially in Durham and Yorkshire WR, by Spiegelhalter in Devon, and by MacLysaght in Ulster.

In Newfoundland:

Early instances: Cornelius, married at St. John's, 1815 (Nfld. Archives BRC); William, carpenter of Carbonear, 1822 (DPHW 48); Eliza, of Harbour Grace, 1866 (Nfld. Archives HGRC).

Modern status: Scattered.

WILLAR, a variant of the surname of England Willer from Old English *wilige* – basket (-maker). (Reaney).

In Newfoundland:

Early instances: Ann Willer, of St. John's, 1828 (Nfld. Archives BRC); William, planter of Lower Island Cove, 1850 (DPHW 55); Thomas, of Shoe Cove (Twillingate district), 1854 (DPHW 86); Edward, of Tickle Cove (Bonavista B.), 1865 (Nfld. Archives KCRC).

Modern status: At Harbour Grace (*Electors* 1955), Grand Falls and St. John's.

WILLCOTT, a surname of England from the English place names Wilcot (Wiltshire), Wilcote (Oxfordshire), Wilcott (Shropshire), or (dweller in the) cottage (by the) well, spring, stream, or confused with WILCOX or Woolcott. (Ekwall).

Traced by Matthews in Devon and Dorset.

In Newfoundland:

Early instances: George Willecott, Willicott or Willcott, of Bay Bulls, 1677, "14 years an inhabitant in 1680," that is, since 1676 (CO 1); John Willecutt, of St. John's, 1705 (CO 194.22); Stephen Woolcock, miner of Shoal Bay (unspecified), 1778, of St. John's, given possession of fishing room at Fleur de Lys, 1805 (CO 194.34, D'Alberti 15); William Woolcott, merchant of Placentia Bay, 1804 (D'Alberti 14); John Willcocks, of Brigus, 1806 (DPHW 34); John Woolcot, granted land at Man of War's Cove, Grand Jervis (Hermitage B.), 1863 (Nfld. Archives, Registry Crown Lands).

Modern status: In the Fortune Bay-Hermitage district especially at St. Albans.

Place name: Dave Woolcott Point 47-47 55-47.

WILLETT, a surname of England from Middle English *Wilot*, *Wilet*, diminutives of Will(iam), with a French suffix (*see* WILLIAMS), or from the English river and place name Willett (Somerset), or a variant of such English surnames as Willard and Waylatt. (Reaney, Cottle). *See also* WILKINS.

Guppy traced Willet(t)s in Worcestershire; Spiegelhalter traced Willett(s) in Devon.

In Newfoundland:

Early instance: Edward, soldier of St. John's, 1816 (DPHW 26B).

Modern status: Rare, at St. John's.

WILLETTE, a surname of France, a matronym equivalent to *Guillette*, a feminine pet-form of Guillaume (William) (*see* WILLIAMS), or a regional variant of the surname Villette. (Dauzat).

In Newfoundland:

Modern status: Rare, at Winterhouse Brook and Corner Brook (*Electors* 1955).

WILLEY, a surname of England from the English place name Willey (Cheshire, Devon, Herefordshire, Shropshire, Warwickshire) or (dweller by the) willow or withy wood, or ? a diminutive of the baptismal name William (*see* WILLIAMS). (Cottle).

Traced by Guppy only, and oddly enough as Cottle points out, in Lincolnshire.

In Newfoundland:

Early instances: Robert, of Water Street (St. John's), 1820 (D'Alberti 30); Richard Willie, of Burin district, 1855 (*Newfoundlander* 6 Sep 1855).

Modern status: Rare, at Carbonear (*Electors* 1955).

Place name (not necessarily from the surname): Willey Shoal 49-05 53-34.

WILLIAMS, a surname of England, Wales, Ireland and the Channel Islands, – son of William, a baptismal name from the Old German personal name *Willahelm* containing the elements *vilja* – will and *helma* – helmet, which became *Guihielm* and later *Guillaume* in French and was introduced into England by the Normans. Surnames derived from William and its diminutives include: WILLIAMS, Williamson, WILLS, WILSON, WILCOX, WILLMOTT, WILLETT, WILKINS, GILL(I)AM. (Withycombe, Reaney, Cottle, MacLysaght, Turk). *See also* PARSONS.

Found widespread by Guppy in the Midlands and southwest, especially in Monmouthshire, and in North and South Wales, and by MacLysaght numerous in all provinces of Ireland.

In Newfoundland:

Family traditions: The Williams family of Bay Bulls is thought to have descended from Vaughan's Welsh colonists (Dillon). George, from Silverdale near Swansea, Wales, chief magistrate and judge in Newfoundland about 1763 (Nfld. Archives Z42). Two Williams brothers, from England, settled at Woody Island (Placentia B.) about 1845; one of the brothers, Samuel, moved to Pools Cove (Fortune B.) (MUN Hist.). ——, from Wales, settled at Pouch Cove in the early 1800s (MUN Hist.). Mary Williams Pike (1827–1918), of Carbonear (MUN Geog.). ——, from the west coast of England, a deserter from the Royal Navy, settled at Diamond Cove and changed his name to Parsons (MUN Folklore).

Early instances: Richard, of Fermeuse, 1676, of Renews, 1681 (CO 1); Benjamin, of St. John's Harbour, 1703 (CO 194.3); James William, of Newfoundland, 1704 (CO 194.3); Thomas Williams, of Conception Bay, [1706], (CO 194.4); Thomas, of Carbonear, 1708–9 (CO 194.4); Thomas, constable of Trinity district, ? 1730, 1732 (CO 194.9); Thomas, of Bay de Verde, 1730 (CO 194.23); George, of Placentia ? district, 1744 (CO 194.24); John, in possession of property in fishery at Petty Harbour, 1794–5, "38 years in Newfoundland," that is, 1756–7 (Census 1794–5); John, of Trinity Bay, 1769 (DPHW 64); Thomas, of Bay Bulls, 1786 (CO 194.36); Thomas, from Beminster (Dorset), of Aquaforte, 1797, aged 28 (D'Alberti 6); Eliza and Ann, of Woolwich (Kent), owners of house at King's Road, St. John's, 1798 (D'Alberti 8); Sara, from Crumarden, married at St. John's, 1798 (Nfld. Archives BRC); John, proprietor and occupier of fishing room, Old Perlican, Winter 1800–01 (Census Trinity B.); William, of Manuels, 1803 (CO 199.18); Stephen, from Anaglin (Co. Waterford), planter of Ferryland, deceased 1810 (*Royal Gazette* 6 Sep 1810); George, established ? Sunday school at Bay Roberts, 1810 (Anspach); John, of Harbour Grace, 1811 (Nfld. Archives HGRC); George, of Bay Roberts, appointed coroner within Conception Bay, 1813 (D'Alberti 23); John, from Cloyne (Co. Cork), tailor and planter of Harbour Grace, deceased 1815 (*Royal Gazette* 24 Aug 1815); Mathias, English adventurer from Great Britain, planter of Trinity (unspecified), 1815 (D'Alberti 25); William, from Cornwall, England, deserted from the employ of George Allen, St. John's, 1818 (*Nfld. Mercantile Journal* 26 Jun 1818); Martin, married at Bauline, 1818 (Nfld. Archives BRC); Elizabeth, daughter of John, from Newton Abbot (Devon), married at St. John's, 1819 (*Nfld. Mercantile Journal* 9 May 1819); William, of Pouch Cove, 1823 (DPHW 26B); Thomas William(s), planter of New Harbour (Trinity B.), 1823 (DPHW 64); George Williams, planter of Mosquitto (now Bristol's Hope), 1832 (DPHW 48); John, of Woody Island (Placentia B.), 1835 (DPHW 30); Nicholas, of Great Codroy River, 1835 (DPHW 30); William, from Broadhempston (Devon), resident of St. John's for many years, deceased 1845, aged 62 (*Newfoundlander* 23 Oct 1845, *Royal Gazette* 28 Oct 1845); Martin, of Placentia Bay, 1856 (*Newfoundlander* 14 Feb 1856); George William, son of John of Holyhead (Anglesey), North Wales, married at St. John's, 1857 (*Newfoundlander* 13 Aug 1857); Charles Williams (1830–98), of Woody Island (Placentia B.), married 1859, of Grand Bank, 1860 (MUN Hist., DPHW 106); widespread in Lovell 1871.

Modern status: Widespread, especially at Woody Island (Placentia B.) (*Electors* 1955), St. John's, Bay Bulls, New Harbour (Trinity B.), Pouch Cove, Pools Cove (Fortune B.) and Corner Brook.

Place names (not necessarily from the surname): William Point 47-46 54-59; Williams 47-26 52-46; Cape —— (Labrador) 56-37 61-54; —— Cove 47-18 52-47; —— Harbour (Labrador) 52-33 55-47, 60-00 64-16: —— Hill 47-19 52-49, 47-24 52-45; Mount —— (Labrador) 60-02 64-16; —— Pond 47-20 53-19, 47-43 52-48; —— Rock 47-44 54-07; —— Harbour Run (Labrador) 53-34 55-49; Williamsport 50-32 56-19.

WILLIS, a surname of England, Scotland and Ireland – son of Will(ie) (*see* WILLIAMS), or from Old English *wylig*, *welig* – (dweller among the) willow(s), or from Old English *wella* – (dweller by the) well, spring or stream. (Cottle, Black, MacLysaght). *See also* WELLS, WITHERS, WYLIE, WITHYCOMBE.

Found scattered by Guppy in nine counties, especially in Berkshire, Essex and Wiltshire, and including Devon; and by MacLysaght in Ulster.

In Newfoundland:

Early instances: ——, of Quidi Vidi, 1703 (CO 194.3); William, soldier of St. John's, 1766 (DPHW 26C); Josiah, of Kiers Cove (Labrador), 1787, of Caribou Tickle (Labrador), 1789 (MUN Hist.); Robert, carpenter of Renews, 1821 (DPHW 31); John, of Little Bay (Burin district), 1830 (DPHW 106); Louis, of Catalina, 1842 (DPHW 67); Julian, of Harbour Grace, 1866 (Nfld. Archives HGRC); Bernard and Charles, of Fogo, 1871 (Lovell).

Modern status: Scattered, especially at Dover (Bonavista B.) and Fogo.

Place names: Willis Cove 47-38 56-22; —— Island, —— Reach 48-48 53-43; —— Rocks (Labrador) 56-56 61-20.

WILLMONT, ? an unrecorded ? Newfoundland variant of Willman or WILLMOTT, all three occurring in or near Bay d'Espoir in *Electors* 1955.

In Newfoundland:

Modern status: At McCallum, Morrisville and Head of Bay d'Espoir (Fortune Bay and Hermitage district).

WILLMOTT, a surname of England and Ireland, Wilmotte of France; in England a pet-form of *Willelm* (William) (*see* WILLIAMS) with a French diminutive suffix; in France a contraction of *Willemotte*, a regional form of the matronym Guillemotte, which is retained in the name of the sea-bird, the guillemot. (Reaney, Cottle, MacLysaght). *See also* WILLMONT.

Guppy traced Wilmot in Derbyshire and Wilmott in Hertfordshire and Somerset; Spiegelhalter traced Wilmot in Devon; and MacLysaght found Wilmot in Ireland since the end of the sixteenth century and in Co. Kerry in 1614.

In Newfoundland:

Early instance: Henry Wilmot, fisherman of Bay de Este, 1871 (Lovell).

Modern status: At Head of Bay d'Espoir (*Electors* 1955) and St. Albans.

WILLS, a surname of England – son of Will(iam) (*see* WILLIAMS) or a variant of WELLS (Reaney, Cottle).

Traced by Guppy in Devon, Cornwall and Somerset.

In Newfoundland:

Early instances: Richard, fisherman of St. John's, 1794–5, "38 years in Newfoundland," that is, 1756–7 (Census 1794–5); William, of English Harbour (Trinity B.), 1802 (DPHW 64); Henry, of Bonavista, 1811 (DPHW 70); Sarah, of Old Perlican, 1820 (DPHW 58); William, fisherman of Adams Cove, 1827 (DPHW 52A); William, fisherman of Pouch Cove, 1828 (DPHW 52A); —— of Port de Grave, 1829 (*Newfoundlander* 14 May 1829); Henry, from Littlehempston (Devon), of St. John's, 1834 (DPHW 26D); Richard, planter of Bay (? for Barrow) Harbour (Bonavista B.), 1838 (DPHW 72); Robert, mason of Trinity (Trinity B.), 1840 (DPHW 64B); John, of Fogo, 1842 (DPHW 83); Thomas, of Greenspond, 1843 (*Newfoundlander* 31 Aug 1843); Robert, of Lower Burgeo, 1846 (DPHW 101); —— on the *Thomas* in the seal fishery out of Catalina, 1848 (*Newfoundlander* 30 Mar 1848); Robert, fisherman of Hunts Island (Burgeo-La Poile district), 1849 (DPHW 101); Thomas, fisherman of Little

Harbour (Fortune B.), 1852 (DPHW 102); Robert, of Dawson's Cove (Fortune B.), 1857 (DPHW 102); William, of Harbour Grace, 1859 (DPHW 43); Horatio B., Twillingate, 1861 (Centre for Nfld. Studies, per W. Kirwin); scattered in Lovell 1871.

Modern status: At St. John's.

Place name (not necessarily from the surname): Wills Rock 49-43 55-53.

WILSON, a surname of England, Scotland and Ireland – son of Will(iam) (*see* WILLIAMS), or from the English place name Wilson (Leicestershire, Devon). (Reaney, Cottle, Black, MacLysaght).

Found widespread by Guppy especially in the north of England and south of the Forth and Clyde; and by MacLysaght "the most numerous English surname in Ireland," mainly in Ulster.

In Newfoundland:

Early instances: Richard, of St. Johns Harbour, 1703 (CO 194.3); Richard, of Petty Harbour, 1708–09 (CO 194.4); Thomas, of Placentia, 1725 (CO 194.8); John, of Trinity (Trinity B.), 1805 (DPHW 64); John, from Yorkshire, victualler of St. John's, deceased 1813 (*Royal Gazette* 2 Dec 1813); William, Wesleyan Missionary of Bonavista, 1829 (DPHW 72); Catheren [sic], of Harbour Grace Parish, 1831 (Nfld. Archives HGRC); George Harrison, 2nd son of George Harrison of Glasnevin (Co. Dublin), of the firm Messrs. Wilson and Meynel, of St. John's, 1845 (*Times* 2 Jul 1845); Joseph, of Greenspond, 1655 (Nfld. Archives KCRC); Robert, from Edinburgh, of St. John's, 1857 (*Newfoundlander* 5 Oct 1857); Carl, of Harbour Grace, 1868 (Nfld. Archives HGRC).

Modern status: Scattered, especially at Merasheen (*Electors* 1955) and St. John's.

WILTON, a surname of England and Scotland from the English place name Wilton (Wiltshire, Somerset, Hereford, Norfolk, Cumberland, Yorkshire) or the Scots place name Wilton (Roxburghshire). (Cottle, Black).

Traced by Guppy in Cornwall and Derbyshire and by Spiegelhalter in Devon.

In Newfoundland:

Early instance: Solomon, fisherman of Burnt Island (Burgeo-La Poile district), 1845, of Bonne Bay (St. Barbe district), 1864 (DPHW 93, 101).

Modern status: At St. John's and in the St. Barbe, Humber East and West districts.

Place name: Wiltondale or Wiltonvale 49-24 57-37.

WILTSHIRE, a surname of England – (the man from) Wiltshire. Reaney records seventeen variants of the name. (Reaney, Cottle). *See also* WELCHER.

Traced by Guppy in Gloucestershire and (oddly enough) Wiltshire, and by Spiegelhalter in Devon.

In Newfoundland:

Early instances: William, of Trinity Bay, 1769 (DPHW 64); William Wiltshire or Wiltsheir, of Bonavista, 1796 (DPHW 70); John Wiltshaw, of Carbonear, 1816 (DPHW 48); William Wiltshire, planter of Trinity (Trinity B.), 1829 (DPHW 64B); John, of Catalina, 1833 (DPHW 70); Elizabeth Wilshord (? for Wiltshire), of King's Cove, 1834 (Nfld. Archives KCRC); George Wiltshire, of St. John's, 1838 (DPHW 26D); Ava, from Stratford (Somerset), married at Catalina, 1842 (DPHW 67); Moses Wiltshear, of Carbonear Natives Society, 1848 (*Nfld. Almanac*); Joseph, planter of Lower Island Cove, 1851 (DPHW 55).

Modern status: At St. John's, Lower Island Cove and Port Union.

WIMBLETON, a surname of England, ? from the English place names Wimbledon (Surrey) or Wimblington (Cambridgeshire).

In Newfoundland:

Early instances: Charles Wimbledon, of Shoe Cove (Green B.), 1844 (DPHW 86); William Wimbleton, of Snooks Arm (Green B.), 1874 (DPHW 90).

Modern status: At Shoe Cove (Green B.).

WINDSOR, and **WINSOR** which reflects the pronunciation, surnames of England from the English place names Windsor (Berkshire), Little Windsor, Broadwindsor (Dorset), Windsor Farm (Devon), Winser (Devon, Hampshire). (Reaney, Cottle, Spiegelhalter). The two forms have been confused in Newfoundland.

Guppy traced Windsor in Cheshire and Shropshire; Spiegelhalter traced Win(d)sor in Devon.

In Newfoundland:

Family traditions: William Windsor (1785–), of Swain's Island (Bonavista B.), 1830 (MUN Hist.).
—— Windsor or Winser, from Devon, settled at Swain's Island (Bonavista B.), about 1800 (MUN Folklore).

Early instances: Richard Windsor, "80 years of Carbonear," 1675 (CO 1); Sam, of Bay Bulls, 1708 (CO 194.4); Peter Winser, in possession of property at St. John's, 1794–5, "23 years in Newfoundland," that is, 1771–2 (Census 1794–5); John Windsor, of Greenspond, in possession of fishing room, Pond Island, Greenspond Harbour, 1799 (Bonavista

Register 1806); John, born at Swain's Island, 1813, baptized 1830 (DPHW 76); Peter Winsor, merchant of Aquaforte, 1821 (DPHW 31); William Windsor, of Cape Ray, 1822 (Cormack); John Win(d)sor, of Petty Harbour, 1841 (DPHW 31); Solomon Windsor, of Tilt Cove (Twillingate district), 1849, of Round Harbour (Twillingate district), 1849 (DPHW 86); John, of Stadin's [sic] Island (Bonavista North district), 1850 (DPHW 76); Robert, of Triton Harbour (now Triton), 1851 (DPHW 86); Henry Winsor, of Ferryland, 1855 (DPHW 31); William, fisherman of Brigus, 1855 (DPHW 35); James and Benjamin Windsor, granted land at Swain's Island (Bonavista B.), 1863 (Nfld. Archives, Registry Crown Lands); John, of Lower Burgeo, 1871 (Lovell); Thomas A. Winsor, merchant of Exploits Burnt Island, 1871 (Lovell); Simon, of Moreton's Harbour, 1871 (Lovell).

Modern status: Windsor, at St. John's, Aquaforte, Carbonear, Harbour Mille (Fortune B.) and Corner Brook; Winsor, widespread, especially at St. John's, Wesleyville, Triton and Corner Brook.

Place names: Windsor 48-57 55-40; —— Cove 49-41 55-58; —— Lake 47-36 52-48, 49-53 55-38; —— Point 47-37 59-15, 49-40 56-00; —— Shoal (Labrador) 57-24 61-34; —— Heights 47-36 52-49; —— Lookout 49-35 55-36; Windsor's Island 49-09 53-33; Winsor Point (Labrador), Winsors Harbour Point 55-21 59-44; —— Harbour Island (Labrador) 55-20 59-45.

WING, a surname of England, and of China; in England ? from the English place name Wing (Buckinghamshire, Rutlandshire); in China – eternal, perpetual; glorious, honourable, prosperous. (Ekwall, F.W So).

In Newfoundland:

Early instance: William Wyng, of Bonavista, 1698 (Prowse).

Modern status: At Bell Island, Corner Brook (*Electors* 1955) and St. John's.

Place names (not necessarily from the surname): Wing Pond 49-00 54-08; Wings Brook 48-38 53-55; —— Point 49-20 54-29; —— Pond 48-37 53-53.

WINSLOW, a surname of England and ? of Ireland, though not recorded by MacLysaght, from the English place name Winslow (Buckinghamshire). (Cottle).

In Newfoundland:

Early instances: George Winslaw or Winslow, from Ireland, of Harbour Grace Parish, 1872 (MUN Folklore, Nfld. Archives HGRC); Eliza Winslow, of Harbour Grace, 1891 (Nfld. Archives HGRC).

Modern status: At St. John's and Grand Falls.

WINSOR. *See* WINDSOR

WINTER, a surname of England from the Old German personal name *Wintar* or Old English *Winter*, *Wintra*, or a nickname for one born in a hard winter, or for one with white hair, or for one of a lugubrious nature. (Reaney, Cottle).

Traced by Guppy in Durham, Lincolnshire, Norfolk and Somerset, and by Spiegelhalter in Devon.

In Newfoundland:

Family tradition: —— Winter formerly Winterhay, from England, settled in the Burin district (MUN Folklore).

Early instances: James, merchant in possession of property at St. John's, 1794–5, "50 years in Newfoundland," that is, 1744–5 (Census 1794–5); Winter, Nicholl and Co., operated salmon fishery at Harbour Breton, 1808 (CO 194.48); James John, of Fools (now Pools) Island, 1827 (DPHW 76); George, from Demerara, married at St. John's, 1834 (*Royal Gazette* 29 Jul 1834); John, from Greenspond, married at St. John's, 1840 (DPHW 26D); James, of Fogo, 1842 (DPHW 83); Sir James Spearman (1845–), born at Lamaline (Mott); John, of Burgeo, deceased (*Newfoundlander* 27 Apr 1857); Charles, of Bonne Bay (St. Barbe district), 1869 (DPHW 93); Thomas, of Burin, 1871 (Lovell).

Modern status: Scattered, especially at St. John's, Valleyfield and Badger's Quay.

Place names (not necessarily from the surname): Winter Bank 47-35 52-40; —— Brook 48-25 53-45; —— Cove, —— Flat 51-13 56-46; —— Island (Labrador) 54-27 57-26; —— —— Tickle 49-23 55-13; —— —— (Labrador) 52-36 55-50; Winterland 47-09 55-18; Winter's Point 49-08 53-39; Winters Point (Labrador) 53-39 57-04; —— Tickle Lake 49-24 55-15; Winterton, —— Cove 47-58 53-20.

WINTERS, a surname of England and Ireland, – son of Winter (*see* WINTER), also in Ireland a synonym of MacAlivery, *Mac Giolla Gheimhridh*, Ir. *geimhreadh* – winter. (Reaney, MacLysaght).

Traced by MacLysaght in Co. Tyrone.

In Newfoundland:

Early instances: James, in possession of property at St. John's and Petty Harbour, 1794–5 (Census 1794–5); Catherine, of Harbour Grace Parish, 1831 (Nfld. Archives HGRC); James, of Fools (now Pools) Island, 1835 (DPHW 76).

Modern status: At Wesleyville and St. John's.

WISCOMBE, a surname of England from the English place name Wiscombe Park (Devon). (Spiegelhalter).

Traced by Spiegelhalter in Devon.

In Newfoundland:

Family tradition: Samuel, from Surrey, England, settled in Newfoundland; his descendants settled at Creston (Placentia B.) (MUN Folklore).

Early instances: Samuel, fisherman of Rock Harbour (Burin district), 1860 (DPHW 100); Samuel Wiscomb, servant of Butter's Cove (? now Creston), 1871 (Lovell); Samuel Wiscombe, of Mortier Bay, 1874 (DPHW 105).

Modern status: At Jerseyside (Placentia B.), Creston, Burin Bay Arm and St. John's.

WISE, a surname of England, WYSE of Ireland, from Old English *wīs* – wise, learned, though in England sometimes a German-Jewish name from German *weiss* – white. (Reaney, Cottle, MacLysaght).

Wise traced by Guppy in Cornwall, Hertfordshire, Yorkshire NR and ER, and by Spiegelhalter in Devon; Wyse traced by MacLysaght in Waterford city and county.

In Newfoundland:

Early instances: Robert, of Bay Bulls, 1681 (CO 1); Maurice Wise, of Trinity Bay, 1773 (DPHW 64); Peter Wyse, of St. John's, 1796 (CO 194.39); James Wise, from Golden (Co. Tipperary), married at St. John's, 1813 (Nfld. Archives BRC); Thomas Wise or Wyse, of Harbour Grace, 1819 (Nfld. Archives HGRC); Michael Wise or Wyse, of Greenspond, 1824 (Nfld. Archives KCRC); Mary Wyse, of Trinity (unspecified), 1826 (Nfld. Archives KCRC); James, of Placentia, 1841 (*Newfoundlander* 4 Feb 1841).

Modern status: Wise, at Black Duck (St. George's district) (*Electors* 1955); Wyse, at Southern Harbour (Placentia B.) (*Electors* 1955), Placentia and St. John's.

WISEMAN, a surname of England, Scotland and Ireland from Old English *wīs* – wise and *mann* – man – the wise, discreet man, or ironically a fool, or magician, wizard, sorcerer. (Reaney, Cottle, Black, MacLysaght 73).

Traced by Guppy in Essex and Norfolk, by Spiegelhalter in Devon; by Black in Angus and Moray; and by MacLysaght in Ireland since the sixteenth century and mainly in Co. Cork.

In Newfoundland:

Family tradition: ——, from the British Isles, was the first settler of Newmans Cove (Bonavista B.) (MUN Folklore).

Early instances: John, of Trinity Bay, 1774 (DPHW 64); Peter, of St. John's, 1797 (DPHW 26D); William, of Bonavista, 1798 (DPHW 70); John,

proprietor and occupier of fishing room, Trinity (Trinity B.), Winter 1800–01 (Census Trinity B.); John, of Fogo, 1803–05 (D'Alberti 13, 15); Henry, of Harbour Grace, 1807 (Nfld. Archives HGRC); Thomas, of Cuckold's Cove (now Dunfield), 1811 (DPHW 64); Philip, planter of Tizzard's Harbour, 1821 (USPG); James, planter of Herring Neck, 1820 (USPG): William, planter of Old Bonaventure, 1822 (DPHW 64); James, of Heart's Desire, 1832 (Nfld. Archives KCRC); William, of Little Bay Islands, 1844 (DPHW 86); J., Inspector of pickled fish at Heart's Content, 1844 (*Nfld. Almanac*); Stephen, of Triton Harbour (now Triton), 1851 (DPHW 86); John, fisherman of Spaniards Bay (now Spaniards Cove), (Trinity B.), 1852 (DPHW 64B); James, of Filthy (now British) Harbour, 1855 (Nfld. Archives KCRC); John, fisherman of Pope's Harbour, 1857 (DPHW 64B); James, of New Perlican, 1857 (*Newfoundlander* 8 Oct 1857); Nathaniel, fisherman of Trouty, 1857 (DPHW 64B); John, fisherman of Delby's Cove (Trinity B.), 1860 (DPHW 64B); William, of Indian Bight, 1860 (DPHW 92); Robert, of Greenspond, 1863 (DPHW 77); scattered in Lovell 1871.

Modern status: Widespread, especially at St. John's, Corner Brook, Little Bay Islands and Bloomfield.

Place names: Wiseman Beach 49-36 55-53; —— Cove 49-39 55-48; —— Head 49-14 55-13; —— —— (Labrador) 51-45 56-20; —— Point 49-40 55-48; Wiseman's Cove 47-47 56-36.

WISHARD, a surname of England and Scotland from Old Norse *vizkr* – wise with the French suffix (*-hard*), giving the Old Norman French personal name *Wisc(h)ard*, Old French *Guisc(h)ard*, *Guiscart*. (Reaney, Black). *See also* WITCHER with which confusion may have occurred.

In Newfoundland:

Early instances: Alexander Wishard, soldier of St. John's, 1778 (DPHW 26C); Thomas Witchard, planter of Twillingate, 1871 (Lovell).

Modern status: Rare, at Catalina (*Electors* 1955) and St. John's.

Place names: Wishart Creek (Labrador) 54-44 66-46; —— Lake (Labrador) 54-44 66-51.

WITCHER, a surname of England from Old English *hwicce* – (maker or seller of) chest(s), or from Old English *wīc* (*see* WEEKS), or dweller by the enclosure of wych-elms. (Reaney). *See also* WISHARD.

In Newfoundland:

Family tradition: John, from Dorset or Somerset,

settled at Barr'd Islands about 1807–1808 (MUN Hist.).

Early instances: John, planter of Barr'd Islands, 1821 (USPG); William Wicher, fisherman of Shoe Cove (Fogo district), 1871 (Lovell).

Modern status: At Barr'd Islands (Fogo district) and Birchy Bay North.

WITHERALL, ? a variant of the surname of England Wetheral, etc. from the English place name Wetherall (Cumberland). (Reaney, Cottle).

Guppy traced We(a)therill, Wetherell in Yorkshire NR and ER, Wetherall, Wetherill in Yorkshire WR, and Weatherall in Nottinghamshire; Spiegelhalter traced Weatherall, Wetherall in Devon.

In Newfoundland:

Early instances: Peddle and Weatheral, Trinity (Trinity B.), Winter 1800–01 (Census Trinity B.); Simeon Wetherall, of Fortune, 1843 (DPHW 109); John Withell, of St. John's, 1854 (*Newfoundlander* 28 Sep 1854).

Modern status: At Fortune.

WITHERS, a surname of England from Old English *wīthig* – (dweller by the) willow(s). (Reaney). *See also* WILLIS, WITHYCOMBE, WYLIE.

Traced by Guppy in Berkshire, Hampshire and Nottinghamshire.

In Newfoundland:

Early instances: ——, of St. John's, 1832 (*Newfoundlander* 20 Dec 1832); Joseph, of Mortier Bay, 1871 (DPHW 105); Joseph and Peter, fishermen of Muddy Hole (Burin district), 1871 (Lovell); Nicholas, fisherman of Rock Harbour (Placentia B.), 1871 (Lovell).

Modern status: At Wreck Cove (Fortune B.) (*Electors* 1955), St. John's and in the Placentia West district.

WITHYCOMBE, a surname of England from the English place names Widdacombe, Widdecombe, Widdicombe (Devon), or Withycombe (Devon, Somerset) – the valley where the withies, willows grow. (Reaney). *See also* WITHERS, WILLIS, WYLIE.

Spiegelhalter traced Withycombe, Widdicombe in Devon.

In Newfoundland:

Early instances: Hugh Wriddycomb, of St. John's, 1769 (DPHW 26D); John Widdicomb, publican of St. John's, 1794–5, "24 years in Newfoundland," that is, 1774–5 (Census 1794–5); Peter Witthycombe, carpenter of St. John's, 1839 (DPHW 26B); John Withycombe, carpenter of Harbour Grace, 1851 (DPHW 43).

Modern status: Rare, at St. John's.

Place names: Withecombe Cove (Labrador), —— Point (Labrador) 53-30 55-46.

WONG, a surname of China – king, prime, ruler; yellow. (F.W. So).

In Newfoundland:

Modern status: At St. John's and Botwood.

WOOD, a surname of England, Scotland and Ireland – (dweller in or near a) wood, or from Old English *wōd* – mad, frenzied; in Ireland often confused with WOODS. (Reaney, Cottle, Black, MacLysaght).

Found widespread by Guppy, especially in Yorkshire, Kent and Sussex, and over a large part of Scotland except in the north.

In Newfoundland:

Early instances: Widow, of Quidi Vidi, 1676 (CO 1); Richard, boatkeeper of St. John's Harbour, 1682 (CO 1); Richard, of Newfoundland, 1704 (CO 194.3); Rev. Henry, of Bay Bulls, 1802 (D'Alberti 12); Eliza, of Harbour Grace, 1816 (Nfld. Archives HGRC); Richard, of Magotty Cove (St. John's), 1820 (DPHW 26B); James, from Carrick-on-Suir (Co. Tipperary), married at St. John's, 1827 (Nfld. Archives BRC); Rev. Thomas Martyn, from Glastonbury (Somerset), married at Port de Grave, 1833, of Petty Harbour, 1835, of Greenspond, 1838, of Bonavista, 1841 (DPHW 70,76, 31, *Royal Gazette* 29 Jan 1833); Benjamin, from Penrith (Cumberland), married in St. John's, 1847 (*Newfoundlander* 7 Oct 1847); Peter, assistant lighthouse keeper of Catalina, 1871 (Lovell); Benjamin, fisherman of Grand Bank, 1871 (Lovell).

Modern status: Scattered.

Place names: (There are many place names containing the specific Wood, only a few of which seem to be derived from the surname): Woods (or Woods Island) Harbour, —— Island 49-06 58-13; —— Lake (Labrador) 54-30 65-13.

WOODEN, a surname of England, a variant of Wooding, from Old English *wudung* – cutting of wood, hence (dweller at a) place where wood has been, or is, cut. (Reaney).

Guppy traced Woodings in Staffordshire.

In Newfoundland:

Modern status: At Grand Bank.

WOODFINE, a surname of England – (dweller at or by the) wood-heap. (Weekley *Surnames*).

Traced by Matthews at Broadhempston (Devon).

In Newfoundland:

Early instances: Richard, of St. John's, 1783 (DPHW 26C); Richard, of Devil's (now Job's) Cove, 1821 (*Royal Gazette* 11 Jun 1812); William, of Northern Bay, born in Newfoundland, 1815 (*Nfld. Quarterly* Sep 1902); Richard, planter of Long Beach (North Shore, Conception B.), 1817 (DPHW 52A); John, of Torbay, 1820 (DPHW 26B); John Woodfin, of Harbour Grace Parish, 1836 (Nfld. Archives HGRC); Joseph and William Woodpine, of Gull Island (Conception B.), 1871 (Lovell).

Modern status: At St. John's, Stephenville, Torbay and Long Beach (North Shore, Conception B.).

WOODFORD, a surname of England and Scotland from the English place name Woodford in ten counties or the Scots place name in Roxburghshire, or (dweller by the) ford in the wood. (Cottle, Black).

Traced by Spiegelhalter in Devon.

In Newfoundland:

Early instances: John, witness in Kelly murder at Harbour Main, 1750 (CO 194.12); William, of Harbour Main, 1771 (CO 199.18); William, of St. John's, 1774 (DPHW 26C); Thomas, of Bonavista, lessee of fishing room, Newman's Point, Bonavista, 1805 (Bonavista Register 1806); Mary, of Harbour Grace, 1806 (Nfld. Archives HGRC); William, planter of Fogo, 1816 (MUN Hist.); William, planter of Herring Neck, 1821 (USPG); Betsy, of King's Cove, 1828 (Nfld. Archives KCRC); ——, on the *Argo* in the seal fishery out of Brigus, 1847 (*Newfoundlander* 25 Mar 1847); William, of Stone Harbour (Twillingate district), 1853, of Gut Arm (Twillingate district), 1856 (DPHW 85); Thomas, of Plate Cove, 1857 (Nfld. Archives KCRC); James, planter of Cat's Cove (now Conception Harbour), 1871 (Lovell); Edmond, of Chapel's Cove (Conception B.), 1871 (Lovell); Joseph, of Flowers Cove to Point Ferole area, 1871 (Lovell); John, of Heart's Content, 1871 (Lovell); Michael, farmer of North Arm, Holyrood, 1871 (Lovell).

Modern status: Scattered, especially at Harbour Main and St. John's.

Place names: Woodford Cove 49-37 55-52; —— Lookout 49-37 55-41; Woodfords 47-24 53-09; —— Arm 49-31 55-52.

WOODLAND, a surname of England from the common English place name Woodland(s) which occurs twelve times in Devon alone, – (dweller by, or worker in, the) woodland. (Reaney, Cottle, Spiegelhalter).

Traced by Guppy in Middlesex and by Spiegelhalter in Devon.

In Newfoundland:

Early instances: Uriah, late 1700s, bequeathed property in Newfoundland to son John ? Old Perlican. (Copy of Will in Registry of Archdeaconry of Exeter from Jeffrey Woodland of Exeter, Devon); John Woodlands, proprietor and occupier of fishing room, Old Perlican, Winter 1800–01 (Census Trinity B.); James, married at Greenspond October 1823 (Parish Records); Thomas Woodland, planter of Flat Rock (Carbonear), 1838 (DPHW 48); James, of Greenspond, 1855 (DPHW 76).

Modern status: Scattered, especially at St. John's.

WOODLEY, a surname of England from the English place names Woodley, Woodleigh (Devon, Berkshire, Cheshire), or (dweller in the) field or clearing in the wood.

Traced by Guppy in Cornwall and by Spiegelhalter in Devon.

In Newfoundland:

Early instances: Mary, in possession of property at Torbay, 1794–5, "7 years in Newfoundland," that is, 1787–8 (Census 1794–5); N. and Samuel, of St. John's, 1826 (Dispatches 1825–6); Samuel, of Maggoty Cove, 1828 (*Newfoundlander* 14 Aug 1828); Nathaniel, from Coffinswell (Devon), planter of St. John's, deceased 1833 (Nfld. Archives T68).

Modern status: At St. John's.

WOODMAN, a surname of England, Scotland and Ireland from the Old English personal name *Wudumann* from **wudumann* – woodman, woodcutter, dweller or worker in the wood. (Reaney, Cottle, Spiegelhalter, MacLysaght, Black).

Traced by Guppy in Middlesex and Northumberland, by Spiegelhalter in Devon, and by MacLysaght in Co. Louth.

In Newfoundland:

Family traditions: ——, from southern England, settled at Trinity (Trinity B.), about 1850; later moved to New Harbour (Trinity B.) (MUN Folklore). Robert (about 1789–1860), from Devon, settled in New Harbour (Trinity B.) via Trinity (Trinity B.), about 1812 (MUN Geog.).

Early instances: —— Woodmann, of St. John's, 1708 (CO 194.4); Robert Woodman, planter of New Harbour (Trinity B.), 1824 (DPHW 64B); John, of King's Cove Parish, 1848 (Nfld. Archives KCRC); John, fisherman of North Side, Trinity (Trinity B.), 1855 (DPHW 64B).

Modern status: Scattered, especially at New Harbour (Trinity B.).

WOODROW, a surname of England from the English place name Woodrow (Wiltshire, Worcestershire, Devon) or from Old English *wudu* – wood and *rāw* – row (dweller in the) row (of cottages in the) wood. (Reaney, Cottle, Spiegelhalter).

Traced by Spiegelhalter in Devon.

In Newfoundland:

Early instances: John Woodroof, of Harbour Grace, 1813 (Nfld. Archives HGRC); John Woodrow, of Harbour Grace, 1818 (Nfld. Archives HGRC); Richard, ? of Northern Bay, 1839 (DPHW 54); James Woodrou and Richard Woodrow, planters of Bay de Verde, 1871 (Lovell).

Modern status: Scattered, especially at Bay de Verde and Northern Bay.

WOODS, a surname of England and Ireland – of (at) the wood, or a plural (*see* WOOD); in Ireland also for a number of Irish names believed rightly or wrongly to contain Ir. *coill* – wood, and often confused with WOOD. (Cottle, MacLysaght).

Traced by Spiegelhalter in Devon and by MacLysaght throughout Ireland, especially in Ulster.

In Newfoundland:

Family tradition: Andrew (1831–1900), from Stonehaven, Scotland, of Grand Bank (MUN Hist.).

Early instances: Edward, of St. John's, 1786 (DPHW 26C); Joseph, of Bonavista, 1803 (DPHW 70); Margaret, died at Grand Bank, 1817 (MUN Hist.); Richard, of Trinity Bay, 1822 (Nfld. Archives BRC); Mary, of Harbour Grace Parish, 1833 (Nfld. Archives HGRC); ——, on the *Montezuma* in the seal fishery out of Bay Roberts, 1849 (*Newfoundlander* 5 Apr 1849); Henry, of Clark's Cove, 1860 (DPHW 85); Thomas, of Harbour Grace, 1869 (Nfld. Archives HGRC); Thomas, tinware of Carbonear, 1871 (Lovell); Thomas, of Hermitage Cove (Fortune B.), 1871 (Lovell).

Modern status: Scattered, especially at St. John's.

Place names: There are many place names containing the specifics Wood and Woods, none apparently from the surname.

WOODWARD, a surname of England from Old English *wuduweard* – forester. (Reaney, Cottle).

Traced by Guppy in the Midlands, especially in Worcestershire, but also in Essex, Suffolk and Yorkshire NR and ER.

In Newfoundland:

Family tradition: Joseph, an English youngster, was the first permanent settler of Boat Harbour (White B.), in the late 1800s (MUN Hist.).

Early instance: Joseph, of French Island (Western Newfoundland), 1873 (MUN Hist.).

Modern status: At Corner Brook and Boat Harbour (White B.).

WOODWORTH, a surname of England from ? Old English *wudu* – wood and *worth* – enclosure, homestead – (dweller or worker at the) outlying farm in the wood or ? a variant of WOODWARD. (E.C. Smith).

In Newfoundland:

Early instances: Thomas Worlwart, of King's Cove, 1850 (Nfld. Archives KCRC); A.W. Woodsworth, teacher of St. John's, 1871 (Lovell).

Modern status: At McKay's, Botwood (*Electors* 1955), Cupids, and Point Leamington.

WOOL(D)RIDGE, surnames of England from the Old English personal name *Wulfrīc* containing the elements *wolf* and *powerful*, or from the English place name Woolridge (Devon). (Reaney, Cottle, Spiegelhalter).

Traced by Spiegelhalter in Devon.

In Newfoundland:

Family tradition: Thomas Woolridge, from England, settled at Seldom in the late 1700s or early 1800s (MUN Folklore).

Early instances: Richard Woolridge, Woldridge or Woolldridge, of Trinity (Trinity B.), 1791 (DPHW 64); Thomas Woolridge, fisherman of Fogo, 1853 (DPHW 83); Richard, fisherman of Cuckold's Cove (now Dunfield), 1854, ? of Silly Cove (now Winterton), 1860 (DPHW 64B); Richard Wooldridge, fisherman of Sulley's Cove (Trinity B.), 1871 (Lovell).

Modern status: Wooldridge, rare, at Burnside (Bonavista B.) (*Electors* 1955); Woolridge, scattered, especially at St. John's and Botwood.

WOOLFREY, a surname of England from the Old English personal name *Wulffrith* containing the elements *wolf* and *peace*. (Reaney).

Traced by Spiegelhalter in Devon.

In Newfoundland:

Family tradition: M. Woolfreys (1800–), of English descent, of Moreton's Harbour (MUN Folklore).

Early instances: George Wo(o)lfrey, of Trinity (Trinity B.), 1772 (DPHW 64); William Wolfrey, of Heart's Delight, 1785 (DPHW 64); Thomas Woolfrey, of Harbour Grace, 1810 (D'Alberti 20); Samuel Wolfrey, missionary of Moreton's Harbour, ? 1815, 1824 (CO 194.56, D'Alberti 33); Marta [*sic*] Woolfrey or Woolfree, of Harbour Grace Parish, 1834 (Nfld. Archives HGRC); Thomas Woolfrey, of Harbour Grace, 1857 (*Newfoundlander* 23 Apr 1857);

Joseph Woolfreys, fisherman of Exploits, 1859 (DPHW 42).

Modern status: Scattered, especially at Lewisporte.

WOOLGAR, a surname of England from the Old English personal name *Wulfgar* containing the elements *wolf* and *spear*. (Reaney, Cottle).
In Newfoundland:
Modern status: At St. John's.

WOOLRIDGE. *See* WOOLDRIDGE

WOOTTON, a surname of England from the English place name Wootton, traced by Cottle in at least fifteen counties, or from Old English **wudu-tūn* – (dweller or worker at the) farm (in or near the) wood. (Reaney, Cottle).
Traced by Guppy in the Midlands, Kent and Wiltshire.
In Newfoundland:
Early instances: James Wooton, of Newfoundland, ? 1706 (CO 194.24); Theo Wotton, fisherman of St. John's or Petty Harbour about 1739–43 (CO 194.11, 24); Thomas, member of court at St. John's, 1751 (CO 194.13); James Sr., from Broadhempston (Devon), and James Jr., from Totnes (Devon), of St. John's, 1777 (CO 194.33); Edward Wotton, of Battle Harbour (Labrador), 1787, of Twillingate, 1789 (MUN Hist.).
Modern status: Rare, at Gander (*Electors* 1955).

WORNELL, a surname of England, ? from an unidentified place name ? Warnell (Cumberland). MacLysaght, however, comments on the surname of Ireland Marnell, that it was originally Warnell, a derivative of Warner – warrener, (game-) parkkeeper. (MacLysaght 73, Cottle).
In Newfoundland:
Early instances: Edward Wornail, fisherman of Trinity (Trinity B.), 1761 (DPHW 64); Charles Wornel, of Greenspond, 1845 (DPHW 76); James F. Worwell, foreman of St. John's, 1871 (Lovell).
Modern status: At Lewisporte (*Electors* 1955), Greenspond and St. John's.

WORRALL, a surname of England from the English place names Worrall (Yorkshire WR) or Wirral (Cheshire), or from Old English *wir* – bog myrtle and *halh* – ? river meadow. (Cottle).
In Newfoundland:
Early instances: Samuel Worrell, soldier of St. John's, 1826 (DPHW 26B); James, clerk of Harbour Grace, 1871 (Lovell); John William Worral, lumberman of Bay of Islands, 1875 (DPHW 95).

Modern status: Rare, at St. John's.

WORTHMAN, a surname of ? England, untraced elsewhere, ? a variant of Wortman from Old English *wyrt* – vegetable(s) and *mann* – man, a seller or grower of vegetables, or ? from Old English *wor* – enclosure, homestead and *mann* – man, hence a dweller or worker at an outlying farm, or from the English place name Worth in several counties.
In Newfoundland:
Early instances: Robert Worsman, planter of New Harbour (Trinity B.), 1823 (DPHW 64); Peter Worthmond, planter of Heart's Delight, 1823 (DPHW 64B); Dr. Worthman (and others), of Heart's Delight, 1871 (Lovell).
Modern status: At Green's Harbour (*Electors* 1955), Heart's Delight and St. John's.

WRIGHT, a surname of England, Scotland, Ireland and the Channel Islands from Old English *wyrhta, wryhta* – maker, craftsman, especially carpenter, joiner. (Reaney, Cottle, Black, MacLysaght, Turk). *See also* WRIXON.
Found widespread by Guppy in England and over a large part of Scotland though rare in the north; and by MacLysaght especially in Ulster and Dublin.
In Newfoundland:
Early instances: John, of Newfoundland, 1730 (CO 194.23); John, of St. John's, 1790 (DPHW 26D); William Ward, of Bonavista, 1791 (USPG); James, of Harbour Grace, 1801 (USPG); Daniel, from Tralee (Co. Kerry), married at St. John's, 1808 (Nfld. Archives BRC); Robert, from Paisley, Scotland, aged 32, left the ship *Cornwall* in Newfoundland and disappeared, 1813 (*Nfld. Mercantile Journal* 13 May 1824); Nathaniel, of Greenspond, 1829 (DPHW 76); John, of Portugal Cove, 1830 (DPHW 30); ——, of Brigus, 1830 (*Newfoundlander* 27 May 1830); John, planter of Broad Cove (North Shore, Conception Bay), 1838 (DPHW 52A); John, ? of Northern Bay, 1846 (DPHW 54); Dr., Commissioner of Grammar School at Carbonear, 1847 (*Nfld. Almanac*); Robert, fisherman of Burin, 1860 (DPHW 100); Charles, fisherman of Butter's Cove (? now Creston), 1871 (Lovell); Charles, of Cat Harbour (now Lumsden), 1871 (Lovell); Esther, of Hearts Content, 1871 (Lovell).
Modern status: Scattered, especially at Greenspond and St. John's.

WRIXON, a surname of England and Ireland – ? son of the wright (*see* WRIGHT), different from RIXON. (Reaney, MacLysaght).

Traced by Guppy in Dorset, and by MacLysaght in Cos. Cork since the end of the seventeenth century.

In Newfoundland:

Modern status: Rare, at Epworth (Burin district).

WYATT, WHYATT, surnames of England from the Old German personal name *Wido*, Old French *Guy* with the diminutive suffix *-ot*. *See* GUY. (Reaney, Cottle).

Wyatt traced by Guppy in Devon, Gloucestershire, Hampshire, Norfolk and Somerset.

In Newfoundland:

Early instances: Walter Wyatt, of Salvage, 1681 (CO 1); William Wiett, fisherman of St. John's or Petty Harbour about 1738–43 (CO 194.11, 44); John Wyatt, of St. John's, 1753 (DPHW 26C); John, from Plymouth, cooper of St. John's, 1813 (*Royal Gazette* 18 Mar 1813); Ann Wiatt, of Harbour Grace, 1822 (Nfld. Archives HGRC); Thomas and William Wyatt, of Twillingate, 1871 (Lovell); Herbert Ernest (1891–), from Edge Hill, Liverpool, settled at Heart's Content in 1915 (*Nfld. Who's Who* 1930); Henry John (1871–), from Highfield, Prince Edward Island, settled at St. John's in the early 20th century (*Nfld. Who's Who* 1930).

Modern status: Whyatt, rare, at Corner Brook; Wyatt, scattered.

WYLIE, a surname of England, Scotland and Ireland, ? from Old English *wylig*, *welig* – (dweller by the) willow(wood); or ? from the English river name and place name Wylye or Wiley (Wiltshire); in Scotland a diminutive of William (*see* WILLIAMS). (Black, MacLysaght). *See* WILLIS, WITHERS, WITHYCOMBE.

Spiegelhalter traced Wiley, Wyley, Wylie in Devon; Guppy traced Wyl(l)ie over a large part of Scotland though rare in the north; and MacLysaght traced Wylie and Wiley especially in Co. Antrim and also in Co. Clare.

In Newfoundland:

Early instances: Robert Wily, from Ross (unspecified) (Co. Wexford), married at St. John's, 1809 (Nfld. Archives BRC); ——, of St. John's, 1832 (*Newfoundlander* 20 Dec 1832); James Wyles, planter of Twillingate, 1871 (Lovell).

Modern status: At Bridgeport (Twillingate district) and St. John's.

WYSE. *See* WISE

Y, Z

YABSLEY, a surname of England, ? from an unidentified place name.

Traced to Kingskerswell and the Newton Abbott district of Devon since about 1600. (R. H. Yabsley).

In Newfoundland:

Family tradition: Richard, cooper from Kingskerswell to St. John's about 1830.

Early instance: Richard L. Yabsley, of St. John's, 1848 (DPHW 26D).

Modern status: At St. John's.

YARD, a surname of England from the English place names Yard(e) (Devon), or from Old English *gerd, gyrd* – (holder of a) virgate, thirty acres. (Reaney, Cottle).

Traced by Guppy in Devon.

In Newfoundland:

Early instances: John, of Ferryland, 1675 (CO 1); George, Samuel and Christopher, of Bay Bulls, 1793 (USPG); John, of Witless Bay, 1804 (Nfld. Archives BRC); Stephen, fisherman of Cape Broyle, 1871 (Lovell).

Modern status: At Calvert (*Electors* 1955), Witless Bay and St. John's.

YARN, a surname of England, apparently not recorded elsewhere, ? a nickname from Old English *earn* – eagle, as in such Devon place names as Yarnacombe Cross, Yarnicombe, Yarnscombe.

In Newfoundland:

Early instances: Martha, of Coomb's Cove (Burin district), 1830 (DPHW 106); Thomas, fisherman of Grole, 1845 (DPHW 102); Luke, of Bonne Bay, 1871 (Lovell); John and Philip, of English Harbour West, 1871 (Lovell); James (and others), of Mose Ambrose, 1871 (Lovell); Kester [sic] and William, of Renews, 1871 (Lovell); William, of Rose Blanche, 1871 (Lovell); Henry, of Belleoram, 1871 (Lovell).

Modern status: Scattered, especially in the Fortune Bay-Hermitage district.

YATES, a surname of England and Ireland from Old English *geat* – (keeper of or dweller by the) gate, or from the English place names Yate, Yeat(t) (Devon) or Yate (Gloucestershire). (Reaney, Cottle, Spiegelhalter, MacLysaght). *See also* YETMAN.

Traced by Guppy in Buckinghamshire, Cheshire, Derbyshire, Herefordshire, Lancashire, Shropshire and Staffordshire, and especially as Yeats by MacLysaght in Co. Sligo since the end of the seventeenth century.

In Newfoundland:

Early instances: John Yate(s), of Scilly Cove (now Winterton), 1708–09 (CO 194.4); William Yates, carpenter of Twillingate, 1817 (USPG); Wm. L. Yeates, from Bristol, of Newfoundland, died on board the *American Lass*, 1843 (*Star and Nfld. Advocate* 7 Sep 1843).

Modern status: Scattered, especially at Corner Brook, St. John's and in the Green Bay district.

Place name: Yates Point 49-28 55-17.

YEO, a surname of England from the English place name Yeo (Devon) or from Old English *ēa* – (dweller near the) stream. (Reaney, Cottle, Spiegelhalter).

Traced by Guppy in Cornwall and Devon.

In Newfoundland:

Family tradition: "Daddy Yeo," from Ireland, in possession of property at King's Cove before 1804 (Devine *Old King's Cove*).

Early instance: John Yow, from Plymouth, married at St. John's, 1820 (DPHW 26D).

Modern status: At Torbay.

YETMAN, a surname of England from Old English *geat* – gate and *mann* – gate-man, gate-keeper. (Reaney). *See also* YATES.

Spiegelhalter traced Yeatman in Devon.

In Newfoundland:

Family traditions: Thomas, of Bryants Cove (Conception B.), between 1750–1775 (MUN Hist.). John Yeatman, of Devon ancestry, born at Harbour Grace in the 18th century (MUN Folklore).

Early instances: William, of Harbour Grace, 1792 (USPG); Archer, of Greenspond, 1817 (Nfld. Archives KCRC); Elizabeth, of King's Cove, 1825 (Nfld. Archives KCRC); William, of Keels, 1836 (DPHW 73); William, planter of Carbonear, 1837 (DPHW 48); —— Yeatman, from Dorset, of Red Bay, Straits of Belle Isle, 1849 (Feild); William, of Middle Bill Cove (Bonavista B.), 1851 (DPHW 76); Henry (and others) Yetman, of Bryant's Cove, 1871 (Lovell); William Sr. and Jr., of Ferryland, 1871

(Lovell); Henry, of Southern Bay (Bonavista B.), 1871 (Lovell); John and Robert, of St. Mary's (St. Mary's B.), 1871 (Lovell).

Modern status: Widespread, especially at St. John's, Harbour Grace, Bryant's Cove and St. Mary's (St. Mary's B.).

Place names: Yetman's Cove (Labrador), —— Point (Labrador) 55-13 59-08.

YICK, a surname of China – benefit, profit; to add, to overflow. (F.W. So).

In Newfoundland:

Modern status: Rare, at Bell Island.

YOUDEN, ? a variant of the surnames of England Youlden, Youldon, from the English place names Youlden, Youldon (Devon), or (dweller on the) old (? long-cultivated) hill. (Reaney, Cottle).

Spiegelhalter traced Youlden in Devon.

In Newfoundland:

Family tradition: Thomas (1794–1876) from London, England, of Bull Cove (Conception B.) (MUN Hist.).

Early instance: Henry, fisherman of Bull Cove (Conception B.), 1850 (DPHW 34)

Modern status: Scattered, especially at Georgetown (Port de Grave district) and Lark Harbour (Humber West district).

YOUNG, a surname of England, Scotland, Ireland and the Channel Islands from Old English *geong* – young, perhaps in the sense of junior to one's father. (Reaney, Cottle, Black, MacLysaght, Turk).

Found widespread by Guppy in England and Scotland, but most frequent south of the Forth and Clyde, and by MacLysaght numerous especially in Ulster.

In Newfoundland:

Family traditions: ——, from Poole (Dorset), settled at Old Perlican in the 1700s (MUN Hist.).

——, from England, settled at Placentia about 1710 (MUN Folklore). Some Young families, of Acadian or French descent in the St. George's Bay area, have changed their name from Lejeune (MUN Geog.). Alexis Le Jeune, from Bras d'Or, N.S., settled in St. George's about 1830 and moved later to Sandy Point. Two Ross brothers, of Scottish origin, from Chéticamp, N.S., settled at Kippens and Point à Luc and changed their name to Young, 1870–1880 (MUN Geog.). ——, from England, one of the earliest settlers of Twillingate, settled at South Side (*Nfld. Quarterly* Dec 1905).

Early instances: John Youngs, of (Upper) Island Cove, 1780, property "in possession of the Family

for 90 years," that is, 1690 (CO 199.18); Joseph Young, fisherman of Trinity (Trinity B.), 1763 (DPHW 64); William, soldier of St. John's, 1783 (DPHW 26D); William and son, occupiers of fishing room, Old Perlican, Winter 1800–01 (Census Trinity B.); William, planter of Fogo, 1808 (MUN Hist.); John Youngs, of Harbour Grace, 1814 (Nfld. Archives HGRC); John Young, of Greenspond, 1815 (DPHW 76); William, planter of Old Perlican Island, 1818 (DPHW 58); William Yonge, of Waterford City, married at St. John's, 1818 (Nfld. Archives BRC); John, planter of Twillingate, 1821 (USPG); John Younges, planter of Heart's Content, 1823 (DPHW 64B); Christiana Young, of Hants Harbour, 1825 (DPHW 59); James, of Fortune, 1825 (DPHW 109); John, planter of British Harbour (Trinity B.), 1827 (DPHW 64B); William, of Grand Bank, 1828 (DPHW 109); James, of Codroy Islands, 1835 (DPHW 30); William Youngs, of Round Harbour (Twillingate district), 1843 (DPHW 86); James Young, fisherman of Fox Island (Burgeo-La Poile district), 1844 (DPHW 101); John, of Petites, 1859 (DPHW 98); William, of St. John's Island (St. Barbe district), 1862 (MUN Hist.); Thomas, of Bonne Bay, 1867 (DPHW 93); widespread in Lovell 1871.

Modern status: Widespread, especially at St. John's, Upper Island Cove, Grey River, Glenburnie, Boswarlos, Lourdes, Stephenville Crossing, St. Teresa, Twillingate, Corner Brook, Deer Lake and Curling.

Place names: Young Bight 47-43 55-00; —— Cove, —— Head 49-44 56-00; —— Point 49-39 54-46; Youngs Cove 48-24 58-38; —— Harbour (Labrador) 56-38 61-04.

ZILLMAN, ? a West Country variant, untraced elsewhere, of the surnames of England Sellman or Sillman from Old English *sælig* – happy and *mann* – man, occasionally a personal name, or *Sely*'s man, servant.

In Newfoundland:

Modern status: Rare, at Port aux Basques.

ZIMMERMANN, a surname of Germany – carpenter, joiner.

In Newfoundland:

Modern status: Rare, at St. John's.

ZWICKER, a surname of Germany from the German place name Zwickau (Saxony).

In Newfoundland:

Modern status: At St. John's (*Electors* 1955) and Gander.

Appendices

1. THE ORDER OF COMMON SURNAMES

The following list shows 816 surnames of Newfoundland with fifty or more entries in the *Official List of Electors* 1955 in descending order. Variants of these names with less than fifty entries have been excluded. Surnames having the same number of entries are given the same rank but are distinguished by a, b, c, etc. Cross references show variants or associated names with more than fifty entries.

Rank	Surname	Number	Rank	Surname	Number
1	White	1835	34	Green	618
2	Parsons	1807		(See No. 84)	
3	Smith	1521	35	Barnes	613
4	Power	1490	36	Kennedy	600
5	Walsh	1408	37	Wells	584
	(See No. 453e)		38	Bishop	572
6	King	1224	39	Squires	567
7	Murphy	1146		(See No. 729h)	
8	Brown	1140	40	Janes	535
9	Ryan	1085	41	Osmond	524
10	Young	1003	42	Payne	520
11	Penney	977	43	Hillier	518
	(See No. 207d)		44	Morgan	514
12	Butler	963	45	Hiscock	503
13	Mercer	953	46	O'Brien	494
14	Reid	942		(See No. 751a)	
15	Clarke	934	47	Peddle	484
	(See No. 331b)		48	Andrews	481
16	Martin	871	49	Miller	480
17	Sheppard	848	50	Baker	473
18	Taylor	839	51	Saunders	472
19	Noseworthy	805	52	Russell	466
20	Butt	803	53	Simms	463
21	Snow	774	54	Hodder	461
22	Pike	747	55	Cooper	456
23	Dawe	735	56	Barrett	447
24	Abbott	732	57	Gosse	446
25	Rose	711	58	Hunt	444
26	Collins	706	59	Piercey	436
27	Williams	705		(See No. 681e)	
28	Tucker	698	60	Davis	429
29	Kelly	697	61	Warren	427
30	Hynes	688	62	Pittman	422
31	Bennett	686	63	Jones	413
	(See No. 88)		64	Lewis	412
32	Roberts	685	65	Hickey	411
33	Rideout	673	66	Harris	403

Rank	Surname	Number	Rank	Surname	Number
67	Pardy	397	112	Dwyer	309
68	Randell	388	113	Rowsell	307
69	Crocker	386	114a	Bailey	306
70	Burton	385	114b	Farrell	306
71	Tobin	380	116a	Hutchings	304
72	Porter	378	116b	Morris	304
73a	Byrne	366	118	Winsor	303
73b	Fitzgerald	366		(See No. 681h)	
75a	Lane	363	119	House	300
75b	Moore	363		(See No. 324a)	
	(See No. 109)		120	Dalton	299
77	Wheeler	355	121	Flynn	298
78	Rowe	354	122	Gillingham	295
79	Whalen	353	123	Anderson	294
	(See No. 99)		124	Howell	291
80a	Hollett	352	125a	Day	290
80b	Johnson	352	125b	Holloway	290
82	Chafe	350	125c	Matthews	290
83	Elliott	346	128a	Pelley	285
84	Greene	345	128b	Tilley	285
	(See No. 34)		130	Spurrell	283
85a	Drover	344	131a	Best	282
85b	Hicks	344	131b	Boone	282
87	Earle	343	133	Skinner	281
88	Benoit	341	134a	Ivany	278
	(See No. 31)		134b	Stone	278
89a	Burt	338	136	Chaulk	275
89b	Evans	338	137	Keeping	274
89c	Goodyear	338	138	Rogers	273
89d	Thorne	338		(See No. 157)	
93	Adams	337	139	Powell	272
94	Strickland	334	140	Churchill	270
95	Hann	332	141	Cook	269
96	Brake	330	142	Ford	267
97a	Bursey	326	143a	Burke	265
97b	Cole	326	143b	Hancock	265
	(See No. 215b)		145	Rice	264
99	Whelan	324	146	Wall	263
	(See No. 79)		147a	Burry	262
100a	French	323	147b	Yetman	262
100b	Fudge	323	149	March	260
102a	Perry	321		(See No. 738g)	
102b	Wiseman	321	150	Keats	259
104	Mouland	320	151	Caines	257
105	Norman	319		(See Nos. 215c, 708f)	
106a	Coombs	318	152	Budgell	255
106b	Doyle	318	153a	Lee	252
106c	Sullivan	318	153b	Ralph	252
109	Moores	317	153c	Slade	252
	(See No. 75b)		156	O'Keefe	250
110	Mitchell	316		(See No. 626c)	
111	Legge	315			

Rank	Surname	Number		Rank	Surname	Number
157	Rodgers	249		207a	Delaney	203
	(See No. 138)			207b	Fowler	203
158	Fitzpatrick	248		207c	Hart	203
159	Short	247		207d	Penny	203
160	Anstey	245			(See No. 11)	
161	Foley	243		211a	Dicks	202
162	Connors	241		211b	Norris	202
163	Noel	240		213a	Anthony	201
164	Kavanagh	239		213b	Marshall	201
165a	LeDrew	238		215a	Bradbury	200
165b	Newhook	238		215b	Coles	200
167a	Collier	236			(See No. 97b)	
167b	Tulk	236		215c	Kean	200
169	Dyke	235			(See Nos. 151, 708f)	
170	Patey	233		218	Jenkins	199
171	Carter	232		219a	Pearce	198
172a	Hussey	231			(See No. 681f)	
172b	Sparkes	231		219b	Snook	198
174a	Coady	230		221	Pitcher	196
174b	Murray	230		222a	O'Reilly	195
176	Canning	229		222b	Richards	195
177a	Lynch	227		224a	Carew	194
177b	Scott	227		224b	Critch	194
179a	Barry	223		224c	Keough	194
179b	Gale	223		227	Nolan	193
179c	Locke	223		228a	Edwards	191
182a	Grandy	222		228b	Maloney	191
182b	Stuckless	222		228c	Pennell	191
184a	Foote	221		228d	Sharpe	191
184b	Harvey	221		232a	Furlong	190
184c	Molloy	221		232b	Hayward	190
187a	Thomas	219		234	Gill	189
187b	Vincent	219		235	Spencer	188
189a	Park	217		236a	Carroll	187
189b	Way	217		236b	Decker	187
191a	Crane	216		236c	Maher	187
191b	Lundrigan	216		236d	Thistle	187
191c	Moss	216		240	Boland	184
194	Oldford	215		241	Healey	181
195	Mills	214		242a	Dunphy	180
196a	Antle	212		242b	Greening	180
196b	Fleming	212		244a	Ash	179
196c	Pynn	212		244b	Hurley	179
199	Feltham	211		244c	Lush	179
200	Curtis	210		244d	Newman	179
201a	Downey	208		248	Sutton	178
201b	Hall	208		249	Conway	176
203	Cox	206		250a	Gibbons	175
204a	Hobbs	205		250b	Loder	175
204b	Manuel	205		250c	Mugford	175
204c	Walters	205		250d	Oliver	175

Rank	Surname	Number	Rank	Surname	Number
254a	Aylward	174	302b	Coates	150
254b	Garland	174	302c	Lake	150
256a	Hammond	173	305a	Hearn	149
256b	Lawrence	173	305b	Hoskins	149
256c	Shea	173	305c	Kelloway	149
259a	Jackman	171	305d	Pope	149
259b	Kent	171	309a	Campbell	148
259c	Langdon	171	309b	Hatcher	148
259d	Manning	171	311a	Burden	147
263	Colbourne	170	311b	Legrow	147
264	Diamond	169	311c	Morrissey	147
265	Barron	168	311d	Warford	147
266a	Griffin	166	315a	Head	146
266b	Noble	166	315b	Samson	146
268	Coish	165		(See No. 788i)	
269a	Button	164	315c	Strong	146
269b	Hayes	164	318	Hogan	145
271a	Brennan	163	319a	Bragg	144
271b	Fifield	163	319b	Hanlon	144
271c	Hawco	163	319c	Harding	144
271d	O'Neill	163	319d	Poole	144
	(See Nos. 395d, 462f)		319e	Woodford	144
275a	Blackmore	162	324a	Howse	143
275b	Blanchard	162		(See No. 119)	
275c	Pilgrim	162	324b	Lawlor	143
278a	Follett	160	326	Blackwood	142
278b	Jacobs	160	327a	Drake	141
278c	Roche	160	327b	Wicks	141
	(See No. 569g)		329a	Benson	140
278d	Stacey	160	329b	Hibbs	140
282	Petten	159	331a	Avery	138
283a	Batten	158	331b	Clark	138
283b	Mullins	158		(See No. 15)	
285a	English	157	331c	Slaney	138
285b	Gillard	157	331d	Whitten	138
285c	Kearley	157	335a	Badcock	137
288a	Cull	156	335b	Lockyer	137
288b	Lambert	156	335c	Organ	137
290a	Blake	155	335d	Phillips	137
290b	Bungay	155	335e	Pretty	137
290c	Marsh	155	335f	Thornhill	137
293	Costello	154	341a	Dunne	136
294	Knight	153		(See No. 535b)	
295a	Blundon	152	341b	Hewitt	136
295b	Connolly	152	341c	Pinsent	136
295c	Milley	152	341d	Thompson	136
295d	Moulton	152	341e	Wade	136
295e	Rees	152	346a	Alexander	135
300a	Guy	151	346b	Coffin	135
300b	Stanley	151	348	Tremblett	134
302a	Ball	150	349a	Baird	133

Rank	Surname	Number	Rank	Surname	Number
349b	Cuff	133	395d	Neil	118
349c	Hudson	133		(See Nos. 271d, 462f)	
352a	Paul	132	395e	Turner	118
352b	Stagg	132	400a	Greeley	117
354a	Baggs	131	400b	Kirby	117
354b	Fisher	131	400c	Philpott	117
354c	Kendell	131	400d	Quinlan	117
	(See No. 555b)		400e	Vaters	117
354d	Mahoney	131	400f	Ward	117
358a	Brett	129	406a	Cutler	116
358b	Oake	129	406b	Dobbin	116
358c	Sellars	129	406c	Durnford	116
361a	Fagan	128	409a	Goulding	115
361b	Hopkins	128	409b	Harnum	115
361c	Soper	128	409c	Whiteway	115
364a	Fry	127	412a	Cahill	114
364b	Higdon	127	412b	Skanes	114
364c	Simmonds	127	414a	Breen	113
	(See No. 433a)		414b	Durdle	113
367a	Allen	126	414c	Meaney	113
367b	Hawkins	126	414d	Peckford	113
367c	Miles	126	414e	Purchase	113
	(See No. 595c)		419a	Gaulton	112
367d	Parrott	126	419b	Humphries	112
367e	Pickett	126	419c	Ricketts	112
367f	Vokey	126	422a	Fewer	111
373a	Cluett	125	422b	Long	111
373b	Genge	125	422c	Stockley	111
373c	Gould	125	425a	Banfield	110
373d	Keating	125	425b	Dillon	110
373e	Newell	125	425c	Edison	110
373f	Quinton	125	4215d	Picco	110
379a	Snelgrove	124	429a	Finn	109
379b	Watkins	124	429b	Hoddinott	109
381a	Eddy	123	429c	Seymour	109
381b	Emberley	123	429d	Vardy	109
381c	Leonard	123	433a	Simmons	108
381d	O'Leary	123		(See No. 364c)	
385a	Grant	122	433b	Stead	108
385b	Verge	122	435a	Cassell	107
387a	Billard	121	435b	Forsey	107
387b	Reynolds	121	435c	Hounsell	107
387c	Sturge	121	435d	Mullett	107
390a	Callahan	120	435e	Pottle	107
390b	Gushue	120	435f	Stratton	107
390c	Hamlyn	120	441a	Frampton	106
393a	Fillier	119	441b	Hill	106
393b	Seaward	119	441c	Nash	106
395a	Dooley	118	441d	Peach	106
395b	Janes	118	441e	Reddy	106
395c	Mackey	118	441f	St. Croix	106

Rank	Surname	Number	Rank	Surname	Number
447a	Barbour	105	492b	Harnett	96
447b	Bugden	105	492c	Hartery	96
447c	Hulan	105	492d	Hewlett	96
447d	Humby	105		(See No. 486d)	
447e	Lahey	105	492e	Kenny	96
447f	Wheaton	105		(See No. 761d)	
453a	Dinn	104	492f	Oxford	96
453b	Jesso	104	492g	Reardon	96
453c	O'Quinn	104	499	Gallant	95
	(See No. 767b)		500a	Blagdon	94
453d	Stamp	104	500b	Chislett	94
453e	Welsh	104	500c	Mayo	94
	(See No. 5)		500d	Regular	94
458a	Jennings	103	504a	Compton	93
458b	May	103	504b	Devereux	93
458c	Stokes	103	504c	Murrin	93
458d	Traverse	103	507a	Beck	92
462a	Bonnell	102	507b	Flight	92
462b	Bruce	102	507c	Noftall	92
462c	Chaffey	102	507d	Toope	92
462d	Chaytor	102	511a	Budden	91
462e	Knee	102	511b	Meade	91
462f	O'Neil	102	513a	Baldwin	90
	(See Nos. 271d, 395d)		513b	Cheeseman	90
462g	West	102	513c	Ezekiel	90
469a	Gillam	101	513d	Jackson	90
469b	Penton	101	513e	Nugent	90
471a	Gilbert	100	513f	Vallis	90
471b	Horwood	100	519a	Brenton	89
471c	Morey	100	519b	Cramm	89
471d	Osborne	100	519c	Gillis	89
	(See No. 681d)		519d	Higgins	89
471e	Somerton	100	523a	Batstone	88
476a	Eveleigh	99	523b	Hunter	88
476b	Fowlow	99	523c	Jewer	88
476c	Hennessey	99	523d	Joyce	88
476d	Humber	99	523e	Pond	88
476e	Joy	99	523f	Tizzard	88
476f	Little	99	523g	Waterman	88
476g	Pritchett	99	530a	Cormier	87
483a	Loveless	98	530b	Furey	87
483b	Small	98	530c	Hayden	87
483c	Templeman	98	530d	Parrell	87
486a	Brazil	97	530e	Whiffen	87
486b	Dean	97	535a	Brinson	86
486c	Dove	97		(See No. 569b)	
486d	Howlett	97	535b	Dunn	86
	(See No. 492d)			(See No. 341a)	
486e	Mason	97	535c	Hardy	86
486f	Strowbridge	97	535d	Meadus	86
492a	Brushett	96	535e	Neville	86

Rank	Surname	Number	Rank	Surname	Number
535f	Pomeroy	86	582e	O'Driscoll	78
535g	Pye	86		(See No. 612e)	
542a	Boyd	85	582f	Quigley	78
	(See No. 569a)		588a	Curran	77
542b	Foster	85	588b	Fahey	77
542c	Lacey	85	588c	Fiander	77
542d	Rumbolt	85	588d	Hennebury	77
542e	Winter	85	588e	Mulrooney	77
547a	Belbin	84	588f	Sacrey	77
547b	Galway	84	588g	Starkes	77
549a	Downton	83	595a	Bradley	76
549b	Forward	83	595b	Jarvis	76
549c	O'Toole	83	595c	Myles	76
549d	Spracklin	83		(See No. 367c)	
549e	Steele	83	598a	Adey	75
549f	Tarrant	83	598b	Bowers	75
555a	Corbett	82	598c	Coleman	75
555b	Kendall	82	598d	Corcoran	75
	(See No. 354c)		598e	Kinsella	75
555c	Simon	82	598f	Samms	75
555d	Sweeney	82	598g	Stoyles	75
555e	Vivian	82	589h	Sweetapple	75
560a	Bussey	81	606a	Barter	74
560b	Cantwell	81	606b	Cave	74
560c	Coffey	81	606c	Drodge	74
560d	Field	81	606d	Froude	74
560e	Granter	81	606e	Walker	74
560f	Ingram	81	606f	Whittle	74
560g	Oates	81	612a	Brace	73
560h	Riggs	81	612b	Bridger	73
560i	Willcott	81	612c	Dalley	73
569a	Boyde	80		(See No. 641e)	
	(See No. 542a)		612d	Dowden	73
569b	Brinston	80	612e	Driscoll	73
	(See No. 535a)			(See No. 582e)	
569c	Chambers	80	612f	Faulkner	73
569d	Ellsworth	80	612g	Holwell	73
569e	Gregory	80	612h	Tiller	73
569f	Hackett	80	620a	Crummey	72
569g	Roach	80	620b	Glover	72
	(See No. 278c)		620c	Greenham	72
569h	Torraville	80	620d	Myers	72
577a	Broderick	79	620e	Rendell	72
577b	Ellis	79	620f	Robbins	72
577c	Jerrett	79	626a	Arnold	71
577d	Turpin	79	626b	Duke	71
577e	Weir	79	626c	Keefe	71
582a	Chatman	78		(See No. 156)	
582b	Hoyles	78	626d	Maidment	71
582c	Lidstone	78	626e	Upshall	71
582d	Lilly	78	626f	Woodman	71

Rank	Surname	Number	Rank	Surname	Number
632a	Caravan	70	674f	Sceviour	65
632b	Colbert	70	674g	Toms	65
632c	Grouchy	70	681a	Goobie	64
632d	Hull	70	681b	Holmes	64
632e	Kettle	70	681c	Kearney	64
632f	Nippard	70	681d	Osbourne	64
632g	Skiffington	70		(See No. 471d)	
	(See No. 641h)		681e	Pearcey	64
632h	Stewart	70		(See No. 59)	
632i	Troke	70	681f	Pierce	64
641a	Austin	69		(See No. 219a)	
641b	Chapman	69	681g	Puddester	64
641c	Cleary	69	681h	Windsor	64
641d	Curnew	69		(See No. 118)	
641e	Daley	69	689a	Bannister	63
	(See No. 612c)		689b	Buffett	63
641f	Grace	69	689c	Carpenter	63
641g	Laing	69	689d	Ginn	63
641h	Skeffington	69	689e	Goosney	63
	(See No. 632g)		689f	Hanrahan	63
641i	Stringer	69	689g	Hickman	63
641j	Wight	69	689h	Luscombe	63
651a	Bickford	68	689i	Mews	63
651b	Brophy	68	689j	Newbury	63
651c	Buckle	68	689k	Robinson	63
651d	Courtney	68	689l	Savoury	63
651e	Dodge	68	689m	Senior	63
651f	Normore	68	689n	Stevenson	63
651g	Stapleton	68	689o	Sweetland	63
651h	Tibbo	68	689p	Wilson	63
659a	Costigan	67	705a	Brewer	62
659b	Cross	67	705b	Casey	62
659c	Ducey	67	705c	Lomond	62
659d	Griffiths	67	708a	Barker	61
659e	Halleran	67	708b	Bond	61
659f	Hannon	67	708c	Christopher	61
659g	Leyte	67	708d	Hilliard	61
	(See No. 776d)		708e	Hooper	61
659h	Linegar	67	708f	Kane	61
659i	Noonan	67		(See Nos. 151, 215c)	
668a	Giles	66	708g	Peters	61
668b	Gorman	66	708h	Peyton	61
668c	Keel	66	708i	Street	61
668d	Renouf	66	708j	Swyers	61
668e	Stoodley	66	708k	Temple	61
668f	Woolridge	66	708l	Vey	61
674a	Carey	65	708m	Woods	61
674b	Eastman	65	721a	Cashin	60
674c	Gray	65	721b	Croucher	60
674d	Jeans	65	721c	Haines	60
674e	Oram	65	721d	Hinks	60

Rank	Surname	Number	Rank	Surname	Number
721e	Holden	60	767c	Carberry	55
721f	Lambe	60	767d	Case	55
721g	Lannon	60	767e	Currie	55
721h	Stanford	60	767f	Fizzard	55
729a	Hamilton	59	767g	Gillett	55
729b	Hatch	59	767h	Mitchelmore	55
729c	Hoffe	59	776a	Burgess	54
729d	Nichols	59		(See No. 738b)	
729e	Oakley	59	776b	Duff	54
729f	Percy	59	776c	Hepditch	54
729g	Smart	59	776d	Laite	54
729h	Squire	59		(See No. 659g)	
	(See No. 39)		780a	Cumby	53
729i	Summers	59	780b	Elms	53
738a	Balsom	59	780c	England	53
738b	Bourgeois	58	780d	Ennis	53
	(See No. 776a)		780e	Linthorne	53
738c	Childs	58	780f	Lodge	53
738d	Duffett	58	780g	Madore	53
738e	Halfyard	58	780h	Pippy	53
738f	Mansfield	58	788a	Crant	52
738g	Marche	58	788b	Cummings	52
	(See No. 149)		788c	Dawson	52
738h	Purcell	58	788d	Hayter	52
738i	Stevens	58	788e	Lear	52
738j	Stickland	58	788f	Maynard	52
738k	Tapper	58	788g	O'Connell	52
738l	Trask	58	788h	Pink	52
738m	Webber	58	788i	Sansome	52
751a	Bryant	57		(See No. 315b)	
	(See No. 46)		788j	Tippett	52
751b	Crawley	57	788k	Trickett	52
751c	Deering	57	799a	Bath	51
751d	Doucette	57	799b	Careen	51
751e	Lucas	57	799c	Carnell	51
751f	Freeman	57	799d	Caul	51
751g	Neary	57	799e	Finlay	51
751h	Ploughman	57	799f	Musseau	51
751i	Pollard	57	799g	Tuff	51
751j	Swain	57	799h	Wakeham	51
761a	Alley	56	799i	Wellon	51
761b	Beaton	56	808a	Dyer	50
761c	Cranford	56	808b	Gabriel	50
761d	Kenney	56	808c	Hapgood	50
	(See No. 492e)		808d	Hefford	50
761e	Watton	56	808e	Northcott	50
761f	Woodland	56	808f	O'Grady	50
767a	Alcock	55	808g	Quilty	50
767b	Aucoin	55	808h	Rossiter	50
	(See No. 453c)		808i	Stride	50

2. THE COMPARATIVE ORDER OF THE PRINCIPAL SURNAMES OF NEWFOUNDLAND, ENGLAND AND WALES, IRELAND AND SCOTLAND

The order for England and Wales, Ireland and Scotland is taken from Matheson; the order for Canada does not appear to be available.

Rank	Newfoundland (1955)	England and Wales (1853)	Ireland (1890)	Scotland (1863)
1	White	Smith	Murphy	Smith
2	Parsons	Jones	Kelly	M'Donald
3	Smith	Williams	Sullivan	Brown
4	Power	Taylor	Walsh	Thomson
5	Walsh	Davies	Smith	Robertson
6	King	Brown	O'Brien	Stewart
7	Murphy	Thomas	Byrne	Campbell
8	Brown	Evans	Ryan	Wilson
9	Ryan	Roberts	Connor	Anderson
10	Young	Johnson	O'Neill	Scott
11	Penney	Wilson	Reilly	Miller
12	Butler	Robinson	Doyle	McKenzie
13	Mercer	Wright	McCarthy	Reid
14	Reid	Wood	Gallagher	Ross
15	Clarke	Thompson	Doherty	M'Kay
16	Martin	Hall	Kennedy	Johnston
17	Sheppard	Green	Lynch	Murray
18	Taylor	Walker	Murray	Clark
19	Noseworthy	Hughes	Quinn	Paterson
20	Butt	Edwards	Moore	Young
21	Snow	Lewis	McLaughlin	Fraser
22	Pike	White	Carroll	M'Lean
23	Dawe	Turner	Connolly	Henderson
24	Abbott	Jackson	Daly	Mitchell
25	Rose	Hill	Connell	Morris

3. SURNAMES RECORDED BEFORE 1700

Surnames are given in their modern form. Baptismal names, occupations, locations and authorities will be found in the appropriate entries in the Dictionary. The years are as given in, or deduced from, the records. Two or more dates for one name indicate that it occurs in different locations. A date followed by a numeral in parentheses indicates occurrences of the name in more than one location in the same year.

Adams 1675, 1676, Ackerman 1680, Andrews before 1658, before 1675, 1681, Anthony 1682, Ash before 1678, Atkins 1675, Aylward 1681, 1682, Ayres 1681

Babb 1681, Badcock before 1663, Bailey 1675, 1676, Baird 1677, 1681, Baker 1675, 1681, Barnes 1676, Batten 1675, Bearnes 1681, Benger 1690, Bennett 1675, 1676, Bickford 1681 (2), 1682, Bishop 1681, before 1689, Boone 1675, Bowden 1677, Bradley 1675, Brent 1677, 1681, Brookes 1681, Brown 1676, Browne 1676, Buckler 1681, Buckley 1676, Bugler 1697, Burt 1675, 1680, 1681, Butler 1662, Butt 1675

Caines 1646, Card 1682, Carter 1675, Chambers 1676, Chapman 1681, Cheeke 1682, Clouter 1682, Codner 1676, Colbourne 1682, Cole 1675, 1676, Collins 1675, 1681, Cooke 1675, 1676, Coombes 1676, Corbin 1675, Cornish 1677, Cotton 1675, Cox 1675, Crane 1699, Crewes 1675, 1676, Curtis 1675, 1677

Davies or Davis 1675, 1677, Davies 1677, Davis 1675, Dawe 1595, Deare 1681, Dick 1682, Down 1681, Downing 1650, Drew 1682

Earl before 1662, 1676, Earle 1696-7, Earles 1681, Edwards 1675, Elliott 1675, Ellis 1677, England 1673, Evans 1664

Feild 1675, 1680, Field 1677, 1681, Fillier before 1670, Fillmore 1681, Ford 1675, Fost 1680, French before 1634

Gabriel 1675, 1681, Garland 1675, Garrett 1681, Genge 1675, Gifford 1675, 1677, Gillespie before 1695, Godfrey 1675, Good 1675, Gordon 1669, Gould 1682, Gray 1676, Green 1676, 1677, Gregory 1675, Guy 1675 (2)

Hall 1681, 1682, Haman 1677, Harris 1681, Harvey 1681, Hayman 1682, Hefford 1675, Hibbs 1675, 1676, Hill 1675, 1682, Hilliard 1666, 1678, Hinds 1675, Hoare 1682 (2), Holloway 1675, Holman 1682, Holwell 1675, Hooper 1676, Hopen 1675, Hopkins 1675 (2), 1681, Horton 1675 (2), 1676, House 1676, Howard 1675, 1681, Howell 1681, before 1684, Hudson 1677, Hunt 1675, Hussey 1688, Hutchens 1682

James 1681, Jefferies 1676, Jenkins 1685, Jewer before 1665, Johnson 1666, Jones 1676

Kearley 1682, Kennedy before 1680, Kent 1676, Keyes 1675, King 1675, 1676, 1681 (2), 1682, Kirk 1675, 1676, 1677, Knight before 1675, 1676

Lane 1675, 1681, Lawrence 1676, Lee 1675, 1676, Lucas 1682, Luther 1681

Maddox 1675, Mahon 1675, Marsh 1681, Marshall before 1670, before 1680, 1681 (3), Martin 1675, 1681 (2), Masters 1687, Matthews 1641, 1650, 1675, May 1675, 1696-7, Maynard 1682, Mayne 1678, Menchions 1681, Mercer before 1682, Middleton 1681, Miller 1675, Mitchell 1680, Mollon 1681, Moores before 1668, 1698, Morris 1676, Mugford 1674

Newell 1675 (2), 1676, Newman 1675, Nolan 1681

Oliver 1681 (2)

Parsons before 1665, 1667, 1673, Patten 1681, Pearce 1668, 1677, Pearcey 1675, Petten 1681, Pike 1681, Pollard 1675, Poole 1675, 1677, Powell before 1641, Pritchard 1676, Prowse 1682, Pynn 1675

Rawlins 1682, Richards before 1692, Robbins 1668, Roberts 1657, 1675, 1691, Robinson 1677, 1681, Rodden 1682, Rolands 1675, Rowley 1681, Russell 1681 (2), Ryder 1681

Sargent 1670, Shambler 1675, 1676, 1681, Shepherd 1681, before 1685, Sibley 1679, 1681, Simmonds 1682, Smith 1675 (2), 1676 (2), Snook 1677, Snow before 1675, 1678, Sparkes 1676, 1677, Spingle 1675, Spurvey 1681, Stephens 1670, 1681, Stone 1675, Strange 1677, Strong 1682, Swain 1675

Talbot 1675, Tapper 1682, Tavernor 1675, Taylor 1675, 1677, Thistle 1663, Thomas before 1685, Thoms 1675, Tilley 1675 (2), Traverse 1681, Tucker 1671, before 1683

Vicars 1681

Wakeham 1681, Wallis 1675, Warren 1669, 1676, Waterman 1681, Webb 1675 (2), Webber before 1677, 1681, Welshman 1675, Weymouth 1676, 1680, 1682, White 1676, 1677, Whiteway 1682, Willcott 1676, Windsor 1675, Wing 1698, Wise 1681, Wood 1676, 1682, Wyatt 1681

Yard 1675, Young 1690